Human Development Index: Rajasthan

By the Same Author

- Health Status Index : Rajasthan

About the Author

Prof. Hemlata Joshi, Department of Geography, Mohanlal Sukhadia University, Udaipur (Rajasthan), was earlier on deputation at the Institute of Development Studies, Jaipur and is presently UGC Research Awardee at Rajasthan University, Jaipur (host institution). She obtained her B.A. (Honours), M.A. and Ph.D. Degrees from the University of Rajasthan, Jaipur. Besides, being a Gold Medalist, she is also the recipient of prestigious *'Chancellor's Gold Medal'* from the University of Rajasthan, Jaipur. Her area of specialization is Human Development Studies, Industrial Geography and Remote Sensing. She has completed research projects on "Fertilizer Industry of India" (UGC), "A Geographical Appraisal of Textile Mill Industry—Banswara District" (UGC), "Fairs of Vagad Region" (TRI - Udaipur), "Education Development Index of Panchayat Samities, Rajasthan, 1991-2000", "Economic Development Index", " Health Status Index" and "Human Development Index - Spatio-Temporal and Gender Appraisal at Panchayat Samiti/Block Level" (all of IDSJ). Besides, having contributed articles to various journals, she has also written books entitled "Fertilizer Industry of India", "Bhartiya Suti Vastra Udyog", "Janjation Ka Bhaugolik Adhyayan", "Perspective in Industrial Geography—A Case Study of Sugar Industry of Rajasthan", "Geographical Appraisal of Textile Mill Industry", "Jansankhya: Ek Bhaugolic Adhyayan", "Vastra Udyog: Ek Bhaugolik Vishleshan". "Education Development Index: Rajasthan", "Economic Development Index (Spatio-Temporal & Gender Appraisal at Panchayat Samiti/Block Level)" and Health Status Index: Rajasthan.

Human Development Index Rajasthan

Spatio-Temporal and Gender Appraisal at Panchayat Samiti/Block Level (1991–2001)

Hemlata Joshi

Published for

Institute of Development Studies, Jaipur

by

CONCEPT PUBLISHING COMPANY, NEW DELHI-110059

Cataloging in Publication Data—DK
Courtesy: D.K. Agencies (P) Ltd. <docinfo@dkagencies.com>

Joshi, Hemlata, 1956-
Human development index, Rajasthan : spatio-temporal and gender appraisal at panchayat samiti/block level, 1991-2001 / Hemlata Joshi.
p. cm.
Includes bibliographical references (p.)
Includes index.
ISBN-13: 9788180694349
ISBN-10: 8180694348

1. Economic indicators—India—Rajasthan. 2. Social indicators—India—Rajasthan. 3. Health status indicators—India—Rajasthan. 4. Education—India—Rajasthan. 5. Women in development—India—Rajasthan. 6. Rural development—India—Rajasthan. 7. Quality of life— India—Rajasthan.
I. Title.

DDC 330.954 4 22

ISBN -13: 978-81-8069-434-9
ISBN -10: 81-8069-434-8

First Published 2008

Published and Printed by
Ashok Kumar Mittal
Concept Publishing Company
A/15-16, Commercial Block, Mohan Garden, New Delhi-110 059

Phones : 25351460, 25351794
Fax : 091-11-25357103
E-mail : publishing@conceptpub.com

Dedicated to

My Beloved Son

Himanshu Joshi

Prof. V. S. VYAS
"Padma Vibhushan Awardee"

विकास अध्ययन संस्थान

INSTITUTE OF DEVELOPMENT STUDIES

8-B, Jhalana Institutional Area, JAIPUR-302 004 (INDIA)
Phone : (0141) 515348, 519825 • Fax : 91-141-515346
Gram : IDEAS • e-mail-vsvyas@idsj.org
visit us at : www.idsj.org

FOREWORD

Two major developments have taken place in our understanding of economic progress in recent years. With the publication of the Human Development Reports by the United Nations Development Programme (UNDP) since 1990, the concept of economic development is widened to encompass, apart from the per capita income, other aspects of well-being such as education and health. Using a rigorous methodology UNDP's successive reports have presented a series of indicators to provide a comparative picture of development—understood in the wider sense—over a period of time and across the nations. An equally important development which has a particular significance for India is the devolution of powers as well as responsibilities to the lower units of administration.

Following UNDP's pioneering efforts many countries, including our own, have attempted to bring out Human Development Index year after year, and for different administrative units; in case of large countries for the constituent units such as states or provinces. In India, several states, in turn have brought out Human Development Reports on the pattern of the country level reports encompassing income, education, health and other indicators of welfare. However, the Index Number of Human Development reported in these publications do not go below the district level. With the devolution of power at the levels lower than a district i.e. at *Panchayat Samitis* and even *panchayats,* assessment of development at the decentralized levels has become necessary.

In her report on **"Human Development Index: Rajasthan"** ***Dr. Hemlata Joshi*** has filled this very important gap for the state of Rajasthan. Mainly because of the statistical reasons, it is difficult to prepare a report for a state, much less for a district or a unit below the district. To construct Human Development Index at the *Panchayat Samiti* level is truly a herculean task. It requires not only lot of labour but also imaginative handling of sparse data. Dr. Joshi has largely succeeded in overcoming these difficulties. The result is a report, which gives a comparative picture of development in terms of health, education and per capita income and also brings out, most importantly, the gender dimension of the developmental process. Latter is extremely important in a conservative society like that of Rajasthan.

The results obtained by Dr. Joshi are quite illuminating. For example, she has shown that in overall terms each *Panchayat Samiti* of Rajasthan has improved its Human Development Indicators over the course of the decade, 1991 to 2001. However, some *Panchayat Samities* have done much better than others. This raises the question as to why certain parts of state have shown better results than others, especially when these are contiguous areas. For example, *Panchayat Samities* in Bikaner division and those in the adjoining Jodhpur division have fared differently in their quest for development. A disturbing trend noted in the study is the widening regional inequality in terms of different indicators, and also in terms of overall development, among the *Panchayat Samities*. This, again, requires further probe.

This book will be of use not only to the Policy Makers and planners at the state and district levels, but also for people at the *Panchayat Samities* level. Specialists as much as the enlightened citizens will benefit by the analysis and the conclusions of the book. For all those who are concerned with human development at the grassroot level findings of Dr. Joshi's research will prove highly valuable and instructive.

V S. Vyas

Jaipur, March 22, 2006.

V.S.Vyas

Prof. (Mrs.) HEMLATA JOSHI

विकास अध्ययन संस्थान

INSTITUTE OF DEVELOPMENT STUDIES

8-B, Jhalana Institutional Area, JAIPUR-302 004 (INDIA)
Phone : (0141) 515348, 519825 • Fax : 91-141-515346
Gram : IDEAS • e-mail-vsvyas@idsj.org
visit us at : www.idsj.org

PREFACE

The first Human Development Report brought out by the United Nations Development Programme (UNDP) in 1990 started with a simple statement of far-reaching significance and consequence: "People are the real wealth of a nation. The basic objective of development is to create an enabling environment for people to enjoy long, healthy and creative lives. Human development is a process of enlarging people's choices." Since then, UNDP has been bringing out Human Development Report (HDR) every year by adding additional criteria for the measurement of human progress and well-being of the people of various nations. In 1997, it introduced Human Poverty Index (HPI) which is a multi-dimensional measure of human deprivation. In addition, other indicators like Gender-related Development Index (GDI) and Gender Empowerment Measure (GEM) were also introduced and countries were ranked accordingly. India with HDI value of 0.611 is placed at the 126th rank amongst 177 countries of the world (HDR—2006).

Though global in their perspective, the HDRs have encouraged the preparation of about 275 national HDRs in some 135 countries. In a few cases, HDRs have been prepared at sub-national levels, too. Rajasthan is the first state in India to prepare HDR at panchayat samiti level. The first and the second phases of this work covering educational and economic aspects of human development are already published (IDSJ, 2003 and 2005). The third phase covered the health aspect of human development is under publication.

This report presents composite index of Human Development covering all the above three phases. This report thrusts on spatio-temporal appraisal of Human Development Index at panchayat samiti (block) level during the 1991-2001 period in Rajasthan. The report presents the kind of analysis that is at the core of human development status. It examines the facts and interprets a wide variety of data through Geographic Information System (GIS) and statistical techniques. It is believed that the information contained herein would help in the proper planning and future growth of human development status and in the removal of regional disparities in the state. I hope that this research would prove to be a milestone in the human development agenda for the state.

I am profoundly beholden to Professor V.S. Vyas (Chairman, IDSJ), Professor Sarthi Acharya (Director, IDSJ) and Professor S.S. Acharya (former Director, IDSJ) for their advice, motivation and intellectual support as also for extending all facilities throughout the course of the present investigation.

I am deeply indebted to my father Mr. Sampat Raj Sharma for his constant inspiration and moral support in the successful completion of this comprehensive study. My son Himanshu Joshi deserves a special mention for his dedicated and valuable help throughout the course of the research. My husband Professor C.P. Joshi (Former Minister of Education, Rural Development & Panchayati Raj, GoR) and brother Mr. B.N. Sharma (IAS) deserve a special mention for the intellectual encouragement, constructive criticism and assistance during the critical phases of this study in spite of their demanding political and administrative involvements respectively.

I would like to acknowledge with great appreciation the dedicated, untiring and valuable support of Mr. Manoj Verma and Mr. Nitin Bhatia (Research Assistants).

I am very much grateful to Dr. P.R. Binda (Cartographer, Department of Geography, UoR, Jaipur) especially for preparing meticulous **"ISOHDI"**, **"ISOHSI"**, **"ISOEDI"**, **"ISOGEDI"**, **"ISOINI"** and *"ISOGINI"* maps using latest GIS technique. I am also very much thankful to Mr. Ashok Kumar Mittal (Concept Publishing Company, New Delhi) for taking keen interest in timely publishing of this report.

I would like to acknowledge with great appreciation the intellectual encouragement and constructive criticism of the IDSJ faculty especially Professor: Surjit Singh, Sunil Ray, Vidya Sagar, M.S. Rathore and Pradeep Bhargav.

My sincere thanks are also due to Mr. R. Harikishan (Joint Director, Census Deptt.), Mr Harish Sharma and Mrs. Jyoti Luhadia (Assistant Directors, Census Deptt.), Mr. G. Fernandes and Mr. Roy (Sr. Investigators Grade-I, Census Deptt), Mr. M.I. Khan, Mrs. Puspa Kripalani, Mrs. Asha Tekchandani and Mr. G.G. Rajan (all of IDSJ), Mr. Narayan Paliwal (Statistical Officer, FWD), Dr. Mohan Shhotriya, Dr. D.P.Jaroli, Dr. Subhash Garg, Mr. Anil Chaplot, Mr. Pankaj Mathur, Mr.Suresh Saini, Mr. S.C. Gupta, Mr. Nitin Sharma, Mr. Pradeep Saini and Mr. Sita Ram Sharma who assisted me in various ways.

H. Joshi

Prof. (Mrs.) Hemlata Joshi

CONTENTS

LIST OF FIGURES

LIST OF TABLES

LIST OF MODELS/CHARTS/BOXES

MODELS

CHARTS

BOXES

ABBREVIATIONS

ABER	Annual Blood Examination Rate
ADB	Asian Development Bank
Agri	Agriculture
AIDS	Acquired Immunity Deficiency Syndrome
AIIMS	All India Institute of Medical Sciences
AIR	All India Radio
Aj	Ajmer Division/District
Al	Alwar District
ALC	Adult Literacy Centre
ANC	Ante-natal Care
ANCD	Annual New Case Detection
ANM	Auxiliary Nurse-Midwife
ANMTC	Auxiliary Nurse-Midwife Training Centre
API	Annual Parasite Incidence
ARI	Acute Respiratory Infection
ASST	Assistant
Bans	Banswara District
BH	Behaviour Surveillance
Bha	Bharatpur District
Bhil	Bhilwara District
Bk	Bikaner Division/District/PS
Bln	Billion
Bmr	Barmer District/PS
BPL	Below Poverty Line
Brm	Baran District/PS
Brn	Baran District/PS
Bun	Bundi District
CBR	Crude Birth Rate
CHC	Community Health Centre
Chitt	Chittaurgarh District
Chu	Churu District/PS
CII	Confederation of Indian Industries
CINI	Child In Need Institute
CM & HO	Chief Medical and Health Officer
CMO	Chief Medical Officer
CNAA	Community Needs Assessment Approach
CSB	Central Supervisory Board
CSSM	Child Survival and Safe Motherhood
CTP	Comprehensive Training Plans
CuT	Copper T
DANIDA	Danish International Development Agency
DCO	Directorate of Census Operation
DDP	Drug De-abdicate Programme
DEMO	Demonstrator
DES	Directorate of Economics and Statistics
DFID	Department For International Development
Dg	Dungarpur District/PS
DGHS	Directorate General of Health Services
Dhaul	Dhaulpur District/PS
DHO	District Health Officer
DIET	District Institute of Education and Training
Distt./Distts	District/Districts
DMHS	Directorate of Medical and Health Services
DoFW	Department of Family Welfare
DOTS	Directly Observed Treatment Short Course Chemotherapy Strategy
DP	District Panchayat
DPC	District Planning Committee
DPEP	District Primary Education Programme
DRDA	District Rural Development Agency
Ds	Dausa District/PS
DY. DIR.	Deputy Director
EA_{fi}	Female Percentage Share to Economically Active Population in ith PS
EAG	Empowered Action Group
EA_i	Percentage Share of ith Panchyat Samiti in District Rural Economically Active Population, 1991
EA_{mi}	Male Percentage Share to Economically Active Population in ith PS
EA_{rd}	Rural Percentage Share to Economically Active Population in District
EA_{ud}	Urban Percentage Share to Economically Active Population in District
EDI	Education Index
EL	Extremely Low Level/Group
ETCT	Enhancing Training Competence of Trainers

FHAC	Family Health Awareness Campaign
FICCI	Federation of Indian Chamber of Commerce and Industries
FLI	Female Literacy Index
FLR	Female Literacy Rate
FPI	Female Population Index
FRU	First Referral Unit
FW	Family Welfare
FWD	Family Welfare Department
FWFW	Family Welfare Field Workers
FWTRC	Family Welfare Training and Research Centre
FYPs	Five Year Plans
GA	General Annex
GDI	Gender-Related Development Index
GDP	Gross Domestic Product
GEDI	Gender – Related Education Index
GEM	Gender Empowerment Measure
Gg	Ganganagar District/PS
GINI	Gender Related Income Index
GoI	Government of India
GoR	Government of Rajasthan
GOVT	Government
GP	Gram Panchayat
GW	Guineaworm
GWEP	Guineaworm Eradication Programme
H	High Level/Group
HA(M)	Health Assistant (Mate)
HDI	Human Development Index
HDR	Human Development Report
HFWTC	Health and Family Welfare Training Centre
HMIS	Health Management Information System
Hn	Hanumangarh District/PS
HPI	Human Poverty Index
HRD	Human Resource Development
HSDM	Health Sector Disaster Management
HSI	Health Status Index
ICDS	Integrated Child Development Scheme
ICMR	Indian Council of Medical Research
IDSJ	Institute of Development Studies, Jaipur
IEC	Information, Education and Communication
IIPS	Indian Institute of Population Science
IIT	Indian Institute of Technology
IMA	Indian Medical Association
IMR	Infant Mortality Rate
INI	Income Index
IOD	Index of Deprivation
IPD	Integrated Population and Development
ISM	Indian System of Medicine
ISOEDI	See Terminology
ISOGEDI	See Terminology
ISOGINI	See Terminology
ISOHDI	See Terminology
ISOHSI	See Terminology
ISOINI	See Terminology
IT	Information Technology
IUD	Intrauterine device
Jais	Jaisalmer District/PS
Jhal	Jhalawar District
Jhun	Jhunjhunun District/PS
JL	Jalor District/PS
JM	Jan Mangal
Jodh	Jodhpur Division/District
Jp	Jaipur Division/District
JT. DIR.	Joint Director
JUN.	Junction
Kg	Kilogram
Kr	Karauli District/PS
Kt	Kota Division/District
kWh	Kilowatt-hour
L	Low Level/Group
LEC	Leprosy Eliminations Campaign for Urban Area
LEM	Leprosy Eradication Monitoring
LJ/LJP	Lok Jumbish/Lok Jumbish Parishad
M	Medium Level/Group
MCH	Mother and Child Health
MCW	Mother and Child Department
MDT	Multi Drug Therapy
MEM	Mass Education and Media Wing
MIS	Management Information System
MLEC	Modified Leprosy Elimination Campaign
MLI	Male Literacy Index
MLL	Minimum Levels of Learning
Mln	Million
MNGO	Mother Non-Government Organisation
MOHFW	Ministry of Health and Family Welfare
MPI	Male Population Index
MPW	Multipurpose Worker
MPW(M)	Multi Purpose Worker (Mate)
MSS	Mahila Swasthya Sangha
MTP	Medical Termination of Pregnancy
NA	Not Available/Not Applicable
NACO	National AIDS Control Organisation
NACP	National AIDS Control Programme
NDC	National Document Centre
NDDP	Net District Domestic Product

NDRDP Net District Rural Domestic Product
NDUDP Net District Urban Domestic Product
NFEC/NFC Non-formal Education Centre
NFHS National Family Health Survey
Ng Nagaur District/PS
NGO Non-Governmental Organisation
NHDR National Human Development Report
NHP National Health Policy
N_i Total population of the ith PS
NIC National Information Centre
NID National Immunization Day
NIEPA National Institute of Educational Planning and Administration
NIFP National Institute of Family Planning
NIHFW National Institute of Health and Family Welfare
NIRD National Institute of Rural Development
NLM National Literacy Mission
N_{mi} Total Male Population of the ith PS
NNF National Neonatology Forum
No. Number
NPDP Net Panchayat Samiti Domestic Product
NPSF National Population Stabilization Fund
NPSP National Polio Surveillance Project
NPVP National Polio Vaccination Programme
NSDP Net State Domestic Product
NSPCD National Surveillance Programme for Communicable Diseases
NSSO National Sample Survey Organisation
NSV Non-Scalped Vasectomy
NWC No Where Children
NYK Nehru Yuvak Kendra
OPV Oral Polio Vaccine
ORT Oral Rehydration Therapy
PC,VD Personal Computer, Video
PCY Estimated Per Capita Net Domestic Product of the ith PS
PDS Population and Development Strategy
PHC Primary Health Centre
Pl Pali District/PS
PM Prime Minister
PMGY Pradhan Mantri Gramodaya Yojana
PMSSY Pradhan Mantri Swasthya Suraksha Yojana
PMTCT Prevention of Mother to Child Transmission of HIV
PNDT Prenatal Diagnostic Techniques (Regulation and Prevention of Misuse)
Pop Population
PPI Pulse Polio Programme
PPP Purchasing Power Parity
PR Prevalence Rate
Pr Sc Primary School
PRIs Panchayati Raj Institutions
PS/PSs Panchayat Samiti/Samities, Samitis
R&D Research and Development
Raj Rajasthan
Rajs Rajsamand District/PS
RCH Reproductive and Child Health
RFWC Rural Family Welfare Centre
RGSJP Rajiv Gandhi Swarn Jayanti Pathshala
RHS Rapid Household Survey
RHTC Rural Health Training Centre
RIICO Rajasthan State Industrial Development Corporation
RNTCP Revised National TB Control Programme
RRC Regional Resource Centre
RRPPM Rajasthan Rajya Patthya Pustak Mandal
RRTS Rapid Response Teams
RSACS Rajasthan State AIDS Control Society
RSBTC Rajasthan State Blood Transfusion Committee
RTI/STI Reproductive Tract Infection/Sexually Transmitted Infections
SAP Structural Adjustment Programme
SAPEL Special Action Project for Elimination of Leprosy
SC Scheduled Castes
SCOVA Standing Committee on Voluntary Action
SET Survey, Education and Treatment
SEWA Society for Empowerment of Women
SEZ Special Economic Zone
SFC State Finance Commission
S_{fi} Female Share to Total Wage Bill in ith PS
SGHS State Government Health Services
SHC Sub-Health Centre
SHEB State Health Education Bureau
SHG Self-Help Groups
SIDA Swedish International Development Authority
SIERT State Institute of Educational Research and Training
SIFPSA State Innovation in Family Planning Services Agency
SIHFW State Institute of Health and Family Welfare
Sk Sikar District
SKP/B Shiksha Karmi Project/Board
SKPS Shiksha Karmi Primary School
SM Sawai Madhopur District/PS
SNA System of National Accounts

SOHS School of Health Sciences
SPR Slide Positive Rate
Sr Sirohi District/PS
SRS Sample Registration System
SS/SSs Secondary School/Schools
SSS/SSSs Senior Secondary School/Schools
STs Scheduled Tribes
STD Sexually Transmitted Disease
TAG Technical Advisory Group
Targ. Target
TB Tuberculosis
TBA/DAIS Trained Birth Attendant
TFA Target Free Approach
TFR Total Fertility Rate
Tk Tonk District/PS
TLC Total Literacy Campaign
TLI Total Literacy Index
TLR Total Literacy Rate
TOT Training of Trainers
Ud Udaipur Division/District
UIP Universal Immunization Programme
UNDP United Nations Development Programme
UNESCO United Nations Educational Scientific and Cultural Organisation
UNFPA United Nations Funds on Population Activities
UNICEF United Nations International Children Education Fund
UPE Universalisation of Primary Education
UPS/UPSs Upper Primary School/Schools
USAID US Agency for International Development
VCTCs Voluntary Counselling and Testing Centers
VES Village Education Committee
Vg/Vgs Village/Villages
VH Very High Level/Group
VHAI Voluntary Health Association of India
VL Very Low Level/Group
VPDs Vaccine Preventable Diseases
W_{f}/W_{m} Ratio of Female Agricultural Wage to Male Agricultural Wage
WHO World Health Organisation
W_{r}/W_{u} Ratio of Rural Wage to Urban Wage
Y_{d} Net District Domestic Product (NDDP) at Constant (1993-94), Prices
Yd_{r} Estimated Net District Rural Domestic Product (NDRDP), at Constant (1993-94), Prices
Yd_{u} Estimated Net District Urban Domestic Product (NDUDP), at Constant (1993-94), Prices
Y_{fi} Estimated Female Earned Income in ith PS
Y_{mi} Estimated Male Earned Income in ith PS
Y_{i} Estimated Net Panchayat Samiti Domestic Product (NPDP), at Constant (1993-94), Prices

TERMINOLOGY

Age Specific Fertility Rate (ASFR) The number of live births per 1000 women of a particular/specific age group in a given year. (Number of births to woman of a given age group per 1000 women in that age group.)

Age Specific Marital Fertility Rate (ASMFR) The number of live births per 1000 married women of a particular/specific age group in a given year.

API Annual Parasitic Index.

Average Annual Growth Rate The rate at which a population is increasing (or decreasing) in a given year, Expressed as a percentage of the base population.

Births attended by skilled health staff The percentage of deliveries attended by a doctor, nurse or midwife or trained traditional birth attendant.

Contraceptive prevalence The percentage of married women aged 15-49 who are using, or whose partners are using, any form of contraception, whether modern or traditional.

Crude Birth Rate (CBR) Number of live births per 1000 population in the given years. The CBR depends on both the level of fertility and age distribution of population.

Crude Death Rate (CDR) Annual number of deaths per 1000 population.

Cumulative Percent Marital Fertility It is defined as the ratio of the age specific Marital Fertility rate to total Marital Fertility multiplied by 100.

Full Immunisation BCG, Measles and Three Doses Each of DPT and Polio Vaccines.

General Fertility Rate (GFR) Number of live births per 1000 women in the reproductive age group (15-49 years) in a given year.

General Marital Fertility Rate (GMFR) Number of live births per 1000 married women in the reproductive age group (15-49 years) in a given year.

HIV/AIDS, people living with The estimated number of people living with HIV/AIDS at the end of the year specified.

Human Development Index (HDI) A composite index measuring average achievement in three basic dimensions of human development—a long and healthy life, knowledge and a decent standard of living.

Improved Drinking Water Based on the improved water sources, drinking water supply has been classified as 'Improved' or otherwise. If the household has access to drinking water supplied from a tap or hand pump/tube well situated within or outside the premises it is considered as having access to 'Improved drinking water source'. However, the concept of improved drinking water is state specific and this is to be considered accordingly.

Infant Mortality Rate (IMR) Annual number of deaths of infants under one year of age per 1000 live births. More specifically this is the probability of dying between birth and exactly one year of age.

Lakh 100 thousand

Life expectancy at birth The number of years a new born infant would live if prevailing patterns of age specific mortality rates at the time of birth were to stay the same throughout the child's life.

Low-birth Weight The percentage of infants with a birth-weight of less than 2,500 grams.

Maternal Mortality Rate (MMR) Annual number of deaths of women from pregnancy related causes per 1000 live births.

Neo-natal Mortality Rate (NMR) Annual number of infants dying within the first month of life (technically 4 weeks, i.e. under 28 days) per 1000 live births.

Oral rehydration therapy use rate The percentage of ill cases of diarrhoea in children under age five treated with oral rehydration salts or recommended home fluids, or both.

Panchayat Samiti Elected body responsible for local government at the block level.

Peri-Natal Mortality (Peri-NM) Death of foetus after seven months of Conception and death of Infants with in seven days of birth.

Post-Neo-Natal Mortality (Post NNM) Infants Dying after one month and before one year of life. (NNM + Post NNM = IMR).

Probability at birth of not surviving to specified age Calculated as 1 minus the probability of surviving to a specified age for a given cohort.

Probability at birth of surviving to a specified age The probability of a new born infant surviving to a specified age, if subject to prevailing patterns of age-specific mortality rates.

Sex-Ratio The number of females per 1000 males.

SFR Slide Falciparum Positivity Rate.

SPR Slide Positivity Rate

Total Fertility Rate The average number of children a woman would bear if age-specific fertility rates remained unchanged during her lifetime. Average number of children that would be born to a woman if she experiences the current fertility pattern throughout her reproductive span (15-49).

Total Marital Fertility Rate (TMFR) The number of children that would have been born alive per married woman during her life time, if she were to pass through her child bearing years and bear children at each age in accordance with prevailing age-specific fertility rates. Average number of children that would be born to a married woman if she experiences the current fertility pattern throughout her reproductive span (15-49).

FORMULAS*

$$\textbf{Crude Birth Rate (CBR)} = \frac{\text{Number of live births during the year}}{\text{Mid - Year Population}} \times 1000$$

$$\textbf{Total Fertility Rate (TFR)} = \frac{5 \times \sum_{15-19}^{45-49} \text{ASFR}}{1000}$$

$$\textbf{General Fertility Rate (GFR)} = \frac{\text{Number of live births in a year}}{\text{Mid - year female pop. in the age - group (15 - 49) years}} \times 1000$$

$$\textbf{Age - Specific Fertility Rate (ASFR)} = \frac{\text{Number of live births in a particular age - group}}{\text{Mid - year female pop. of the same age - group}} \times 1000$$

$$\textbf{General Marital Fertility Rate (GMFR)} = \frac{\text{Number of live births in a year}}{\text{Mid-year married female pop. in the age-group (15-49) years}} \times 1000$$

$$\textbf{Age-Specific Marital Fertility Rate (ASMFR)} = \frac{\text{Number of live births in a particular age-group}}{\text{Mid-year married female pop. of the same age-group}} \times 1000$$

$$\textbf{Total Marital Fertility Rate (TMFR)} = \frac{5 \times \sum_{15-19}^{45-49} \text{ASMFR}}{1000}$$

Mean age at effective marriage = Average age at which females start living with their husband

$$\textbf{Crude Death Rate (CDR)} = \frac{\text{Number of deaths during the year}}{\text{Mid - Year Population}} \times 1000$$

$$\textbf{Infant Mortality Rate} = \frac{\text{Number of infant deaths during the year}}{\text{Number of live births during the year}} \times 1000$$

$$\textbf{Maternal Mortality Rate (MMR)} = \frac{\text{Number of maternal deaths to women in the age group 15-49}}{\text{Number of live births}} \times 100{,}000$$

* Compedium of India's Fertility & Mortality Indicators, 1971-97, Based on The SRS, RGI, New Delhi, 1999, pp. xxvii.

$$\textbf{Age - Specific Mortality Rate (ASMR)} = \frac{\text{Number of deaths in a particular age - group}}{\text{Mid - year pop. of the same age - group}} \times 1000$$

$$\textbf{Neo - natal Mortality Rate (NMR)} = \frac{\text{Number of infant deaths of less than 29 days during the year}}{\text{Number of live births during the year}} \times 1000$$

$$\textbf{Early Neo - natal Mortality Rate} = \frac{\text{Number of infant deaths of less than 7 days during the year}}{\text{Number of live births during the year}} \times 1000$$

$$\textbf{Gross Reproduction Rate (GRR)} = \frac{5 \times \sum_{15-19}^{45-49} \text{ASFR for female live births}}{1000}$$

$$\textbf{Late Neo-natal Mortality Rate} = \frac{\text{Number of infant deaths of less than 7 days to less 29 days during the year}}{\text{Number of live births during the year}} \times 1000$$

$$\textbf{Post Neo-natal Mortality Rate (PNMR)} = \frac{\text{Number of deaths of 29 days to less than one year during the year}}{\text{Number of live births during the year}} \times 1000$$

$$\textbf{Peri-natal Mortality Rate (PMR)} = \frac{\text{Number of still births and infant deaths of less than 7 days during the year}}{\text{Number of live births and still births during the year}} \times 1000$$

$$\textbf{Still - Birth Rate (SBR)} = \frac{\text{Number of still - births during the year}}{\text{Number of live births and still - births during the year}} \times 1000$$

LIST OF ANNEXURES

(A) GENERAL ANNEXURES

(B) CHAPTER ANNEXURES

(C) LATEST UPDATE

1

IMPORTANCE AND METHODOLOGY

The Human Development Index (HDI) developed by the United Nations Development Programme (UNDP) is often regarded as an alternative to income-based measure of welfare. It is based on three indicators: longevity, education and standard of living. Thus merely raising income-levels is not the central concern of human development.

The first Human Development Report, 1990 started with the simple but far-reaching statement: "People are the real wealth of a nation. The basic objective of development is to create an enabling environment for people to enjoy long, healthy and creative lives. Human development is a process of enlarging people's choices."

Since then, UNDP has been bringing out Human Development Reports (HDRs) every year by adding additional criteria for measuring human progress and well-being of the people of various nations. In 1997, it introduced Human Poverty Index (HPI) which is a multi-dimensional measure of human deprivation. In addition, other indicators like Gender-related Development Index (GDI) and Gender Empowerment Measure (GEM) were also introduced and countries were ranked on these bases. India with Human Development Index (HDI) value of 0.611 is placed at the 126th rank amongst 177 countries of the world (HDR–2006).

Though global in their perspective, the HDRs have encouraged the preparation of about 275 national HDRs in some 135 countries. In a few cases, HDRs have been prepared at sub-national level too. It is being gradually recognized that socio-economic issues of importance at macro, meso and micro levels could be effectively addressed by human development profile of spatial units such as district/panchayat samiti/village. In India, NCAER undertook a comprehensive exercise in this area. Amongst states, MP, Karnataka and Rajasthan have done pioneering work. Other than these attempts not much work has been done in India in the field of human development, and at panchayat samiti (block) level it is almost negligible. Rajasthan henceforth became the first state in India to prepare a HDR at panchayat samiti level.

Rajasthan was the first state to start 'Panchayati Raj' in India. The dream of democratic decentralization was materialized with the inauguration of the 'Panchayati Raj' by the then Prime Minister, Pandit Jawaharlal Nehru at Nagaur on 2nd Oct., 1959. Presently, the Panchayati Raj is a well knit system organised into 32 Zila Parishads, 237 Panchayat Samitis (Development Blocks) and 9189 Gram Panchayats.

April 24, 1993 is a landmark day in the history of Panchayati Raj in India. On this day, the 73rd Amendment Act, 1992 of the Constitution came into force to provide constitutional status to the Panchayati Raj Institutions (PRIs). With the growing thrust on decentralised planning and devolution of development functions and financial resources to PRIs at different levels, there is a need for evolving objective criteria for directing resources to most deserving areas (with the need of various micro administrative and planning units). Due to wide ranging disparities amongst districts and amongst panchayat samitis within the same district, there is an urgent need for constructing HDI for all the three levels of PRIs viz. districts, panchayat samitis and gram panchayats. The second step for assessment of human development at disaggregated level is to measure the levels of development in different panchayat samities.

Rajasthan is not only India's largest state, but also among the poorest. More than 61 per cent area of the state falls under harsh desert and semi-desert region which is known as the Great Indian Desert, *'The Thar'*. The state with its meagre water resources and perilous dependence on scanty, low and uncertain rainfall is highly vulnerable to drought and famine conditions.

Drought is synonymous with Rajasthan, as the state has experienced the pangs of thirst for 40 out of 49 years of its existence since 1956. Fortunately, with concerted efforts of the state government, various financial institutions, NGOs etc., the state registered significant improvement in agriculture, law and order, education and infrastructure amongst 19 major states in India (Table 1.1). These states were evaluated on 46 parameters across 8 categories.

TABLE 1.1: Improving Performance of Rajasthan Amongst Major Indian States, 1991-01

S. No.	*Particulars*	*Rank in India*		
		1991	*2001*	*Change*
1.	Agriculture	18	12	6
2.	Law and Order	7	5	2
3.	Education	18	17	1
4.	Infrastructure	14	13	1
5.	Health	14	14	0

Souce: Compiled from India Today, May 19, 2003.

The committee of the Planning Commission in its report praised Rajasthan highly for its achievements in human resource development. The report had assessed the overall progress of states in the last three decades. It said that Rajasthan, which was at 11th position among the 15 developing states, has scaled up to the 9th position. Tables 1.2 and 1.3 present position of Rajasthan in India with respect to key indicators of human development.

Keeping this in mind an attempt has been made to present an indepth study of human development status at panchayat samiti level in Rajasthan. Studies on educational* aspect (phase I), economic** aspect (phase II) and health*** aspect (phase III) have already been carried out and published by the author.

Various geographical factors viz. physical, economic, human, historical, technological, political etc. affect human development of an area. There are three essential components of the human development paradigm namely, Equity, Sustainability and Empowerment as depicted in Model 1.1.

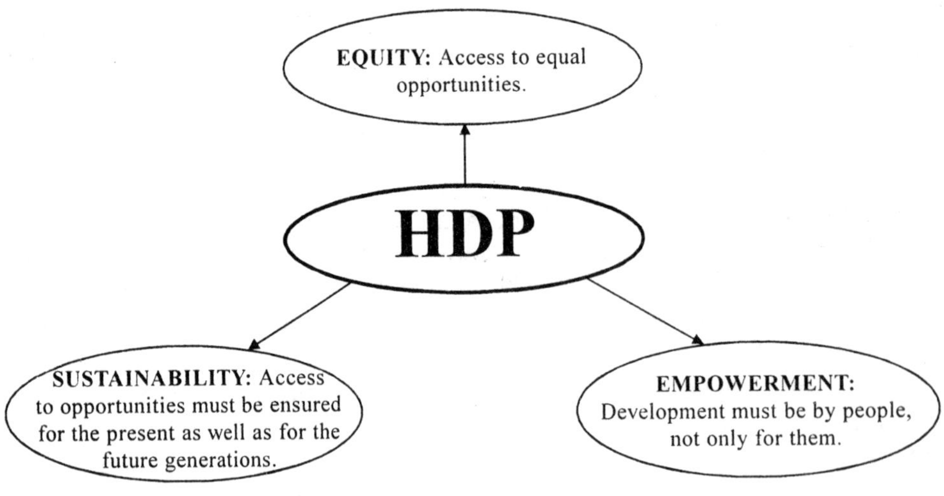

MODEL 1.1: Components of the Health Development Paradigm (HDP)

* Hemlata Joshi, 2003. *'Educational Development Index-Rajasthan (Spatio-Temporal Appraisal at Panchayat Samiti/Block Level)'*, Published Research Report, IDSJ, University Book House, Jaipur.

** Hemlata Joshi, 2005. *'Economic Development Index, Rajasthan (Spatio-Temporal & Gender Appraisal at Panchayat Samiti/Block Level)'*, Published Research Report, IDSJ, University Book House, Jaipur.

*** Hemlata Joshi, 2007. *'Health Status Index-Rajasthan (Spatio-Temporal Appraisal at Panchayat Samiti/Block Level)'*, Published Research Report, IDS Jaipur, Concept Publishing Company, New Delhi.

TABLE 1.2: Key Indicators of Human Development : Rajasthan *Vis-a-Vis* India

	Indicators		*Rajasthan*	*India*
1.	Geographical Area (Lakh sq. kms.)		3.42	32.87
2.	Population 2001 (Million No.)		56.5	1028.6
3.	Percentage Decadal Population Growth Rate (1991-01)		28.33	21.34
4.	Density of Population per sq. km. (2001)		165	324
5.	Percentage of Urban Population to Total Population 2001		23.4	27.8
6.	Percentage of SC Population to Total Population (2001)		17.2	16.2
7.	Percentage of ST Population to Total Population (2001)		12.6	8.2
8.	Literacy Rate 2001		60.4	64.8
9.	Sex Ratio (2001)		922	933
10.	Life Expectancy at Birth (2001-06)	(i) Male	62.17	63.87
		(ii) Female	62.8	66.91
11.	Infant Mortality Rate (per 1000 live births, 2002)		78	63
12.	Birth Rate (per 1000), 2002 (P)		30.6	25
13.	Death Rate (per 1000), 2002 (P)		7.7	8.1
14.	Access to Safe Drinking Water in Rural Areas (%, 2001)	(i) Rural	60.4	73.2
		(ii) Urban	93.5	90.8
		(iii) Total	68.2	77.9
15.	Per Capita Consumption of Electricity (kWh, 2002-03)		291	373
16.	Percentage of Electrified Villages to Total Villages (March 2003)		97.4	84
17.	Percentage of Household having electricity within house	(i) Rural	44	44
		(ii) Urban	90	88
		(iii) Total	55	56
18.	Gross Domestic Product at Constant (1993-94) Prices, 2004-05 (Billion Rs.)		657.8	15293.7
19.	Gross Domestic Product at Current Prices, 2004-05 (Billion Rs.)		1087.3	28381.2
20.	Per Capita Income at Constant (1993-94) Prices (Rs. 2004-05)		9603	12414
21.	Per Capita NSDP at Current Prices (Rs. 2004-05)		15673	23308
22.	Total No. of Registered Educational Institution, 2002-03	(i) Primary	32953	651382
		(ii) Upper Primary	23181	245274
		(iii) Hr. Secondary	8531	137207
		(iv) College for general education	334	9166
		(v) Professional Education	76	2610
		(vi) University/Deemed Uni. etc.	15	385
23.	Gross Enrolment Ratio, 2002-03			
	(1) Class I-V (6-11) Yrs	(i) Boys	102	98
		(ii) Girls	92	93
		(iii) Total	97	95
	(2) Class VI-VIII (11-14) Yrs	(i) Boys	69	65
		(ii) Girls	41	56
		(iii) Total	56	61
	(3) Class I-VIII (6-14) Yrs	(i) Boys	90	85
		(ii) Girls	74	79
		(iii) Total	82	83
24.	Average Size of Holdings (Hect., 1995-96)		3.96	1.41
25.	Consumption of Fertilizer Per Hectare of Cropped Area (kg, 2000-01)		29.78	87.56
26.	Average Daily Employment of Factory Workers Per Lakh of Population (No., 1999)		663	1119
27.	Per Capita Value Added in Industries (Rs. 2001-02)		842	1379
28.	Number of Motor Vehicals Per Lakh of Population (31.03.02)		5507	5617
29.	Total Road Length (per 100 sq. km of area, km, Mar. 1999)		48	77
30.	No. of Banking Offices Per Lakh of Population (Sep. 04)		5.5	6.2
31.	Total No. of Banks at the end of June, 2004		2050	46715
32.	Total Public Sector Bank Deposits (Million Rs., at the end of June 2004)		295.23	11392.14
33.	Total Credit of Public Sector Banks (Million Rs., at the end of June 2004)		185.54	6196.6
34.	Per Capita Bank Deposit (Rs., Sep, 2004)		5594	14380
35.	Per Capita Bank Credit (Rs., Sep, 2004)		3987	8617
36.	10th Plan Projected Outlay at Constant (2001-02) Prices (Billion Rs.)		273.18	5909.48

(P)—Provisional

Source: 1. *Economic Review,* Rajasthan 2004-05, DES, Jaipur. 2. *Economic Survey,* 2004-05, GoI.

3. Hemlata Joshi. 2007. *'Health Status Index-Rajasthan (Spatio-Temporal Appraisal at Panchayat Samiti / Block Level),* Published Research Report, IDS Jaipur, Concept Publishing Company, New Delhi.

TABLE 1.3: Rank of Rajasthan in India (Key Indicators of Human Development)

Rank	*Indicators*	*Rank*	*Indicators*
1	• Area	12	• Life Expectancy at Birth (2001-06)
	• Average Size of Holdings		• Rural Still Birth Rate#
2	• GFR#		• %age of Neo-natal Deaths to Infant Deaths-Rural#
3	• Female IMR (2002)		• Bank Deposits, June (2004)
	• Birth Rate (2002)		• Per Capita Consumption of Electricity (2002-03)
	• TFR (SRS, 1998)		• Per Capita Revenue (2004-05)*
	• GRR (SRS, 1998)		• Per Capita Development Expenditure Revenue (2004-05) *
4	• Male IMR (2002)		• Per Capita Bank Credit (Sep. 04)*
	• IMR,Total (2002)	14	• Per Capita Bank Deposits (Sep. 04)*
	• Rural IMR (2001)		• Per Capita Revenue Expenditure (2004-05)*
	• Rural Neo-natal Mortality Rate#		• No. of Banking Offices Per Lakh Pop.(2002)
5	• No. of Registered Higher Sec. Schools	16	• Total Road Length Per 100 sq. km (1999) *
	• TMFR#	17	• PCI at Current Prices 2002-03
6	• No. of Registered UPS, 2002-03		• Consumption of Fertilizer Per Hectare of Cropped Area*
7	• Death Rate (2002)	19	• Sex-Ratio (2001)
	• Rural Peri-natal Mortality Rate#	22	• Enrolment-Ratio (Male and Total), Class I to V(6-11 yrs.), 2002-03
8	• Total Population (2001),		
	• Gross Domestic Product at Constant (1993-94) Prices		• %age of Currently Married Women With Any Reproductive Health Problem# #
	• Per Capita Bank Credit,		
	• Average Daily Employment of Factory Workers Per Lakh of Population (1999)	23	• Male Enrolment-Ratio (11-14 Yrs.) Class VI to VIII, 2002-03
		24	• Density of Population Per sq. km. (2001*),
	• 10th Plan Projected Outlay at Constant Prices		• Male Enrolment Ratio Class I to VIII (6-14 Yrs.), 2002-03
9	• %age of Electrified Villages to Total Villages (2003)	25	• Female Enrolment-Ratio, Class I to V (6-11 Yrs.), 2002-03
	• Number of Motor Vehicals Per lakh of Population (2002)		• Access to Safe Drinking Water in Rural Areas (%, 2001)
	• No. of Registered Primary Schools (2002-03)		• %age of Deliveries Assisted by Health Professionals *
	• Per Capita Share in Central Taxes	27	• Female Enrolment- Ratio Class I to VIII (6-11 Yrs.)
10	• Per Capita NSDP at Current Prices (2002-03) *		• %age of Rural Households Having Electricity Within House (2001)
	• Per Capita Tax Revenue (2004-05) *		
	• No. of Registered Professional Institutes 2002-03	28	• Literacy Rate
	• Infants Immunised Under 20-Point Programme		• %age of Live Births Delivered in Medical Institutions# #
11	• No. of Commercial Banks (Sep. 2004),		• %age of Live Births Receiving 2 Doses of TT Vaccine#**
	• Per Capita Value Added in Industries (2001-02) *	29	• Couple Protection Rate, (NFHS-2, 1998-99)
	• Bank Credits (June 2004) *,	30	• Enrolment-Ratio, Class VI to VIII (11-14 Yrs.)
	• No. of Universities/Deemed Universities	32	• Female Enrolment-Ratio, Class VI to VIII (2002-03)
	• No. of Colleges for General Education 2002-03		• %age of Children Age 12-23 Months Who Received Full Immunisation, **# #
	• Female Age at Effective Marriage#		
12	• %age of Urban Population to Total Population (2001),	33	• %age of Live Birth Receiving Iron/Folic Tablets##
	• %age Decadal Growth of Population (1991-01)	34	• %age of Live Births Receiving Antenatal Care##

* Rank Amongst Major States. # SRS, 1998, ## NFHS-2, 1998-99

Source: 1. *Economic Review,* Rajasthan, 2004-05, DES, Jaipur.

2. *Economic Survey* 2004-05, GoI.

3. Hemlata Joshi. 2007. *'Health Status Index-Rajasthan (Spatio-Temporal Appraisal at Panchayat Samiti / Block Level),* Published Research Report, IDS Jaipur, Concept Publishing Company, New Delhi.

Health care facilities include Prevention and Cure of Diseases, Control of Communicable Diseases, Family Planning and Care of Mother & Child, Health Insurance, Nutrition, Safe Drinking Water, Sanitation etc. (Model 1.2).

The Study Region

The present research study entitled 'Human Development Index: Rajasthan (Spatio-Temporal and Gender Appraisal at Panchayat Samiti/Block Level, 1991-2001)', covers all the 237 Panchayat Samitis (PSs) of Rajasthan (India) which are spread over 32 districts and 6 divisions (Fig. 1.1 & 1.2).

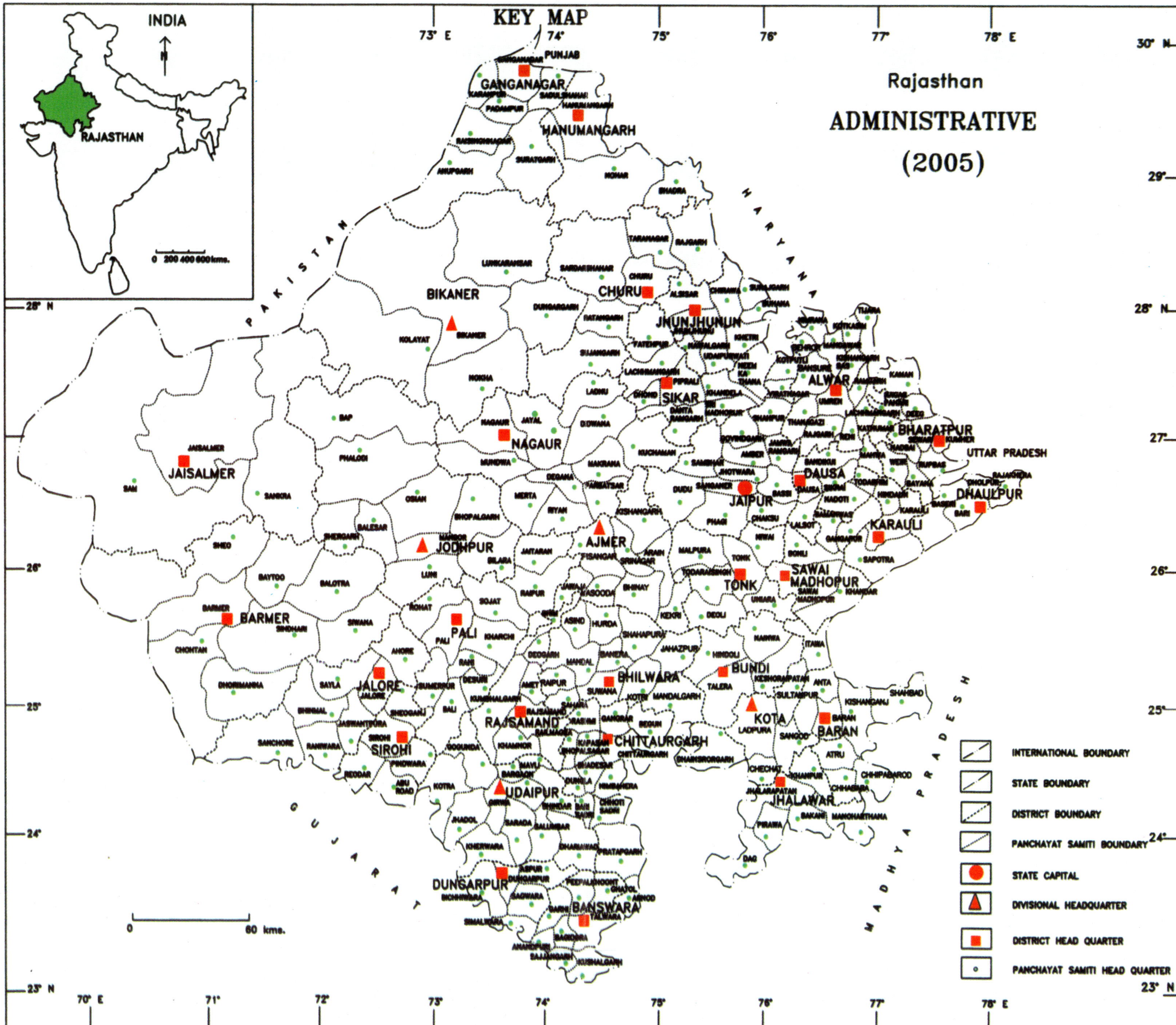

Note: Dungargarh Panchayat Samiti Shifted from Churu of Bikaner District on 1st April 2001.

FIG. 1.1

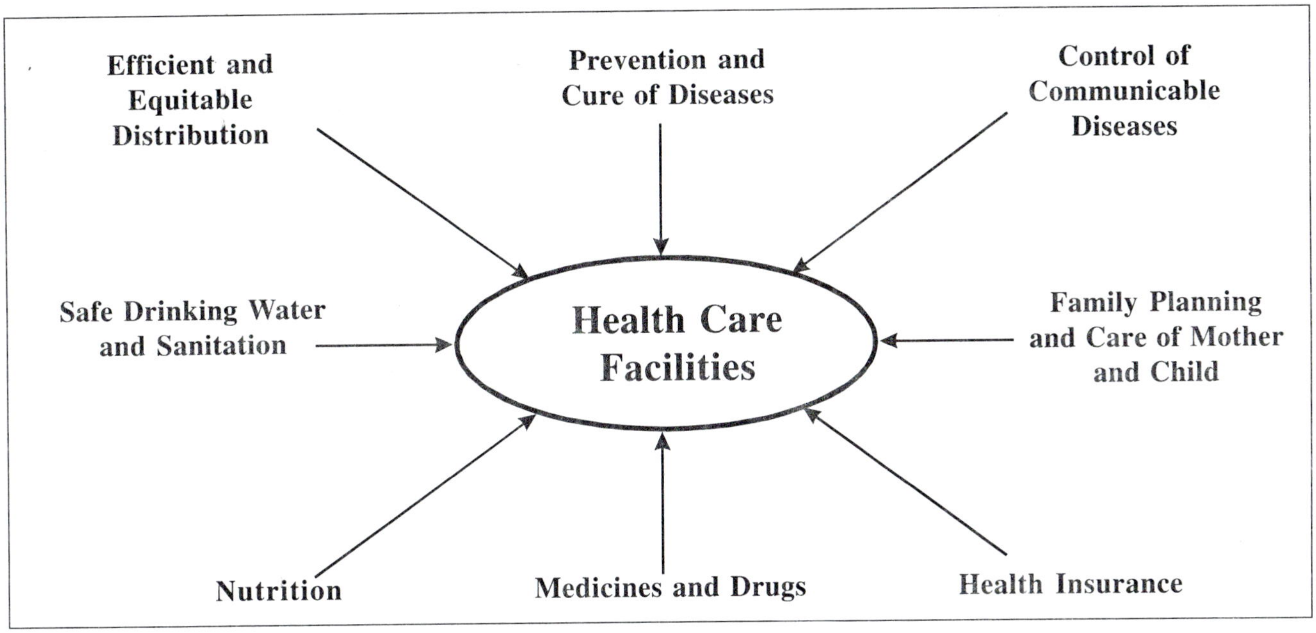

MODEL 1.2: Health Care Facilities

Universalisation of Elementary Education (UEE) has been accepted as the basic objective of the State Education Policy. Now the elementary education system in Rajasthan has become one of the largest in the country. The UEE has following three parameters as presented in Model 1.3

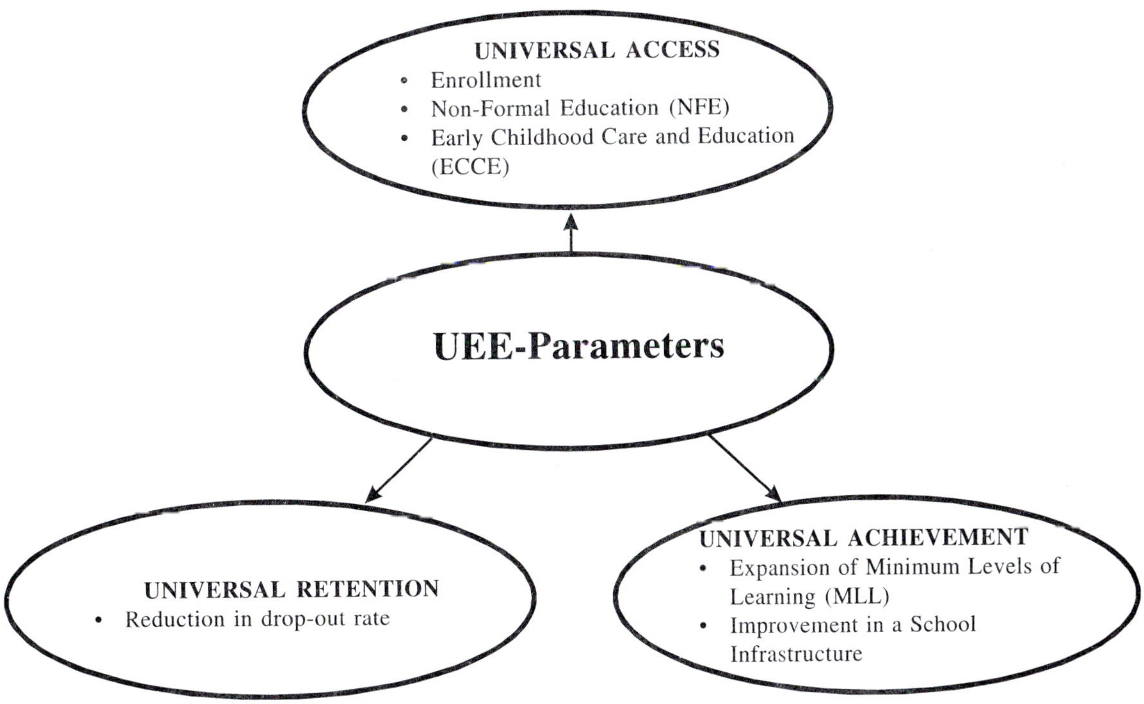

MODEL 1.3: Universalisation of Elementary Education (UEE)

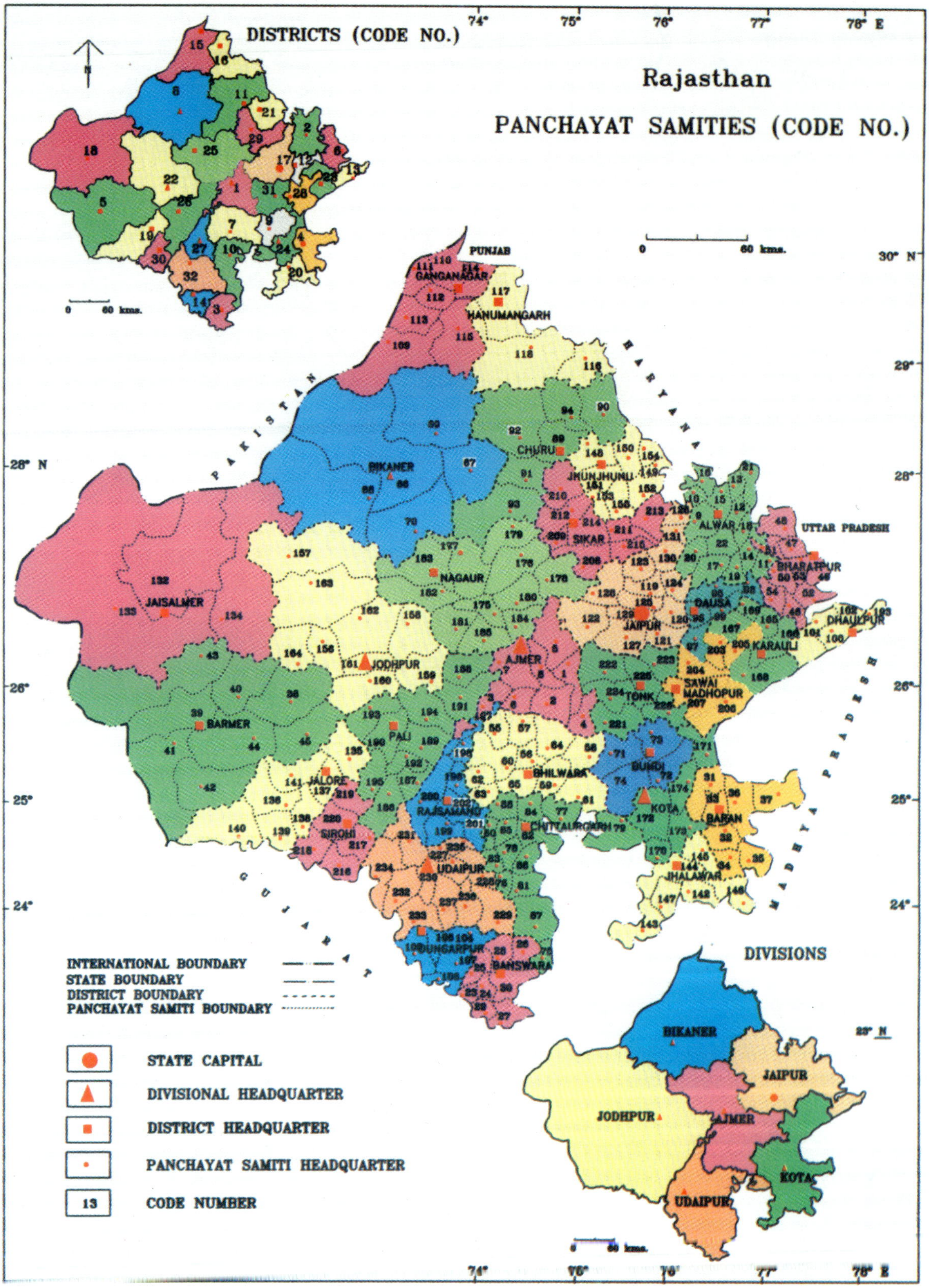

Note: Dungargarh Panchayat Samiti (Code No. 67) Shifted from Churu to Bikaner District on 1st April 2001.

FIG. 1.2

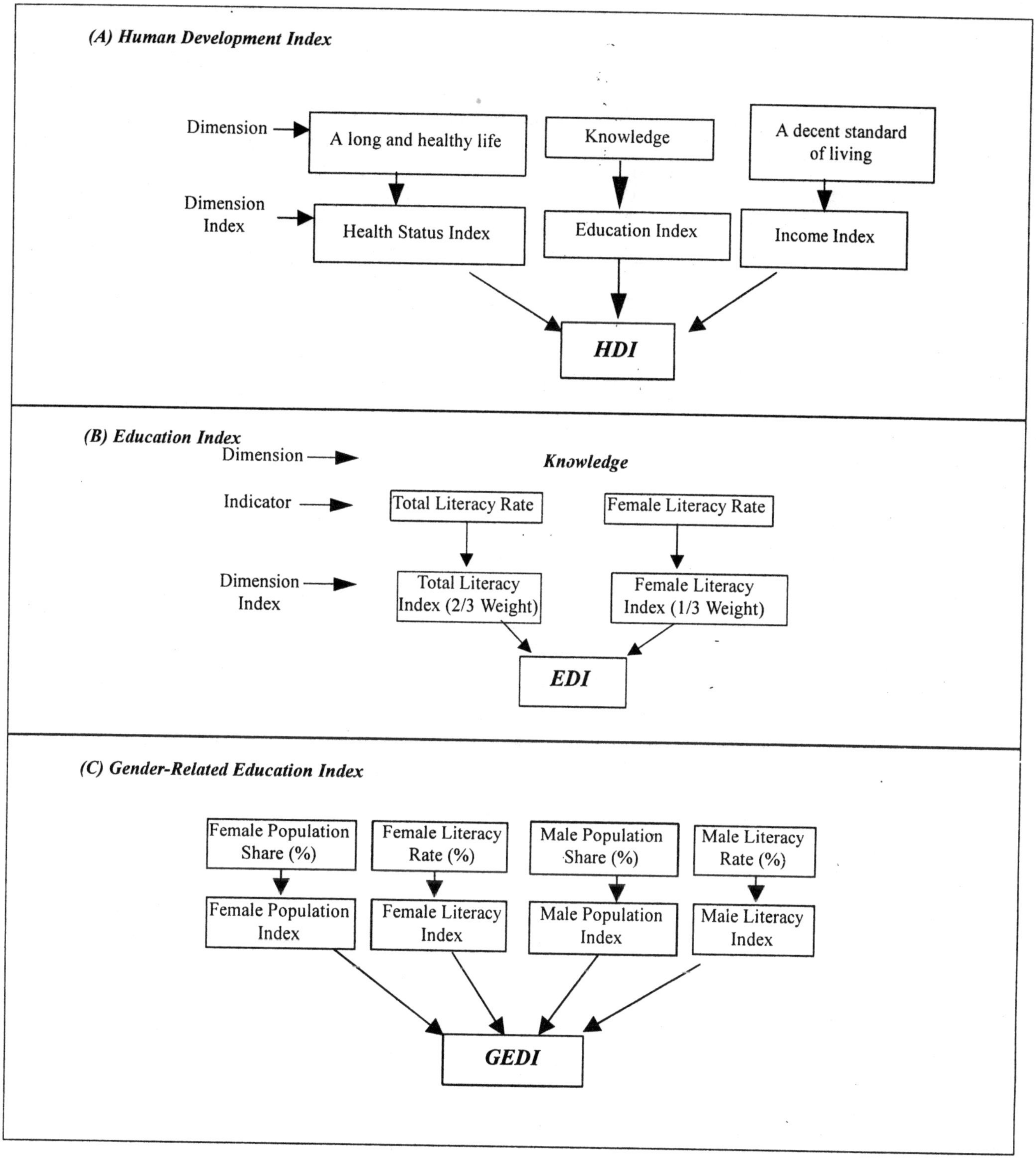

MODEL 1.4: Calculating HDI, EDI and GEDI

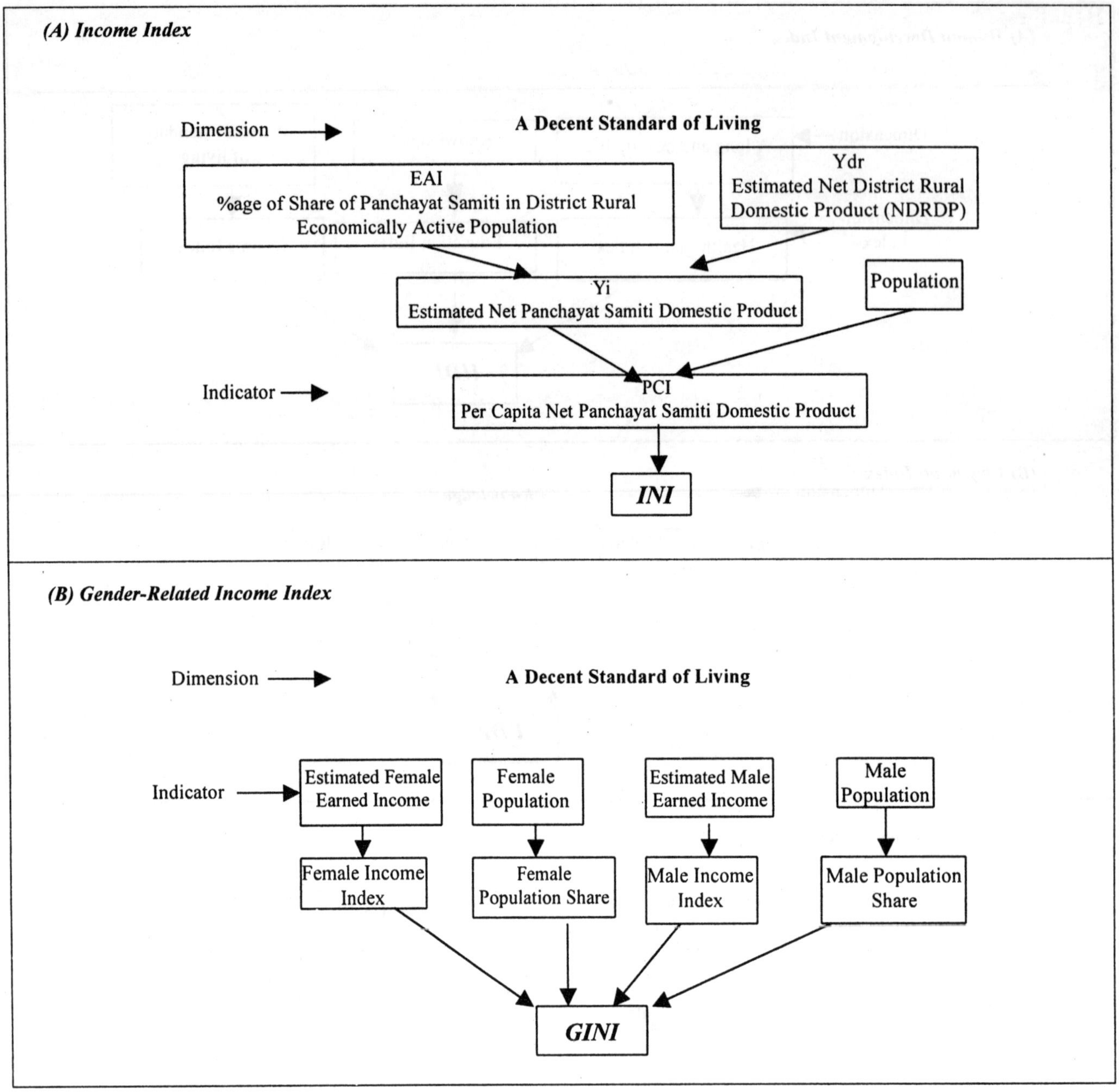

MODEL 1.5: Calculating INI and GINI

Objectives

The main objective of the research is to present spatio-temporal and gender appraisal of human development index at Panchayat Samiti level in Rajasthan. The specific objectives of the study are:

1. To interpret spatial distribution pattern of HDI at PS level.
2. To present temporal appraisal of HDI in two points of time *viz.* 1991 and 2001.
3. To present gender appraisal of HDI.
4. To present Growth Trends and
5. To present Plan of Action.

Hypotheses

The research is based on the following hypotheses:

1. Although during 1991-01 period, the HSI in the state increased significantly, the index of deprivation (IOD) is still high and the state has to travel a long way.
2. There is a great deal of spatial variation in HSI among the PSs across the state.
3. Western arid and southern tribal areas are the most deprived areas in the state.

Methodology

The methodology is mainly based on UNDP-HDR* framework. However, it has been modified wherever necessary, depending on the availability of data at Panchayat Samiti (PS) level. Human Development Index is a measure of how far a panchayat samiti has travelled from a minimum level of achievement and how far it has still to go (Model 1.4).The HDI value ranges between 1 (best) and 0 (worst). The HDI is a summary measure of human development. It measures the average achievements in a panchayat samiti in three key dimensions of human development:

1. A long and healthy life, as measured by Health Status Index (HSI).
2. Knowledge, as measured by Total Literacy Rate (with 2/3 weight) and Female Literacy Rate (with 1/3 weight).
3. A decent standard of living, as measured by Estimated Per Capita Net Panchayat Samiti Domestic Product.

An index was created for each of these dimensions before the calculation of HDI. To calculate these dimension indices goalposts (minimum and maximum values) are choosen as presented in Table 1.4. Performance of each dimension (Table 1.5) is expressed as a value between 0 and 1 by applying the following general formula. The HDI is then calculated as a simple average of the three dimension indices.

$$\text{Dimension Index} = \frac{\text{Actual Value} - \text{Minimum Value}}{\text{Maximum Value} - \text{Minimum Value}}$$

$$\text{HDI} = \frac{\text{HSI} + \text{EDI} + \text{INI}}{3}$$

TABLE 1.4: Goalposts for Calculating the HDI

	Variables	*Maximum Value*	*Minimum Value*
1.	Estimated Per Capita Net Panchayat Samiti Domestic product at constant prices (NPDP, Rs.)	17000** (25000)***	2000** (100)***
2.	Literacy rate (%)		
3.	Percentage of rural population served by medical amenities		
4.	Percentage of villages having medical amenities		
5.	Percentage of rural population served by drinking water amenities	100	0
6.	Percentage of rural population served by educational amenities		
7.	Percentage of rural population approached by pucca road		
8.	Percentage of rural population served by power amenities		
9.	Sex ratio	1080	760

* UNDP, 2005, Human Development Report,
** For Calculation of INI
*** For Calculation of GINI

With respect to sex ratio, the maximum and minimum values taken are 1080 and 760. The basis for this is that Sagwara PS of Dungarpur district (P. Code 107) had the highest 1074 sex ratio in the year 2001 while, Bari PS of Dhaulpur (P. Code 100) had the lowest 763 sex ratio in 1991.

TABLE 1.5: Calculating HDI at PS Level (2001)

P. Code	*Panchayat Samiti*	*HSI*	*EDI*	*INI*	*HDI (Col. 3+4+5)/3*	*Remark*
1	*2*	*3*	*4*	*5*	*6*	*7*
170 28	Chechat Peepalkhoont	0.6970 0.5685	0.6320 0.2110	0.9466 0.3760	0.7585 0.3852	Top PS Bottom PS

Source: Annex 17.1

Education Index (Model 1.4B and Table 1.4)

The EDI is a composite index comprising two parameters (1) Total Literacy Rate (2/3 weight) and (2) Female Literacy Rate (1/3 weight).

Total Litercy Rate does not indicate the gender inequalities arising out of historically perpetuated deprivations. Therefore, for the calculation of EDI in the Panchayat Samiti (PS), female literacy rate is explicitly included as a separate component for the construction of EDI. A higher weight for female literacy was taken to give importance to this most essential criterion. Hence, the following two parameters were taken for measuring EDI for each PS of the State.

$$\text{(i) Total Literacy Rate (TLR)} = \frac{\text{Total Literates}}{\text{Total Population (excluding 0 - 6 age group)}}$$

$$\text{(ii) Female Literacy Rate (FLR)} = \frac{\text{Total Female Literates}}{\text{Total Female Population (excluding 0 - 6 age group)}}$$

TABLE 1.6: Calculating EDI at PS Level (2001)

P. Code	*Panchayat Samiti*	*Total Literacy Index (A)*	*Female Literacy Index (B)*	*EDI (2*A+1*B)/3*	*Remark*
1	*2*	*3*	*4*	*5*	*6*
10 234	Behror Kotra	0.9319 0.066	0.7218 0.2452	0.862 0.201	Top PS Bottom PS

Source: Annex 8.1

Gender-Related Education Index (Model 1.4C and Table 1.5)

The Gender-Related Education Index (GEDI) measures achievement in the same basic capabilities as the EDI does, but takes note of inequality in achievement between women and men. The methodology used imposes a penalty for inequality, such that the GEDI falls when the achievement levels of both women and men in a Panchayat Samiti go down or when the disparity between their achievements increases.

The GEDI calculations are based on $\epsilon^{*} = 2$, the harmonic mean of female and male achievements. The incremental achievement of women has four times the weight of men's if the ratio of male to female achievement is two and $\epsilon = 2$. GEDI value of 1.0 reflects a maximum achievement in basic capabilities with perfect gender equality. But no society achieves such a value.

* An adjustable parameter used in calculation of GEDI to represent weight given to the objective of achieving equality.

The methodology adopted for the computation of GEDI 1991 and 2001 is presented below:

I. Female Population Share
II. Male Population Share
III. FLI, (Female Literacy Index)
IV. MLI, (Male Literacy Index)

$$GEDI = [\{I\} \times \{III\}^{-1} + \{II\} \times \{IV\}^{-1}]^{-1}$$

TABLE 1.7: Calculating GEDI at PS Level (2001)

P. Code	*Panchayat Samiti*	*Female Population Share*	*Male Population Share*	*FLI*	*MLI*	*GEDI*	*Remark*
1	*2*	*3*	*4*	*5*	*6*	*7*	*8*
10	Behror	0.478	0.522	0.722	0.898	0.804	Top PS
234	Kotra	0.495	0.505	0.111	0.376	0.172	Bottom PS

Source: Annex 10.1

Income Index (Model 1.5 A & Table 1.6)

Dimension — A decent standard of living
Indicator — NPDP per capita (Rs.)

↓

INI (NPDP Index)

$$INI = \frac{\log(\text{actual value}) - \log(\text{minimum value})}{\log(\text{maximum value}) - \log(\text{minimum value})}$$

$$= \frac{\log(\text{actual value}) - \log 2000\ (100^{*})}{\log 17{,}000\ (25{,}000^{*}) - \log 2000\ (100^{*})}$$

IOD = 1- Index Value.

Keys

Y_d = Net District Domestic Product Keys (NDDP) at constant (1993-94) prices.
Yd_r = Estimated Net District Rural Domestic Product (NDRDP) at constant (1993-94) prices.
Yd_u = Estimated Net District Urban Domestic Product (NDUDP) at constant (1993-94) prices.
Y_i = Estimated Net Panchyat Samiti Domestic Product (NPSDP) at constant (1993-94) prices.
PCY_i = Estimated Per Capita Net Panchayat Samiti Domestic Product of the ith PS (NPDP per capita).
EA_i = %age share of ith panchyat samiti in district rural economically active Population, 1991.
W_r/W_u = Ratio of Rural wage to Urban wage.
W_f/W_m = Ratio of female agricultural wage to male agricultural wage.
EA_{rd} = Rural percentage share of economically active population in district.
EA_{ud} = Urban percentage share of economically active population in district.
EA_{fi} = Female percentage share of economically active population in ith PS.
EA_{mi} = Male percentage share of economically active population in ith PS.
S_{fi} = Female share of wage bill in ith PS.
N_i = Total population of the ith PS.

* For calculation of GINI at PS level

N_{fi} = Total female population of the ith PS.
N_{mi} = Total male population of the ith PS.
Y_{fi} = Estimated female earned income of ith PS.
Y_{mi} = Estimated male earned income of ith PS.

(I) Net District Domestic Product (Yd)

The data related to NDDP at constant prices (1993-94) for the year 1991-92 and 1998-99 as received from the Directorate of Economics & Statistics, Jaipur (Raj.).

(II) Calculating Ydr [Estimated Net District Rural Domestic Product (NDRDP)]

Assumption: Since separate data for rural and urban NSDP at district level is not available, it has been assumed that all India rural and urban income ratio (1.29:1) and wage ratio (0.73) is applicable to Rajasthan.

Yd_r is calculated by three different methods as presented in Table 1.2. These methods are:

(a) Based on All India Rural : Urban Income Ratio, 1.29:1* (Annex 1.1)

$$Ydr = \frac{1.29}{2.9} \times Yd$$

(b) Based on All India Rural : Urban Wages Ratio, 0.73** (Annex 1.5)

$$Yd_r = \frac{W_r / W_u(EA_{rd})}{[W_r / W_u(EA_{rd})] + EA_{ud}} \times Yd$$

(c) Based on assumed Rural: Urban Wages Ratio for Rajasthan, 0.65 (Annex 1.7)

$$Yd_r = \frac{W_r / W_u(EA_{rd})}{[W_r / W_u(EA_{rd})] + EA_{ud}} \times Yd$$

It is worthwhile to mention here that for academic purposes although Ydr is calculated from the above three methods, method I, which is more authentic and reliable, is used in this research for interpretation and mapping of INI/GINI at panchayat samiti level.

(III) Calculating Ydu (Estimated Net District Urban Domestic Product – NDUDP, Annex-1.1, 1.5 & 1.7)

$$Yd_u = Yd - Yd_r$$

(IV) Calculating Yi (Estimated Net Panchyat Samiti Domestic Product – NPDP, Annex 1.2, 1.6 & 1.7)

$$Yi = EA_i \times Yd_r$$

Assumption: Since PS-wise Eai data for the year 1998-99 is not available, it has been assumed that Eai census data 1991 is applicable for the year 1998-99.

(V) Calculating Estimated Per Capita Net Domestic Product (Annex 1.2, 1.6 & 1.7)

$$PCY_i = \frac{Yi}{N_i}$$

* Rural-Urban income series: Some Estimates by Deepak Mohanty and A. George. Reserve Bank of India, Occasional Papers. Vol. 10, No. 4, Dec. 1989 pp. 397-399.

** *Servekshana,* (July 1993-June 1994), Table No. 55, NSS 50th Round, Report No. 409.

TABLE 1.8: Calculating PCI & INI at PS Level (1998-99)
(Based On Rural and Urban Income Ratio, India : 1.29:1)

PS (P. Code)	*EAi (%)*	*Ydr ('000 Rs.)*	*Yi (Col. 2 X Col. 3)/ 100 ('000 Rs.)*	*Projected Population, as on Oct. 1998 ('000)*	*PCI (Col. 4/Col. 5) (Rs.)*	*INI*	*Remark*
1	*2*	*3*	*4*	*5*	*6*	*7*	*8*
Sanganer (129)	7.4	28378761	2100028.3	121.86	17233	1.0065	Top PS
Aspur (104)	16.2	3109407	503723.9	174.78	2882	0.1708	Bottom PS

Source: Hemlata Joshi. 2005. *'Economic Development Index, Rajasthan* (Spatio-Temporal & Gender Appraisal at PS Level), Published Research Report, IDSJ, University Book House, Jaipur, pp. 188-190.

Gender-Related Income Index (Model 1.5B & Table 1.7)

(I) Estimated Female and Male Earned Income: Calculating S_{fi} (female share of wage bill in the ith PS, Table 1.4)

Assumption: As separate data for wage rate of female and male are not available it has been assumed that female agricultural wage rate is 67 per cent of male agricultural wage rate based upon a recently conducted poverty assessment survey[1]. It is also assumed that the ratio of female wages to male wages in the agricultural sector applies to the rest of the economy.

$$(S_{fi})\ \frac{W_f / W_m\,(EA_{fi})}{[W_f / W_m\,(EA_{fi})]\ EA_{mi}}$$

Calculating Yfi & Ymi (female and male earned income in ith PS): An assumption has to be made that the female share of the wage bill is equal to the female share of Yi (NPDP).

Female population of the ith PS (Nf_i)

Estimated female earned income of ith PS

$$\text{Male population of the ith PS } (Y_{fi}) = \frac{S_{fi}\,(Y_i)}{N_{fi}}$$

$$\text{Estimated male earned income of ith PS } (Y_{mi}) = \frac{Y_i - S_{fi}\,(Y_i)}{N_{mi}}$$

$$\text{GINI} = \frac{\log(\text{actual value}) - \log(\text{minimum value})}{\log(\text{maximum value}) - \log(\text{minimum value})} = \frac{\log(\text{actual value}) - \log(100)}{\log(25000) - \log(100)}$$

TABLE 1.9: Calculating GINI at PS Level (1998-99)

PS (P.Code)	*%age Share of Total Workers (Main + Marginal)*		*Yi ('000 Rs.)*	*Sfi (Wf/Wm = 67%)*	*Yfi (Rs.)*	*Ymi (Rs.)*	*INI*		*GINI*
	Male (Eami)	*Female (Eafi)*					*Female*	*Male*	
1	*2*	*3*	*4*	*5*	*6*	*7*	*8*	*9*	*10*
Sanganer* (129)	64.27	35.73	2100028.3	0.271	9790	24022	0.830	0.993	0.9081
Siwana# (45)	60.94	39.06	570399.9	0.300	1798	3893	0.523	0.663	0.5875

* Top PS # Bottom PS

Source: Hemlata Joshi. 2005. *'Economic Development Index, Rajasthan* (Spatio-Temporal & Gender Appraisal at PS Level), Published Research Report, IDSJ, University Book House, Jaipur, pp. 213-217.

1. Rajasthan Human Development Report, 2002, GoR, Jaipur.

Health Status Index (Model 1.6 and Table 1.8)

The Health Status Index (HSI) is a composite index comprising 8 parameters/variables namely, percentage of rural population served by medical amenities (V1), percentage of villages having medical amenities (V2), percentage of rural population served by drinking water amenities (V3), sex-ratio (V4), Female Literacy Rate (V5), percentage of rural population served by educational amenities (V6), percentage of rural population approached by pucca road (V7) and percentage of rural population served by power amenities (V8).

The health status index is the average of all the eight indicators. The maximum value of HSI is **one (best)** and the minimum is zero (worst).

TABLE 1.10: Calculating HSI at PS Level (2001)

PS (P.Code)	*%age Rural Pop. Served by Medical Amenities (V1)*	*%age of Rural Pop. Served by Drinking Water Amenities (V2)*	*Sex-Ratio (V3)*	*Female LR (%) (V4)*	*%age of Villages Having Medical Amenities (V5)*	*%age of Rural Population Having Amenities of*			*HSI*
						Education (V6)	*Pucca Road (V7)*	*Power (V8)*	
1	*2*	*3*	*4*	*5*	*6*	*7*	*8*	*9*	*10*
Udai—purwati* (155)	80.1	99.8	963	68.0	64.2	100.0	89.9	99.1	0.8307
Sam# (133)	47.3	83.5	787	24.0	17.1	95.1	65.0	39.5	0.4749

* Top PS # Bottom PS

Source: Hemlata Joshi. 2005. *'Health Status Index-Rajasthan* (Spatio-Temporal Appraisal at Panchayat Samiti/Block Level), Research Report, IDS Jaipur, pp. 288-291.

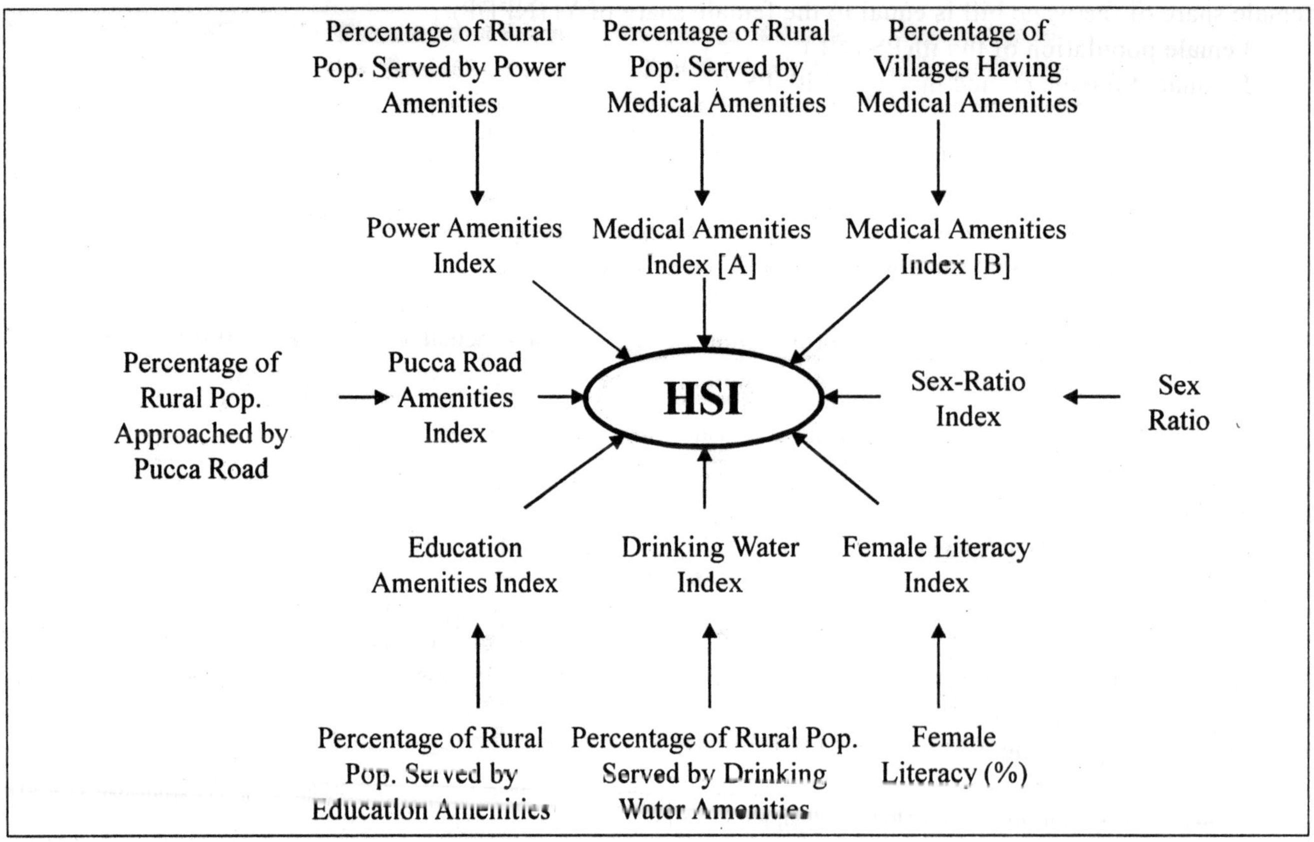

MODEL 1.6: Calculating Health Status Index

Gender Empowerment Measure (Model 1.7 & Table 1.9)

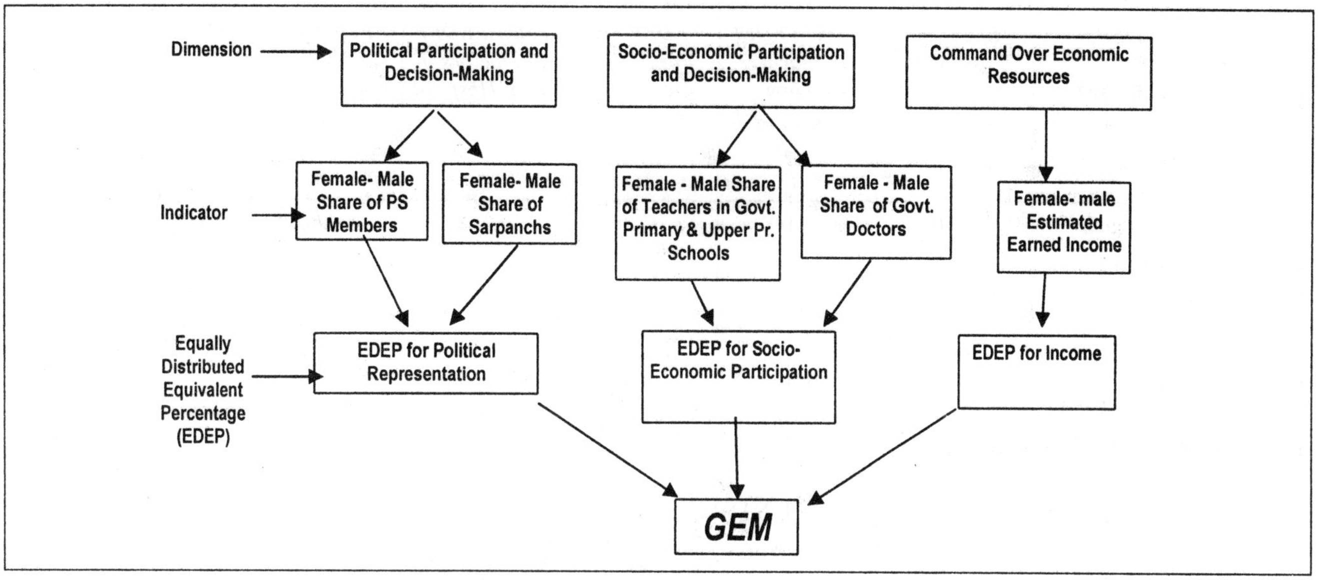

MODEL 1.7: Calculating Gender Empowerment Measure*

Focusing on women's opportunities rather than their capabilities, the GEM captures gender inequality in three key areas:

- Political participation and decision-making power, as measured by women's and men's percentage share of PS members and Sarpanchs.
- Socio-economic participation and decision-making power, as measured by two indicators-women's and men's percentage share of teachers in government primary and upper primary Schools and women's and men's percentage share of government doctors.
- Command over economic resources, as measured by women's and men's estimated earned income (Rs.).

For each of these three dimensions, an equally distributed equivalent percentage (EDEP) is calculated, as a population-weighted average, according to the following general formula:

$$\text{EDEP} = \frac{1}{\left\{\left[\text{Female Population Share (Female Index} \times {}^{1-}\in)\right] + \left[\text{Male Population Share (Male Index}^{1-}\in)\right]^{1/1-}\in\right\}}$$

$\in$ measures the aversion to inequality. In the GEM $\in$ =2, which places a moderate penalty on inequality. The formula is thus:

$$\text{EDEP} = \frac{1}{\dfrac{\text{Female Population Share}}{\text{Female Index}} + \dfrac{\text{Male Population Share}}{\text{Male Index}}}$$

For political and socio-economic participation and decision-making, the EDEP is then indexed by dividing it by 50. The rationale for this indexation: in an ideal society, with equal empowerment of the sexes, the GEM variables would equal 50 per cent—that is, women's share would equal men's share for each variable. Finally, the GEM is calculated as a simple average of the three indexed EDEPs. The GEM value lies between 0 (minimum) and 1 (maximum), which shows the worst and best position respectively.

* Since there is 33 per cent reservation in effect for females at all the three levels of elected representation in PRIs' (Panchayti Raj Institutions viz. Zila Parishad, Panchayat Samiti and Gram Panchayat), therefore, EDEP for political participation in the calculation of GEM is almost a constant factor all over the state.

TABLE 1.11: Calculating GEM at PS Level. (2001)

PS (P. Code)	*EDEP for Political Repre* (A)*	*EDEP for Position as Teachers in Govt. Pr. and UPS*	*Indexed EDEP for Teachers in Govt. Primary and UPS*	*EDEP for Position as Doctors in Govt. Hospital*	*Indexed EDEP for Doctors in Govt. Hospital*	*EDEP for Socio-Eco. Participation (B)*	*EDEP for Income (C)*	*GEM (A+B+C)/3*
1	*2*	*3*	*4*	*5*	*6*	*7*	*8*	*9*
Chechat* (170)	0.981	40.0	0.800	47.6	0.952	0.876	0.887	0.915
Sheo# (43)	0.946	11.2	0.225	0.0	0.000	0.112	0.613	0.557

Source: Annex 15.1. * Top PS # Bottom PS UPS = Upper Primary School

Limitations of the Methodology

It will be pertinent to mention here that the UNDP has used 'life-expectancy at birth' for assessing the level of health status in human development index. Since, data related to life-expectancy at PS level is not calculated or estimated in Rajasthan as well as in India, HSI in the presented study is based on the available data at PS level *viz.* medical and other related amenities#, sex-ratio and female literacy data. Similarly, UNDP has used adult literacy rate and gross enrollment ratio for the calculation of Education Index. Since data related to gross enrollment ratio at PS level for the year 1991 and 2001 is not available, EDI in this research is a composite index based on total literacy rate (2/3 weight) and female literacy rate (1/3 weight).

Source of Data

This study is mainly based on secondary data, which are compiled from the following sources:

1. Directorate of Medical & Health, GoR, Jaipur.
2. Directorate of Medical, Health and Family Welfare, GoR, Jaipur.
3. Directorate of Census Operations, Jaipur.
4. Directorate of Economics & Statistics-DES, GoR, Jaipur.
5. Education Department, GoR, Jaipur.
6. Census of India 2001, Series 9, Rajasthan, Final Population Totals.

It may be pointed out here that in 1991, there were 237 PSs distributed over 27 districts. After the 1991 census, five new districts viz. Baran, Dausa, Hanumangarh, Karauli and Rajsamand, have been created. Hence, for temporal appraisal, data of the concerning PSs of these new districts (for the year 1991) has been taken from the parent districts namely, Kota, Jaipur, Hanumangarh, Sawai Madhopur and Udaipur respectively.

Code Number of PSs

The code number of 237 PSs (Fig. 1.2) are given as follows:

I Alphabetical coding of 32 districts that existed in the year 2001.
II District-wise alphabetical coding of the PSs of these 32 districts.

It is worthwhile to mention here that these code numbers of PSs are different from census code numbers. Annex 1.1 reveals both the code numbers for the planning purpose.

having direct bearing on health status

Organisation

The present volume contains eighteen Chapters. The first two are introductory Chapters and are devoted to importance of the research and the methodology adopted and geographical profile of Rajasthan. Chapters three and four deal with infrastructure status for the years 1991 and 2001 respectively. Chapters five and six present Health Status Index (HSI) for the years 1991 and 2001. The next two Chapters focus on Education Index (EDI) for the years 1991 and 2001. Gender-Related Education Index (GEDI) for the years 1991 and 2001 has been presented in Chapters nine and ten respectively. The Income Index (INI) for the year 1991-92 is discussed in Chapter eleven while Income Index for the year 1998-99 is discussed in Chapter twelve. The Gender-Related Income Index (GINI) for the years 1991-92 and 1998-99 has been presented in Chapter thirteen and fourteen. Gender Empowerment Measure (GEM) for the year 2001 is discussed in Chapter fifteen.

Human Development Index for the years 1991 and 2001 is presented in Chapters sixteen and seventeen. Growth Trends and Action Plan are discussed in the last Chapter.

2

GEOGRAPHICAL PROFILE OF RAJASTHAN

Rajasthan is the largest state of India with 10.4 per cent of the geographical area. It constitutes 5.5 per cent (56.5 million) of the country's population and occupies eight position among the states and union territories. It is located between 23°3' and 30°12' North latitudes and between 69°30' and 78°17' East longitudes. The Tropic of Cancer passing through the southern-most tip of the state places the state into sub-tropical and tropical zones of the Northern Hemisphere.

BOX 2.1: Peculiar geographical characteristics of Rajasthan

- Two-thirds area of the state comes under arid, semi-arid and under hilly region. These vast tracts coupled with sparse population renders the task of development of socio-economic infrastructure very costly.
- Predominantly an agrarian state, about 70 per cent of the population depends on agriculture and about 32 per cent of the NSDP is generated by primary sector.
- Agriculture is essentially rainfed and continues to be vulnerable to the vagaries of monsoon.
- Great spatial variation in physical and cultural environment.
- Recurring drought and scarcity of water.
- Abundance of natural resources, still to emerge as an industrially developed state.
- High fertility, mortality and morbidity indicators. The situation is very grave in tribal, backward and remote areas and in vulnerable groups.
- Very high percentage of rural population (77%).
- Very high population growth rate (28.33%) during 1991-2001.
- Children below 6 years constitute approximately 17 per cent of the total population.
- High percentage of SC (17.16) and ST (12.56) population.
- Low female literacy rate (44%), female work participation rate (38%) and low female age at marriage. 25 per cent females are married in the 10-14 age group in rural Rajasthan.
- Very low CPR (43%).
- Very low sex-ratio (922) especially child sex-ratio (909) with decreasing trend.
- Dominance of small villages.
- Great gender disparity (Very low status of girls and women).
- Rajasthan is one of the highly guineaworm endemic states, contributing more than 68 per cent of total affected villages and 78 per cent of total cases in India.
- The prevalence rate of blindness is very high (2.24%) as compared to national average (1.49%).
- 70-75 per cent births in Rajasthan happen out-side hospitals.
- Percentage of never married males is higher than that of females in both rural and urban areas.
- 78 per cent rural households are deprived of tap water amenity*.
- 69 per cent rural households are without hand pumps facility*.
- 56 per cent rural households are deprived of electricity amenity*.
- 51 per cent villages are without road connectivity*.
- 40 per cent rural households are deprived of safe drinking water amenity*. 76 per cent are deprived of bank account facility* and 47 per cent are deprived of specified assets*.

* Rapid Households Survey under the RCH Programme 1998-99, Ministry of Health & Family Welfare, GoI, New Delhi

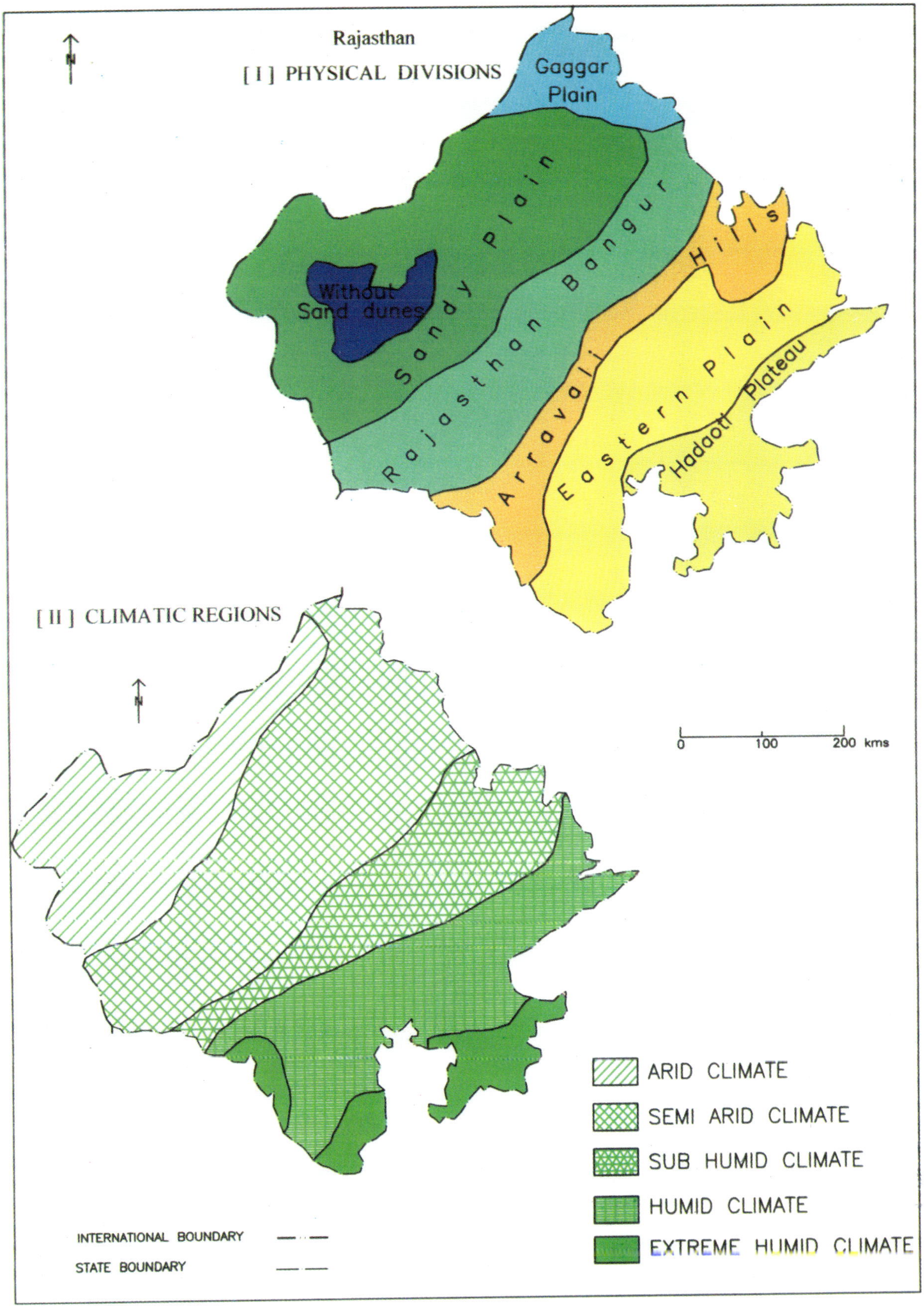
Rajasthan
[I] PHYSICAL DIVISIONS
N
Gaggar Plain
Sandy Plain
Without Sand dunes
Rajasthan Bangur
Arravali Hills
Eastern Plain
Hadaoti Plateau
[II] CLIMATIC REGIONS
N
0 100 200 kms
ARID CLIMATE
SEMI ARID CLIMATE
SUB HUMID CLIMATE
HUMID CLIMATE
EXTREME HUMID CLIMATE
INTERNATIONAL BOUNDARY
STATE BOUNDARY

FIG. 2.1

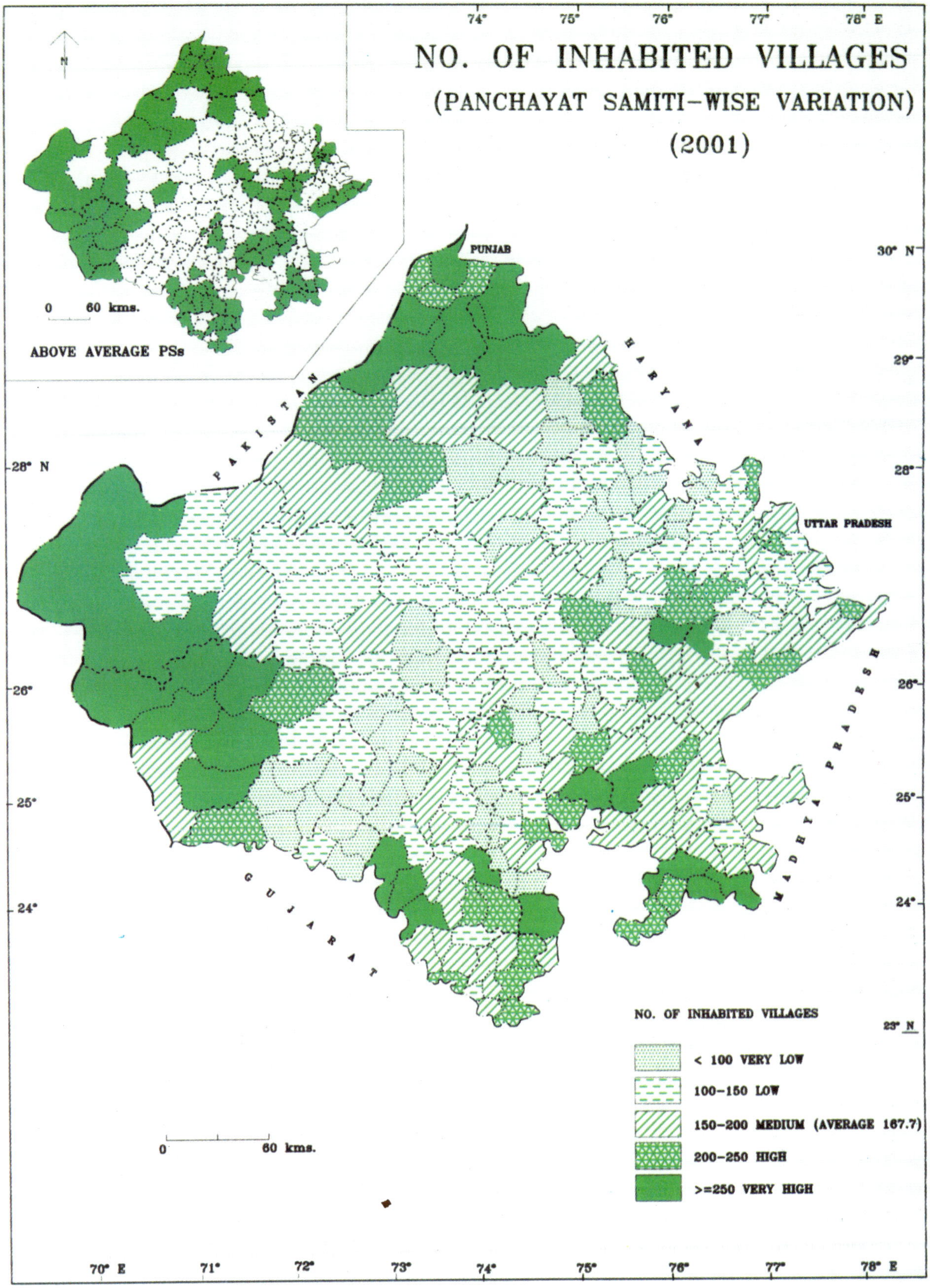
NO. OF INHABITED VILLAGES
(PANCHAYAT SAMITI-WISE VARIATION)
(2001)
ABOVE AVERAGE PSs
0 60 kms.
PUNJAB
HARYANA
PAKISTAN
UTTAR PRADESH
MADHYA PRADESH
GUJARAT
NO. OF INHABITED VILLAGES
< 100 VERY LOW
100-150 LOW
150-200 MEDIUM (AVERAGE 167.7)
200-250 HIGH
>=250 VERY HIGH
0 60 kms.
70° E
71°
72°
73°
74°
75°
76°
77°
78° E
30° N
29°
28° N
26°
25°
24°
23° N

FIG. 2.2

The state is situated in the north-western part of the Indian Union covering the complete Arid 'Great Indian Desert' and parts of semi-arid climatic zone. Rajasthan is surrounded by Punjab, Uttar Pradesh, Haryana and the Union Territory of Delhi in the north; part of Uttar Pradesh and Madhya Pradesh in the east; Gujarat and Madhya Pradesh in the south and Pakistan in the west. Its location in the western fringe of the Indian landmass has placed the state on the route of hot western winds during summers and mediterranean cyclones during the winters. The state stretches 826 kms from north to south and 869 kms from east to west. The overall length of the state boundary is 5920 kms, of which 1070 kms is the international boundary, separating India from Pakistan on its western flank. Thus, the state has a special status in the matters of defence, political interaction and security arrangements.

TABLE 2.1: Administrative Structure: Rajasthan

S. No.	*Districts*	*Sub-Divisions*	*Tahsils*	*PSs*	*Gram Panchayats*	*Villages*	
						Revenue	*Inhabited*
1	Ajmer	6	9	8	276	1038	1025
2	Alwar	12	12	14	478	1994	1954
3	Banswara	3	5	8	325	1504	1476
4	Baran	6	8	7	215	1207	1089
5	Barmer	4	8	8	380	1941	1933
6	Bharatpur	9	10	9	371	1472	1366
7	Bhilwara	8	12	11	381	1745	1693
8	Bikaner	5	8	5*	219	875*	804*
9	Bundi	5	5	4	181	849	839
10	Chittaurgarh	8	13	14	391	2395	2201
11	Churu	5	6	6**	249**	882**	854**
12	Dausa	5	5	5	223	1058	1025
13	Dhaulpur	4	5	4	153	802	786
14	Dungarpur	3	4	5	237	858	854
15	Ganganagar	6	9	7	320	3014	2830
16	Hanumangarh	7	7	3	251	1905	1773
17	Jaipur	13	13	13	488	2131	2077
18	Jaisalmer	3	3	3	128	637	600
19	Jalor	5	7	7	264	706	697
20	Jhalawar	5	7	6	252	1600	1477
21	Jhunjhunu	5	7	9	288	1063	855
22	Jodhpur	5	6	8	339	859	1058
23	Karauli	5	6	5	224	798	755
24	Kota	5	5	5	162	892	812
25	Nagaur	9	10	11	461	1500	1480
26	Pali	6	9	10	320	949	936
27	Rajsamand	4	7	7	206	987	973
28	Sawai Madhopur	4	7	5	197	794	719
29	Sikar	6	6	8	329	992	986
30	Sirohi	3	5	5	151	462	455
31	Tonk	7	7	6	231	1093	1032
32	Udaipur	7	10	11	498	2351	2339
	Total (32)	**188**	**241**	**237**	**9188**	**41353**	**39753**

Note: * Including Dungargarh PS ** Excluding Dungargarh PS
Source: 1. General Annex VII & VIII 2. Directorate of Census Operation, Jaipur.

Administratively, the state comprises of 6 divisions, 32 districts, 188 sub-divisions, 183 municipalities, 241 tehsils, 237 panchayat samitis/blocks, 9189 gram panchayats and 41353 revenue villages (39753 inhabited and 1600 uninhabited) as highlighted in table 2.3. It is appropriate to mention here that after the 1991 Census, five more districts have come into existence namely—(1) Dausa carved out of Jaipur and Sawai Madhopur districts, (2) Hanumangarh out of Ganganagar district, (3) Rajsamand out of Udaipur district, (4) Baran out of Kota district, and (5) Karauli carved out of Sawai Madhopur district. The total number of districts in the state has thus, gone upto 32. Similarly, 28 new tehsils have been created by the state government after 1991, raising the total number to 241. The number of revenue villages has also increased from 39810 to 41353 during the decade. However, the number of urban units has remained the same at 222.

Division-wise distribution of districts and Panchayat Samities (PSs) is presented in Table 2.2. Jaipur is the biggest division comprising of 7 districts and 61 PSs while, Bikaner is the smallest division with 4 districts and 21 PSs.

TABLE 2.2: Division-wise Distribution of Districts and PSs: Rajasthan

S.No.	*Division*	*Included Districts*			*Panchayat Samities*	
		No.	*%*	*Name*	*No.*	*%*
1	Jaipur	7	21.88	Jaipur, Dausa, Alwar, Bharatpur, Dhaulpur, Sikar and Jhunjhunun	61	25.74
2	Bikaner	4	12.50	Bikaner, Ganganagar, Hanumangarh and Churu	21	8.86
3	Ajmer	4	12.50	Ajmer, Nagaur, Bhilwara and Tonk	36	15.19
4	Jodhpur	6	18.75	Jodhpur, Jaisalmer, Jalor, Barmer, Sirohi and Pali	42	17.72
5	Udaipur	5	15.63	Udaipur, Rajsamand, Banswara, Dungarpur and Chittaurgarh	45	18.99
6	Kota	6	18.75	Kota, Bundi, Jhalawar, Baran, Sawai Madhopur and Karauli	32	13.50
	Rajasthan	**32**	**100.00**		**237**	**100.00**

Table 2.3 shows classification of districts on the basis of number of Panchayat Samities (PSs). Both Alwar and Chittaurgarh districts have the highest (14 each) number of PSs followed by Jaipur (13); Bhilwara, Nagaur, Udaipur (11 each); Pali (10) etc. respectively. On the otherside, Jaisalmer and Hanumangarh districts have the lowest number of PSs (3 each).

TABLE 2.3: Classification of Districts on the Basis of No. of PSs: Rajasthan

No. of PSs	*Districts*	
	No.	*Name*
14	2	Alwar and Chittaurgarh
13	1	Jaipur
11	3	Bhilwara, Nagaur and Udaipur
10	1	Pali
9	2	Bharatpur and Jodhpur
8	5	Ajmer, Banswara, Barmer, Jhunjhunun and Sikar
7	4	Ganganagar, Jalor, Baran and Rajsamand
6	3	Churu*, Jhalawar and Tonk
5	7	Bikaner*, Dungarpur, Kota, Sawai Madhopur, Sirohi, Dausa and Karauli
4	2	Bundi and Dhaulpur
3	2	Jaisalmer and Hanumangarh
237	32	

Note: * Dungargarh PS shifted from Churu to Bikaner district on 1st April 2001.

Classification of PSs by total rural population, percentage of 0-6 population, total number of revenue and inhibited villages and number of Gram Panchayats is expressed in Table 2.4. There are five group viz. Very High, High, Medium, Low and Very Low groups. With respect to total rural population the state has dominance of VH group PSs (Pop. > 160,000) followed by H, M, L and VL group PSs.

Similarly, with respect to percentage of 0-6 population to total population, maximum 97 PSs are in Medium (18-20%) group while only 5 PSs are in VL (< 16%) group. With respect to the total number of revenue villages as well as inhabited villages, the state is dominated by Low group (100-150 villages) PSs followed by Medium, High, Very Low and Very High group PSs. With regard to total number of Gram Panchayats, Medium group (30-40 GPs) PSs led in the state followed by H, L, VH and VL group PSs.

Hanumangarh PS (Hn dist.) had the highest (628123) rural population in the state. It is followed by Osian, Anupgarh, Bikaner, Nohar, Sanchore, Neem ka Thana, Didwana, Nokha and Govindarh PSs respectively.

On the other hand, Bhopalsagar PS (Jodh dist.) had the lowest (72675) population preceded by Rashmi, Deogarh, Bhainsrorgarh, Raipur, Kapasan, Amet, Gangrar, Bari Sadri and Jhotwara PSs.

TABLE 2.4: Classification of PSs by total Rural Pop., 0-6 Pop. Villages and Gram Panchayat

	Total Rural Population		*%age of 0-6 pop. to total population*		*Total No. of Villages*			*No. of Gram Panchayats*	
	Group	*PSs%*	*Group*	*PSs%*	*Group*	*Revenue*	*Inhabited*	*Group*	*PSs%*
	(000' No)		*%*		*No.*	*PSs %*	*PSs %*	*No.*	
VH	>160	61.6	>22	17.3	>250	11.8	10.1	>50	11.8
H	140-160	15.2	20-22	22.8	200-250	16.5	12.7	40-50	28.3
M	120-140	9.7	18-20	40.9	150-200	25.3	25.3	30-40	41.8
L	100-120	6.8	16-18	16.9	100-150	31.2	34.6	20-30	16.9
VL	<100	6.8	<16	2.8	<100	15.2	17.3	<20	1.3
	Total	**100**	**Total**	**100**	**Total**	**100**	**100**	**100**	**100**

Source: Annex 2.1 to 2.5 and K2.

With respect to percentage of 0-6 population to total population, Kaman (25.1%) PS of Bharatpur district is at the top rank, followed by Kotra, Abu Road, Bari, Kushalgarh, Bap, Dungargarh, Sankra, Sheo and Dhorimanna PSs. On the other side, Kapasan (15.2%) PS of Chittaurgarh district is at the bottom preceded by Bhopalsagar, Sadulshahar, Railmagra, Ganganagar, Karanpur, Rashmi, Padampur, Mavli and Dungla PSs.

With respect to the total number of revenue villages, Hanumangarh PS (Hn Dist.) is at the first rank with 1152 villages. The other dominating PSs are Anupgarh, Nohar, Suratgah, Raisinghnagar, Pratapgarh, Bakani, Baytoo and Lalsot. On the other hand, Sumerpur PS of Pali district is at the last rank with only 65 villages. The other bottom PSs are Sawai Madhopur, Jalor, Sheoganj, Hurda, Jhotwara, Jaswantpura, Rani Station, Sayla and Desuri.

Anupgarh PS of Ganganagar district has the maximum 1090 inhabited villages in the state (Fig. 2.2). It is followed by Hanumangarh, Nohar, Suratgarh, Raisinghnagar, Pratapgarh, Baytoo, Barmer, Kotra and Lalsot PSs. Sumerpur PS of Pali District, on the other side, has the minimum 63 inhabited villages. It is preceded by Sawai Madhopur, Jalor, Sheoganj, Hurda, Jhotwara, Jaswantpura, Rani Station, Sayla, Abu Road and Desuri PSs.

With respect to the total number of gram panchayats and households, Hanumangarh PS is again at the top with 121 Gram Panchayats and 101573 households. Anupgarh, Nohar, Osian, Bikaner, Sanchore, Kherwara, Talera and Neem Ka Thana are the other leading PSs. Jhotwara PS of Jaipur district, on the other side, is at the bottom with only 16 Gram Panchayats and 11998 households. Deogarh, Bhopalsagar, Hurda, Amet, Gangrar, Raipur, Rohat, Rashmi, Pali, Kapasan, Bhainsrorgarh, Bari Sadri, Sheoganj, Kotkasim, Desuri and Chhoti Sadri are the other bottom PSs.

Karanpur PS of Ganganagar has the highest (47) percentage of SC population to total population while, Kushalgarh of Banswara has the lowest (1%). In ST population, Kushalgarh PS is at the top (94.5%) while Rajakhera (Dhaulpur) is at the bottom (absence) (Table 2.5).

TABLE 2.5: Classification of PSs by Percentage of SC and ST Population to Total Population: Raj. (2001)

	SC Pop.		*ST Pop.*	
	Group (%age of SC Pop.)	*PSs %*	*Group (%age of ST Pop.)*	*PSs %*
VH	>25	8.4	>40	10.5
H	20-25	22.8	30-40	5.9
M	15-20	41.8	20-30	8.9
L	10-15	13.9	10-20	18.1
VL	<10	13.1	<10	56.6

Source: Annex K11 and K12.

District-wise distribution of top and bottom PSs by total rural population, percentage of 0-6 population to total population, number of revenue/inhabited villages and total number of Gram Panchayats is shown in Table 2.6.

Physiographically, the state is divided into 4 major and 11 meso divisions as shown in Fig. 2.1 and Chart 2.1. The western desert accounts for 58 per cent of the total area and 40 per cent of the population of the state. It comprises of 12 districts viz. Jaisalmer, Barmer, Jalor, Pali, Jodhpur, Nagaur, Jhunjhunu, Churu, Sikar, Bikaner, Hanumangarh and Ganganagar.

The Aravalli range of hills, one of the oldest mountain systems of the world, is the most conspicuous physiographic feature of the state. It consists of parallel hills with high dimensions of folds, stretching diagonally across the state from the south-west to the north-east direction over a distance of about 690 kms. This division comprises of 9 districts, namely, Sirohi, Banswara, Dungarpur, Chittaurgarh, Udaipur, Rajsamand, Ajmer, Jaipur and Alwar. The Aravalli ranges divide Rajasthan into two natural divisions viz., the northwest, which comprises of about three-fifths of the state, and the south-east, which covers about two-fifths.

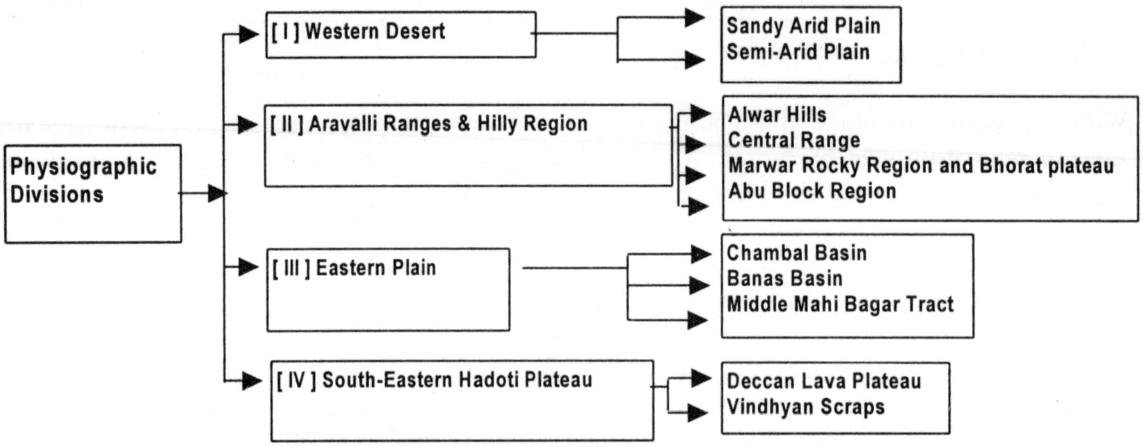

CHART 2.1: Physiographic Divisions: Rajasthan

The eastern plain accounts for 24 per cent of area and 42 per cent of the total population of the state. It is mostly tabular to plain ground surface through which flow the important river courses of the state like Banas, Berach, Gambhiri, Chambal, etc. This region comprises of Bharatpur, Dhaulpur, Karauli, Dausa, Sawai Madhopur and Tonk districts and plainy areas of Jaipur, Alwar, Bhilwara, Kota and Bundi districts.

The south-eastern Hadoti plateau region comprising of Kota, Jhalawar, Baran and Bundi districts contains 9.6 per cent of the area of the state. The tableland has a very diverse topography, broad depressions and level stretches of deep black soil.

Out of the total population, 52 per cent are males. Rural-urban population ratio in the state is 77 : 23. The decadal percentage growth rate of the state has declined from 28.44 in 1981-91 to 28.41 in 1991-2001 (Table 2.7).

The sex-ratio in the state is highly adverse *i.e.,* 1000 male to 922 female, whereas for the country as a whole it is 933. Except Dungarpur, Banswara, Udaipur, Sirohi, Sikar, Nagaur, Jhunjhunu and Churu districts, the state continues to be a male dominated state. This is an important indicator of gender status. Obviously, there is neglect of the girl child. There are various structural and institutional dimensions, which have created inequality between male and female in Rajasthan. The purdah system, child marriage, widowhood, dowry and sati practices have been responsible for the low status of women in Rajasthan.

TABLE 2.6: District-wise Top and Bottom PSs by Total Rural Pop., 0-6 Pop., Villages and Gram Panchayats

District	*(A) Total Rural Pop.*		*(B) % Share of 0-6 Pop. To Total Pop*		*(C) No. of Revenue/ Inhabited Villages*		*(D) Total No. of Gram Panchayats*	
	Top	*Bottom*	*Top*	*Bottom*	*Top*	*Bottom*	*Top*	*Bottom*
Ajmer	Pisangan*	Arian*	Jawaja*	Kekri	Jawaja	Srinagar	Pisangan	Arian
Alwar	Tijara*	Kotkasim*	Tijara*	Behror	Tijara	Nimrana	Lachmangarh	Kotkasim
Banswara	Garhi*	Anandpuri*	Kushalgarh	Garhi	Ghatol, Talwara #	Anandpuri	Garhi and Talwara	Anandpuri
Baran	Anta*	Chhabra	Shahbad	Baran	Shahbad, Chhabra##	Baran	Anta	Baran, Chhabra and Shahbad
Barmer	Balotra*	Sheo	Sheo	Siwana*	Baytoo	Siwana	Balotra	Siwana
Bharatpur	Nagar Pharai*	Deeg	Kama	Nadbai*	Nagar Pharai	Nadbai	Nagar Pharai	Sewar
Bhilwara	Mandalgarh*	Raipur	Asind	Sahara	Mandalgarh	Hurda	Mandalgarh	Hurda
Bikaner	Bikaner*	Kolayat	Nokha*	Bikaner	Bikaner	Nokha	Bikaner	Dungargarh
Bundi	Talera*	Nainwa*	Hindoli	Keshoraipatan	Talera	Hindoli	Talera	Nainwa
Chittaurgarh	Pratapgarh*	Bhopalsagar*	Arnod	Kapasan	Pratapgarh	Rashmi*, Bhopalsagar	Pratapgarh	Bhopalsagar
Churu	Rajgarh*	Taranagar*	Dungargarh*	Rajgarh	Rajgarh	Dungargarh	Rajgarh	Taranagar
Dausa	Dausa*	Mahwa*	Lalsot*	Bandikui	Lalsot	Sikrai	Dausa	Sikrai, Mahwa
Dhaulpur	Dhaulpur*	Bari*	Bari	Rajakhera	Dhaulpur	Bari	Dhaulpur	Bari
Dungarpur	Simalwara*	Dungarpur*	Simalwara	Sagwara	Simalwara	Aspur	Simalwara	Dungarpur
Ganganagar	Anupgarh*	Karanpur*	Anupgarh	Sadulshahar	Anupgarh	Karanpur	Anupgarh	Sadulshahar
Hanumangarh	HN*	Bhadra*	Nohar	Bhadra	HN	Bhadra	HN	Bhadra
Jaipur	Govindgarh	Jhotwara*	Viratnagar	Sambhar	Chaksu	Jhotwara	Dudu	Jhotwara
Jaisalmer	Sankra*	Jaisalmer*	Sankra	Jaisalmer	Sam*	Jaisalmer	Sam	Sankra
Jalor	Sanchore*	Jaswantpura	Bhinmal	Ahore	Sanchore	Jalore*	Sanchore	Jalore
Jhalawar	Jhalrapatan	Bakani	Manohar—thana	Dag	Bakani	Khanpur	Jhalrapatan	Khanpur
Jhunjhunun	Udaipurwati*	Alsisar	Udaipurwati	Buhana*	Jhunjhunun	Udaipurwati	Buhana	Chirawa
Jodhpur	Osian*	Mandore*	Bap	Bilara	Osian	Bhopalgarh	Osian	Mandore
Karauli	Hindaun*	Nadouti*	Karauli	Nadoti	Sapotra	Nadauti	Sapotra	Nadoti
Kota	Itawa*	Chechat*	Chechat	Itawa	Sangod*	Chechat	Chechat and Sangod	Ladpura
Nagaur	Didwana*	Ladnu*	Nagaur	Riyan	Kuchaman	Ladnu	Didwana	Ladnu
Pali	Jaitaran	Pali*	Rohat*	Rani Station	Kharchi/ Marwar*	Sumerpur	Kharchi/ Marwar	Rohat and Pali
Rajsamand	Khamnor*	Deogarh*	Bhim	Railmagra*	Khamnor	Railmagra	Khamnor	Deogarh
Sawai Madhopur	S. M*	Bamanwas*	Gangapur*	Bamanwas	Bonli, Khandar*# #	Gangapur	S. Madhopur	Khandar
Sikar	Neem Ka Thana*	Fatehpur*	Khendala	Dhond	Danta Ramgarh	Sri Madhopur*	Neem Ka Thana	Sri Madhopur
Sirohi	Pindwara	Sheoganj*	Abu Road*	Sheoganj	Reodar*	Sheoganj	Reodar	Sheoganj
Tonk	Tonk*	Todarai-singh*	Niwai	Todarai-singh	Tonk	Todarai-singh	Tonk	Todarai-singh*
Udaipur	Kherwara*	Bargaon*	Kotra*	Mavli	Kotra	Bargaon	Kherwara	Bargaon

Source: Annex 2.1 to 2.5

\# PS having Top only in Total No. of Revenue Villages

\# # PS having Top only in Total No. of Inhabited Villages

* Prominent PS having Top/Bottom in two or more than two indicators

TABLE 2.7: Growth of Population in Rajasthan

S.No.	*Year*	*Population (million No.)*	*Decennial Growth (%)*
1	*2*	*3*	*4*
1	1951	16.0	15.20
2	1961	20.2	26.20
3	1971	25.8	27.83
4	1981	34.3	32.97
5	1991	44.0	28.44
6	2001	56.5	28.41

Source: *Economic Review*, 2004-05.

BOX 2.2: Important Health Indicators: Rajasthan *Vis-a-Vis* India

Indicators		*Rajasthan*	*India*
Sex Ratio (2001)	0-6 Population	909	927
Life Expectancy at Birth (2001-06)	Female	62.8	66.91
	Male	62.17	63.87
Infant Mortality Rate (per 1000 live births, 2002)	Female	80	65
	Male	75	62
	Rural	81	69
	Urban	55	40
Crude Death Rate (per 1000), 2002 (Provisional)	Rural	8.0	NA
	Urban	6.4	NA
Crude Birth Rate (per 1000), 2002 (Provisional)	Rural	31.9	26.6
	Urban	24.2	19.9
Female Age at Effective Marriage, SRS, 2002	Rural	19.1	19.4
	Urban	20.5	21.1
GFR (General Fertility Rate), SRS, 1998	Rural	142.8	115.2
	Urban	97.8	79.2
TFR (Total Fertility Rate)*	Rural	4.4	3.5
	Urban	2.9	2.3
TMFR (Total Marital Fertility Rate)*	Rural	5.2	5.0
	Urban	4.1	4.2
GRR (Gross Reproduction Rate)*	Rural	2.1	1.7
	Urban	1.4	1.1
Neo-natal Mortality Rates*	Rural	52	49
	Urban	32	27
Peri-natal Mortality Rates*	Rural	40	44
	Urban	30	26
Still birth Rates*	Rural	6	9
	Urban	9	7
%age of Neo-natal Deaths to Infant Deaths*	Rural	63.1	65.8
	Urban	54.4	63.0
%age of Live Births by Various Maternal Care Indicators **			
• % Receiving Antenatal Care		48	65
• % Receiving 2 Doses of TT Vaccine		52	67
• % Receiving Iron/Folic Tablets		39	58
• % of Births Delivered in Medical Institutions		22	34
• % of Deliveres Assisted by Health Professionals		36	42
%age of Children Age, 12-23 Months who Received Full Immunisation, ##	17.3	42	
CPR (Couple Protection Rate)**		40.3	48.2
ANC (Ante Natal Care)**		47.5	65.4
%age of Currently Married Women with any Reproductive Health problem**		43.2	39.2

BCG, Measles and Three Doses Each of DPT and Polio Vaccines. * SRS, 2000, ** NFHS-2, 1998-99

Source: 1. *'SRS Bulletin'* Oct 2002 & 2003 Vol. 36 & 37, No. 2, RGI, New Delhi, 2. 'NFHS-2', Oct. 2000, IIPS, Mumbai. 3. Hemlata Joshi. 2007. *'Health Status Index-Rajasthan* (Spatio-Temporal Appraisal at Panchayat Samiti/Block Level), Published Research Report, IDS, Jaipur, Concept Publishing Company, New Delhi.

BOX 2.3: Medical and Health Scenario: Rajasthan

(A) Medical Institutions, Beds & Doctors (2004-05)

Particulars	*(No.)*	*Particulars*	*(No.)*
Hospitals (No. of CHC)	215(95)	No.of Beds	38873
Dispensaries	209	No.of Doctors	6176
Mother & Child Welfare Centres	118	Population (in million No.)	56.507
Primary Health Centres (Upgraded PHC)	1677(203)	Budget (in million Rs.)	11448.928
Urban Primary Health Centres	29	Per Person Budget (Rs.)	202.61
Sub Centres	10387	Population Served Per Bed	1454
Total No. of Medical Institutions	12635	Population Served Per Doctor	9149
Family Welfare Centres	293	Population Served Per Medical Inst.	4468

(B) Achievements of FWPs: Raj., 1985-04 ('000 No.)

Year	Sterilisation	IUD Inserted	OP Users	Nirodh Users
1985-86	267.9	95.6	13.6	178.0
2003-04	300.1	265.8	713.7	1459.8
2004-05 (Upto Jan. 05)	233.1	226.2	399.3 (New Users)	446.0 (New Users)

(C) Ayurvedic/Unani/Homeopathic and Prakritik Institutions, 2003-04 (Nos.)

Hospitals	: 85	Vaidyas/Hakeems	: 3838
Dispensaries	: 3648	Nurses/Compounders	: 3980
Mobile Units	: 7	Patients treated, 2001	: 5761
Beds	: 1186		

Source: 1. *'Pragati Prativedan'*, 2004-05, Directorate of Medical and Health, GoR, Jaipur.
2. *Pragati Prativedan,* 2004-05, Directorate of Medical, Health and Family Welfare Services Raj., Jaipur.
3. Some facts about Raj., 2004, DES, Jaipur.

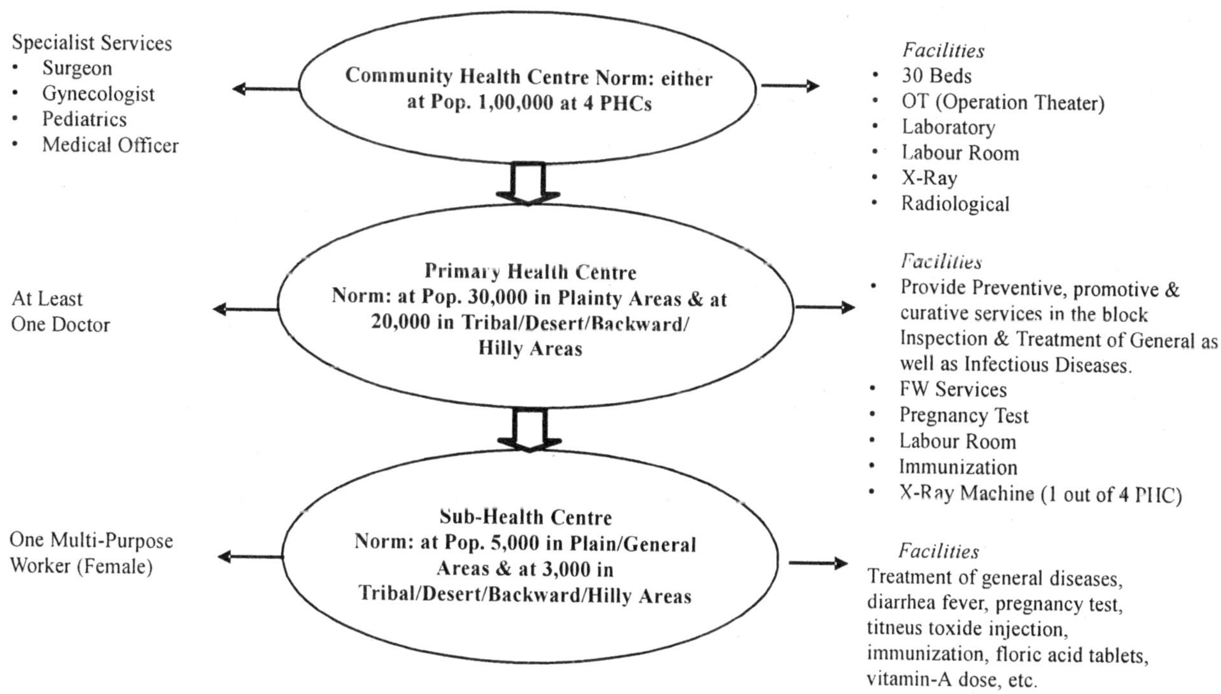

MODEL 2.1: 3-Tier Structure of Rural Health System

BOX 2.4: Educational Scenario: Rajasthan

(A) Literacy Rate

	1951	*1991*	*2001*
Total	8.5	38.6	60.4
Male	13.9	55.0	75.7
Female	2.7	20.4	43.9

(B) Educational Institutions (2004-05)

Institutions	*Number*	*Enrollment (in Mln No.)*	*Teachers (in '000 No.)*
Pre- Primary & Primary Schools	34743	9.97	120.37
Upper Primary Schools	28414	2.7	154.92
Secondary/Sr. Hr. Secondary Schools	9752	3.5	114.25
College Education #(Arts, Science & Commerce Colleges)	509	286	3.9*

(C) Adult Education

Particulars	*Enrollment (Mln No.)*
Total literacy Campaign	8.1
Post Literacy programme	5.4
Continuing Education	2.8
No. of Neo-literates	6.5

for the year 2003-04, * Govt. Degree & P.G. Colleges

Source: 1. *Economic Review,* 2004-05

2. Some Facts About Raj., 2004, DES, Jaipur.

3. Annex K-7 & K-10.

Rajiv Gandhi Prarambhic Shiksha and Saksharta Mission (RGPSSM) was established in the state in the year 2000-01. Model 2.2 presents its structure. The specific objective of RGPSSM are as under :

- To act as an apex body for implementation of Elementary Education and Literacy activities in the state.
- To extend the activities of the Mission in the whole of the State through Directorate of Elementary Education, Directorate of Literacy and Continuing Education, Directorate of Panchayati Raj and Projects like DPEP, LJP and SKB.
- To function as a Social Mission for bringing about a fundamental change in the Elementary Education System and through it, in the overall Socio-cultural situation.
- Universalisation of Elementary Education for the age group of 6-14 years through :
  * Improving access to elementary education for all children upto 14 years of age, by making a primary school available within a radius of 1 km. and an upper primary school in each Gram Panchayat.
  * Increasing real enrollment in primary classes to 100 per cent and retention to 90 per cent.
  * Ensuring that 80 per cent of the children complete minimum levels of learning.
  * Making primary education compulsory.
  * Universalizing participation till children complete primary stage through formal and non-formal education programmes.
- To make all the people in age group of 15-35 years literate under Total Literacy Campaign and arrange for their continuing education.

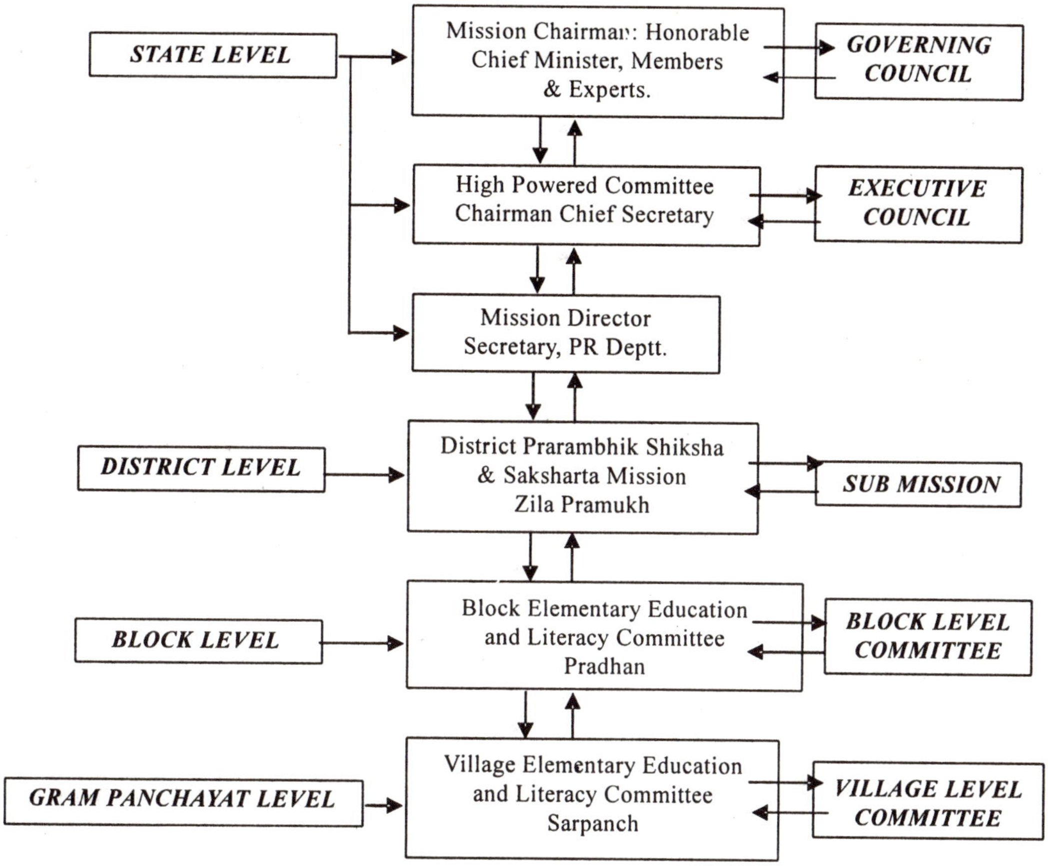

MODEL 2.2: Structure of Rajiv Gandhi Prarambhic Shiksha and Saksharta Mission (RGPSSM)

The human settlement in the state is scattered. Low density of population, vast area and segmented pattern of human settlement are some of the constraints in the development of the state's human development status. Besides higher initial investment for creating infrastructural facilities, the state requires higher per unit expenditure for providing basic services and necessities.

The Chambal is the only large and perennial river of the state. Similarly, the Luni and a large number of tributaries originating in the Aravalli ranges form drainage of the arid region. The Mahi and the Sabi river systems have dissected the southern region into a maze of innumerable valleys. The drainage of the lower area in the south-east of the Aravalli is through various rivers and rivulets flowing in the north-easterly direction.

The state has an amalgamation of arid, semi-arid and sub-humid climates. As mentioned earlier, western Rajasthan has arid climate. Here rainfall is low and varies highly year after year, creating in hospitable living conditions for both human and livestock population. True desert conditions prevail in the extreme western part of the state. The semi-arid region includes the districts of Alwar, Jaipur, Bharatpur, Ajmer, Tonk, Sawai Madhopur, Bhilwara, Bundi, Kota, Chittaurgarh, Udaipur, Sirohi, Dungarpur and part of Jhalawar. While, the sub-humid region covers parts of Jhalawar and Banswara districts of the state.

A short spell of monsoon with low, erratic and scanty rainfall has made Rajasthan the most water-deficient state in the country. The climate of the state with a large variation from region to region is, thus, the driest in the country. The average rainfall in the state is 57.5 cms which is not only meagre but also varies significantly from year to year and from one place to another leading to frequent droughts.

Till now, 37,680 villages and all the 222 cities have been covered under safe drinking water supply. Besides, drinking water has also been made available to about 56, 057 dhanies. During the year 2004-05 (upto December 2004), 7,416 habitations benefited from the drinking water facility.

In the year 2004-05, total cultivable area and agricultural production in the state was 25.4 million hectares and 28.02 million tonnes (excluding 6.5 lakh bales of cotton) respectively. Principal crops cultivated in the state are barley, jowar, millet, maize, gram, wheat, oilseeds, pulses, cotton and tobacco. Cultivation of vegetables and citrus fruits such as orange and malta has also picked up over the last few years. Other crops are red chillies, mustard, cuminseed, methi and hing.

There are four major sources of irrigation viz. canals, tanks, wells and tube-wells. In the year 2002-03, the gross irrigated area in the state was 5.27 million hectares which was only 32.4 per cent of gross cropped area. Out of this gross irrigated area, 73.7 per cent was irrigated by wells and tube-wells, 25.6 per cent by canals, 0.1 per cent by tanks and remaining 0.6 per cent by other sources.

The state has rich deposits of zinc concentrates, lead, emerald, garnet, gypsum, silver ore, asbestos, felspar, mica, salt, rock phosphate, marble, red stone, beryl, quartz, tantanite, lime stone, sand stone and copper. The first Export Promotion Industrial Park (EPIP) of the country has been established and made operational at Sitapura, Jaipur.

BOX 2.5: Economic Scenario: Rajasthan

• Gross Domestic Product at Constant (1993-94) Prices, 2004-05 (Billion Rs.)	657.8
• Gross Domestic Product at Current Prices, 2004-05 (Billion Rs.)	1087.3
• Per Capita Income at Constant (1993-94) Prices (Rs., 2004-05)	9603
• Per Capita NSDP at Current Prices (Rs., 2004-05)	15673
• Gross irrigated area to gross cropped area (%) *	39.89
• Net irrigated area to net area sown (%) *	40.45
• Net area sown to total reporting area (%) *	31.54
• Consumption of fertilizers per hectare of cropped area (kg.) *	41.89
• Per capita foodgrain production (kg.) *	127.47
• Average yield per hectare of principal crops *	
(i) Foodgrains	873
(ii) Oil Seeds	716
(iii) Sugarcane	42226
(iv) Cotton (Lint)	111
• Index No. of agricultural production (Base year 1979-80 to 1981-82 = 100) **	321
• Index No. of industrial production, 2004 (Base year 1993-94)	
(i) Manufacturing	204
(ii) Electricity	157
(iii) Minning	277
• Index No.of wholesale prices, 2004 (Base year 1952-53 = 100)	2734
• Small scale industrial units **	
(i) Total registered ('000 No.)	251
(ii) Total investment (Billion Rs.)	38.35
(iii) Total employment ('000)	963
• Total Road length * ('000)	1529
• Road length per 100 sq. km of agea *	44.7
• Road length per Lakh of population	270.58
• Total rail length, 2001-02 ('000)	5.9
• Post offices **	10450
• Telegraph offices **	702
• Telephone exchanges**	2338
• Telephone Density (sq. km) **	5.94
• Telephone Density (per 100 pop) **	3.6
• Total tourist traffic, 2003 (million No.s)	13.2

* For the year 2002-03, ** For the year 2003-04
Source: Economic Review, 2004-05 and Some facts about Rajasthan, 2004, DES, Jaipur.

Rajasthan is the first state in India to have restructured its entire power sector in one phase. The reforms changed it all. Power generation increased mainfold, transmission and distribution losses came down and revenues shot up sharply. The installed capacity of power in the state upto December 2004 was 5278 MW. Kota and Suratgarh Thermal Power Plants, Mahi Hydel Project, Bhakra, Beas, Chambal and Satpura Projects are the main sources of power supply to the state. Besides, Rajasthan Atomic Power Plant, Singrauli, Rihand,

Anta, Auraiya, Narora, Dadari Gas, Unchahar Thermal and Tanakpur, Salal, Chamera and Uri Projects in central sector are also sharing power with the state.

The state government launched the Industrial Policy 1998 with the aim of rapid industrialisation and for making Rajasthan a preferred destination for investment in the identified sectors so that it could eventually achieve global competitiveness. Major industries identified for this purpose are: textiles and woollens, sugar, cement, glass, oxygen, vegetable dyes, pesticides, zinc, fertilizers, railway wagons, ball bearings, water and electricity metres, sulfuric acid, television sets, synthetic yarn and insulating bricks. Around 220 thousand industrial units were registered with a total investment of Rs. 31000 million and one million persons were employed therein. Some of the important central undertakings are: Zinc Smelter Plant at Debari (Udaipur), Copper Plant at Khetri Nagar (Jhunjhunun) and Instrumentation Limited at Kota.

Rajasthan is an under-developed state in respect of transport and communication. In the absence of internal waterways and inadequate expansion of railways, roads provide a major infrastructural link in the state. The total road length in the state is 1.64 lakh kms as on March, 2005.

The total length of railway routes in the state by the end of March, 2002 was 5894 kms (9.4% of India). Out of the total railway route length in the state, 51 per cent was under broad gauge, 47.4 per cent under metre gauge and 1.5 per cent under narrow gauge. Regular air services connect Jaipur, Jodhpur and Udaipur cities with Delhi and Mumbai.

Rajasthan is one of the most attractive destinations in India for both domestic and international tourists. Many forts and palaces, heritage hotels and the fascination of travelling on the 'Palace on Wheels' have been the unique selling propositions for tourists coming to the state. Visitors also appreciate the colourful fairs and festivals. The variety of ethnic cultures of the people has proved to be a major attraction for the visitors, alongwith the unique desert environment in western Rajasthan. The total arrival of tourists in Rajasthan was 13.2 million (95% domestic and 5% foreign) in the year 2003.

The State Government had worked out a new concept of linking drought relief works with development and utilised the funds on the construction of roads in villages. This helped lakhs of drought victims to secure employment. It also helped in connecting hundreds of villages in the State by link roads.

The National Highway Authority of India (NHAI) has completed work for making the 93 km long Jaipur-Kishangarh (National Highway No. 8) into a 6 lane highway and 431 km long Kishangarh-Chittaurgarh-Udaipur-Ratanpur Highway into a four lane highway. Similarly work on 641 km long East-West corridor Pindwara-Udaipur-Chittaurgarh-Kota, Baran-Shivpur highway into 4-lane highway will be completed by May 2007.

Upto December 2004, sanction of Rs 17.4 billion had been received from the GoI under PMGSY (Pradhan Mantri Gram Sarak Yojana) for connecting 4015 villages by constructing 14 thousand km BT (Black Top) roads against which 2613 villages have already been connected by constructing 9205 km BT roads.

Almost 4,000 km of new roads are being built in nearly 1,200 villages at a cost of Rs. 4 billions. This is besides up-gradation and renewal of 24,000 km of older roads and four-laning of Delhi-Mumbai Highway at a cost of over Rs. 15 billions. by NHAI through Rajasthan.

Various benefits have been provided to diversify rural livelihoods especially in the non-farm sector. Over 24,000 small shops have been constructed under the Swarn Jayanti Gram Swarojgar Yojna and 23,000 have been allotted to BPL beneficiaries, who, with an infusion of credit and subsidy, are running their shops.

Today there are over 84 thousand Self-Help Group (SHGs) in the state with a membership over 8 lakh. About 60 per cent of these groups are of women and 32 per cent groups are of BPL families. Under the Swaran Jayanti Gram Swarojgar Yojana provision has been made to set-up at least two self-help groups at each Gram Panchayat area.

A computer revolution that will make the e-governance dream come true was recently started in the villages of Rajasthan. With STD and ISD rates slashed, the focus is now to provide additional services. Similarly, with the introduction of net telephony, teledensity has been increased significantly.

The State Government in a major drive launched *'Prashasan Gaon Ke Sang Campaign'* (administration at the doorsteps of the villages) in rural areas, benefiting over 7 million population. It has played a vital role in identifying and solving the rural problems. In the rural areas of the state more than 25 centrally and state sponsored schemes are being implemented to eradicate poverty, generate additional employment opportunities, develop basic amenities and to remove regional disparities.

Table 2.8 presents five year plan-wise outlay and expenditure in the state. Since the commencement of First Five Year Plan in 1951, Ninth Five Year Plans and 6 annual plans are already completed. At present, Tenth Five Year Plan (2002-07) is running. The total outlay of this FYP is to the tune of Rs. 318317.5 millions at current prices and Rs. 273180 millions at constant prices.

TABLE 2.8: Five Year Planwise Outlay and Expenditure: Rajasthan

(Million Rs.)

Five Year Plans		*Outlay*	*Total Expenditure*	
			Expenditure	*%age Share to Plan Outlay*
I	(1951-56)	645.0	541.5	84
II	(1956-61)	1052.7	1027.4	98
III	(1961-66)	2360.0	2127.0	90
3 Annual Plans	(1966-69)	1327.2	1367.6	103
IV	(1969-74)	3062.1	3087.9	101
V	(1974-79)	8471.6	8576.2	101
Annual Plan	(1979-80)	2750.0	2901.9	106
VI	(1980-85)	20250.0	21204.5	105
VII	(1985-90)	30000.0	31061.8	104
Annual Plan	(1990-91)	9615.3	9732.2	101
Annual Plan	(1991-92)	11700.0	11844.1	101
VIII	(1992-97)	115000.0	119989.7	104
IX	(1997-02)	276500.0	195668.2 R	71
X	(2002-07)	318317.5 #	44310.7*	13.9*
		273180.0 @	—	—

At Current Prices, @—At Constant Prices, R—Revised, * For the Year 2002-03
Source: Some Facts About Rajasthan, 2004, Directorate of Economics & Statistics, Rajasthan, Jaipur

Details of the Tenth Five Year Plan plan outlay and annual plan 2004-05 is shown in Table 2.9. Out of the total Tenth Five Year Plan outlay, Rs. 67975 millions (21.35%) is earmarked for the above annual plan. Of which, 35.81 per cent share is allotted for social and community services, 28.2 per cent for power and 9.8 per cent is allotted for rural development, agriculture and for special area programme.

TABLE 2.9: Tenth Five Year Plan Outlay and Annual Plan 2004-05

(Million Rs.)

	Sectors	*Plan Outlay*			
		*Tenth Plan (2002-07)**	*(%)*	*Annual Plan*	*(%)*
1.	Agriculture and Allied Services	19340.2	(6.08)	1422.3	(2.09)
2.	Rural Development	26836.9	(8.43)	4911.5	(7.23)
3.	Special Area Programme	1971.8	(0.62)	329.4	(0.48)
4.	Irrigation and Flood Control	34754.4	(10.92)	8647.7	(12.72)
5.	Power	84604.3	(26.58)	19143.7	(28.16)
6.	Industry and Minerals	11135.6	(3.50)	827.8	(1.22)
7.	Transport	29501.0	(9.27)	5317.9	(7.82)
8.	Scientific Services and Research	141.8	(0.04)	10.2	(0.02)
9.	Social and Community Services	96428.0	(30.29)	24339.3	(35.81)
10.	Economic Services	12583.2	(3.95)	2616.3	(3.85)
11.	General Services	1020.3	(0.32)	408.9	(0.60)
	TOTAL	318317.5	(100)	67975.0	(100)

Source: *Economic Review*, 2004-05 * At Current Prices

3

INFRASTRUCTURE STATUS (1991)

Medical Amenities

	%age of Rural Pop Served by	*%age of Villages# Having Amenities*	*No. of Medical Institutions**
State Average (Rural Raj.)	46	22.7	Per PS 42.4 (Total 10050)
Percentage of AAPs	48	56	44
Top PS	Govindgarh (78.5)	Navalgarh (54.3)	Garhi (104)
Bottom PS	Abu Road (4.4)	Choti Sadri (6.4)	Karanpur (12)

TABLE 3.1: Classification of PSs by Medical Amenities (1991)

(A) %age of Rural Pop Served by			*(B) %age of Villages# Having Amenities*			*(C) Total No. of Medical Institutions**		
Group	*No. of PSs*	*%*	*Group*	*No. of PSs*	*%*	*Group*	*No. of PSs*	*%*
>=60	36	15.2	>=50	2	0.8	>=80	4	1.7
50-60	47	19.8	40-50	14	5.9	60-80	22	9.3
40-50	74	31.2	30-40	35	14.8	40-60	102	43.0
30-40	56	23.6	20-30	88	37.1	20-40	99	41.8
<30	24	10.1	<20	98	41.4	<20	10	4.2
Total	**237**	**100**	**Total**	**237**	**100**	**Total**	**237**	**100**

Source: Annex 3.1 to 3.3

TABLE 3.2: District-wise First and Last PSs by Medical Amenities (1991)

District	*(A) %age of Rural Pop Served by*		*(B) %age of Villages# Having Amenities*		*(C) Total No. of Medical Institutions**	
	First Rank	*Last Rank*	*First Rank*	*Last Rank*	*First Rank*	*Last Rank*
Ajmer	Kekri	Jawaja	Pisangan	Jawaja	Pisangan	Arian
Alwar	Thanagazi	Tijara	Nimrana	Tijara	Kathumar	Kishangah Bas
Banswara	Garhi	Kushalgarh	Garhi	Kushalgarh	Garhi	Sajjangarh
Baran	Atru	Chhabra	Atru	Shahbad	Atru	Shahbad
Barmer	Siwana	Baytoo	Siwana	Baytoo	Siwana	Sheo
Bharatpur	Kumher	Nagar Pharai	Kumher	Nagar Pahari	Rupbas	Kaman
Bhilwara	Banera	Kotri	Banera	Mandalgarh	Mandalgarh	Raipur
Bikaner	Bikaner	Kolayat	Bikaner	Kolayat	Bikaner	Lunkaransar
Bundi	Nainwa	Hindoli	Talera	Hindoli	Talera	Nainwa
Chittaurgarh	Rashmi	Chhoti Sadri	Rashmi	Chhoti Sadri	Pratapgarh	Nimbahera
Churu	Dungargarh	Sardarshahar	Dungargarh	Rajgarh	Sujangarh	Sardarshahar
Dausa	Sikrai	Lalsot	Sikrai	Lalsot	Mahwa	Lalsot
Dhaulpur	Dhaulpur	Rajakhera	Dhaulpur	Rajakhera	Dhaulpur	Rajakhera
Dungarpur	Sagwara	Dungarpur	Sagwara	Simalwara	Aspur	Simalwara
Ganganagar	Ganganagar	Anupgarh	Gangangar	Anupgarh	Raisinghnagar	Karanpur
Hanumangarh	Hanumangarh	Nohar	Bhadra	Hanumangarh	Nohar	Bhadra
Jaipur	Govindgarh	Jhotwara	Govindgarh	Sanganer	Govindgarh	Jhotwara
Jaisalmer	Jaisalmer	Sam	Sankra	Sam	Sankra	Jaisalmer
Jalor	Jalor	Raniwara	Jalor	Raniwara	Ahore	Raniwara
Jhalawar	Khanpur	Manoharthana	Pirawa	Bakani	Dag	Khanpur
Jhunjhunun	Nawalgarh	Surajgarh	Nawalgarh	Alsisiar	Jhunjhunun	Surajgarh
Jodhpur	Bilara	Bap	Bilara	Mandor	Osian	Bap
Karauli	Nadoti	Karauli	Hindaun	Sapotra	Karauli	Hindaun
Kota	Chechat	Sangod	Chechat	Sangod	Itawa	Ladpura
Nagaur	Merta	Didwana	Ladnu	Makrana	Kuchaman	Mundwa
Pali	Bali	Rohat	Sumerpur	Rohat	BaliandKharchi	Rohat
Rajsamand	Khamnor	Deogarh	Khamnor	Deogarh	Khamnor	Deogarh
Sawai Madhopur	Gangapur	Bonli	Gangapur	Bonli	Sawai Madhopur	Bamanwas
Sikar	Dhond	Lachhmangarh	Dhond	Lachhmangarh	Danta Ramgarh	Khandela
Sirohi	Sheoganj	Abu Road	Sheoganj	Reodar	Pindwara	Abu Road
Tonk	Deoli	Uniara	Malpura	Niwai	DeoliandTonk	Todaraisingh
Udaipur	Girwa	Kotra	Mavli	Kotra	JhadolandKherwara	Kotra

Source: General Annex II, III and IV   * Include despensary, hospital, MCWC, PHC and SHC   # Inhabited villages

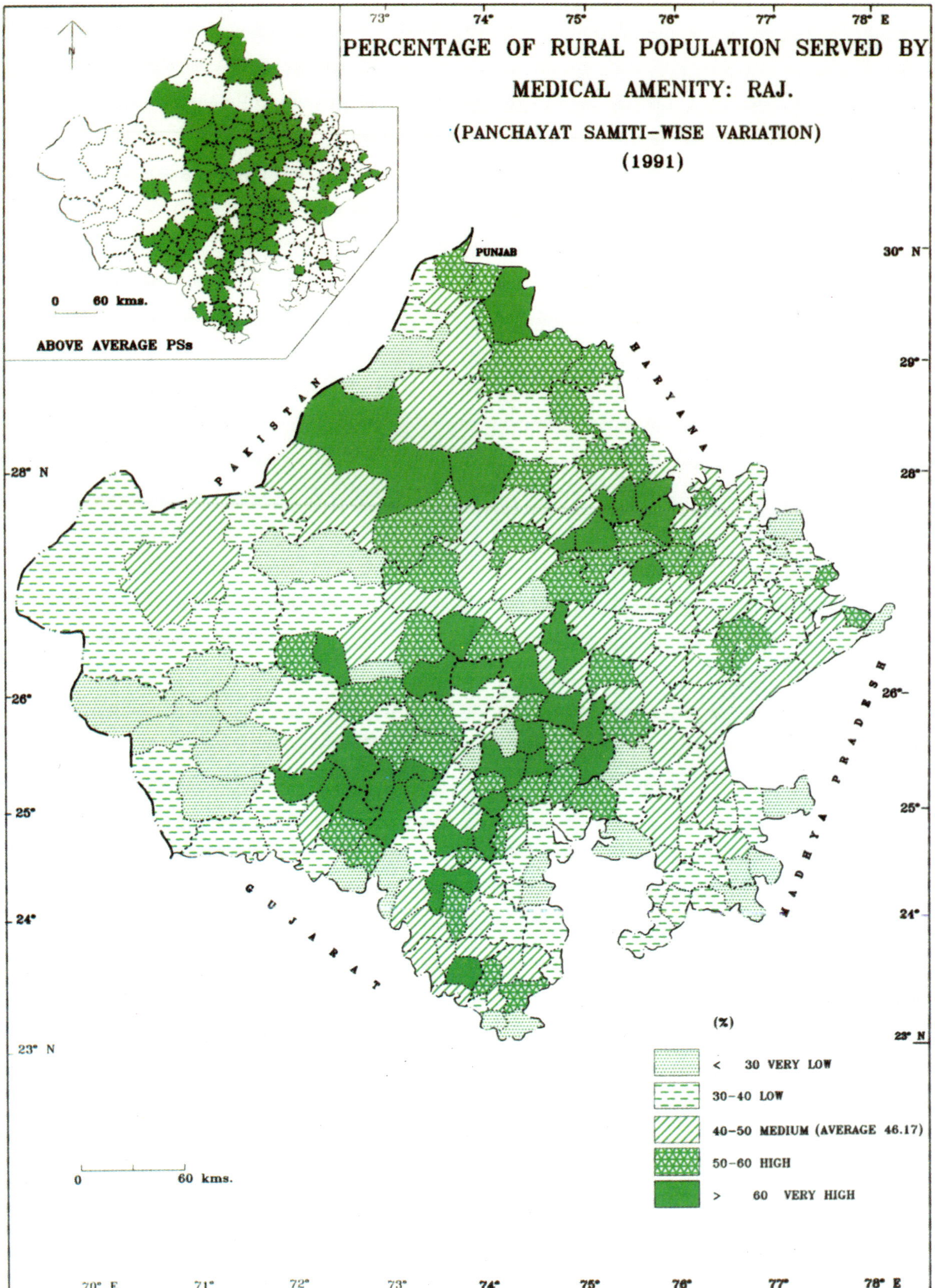
PERCENTAGE OF RURAL POPULATION SERVED BY
MEDICAL AMENITY: RAJ.
(PANCHAYAT SAMITI-WISE VARIATION)
(1991)
ABOVE AVERAGE PSs
0 60 kms.
PUNJAB
HARYANA
PAKISTAN
GUJARAT
MADHYA PRADESH
(%)
< 30 VERY LOW
30-40 LOW
40-50 MEDIUM (AVERAGE 46.17)
50-60 HIGH
> 60 VERY HIGH
0 60 kms.

FIG. 3.1

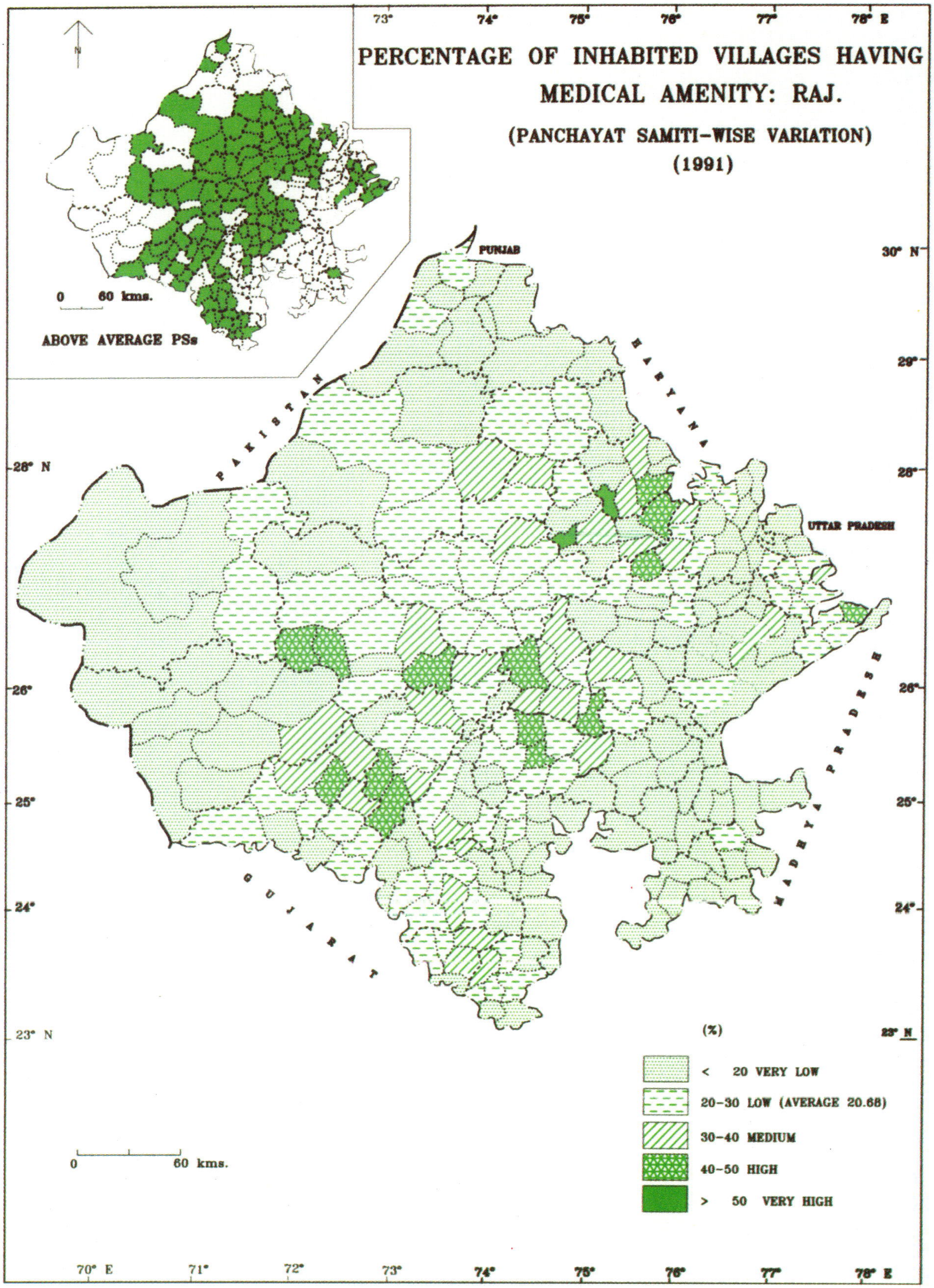
PERCENTAGE OF INHABITED VILLAGES HAVING MEDICAL AMENITY: RAJ.
(PANCHAYAT SAMITI-WISE VARIATION)
(1991)
ABOVE AVERAGE PSs
0 60 kms.
PUNJAB
HARYANA
UTTAR PRADESH
MADHYA PRADESH
GUJARAT
PAKISTAN
(%)
< 20 VERY LOW
20-30 LOW (AVERAGE 20.68)
30-40 MEDIUM
40-50 HIGH
> 50 VERY HIGH
0 60 kms.
70° E
71°
72°
73°
74°
75°
76°
77°
78° E
30° N
29°
28° N
26°
25°
24°
23° N

FIG. 3.2

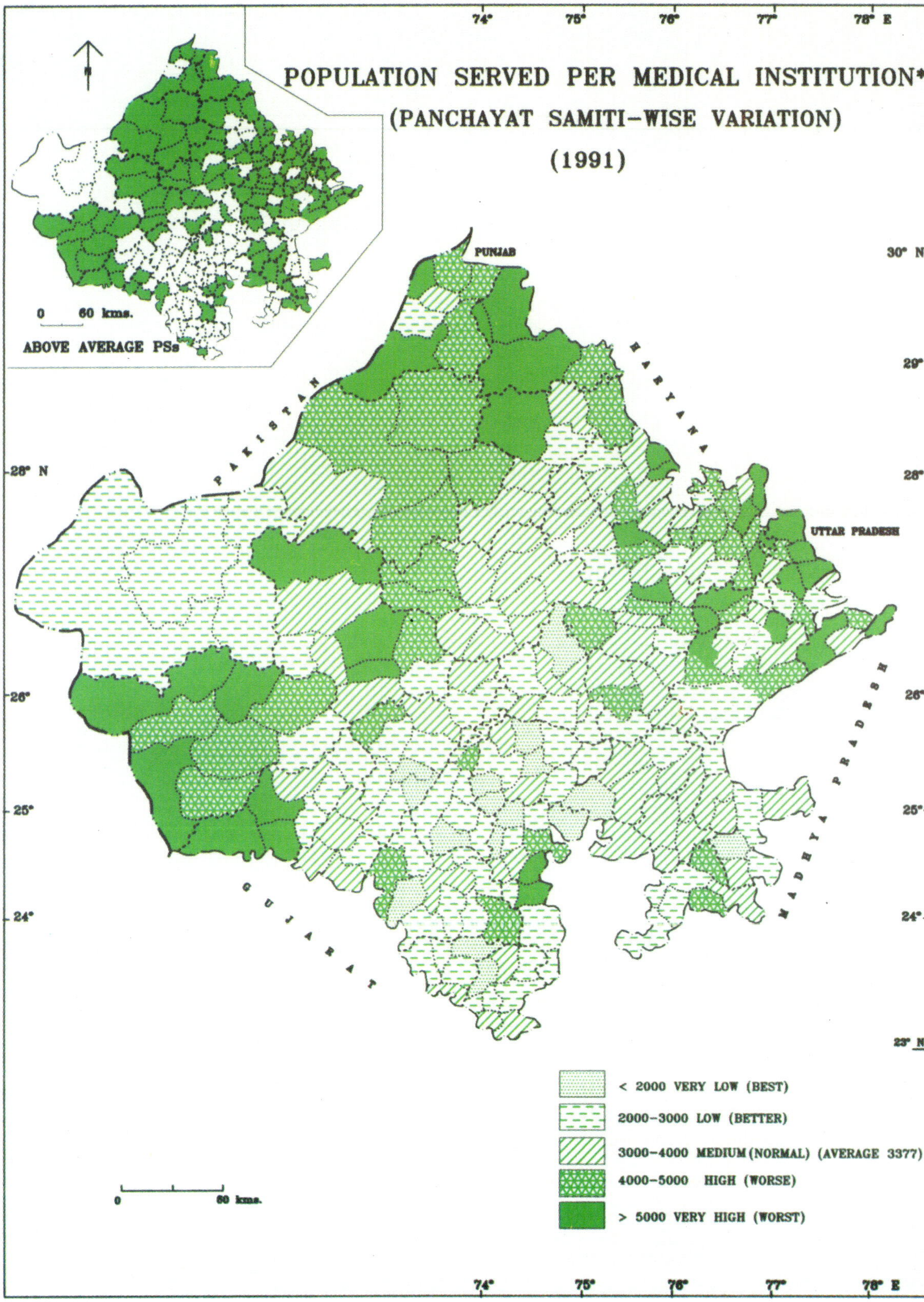

Note: *Medical Institution Includes Hospital, Dispensary , PHC, CHC and MCW Centre.

FIG. 3.3

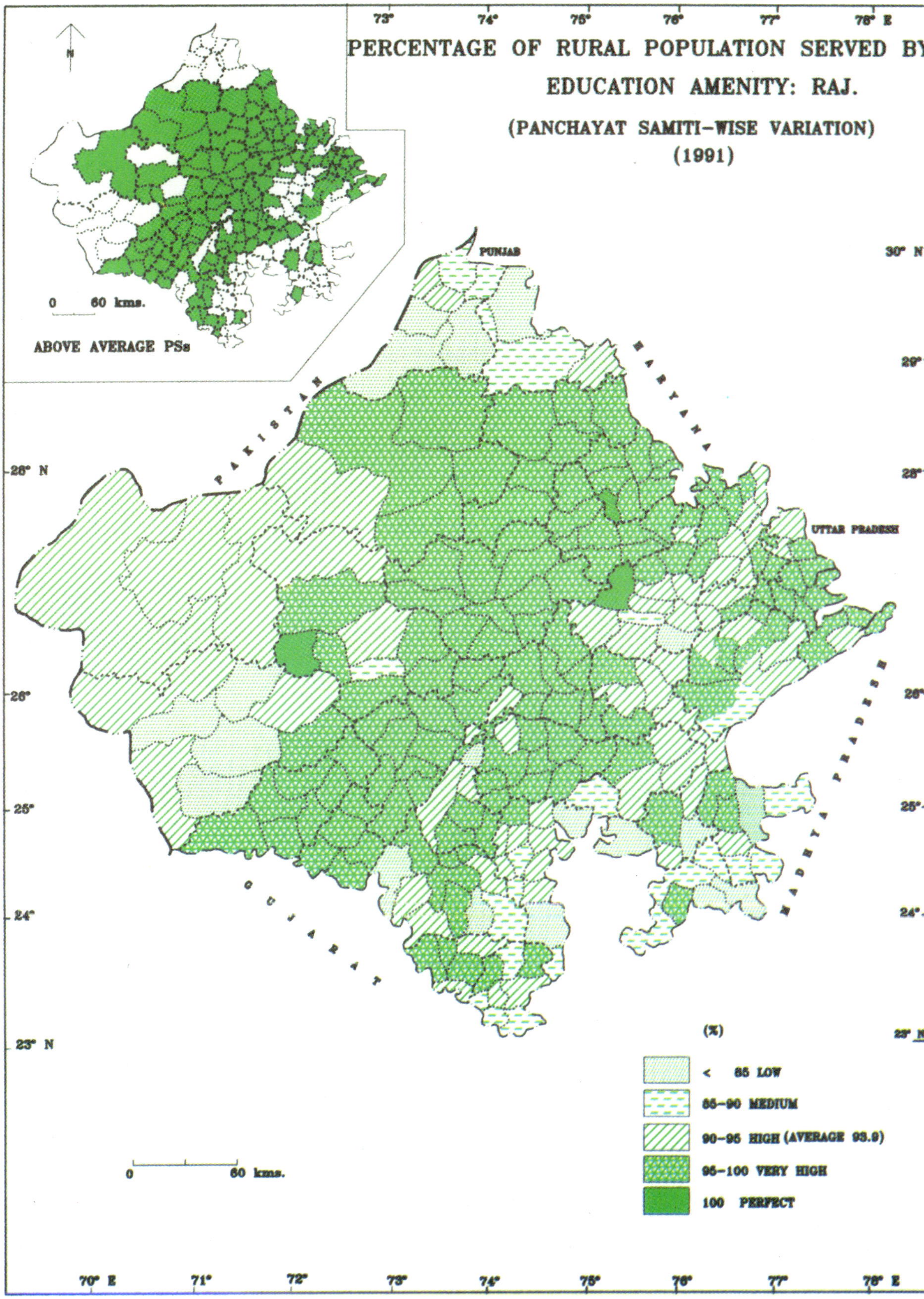
PERCENTAGE OF RURAL POPULATION SERVED BY EDUCATION AMENITY: RAJ.
(PANCHAYAT SAMITI-WISE VARIATION)
(1991)
ABOVE AVERAGE PSs
0 60 kms.
N
PUNJAB
HARYANA
UTTAR PRADESH
MADHYA PRADESH
GUJARAT
PAKISTAN
(%)
< 85 LOW
85-90 MEDIUM
90-95 HIGH (AVERAGE 93.9)
95-100 VERY HIGH
100 PERFECT
0 60 kms.
70° E
71°
72°
73°
74°
75°
76°
77°
78° E
30° N
29°
28° N
26°
25°
24°
23° N

FIG. 3.4

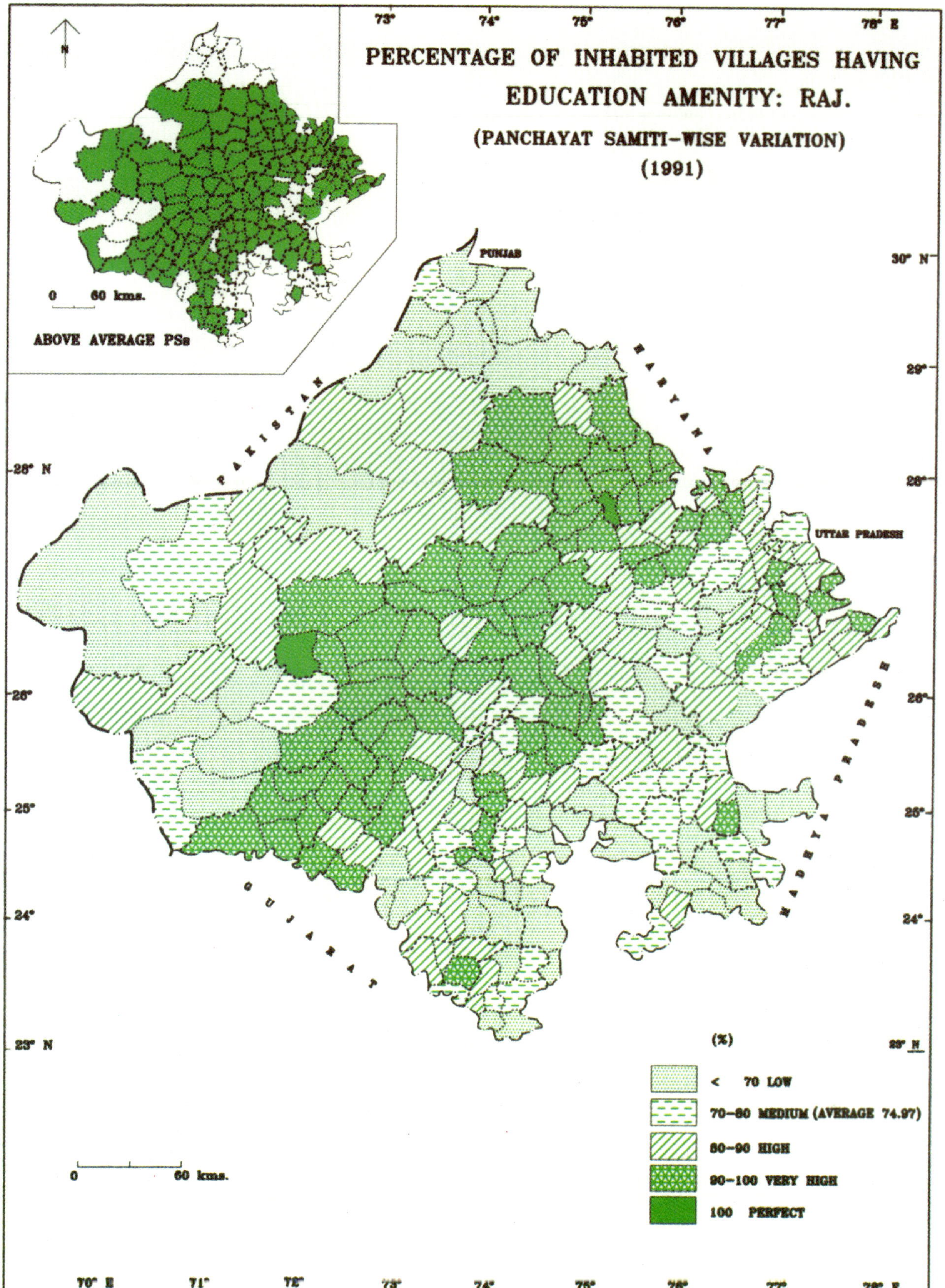
PERCENTAGE OF INHABITED VILLAGES HAVING EDUCATION AMENITY: RAJ.
(PANCHAYAT SAMITI-WISE VARIATION)
(1991)
ABOVE AVERAGE PSs
0 60 kms.
PUNJAB
HARYANA
UTTAR PRADESH
MADHYA PRADESH
GUJARAT
PAKISTAN
(%)
< 70 LOW
70-80 MEDIUM (AVERAGE 74.97)
80-90 HIGH
90-100 VERY HIGH
100 PERFECT
0 60 kms.

FIG. 3.5

Education Amenities

	%age of Rural Pop Served by	*%age of Villages# Having Amenities*	*No. of Pr. Schools*
State Average (Rural Raj.)	94	75	Per PS 129.4 (Total 30667)
Percentage of AAPs	64	74	48.5
Top PS	Navalgarh and Shergarh (100)	Navalgarh and Shergarh (100)	Anupgarh (293)
Bottom PS	Anupgarh (56.5)	Hanumangarh (25.8)	Sumerpur (55)

TABLE 3.3: Classification of PSs by Education Amenities (1991)

(A) %age of Rural Pop Served by			*(B) %age of Villages# Having Amenities*			*(C) Total No. of Pr. Schools*		
Group	*No. of PSs*	*%*	*Group*	*No. of PSs*	*%*	*Group*	*No. of PSs*	*%*
100	2	0.8	100	2	0.8	>=400	—	—
95-100	134	56.5	90-100	82	34.6	300-400	—	—
90-95	60	25.3	80-90	62	26.2	200-300	6	2.5
85-90	22	9.3	70-80	41	17.3	100-200	180	75.9
< 85	19	8.0	< 70	50	21.1	< 100	51	21.5
Total	**237**	**100**	**Total**	**237**		**Total**	**237**	**100**

Source: Annex 3.4 to 3.6

TABLE 3.4: District-wise First and Last PSs by Education Amenities (1991)

District	*(A) %age of Rural Pop Served by*		*(B) %age of Villages# Having Amenities*		*(C) Total No. of Pr. Schools*	
	First Rank	*Last Rank*	*First Rank*	*Last Rank*	*First Rank*	*Last Rank*
Ajmer	Srinagar	Jawaja	Srinagar	Jawaja	Pisangan	Srinagar
Alwar	Behror	Tijara	Mandawar	Rajgarh	Lacchmangarh	Nimrana
Banswara	Garhi	Peepalkhoont	Garhi	Peepalkhoont	Ghatol and Talwara	Anandpuri
Baran	Baran	Kishanganj	Baran	Kishanganj	Chhabara	Baran and Shahbad
Barmer	Siwana	Baytoo	Siwana	Baytoo	Barmer	Siwana
Bharatpur	Kumher	Kaman	Kumher	Kaman	Nagar Pahari	Nadbai
Bhilwara	Hurda	Mandalgarh	Hurda	Mandalgarh	Asind	Hurda
Bikaner	Nokha	Kolayat	Lunkaransar	Kolayat	Bikaner	Kolayat
Bundi	Hindoli	Talera	Nainwa	Keshoraipatan	Talera	Hindoli
Chittaurgarh	Rashmi	Bhainsrorgarh	Rashmi	Bhainsrorgarh	Pratapgarh	Rashmi
Churu	Churu	Sardarshahar	Dungargarh	Taranagar	Rajgarh	Ratangarh
Dausa	Sikrai	Bandikui	Mahwa	Lalsot	Lalsot	Sikrai
Dhaulpur	Dhaulpur	Bari	Dhaulpur	Basari	Dhaulpur	Bari
Dungarpur	Sagwara	Aspur	Sagwara	Simalwara	Simalwara	Aspur
Ganganagar	Padampur	Anupgarh	Karanpur	Anupgarh	Anupgarh	Sadulshahar
Hanumangarh	Bhadra	Hanumangarh	Bhadra	Hanumangarh	Nohar	Bhadra
Jaipur	Shahpura	Chaksu	Shahpura	Chaksu	Jamwa Ramgarh	Jhotwara
Jaisalmer	Sankra	Sam	Sankra	Sam	Sam	Jaisalmer
Jalor	Raniwara	Bhinmal	Raniwara	Sanchore	Sanchore	Jaswantpura
Jhalawar	Pirawa	Manoharthana	Pirawa	Bakani	Jhalrapatan	Khanpur
Jhunjhunun	Nawalgarh*	Jhunjhunun	Nawalgarh	Jhunjhunun	Jhunjhunun	Chirawa
Jodhpur	Shergarh*	Osian	Shergarh	Bap	Osian	Shergarh
Karauli	Hindaun	Karauli	Hindaun	Sapotra	Sapotra	Nadoti
Kota	Ladpura	Sangod	Ladpura	Sangod	Sangod	Ladpura
Nagaur	Degana	Merta	Parabatsar	Merta	Didwana	Merta
Pali	Bali	Raipur	Bali	Raipur	Kharchi/Marwar	Sumerpur
Rajsamand	Rajsamand	Deogarh	Railmagra	Deogarh	Kumbhalgarh	Deogarh
Sawai Madhopur	Gangapur	Khandar	Gangapur	Khandar	Sawai Madhopur	Khandar
Sikar	Sri Madhopur	Neem Ka Thana	Fatehpur	Khandela	Danta Ramgarh	Sri Madhopur
Sirohi	Abu Road	Reodar	Abu Road	Sirohi	Reodar	Sheoganj
Tonk	Malpura	Uniara	Malpura	Uniara	Tonk	Todarisingh
Udaipur	Mavli	Kotra	Mavli	Kotra	Kherwara	Gogunda

Source: General Annex-II, III and V * PS having almost Perfect (100%) Education Amenities. # Inhabited villages

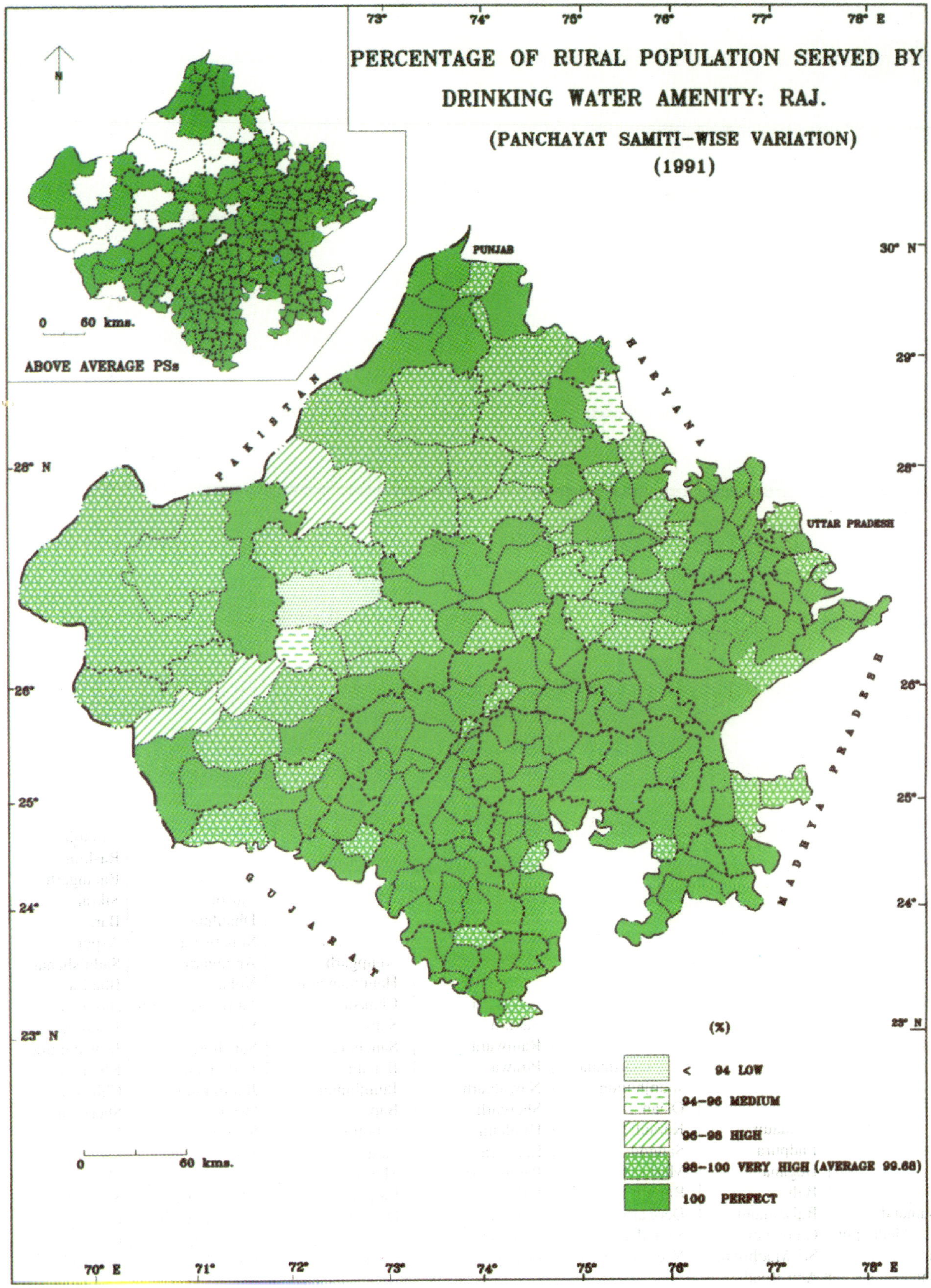
PERCENTAGE OF RURAL POPULATION SERVED BY DRINKING WATER AMENITY: RAJ.
(PANCHAYAT SAMITI-WISE VARIATION)
(1991)
ABOVE AVERAGE PSs
0 60 kms.
PUNJAB
HARYANA
UTTAR PRADESH
MADHYA PRADESH
GUJARAT
PAKISTAN
(%)
< 94 LOW
94-96 MEDIUM
96-98 HIGH
98-100 VERY HIGH (AVERAGE 99.68)
100 PERFECT

FIG. 3.6

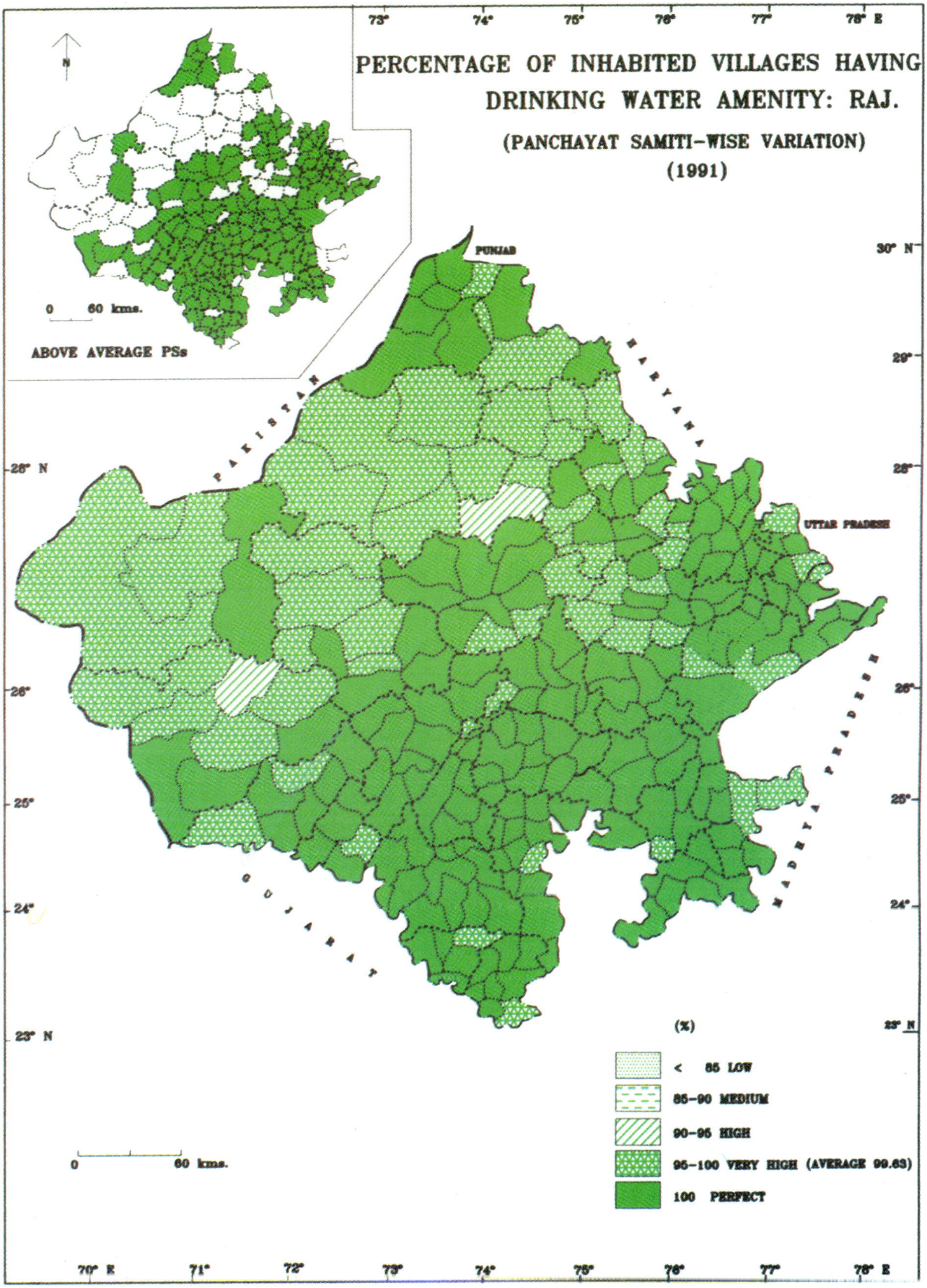
PERCENTAGE OF INHABITED VILLAGES HAVING DRINKING WATER AMENITY: RAJ.
(PANCHAYAT SAMITI-WISE VARIATION)
(1991)
ABOVE AVERAGE PSs
0 60 kms.
N
PUNJAB
HARYANA
UTTAR PRADESH
MADHYA PRADESH
GUJARAT
PAKISTAN
(%)
< 85 LOW
85-90 MEDIUM
90-95 HIGH
95-100 VERY HIGH (AVERAGE 99.63)
100 PERFECT
0 60 kms.
70° E
71°
72°
73°
74°
75°
76°
77°
78° E
30° N
29°
28° N
28°
26°
25°
24°
23° N

FIG. 3.7

Drinking Water Amenities

	%age of Rural Pop Served by	%age of Villages# Having Amenities
State Average (Rural Raj.)	99.7	99.6
Percentage of AAPs	88	76.4
Top PS	180 PSs (100)	181 PSs (100)
Bottom PS	Phalodi (93)	Sujangarh (93.5)

TABLE 3.5: Classification of PSs by Drinking Water Amenities (1991)

(A) %age of Rural Pop Served by			(B) %age of Villages# Having Amenities		
Group	No. of PSs	%	Group	No. of PSs	%
100	180	75.9	100	181	76.4
98-100	51	21.5	95-100	54	22.8
96-98	3	1.3	<95	2	0.8
94-96	2	0.8	—	—	—
<94	1	0.4	—	—	—
Total	**237**	**100**	**Total**	**237**	**100**

Source: Annex 3.7 and 3.8

TABLE 3.6: District-wise First and Last PSs by Drinking Water Amenities (1991)

District	(A) %age of Rural Pop Served by		(B) %age of Villages# Having Amenities	
	First Rank	Last Rank	First Rank	Last Rank
Ajmer	7 PSs*	Jawaja	7 PSs*	Jawaja
Alwar	All PSs*	—	All PSs*	—
Banswara	7 PSs*	Kushalgarh	7 PSs*	Kushalgarh
Baran	5 PSs*	Shahbad	5 PSs*	Shahbad
Barmer	3 PSs*	Baytoo	3 PSs*	Baytoo
Bharatpur	6 PSs*	Kumher	6 PSs*	Kumher
Bhilwara	All PSs*	—	All PSs*	—
Bikaner	Lunkaransar	Kolayat	Lunkaransar	Bikaner
Bundi	All PSs*	—	All PSs*	—
Chittaurgarh	13 PSs*	Nimbahera	13 PSs*	Nimbahera
Churu	Taranagar*	Rajgarh	Sardarshahar	Sujangarh
Dausa	All PSs*	—	All PSs*	—
Dhaulpur	All PSs*		All PSs*	—
Dungarpur	4 PSs*	Aspur	4 PSs*	Aspur
Ganganagar	6 PSs*	Sadulshahar	6 PSs*	Sadulshahar
Hanumangarh	Bhadra and Hn	Nohar	Bhadra and Hn	Nohar
Jaipur	6 PSs*	Phagi	6 PSs*	Sambhar
Jaisalmer	Sankra*	Jaisalmer	Sankra	Jaisalmer
Jalor	5 PSs*	Sanchore	5 PSs*	Sanchore
Jhalawar	All PSs*	—	All PSs*	—
Jhunjhunun	5 PSs*	Surajgarh	5 PSs*	Surajgarh
Jodhpur	Bilara and Jodhpur	Phalodi	4 PSs*	Shehgarh
Karauli	4 PSs*	Sapotra	4 PSs*	Sapotra
Kota	4 PSs*	Chechat	4 PSs*	Chechat
Nagaur	8 PSs*	Parbatsar	8 PSs*	Kuchaman
Pali	All PSs*	—	All PSs*	—
Rajsamand	All PSs*	—	All PSs*	—
Sawai Madhopur	4 PSs*	Bonli	4 PSs*	Bonli
Sikar	5 PSs*	Neem Ka Thana	5 PSs*	Dhond
Sirohi	4 PSs*	Pindwara	4 PSs*	Pindwara
Tonk	All PSs*	—	All PSs*	—
Udaipur	All PSs*	—	All PSs*	—

Source: General Annex-II and III. * PS/PSs having Almost perfect (100%) Drinking Water Amenities. # Inhabited villages

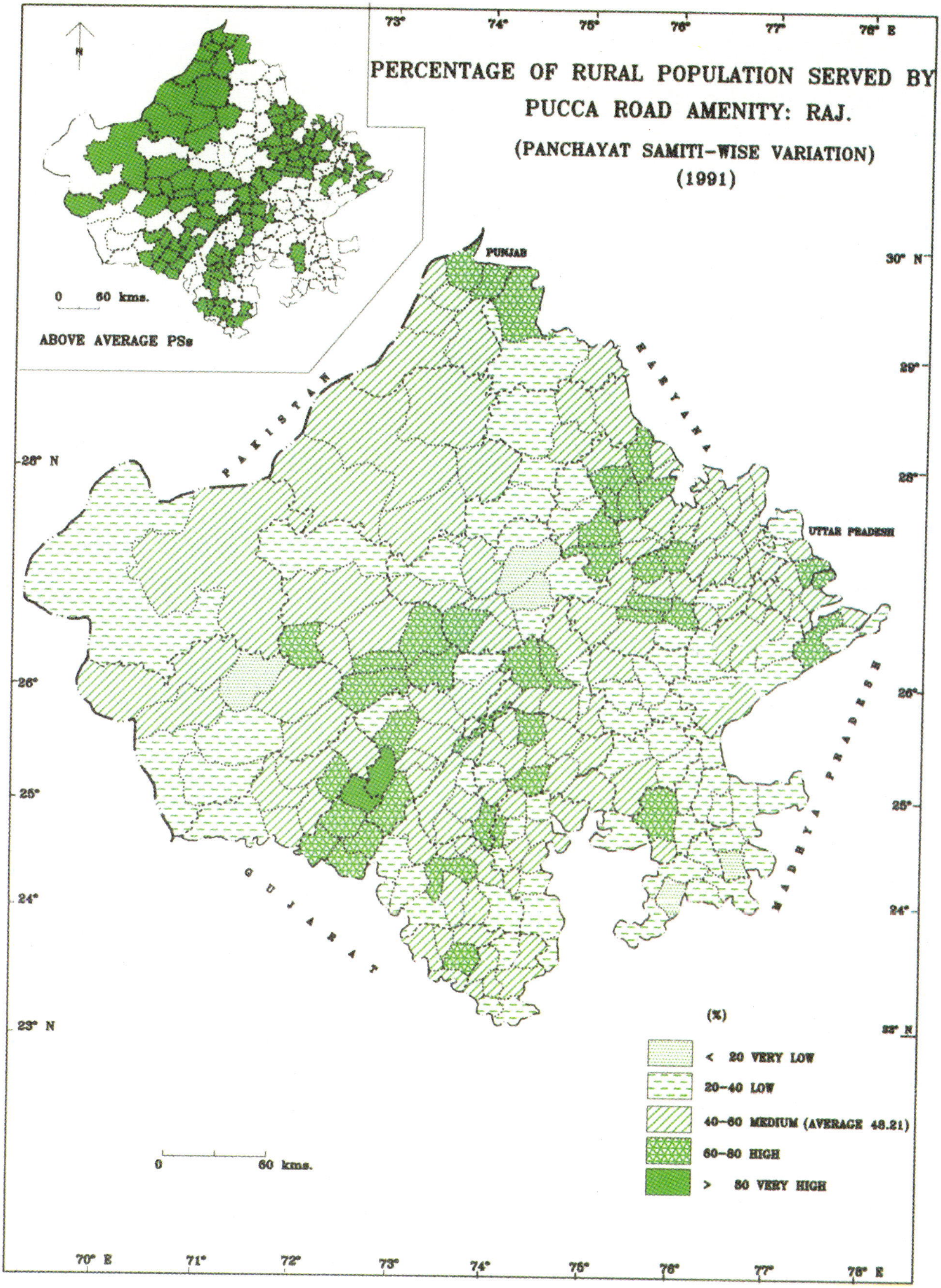
PERCENTAGE OF RURAL POPULATION SERVED BY
PUCCA ROAD AMENITY: RAJ.
(PANCHAYAT SAMITI-WISE VARIATION)
(1991)
ABOVE AVERAGE PSs
0 60 kms.
PUNJAB
HARYANA
UTTAR PRADESH
MADHYA PRADESH
GUJARAT
PAKISTAN
(%)
< 20 VERY LOW
20–40 LOW
40–60 MEDIUM (AVERAGE 48.21)
60–80 HIGH
> 80 VERY HIGH
0 60 kms.

FIG. 3.8

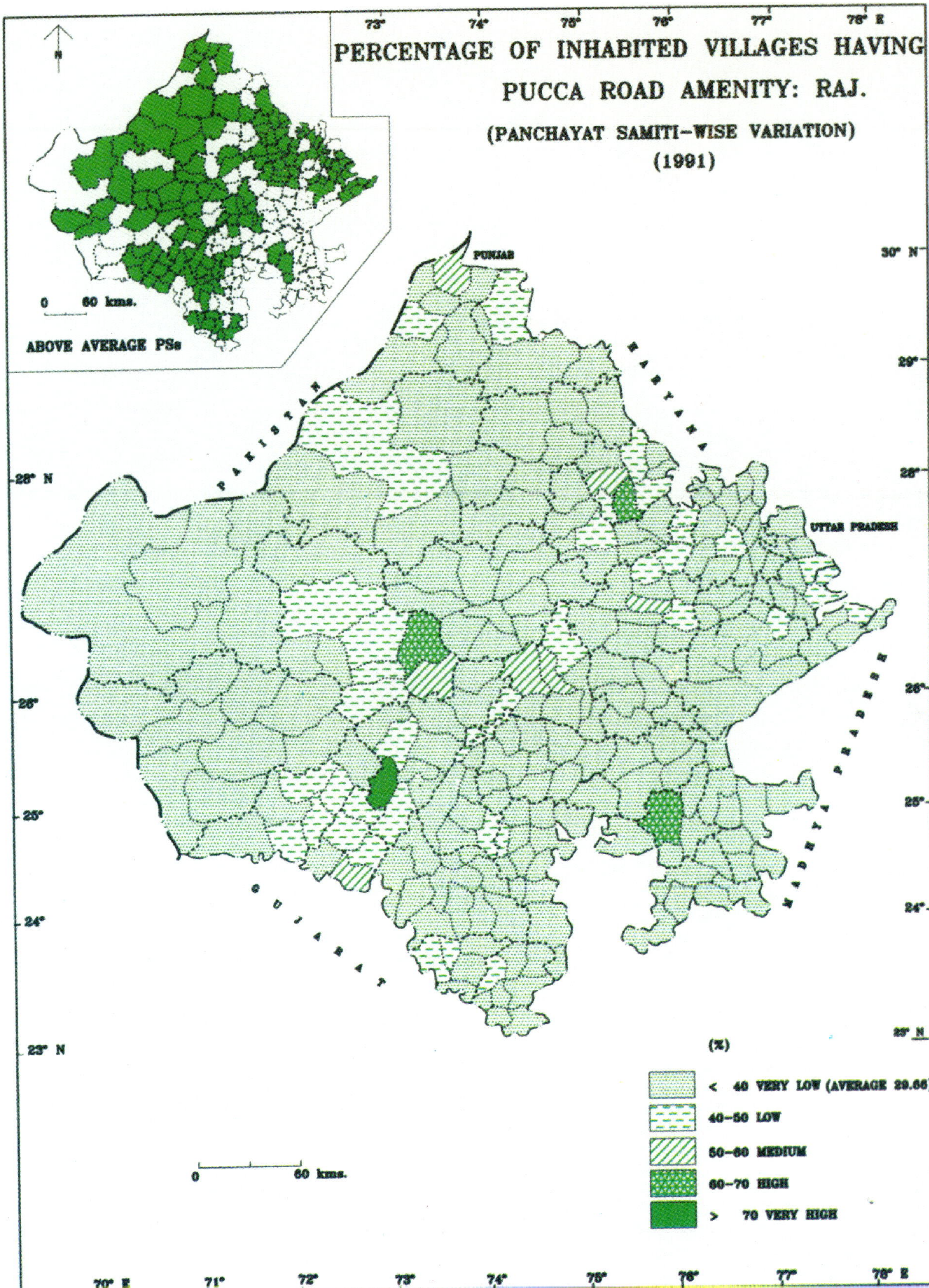
PERCENTAGE OF INHABITED VILLAGES HAVING PUCCA ROAD AMENITY: RAJ.
(PANCHAYAT SAMITI-WISE VARIATION)
(1991)
ABOVE AVERAGE PSs
0 60 kms.
PUNJAB
HARYANA
PAKISTAN
UTTAR PRADESH
MADHYA PRADESH
GUJARAT
(%)
< 40 VERY LOW (AVERAGE 29.66)
40-50 LOW
50-60 MEDIUM
60-70 HIGH
> 70 VERY HIGH
0 60 kms.
70° E 71° 72° 73° 74° 75° 76° 77° 78° E
23° N 24° 25° 26° 27° 28° N 29° 30° N

FIG. 3.9

Pucca Road Amenities

	%age of Rural Pop Served by	*%age of Villages# Having Amenities*
State Average (Rural Raj.)	48	29.7
Percentage of AAPs	49	56.5
Top PS	Sheoganj (98)	Sumerpur (74.6)
Bottom PS	Didwana (4.8)	Makrana (8.3)

TABLE 3.7: Classification of PSs by Pucca Road Amenities (1991)

(A) %age of Rural Pop Served by			***(B) %age of Villages# Having Amenities***		
Group	*No. of PSs*	*%*	*Group*	*No. of PSs*	*%*
>80	3	1.3	>70	1	0.4
60-80	40	16.9	60-70	3	1.3
40-60	120	50.6	50-60	7	3.0
20-40	69	29.1	40-50	40	16.9
<20	5	2.1	<40	186	78.5
Total	**237**	**100**	**Total**	**237**	**100**

Source: Annex 3.9 and 3.10.

TABLE 3.8: District-wise First and Last PSs by Pucca Road Amenities (1991)

District	*(A) %age of Rural Pop Served by*		*(B) %age of Villages# Having Amenities*	
	First Rank	*Last Rank*	*First Rank*	*Last Rank*
Ajmer	Pisangan	Arian	Pisangan	Arian
Alwar	Thanagazi	Tijara	Umrain	Reni
Banswara	Talwara	Kushalgarh	Garhi	Kushalgarh
Baran	Baran	Chhabra	Baran	Chhabra
Barmer	Sheo	Baytoo	Sheo	Baytoo
Bharatpur	Kumher	Kaman	Kumher	Kaman
Bhilwara	Hurda	Raipur	Suwana	Raipur
Bikaner	Bikaner	Nokha	Bikaner	Kolayat
Bundi	Talera	Keshoraipatan	Talera	Nainwa
Chittaurgarh	Bhopalsagar	Pratapgarh	Bhopalsagar	Arnod
Churu	Dungargarh	Sujangarh	Dungargarh	Sujangarh
Dausa	Sikrai	Bandikui	Sikrai	Bandikui
Dhaulpur	Baseri	Bari	Dhaulpur	Rajakhera
Dungarpur	Sagwara	Siamalwara	Dungarpur	Siamalwara
Ganganagar	Ganganagar	Padampur	Ganganagar	Anupgarh
Hanumangarh	Hanumangarh	Nohar	Hanumangarh	Nohar
Jaipur	Jhotwara	Chaksu	Jhotwara	Chaksu
Jaisalmer	Jaisalmer	Sam	Jaisalmer	Sam
Jalor	Jalor	Sanchore	Jalor	Ahore
Jhalawar	Bakani	Pirawa	Jhalrapatan	Pirawa
Jhunjhunun	Udaipurwati	Buhana	Udaipurwati	Alsisar
Jodhpur	Bhopalgarh	Bap	Bhopalgarh	Bap
Karauli	Hindaun	Karauli	Hindaun	Karauli
Kota	Ladpura	Sultanpur	Ladpura	Itawa
Nagaur	Merta	Didwana	Riyan	Makrana
Pali	Sumerpur	Jaitaran	Sumerpur	Jaitaran
Rajsamand	Railmagra	Amet	Bhim	Deogarh
Sawai Madhopur	Bamanwas	Sawai Madhopur	Gangapur	Sawai Madhopur
Sikar	Piprali	Fatehpur	Piprali	Fatehpur
Sirohi	Sheoganj	Reodar	Abu Road	Reodar
Tonk	Malpura	Niwai	Tonk	Niwai
Udaipur	Girwa	Kotra	Mavli	Jhadol

Source: General Annex-II and III. # Inhabited villages

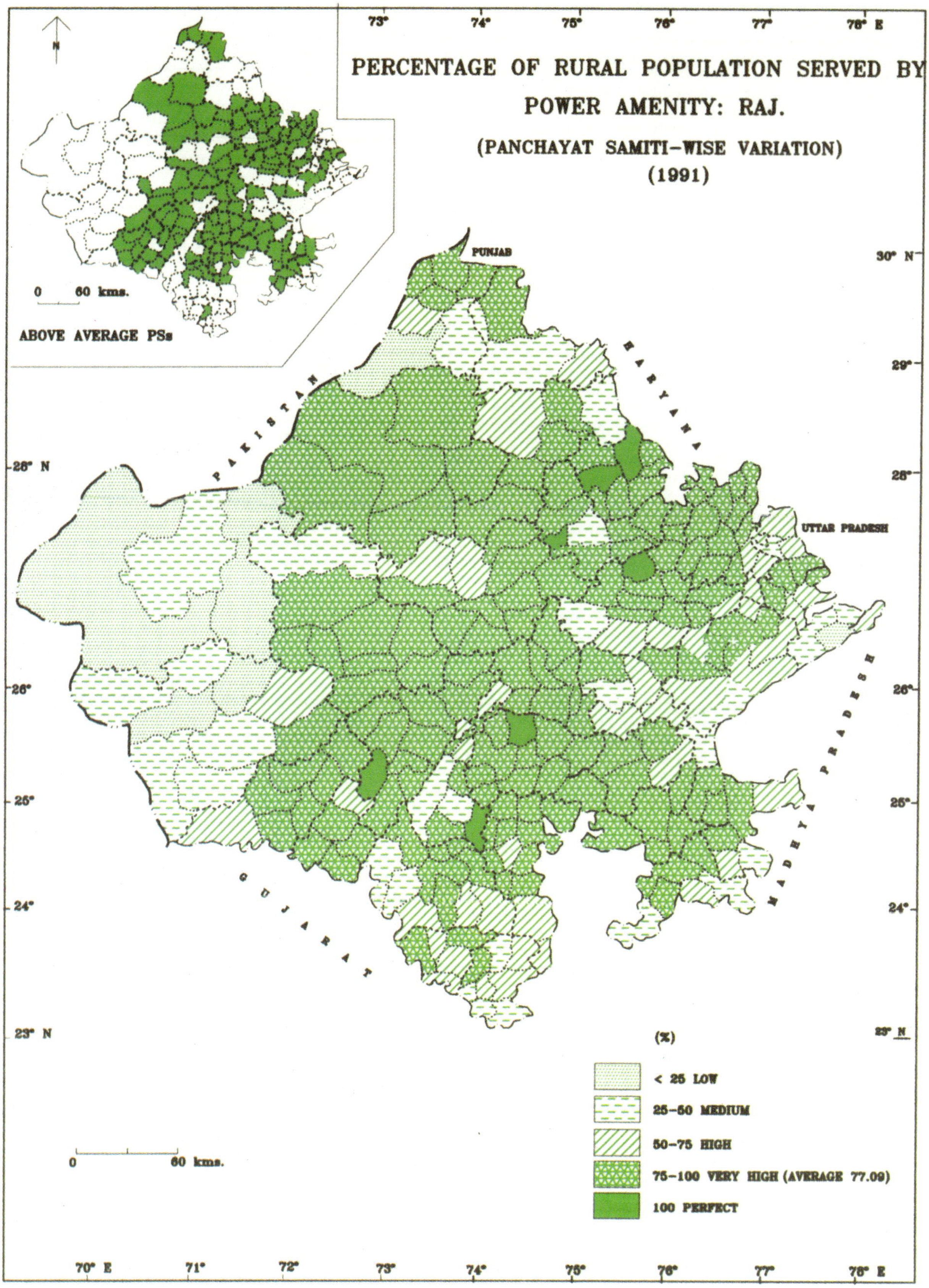
PERCENTAGE OF RURAL POPULATION SERVED BY POWER AMENITY: RAJ.
(PANCHAYAT SAMITI-WISE VARIATION)
(1991)
ABOVE AVERAGE PSs
0 60 kms.
PUNJAB
HARYANA
PAKISTAN
UTTAR PRADESH
MADHYA PRADESH
GUJARAT
(%)
< 25 LOW
25-50 MEDIUM
50-75 HIGH
75-100 VERY HIGH (AVERAGE 77.09)
100 PERFECT
0 60 kms.

FIG. 3.10

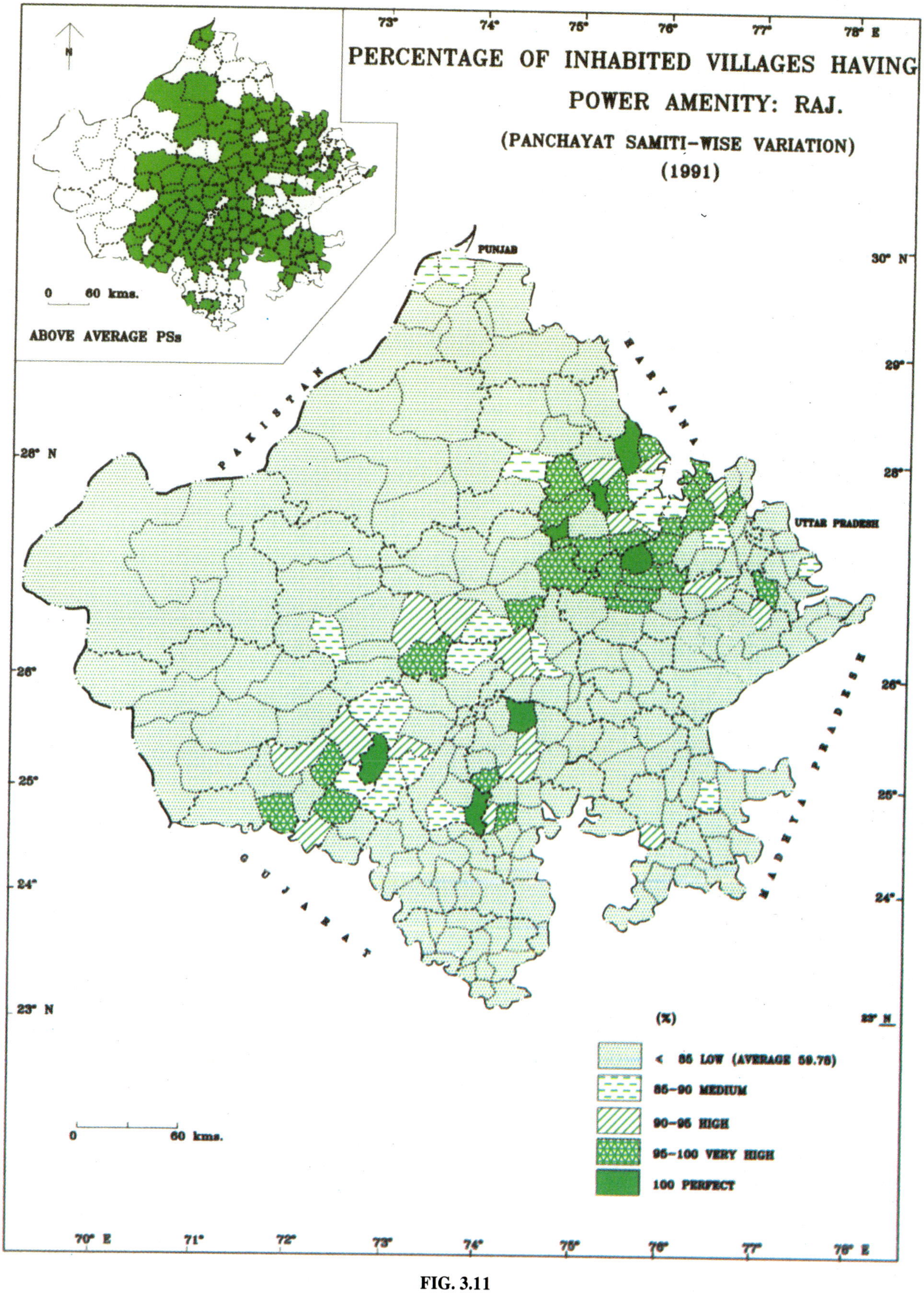
PERCENTAGE OF INHABITED VILLAGES HAVING POWER AMENITY: RAJ.
(PANCHAYAT SAMITI-WISE VARIATION)
(1991)
ABOVE AVERAGE PSs
0 60 kms.
PUNJAB
HARYANA
PAKISTAN
UTTAR PRADESH
MADHYA PRADESH
GUJARAT
(%)
< 85 LOW (AVERAGE 59.75)
85-90 MEDIUM
90-95 HIGH
95-100 VERY HIGH
100 PERFECT
0 60 kms.

FIG. 3.11

Power Amenities

	%age of Rural Pop Served by	%age of Villages# Having Amenities
State Average (Rural Raj.)	77	59.8
Percentage of AAPs	62.9	68.8
Top PS	7 PSs had perfect (100%) Amenities	7 PSs had perfect (100%) Amenities
Bottom PS	Sam (1.5)	Sam (0.4)

TABLE 3.9: Classification of PSs by Power Amenities (1991)

(A) %age of Rural Pop Served by			*(B) %age of Villages# Having Amenities*		
Group	*No. of PSs*	*%*	*Group*	*No. of PSs*	*%*
100	7	3.0	100	7	3.0
75-100	151	63.7	95-100	25	10.5
50-75	45	19.0	90-95	20	8.4
25-50	29	12.2	85-90	19	8.0
<25	5	2.1	<85	166	70.4
Total	**237**	**100**	**Total**	**237**	**100**

Source: Annex 3.11 and 3.12

TABLE 3.10: District-wise First and Last PSs by Power Amenities (1991)

District	*(A) %age of Rural Pop Served by*		*(B) %age of Villages# Having Amenities*	
	First Rank	*Last Rank*	*First Rank*	*Last Rank*
Ajmer	Pisangan	Jawaja	Pisangan	Jawaja
Alwar	Nimrana	Lachhmangarh	Nimrana	Lachhmangarh
Banswara	Grahi	Peepalkhoont	Grahi	Peepalkhoont
Baran	Baran	Chhipabarod	Baran	Chabra
Barmer	Siwana	Barmer	Siwana	Barmer
Bharatpur	Weir	Nagar Pahari	Weir	Nagar Pahari
Bhilwara	Hurda	Kotri	Hurda *	Jahazpur
Bikaner	Nokha	Kolayat	Nokha	Kolayat
Bundi	Hindoli*	Keshoraipatan	Hindoli	Keshoraipatan
Chittaurgarh	Kapasan	Pratapgarh	Kapasan	Pratapgarh
Churu	Ratangarh	Rajgarh	Ratangarh	Rajgarh
Dausa	Bandikui	Mahwa	Bandikui	Mahwa
Dhaulpur	Rajakhera	Bari	Rajakhera	Bari
Dungarpur	Aspur	Dungarpur	Bichhiwara	Dungarpur
Ganganagar	Karanpur	Anupgarh	Ganganagar	Anupgarh
Hanumangarh	Hanumangarh	Nohar	Hanumangarh	Nohar
Jaipur	Govindgarh*	Dudu	Govindgarh*	Phagi
Jaisalmer	Jaisalmer	Sam	Jaisalmer	Sam
Jalor	Raniwara	Sanchore	Raniwara	Sanchore
Jhalawar	Jhalrapatan	Manoharthana	Pirawa	Manoharthana
Jhunjhunun	Chirawa* and Nawalgarh*	Alsisar	Chirawa* and Nawalgarh*	Alsisar
Jodhpur	Bilara	Bap	Bilara	Bap
Karauli	Hindaun	Karauli	Hindaun	Karauli
Kota	Chechat	Itawa	Chechat	Itawa
Nagaur	Kuchaman	Jayal	Kuchaman	Jayal
Pali	Sumerpur*	Raipur	Sumerpur*	Raipur
Rajsamand	Railmagra*	Rajsamand	Railmagra*	Deogarh
Sawai Madhopur	Gangapur	Khandar	Gangapur	Khandar
Sikar	Dhond*	Piprali	Dhond*	Piprali
Sirohi	Sirohi	Sheoganj	Sirohi	Abu Road
Tonk	Niwai	Todraisingh	Niwai	Deoli
Udaipur	Bargaon	Kotra	Bargaon	Kotra

* PS/PSs having Almost perfect (100%) Power Amenities. *Source*: General Annex-II and III. # Inhabited villages

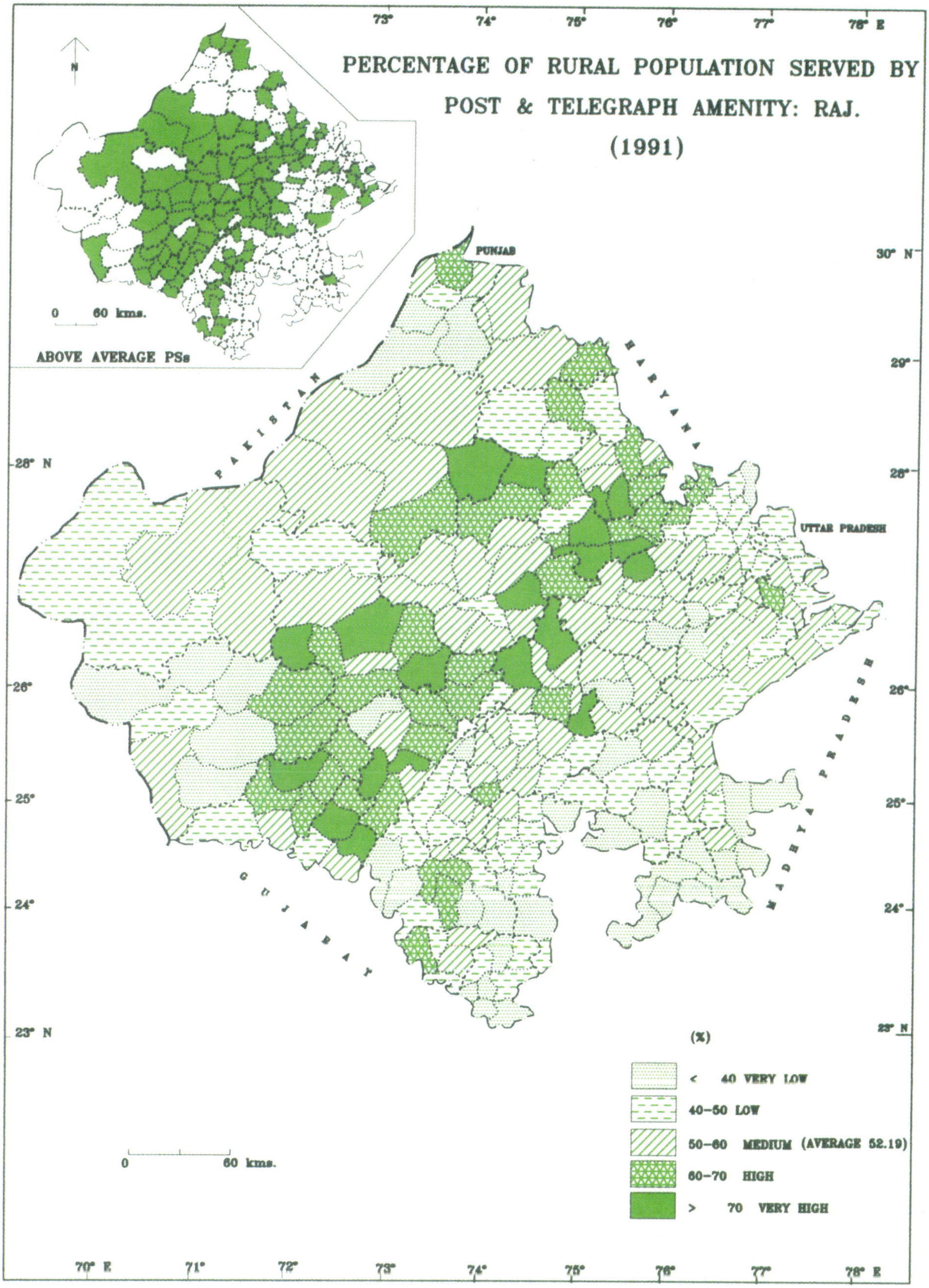
PERCENTAGE OF RURAL POPULATION SERVED BY POST & TELEGRAPH AMENITY: RAJ. (1991)
ABOVE AVERAGE PSs
0 60 kms.
PUNJAB
HARYANA
PAKISTAN
UTTAR PRADESH
MADHYA PRADESH
GUJARAT
(%)
< 40 VERY LOW
40-50 LOW
50-60 MEDIUM (AVERAGE 52.19)
60-70 HIGH
> 70 VERY HIGH
0 60 kms.

FIG. 3.12

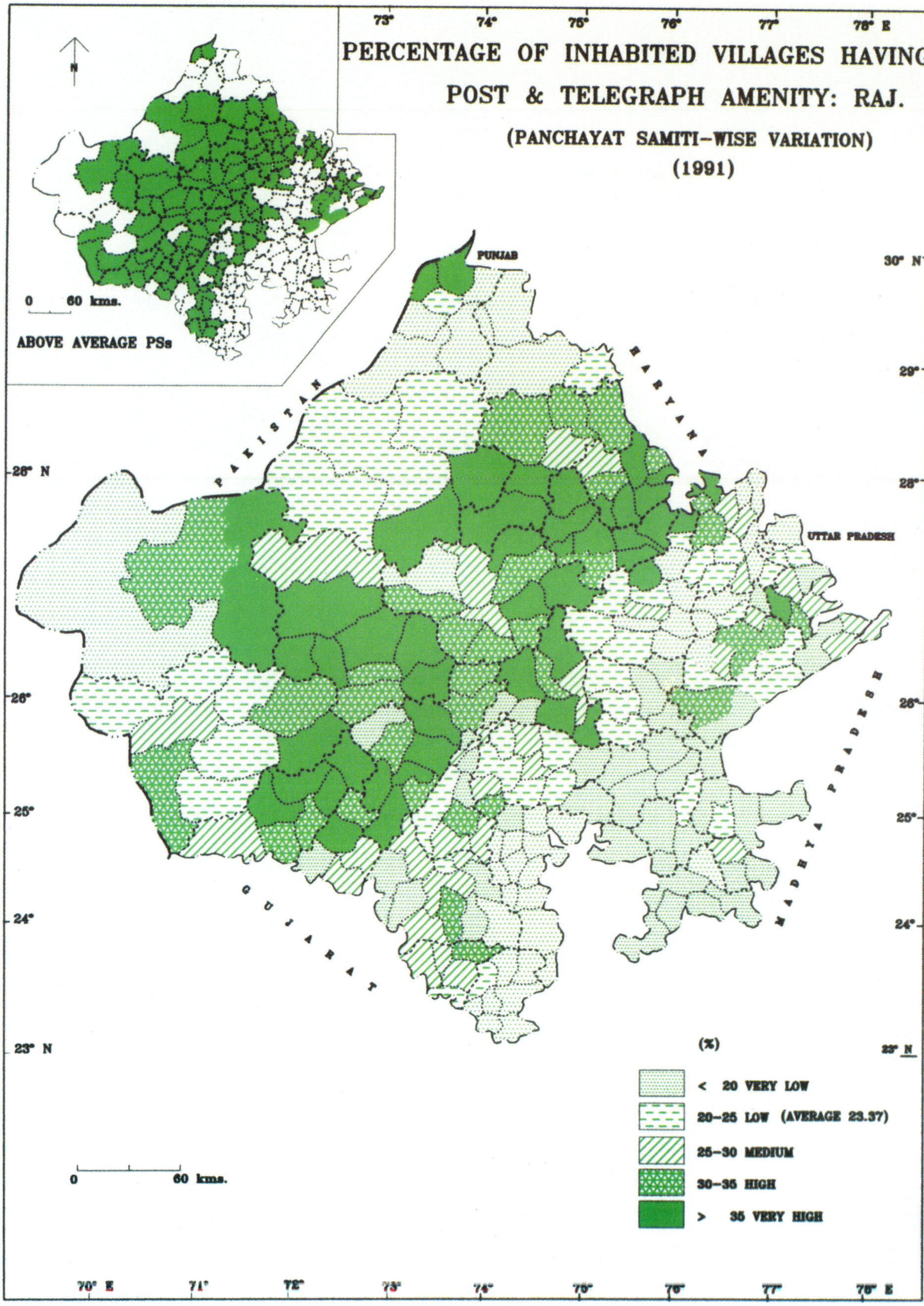
PERCENTAGE OF INHABITED VILLAGES HAVING
POST & TELEGRAPH AMENITY: RAJ.
(PANCHAYAT SAMITI-WISE VARIATION)
(1991)
N
0 60 kms.
ABOVE AVERAGE PSs
73° 74° 75° 76° 77° 78° E
30° N
29°
28° N
28°
26°
25°
24°
23° N
PUNJAB
HARYANA
UTTAR PRADESH
MADHYA PRADESH
PAKISTAN
GUJARAT
(%)
< 20 VERY LOW
20–25 LOW (AVERAGE 23.37)
25–30 MEDIUM
30–35 HIGH
> 35 VERY HIGH
0 60 kms.
70° E 71° 72° 73° 74° 75° 76° 77° 78° E

FIG. 3.13

Post and Telegraph Amenities

	%age of Rural Pop Served by	*%age of Villages# Having Amenities*
State Average (Rural Raj.)	52.2	23.4
Percentage of AAPs	48.1	56.1
Top PS	Sumerpur (82.5)	Sumerpur (60.3)
Bottom PS	Todaraising (0.4)	Kushalgarh (5.3)

TABLE 3.11: Classification of PSs by Post and Telegraph Amenities (1991)

(A) %age of Rural Pop Served by			*(B) %age of Villages# Having Amenities*		
Group	*No. of PSs*	*%*	*Group*	*No. of PSs*	*%*
>70	20	8.4	>35	49	20.7
60-70	42	17.7	30-35	34	14.3
50-60	67	28.3	25-30	36	15.2
40-50	69	29.1	20-25	48	20.3
<40	39	16.5	<20	70	29.5
Total	**237**	**100**	**Total**	**237**	**100**

Source: Annex 3.11 and 3.12

TABLE 3.12: District-wise First and Last PSs by Post and Telegraph Amenities (1991)

District	*(A) %age of Rural Pop Served by*		*(B) %age of Villages# Having Amenities*	
	First Rank	*Last Rank*	*First Rank*	*Last Rank*
Ajmer	Kekri	Jawaja	Pisangan	Jawaja
Alwar	Nimrana	Tijara	Nimrana	Tijara
Banswara	Garhi	Kushalgarh	Garhi	Kushalgarh
Baran	Atru	Chhabra	Atru	Chhabra
Barmer	Siwana	Baytoo	Siwana	Baytoo
Bharatpur	Weir	Sewar	Weir	Sewar
Bhilwara	Sahara	Mandalgarh	Sahara	Mandalgarh
Bikaner	Nokha	Lunkaransar	Nokha	Kolayat
Bundi	Keshoraipatan	Hindoli	Keshoraipatan	Hindoli
Chittaurgarh	Rashmi	Bhainrorgarh	Rashmi	Bhainsrorgarh
Churu	Ratangarh	Churu	Dungargarh	Churu
Dausa	Mahwa	Lalsot	Sikrai	Lalsot
Dhaulpur	Baseri	Bari	Rajakhera	Baseri
Dungarpur	Bichhiwara	Dungarpur	Aspur	Simalwara
Ganganagar	Ganganagar	Anupgarh	Ganganagar	Anupgarh
Hanumangarh	Bhadra	Nohar	Bhadra	Nohar
Jaipur	Govindgarh	Chaksu	Govindgarh	Chaksu
Jaisalmer	Jaisalmer	Sam	Sankra	Sam
Jalor	Sayla	Sanchore	Sayla	Sanchore
Jhalawar	Bakani	Manoharthana	Pirawa	Manoharthana
Jhunjhunun	Nawalgarh	Jhunjhunun	Nawalgarh	Alsisar
Jodhpur	Bilara	Bap	Shergarh	Bap
Karauli	Nadoti	Karauli	Nadoti	Karauli
Kota	Itawa	Ladpura	Sultanpur	Ladpura
Nagaur	Makrana	Degana	Makrana	Nagaur
Pali	Sumerpur	Rohat	Sumerpur	Rohat
Rajsamand	Rajsamand	Deogarh	Rajsamand	Deogarh
Sawai Madhopur	Gangapur	Khandar	Sawai Madhopur	Khandar
Sikar	Piprali	Lachmangarh	Sri Madhopur	Lachmangarh
Sirohi	Pindwara	Reodar	Sirohi	Reodar
Tonk	Malpura	Todaraisingh	Malpura	Uniara
Udaipur	Sarada	Kotra	Sarada	Jhadol

Source: General Annex-II and III.

Inhabited Villages

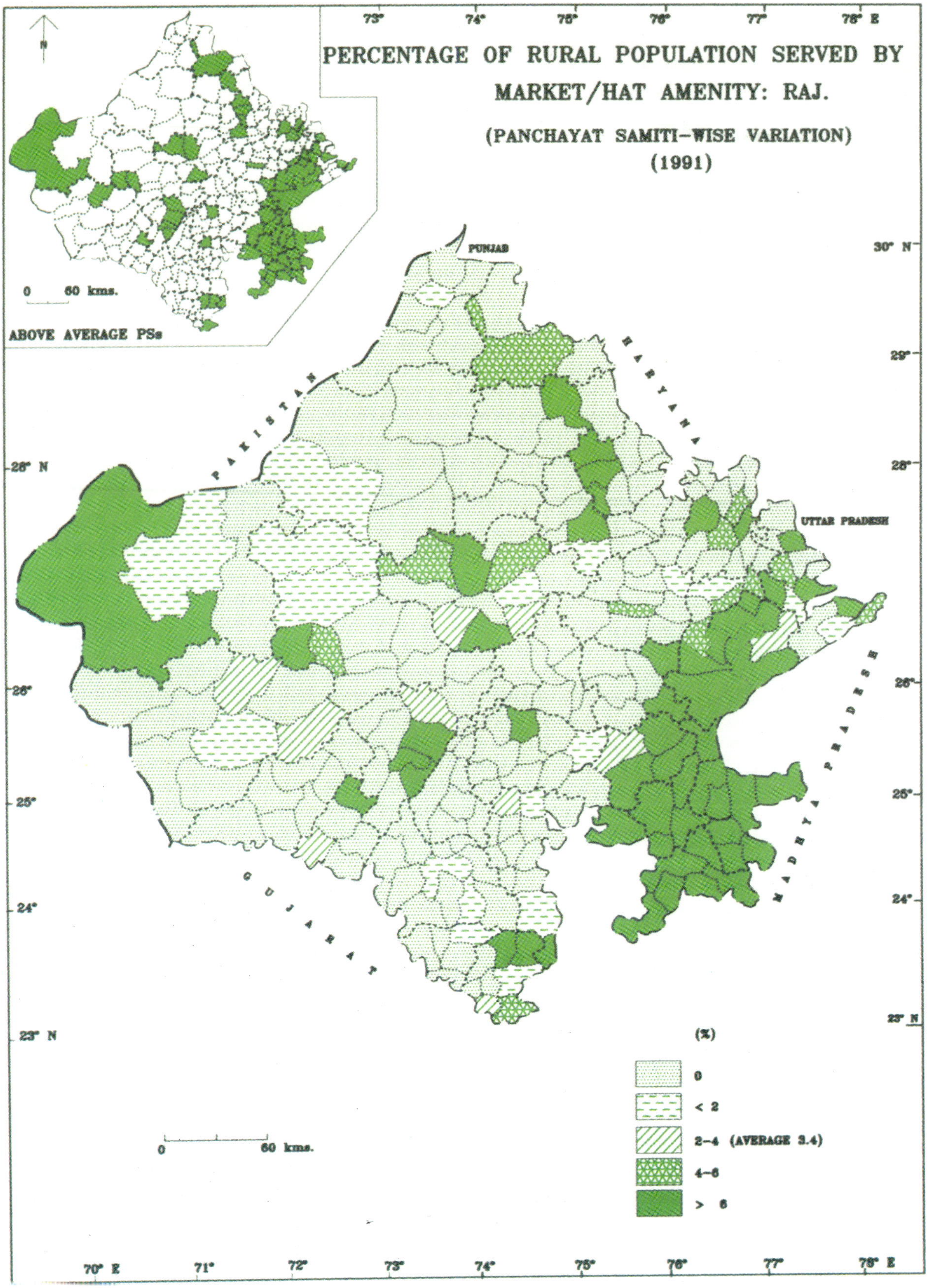
PERCENTAGE OF RURAL POPULATION SERVED BY
MARKET/HAT AMENITY: RAJ.
(PANCHAYAT SAMITI-WISE VARIATION)
(1991)
ABOVE AVERAGE PSs
0 60 kms.
PUNJAB
HARYANA
UTTAR PRADESH
MADHYA PRADESH
GUJARAT
PAKISTAN
(%)
0
< 2
2-4 (AVERAGE 3.4)
4-6
> 6
0 60 kms.
70° E
71°
72°
73°
74°
75°
76°
77°
78° E
30° N
29°
28° N
26°
25°
24°
23° N

FIG. 3.14

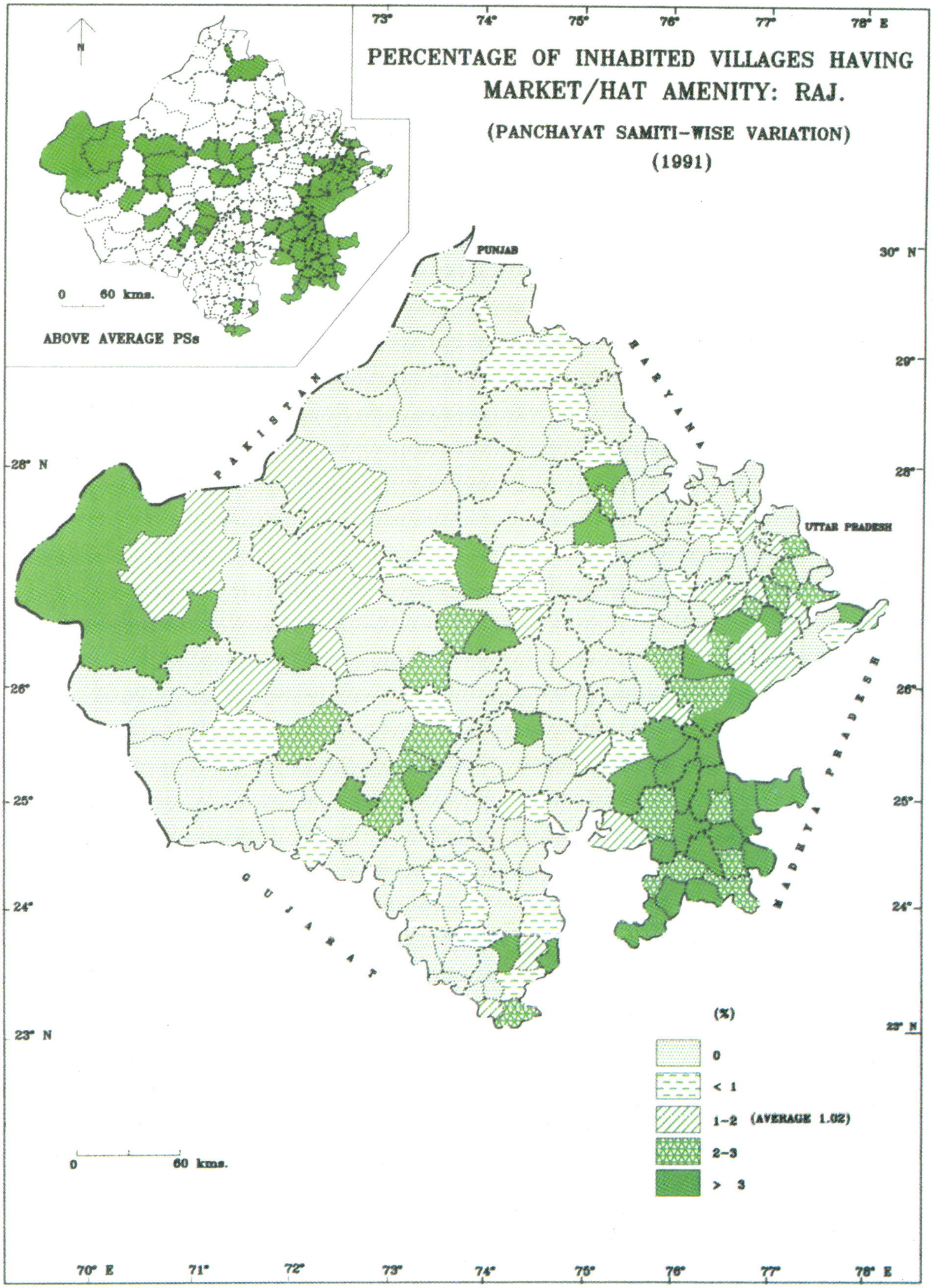
PERCENTAGE OF INHABITED VILLAGES HAVING MARKET/HAT AMENITY: RAJ.
(PANCHAYAT SAMITI-WISE VARIATION)
(1991)
ABOVE AVERAGE PSs
0 60 kms.
PUNJAB
HARYANA
UTTAR PRADESH
MADHYA PRADESH
GUJARAT
PAKISTAN
(%)
0
< 1
1-2 (AVERAGE 1.02)
2-3
> 3
0 60 kms.
70° E
71°
72°
73°
74°
75°
76°
77°
78° E
30° N
29°
28° N
26°
25°
24°
23° N

FIG. 3.15

Market/Hat Amenities

	%age of Rural Pop Served by	*%age of Villages# Having Amenities*
State Average (Rural Raj.)	3.4	1.0
Percentage of AAPs	30.4	29.1
Top PS	Itawa (37.5)	Shergarh (28)
Bottom PS	138 PSs (Absence of Amenities)	137 PSs (Absence of Amenities)

TABLE 3.13: Classification of PSs by Market/Hat Amenities (1991)

(A) %age of Rural Pop Served by			*(B) %age of Villages# Having Amenities*		
Group	*No. of PSs*	*%*	*Group*	*No. of PSs*	*%*
>6	56	23.6	>3	32	13.5
4-6	11	4.6	2-3	22	9.3
2-4	12	5.1	1-2	15	6.3
<2	20	8.4	<1	31	13.1
0	138	58.2	0	137	57.8
Total	**237**	**100**	**Total**	**237**	**100**

Source: Annex 3.11 and 3.12

TABLE 3.14: District-wise First and Last PSs by Market/Hat Amenities (1991)

District	*(A) %age of Rural Pop Served by*		*(B) %age of Villages# Having Amenities*	
	First Rank	*Last Rank*	*First Rank*	*Last Rank*
Ajmer	—	All PSs*	—	All PSs*
Alwar	Ramgarh	10 PSs*	Ramgarh	10 PSs*
Banswara	Pipalkhoont	3 PSs*	Pipalkhoont	3 PSs*
Baran	Atru	Chhabra	Atru	Baran
Barmer	Baytoo	5 PSs*	Siwana	5 PSs*
Bharatpur	Rupbas	3 PSs*	Rupbas	3 PSs*
Bhilwara	Hurda	9 PSs*	Hurda	9 PSs*
Bikaner	Kolayat	3 PSs*	Kolayat	3 PSs*
Bundi	Talera	Hindoli	Talera	Hindoli
Chittaurgarh	Arnod	9 PSs*	Arnod	9 PSs*
Churu	Taranagar	6 PSs*	Taranagar	6 PSs*
Dausa	Sikrai	Dausa*	Mahwa	Dausa*
Dhaulpur	Dhaulpur	Baseri*	Dhaulpur	Baseri*
Dungarpur	Aspur	4 PSs*	Aspur	4 PSs*
Ganganagar	Padampur	6 PSs*	Padampur	6 PSs*
Hanumangarh	Nohar	Bhadra* and Hn*	Nohar	Bhadra* and Hn*
Jaipur	Sanganer	11 PSs*	Sanganer	11 PSs*
Jaisalmer	Sam	Sankra*	Sam	Sankra*
Jalor	—	All PSs*	—	All PSs*
Jhalawar	Bakani	Jhalrapatan	Pirawa	Jhalrapatan
Jhunjhunun	Nawalgarh	5 PSs*	Jhunjhunun	5 PSs*
Jodhpur	Shergarh	5 PSs*	Shergarh	5 PSs*
Karauli	Nadoti	Karauli	Nadoti	Karauli
Kota	Itawa	Ladpura	Itawa	Ladpura
Nagaur	Jayal	4 PSs*	Riyan	4 PSs*
Pali	Desuri	6 PSs*	Desuri	5 PSs*
Rajsamand	—	All PSs*	—	All PSs*
Sawai Madhopur	Bonli	Gangapur	Bonli	Gangapur
Sikar	Piprali	6 PSs*	Piprali	6 PSs*
Sirohi	Sheoganj	3 PSs*	Sheoganj	3 PSs*
Tonk	Uniara	4 PSs*	Niwai	4 PSs*
Udaipur	Salumber	9 PSs*	Girwa	9 PSs*

* Absence of Amenities *Source*: General Annex-II and III. # Inhabited Villages

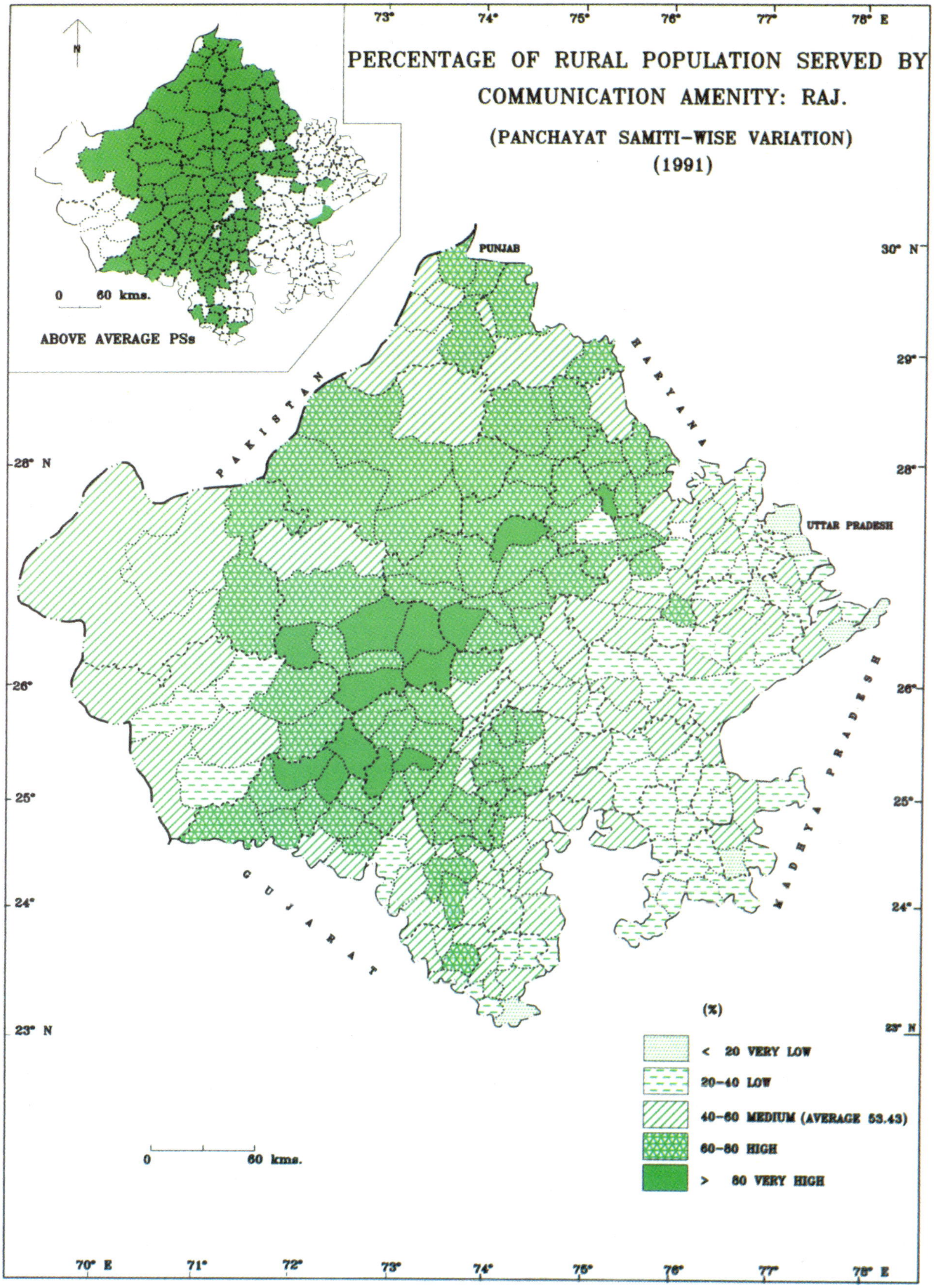
PERCENTAGE OF RURAL POPULATION SERVED BY COMMUNICATION AMENITY: RAJ.
(PANCHAYAT SAMITI-WISE VARIATION)
(1991)
ABOVE AVERAGE PSs
0 60 kms.
N
PUNJAB
HARYANA
UTTAR PRADESH
MADHYA PRADESH
GUJARAT
PAKISTAN
(%)
< 20 VERY LOW
20-40 LOW
40-60 MEDIUM (AVERAGE 53.43)
60-80 HIGH
> 80 VERY HIGH
0 60 kms.
70° E
71°
72°
73°
74°
75°
76°
77°
78° E
30° N
29°
28° N
26°
25°
24°
23° N

FIG. 3.16

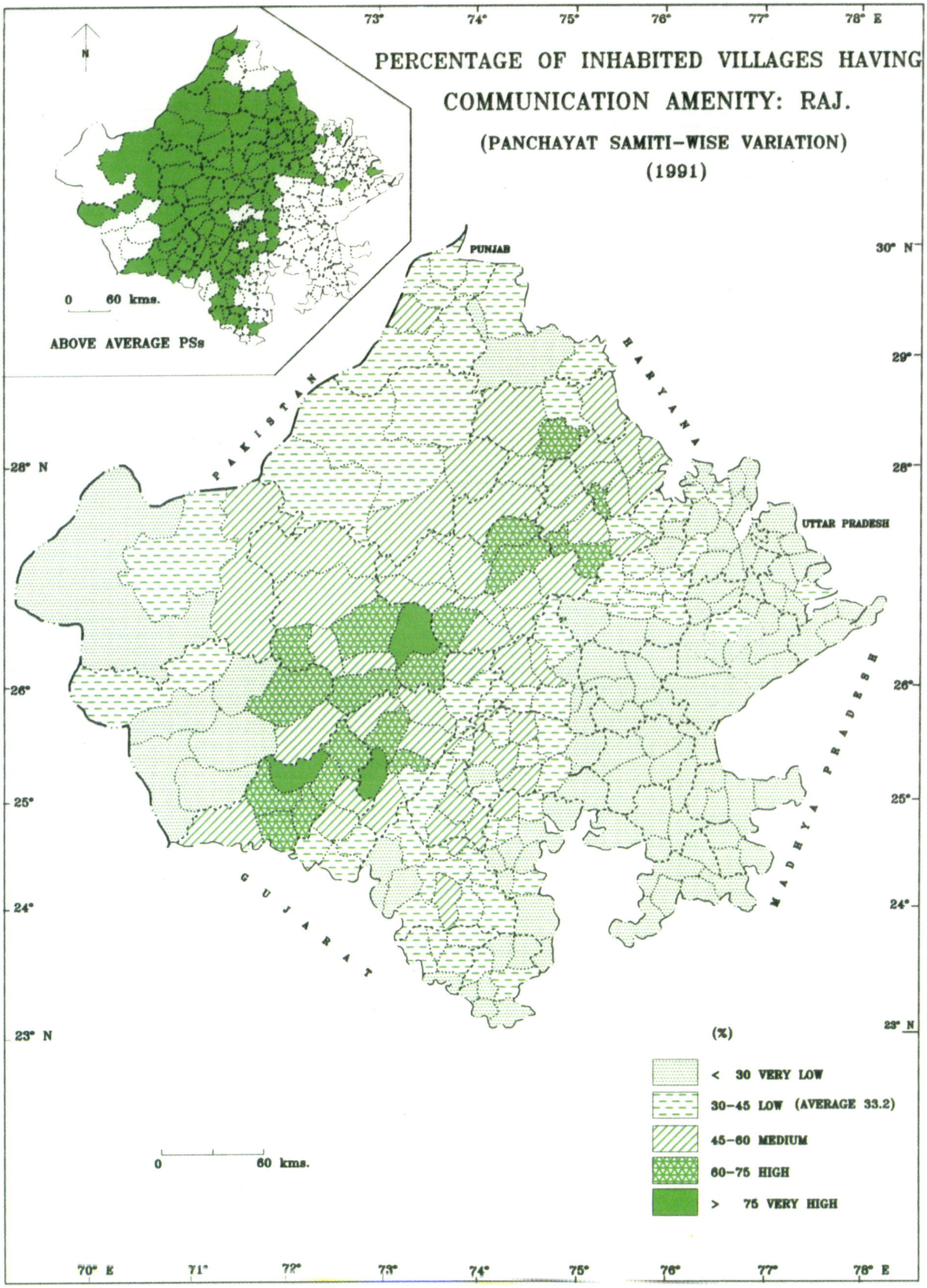
PERCENTAGE OF INHABITED VILLAGES HAVING
COMMUNICATION AMENITY: RAJ.
(PANCHAYAT SAMITI-WISE VARIATION)
(1991)
0 60 kms.
ABOVE AVERAGE PSs
PUNJAB
HARYANA
PAKISTAN
UTTAR PRADESH
MADHYA PRADESH
GUJARAT
(%)
< 30 VERY LOW
30-45 LOW (AVERAGE 33.2)
45-60 MEDIUM
60-75 HIGH
> 75 VERY HIGH
0 60 kms.

FIG. 3.17

COMMUNICATION AMENITIES

	%age of Rural Pop Served by	*%age of Villages# Having Amenities*
State Average (Rural Raj.)	53.4	33.2
Percentage of AAPs	50.2	51.1
Top PS	Osian (97.1)	Bhopalgarh (79.8)
Bottom PS	Deeg (10.8)	Deeg (6.7)

TABLE 3.15: Classification of PSs by Communication Amenities (1991)

(A) %age of Rural Pop Served by			*(B) %age of Villages# Having Amenities*		
Group	*No. of PSs*	*%*	*Group*	*No. of PSs*	*%*
>80	13	5.5	<75	3	1.3
60-80	75	31.6	60-75	19	8.0
40-60	86	36.3	45-60	54	22.8
20-40	56	23.6	30-45	62	26.2
<20	7	3.0	<30	99	41.8
Total	**237**	**100**	**Total**	**237**	**100**

Source: Annex 3.17 and 3.18

TABLE 3.16: District-wise First and Last PSs by Communication Amenities (1991)

District	*(A) %age of Rural Pop Served by*		*(B) %age of Villages# Having Amenities*	
	First Rank	*Last Rank*	*First Rank*	*Last Rank*
Ajmer	Srinagar	Kekri	Pisangan	Kekri
Alwar	Thanagazi	Tijara	Mandawar	Reni
Banswara	Garhi	Kushalgarh	Garhi	Kushalgarh
Baran	Kishanganj	Chhabra	Atru	Shahbad
Barmer	Balotra	Dhorimanna	Balotra	Baytoo
Bharatpur	Rupbas	Deeg	Rupbas	Deeg
Bhilwara	Hurda	Jahazpur	Hurda	Mandalgarh
Bikaner	Nokha	Lunkaransar	Nokha	Lunkaransar
Bundi	Nainwa	Talera	Keshoraipatan	Hindoli
Chittaurgarh	Rashmi	Arnod	Rashmi	Arnod
Churu	Ratangarh	Rajgarh	Churu	Taranagar
Dausa	Dausa	Mahwa	Dausa	Mahwa
Dhaulpur	Baseri	Rajakhera	Baseri	Rajakhera
Dungarpur	Sagwara	Dungarpur	Sagwara	Aspur
Ganganagar	Sadulshahar	Karanpur	Raisinghnagar	Suratgarh
Hanumangarh	Hanumangarh	Nohar	Bhadra	Nohar
Jaipur	Govindgarh	Chaksu	Jhotwara	Chaksu
Jaisalmer	Sankra	Sam	Sankra	Sam
Jalor	Sayla	Sanchore	Sayla	Sanchore
Jhalawar	Dag	Manoharthana	Dag	Khanpur
Jhunjhunun	Nawalgarh	Surajgarh	Nawalgarh	Surajgarh
Jodhpur	Osian	Bap	Bhopalgarh	Bap
Karauli	Nadoti	Todabhim	Nadoti	Karauli
Kota	Itawa	Ladpura	Chechat	Ladpura
Nagaur	Merta	Parabatsar	Ladnu	Jayal
Pali	Sumerpur	Raipur	Sumerpur	Raipur
Rajsamand	Rajsamand	Deogarh	Amet	Deogarh
Sawai Madhopur	Khandar	Bamanwas	Khandar	Sawai Madhopur
Sikar	Danta Ramgarh	Piprali	Dhond	Neem ka Thana
Sirohi	Sheoganj	Abu Road	Sirohi	Abu Road
Tonk	Todaraisingh	Tonk	Malpura	Tonk
Udaipur	Mavli	Kotra	Sarada	Kotra

Source: General Annex-II and III.

\# Inhabited Villages

4

INFRASTRUCTURE STATUS (2001)

Medical Amenities

	%age of Rural Pop. Served by	*%age of Villages# Having Amenities*	*No. of Medical Institutions**
State Average (Rural Raj.)	57	29.2	Per PS 60.05 (Total 14231)
Percentage of AAPs	47	58	45.2
Top PS	Sirohi (88%)	Bilara (69.7%)	Aspur and Hn (137)
Bottom PS	Chhabra (14.8%)	Chhabra (7.5%)	Bari Sadri, Chhabraand Kapasan (14)

TABLE 4.1: Classification of PSs by Medical Amenities (2001)

(A) %age of Rural Pop Served by			*(B) %age of Villages# Having Amenities*			*(C) Total No. of Medical Institutions**		
Group	*No. of PSs*	*%*	*Group*	*No. of PSs*	*%*	*Group*	*No. of PSs*	*%*
>=60	91	38.4	>=50	28	11.8	>=80	50	21.1
50-60	65	27.4	40-50	38	16.0	60-80	62	26.2
40-50	54	22.8	30-40	61	25.7	40-60	77	32.5
30-40	21	8.9	20-30	64	27.0	20-40	43	18.1
<30	6	2.5	<20	46	19.4	<20	5	2.1
Total	**237**	**100**	**Total**	**237**	**100**	**Total**	**237**	**100**

Source: Annex 4.1 to 4.3

TABLE 4.2: District-wise First and Last PSs by Medical Amenities (2001)

District	*(A) %age of Rural Pop Served by*		*(B) %age of Villages# Having Amenities*		*(C) Total No. of Medical Institutions**	
	First Rank	*Last Rank*	*First Rank*	*Last Rank*	*First Rank*	*Last Rank*
Ajmer	Kekri	Jawaja	Pisangan	Masooda	Pisangan	Arian [1]
Alwar	Nimrana	Kishangarh Bas	Nimrana	Kotkasim	Mandawar	Kotkasim
Banswara	Garhi	Kushalgarh	Garhi	Ghatol	Garhi	Anandpuri
Baran	Atru	Chhabra	Baran	Chhabra	Anta	Chhabra
Barmer	Siwana	Baytoo	Siwana	Sheo	Sindhari	Sheo
Bharatpur	Bayana	Nagar Pahari	Nadbai	Nagar Pahari	Rupbas	Kaman
Bhilwara	Banera	Kotri	Banera	Mandal	Mandalgarh	Hurda
Bikaner	Nokha	Bikaner	Nokha	Kolayat	Bikaner	Nokha
Bundi	Hindoli	Keshoraipatan	Hindoli	Nainwa	Hindoli [2]	Nainwa
Chittaurgarh	Rashmi	Kapasan	Dungla	Kapasan	Pratapgarh	Bari Sadri [3]
Churu	Ratangarh	Sardarshahar	Ratangarh	Taranagar	Ratangarh	Sardarshahar
Dausa	Dausa	Lalsot	Mahwa	Lalsot	Dausa	Bandikui
Dhaulpur	Bari	Rajakhera	Bari	Rajakhera	Dhaulpur	Rajakhera
Dungarpur	Sagwara	Simalwara	Sagwara	Simalwara	Aspur	Dungarpur
Ganganagar	Sadulshahar	Anupgarh	Padampura	Anupgarh	Anupgarh	Padampur
Hanumangarh	Bhadra	Nohar	Bhadra	Nohar	Hanumangarh	Bhadra
Jaipur	Govindgarh	Chaksu	Govindgarh	Chaksu	Dudu	Jhotwara
Jaisalmer	Jaisalmer	Sam	Jaisalmer	Sam	Sankra	Jaisalmer
Jalor	Ahore	Sanchore	Jalor	Sanchore	Sanchore	Raniwara
Jhalawar	Khanpur	Manoharthana	Khanpur	Manoharthana	Khanpur	Manoharthana
Jhunjhunun	Udaipurwati	Surajgarh	Udaipurwati	Alsisar	Buhana	Surajgarh
Jodhpur	Balesar	Bap	Bilara	Bap	Osian	Mandor
Karauli	Hindaun	Karauli	Hindaun	Sapotra	Sapotra	Nadoti
Kota	Sultanpur	Sangod	Sultanpur	Itawa	Sangod	Chechat
Nagaur	Ladnu	Kuchaman	Parbatsar	Kuchamana	Degana	Merta, Mundwa
Pali	Bali	Rohat	Sumerpur	Rohat	Sojat	Pali
Rajsamand	Railmagara	Deogarh	Railmagra	Deogarh	Kumbhalgarh	Deogarh
Sawai Madhopur	Gangapur	Bamanwas	Gangapur	Bonli	Sawai Madhopur	Bamanwas
Sikar	Dhond	Lachhmangarh	Dhond	Lachhmangarh	Danta Ramgarh	Sri Madhopur
Sirohi	Sirohi	Abu Road	Sirohi	Abu Road	Sirohi	Abu Road
Tonk	Tonk	Niwai	Tonk	Uniara	Tonk	Uniara
Udaipur	Mavli	Kotra	Mavli	Kotra	Sarada	Bargaon

Source : General Annex VII, VIII and IX

\# Inhabited Villages

* Include despensary, hospital, MCWC, PHC and SHC,[1] and Sri Nagar,[2] and Talera,[3] and Kapasan

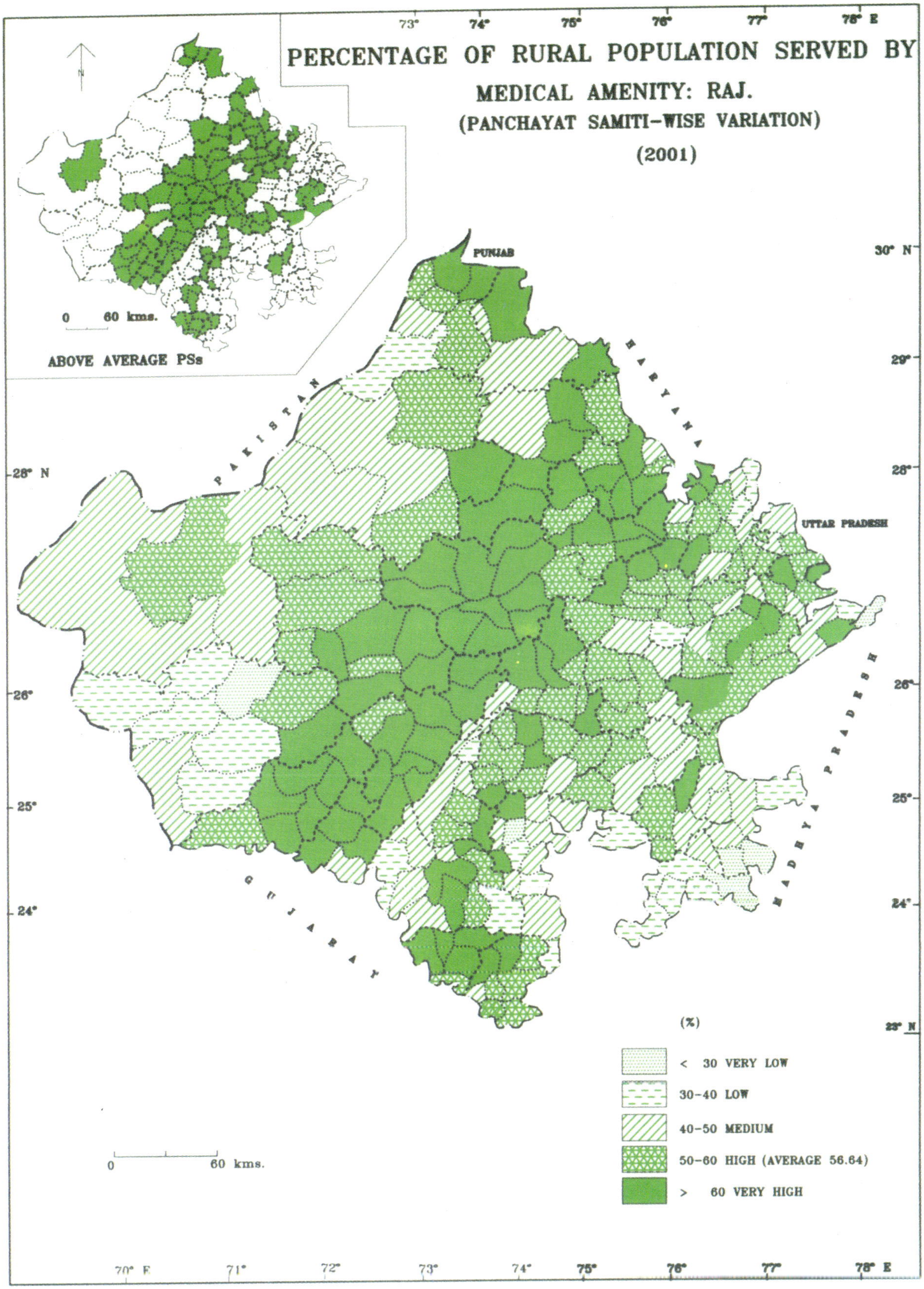
PERCENTAGE OF RURAL POPULATION SERVED BY
MEDICAL AMENITY: RAJ.
(PANCHAYAT SAMITI-WISE VARIATION)
(2001)
ABOVE AVERAGE PSs
0 60 kms.
PUNJAB
HARYANA
UTTAR PRADESH
MADHYA PRADESH
GUJARAT
PAKISTAN
(%)
< 30 VERY LOW
30-40 LOW
40-50 MEDIUM
50-60 HIGH (AVERAGE 56.64)
> 60 VERY HIGH
0 60 kms.
70° E
71°
72°
73°
74°
75°
76°
77°
78° E
30° N
29°
28° N
26°
25°
24°
23° N

FIG. 4.1

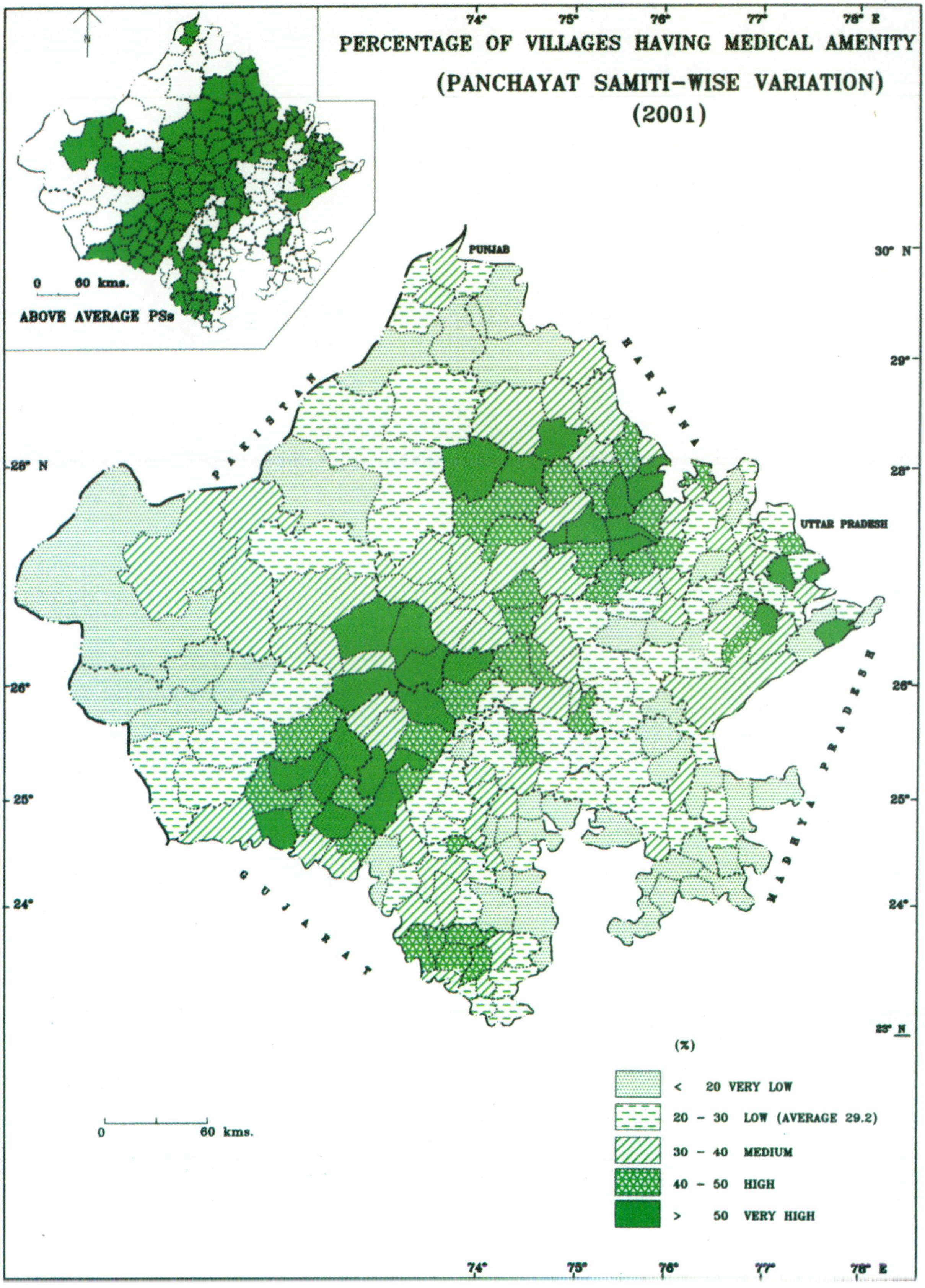
PERCENTAGE OF VILLAGES HAVING MEDICAL AMENITY
(PANCHAYAT SAMITI-WISE VARIATION)
(2001)
ABOVE AVERAGE PSs
0 60 kms.
PUNJAB
HARYANA
UTTAR PRADESH
MADHYA PRADESH
GUJARAT
PAKISTAN
(%)
< 20 VERY LOW
20 - 30 LOW (AVERAGE 29.2)
30 - 40 MEDIUM
40 - 50 HIGH
> 50 VERY HIGH
74° 75° 76° 77° 78° E
30° N
29°
28° N
26°
25°
24°
23° N

FIG. 4.2

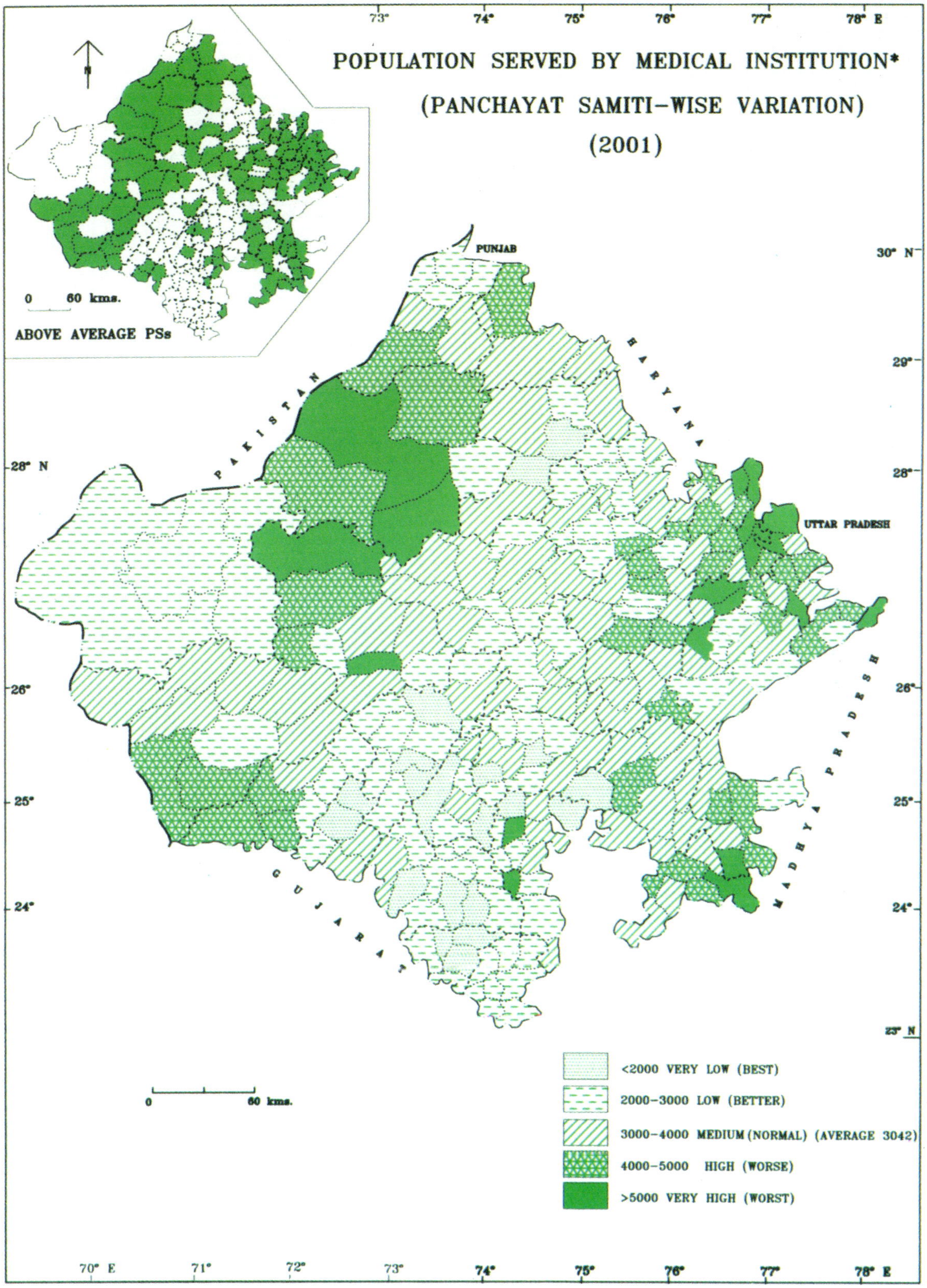

Note: *Medical Institution Includes Hospital, Dispensary , PHC, CHC and MCW Centre.

FIG. 4.3

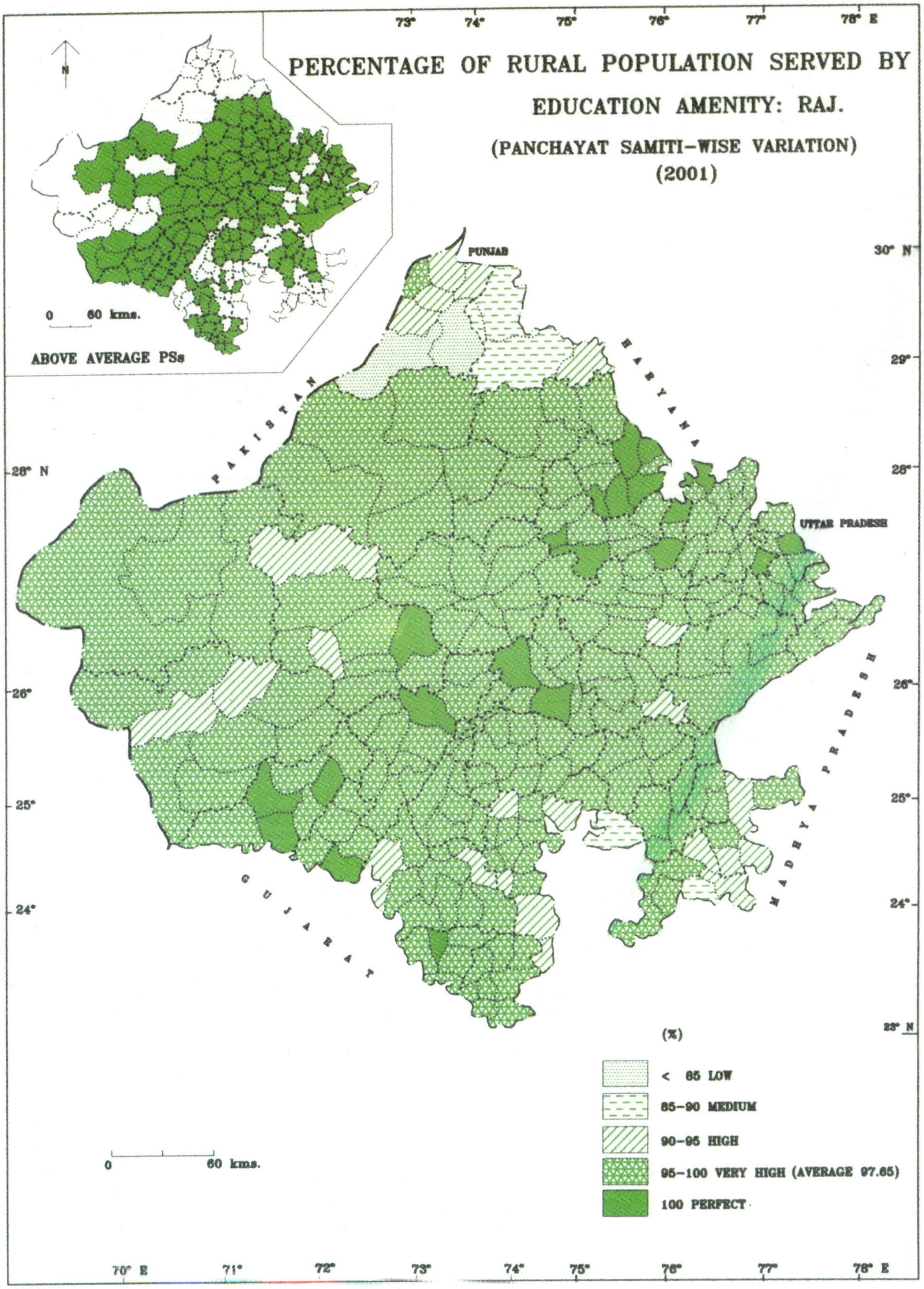
PERCENTAGE OF RURAL POPULATION SERVED BY EDUCATION AMENITY: RAJ.
(PANCHAYAT SAMITI-WISE VARIATION)
(2001)
ABOVE AVERAGE PSs
0 60 kms.
PUNJAB
HARYANA
PAKISTAN
UTTAR PRADESH
MADHYA PRADESH
GUJARAT
(%)
< 85 LOW
85-90 MEDIUM
90-95 HIGH
95-100 VERY HIGH (AVERAGE 97.65)
100 PERFECT
0 60 kms.

FIG. 4.4

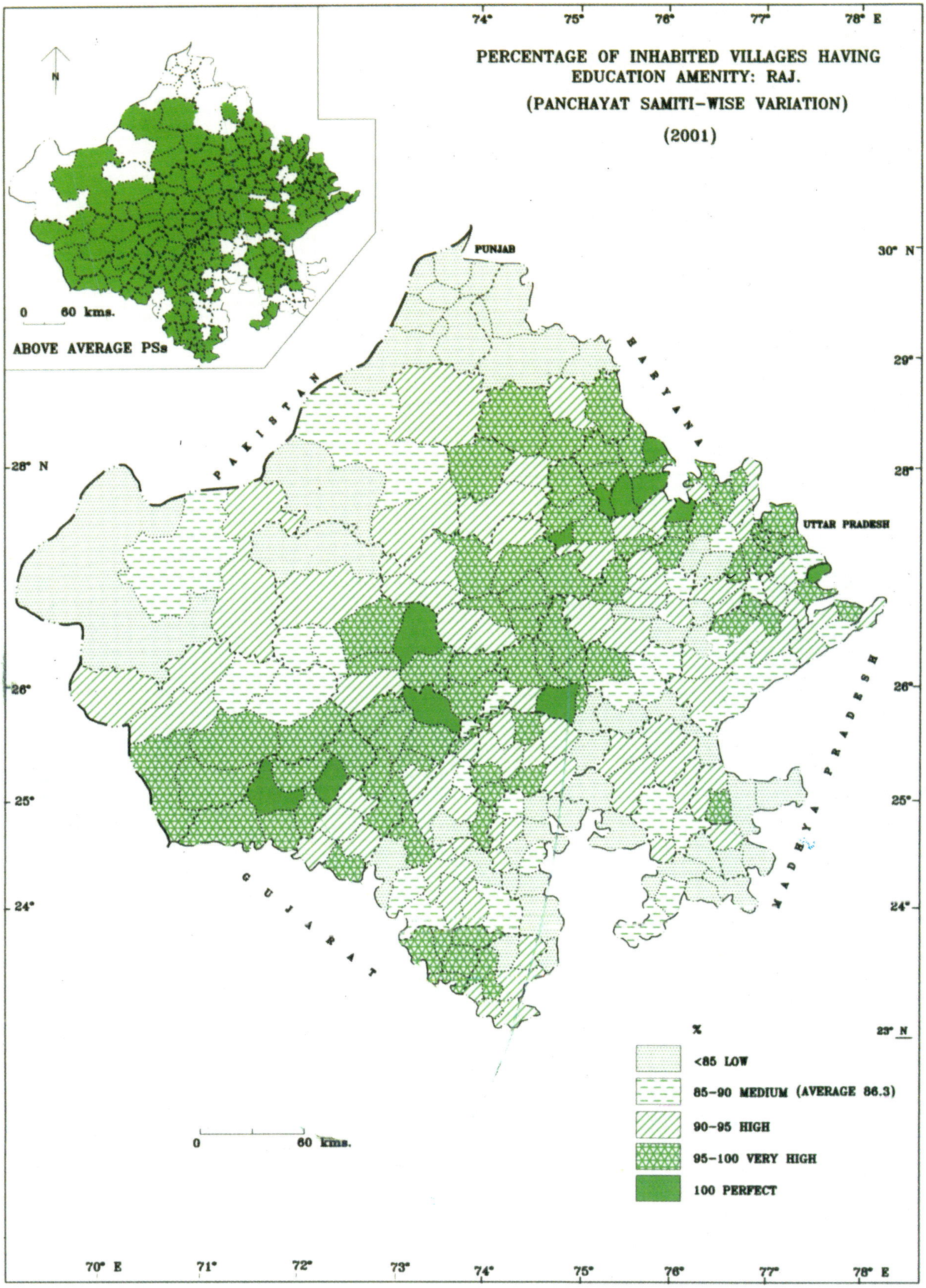
PERCENTAGE OF INHABITED VILLAGES HAVING EDUCATION AMENITY: RAJ.
(PANCHAYAT SAMITI-WISE VARIATION)
(2001)
ABOVE AVERAGE PSs
0 60 kms.
PUNJAB
HARYANA
PAKISTAN
UTTAR PRADESH
MADHYA PRADESH
GUJARAT
%
<85 LOW
85-90 MEDIUM (AVERAGE 86.3)
90-95 HIGH
95-100 VERY HIGH
100 PERFECT
70° E
71°
72°
73°
74°
75°
76°
77°
78° E
30° N
29°
28° N
26°
25°
24°
23° N

FIG. 4.5

Education Amenities

	%age of Rural Pop. Served by	%age of Villages# Having Amenities	No. of Pr. Schools**
State Average (Rural Raj.)	98	86.3	Per PS 211.9 (Total 50219)
Percentage of AAPs	71	81	42.6
Top PS	21 PS had Perfect Amenities	11 PS had Perfect (100%) Amenities	Osian (585)
Bottom PS	Anupgarh (78%)	Hanumangarh (36.6%)	Sheoganj (76%)

TABLE 4.3: Classification of PSs by Education Amenities (2001)

(A) %age of Rural Pop. Served by			(B) %age of Villages# Having Amenities			(C) Total No. of Pr. Schools**		
Group	No. of PSs	%	Group	No. of PSs	%	Group	No. of PSs	%
100	21	8.9	100	11	4.6	>=400	6	2.5
95-100	189	79.7	95-100	79	33.3	300-400	28	11.8
90-95	21	8.9	90-95	74	31.2	200-300	82	34.6
85-90	4	1.7	85-90	29	12.2	100-200	114	48.1
<85	2	0.8	<85	44	18.6	<100	7	3.0
Total	**237**	**100**	**Total**	**237**	**100**	**Total**	**237**	**100**

Source: Annex 4.4 to 4.6

TABLE 4.4: District-wise First and Last PSs by Education Amenities (2001)

District	(A) %age of Rural Pop. Served by		(B) %age of Villages# Having Amenities		(C) Total No. of Pr. Schools**	
	First Rank	Last Rank	First Rank	Last Rank	First Rank	Last Rank
Ajmer	Bhinay*[1]	Jawaja	Bhinay*	Jawaja	Jawaja	Arain
Alwar	Kathumar*[2]	Rajgarh	Bansure	Thanagazi	Bansure	Kotkasim
Banswara	Garhi	Peepalkhoont	Garhi	Peepalkhoont	Ghatol	Anandpuri
Baran	Baran	Chabra	Baran	Chhipabarod	Kishanganj	Baran
Barmer	Sindhari	Barmer	Sindhari	Baytoo	Barmer	Siwana
Bharatpur	Deeg*	Sewar	Kumher	Sewar	Nagar Pahari	Nadbai
Bhilwara	Banera	Mandalgarh##	Raipur	Mandalgarh	Mandal	Raipur
Bikaner	Kolayat	Lunkaransar	Lunkaransar	Kolayat	Bikaner	Lunkaransar
Bundi	Talera	Hindoli	Talera	Keshoraipatan	Talera	Nainwa
Chittaurgarh	Bhopalsagar	Bhainsrorgarh	Dungla	Begun	Pratapgarh	Bhopalsagar
Churu	Dungargarh	Sardarshahar	Churu, Rajgarh	Taranagar	Sujangarh	Taranagar
Dausa	Sikrai	Mahwa	Sikrai	Lalsot	Lalsot	Sikrai
Dhaulpur	Dhaulpur	Bari	Aspur	Bari	Dhaulpur	Bari
Dungarpur	Dungarpur*	Aspur	Dungarpur	Anupgarh	Simalwara	Dungarpur
Ganganagar	Karanpur	Anupgarh	Karanpur	Suratgarh	Anupgarh	Sadulshahar
Hanumangarh	Bhadra	Hanumangarh	Bhadra	Hanumangarh	Hanumangarh	Bhadra
Jaipur	Kotputli*[3]	Chaksu	Kotputli*	Chaksu	Dudu	Jhotwara
Jaisalmer	Sankra	Sam	Sankra	Sam	Sankra	Jaisalmer
Jalor	Bhinmal*[4]	Sanchhore	Bhinmal*, Jalor*	Ahore	Sanchore	Jalor
Jhalawar	Pirawa	Bakani	Pirawa	Bakani	Jhalrapatan	Khanpur
Jhunjhunun	Chirawa*[5]	Alsisar	Khetri*,[9]	Alsisar	Udaipurwati	Chirawa
Jodhpur	Bhopalsagar*	Bap	Bhopalgarh*	Bap	Osian	Mandor
Karauli	Todabhim	Sapotra	Hindaun	Sapotra	Karauli	Nadauti
Kota	Chechat,[6]	Itawa	Sultanpur	Itawa	Sultanpur	Ladpura
Nagaur	Degana	Merta,[7]	Didwana, Parbatsar	Ladnu, Merta	Kuchaman	Ladnu
Pali	Sojat*	Pali	Sojat*	Desuri	Raipur	Rani Station
Rajsamand	Bhim	Deogarh	Bhim	Khamnor	Khamnor	Deogarh
Sawai Madhopur	Gangapur	Khandar	Sawai Madhopur	Khandar	Bamanwas	Khandar
Sikar	Dhond, *[8]	Neem Ka Thana	Dhond*	Khandela	Neem ka Thana	Fatehpur
Sirohi	Abu Road*	Reodar	Abu Road	Reodar	Pindwara	Sheoganj
Tonk	Malpura	Uniara	Malpura	Uniara	Niwai and Tonk	Todarai Singh
Udaipur	Gogunda	Kotra	Gogunda	Kotra	Kherwara	Bargaon

and Jahajpur, * PS/PSs having almost Perfect (100%) Education Amenity. ** for the year 2000

Source : General Annex-VII, VIII and XIV

1 and Pisangan*, 2 and Nimrana*, 3 and Shahpura*, 4 and Jalor*, Raniwara 5 and Khetri * Nawalgarh* Surajgarh* Udaipurwati*, 6 and Sultanpur 7 Mundwa, Riyan 8 and Sawai Madhopur* 9 Nawalgarh, Surajgarh, Udaipurwati # Inhabited Villages

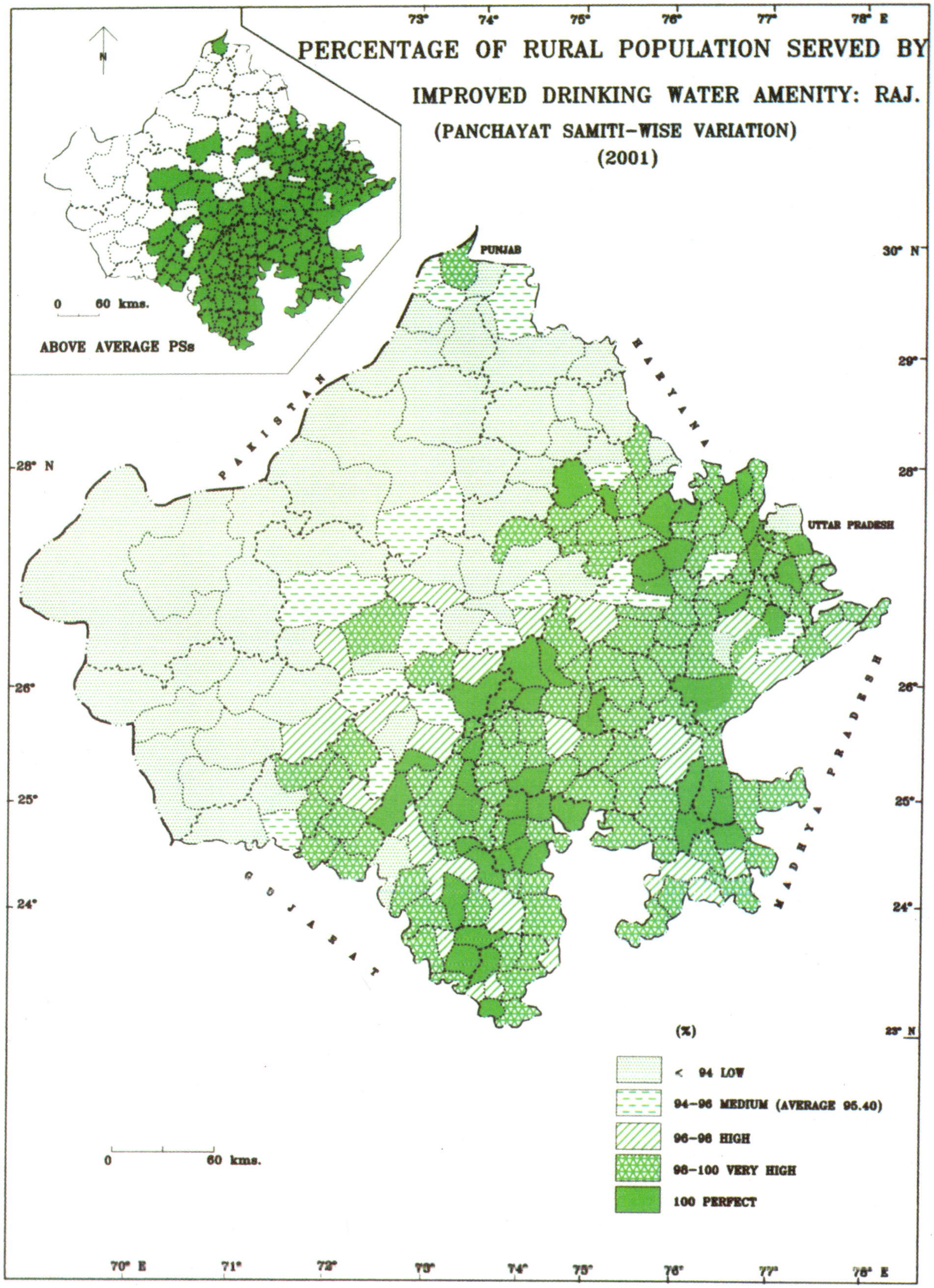

PERCENTAGE OF RURAL POPULATION SERVED BY
IMPROVED DRINKING WATER AMENITY: RAJ.
(PANCHAYAT SAMITI-WISE VARIATION)
(2001)
N
0 60 kms.
ABOVE AVERAGE PSs
PUNJAB
HARYANA
PAKISTAN
UTTAR PRADESH
MADHYA PRADESH
GUJARAT
(%)
< 94 LOW
94-96 MEDIUM (AVERAGE 95.40)
96-98 HIGH
98-100 VERY HIGH
100 PERFECT
0 60 kms.
70° E
71°
72°
73°
74°
75°
76°
77°
78° E
30° N
29°
28° N
28°
26°
25°
24°
23° N

FIG. 4.6

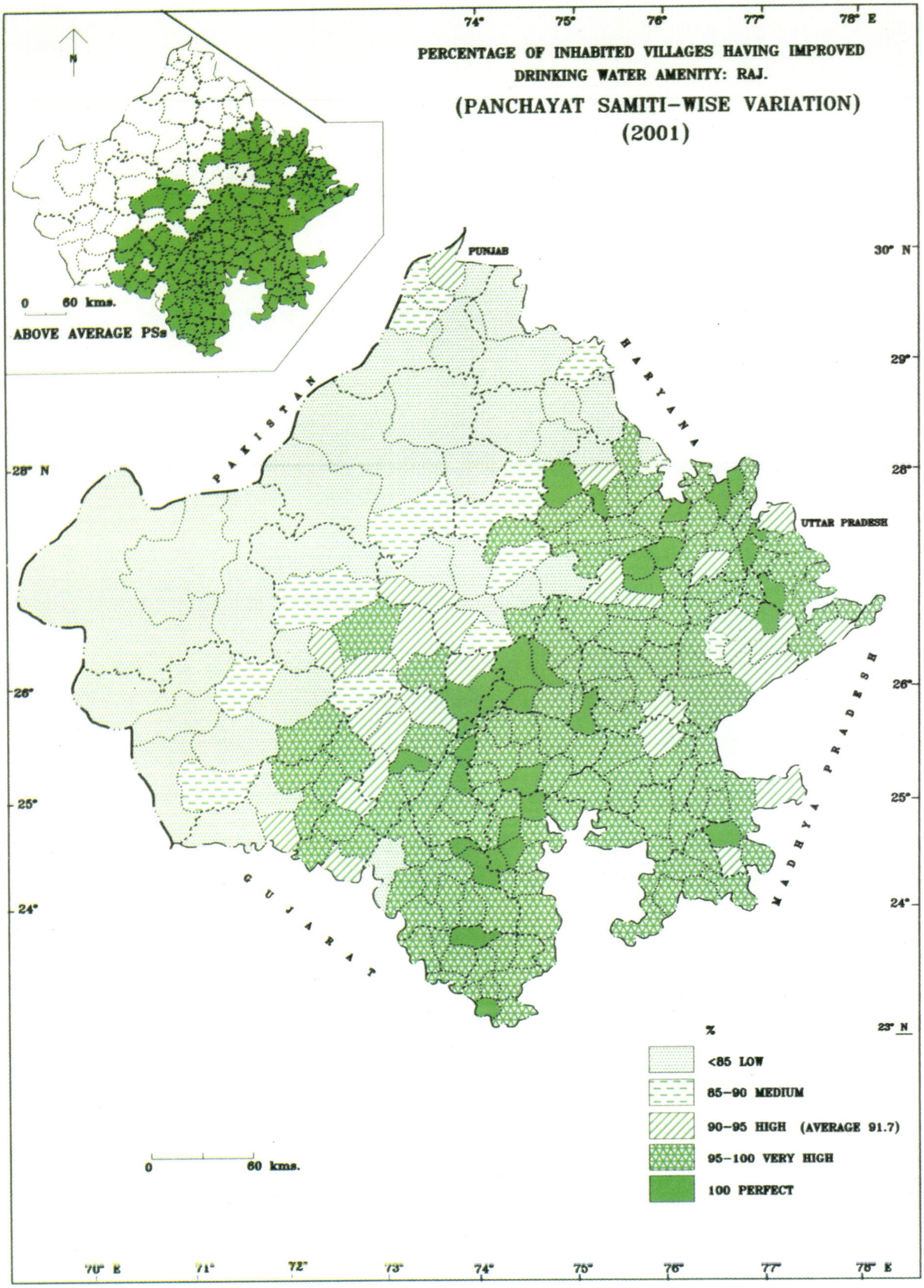
PERCENTAGE OF INHABITED VILLAGES HAVING IMPROVED DRINKING WATER AMENITY: RAJ.
(PANCHAYAT SAMITI-WISE VARIATION)
(2001)
N
0 60 kms.
ABOVE AVERAGE PSs
PUNJAB
HARYANA
PAKISTAN
UTTAR PRADESH
MADHYA PRADESH
GUJARAT
%
<85 LOW
85-90 MEDIUM
90-95 HIGH (AVERAGE 91.7)
95-100 VERY HIGH
100 PERFECT
0 60 kms.
70° E
71°
72°
73°
74°
75°
76°
77°
78° E
30° N
29°
28° N
26°
25°
24°
23° N

FIG. 4.7

Improved Drinking Water Amenities

	%age of Rural Pop Served by	*%age of Villages# Having Amenities*
State Average (Rural Raj.)	95.4	91.7
Percentage of AAPs	77	75.9
Top PS	47 PSs had Perfect (100%) Amenities	30 PSs had Perfect (100%) Amenities
Bottom PS	Sardarshahar (52.5%)	Sardarshahar (47%)

TABLE 4.5: Classification of PSs by Improved Drinking Water Amenities (2001)

(A) %age of Rural Pop Served by			*(B) %age of Villages# Having Amenities*		
Group	*No. of PSs*	*%*	*Group*	*No. of PSs*	*%*
100	47	19.8	100	30	12.6
98-100	105	44.3	95-100	131	55.3
96-98	24	10.1	90-95	30	12.7
94-96	18	7.6	85-90	13	5.5
<94	43	18.1	<85	33	13.9
Total	**237**	**100**	**Total**	**237**	**100**

Source: Annex 4.7 and 4.8

TABLE 4.6: District-wise First and Last PSs by Improved Drinking Water Amenities (2001)

District	*(A) %age of Rural Pop Served by*		*(B) %age of Villages# Having Amenities*	
	First Rank	*Last Rank*	*First Rank*	*Last Rank*
Ajmer	Jawaja,* Kekri,* Masooda,* Pisangan,* Srinagar*	Bhinay	Jawaja*, Kekri*, Masooda*, Pisangan*, Srinagar*	Arain
Alwar	Kotkasim,* Lachhmangarh,* Mandawar*, Ramgarh*	Rajgarh	Kotkasim*, Lachhmangarh,* Mandawar*, Ramgarh*	Rajgarh
Banswara	Garhi*, Sajjangarh*	Anandpuri	Sajjangarh*	Peepalkhoont
Baran	Anta, * Atru, * Baran*	Chhabra	Atru*	Shahbad
Barmer	Siwana	Barmer	Siwana	Barmer
Bharatpur	Deeg*, Nadbai*	Kaman	Nadbai*	Kaman
Bhilwara	Suwana*	Shahpura	Suwana*	Shahpura
Bikaner	Nokha	Kolayat	Nokha	Kolayat
Bundi	Talera	Keshoraipatan	Talera	Nainwa
Chittaurgarh	Begun*, Bhadesar*, Dungla*, Kapasan*, Nimbahera*, Rashmi*	Arnod	Bhadesar*, Dungla*, Gangrar*, Kapasan*	Arnod, Chhotisadri
Churu	Ratangarh	Sardarshahar	Ratangarh	Sardarshahar
Dausa	Sikrai*	Dausa	Sikrai	Lalsot
Dhaulpur	Dhaulpur	Bari	Rajakhera	Bari
Dungarpur	Aspur*, Sagwara*	Dungarpur	Aspur*	Dungarpur
Ganganagar	Ganganagar	Suratgarh	Ganganagar	Sadulshahar
Hanumangarh	Bhadra	Nohar	Bhadra	Nohar
Jaipur	Amber*, Govindgarh*, Kotputli, * Shahpura*	Jhotwara	Amber*, Govindgarh*, Kotputli, * Shahpura*	Jhotwara
Jaisalmer	Sankra	Jaisalmer	Sankra	Jaisalmer
Jalor	Ahore, Jalor	Bhinmal	Jalor	Bhinmal
Jhalawar	Pirawa	Bakani	Dag	Bakani
Jhunjhunun	Nawalgarh	Alsisar	Nawalgarh*	Alsisar
Jodhpur	Bilara	Bap	Bilara	Bap
Karauli	Hindaun*	Karauli	Hindaun*	Karauli
Kota	Sangod*, Sultanpur*	Chechat	Sangod	Chechat
Nagaur	Ladnu	Jayal	Parabatsar	Jayal
Pali	Bali, * Raipur*, Rani Station*	Pali	Raipur*, Rani Station*	Jaitaran
Rajsamand	Amet*, Deogarh*, Rajsamand*	Bhim	Amet*, Deogarh*	Bhim
Sawai Madhopur	Sawai Madhopur*	Bamanwas	Sawai Madhopur	Bamanwas
Sikar	Fatehpur*, Neem ka Thana*	Danta Ramgarh	Fatehpur*	Piprali
Sirohi	Reodar	Sheoganj	Reodar	Sheoganj
Tonk	Todaraisingh	Uniara	Deoli	Uniara
Udaipur	Bhinder*, Mavli*, Sarada*	Kotra	Bhinder*, Mavli*	Kotra

Source: General Annex-VII and VIII. * PS/PSs having almost perfect (100%) Drinking Water amenity. # Inhabited Villages

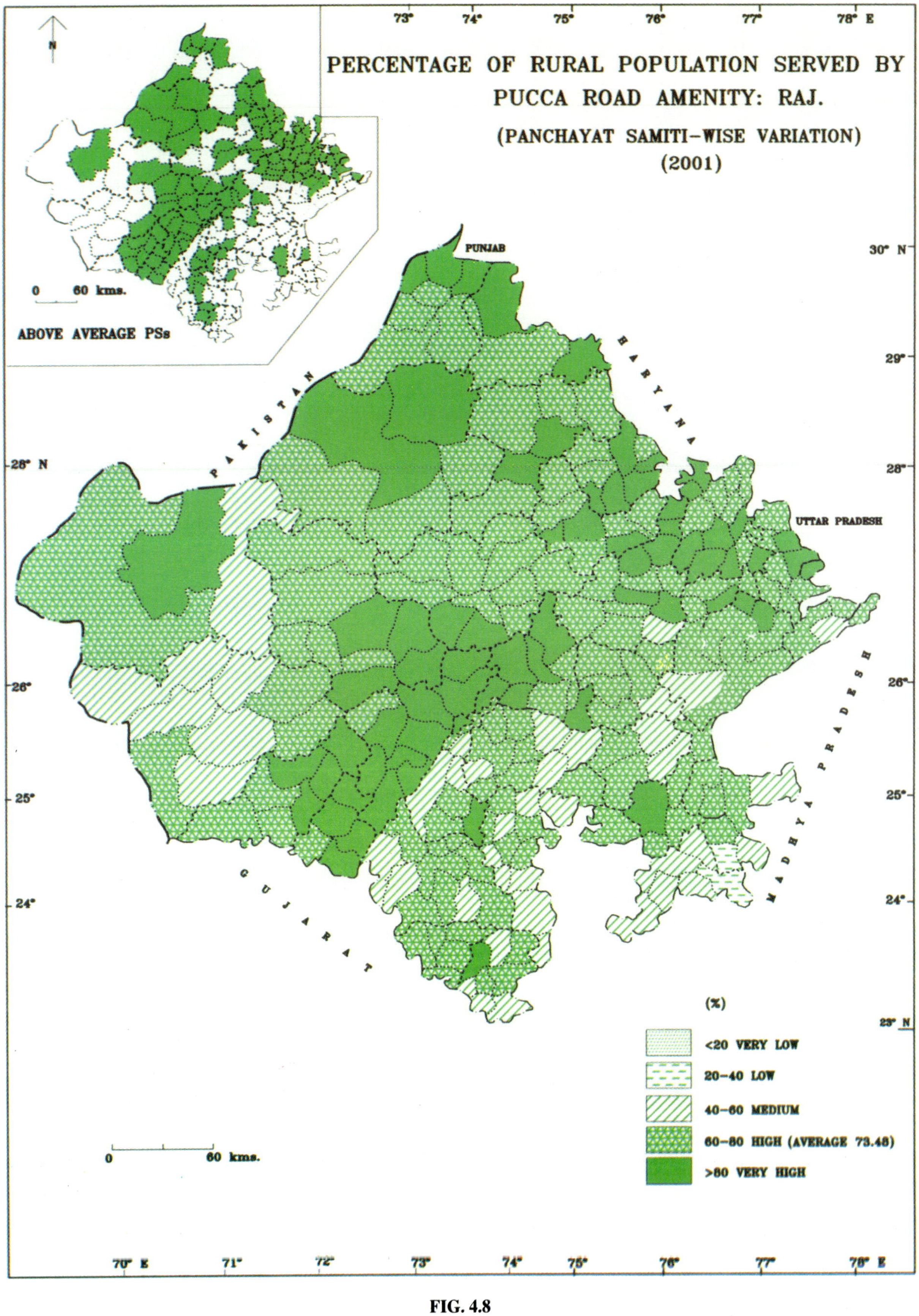
PERCENTAGE OF RURAL POPULATION SERVED BY PUCCA ROAD AMENITY: RAJ.
(PANCHAYAT SAMITI-WISE VARIATION)
(2001)
ABOVE AVERAGE PSs
0 60 kms.
N
PUNJAB
HARYANA
UTTAR PRADESH
MADHYA PRADESH
GUJARAT
PAKISTAN
(%)
<20 VERY LOW
20-40 LOW
40-60 MEDIUM
60-80 HIGH (AVERAGE 73.48)
>80 VERY HIGH
0 60 kms.
70° E
71°
72°
73°
74°
75°
76°
77°
78° E
30° N
29°
28° N
28°
26°
25°
24°
23° N

FIG. 4.8

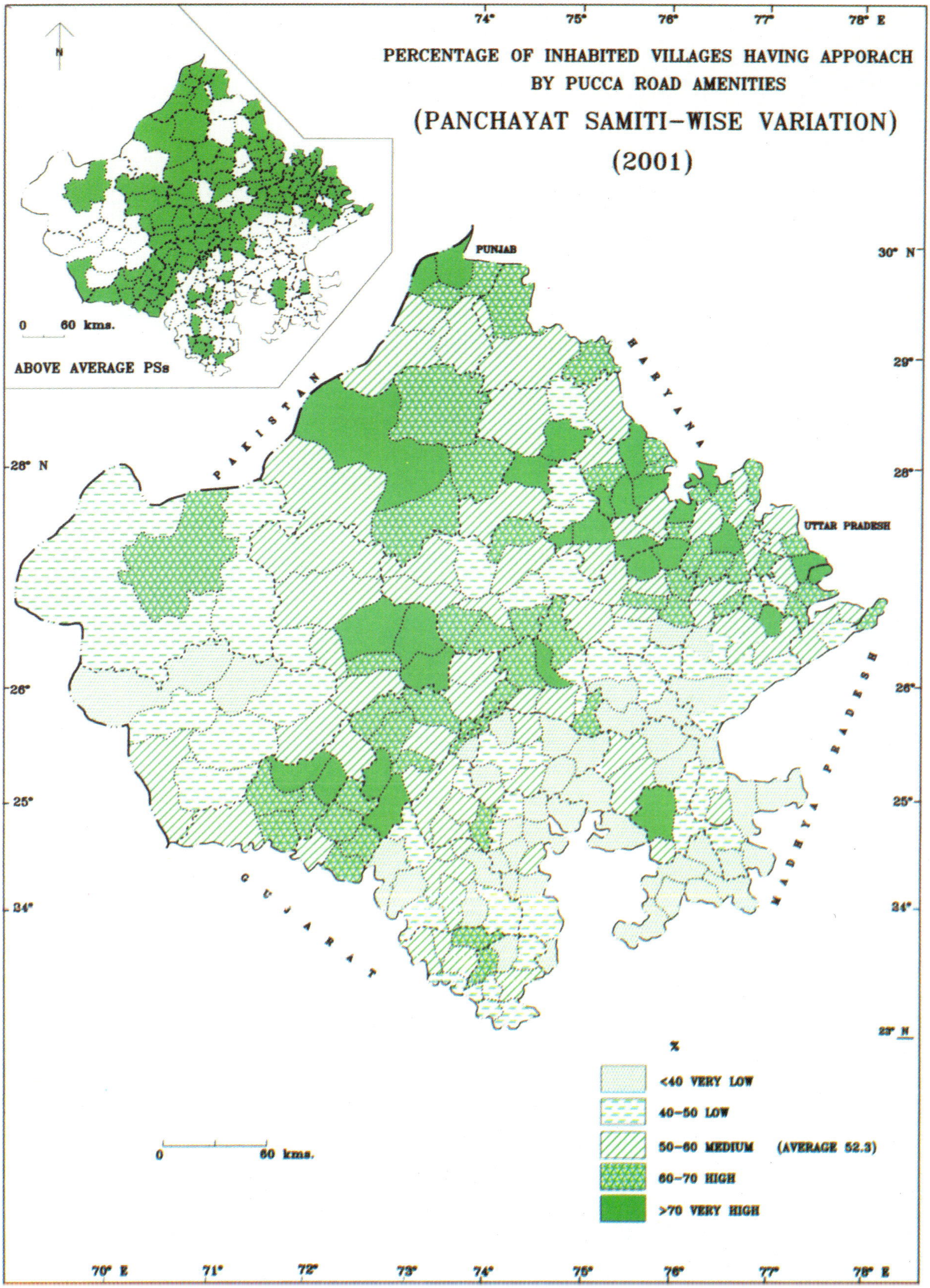
PERCENTAGE OF INHABITED VILLAGES HAVING APPORACH BY PUCCA ROAD AMENITIES
(PANCHAYAT SAMITI–WISE VARIATION)
(2001)
ABOVE AVERAGE PSs
0 60 kms.
PUNJAB
HARYANA
UTTAR PRADESH
MADHYA PRADESH
GUJARAT
PAKISTAN
%
<40 VERY LOW
40–50 LOW
50–60 MEDIUM (AVERAGE 52.3)
60–70 HIGH
>70 VERY HIGH
0 60 kms.
70° E
71°
72°
73°
74°
75°
76°
77°
78° E
30° N
29°
28° N
28°
26°
25°
24°
23° N

FIG. 4.9

Pucca Road Amenities

	%age of Rural Pop. Served by	%age of Villages# Having Amenities
State Average (Rural Raj.)	73	52.3
Percentage of AAPs	54	57.4
Top PS	Sumerpur (99.8%)	Sumerpur (98.4%)
Bottom PS	Manoharthana (31%)	Manoharthana (21.8%)

TABLE 4.7: Classification of PSs by Pucca Road Amenities (2001)

(A) %age of Rural Pop. Served by			*(B) %age of Villages# Having Amenities*		
Group	*No. of PSs*	*%*	*Group*	*No. of PSs*	*%*
>80	69	29.1	>70	29	12.2
60-80	125	52.7	60-70	53	22.4
40-60	41	17.3	50-60	67	28.3
<40	2	0.8	40-50	45	19.0
—	—	—	<40	43	18.1
Total	**237**	**100**	**Total**	**237**	**100**

Source: Annex 4.9 and 4.10

TABLE 4.8: District-wise First and Last PSs by Pucca Road Amenities (2001)

District	*(A) %age of Rural Pop. Served by*		*(B) %age of Villages# Having Amenities*	
	First Rank	*Last Rank*	*First Rank*	*Last Rank*
Ajmer	Srinagar	Arain	Srinagar	Arain
Alwar	Nimrana	Kotkasim	Nimrana	Kotkasim
Banswara	Garhi	Kushalgarh	Garhi	Peepalkhoont
Baran	Baran	Chhabra	Baran	Chhabra
Barmer	Siwana	Baytoo	Chohtan	Baytoo
Bharatpur	Sewar	Weir	Sewar	Weir
Bhilwara	Hurda	Raipur	Hurda	Raipur
Bikaner	Bikaner	Kolayat	Bikaner	Kolayat
Bundi	Talera	Keshoraipatan	Hindoli	Nainwa
Chittaurgarh	Rashmi	Kapasan	Nimbahera	Dungla
Churu	Ratangarh	Sardarshahar	Churu	Taranagar
Dausa	Sikrai	Lalsot	Sikrai	Lalsot
Dhaulpur	Dhaulpur	Bari	Rajakhera	Bari
Dungarpur	Aspur, Sagwara	Dungarpur	Dungarpur, Anupgarh	Simalwara
Ganganagar	Ganganagar	Raisinghnagar	Karanpur	Raisinghnagar
Hanumangarh	Hanumangarh	Nohar	Hanumangarh	Nohar
Jaipur	Govindgarh	Chaksu	Kotputli	Chaksu
Jaisalmer	Jaisalmer	Sankra	Jaisalmer	Sankra
Jalor	Jalor	Sanchore	Jalor	Sanchore
Jhalawar	Khanpur	Manoharthana	Jhalrapatan	Manoharthana
Jhunjhunun	Chirawa	Surajgarh	Udaipurwati	Alsisar
Jodhpur	Bhopalgarh	Shergarh	Bhopalgarh	Shergarh
Karauli	Hindaun	Sapotra	Hindaun	Sapotra
Kota	Ladpura	Sangod	Ladpura	Itawa
Nagaur	Merta	Kuchaman	Merta	Makrana
Pali	Sumerpur	Rohat	Sumerpur	Desuri
Rajsamand	Railmagra	Deogarh	Bhim	Deogarh
Sawai Madhopur	Gangapur	Sawai Madhopur	Gangapur	Sawai Madhopur
Sikar	Sri Madhopur	Fatehpur	Sawai Madhopur	Lachhmangarh
Sirohi	Sirohi	Reodar	Sheoganj	Reodar
Tonk	Malpura	Uniara	Tonk	Deoli
Udaipur	Girwa	Kotra	Sarada	Kotra

Source: General Annex-VII and VIII. # Inhabited Villages

Bank Amenities

	%age of Rural Pop. Served by	*%age of Villages# Having Amenities*
State Average (Rural Raj.)	19.3	5.3
Percentage of AAPs	50.2	50.2
Top PS	Pali (41.2%)	Pali (17.5%)
Bottom PS	Rajakhera (3.3%)	Anupgarh (1.2%)

TABLE 4.19: Classification of PSs by Bank Amenities (2001)

(A) %age of Rural Pop. Served by			*(B) %age of Villages# Having Amenities*		
Group	*No. of PSs*	*%*	*Group*	*No. of PSs*	*%*
>=25	52	21.9	>=7	80	33.8
20-25	61	25.7	6-7	19	8.0
15-20	51	21.5	5-6	25	10.5
10-15	45	19.0	4-5	47	19.8
<10	28	11.8	<4	66	27.8
Total	**237**	**100**	**Total**	**237**	**100**

Source: Annex 4.21 and 4.22

TABLE 4.20: District-wise First and Last PSs by Bank Amenities (2001).

District	*(A) %age of Rural Pop. Served by*		*(B) %age of Villages# Having Amenities*	
	First Rank	*Last Rank*	*First Rank*	*Last Rank*
Ajmer	Kishangarh	Jawaja	Arain	Jawaja
Alwar	Reni	Kishagarh Bas	Nimrana	Lachhmangarh
Banswara	Garhi	Kushalgarh	Garhi	Anandpuri
Baran	Anta	Chhabra	Anta	Chhabra
Barmer	Siwana	Barmer	Siwana	Barmer
Bharatpur	Kumher	Kaman	Kumher	Kaman
Bhilwara	Hurda	Jahazpur	Hurda	Kotri
Bikaner	Bikaner	Kolayat	Nokha	Kolayat
Bundi	Talera	Keshoraipatan	Talera	Keshoraipatan
Chittaurgarh	Bhopalsagar	Rashmi	Bhopalsagar	Bhainsrorgarh
Churu	Taranagar	Sardarshahar	Dungargarh	Rajgarh
Dausa	Sikrai	Mahwa	Sikrai	Mahwa
Dhaulpur	Dhaulpur	Rajakhera	Baseri	Rajakhera
Dungarpur	Sagwara	Dungarpur	Sagwara	Dungarpur
Ganganagar	Ganganagar	Raisinghnager	Ganganagar	Anupgarh
Hanumangarh	Bhadra	Nohar	Bhadra	Hanumangarh
Jaipur	Govindgarh	Jhotwara	Govindgarh	Jhotwara
Jaisalmer	Jaisalmer	Sankra	Jaisalmer	Sam
Jalor	Ahore	Sanchore	Sayla	Raniwara
Jhalawar	Khanpur	Manoharthana	Pirwa	Manoharthana
Jhunjhunun	Alsisar	Jhunjhunun	Udaipurwati	Jhunjhunun
Jodhpur	Bhopalgarh	Balesar	Phalodi	Balesar
Karauli	Nadoti	Todabhim	Nadoti	Karauli
Kota	Sultanpur	Ladpura	Sultanpur	Sangod
Nagaur	Merta	Nagaur	Merta	Nagaur
Pali	Pali	Rohat	Pali	Bali
Rajsamand	Railmagara	Amet	Railmagara	Amet
Sawai Madhopur	Sawai Madhopur	Khandar	Gangapur	Khandar
Sikar	Piprali	Fatehpur	Sri Madhopur	Fatehpur
Sirohi	Sirohi	Reodar	Sirohi	Reodar
Tonk	Malpura	Todaraisingh	Malpura	Uniara
Udaipur	Bargaon	Kherwara	Bargaon	Dhariawad

Source: Annex-VII and VIII

Inhabited Villages

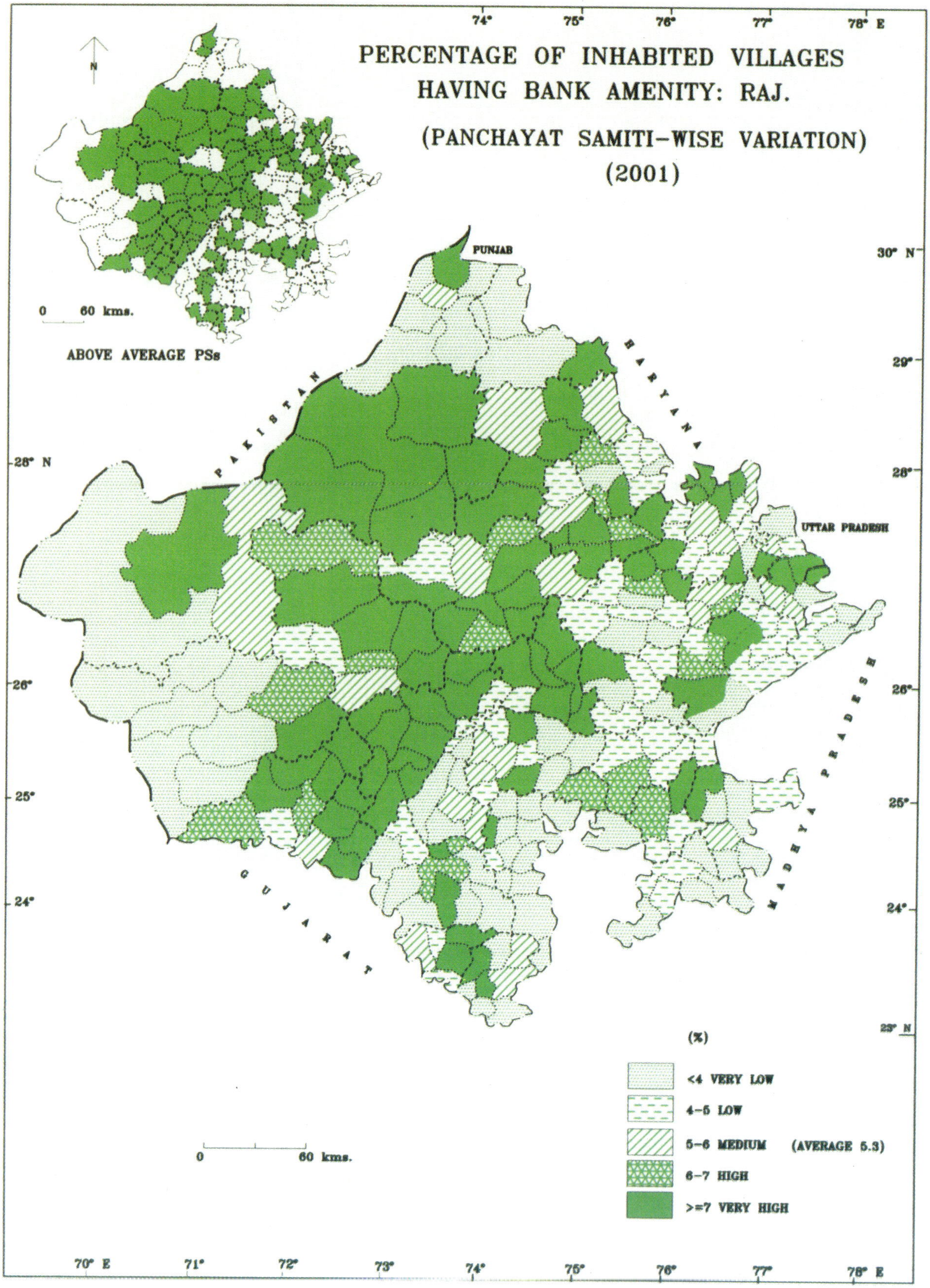
PERCENTAGE OF INHABITED VILLAGES
HAVING BANK AMENITY: RAJ.
(PANCHAYAT SAMITI-WISE VARIATION)
(2001)
N
0 60 kms.
ABOVE AVERAGE PSs
PUNJAB
HARYANA
PAKISTAN
UTTAR PRADESH
MADHYA PRADESH
GUJARAT
(%)
<4 VERY LOW
4-5 LOW
5-6 MEDIUM (AVERAGE 5.3)
6-7 HIGH
>=7 VERY HIGH
0 60 kms.
70° E
71°
72°
73°
74°
75°
76°
77°
78° E
30° N
29°
28° N
28°
26°
25°
24°
23° N

FIG. 4.21

5

HEALTH STATUS INDEX (HSI) (1991)

Highlights

- Rural HSI—Rajasthan : 0.559
- Percentage of AAPs: 52.74
- 39 PSs had HSI below 0.5

	Panchayat Samiti	District	Division
• **Top**	Sumerpur (HSI 0.729)	Pali	Jodhpur
• **Bottom**	Sam (HSI 0.346)	Jaisalmer	Jodhpur

The Health Status Index (HSI) of rural Rajasthan in the year 1991 was 0.559. There were 125 PSs having HSI above the state average. A great deal of regional disparity is observed in HSI across the state. Whereas, 50 per cent PSs of Jodhpur division, 44 per cent of Ajmer and 39 per cent PSs of Jaipur division had medium to high level of HSI (>0.6), 100 per cent PSs of Kota division, 86 per cent of Bikaner and more than 70 per cent PSs of Udaipur division had low to very low of HSI (Fig. 5.1). The HSI level in the state increases mainly from the South-East and South to the South-West, Central and North-East direction.

TABLE 5.1: Distribution of First and Last Ten Panchayat Samities by HSI, 1991 : Rajasthan

S. No.	*First Ten PSs (Descending Order)*						*Last Ten PSs (Ascending Order)*						
	Districts/ PSs						*Districts/ PSs*						
	Pali	*Jhun*	*Jodh*	*Jp*	*Ajmer*	*Sikar*	*Barmer*	*Jhal*	*Jodh*	*Udaipur*	*Gg*	*Dhaul*	*Jais*
	(4)	*(2)*	*(1)*	*(1)*	*(1)*	*(1)*	*(4)*	*(1)*	*(1)*	*(1)*	*(1)*	*(1)*	*(1)*
1	Sumerpur	Nawal[1]	Bilara	Govind	Pisangan	Dhond	Baytoo	Mano[3]	Bap	Kotra	Anup[4]	Bari	Sam
2	Bali	Udaip[2]	—	—	—	—	Barmer	—	—	—	—	—	—
3	Rani Station	—	—	—	—	—	Sheo	—	—	—	—	—	—
4	Desuri	—	—	—	—	—	Sindhari	—	—	—	—	—	—

Source: Annex 5.1 [1] Nawalgarh [2] Udaipurwati [3] Manoharthana [4] Anupgarh.

Sumerpur PS of Pali district had the maximum HSI (0.7291) followed by Nawalgarh, Bali, Bilara, Udaipurwati, Govindgarh, Pisangan, Rani Station, Dhond and Desuri PSs (in descending order, Annex 5.2). These top ten PSs were spread over six districts. Pali led with four PSs followed by Jhunjhunun (2) and Jodhpur, Jaipur, Ajmer and Sikar (one each) districts (Table 5.1). Sam PS of Jaisalmer district, on the other hand, had the minimum (0.346) HSI. It was preceded by Baytoo, Barmer, Bari, Anupgarh, Kotra, Bap, Sheo, Manoharthana, and Sindhari PSs (in ascending order).

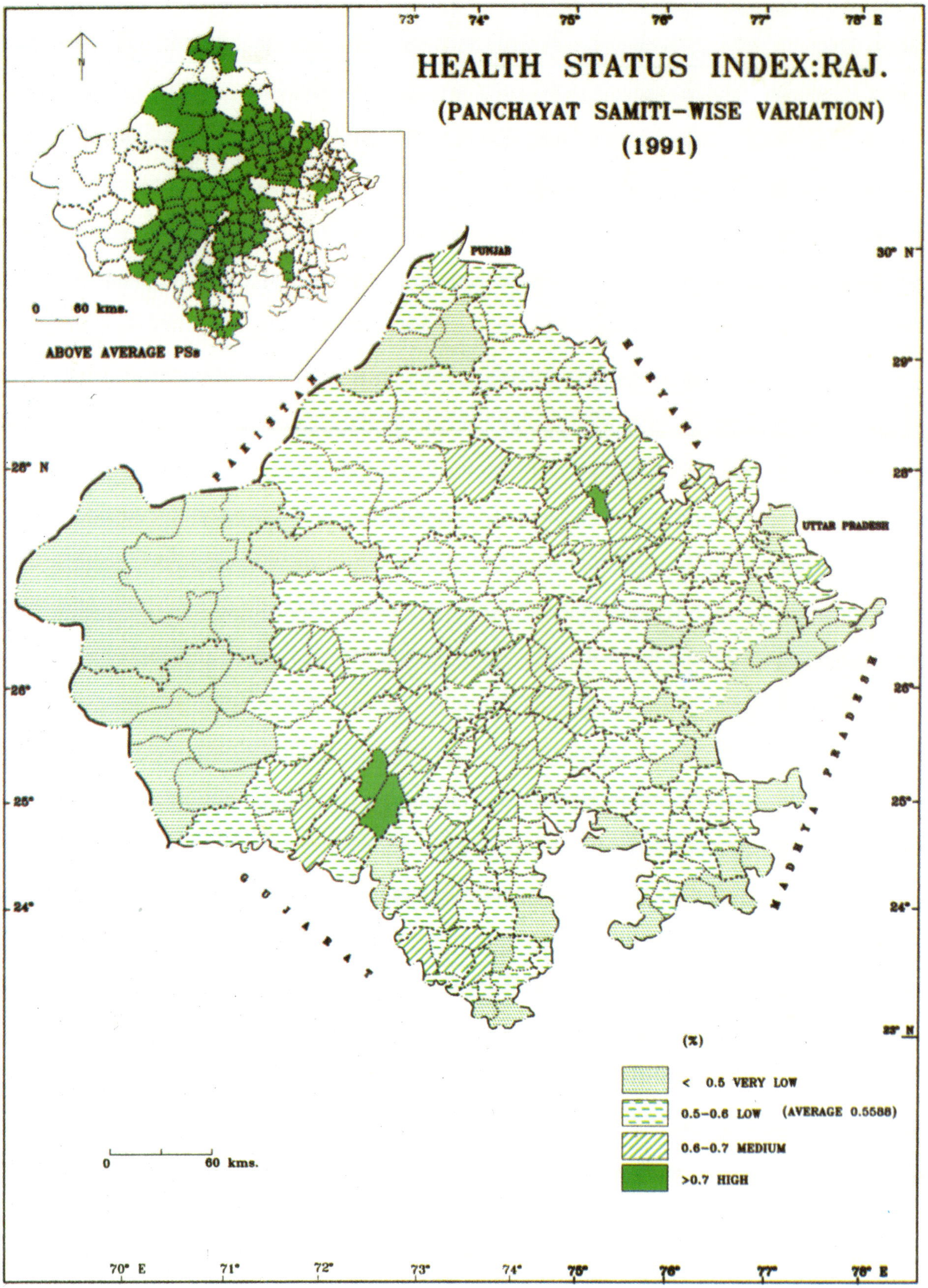
HEALTH STATUS INDEX:RAJ.
(PANCHAYAT SAMITI-WISE VARIATION)
(1991)
ABOVE AVERAGE PSs
0 60 kms.
PUNJAB
HARYANA
UTTAR PRADESH
MADHYA PRADESH
GUJARAT
PAKISTAN
(%)
< 0.5 VERY LOW
0.5-0.6 LOW (AVERAGE 0.5588)
0.6-0.7 MEDIUM
>0.7 HIGH
0 60 kms.

FIG. 5.1

These last ten PSs were concentrated in seven districts. Barmer dominated with 4 PSs while Jhalawar, Jodhpur, Udaipur, Ganganagar, Dhaulpur and Jaisalmer districts had one PS each. Similarly, district-wise first and the last PSs by HSI are shown in Table 5.2.

TABLE 5.2: District-wise First and Last PSs by HSI (1991)

District	*First Rank*	*Last Rank*	*District*	*First Rank*	*Last Rank*
Ajmer	Pisangan	Jawaja	Jaipur	Govindgarh	Chaksu
Alwar	Nimrana	Lachmangarh	Jaisalmer	Jaisalmer	Sam
Banswara	Garhi	Kushalgarh	Jalor	Jalor	Sanchore
Baran	Atru	Chhipabarod	Jhalawar	Jhalrapatan	Manoharthana
Barmer	Siwana	Bayatoo	Jhunjhunun	Nawalgarh	Surajgarh
Bharatpur	Kumher	Nagar Pahari	Jodhpur	Bilara	Bap
Bhilwara	Hurda	Mandalgarh	Karauli	Hindaun	Karauli
Bikaner	Nokha	Kolayat	Kota	Ladpura	Itawa
Bundi	Nainwa	Keshoraipatan	Nagaur	Merta	Didwana
Chittaurgarh	Bhopalsagar	Bhainsrorgarh	Pali	Sumerpur	Rohat
Churu	Ratangarh	Rajgarh	Rajsamand	Railmagra	Kumbhalgarh
Dausa	Dausa	Lalsot	Sawai Madhopur	Gangapur	Khandar
Dhaulpur	Dhaulpur	Bari	Sikar	Dhond	Piprali
Dungarpur	Sagwara	Simalwara	Sirohi	Sirohi	Abu Road
Ganganagar	Ganganagar	Anupgarh	Tonk	Malpura	Uniara
Hanumangarh	Hanumangarh	Nohar	Udaipur	Mavli	Kotra

Source: Annex 6.1

Classification of PSs by HSI

Table 5.3 presents classification of PSs by HSI. The state had dominance of Low Level PSs (51.1%) followed by Medium (30.8%), Very Low (16.5%), and High (1.3%) level PSs.

TABLE 5.3: Classification of PSs on the Basis of HSI (1991) : Rajasthan

Group	*Included PSs*			
	No.	*%*	*Distributed in*	
			Districts	*Divisions*
High (H), (0.7-0.8)	3	1.3	2	2
Medium (M), (0.6-0.7)	73	30.8	19	6
Low (L), (0.5-0.6)	122	51.5	31	6
Very Low (VL), (<0.5)	39	16.5	18	6
Total	**237**	**100**		

Source: Annex 5.1.

If we look at division-wise classification and distribution of PSs by HSI (Table 5.4) following interpretations can be made:

- Both Jaipur and Jodhpur divisions had PSs of all the four levels, while Ajmer, Bikaner and Udaipur divisions had PSs of 3 levels. Kota was the only division having PSs of 2 levels.
- Jodhpur division secured the top position in the state with 67 per cent share of High level PSs.

Table 5.4: Division-wise Classification and Distribution of PSs on the Basis of HSI Level (2001)

Divisions	*Classification*					*Distribution (% Share)*			
	HSI Level					*HSI Level*			
	High	*Medium*	*Low*	*Very Low*	*Total PSs*	*High*	*Medium*	*Low*	*Very Low*
Jaipur	1 (1.6)	24 (39.3)	31 (50.8)	5 (8.2)	61 (100.0)	16.7	30.4	25.6	—
Bikaner	1 (4.8)	6 (28.6)	9 (42.9)	5 (23.8)	21 (100.0)	16.7	7.6	7.4	—
Ajmer	— —	15 (41.7)	21 (58.3)	— —	36 (100.0)	—	19.0	17.4	—
Kota	— —	3 (9.4)	22 (68.8)	7 (21.9)	32 (100.0)	—	3.8	18.2	—
Jodhpur	4 (9.5)	19 (45.2)	10 (23.8)	5 (11.9)	42 (100.0)	66.7	24.1	8.3	80.0
Udaipur	— —	12 (26.7)	28 (62.2)	4 (8.9)	45 (100.0)	—	15.2	23.1	20.0
Total	**6 (2.5)**	**79 (33.3)**	**121 (51.1)**	**26 (11.0)**	**237 (100.0)**	**100**	**100**	**100**	**100**

Figure in brackets shows percentage share to total Panchayat Samities.
Source: Annex 5.1
Note: HSI Level H: (>0.7), M : (0.6-0.7), L : (0.5-0.6), VL : (<0.5)

- Kota divison was the most deprived led in PSs having VL (28.2%) HSI level while, Jaipur division led in M (30%) as well as L (23.8%) level PSs.
- Except Jodhpur, all the divisions have dominance of L level PSs. Jodhpur division had dominance of M level PSs.
- The percentage of H level PSs in Jodhpur and Jaipur divisions; M level in Jodhpur, Ajmer and Jaipur divisions; L level in Bikaner, Udaipur, Kota and Ajmer, divisions and VL level in Kota and Jodhpur divisions was higher than the state average.

High and Medium HSI Region

There were only 3 PSs viz. Sumerpur and Bali of Pali District and Nawalgarh of Jhunjhunun having High HSI both these districts had greater percentage of H level PSs in comparison to the state average (1.3). The percentage ranged from 20 in Pali district to 12.5 in Jhunjhunun (Tables 5.5 & 5.6).

Medium HSI area was widely distributed in 5 divisions (Except Kota) and 19 districts. There were total 73 M level PSs. Jaipur division with 30.1 per cent share had the maximum concentration of these PSs follwed by Jodhpur (26%), Ajmer (21.9%), Udaipur (17.8%), and Bikaner (4.1%) divisions. The percentage share of M level PSs to total PSs was the highest in Jodhpur with 45.2 per cent, 44.4 in Ajmer, 36.1 in Jaipur, 28.9 in Udaipur, and the lowest 14.3 in Bikaner division.

District-wise distribution of these PSs makes it clear that Bhilwara secured the top rank with 8 PSs followed by Sikar (7); Ajmer, Jhunjhunun and Pali (6 each); Jaipur and Jodhpur (5 each); Jalor, Sirohi and Udaipur (4 each); Alwar Dungarpur and Rajsamand (3 each); Chittaurgarh, Churu and Nagaur (2 each); and Banswara, Bharatpur and Ganganagar (1each) respectively. All the above districts, except Alwar, Banswara, Bharatpur, Chittaurgarh, Churu, Ganganagar, and Nagaur had higher percentage of Medium level PSs in comparison to the state average (30.8). Sikar district had the highest percentage (87.5) of M level PSs while, Bharatpur had the lowest (11.1).

TABLE 5.5: District-wise Classification of PSs on the Basis of HSI Level, 1991

DISTRICT	*H*	*M*	*L*	*VL*	*TOTAL*
Ajmer	—	6	2	—	8
	—	(75.0)	(25.0)	—	(100.0)
Alwar	—	3	11	—	14
	—	(21.4)	(78.6)	—	(100.0)
Banswara	—	1	4	3	8
	—	(12.5)	(50.0)	(37.5)	(100.0)
Baran	—	—	4	3	7
	—	—	(57.1)	(42.9)	(100.0)
Barmer	—	—	2	6	8
	—	—	(25.0)	(75.0)	(100.0)
Bharatpur	—	1	5	3	9
	—	(11.1)	(55.6)	(33.3)	(100.0)
Bhilwara	—	8	3	—	11
	—	(72.7)	(27.3)	—	(100.0)
Bikaner	—	—	4	—	4
	—	—	(100.0)	—	(100.0)
Bundi	—	—	3	1	4
	—	—	(75.0)	(25.0)	(100.0)
Chittaurgarh	—	2	10	2	14
	—	(14.3)	(71.4)	(14.3)	(100.0)
Churu	—	2	5	—	7
	—	(28.6)	(71.4)	—	(100.0)
Dausa	—	—	3	2	5
	—	—	(60.0)	(40.0)	(100.0)
Dhaulpur	—	—	1	3	4
	—	—	(25.0)	(75.0)	(100.0)
Dungapur	—	3	2	—	5
	—	(60.0)	(40.0)	—	(100.0)
Ganganagar	—	1	4	2	7
	—	(14.3)	(57.1)	(28.6)	(100.0)
Hanumangarh	—	—	3	—	3
	—	—	(100.0)	—	(100.0)
Jaipur	—	5	7	1	13
	—	(38.5)	(53.8)	(7.7)	(100.0)
Jaisalmer	—	—	—	3	3
	—	—	—	(100.0)	(100.0)
Jalor	—	4	3	—	7
	—	(57.1)	(42.9)	—	(100.0)
Jhalawar	—	—	3	3	6
	—	—	(50.0)	(50.0)	(100.0)
Jhunjhunun	1	6	1	—	8
	(12.5)	(75.0)	(12.5)	—	(100.0)
Jodhpur	—	5	3	1	9
	—	(55.6)	(33.3)	(11.1)	(100.0)
Karauli	—	—	3	2	5
	—	—	(60.0)	(40.0)	(100.0)
Kota	—	—	4	1	5
	—	—	(80.0)	(20.0)	(100.0)
Nagaur	—	2	9	—	11
	—	(18.2)	(81.8)	—	(100.0)
Pali	2	6	2	—	10
	(20.0)	(60.0)	(20.0)	—	(100.0)
Rajsamand	—	3	4	—	7
	—	(42.9)	(57.1)	—	(100.0)
Sawai Madhopur	—	—	4	1	5
	—	—	(80.0)	(20.0)	(100.0)
Sikar	—	7	1	—	8
	—	(87.5)	(12.5)	—	(100.0)
Sirohi	—	4	1	—	5
	—	(80.0)	(20.0)	—	(100.0)
Tonk	—	—	5	1	6
	—	—	(83.3)	(16.7)	(100.0)
Udaipur	—	4	6	1	11
	—	(36.4)	(54.5)	(9.1)	(100.0)
Rajasthan	**3**	**73**	**122**	**39**	**237**
	(1.3)	**(30.8)**	**(51.5)**	**(16.5)**	**(100.0)**

Note: HSI Level H: (>0.7-0.8), M : (0.6-0.7), L : (0.5-0.6), VL : (<0.5) Figures in brackets show percentage share of total Panchayat Samities.
Source: Annex 6.1.

TABLE 5.6: Distribution of PSs Having High and Medium HSI Level, 1991

S. No.	*District*	*No. & Name of PSs in Descending Order*
		(A) High Level (3)
1	Pali	2—Sumerpur and Bali
2	Jhunjhunun	1—Nawalgarh
		(B) Medium Level (73)
1	Bhilwara	8—Hurda, Sahara, Banera, Mandal, Raipur, Suwana, Sahahpura and Asind
2	Sikar	7—Dhond, Danta Ramgarh, Sri Madhopur, Khandela, Neem ka Thana, Lachhmangarh and Fatehpur
3	Ajmer	6—Pisangan, Kekri, Srinagar, Bhinay, Kishangarh and Masooda
4	Jhunjhunun	6—Udaipurwati, Chirawa, Jhunjhunun, Khetri, Alsisar and Buhana
5	Pali	6—Rani Station, Desuri, Sojat, Kharchi, Pali and Jaitaran
6	Jaipur	5—Govindgarh, Shahpura, Viratnagar, Sambhar and Kotputli
7	Jodhpur	5—Bilara, Bhopalgarh, Baleasr, Luni and Shergarh
8	Jalor	4—Jalor, Sayal, Ahore and Jaswantpura
9	Sirohi	4—Sirohi, Sheoganj, Pindwara and Reodar
10	Udaipur	4—Mavli, Sarda, Girwa and Bargaon
11	Alwar	3—Nimrana, Behror and Mandawar
12	Dungarpur	3—Sagwara, Aspur and Bichhiwara
13	Rajsamand	3—Railmagra, Khamnor and Bhim
14	Chittaurgarh	2—Bhopalsagar and Rashmi
15	Churu	2—Dungargarh and Ratangarh
16	Nagaur	2—Merta and Riyan
17	Banswara	1—Garhi
18	Bharatpur	1—Kumher
19	Bikaner	1—Dungarpur
20	Ganganagar	1—Ganganagar

Source: Annex- 5.1

Low HSI Region

Low HSI area was widely spread over all the 6 divisions and 31 districts (except Jailsalmer). There were total 122 PSs in this category. Jaipur division led with 23.8 per cent share followed by Udaipur (21.3 %), Kota (17.2 %), Ajmer (15.6%), Bikaner (13.6%) and Jodhpur (9.0%) divisions. Among the districts, Alwar dominated with 11 PSs followed by Chittarugarh (10); Nagaur (9); Jaipur (7), Udaipur (6), Bharatpur, Chittaurgarh, Tonk (5 each); Banswara, Baran, Bikaner, Ganganagar, Kota, Rajsamand and Sawai Madhopur (4 each); Bhilwara, Bundi, Dausa, Hanumangarh, Jalor, Jhalawar, Jodhpur and Karauli (3 each); Ajmer Barmer, Dungarpur and Pali (2 each) and Dhaulpur, Jhunjhunun, Sikar and Sirohi (1each) districts respectively (Table 5.7). All the above districts, except Banswara, Barmer, Bhilwara, Dhaulpur, Dungarpur, Jhunjhunun, Jodhpur, Pali, Sikar and Sirohi had greater percentage of L level PSs as compared to the state average (51.5). Tonk district had the maximum percentage (83.3) of Low level PSs while, Jhunjhunun had the minimum (12.5%).

Very Low HSI Area

Very low HSI area was also widely distributed in all the 6 divisions and 18 districts. There were 39 PSs in this category. Kota divisions was the most deprived having 28.2 share preceded by Jodhpur (25.6%), Jaipur (23.14), Udaipur (15.4), Bikaner (5.1%) and Ajmer (2.6%) divisions. If we look at district-wise distribution of these PSs, it is clear that, Barmer led with 6 PSs followed by Banswara, Baran, Bharatpur, Dhaulpur, Jaisalmer, Jodhpur (3 each); Churu, Dausa, Ganganager, Karauli (2 each) and Bundi, Jaipur, Jodhpur, Kota, Sawai Madhopur, Tonk and Udaipur (one each) respectively (Table 5.8). All the above districts except Chittaurgarh, Jaipur, Jodhpur and Udaipur had higher percentage of VL level PSs than the state average (16.5). Jaisalmer district had the maximum percentage (100%) of these PSs, while Jaipur had the minimum (7.7%).

TABLE 5.7: Distribution of PSs having Low HSI Level, 1991

S. No.	*District*	*No. & Name of PSs in Descending Order*
		Low Level (122)
1	Alwar	11—Kishangar Bas, Bansur, Thanagazi, Kotkasim, Rajgarh, Ramgarh, Umren, Reni, Khatumber, Tijara and Lachhmangarh
2	Chittaurgarh	10—Kapasan, Chittaurgarh, Nimbhera, Dungla, Bari Sadri, Begun, Gangrar, Arnod, Chhoti Sadri and Bhadesar
3	Nagaur	9—Kuchaman, Degana, Ladnu, Parbatsar, Mundwa, Makrana, Nagaur, Jayal and Didwana
4	Jaipur	7—Jhotwara, Amber, Jamwa Ramgarh, Bassi, Sanganer, Phagi and Dudu
5	Udaipur	6—Bhindar, Salumber, Gogunda, Kherwara, Jhadol and Dhariawad
6	Tonk	5—Malpura, Deoli, Niwai, Todaraisingh and Tonk
7	Churu	5—Taranagar, Churu, Sujangarh, Sardarshahar and Rajgarh
8	Bharatpur	5—Weir, Sewar, Nadbai, Rupbas and Deeg
9	Sawai Madhopur	4—Gangapur, Bamanwas, Bonli and Sawai Madhopur
10	Rajsamand	4—Amet, Rajsamand, Deogarh and Khumbalgarh
11	Kota	4—Ladpura, Chechat, Sultanpur and Sangod
12	Ganganagar	4—Karanpur, Sadulshahar, Padampura and Raisinghnagar
13	Bikaner	4—Nokha, Bikaner, Lunkaransar and Kolayat
14	Baran	4—Atru, Baran, Anta and Kishanganj
15	Banswara	4—Talwara, Bagidora, Ghatol and Anandpuri
16	Karauli	3—Hindaun, Nadoti and Todabhim
17	Jodhpur	3—Osian, Mandor and Phalodi
18	Jhalawar	3—Jhalrapatan, Khanpur and Piprali
19	Jalor	3—Raniwara, Bhinmal and Sanchore
20	Hanumangarh	3—Hanumangarh, Bhadra and Nohar
21	Dausa	3—Dausa, Sikrai and Bandikui
22	Bundi	3—Nainwa, Talera and Hindoli
23	Bhilwara	3—Jahazpur, Kotri and Mandalgarh
24	Pali	2—Raipur and Rohat
25	Dungarpur	2—Dungarpur and Simalwara
26	Barmer	2—Siwana and Balotra
27	Ajmer	2—Arian and Jawaja
28	Sirohi	1—Abu Road
29	Sikar	1—Piprali
30	Jhunjhunun	1—Surajgarh
31	Dhaulpur	1—Dhaulpur

Source: Annex- 5.1

TABLE 5.8: Distribution of PSs Having Very Low HSI Level, 1991

S. No.	*District*	*No. & Name of PSs in Descending Order*
		Very Low Level (39)
1	Barmer	6—Chohtan, Dhorimanna, Sindhari, Sheo, Barmer and Baytoo
2	Jhalawar	3—Bakani, Dag and Manoharthana
3	Jaisalmer	3—Jaisalmer, Sankra and Sam
4	Dhaulpur	3—Baseri, Rajakhera and Bari
5	Dausa	3—Mahwa and Lalsot
6	Bharatpur	3—Bayana, Kaman and Nagar Pharai
7	Baran	3—Shahbad, Chhabra and Chhipabarod
8	Banswara	3—Peepalknoont, Sajjangarh and Kushalgarh
9	Karauli	2—Sapotra and Karauli
10	Ganganagar	2—Suratgarha nd Anupgarh
11	Chittaurgarh	2—Pratapgarh and Bhainsrorgarh
12	Udaipur	1—Kotra
13	Tonk	1—Uniara
14	Sawai Madhopur	1—Khandar
15	Kota	1—Itawa
16	Jodhpur	1—Bap
17	Jaipur	1—Chaksu
18	Bundi	1—Keshoraipatan

Source: Annex- 5.1

6

HEALTH STATUS INDEX (HSI) (2001)

Highlights

- Rural HSI-Raj. : 0.6684
- Percentage of AAPs: 56
- 14% PSs had HSI above 0.75

	Panchayat Samiti	**District**	**Division**
• **Top**	Udaipurwati (0.8307)	Jhunjhunun	Jaipur
• **Bottom**	Sam (0.4749)	Jaisalmer	Jodhpur

Health Status Index of rural Rajasthan rose to 0.6684 in the year 2001. There were 132 PSs having HSI above the state average. Whereas, Jodhpur division led not only in PSs having very high HSI (66.7%) but also in PSs having very low HSI (80%). Jaipur division dominated in PSs having high (30.4%) as well as Medium (25.6%) HSI while Kota division led in low HSI level PSs.

Figure 6.1 depicts spatial distribution pattern of HSI at PS level. It is interesting to note that the PSs having High and Very High HSI are mainly concentrated in a belt along with Aravalli hills area from South-West (Sirohi dist.) to North-East (Jhunjhunun/Alwar dist.) direction. The HSI level decreases towards both sides mainly towards Western arid and semi-arid areas. Udaipurwati PS of Jhunjhunun district had the maximum 0.8307 HSI followed by Ratangarh, Rani Station, Sumerpur, Sirohi, Bali, Dhond, Ahore, Piprali and Bilara PSs (Descending order, Annex 6.1). These top ten PSs are spread over seven districts. Pali district led with three PSs followed by Sikar (2), Sirohi, Jodhpur, Jalor, Jhunjhunun and Churu (one each) respectively (Table 6.1).

TABLE 6.1: Distribution of First and Last Ten PSs HSI: Rajasthan (2001)

S. No.	*First Ten PSs (Descending Order)*							*Last Ten PSs (Ascending Order)*					
	Districts/ PSs							*Districts/ PSs*					
	Pali	*Sikar*	*Sirohi*	*Jodh*	*Jalor*	*Jhun*	*Churu*	*Barmer*	*Jais*	*Jhal*	*Ud*	*Gg*	*Baran*
	(3)	*(2)*	*(1)*	*(1)*	*(1)*	*(1)*	*(1)*	*(3)*	*(2)*	*(2)*	*(1)*	*(1)*	*(1)*
1	Rani Station	Dhond	Sirohi	Bilara	Ahore	Udaip[1]	Ratan-garh	Barmer	Sam	Mano[2]	Kotra	Surat-garh	Chha-bra
2	Sumerpur	Piprali	—	—		—	—	Sheo	Sankra	Bakani	—	—	—
3	Bali	—	—	—		—	—	Baytoo	—	—	—	—	—
4	—	—	—	—		—	—	—	—	—	—	—	—

Source: Annex 6.2, 1. Udaipurwati, 2. Manoharthana

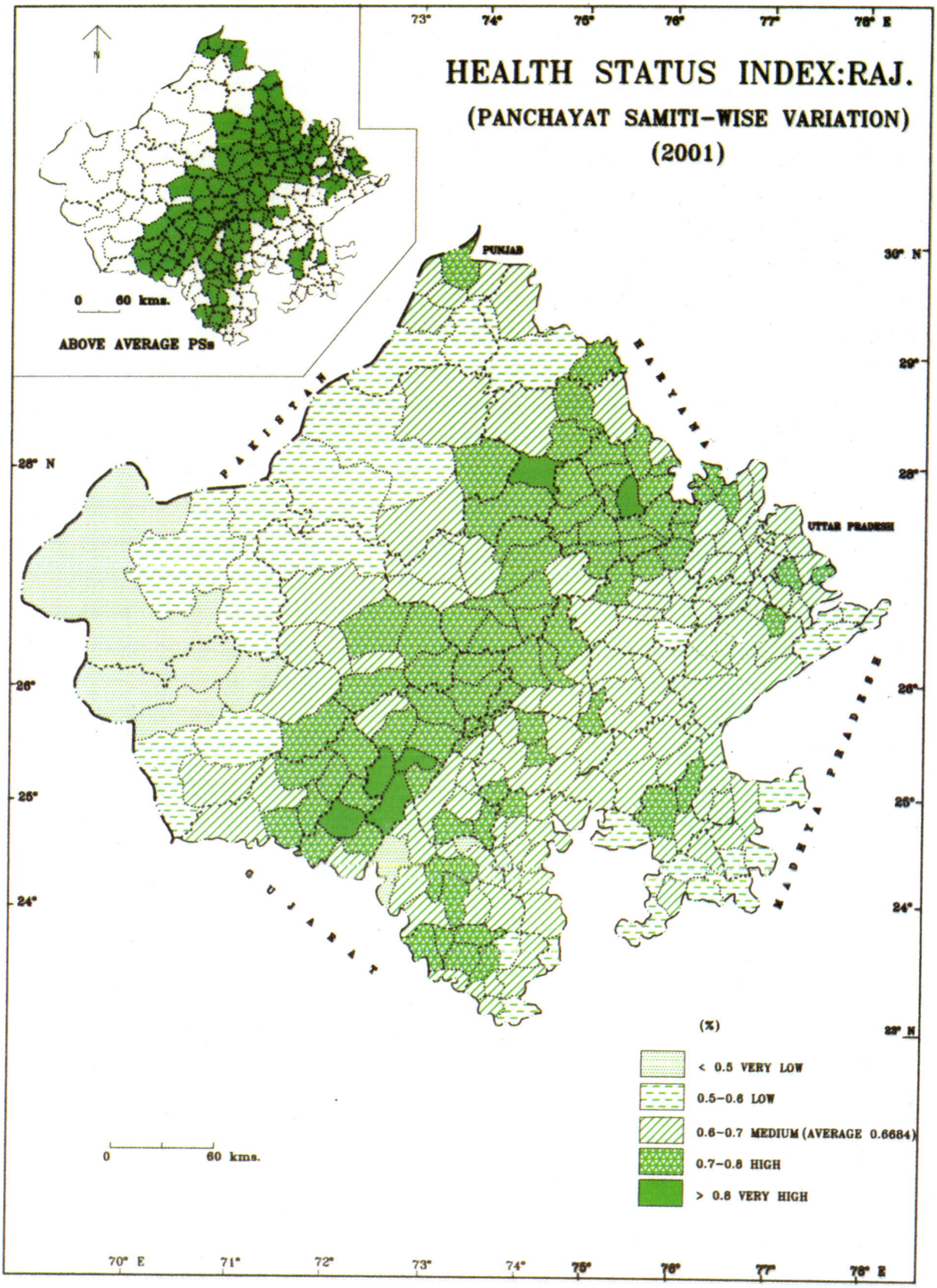

HEALTH STATUS INDEX:RAJ.
(PANCHAYAT SAMITI-WISE VARIATION)
(2001)
ABOVE AVERAGE PSs
0 60 kms.
PUNJAB
HARYANA
PAKISTAN
UTTAR PRADESH
MADHYA PRADESH
GUJARAT
(%)
< 0.5 VERY LOW
0.5-0.6 LOW
0.6-0.7 MEDIUM (AVERAGE 0.6684)
0.7-0.8 HIGH
> 0.8 VERY HIGH
0 60 kms.

FIG. 6.1

TABLE 6.2: District-wise First and Last PSs by HSI (2001)

District	*First Rank*	*Last Rank*	*District*	*First Rank*	*Last Rank*
Ajmer	Pisangan	Arain	Jaipur	Govindgarh	Chaksu
Alwar	Behror	Tijara	Jaisalmer	Jaisalmer	Sam
Banswara	Garhi	Kushalgarh	Jalor	Ahore	Sanchore
Baran	Baran	Chhabra	Jhalawar	Khanpur	Manoharthana
Barmer	Siwana	Barmer	Jhunjhunun	Udaipurwati	Surajgarh
Bharatpur	Kumher	Bayana	Jodhpur	Bilara	Bap
Bhilwara	Banera	Kotri	Karauli	Hindaun	Sapotra
Bikaner	Nokha	Kolayat	Kota	Sultanpur	Itawa
Bundi	Hindoli	Nainwa	Nagaur	Ladnu	Nagaur
Chittaurgarh	Rashmi	Bhainsrorgarh	Pali	Rani Station	Rohat
Churu	Ratangarh	Sardarshahar	Rajsamand	Railmagra	Deogarh
Dausa	Bandikui	Lalsot	S. Madhopur	Gangapur	Khandar
Dhaulpur	Dhaulpur	Baseri	Sikar	Dhond	Lachhmangarh
Dungarpur	Sagwara	Simalwara	Sirohi	Sirohi	Abu Road
Ganganagar	Ganganagar	Suratgarh	Tonk	Todaraisingh	Uniara
Hanumangarh	Bhadra	Nohar	Udaipur	Mavli	Kotra

Source: Annex 6.1

Sam PS of Jaisalmer district, on the other hand, was at the bottom with 0.4749 HSI. It was followed by Barmer, Sheo, Baytoo, Kotra, Manoharthana, Suratgarh, Chhabra, Sankra and Bakani PSs (Ascending order). These last ten PSs were concentrated in six districts viz. Barmer (3); Jaisalmer and Jhalawar (2 each); Udaipur, Ganganagar and Baran (one each) respectively. District-wise PSs with highest and lowest HSI is shown in Table 6.2.

TABLE 6.3: Classification of PSs on the Basis of HSI (2001): Rajasthan

Group	*Included PSs*			
	No.	*%*	*Distributed in*	
			Districts	*Divisions*
Very High (VH), (>0.8)	6	2.5	4	3
High (H), (0.7-0.8)	79	33.3	23	6
Medium (M), (0.6-0.7)	121	51.1	29	6
Low (L), (0.5-0.6)	26	11.0	12	5
Very Low (VL), (<0.5)	5	2.1	3	2
Total	**237**	**100**		

Source: Annex 6.2.

Classification of PSs by HSI

Table 6.3 presents classification of PSs by HSI. There is a clearcut dominance of Medium level PSs (51.1%) followed by High (33.3%), Low (11%), Very High (2.5%) and Very Low (2.1%) level PSs.

If we look at division-wise classification and distribution of PSs by HSI (Table 6.4) following conclusions can be drawn:

- Jodhpur is the only division having PSs with all the five levels of HSI while, Ajmer had PSs with only two levels. PSs in Jaipur, Bikaner and Udaipur divisions had four levels while Kota had three.
- Jodhpur division led in PSs having Very High as well as Very Low HSI level while Jaipur in High and Medium and Kota led in PSs having Low HSI level.
- Medium level PSs were dominating in all the divisions except Jodhpur.

- The percentage share of VH level PSs in Jodhpur and Bikaner divisions; H level in Jaipur, Ajmer and Jodhpur divisions; M level in Ajmer, Kota and Udaipur divisions; L level in Bikaner, Kota and Jodhpur divisions and VL level in Jodhpur and Udaipur divisions was higher than the state average.

TABLE 6.4: Division-wise Classification and Distribution of PSs on the Basis of HSI Level (2001)

Divisions	*Classification*						*Distribution (% Share)*				
	HSI Level						*HSI Level*				
	Very High	*High*	*Medium*	*Low*	*Very Low*	*Total PSs*	*Very High*	*High*	*Medium*	*Low*	*Very Low*
Jaipur	1	24	31	5	—	61	16.7	30.4	25.6	19.2	—
	(1.6)	(39.3)	(50.8)	(8.2)	—	(100.0)					
Bikaner	1	6	9	5	—	21	16.7	7.6	7.4	19.2	—
	(4.8)	(28.6)	(42.9)	(23.8)	—	(100.0)					
Ajmer	—	15	21	—	—	36	—	19.0	17.4	—	—
	—	(41.7)	(58.3)	—	—	(100.0)					
Kota	—	3	22	7	—	32	—	3.8	18.2	26.9	—
	—	(9.4)	(68.8)	(21.9)	—	(100.0)					
Jodhpur	4	19	10	5	4	42	66.7	24.1	8.3	19.2	80.0
	(9.5)	(45.2)	(23.8)	(11.9)	(9.5)	(100.0)					
Udaipur	—	12	28	4	1	45	—	15.2	23.1	15.4	20.0
	—	(26.7)	(62.2)	(8.9)	(2.2)	(100.0)					
Total	**6**	**79**	**121**	**26**	**5**	**237**	**100**	**100**	**100**	**100**	**100**
	(2.5)	**(33.3)**	**(51.1)**	**(11.0)**	**(2.1)**	**(100.0)**					

Note: Figure in brackets shows percentage share to total Panchayat Samities.
HSI Level VH : (>0.8), H: (0.7-0.8), M : (0.6-0.7), L : (0.5-0.6), VL : (<0.5)
Source: Annex 6.1

Different HSI Regions

Very High HSI Region

There were only 6 VH level PSs which were concentrated in four districts (Pali, Sirohi, Jhunjhunun and Churu) falling under three divisions (Jodhpur, Jaipur and Bikaner). Jodhpur division had 4 PSs while Jaipur and Bikaner divisions each had one PS. It is sad that, no PS of Ajmer, Kota and Udaipur divisions found mention in this category. The percentage share of VH level PSs to total PSs ranged from a maximum of 9.5 in Jodhpur to a minimum of 1.6 in Jaipur division.

Among the districts, Pali had 3 PSs while Churu, Jhunjhunun and Sirohi each had one PS. All the above four districts had higher percentage of VH level PSs than the state average (2.5%, Tables 6.5 and 6.6). The percentage varied from a maximum of 30 in Pali to a minimum of 12.5 in Jhunjhunun district.

High HSI Region

High HSI region was spread over 23 districts and all the six divisions. There were 79 High level PSs in all. Jaipur division topped with 30.4 per cent PSs followed by Jodhpur (24.1%), Ajmer (19%), Udaipur (15.2%), Bikaner (7.6%) and Kota (3.8%) divisions. The highest percentage of H level PSs is 45.2 which is in Jodhpur, 41.7 in Ajmer, 39.3 in Jaipur, 28.6 in Bikaner, 26.7 in Udaipur and the lowest 9.4 in Kota division. Jodhpur, Ajmer and Jaipur divisions had higher percentage of M level PSs in comparison to the state average (33.3%). Among the districts, Sikar led with 8 PSs followed by Nagaur (7); Jhunjhunun, Pali (6 each); Ajmer, Jaipur, Jalor (5 each); Churu, Dungarpur, Jodhpur (4 each); Alwar, Bhilwara, Rajsamand, Sirohi, Udaipur (3 each); Bharatpur, Kota (2 each) and Banswara, Barmer, Bikaner, Chittaurgarh, Ganganagar, Hanumangarh and Karauli (one each) districts respectively (Table 6.7). Except Alwar, Banswara, Barmer, Bharatpur, Bhilwara, Chittaurgarh, Ganganagar, Karauli and Udaipur, all the above districts had greater percentage of H level PSs in comparison to the state average.

TABLE 6.5: District-wise Classification of PSs on the Basis of HSI Level, 2001

District	*HSI Level*					*Total*
	VH	*H*	*M*	*L*	*VL*	
Ajmer	—	5	3	—	—	8
	—	(62.5)	(37.5)	—	—	(100.0)
Alwar	—	3	11	—	—	14
	—	(21.4)	(78.6)	—	—	(100.0)
Banswara	—	1	5	2	—	8
	—	(12.5)	(62.5)	(25.0)	—	(100.0)
Baran	—	—	4	3	—	7
	—	—	(57.1)	(42.9)	—	(100.0)
Barmer	—	1	2	2	3	8
	—	(12.5)	(25.0)	(25.0)	(37.5)	(100.0)
Bharatpur	—	2	7	—	—	9
	—	(22.2)	(77.8)	—	—	(100.0)
Bhilwara	—	3	8	—	—	11
	—	(27.3)	(72.7)	—	—	(100.0)
Bikaner	—	—	2	2	—	4
	—	—	(50.0)	(50.0)	—	(100.0)
Bundi	—	—	4	—	—	4
	—	—	(100.0)	—	—	(100.0)
Chittaurgarh	—	1	11	2	—	14
	—	(7.1)	(78.6)	(14.3)	—	(100.0)
Churu	1	4	2	—	—	7
	(14.3)	(57.1)	(28.6)	—	—	(100.0)
Dausa	—	—	5	—	—	5
	—	—	(100.0)	—	—	(100.0)
Dhaulpur	—	—	—	4	—	4
	—	—	—	(100.0)	—	(100.0)
Dungarpur	—	4	1	—	—	5
	—	(80.0)	(20.0)	—	—	(100.0)
Ganganagar	—	1	4	2	—	7
	—	(14.3)	(57.1)	(28.6)	—	(100.0)
Hanumangarh	—	1	1	1	—	3
	—	(33.3)	(33.3)	(33.3)	—	(100.0)
Jaipur	—	5	7	1	—	13
	—	(38.5)	(53.8)	(7.7)	—	(100.0)
Jaisamer	—	—	—	2	1	3
	—	—	—	(66.7)	(33.3)	(100.0)
Jalor	—	5	2	—	—	7
	—	(71.4)	(28.6)	—	—	(100.0)
Jhalawar	—	—	2	4	—	6
	—	—	(33.3)	(66.7)	—	(100.0)
Jhunjhunun	1	6	1	—	—	8
	(12.5)	(75.0)	(12.5)	—	—	(100.0)
Jodhpur	—	4	4	1	—	9
	—	(44.4)	(44.4)	(11.1)	—	(100.0)
Karauli	—	1	4	—	—	5
	—	(20.0)	(80.0)	—	—	(100.0)
Kota	—	2	3	—	—	5
	—	(40.0)	(60.0)	—	—	(100.0)
Nagaur	—	7	4	—	—	11
	—	(63.6)	(36.4)	—	—	(100.0)
Pali	3	6	1	—	—	10
	(30.0)	(60.0)	(10.0)	—	—	(100.0)
Rajsamand	—	3	4	—	—	7
	—	(42.9)	(57.1)	—	—	(100.0)
Sawai Madhopur	—	—	5	—	—	5
	—	—	(100.0)	—	—	(100.0)
Sikar	—	8	—	—	—	8
	—	(100.0)	—	—	—	(100.0)
Sirohi	1	3	1	—	—	5
	(20.0)	(60.0)	(20.0)	—	—	(100.0)
Tonk	—	—	6	—	—	6
	—	—	(100.0)	—	—	(100.0)
Udaipur	—	3	7	—	1	11
	—	(27.3)	(63.6)	—	(9.1)	(100.0)
Rajasthan	**6**	**79**	**121**	**26**	**5**	**237**
	(2.5)	**(33.3)**	**(51.1)**	**(11.0)**	**(2.1)**	**(100.0)**

Note : Figures in brackets show percentage share to total Panchayat Samities
HSI Level VH : (>0.8), H: (0.7-0.8), M : (0.6-0.7), L : (0.5-0.6), VL : (<0.5)

Source: Annex 6.1

TABLE 6.6: Distribution of PSs having Very High HSI Level, 2001

S. No.	*District*	*No. & Name of PSs in Descending Order*
		Very High (6)
1	Pali	3—Rani Station, Sumerpur and Bali
2	Churu	1—Ratangarh
3	Jhunjhunun	1—Udaipurwati
4	Sirohi	1—Sirohi

Source: Annex 6.2

TABLE 6.7: Distribution of PSs having High HSI Level, 2001

S. No.	*District*	*No. & Name of PSs in Descending Order*
		High (79)
1	Sikar	8—Dhond, Piprali, Sri Madhopur, Khandela, Danta Ramgarh, Fatehpur, Neem ka Thana and Lachhmangarh
2	Nagaur	7—Ladnu, Didwana, Parbatsar, Merta, Riyan, Degana and Makrana
3	Jhunjhunun	6—Khetri, Chirawa, Nawalgarh, Buhana, Jhunjhunun and Alsisar
4	Pali	6—Desuri, Sojat, Kharchi, Jaitaran, Raipur and Pali
5	Ajmer	5—Pisangan, Kekri, Jawaja, Kishangarh and Srinagar
6	Jaipur	5—Govindgarh, Shahpura, Sambhar, Viratnagar and Kotputli
7	Jalor	5—Ahora, Jalor, Sayal, Jaswantpura and Rasniwara
8	Churu	4—Churu, Dungargarh, Sujangarh and Taranagar
9	Dungarpur	4—Sagwara, Aspur, Bichhiwara and Dungarpur
10	Alwar	3—Behror, Nimrana and Mandawar
11	Bhilwara	3 Banera, Sahara and Hurda
12	Jodhpur	4—Bilara, Bhopalgarh, Luni and Osian
13	Rajsamand	3—Railmagra, Khamnor and Bhim
14	Sirohi	3—Sheoganj, Pindwara and Reodar
15	Udaipur	3—Mavli, Sarada and Girwa
16	Bharatpur	2—Kumher and Nadbai
17	Kota	2—Sultanpur and Ladpura
18	Banswara	1—Garhi
19	Barmer	1—Siwana
20	Chittaurgarh	1—Rashmi
21	Ganganagar	1—Ganganagar
22	HN	1—Bhadra
23	Karauli	1—Hindaun

Source: Annex 6.2

Medium HSI Region

Medium HSI region was widely distributed in 29 districts and all the six divisions. There were 121 PSs in this category. As explained earlier, Jaipur division had the maximum concentration of these PSs (25.6% share) in the state. It was followed by Udaipur (23.1%), Kota (18.2%), Ajmer (17.4%), Jodhpur (8.3%) and Bikaner (7.4%) divisions. The highest percentage share of M level PSs to total PSs was 68.8 in Kota division followed by 62.2 in Udaipur, 58.3 in Ajmer, 50.8 in Jaipur, 42.9 in Bikaner and the lowest 23.8 in Jodhpur division. Kota, Udaipur and Ajmer divisions had greater percentage of M level PSs than the state average (51.1). If we see district-wise distribution of these PSs, it is clear that Alwar and Chittaurgarh secured the top position with 11 PSs each followed by Bhilwara (8); Bharatpur, Jaipur and Udaipur (7 each); Tonk (6); Banswara, Dausa, Sawai Madhopur (5 each); Baran, Bundi, Ganganagar, Jodhpur, Karauli, Nagaur, Rajsamand (4 each); Ajmer, Kota (3 each); Barmer, Bikaner, Churu, Jalor, Jhalawar (2 each); Dungarpur, Hanumangarh, Jhunjhunun, Pali and Sirohi (1 each) districts respectively (Table 6.8). Alwar, Banswara, Baran, Bharatpur, Bhilwara, Bundi, Chittaurgarh, Dausa, Ganganagar, Karauli, Kota, Rajsamand, Sawai Madhopur, Tonk and Udaipur districts had higher percentage of Medium level PSs than the state average. Moreover four districts, namely, Bundi, Dausa, Sawai Madhopur and Tonk had 100 per cent of their PSs in Medium category while Pali had the minimum (10) percentage of these PSs.

TABLE 6.8: Distribution of PSs having Medium HSI Level, 2001

S. No.	*District*	*No. & Name of PSs in Descending Order*
		Medium (121)
1	Alwar	11—Reni, Bansur, Umren, Thanagazi, Lachhmangarh, Kathumar, Kotkasim, Ramgarh, Rajgarh, Kishangar Bas and Tijara
2	Chittaurgarh	11—Dungla, Nimbahera, Bhopalsagar, Gangrar, Chittaurgarh, Bari Sadri, Bhadesar, Begun, Pratapgarh, Chhoti Sadri and Kapasan
3	Bhilwara	8—Suwana, Raipur, Mandal, Asind, Shahapura, Jahazpur, Mandalgarh and Kotri
4	Bharatpur	7—Deeg, Sewar, Rupbas, Weir, Nagar Pahari, Kaman and Bayana
5	Jaipur	7—Jamwa Ramgarh, Amber, Bassi, Jhotwara, Dudu, Sanganer and Phagi
6	Udaipur	7—Bargaon, Bhinder, Salumber, Gogunda, Kherwara, Jhadol and Dhariawad
7	Tonk	6—Todaraisingh, Malpura, Tonk, Niwai, Deoli and Uniara
8	Banswara	5—Talwara, Ghatol, Bagidora, Anandpuri and Sajjangarh
9	Dausa	5—Bandikui, Dausa, Sikari, Mahwa and Lalsot
10	Sawai Madhopur	5—Gangapur, Sawai Madhopur, Bonli, Bamanwas and Khandar
11	Baran	4—Baran, Atru, Anta and Kishanganj
12	Bundi	4—Hindoli, Talera, Keshoraipatan and Nainwa
13	Ganganagar	4—Padampur, Karanpur, Sadulshahar and Raisinghnagar
14	Jodhpur	4—Mandor, Phalodi, Balesar and Shergarh
15	Karauli	4—Todabhim, Nadoti, Karauli and Sapotra
16	Nagaur	4—Mundwa, Jayal, Kuchaman and Nagaur
17	Rajsamand	4—Rajsamandh, Kumbhalgarh, Amet and Deogarh
18	Ajmer	3—Masooda, Bhinay and Arian
19	Kota	3—Chechat, Sangod and Itawa
20	Barmer	2—Balotra and Dhorimanna
21	Bikaner	2—Nokha and Lunkaransar
22	Churu	2—Rajgarh and Sardarshahar
23	Jalor	2—Bhinmal and Sanchore
24	Jhalawar	2—Khanpur and Pirawa
25	Dungarpur	1—Simalwara
26	Hanumangarh	1—Hanumangarh
27	Jhunjhunun	1—Surajgarh
28	Pali	1—Rohat
29	Sirohi	1—Abu Road

Source: Annex 6.2

TABLE 6.9: Distribution of PSs Having Low to Very Low HSI Level, 2001

S. No.	*District*	*No. & Name of PSs in Descending Order*
		[A] Low (26)
1	Dhaulpur	4—Dhaulpur, Bari, Rajakhera and Baseri
2	Jhalawar	4—Jhalrapatan, Dag, Bakani and Manoharthana
3	Baran	3—Shahbad, Chhipabarod and Chhabra
4	Banswara	2—Peepalkhoont and Kushalgarh
5	Barmer	2—Chohtan and Sindhari
6	Bikaner	2—Bikaner and Kolayat
7	Chittaurgarh	2—Arnod and Bhainsrogarh
8	Ganganagar	2—Anupgarh and Suratgarh
9	Jaisalmer	2—Jaisalmer and Sankra
10	Hanumangarh	1—Nohar
11	Jaipur	1—Chaksu
12	Jodhpur	1—Bap
		[B] Very Low (5)
1	Barmer	3—Baytoo, Sheo and Barmer
2	Jaisalmer	1—Sam
3	Udaipur	1—Kotra

Source: Annex 6.2

Low and Very Low HSI Region

This region was spread over 12 districts and 5 divisions. There were 26 PSs having Low HSI. Kota division led with 26.9 per cent share followed by Jaipur, Bikaner, Jodhpur (19.2% each) and Udaipur (15.4%) divisions. Bikaner, Kota and Jodhpur divisions had higher percentage of these PSs in comparison to the state average (11%). Among the districts, Dhaulpur and Jhalawar led with 4 PSs each followed by Baran (3); Banswara, Barmer, Bikaner, Chittaurgarh, Ganganagar, Jaisalmer (2 each), Hanumangarh, Jaipur and Jodhpur (1each) respectively (Table 6.9). All the above districts, except Jaipur had higher percentage of these PSs in comparison to state average. Moreover, Dhaulpur district had 100 per cent of its PSs in this category.

Sam PS of Jaisalmer, Kota of Udaipur and Baytoo, Sheo and Barmer PSs of Barmer district were the only PSs of the state in this category.

7

EDUCATION INDEX (1991)

Highlights

- Rural EDI-Raj. : 0.2413
- Percentage of AAPs: 47
- No PS had crossed 0.5 EDI

	Panchayat Samiti	District	Division
• **Top**	Nimrana (EDI 0.465)	Alwar	Jaipur
• **Bottom**	Kotra (EDI 0.066)	Udaipur	Udaipur

The Education Index (EDI) of rural Rajasthan in the year 1991 was 0.2413. There were 111 PSs having EDI above the state average. A great deal of regional disparity is observed in EDI across the state. Whereas, 49 per cent PSs of Jaipur division had Medium to High level of EDI, 100 per cent PSs of Udaipur and Jodhpur divisions had Low to Very low of EDI (Fig. 7.1). The EDI level in the state increases from the South-West and South to the North-East and North direction.

Nimrana PS of Alwar district had the maximum EDI (0.465) followed by Behror, Kotkasim, Buhana, Mandawar, Jhunjhunun, Ganganagar, Padampur, Chirawa, and Nawalgarh PSs (in descending order, Annex 7.2). These top ten PSs were concentrated in three districts. Both Alwar and Jhunjhunun had four PSs each while Ganganagar had 2 PSs (Table 7.1).

TABLE 7.1: Distribution of First and Last Ten PSs by EDI: Rajasthan (1991)

S. No.	*First Ten PSs (Descending Order)*			*Last Ten PSs (Ascending Order)*				
	Districts/ PSs			*Districts/ PSs*				
	Alwar	Jhun	Gg	Barmer	Banswara	Jalor	Udaipur	Jhalawar
	(4)	*(4)*	*(2)*	*(3)*	*(2)*	*(2)*	*(2)*	*(1)*
1	Nimrana	Buhana	Gg	Chohtan	Peepalkhoont	Bhinmal	Kotra	Manoharthana
2	Behror	Jhun	Padampur	Dhorimanna	Kushalgarh	Sanchore	Dhariawad	—
3	Kotkasim	Chirawa	—	Sindhari	—	—	—	—
4	Mandawar	Nawalgarh	—	—	—	—	—	—

Source: Annex 7.1

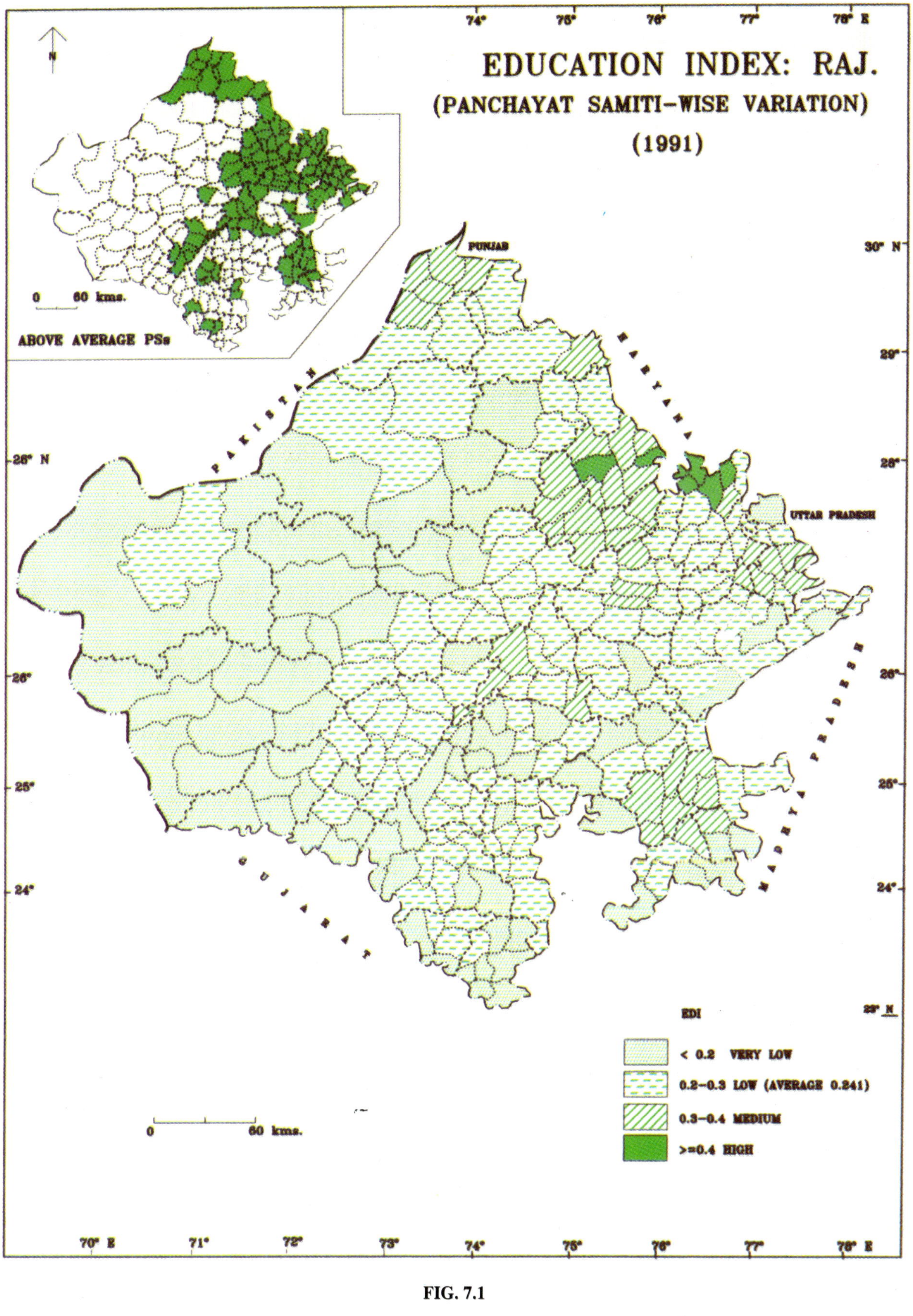
EDUCATION INDEX: RAJ.
(PANCHAYAT SAMITI-WISE VARIATION)
(1991)
ABOVE AVERAGE PSs
0 60 kms.
PUNJAB
HARYANA
PAKISTAN
UTTAR PRADESH
MADHYA PRADESH
GUJARAT
EDI
< 0.2 VERY LOW
0.2–0.3 LOW (AVERAGE 0.241)
0.3–0.4 MEDIUM
>=0.4 HIGH
0 60 kms.
70° E
71°
72°
73°
74°
75°
76°
77°
78° E
30° N
29°
28° N
26°
25°
24°
23° N

FIG. 7.1

Kotra PS of Udaipur district, on the other hand, had the minimum (0.066) EDI. It was preceded by Kotra, Peepalkhoont, Chohtan, Kushalgarh, Dhariwad, Manoharthana, Dhorimanna, Sindhari, Bhinmal, Sanchore and Sajjangarh, PSs (in ascending order). These last ten PSs were spread over seven districts. Barmer dominated with 3 PSs while Banswara, Jalore, Udaipur (2 PSs each) and Jhalawar (1) districts. Similarly, district-wise first and the last PSs by EDI is shown in Table 7.2.

TABLE 7.2: District-wise First and Last PSs by EDI (1991)

District	*First Rank*	*Last Rank*	*District*	*First Rank*	*Last Rank*
Ajmer	Kekri	Arain	Jaipur	Govindgarh	Chaksu
Alwar	Nimrana	Thanagazi	Jaisalmer	Jaisalmer	Sam
Banswara	Garhi	Peepalkhoont	Jalor	Ahore	Bhinmal
Baran	Anta	Chhabra	Jhalawar	Khanpur	Manoharthana
Barmer	Balotra	Chohtan	Jhunjhunun	Buhana	Udaipurwati
Bharatpur	Kumher	Kaman	Jodhpur	Bilara	Bap
Bhilwara	Hurda	Shahpura	Karauli	Hindaun	Karauli
Bikaner	Bikaner	Nokha	Kota	Sultanpur	Itawa
Bundi	Keshoraipatna	Hindoli	Nagaur	Degana	Mundwa
Chittaurgarh	Nimbahera	Kapasan	Pali	Rani Station	Jaitaran
Churu	Rajgarh	Sardarshahar	Rajsamand	Railmagra	Deogarh
Dausa	Mahwa	Lalsot	Sawai Madhopur	Gangapur	Khandar
Dhaulpur	Dhaulpur	Rajakhera	Sikar	Sri Madhopur	Fatehpur
Dungarpur	Sagwara	Simalwara	Sirohi	Sirohi	Abu Road
Ganganagar	Ganganagar	Anupgarh	Tonk	Deoli	Tonk
Hanumangarh	Bhadra	Nohar	Udaipur	Bargaon	Kotra

Source: Annex 8.1

TABLE 7.3: Classification of PSs on the Basis of EDI (1991): Rajasthan

Group	*EDI*			
	Included PSs			
	No.	*%*	*Distributed in*	
			Districts	*Divisions*
High (H), (0.4-0.5)	6	2.5	2	1
Medium (M), (0.3-0.4)	41	17.3	12	4
Low (L), (0..2-0.3)	120	50.6	29	6
Very Low (VL), (<0.2)	70	29.5	23	6
Total	**237**	**100**	—	—

Source: Annex 7.1

Classification of PSs by EDI

Table 7.3 presents classification of PSs by EDI. The state had dominance of Low Level PSs (50.6%) followed by Very Low (29.5%), Medium (17.3%), and High (2.5%) level PSs.

If we look at division-wise classification and distribution of PSs by EDI (Table 7.4) following conclusions can be drawn:

- Jaipur was the only division having PSs of all the four levels, while Bikaner, Ajmer, and Kota divisions had PSs of 3 levels. Jodhpur and Udaipur divisions having PSs of 2 levels.
- Jaipur division was at the best position with 100 per cent share of High level and 58.5 per cent share of medium level PSs.

- Jodhpur divison was the most deprived, leading in PSs having VL (35.7% share) EDI level followed by Udaipur (27.1%) division.
- Except Jodhpur, all divisions had dominance of L level PSs. Jodhpur division had dominance of VL level PSs.
- The percentage of H level PSs in Jaipur division; M level in Jaipur, Bikaner and Kota divisions; L level in Bikaner, Jaipur and Udaipur, divisions and VL level in Jodhpur and Udaipur divisions was higher than the state average.

TABLE 7.4: Division-wise Classification and Distribution of PSs on the Basis of EDI Level (1991)

Divisions	*Classification*					*Distribution (% Share)*			
	EDI Level					*EDI Level*			
	High	*Medium*	*Low*	*Very Low*	*Total PSs*	*High*	*Medium*	*Low*	*Very Low*
Jaipur	6 (9.8)	24 (39.3)	29 (47.5)	2 (3.3)	61 (100.0)	100.0	58.5	24.2	2.9
Bikaner	— —	6 (28.6)	10 (47.6)	5 (23.8)	21 (100.0)	—	14.6	8.3	7.1
Ajmer	— —	3 (8.3)	23 (63.9)	10 (27.8)	36 (100.0)	—	7.3	19.2	14.3
Kota	— —	8 (25.0)	15 (46.9)	9 (28.1)	32 (100.0)	—	19.5	12.5	12.9
Jodhpur	— —	— —	17 (40.5)	25 (59.5)	42 (100.0)	—	—	14.2	35.7
Udaipur	— —	— —	26 (57.8)	19 (42.2)	45 (100.0)	—	—	21.7	27.1
Total	**6** **(2.5)**	**41** **(17.3)**	**120** **(50.6)**	**70** **(29.5)**	**237** **(100.0)**	**100**	**100**	**100**	**100**

Figure in brackets shows percentage share to total Panchayat Samities.
Note: EDI Level H : (>0.4), M : (0.3-0.4), L : (0.2-0.3), VL : (<0.2).
Source: Annex 7.1

High EDI Region

There were only 6 PSs having High EDI concentrated in Alwar and Jhunjhunun districts of Jaipur division. These PSs were: Nimrana, Behror, Kotkasim and Mandawar (all of Alwar Dist.), Buhana and Jhunjhunun (both of Jhun). Both these districts had greater percentage of H level PSs in comparison to the state average (2.5). The percentage ranged from 28.6 in Alwar district to 25 in Jhunjhunun (Tables 7.5 and 7.6).

Medium EDI Region

PSs having Medium EDI were distributed in 4 divisions (Except Jodhpur and Udaipur) and 12 districts. There were total 41 M level PSs. Jaipur division with 58.5 per cent share had the maximum concentration of these PSs follwed by Kota (19.5%), Bikaner (14.6%) and Ajmer (7.3%) divisions. The per cent share of M level PSs to total PSs was the highest 39.3 in Jaipur, 28.6 in Bikaner, 25 in Kota and the lowest 8.3 in Ajmer division.

District-wise distribution of these PSs makes it clear that Sikar secured the top rank with 8 PSs followed by Jhunjhunun (6); Bhilwara and Ganganagar (5 each); Kota (4); Ajmer, Baran and Jaipur (1 each) and Alwar, Dausa, Hanumangarh and Jhalawar (1 each); respectively. All the above districts, except Alwar and Jhalawar had higher percentage of Medium level PSs in comparison to the state average (17.3). Sikar district had the highest percentage (100) of M level PSs while, Alwar had the lowest (7.1).

TABLE 7.5: District-wise Classification of PSs on the Basis of EDI Level (1991)

District	*EDI Level*				*Total PSs*
	H	*M*	*L*	*VL*	
Ajmer	—	3 (37.5)	5 (62.5)	—	8 (100.0)
Alwar	4 (28.6)	1 (7.1)	9 (64.3)	—	14 (100.0)
Banswara	—	—	1 (12.5)	7 (87.5)	8 (100.0)
Baran	—	3 (42.9)	2 (28.6)	2 (28.6)	7 (100.0)
Barmer	—	—	—	8 (100.0)	8 (100.0)
Bharatpur	—	5 (55.6)	3 (33.3)	1 (11.1)	9 (100.0)
Bhilwara	—	—	5 (45.5)	6 (54.5)	11 (100.0)
Bikaner	—	—	2 (50.0)	2 (50.0)	4 (100.0)
Bundi	—	—	2 (50.0)	2 (50.0)	4 (100.0)
Chittaurgarh	—	—	12 (85.7)	2 (14.3)	14 (100.0)
Churu	—	—	4 (57.1)	3 (42.9)	7 (100.0)
Dausa	—	1 (20.0)	4 (80.0)	—	5 (100.0)
Dhaulpur	—	—	3 (75.0)	1 (25.0)	4 (100.0)
Dungarpur	—	—	3 (60.0)	2 (40.0)	5 (100.0)
Ganganagar	—	5 (71.4)	2 (28.6)	—	7 (100.0)
Hanumangarh	—	1 (33.3)	2 (66.7)	—	3 (100.0)
Jaipur	—	3 (23.1)	10 (76.9)	—	13 (100.0)
Jaisalmer	—	—	1 (33.3)	2 (66.7)	3 (100.0)
Jalor	—	—	2 (28.6)	5 (71.4)	7 (100.0)
Jhalawar	—	1 (16.7)	2 (33.3)	3 (50.0)	6 (100.0)
Jhunjhunun	2 (25.0)	6 (75.0)	—	—	8 (100.0)
Jodhpur	—	—	4 (44.4)	5 (55.6)	9 (100.0)
Karauli	—	—	4 (80.0)	1 (20.0)	5 (100.0)
Kota	—	4 (80.0)	1 (20.0)	—	5 (100.0)
Nagaur	—	—	8 (72.7)	3 (27.3)	11 (100.0)
Pali	—	—	9 (90.0)	1 (10.0)	10 (100.0)
Rajsamand	—	—	4 (57.1)	3 (42.9)	7 (100.0)
Sawai Madhopur	—	—	4 (80.0)	1 (20.0)	5 (100.0)
Sikar	—	8 (100.0)	—	—	8 (100.0)
Sirohi	—	—	1 (20.0)	4 (80.0)	5 (100.0)
Tonk	—	—	5 (83.3)	1 (16.7)	6 (100.0)
Udaipur	—	—	6 (54.5)	5 (45.5)	11 (100.0)
Rajasthan	**6 (2.5)**	**41 (17.3)**	**120 (50.6)**	**70 (29.5)**	**237 (100.0)**

Figures in brackets show percentage share to total Panchayat Samities

Note: EDI Level H : (>0.4), M : (0.3-0.4), L : (0.2-0.3), VL : (<0.2). *Source*: Annex 8.1

TABLE 7.6: Distribution of PSs Having High and Medium EDI Level, 1991

S. No.	*District*	*No. & Name of PSs in Descending Order*
		[I] High Level (6)
1	Alwar	4—Nimrana, Behror, Kotkasim and Mandawar
2	Jhunjhunun	2—Buhana and Jhunjhunun
		[I] Medium Level (41)
1	Sikar	8—Sri Madhopur, Piprali, Neem ka Thana, Khandela, Lachhmangarh, Dhond, Danta Ramgarh and Fatehpur
2	Jhunjhunun	6—Chirawa, Nawalgarh, Surajgarh, Alsisar, Khetri and Udaipurwati
3	Bharatpur	5—Kumher, Rupbas, Nadbai, Sewar and Weir
4	Ganganagar	5—Ganganagar, Padampur, Karanpur, Sadulshahar and Raisinghnagar
5	Kota	4—Sultanpur, Sangod, Ladpura and Chechat
6	Ajmer	3—Kekri, Pisangan and Jawaja
7	Baran	3—Anta, Baran and Atru
8	Jaipur	3—Govindgarh, Jhotwara and Sanganer
9	Alwar	1—Kishangarbas
10	Dausa	1—Mahwa
11	Hanumangarh	1—Bhadra
12	Jhalawar	1—Khanpur

Source: Annex 7.1

TABLE 7.7: Distribution of PSs Having Low EDI Level, 1991

S. No.	*District*	*No. & Name of PSs in Descending Order*
		Low Level (120)
1	Chittaurgarh	12—Arnod, Nimbhera, Chhoti Sadri, Bhopalsagar, Chittaurgarh, Rashmi, Parbatsar, Dungla, Bari Sadri, Begun, Bhadesar and Gangrar
2	Jaipur	10—Shahpura, Kotputli, Sambhar, Amber, Viratnagar, Dudu, Bassi, Jamwa Ramgarh, Phagi & Chaksu
3	Alwar	9—Kathumar, Rajgarh, Ramgarh, Tijara, Bansure, Lachhmangarh, Reni, Umren & Thanagazi
4	Pali	9—Rani Station, Sumerpur, Bali, Desuri, Sojat, Kharchi, Raipur, Pali and Rohat
5	Nagaur	8—Degana, Ladnu, Merta, Makrana, Didwana, Kuchaman, Riyan and Parbatsar
6	Udaipur	6—Bargaon, Kherwara, Mavli, Bhindar, Girwa and Sarda
7	Ajmer	5—Masooda, Srinagar, Bhinay, Kishangarh and Arian
8	Bhilwara	5—Hurda, Banera, Jahazpur, Kotri and Sahara
9	Tonk	5—Deoli, Niwai, Todaraisingh, Malpura and Uniara
10	Churu	4—Churu, Rajgarh, Taranagar and Ratangarh
11	Dausa	4—Bandikui, Dausa, Sikrai and Lalsot
12	Jodhpur	4—Bilara, Luni, Mandor and Bhopalgarh
13	Karauli	4—Hindaun, Nadoti, Todabhim and Sapotra
14	Rajsamand	4—Railmagra, Rajsamand, Khamnor and Bhim
15	Sawai Madhopur	4—Bamanwas, Gangapur, Sawai Madhopur and Bonli
16	Bharatpur	3—Deeg, Bayana and Nagar Pahari
17	Dhaulpur	3—Dhaulpur, Baseri, Rajakhera
18	Dungarpur	3—Aspur, Sagwara and Dungarpur
19	Baran	2—Shahbad and Kishanganj
20	Bikaner	2—Bikaner and Lunkaransar
21	Bundi	2—Keshoraipatan and Talera
22	Ganganagar	2—Suratgarh and Anupgarh
23	Hanumangarh	2—Hanumangarh and Nohar
24	Jalor	2—Ahore and Jalor
25	Jhalawar	2—Pirawa and Jhalarapatan
26	Banswara	1—Garhi
27	Jaisalmer	1—Jaisalmer
28	Kota	1—Itawa
29	Sirohi	1—Sirohi

Source: Annex 7.1

Low EDI Region

Low EDI area was widely spread over all the 6 divisions and 29 districts (except Barmer, Sikar and Jhun). There were total 120 PSs in this category. Jaipur division led with 24.2 per cent share followed by Udaipur (21.6 %), Ajmer (19.2 %), Jodhpur (14.2%), Kota (12.5%) and Bikaner (8.3%) divisions.

Among the districts, Chittarugarh dominated with 12 PSs followed by Jaipur (10); Alwar and Pali (9 each); Nagaur (8), Udaipur (6), Ajmer, Bhilwara, Tonk (5 each); Churu, Dausa Jodhpur Karauli, Rajsamand and Sawai Madhopur (4 each); Bharatpur, Dhaulpur, Dungarpur (3 each); Baran, Bikaner, Bundi, Ganganagar, Hanumangarh, Jalore and Jhalawar (2 each) and Banswara, Jaisalmer and Sirohi (1 each) districts respectively. All the above districts, except Banswara, Baran, Bharatpur, Ganganagar, Jaisalmer, Jalore, Jhalawar, and Jodhpur. Kota and Sirohi had greater percentage of L level PSs in comparison to the state average (50.6). Pali district had the maximum percentage (90) of Low level PSs while, Banswara had the minimum (12.5).

TABLE 7.8: Distribution of PSs Having Very Low EDI Level, 1991

S. No.	*District*	*No. & Name of PSs in Descending Order*
		Very Low Level (70)
1	Barmer	8—Balotra, Siwana, Baytoo, Barmer, Sheo, Sindhari, Dhorimanna and Chohtan
2	Banswara	7—Bagidora, Talwara, Ghatol, Anandpuri, Sajjangarh, Kushalgarh and Peepalkhoont
3	Bhilwara	6—Raipur, Suwana, Asind, Mandal, Mandalgarh and Sahahpura
4	Jalor	5—Jaswantpura, Sayla, Raniwara, Sanchore and Bhinmal
5	Jodhpur	5—Osian, Balesar, Phalodi, Shergarh and Bap
6	Udaipur	5—Gogunda, Salumbar, Jhadol, Dhariadwad and Kotra
7	Sirohi	4—Sheoganj, Pindwara, Reodar and Abu Road
8	Churu	3—Sujangarh, Dungargarh and Sardarshahar
9	Nagaur	3—Nagaur, Jayal and Mundwa
10	Rajsamand	3—Kumbhalgarh, Amet and Deogarh
11	Baran	2—Chhipabarod and Chhabra
12	Bikaner	2—Kolyat, Nokha
13	Bundi	2—Nainwa and Hindoli
14	Chittaurgarh	2—Bhainsrorgarh and Kapasan
15	Dungarpur	2—Bichhiwara and Simalwara
16	Jaisalmer	2—Sankra and Sam
17	Jhalawar	2—Dag and Manoharthana
18	Dhaulpur	1—Bari
19	Bharatpur	1—Kaman
20	Karauli	1—Karauli
21	Pali	1—Jaitaran
22	Sawai Madhopur	1—Khandar
23	Tonk	1—Tonk

Source: Annex 7.1

Very Low EDI Area

Very low EDI area was also widely distributed in all the 6 divisions and 24 districts. There were 70 PSs in this category. Jodhpur division was the most deprived in EDI having 35.7 share of low level PSs preceded by Udaipur (27.1%), Ajmer (14.3), Kota (12.9), Bikaner (7.1%) and Jaipur (2.9%) divisions. If we look at district-wise distribution of these PSs, it is clear that, Barmer led with 8 PSs followed by Banswara (7), Bhilwara (6); Jalore, Jodhpur and Udaipur (5 each), Churu, Jhalawar, Nagaur (3 each); Baran, Bikaner, Bundi, Chittaurgarh (2 each) and Bharatpur, Dhaulpur, Dungarpur, Jaisalmer, Karauli, Pali, Rajasmand, Sawai Madhopur, Sirohi and Tonk (one each) respectively. All the above districts except Baran, Bikaner, Chittaurgarh, Dhaulpur, Karauli, Nagaur, Pali, Sawai Madhopur, and Tonk had higher percentage of VL level PSs than the state average (29.5). Bundi district had the maximum percentage (100) of these PSs, while Pali had the minimum (10).

8

EDUCATION INDEX (2001)

Highlights

- Rural EDI-Raj. : 0.4991
- Percentage of AAPs: 42

	Panchayat Samiti	District	Division
• **Top**	Behror (0.862)	Alwar	Jaipur
• **Bottom**	Kotra (0.201)	Udaipur	Udaipur

Education Index of rural Rajasthan rose to 0.499 in the year 2001. There were 99 PSs having EDI above the state average. Whereas, Jaipur division led in PSs having Very High EDI (61%) Udaipur being the most deprived led in PSs having Medium to Low EDI (34.1%).

Figure 8.1 Annex 8.1 depict spatial distribution pattern of EDI at PS level. Most of the North-Eastern, Northern and South-Eastern economically developed regions have concentration of PSs having Very High EDI. On the other hand Southern tribal-hilly, Western desert and central regions were dominating in PSs having Low to Medium EDI.

Behror PS of Alwar district had the maximum 0.862 EDI followed by Udaipurwati, Bhuna, Jhunjhunun, Fatehpur, Lachhmangarh, Chirawa, Alsisar, Jawaja, Taranagar, (Descending order, Annex 8.2). These top ten PSs were distributed in five districts. Jhunjhunun district led with five PSs followed by Sikar (2), Alwar, Ajmer, and Churu (one each) respectively (Table 8.1).

TABLE 8.1: Distribution of First and Last Ten Panchayat Samities by EDI: Rajasthan, (2001)

S. No.	*First Ten PSs (Descending Order)*					*Last Ten PSs (Ascending Order)*				
	Districts/ PSs					*Districts/ PSs*				
	Jhunjhunun	*Sikar*	*Alwar*	*Ajmer*	*Churu*	*Banswara*	*Udaipur*	*Jalor*	*Bhilwara*	*Jodhpur*
	(5)	*(2)*	*(1)*	*(1)*	*(1)*	*(4)*	*(2)*	*(2)*	*(1)*	*(1)*
1.	Udaipurwati	Fatehpur	Behror	Jawaja	Taranagar	Peepalkhoont	Kotra	Jaswantpura	Kotri	Shergarh
2.	Buhana	Lachhman-garh	—	—	—	Kushalgarh	Dhariawad	Bhinmal	—	—
3.	Jhunjhunun	—	—	—	—	Sajjangarh	—	—	—	—
4.	Chirawa	—	—	—	—	Ghatol	—	—	—	—
5.	Alsisar	—	—	—	—	—	—	—	—	—

Source: Annex 8.3

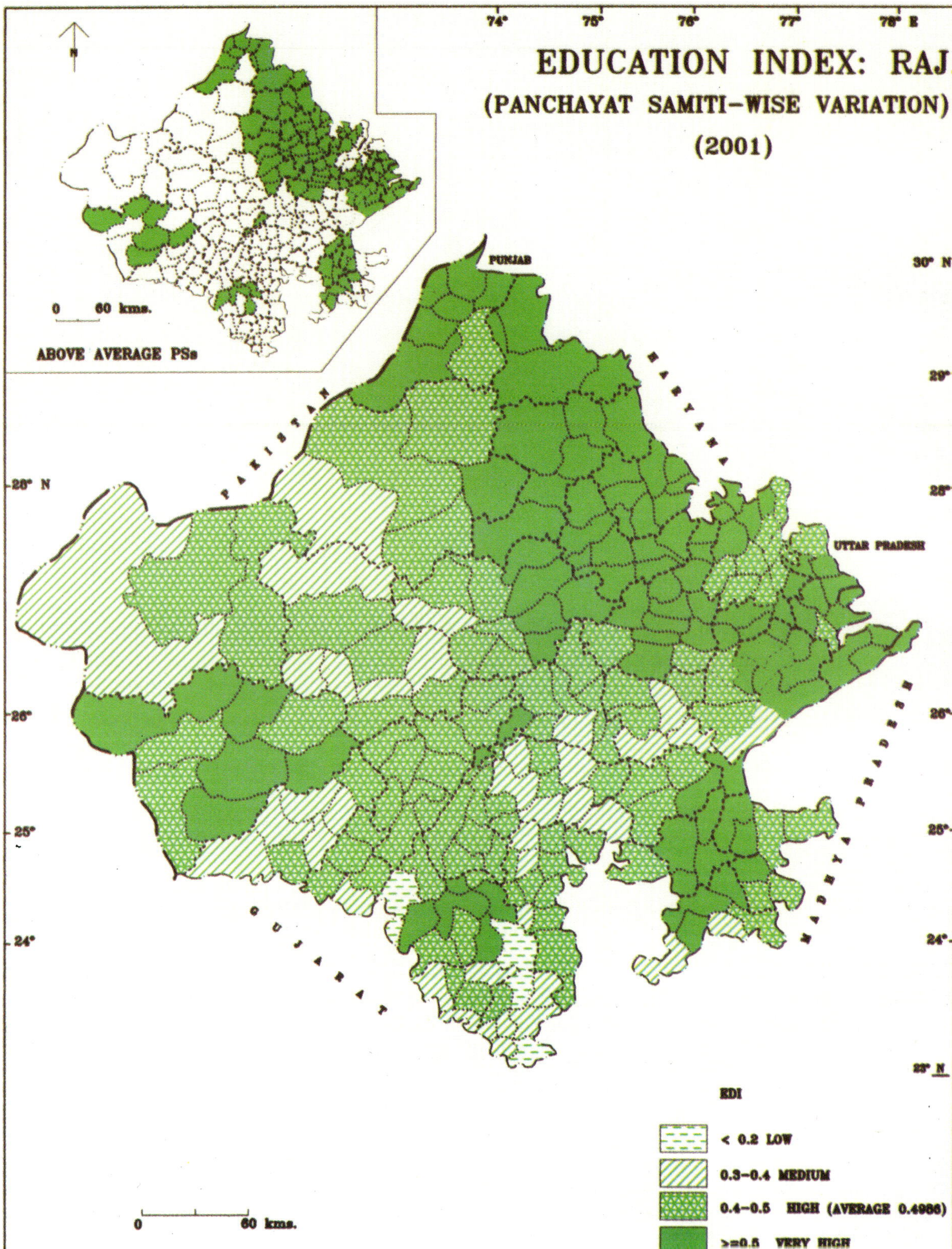
EDUCATION INDEX: RAJ.
(PANCHAYAT SAMITI-WISE VARIATION)
(2001)
ABOVE AVERAGE PSs
0 60 kms.
PUNJAB
PAKISTAN
HARYANA
UTTAR PRADESH
MADHYA PRADESH
GUJARAT
EDI
< 0.2 LOW
0.3-0.4 MEDIUM
0.4-0.5 HIGH (AVERAGE 0.4986)
>=0.5 VERY HIGH
0 60 kms.
70° E
71°
72°
73°
74°
75°
76°
77°
78° E
30° N
29°
28° N
26°
25°
24°
23° N

FIG. 8.1

Kotra PS of Udaipur district, on the other hand, had the manimum 0.201 EDI. It was followed by Peepalkhoont, Kushalgarh, Dhariawad, Sajjangarh, Jaswantpura, Bhinmal, Kotri, Ghatol and Shergarh PSs (ascending order). These last ten PSs were also concentrated in five districts. Banswara district dominated with 4 PSs while both Udaipur and Jalore had 2 PSs each and both Jalore and Jodhpur had one PS each. District-wise PSs with highest and lowest EDI is shown in Table 8.2.

TABLE 8.2: District-wise First and Last PSs by EDI (2001)

District	*First Rank*	*Last Rank*	*District*	*First Rank*	*Last Rank*
Ajmer	Jawaja	Bhinay	Jaipur	Kotputli	Chaksu
Alwar	Behror	Thanagazi	Jaisalmer	Sankra	Sam
Banswara	Garhi	Peepalkhoont	Jalor	Ahore	Jaswantpura
Baran	Baran	Chhipabarod	Jhalawar	Pirawa	Bakani
Barmer	Dhorimanna	Chohtan	Jhunjhunun	Udaipurwati	Khetri
Bharatpur	Nadbai	Kaman	Jodhpur	Luni	Shergarh
Bhilwara	Hurda	Kotri	Karauli	Hindaun	Karauli
Bikaner	Nokha	Kolayat	Kota	Sultanpur	Itawa
Bundi	Keshoraipatna	Hindoli	Nagaur	Didwana	Mundwa
Chittaurgarh	Nimbahera	Rashmi	Pali	Rani Station	Jaitaran
Churu	Taranagar	Sardarshahar	Rajsamand	Railmagra*	Kumbhalgarh
Dausa	Bandikui	Lalsot	Sawai Madhopur	Bamanwas	Khandar
Dhaulpur	Baseri	Bari	Sikar	Fatehpur	Sri Madhopur
Dungarpur	Sagwara	Simalwara	Sirohi	Pindwara	Abu Road
Ganganagar	Raisinghnagar	Suratgarh	Tonk	Todaraisingh	Tonk
Hanumangarh	Bhadra	Hanumangarh	Udaipur	Bargaon	Kotra

Source: Annex 8.1 * and Rajasmand

TABLE 8.3: Classification of PSs on the Basis of EDI (2001): Rajasthan

Group	*Included PSs*			
	No.	*%*	*Distributed in*	
			Districts	*Divisions*
Very High (VH), (>0.5)	98	41.4	19	6
High (H), (0.4-0.5)	95	40.1	25	6
Medium (M), (0.3-0.4)	40	16.9	14	5
Low (L), (0.2-0.3)	4	1.7	2	1
Total	**237**	**100**		

Source: Annex 8.3

Classification of PSs by EDI

Classification of PSs in to four groups by EDI is shown in Table 8.3. Very High level PSs were dominated with 41.1 per cent share followed by High (40.1%), Medium (8.9%) and Low (11%) level PSs.

If we look at division-wise classification and distribution of PSs by EDI (Table 8.4) following conclusions can be drawn:

- Jodhpur and Udaipur were the only divisions having PSs with all the five levels of EDI while, Jaipur had PSs with only two levels. PSs in Bikaner, Ajmer and Kota divisions had four levels while Kota had three.
- Jaipur division dominated (49% share) in PSs, having Very High EDI and both Jodhpur and Udaipur in PSs having High (26.3% each) EDI while Ajmer division dominated in PSs having Medium (32.5 %) EDI.
- Very High level PSs were dominated in Jaipur (79%), Bikaner (76%) and Kota (56%) while High level PS were dominated in remaining divisions.

- **The percentage share of VH level PSs in Jaipur, Bikaner and Kota divisions; H level in, Ajmer, Jodhpur and Udaipur divisions; M level in Ajmer division and L level in both Udaipur and Jodhpur divisions was higher than the state average.**

TABLE 8.4: Division-wise Classification and Distribution of PSs on the Basis of EDI Level (2001)

Divisions	*Classification*					*Distribution (% Share)*			
	EDI Level					*EDI Level*			
	Very High	*High*	*Medium*	*Low*	*Total PSs*	*Very High*	*High*	*Medium*	*Low*
Jaipur	48	13	—	—	61	49.0	13.7	—	—
	(78.7)	(21.3)	—	—	(100.0)				
Bikaner	16	4	1	—	21	16.3	4.2	2.5	—
	(76.2)	(19.0)	(4.8)	—	(100.0)				
Ajmer	6	17	13	—	36	6.1	17.9	32.5	—
	(16.7)	(47.2)	(36.1)	—	(100.0)				
Kota	18	11	3	—	32	18.4	11.6	7.5	—
	(56.3)	(34.4)	(9.4)	—	(100.0)				
Jodhpur	5	25	12	—	42	5.1	26.3	30.0	—
	(11.9)	(59.5)	(28.6)	—	(100.0)				
Udaipur	5	25	11	4	45	5.1	26.3	27.5	100.0
	(11.1)	(55.6)	(24.4)	(8.9)	(100.0)				
Total	**98**	**95**	**40**	**4**	**237**	**100**	**100**	**100**	**100**
	(41.4)	**(40.1)**	**(16.9)**	**(1.7)**	**(100.0)**				

Figure in brackets shows percentage share to total Panchayat Samities.
Note : EDI Level VH: (>0.5), H : (0.4-05), M : (0.3-0.4), L : (0.2-0.3), VL : (<0.2).
Source : Annex 8.3

Different EDI Regions

Very High EDI Region

There were only 98 VH level PSs which were spread over 19 districts and all the 6 divisions. Jaipur division dominated with 49 per cent share followed by Kota (18.4%), Bikaner (16.3%), Ajmer (6.1%) and both Jodhpur and Udaipur divisions (5.1% each). The percentage share of VH level PSs to total PSs ranged from a maximum of 78.7 in Jaipur to a minimum of 11.1 in Udaipur division. Among the districts, Jaipur dominated with 11 PSs followed by Jhunjhunun and Sikar (8 each); Bharatpur and Churu (7 each); Alwar and Ganganager (6 each); Barmer, Karauli, Kota, Nagaur and Udaipur (5 each); Dausa and Dhaulpur (4 each); Baran, Hanumangarh and Jhalawar (3 each), Sawai Madhopur (2) and Ajmer (1) districts respectively. All the above districts except Ajmer and Sawai Madhopur had higher percentage of VH level PSs than the state average (2.5%). The percentage varied from a maximum of 100 in Churu, Dhaulpur, Hanumangarh, Jhunjhunun, Karauli, Kota and Sikar districts to a minimum of 12.5 in Ajmer district. (Tables 8.4 to 8.6).

High EDI Region

High EDI region was spread over 25 districts and all the six divisions. There were 95 High level PSs in all. Jodhpur and Udaipur divisions topped with 26.3 per cent PSs each followed by Ajmer (17.9%), Jaipur (13.7%), Kota (11.6%) and Bikaner (4.2%) divisions. The highest percentage of H level PSs of total PSs was 59.5 which is in Jodhpur, 55.6 in Udaipur, 47.2 in Ajmer, 34.4 in Kota, 21.3 in Jaipur and the lowest 19 in Bikaner division. Among the districts, Chittaurgarh led with 11 PSs followed by Pali (10); Alwar (8); Rajsamand (7); Baran, Bundi, Jodhpur, Sirohi and Udaipur (4 each); Barmer, Bhilwara, Bikaner and Tonk (3 each); Bharatpur, Dungarpur, Jaipur, Jaisalmer, Jalor and Sawai Madhopur (2 each) and Banswara, Dausa, Ganganagar and Jhalawar (one each) districts respectively. Except Banswara, Bharatpur, Bhilwara, Dausa, Dungarpur,

TABLE 8.5: District-wise Classification of PSs on the Basis of EDI Level (2001)

District	*EDI Level*				*Total PSs*
	H	*M*	*L*	*VL*	
Ajmer	1 (12.5)	6 (75.0)	1 (12.5)	—	8 (100.0)
Alwar	6 (42.9)	8 (57.1)	—	—	14 (100.0)
Banswara	—	1 (12.5)	5 (62.5)	2 (25.0)	8 (100.0)
Baran	3 (42.9)	4 (57.1)	—	—	7 (100.0)
Barmer	5 (62.5)	3 (37.5)	—	—	8 (100.0)
Bharatpur	7 (77.8)	2 (22.2)	—	—	9 (100.0)
Bhilwara	—	3 (27.3)	8 (72.7)	—	11 (100.0)
Bikaner	—	3 (75.0)	1 (25.0)	—	4 (100.0)
Bundi	—	4 (100.0)	—	—	4 (100.0)
Chittaurgarh	—	11 (78.6)	3 (21.4)	—	14 (100.0)
Churu	7 (100.0)	—	—	—	7 (100.0)
Dausa	4 (80.0)	1 (20.0)	—	—	5 (100.0)
Dhaulpur	4 (100.0)	—	—	—	4 (100.0)
Dungarpur	—	2 (40.0)	3 (60.0)	—	5 (100.0)
Ganganagar	6 (85.7)	1 (14.3)	—	—	7 (100.0)
Hanumangarh	3 (100.0)	—	—	—	3 (100.0)
Jaipur	11 (84.6)	2 (15.4)	—	—	13 (100.0)
Jaisalmer	—	2 (66.7)	1 (33.3)	—	3 (100.0)
Jalor	—	2 (28.6)	5 (71.4)	—	7 (100.0)
Jhalawar	3 (50.0)	1 (16.7)	2 (33.3)	—	6 (100.0)
Jhunjhunun	8 (100.0)	—	—	—	8 (100.0)
Jodhpur	—	4 (44.4)	5 (55.6)	—	9 (100.0)
Karauli	5 (100.0)	—	—	—	5 (100.0)
Kota	5 (100.0)	—	—	—	5 (100.0)
Nagaur	5 (45.5)	5 (45.5)	1 (9.1)	—	11 (100.0)
Pali	—	10 (100.0)	—	—	10 (100.0)
Rajsamand	—	7 (100.0)	—	—	7 (100.0)
Sawai Madhopur	2 (40.0)	2 (40.0)	1 (20.0)	—	5 (100.0)
Sikar	8 (100.0)	—	—	—	8 (100.0)
Sirohi	—	4 (80.0)	1 (20.0)	—	5 (100.0)
Tonk	—	3 (50.0)	3 (50.0)	—	6 (100.0)
Udaipur	5 (45.5)	4 (36.4)	—	2 (18.2)	11 (100.0)
Rajasthan	**98 (41.4)**	**95 (40.1)**	**40 (16.9)**	**4 (1.7)**	**237 (100.0)**

Figures in brackets show percentage share to total Panchayat Samities.

Note: EDI LevelVH: (>0.5), H : (0.4-05), M : (0.3-0.4), L : (0.2-0.3), VL : (<0.2).

Source: Annex 8.2

TABLE 8.6: Distribution of PSs Having Very High EDI Level-2001

S. No.	*District*	*No. & Name of PSs in Descending Order*
		Very High Level (98)
1	Jaipur	11—Kotputli, Viratnagar, Sambhar, Jhotwara, Govindgarh, Shahpura, Jamwaramgarh, Sanganer, Phagi, Amber and Bassi
2	Jhunjhunun	8—Udaipurwati , Buhana, Jhunjhunun , Chirawa, Alsisar, Surajgarh, Nawalgarh and Khetri
3	Sikar	8—Fatehpur, Lachhmangarh, Khandela, Danta ramgarh, Piprali, Dhond, Neem ka Thana and Sri Madhopur
4	Bharatpur	7—Nadbai , Rupbas, Sewar, Kumher, Weir, Nagarpahari and Deeg
5	Churu	7—Taranagar, Rajgarh, Churu, Ratangarh, Sujangarh, Sardarshahar and Dungargarh
6	Alwar	6—Behror, Kotkasim, Mandawar, Nimrana, Bansure and Kathumar
7	Ganganagar	6—Raisinghnagar and Ganganagar, Padampur, Sadulshahar, Karanpur and Anupgarh
8	Barmer	5—Dhorimanna, Sindhari, Siwana, Baytoo and Sheo
9	Karauli	5—Hindaun, Nadoti , Todabhim, Sapotra and Karauli
10	Kota	5—Sultanpur, Sangod, Chechat, Ladpura and Itawa
11	Nagaur	5—Didwana, Kuchaman, Makrana, Ladnu and Parbatsar
12	Udaipur	5—Bargaon, Bhinder, Jhadol, Girwa and Salumbar
13	Dausa	4—Bandikui, Mahwa, Sikrai and Dausa
14	Dhaulpur	4—Baseri, Dhaulpur, Rajakhera and Bari
15	Baran	3—Baran, Anta and Atru
16	Hanumangarh	3—Bhadra, Nohar and Hanumangarh
17	Jhalawar	3—Pirawa, Khanpur and Jhalrapatan
18	Sawai Madhopur	2—Bamanwas and Gangapur
19	Ajmer	1—Jawaja

Source: Annex- 8.3

TABLE 8.7: Distribution of PSs Having High EDI Level-2001

S. No.	*District*	*No. & Name of PSs in Descending Order*
		High Level (95)
1	Chittaurgarh	11—Nimbahera, Pratapgarh, Chhotisadri, Bhopalsagar, Chittaurgarh, Begun, Dungla, Arnod, Bhadesar, Gangrar and Bhainsrorgarh
2	Pali	10—Rani Station, Sumerpur, Sojat, Bali, Desuri, Rohat , Kharchi/Marwar Jun., Raipur, Pali and Jaitaran
3	Alwar	8—Reni, Kishangarh Bas, Lachhmangarh, Rajgarh, Ramgarh, Umren, Tijara and Thanagazi
4	Rajsamand	7—Railmagra, Rajsamand, Bhim, Khamnor, Deogarh, Amet and Kumbhalgarh
5	Ajmer	6—Masuda, Kishangarh, Pisangan, Srinagar, Arian and Kekri
6	Nagaur	5—Merta, Degana, Riyan, Jayal and Nagaur
7	Baran	4—Kishanganj, Chhabra, Shahbad and Chhipabrod
8	Bundi	4—Keshoraipatan, Talera , Nainwa and Hindoli
9	Jodhpur	4—Luni, Bilara, Osian and Phalodi
10	Sirohi	4—Pindwara, Sheoganj, Sirohi and Reodar
11	Udaipur	4—Kherwara, Sarada, Mavli and Gogunda
12	Barmer	3—Balotra, Barmer and Chohtan
13	Bhilwara	3—Hurda, Banera and Jahazpur
14	Bikaner	3—Nokha, Bikaner and Lunkaransar
15	Tonk	3—Todaraisingh, Niwai and Malpura
16	Bharatpur	2—Bayana and Kaman
17	Dungarpur	2—Sagwara and Dungarpur
18	Jaipur	2—Dudu and Chaksu
19	Jaisalmer	2—Sankra and Jaisalmer
20	Jalor	2—Ahore and Raniwara
21	Sawai Madhopur	2—Bonli and Sawai Madhopur
22	Banswara	1—Garhi
23	Dausa	1 Lalsot
24	Ganganagar	1—Suratgarh
25	Jhalawar	1—Manoharthana

Source: Annex- 8.3’

Ganganagar, Jaipur, Jalore, Jhalawar and Udaipur all the above districts had greater percentage of H level PSs in comparison to the state average (40.1). Moreover three districts, namely, Bundi, Pali and Rajsamand had 100 per cent of their PSs in High category while Banswara had the minimum (12.5) percentage of these PSs.

TABLE 8.8: Distribution of PSs Having Medium and Low EDI Level-2001

S. No.	*District*	*No. & Name of PSs in Descending Order*
		[A] Medium (40)
1	Bhilwara	8—Suwana, Sahara, Mandalgarh, Mandal, Shahpura, Raipur, Asind and Kotri
2	Banswara	5—Talwara, Bagidora, Anandpuri, Ghatol and Sajjangarh
3	Jalor	5—Sanchore, Jalor, Sayla, Bhinmal and Jaswantpura
4	Jodhpur	5—Bhopalgarh, Bap, Mandor, Balesar and Shergarh
5	Chhittaurgarh	3—Kapasan, Barisadri and Rashmi
6	Dungarpur	3—Bichhiwara, Aspur and Simalwara
7	Tonk	3—Uniara, Deoli and Tonk
8	Jhalawar	2—Dag and Bakani
9	Bikaner	1—Kolayat
10	Jaisalmer	1—Sam
11	Jhunjhunun	1—Luni
12	Nagaur	1—Mundwa
13	Sawai Madhopur	1—Khandar
14	Sirohi	1—Abu Road
		[B] Low Level (4)
1	Banswara	2—Kushalgarh and Peepalkhoont
2	Udaipur	2—Dhariwad and Kotra

Source: Annex- 8.3

Medium EDI Region

Medium EDI region was widely distributed in 14 districts and 5 divisions (except Jaipur). There were 40 PSs in this category. Ajmer division had the maximum concentration of these PSs (32.5% share) followed by Jodhpur (30%), Udaipur (27.5%), Kota (7.5%), and Bikaner (2.5%) divisions. The highest percentage share of M level PSs to total PSs was 36.1 in Ajmer division followed by 28.9 in Udaipur, 23.8 in Jodhpur, 9.4 in Kota and the lowest 4.8 in Bikaner division. Ajmer, Jodhpur and Udaipur divisions had greater percentage of M level PSs than the state average (8.9). If we analyse district-wise distribution of these PSs, it is clear that Bhilwara secured the top position with 8 PSs followed by Banswara, Jalore, and Jodhpur (5 each); Chittaurgarh, Dungarpur, and Tonk (3 each); Jhalawar (2); Ajmer, Bikaner, Jaisalmer, Nagaur, Sawai Madhopur, Sirohi and Udaipur (1 each) districts respectively. Except Ajmer and Nagaur all the above districts had higher percentage of Medium level PSs than the state average. Bhilwara had the highest 72.7 per cent of these PSs while Nagaur had the Lowest (9.1%).

Low EDI Region

Kotra and Dhariwad PSs of Udaipur district and Banswara and Kushalgarh of Banswara district were the only PSs having Low EDI. Both Banswara (25%) and Udaipur (18%) districts had greater percentage of these PSs than the state average (17%).

9

GENDER-RELATED EDUCATION INDEX (1991)

Highlights

- Rural GEDI-Raj. : 0.192
- Percentage of AAPs : 41
- 20 PSs had GEDI below 0.1

	Panchayat Samiti	District	Division
• **Top**	Nimrana (0.452)	Alwar	Jaipur
• **Bottom**	Chohtan (0.042)	Barmer	Jodhpur

The Gender-Related Education Index (GEDI) of rural Rajasthan in the year 1991 was not only low (0.192) but also had a great spatial variation. Fig. 9.1 presents panchayat samiti-wise variation in GEDI value across the state. Whereas, 44 per cent PSs of Bikaner, 36 per cent of Jaipur, 22 per cent of Kota and 9 per cent PSs of Ajmer divisions had Very High to High level of GEDI, no PS of Jodhpur and Udaipur divisions qualified for a place in this category. Morever, more than 90 per cent PSs of Jodhpur and 80 per cent of Udaipur divisions had Low to Extremely Low level of GEDI.

Jaipur division led not only in PSs (62.5% share) having Very High GEDI, but also in PSs having High (48%) and Medium (51%) GEDI. On the other hand, Jodhpur was the most deprived division, dominating in PSs having Extemely Low (75% share) and Very Low (27%) GEDI followed by Udaipur division, which led in PSs (26%) having Low GEDI.

Nimrana PS of Alwar district had the highest (0.452) GEDI followed by Behror, Ganganagar, Kotkasim, Padampur, Buhana, Mandawar, Jhunjhunun, Karanpur and Chirawa PSs respectively (Annex 9.2). These (first ten) PSs were distributed in three districts. Alwar had maximum four PSs followed by Jhunjhunun and Ganganagar (3 each) districts respectively (Table 9.1). On the other side, Chohtan PS of Barmer district had

Table 9.1: Distribution of First and Last Ten Panchayat Samities: GEDI Value (1991)

S. No.	*First Ten PSs (Descending Order)*			*Last Ten PSs (Ascending Order)*				
	Districts/ PSs			*Districts/ PSs*				
	Alwar	*Jhunjhunun*	*Ganganagar*	*Barmer*	*Jalor*	*Udaipur*	*Banswara*	*Jhalawar*
1	Nimrana	Buhana	Ganganagar	Chohtan	Sanchore	Kotra	Peepalkhoont	Manoharthana
2	Behror	Jhunjhunun	Padampur	Sindhari	Bhinmal	—	—	—
3	Kotkasim	Chirawa	Karanpur	Dhorimanna	—	—	—	—
4	Mandawar	—	—	Sheo	—	—	—	—
5	—	—	—	Barmer	—	—	—	—
Total	**4**	**3**	**3**	**5**	**2**	**1**	**1**	**1**

Source: Annex 9.1

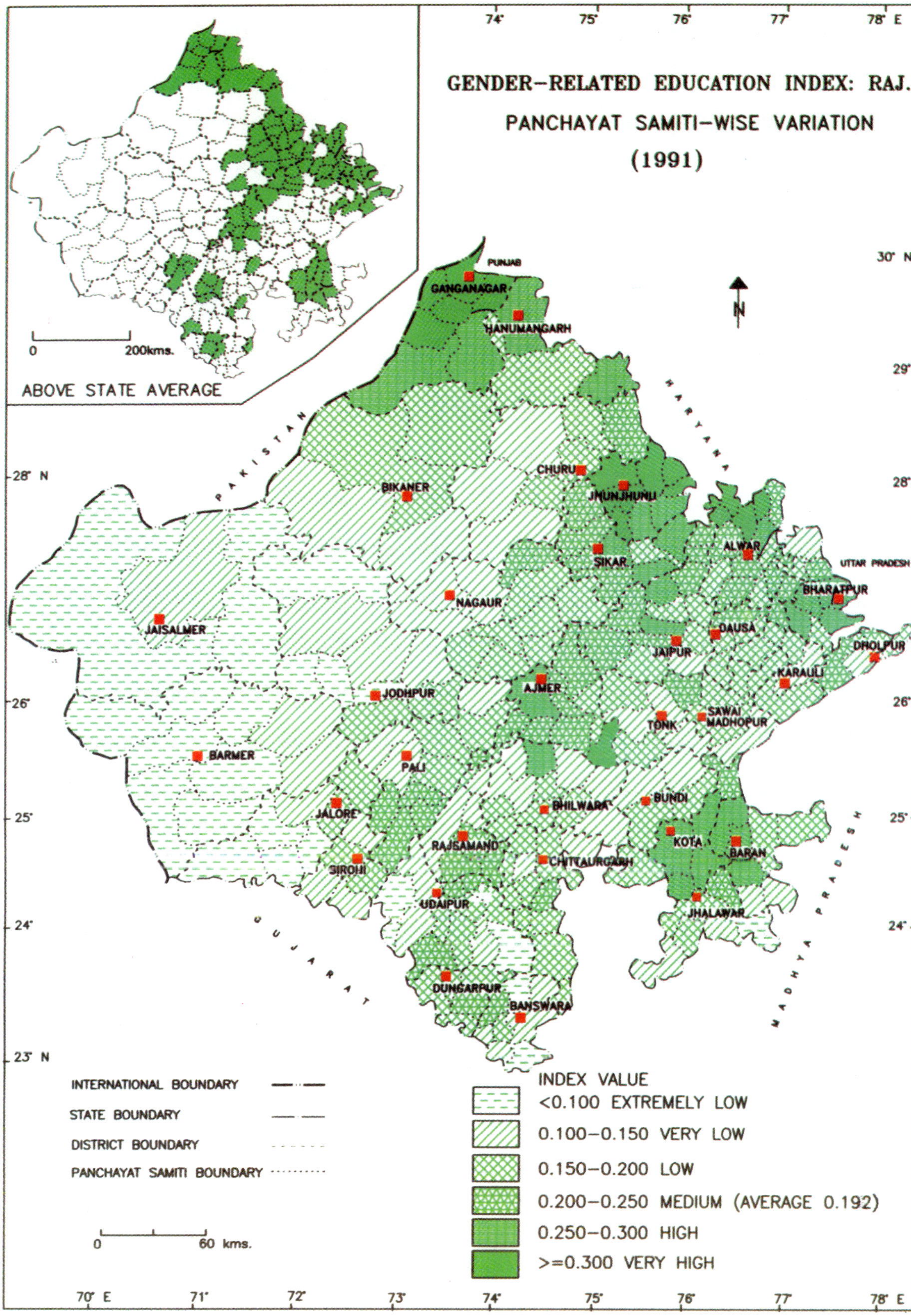
GENDER–RELATED EDUCATION INDEX: RAJ.
PANCHAYAT SAMITI–WISE VARIATION
(1991)
ABOVE STATE AVERAGE
0 200kms.
PUNJAB
GANGANAGAR
HANUMANGARH
HARYANA
PAKISTAN
CHURU
JHUNJHUNU
BIKANER
SIKAR
ALWAR
UTTAR PRADESH
BHARATPUR
NAGAUR
JAISALMER
DAUSA
JAIPUR
DHOLPUR
KARAULI
AJMER
JODHPUR
TONK
SAWAI MADHOPUR
BARMER
PALI
BHILWARA
BUNDI
JALORE
KOTA
BARAN
RAJSAMAND
SIROHI
CHITTAURGARH
UDAIPUR
JHALAWAR
GUJARAT
MADHYA PRADESH
DUNGARPUR
BANSWARA
INTERNATIONAL BOUNDARY
STATE BOUNDARY
DISTRICT BOUNDARY
PANCHAYAT SAMITI BOUNDARY
0 60 kms.
INDEX VALUE
<0.100 EXTREMELY LOW
0.100–0.150 VERY LOW
0.150–0.200 LOW
0.200–0.250 MEDIUM (AVERAGE 0.192)
0.250–0.300 HIGH
>=0.300 VERY HIGH
70° E
71°
72°
73°
74°
75°
76°
77°
78° E
30° N
29°
28° N
26°
25°
24°
23° N

FIG. 9.1

the lowest (0.042) GEDI preceded by Kotra, Peepalkhoont, Sindhari, Dhorimanna, Sanchore, Manoharthana, Bhinmal, Sheo and Barmer (ascending order) PSs. These last ten PSs were spread over five districts. Barmer led with five PSs followed by Jalor (2), Udaipur, Banswara and Jhalawar (one each) districts respectively.

The PSs which secured the top spot in GEDI value in their respecitve districts were : Kekri (Aj), Nimrana (Al), Garhi (Bans), Siwana (Bmr), Rupbas (Bharat), Hurda (Bhil), Lunkaransar (Bk), Keshoraipatan (Bun), Nimbahera (Chitt), Rajgarh (Chu), Baseri (Dhaul), Sagwara (Dg), Ganganagar (Gg), Govindgarh (Jp), Jaisalmer (Jais), Ahore (Jl), Khanpur (Jhala), Buhana (Jhun), Luni (Jodh), Sultanpur (Kt), Ladnu (Ng), Rani Station (Pl), Gangapur (SM), Siri Madhopur (Sk), Sirohi (Sr), Niwai (Tk), Bargaon (Ud), Anta (Brn), Mahwa (Ds), Railmagra (Rajs), Hanumangarh (Hn) and Nadoti (Kr) as shown in Table 9.2.

On the other side, the PSs which had the bottom spot in their respective districts were : Arain, Thanagazi, Peepalkhoont, Chohtan, Kaman, Shahpura, Nokha, Nainwa, Kapasan, Sardarshahar, Bari, Bichhiwara, Suratgarh, Chaksu, Sam, Sanchore, Manoharthana, Udaipurwati, Shergarh, Itawa, Mundwa, Rohat, Khandar, Khandela, Abu Road, Tonk, Kotra, Chhabra, Sikrai, Deogarh, Nohar and Karauli.

TABLE 9.2: District-wise First and Last PSs by GEDI (1991)

District	*First Rank*	*Last Rank*	*District*	*First Rank*	*Last Rank*
Ajmer	Kekri	Arian	Jaipur	Govindgarh	Chaksu
Alwar	Nimrana	Thanagagi	Jaisalmer	Jaisalmer	Sam
Banswara	Garhi	Peepalkhoont	Jalor	Ahore	Sanchore
Baran	Anta	Chhabra	Jhalawar	Khanpur	Manoharthana
Barmer	Siwana	Chhohtan	Jhunjhunun	Buhana	Udaipurwati
Bharatpur	Rupbas	Kaman	Jodhpur	Luni	Shergarh
Bhilwara	Hurda	Shahpura	Karauli	Nadoti	Karauli
Bikaner	Lunkaransar	Nokha	Kota	Sultanpur	Itawa
Bundi	Keshoraipatan	Nainwa	Nagaur	Ladnu	Mundwa
Chittaurgarh	Nimbahera	Kapasan	Pali	Rani Station	Rohat
Churu	Rajgarh	Sardarshahar	Rajsamand	Railmagra	Deogarh
Dausa	Mahwa	Sikrai	Sawai Madhopur	Gangapur	Khandar
Dhaulpur	Baseri	Bari	Sikar	Sri Madhopur	Khandela
Dungarpur	Sagwara	Bichhiwara	Sirohi	Sirohi	Abu Road
Ganganagar	Ganganagar	Suratgarh	Tonk	Niwari	Tonk
Hanumangarh	Hanumangarh	Nohar	Udaipur	Bargaon	Kotra

Source: Annex 10.1, Col. 7

The GEDI range (difference between GEDI value of the top and the bottom PSs) in the state was 0.410. Among the districts, Alwar had the highest (0.297) range followed by Banswara, Jhalawar, Udaipur, Bharatpur, Baran, Bhilwara and Ganganagar districts respectively (Table 9.2). On the other side, Sikar district had the lowest (0.033) range preceded by Jaisalmer, Bundi, Bikaner, Sirohi and Kota districts respectively.

TABLE 9.3: GEDI (1991) : Classification of Districts on the Basis of percentage of AAPs

%age of Above Average PSs	*Districts*		
	No.	*%*	*Name*
Absence (0)	7	21.9	Barmer, Bikaner, Bundi, Jaisalmer, Jalor, Jodhpur and Sirohi
Very Low (1 -25)	9	28.1	Banswara, Bhilwara, Chittaurgarh, Churu, Jhalawar, Nagaur, Sawai Madhopur, Tonk and Karauli
Low (25 - 50)	6	18.8	Dungarpur, Pali, Udaipur, Baran, Dausa and Rajsamand
Medium (50 - 75)	3	9.4	Bharatpur, Dhaulpur and Jaipur
High (75 - 100)	2	6.3	Ajmer and Alwar
Perfect (100)	5	15.6	Ganganagar, Jhunjhunun, Kota, Sikar and Hanumangarh
Total	**32**	**100.0**	

Source: Annex 10.1

Above Average PSs (AAPs)

Unfortunately, there were 59 per cent PSs having GEDI value below the state average. The inset map (Fig. 9.1) depicts spatial distribution of AAPs in the state. These PSs were spread over 25 districts. It is understood that GEDI in the north-eastern region, being high level these PSs were also concentrated mainly in this region followed by northern, central and south-eastern regions respectively.

On the basis of percentage of AAPs, districts can be classified in to five groups (Table 9.3). Unfortunately, 7 districts viz. Barmer, Bikaner, Bundi, Jaisalmer, Jalor, Jodhpur and Sirohi had 0 per cent AAPs and 15 others had <50 per cent AAPs. On the otherside, only 5 districts namely, Ganganagar, Jhunjhunun, Kota, Sikar and Hanumangarh had 100 per cent and five others had >50 per cent AAPs.

GEDI Levels

PSs of the state can be classified into six groups on the basis of GEDI levels viz. Very High (VH), High (H), Medium (M), Low (L), Very Low (VL) and Extremely Low (EL) levels (Table 9.4).

TABLE 9.4: Classification of PSs on the Basis of GEDI (1991): Rajasthan

Group *GEDI Level*	*Included PSs*			
	No.	*%*	*Distributed in*	
			Districts	*Divisions*
Very High (VH), (>0.3)	16	6.8	4	3
High (H), (0.25-0.3)	25	10.5	11	4
Medium (M), (0.2-0.25)	47	19.8	18	6
Low (L), (0.15-0.2)	77	32.5	26	6
Very Low (VL), (0.1-0.15)	52	22.0	23	6
Extremely Low (EL), (<0.1)	20	8.4	7	3
Total	**237**	**100**		

Source: Annex 9.1

TABLE 9.5: Division-wise Classification and Distribution of PSs on the Basis of GEDI Level (1991)

Divisions	*Classification*							*Distribution (% Share)*					
	GEDI Level							*GEDI Level*					
	VH	*H*	*M*	*L*	*VL*	*EL*	*Total PSs*	*VH*	*H*	*M*	*L*	*VL*	*EL*
Jaipur	10	12	24	12	3	—	61	62.5	48.0	51.1	15.6	5.8	—
	(16.4)	(19.7)	(39.3)	(19.7)	(4.9)	—	(100.0)						
Bikaner	5	4	1	6	5	—	21	31.3	16.0	2.1	7.7	9.6	—
	(23.8)	(19.0)	(4.8)	(28.6)	(23.8)	—	(100.0)						
Ajmer	1	2	7	16	10	—	36	6.2	8.0	14.9	20.8	19.2	—
	(2.8)	(5.6)	(19.4)	(44.4)	(27.8)	—	(100.0)						
Kota	—	7	2	14	8	1	32	—	28.0	4.3	18.2	15.4	5.0
	—	(21.9)	(6.2)	(43.8)	(25.0)	(3.1)	(100.0)						
Jodhpur	—	—	4	9	14	15	42	—	—	8.5	11.7	26.9	75.0
	—	—	(9.5)	(21.5)	(33.3)	(35.7)	(100.0)						
Udaipur	—	—	9	20	12	4	45	—	—	19.1	26.0	23.1	20.0
	—	—	(20.0)	(44.4)	(26.7)	(8.9)	(100.0)						
Total	**16**	**25**	**47**	**77**	**52**	**20**	**237**	**100**	**100**	**100**	**100**	**100**	**100**
	(6.8)	**(10.5)**	**(19.8)**	**(32.5)**	**(22.0)**	**(8.4)**	**(100.0)**						

Figure in brackets shows percentage share to total Panchayat Samities.
Note: GEDI Level VH : (>0.3), H : (0.25-0.3), M : (0.2-0.25), L : (0.15-0.2), VL : (0.1 0.15), EL : (<0.1)
Source: Annex 9.1

TABLE 9.6: District-wise Classification of PSs on the Basis of GEDI Level (1991)

District	*GEDI Level*						
	VH	*H*	*M*	*L*	*VL*	*EL*	*Total PSs*
Ajmer	1	1	5	1	—	—	8
	(12.5)	(12.5)	(62.5)	(12.5)	—	—	(100.0)
Alwar	4	1	7	2	—	—	14
	(28.6)	(7.1)	(50.0)	(14.3)	—	—	(100.0)
Banswara	—	—	1	1	4	2	8
	—	—	(12.5)	(12.5)	(50.0)	(25.0)	(100.0)
Baran	—	3	—	2	2	—	7
	—	(42.9)	—	(28.6)	(28.6)	—	(100.0)
Barmer	—	—	—	—	2	6	8
	—	—	—	—	(25.0)	(75.0)	(100.0)
Bharatpur	—	4	2	2	1	—	9
	—	(44.4)	(22.2)	(22.2)	(11.1)	—	(100.0)
Bhilwara	—	1	—	5	5	—	11
	—	(9.1)	—	(45.5)	(45.5)	—	(100.0)
Bikaner	—	—	—	2	2	—	4
	—	—	—	(50.0)	(50.0)	—	(100.0)
Bundi	—	—	—	2	2	—	4
	—	—	—	(50.0)	(50.0)	—	(100.0)
Chittaurgarh	—	—	1	11	2	—	14
	—	—	(7.1)	(78.6)	(14.3)	—	(100.0)
Churu	—	—	1	3	3	—	7
	—	—	(14.3)	(42.9)	(42.9)	—	(100.0)
Dausa	—	—	2	3	—	—	5
	—	—	(40.0)	(60.0)	—	—	(100.0)
Dhaulpur	—	—	2	1	1	—	4
	—	—	(50.0)	(25.0)	(25.0)	—	(100.0)
Dungarpur	—	—	1	4	—	—	5
	—	—	(20.0)	(80.0)	—	—	(100.0)
Ganganagar	5	2	—	—	—	—	7
	(71.4)	(28.6)	—	—	—	—	(100.0)
Hanumangargh	—	2	—	1	—	—	3
	—	(66.7)	—	(33.3)	—	—	(100.0)
Jaipur	—	2	6	4	1	—	13
	—	(15.4)	(46.2)	(30.8)	(7.7)	—	(100.0)
Jaisalmer	—	—	—	—	1	2	3
	—	—	—	—	(33.3)	(66.7)	(100.0)
Jalor	—	—	—	2	1	4	7
	—	—	—	(28.6)	(14.3)	(57.1)	(100.0)
Jhalawar	—	—	1	2	2	1	6
	—	—	(16.7)	(33.3)	(33.3)	(16.7)	(100.0)
Jhunjhunun	6	2	—	—	—	—	8
	(75.0)	(25.0)	—	—	—	—	(100.0)
Jodhpur	—	—	—	2	4	3	9
	—	—	—	(22.2)	(44.4)	(33.3)	(100.0)
Karauli	—	—	—	4	1	—	5
	—	—	—	(80.0)	(20.0)	—	(100.0)
Kota	—	4	1	—	—	—	5
	—	(80.0)	(20.0)	—	—	—	(100.0)
Nagaur	—	—	1	7	3	—	11
	—	—	(9.1)	(63.6)	(27.3)	—	(100.0)
Pali	—	—	4	3	3	—	10
	—	—	(40.0)	(30.0)	(30.0)	—	(100.0)
Rajsamand	—	—	3	1	3	—	7
	—	—	(42.9)	(14.3)	(42.9)	—	(100.0)
Sawai Madhopur	—	—	—	4	1	—	5
	—	—	—	(80.0)	(20.0)	—	(100.0)
Sikar	—	3	5	—	—	—	8
	—	(37.5)	(62.5)	—	—	—	(100.0)
Sirohi	—	—	—	2	3	—	5
	—	—	—	(40.0)	(60.0)	—	(100.0)
Tonk	—	—	1	3	2	—	6
	—	—	(16.7)	(50.0)	(33.3)	—	(100.0)
Udaipur	—	—	3	3	3	2	11
	—	—	(27.3)	(27.3)	(27.3)	(18.2)	(100.0)
Rajasthan	**16**	**25**	**47**	**77**	**52**	**20**	**237**
	(6.8)	**(10.5)**	**(19.8)**	**(32.5)**	**(22.0)**	**(8.4)**	**(100.0)**

Figures in brackets show percentage share to total Panchayat Samities

Note: GEDI Level VH : (>0.3), H : (0.25-0.3), M : (0.2-0.25), L : (0.15-0.2), VL : (0.1-0.15), EL : (<0.1)

Source: Annex 10.1, Col. 7

There was a clear cut dominance of L level PSs (32.5%), followed by VL (22%), M (19.8%), H & VH (17.3%) and EL (8.4%) level PSs in the state. Whereas, M, L and VL level PSs were spread over all the six divisions, the others were concentrated only in few divisions.

Division-wise and district-wise classification and distribution of PSs on the basis of GEDI level is shown in Table 9.5 and 9.6 respectively. It is clear that no division had all the six GEDI levels. Whereas, Jaipur, Bikaner, Ajmer and Kota divisions had PSs of five levels, Jodhpur and Udaipur divisions had PSs of four levels. As mentioned earlier, Jaipur division (north-eastern region) led in very high to medium level PSs, Jodhpur and Udaipur were the most deprived divisions.

Based on the analysis of the division-wise classification of PSs (on the basis of different GEDI levels), we can conclude that whereas, M level PSs (39.3% share) were dominating in Jaipur division and Low level in Udaipur (44.4%), Ajmer (44.4%), Kota (43.8%) and Bikaner (28.6%) divisions while EL level PSs were leading in Jodhpur (35.7%) division.

The percentage of VH, H and M level PSs in Jaipur division was higher than the state average. Similarly, the percentage of VH, H and VL in Bikaner division; L and VL in Ajmer; H, L and VL in Kota; VL and EL in Jodhpur and M, L, VL and EL level PSs in Udaipur division was above the state average.

Jaipur division secured the top rank not only in VH (62.5%) and H (48%) level PSs but also in M (51.1%) level PSs in the state. Jodhpur dominated in both EL (75%) and VL (27%) level PSs while, Udaipur division led in L level (26%) PSs. The indepth account of different GEDI areas is presented here:

Very High and High GEDI Areas

As mentioned earlier, Very High and High GEDI areas were mainly concentrated in Jaipur division followed by some part of Bikaner, Ajmer and Kota divisions. There were 16 VH level PSs distributed in 4 districts. Jaipur division accounted the highest 62.5 per cent share followed by Bikaner (31.3%) and Ajmer (6.2%) divisions respectively. Among the districts, Jhunjhunun had the maximum 6 PSs followed by Ganganagar (5), Alwar (4) and Ajmer (1) districts respectively. The percentage of VH level PSs varied from maximum 75 in Jhunjhunun to minimum 12.5 in Ajmer district (Table 9.7).

TABLE 9.7: Distribution of PSs having Very High and High Level of GEDI (1991)

S. No.	*District*	*No. & Name of PSs (in Descending Order)*
		[I] Very High Level (16)
1	Jhunjhunun	6—Buhana, Jhunjhunun, Chirawa, Nawalgarh, Surajgarh and Alsisar
2	Ganganagar	5—Ganganagar, Padampur, Karanpur, Sadulshahar and Raisinghnagar
3	Alwar	4—Nimrana, Behror, Kotkasim and Mandawar
4	Ajmer	1—Kekri
		[II] High Level (25)
1	Bharatpur	4—Rupbas, Kumher, Sewar and Nadbai
2	Kota	4—Sultanpur, Sangod, Ladpura and Chechat
3	Sikar	3—Sri Madhopur, Piprali and Neem ka Thana
4	Baran	3—Anta and Both, Atru and Baran
5	Ganganagar	2—Anupgarh and Suratgarh
6	Jaipur	2—Govindgarh and Jhotwara
7	Jhunjhunun	2—Khetri and Udaipurwati
8	Hanumangarh	2—Hanumangarh and Bhadra
9	Ajmer	1—Pisangan
10	Alwar	1—Kishangarh Bas
11	Bhilwara	1—Hurda

Source: Annex 9.1

High level 25 PSs were also concentrated mainly in Jaipur (48%) division followed by Kota (28%), Bikaner (16%) and Ajmer (8%) divisions respectively. These PSs were spread over in 11 districts. Bharatpur and Kota districts had 4 PSs followed by Sikar and Baran (3 each); Ganganagar, Jaipur, Jhunjhunun and Hanumangarh (2 each); Ajmer, Alwar and Bhilwara (1 each) districts respectively. The percentage of H level PSs varied from maximum 80 in Kota to minimum 7 in Alwar district.

Medium GEDI Areas

There were 47 M level PSs distributed in 18 districts of all the six divisions. Jaipur division dominated with 51.1 per cent share followed by Udaipur (19.1%), Ajmer (14.9%), Jodhpur (8.5%), Kota (4.3%) and Bikaner (2.1%) divisions respectively. Among the districts, Alwar led with 7 PSs followed by Jaipur (6); Ajmer, Sikar (5 each); Pali (4); Udaipur and Rajsamand (3 each); Bharatpur, Dhaulpur, Dausa (2 each); Banswara, Chittaurgarh, Churu, Dungarpur, Jhalawar, Kota, Nagaur and Tonk (one each) districts respectively (Table 9.8). The percentage of M level PSs varied from maximum 62.5 in both Sikar and Ajmer to minimum 7.1 in Chittaurgarh district.

TABLE 9.8: Distribution of PSs having Medium Level of GEDI (1991)

S. No.	*District*	*No. & Name of PSs (in Descending Order)*
		[I] Medium Level (47)
1	Alwar	7—Ramgarh, Tijara, Bansure, Rajgarh, Lachhmangarh, Umren and Kathumar
2	Jaipur	6—Sanganer, Shahpura, Kotputli, Sambhar, Viratnagar and Dudu
3	Ajmer	5—Bhinay, Srinagar, Jawaja, Kishangarh and Masooda
4	Sikar	5—Lachhmangarh, Danta Ramgarh, Fatehpur, Dhond and Khandela
5	Pali	4—Rani Station, Bali, Sumerpur and Desuri
6	Udaipur	3—Bargaon, Mavli and Kherwara
7	Rajsamand	3—Railmagra, Khamnor and Rajsamand
8	Bharatpur	2—Weir and Deeg
9	Dhaulpur	2—Baseri and Dhaulpur
10	Dausa	2—Mahwa and Bandikui
11	Banswara	1—Garhi
12	Chittaurgarh	1—Nimbahera
13	Churu	1—Rajgarh
14	Dungarpur	1—Sagwara
15	Jhalawar	1—Khanpur
16	Kota	1—Itawa
17	Nagaur	1—Ladnu
18	Tonk	1—Niwai

Source: Annex 9.1

Low, Very Low and Extremely Low GEDI Areas

It is a matter of great concern that 91.5 per cent PSs of Jodhpur, 80 per cent of Udaipur, 78 per cent of Kota, 72 per cent of Ajmer and 52 per cent PSs of Kota divisions had Low to Extremely Low GEDI level.

There were 77 PSs having Low GEDI. These PSs were widely spread over in 26 districts of all the six divisions. Udaipur division dominated with 26 per cent share following by Ajmer (20.8%), Kota (18.2%), Jaipur (15.6%), Jodhpur (11.7%) and Bikaner (7.7%) divisions. Among the districts, Chittaurgarh had a leading position with 11 PSs followed by Nagaur (7); Bhilwara (5); Dungarpur, Jaipur, Sawai Madhopur and Karauli (4 each); Churu, Pali, Tonk, Udaipur and Dausa (3 each); Alwar, Bharatpur, Bikaner, Bundi, Jalor, Jhalawar, Jodhpur, Sirohi; Baran (2 each); Ajmer, Banswara, Dhaulpur, Rajsamand, and Hanumangarh (one each) districts respectively. The percentage of Low level PSs varied from maximum 80 in Dungarpur, SM and Karauli to minimum 12.5 in Ajmer and Banswara districts (Table 9.9).

The 52 VL level PSs were also widely distributed in 23 districts and 6 divisions. Jodhpur division secured the top position with 26.9 per cent share followed by Udaipur (23%), Ajmer (19.2%), Kota (15.4%), Bikaner (9.6%) and Jaipur (5.8%) divisions respectively. Among the districts, Bhilwara dominated with 5 PSs followed

TABLE 9.9: Distribution of PSs having L, VL and EL Level of GEDI (1991)

S. No.	*District*	*No. & Name of PSs (in Descending Order)*
		Low Level (77)
1	Chittaurgarh	11—Arnod and Chhoti Sadri, Bhopalsagar, Chittaurgarh, Pratapgarh and Rashmi, Gangrar, Dungla, Bhadesar, Bari Sadri and Bhainsrorgarh
2	Nagaur	7—Makrana, Merta, Kuchaman, Didwana, Parbatsar, Riyan and Degana
3	Bhilwara	5—Kotri, Banera, Sahara, Raipur and Suwana
4	Dungarpur	4—Aspur, Dungarpur, Simalwara and Bichhiwara
5	Jaipur	4—Amber, Phagi, Bassi and Jamwa Ramgarh
6	Sawai Madhopur	4—Gangapur, Bonli, Bamanwas and Sawai Madhopur
7	Karauli	4—Nadoti, Hindaun, Sapotra and Todabhim
8	Churu	3—Churu, Taranagar and Ratangarh
9	Pali	3—Sojat, Kharchi/Marwar Jun. and Raipur
10	Tonk	3—Deoli, Malpura and Todaraisingh
11	Udaipur	3—Girwa, Bhinder and Sarada
12	Dausa	3—Dausa, Lalsot and Sikrai
13	Alwar	2—Reni and Thanagazi
14	Bharatpur	2—Bayana and Nagar Pahari
15	Bikaner	2—Lunkaransar and Bikaner
16	Bundi	2—Keshoraipatan and Talera
17	Jalor	2—Ahore and Jalor
18	Jhalawar	2—Jhalrapatan and Pirawa
19	Jodhpur	2—Luni and Bilara
20	Sirohi	2—Sirohi and Pindwara
21	Baran	2—Shahbad and Kishanganj
22	Ajmer	1—Arain
23	Banswara	1—Bagidora
24	Dhaulpur	1—Rajakhera
25	Rajsamand	1—Bhim
26	Hanumangarh	1—Nohar
		Very Low Level (52)
1	Bhilwara	5—Jahazpur, Mandal and Mandalgarh, Asind and Shahpura
2	Banswara	4—Talwara, Ghatol, Anandpuri and Sajjangarh
3	Jodhpur	4—Mandor, Bhopalgarh, Osian and Phalodi
4	Churu	3—Dungargarh, Sujangarh and Sardarshahar
5	Nagaur	3—Both Nagaur and Jayal and Mundwa
6	Pali	3—Pali, Jaitaran and Rohat
7	Sirohi	3—Sheoganj, Reodar and Abu Road
8	Udaipur	3—Gogunda, Salumbar and Jhadol
9	Rajsamand	3—Kumbhalgarh, Amet and Deogarh
10	Barmer	2—Siwana and Balotra
11	Bikaner	2 Kolayat and Nokha
12	Bundi	2—Hindoli and Nainwa
13	Chittaurgarh	2—Begun and Kapasan
14	Jhalawar	2 Bakani and Dag
15	Tonk	2—Uniara and Tonk
16	Baran	2—Chhipabarod and Chhabara
17	Bharatpur	1—Kaman
18	Dhaulpur	1—Bari
19	Jaipur	1—Chaksu
20	Jaisalmer	1—Jaisalmer
21	Jalor	1—Sayla
22	Sawai Madhopur	1—Khandar
23	Karauli	1—Karauli
		Extremely Low Level (20)
1	Barmer	6—Baytoo, Barmer, Sheo, Dhorimanna, Sindhari and Chohtan
2	Jalor	4—Jaswantpura, Raniwara, Bhinmal and Sanchore
3	Jodhpur	3—Balesar, Bap and Shergarh
4	Banswara	2—Kushalgarh and Peepalkhoont
5	Jaisalmer	2—Sankra and Sam
6	Udaipur	2—Dhariawad and Kotra
7	Jhalawar	1—Manoharthana

Source: Annex 9.1

by Banswara and Jodhpur (4 each); Churu, Nagaur, Pali, Sirohi, Udaipur and Rajsamand (3 each); Barmer, Bikaner, Bundi, Chittaurgarh, Jhalawar, Tonk, Baran (2 each); Bharatpur, Dhaulpur, Jaipur, Jaisalmer, Jalor, SM and Karauli (one each) districts respectively. The percentage of VL level PSs ranged from maximum 60 in Sirohi to minimum 7.7 in Jaipur district.

Twenty EL level PSs were concentrated in 7 districts of 3 divisions. Jodhpur division had maximum 75 per cent share followed by Udaipur (20%) and Kota (5%) divisions. Among the districts, Barmer had the highest 6 PSs followed by Jalor (4), Jodhpur (3), Banswara, Jaisalmer, Udaipur (2 each) and Jhalawar (1) districts. The percentage of EL level PSs varied from maximum 75 in Barmer to 16.7 in Jhalawar district.

10

GENDER-RELATED EDUCATION INDEX (2001)

Highlights

- Rural GEDI-Raj. : 0.503
- Percentage of AAPs: 40.9

	Panchayat Samiti	**District**	**Division**
• **Top**	Behror (0.804)	Alwar	Jaipur
• **Bottom**	Kotra (0.172)	Udaipur	Udaipur

Gender-Related Education Index (GEDI) of rural Rajasthan rose to 0.503 in the year 2001. There were total 97 PSs having GEDI above the state average. Spatial distribution pattern of GEDI at PS level is depicted in Fig. 10.1 and Annex 10.1. Whereas, 49 per cent of PSs of Jaipur division, 43 per cent of Bikaner and 28 per cent PSs of Kota divisions had above 0.6 GEDI, less than 3 per cent PSs of Jodhpur, Ajmer and Udaipur divisions qualified for this category. The GEDI level in the state increases from the SW and South to the NE, North and SE direction.

Behror PS of Alwar district had the highest 0.804 GEDI followed by Udaipurwati, Buhana, Jhunjhunun, Fatehpur, Chirawa, Lachhmangarh, Alsisar, Jawaja, and Hindaun PSs, (Descending order, Annex 10.1). These top ten PSs were distributed in five districts. Jhunjhunun led with five PSs followed by Sikar (2), Ajmer, Alwar, and Karauli (one each) districts respectively (Table 10.1).

TABLE 10.1: Distribution of First and Last Ten Panchayat Samities by GEDI: Rajasthan, (2001)

S. No.	*First Ten PSs (Descending Order)*					*Last Ten PSs (Ascending Order)*			
	Districts/ PSs					*Districts/ PSs*			
	Jhun	*Sikar*	*Ajmer*	*Alwar*	*Karauli*	*Banswara*	*Jodh*	*Jalor*	*Udaipur*
	(5)	*(2)*	*(1)*	*(1)*	*(1)*	*(4)*	*(2)*	*(2)*	*(2)*
1	Udaipurwati	Fatehpur	Jawaja	Behror	Hindaun	Peepalkhoont	Shergarh	Bhinmal	Kotra
2	Buhana	Lachhmangarh	—	—	—	Kushalgarh	Balesar	Jasawantpura	Dhariawad
3	Jhunjhunun	—	—	—	—	Sajjangarh	—	—	—
4	Chirawa	—	—	—	—	Ghatol	—	—	—
5	Alsisar	—	—	—	—	—	—	—	—

Source: Annex 10.3

Kotra PS of Udaipur district, on the other hand, had the lowest 0.172 GEDI. It was preceded by Peepalkhoont, Kushalgarh, Dhariwad, Bhinder, Shergarh, Sajjangarh, Jaswantpura, Balesar and Ghatol, PSs

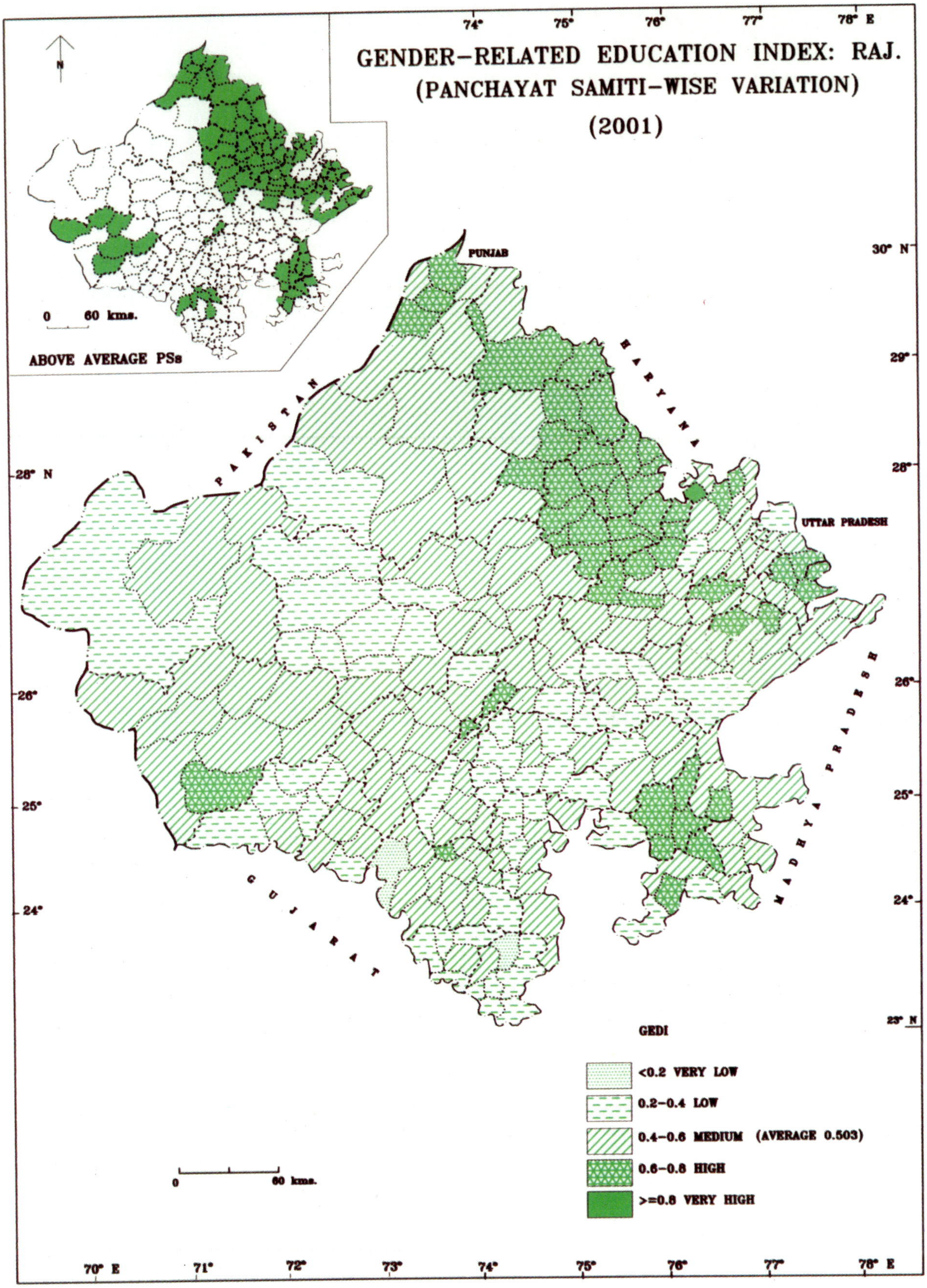
GENDER-RELATED EDUCATION INDEX: RAJ.
(PANCHAYAT SAMITI-WISE VARIATION)
(2001)
ABOVE AVERAGE PSs
0 60 kms.
N
PUNJAB
HARYANA
UTTAR PRADESH
MADHYA PRADESH
GUJARAT
PAKISTAN
GEDI
<0.2 VERY LOW
0.2-0.4 LOW
0.4-0.6 MEDIUM (AVERAGE 0.503)
0.6-0.8 HIGH
>=0.8 VERY HIGH
0 60 kms.
70° E
71°
72°
73°
74°
75°
76°
77°
78° E
30° N
29°
28° N
28°
26°
25°
24°
23° N

FIG. 10.1

(ascending order). These last ten PSs were concentrated in four districts. Banswara dominated with 4 PSs while Jodhpur, Jalor and Udaipur had 2 PSs each. District-wise PSs having the highest and the lowest GEDI is shown in Table 10.2.

TABLE 10.2: District-wise First and Last PSs by GEDI (2001)

District	*First Rank*	*Last Rank*	*District*	*First Rank*	*Last Rank*
Ajmer	Jawaja	Bhinay	Jaipur	Kotputli	Chaksu
Alwar	Behror	Thanagaji	Jaisalmer	Sankra	Sam
Banswara	Garhi	Peepalkhoont	Jalor	Ahore	Bhinmal
Baran	Baran	Chipabarod	Jhalawar	Pirawa	Bakani
Barmer	Dhorimanna	Chohtan	Jhunjhunun	Udaipurwati	Khetri
Bharatpur	Nadbai	Kaman	Jodhpur	Luni	Shergarh
Bhilwara	Hurda	Kotri	Karauli	Hindaun	Karauli
Bikaner	Bikaner	Kolayat	Kota	Sultanpur	Itawa
Bundi	Keshoraipatan	Hindoli	Nagaur	Didwana	Mundwa
Chittaurgarh	Pratapgarh	Rashmi	Pali	Rani Station	Jaitaran
Churu	Taranagar	Dungargarh	Rajsamand	Railmagra	Kumbhalgarh
Dausa	Bandikui	Lalsot	Sawai Madhopur	Bamanwas	Khandar
Dhaulpur	Baseri	Bari	Sikar	Fatehpur	Sri Madhopur
Dungarpur	Sagwara	Simalwara	Sirohi	Pindwara	Abu Road
Ganganagar	Raisinghnagar	Suratgarh	Tonk	Todaraisingh	Tonk
Hanumangarh	Bhadra	Hanumangarh	Udaipur	Bargaon	Kotra

Source: Annex 10.1

TABLE 10.3: Classification of PSs on the Basis of GEDI (2001)

Group	*Included PSs*			
	No.	*%*	*Distributed in*	
			Districts	*Divisions*
Very High (VH), (≥0.8)	1	0.4	1	1
High (H), (0.6-0.8)	50	21.1	16	6
Medium (M), (0.4-0.6)	127	53.3	30	6
Low (L), (0.2-0.4)	57	24.1	20	6
Very Low (VL), (<0.2)	2	0.8	2	1
Total	**237**	**100**		

Source: Annex 10.3

Classification of PSs by GEDI

Table 10.3 reveals classification of PSs in to five groups by GEDI. Medium Level PSs dominated with 53.6 per cent share followed by Low (24.1 %), High (21.2%), Very Low (0.8%) and Very High (0.4 %) level PSs.

If we look at division-wise classification and distribution of PSs by GEDI (Table10.4) following conclusions can be drawn:

- No division had PSs of all the five GEDI levels. Jaipur and Udaipur divisions had PSs of four levels while remaining divisions had PSs of three levels.
- Jaipur division was in the best position, led in PSs having Very High (100% share), High (58%) as well as medium (22.8%) GEDI Udaipur division on the other side, was the most deprived and led in PSs having Low (31.6%) as well as Very Low (100%) GEDI.
- Medium Level PSs dominated in all the divisions except Jaipur. In Jaipur division both High as well as Medium level PSs were dominated.

- The percentage of VH level PSs in Jaipur division; H level in Jaipur, Bikaner and Kota divisions; M level in Jodhpur and Kota divisions and L level in Ajmer, Jodhpur and Udaipur divisions and Very Low level in Udaipur division was higher than the state average.

TABLE 10.4: Division-wise Classification and Distribution of PSs on the Basis of GEDI Level (2001)

Divisions	*Classification*						*Distribution (% Share)*				
	GEDI Level						*GEDI Level*				
	Very High	*High*	*Medium*	*Low*	*Very Low*	*Total PSs*	*Very High*	*High*	*Medium*	*Low*	*Very Low*
Jaipur	1	29	29	2	—	61	100.0	58.0	22.8	3.5	—
	(1.6)	(47.5)	(47.5)	(3.3)	—	(100.0)					
Bikaner	—	9	11	1	—	21	—	18.0	8.7	1.8	—
	—	(42.9)	(52.4)	(4.8)	—	(100.0)					
Ajmer	—	1	19	16	—	36	—	2.0	15.0	28.1	—
	—	(2.8)	(52.8)	(44.4)	—	(100.0)					
Kota	—	9	18	5	—	32	—	18.0	14.2	8.8	—
	—	(28.1)	(56.3)	(15.6)	—	(100.0)					
Jodhpur	—	1	26	15	—	42	—	2.0	20.5	26.3	—
	—	(2.4)	(61.9)	(35.7)	—	(100.0)					
Udaipur	—	1	24	18	2	45	—	2.0	18.9	31.6	100.0
	—	(2.2)	(53.3)	(40.0)	(4.4)	(100.0)					
Total	**1**	**50**	**127**	**57**	**2**	**237**	**100.0**	**100.0**	**100**	**100**	**100**
	(0.4)	**(21.1)**	**(53.6)**	**(24.1)**	**(0.8)**	**(100.0)**					

Figure in brackets shows percentage share to total Panchayat Samities.
Note: GEDI Level VH : (>0.8) H : (0.6-0.8), M : (0.4-0.6), L : (0.2-0.4), VL : (<0.2).
Source: Annex 10.3

Different GEDI Regions

Very High GEDI Region

Behror PS of Alwar district was the only PS in the state having Very High Level of GEDI.

High GEDI Region

High GEDI region was spread over 16 districts and all the six divisions. There were 50 High level PSs. Jaipur division topped with 58 per cent share followed by Bikaner and Kota (18 % each), Ajmer, Jodhpur and Udaipur (2% each) divisions. The highest percentage of H level PSs of total PSs was 47.5 which was in Jaipur followed by 42.9 in Bikaner, 28.1 in Kota, 2.8 in Ajmer, 2.4 in Jodhpur and the lowest 2.2 in Udaipur division. Among the districts. Jhunjhunun and Sikar led with 8 PSs each follwed by Jaipur (6); Bharatpur, Churu and Kota (4 each); Ganganager (3); Alwar, Hanumangarh, Jhalawar and Karauli (2 each) and Ajmer, Banswara, Baran, Barmer, Dausa and Udaipur (1 each) districts respectively. Churu, Ganganager, Hanumangarh, Jaipur, Jhalawar, Jhunjhunun, Karauli, and Sikar districts had greater percentage of High Level PSs in comparison to the state average (21.1). Moreover, Jhunjhunun and Sikar had 100 per cent of their PSs in High category while Udaipur had the minimum (9.1) percentage of these PSs.

TABLE 10.5: District-wise Classification of PSs on the Basis of GEDI Level (2001)

District	*EDI Level*					*Total PSs*
	VH	*H*	*M*	*L*	*VL*	
Ajmer	—	1	4	3	—	8
	—	(12.5)	(50.0)	(37.5)	—	(100.0)
Alwar	1	2	10	1	—	14
	(7.1)	(14.3)	(71.4)	(7.1)	—	(100.0)
Banswara	—	—	1	6	1	8
	—	—	(12.5)	(75.0)	(12.5)	(100.0)
Baran	—	1	6	—	—	7
	—	(14.3)	(85.7)	—	—	(100.0)
Barmer	—	1	7	—	—	8
	—	(12.5)	(87.5)	—	—	(100.0)
Bharatpur	—	4	4	1	—	9
	—	(44.4)	(44.4)	(11.1)	—	(100.0)
Bhilwara	—	—	3	8	—	11
	—	—	(27.3)	(72.7)	—	(100.0)
Bikaner	—	—	3	1	—	4
	—	—	(75.0)	(25.0)	—	(100.0)
Bundi	—	—	3	1	—	4
	—	—	(75.0)	(25.0)	—	(100.0)
Chittaurgarh	—	—	8	6	—	14
	—	—	(57.1)	(42.9)	—	(100.0)
Churu	—	4	3	—	—	7
	—	(57.1)	(42.9)	—	—	(100.0)
Dausa	—	1	4	—	—	5
	—	(20.0)	(80.0)	—	—	(100.0)
Dhaulpur	—	—	4	—	—	4
	—	—	(100.0)	—	—	(100.0)
Dungarpur	—	—	1	4	—	5
	—	—	(20.0)	(80.0)	—	(100.0)
Ganganagar	—	3	4	—	—	7
	—	(42.9)	(57.1)	—	—	(100.0)
Hanumangarh	—	2	1	—	—	3
	—	(66.7)	(33.3)	—	—	(100.0)
Jaipur	—	6	7	—	—	13
	—	(46.2)	(53.8)	—	—	(100.0)
Jaisalmer	—	—	2	1	—	3
	—	—	(66.7)	(33.3)	—	(100.0)
Jalor	—	—	2	5	—	7
	—	—	(28.6)	(71.4)	—	(100.0)
Jhalawar	—	2	2	2	—	6
	—	(33.3)	(33.3)	(33.3)	—	(100.0)
Jhunjhunun	—	8	—	—	—	8
	—	(100.0)	—	—	—	(100.0)
Jodhpur	—	—	2	7	—	9
		—	(22.2)	(77.8)	—	(100.0)
Karauli	—	2	3	—	—	5
	—	(40.0)	(60.0)	—	—	(100.0)
Kota	—	4	1	—	—	5
	—	(80.0)	(20.0)	—	—	(100.0)
Nagaur	—	—	10	1	—	11
	—	—	(90.9)	(9.1)	—	(100.0)
Pali	—	—	9	1	—	10
	—	—	(90.0)	(10.0)	—	(100.0)
Rajsamand	—	—	6	1	—	7
	—	—	(85.7)	(14.3)	—	(100.0)
Sawai Madhopur	—	—	3	2	—	5
	—	—	(60.0)	(40.0)	—	(100.0)
Sikar	—	8	—	—	—	8
	—	(100.0)	—	—	—	(100.0)
Sirohi	—	—	4	1	—	5
	—	—	(80.0)	(20.0)	—	(100.0)
Tonk	—	—	2	4	—	6
	—	—	(33.3)	(66.7)	—	(100.0)
Udaipur	—	1	8	1	1	11
	—	(9.1)	(72.7)	(9.1)	(9.1)	(100.0)
Rajasthan	**1**	**50**	**127**	**57**	**2**	**237**
	(0.4)	**(21.1)**	**(53.6)**	**(24.1)**	**(0.8)**	**(100.0)**

Figures in brackets show percentage share to total Panchayat Samities.

Note: GEDI Level VH : (>=0.8) H : (0.6-0.8), M : (0.4-0.6), L : (0.2-0.4), VL : (<0.2). *Source*: Annex 10.3

TABLE 10.6: Distribution of PSs having Very High and High GEDI Level, 2001

S. No.	District	No. & Name of PSs (in Descending Order)
		[A] Very High Level (1)
1	Alwar	1—Behror
		[B] High (50)
1	Jhunjhuunun	8—Udaipurwati, Buhana, Jhunjhunun, Chirawa, Alsisar, Surajgarh, Nawalgarh and Kheiri
2	Sikar	8—Fatehpur, Lachhmangarh, Khandela, Danta Ramgarh, Piprali, Dhond, Neem ka Thana and Sawai Madhopur
3	Jaipur	6—Kotputli, Viratnagar, Sambhar, Jhotwara, Govindgarh and Shahpura
4	Bharatpur	4—Nadbai, Rupbas, Sewar and Kumher
5	Churu	4—Taranagar, Rajgarh, Churu and Ratangarh
6	Kota	4—Sultanpur, Sangod, Chechat and Ladpura
7	Ganganagar	3—Raisinghnagar, Ganganagar and Padampur
8	Alwar	2—Kotkasim, Mandawar
9	Hanumangarh	2—Bhadra and Nohar
10	Jhalawar	2—Pirawa and Khanpur
11	Karauli	2—Hindaun and Nadoti
12	Ajmer	1—Jawaja
13	Banswara	1—Garhi
14	Baran	1—Baran
15	Barmer	1—Dhorimanna
16	Dausa	1—Bandikui
17	Udaipur	1—Bargaon

Source: Annex 10.3

TABLE 10.7: Distribution of PSs having Medium GEDI Level, 2001

S. No.	District	No. & Name of PSs (in Descending Order)
		Medium (127)
1	Alwar	10—Nimrana, Bansure, Kathumar, Kishangarhbas, Reni, Lachhmangarh, Rajgarh, Ramgarh, Tizara and Umren
2	Nagaur	10—Didwana, Kuchaman, Makrana, Ladnu, Parbatsar, Merta, Degana, Riyan, Jayal and Nagaur
3	Pali	9—Rani Station, Sumerpur, Bali, Desuri, Sojat, Rohat, Kharchi-Marwar Junction, Raipur and Pali
4	Chittaurgarh	8—Pratapgarh, Nimbahera, Chootisadri, Bhopalgarh, Chittaurgarh Arnod, Begun and Dungla
5	Udaipur	8—Bhinder, Jhadol, Salumbar, Girwa, Sarada, Kherwara, Mavli and Gogunda
6	Barmer	7—Sindhari, Siwana, Baytoo, Sheo, Balotra, Barmer and Chohtan
7	Jaipur	7—Jamwaramgarh, Sanganer, Phagi, Amber, Bassi, Dudu and Chaksu
8	Baran	6—Anta, Atru, Kishanganj, Shahbad, Chabra and Chhipabarod
9	Rajsamand	6—Railmagra, Rajsamand, Bhim, Khamnor, Deogarh and Amet
10	Ajmer	4—Kishangarh, Masooda, Pisanagan and Srinagar
11	Bharatpur	4—Weir, Nagar Pahari, Deeg and Bayana
12	Dausa	4—Mahwa, Sikrai, Dausa and Lalsot
13	Dhaulpur	4—Baseri, Dhaulpur, Rajakhera and Bari
14	Ganganagar	4—Sadulshahar, Karanpur, Anupgarh and Suratgarh
15	Sirohi	4—Pindwara, Sheoganj, Sirohi and Reodar
16	Bhilwara	3—Hurda, Banera and Jahazpur
17	Bikaner	3—Bikaner, Lunkarnsar and Nokha
18	Bundi	3—Keshoraipatan, Talera and Nainwa
19	Churu	3—Sujangarh, Sardarshahar and Dungargarh
20	Karauli	3—Todabheem, Sapotra and Karauli
21	Sawai Madhopur	3—Bamanwas, Gangapur and Bonli
22	Jaisalmer	2—Sankra, Jaisalmer
23	Jalor	2—Ahore and Raniwara
24	Jhalawar	2—Jhalrapatan and Manoharthana
25	Jodhpur	2—Luni and Bilara
26	Tonk	2—Todarisingh and Niwai
27	Banswara	1—Garhi
28	Dungarpur	1—Sagwara
29	Hanumangarh	1—Hanumangarh
30	Kota	1—Itawa

Source: Annex 10.3

Medium GEDI Region

Medium GEDI region was widely distributed in 30 districts and all the 6 divisions. There were 127 PSs in this category. Jaipur division had the maximum concentration of these PSs (22.8 % share) followed by Jodhpur (20.5%), Udaipur (18.9%), Ajmer (15%), Kota (14.2%) and Bikaner (8.7%) divisions. The highest percentage share of M level PSs to total PSs was 61.9 in Jodhpur division followed by 56.3 in Kota, 53.3 in Udaipur, 52.8 in Ajmer, 52.4 in Bikaner and the lowest 47.5 in Jaipur division. Jodhpur and Kota divisions had greater percentage of M level PSs than the state average (53.6). If we see district-wise distribution of these PSs, it will be clear that both Alwar and Nagaur secured the top position with 10 PSs each followed by Pali (9); Chittaurgarh and Udaipur (8 each); Barmer and Jaipur (7 each); Baran and Rajasmand (6 each); Ajmer, Bahartpur, Dausa, Dhaulpur, Ganganagar, Sirohi (4 each); Bhilwara, Bikaner, Bundi, Churu, Karauli and Sawai Madhopur (3 each); Jaisalmer, Jhalawar, Jalor, Jodhpur and Tonk (2 each); Banswara, Dungarpur, Hanumangarh and Kota (1 each) districts respectively. Except Ajmer, Banswara, Bhilwara, Churu, Dungarpur, Hanumangarh, Jalor, Jhalawar, Jodhpur and Kota all the above districts had higher percentage of Medium level PSs than the state average. Dhaulpur had the highest percentage (100 %) of these PSs while, Banswara had the lowest (12.5 %).

TABLE 10.8: Distribution of PSs having Low and Very Low GEDI Level, 2001

S. No.	*District*	*No. & Name of PSs (in Descending Order)*
		Low (57)
1	Bhilwara	8—Suwana, Saharam Mandalgarh, Shahpura, Mandal, Raipur, Asind and Kotri
2	Jodhpur	7—Phalodi, Osian, Bap, Bhopalgarh, Mandore, Balesar and Shergarh
3	Banswara	6—Talwara, Bagidora, Anandpuri, Ghatol, Sajjangarh and Kushalgarh
4	Chittaurgarh	6—Bhadesar, Gangrar, Bhainsrorgarh, Kapasan, Bari Sadari and Rashmi
5	Jalor	5—Jalore, Sanchore, Sayla, Jaswantpura and Bhinmal
6	Dungarpur	4—Bichhiwara, Dungarpur, Aspur and Simalwara
7	Tonk	4—Malpura, Deoli, Uniara and Tonk
8	Ajmer	3—Arian, Kekri and Bhinay
9	Jhalawar	2—Dag and Bakani
10	Sawai Madhopur	2—Sawai Madhopur and Khandar
11	Alwar	1—Thanagazi
12	Bharatpur	1—Kaman
13	Bikaner	1—Kolayat
14	Bundi	1—Hindoli
15	Jaisalmer	1—Sam
16	Nagaur	1 Mundwa
17	Pali	1—Jaitaran
18	Rajsamand	1—Kumbhalgarh
19	Sirohi	1—Abu Road
20	Udaipur	1—Dhariawad
		[B] Very Low (2)
1	Banswara	1—Peepalkhoont
2	Udaipur	1—Kotra

Source: Annex-10.3

Low GEDI Region

There were 57 PSs having Low GEDI. These PSs were also widely spread over 20 districts and all the 6 divisions. Udaipur division with 31.6 per cent share had the highest concentration of these PSs followed by Ajmer (28.1%), Jodhpur (26.3%), Kota (8.8%), Jaipur (3.5%) and Bikaner (1.8%) divisions. The maximum percentage of Low level PSs to total PSs was 44.4 in Ajmer division followed by Udaipur (40%), Jodhpur (35.7%), Kota (15.6%), Bikaner (4.8%) and Jaipur (3.3%) divisions. Ajmer, Udaipur and Jodhpur divisions had higher percentage of these PSs in comparison to the State average (24.1). If we see district-wise distribution of these PSs it is clear that Bhilawara dominated with 8 PSs followed by Jodhpur (7); Banswara and Chittaurgarh (6 each); Jalor (5); Dungarpur and Tonk (4 each); Ajmer (3); Jhalawar and Sawai Madhopur (2 each) and Bharatpur, Bikaner, Bundi, Jaisalmer, Nagaur, Pali, Rajsamand and Sirohi (1 each) districts respectively. All the above districts except Alwar, Bharatpur, Nagaur, Pali, Rajsamand, Sirohi, and Udaipur had greater percentage of these PSs in comparison to the state average Dungarpur district had the highest (80) percentage of these PSs while Alwar had the lowest (7.1%).

Very Low GEDI Region

Kotra PS of Udaipur district and Peepalkhoont of Banswara were the only PSs in the state having Very Low GEDI. The percentage of L level PSs in both Banswara (12.5%) and Udaipur (9.1%) districts was greater than the state average (0.8%).

11

INCOME INDEX (1991-92)

Highlights

- Rural PCI-Raj. : Rs. 4523/-
- Rural INI-Raj : 0.3813
- Percentage of AAPs : 41
- Only 16 per cent PSs achieved above 0.5 INI level

	Panchayat Samiti	District	Division
• **Top**	Sangod, 0.7641	Kota	Kota
• **Bottom**	Aspur, 0.0319	Dungarpur	Udaipur

In the year 1991-92, per capita income (PCI) and income index (INI) of rural Rajasthan was Rs. 4523 and 0.3813 respectively and there were only 96 (41%) Panchayat Samities (PSs) having PCI/INI above the state average. A great deal of regional disparity is observed in INI among the 237 PSs spread over 32 districts and 6 divisions of Rajasthan (Fig 11.1). Jaipur division had maximum concentration (41%) of PSs having High INI followed by Kota (35%) and Bikaner (24%) divisions. On the other hand, 100 per cent PSs of Jodhpur and Udaipur divisions had Medium to Very Low INI. The INI level in the state increases from SW and South to NE, SE and North direction.

Sangod PS of Kota district had the maximum PCI as well as INI (Rs. 10261 and 0.7641) followed by Chechat, Chaksu, Itawa, Ladpura, Sultanpur, Karanpur, Phagi, Bassi and Raisinghnagar PSs (Descending order). These top ten PSs were concentrated in three districts *viz.* Kota (5), Jaipur (3) and Ganganagar (2) as shown in Table 11.1.

TABLE 11.1: Distribution of First and Last Ten Panchayat Samities by PCI and INI: Rajasthan (1991-92)

S. No.	*First Ten PSs (Descending Order)*			*Last Ten PSs (Ascending Order)*		
	Districts/ PSs			*Districts/ PSs*		
	Kota	*Jaipur*	*Ganganagar*	*Dungarpur*	*Jhunjhunun*	*Barmer*
	(5)	*(3)*	*(2)*	*(5)*	*(3)*	*(3*
1	Sangod	Chaksu	Karanpur	Aspur	Nawalgarh	Siwana
2	Chechat	Phagi	Raisinghnagar	Sagwara	Khetri	Sheo
3	Itawa	Bassi	—	Bichhiwara	Chirawa	—
4	Ladpura	—	—	Dungarpur	—	—
5	Sultanpur	—	—	Simalwara	—	—

Source: Annex 11.1 and 11.2

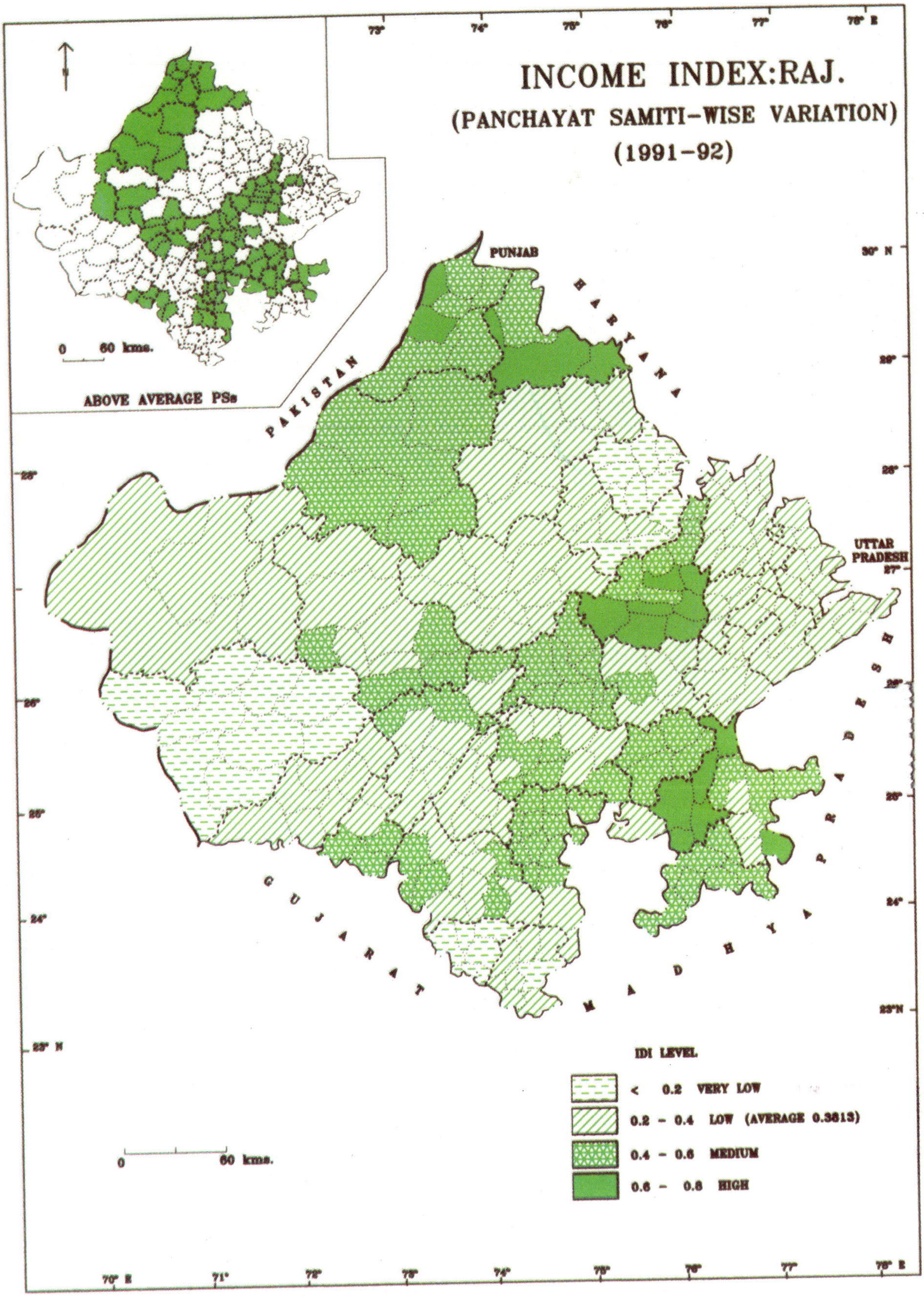
INCOME INDEX:RAJ.
(PANCHAYAT SAMITI-WISE VARIATION)
(1991-92)
ABOVE AVERAGE PSs
0 60 kms.
PUNJAB
HARYANA
UTTAR PRADESH
MADHYA PRADESH
GUJARAT
PAKISTAN
IDI LEVEL
< 0.2 VERY LOW
0.2 - 0.4 LOW (AVERAGE 0.3813)
0.4 - 0.6 MEDIUM
0.6 - 0.8 HIGH
0 60 kms.

FIG. 11.1

Aspur PS (Dungarpur district) on the other hand, was the most deprived having PCI Rs. 2141 and INI 0.0319. It was followed by Nawalgarh, Sagwara, Siwana, Sheo, Bichhiwara, Khetri, Dungarpur, Chirawa and Simalwara PSs (Ascending order). These last ten PSs were also located in three districts namely, Dungarpur (5), Jhunjhunun (3) and Barmer (3). Similarly, district-wise first and the last PSs by INI is shown in Table 11.2.

TABLE 11.2: District-wise First and Last PSs by INI (1991-92)

District	*First Rank*	*Last Rank*	*District*	*First Rank*	*Last Rank*
Ajmer	Arain	Jawaja	Jaipur	Chaksu	Govindgarh
Alwar	Reni	Nimrana	Jaisalmer	Sankra	Jaisalmer
Banswara	Anandpuri	Talwara	Jalor	Ahore	Sayla
Baran	Chhipabarod	Chhabra	Jhalawar	Manoharthana	Dag
Barmer	Baytoo	Siwana	Jhunjhunun	Buhana	Nawalgarh
Bharatpur	Deeg	Rupbas	Jodhpur	Bhopalgarh	Bap
Bhilwara	Sahara	Raipur	Karauli	Sapotra	Hindaun
Bikaner	Nokha	Lunkaransar	Kota	Sangod	Sultanpur
Bundi	Hindoli	Talera	Nagaur	Riyan	Kuchaman
Chittaurgarh	Kapasan	Arnod	Pali	Sojat	Desuri
Churu	Dungargarh	Sardarshahar	Rajsamand	Kumbhalgarh	Rajsamand
Dausa	Sikrai	Bandikui	Sawai Madhopur	Bonli	Sawai Madhopur
Dhaulpur	Baseri	Rajakhera	Sikar	Fatehpur	Sri Madhopur
Dungarpur	Simalwara	Aspur	Sirohi	Pindwara	Sirohi
Ganganagar	Karanpur	Padampur	Tonk	Todaraisingh	Uniara
Hanumangarh	Bhadra	Hanumangarh	Udaipur	Bhinder	Kherwara

Source: Annex 12.1, Col. 6.

Classification of PSs by PCI and INI

On the basis of PCI and INI, PSs of the state are classified in to 4 groups as presented in Table 11.3. It is a matter of great concern that 93 per cent PSs of the state had Medium to Very Low INI level.

TABLE 11.3: Classification of PSs on the Basis of PCI and INI (1991-92): Rajasthan

	[I] PCI			
Group (in Rs.)	*Included PSs*		*Distributed in*	
	No.	*%*	*Districts*	*Divisions*
High (H), (>8000)	10	4.2	3	3
Medium (M), (6000-8000)	27	11.4	8	4
Low (M), (4000-6000)	105	44.3	22	6
Very Low (VL), (< 4000)	95	40.1	7	3
Total	237	100		
	[II] INI			
Group	*Included PSs*		*Distributed in*	
	No.	*%*	*Districts*	*Divisions*
High (H), (>=0.6)	17	7.2	5	3
Medium (M), (0.4-0.6)	62	26.2	15	6
Low (L), (0.2-0.4)	133	56.1	22	6
Very Low (VL), (<0.2)	25	10.5	5	3
Total	237	100		

Source: Annex 11.1 and 11.2.

Division-wise classification and distribution of PSs by INI level is shown in Table 11.4, leading to following conclusions :

- Only Jaipur division had PSs of all the four INI levels. Ajmer division had PSs of 2 levels, while the others had PSs of 3 levels.
- Jaipur division dominated not only in H level PSs (41.2% share) but also in L (27%) and VL (44%) level PSs. Udaipur division dominated in M level PSs (24.2%).
- Low level PSs were leading in all the divisions except Bikaner, where M level PSs were dominating.
- Whereas, H and VL level PSs were concentrated only in 3 divisions, M and L level PSs were widely spread over the state.
- The percentage share of H level PSs to total PSs in Jaipur, Bikaner and Kota divisions; M level in Bikaner, Ajmer, Jodhpur and Udaipur divisions; L level in Jaipur, Ajmer, Kota and Jodhpur divisions and VL level PSs in Jaipur, Jodhpur and Udaipur divisions was higher than the state average.

TABLE 11.4: Division-wise Classification and Distribution of PSs on the Basis of INI Level (1991-92)

Divisions	*Classification*					*Distribution (% Share)*			
	INI Level					*INI Level*			
	High	*Medium*	*Low*	*Very Low*	*Total PSs*	*High*	*Medium*	*Low*	*Very Low*
Jaipur	7 (11.5)	7 (11.5)	36 (59.0)	11 (18.0)	61 (100.0)	41.2	11.3	27.1	44.0
Bikaner	4 (19.0)	10 (47.6)	7 (33.3)	— —	21 (100.0)	23.5	16.1	5.3	—
Ajmer	— —	14 (38.9)	22 (61.1)	— —	36 (100.0)	—	22.6	16.5	—
Kota	6 (18.8)	6 (18.8)	20 (62.5)	— —	32 (100.0)	35.3	9.7	15.0	—
Jodhpur	— —	10 (23.8)	24 (57.1)	8 (19.0)	42 (100.0)	—	16.1	18.0	32.0
Udaipur	— —	15 (33.3)	24 (53.3)	6 (13.3)	45 (100.0)	—	24.2	18.0	24.0
Total	**17 (7.2)**	**62 (26.2)**	**133 (56.1)**	**25 (10.5)**	**237 (100.0)**	**100**	**100**	**100**	**100**

Figure in brackets shows percentage share to total Panchayat Samities.
Note: INI Level H : (>=0.6), M : (0.4-0.6), L : (0.2-0.4), VL : (<0.2)
Source: Annex 11.1

Similarly, district-wise classification of PSs on the basis of INI is presented in Table 11.5. It is interesting to note that 100 per cent PSs of 18 districts were fully entered in either of any one group. For example: all the PSs of Kota district had High INI; Ajmer, Bikaner and Bundi had Medium INI; Bharatpur, Churu, Dausa, Dhaulpur, Jaisalmer, Jalor, Jhalawar, Karauli, Nagaur, Rajsamand and Sawai Madhopur had Low INI and Brmer (Table 11.6), Dungarpur and Jhunjhunun had Very Low INI.

High INI Region

High INI region was concentrated in five districts of three divisions. There were total 17 H level PSs. As mentioned earlier, Jaipur division topped with 41.2 per cent share followed by Kota (35.3%) and Bikaner (23.5%) divisions. It is really unfortunate that no PSs of Ajmer, Jodhpur and Udaipur divisions found mention in this category. The percentage share of H level PSs to total PSs was 11.5 in Jaipur, 19 in Bikaner and 18.8 in Kota division which was above the state average (7.2%). Among the districts, Jaipur dominated with 7 PSs followed by Kota (5); Ganganagar, Hanumangarh (2 each) and Baran (1) districts (Table 11.6).

TABLE 11.5: District-wise Classification of PSs on the Basis of INI Level (1991-92)

District	*INI Level*				*Total PSs*
	H	*M*	*L*	*VL*	
Ajmer	—	8	—	—	8
	—	(100.0)	—	—	(100.0)
Alwar	—	1	13	—	14
	—	(7.1)	(92.9)	—	(100.0)
Banswara	—	—	7	1	8
	—	—	(87.5)	(12.5)	(100.0)
Baran	1	2	4	—	7
	(14.3)	(28.6)	(57.1)	—	(100.0)
Barmer	—	—	—	8	8
	—	—	—	(100.0)	(100.0)
Bharatpur	—	—	9	—	9
	—	—	(100.0)	—	(100.0)
Bhilwara	—	5	6	—	11
	—	(45.5)	(54.5)	—	(100.0)
Bikaner	—	4	—	—	4
	—	(100.0)	—	—	(100.0)
Bundi	—	4	—	—	4
	—	(100.0)	—	—	(100.0)
Chittaurgarh	—	11	3	—	14
	—	(78.6)	(21.4)	—	(100.0)
Churu	—	—	7	—	7
	—	—	(100.0)	—	(100.0)
Dausa	—	—	5	—	5
	—	—	(100.0)	—	(100.0)
Dhaulpur	—	—	4	—	4
	—	—	(100.0)	—	(100.0)
Dungarpur	—	—	—	5	5
	—	—	—	(100.0)	(100.0)
Ganganagar	2	5	—	—	7
	(28.6)	(71.4)	—	—	(100.0)
Hanumangarh	2	1	—	—	3
	(66.7)	(33.3)	—	—	(100.0)
Jaipur	7	6	—	—	13
	(53.8)	(46.2)	—	—	(100.0)
Jaisalmer	—	—	3	—	3
	—	—	(100.0)	—	(100.0)
Jalor	—	—	7	—	7
	—	—	(100.0)	—	(100.0)
Jhalawar	—	—	6	—	6
	—	—	(100.0)	—	(100.0)
Jhunjhunun	—	—	—	8	8
	—	—	—	(100.0)	(100.0)
Jodhpur	—	4	5	—	9
	—	(44.4)	(55.6)	—	(100.0)
Karauli	—	—	5	—	5
	—	—	(100.0)	—	(100.0)
Kota	5		—	—	5
	(100.0)	—	—	—	(100.0)
Nagaur	—	—	11	—	11
	—	—	(100.0)	—	(100.0)
Pali	—	3	7	—	10
	—	(30.0)	(70.0)	—	(100.0)
Rajsamand	—	—	7	—	7
	—	—	(100.0)	—	(100.0)
Sawai Madhopur	—	—	5	—	5
	—	—	(100.0)	—	(100.0)
Sikar	—	—	5	3	8
	—	—	(62.5)	(37.5)	(100.0)
Sirohi	—	3	2	—	5
	—	(60.0)	(40.0)	—	(100.0)
Tonk	—	1	5	—	6
	—	(16.7)	(83.3)	—	(100.0)
Udaipur	—	4	7	—	11
	—	(36.4)	(63.6)	—	(100.0)
Rajasthan	**17**	**62**	**133**	**25**	**237**
	(7.2)	**(26.2)**	**(56.1)**	**(10.5)**	**(100.0)**

Figures in brackets show percentage share of total Panchayat Samities

Note: INI Level H : (0.6-0.8), M : (0.4-0.6), L : (0.2-0.4), VL : (<0.2)

Source: Annex 11.3

Medium INI Region

M level 62 PSs were distributed in 15 districts and all the divisions. Udaipur division led with 24.2 per cent share followed by Ajmer (22.6%), Jodhpur and Bikaner (16.1% each), Jaipur (11.3%) and Kota (9.7%) divisions. The percentage share of M level PSs to total PSs was the highest 47.6 in Bikaner, 38.9 in Ajmer, 33.3 in Udaipur, 23.8 in Jodhpur, 18.8 in Kota and the lowest 11.5 in Jaipur division. Except Jaipur and Kota, all these divisions had higher percentage of M level PSs than the state average (26.2%). Among the districts, Chittaurgarh topped with 11 PSs followed by Ajmer (8); Jaipur (6); Bhilwara, Ganganagar (5 each); Bikaner, Bundi, Jodhpur, Udaipur (4 each); Pali, Sirohi (3 each); Baran (2) and Alwar, Hanumangarh and Tonk (1 each) districts respectively. Except Alwar and Tonk, all these districts had percentage of these PSs above the state average.

TABLE 11.6: Distribution of PSs having High INI Level 1991-92

S. No.	*District*	*No. & Name of PSs (in Descending Order)*
		High Level (17)
1	Jaipur	7—Chaksu, Phagi, Bassi, Amber, Dudu, Jamwa Ramgarh and Sanganer
2	Kota	5—Sangod, Chechat, Itawa, Ladpura and Sultanpur
3	Ganganagar	2—Karanpur and Raisinghnagar
4	Hanumangarh	2—Bhadra and Nohar
5	Baran	1—Chhipabarod

Source: Annex 11.1

TABLE 11.7: Distribution of PSs having Medium INI Level 1991-92

S. No.	*District*	*No. & Name of PSs (in Descending Order)*
		Medium Level (62)
1	Chittaurgarh	11—Kapasan, Gangrar, Bhadesar, Chhoti Sadri, Bari Sadri, Begun, Chittaurgarh, Rashmi, Dungla, Nimbahera and Bhopalsagar
2	Ajmer	8—Arian, Bhinay, Kekri, Srinagar, Masooda, Pisangan, Kishangarh and Jawaja
3	Jaipur	6—Kotputli, Shahpura, Jhotwara, Sambhar, Viratnagar and Govindgarh
4	Bhilwara	5—Sahara, Mandal, Suwana, Banera and Mandalgarh
5	Ganganagar	5—Anupgarh, Suratgarh, Ganganagar, Sadulshahar and Padampur
6	Bikaner	4—Nokha, Bikaner, Kolayat and Lunkaransar
7	Bundi	4—Hindoli, Nainwa, Keshoraipatan and Talera
8	Jodhpur	4—Bhopalgarh, Bilara, Shergarh and Luni
9	Udaipur	4—Bhinder, Salumbar, Kotra and Jhadol
10	Pali	3—Sojat, Rohat and Jaitaran
11	Sirohi	3—Pindwara, Reodar and Abu Road
12	Baran	2—Shahbad and Kishanganj
13	Alwar	1—Reni
14	Hanumangarh	1—Hanumangarh
15	Tonk	1—Todaraisingh

Source: Annex 11.1

Low INI Region

Low INI region was widely spread over 22 districts and all the 6 divisions. There were total 133 L level PSs. Jaipur division dominated with 27 per cent share followed by Jodhpur, Udaipur (18% each); Ajmer (16.5%); Kota (15%) and Bikaner (5.3%) divisions. Jaipur, Ajmer, Kota and Jodhpur divisions had higher percentage of L level PSs than the state average (56.1%). Among the districts, Alwar led with 13 PSs followed by Nagaur (11); Bharatpur (9); Banswara, Churu, Jalor, Pali, Rajsamand and Udaipur (7 each); Bhilwara, Jhalawar

(6 each); Dausa, Jodhpur, Karauli, Sawai Madhopur, Sikar, Tonk (5 each); Baran, Dhaulpur (4 each); Chittaurgarh and Jaisalmer (3 each) and Sirohi (2) districts. All the above districts, except Bhilwara, Chittaurgarh, Jodhpur and Sirohi had higher percentage of Low level PSs in comparison to the state average.

TABLE 11.8: Distribution of PSs having Low INI Level 1991-92

S. No.	*District*	*No. & Name of PSs in Descending Order*
		Low Level (133)
1	Alwar	13—Rajgarh, Lachhmangarh, Behror, Khathumar, Thanagazi, Tijara, Bansure, Umren, Kishangarh Bas, Ramgarh, Kotkasim, Mandawar and Nimrana
2	Nagaur	11—Riyan, Mundwa, Degana, Parbatsar, Jayal, Merta, Nagaur, Ladnu, Makrana, Didwana and Kuchaman
3	Bharatpur	9—Deeg, Kaman, Kumher, Nadbai, Nagar Pahari, Weir, Bayana, Sewar and Rupbas
4	Banswara	7—Anandpuri, Bagidora, Sajjangarh, Kushalgarh, Peepalkhoont, Ghatol, Grahi and Talwara
5	Churu	7—Dungargarh, Taranagar, Rajgarh, Sujangarh, Ratangarh, Churu and Sardarshahar
6	Jalor	7—Ahore, Sanchore, Bhinmal, Jaswantpura, Raniwara, Jalor and Sayla
7	Pali	7—Pali, Raipur, Kharchi/Marwar Jun., Bali, Rani Station, Sumerpur and Desuri
8	Rajsamand	7—Kumbhalgarh, Railmagra, Khamnor, Amet, Bhim, Deogarh and Rajsamand
9	Udaipur	7—Bargaon, Dhariawad, Gogunda, Mavli, Sarada, Girwa and Kherwara
10	Bhilwara	6—Asind, Kotri, Shahpura, Hurda, Jahazpur and Raipur
11	Jhalawar	6—Manoharthana, Bakani, Pirawa, Jhalrapatan, Khanpur and Dag
12	Dausa	5—Sikrai, Dausa, Lalsot, Mahwa and Bandikui
13	Jodhpur	5—Phalodi, Balesar, Mandor, Osian and Bap
14	Karauli	5—Sapotra, Karauli, Nadoti, Todabhim and Hindaun
15	Sawai Madhopur	5—Bonli, Khandar, Bamanwas, Gangapur and Sawai Madhopur
16	Sikar	5—Fatehpur, Lachhmangarh, Dhond, Piprali and Khandela
17	Tonk	5—Deoli, Niwai, Tonk, Malpura nad Uniara
18	Baran	4—Baran, Atru, Anta and Chhabra
19	Dhaulpur	4—Baseri, Bari, Dhaulpur and Rajakhera
20	Chittaurgarh	3—Bhainsrorgarh, Partapgarh and Arnod
21	Jaisalmer	3—Sankra, Sam and Jaisalmer
22	Sirohi	2—Sheoganj and Sirohi

TABLE 11.9: Distribution of PSs having Very Low INI Level 1991-92

S. No.	*District*	*No. & Name of PSs in Descending Order*
		Very Low Level (25)
1	Barmer	8—Baytoo, Sindhari, Chohtan, Dhorimanna, Balotra, Barmer, Sheo and Siwana
2	Jhunjhunun	8—Buhana, Surajgarh, Jhunjhunun, Alsisar, Udaipurwati, Chirawa, Khetri and Nawalgarh
3	Dungarpur	5—Simalwara, Dungarpur, Bichhiwara, Sagwara and Aspur
4	Sikar	3—Danta Ramgarh, Neem ka Thana and Sri Madhopur
5	Banswara	1—Talwara

Source: Annex 11.1

Very Low INI Region

Very Low INI area was concentrated in 5 districts of 3 divisions. There were 25 PSs having Very Low INI. Jaipur division had the highest 11 PSs while Jodhpur had 8 and Udaipur had 6 PSs in this group. With respect to district-wise distribution of these PSs, it is clear that both Barmer and Jhunjhunun led by 8 PSs each followed by Dungarpur (5), Sikar (3) and Banswara (1) districts. The percentage share of these PSs to total PSs in the above divisions and district was higher than the state average (10.5%).

12

INCOME INDEX (1998-99)

Highlights

- Rural PCI-Raj. : Rs. 6432/-
- Rural INI-Raj : 0.5458
- Percentage of AAPs : 34
- 55 per cent PSs achieved above 0.5 INI level

	Panchayat Samiti	**District**	**Division**
• **Top**	Sanganer, 1.0065	Jaipur	Jaipur
• **Bottom**	Aspur, 0.1708	Dungarpur	Udaipur

In the year 1998-99, the PCI and INI of rural Rajasthan became Rs. 6432 and 0.5458 respectively. There were only 34 per cent PSs having PCI/INI above the state average, while Jaipur division dominated in PSs having Very High (47%) and Medium (30%) INI, Udaipur (31%) and Jodhpur (35%) divisions dominated in PSs having High and Low INI respectively. The INI level in the state increases from South to North as well as from West to East direction (Fig 12.1 & Annex 12.1).

Table 12.1: Distribution of First and Last Ten PSs by PCI and INI (1998-99)

S. No.	*First Ten PSs (Descending Order)*			*Last Ten PSs (Ascending Order)*	
	Districts/ PSs			*Districts/ PSs*	
	Jaipur	*Kota*	*Ganganagar*	*Dungarpur*	*Barmer*
	(4)	*(4)*	*(2)*	*(5)*	*(5)*
1	Sanganer	Chechat	Sadulshahar	Aspur	Siwana
2	Jhotwara	Sangod	Suratgarh	Bichhiwara	Sheo
3	Chaksu	Itawa	—	Sagwara	Barmer
4	Phagi	Sultanpur	—	Dungarpur	Balotra
5	—	—	—	Simalwara	Dhorimanna

Source: Annex 12.2 & 12.3.

Ranking of PSs by PCI and INI is presented in Annex 12.2 and 12.3 respectively. Sanganer PS of Jaipur district had the maximum PCI and INI (Rs. 17233, 1.0065) followed by Jhotwara, Chechat, Sangod, Chaksu, Phagi, Sadulshahar, Itawa, Sultanpur and Suratgarh PSs (Descending order). These top ten PSs were concentrated in three districts. Jaipur and Kota districts were leading with four PSs each while Ganganagar had 2 PSs (Table 12.1). Aspur PS of Dungarpur district, on the other hand, was at the bottom with PCI Rs. 2882 and INI 0.1708. It was followed by Siwana, Bichhiwara, Sheo, Sagwara, Dungarpur, Simalwara, Barmer, Balotra and Dhorimanna PSs (ascending order). These last ten PSs were equally distributed (5 each) in Dungarpur and Barmer districts. Similarly, district-wise first and last PSs by INI is shown in Table 12.2.

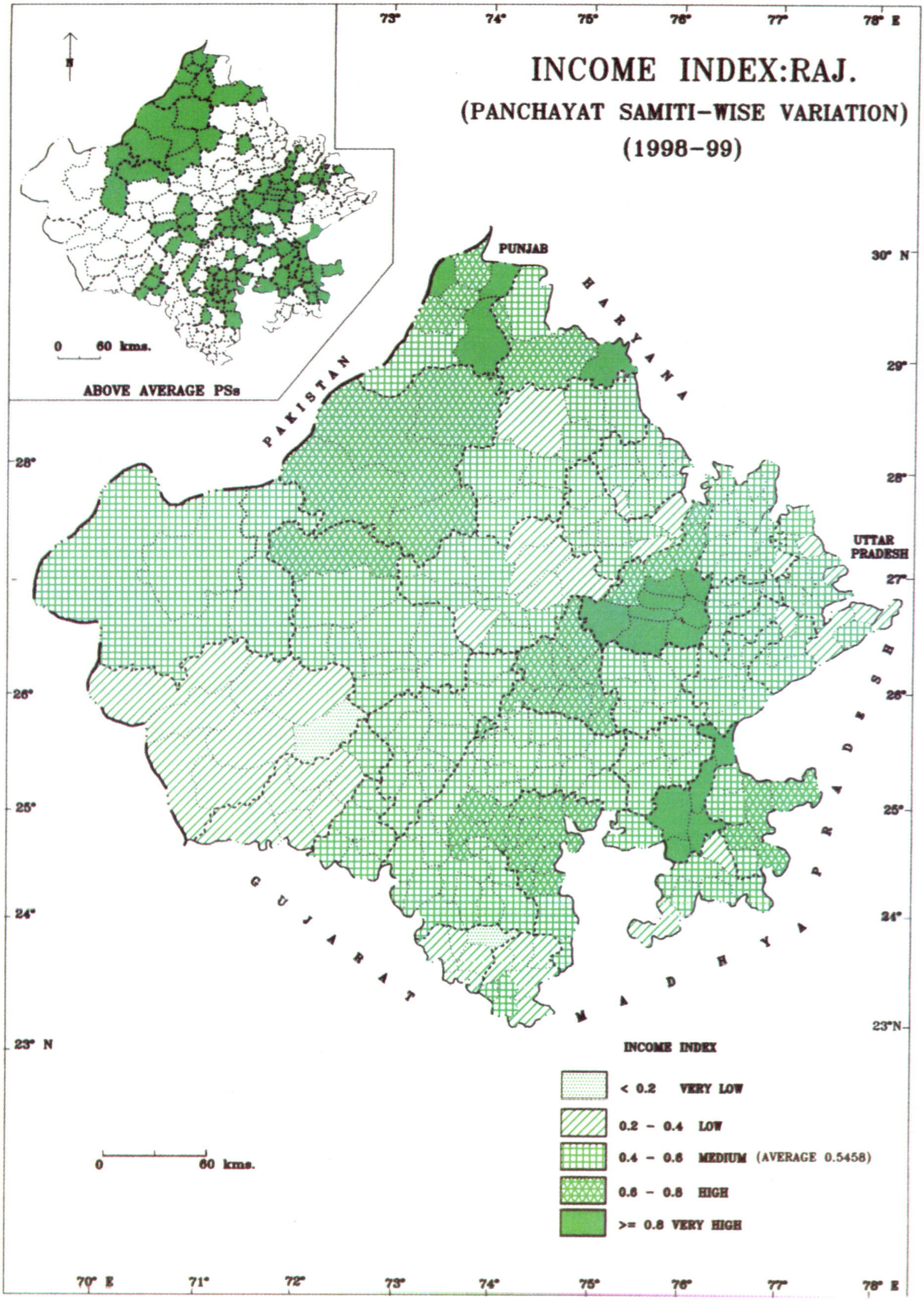
INCOME INDEX:RAJ.
(PANCHAYAT SAMITI-WISE VARIATION)
(1998-99)
ABOVE AVERAGE PSs
0 60 kms.
PUNJAB
HARYANA
PAKISTAN
UTTAR PRADESH
MADHYA PRADESH
GUJARAT
INCOME INDEX
< 0.2 VERY LOW
0.2 - 0.4 LOW
0.4 - 0.6 MEDIUM (AVERAGE 0.5458)
0.6 - 0.8 HIGH
>= 0.8 VERY HIGH
0 60 kms.

FIG. 12.1

TABLE 12.2: District-wise First and Last PSs by INI (1998-99)

District	*First Rank*	*Last Rank*	*District*	*First Rank*	*Last Rank*
Ajmer	Arain	Jawaja	Jaipur	Sanganer	Viratnagar
Alwar	Reni	Ramgarh	Jaisalmer	Sankra	Jaisalmer
Banswara	Anandpuri	Talwara	Jalor	Ahore	Raniwara
Baran	Chhipabarod	Anta	Jhalawar	Bakani	Khanpur
Barmer	Baytoo	Siwana	Jhunjhunun	Buhana	Nawalgarh
Bharatpur	Deeg	Rupbas	Jodhpur	Bap	Phalodi
Bhilwara	Sahara	Jahazpur	Karauli	Nadoti	Hindaun
Bikaner	Nokha	Bikaner	Kota	Chechat	Ladpura
Bundi	Hindoli	Talera	Nagaur	Riyan	Kuchaman
Chittaurgarh	Kapasan	Arnod	Pali	Pali	Desuri
Churu	Dungargarh	Sardarshahar	Rajsamand	Railmagra	Khamnor
Dausa	Mahwa	Bandikui	S. Madhopur	Khandar	Gangapur
Dhaulpur	Bari	Dhaulpur	Sikar	Fatehpur	Sri Madhopur
Dungarpur	Simalwara	Aspur	Sirohi	Reodar	Abu Road
Ganganagar	Sadulshahar	Anupgarh	Tonk	Todaraisingh	Uniara
Hanumangarh	Bhadra	Hanumangarh	Udaipur	Baragaon	Kherwara

Source: Annex 12.1

Classification of PSs by PCI and INI

Table 12.3 presents classification of PSs by PCI and INI. There is a visible dominance of Medium level PSs. In PCI, 43.9 per cent PSs were in Medium level followed by High (33.8%), Very High (17.3%) and Low (5%) level PSs. Likewise, in INI, 58.6 per cent PSs entered in Medium level followed by High (17.7%), Low (15.6%), Very High (7.2%) and Very Low (0.8%) level PSs.

TABLE 12.3: Classification of PSs on the Basis of PCI and INI (1998-99): Rajasthan

	[I] PCI			
Group (Rs.)	*Included PSs*			
	No.	*%*	*Distributed in*	
			Districts	*Divisions*
Very High (VH), (>=8000)	41	17.3	10	6
High(H), (6000-8000)	80	33.8	19	6
Medium (M), (4000-6000)	104	43.9	20	6
Low (L), (< 4000)	12	5.1	3	2
Total	**237**	**100**		
	[II] INI			
Group	*Included PSs*			
	No.	*%*	*Distributed in*	
			Districts	*Divisions*
Very High (VH), (>=0.8)	17	7.2	4	3
High (H), (0.6-0.8)	42	17.7	9	6
Medium (M), (0.4-0.6)	139	58.6	27	6
Low (L), (0.2-0.4)	37	15.6	11	6
Very Low (VL), (<0.2)	2	0.8	2	2
Total	**237**	**100**		

Source: Annex 12.1 and 12.2.

TABLE 12.4: Division-wise Classification and Distribution of PSs on the Basis of INI Level

Divisions	*Classification*						*Distribution (% Share)*				
	INI Level						*INI Level*				
	Very High	*High*	*Medium*	*Low*	*Very Low*	*Total PSs*	*Very High*	*High*	*Medium*	*Low*	*Very Low*
Jaipur	8	5	42	6	—	61	47.1	11.9	30.2	16.2	—
	(13.1)	(8.2)	(68.9)	(9.8)	—	(100.0)					
Bikaner	4	8	8	1	—	21	23.5	19.0	5.8	2.7	—
	(19.0)	(38.1)	(38.1)	(4.8)	—	(100.0)					
Ajmer	—	8	23	5	—	36	—	19.0	16.5	13.5	—
	—	(22.2)	(63.9)	(13.9)	—	(100.0)					
Kota	5	5	19	3	—	32	29.4	11.9	13.7	8.1	—
	(15.6)	(15.6)	(59.4)	(9.4)	—	(100.0)					
Jodhpur	—	3	25	13	1	42	—	7.1	18.0	35.1	50.0
	—	(7.1)	(59.5)	(31.0)	(2.4)	(100.0)					
Udaipur	—	13	22	9	1	45	—	30.9	15.1	24.3	50.0
	—	(28.9)	(48.9)	(20.0)	(2.2)	(100.0)					
Total	**17**	**42**	**139**	**37**	**2**	**237**	**100**	**100**	**100**	**100**	**100**
	(7.2)	**(17.7)**	**(58.6)**	**(15.6)**	**(0.8)**	**(100.0)**					

Figure in brackets shows percentage share to total Panchayat Samities
Note: INI Level VH: (>0.08), H : (0.6-0.8), M : (0.4-0.6), L : (0.2-0.4), VL : (<=0.02)
Source: Annex 12.2.

If we see division-wise classification and distribution of PSs by INI (Table 12.4) following conclusions can be drawn:

- No division had PSs of all the 5 INI levels. Except Ajmer (3), all divisions had PSs of 4 levels.
- Jaipur division led in VH (47% share) as well as Medium (30.2%) level PSs and Udaipur in H level (31 %) while Jodhpur division was the most deprived leading in L (35 %) level PSs.
- Medium level PSs were dominating in all the divisions except Bikaner.
- The percentage share of VH level PSs in Kota, Jaipur and Bikaner divisions; H level in Bikaner, Ajmer and Udaipur divisions; M level in Jaipur, Ajmer, Jodhpur and Kota divisions; L level in Jodhpur and Udaipur divisions and VL level in Jodhpur and Udaipur divisions was higher than the state average.

Very High INI Region

Very High INI region was concentrated in four districts of three divisions. There were total 17 VH level PSs. Among the divisions, Jaipur was leading with 47.1 per cent PSs followed by Kota (29.4%) and Bikaner (23.5%) divisions. It is sad that no PSs of Ajmer, Jodhpur and Udaipur divisions found mention in this category. The percentage share of VH level PSs to total PSs ranged from a maximum of 19 in Bikaner to a minimum 13.1 in Jaipur division. Among the districts, Jaipur was dominating with 8 PSs followed by Kota (5), Ganganagar (3) and Hanumangarh (1) districts. All the above three districts had higher percentage of VH level PSs than the state average (7.2%). The percentage ranged from a maximum of 100 in Kota to a minimum of 33.3 in Hanumangarh district (Table 12.4 to 12.6).

TABLE 12.5: District-wise Classification of PSs on the Basis of INI Level (1998-99)

Districts	*INI Level*					
	VH	*H*	*M*	*L*	*VL*	*Total PSs*
Ajmer	—	8 (100.0)	—	—	—	8 (100.0)
Alwar	—	—	14 (100.0)	—	—	14 (100.0)
Banswara	—	—	3 (37.5)	5 (62.5)	—	8 (100.0)
Baran	—	5 (71.4)	2 (28.6)	—	—	7 (100.0)
Barmer	—	—	—	7 (87.5)	1 (12.5)	8 (100.0)
Bharatpur	—	—	9 (100.0)	—	—	9 (100.0)
Bhilwara	—	—	11 (100.0)	—	—	11 (100.0)
Bikaner	—	4 (100.0)	—	—	—	4 (100.0)
Bundi	—	—	4 (100.0)	—	—	4 (100.0)
Chittaurgarh	—	11 (78.6)	3 (21.4)	—	—	14 (100.0)
Churu	—	—	6 (85.7)	1 (14.3)	—	7 (100.0)
Dausa	—	—	5 (100.0)	—	—	5 (100.0)
Dhaulpur	—	—	1 (25.0)	3 (75.0)	—	4 (100.0)
Dungarpur	—	—	—	4 (80.0)	1 (20.0)	5 (100.0)
Ganganagar	3 (42.9)	3 (42.9)	1 (14.3)	—	—	7 (100.0)
Hanumangarh	1 (33.3)	1 (33.3)	1 (33.3)	—	—	3 (100.0)
Jaipur	8 (61.5)	5 (38.5)	—	—	—	13 (100.0)
Jaisalmer	—	—	3 (100.0)	—	—	3 (100.0)
Jalor	—	—	1 (14.3)	6 (85.7)	—	7 (100.0)
Jhalawar	—	—	4 (66.7)	2 (33.3)	—	6 (100.0)
Jhunjhunun	—	—	7 (87.5)	1 (12.5)	—	8 (100.0)
Jodhpur	—	3 (33.3)	6 (66.7)	—	—	9 (100.0)
Karauli	—	—	4 (80.0)	1 (20.0)	—	5 (100.0)
Kota	5 (100.0)	—	—	—	—	5 (100.0)
Nagaur	—	—	6 (54.5)	5 (45.5)	—	11 (100.0)
Pali	—	—	10 (100.0)	—	—	10 (100.0)
Rajsamand	—	1 (14.3)	6 (85.7)	—	—	7 (100.0)
Sawai Madhopur	—	—	5 (100.0)	—	—	5 (100.0)
Sikar	—	—	6 (75.0)	2 (25.0)	—	8 (100.0)
Sirohi	—	—	5 (100.0)	—	—	5 (100.0)
Tonk	—	—	6 (100.0)	—	—	6 (100.0)
Udaipur	—	1 (9.1)	10 (90.9)	—	—	11 (100.0)
Rajasthan	**17 (7.2)**	**42 (17.7)**	**139 (58.6)**	**37 (15.6)**	**2 (0.8)**	**237 (100.0)**

Note: Figures in brackets show percentage share to total Panchayat Samities.
INI Level VH: (>0.08), H : (0.6-0.8), M : (0.4-0.6), L : (0.2-0.4), VL : (<=0.02) *Source* : Annex 12.2

TABLE 12.6: Distribution of PSs having Very High INI Level (1998-99)

S. No.	*District*	*No. & Name of PSs in Descending Order*
		Very High Level (17)
1	Jaipur	8—Sanganer, Jhotwara, Chaksu, Phagi, Amber, Dudu, Jamwa Ramgarh and Bassi
2	Kota	5—Chechat, Sangod, Itawa, Sultanpur and Ladpura
3	Ganganagar	3—Sadulshahar, Suratgarh and Karanpur
4	Hanumangarh	1—Bhadra

Source: Annex 12.2

High INI Region

High INI region was spread over 9 districts and all the six divisions. There were total of 42 High level PSs. Udaipur division topped with 30.9 per cent PSs followed by Ajmer and Bikaner (19% each), Jaipur and Kota (11.9% each) and Jodhpur (7.1%) divisions. The percentage share of H level PSs to total PSs is the highest 38.1 in Bikaner, 28.9 in Udaipur, 22.2 in Ajmer, 15.6 in Kota, 8.2 in Jaipur and the lowest 7.1 in Jodhpur division. Bikaner, Udaipur and Ajmer divisions had higher percentage of M level PSs in comparison to the state average (17.7%). Among the districts, Chittaurgarh led with 11 PSs followed by Ajmer (8); Baran, Jaipur (5 each); Bikaner (4); Ganganagar and Jodhpur (3 each); Hanumangarh, Rajsamand and Udaipur (1 each) districts respectively (Table 12.7). Except Rajsamand and Udaipur, all the above districts had greater percentage of H level PSs in comparison to the state average.

TABLE 12.7: Distribution of PSs having High INI Level (1998-99)

S. No.	*District*	*No. and Name of PSs in Descending Order*
		High Level (42)
1	Chittaurgarh	11—Kapasan, Bari Sadri & Gangrar, Chhoti Sadri, Rashmi, Dungla, Begun, Bhadesar, Bhopalsagar, Chittaurgarh and Nimbhera
2	Ajmer	8—Arian, Bhinay, Kekri, Masooda, Srinagar, Kishangarh, Pisangan and Jawaja
3	Baran	5—Chhipabarod, Chhabra, Kishanganj, Atru and Shahbad
4	Jaipur	5—Kotputli, Sambhar, Govindgarh, Shahpura and Viratnagar
5	Bikaner	4—Nokha, Lunkaransar, Kolayat and Bikaner
6	Ganganagar	3—Raisinghnagar, Ganganagar and Padampur
7	Jodhpur	3—Bap, Bilara and Bhopalgarh
8	Hanumangarh	1 Nohar
10	Rajsamand	1—Railmagra
11	Udaipur	1—Bargaon

Source:Annex 12.2

Medium INI Region

Medium INI region was widely distributed in 27 districts and all the six divisions. There were 139 PSs in this category. As explained earlier, Jaipur division had the maximum concentration of these PSs (30.2%). It was followed by Jodhpur (18%), Ajmer (16.5%), Udaipur (15.8%), Kota (13.7%) and Bikaner (5.8%) divisions. The percentage share of M level PSs to total PSs was the highest 68.9 in Jaipur division, 63.9 in Ajmer, 59.5 in Jodhpur and Kota, 48.9 in Udaipur and the lowest 38.1 in Bikaner division. Jaipur, Ajmer, Kota and Jodhpur divisions had percentage of these PSs higher than the state average (58.6). If we see district-wise distribution of these PSs (Table 12.8), it will be clear that Alwar secured the top position with 14 PSs followed by Bhilwara (11); Pali and Udaipur (10 each); Bharatpur (9); Jhunjhunun (7), Churu, Jodhpur, Nagaur, Rajsamand, Sikar and Tonk (6 each); Dausa, Sawai Madhopur and Sirohi (5 each); Bundi, Jhalawar and Karauli

(4 each); Banswara, Chittaurgarh and Jaisalmer (3 each); Baran (2); Dhaulpur, Ganganagar, Hanumangarh and Jalor (1 each) respectively. Except Banswara, Baran, Chittaurgarh, Dhaulpur, Ganganagar, Hanumangarh, Jalor and Nagaur, all the above districts had higher percentage of Medium level PSs than the state average. Moreover ten districts, namely Alwar, Bharatpur, Bhilwara, Bundi, Dausa, Jaisalmer, Pali, Sawai Madhopur, Sirohi and Tonk had 100 per cent of their PSs in Medium category while Ganganagar and Jalor had the minimum 14 per cent share of these PSs.

TABLE 12.8: Distribution of PSs having Medium INI Level (1998-99)

S. No.	*District*	*No. and Name of PSs in Descending Order*
		Medium Level (139)
1	Alwar	14—Reni, Rajgarh, Behror, Lachhmangarh, Kathumer, Thanagazi, Umren, Kishangarh Bas, Bansure, Kotkasim, Mandawar, Nimrana, Tijara and Ramgarh
2	Bhilwara	11—Sahara, Banera, Kotri, Asind, Shahpura, Suwana, Mandalgarh, Hurda, Mandal, Raipur and Jahazpur
3	Pali	10—Pali, Sojat, Rani Station, Rohat, Kharchi/Marwar Junction, Jaitaran, Bali, Sumerpur, Raipur and Desuri
4	Udaipur	10—Bhindar, Salumbar, Mavli, Jhadol, Gogunda, Dhariadwad, Sarada, Kotra, Girwa and Kherwara
5	Bharatpur	9—Deeg, Kumher, Kaman, Nadbai, Weir, Bayana, Nagar Pahari, Sewar and Rupbas
6	Jhunjhunun	7—Buhana, Jhunjhunun, Surajgarh, Alsisar, Chirawa, Udaipurwati and Khetri
7	Churu	6—Dungargarh, Taranagar, Rajgarh, Ratangarh, Churu and Sujangarh
8	Jodhpur	6—Luni, Shergarh, Balesar, Osian, Mandor and Phalodi
9	Nagaur	6—Riyan, Degana, Mundwa, Nagaur, Jayal and Parbatsar
10	Rajsamand	6—Kumbhalgarh, Amet, Deogarh, Bhim, Rajsamand and Khamnor
11	Sikar	6—Fatehpur, Lachhmangarh, Piprali, Khandela, Dhond and Danta Ramgarh
12	Tonk	6—Todaraisingh, Niwai, Malpura, Tonk, Deoli and Uniara
13	Dausa	5—Mahwa, Dausa, Sikrai, Lalsot and Bandikui
14	Sawai Madhopur	5—Khandar, Bonli, Bamanwas, Sawai Madhopur and Gangapur
15	Sirohi	5—Reodar, Pindwara, Sirohi, Sheogang and Abu Road
16	Bundi	4—Hindoli, Nainwa, Keshoraipatan and Talera
17	Jhalawar	4—Bakani, Manoharthana, Pirawa and Jhalrapatan
18	Karauli	4—Nadoti, Sapotra, Karauli and Todabhim
19	Banswara	3—Anandpuri, Bagidora and Sajjangarh
20	Chittaurgarh	3—Bhainsrorgarh, Partapgarh and Arnod
21	Jaisalmer	3—Sankra, Sam and Jaisalmer
22	Baran	2—Baran and Anta
23	Dhaulpur	1—Bari
24	Ganganagar	1—Anupgarh
25	Hanumangarh	1—Hanumangarh
26	Jalor	1—Ahore

Source: Annex 12.2

Low INI Region

This region was spread over 11 districts and 6 divisions. There were 37 PSs having Low INI. Jodhpur division led with 35.1 per cent share followed by Udaipur (24.3%), Jaipur (16.2%), Ajmer (13.5%), Kota (8.1%) and Bikaner (2.7%) divisions. Jodhpur and Udaipur divisions had higher percentage of these PSs in comparison to the state average (15.6%). Among the districts, Barmer had the highest PSs (7) in this group followed by Jalor (6); Banswara and Nagaur (5 each); Dungarpur (4); Dhaulpur (3); Jhalawar and Sikar (2 each); Churu, Jhunjhunun and Karauli (1 each) districts (Table 12.9).

Very Low INI Region

Aspur PS of Dungarpur district and Siwana of Barmer were the only PSs found mention in this category.

TABLE 12.9: Distribution of PSs having Low and Very Low INI Level (1998-99)

S. No.	*District*	*No. and Name of PSs in Descending Order*
		[A] Low Level (37)
1	Barmer	7—Baytoo, Chohtan, Sindhari, Dhorimanna, Balotra, Barmer and Sheo
2	Jalor	6—Bhinmal, Jaswantpura, Jalor, Sanchore, Sayla and Raniwara
3	Banswara	5—Kushalgarh, Peepalkhoont, Garhi, Ghatol and Talwara
4	Nagaur	5—Merta, Ladnu, Makrana, Didwana and Kuchaman
5	Dungarpur	4—Simalwara, Dungarpur, Sagwara and Bichhiwara
6	Dhaulpur	3—Baseri, Rajakhera and Dhaulpur
7	Jhalawar	2—Dag and Khanpur
8	Sikar	2—Neem ka Thana and Sri Madhopur
9	Churu	1—Sardarshahar
10	Jhunjhunun	1—Nawalgarh
11	Karauli	1—Hindaun
		[A] Very Low Level (2)
1	Barmer	1—Siwana
2	Dungarpur	1—Aspur

Source: Annex 12.2.

13

GENDER-RELATED INCOME INDEX (1991-92)

Highlights

- GINI Rural Raj.: 0.6680
- Percentage of AAPs: 41.4%
- Only 42 (17.7%) PSs had GINI above 0.7

	Panchayat Samiti	District	Division
• **Top**	Sangod (0.8196)	Kota	Kota
• **Bottom**	Rajakhera (0.2323)	Dhaulpur	Jaipur

In the year 1991-92, the Gender-Related Income Index (GINI) of rural Rajasthan was moderate (0.6680). There were 98 (41.4%) PSs having GINI above the state average. Jaipur division dominated not only in PSs having Very High GINI (41.2%) but also in PSs having Low (29.2%) and Very Low (47.4%) GINI. Similarly, Ajmer division led in PSs having high (28%) GINI while, Udaipur (26%) division led in Low GINI (Fig 13.1).

Sangod PS of Kota district had the maximum 0.8196 GINI followed by Chaksu, Chechat, Karanpur, Itawa, Bassi, Phagi, Ladpura, Amber and Bhadra PSs (descending order, Annex 13.1 & 13.2). These top ten PSs were distributed in four districts. Both Jaipur and Kota districts dominated with 4 PSs each. Similarly, Ganganagar and Hanumangarh each had 1 PS as shown in Table 13.1.

TABLE 13.1: Distribution of First and Last Ten Panchayat Samities by GINI: Rajasthan, (1991-92)

S. No.	*First Ten PSs (Descending Order)*				*Last Ten PSs (Ascending Order)*				
	Districts/ PSs				*Districts/ PSs*				
	Jaipur	*Kota*	*Gg*	*Hn*	*Dhaulpur*	*Jhun*	*Sikar*	*Barmer*	*Dg*
	(4)	*(4)*	*(1)*	*(1)*	*(3)*	*(3)*	*(2)*	*(')*	*(')*
1	Chaksu	Sangod	Karanpur	Bhadra	Rajakhera	Nawalgarh	Sri Madhopur	Sheo	Aspur
2	Bassi	Chechat	—	—	Dhaulpur	Khetri	Neem ka Thana	—	—
3	Phagi	Itawa	—	—	Bari	Chirawa	—	—	—
4	Amber	Ladpura	—	—	—	—	—	—	—

Source: Annex 13.1

Rajakhera PS of Dhaulpur district, on the other hand, was the most deprived having GINI 0.2323. It was followed by Dhaulpur, Nawalgarh, Aspur, Bari, Sri Madhopur, Neem ka Thana, Khetri, Sheo and Chirawa

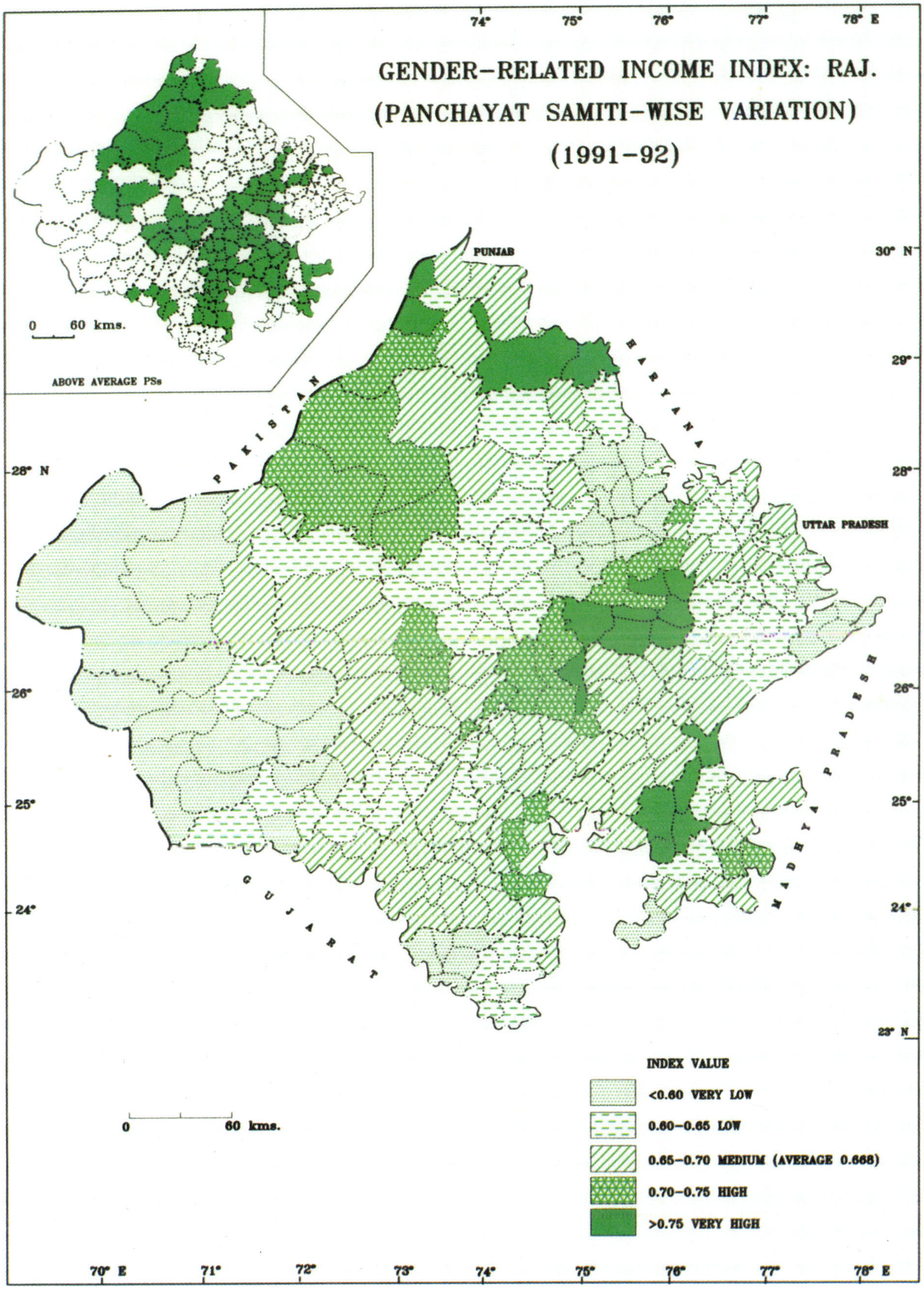
GENDER–RELATED INCOME INDEX: RAJ.
(PANCHAYAT SAMITI–WISE VARIATION)
(1991–92)
ABOVE AVERAGE PSs
0 60 kms.
PUNJAB
HARYANA
UTTAR PRADESH
MADHYA PRADESH
GUJARAT
PAKISTAN
74° 75° 76° 77° 78° E
30° N
29°
28° N
28°
26°
25°
24°
23° N
70° E 71° 72° 73° 74° 75° 76° 77° 78° E
INDEX VALUE
<0.60 VERY LOW
0.60–0.65 LOW
0.65–0.70 MEDIUM (AVERAGE 0.668)
0.70–0.75 HIGH
>0.75 VERY HIGH

Fig. 13.1

PSs (in ascending order). These last ten PSs were spread over five districts. Dhaulpur and Jhunjhunun topped with 3 PSs each followed by Sikar (2), Barmer and Dungarpur (1 each) districts. Similarly, district-wise first and last PSs by GINI is presented in Table 13.2.

TABLE 13.2: District-wise First and Last PSs by GINI (1991-92)

District	*First Rank*	*Last Rank*	*District*	*First Rank*	*Last Rank*
Ajmer	Arain	Jawaja	Jaipur	Chaksu	Viratnagar
Alwar	Reni	Nimrana	Jaisalmer	Sankra	Jaisalmer
Banswara	Anandpuri	Talwara	Jalor	Ahore	Sayla
Baran	Chhipabarod	Anta	Jhalawar	Manoharthana	Dag
Barmer	Baytoo	Sheo	Jhunjhunun	Buhana	Nawalgarh
Bharatpur	Deeg	Rupbas	Jodhpur	Bhopalgarh	Bap
Bhilwara	Sahara	Raipur	Karauli	Nadoti	Hindaun
Bikaner	Nokha	Lunkaransar	Kota	Sangod	Sultanpur
Bundi	Hindoli	Talera	Nagaur	Riyan	Kuchaman
Chittaurgarh	Kapasan	Bhainsrorgarh	Pali	Sojat	Sumerpur
Churu	Dungargarh	Sardarshahar	Rajsamand	Kumbhalgarh	Rajsamand
Dausa	Sikrai	Bandikui	Sawai Madhopur	Bonli	Gangapur
Dhaulpur	Baseri	Rajakhera	Sikar	Fatehpur	Sri Madhopur
Dungarpur	Simalwara	Aspur	Sirohi	Pindwara	Sirohi
Ganganagar	Karanpur	Padampur	Tonk	Todaraisingh	Uniara
Hanumangarh	Bhadra	Hanumangarh	Udaipur	Bhinder	Gogunda

Source: Annex 14.1, Col. 3

Classification of PSs by GINI

On the basis of GINI, PSs of the state are classified into 5 groups viz. Very High (VH), High (H), Medium (M), Low (L) and Very Low (VL) as presented in Table 13.3. The state had clear-cut dominance of M (38.9%) level PSs followed by L (27.4%), VL (16%), H (10.5%) and VH (7.2%) level PSs.

TABLE 13.3: Classification of PSs on the Basis of GINI (1991-92): Rajasthan

Group	*Included PSs*			
	No.	*%*	*Distributed in*	
			Districts	*Divisions*
Very High (VH), (>=0.75)	17	7.2	5	4
High (H), (0.70-0.75)	25	10.5	7	6
Medium (M), (0.65-0.70)	92	38.9	23	6
Low (L), (0.60-0.65)	65	27.4	20	6
Very Low (VL), (<0.60)	38	16.0	11	5
Total	**237**	**100**		

Source: Annex 13.1.

Division-wise classification and distribution of PSs by GINI level is shown in Table 13.4. Following conclusions can be drawn:

- While the PSs having VH GINI were concentrated in four divisions and VL level in five divisions, the PSs having H, M and L GINI were widley spread over all the six divisions.
- Jaipur, Ajmer and Kota were the only divisions having PSs of all the five levels while the remaining divisions had PSs of 4 levels.
- As explained earlier, Jaipur, division had secured the first rank in PSs having Very High, Low and Very Low GINI while, Ajmer and Udaipur division topped in High and Medium level PSs respectively.
- Medium level PSs led in all the divisions except Jaipur where Low level PSs led.

- The percentage of VH level PSs in Jaipur, Bikaner and Kota divisions; H level in Bikaner, Ajmer and Udaipur divisions; M level in Ajmer, Jodhpur, Kota and Udaipur divisions; L level in Jaipur, Bikaner, Ajmer and Kota divisions and VL level in Jaipur and Jodhpur divisions were higher than the state average.

TABLE 13.4: Division-wise Classification and Distribution of PSs on the Basis of GINI Level (1991-92)

Divisions	*Classification*						*Distribution (% Share)*				
	GINI Level						*GINI Level*				
	Very High	*High*	*Medium*	*Low*	*Very Low*	*Total PSs*	*Very High*	*High*	*Medium*	*Low*	*Very Low*
Jaipur	7	5	12	19	18	61	41.2	20.0	13.0	29.2	47.4
	(11.5)	(8.2)	(19.7)	(31.1)	(29.5)	(100.0)					
Bikaner	4	4	7	6	—	21	23.5	16.0	7.6	9.2	—
	(19.0)	(19.0)	(33.3)	(28.6)	—	(100.0)					
Ajmer	1	7	16	11	1	36	5.9	28.0	17.4	16.9	2.6
	(2.8)	(19.4)	(44.4)	(30.6)	(2.8)	(100.0)					
Kota	5	2	15	9	1	32	29.4	8.0	16.3	13.8	2.6
	(15.6)	(6.3)	(46.9)	(28.1)	(3.1)	(100.0)					
Jodhpur	—	2	18	10	12	42	—	8.0	19.6	15.4	31.5
	—	(4.8)	(42.9)	(23.8)	(28.6)	(100.0)					
Udaipur	—	5	24	10	6	45	—	20.0	26.0	15.4	15.8
	—	(11.1)	(53.3)	(22.2)	(13.3)	(100.0)					
Total	**17**	**25**	**92**	**65**	**38**	**237**	**100**	**100**	**100**	**100**	**100**
	(7.2)	**(10.5)**	**(38.9)**	**(27.4)**	**(16.0)**	**(100.0)**					

Figure in brackets shows percentage share to total Panchayat Samities.
Note: GINI Level VH : (>=0.75), H : (0.70-0.75), M : (0.65-0.70), L : (0.60-0.65), VL : (<0.60)
Source: Annex 13.1.

Different GINI Areas

Very High GINI Area

Very High GINI area was concentrated in five districts and four divisions (except Jodhpur and Udaipur). There were total 17 PSs in this group. Jaipur division led with 41.2 per cent share followed by Kota (29.4%), Bikaner (23.5%) and Ajmer (5.9%) divisions. The percentage share of VH level PSs to total PSs ranged between a maximum of 19 in Bikaner and a minimum of 2.8 in Ajmer division. Among the districts, Jaipur dominated with 7 PSs followed by Kota (5), Ganganagar and Hanumangarh (2 each) and Ajmer (1) districts (Table 13.5 & 13.6}. All these districts had higher percentage share of VH level PSs than state average (7.2%). The percentage ranged between a maximum of 100 in Kota district and a minimum of 12.5 in Ajmer.

High GINI Area

High GINI area was distributed in 7 districts and all the 6 divisions. There were total 25 PSs in this category. Ajmer division topped with 28 per cent share followed by Jaipur and Udaipur (20% each), Bikaner (16%), Kota and Jodhpur (8% each) divisions. The percentage of H level PSs to total PSs was the highest 19 in Ajmer and Bikaner, 11 in Udaipur, 8 in Jaipur, 6 in Kota and the lowest 5 in Jodhpur division. Bikaner, Ajmer and Udaipur divisions had percentage share of H level PSs higher than the state average (10.5%). In view of district-wise distribution, it is clear that Ajmer dominated with 7 PSs followed by Chittaurgarh and Jaipur (5 each); Bikaner (3); Baran and Jodhpur (2 each) and Ganganagar (1) districts. All these districts had higher percentage of H level PSs than the state average. The percentage ranged from the highest 87.5 in Ajmer district to the lowest 14 in Ganganagar.

TABLE 13.5: District-wise Classification of PSs on the Basis of GINI Level (1991-92)

District	*EDI Level*					*Total PSs*
	VH	*H*	*M*	*L*	*VL*	
Ajmer	1 (12.5)	7 (87.5)	—	—		8 (100.0)
Alwar	—	—	7 (50.0)	7 (50.0)	—	14 (100.0)
Banswara	—	—	—	7 (87.5)	1 (12.5)	8 (100.0)
Baran	—	2 (28.6)	4 (57.1)	1 (14.3)	—	7 (100.0)
Barmer	—	—	—	1 (12.5)	7 (87.5)	8 (100.0)
Bharatpur	—	—	2 (22.2)	6 (66.7)	1 (11.1)	9 (100.0)
Bhilwara	—	—	10 (90.9)	1 (9.1)	—	11 (100.0)
Bikaner	—	3 (75.0)	1 (25.0)	—	—	4 (100.0)
Bundi	—	—	4 (100.0)	—	—	4 (100.0)
Chittaurgarh	—	5 (35.7)	9 (64.3)	—	—	14 (100.0)
Churu	—	—	2 (28.6)	5 (71.4)	—	7 (100.0)
Dausa	—	—	1 (20.0)	4 (80.0)	—	5 (100.0)
Dhaulpur	—	—	—	—	4 (100.0)	4 (100.0)
Dungarpur	—	—	—	—	5 (100.0)	5 (100.0)
Ganganagar	2 (28.6)	1 (14.3)	3 (42.9)	1 (14.3)	—	7 (100.0)
Hanumangarh	2 (66.7)	—	1 (33.3)	—	—	3 (100.0)
Jaipur	7 (53.8)	5 (38.5)	1 (7.7)	—	—	13 (100.0)
Jaisalmer	—	—	1 (33.3)	—	2 (66.7)	3 (100.0)
Jalor	—	—	1 (14.3)	3 (42.9)	3 (42.9)	7 (100.0)
Jhalawar	—	—	3 (50.0)	2 (33.3)	1 (16.7)	6 (100.0)
Jhunjhunun	—	—	—	1 (12.5)	7 (87.5)	8 (100.0)
Jodhpur	—	2 (22.2)	6 (66.7)	1 (11.1)	—	9 (100.0)
Karauli	—	—	—	5 (100.0)	—	5 (100.0)
Kota	5 (100.0)	—	—	—	—	5 (100.0)
Nagaur	—	—	—	10 (90.9)	1 (9.1)	11 (100.0)
Pali	—	—	6 (60.0)	4 (40.0)	—	10 (100.0)
Rajsamand	—	—	4 (57.1)	3 (42.9)	—	7 (100.0)
Sawai Madhopur	—	—	4 (80.0)	1 (20.0)	—	5 (100.0)
Sikar	—	—	1 (12.5)	1 (12.5)	6 (75.0)	8 (100.0)
Sirohi	—	—	4 (80.0)	1 (20.0)	—	5 (100.0)
Tonk	—	—	6 (100.0)	—	—	6 (100.0)
Udaipur	—	—	11 (100.0)	—	—	11 (100.0)
Rajasthan	**17 (7.2)**	**25 (10.5)**	**92 (38.8)**	**65 (27.4)**	**38 (16.0)**	**237 (100.0)**

Figures in brackets show percentage share to total Panchayat Samities

Note : GINI Level VH : (0.75), H : (0.70-0.75), M : (0.65-0.70), L : (0.60-0.65), VL : (<0.60) *Source*: Annex 13.1.

TABLE 13.6: Distribution of PSs having Very High and High GINI Level (1991-92)

S. No.	*District*	*No. & Name of PSs in Descending Order*
		[A] Very High Level (17)
1	Jaipur	7—Chaksu, Bassi, Phagi, Amber, Jamwa Ramgarh, Dudu and Sanganer
2	Kota	5—Sangod, Chechat, Itawa, Ladpura and Sultanpur
3	Ganganagar	2—Karanpur and Raisinghnagar
4	Hanumangarh	2—Bhadra and Nohar
5	Ajmer	1—Arian
		[B] High Level (25)
1	Ajmer	7—Bhinay, Kekri, Srinagar, Masooda, Pisangan, Kishangarh and Jawaja
2	Chittaurgarh	5—Kapasan, Chhoti Sadri, Gangrar, Bari Sadri and Bhadesar
3	Jaipur	5—Shahpura, Kotputli, Sambhar, Jhotwara and Govindgarh
4	Bikaner	3—Nokha, Bikaner and Kolayat
5	Baran	2—Chhipabarod and Chhabra
6	Jodhpur	2—Bhopalgarh and Bilara
7	Ganganagar	1—Anupgarh

Source: Annex 13.1

TABLE 13.7: Distribution of PSs having Medium GINI Level (1991-92)

S. No.	*District*	*No. & Name of PSs in Descending Order*
		Medium Level (92)
1	Udaipur	11—Bhinder, Kotra, Jhadol, Salumbar, Dhariadwad, Bargaon, Kherwara, Mavli, Gogunda, Sarda and Girwa
2	Bhilwara	10—Sahara, Mandal, Asind, Suwana, Banera, Shahpura, Kotri, Mandalgarh, Hurda and Jhahazpur
3	Chittaurgarh	9—Chittaurgarh, Dungla, Rashmi, Begun, Nimbhera, Bhopalsagar, Arnod, Pratapgarh and Bhainsrorgarh
4	Alwar	7—Reni, Rajgarh, Behror, Lachhmangarh, Khathumar, Tijara and Thanagazi
5	Jodhpur	6—Shergarh, Luni, Phalodi, Balesar, Mandor and Osian
6	Pali	6—Sojat, Rohat, Jaitaran, Raipur, Pali and Kharchi/Marwar Jun.
7	Tonk	6—Todaraisingh, Niwai, Deoli, Tonk, Malpura and Uniara
8	Baran	4—Shahbad, Kisanganj, Baran and Atru
9	Bundi	4—Hindoli, Nainwa, Keshoraipatan and Talera
10	Rajsamand	4—Kumbhalgarh, Railmagra, Bhim and Khamnor
11	Sawai Madhopur	4—Bonli, Khandar, Bamanwas and Sawai Madhopur
12	Ganganagar	3—Suratgarh, Ganganagar and Sadulshahar
13	Jhalawar	3—Manoharthana, Bakani and Pirawa
14	Sirohi	3 Pindwara, Reodar and Abu Road
15	Bharatpur	2—Deeg and Kaman
16	Churu	2—Dungargarh and Taranagar
17	Bikaner	1—Lunkaransar
18	Dausa	1—Sikrai
19	Hanumangarh	1—Hanumangarh
20	Jaipur	1—Viratnagar
21	Jaisalmer	1—Sankara
22	Jalor	1—Ahore
23	Sikar	1—Fatehpur

Source: Annex 13.1

Medium GINI Area

This area was widely spread over 23 districts and all the 6 divisions. As mentioned earlier, the state had dominance of M level PSs. There were total 92 PSs in this group. Udaipur division with 26 per cent share had the maximum concentration of these PSs followed by Jodhpur (19.6%), Ajmer (17.4%), Kota (16.3%), Jaipur (13%) and Bikaner (7.6%) divisions. The percentage of M level PSs to total PSs was the highest 53 in Udaipur,

47 in Kota, 44 in Ajmer, 43 in Jodhpur, 33 in Bikaner and the lowest 20 in Jaipur division. All the divisions except Jaipur and Bikaner had higher percentage of these PSs than the state average (39 %).

Among the districts, Udaipur topped with 11 PSs followed by Bhilwara (10); Chittaurgarh (10 each); Alwar (7); Jodhpur and Tonk (6 each); Pali (5); Sawai Madhopur, Baran Bundi, Rajsamand and Sirohi (4 each); Jhalawar and Ganganagar (3 each), Bharatpur and Churu (2 each) and Bikaner, Hanumangarh, Jaipur, Jaisalmer, Jalor and Sikar (one each) districts respectively (Table 13.7). All these districts, except Bharatpur, Bikaner, Churu, Dausa, Hanumangarh, Jaipur, Jaisalmer, Jhalawar and Sikar had higher percentage of these PSs in comparison to state average. The percentage ranged between a maximum of 100 in Bundi, Tonk and Udaipur districts and a minimum of 8 in Jaipur.

TABLE 13.8: Distribution of PSs having Low GINI Level (1991-92)

S. No.	*District*	*No. & Name of PSs in Descending Order*
		Low Level (66)
1	Nagaur	10—Riyan, Mundwa, Degana, Parbatsar, Jayal, Merta, Ladnu, Nagaur, Didwana and Makrana
2	Alwar	7—Bansure, Umren, Kotkasim, Kishangarh Bas, Mandawar, Ramgarh and Nimrana
3	Banswara	7—Anandpuri, Bagidora, Sajjangarh, Kushalgarh, Peepalkhoont, Ghatol and Garhi
4	Bharatpur	6—Kumher, Nadbai, Weir, Nagar Pahari, Sewar and Bayana
5	Churu	5—Rajgarh, Sujangarh, Ratangarh, Churu and Sardarshahar
6	Karauli	5—Nadoti, Sapotra, Karauli, Todabhim and Hindaun
7	Dausa	4—Dausa, Mahwa, Lalsot and Bandikui
8	Pali	4—Rani Station, Bali, Desuri and Sumerpur
9	Jalor	3—Bhinmal, Sanchore and Jaswantpura
10	Rajsamand	3—Amet, Deogarh and Rajsamand
11	Jhalawar	2—Jhalarapatan and Khanpur
12	Sirohi	2—Sheoganj and Sirohi
13	Baran	1—Anta
14	Barmer	1—Baytoo
15	Bhilwara	1—Raipur
16	Ganganagar	1—Padampur
17	Jhunjhunun	1—Buhana
18	Jodhpur	1—Bap
19	Sawai Madhopur	1—Gangapur
20	Sikar	1—Lachhmangarh
21	Sirohi	1—Sirohi

Source: Annex 13.1

Low GINI Area

Low GINI area was spread over 21 districts and 6 divisions. There were total 65 PSs in this group. Jaipur division led with 29.2 per cent share followed by Ajmer (16.9), Jodhpur and Udaipur (15.4% each), Kota (13.8%) and Bikaner (9.2%) divisions. Except Jodhpur and Udaipur, all the divisions had higher percentage of L level PSs in comparison to the state average (27.4).

In view of district-wise distribution of these PSs it is clear that Nagaur stood at the first rank (10 PSs), followed by Alwar and Banswara (7 each); Bharatpur (6); Churu and Karauli (5 each); Dausa and Pali (4 each); Jalor and Rajsamand (3 each); Jhalawar (2); Baran, Barmer, Bhilwara, Ganganagar, Jhunjhunun, Jodhpur, Sawai Madhopur, Sikar and Sirohi (one each) districts respectively (Table 13.8). Except Baran, Barmer, Bharatpur, Bhilwara, Ganganagar, Jhunjhunun, Jodhpur, Sawai Madhopur, Sikar and Sirohi all these districts had greater percentage of L level PSs than the state average. The percentage ranged between a maximum of 100 in Karauli district and a minimum of 9 in Bhilwara.

TABLE 13.9: Distribution of PSs having Very Low GINI Level (1991-92)

S. No.	*District*	*No. & Name of PSs (in Descending Order)*
		Very Low Level (38)
1	Barmer	7—Sindhari, Dhorimanna, Chohtan, Balotra, Barmer, Siwana and Sheo
2	Jhunjhunun	7—Jhunjhunun, Surajgarh, Alsisar, Udaipurwati, Chirawa, Khetri and Nawalgarh
3	Sikar	6—Khandela, Piprali, Dhond, Danta Ramgarh, Neem ka Thana and Sri Madhopur
4	Dungarpur	5—Simalwara, Dungarpur, Bichhiwara, Sagwara and Aspur
5	Dhaulpur	4—Baseri, Bari, Dhaulpur and Rajakhera
6	Jalor	3—Raniwara, Jalor and Sayla
7	Jaisalmer	2—Sam and Jaisalmer
8	Banswara	1—Talwara
9	Bharatpur	1—Rupbas
10	Jhalawar	1—Dag
11	Nagaur	1—Kuchaman

Source: Annex 13.1.

Very Low GINI Area

This area was concentrated in 11 districts and 5 divisions (except Bikaner). There were 38 PSs having Very Low GINI. As mentioned earlier, Jaipur division dominated with 47.4 per cent share followed by Jodhpur (31.6%), Udaipur (15.8%), Ajmer and Kota (2.6% each) divisions. The percentage of VL level PSs to total PSs was the maximum 29.5 in Jaipur and the minimum 2.8 in Ajmer division. Both Jaipur and Jodhpur divisions had higher percentage of these PSs in comparison to the state average (16). If we see district-wise distribution of these PSs, it will be clear that both Barmer and Jhunjhunun topped with 7 PSs each followed by Sikar (6); Dungarpur (5); Dhaulpur (4); Jalor (3); Jaisalmer (2) Banswara, Bharatpur and Nagaur (one each) districts respectively (Table 13.9). All the above districts, except Banswara, Bharatpur and Nagaur had higher percentage of VL level PSs than the state average. The percentage ranged between a maximum of 100 in Dhaulpur and Dungarpur districts and a minimum of 9 in Nagaur district.

14

GENDER-RELATED INCOME INDEX (1998-99)

Highlights

- GINI, Rural Raj.: 0.7390
- Percentage of AAPs: 40%
- 72 per cent PSs had GINI above 0.7

	Panchayat Samiti	District	Division
• **Top**	Sanganer, 0.9081	Jaipur	Jaipur
• **Bottom**	Siwana, 0.5875	Barmer	Jodhpur

Although the GINI of rural Rajasthan reached 0.7390 in the year 1998-99 and IOD came down to 0.2610 still, the state has to travel a long way to achieve the targeted value 1.0. There were only 95 PSs (40%) having GINI above the state average. Panchayat samiti-wise variation in the distribution of GINI is presented in Fig 14.1 & Annex 14.1. Jaipur division dominated not only in VH level PSs (24.7%) but also in H (31%) level PSs. On the other hand, Jodhpur division was the most deprived, and led in M to VL (28%) level PSs.

Sanganer PS of Jaipur district had the maximum 0.9081 GINI followed by Jhotwara, Chaksu, Chechat, Sangod, Phagi, Sadulshahar, Bhadra, Jamwa Ramgarh and Dudu PSs (in descending order, Annex 14.2). These top ten PSs were distributed in four districts. Jaipur dominated with 6 PSs followed by Kota (2), Ganganagar and Hanumangarh (one each) districts (Table 14.1).

TABLE 14.1: Distribution of First and Last Ten PSs by GINI: Rajasthan, (1998-99)

S. No.	*First Ten PSs (Descending Order)*				*Last Ten PSs (Ascending Order)*		
	Districts/ PSs				*Districts/ PSs*		
	Jaipur	*Kota*	*Gg*	*Hn*	*Dg*	*Barmer*	*Ng*
	(6)	*(2)*	*(1)*	*(1)*	*(5)*	*(4)*	*(1)*
1	Sanganer	Chechat	Sadulshahar	Bhadra	Aspur	Siwana	Kuchaman
2	Jhotwara	Sangod	—	—	Bichhiwara	Sheo	—
3	Chaksu	—	—	—	Sagwara	Barmer	—
4	Phagi	—	—	—	Dungarpur	Balotra	—
5	Dudu	—	—	—	Simalwara	—	—
6	Jamwa Ramgarh	—	—	—	—	—	—

Source: Annex 14.2.

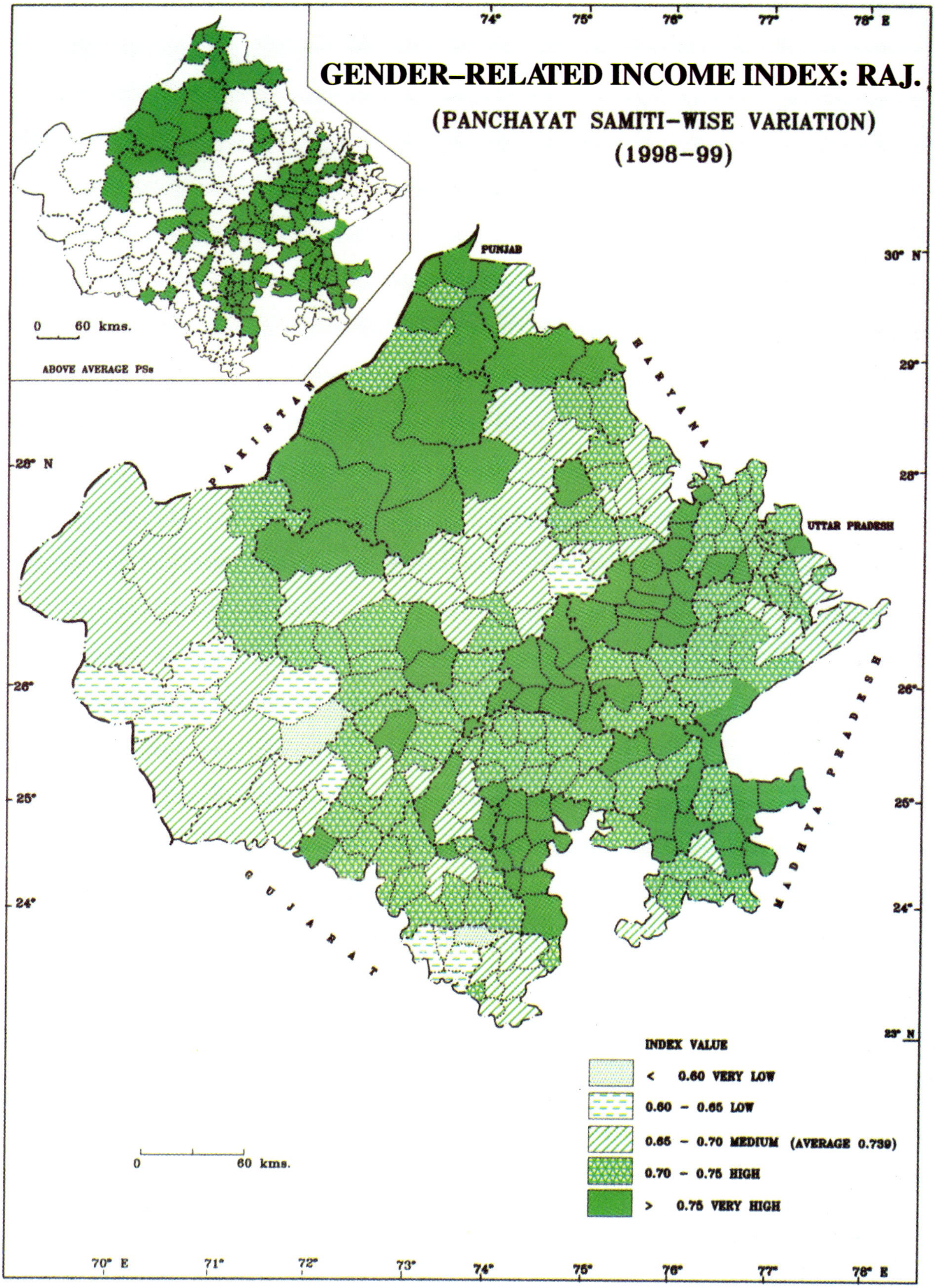
GENDER-RELATED INCOME INDEX: RAJ.
(PANCHAYAT SAMITI-WISE VARIATION)
(1998-99)
ABOVE AVERAGE PSs
0 60 kms.
PUNJAB
HARYANA
UTTAR PRADESH
MADHYA PRADESH
GUJARAT
PAKISTAN
INDEX VALUE
< 0.60 VERY LOW
0.60 - 0.65 LOW
0.65 - 0.70 MEDIUM (AVERAGE 0.739)
0.70 - 0.75 HIGH
> 0.75 VERY HIGH
0 60 kms.
70° E
71°
72°
73°
74°
75°
76°
77°
78° E
30° N
29°
28° N
26°
25°
24°
23° N

FIG. 14.1

Siwana PS of Barmer district, on the other hand, was the most deprived having GINI 0.5875. It was followed by Aspur, Sheo, Bichhiwara, Sagwara, Dungarpur, Simalwara, Barmer, Kuchaman and Balotra PSs (in ascending order). These last ten PSs were concentrated in 3 districts. Dungarpur led with 5 PSs while Barmer had 4 and Nagaur had 1 PS. Similarly, district-wise first and the last PSs by GINI is presented in Table 14.2.

TABLE 14.2: District-wise First and Last PSs by GINI (1998-99)

District	*First Rank*	*Last Rank*	*District*	*First Rank*	*Last Rank*
Ajmer	Arian	Srinagar	Jaipur	Sanganer	Govindgarh
Alwar	Reni	Ramgarh	Jaisalmer	Sankra	Jaisalmer
Banswara	Anandpuri	Talwara	Jalor	Ahore	Jalor
Baran	Chhipabarod	Anta	Jhalawar	Bakani	Dag
Barmer	Baytoo	Siwana	Jhunjhunun	Buhana	Nawalgarh
Bharatpur	Deeg	Sewar	Jodhpur	Bap	Phalodi
Bhilwara	Sahara	Jahazpur	Karauli	Nadoti	Hindaun
Bikaner	Nokha	Bikaner	Kota	Chechat	Ladpura
Bundi	Hindoli	Talera	Nagaur	Degana	Kuchaman
Chittaurgarh	Kapasan	Arnod	Pali	Pali	Sumerpur
Churu	Dungargarh	Sardarshahar	Rajsamand	Kumbhalgahr	Rajsamand
Dausa	Dausa	Bandikui	Sawai Madhopur	Khandar	Gangapur
Dhaulpur	Bari	Dhaulpur	Sikar	Fatehpur	Sri Madhopur
Dungarpur	Simalwara	Aspur	Sirohi	Reodar	Sheoganj
Ganganagar	Sadulshahar	Padampur	Tonk	Todaraisingh	Uniara
Hanumangarh	Bhadra	Hanumangarh	Udaipur	Bargaon	Girwa

Source: Annex 14.1, Col. 4

TABLE 14.3: Classification of PSs on the Basis of GINI (1998-99): Rajasthan

Groups	*Included PSs*			
	No.	*%*	*Distributed in*	
			Districts	*Divisions*
Very High (VH), (>=0.75)	73	30.8	21	6
High (H), (0.70-0.75)	97	40.9	24	6
Medium (M), (0.65-0.70)	56	23.6	17	6
Low (L), (0.60-0.65)	9	3.8	4	3
Very Low (VL), (<=0.60)	2	0.8	2	2
Total	**237**	**100**		

Source: Annex 14.2.

Classification of PSs by GINI

On the basis of GINI, PSs of the state are classified into five groups viz. Very High (VH), High (H), Medium (M), Low (L) and Very Low (VL) as presented in Table 14.3. The state had clear-cut dominance of H (40.9 %) level PSs followed by VH (30.8%), M (23.6%), L (3.8%) and VL (0.8%) level PSs.

Division-wise classification and distribution of PSs by GINI levels is shown in Table 14.4. Following conclusions can be drawn:

- Jaipur division dominated not only in VH level PSs (24.7%) but also in H (31%) level PSs. On the other hand, Jodhpur division was the most deprived, and led in M to VL (29%) level PSs.
- Jodhpur and Udaipur were the only devisions having PSs in all the 5 levels. Ajmer division had PSs in 4 levels while Jaipur and Bikaner division had PSs in 3 levels.
- While the PSs having VH, H and M GINI were widely spread over all the 6 divisions, the PSs having L and VL GINI were concentrated in 3 and 2 divisions respectively.
- VH level PSs were leading in both Bikaner (57%) and Udaipur (33%) divisions while H level PSs were leading in Jaipur (49%), Ajmer (47%), Kota (44%) and Jodhpur (43%) divisions.

- The percentage of VH level PSs in Bikaner, Kota and Udaipur divisions; H level in Jaipur, Ajmer and Jodhpur divisions; M level in Bikaner and Jodhpur divisions, L as well as VL level in both Jodhpur and Udaipur divisions were higher than the state average.

TABLE 14.4: Division-wise Classification and Distribution of PSs on the Basis of GINI Level (1998-99)

Divisions	*Classification*						*Distribution (% Share)*				
	GINI Level						*GINI Level*				
	Very High	*High*	*Medium*	*Low*	*Very Low*	*Total PSs*	*Very High*	*High*	*Medium*	*Low*	*Very Low*
Jaipur	18	30	13	—	—	61	24.7		23.2	—	—
	(29.5)	(49.2)	(21.3)	—	—	(100.0)					
Bikaner	12	4	5	—	—	21	16.4	4.1	8.9	—	—
	(57.1)	(19.0)	(23.8)	—	—	(100.0)					
Ajmer	10	17	8	1	—	36	13.7	17.5	14.3	11.1	—
	(27.8)	(47.2)	(22.2)	(2.8)	—	(100.0)					
Kota	13	14	5	—	—	32	17.8	14.4	8.9	—	—
	(40.6)	(43.8)	(15.6)	—	—	(100.0)					
Jodhpur	5	18	14	4	1	42	6.8	18.6	25.0	44.4	50.0
	(11.9)	(42.9)	(33.3)	(9.5)	(2.4)	(100.0)					
Udaipur	15	14	11	4	1	45	20.5	14.4	19.6	44.4	50.0
	(33.3)	(31.1)	(24.4)	(8.9)	(2.2)	(100.0)					
Total	**73**	**97**	**56**	**9**	**2**	**237**	**100**	**100**	**100**	**100**	**100**
	(30.8)	**(40.9)**	**(23.6)**	**(3.8)**	**(0.8)**	**(100.0)**					

Figure in brackets shows percentage share to total Panchayat Samities
Note: GINI Level VH : (>=0.75), H : (0.70-0.75), M : (0.65-0.70), L : (0.60-0.65), VL : (<0.60)
Source: Annex 14.2

Very High GINI Area

Very High GINI area was distributed in 21 districts and all the 6 divisions. There were total 73 PSs in this group. As mentioned earlier, Jaipur division led with 24.7 per cent share followed by Udaipur (20.5%), Kota (17.8%), Bikaner (16.4%), Ajmer (13.7%) and Jodhpur (8%) divisions. The percentage share of VH level PSs to total PSs ranged between a maximum of 57.1 in Bikaner and a minimum of 11.9 in Jodhpur division. Among the districts, Jaipur dominated with 13 PSs followed by Chittaurgarh (12); Ajmer (8); Baran, Ganganagar and Kota (5 each); Bikaner (4); Alwar and Jodhpur (3 each); Bundi, Hanumangarh and Rajsamand (2 each); Bharatpur, Bhilwara, Churu, Pali, Sawai Madhopur, Sikar, Sirohi, Tonk and Udaipur (1 each) districts. Ajmer, Baran, Bikaner, Bundi, Chittaurgarh, Ganganagar, Hanumangarh, Jaipur, Jodhpur and Kota districts had higher percentage of these PSs than the state average (30.8%). The percentage ranged between a maximum of 100 in Ajmer, Bikaner, Jaipur and Kota districts and a minimum of 9 in Bhilwara and Udaipur.

High GINI Area

High GINI area was widely spread over 24 districts and over all the six divisions. As mentioned earlier, the state had dominance (41%) of H level PSs. There were total 97 PSs in this category. Jaipur division topped with 30.9 per cent share followed by Jodhpur (18.6%), Ajmer (17.5%), Kota and Udaipur (14.4% each) and Bikaner (4.1%) divisions respectively.

The percentage of H level PSs to total PSs was the highest 49.2 in Jaipur, 47.2 in Ajmer, 43.8 in Kota, 42.9 in Jodhpur, 31.1 in Udaipur and was the lowest 19 in Bikaner division. Jaipur, Ajmer, Kota and Jodhpur divisions had percentage share of H level PSs higher than the state average (40.9%). Among the districts, Alwar led with 11 PSs followed by Bhilwara (10); Udaipur (9); Pali (7); Bharatpur (6); Dausa, Jodhpur and Tonk (5 each); Jhalawar, Jhunjhunun, Sawai Madhopur, Sikar and Sirohi (4 each); Baran, Bundi, Chittaurgarh, Churu, Ganganagar, Karauli, Nagaur, Rajsamand (2 each) and Banswara, Jaisalmer and Jalor (one each) districts respectively (Table 14.7). All these districts, except Banswara, Baran, Chittaurgarh, Churu, Ganganagar, Jaisalmer, Jalor, Karauli, Nagaur and Rajsamand had higher percentage of H level PSs than the state average. The percentage ranged between the highest 100 in Dausa district and the lowest 14 in and Jalor.

TABLE 14.5: District-wise Classification of PSs on the Basis of GINI Level (1998-99)

District	*GINI Level*					*Total PSs*
	VH	*H*	*M*	*L*	*VL*	
Ajmer	8 (100.0)	—	—	—	—	8 (100.0)
Alwar	3 (21.4)	11 (78.6)	—	—	—	14 (100.0)
Banswara	—	1 (12.5)	7 (87.5)	—	—	8 (100.0)
Baran	5 (71.4)	2 (28.6)	—	—	—	7 (100.0)
Barmer	—	—	4 (50.0)	3 (37.5)	1 (12.5)	8 (100.0)
Bharatpur	1 (11.1)	6 (66.7)	2 (22.2)	—	—	9 (100.0)
Bhilwara	1 (9.1)	10 (90.9)	—	—	—	11 (100.0)
Bikaner	4 (100.0)	—	—	—	—	4 (100.0)
Bundi	2 (50.0)	2 (50.0)	—	—	—	4 (100.0)
Chittaurgarh	12 (85.7)	2 (14.3)	—	—	—	14 (100.0)
Churu	1 (14.3)	2 (28.6)	4 (57.1)	—	—	7 (100.0)
Dausa	—	5 (100.0)	—	—	—	5 (100.0)
Dhaulpur	—	—	4 (100.0)	—	—	4 (100.0)
Dungarpur	—	—	—	4 (80.0)	1 (20.0)	5 (100.0)
Ganganagar	5 (71.4)	2 (28.6)	—	—	—	7 (100.0)
Hanumangarh	2 (66.7)	—	1 (33.3)	—	—	3 (100.0)
Jaipur	13 (100.0)	—	—	—	—	13 (100.0)
Jaisalmer	—	1 (33.3)	2 (66.7)	—	—	3 (100.0)
Jalor	—	1 (14.3)	5 (71.4)	1 (14.3)	—	7 (100.0)
Jhalawar	—	4 (66.7)	2 (33.3)	—	—	6 (100.0)
Jhunjhunun	—	4 (50.0)	4 (50.0)	—	—	8 (100.0)
Jodhpur	3 (33.3)	5 (55.6)	1 (11.1)	—	—	9 (100.0)
Karauli	—	2 (40.0)	3 (60.0)	—	—	5 (100.0)
Kota	(5) (100.0)	—	—	—	—	5 (100.0)
Nagaur	—	2 (18.2)	8 (72.7)	1 (9.1)	—	11 (100.0)
Pali	1 (10.0)	7 (70.0)	2 (20.0)	—	—	10 (100.0)
Rajsamand	2 (28.6)	2 (28.6)	3 (42.9)	—	—	7 (100.0)
Sawai Madhopur	1 (20.0)	4 (80.0)	—	—	—	5 (100.0)
Sikar	1 (12.5)	4 (50.0)	3 (37.5)	—	—	8 (100.0)
Sirohi	1 (20.0)	4 (80.0)	—	—	—	5 (100.0)
Tonk	1 (16.7)	5 (83.3)	—	—	—	6 (100.0)
Udaipur	1 (9.1)	9 (81.8)	1 (9.1)	—	—	11 (100.0)
Rajasthan	**73 (30.8)**	**97 (40.9)**	**56 (23.6)**	**9 (3.8)**	**2 (0.8)**	**237 (100.0)**

Figures in brackets show percentage share of total Panchayat Samities

Note: GINI Level VH : (>=0.75), H : (0.70-0.75), M : (0.65-0.70), L : (0.60-0.65), VL : (<0.60)

Source: Annex 14.2.

TABLE 14.6: Distribution of PSs having Very High GINI Level 1998-99

S. No.	*District*	*No. & Name of PSs (in Descending Order)*
		Very High Level (73)
1	Jaipur	13—Sanganer, Jhotwara, Chaksu, Phagi, Jamwa Ramgarh, Dudu, Amber, Bassi, Kotputli, Viratnagar, Sambhar, Shahpura and Govindgarh
2	Chittaurgarh	12—Kapasan, Bari Sadari, Chhoti Sadri, Dungla, Rashmi, Begun, Bhadesar, Gangrar, Bhopalsagar, Nimbahera, Chittaurgarh and Pratapgarh
3	Ajmer	8—Arian, Bhinay, Kekri, Masooda, Kishangarh, Pisangan, Jawaja and Srinagar
4	Baran	5—Chhipabarod, Chhabra, Kishanganj, Shahbad and Atru
5	Ganganagar	5—Sadulshahar, Karanpur, Suratgarh, Raisinghnagar and Ganganagar
6	Kota	5—Chechat, Sangod, Itawa, Sultanpur and Ladpura
7	Bikaner	4—Nokha, Lunkaransar, Kolayat and Bikaner
8	Alwar	3—Reni, Behror and Rajgarh
9	Jodhpur	3—Bap, Bilara and Bhopalgarh
10	Bundi	2—Hindoli and Nainwa
11	Hanumangarh	2—Bhadra and Nohar
12	Rajsamand	2—Kumbhalgarh and Railmagra
13	Bharatpur	1—Deeg
14	Bhilwara	1—Sahara
15	Churu	1—Dungargarh
16	Pali	1—Pali
17	Sawai Madhopur	1—Khandar
18	Sikar	1—Fatehpur
19	Sirohi	1—Reodar
20	Tonk	1—Todaraisingh
21	Udaipur	1—Bargaon

Source: Annex 14.2

TABLE 14.7: Distribution of PSs having High GINI 1998-99

S. No.	*District*	*No. & Name of PSs (in Descending Order)*
		High Level (97)
1	Alwar	11—Kathumar, Lachhmangarh, Thanagazi, Kishangarh Bas, Kotkasim, Mandawar, Bansure, Nimrana, Umren, Tijara and Ramgarh
2	Bhilwara	10—Asind, Banera, Kotri, Shahpura, Suwana, Mandalgarh, Mandal, Hurda, Raipur and Jahazpur
3	Udaipur	9—Salumber, Bhinder, Dhariadwad, Jhadol, Gogunda, Kotra, Mavli, Kherwara Sarada
4	Pali	7—Sojat, Rohat, Kharchi/Marwar Jun., Rani Station, Jaitaran, Bali and Raipur
5	Bharatpur	6—Kaman, Kumher, Nadbai, Weir, Nagar Pahari and Bayana
6	Dausa	5—Dausa, Sikarai, Mahwa, Lalsot and Bandikui
7	Jodhpur	5—Luni, Osian, Shergarh, Balesar and Mandor
8	Tonk	5—Niwai, Tonk, Deoli, Malpura and Uniara
9	Jhalawar	4—Bakani, Manoharthana, Pirawa and Jhalarapatan
10	Jhunjhunun	4—Buhana, Jhunjhunun, Surajgarh and Alsisar
11	SMr	4—Bonli, Bamanwas, Sawai Madhopur and Gangapur
12	Sikar	4—Lachhmangarh, Piprali, Khandela and Dhond
13	Sirohi	4—Pindwara, Sirohi, Abu Road and Sheoganj
14	Baran	2—Baran and Anta
15	Bundi	2—Keshoraipatan and Talera
16	Chittaurgarh	2—Bhainsorgarh and Arnod
17	Churu	2—Taranagar and Rajgarh
18	Ganganagar	2—Anupgarh and Padampur
19	Karauli	2—Nadoti and Sapotra
20	Nagaur	2—Degana and Riyan
21	Rajsamand	2—Deogarh and Bhim
22	Banswara	1—Anandpuri
23	Jaisalmer	1—Sankra
24	Jalor	1—Ahore

Source: Annex 14.2

Medium GINI Area

This area was distributed in 17 districts and in all the 6 divisions. There were total 56 PSs in this group. Jodhpur division with 25 per cent share had the maximum concentration of these PSs followed by Jaipur (23.2%), Udaipur (19.6%), Ajmer (14.3%) and Bikaner and Kota (8.9% each) divisions. The percentage of M level PSs to total PSs was the highest 33.3 in Jodhpur, 24.4 in Udaipur, 23.8 in Bikaner, 22.2 in Ajmer, and the lowest 15.6 in Kota division. Bikaner, Jodhpur and Udaipur divisions had percentage of these PSs higher than the state average (23.6%). If we see district-wise distribution of these PSs it will be clear that Nagaur topped with 8 PSs followed by Banswara (7); Jalor (5); Barmer, Churu, Dhaulpur and Jhunjhunun (4 each); Karauli, Rajsamand and Sikar (3 each); Bharatpur, Jaisalmer, Jhalawar and Pali (2 each); and Hanumangarh, Jodhpur and Udaipur (one each) districts (Table 14.8). All these districts, except Bharatpur, Jodhpur and Pali had higher percentage of these PSs in comparison to the state average.

TABLE 14.8: Distribution of PSs having Medium GINI Level 1998-99

S. No.	*District*	*No. & Name of PSs (in Descending Order)*
		Medium Level (56)
1	Nagaur	8—Jayal, Mundwa, Nagaur, Merta, Ladnu, Parbatsar, Didwana and Makrana
2	Banswara	7—Bagidora, Sajjangarh, Kushalgarh, Peepalkhoont, Ghatol, Garhi and Talwara
3	Jalor	5—Bhinmal, Sanchore, Jaswantpura, Sayla and Raniwara
4	Barmer	4—Baytoo, Chohtan, Sindhari and Dhorimanna
5	Churu	4—Ratangarh, Churu, Sujangarh and Sardarshahar
6	Dhaulpur	4—Bari, Baseri, Rajakhera and Dhaulpur
7	Jhunjhunun	4—Chirawa, Khetri, Udaipurwati and Nawalgarh
8	Karauli	3—Todabhim, Karauli and Hindaun
9	Rajsamand	3—Amet, Khamnor, Rajsamand
10	Sikar	3—Danta Ramgarh, Neem ka Thana and Sri Madhopur
11	Bharatpur	2—Rupbas and Sewar
12	Jaisalmer	2—Sam and Jaisalmer
13	Jhalawar	2—Khanpur and Dag
14	Pali	2—Desuri and Sumerpur
15	Hanumangarh	1—Hanumangarh
16	Jodhpur	1—Phalodi
17	Udaipur	1—Girwa

Source: Annex 14.2

TABLE 14.9: Distribution of PSs having Low to Very Low GINI Level 1998-99

S. No.	*District*	*No. & Name of PSs (in Descending Order)*
		[A] Low Level (9)
1	Dungarpur	4—Simalwara, Dungarpur, Sagwara and Bichhiwara
2	Barmer	3—Balotra, Barmer and Sheo
3	Jalor	1—Jalor
4	Nagaur	1—Kuchaman
		[B] Very Low Level (2)
1	Barmer	1—Siwana
2	Dungarpur	1—Aspur

Source: Annex 14.2

Low and Very Low GINI Area

There were 9 Low GINI PSs concentrated in 4 districts and 3 divisions. Dungarpur district topped with 4 PSs followed by Barmer (3); Jalor and Nagaur (1 each) districts (Table 14.9). Siwana PS of Barmer district and Aspur of Dungarpur were the only 2 PSs having Very Low GINI.

15

GENDER EMPOWERMENT MEASURE (2001)

Highlights

- GEM Value, Rural Raj. : 0.759
- Percentage of AAPs 36.7%

	Panchayat Samiti	District	Division
• **Top**	Chechat, 0.915	Kota	Kota
• **Bottom**	Sheo, 0.557	Barmer	Jodhpur

The Gender Empowerment Measure (GEM) of Rural Rajasthan in the year 2001 was 0.759 and the index of deprivation (IOD) was 0.241. There were only 87 PSs (36.7%) having GEM above the state average. A great deal of spatial variation at PS level is seen in GEM value across the state as depicted in Fig 15.1 and Annex 15.1. While more than 38 per cent PSs of Bikaner and 33 per cent of Ajmer division had High to Very High Level (>0.8) of GEM, less than 5 per cent PSs of Jodhpur division found mention in this category. Jaipur division led (50% share) not only in having VH level of GEM but also in PSs having M (27.2%) and L (31.1%) level of GEM. On the other hand, Jodhpur division being the most deprived dominated (62.5% share) in VL level PSs. Ajmer division dominated (33.3%) in H level PSs. Barring a few exceptions, increase in the GEM level in the state sprang mainly from western and southern Rajasthan to northern, south-eastern and north-eastern Rajasthan.

TABLE 15.1: Distribution of First and Last Ten Panchayat Samities by GEM

S. No.	*First Ten PSs (Descending Order)*						*Last Ten PSs (Ascending Order)*					
	Districts/ PSs						*Districts/ PSs*					
	Kota	*Gg*	*Jp*	*Bhil*	*Chitt*	*Udaipur*	*Barmer*	*Karauli*	*Sikar*	*Dhaul*	*Jais*	*Jalor*
	(3)	*(2)*	*(3)*	*(1)*	*(1)*	*(1)*	*(3)*	*(2)*	*(2)*	*(1)*	*(1)*	*(1)*
1	Chechat	Gg	Sanganer	Mandalgarh	Bhain[1]	Bargaon	Sheo	Sapotra	Neem[2]	Baseri	Sam	Raniwara
2	Sultanpur	Suratgarh	Jhotwara	—	—	—	Chohtan	Todabhim	Khandela	—	—	—
3	Ladpura	—	Amber	—	—	—	Dhori-manna	—	—	—	—	—

Source: Annex 15.2 1 Bhainsrorgarh, 2 Neem ka Thana

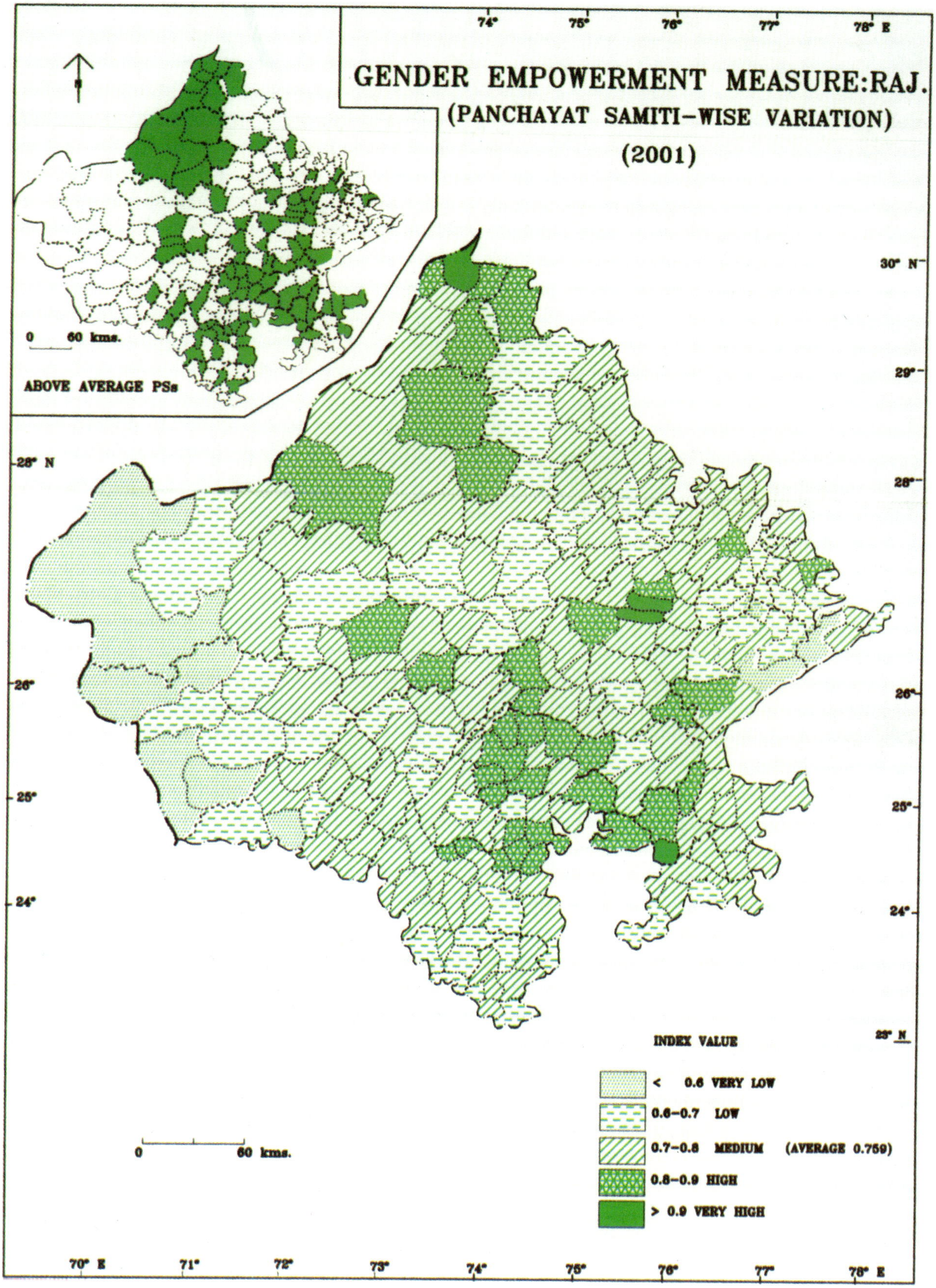
GENDER EMPOWERMENT MEASURE:RAJ.
(PANCHAYAT SAMITI-WISE VARIATION)
(2001)
ABOVE AVERAGE PSs
0 60 kms.
INDEX VALUE
< 0.6 VERY LOW
0.6-0.7 LOW
0.7-0.8 MEDIUM (AVERAGE 0.759)
0.8-0.9 HIGH
> 0.9 VERY HIGH
0 60 kms.
70° E
71°
72°
73°
74°
75°
76°
77°
78° E
30° N
29°
28° N
26°
25°
24°
23° N

FIG. 15.1

Chechat PS of Kota district had the maximum 0.915 GEM value followed by Sanganer, Jhotwara, Ganganagar, Bhainsrorgarh, Sultanpur, Ladpura, Suratgarh, Bargaon, Mandalgarh and Amber PSs (in descending order, Annex 15.2). These PSs were distributed in six districts. Kota dominated with 3 PSs followed by Ganganagar and Jaipur (2 each), Bhilwara, Chittaurgarh and Udaipur (one each) districts (Table 15.1). Sheo PS of Barmer district, on the other hand, had the minimum 0.557 GEM value preceded by Chohtan, Sam, Raniwara, Baseri, Dhorimanna, Sapotra, Todabhim, Neem ka Thana and Khandela PSs (ascending order). These last ten PSs were also concentrated in 6 districts. Barmer led with 3 PSs while Karauli and Sikar had 2 PSs each and Dhaulpur, Jaisalmer and Jalor had 1 PS. Similarly, district-wise first and the last PSs by GEM are presented in Table 15.2.

TABLE 15.2: District-wise First and Last PSs by GEM (2001)

District	*First Rank*	*Last Rank*	*District*	*First Rank*	*Last Rank*
Ajmer	Masooda	Bhinay	Jaipur	Sanganer	Phagi
Alwar	Umren	Kathumar	Jaisalmer	Sankra	Sam
Banswara	Garhi	Anandpuri	Jalor	Jalor	Raniwara
Baran	Chhipabarod	Atru	Jhalawar	Jhalrapatan	Bakani
Barmer	Balotra	Sheo	Jhunjhunun	Nawalgarh	Udaipurwati
Bharatpur	Sewar	Kaman	Jodhpur	Osian	Shergarh
Bhilwara	Mandalgarh	Banera	Karauli	Hindaun	Sapotra
Bikaner	Lunkaransar	Nokha	Kota	Chechat	Itawa
Bundi	Talera	Hindoli	Nagaur	Parbatsar	Ladnu
Chittaurgarh	Bhainsrorgarh	Arnod	Pali	Bali	Desuri
Churu	Dungargarh	Ratangarh	Rajsamand	Kumbhalgarh	Rajsamand
Dausa	Sikrai	Dausa	Sawai Madhopur	Sawai Madhopur	Bonli
Dhaulpur	Bari	Baseri	Sikar	Fatehpur	Neem ka Thana
Dungarpur	Dungarpur	Bichhiwara	Sirohi	Pindwara	Sheoganj
Ganganagar	Ganganagar	Padampur	Tonk	Uniara	Todaraisingh
Hanumangarh	Hanumangarh	Nohar	Udaipur	Bargaon	Dhairawad

Source: Annex 15.1, Col. 26.

TABLE 15.3: Classification of PSs on the Basis of GEM (2001): Rajasthan

Group	*Included PSs*			
	No.	*%*	*Distributed in*	
			Districts	*Divisions*
Very High (VH), (>=0.9)	4	1.7	3	3
High (H), (0.8-0.9)	36	15.2	15	6
Medium (M), (0.7-0.8)	125	52.7	31	6
Low (L), (0.6-0.7)	64	27.0	24	6
Very Low (VL) <0.6	8	3.4	5	3
Total	**237**	**100**		

Source: Annex 15.2.

Classification of PSs by GEM

On the basis of GEM value, PSs of the state are classified into five groups viz. Very High (VH), High (H), Medium (M), Low (L) and Very Low (VL) as presented in Table 15.3. As mentioned earlier, the state had clear-cut dominance of M (52.7 %) level PSs followed by L (27%), H (15.21%), VL (3.4%) and VH (1.7%) level PSs. If we look at division-wise classification and distribution of PSs by GEM (Table 15.4) following conclusions can be drawn:

- Jaipur division topped not only in PSs having VH GEM level (50% share) but also in PSs having

M (27.2%) and L (31.1%) level PSs. Similarly, Ajmer division dominated in H (33.3%) level PSs. On the other hand, Jodhpur division was the most deprived, and led in PSs having VL (62.5%) GEM level.

- Jaipur and Kota were the only divisions having PSs of all the five GEM value levels. Bikaner and Jodhpur divisions had PSs of 4 levels while, Ajmer and Udaipur divisions had PSs of 3 levels.
- While the PSs having H, M and L GEM value were widely spread over all the 6 divisions, the PSs having VH as well as VL GEM were concentrated each in 3 divisions.
- It is obvious that the percentage share of M level PSs to total PSs in all divisions ranged between a maximum of 59.4 per cent in Kota division and a minimum of 41.7 per cent in Ajmer division. The percentage of VH level PSs in Jaipur, Bikaner and Kota divisions; H level in Bikaner, Ajmer and Udaipur divisions; M level in Jaipur, Kota and Udaipur divisions; L level Jaipur, Jodhpur and Udaipur divisions and VL level in both Kota and Jodhpur divisions were higher than the state average.

TABLE 15.4: Division-wise Classification and Distribution of PSs on the Basis of GEM Level (2001)

Divisions	*Classification*						*Distribution (% Share)*				
	GINI Level						*GINI Level*				
	Very High	*High*	*Medium*	*Low*	*Very Low*	*Total PSs*	*Very High*	*High*	*Medium*	*Low*	*Very Low*
Jaipur	2	4	34	20	1	61	50.0	11.1	27.2	31.3	12.5
	(3.3)	(6.6)	(55.7)	(32.8)	(1.6)	(100.0)					
Bikaner	1	7	10	3	—	21	25.0	19.4	8.0	4.7	—
	(4.8)	(33.3)	(47.6)	(14.3)	—	(100.0)					
Ajmer	—	12	15	9	—	36	—	33.3	12.0	14.1	—
	—	(33.3)	(41.7)	(25.0)	—	(100.0)					
Kota	1	3	19	7	2	32	25.0	8.3	15.2	10.9	25.0
	(3.1)	(9.4)	(59.4)	(21.9)	(6.3)	(100.0)					
Jodhpur	—	2	22	13	5	42	—	5.6	17.6	20.3	62.5
	—	(4.8)	(52.4)	(31.0)	(11.9)	(100.0)					
Udaipur	—	8	25	12	—	45	—	22.2	20.0	18.8	—
	—	(17.8)	(55.6)	(26.7)	—	(100.0)					
Total	**4**	**36**	**125**	**64**	**8**	**237**	**100**	**100**	**100**	**100**	**100**
	(1.7)	**(15.2)**	**(52.7)**	**(27.0)**	**(3.4)**	**(100.0)**					

Figure in brackets shows percentage share to total Panchayat Samities

Note: GEM Level VH: (=>0.09), H : (0.8-0.9), M : (0.7-0.8), L : (0.6-0.7), VL : (<0.06)

Source: Annex 15.2.

Very High & High GEM Area

There were only 4 PSs namely Sanganer, Jhotwara (both of Jaipur dist.), Ganganagar (Gg) and Chechat (Kt) having VH level of GEM. The percentage of these PSs in Jaipur, Bikaner and Kota divisions as well as Jaipur, Ganganagar and Kota districts was higher than the state average (1.7%). The percentage of VH level PSs to total PSs ranged between a maximum of 4.8 in Bikaner and a minimum of 3.1 in Kota division and 20 in Kota district to 14.3 in Ganganagar.

High GEM area was widely spread over 15 districts and over all the six divisions. There were total 39 PSs in this category. Ajmer division topped with 33 per cent share followed by Udaipur (22.2%), Bikaner (19.4%), Jaipur (11.1%), Kota (8.3%) and Jodhpur (5.6%) divisions respectively. The percentage of H level PSs to total PSs was the highest 33.3 in both Bikaner and Ajmer divisions, 17.8 in Udaipur, 9.4 in Kota, 6.6 in Jaipur and was the lowest 4.8 in Jodhpur division. Bikaner, Ajmer and Udaipur divisions had percentage share of H level PSs higher than the state average (15.2%). Among the districts, Bhilwara led with 9 PSs followed by Chittaurgarh (6), Ganganagar (3), Ajmer, Bikaner, Jaipur, Jodhpur, Kota and Udaipur (2 each) and Alwar, Bharatpur, Churu, Hanumangarh, Sawai Madhopur and Tonk (1 each) respectively. All these districts, except Alwar, Bharatpur and Churu had higher percentage of H level PSs than the state average (15.2). The percentage ranged between the highest 81.8 in Bhilwara district to the lowest 7.1 in Alwar.

TABLE 15.5: District-wise Classification of PSs on the Basis of GEM Level (2001)

District	*GEM Level*					*Total PSs*
	VH	*H*	*M*	*L*	*VL*	
Ajmer	—	2 (25.0)	6 (75.0)	—	—	8 (100.0)
Alwar	—	1 (7.1)	9 (64.3)	4 (28.6)	—	14 (100.0)
Banswara	—	—	4 (50.0)	4 (50.0)	—	8 (100.0)
Baran	—	—	7 (100.0)	—	—	7 (100.0)
Barmer	—	—	1 (12.5)	4 (50.0)	3 (37.5)	8 (100.0)
Bharatpur	—	1 (11.1)	2 (22.2)	6 (66.7)	—	9 (100.0)
Bhilwara	—	9 (81.8)	2 (18.2)	—	—	11 (100.0)
Bikaner	—	2 (50.0)	2 (50.0)	—	—	4 (100.0)
Bundi	—	—	3 (75.0)	1 (25.0)	—	4 (100.0)
Chittaurgarh	—	6 (42.9)	6 (42.9)	2 (14.3)	—	14 (100.0)
Churu	—	1 (14.3)	4 (57.1)	2 (28.6)	—	7 (100.0)
Dausa	—	—	2 (40.0)	3 (60.0)	—	5 (100.0)
Dhaulpur	—	—	2 (50.0)	1 (25.0)	1 (25.0)	4 (100.0)
Dungarpur	—	—	1 (20.0)	4 (80.0)	—	5 (100.0)
Ganganagar	1 (14.3)	3 (42.9)	3 (42.9)	—	—	7 (100.0)
Hanumangarh	—	1 (33.3)	1 (33.3)	1 (33.3)	—	3 (100.0)
Jaipur	2 (15.4)	2 (15.4)	9 (69.2)	—	—	13 (100.0)
Jaisalmer	—	—	1 (33.3)	1 (33.3)	1 (33.3)	3 (100.0)
Jalor	—	—	4 (57.1)	2 (28.6)	1 (14.3)	7 (100.0)
Jhalawar	—	—	4 (66.7)	2 (33.3)	—	6 (100.0)
Jhunjhunun	—	—	7 (87.5)	1 (12.5)	—	8 (100.0)
Jodhpur	—	2 (22.2)	5 (55.6)	2 (22.2)	—	9 (100.0)
Karauli	—	—	—	3 (60.0)	2 (40.0)	5 (100.0)
Kota	1 (20.0)	2 (40.0)	2 (40.0)	—	—	5 (100.0)
Nagaur	—	—	3 (27.3)	8 (72.7)	—	11 (100.0)
Pali	—	—	6 (60.0)	4 (40.0)	—	10 (100.0)
Rajsamand	—	—	6 (85.7)	1 (14.3)	—	7 (100.0)
Sawai Madhopur	—	1 (20.0)	3 (60.0)	1 (20.0)	—	5 (100.0)
Sikar	—	—	3 (37.5)	5 (62.5)	—	8 (100.0)
Sirohi	—	—	5 (100.0)	—	—	5 (100.0)
Tonk	—	1 (16.7)	4 (66.7)	1 (16.7)	—	6 (100.0)
Udaipur	—	2 (18.2)	8 (72.7)	1 (9.1)	—	11 (100.0)
Rajasthan	**4 (1.7)**	**36 (15.2)**	**125 (52.7)**	**64 (27.0)**	**8 (3.4)**	**237 (100.0)**

Figures in brackets show percentage share to total Panchayat Samities

Note: GEM Level VH: (=>0.09), H : (0.8-0.9), M : (0.7-0.8), L : (0.6-0.7), VL : (<0.06) *Source*: Annex 15.2.

TABLE 15.6: Distribution of PSs having Very High and High Level of GEM (2001)

S. No.	*District*	*No. & Name of PSs (in Descending Order)*
		[I] Very High Level (4)
1	Jaipur	2—Sanganer and Jhotwara
2	Ganganagar	1—Ganganagar
3	Kota	1—Chechat
		[II] High Level (36)
1	Bhilwara	9—Mandalgarh, Mandal, Shahpura, Hurda, Sahara, Asind, Raipur, Suwana and Jahazpur
2	Chittaurgarh	6—Bhainsrorgarh, Bhadesar, Kapasan, Nimbahera, Chittaurgarh and Dungla
3	Ganganagar	3—Suratgarh, Karanpur and Sadulshahar
4	Jaipur	2—Amber and Dudu
5	Ajmer	2—Masooda and Pisangan
6	Bikaner	2—Kolayat and Lunkaransar
7	Jodhpur	2—Bilara and Osian
8	Kota	2—Sultanpur and Ladpura
9	Udaipur	2—Bargaon and Mavli
10	Alwar	1—Umren
11	Bharatpur	1—Sewar
12	Churu	1—Dungargarh
13	Hanumangarh	1—Hanumangarh
14	Sawai Madhopur	1—Sawai Madhopur
15	Tonk	1—Uniara

Source: Annex 15.2

Medium GEM Area

This area was spread over the entire state except Karauli district. There were total 125 PSs in this group. Jaipur division with 27.2 per cent share had the maximum concentration of these PSs followed by Udaipur (20%), Jodhpur (17.6%), Kota (15.2%), Ajmer (12%) and Bikaner (8%) divisions. The percentage of M level PSs to total PSs was the highest 59.4 in Kota, 55.7 in Jaipur, 55.6 in Udaipur, 52.4 in Jodhpur, 47.6 in Bikaner and the lowest 41.7 in Ajmer division. Jaipur, Kota, and Udaipur divisions had percentage of these PSs higher than the state average (52.7%). If we see district-wise distribution of these PSs it is clear that both Alwar and Jaipur topped with 9 PSs each followed by Udaipur (8); Jhunjhunun and Baran (7 each); Ajmer, Chittaurgarh, Pali and Rajsamand (6 each); Jodhpur and Sirohi (5 each); Banswara, Churu, Jalor, Jhalawar and Tonk (4 each); Bundi, Dungarpur, Ganganagar, Nagaur, Sawai Madhopur and Sikar (3 each); Bharatpur, Dausa, Bhilwara, Bikaner, Dhaulpur, Dungarpur, Kota (2 each) and Barmer, Dausa, Hanumangarh and Jaisalmer (1 each) respectively. Sixteen districts namely Ajmer, Alwar, Baran, Bundi, Churu, Jaipur, Jalor, Jhalawar, Jhunjhunun, Jodhpur, Rajsamand, Sawai Madhopur, Sirohi, Tonk and Udaipur had higher percentage of M level PSs than by the state average. The percentage of these PSs ranged between 100 in both Baran and Sirohi districts and 12.5 in Barmer.

Low and Very Low GEM Area

There were 64 Low GEM PSs distributed in 24 districts and all the 6 divisions. As mentioned earlier, Jaipur division with 31.3 per cent share had the highest concentration of these PSs followed by Jodhpur (20.3%), Udaipur (18.8%), Ajmer (14.1%), Kota (10.9%) and Bikaner (4.7%) divisions. The percentage of L level PSs to total PSs was also highest 32.8 in Jaipur division, 31 in Jodhpur, 26.7 in Udaipur, 25 in Ajmer, 21.9 in Kota and the lowest 14.3 in Bikaner division. Jaipur, Jodhpur and Udaipur divisions had higher percentage of these PSs than the state average (27%).

Among the districts, Nagaur led with 9 PSs followed by Bharatpur (6); Sikar (5); Alwar, Banswara, Barmer and Pali (4 each); Dausa, Dungarpur and Karauli (3 each); Chittaurgarh, Churu, Dhaulpur, Jalor,

Jhalawar and Jodhpur (2 each); and Bundi, Hanumangarh, Jaisalmer, Jhunjhunun, Rajsamand, Sawai Madhopur, Tonk and Udipur (1 each) districts respectively. Fourteen districts viz. Alwar, Banswara, Barmer, Bharatpur, Churu, Dungarpur, Hanumangarh, Jaisalmer, Jalor, Jhalawar, Karauli, Nagaur, Pali and Sikar had higher percentage of L level PSs than the state average. The percentage of these PSs ranged between 80 in Dungarpur district and 9.1 in Udaipur.

TABLE 15.7: Distribution of PSs having Medium Level of GEM (2001)

S. No.	*District*	*No. & Name of PSs (in Descending Order)*
		High Level (97)
1	Alwar	9—Kishangarh Bas, Lachhmangarh, Thanagazi, Behror, Bensure, Mandawar, Rajgarh, Ramgarh and Nimrana
2	Jaipur	9—Kotputli, Bassi, Jamwa Ramgarh, Shahpura, Govindgarh, Chaksu, Sambhar, Phagi and Viratnagar
3	Udaipur	8—Girwa, Bhinder, Kherwara, Salumbar, Kotra, Jhadol, Gogunda and Sarada
4	Baran	7—Chhipabarod, Baran, Kishanganj, Shahbad, Anta, Chabra and Atru
5	Jhunjhunun	7—Nawalgarh, Chirawa, Surajgarh, Jhunjhunun, Buhana, Khetri and Alsisar
6	Ajmer	6—Kekri, Jawaja, Kishangarh, Arian, Srinagar and Bhinay
7	Chittaurgarh	6—Pratapgarh, Bhopalsagar, Chhoti Sadri, Bari Sadri, Begun and Gangrar
8	Pali	6—Bali, Sumerpur, Raipur, Jaitaran, Pali and Sojat
9	Rajsamand	6—Kumbhalgarh, Amet, Railmagra, Bhim, Deogarh and Khamnor
10	Jodhpur	5—Luni, Mandor, Bhopalgarh, Bap and Balesar
11	Sirohi	5—Pindwara, Abu Road, Reodar, Sirohi and Sheoganj
12	Banswara	4—Garhi, Talwara, Bagidora and Ghatol
13	Churu	4—Churu, Rajgarh, Sujangarh and Taranagar
14	Jalor	4—Jalor, Sayla, Bhinmal and Ahore
15	Jhalawar	4—Jhalrapatan, Manoharthana, Khanpur and Pirwara
16	Tonk	4—Deoli, Tonk, Niwai and Malpura
17	Bundi	3—Talera, Keshoraipatan and Nainwa
18	Ganganagar	3—Anupgarh, Raisinghnagar and Padampur
19	Nagaur	3—Parbatsar, Kuchaman and Jayal
20	Sawai Madhopur	3—Gangapur, Khandar and Bamanwas
21	Sikar	3—Fatehpur, Piprali and Danta Ramgarh
22	Bharatpur	2—Nadbai and Nagar Pahari
23	Bhilwara	2—Kotri and Banera
24	Bikaner	2—Bikaner and Nokha
25	Dausa	2—Sikrai and Lalsot
26	Dhaulpur	2—Bari and Dhaulpur
27	Kota	2—Sangod and Itawa
28	Barmer	1—Balotra
29	Dungarpur	1—Dungarpur
30	Hanumangarh	1—Bhadra
31	Jaisalmer	1—Sankra

Source: Annex 15.2

There were only 8 PSs in the VL category concentrated in 5 districts and 3 divisions. Jodhpur division led with 5 PSs followed by Kota (2) and Jaipur (1) divisions. Jodhpur and Kota divisions had higher percentage of these PSs than the state average (3.4%). If we see district-wise distribution of these PSs, it will be clear that Barmer was at the top rank with 3 PSs, Karauli had 2 while, Dhaulpur, Jaisalmer and Jalor had 1 PS each. All these districts had higher percentage of these PSs than the state average. The percentage of these PSs ranged between 40 in Karauli district and 14.3 in Jalor.

TABLE 15.8: Distribution of PSs having Low and Very Low Level of GEM (2001)

S. No.	*District*	*No. & Name of PSs (in Descending Order)*
		[A] Low Level (64)
1	Nagaur	8—Riyan, Merta, Makrana, Nagaur, Mundwa, Degana, Didwana and Ladnu
2	Bharatpur	6—Weir, Kumher, Bayana, Rupbas, Deeg and Kaman
3	Sikar	5—Sri Madhopur, Lachhmangarh, Dhond, Khandela and Neem ka Thana
4	Alwar	4—Tijara, Kotkasim, Reni, and Kathumar
5	Banswara	4—Kushalgarh, Sajjangarh, Peepalkhoont and Anandpuri
6	Barmer	4—Siwana, Bayatoo, Barmer and Sindhari
7	Dungarpur	4—Sagwara, Simalwara, Aspur and Bichhiwara
8	Pali	4—Rohat, Kharchi/Marwar Jun., Rani Station and Desuri
9	Dausa	3—Bandikui, Mahwa and Dausa
10	Karauli	3—Hindaun, Nadoti and Karauli
11	Chittaurgarh	2—Rashmi and Arnod
12	Churu	2—Sardarshaher and Ratangarh
13	Jalor	2—Jaswantpura and Sanchore
14	Jhalawar	2—Dag and Bakani
15	Jodhpur	2—Phalodi and Shergarh
16	Bundi	1—Hindoli
17	Dhaulpur	1—Rajakhera
18	Hanumangarh	1—Nohar
19	Jaisalmer	1—Jaisalmer
20	Jhunjhunun	1—Udaipurwati
21	Rajsamand	1—Rajsamand
22	Sawai Mdhopur	1—Bonli
23	Tonk	1—Todaraisingh
24	Udaipur	1—Dhariawad
		[B] Very Low Level (8)
1	Barmer	3—Dhorimanna, Chohtan and Sheo
2	Karauli	2—Todhabhim and Sapotra
3	Dhaulpur	1—Baseri
4	Jaisalmer	1—Sam
5	Jalor	1—Raniwara

Source: Annex 15.2

16

HUMAN DEVELOPMENT INDEX (1991)

Highlights

- Rural HDI-Raj. : 0.3938
- Percentage of AAPs: 42.2
- 94.5 PSs had HDI below 0.5

	Panchayat Samiti	District	Division
• **Top**	Chechat (0.5464)	Kota	Kota
• **Bottom**	Sheo (0.2148)	Barmer	Jodhpur

The Human Development Index (HDI) of rural Rajasthan in the year 1991 was 0.3938. There were 100 PSs having HDI above the state average. A great deal of regional disparity is observed in HDI across the state. Both Jaipur and Kota divisons dominated in PSs having High HDI (30.8% share each) followed by Bikaner (23.1%), Ajmer (5.6%) divisions, no PS of Udaipur and Jodhpur divisions qualified for a place in this category. Jodhpur and Udaipur divisions accounted 45.5 per cent and 36.4 per cent PSs having VL HDI.

Chechat PS of Kota district had the maximum HDI (0.5464) followed by Karanpur, Sangod, Ladpura, Sultanpur, Govindgarh, Ganganagar, Kekri, Shahpura, and Pisangan PSs (in descending order, Annex 16.2). These top ten PSs were concentrated in four districts. Kota had four PSs while Ganganagar, Jaipur and Ajmer each had 2 PSs (Table 16.1).

TABLE 16.1: Distribution of First and Last Ten Panchayat Samities by HDI, (1991)

S. No.	*First Ten PSs (Descending Order)*				*Last Ten PSs (Ascending Order)*		
	Districts/ PSs				*Districts/ PSs*		
	Kota	*Gg*	*Jaipur*	*Ajmer*	*Barmer*	*Banswara*	*Jais*
	(4)	*(2)*	*(2)*	*(2)*	*(7)*	*(2)*	*(1)*
1	Chechat	Karanpur	Govindgarh	Kekri	Sheo	Kushalgarh	Sam
2	Sangod	Ganganagar	Shahpura	Pisangan	Barmer	Peepalkhoont	—
3	Ladpura	—	—	—	Chohtan	—	—
4	Sultanpur	—	—	—	Baytoo	—	—
5.		—	—	—	Dhorimanna	—	—
6.		—	—	—	Sindhari	—	—
7.		—	—	—	Balotra	—	—

Source: Annex 16.1

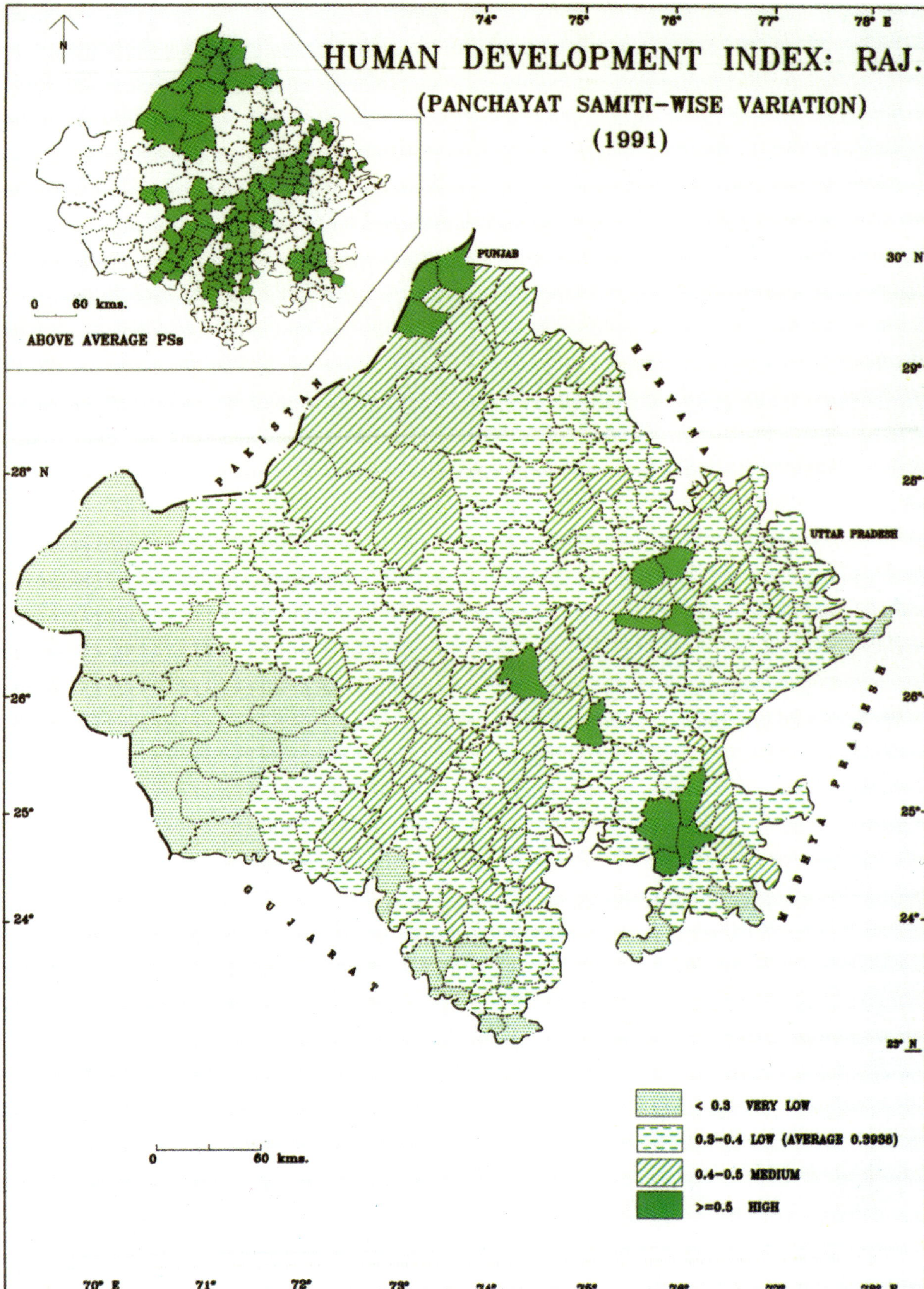
HUMAN DEVELOPMENT INDEX: RAJ.
(PANCHAYAT SAMITI-WISE VARIATION)
(1991)
N
0 60 kms.
ABOVE AVERAGE PSs
PUNJAB
PAKISTAN
HARYANA
UTTAR PRADESH
MADHYA PRADESH
GUJARAT
< 0.3 VERY LOW
0.3-0.4 LOW (AVERAGE 0.3938)
0.4-0.5 MEDIUM
>=0.5 HIGH
0 60 kms.
70° E 71° 72° 73° 74° 75° 76° 77° 78° E
30° N 29° 28° N 26° 25° 24° 23° N

FIG. 16.1

Sheo PS of Barmer district, on the other hand, had the minimum (0.2148) HDI. It was preceded by Barmer, Chohtan, Baytoo, Dhorimanna, Sindhari, Kushalgarh, Sam, Peepalkhoont and Balotra PSs (in ascending order). These last ten PSs were located in three districts. Barmer dominated with 7 PSs while Banswara had 2, and Jaisalmer had 1 PS. Similarly, district-wise first and the last PSs by HDI are shown in Table 16.2.

TABLE 16.2: District-wise First and Last PSs by GEM (2001)

District	*First Rank*	*Last Rank*	*District*	*First Rank*	*Last Rank*
Ajmer	Kekri	Jawaja	Jaipur	Govindgarh	Dudu
Alwar	Behror	Umren	Jaisalmer	Sankra	Sam
Banswara	Garhi	Kushalgarh	Jalor	Ahore	Sanchore
Baran	Atru	Chhabra	Jhalawar	Pirawa	Dag
Barmer	Balotra	Siwana	Jhunjhunun	Jhunjhunun	Khetri
Bharatpur	Kumher	Nagar Pahari	Jodhpur	Bilara	Bap
Bhilwara	Hurda	Mandalgarh	Karauli	Nadauti	Karauli
Bikaner	Bikaner	Kolayat	Kota	Chechat	Itawa
Bundi	Nainwa	Hindoli	Nagaur	Merta	Nagaur
Chittaurgarh	Bhopalsagar	Bhainsrorgarh	Pali	Sumerpur	Raipur
Churu	Taranagar	Sardarshahar	Rajsamand	Railmagra	Deogarh
Dausa	Dausa	Lalsot	Sawai Madhopur	Bonli	Khandar
Dhaulpur	Baseri	Bari	Sikar	Fatehpur	Neem ka Thana
Dungarpur	Sagwara	Simalwara	Sirohi	Pindwara	Abu Road
Ganganagar	Karanpur	Anupgarh	Tonk	Malpura	Uniara
Hanumangarh	Bhadra	Nohar	Udaipur	Mavli	Kotra

Source: Annex 17.1, Col. 6.

TABLE 16.3: Classification of PSs on the Basis of HDI (1991): Rajasthan

Group	*HDI*			
	No.	*%*	*Distributed in*	
			Districts	*Divisions*
High (H), (>=0.5)	13	5.5	4	4
Medium (M), (0.4-0.5)	76	32.1	18	6
Low (L), (0.3-0.4)	126	53.2	25	6
Very Low (VL), (<0.3)	22	9.3	8	4
Total	**237**	**100**		

Source: Annex 16.1

Classification of PSs by HDI

Table 16.3 presents the classification of PSs by HDI. The state had dominance of Low Level PSs (53.2%) followed by Medium (32.1%), Very Low (9.3%), and High (5.5%) level PSs. If we look at division-wise classification and distribution of PSs by HDI (Table 16.4) following conclusions can be drawn:

- Both Jaipur and Kota divisions had PSs of all the four levels, while other divisions had PSs of 3 levels.
- Jaipur division was at the top position with 30.3 per cent share of PSs having High to Medium level of HDI.
- Jodhpur division was the most deprived, and led in PSs having VL (45.5%) HDI level followed by Udaipur (36.4%) division.
- Except Bikaner, all divisions had dominance of L level PSs. Bikaner division had dominance of M level PSs.
- The percentage of H level PSs in Jaipur, Bikaner, Ajmer and Kota divisions; M level in Jaipur, Bikaner and Jodhpur divisions; L level in Jaipur, Ajmer and Kota, divisions and VL level in Jodhpur and Udaipur divisions was higher than the state average.

TABLE 16.4: Division-wise Classification and Distribution of PSs by HDI (1991)

Divisions	*Classification*					*Distribution (% Share)*			
	HDI Level					*HDI Level*			
	High	*Medium*	*Low*	*Very Low*	*Total PSs*	*High*	*Medium*	*Low*	*Very Low*
Jaipur	4 (6.6)	23 (37.7)	32 (52.5)	2 (3.3)	61 (100.0)	30.8	30.3	25.4	9.1
Bikaner	3 (14.3)	11 (52.4)	7 (33.3)	— —	21 (100.0)	23.1	14.5	5.6	—
Ajmer	2 (5.6)	11 (30.6)	23 (63.9)	— —	36 (100.0)	15.4	14.5	18.3	—
Kota	4 (12.5)	5 (15.6)	21 (65.6)	2 (6.3)	32 (100.0)	30.8	6.6	16.7	9.1
Jodhpur	— —	15 (35.7)	17 (40.5)	10 (23.8)	42 (100.0)	—	19.7	13.5	45.5
Udaipur	— —	11 (24.4)	26 (57.8)	8 (17.8)	45 (100.0)	—	14.5	20.6	36.4
Total	**13 (5.5)**	**76 (32.1)**	**126 (53.2)**	**22 (9.3)**	**237 (100.0)**	**100.0**	**100**	**100**	**100**

Figures in brackets show percentage share to total Panchayat Samities.
Note: HDI Level H : (>=0.5), M : (0.4-0.5), L : (0.3-0.4), VL : (<0.3).
Source: Annex 16.1

High HDI Region

There were only 13 PSs having High HDI which were concentrated in 4 districts falling under 4 divisions. Both Jaipur and Kota districts had 4 PSs each while Ganganagar had 3 and Ajmer had 1 PS in this group. All these 4 districts had greater percentage of H level PSs in comparison to the state average (5.5). The percentage ranged between 80 in Kota district and 25 in Ajmer (Table 16.5 and 16.6).

Medium HDI Region

PSs having Medium HDI were distributed in 18 districts and 6 divisions. There were total 76 M level PSs. Jaipur division with 30.3 per cent share had the maximum concentration of these PSs followed by Jodhpur (19.7%), Bikaner, Ajmer and Udaipur (14.5% each) and Kota (6.6%) divisions. The percentage share of M level PSs to total PSs was the highest 52.5 in Bikaner, 37.7 in Jaipur, 35.7 in Jodhpur, 30.6 in Ajmer, 24.4 in Udaipur and the lowest 15.6 in Kota division.

District-wise distribution of these PSs makes it clear that Jaipur secured the top rank with 9 PSs followed by Pali (8); Alwar (7); Ajmer (6); Chittaurgarh (5); Baran, Bikaner, Ganganagar, Jodhpur and Udaipur (4 each). Hanumangarh, Sikar and Sirohi (3 each) and Bharatpur, Jhunjhunun and Rajsamand (2 each) and Kota (1) districts respectively. All the above districts, except Bharatpur, Jhunjhunun, Kota and Rajsamand had higher percentage of Medium level PSs in comparison to the state average (32.1). Bikaner and Hanumangarh districts had the highest percentage (100) of M level PSs while, Kota had the lowest (20).

Low HDI Region

Low HDI area was widely spread over all the 6 divisions and 25 districts (except Ajmer, Barmer, Bikaner, Ganganagar, Hanumangarh, Jaipur and Kota). There were total 126 PSs in this category. Jaipur division again led with 25.4 per cent share followed by Udaipur (20.6 %), Ajmer (18.3 %), Kota (16.7%), Jodhpur (13.5%) and Bikaner (5.6%) divisions.

Among the districts, Nagaur dominated with 11 PSs followed by Chittaurgarh (9); Alwar, Bharatpur and Churu (7 each); Bhilwara, Jalor, Jhunjhunun, Tonk and Udaipur (6 each), Banswara, Dausa, Jodhpur, Rajsamand, Sawai Madhopur and Sikar (5 each); Bundi and Jhalawar and Karauli (4 each); Baran (3), Dhaulpur, Jaisalmer, Pali and Sirohi (2 each) and Dungarpur (1) districts respectively.

TABLE 16.5: District-wise Classification of PSs by HDI (1991)

District	*HDI Level*				*Total PSs*
	VH	*H*	*M*	*L*	
Ajmer	2 (25.0)	6 (75.0)	—	—	8 (100.0)
Alwar	—	7 (50.0)	7 (50.0)	—	14 (100.0)
Banswara	—	—	5 (62.5)	3 (37.5)	8 (100.0)
Baran	—	4 (57.1)	3 (42.9)	—	7 (100.0)
Barmer	—	—	—	8 (100.0)	8 (100.0)
Bharatpur	—	2 (22.2)	7 (77.8)	—	9 (100.0)
Bhilwara	—	5 (45.5)	6 (54.5)	—	11 (100.0)
Bikaner	—	4 (100.0)	—	—	4 (100.0)
Bundi	—	—	4 (100.0)	—	4 (100.0)
Chittaurgarh	—	5 (35.7)	9 (64.3)	—	14 (100.0)
Churu	—	—	7 (100.0)	—	7 (100.0)
Dausa	—	—	5 (100.0)	—	5 (100.0)
Dhaulpur	—	—	2 (50.0)	2 (50.0)	4 (100.0)
Dungarpur	—	—	1 (20.0)	4 (80.0)	5 (100.0)
Ganganagar	3 (42.9)	4 (57.1)	—	—	7 (100.0)
Hanumangarh	—	3 (100.0)	—	—	3 (100.0)
Jaipur	4 (30.8)	9 (69.2)	—	—	13 (100.0)
Jaisalmer	—	—	2 (66.7)	1 (33.3)	3 (100.0)
Jalor	—	—	6 (85.7)	1 (14.3)	7 (100.0)
Jhalawar	—	—	4 (66.7)	2 (33.3)	6 (100.0)
Jhunjhunun	—	2 (25.0)	6 (75.0)	—	8 (100.0)
Jodhpur	—	4 (44.4)	5 (55.6)	—	9 (100.0)
Karauli	—	—	5 (100.0)	—	5 (100.0)
Kota	4 (80.0)	1 (20.0)	—	—	5 (100.0)
Nagaur	—	—	11 (100.0)	—	11 (100.0)
Pali	—	8 (80.0)	2 (20.0)	—	10 (100.0)
Rajsamand	—	2 (28.6)	5 (71.4)	—	7 (100.0)
S. Madhopur	—	—	5 (100.0)	—	5 (100.0)
Sikar	—	3 (37.5)	5 (62.5)	—	8 (100.0)
Sirohi	—	3 (60.0)	2 (40.0)	—	5 (100.0)
Tonk	—	—	6 (100.0)	—	6 (100.0)
Udaipur	—	4 (36.4)	6 (54.5)	1 (9.1)	11 (100.0)
Rajasthan	**13** **(5.5)**	**76** **(32.1)**	**126** **(53.2)**	**22** **(9.3)**	**237** **(100.0)**

Figures in brackets show percentage share to total Panchayat Samities.
Source: Annex 16.1

Note: HDI Level H : (>=0.5), M : (0.4-0.5), L : (0.3-0.4), VL : (<0.3).

TABLE 16.6: Distribution of PSs having High and Medium HDI Level (1991)

S. No.	*District*	*No. & Name of PSs (in Descending Order)*
		[I] High Level (13)
1	Jaipur	4—Govindgarh, Shahpura, Bassi and Sanganer
2	Kota	4—Chechat, Sangod, Ladpura and Sultanpur
3	Ganganagar	3—Karanpur, Ganganagar and Raisinghnagar
4	Ajmer	2—Kekri, Pisangan
		[I] Medium Level (76)
1	Jaipur	9—Amber, Jhotwara, Kotputli, Jamwa Ramgarh, Sambhar, Phagi, Viratnagar, Chaksu and Dudu
2	Pali	8—Sumerpur, Rani Station, Sojat, Bali, Desuri, Kharchi-Marwar Junction, Pali and Jaitaran
3	Alwar	7—Behror, Nimrana, Mandawar, Kotkasim, Rajgarh, Reni and Kishangarh Bas
4	Ajmer	6—Bhinay, Srinagar, Masooda, Kishangarh, Arian and Jawaja
5	Bhilwara	5—Hurda, Sahara, Banera, Mandal and Suwana
6	Chittaurgarh	5—Bhopalgarh, Rashmi, Nimbahera, Kapasan and Chhoti Sadri
7	Baran	4—Atru, Baran, Chipabarod and Anta
8	Bikaner	4—Bikaner, Nokha, Lunkaransar and Kolayat
9	Ganganagar	4—Sadulshahar, Padampur, Suratgarh and Anupgarh
10	Jodhpur	4—Bilara, Bhopalgarh, Luni and Balesar
11	Udaipur	4—Mavli, Bargaon, Bhinder and Sarada
12	Hanumangarh	3—Bhadra, Hanumangarh and Nohar
13	Sikar	3—Fatehpur, Dhond and Lachhmangarh
14	Sirohi	3—Pindwara, Sirohi and Sheoganj
15	Bharatpur	2—Kumher and Weir
16	Jhunjhunun	2—Jhunjhunun and Buhana
17	Rajsamand	2—Railmagra and Khamnor
18	Kota	1—Itawa

Source: Annex 16.1

TABLE 16.7: Distribution of PSs having High and Medium HDI Level (1991)

S. No.	*District*	*No. & Name of PSs (in Descending Order)*
		Low Level (126)
1	Nagaur	11—Merta, Riyan, Ladnu, Degana, Parbatsar, Kuchaman, Mundwa, Makrana, Didwana, Jayal and Nagaur
2	Chittaurgarh	9—Chittaurgarh, Dungla, Gangrar, Bari Sadari, Begun, Bhadesar, Arnod, Pratapgarh and Bhainsrorgarh
3	Alwar	7—Bansure, Kathumar, Thanagazi, Lachhmangarh, Tijara, Ramgarh and Umren
4	Bharatpur	7—Nadbai, Deeg, Sewar, Rupbas, Bayana, Kaman and Nagar Pahari
5	Churu	7—Dungargarh, Taranagar, Ratangarh, Rajgarh, Churu, Sujangarh and Sardarshahar
6	Bhilwara	6—Asind, Kotri, Shahpura, Raipur, Jahazpur and Mandalgarh
7	Jalor	6—Ahore, Jalor, Sayla, Jaswantpura, Raniwara and Bhinmal
8	Jhunjhunun	6—Udaipurwati, Nawalgarh, Chirawa, Alsisar, Surajgarh and Khetri
9	Tonk	6—Malpura, Deoli, Niwai, Todaraisingh, Tonk and Uniara
10	Udaipur	6—Girwa, Kherwara, Salumbar, Gogunda, Jhadol and Dhariawad
11	Banswara	5—Garhi, Bagidora, Anandpuri, Ghatol and Talwara
12	Dausa	5—Dausa, Mahwa, Bandikui, Sikrai and Lalsot
13	Jodhpur	5—Shergarh, Mandor, Osian, Phalodi and Bap
14	Rajsamand	5—Bhim, Amet, Rajsamand, Kumbhalgarh and Deogarh
15	Sawai Madhopur	5—Bonli, Gangapur, Bamanwas, Sawai Madhopur and Khandar
16	Sikar	5—Khandela, Danta Ramgarh, Sri Madhopur, Piprali and Neem ka Thana
17	Bundi	4—Nainwa, Talera, Keshoraipatan and Hindoli
18	Jhalawar	4—Pirawa, Khanpur, Jhalrapatan and Bakani
19	Karauli	4—Nadoti, Hindaun, Todabhim and Sapotra
20	Baran	3—Kishanganj, Shahbad and Chhabra
21	Dhaulpur	2—Baseri and Dhaulpur
22	Jaisalmer	2—Sankara and Jaisalmer
23	Pali	2—Rohat and Raipur
24	Sirohi	2—Reodar and Abu Road
25	Dungarpur	1—Sagwara

Source: Annex 16.1

All the above districts, except Baran, Dhaulpur, Dungarpur, Pali, Sirohi had greater percentage of L level PSs in comparison to the state average (53.2). Six districts viz. Bundi, Churu, Dausa, Nagaur, Sawai Madhopur and Tonk had the maximum percentage (100) of Low level PSs while, Dungarpur and Pali had the minimum (20%).

TABLE 16.8: Distribution of PSs having Very Low HDI Level (1991)

S. No.	*District*	*No. & Name of PSs (in Descending Order)*
		Very Low Level (22)
1	Barmer	8—Siwana, Balotra, Sindhari, Dhorimanna, Baytoo, Chohtan, Barmer and Sheo
2	Dungarpur	4—Dungarpur, Bichhiwara, Aspur and Simalwara
3	Banswara	3—Sajjangarh, Peepalkhoont and Kushalgarh
4	Dhaulpur	2—Rajakhera and Bari
5	Jhalawar	2—Manoharthana and Dag
6	Jaisalmer	1—Sam
7	Jalor	1—Sanchore
8	Udaipur	1—Kotra

Source: Annex 16.1

Very Low HDI Area

Very low HDI area was also widely distributed in divisions (Except Bikaner and Ajmer) and 8 districts. There were 126 PSs in this category. Jodhpur divisions led with 45.5 per cent share followed by Udaipur (36.4%), Jaipur and Kota (9.1% each) divisions. If we look at district-wise distribution of these PSs, it will be clear that, Barmer led with 8 PSs followed by Banswara (3), Dhaulpur and Jhalawar (2 each) and Jaisalmer, Jalor, and Udaipur (one each) respectively. All the 8 districts had higher percentage of VL level PSs than the state average (9.3). Barmer district had the maximum percentage (100) of these PSs, while Udaipur had the minimum (9.1%).

17

HUMAN DEVELOPMENT INDEX (2001)

Highlights

- Rural HDI-Raj. : 0.571
- Percentage of AAPs: 41.8

	Panchayat Samiti	District	Division
• **Top**	Chechat (0.759)	Kota	Kota
• **Bottom**	Peepalkhoont (0.385)	Banswara	Udaipur

The Human Development Index (HDI) of rural Rajasthan rose to 0.571 in the year 2001. There were 99 PSs having HDI above the state average. Figure 17.1 depicts spatial distribution pattern of HDI at PS level. Where as, 67 per cent PSs of Bikaner and 51 per cent PSs of Jaipur division had Very High Level of HDI only, 5 PSs of Jodhpur division and 7 per cent of Udaipur division entered in this category. Jaipur division led in PSs (47.1% share) having Very High as well as High (20.3%) HDI Jodhpur and Udaipur are the most deprived led in PSs having Medium to Low HDI. The HDI Level in the state rises from the West and the South-West to the North East, North and the Sourth-East Direction.

Chechut PS of Kota district had the maximum 0.759 HDI followed by Jhotwara, Sanganer, Sangod, Sultanpur, Behror, Bhadra, Kotputli, Ladpura and Sadulshahar PSs (descending order, Annex 17.1). These top ten PSs were distributed in five districts. Kota led with four PSs followed by Jaipur (3), Alwar, Ganganagar, and Hanumangarh (one each) districts respectively (Table 17.1).

TABLE 17.1: Distribution of First and Last Ten PSs by HDI: Rajasthan, (2001)

S. No.	*First Ten PSs (Descending Order)*					*Last Ten PSs (Ascending Order)*				
	Districts/ PSs					*Districts/ PSs*				
	Kota	*Jaipur*	*Alwar*	*Gg*	*Hn*	*Banswara*	*Dg*	*Barmer*	*Jais*	*Udaipur*
	(4)	*(3)*	*(1)*	*(1)*	*(1)*	*(3)*	*(3)*	*(2)*	*(1)*	*(1)*
1	Chechat	Jhotwara	Behror	Sadulshahar	Bhadra	Peepalkhoont	Simalwara	Sheo	Sam	Kotra
2	Sangod	Sanganer	—	—	—	Kushalgarh	Aspur	Barmer	—	—
3	Sultanpur	Kotputli	—	—	—	Sajjangarh	Bichhiwara	—	—	—
4	Ladpura	—	—	—	—	—	—	—	—	—

Source: Annex 17.3

Peepalkhoont PS of Banswara district, on the othçr hand, had the minimum (0.385) HDI. It was preceded by Kotra, Sheo, Kushalgarh, Barmer, Simalwara, Sam, Aspur, Sajjangarh and Bichhiwara PSs. These last ten PSs were also concentrated in five districts. Banswara and Dungarpur districts dominated with 3 PSs while Barmer had 2 and Jaisalmer and Udaipur had one PS each. District-wise distribution of PSs having highest and lowest HDI is shown in Table 17.2.

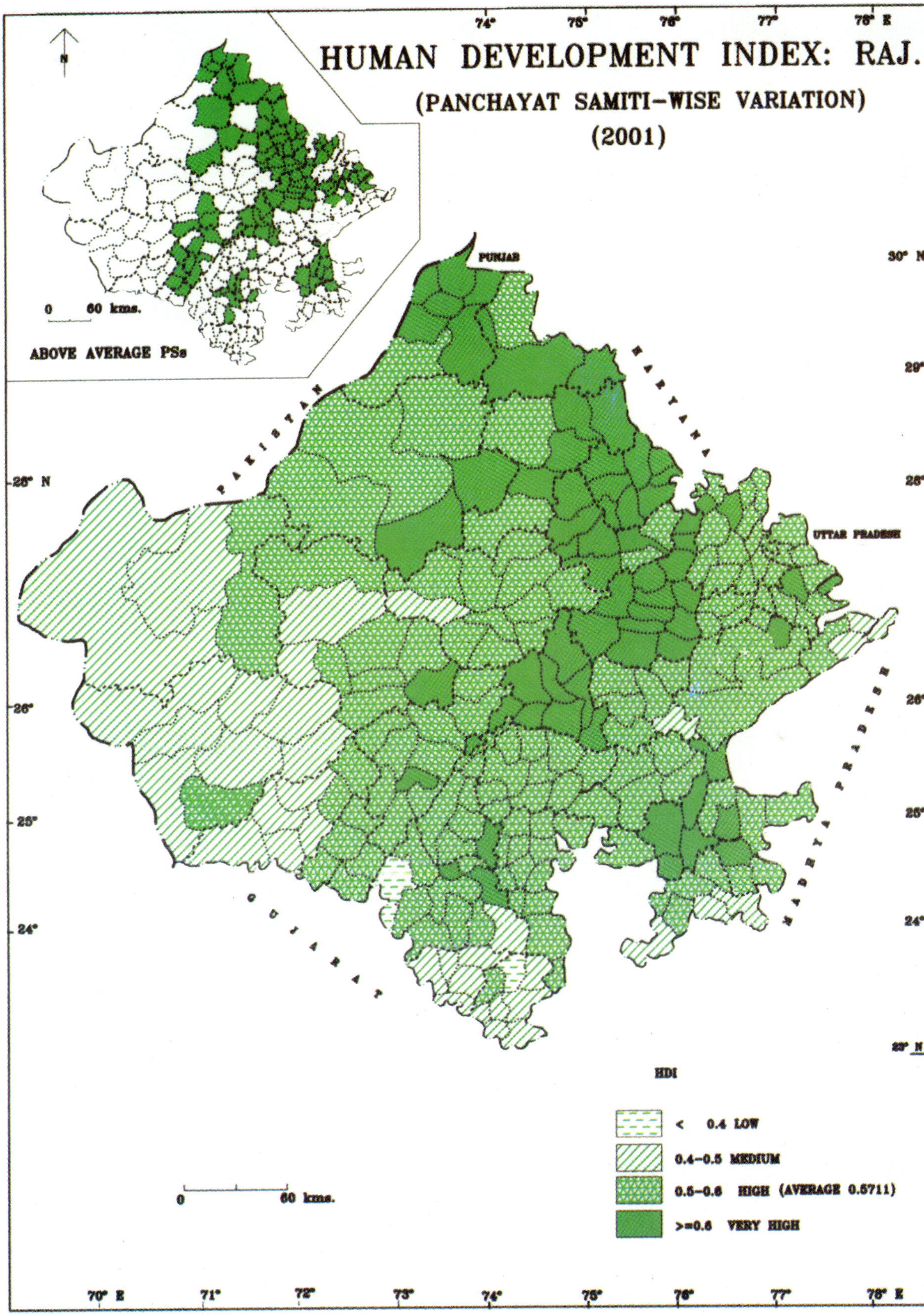
HUMAN DEVELOPMENT INDEX: RAJ.
(PANCHAYAT SAMITI-WISE VARIATION)
(2001)
ABOVE AVERAGE PSs
0 60 kms.
PUNJAB
HARYANA
PAKISTAN
UTTAR PRADESH
MADHYA PRADESH
GUJARAT
HDI
< 0.4 LOW
0.4-0.5 MEDIUM
0.5-0.6 HIGH (AVERAGE 0.5711)
>=0.6 VERY HIGH
0 60 kms.
70° E
71°
72°
73°
74°
75°
76°
77°
78° E
30° N
29°
28° N
26°
25°
24°
23° N

FIG. 17.1

TABLE 17.2: District-wise First and Last PSs by HDI (2001)

District	*First Rank*	*Last Rank*	*District*	*First Rank*	*Last Rank*
Ajmer	Jawaja	Bhinay	Jaipur	Jothwara	Chaksu
Alwar	Behror	Tijara	Jaisalmer	Sankra	Sam
Banswara	Garhi	Peepalkhoont	Jalor	Ahore	Sanchore
Baran	Baran	Chhabra	Jhalawar	Pirawa	Dag
Barmer	Dhorimanna	Sheo	Jhunjhunun	Buhana	Nawalgarh
Bharatpur	Kumher	Kaman	Jodhpur	Bilara	Phalodi
Bhilwara	Banera	Kotri	Karauli	Hindaun	Karauli
Bikaner	Nokha	Kolayat	Kota	Chechat	Itawa
Bundi	Keshoraipatna	Nainwa	Nagaur	Ladnu	Mundwa
Chittaurgarh	Nimbahera	Arnod	Pali	Rani Station	Jaitaran
Churu	Taranagar	Sardarshahar	Rajsamand	Railmagra	Deogarh
Dausa	Mahwa	Lalsot	S. Madhopur	Gangapur	Khandar
Dhaulpur	Baseri	Rajakhera	Sikar	Fatehpur	Neem ka Thana
Dungarpur	Sagwara	Simalwara	Sirohi	Sirohi	Abu Road
Ganganagar	Sadulshahar	Anupgarh	Tonk	Todaraisingh	Uniara
Hanumangarh	Bhadra	Hanumangarh	Udaipur	Bargaon	Kotra

Source: Annex 17.1, Col. 10.

TABLE 17.3: Classification of PSs on the Basis of HDI (2001): Rajasthan

Group	*HDI*			
	No.	*%*	*Distributed in*	
			Districts	*Divisions*
Very High (VH), (>=0.6)	66	27.8	17	6
High (H), (0.5-0.6)	133	56.1	27	6
Medium (M), (0.4-0.5)	36	15.2	11	5
Low (L), (<0.4)	2	0.8	2	1
Total	**237**	**100**		

Source: Annex 17.3

Classification of PSs by HDI

Table 17.3 presents classification of PSs in to four groups by HDI. High Level PSs were dominated with 56.1 per cent share followed by Very High (27.8 %), Medium (15.2%) and Low (0.8%) level PSs.

If we look at division-wise classification and distribution of PSs by HDI (Table 17.4) following conclusions can be drawn:

- Udaipur was the only division having PS, with all the four levels of HDI while other divisions had PSs with three levels of HDI.
- Jaipur division led in PSs, having Very High to High HDI (29 % share), Jodhpur in Medium level (44.4%), while Udaipur division (100%) led in L level PSs.
- Very High level PSs dominated in both Bikaner (66.7% share) and Jaipur (50.8%) divisions while Medium Level PSs dominated in remaining divisions.
- The percentage of VH level PSs in Jaipur and Bikaner divisions; H level in Ajmer, Kota, Jodhpur and Udaipur divisions; M level in Jodhpur and Udaipur divisions and L level in Udaipur division was higher than the state average.

TABLE 17.4: Division-wise Classification and Distribution of PSs on the Basis of HDI (1991)

Divisions	*Classification*					*Distribution (% Share)*			
	HDI Level					*HDI Level*			
	Very High	*High*	*Medium*	*Low*	*Total PSs*	*Very High*	*High*	*Medium*	*Low*
Jaipur	31	27	3	—	61	47.0	20.3	8.3	—
	(50.8)	(44.3)	(4.9)	—	(100.0)				
Bikaner	14	7	—	—	21	21.2	5.3	—	—
	(66.7)	(33.3)	—	—	(100.0)				
Ajmer	8	26	2	—	36	12.1	19.5	5.6	—
	(22.2)	(72.2)	(5.6)	—	(100.0)				
Kota	8	21	3	—	32	12.1	15.8	8.3	—
	(25.0)	(65.6)	(9.4)	—	(100.0)				
Jodhpur	2	24	16	—	42	3.0	18.0	44.4	—
	(4.8)	(57.1)	(38.1)	—	(100.0)				
Udaipur	3	28	12	2	45	4.5	21.1	33.3	100.0
	(6.7)	(62.2)	(26.7)	(4.4)	(100.0)				
Total	**66**	**133**	**36**	**2**	**237**	**100**	**100**	**100**	**100**
	(27.8)	**(56.1)**	**(15.2)**	**(0.8)**	**(100.0)**				

Figure in brackets shows percentage share to total Panchayat Samities.
Note: HDI VH : (>=0.6), H : (0.5-0.6), M : (0.4-0.5), L : (< 0.4).
Source: Annex 17.3

Very High HDI Region

There were 66 VH level PSs which were spread over 17 districts and all the 6 divisions. The percentage of VH level PSs to total PSs ranged between a maximum of 66.7 in Bikaner and a minimum of 4.8 in Jodhpur division. Jaipur division accounted for the highest concentration of those PSs (47 % share) in the state. It was followed by Bikaner (21.2%), Ajmer and Kota (12.1 % each), Udaipur (4.5%) and Jodhpur (3%) divisions.

Among the Districts Jaipur dominated with 13 PSs followed by Ajmer and Jhunjhunun (8 each); Ganganager and Sikar (6 each); Churu and Kota (5 each); Alwar, Baran, Bharatpur, Hanumangarh and Udaipur (2 each) and Bikaner, Jodhpur, Karauli, Alwar and Rajsamand (1 each). All the above districts except Ajmer and Sawai Madhopur had higher percentage of VH level PSs than the state average (2.5%). The percentage of three PSs varied between a maximum of 100 in Ajmer, Jaipur, Jhunjhunun and Kota districts and a minimum of 10 in Pali district.

High HDI Region

High HDI region was spread over 27 districts and all the six divisions. There were total 133 High level PSs. Udaipur division topped with 21.1 per cent share followed by Jaipur (20.3%), Ajmer (19.3%), Jodhpur (18%), Kota (15.8%) and Bikaner (5.3 %) divisions. The highest percentage of H level PSs of total PSs is 72.2 which is in Ajmer followed by 65.6 in Kota, 62.2 in Udaipur, 57.1 in Jodhpur, 44.3 in Jaipur and the lowest 33.3 in Bikaner division. Among the districts, Chittaurgarh led with 14 PSs followed by Alwar (12); Bhilwara (11); Nagaur (10); Pali (9); Bharatpur and Udaipur (7 each); Jodhpur and Rajsamand (6 each); Baran, Dausa, Sawai Madhopur, Sirohi and Tonk (5 each); Bundi and Karauli (4 each); Bikaner and Jhalawar (3 each); Churu, Jalor and Sikar (2 each) and Banswara, Barmer, Dhaulpur, Ganganagar, Hanumangarh and Jaisalmer (1 each) districts respectively.

Ajmer, Baran, Bharatpur, Bhilwara, Bikaner, Bundi, Chittaurgarh, Dausa, Jodhpur, Karauli, Nagaur, Pali, Rajsamand, Sawai Madhopur, Sirohi, Tonk and Udaipur districts had greater percentage of High Level PSs in comparison to the state average (56.1). Moreover, 6 districts, namely Bhilwara, Bundi, Chittaurgarh, Dausa, Sawai Madhopur and Sirohi had 100 per cent of their PSs in High category while Banswara and Barmer had the minimum (12.5) percentage of these PSs.

TABLE 17.5: District-wise Classification of PSs on the Basis of HDI Level (2001)

District	*HDI Level*				*Total PSs*
	VH	*H*	*M*	*L*	
Ajmer	8	—	—	—	8
	(100.0)	—	—	—	(100.0)
Alwar	2	12	—	—	14
	(14.3)	(85.7)	—	—	(100.0)
Banswara	—	1	6	1	8
	—	(12.5)	(75.0)	(12.5)	(100.0)
Baran	2	5	—	—	7
	(28.6)	(71.4)	—	—	(100.0)
Barmer	—	1	7	—	8
	—	(12.5)	(87.5)	—	(100.0)
Bharatpur	2	7	—	—	9
	(22.2)	(77.8)	—	—	(100.0)
Bhilwara	—	11	—	—	11
	—	(100.0)	—	—	(100.0)
Bikaner	1	3	—	—	4
	(25.0)	(75.0)	—	—	(100.0)
Bundi	—	4	—	—	4
	—	(100.0)	—	—	(100.0)
Chittaurgarh	—	14	—	—	14
	—	(100.0)	—	—	(100.0)
Churu	5	2	—	—	7
	(71.4)	(28.6)	—	—	(100.0)
Dausa	—	5	—	—	5
	—	(100.0)	—	—	(100.0)
Dhaulpur	—	1	3	—	4
	—	(25.0)	(75.0)	—	(100.0)
Dungarpur	—	—	5	—	5
	—	—	(100.0)	—	(100.0)
Ganganagar	6	1	—	—	7
	(85.7)	(14.3)	—	—	(100.0)
Hanumangarh	2	1	—	—	3
	(66.7)	(33.3)	—	—	(100.0)
Jaipur	13	—	—	—	13
	(100.0)	—	—	—	(100.0)
Jaisalmer	—	1	2	—	3
	—	(33.3)	(66.7)	—	(100.0)
Jalor	—	2	5	—	7
	—	(28.6)	(71.4)	—	(100.0)
Jhalawar	—	3	3	—	6
	—	(50.0)	(50.0)	—	(100.0)
Jhunjhunun	8	—	—	—	8
	(100.0)	—	—	—	(100.0)
Jodhpur	1	6	2	—	9
	(11.1)	(66.7)	(22.2)	—	(100.0)
Karauli	1	4	—	—	5
	(20.0)	(80.0)	—	—	(100.0)
Kota	5	—	—	—	5
	(100.0)	—	—	—	(100.0)
Nagaur	—	10	1	—	11
	—	(90.9)	(9.1)	—	(100.0)
Pali	1	9	—	—	10
	(10.0)	(90.0)	—	—	(100.0)
Rajsamand	1	6	—	—	7
	(14.3)	(85.7)	—	—	(100.0)
Sawai Madhopur	—	5	—	—	5
	—	(100.0)	—	—	(100.0)
Sikar	6	2	—	—	8
	(75.0)	(25.0)	—	—	(100.0)
Sirohi	—	5	—	—	5
	—	(100.0)	—	—	(100.0)
Tonk	—	5	1	—	6
	—	(83.3)	(16.7)	—	(100.0)
Udaipur	2	7	1	1	11
	(18.2)	(63.6)	(9.1)	(9.1)	(100.0)
Rajasthan	**66**	**133**	**36**	**2**	**237**
	(27.8)	**(56.1)**	**(15.2)**	**(0.8)**	**(100.0)**

Figures in brackets show percentage share to total Panchayat Samities. *Note*: HDI VH : (>=0.6), H : (0.5-0.6), M : (0.4-0.5), L : (< 0.4).

Source: Annex 17.2

TABLE 17.6: Distribution of PSs having Very High HDI Level, 2001

S. No.	*District*	*No. & Name of PSs (in Descending Order)*
		Very High (66)
1	Jaipur	13—Jhotwara, Sanganer, Kotputli, Sambhar, Govindgarh, Jamwa Ramgarh, Phagi, Viratnagar, Shahpura, Amber, Bassi, Dudu and Chaksu
2	Ajmer	8—Jawaja, Kishangarh, Srinagar, Kekri, Pisangan, Masooda, Arian and Bhinay
3	Jhunjhunun	8—Buhana, Udaipurwati, Jhunjhunun, Chirawa, Alsisar, Surajgarh, Khetri and Nawalgarh
4	Ganganagar	6—Sadulshahar, Karanpur, Ganganagar, Raisinghnagar, Padampur and Suratgarh
5	Sikar	6—Fathepur, Lachhmangarh, Khandela, Piprali, Dhond and Danta Ramgarh
6	Churu	5—Taranagar, Dungargarh, Ratangarh, Rajgarh and Churu
7	Kota	5—Chechat, Sangod. Sultanpur, Ladpura and Itawa
8	Alwar	2—Behror, Mandawar
9	Baran	2—Baran, Atru
10	Bharatpur	2—Kumher, Nadbai
11	Hanumangarh	2—Bhadra, Nohar
12	Udaipur	2—Bargaon, Bhinder
13	Bikaner	1—Nokha
14	Jodhpur	1—Bilara
15	Karauli	1—Hindaun
16	Pali	1—Rani Station
17	Rajsamand	1—Railmagra

Source: Annex 17.3

TABLE 17.7: Distribution of PSs having High HDI Level, 2001

S. No.	*District*	*No. & Name of PSs (in Descending Order)*
		High Level (133)
1	Chittaurgarh	14—Nimbahera, Dungla, Bhopalsagar, Rashmi, Chooti Sadri, Gangrar, Chittaurgarh, Begun, Bari Sadri, Bhadesar, Kapasan, Pratapgarh, Bhainsrorgarh, and Arnod
2	Alwar	12—Kotkasim, Reni, Nimrana, Kathumar, Lachhmangarh, Bansure, Rajgarh, Kishangarh Bas, Umren, Thanagazi, Ramgarh and Tijara
3	Bhilwara	11—Banera, Sahara, Hurda, Suwana, Asind, Mandal, Raipur, Shahpura, Jahazpur, Mandalgarh and Kotri
4	Nagaur	10—Ladnu, Didwana, Prabatsar, Makrana, Riyan, Degana, Merta, Kuchaman, Jayal and Nagaur
5	Pali	9—Sojat, Sumerpur, Pali, Bali, Kharchi-Marwar Jun, Desuri, Rohat, Raipur and Jaitaran
6	Bharatpur	7—Sewar, Deeg, Rupbas, Weir, Nagar Pahari, Bayana, Kaman
7	Udaipur	7—Salumbar, Mavli, Girwa, Sarada, Jhadol, Kherwara and Gogunda
8	Jodhpur	6—Luni, Bhopalgarh, Osian, Bap, Mandor and Balesar
9	Rajsamand	6—Kumbhalgarh, Bhim, Rajsamand, Amet, Khamnor and Deogarh
10	Baran	5—Anta, Kishanganj, Chhipabarod, Shahbad, Chhabra
11	Dausa	5—Mahwa, Sikari, Bandikui, Dausa and Lalsot
12	Sawai Madopur	5—Gangapur, Bamanwas, Bonli, Sawai Madhopur and Khandar
13	Sirohi	5—Sirohi, Pindwara, Sheoganj, Reodar and Abu Road
14	Tonk	5—Todaraisingh, Niwai, Malpura, Tonk and Deoli
15	Bundi	4—Keshoraipatan, Talera, Hindoli, Nainwa
16	Karauli	4—Nadoti, Todabhim, Sapotra and Karauli
17	Bikaner	3—Lunkaransar, Bikaner, Kolayat
18	Jhalawar	3—Pirawa, Khanpur, Jhalrapatan
19	Churu	2—Sujangarh, Sardarshahar
20	Jalor	2—Ahore, Jalore
21	Sikar	2—Sri Madhopur, Neem ka Thana
22	Banswara	1—Garhi
23	Barmer	1—Dhorimanna
24	Dhaulpur	1—Baseri
25	Ganganagar	1—Anupgarh
26	Hanumangarh	1—Hanumangarh
27	Jaisalmer	1—Sankra

Source: Annex 17.3

TABLE 17.8: Distribution of PSs having Medium and Low HDI Level, 2001

S. No.	*District*	*No. & Name of PSs (in Descending Order)*
		[A] Medium (36)
1	Barmer	7—Sindhari, Siwana, Balotra, Chohtan, Baytoo, Barmer and Sheo
2	Banswara	6—Talwara, Anandpuri, Bagidora, Ghatol, Sajjangarh and Kushalgarh
3	Dungarpur	5—Sagawara, Dungarpur, Bichhiwara, Aspur and Simalwara
4	Jalor	5—Raniwara, Sayla, Jaswantpura, Bhinmal and Sanchore
5	Dhaulpur	3—Bari, Dhaulpur and Rajakhera
6	Jhalawar	3—Bakani, Manoharthana and Dag
7	Jaisalmer	2—Jaisalmer and Sam
8	Jodhpur	2—Shergarh and Phalodi
9	Nagaur	1—Mundwa
10	Tonk	1—Uniara
11	Udaipur	1—Dhariawad
		[B] Low (2)
1	Banswara	1—Peepalkhoont
2	Udaipur	1—Kotra

Source: Annex 17.3

Medium HDI Region

Medium HDI region was widely distributed in 11 districts and 5 divisions (except Bikaner). There were 36 PSs in this category. Jodhpur division had the maximum concentration of these PSs (44.4% share) followed by Udaipur (33.3%), Jaipur and Kota (8.3% each) and Ajmer (5.6%) divisions. The highest percentage share of M level PSs to total PSs was 38.1 which was in Jodhpur division followed by 26.7 in Udaipur, 9.4 in Kota, 5.6 in Ajmer and the lowest 4.9 in Jaipur division. Jodhpur and Udaipur divisions had higher percentage of M level PSs than the state average (15.2). If we see district-wise distribution of these PSs, it will be clear that Barmer secured the top position with 7 PSs followed by Banswara (6); Jalor and Dungarpur (5 each); Dhaulpur and Jhalawar (3 each); Jaisalmer and Jodhpur (2) and Nagaur, Tonk and Udaipur (1 each) districts respectively. Except Nagaur and Udaipur all the above districts had greater percentage of Medium level PSs than the state average. Dungarpur had the highest (100) percentage of these PSs while Nagaur and Udaipur had the Lowest (9.1%).

Low HDI Region

Peepalkhoont PS of Banswara district and Kotra of Udaipur were the only PSs having Low HDI. The percentage of L level PSs in both Banswara (12.5%) and Udaipur (9.1%) districts was higher than the state average (0.8%).

18

GROWTH TRENDS AND ACTION PLAN

Rajasthan is not only India's largest state but also among the poorest. It is a matter of great pleasure that Planning Commission of India praised Rajasthan highly for its achievements in human development. The commission had assessed the overall progress of states in the last three decades. It said that Rajasthan, which was at Eleventh position among the 15 developing states, has scaled up to the Ninth position. The state is predominantly an agrarian state where about 70 per cent of the population depends on agriculture as a source of livelihood and about 32 per cent of the NSDP is generated by primary sector.

The thrust of this research is on Spatio-Temporal and Gender Appraisal of Human Development Index at Panchayat Samiti/Block level in Rajasthan State (India) during the 1991-2001 period. The study is mainly based on UNDP methodology. However, the same has been changed depending on the availability of data. Human Development Status of Rural Rajasthan is measured through Health Status Index (HSI), Education Index (EDI), Gender-Related Education Index (GEDI), Income Index (INI), Gender-Related Income Index (GINI), Human Poverty Index (HPI) and Gender Empowerment Measure (GEM). The research highlights changing relative status of PSs in these indices, spatial distribution pattern, division-wise as well as district-wise classification and distribution of PSs on the basis of these indices, and areas having Very High, High, Medium, Low and Very Low Human Development Indices. The study brings forth not just analysis but points to possible actions on the Human Development Sector.

Although, the HDI of rural Rajasthan increased 45 per cent from 0.3938 in 1991 to 0.5709 in 2001, still Ihe Index of Deprivation (IOD) is high (0.4291) and there is a long way to go (Chart 18.1). It is also unfortunate that disparity in HDI value among the PSs rose from 0.332 to 0.374. There were only 58 PSs which registered an increase in HDI value above 0.2 during the period.

A great deal of spatial variation is seen in HDI value among the 237 Panchayat Samities (PSs) spread over 32 districts and 6 divisions of Rajasthan. In the year 2001, Chechat PS of Kota district had the maximum 0.759 HDI, while Peepalkhoont of Banswara had the minimum (0.385). While 67 per cent PSs of Northern (Bikaner division), 51 per cent PSs of North-Eastern (Jaipur division), 25 per cent of South-Eastern (Kota division) and 22.2 per cent of Central (Ajmer division) socio-economically developed regions had above 0.6 HDI level (> 0.6), only 4.8 per cent PSs of Western Arid/Semi-Arid (Jodhpur division) and 6.7 per cent PSs of Southern-Tribal/Hilly (Udaipur division) regions qualified for this category. The HDI Level in the state rises from the West and South-West to the North-East, North and Sourth-East direction. The north-eastern, northern, south-eastern and some parts of central regions have various physical, socio-economic, technological, political and historical advantages. On the other hand, the remaining regions have various disadvantages on account of physiographic conditions, socio-cultural traditions, lack of infrastructural facilities, low economic development etc.

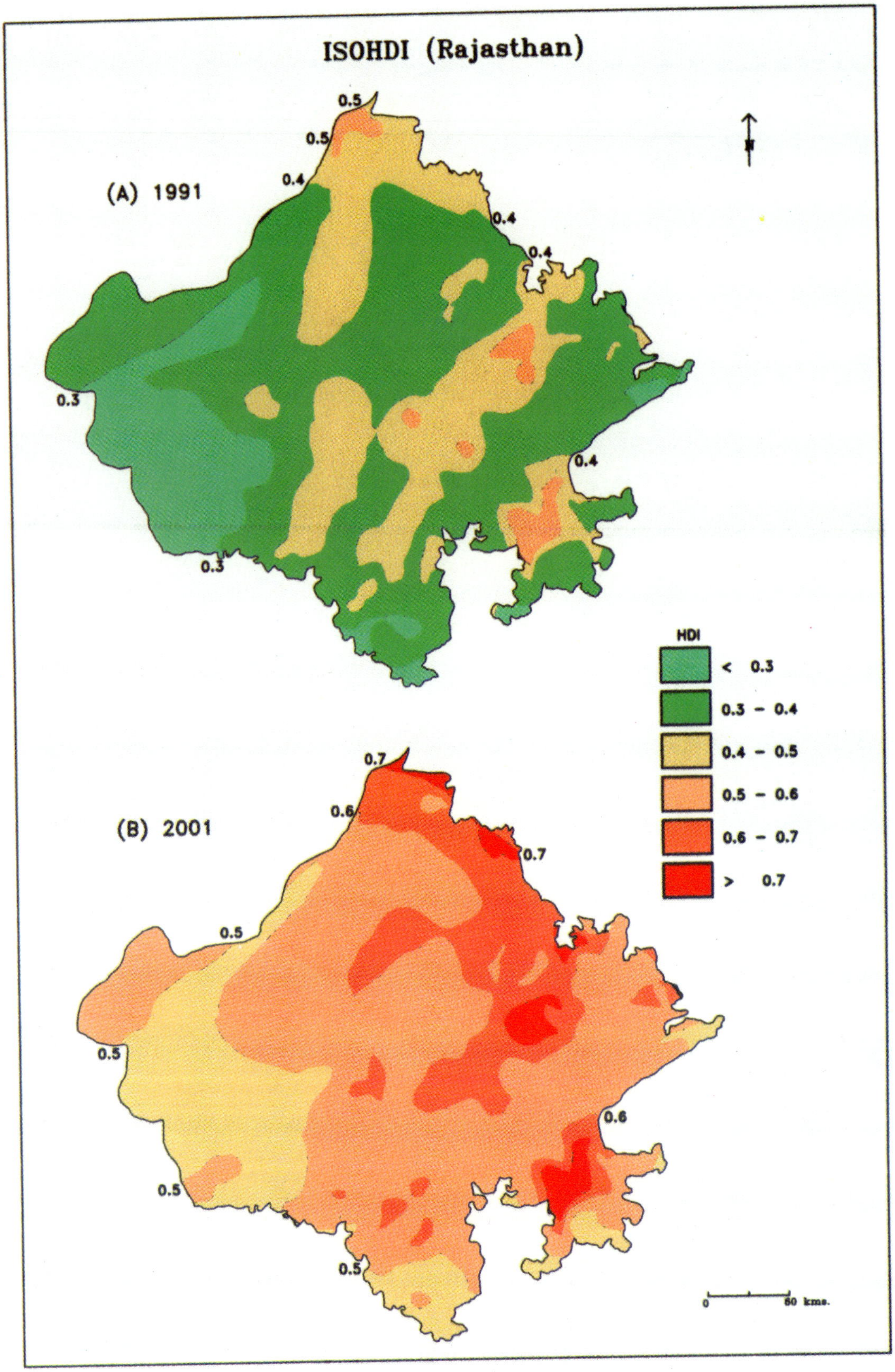

Note: ISOHDI: Line Joins Places Having Equal HDI

FIG 18.1

HDI: Growth Trends at PS Level (Rural Raj. 1991-2001)

- **45 per cent increase in HDI (0.3938 to 0.5709) Still, a Long Way to Go**
- **Disparity Increased (0.332 to 0.374)**
- **Increasing HDI from West & South-West to North-East, North & South-East Direction**
- **Chechat PS (Kt) Maintained its Top Position**
- **Peepalkhoont PS (Bans) came down at the Bottom in place of Sheo (Bmr)**
- **15 PSs Maintained I Rank, While 18 Maintained Last Rank in their Respective Districts**
- **All PSs Registered Increase in HDI Value**
- **Dhorimanna (Bmr, 122%, 0.2814) PS Registered Maximum Increase in HDI, While Kekri (Aj, 23%) and Kotra (Ud, 0.0997) Registered Minimum Increase**
- **42 per cent PSs Registered Higher Increase in HDI Value than the State Average (0.1771)**
- **42.6 per cent (101) PSs Improved their Ranks in the State**
- **Ratangarh PS (Churu) Registered Maximum (123) Improvement in its Rank, While Balesar (Jodh) Registered Maximum (-106) Deteriotion**
- **6 PSs (Baseri, Ahore, Chechat, Sultanpur, Tonk and Gogunda) Maintained their Ranks**

CHART 18.1

The State had dominance of PSs (56.1%) having high level of HDI (0.5-0.6) followed by PSs having Very High (>= 0.6, 27.8%), Medium (0.4-0.5, 15.2%) and Low (< 0.4, 0.8%) level of HDI. Where as, H level PSs were widely spread over 27 districts and VH level over 17 districts, M and L level PSs were concentrated in 11 and 2 districts respectively.

Udaipur was the only division having PSs of all the four levels of HDI, where as other divisions had PSs of three levels of HDI. Jaipur division led (29 % share) in PSs having Very High to High HDI, Jodhpur (44.4%) in Medium level, and Udaipur division led (100%) in PSs having Low HDI. Very High level PSs dominated in both Bikaner (66.7% share) and Jaipur (50.8%) divisions, where as Medium Level PSs dominated in remaining divisions. The percentage of VH level PSs in Jaipur and Bikaner divisions; H level in Ajmer, Kota, Jodhpur and Udaipur divisions; M level in Jodhpur and Udaipur divisions and L level in Udaipur division was higher than the state average.

The percentage of VH level PSs varied between a maximum of 100 in Ajmer, Jaipur, Jhunjhunun and Kota districts and a minimum of 10 in Pali district. Similarly, while Bhilwara, Bundi, Chittaurgarh, Dausa, Sawai Madhopur and Sirohi had 100 per cent of their PSs in High category, Banswara and Barmer had the minimum percentage (12.5) of these PSs. In Medium HDI level, Dungarpur District had the highest (100) percentage of these PSs, where as Nagaur and Udaipur had the Lowest (9.1%). Like-wise, Peepalkhoont PS of Banswara district and Kotra of Udaipur were the only two PSs having Low HDI.

ISOHDI maps (Fig 18.1A & B) depict increased pattern of Human Development Index in Rajasthan during 1991-01 period. ISOHDI denotes the line on a map, which joins the places of equal HDI. In the year 1991, the state was covered by three ISOHDI lines viz. 0.5 (highest), 04 and 0.3 (lowest). More than half portion of the state lay between 0.3 and 0.4 ISOHDI lines. This area is widely spread over 25 districts and all the six divisions. PSs of Jaipur division are in a leading position, followed by Udaipur and Ajmer division.

Nearly 1/3 portion of the state lay between 0.4 and 0.5 ISOHDI lines. This area also widely covers PSs of 18 districts, but prominently those of Jaipur division. 13 PSs lay above 0.5 ISOHDI line. These PSs were: Govindgarh, Shahpura, Bassi and Sanganer of Jaipur district; Chechat, Sangod, Ladpura and Sultanpur of Kota; Karanpur, Ganganagar and Raisinghnagar of Ganganagar and Kekri and Pisangan of Ajmer district.

The area below 0.3 ISOHDI line included almost all the PSs of Barmer; Dungarpur, Bichhiwara, Aspur and Simalwara of Dungarpur; Sajjangarh, Peepalkhoont and Kushalgarh of Banswara; Rajakhera and Bari of Dhaulpur; Sam of Jaisalmer; Sanchore of Jalor and Kotra of Udaipur.

In the year 2001, with the increase in over all human development status in the state, the value of ISOHDI lines also rose viz. 0.7 (highest), 0.6 and 0.5 (lowest). While in the year 1991, more than half of the state lay between 0.3 and 0.4 ISOHDI lines, in the year 2001, more than half of the state jumped in 0.5 and 0.6 ISOHDI lines and more than 1/4 area even jumped above 0.6 ISOHDI line. Chechat, Sangod, Sultanpur and Ladpura PSs of Kota; Jhotwara, Sanganer and Kotputli PSs of Jaipur; Behror of Alwar; Sadulshahar of Ganganagar and Bhadra of Hanumangarh districts even crossed 0.7 ISOHDI line. On the other side, there were only 38 PSs (16%) that remained beneath 0.5 ISOHDI line.

Dhorimanna PS of Barmer district was at the top with 122 per cent increase in HDI value (1991-2001) followed by Chohtan, Sindhari, Baytoo, Sheo, Barmer, Bari, Bap, Rajgarh, Ratangarh, Udaipurwati and Siwana PSs. On the other side, Kekri PS of Ajmer district was at the bottom (23%) preceded by Pisangan, Bhinay, Shergarh, Hurda, Hanumangarh, Khamnor, Karanpur and Mandal PSs.

With respect to absolute increased value of HDI (1991-2001), Dhorimanna PS of Barmer district again secured the first rank (0.2814) followed by Udaipurwati, Buhana, Fatehpur, Piprali, Tananagar, Ratangarh, Khandela, Jhotwara and Rajgarh PSs. Kotra PS of Udaipur, on the other hand, was at the last rank (0.0997) preceded by Shergarh, Kotri, Balesar, Mandal, Hurda, Peepalkhoont, Khamnor, Bagidora, Kekri and Bhinay PSs.

Ratangarh PS of Churu district registered maximum improvement in its rank (+123) followed by Rajgarh, Churu, Taranagar, Piprali, Khetri, Dungargarh, Sujangarh, Surajgarh and Mahwa PSs. On the other side, Balesar PS of Jodhpur registered maximum deterioration (-106) in its rank preceded by Mandal, Shergarh, Khamnor, Kotri, Asind, Deoli, Hurda, Suwana, and Shahpura PSs.

Table 18.1 shows classification of districts in to High, Medium Low groups by per cent increase in HDI value. Barmer district registered highest increase (93%) where as Bhilwara registered the lowest increase (31%). Barmer is the only district joined the High Group and 10 districts namely, Bharatpur, Churu, Dausa, Dhaulpur, Dungarpur, Jaisalmer, Jhunjhunun, Karauli, Nagaur and Sikar entered in Medium group where as remaining 21 districts were in Low group.

TABLE 18.1: Classification of Districts on the Basis of % Increase in HDI Value (1991-2001)

Group	*% Increase*	*Districts*		
		No.	*%*	*Name*
High	>=75	1	3.1	Barmer
Medium	50-75	10	31.3	Bharatpur, Churu, Dausa, Dhaulpur, Dungarpur, Jaisalmer, Jhunjhunun, Karauli, Nagaur and Sikar
Low	<50	21	65.6	Ajmer, Alwar, Banswara, Baran, Bhilwara, Bikaner, Bundi, Chittaurgarh, Ganganagar, Hanumangarh, Jaipur, Jalore, Jhalawar, Jodhpur, Kota, Pali, Rajsamand, SM, Sirohi, Tonk and Udaipur

Source: Annex. 17.2, Col 9

Classification of districts on the basis of HDI growth trends is presented in Table 18.2. Out of 32 districts, 100 per cent PSs of Barmer, Churu, Dausa, Jhunjhunun, Karauli and Sikar and more than 50 per cent PSs of Baran, Bharatpur, Dhaulpur, Hanumangarh, Jaipur, Nagaur and Rajsamand districts registered improvement in both HDI value and their ranks. On the other hand, 100 per cent PSs of Bhilwara, Banswara, Dungarpur, Pali and Sirohi districts and more than 50 per cent PSs of remaining 14 districts had registered increase in HDI value, but at the same time their ranks deteriorated.

TABLE 18.2: Classification of Districts on the Basis of HDI Growth Trends (1991-2001)

Growth Trends	*Districts*		
	No	*%*	*Name*
(A) All Panchayat Samities (100%) registered improvement in both HDI value and Rank	6	18.8	Barmer, Churu, Dausa, Karauli, Jhunjhunun, and Sikar
(B) All Panchayat Samities registered improvement in HDI value but rank deteriorated in			
(a) 100% PSs	5	15.6	Bhilwara, Banswara, Pali, Dungarpur, and Sirohi
(b) >= 50% PSs	14	43.8	Ajmer, Alwar, Bikaner, Jalor, Chittaurgarh, Jhalawar, Bundi, Ganganagar, Jaisalmer, SM Jodhpur, Kota, Tonk and Udaipur
(c) < 50% PSs	7	21.9	Baran, Bharatpur, Dhaulpur, Hanumangarh, Jaipur, Nagaur and Rajsamand.

Source: Annex 17.2, Col. 10.

Classificaton of PSs into five groups (Very High to Very Low) by per cent increased value of HDI and rank difference during 1991-01 period is presented in Table 18.3. In regard to per cent increase in HDI value, maximum PSs (62.9%) were in Low group followed by Medium group. There were only 3 PSs each in VH, H as well as in VL groups.

TABLE 18.3: Classification of PSs by Increased Value of HDI and Rank Difference (1991-2001)

Group	*(A) % Increase in HDI Value*		*(B) Absolute Increase in HDI Value*		*(C) Rank Difference*	
	% Increase	*PSs (%)*	*Value*	*PSs (%)*	*Rank Difference*	*PSs (%)*
Very High	>100	1.3	>=0.25	5.5	> = 50	13.5
High	75-100	1.3	0.20-0.25	19	25 to 50	9.3
Medium	50-75	33.3	0.15-0.20	50.6	0 to 25	22.4
Low	25-50	62.9	0.10-0.15	24.5	0 to -25	31.2
Very Low	<25	1.3	< 0.10	0.4	>-25	23.6
		100		**100**		**100**

Source: Annex 18.1 to 18.3

TABLE 18.4: Upward Movement in the Level of Human Development Indices (1991-2001)

(% share to total PSs)

Group (Level)	*HSI.*		*EDI*		*GEDI*		*INI**		*GINI**		*HDI*	
	1991	*2001*	*1991*	*2001*	*1991*	*2001*	*1991*	*1998*	*1991*	*1998*	*1991*	*2001*
(>=0.75)	—	13.9	—	0.4	—	1.2	0.8	10.1	7.2	30.8	—	0.4
(0.60-0.75)	32	73.0	—	18.6	—	20.3	6.3	14.8	76.8	68.4	—	27.4
(<0.60)	68	13.1	100	81.0	100	78.5	92.8	75.1	16.0	0.8	100	72.2
	100	**100**	**100**	**100**	**100**	**100**	**100**	**100**	**100**	**100**	**100**	**100**

* During 1991-98 period.
Source: Compiled from Annex. 5.1, 6.2, 7.1, 8.3, 9.1, 10.3, 11.1, 12.2, 13.1, 14.2, 15.2, 16.1, 17.3

With regard to absolute increase in HDI value, highest PSs (56%) registered moderate increase (0.15 to 0.20) followed by PSs in L, H and VH groups. Kotra of Udaipur district was the only PS which registered Very Low (<0.10) increase in HDI. Similarly, maximum PSs (31.2%) were in Low group (0 to -25) in regard to rank difference followed by PSs in VL, M, VH and H groups.

In HDI, 15 PSs that maintained the first rank in their respective districts during 1991-2001 period. These PSs were: Behror, Garhi, Kumher, Nimbahera, Taranagar, Baseri, Sagwara, Bhadra, Sankra, Ahore, Pirawa, Bilara, Chechat, Railmagra and Fatehpur. Similarly, 18 PSs namely, Chhabra, Kolayat, Sardarshahar, Lalsot, Simalwara, Anupgarh, Chaksu, Sam, Sanchore, Dag, Karauli, Itawa, Deogarh, Khandar, Neem ka Thana, Abu Road, Uniara and Kotra maintained the last rank.

Table 18.4 reveals upward movement in the level of human development indices during the 1991–2001 period (1991-98 for INI/GINI). In the year 1991, it was sad that 100 per cent PSs in HDI, EDI and GEDI; 93 per cent in INI and 68 per cent PSs in HIS had index value below 0.6. The situation was only good in GINI, where 84 per cent PSs had index value above 0.6. In the year 2001, with the improvement in the level of human development status across the state, 99.2 per cent PSs in GINI, 87 per cent in HSI, 28 per cent in HDI, 25 per cent in INI, 21.5 per cent in GEDI and 19 per cent PSs in EDI jumped up and crossed 0.6 index value.

On the basis of growth pattern in human development indices, PSs of the state can be classified into four groups viz.: (A) PSs, which registered improvement in both value and rank, (B) PSs, which registered improvement in value but their ranks deteriorated, (C) PSs, which registered improvement in value but their ranks remained constant and (D) PSs which registered deterioration in both value and rank (Table 18.5)

TABLE 18.5: Classification of PSs on the Basis of Growth Patterns in Human Development Indices (1991)

(% Share to Total PSs)

Growth Trend	*HSI*	*EDI*	*GEDI**	*INI**	*GINI*	*HDI*
(A) Improvement in Both Value and Rank	46.0	43.0	45.6	40.9	42.6	42.6
(B) Increase in Value but Rank Deteriorated	50.6	54.9	53.6	54.0	55.7	54.9
(C) Increase in Value but Rank Remained Constant	3.0	2.1[b]	0.8[c]	4.6	1.7[e]	2.5[f]
(D) Deterioration in Both Value and Rank.	0.4[a]	—	—	0.4[d]	—	—

a—Only Shergarh PS. b—five PSs viz : Peepalkhoont, Lalsot, Bassi, Sayla and Kotra, c—Talera and Itawa PSs, d—Hanumangarh PS, e—Masoda, Kotputli, Jaisalmer and Desuri PSs, f—six PSs viz Baseri, Ahore, Chechat, Sultanpur, Tonk and Gogunda,
*—During 1991-98 period
Source: Annex. 6.1, 8.2, 10.2, 14.1, and 17.2

It is interesting to note that in all the human development indices, PSs in B group were dominating followed by PSs in A and C groups. In HDI, maximum 54.9 per cent PSs were in B Group 42.6 per cent in A Group and 2.5 per cent in C Group. The percentage of B group PSs ranged between maximum 55.7 in GINI and minimum 50.6 in HSI. The percentage of PSs in A group ranged between highest 45.6 in GEDI and 40.9 in INI. Similarly, the percentage of PSs in C group ranged between maximum 4.6 in INI and minimum 0.8 in GEDI. Shergarh PS (Jodh) in HSI and Hanumangarh (Hn) in INI were the only two PSs in D group. Similarly, district-wise best and the worst PSs by percentage increase in human development indices during 1991-2001 period is presented in Table 18.6.

In spite of being a developing state with weak socio-demographic indicators, Rajasthan registered remarkable achievements in health status during the Five Year Plans (FYP) period. Since the commencement of the first FYP in the year 1951, a multifold increase has been registered in government investment in health sector (1022 times), total number of medical institutions (30 times), number of doctors (7.4 times), beds (580 times), patient treated etc. Health infrastructural facilities have been strengthened and both qualitive and quantitative improvement has been achieved in health services. Various national and state level health programmes and schemes are being launched in the state. Special schemes have been also launched for the arid/semi-arid, tribal, backward and remote areas.

Concerted efforts are being made by the state as well as central government for ensuring availability of health services to people at their door-steps. As a result, life expectancy at birth increased significantly while sharp decline has been registered in fertility, mortality and morbidity indicators. Similarly, as a result of improvement in the health infrastructural facilities, number of population served per bed and per institution came down from 2792 to 1454 and from 38208 to 4468 respectively during 1951-04 period; and number of population served per doctor came down from 22132 to 9149 during 1955-04 period.

TABLE 18.6: DISTRICT-WISE BEST AND THE WORST PSS BY % INCREASE IN HUMAN DEVELOPMENT INDICES (1991-01)

Dists.	% Increase in Human Development Indices.(1991-01)											
	HSI		EDI		GEDI		INI (1991-98)		GINI (1991-98)		HDI	
	Best	Worst	Best	Worst	Best	Worst	Best	Worst	Best	Worst	Best	Worst
AJ	JAWAJA*	PISANGAN*	JAWAJA	KEKRI*	JAWAJA	KEKRI	KEKRI	PISANGAN	KEKRI	SRINAGAR	JAWAJA	KEKRI
AL	LACHHMAN[1]	KISHAN[4]	BEHROR*	NIMRANA*	RENI	NIMRANA*	NIMRANA	TIZARA*	NIMRANA*	TIZARA	BEHROR	NIMRANA
BANS	SAJJANGARH	BAGIDORA*	KUSHAL*[6]	GARHI*	KUSHAL*[6]	GARHI	TALWARA	PEEPAL-KHOONT[13]	TALWARA	KUSHAL*[6]	KUSHAL[6,12]	BAGIDORA
BARAN	CHHIPABAROD*	CHHABRA*	CHHABRA	ANTA*	CHHABRA	ANTA	CHHABRA	CHHIPABAROD	ANTA	CHHIPABAROD	CHHABRA	CHHIPABAROD
BMR	DHORIMANNA*	SHEO*	DHORIMANNA	BALOTRA*	DHORIMANNA	BALOTRA	SHEO*	BAYTOO	CHOHTAN	SIWANA	DHORIMANNA	BALOTRA
BHART	NAGAR PAHARI*	WEIR*	KAMAN*	WEIR	KAMAN	ROOPBAS*	ROOPBAS*	KAMAN	ROOPBAS*	KAMAN	NAGAR PAHARI	WEIR
BHIL	MANDALGARH	SHAHPURA*	SHAHPURA	HURDA*	JHAZPUR	HURDA	RAIPUR*	MANDAL*	RAIPUR	MANDAL	BANERA	HURDA
BK	NOKHA*	BIKANER*	NOKHA	KOLAYAT*	NOKHA	KOLAYAT	NOKHA, LUN[10]	BIKANER	LUN*[10]	BIKANER	NOKHA	BIKANER
BUN	Hindoli	NAINWA*	NAINWA*	KESHO*[8]	NAINWA*	TALERA	KESHO*[8]	NAINWA*	TALERA	NAINWA	KESHO*[8]	NAINWA
CHIT	DUNGLA	KAPASAN*	KAPASAN*	RASHMI*	KAPASAN	RASHMI	BHOPALSAGAR*	ARNOD*	BHOPALSAGAR	ARNOD	PRATAPGARH	ARNOD
CHURU	RAJGARH*	SARDAR*[5]	TARANAGAR	RAJGARH	SARDAR*[5]	RAJGARH	DUNGARGARH*	SUJANGARH	DUNGARGARH	SUJANGARH	RAJGARH	SARDAR*[5]
DAUSA	BANDIKUI*	DAUSA*	SIKRAI*	MAHWA*	SIKRAI	MAHWA	MAHWA	BANDIKUI	LALSOT	BANDIKUI	MAHWA	DUSA
DHAUL	BARI*	DHAULPUR*	BARI	DHAULPUR	BARI	DHAULPUR	RAJAKHERA*	BASERI*	RAJAKHERA	BASERI	BARI	DHAULPUR
DG	SIMALWARA*	SAGWARA*	BICHHIWARA*	SAGWARA	BICHHIWARA	SAGWARA	ASPUR*	SIMALWARA	ASPUR	DUNGARPUR	SIMALWARA	SAGWARA
GG	ANUPGARH*	SURATGARH	ANUPGARH	GANGANAGAR*	ANUPGARH	GG	SADUL-SHAHAR*	ANUPGARH	SADUL-SHAHAR*	RAISINGH-NAGAR	SADUL-SHAHAR	KARANPUR
HN	BHADRA*	HN	NOHAR*	HN	NOHAR	HN	BHADRA	HN	BHADRA	HN	BHADRA	HN
JP	DUDU	GOVINDGARH*	KOTPUTLI, PHAGI	GOVINDGARH	JAMWA RAMGARH	SANGANER	JHOTWARA*	BASSI*	JHOTWARA	BASSI	JHOTWARA	GOVINDGARH
JAIS	SAM*	SANKRA*	SANKRA	JAISALMER*	SAM	JAISALMER	SAM	JAISALMER	SAM	SANKRA	SAM	JAISALMER
JL	BHINMAL	JALOR*	SANCHORE*	JALOR	SANCHORE	JALOR	JALOR	SANCHOR	SAYLA	AHORE	SANCHORE	JALOR
JHAL	MANOHAR*[2]	BAKANI*	MANOHAR*[2]	KHANPUR	MANOHAR*[2]	BAKANI	DAG*	PIRAWA*	DAG	PIRAWA	MANOHAR*[2]	BAKANI
JHUN	BUHANA	NAWALGARH*	UDAIPURWATI*	NAWALGARH	UDAIPURWATI	NAWALGARH	NAWALGARH	BUHANA	NAWALGARH	ALSISAR	UDAIPURWATI	NAWALGARH
JODH	BAP*	SHIVGANJ*	BAP	MADNOR*	PHALODI*	MANDOR	BAP	PHALODI	BAP	PHALODI	BAP	SHERGARH
KR	KARAULI*	NADOTI*	KARAULI	TODABHEEM	HINDAUN*	NADOTI	NADOTI	KARAULI	HINDAUN	KARAULI	HINDAUN[14]	NADOTI
KT	SULTANPUR*	LADPURA*	CHECHAT*	SULTANPUR	ITAWA	SULTANPUR	CHECHAT	LADPURA	SULTANPUR	LADPURA	SULTANPUR	LADPURA
NG	DIDWANA*	MERTA*	JAYAL*	MERTA	JAYAL	MERTA	NAGAUR*	MUNDWA	NAGAUR	PARBATSAR	DIDWANA	MERTA
PL	RAIPUR*	SUMERPUR*	ROHAT*	RANI STATION*	ROHAT	RANI STATION	RANI STATION	JAITARAN	PALI	RAIPUR	ROHAT	SUMERPUR[11]
RAJS	KUMBHAL*[3]	KHAMNOR*	DEOGARH*	KHAMNOR	DEOGARH	KHAMNOR	RAILMAGRA	KHAMNOR	DEOGARH	KHAMNOR	KUMBHAL*[3]	KHAMNOR
SM	KHANDAR*	BAMANWAS*	BAMANWAS*	SM*	BAMANWAS	SM	GANGAPUR	BONLI	KHANDAR	BONLI	KHANDAR	SM
SK	PIPRALI*	DHOND*	FATEHPUR*	SRI M*[9]	FATEHPUR	SRI M*[9]	NEEM KA THANA	FATEHPUR	SRI M*[9]	FATEHPUR	PIPRALI	DHOND
SR	SIROHI*	SHEOGANJ*	ABU ROAD	SIROHI	SHEOGANJ	SIROHI	SIROHI	PINDWARA*	SIROHI	PINDWARA	SIROHI	PINDWARA
TK	TODARAI SINGH*	MALPURA*	TODA[7]	DEOLI*	TODA[7]	DEOLI	MALPURA	UNIARA, DEOLI	MALPURA	DEOLI	TODA[7]	DEOLI
UD	JHADOL*	SARADA*	JHADOL	MAVLI*	JHADOL	MAVLI	BARGAON*	KOTRA*	BARGAON	KOTRA	JHADOL	KOTRA

* Prominent PS/PSs having Best / Worst Position in two or more than two indicators in their respective districts

1. Lachhmangarh, 2. Manogarthan, 3. Kumbhalgarh, 4.Kishangarh Bas, 5.Sardarshahar. 6.Kushalgarh, 7.Tocaraisingh, 8.Keshoraipatan, 9.Sri Madhopur, 10. Lunkaransar. 11.and Bali and Desuri 12.and Sajjangarh 13.and Kushalgarh 14. and Karauli

Source: 1. Hemlata Joshi. 2005. *'Economic Development Index and Health Status Index-Rajasthan* (Spatio-Temporal & Gender Appraisal at Panchayat Samiti / Block Level), Published Reaserch Reports,IDSJ.

2 . Annex 6.1, 8.2, 10.2, 14.1 and 17.2

BOX 18.1: Health Status of Rajasthan in India

[I] Unsatisfactory		[II] Satisfactory
Health Indicators are Higher than National Average	**Health Indicators are Lower than National Average**	
• IMR • CBR • GFR • GRR • Rural TMFR • Neo-natal mortality rate. • Percentage of currently married women with any reproductive problem.	• Life expectancy at birth. • Female age at effective marriage. • Percentage of live birth receiving ante-natal care. • Percentage of live birth receiving 2 doses of TT vaccine. • Percentage of live birth receiving iron/folic tablets. • Percentage of birth delivered in medical institutions. • Percentage of deliveries assisted by health professionals. • Percentage of children age 12-23 months receiving full immunization. • CPR. • ANC. • Sex-ratio (more particularly of 0-6 pop.). • Female literacy rate. • Access to safe drinking water in rural areas.* • Percentage of households having electricity within house in rural areas.*	• Still-birth rate in rural areas. • CDR. • Peri-natal mortality rate in rural area. • Percentage of Neo-natal deaths to infant death. • Achievement in immunization programme (under 20-point programme). • Achievement in villages covered under drinking water facility (under 20-point programme). • Access to safe drinking water in urban areas*. • Percentage of households having electricity within house in urban areas.* • Male literacy rate, 2001. • Percentage increase in female literacy and total literacy rate during 1991-2001.

Note: * Infrastructure related indices having direct bearing on health status. *Source* : Hemlata Joshi. 2005. *'Health Status Index-Rajasthan* (Spatio-Temporal Appraisal at Panchayat Samiti/Block Level), Research Report, IDS, Jaipur.

Growth Trends in HSI at PS Level (1991-2001)

- **20% Increase in HSI (0.5588 to 0.6684)**
- **Increasing HSI From South-East, South and West to North-East and Central Direction**
- **Udaipurwati PS (Jhun, 0.8307) Snatched the First Rank From Sumerpur (Pali, 0.729)**
- **Sam PS Maintained its Bottom Rank**
- **18 PSs Maintained their First / Last Ranks in their Respective Districts**
- **Bari (Dhaul, 47%) and Ratangarh (Churu, 0.2164) PSs Registered Highest Growth.**
- **Shergarh PS of Jodhpur is the Only PS Registered Decrease in HSI Value.**
- **46% (109) PSs Improved their Ranks in the State.**
- **Nadbai PS (Bharat, + 113) Registered Maximum Improvement in Rank, While Shergarh (Jodh, -132) Registered Maximum Deterioration**
- **7 PSs : Anta, Bayana, Sam, Sayla, Chirawa, Nadoti and Ladpura Maintained their Ranks**

CHART 18.2

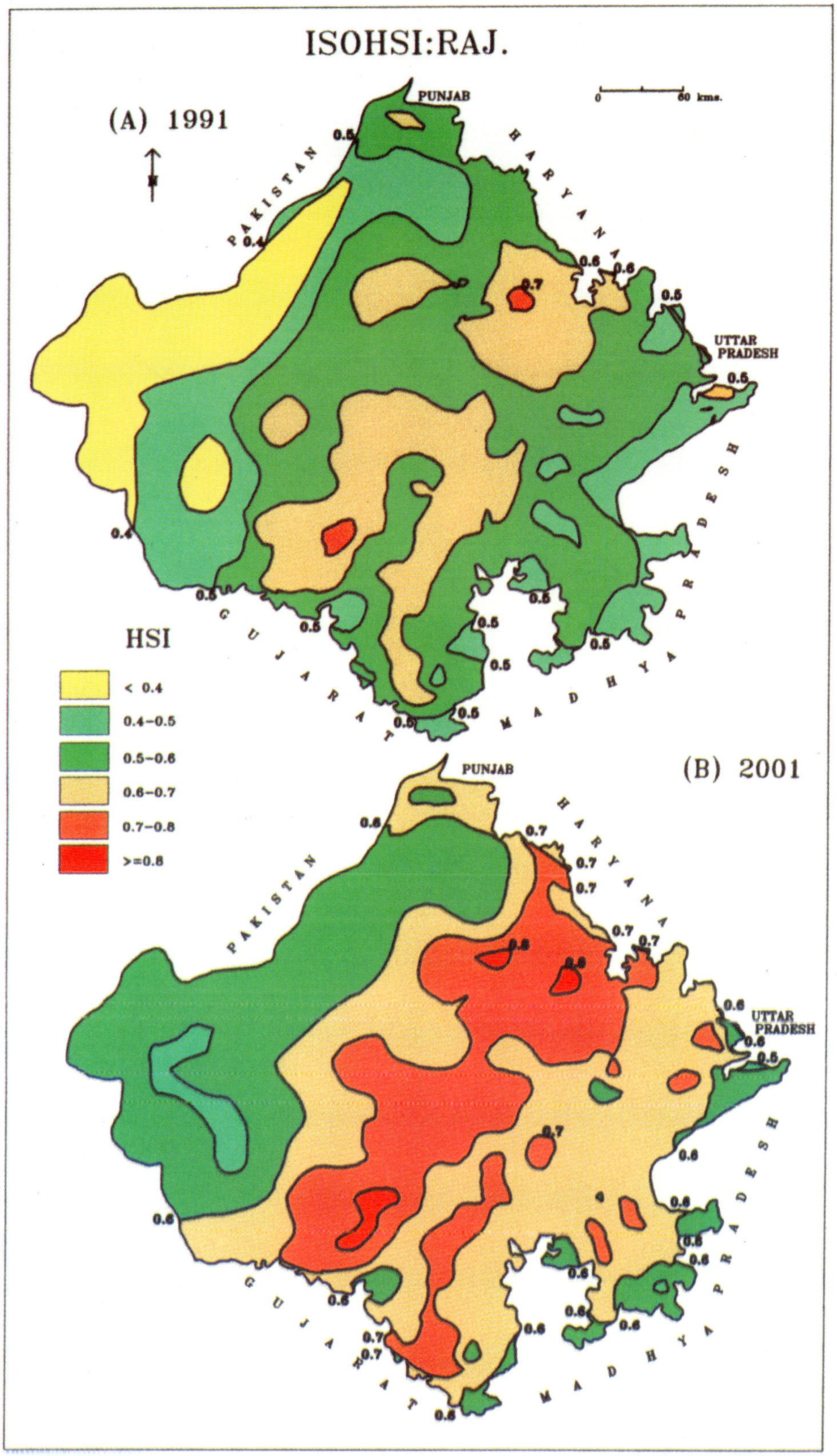

Note: ISOHSI: Line Joins Places Having Equal HSI.

FIG 18.2

The state government has been providing special thrust to strengthen the Ayurvedic, the indigenous system of medicines. At the time of formation of Rajasthan, the state had only 346 Ayurvedic hospitals and homeopathic hospitals with a total bed-strength of 100. By the end of 2000-01, the number has gone up to 3733 hospitals and dispensaries with a total bed strength of 1186. Besides these, the state has 6 mobile dispensaries, 3 Ayurvedic colleges (including two private colleges) and 2 training centres for para-medical staff. The National Institute of Ayurved (NIA) is also located at Jaipur.

The Health Status Index (HSI) of rural Rajasthan increased by 20 per cent from 0.5590 in 1991 to 0.6684 in 2001. It is interesting to note that the PSs having High and Very High HSI are mainly concentrated in a belt along Aravalli hills area from South-West (Sirohi dist.) to North-East (Jhun/Alwar dists.) direction. The HSI level decreases towards both sides mainly towards Western arid and semi-arid areas. Udaipurwati PS of Jhunjhunun district had the highest HSI (0.8307) where as Sam PS of Jaisalmer district had the lowest (0.4749).

ISOHSI maps (Fig 18.2 A & B) depict increased pattern of health status in Rajasthan during 1991-2001 period. ISOHSI denotes the line on a map, which joins the places of equal health status index. In the year 1991, the state was covered by four ISOHSI lines viz. 0.7 (highest), 06, 0.5 and 0.4 (lowest). More than half of the state lay between 0.5 and 0.6 ISOHSI lines. The included PSs in this group were spread over entire Rajasthan except Jodhpur division where only 3 PSs namely Osian, Mandor and Pholodi entered in this group. The main districts covered between 0.5 and 0.6 ISOHSI lines are: Alwar, Bharatpur and Dausa in the NE; Ganganagar, Hanumangarh, Churu and Bikaner in the North; Nagaur in the Central; Kota, Bundi, Jhalawar, Baran, Sawai Madhopur, Karauli and Tonk in the South-East and Banswara, Udaipur, Rajsamand and Chittaurgarh in the Southern Rajasthan.

Nearly 1/3 portion of the state covering Sikar, Jhunjhunun, Jaipur, Ajmer, Bhilwara, Pali, Jodhpur, Jalor, Sirohi, Alwar (Nimrana, Behror and Mandawar PSs), Dungarpur, (Sagwara, Aspur and Bichhiwara PSs) and Rajsamand (Railmagra, Khamnor and Bhim PSs) districts lay between 0.6 and 0.7 ISOHSI lines. Similarly, a small portion of Pali (Sumerpur and Bali PSs) and Jhunjhunun (Nawalgarh PS) had above 0.7 HSI. The remaining area of the state mainly of Jaisalmer, Barmer, Bikaner, Dhaulpur, Jhalawar (Bakani, Dag and Manoharthana PSs), Bharatpur (Bayana, Kaman and Nagar Pahari PSs), Baran (Shahbad, Chhabra and Chhipabarod PSs), Banswara (Peepalkhoont, Sajjangarh and Kushalgarh PSs), Karauli (Sapotra and Karauli PSs), Ganganagar (Suratgarh and Anupgarh PSs) and Chittaurgarh (Pratapgarh and Bhainsrorgarh PSs) districts covered by 0.5 ISOHSI line and a small patch including Sam PS of Jaisalmer, Anupgarh of Ganganagar and Baytoo of Barmer district covered by 0.4 ISOHSI line were in the worst position.

In the year 2001, with the increase in over all health status in the state, the value of ISOHSI lines also rose viz. 0.8 (highest), 0.7, 0.6 and 0.5 (lowest). While in the year 1991, more than half portion of the state lay between 0.5 and 0.6 ISOHSI lines, in the year 2001, more than half portion of the state jumped to 0.6 and 0.7 ISOHSI lines. The districts covered are; Alwar (all PSs, except Behror, Nimrana and Mundawar); Bharatpur (except Kumher and Nadbai PSs), Jaipur (Jamwa Ramgarh, Amber, Jhotwara, Sanganer, Bassi and Phagi PSs), Dausa, Ajmer (Masooda, Bhinay and Arian PSs), Ganganagar (Padampur, Karanpur, Sadulshahar and Raisinghnagar), Bikaner (Nokha and Lunkaransar), Churu (Rajgarh and Sardarshahar), Hanumangarh (Hanumangarh), Chittaurgarh (except Rashmi, Arnod and Bhainsorgarh PSs), Bhilwara (except Banera, Sahara and Hurda PSs), Udaipur (except Girwa, Mavli, Kotra and Sarada PSs), Banswara (except Garhi, Peepalkhoont and Kushalgarh), Rajsamand (Rajsamand, Kumbhalgarh, Amet and Deogarh PSs), Tonk, S. Madhopur, Bundi, Baran (Baran, Atru, Anta and Kishangarh PSs), Karauli (except Hindaun PS), Kota (Sultanpur, Ladpura and Chechat PSs), Jhalawar (Khanpur and Pirawa PSs), Barmer (Balotra and Dhorimanna PSs) and Jalor (Bhinmal and Sanchore PSs) districts.

Similarly, more than 1/3 portion of the state jumped between 0.7 and 0.8 ISOHSI lines covering Jhunjhunun, Jaipur (Govindgarh, Shahpura, Sambhar, Viratnagar and Kotputli PSs), Alwar (Behror, Nimrana and Mandawar PSs), Bharatpur (Kumher and Nadbai PSs), Churu (Churu, Dungargarh, Sujangarh and Taranagar PSs), Dungarpur, Pali, Jalor, Jodhpur (Bilara, Bhopalgarh, Luni and Osian PSs), Bhilwara (Hurda, Banera and Sahara PSs), Rajsamand (Railmagra, Khamnor and Bhim PSs), Sirohi (Reodar, Pindwara, Sheoganj PSs) and Udaipur (Mavli and Girwa PSs) districts. Like-wise, one-tenth part of the state now lay between 0.5 and 0.6

ISOHSI lines encompassing Jaisalmer, Barmer, Bikaner, South Ganganagar, Dhaulpur, Jhalawar, Baran and Chittaurgarh etc. districts. A small patch covering Rani Station, Sumerpur, Sirohi, Jhunjhunun and Ratangarh PSs were covered by 0.8 ISOHSI were in the best health status while Barmer, Baytoo, Sheo (all of Barmer) and Kotra (Udaipur) PSs covered by 0.5 ISOHSI were in the worst health status.

Bari PS of Dhaulpur district was at the top rank with 47 per cent increase in HSI (1991-01) followed by Nagar Pahari, Dhorimanna, Anupgarh, Karauli, Deeg, Nadbai, Sam, Chohtan, Rajgarh and Ratangarh PSs. On the other side, Shergarh PS of Jodhpur district was at the bottom (0%) preceded by Bikaner, Balesar, Kapasan, Shahpura, Bhopalsagar, Hurda, Nawalgarh, Kolayat, Pisangan and Bhinay PSs.

With respect to increased value of HSI, Ratangarh PS of Churu district secured the first rank (0.2164) followed by Nadbai, Churu, Piprali, Deeg, Nagar Phari, Bari, Didwana, Rajgarh and Sultanpur PSs. Shergarh PS, on the other hand, was at the last rank (-0.0008) preceded by Bikaner, Balesar, Kapasan, Shahpura, Kolayat, Hurda, Bhopalsagar, Kotri and Bhinay PSs.

If we look at the change in HSI rank, Nadbai PS of Bharatpur district registered maximum improvement in its rank (+113) followed by Deeg, Didwana, Rajgarh, Churu, Sultanpur, Kumbhalgarh, Bhadra, Raipur and Piprali PSs. On the other side, Shergarh PS registered maximum deterioration (-132) in its rank preceded by Bikaner, Balesar, Kapasan, Shahpura, Jahazpur, Bhopalsagar, Kotri, Kishangar Bas and Bagidora PSs. Anta, Bayana, Sam, Sayla, Chirawa, Nadoti and Ladpura were the seven PSs which registered no change in their ranks. If we analyse district-wise per cent increase in HSI value, Barmer, Bharatpur and Karauli districts registered highest 29 per cent increase while Bikaner registered the lowest 6 per cent increase. Maximum 20 districts registered moderate increase (20 to 30%) while 11 registered low increase (10 to 20%).

If we classify districts on the basis of HSI growth trends it is clear that 100 per cent PSs of Dausa and Dungarpur districts and more than 50 per cent PSs of Baran, Barmer, Bharatpur, Bundi, Churu, Jaisalmer, Jalor, Kota, Karauli, Nagaur, Pali, Sawai Madhopur and Sikar districts registered improvement in both HSI value and their ranks. On the other hand, 100 per cent PSs of Bhilwara and Jhalawar districts and more than 50 per cent PSs of remaining 15 districts had registered increase in HSI value but at the same time their ranks deteriorated.

TABLE 18.7: Classification of PSs by Population Served Per Medical Institution/Per Bed/Per Doctor and Area Served Per Medical Institution (2001)

Group	*Critaria/Panchayat Samities*							
	*Pop. Served Per Medical Institution**		*Area Served Per Medical Institution***		*Pop. Served Per Bed#*		*Pop. Served Per Doctor##*	
	PSs	*%*	*PSs*	*%*	*PSs*	*%*	*PSs*	*%*
Worst	19	8.0	26	11.0	21	8.9	24	10.1
Worse	39	16.5	17	7.2	32	13.5	27	11.4
Normal	70	29.5	49	20.7	109	46.0	63	26.6
Better	89	37.6	109	46.0	72	30.4	89	37.6
Best	20	8.4	36	15.2	3	1.3	34	14.3
Total	**237**	**100**	**237**	**100**	**237**	**100**	**237**	**100**

Note: * Group in ' 000 ' No., Worst (>5), Worse (4-5), Normal (3-4), Better (2-3) and Best (<2)
** Group (sq. kms.), Worst (>40), Worse (30-40), Normal (20-30), Better (10-20) and Best (<10)
# Group in ' 000 ' No., Worst (>4), Worse (3-4), Normal (2-3), Better (1-2) and Best (<1)
Group in ' 000 ' No., Worst (>25), Worse (20-25), Normal (15-20), Better (10-15) and Best (<10)

Source: Annex-6.3 to 6.5

In HSI value, there were 18 PSs that maintained their first/last ranks in their respective districts. The PSs which maintained their first ranks were: Pisangan, Garhi, Siwana, Kumher, Nokha, Ratangarh, Bandikui, Dhaulpur, Sagwara, Ganganagar, Govindgarh, Jaisalmer, Bilara, Hindaun, Railmagra, Gangapur, Dhond, Sirohi and Mavli. Similarly, Kushalgarh, Kolayat, Bhainsrorgarh, Slasot, Simalwara, Nohar, Chaksu, Sam, Sanchore, Manoharthana, Surajgarh, Bap, Itawa, Rohat, Khandar, Abu Road, Uniara and Kotra were the PSs which continued to be at the last rank.

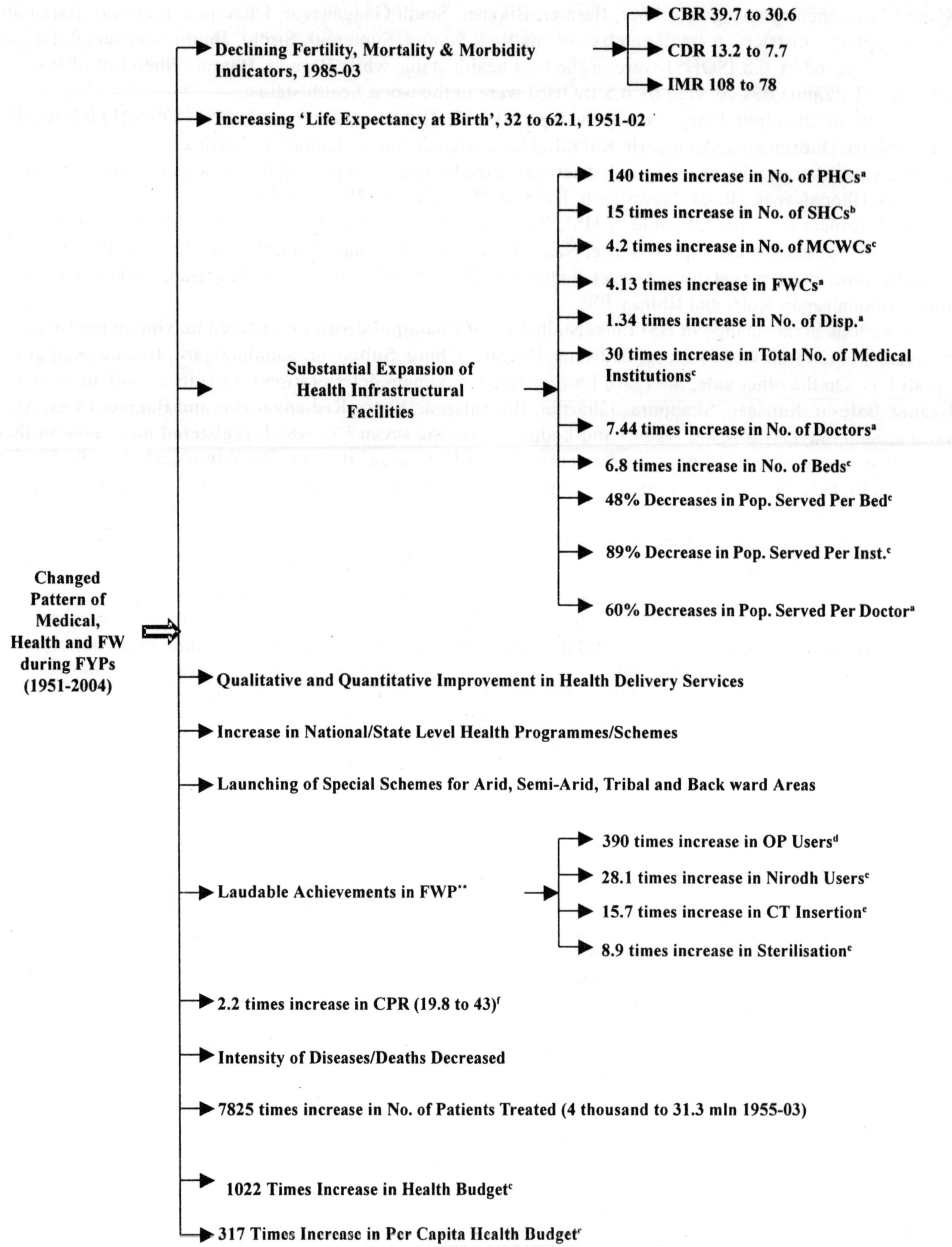

Note: a—During 1955-04, b—During 1965-04, c—During 1951-04, d—During 1981-03, e—During 1971-03, f—During 1985-04.

CHART 18.3

TABLE 18.8: Classification of PSs by Sex-Ratio (2001)

Group	*Sex-Ratio*							
	0-6 Pop.		*Total Pop.*		*SC Pop.*		*ST Pop.*	
	PSs	*%*	*PSs*	*%*	*PSs*	*%*	*PSs*	*%*
Very High (Best, >1000)	1	0.4	27	11.4	12	5.1	17	7.2
High (Better, 950-1000)	31	13.1	69	29.1	49	20.7	52	21.9
Medium (900-950)	138	58.2	92	38.8	132	55.7	78	32.9
Low (Worse, 850-900)	56	23.6	33	13.9	34	14.3	59	24.9
Very Low (Worst<850)	11	4.6	16	6.8	10	4.2	31	13.1
Total	**237**	**100**	**237**	**100**	**237**	**100**	**237**	**100**

Source: Annex-2.6, 2.7, K13 and K14

TABLE 18.9: Classification of PSs by Gender Gap in Literacy Rate (2001)

Group (LR %)	*Literacy Rate*			*Gender Gap in Literacy Rate*	
	Total	*Male*	*Female*		
	PSs (%)	*PSs (%)*	*PSs (%)*	*Group (gap in LR %)*	*PSs (%)*
Best >60	30	92.4	3.4	Worst >40	15.6
Medium 50-60	35	6.3	12.2	Medium 30-40	69.6
Worst <50	35	1.3	84.4	Best <30	14.8
Total	**100**	**100**	**100**		**100**

Source: Annex K- 3 to K-6

Classification of PSs by population served per medical institution/per bed/per doctor and area served per medical institution is presented in Table 18.7. It is sad that in spite of huge investment in health sector during FYPs period, 17 to 24 PSs are still in the worse/worst condition. It is again sad that more than 38 per cent PSs in sex-ratio in ST population and 28 per cent PSs in sex-ratio in 0-6 Pop. are in the worse/worst condition (Table 18.8.). Unfortunately, around 85 per cent PSs of the state had above 30 per cent gender gape in literacy rate and had below 50 per cent female literacy rate (Table 18.9). District-wise Best and the worst PSs by population served per medical institution/per bed/per doctor and area served per medical institution is presented in Table 18.10.

Although, EDI of the state increased 107 per cent from mere 0.2413 in 1991 to 0.4991 in 2001, the index of deprivation is still Very High (0.5009) and the state has to travel a long distance to achieve the targeted value (1.0). Most of the North-Eastern, Northern and South-Eastern economically developed regions have concentration of PSs having Very High EDI. On the other hand Southern tribal-hilly, Western desert and central regions were dominating in PSs having Low to Medium EDI. Behror PS of Alwar district had the maximum 0.862 EDI, while Kotra of Udaipur had the minimum (0.201). The State had dominance of PSs having Very High (> 0.5) level of EDI (41.4% share) followed by PSs having High (0.4-0.5, 40.1%), Medium (0.3-0.4, 8.9%) and Low (0.2-0.3, 11%) level of EDI.

Jodhpur and Udaipur were the only divisions having PSs with all the four levels of EDI while, Jaipur had PSs with only two levels. PSs in Bikaner, Ajmer and Kota divisions had four levels while Kota had three. Jaipur division dominated (49% share) in PSs, having Very High EDI and both Jodhpur and Udaipur in PSs having High (26.3% each) EDI while Ajmer division dominated in PSs having Medium (32.5 %) EDI.Very High level PSs were dominated in Jaipur (79%), Bikaner (76%) and Kota (56%) divisions while High level PS were dominated in remaining divisions. The percentage share of VH level PSs in Jaipur, Bikaner and Kota divisions; H level in, Ajmer, Jodhpur and Udaipur divisions; M level in Ajmer division and L level in both Udaipur and Jodhpur divisions was higher than the state average.

TABLE 18.10: DISTRICT-WISE BEST AND THE WORST PSS BY POPULATION SERVED PER MEDICAL INSTITUTION/ PER BED/ PER DOCTOR AND AREA SERVED PER MEDICAL INSTITUTION (2001)

Districts	Pop. Served Per Medical Institution		Area Served Per Medical Institution		Pop. Served Per Bed		Pop. Served Per Doctor	
	Best	Worst	Best	Worst	Best	Worst	Best	Worst
AJMER	KEKRI*	SRINAGAR*	JAWAJA	Arian	KEKRI	SRINAGAR	KEKRI	SRINAGAR
ALWAR	RENI	KOTKASIM	BEHROR*	RAJGARH	BEHROR	UMREN	BEHROR	RAMGARH
BANSWARA	KUSHALGARH	BAGIDORA	GARHI*	Peepalkhoont	GARHI	TALWARA	GARHI	ANANDPURI
BARAN	SHAHBAD*	CHHABRA*	ANTA*	CHHABRA	SHAHBAD	BARAN	ANTA	BARAN
BARMER	SINDHARI*	CHOHTAN	SIWANA*	SHEO	DHORIMANNA	BARMER	SIWANA	SINDHARI
BHARATPUR	KUMHER	KAMAN	RUPBAS	BAYANA	WEIR*	SEWAR*	WEIR	SEWAR
BHILWARA	MANDALGARH	MANDAL*	RAIPUR	MANDAL	SAHARA	SHAHPURA*	JHAZPUR	SHAHPURA
BIKANER	LUNKARANSAR*	NOKHA*	NOKHA*	KOLAYAT*	BIKANER	LUNKARANSAR*	LUNKARANSAR	KOLAYAT
BUNDI	NAINWA*	TALERA*	NAINWA	TALERA	NAINWA	HINDOLI	KESHORAIPATAN	TALERA
CHITTAURGARH	BEGUN*	BADI SADRI	RASHMI	BHAINSRORGARH	BEGUN	CHITTAURGAH	BEGUN	PRATAPGARH
CHURU	RATANGARH*	SARDARSHAHAR*	RATANGARH	SARDARSHAHAR	CHURU	SARDARSHAHAR	RATANGARH	SARDARSHAHAR
DAUSA	DAUSA*	BANDIKUI	MAHWA*	LALSOT*	DAUSA	SIKRAI	MAHWA	LALSOT
DHAULPUR	BARI*	RAJAKHERA*	DHAULPUR	RAJAKHERA	BARI	DHAULPUR	BARI	BASERI
DUNGARPUR	ASPUR*	BICHHIWARA*	ASPUR	SIMALWARA	SAGWARA*	BICHHIWARA	SAGWARA	BICHHIWARA
GANGANAGAR	SADULSHAHAR*	ANUPGARH*	GANGANAGAR	SURATGARH	KARANPUR*	ANUPGARH	KARANPUR	SADULSHAHAR*
HANUMANGARH	BHADRA	HANUMANGARH*	HANUMANGARH*	NOHAR*	NOHAR*	HANUMANGARH	NOHAR	HANUMANGARH
JAIPUR	SANGANER	AMBER	SHAHPURA	PHAGI	VIRATNAGAR	JHOTWARA	JAMWA RAMGARH	CHAKSU
JAISALMER	JAISALMER*	SANKRA*	SANKRA*	SAM	SANKRA	JAISALMER*	JAISALMER	SANKRA
JALOR	JALOR*	BHINMAL*	JALOR	SANCHORE*	BHINMAL	SAYLA	JASWANTPURA	SANCHORE
JHALAWAR	KHANPUR*	MANOHARTHANA*	KHANPUR	MANOHARTHANA	DAG*	JHALRAPATAN*	DAG	JHALRAPATAN
JHUNJHUNUN	JHUNJHUNUN*	SURAJGARH*	BUHANA	SURAJGARH	JHUNJHUNUN	KHETRI	NAWALGARH	KHETRI
JODHPUR	BILARA*	MANDOR	BILARA*	BAP	BILARA	PHALODI*	BILARA	PHALODI
KARAULI	NADOTI*	HINDAUN	TODABHIM	SAPOTRA	NADOTI	KARAULI	NADOTI	SAPOTRA
KOTA	SANGOD*	CHECHAT	SANGOD	LADPURA *	LADPURA *	ITAWA	Ladpura	SANGOD*
NAGAUR	DEGANA	DIDWANA	PARBATSAR*	MUNDWA	MERTA	NAGAUR	MAKRANA	PARBATSAR*
PALI	RANI STATION *	RAIPUR	RANI STATION	PALI*	DESURI*	PALI	DESURI	PALI
RAJSAMAND	KUMBHALGARH	DEOGARH*	KHAMNOR*	DEOGARH	RAJSAMAND	KHAMNOR*	DEOGARH	AMET
S. MADHOPUR	S.MADHOPUR*	GANGAPUR*	GANGAPUR*	KHANDAR	GANGAPUR	S. MADHOPUR*	GANGAPUR	S. MADHOPUR
SIKAR	DHOND*	SRI MADHOPUR	DANTA RAMGARH	LACHHMANGARH*	FATEHPUR*	LACHHMANGARH	FATEHPUR	DHOND*
SIROHI	SIROHI*	ABU ROAD*	SIROHI	ABU ROAD	ABU ROAD*	PINDWARA*	ABU ROAD	PINDWARA
TONK	TONK*	UNIARA*	TONK	UNIARA	TONK	UNIARA	TODHABHIM	DEOLI
UDAIPUR	JHADOL	KOTRA*	SALUMBER	KOTRA	BHINDER*	GOGUNDA	BHINDER*	KOTRA

* Prominent: PS/PSs having Best/Worst Position in two or more than two indicators in their respective districts.

Source: 1. Hemlata Joshi. 2005. *'Health Status Index-Rajasthan* (Spatio-Temporal Appraisal at Panchayat Samiti / Block Level), Research Report, IDS Jaipur.

2. Annex 6.1, 8.2, 102, 14.1 and 17.2

Growth Trends in EDI at PS Level (1991-2001)

- **Rising EDI From SW and South and West to NE and North Direction**
- **107% Increase in EDI (0.2413 to 0.4991), Still the IOD is Very High (0.5009)**
- **Behror PS (AL, 0.862) Snatched the First Rank from Nimrana (AL, 0.465)**
- **Kotra PS (Ud) maintained its Bottom Rank**
- **12 PSs Maintained First Ranks, while 18 maintained Last Ranks in their Repective Districts**
- **All PSs Registered Increase in EDI Value**
- **Dhorimanna (Bmr, 47%) PS Registered Highest (426%, 0.5188) Growth, while Nimrana (Al, 14%) and Kekri (Aj, 0.063) Registered Lowest Growth**
- **43% PSs (102) Improved their Ranks in the State**
- **Dhorimanna (Bmr, 210) PS Registered Maximum Improvement in EDI Rank, while Kekri (Aj, -174) Registered Maximum Deterioration**
- **5 PSs: Peepalkhoont, Lalsot, Bassi, Sayla and Kotra maintained their Ranks**

CHART 18.4

Behror PS of Alwar district with 0.862 EDI snatched the top position from Nimrana (AL, 0.465), while Kotra of Udaipur remained at the bottom during the 1991-2001 period. While Dhorimanna PS of Barmer registered highest increase (426%, 0.5188) in EDI value, Nimrana (AL, 14%) and Kekri (Aj, 0.063) registered the lowest increase. 12 PSs maintained their first ranks while 18 maintained last ranks in their respective districts.

All PSs registered increase in EDI value. 102 PSs improved their ranks in the state, while 5 PSs maintained their ranks (Chart 18.4). Dhorimanna PS of Barmer registered maximum improvement in its ranks (210), while Kekri of Ajmer registered maximum deterioration (-174). In EDI there were 12 PSs which maintained the first rank in their respective districts during 1991-2001. These PSs were: Garhi, Hurda, Nimbahera, Sagwara, Bhadra, Ahore, Hindaun, Sultanpur, Rani Station, Railmagra and Bargaon. Similarly 17 PSs viz. Peepalkhoont, Chohtan, Hindoli, Sardarshahar, Lalsot, Simalwara, Chaksu, Sam, Karauli, Itawa, Mundwa, Jaitaran, Khandar, Sri Madhopur, Abu Road, Tonk and Kotra maintained their last rank.

ISOEDI maps (Fig 18.3 A & B) depict increased pattern of education index in the state. ISOEDI denotes the line on a map, which joins the places of equal education index. In the year 1991-92, the state was covered by three ISOEDI lines viz. 0.2 (lowest), 0.3 and 0.4 (highest) ISOEDI. It was unfortunate that more than half portion of the state lay between 0.2 and 0.3 ISOEDI lines and nearly 3/10 portion lay beneath 0.2 ISOEDI line. Nimrana, Behror, Kotkasim and Mandawar (all of Alwar dist) and Buhana and Jhunjhunun (both of Jhunjhunun) were the only six PSs lay above 0.4 ISOEDI.

As the overall level of EDI had risen, more than 2/5 portion of the state has crossed 0.5 ISOEDI line. Behror PS of Alwar district has even crossed 0.8 EDI level and Udaipurwati, Buhana, Jhunjhunun and Chirawa (all of Jhun Dist); Lachhmangarh and Fatehpur (Sikar) entered between 0.7 and 0.8 ISOEDI. On the other side, Kotra, Dhariawad (both of Udaipur dist), Peepalkhoont and Kushalgarh (both of Banswara) were the only four PSs remained between 0.2 and 0.3 ISOEDI lines.

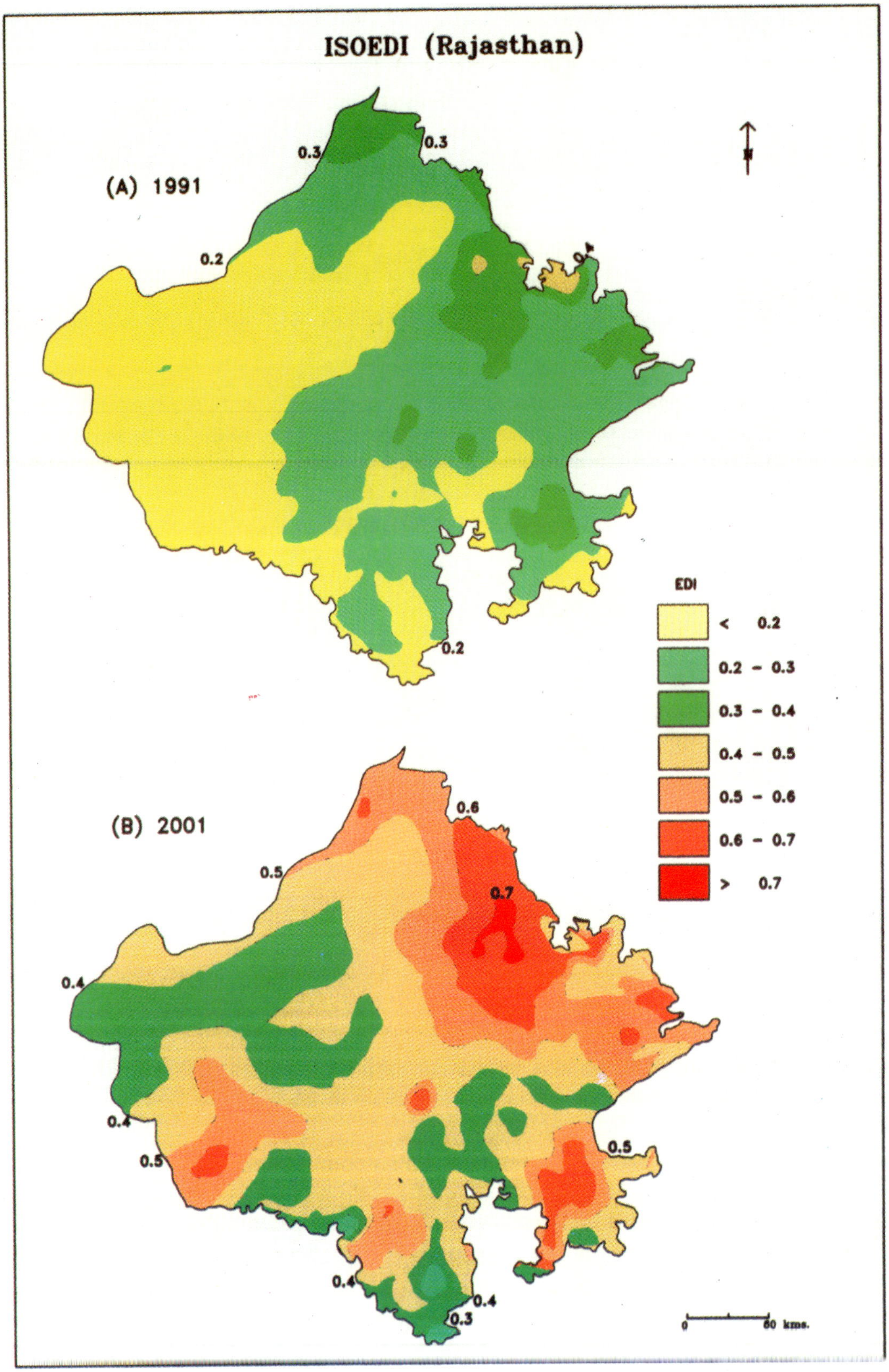

Note: ISOEDI: Line Joins Places Having Equal EDI.

FIG. 18.3

TABLE 18.11: Improvement in Population and Area Served Per Primary School at PS Level : Rajasthan (1991-2001)

(%age share to total PSs)

Group	*(A) Pop. Served Per Primary School*			*(B) Area Served Per Primary School*		
	Population Served	*1991*	*2001*	*Area Served (Sq. Kms)*	*1991*	*2001*
Best	<750	2.5	15.6	<2.5	—	2.5
Better	750-1000	29.1	43.0	2.5-5.0	20.7	46.4
Normal	1000-1250	43.0	32.1	5.0-7.5	28.7	20.7
Worse	1250-1500	20.7	7.6	7.5-10.0	19.0	12.2
Worst	>1500	4.6	1.7	>10	31.7	18.2
	Total	**100**	**100**	**Total**	**100**	**100**

Source: Annex 7.2, 7.3, K-8 and K-9.

Table 18.11 presents improvements in population and area served per primary school during the 1991-2001 periods. In the year 1991, it was extremely bad that in 68.4 per cent PSs, population served per primary school was above 1000 and in 79.3 per cent PSs, area served per primary school was above 5 sq. kms. In the year 2001, with the over all improvement in educational infrastructural facilities, the percentage of PSs in the above categories came down to 41.4 and 51.1 per cent respectively.

BOX 18.2: Important Educational Programmes and Schemes

PROGRAMMES		*SCHEMES*
• Lok Jumbish (LJ) • DPEP	• Total Literacy Campaign • Post-Literacy and Continuing Education	• Non-Formal Education • Border Area Development (Education) Programme • Vocational Education
• Shiksha Karmi Project	• Operation Black Board	• Upgradation of Merit of SC and ST Children
• Rajiv Gandhi Swarn Jayanti Pathshala	• Improvement of Science Education • Class Project for Computer Education Technology • Environmental Education	• Teacher Education • Guru Mitra Yojana

GEDI: Growth Trends at PS Level (1991-2001)

- **162% Increase in GEDI (0.192 to 0.503)**
- **Behror PS (AL, 0.804) Snatched the First Rank From Nimrana (AL, 0.452)**
- **Kotra (Ud, 0.172) PS came down at the Bottom in place of Chohtan (Bmr, 0.042)**
- **Disparity Increased (0.410 to 0.632)**
- **Rising GEDI From SW & South & West to North & NE Direction**
- **11 PSs Maintained their First Ranks While 14 Maintained Last Ranks in their Respective Districts**
- **All PSs Registered Increase in GEDI Value**
- **Dhorimanna (Bmr, 1058%, 0.603) PS Registered Maximum Growth, While Nimrana (AL, 21%) & Kekri (Aj, 0.073) Registered Minimum Growth.**
- **45.6% (108) PSs Improved their Ranks in the State**
- **Dhorimanna (Bmr, +211) PS Registered Maximum Improvement in GEDI Rank While Kekri (Aj, –184) Registered Maximum Deterioration**
- **Talera and Itawa PSs Maintained their Ranks**

CHART 18.5

The GEDI value of the state was only 0.192 in the year 1991. Unfortunately, 59 per cent PSs had GEDI value below average and no PS of the state had even achieved 0.4 GEDI level except Nimrana (0.452) and Behror (0.418) PSs of Alwar district. Chohtan PS of Barmer district had the lowest GEDI. (0.042) Jaipur was the only division whose more than 75 per cent PSs had GEDI above 0.2. On the other side, 91.5 per cent PSs of Jodhpur division, 80 per cent of Udaipur, 78 per cent of Kota, 72 per cent of Ajmer and 52 per cent PSs of Bikaner divisions had GEDI below 0.2. Inter-district variation in PSs having highest and lowest GEDI was maximum in Alwar district followed by Banswara, Jhalawar, Udaipur, Bharatpur and Baran districts respectively.

In the year 2001, the GEDI value rose to 0.503, while 49 per cent PSs of Jaipur division, 43 per cent of Bikaner and 28 per cent PSs of Kota division have above 0.6 GEDI less than 3 per cent PSs of Jodhpur, Ajmer and Udaipur divisions qualified for this category. The GEDI level in the state increases from the SW and South to NE, North and SE direction. Behror PS of Alwar district have the maximum GEDI (0.804) while Kotra of Udaipur had the minimum (0.172). Maximum PSs (53.6%) of the state had medium level of GEDI (0.4-0.6) followed by Low (0.2-0.3, 24.1%), High (0.6-0.8 21.2%) and Very Low (<0.2, 0.8%) level. Behror was the only PS in Very High group (>0.8).

During 1991-2001 period, although the GEDI of the state has increased by 162 per cent (0.192 to 0.503), the index of deprivation is still high (0.497). Behror PS of Alwar district snatched the first rank from Nimrana (AL), while Kotra of Udaipur came down at the bottom in place of Chohtan of Barmer. 11 PSs maintained top ranks while 14 maintained bottom ranks in their respective districts. All PSs registered increase in GEDI value. Dhorimanna PS of Barmer district registered highest increase while Nimrana (AL) and Kekri (Aj) registered the lowest increase.

ISOGEDI maps (Fig 18.4 A & B) depict increased pattern of GEDI in Rajasthan during 1991-01 period. ISOGEDI denotes the line on a map, which joins the places of equal GEDI. In the year 1991, the state was covered by three ISOGEDI lines viz. 0.4 (highest), 03 and 0.2 (lowest). It was unfortunate that more than 3/5 portion (> 60%) of the state lay below 0.2 ISOGEDI line and 1/3 lied between 0.2 and 0.3 ISOGEDI lines. Nimrana and Behror both of Alwar district were the only PSs had GEDI above 0.4. The remaining area comprised of 14 PSs viz. Buhana, Jhunjhunun, Chirawa, Nawalgarh and Alsisar of Jhunjhunun district; Kotkasim and Mandawar of Alwar; Padampur, Karanpur, Sadulshahar, Suratgarh and Raisinghnagar of Ganganagar and Kekri PS of Ajmer lay between 0.3 and 0.4 ISOGEDI lines.

In the year 2001, with the increase in over all educational status of the state and particularly of female educational status, the value and number of ISOGEDI lines rose viz. 0.7 (highest), 0.6, 0.5 and 0.4 (lowest). While in the year 1991, more than 60 per cent portion of the state lay beneath 0.2 ISOGEDI line, in the year 2001, more than half portion of the state rose between 0.4 and 0.6 ISOGEDI lines and more than 2/5 portion even crossed 0.6 ISOGEDI. Behror PS of Alwar district has even crossed 0.8 GEDI level. Now, Kotra PS of Udaipur district and Peepalkhoot of Banswara are the only PSs that have remained beneath 0.2 ISOGEDI line.

There were 11 PSs viz. Garhi, Hurda, Keshoraipatan, Baseri, Sagwara, Ahore, Luni, Sultanpur, Rani Station, Railmagra and Bargaon which were continued to be at the top positions in GEDI in their respective districts during 1991-01 period. Likewise, 14 PSs viz. Thanaganji, Peepalkhoont, Chohtan, Bari, Suratgarh, Chaksu, Sam, Shergarh, Karauli, Itawa, Mundwa, Abu Road, Tonk and Kotra continued to remain at the bottom.

The INI of rural Rajasthan has increased 1.4 times from 0.3813 in 1991-92 to 0.5458 in 1998-99. While more than 90 per cent PSs of Jaipur, Bikaner and Kota divisions had Very High to Medium (0.4 to 1.0) level of INI, 93 per cent PSs of Jodhpur and 71 per cent PSs of Udaipur divisions had Very Low to Medium (0.17 to 0.6) level. The INI level in the state increases from SW and South to North, NE and SE direction. There were only 51 PSs (21.5%) which had registered an increase in INI of above 0.2. Where as, 87 per cent PSs of Jaipur division, 62 per cent of Bikaner and 58 per cent PSs of Udaipur division had an increased value of INI above 0.15, 63 per cent PSs of Kota, 62 per cent Jodhpur and 56 per cent PSs of Ajmer division had an increased value of INI below 0.15. Sanganer PS of Jaipur (0.3860) and Nawalgarh of Jhunjhunun (512%) registered the highest growth in INI, while, Hanumangarh (-0.0059, -1%) is the only PS in the State which registered decrease in INI.

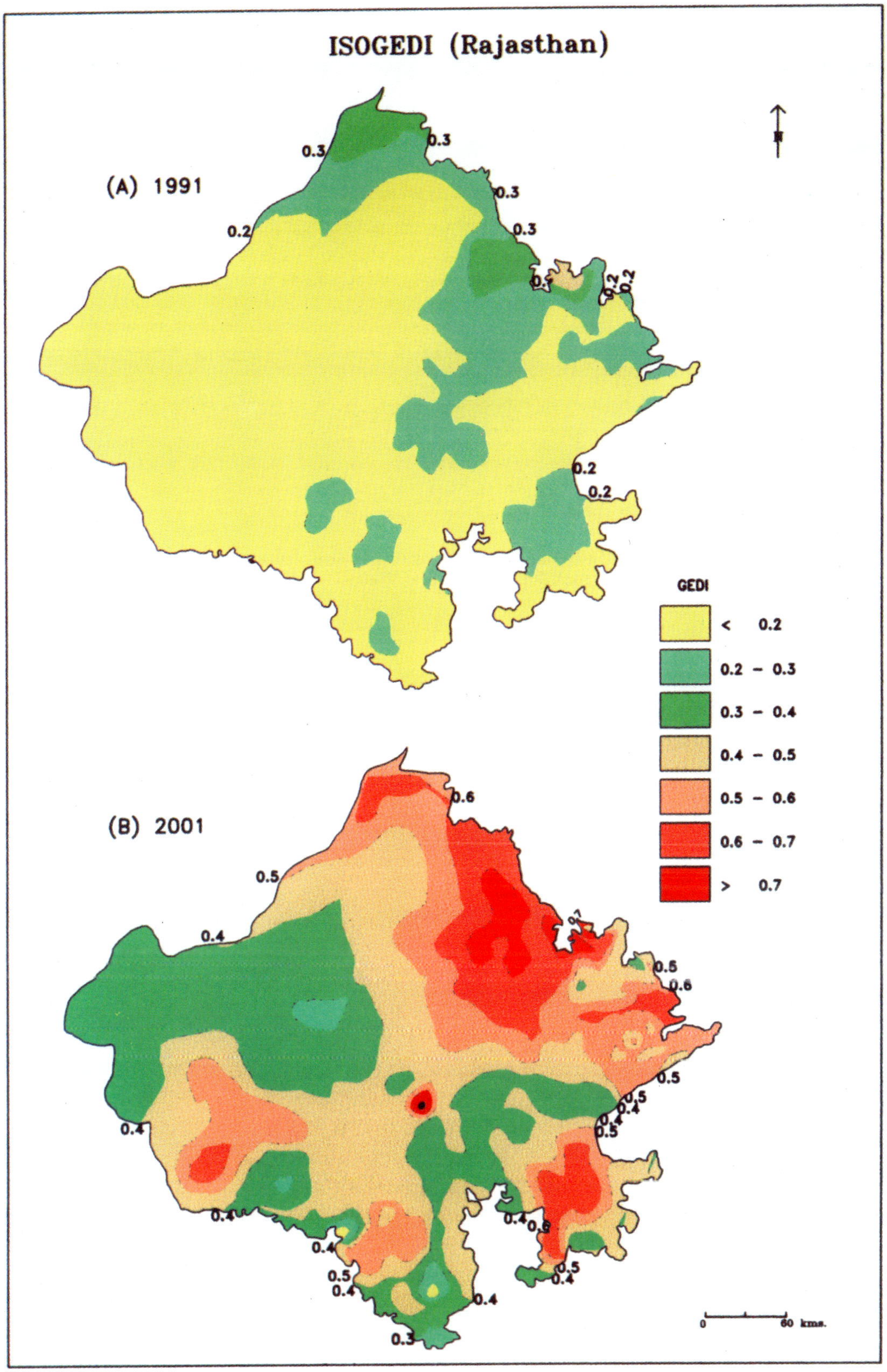

Note: ISOGEDI: Line Joins Places Having Equal GEDI.

Fig. 18.4

INI: Growth Trends at PS Level (1991-98)

- **43% Increase in INI (0.3813 to 0.5458)**
- **Increasing Disparity (0.7322 to 0.8357)**
- **Rising INI From South-West & South to North-East, North & SE Direction**
- **Sanganer PS (Jp, 1.0) Snatched the Ist Rank From Sangod (Kt, 0.7641)**
- **Aspur (Dg) Maintained its Bottom Rank (0.0319 / 0.1708)**
- **19 PSs Maintained I Rank, While 18 Maintained Last Rank in their Respective Districts**
- **Jaipur Division Dominating in PSs Having Very High to Medium INI Increased Value Where as Jodhpur in Low to Very Low**
- **All PSs, Except Hanumangarh (-0.0059, -1%) Registered Increase in INI Value**
- **Sanganer (Jp, 0.3860) and Navalgarh (Jhun, 512%) PSs Registered Maximum Increase INI**
- **46% PSs Registered Higher Increase in INI Value than the State Average (0.1645)**
- **41% PSs (97) Improved their Ranks in the State**
- **11 PSs: Arain, Jawaja, Pisangan, Raipur, Sahara, Aspur, Bhadra, Amber, Dudu, Sambhar and Nagaur Maintained their Ranks**

CHART 18.6

During 1991-98 period, the percentage of PSs having INI above 0.6 and between 0.4 to 0.6 rose from 7.2 to 24.9 and from 26.2 to 58.6 respectively. As a result, the percentage of PSs having INI below 0.4 fell sharply from 66.6 to 16.4. On the basis of increased value of INI, PSs of the state are classified in to five groups viz. Very High (>0.25), High (0.20-0.25), Medium (0.15-0.20), Low (0.10-0.15) and Very Low (<0.10). It is sad that 42.6 per cent PSs had registered low to very low increase in INI followed by PSs which had registered medium (35.9%) and high to very high (21.5%) increase in INI value. The percentage of PSs having Very High INI increased value in Jaipur and Bikaner divisions; High increased value in Jaipur, Ajmer and Udaipur divisions; Medium, increased value in Jaipur, Bikaner and Udaipur divisions; Low increased value in Ajmer, Kota, Jodhpur and Udaipur divisions and Very Low increased value in Bikaner, Kota and Jodhpur divisions was higher than the state average.

ISOINI maps (Fig 18.5 A & B) depict increased pattern of income index in the state. ISOINI denotes the line on a map, which joins the places of equal income index. In the year 1991-92, the state was covered by three ISOINI lines viz. 0.2 (lowest), 0.4 and 0.6 (highest) ISOINI. Barmer, Dungarpur and Jhunjhunun districts, covered by 0.2 ISOINI, were the most deprived areas. On the other hand, Jaipur and Kota districts lay between 0.6 and 0.8 ISOINI lines, were the most developed areas. More than 50 per cent portion of the state mainly arid, semi-arid and southern hilly areas lay between 0.2 and 0.4 ISOINI lines. In the year 1998-99 four ISOINI lines viz 0.35 (lowest), 0.50, 0.65 and 0.8 ISOINI passed through the state. As the overall level of INI had risen, around three-fourth portion of the state fell between 0.35 and 0.65 ISOINI lines. Barmer, Jalor and Dungarpur districts were covered by the lowest 0.35 ISOINI while Kota, central Jaipur and northern Hanumangarh districts were covered by the highest 0.80 ISOINI followed by 0.6 ISOINI.

Nineteen PSs in INI maintained the top positions in their respective districts during 1991-98 period These PSs were: Arain, Reni, Anandpuri, Chhipabarod, Baytoo, Deeg, Sahara, Nokha, Hindoli, Kapasan, Dungargarh, Simalwara, Sadulshahar, Bhadra, Sanganer, Sankra, Ahore, Buhana, Riyan, Fatehpur and Todaraisingh. Similarly, eighteen PSs viz. Jawaja, Ramgarh, Talwara, Siwana, Rupbas, Talera, Arnod, Sardarshahar, Bandikui, Aspur, Hanumangarh, Jaisalmer, Nawalgarh, Hindaun, Kuchaman, Sri Madhopur, Uniara and Kherwara maintainaned the worst position.

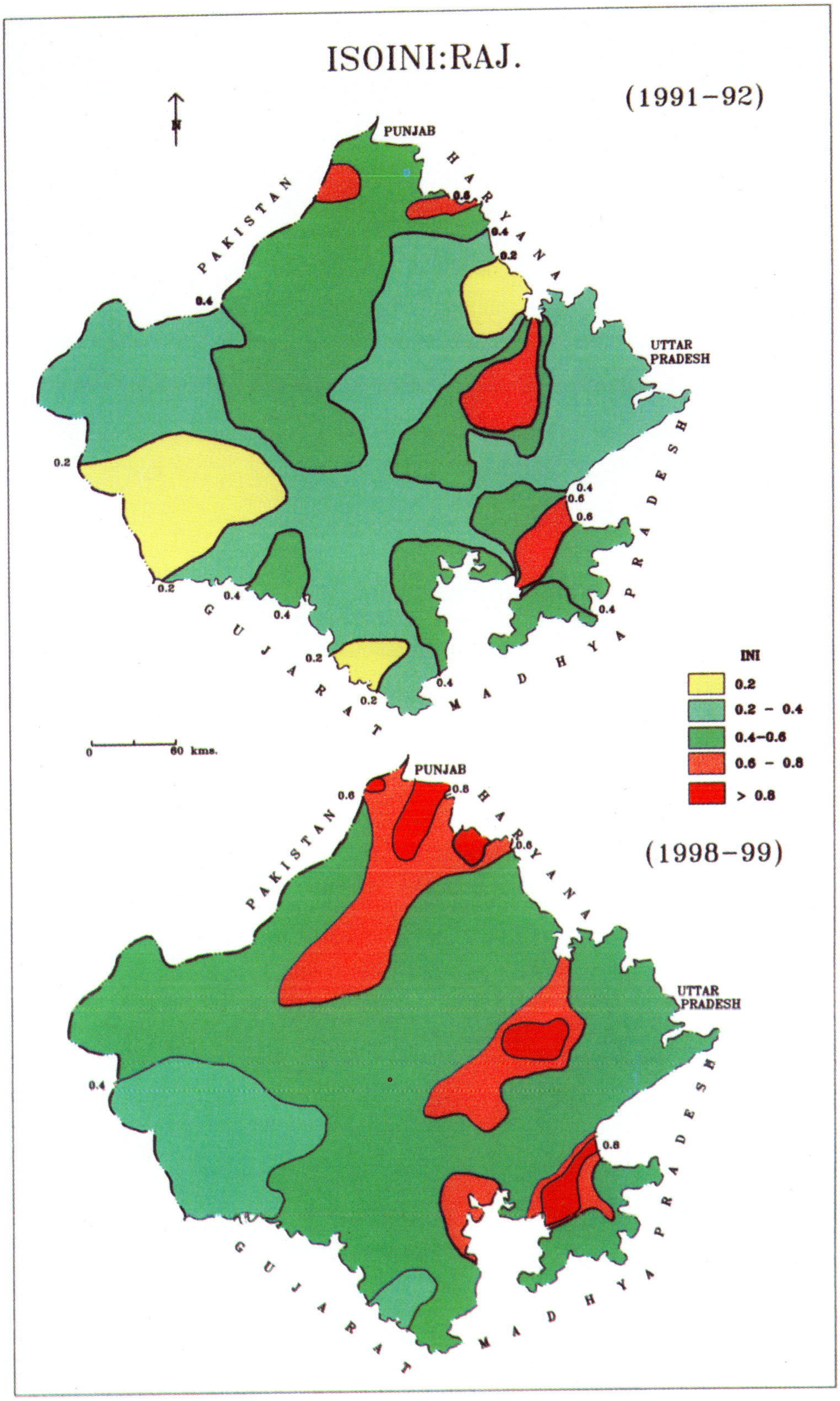

Note: ISOINI: Line Joins Places Having Equal INI.

Fig. 18.5

The Gender-Related Income Index (GINI) of rural Rajasthan in the year 1991-92 was moderate (0.6680). There were only 18 per cent PSs having GINI above 0.7. Jaipur division dominated not only in PSs having Very High GINI (41.2% share) but also in PSs having Low (29.2%) and Very Low (47.4%) GINI. Similarly, Ajmer division led in PSs having High (28%) GINI while, Udaipur (26%) division topped in PSs having Low GINI. Sangod PS of Kota district had the maximum 0.8196 GINI while, Rajakhera of Dhaulpur was the most deprived (0.2323). The state had clear-cut dominance of PSs having medium (0.65-0.7, 38.9%) GINI followed by PSs having Low (0.6-0.65, 27.4%), Very Low (<0.6, 16%), High (0.7-0.75, 10.5%) and Very High (>0.75, 7.2%) GINI.

Growth Trends In GINI (Rural Raj, 1991-98)

- **106% Increase in GINI (0.668 to 0.739)**
- **Disparity Among PSs Decreased (0.5873 to 0.3206)**
- **Rising GINI from South-West & South to North-East, North & SE Direction**
- **Sanganer PS (Jp, 0.9081) Snatched the Ist Rank from Sangod (Kt, 0.8196)**
- **Siwana PS (Bmr, 0.5875) came down at the Bottom in place of Rajakhera (Dhaul, 0.2323)**
- **19 PSs Maintained I Rank While 18 Maintained Last Rank in their Districts**
- **All PSs Registered Increase in GINI Value**
- **Rajakhera PS (Dhaul, 184%, 0.4272) Registered Maximum Increase, While Phalodi (Jodh, 1%, 0.0073) Registered Minimum Increase**
- **49.4% PSs Registered Higher Increase in INI Value than the State Average (0.071)**
- **42.6% PSs (101) Improved their Ranks in the State**
- **Sadulshar PS (Gg) Registered Highest (118) Improvement in its Rank, While Phalodi (Jodh) Registered Highest (-114) Deterioration**

CHART 18.7

In the year 1998-99, although the GINI rose to 0.7390 and simultaneously IOD came down to 0.2610 still, the state has to travel a long way to achieve the targeted value 1.0. The percentage of PSs having GINI above 0.7 had gone up from merely 18 in 1991-92 to 72 in 1998-99. Jaipur division dominated not only in VH level PSs (24.7%) but also in H (31%) level PSs. On the other hand, Jodhpur division was the most deprived led in M to VL (28%) level PSs. Sanganer PS of Jaipur district had the maximum GINI (0.9081) while, Siwana of Barmer had the minimum GINI (0.5875). The state had clear-cut dominance of PSs having High GINI (40.9%) followed by PSs having Very High (30.8%), Medium (23.6%), Low (3.8%) and Very Low (0.8%) GINI.

ISOGINI maps (Fig 18.6 A&B) reveal the changed scenario of gender related economic development in the state. ISOGINI represents the line on a map which joins the places of equal gender related income index. In the year 1991-92, four ISOGINI lines viz. 0.60, 0.65, 0.70 and 0.75 passed through the state. Jaisalmer, Barmer, Jhunjhunun and Dungarpur districts were covered by the lowest 0.6 ISOGINI while most part of Jaipur, Kota and some part of Hanumangarh district was covered by the highest 0.75 ISOGINI line. Around two-third portion of the state lay between 0.65 and 0.7 ISOGINI lines.

In the year 1998-99, the state is again crossed by four ISOGINI with increased minimum and maximum values. These are: 0.65 (minimum), 0.70, 0.75 and 0.80 ISOGINI. The lowest 0.65 ISOGINI passed through Barmer and Dungarpur districts while the highest 0.80 ISOGINI passed through Kota, Hanumangarh, northern Ganganagar and southern Bikaner districts. About two-third portion of the state lay between 0.70 and 0.75 ISOGINI.

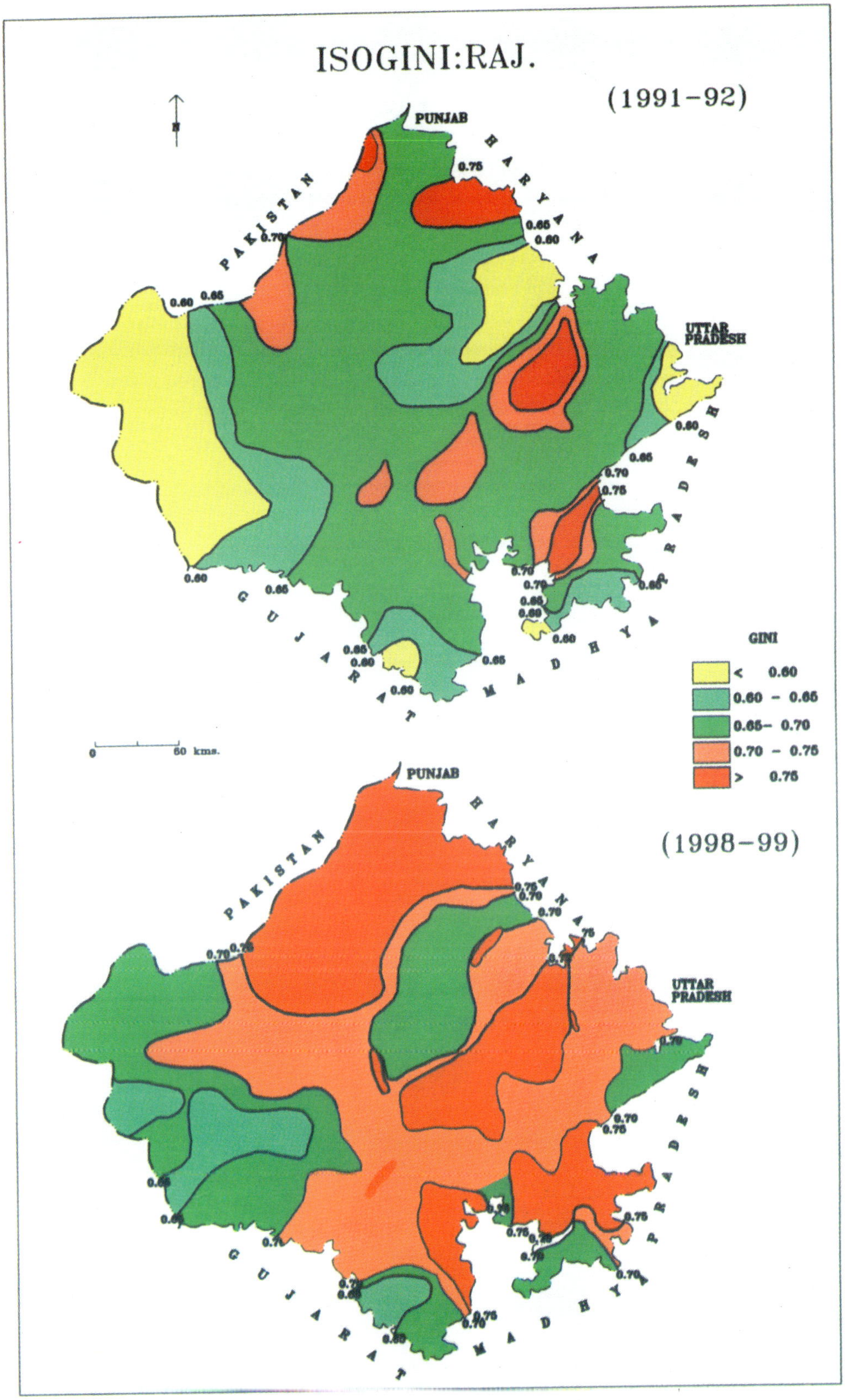

Note: ISOGINI: Line Joins Places Having Equal GINI.

FIG. 18.6

In GINI, twenty-one PSs continued to be at the best position in their respective districts during 1991-98 period. These PSs were: Arain, Reni, Anandpuri, Chhipabarod, Baytoo, Deeg, Sahara, Nokha, Hindoli, Kapasan, Dungargarh, Simalwara, Bhadra, Sankra, Ahore, Buhana, Nadoti, Kumbhalgarh, Fatehpur, Todarsingh and Bhinder. On the other hand, 18 PSs namely Talwara, Anta, Talera, Sardarshahar, Bandikui, Rajakhera, Aspur, Padampur, Hanumangarh, Jaisalmer, Dag, Nawalgarh, Hindaun, Kuchaman, Sumerpur, Rajsamand, Gangapur, Sri Madhopur and Uniara were continued to be remained at the worst position.

The Gender Empowerment Measure (GEM) of Rural Rajasthan in the year 2001 was 0.759.While more than 38 per cent PSs of Bikaner and 33 per cent of Ajmer division had High to Very High Level (>0.8) of GEM, less than 5 per cent PSs of Jodhpur division found mention in this category. Jaipur division led (50% share) not only in having VH level of GEM but also in PSs having M (27.2%) and L (31.1%) level of GEM. On the other hand, Jodhpur division being the most deprived dominated (62.5% share) in VL level PSs. Ajmer division dominated (33.3%) in H level PSs. Chechat PS of Kota district had the maximum GEM (0.915), where as Sheo of Barmer, on the other hand, had the minimum (0.557). Barring a few exceptions, increase in the GEM level in the state sprang mainly from western and southern Rajasthan to northern, south-eastern and north-eastern Rajasthan.

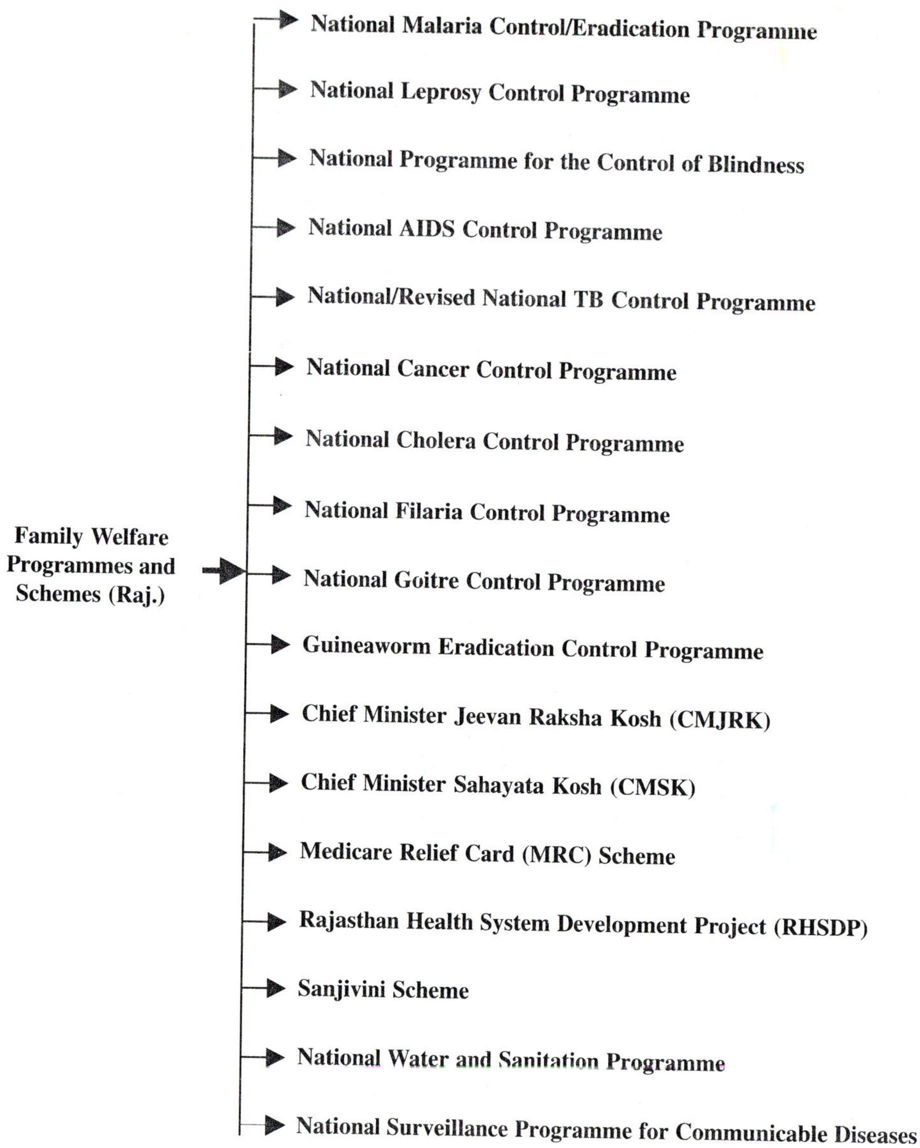

CHART 18.8

Family Welfare Programmes and Schemes (Raj.) →

- **Reproductive and Child Health Programme**
- **Expended Programme of Immunization (EPI)/Universal Immunization Programme (UIP)**
- **Special Pulse Polio Scheme (SPPS)**
- **Pilot Project on Hepatitis-B Vaccine**
- **UNFPA Assisted Area Project (UAAP)**
- **UNFPA Assisted Integrated Population and Development (IPD) Project Phase II**
- **UNICEF Assisted Women's Health Programme**
- **European Commission Assisted Health and FWP**
- **Post-Partum Centre Scheme**
- **Pariwar Seva Sansthan (PSS)**
- **Pariwar Kalyan Pension Yojana (PKPY)**
- **Jan Mangal Scheme (JMS)**
- **National Rural Health Mission***
- **Rajasthan Health Care Project (EAP)**
- **Vikalp Yojana**
- **National Motherhood Benefit Scheme (NMBS)**
- **Raj Laxmi Scheme (RLS)**
- **Minimum Needs Programme (MNP)**
- **Integrated Child Development Services (ICDS) Scheme**
- **Employees State Insurance Scheme (ESIS)**
- **UNICEF Assisted Border Districts Community Strategy Project**
- **Static and FRU Center Scheme**
- **Revamping Scheme**
- **Village Health Guide Scheme (VHGS)**
- **Social Security Scheme (SSS)**

CHART 18.9

BOX 18.3: Latest NFHS Data for Rajasthan: Highlights

- 51.55% of pregnant and lactating mothers in Rajasthan are found to have anaemia.
- 48-49% of working women are anaemic.
- Children below 6 years constitute approximately 17% of the total population.
- About 83 infants out of 1000 live births die before attaining first birth day.
- More than 50% of the children in age group 0 to 6 years suffer from different degree of malnutrition.
- 51% of the children under three years of age are underweight.
- Average 3.8 children are born to a woman.
- Average 2.6 children are desired by a woman.
- Muslim women have the highest unwanted children. They produce 2 children more than they actually want to, followed by Hindu women who have about one unwanted child.
- Jain women have minimum difference (0.3) between the children wanted and produced.
- 75% of Muslim women and 70% of the SC & ST women are not using any FP method which is highest in the state.
- Contraception prevalence is highest (66%) among Jain women followed by Hindu (41%), women belonging to other religion (53%) and the lowest (25%) among Muslim women.
- Use of contraceptive methods increases with increasing education, 37% among illiterate women to 59% among women who have at least complete high school. Three quarters of Hindus and four-fifths of Muslims are illiterate. In contrast, 90% Jain women are literate.
- The use of female sterilization is lower among Muslims than women belonging to other religions.

Poor acceptance of FP methods mainly by Muslims and SC/ST women.

"75% Muslim women and 70% of the SC/ST women are not using any family planning methods. They produce about two children more than they actually want to, followed by Hindu women, who have about one unwanted child. On an average, 3.8 children are born to a woman here, contrary to her desire to have only 2.6 children. The use of female sterilisation is much lower among Musilms than women belonging to other religions."

Source: 1. National Family Health Survey, 1998-99 (NFHS-2) Rajasthan.
2. *Hindustan Times,* 12th April, 2004, Jaipur.

BOX 18.4: Family Welfare and MCH Programmes: Rajasthan

Integrated FWP and MCH programmes are being launched in Rajasthan.

Objectives:

- Population stabilization—to promote responsible parenthood with small family norm through independent choice of family planning method best suits to couple.
- To reduce IMR.
- To reduce MMR.

Changed strategy:

Since 1976-77, Community Need Assessment Approach (CNAA) has been adopted in place of Target Free Approach (TFA). Under CNAA, the worker himself/herself determines target according to the demand of public.

Provision made during X FYP period (2002-07): Rs. 275 million

Progress 2004-05 (up to Dec. 04)

Sterilisation operation performed: 1.81 lakh
IUD inserted: 2.04 lakh
Oral Pills and Conventional Contraceptive Users:

- ➢ Routine users: 3.62 lakh
- ➢ New users: 3.97 lakh

Referral transport services

- ➢ Provided to 3415 pregnant women of BPL families.
- ➢ Amount spent: Rs. 1.6 million

Night deliveries held: 76693
Expenditure occurred made on round-the-clock delivery services: Rs. 23.27 million
National Maternity Benefit Scheme
➢Women benefited: 4977
➢Expenditure incurred: Rs. 2.49 million

Functioning:

Vast institutional infrastructure along with special institutions in the form of ICDS scheme, universal immunization programme and post partum centres are being spread across the state.

Monitoring:

Effective monitoring is done at each level-state, district and block level.

(contd.)

BOX 18.4: FWP and MCH Programmes: Rajasthan: Highlights

TRENDS

- Increased availability of contraceptives in each village through:

➢ AWC	➢ FRU	➢ Jan Mangal Couple
➢ SHC	➢ Hospital	➢ Dairy
➢ PHC	➢ Dispensary	➢ Cooperative Society
➢ CHC	➢ Ayurvedic Hospital	➢ Fair Price Shop

'Condom Vending Machines Established in Jaipur'

- 100 vending machines established across the city in public places such as the sulabh complexes, railway stations and bus stations.
- The machine would dispense a packet containing five condoms once a person inserts a Rs 5 coin.
- Depending on the reaction to these machines, the government plans to install similar machines across the state.

'Parivar Kalyan Pension Scheme' (PKPS)

Rajasthan is the first state in India to implement this scheme. Pension of Rs. 150 per month will be given to men (after the age of 60 years) who had undergone family planning operation after two children. In case of his death, his widow will be given the pension (after the age of 55 years).

MCH special monitoring movement was held during 5th Feb. 2005 to 31st March 2005.

'MCH Day' : Since 4th Oct. 2004, mother and child day (once in a month) is observed across the state with the objective of strengthening MCH services.

TFA/CNNA

- ➢ The family welfare programme was being implemented under the 'Target Free Approach (TFA)' since 1st April 1996 all over India and under the system of decentralized participatory planning.
- ➢ TFA has been renamed as **Community Needs Assessment Approach (CNAA)** from 1997.
- ➢ The preparation of the annual action plans at district and state levels is based on the assessed needs of the people for FW services is one of the most essential and vital activities in the programme.
- ➢ This approach is expected to bring about improvements in the quality of services and client satisfaction.
- ➢ The decentralized participatory planning strategy adopted under this approach involves inter-alia, close association of the community and its leading lights and opinion leaders such as village pradhans, mahila swasthya sanghs, primary school teachers etc. in the formulation of the PHC based family welfare and health care plans.
- ➢ "Guidelines as a supplement to CNAA Manual", a supplementary booklet has also been got printed and circulated across the state.
- ➢ NIC has developed new software for transmission of data from district health officers to the state health office. This software is being download in the computer at district and state level.

BOX 18.5: Causes of High IMR in Rajasthan

- Pre-maturity of birth.
- Low birth weight. 51% of the children under three years of age are underweight. (NFHS – 2)
- Low peri-natal, neo-natal and post-natal care. About 83 infants out of 1000 live births die before attaining first birth day. (NFHS-2)
- Diseases like—acute respiratory infection, diarrhoea, fever.
- Poor birth practices.
- Malnutrition. More than 50% of the children in age group 0 to 6 years suffer from different degree of malnutrition. (NFHS – 2)
- Early age at motherhood.
- Anaemic.
- Low status of women.
- Low level of immunization.
- Lack of awareness and access to the health facilities.

BOX 18.6: Malnutrition in Rajasthan

Chronic nutrition deficiency in children, adolescent girls and pregnant women.

Most Suffering Areas:

- Arid/Semi-arid/hilly.
- Tribal.
- Backward.

Causes:

- Inadequate food supply.
- Lack of knowledge regarding nutritious foods.
- Foods taboos.
- Gender biasness, inequitable distribution of food within the family.
- Inaccessibility to nutritional services.
- Poverty.
- Poor Performance of ICDS.
- Negligence of women.
- Lack of community consciousness.

Effects:

- Stunt growth.
- Increases susceptibility to infections and diseases.
- Impedes physiological maturity.
- Due to Iodine deficiency, women have higher rates of foetal wastages, still-birth and low-birth-weight babies.
- Anemia causes fatigue, poor appetite, poor learning capacity, gastrointestinal and neurological problems.

BOX 18.7: AIDS in Rajhasthan: Highlights

- First case of HIV positive reported in Pushkar (Ajmer Distt.) in 1986.
- Up to Dec 2004, the total cases reported are 1322.
- 50% of the total AIDS cases are registered from five districts viz. Jaipur, Churu, Jhunjhunun, Nagaur and Sikar.
- 70% cases are reported from rural areas.
- Fresh cases of AIDS registered in the year 2004-05 are 463.
- The first community care centre for AIDS opened in Jaipur on the occasion of World Aids Day on 1st Dec. 2005 and the second one is expected soon in Sikar. The GoR is going to open such CCC for AIDS patients in each divisional headquarter.
- As per announcement made by state government, anti-retroviral (ARV) drugs will be included in the essential drug list and will be made available for free to the BPL patients. The kind of ARV drugs offered will depend on the severity of the patient's condition. Other poor patients, who do not fall in the BPL category, will also be offered assistance from the CM's Relief Fund.
- The state government is mooting the proposal of permitting people living with HIV/AIDS to travel free in buses together with an attendant. A pension policy for such persons is also on the cards.
- SOS fund will be created to route the funds donated for tackling Aids.
- Free primary education for boys of HIV/AIDS infected parents is also being planned, as the government already provides free education for all girls.
- Several awards are also being given to organizations and individuals who have made a significant contribution to fight against AIDS.
- Women Join Fight Against AIDS: Wives of migrant labourers in Churu, Jhunjhunun and Sikar districts have now emerged as quiet but fierce campaigners in the struggle against the AIDS. These women have begun stocking condoms at their homes for easy accessibility and teaching others in the area about the virtues of safe sex. Under 'Hamara' a project that covers nearly 24000 migrants wives in 133 villages more than 3 lakhs condoms were distributed during the year 2003-04. India-Canada Collaborative HIV and AIDS Project (ICHAP) communication programme which begin in 2001 and which promoted safe sex without disheveling cultural sensitivity.
- Thrust on Research-ICMR is keenly following the trials on herbal medicine to cure hepatitis B and C, which are on at several places including Jaipur to allowed varied patients profiles. It will enable to reach the poor as it will reduce the cost of vaccines by nearly 50%. This herbal vaccine is derived from Mulethi (*Glycyrrhiza Glabra*) and helps control cirrhosis lung cancer.
- Jaipur to be 'Epicenter of AIDS Research'*—It is a matter of great pleasure that Jaipur will soon get a research centre dedicated to work on various facets of AIDS. The centre excepted to come up in another six months, will focus on the extensive database of the SMS Medical College that has over 1250 registered AIDS patients with their treatment records dating back to as many as four years. One of the possible projects that could be carried out here includes the usage of microbicides, such as the Praneem cream made out of the Neem tree, to destroy the HIV virus. The cream is used as a suppository and applied around the genitals. The centre would consist of a multi-specialty team dedicated to patient care and research.

* *Hindustan Times,* 11th Oct, 2004, Jaipur.

BOX 18.8: Drinking Water and Sanitation Problems in Rajasthan

[I] 'Drinking Water'

- Rajasthan accounts for 5.65 India's population but only 1.28% of available water source.
- There are 74 over-exploited blocks, where annual extraction of groundwater is more than annual recharge*.
- There are 20 dark blocks, where annual extraction is 85—100 per cent of the annual recharge*.

Decline in Ground Water#	**Districts**
Up to 2 metres	Bundi, Banswara, Dhaulpur, Udaipur, Bharatpur, Baran, Dungarpur, Karauli, Alwar and Jhalawar
2 to 4 metres	Sikar, Dausa, Dungarpur, Jhunjhunun and Alwar
More than 4 metres	Jalor, Sirohi, Bhilwara, Jaipur, Pali, Dausa and Tonk

- There are 11000 habitations (10% of India) in Rajasthan, where water level has gone down and water availability for drinking contains fluoride, iron and other impurities.
- 2642 villagers are severely affected by fluoride contamination (>5 ppm, above permissible limit).
- Out of the total 47000 sites identified for water harvesting structures, only 8% structures have been completed so far.

Causes:

- Non-availability of perrential sources of water in major portion of the state.
- Ground water is also available at considerable depth.
- Ground water in many places is not safe for drinking purpose.
- Frequent failure of rain further complicates the situation.
- Lack of public awareness. Wastage and misuse of water is common.

[II] SANITATION

- More than 75% diseases in rural Rajasthan are related to inadequate sanitation which is also one of the major causes of high IMR.
- Poor performance of Total Sanitation Campaign:
  - Only one-fourth of released funds have been utilised during last four years.
  - Against the target of covering 320,000 households under the Individual Household Latrine (IHHL) project, the achievement was only 5% (17,201) in the first two years.
  - Against the target of covering 14,730 schools in the first two years, the achievement was less than 15% (2145).

As per ground water resources estimation made by ground water board for Rajasthan.

BOX 18.9: Alleviation of Hunger and Malnutrition

- Strategy for alleviation of hunger and malnutrition to all sections of society through poverty alleviation measures e.g. Integrated Child Development Scheme (ICDS), Special Nutrition Programme (SNP), Mid-day Meals Programme, Education, Research and Evaluation.
- Improving performance of ICDS programme through:
  - Full capacity utilization of *Anganwari* Centres (AWC) along with their proper training.
  - Ensuring timely and adequately supply of supplementary nutrients (SN) to AWCs.
  - More AWCs should be opened in Saharia area (Baran District) in view of Supreme Court Judgment treating all Saharaias as BPL
  - Alternative SN (Supplementary Nutrients) should be introduced of
  - Effectively monitoring by Panchayats.
  - Community participation and awareness should be effectively generated.
  - Health education to adolescent girls and school students.

BOX 18.10: Tackling HIV/AIDS

- Bold and determined efforts need to be made to achieve zero-level growth of HIV/AIDS through:
  - ➢ Improved surveillance by setting up of more sentinel sites,
  - ➢ Use of primary health centres to monitor HIV/AIDS,
  - ➢ Public awareness campaigns,
  - ➢ Promotion of safe sex by using of condoms,
  - ➢ Prevention of drug abuse and
  - ➢ Distribution of disposable syringes.
- Priority should be given to cost-effective epidemic logical surveillance and vital registration system.
- Intensive efforts for high risk behaviour groups and extensive efforts for the community at large be taken up to create a good understanding of HIV/AIDS.
- NGO should be effectively engaged in supplementing government efforts, particularly for high risk groups.
- Behaviour surveillance (BH) programme should be effectively implemented by state AIDS Control Society (SACs) especially in high risk groups eg: commercial sex workers, intravenous drug users and transport workers.
- BH should include monitoring of 4 key indicators:
  - ➢ Sexual intercourse with multiple partners.
  - ➢ Use of condoms with non-regular sex partners.
  - ➢ Awareness of preventive methods of HIV.
  - ➢ Treatment of STDs.

BOX 18.11: Total Sanitation Campaign (Rajasthan)

Sponsored by	:	GoI Expenditure ratio: GoI : GoR
Partnered by	:	UNICEF 1.85 : 1
Launched in	:	2000 Nodal agency : Panchayati Raj Department
Project cost	:	Rs.1.29 blns Executed through : Village Panchayats
Districts covered	:	Initially 5, at Present 11 (Rajsamand, Jaipur, Kota, Bundi, Jhalawar, Dhaulpur, Tonk, Sawai Madhopur, Sikar, Ajmer, Alwar)

BOX 18.12: Drinking Water Projects (Rajasthan): Highlights

- Rs. 1.51 billion has been earmarked by GoI for drinking water projects to be undertaken in Rajasthan during the year 2005-06.
- Rs. 753 million granted by GoI for drinking water under TGPY (Twarit Gramin Payjal Yojana) to provide potable drinking water in rural areas of the state.
- The public health engineering department launched a campaign to repair hand pumps from Ist of January 2005.

Survey to Assess Drinking Water Problem

Survey is going to be conducted by	:	GoR
Costing	:	Rs. 2.23 billion
Expenditure share (%)	:	Rural : Urban 76 : 24
Objectives	:	To prepare a contingency plan to solve water problem.

'Water Transportation'

Plan to transport water by road to 60 towns and 10,000 villages and *dhanis.* Water will also be transported through rail to eight towns and 27 villages and *dhanis.* In urban areas, 410 tube wells and 1700 hand pumps will be installed. In rural areas, the number of tube wells is 1000 tube wells and 7000 haird pumps will be installed.

'Water Project Under the Vision Document 2005'

Under the Vision Document 2005, priority has been given to complete all pending projects in rural and urban areas. Besides new projects have also been undertaken to improve the surface and underground water situation in the entire state.

'National Fluoride Mitigation Sub-Center'

NFMSC is being set up at Jaipur with an investment of Rs. 650 million. The center will purify water and make it safe for drinking.

Rural Water Supply Scheme

Revenue Expenditure	*million Rs.*
Accounts, 2003-04	2629.85
Revised Estimates, 2004-05	2571.54
Budget Estimates, 2005-06	2286.24

BOX 18.13: Human Development: A Partial Balance Sheet (1991-01)

Achievements	Failures
• ***Human Development Index*** of Rural Rajasthan registered 45% increase from 0.3938 to 0.5709 during 1991-2001 periods. • All PSs registered improvement in HDI value. • 24.5% PSs registered increase in HDI value above 0.2.	• ***Index of deprivation is still high (0.4291)*** and state has to travel a long way to achieve the targeted value 1.0. • ***38 PSs still had HDI value below 0.5.*** • ***Disparity*** in HDI value at PS level increased from 0.332 to 0.374. • 152 (64%) PSs registered less than 50% increase in HDI value. • 21 districts out of 32 registered below 50% increase in HDI value. Bhilwara was at the bottom (31%) followed by Ajmer; Ganganagar and Pali; Bikaner and Hanumangarh; Kota, Jodhpur, Tonk; Jaipur and Sirohi; Alwar and Chittaurgarh; Swai Madhopur, Baswara, Bundi and Udaipur; Rajsamand, Jalor Baran and Jhalawar districts (in ascending order) respectively.
• In ***Health Status Index,*** the state registered 20% increase from 0.5588 to 0.6684.	• ***Sam PS*** of Jaisalmar; ***Barmer, Sheo*** and ***Baytoo*** of Barmer and ***Kotra*** of Udaipur districts still had HSI value below 0.5. • ***Shergarh PS*** of Jodhpur registered decrease in HSI value during the period.
• ***Education Index*** registered 107% increase from 0.2413 to 0.4991.	• ***58.6% PS still had EDI value less than 0.5.***
• Gender - Related Education Index registered 162% increase (0.192 to 0.503).	• ***58% PSs still had GEDI value below 0.5.***
• ***Income Index*** increased 1.4 times from 0.3813 to 0.5458 during 1991-98 period.	• ***45% PSs had INI value below 0.5.***
• ***Gender-Related Income Index*** increased by 106% from 0.6680 in 1991-92 to 0.7390 in 1998-99.	• ***11 PSs still had GINI value below 0.5.***
• ***Human Poverty Index*** decreased from 57% in the year 1991 to 55% in the year 2001. *	• ***157 PSs had HPI value above 50%.***
• The ***Gender Empowerment Measure*** of Rural Rajasthan was 0.759 in the year 2001.	• While more than 38% PSs of Bikaner and 33% of Ajmer division had High to Very High Level (>0.8) of GEM, less than 5% PSs of Jodhpur division found mention in this category.
• 98% ***rural population*** of the state was served by education amenities followed by 95% by improved drinking water amenities, 92% by power amenities, 73% by pucca road amenities, 64% by telephone amenities, 63% by transport communications amenities, 57% by medical and 51% rural population was served by post office amenities.**	• ***81% rural population*** was ***deprived of bank*** amenities and ***70%*** had no ***agricultural credit societies***. **
• 92% ***inhabited villages*** of the state had improved drinking water amenities followed by 86% had education amenities, 81% had power amenities and 52.3% villages had pucca road amenities.**	• 95% ***inhabited villages*** had ***no bank*** amenities, 87% had no ***agricultural credit societies***, 77% had no ***post office*** amenities, 57% had no ***transport communications*** amenities and 56% inhabited villages had no ***telephone*** amenities.**

* Hemlata Joshi. 2005. '*Economic Development Index, Rajasthan* (Spatio-Temporal & Gender Appraisal at Panchayat Samiti/Block Level), Published Research Report, IDSJ, University Book House, Jaipur.

** As per 2001 Census.

BOX 18.14: Challenges Facing Rural Rajasthan

- Frequent Drought
- Poverty
- Illiteracy
- Malnutrition
- Unemployment
- Rainwater Harvesting
- Livelihood Security
- Lack of Socio-Economic Infrastructural Facilities
- Shrinking Resources
- Gender Disparity
- Problems of Deprived Areas (Desert, Hilly, Plateau etc.)
- Problems of Weaker Sections (SC, ST, Women & OBC)

BOX 18.15: Recommendations

- Effective Management of Natural Resources and Ensuring Sustainable Socio- Economic Development in an Eco-Friendly Manner.
- Strengthening Anti-Poverty Programmes. Alleviation of Hunger and Malnutrition at a Priority Basis.
- Strengthening Basic Infrastructural Facilities.
- Improving Quality of Health, Education and Other Socio-Economic Services.
- Thrust on Effective Implementation of Government. Programmes and Schemes.
- Allotment of Adequate Resources for the Upliftment of Deprived Areas (Desert, Hilly and Plateau) and Weaker Sections (SC, ST, OBC etc.)
- Ensuring Equity in Land Holding
- Market and Technology Support for Agriculture and Industrial Development
- Women's Empowerment
- Focus on Govt-NGO Ties. Increasing People's Participation in the Development Process.
- Tackling Drinking Water Crises Effectively. Conservation of Water Through: Integrated Watershed Management, Setting up of Irrigation and Water Structuring Projects and Through Rainwater Harvesting.
- Thrust Towards Modernisation. Launching of Comprehensive and Integrated Training Programmes.
- Effective Role of Public Representatives and PRIs.
- Effective Networking of Insurance Services.
- Promoting Higher Reasearch on Human Development.

MODEL 18.1: Education Expenditure Model

Objectives :

- To reduce areal differentiation in education development
- Upliftment of deprived areas and weaker sections
- To reduce gender disparity in education Development

The inference of this research suggests that for better results following expenditure ratio model should be adopted :

	(a) Tribal/Desert/Hilly Plateau Areas ↓	***(B) NE, Northern and South-Eastern Developed Areas*** ↓
Total Expenditure on Education →	***More thrust should be given on Elementary Education in comparison to the state average***	***More thrust should be given on Higher Education in comparison to the state average***
Expenditure on Elementary *Education* →	***Higher thrust should be given on Achievements and equal thrust on Enrollment and Retention***	***Higher thrust should be given on Achievements in comparison to state average***

Per Capita Expenditure on Education ↓

Base: Female Literacy Rate (%) → ***> 60 /30–60 /<30***

↓ ↓ ↓

Expenditure Ratio Should be → ***1 : 2 : 3***

MODEL 18.2: Health Policy: Thrust Area

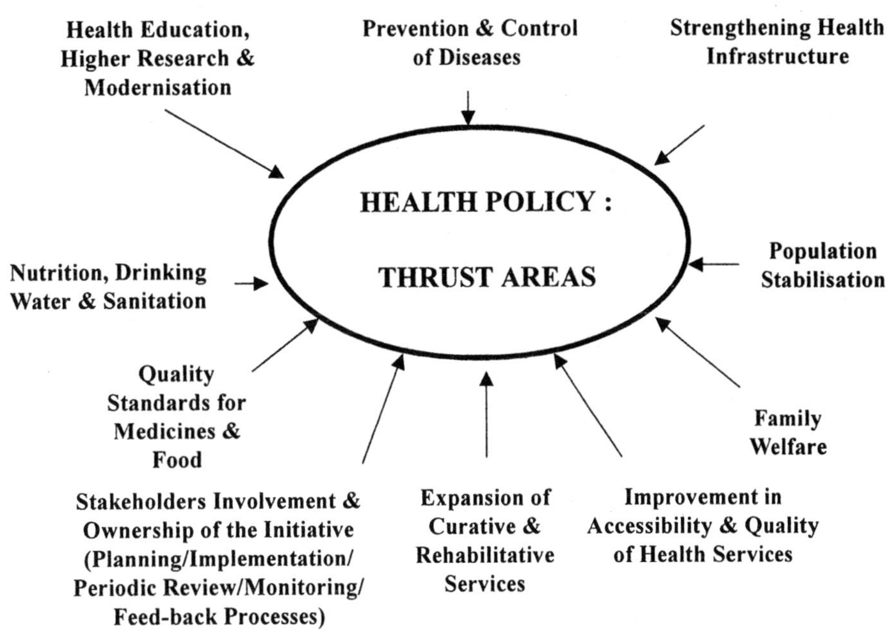

MODEL 18.3: EIA Approach in Improving Human Development Status in Rural Rajasthan

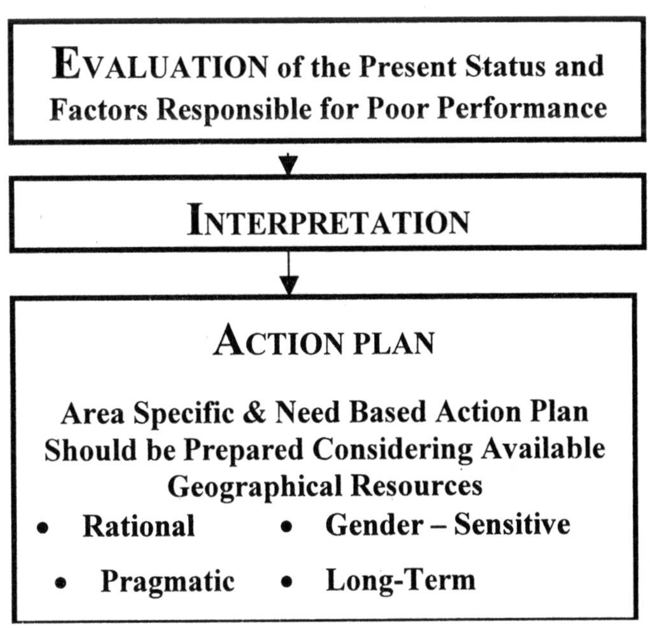

BOX 18.16: ACTION PLAN *(A) STATE LEVEL*

Top Priority should be given for the Improvement in Human Development Status of the following Bottom 50 PSs

Rank	Criteria (2001) / Name of PSs					
	%age of Rural Pop. Served by Medical Amenities	Pop. Served Per Medical Institution	Area Served Per Medical Institution	Pop. Served Per Bed	Pop. Served Per Doctor	Sex-Ratio (0-6)
1	2	3	4	5	6	7
1	CHHABRA	MANOHARTHANA	SAM	SEWAR	SRINAGAR	SADULSHAHAR
2	MANOHARTHANA	RAJAKHERA	JAISALMER	SRINAGAR	SAWAI MADHOPUR	GANGANAGAR
3	KAPASAN	KAMAN	KOLAYAT	JAISALMER	SEWAR	KARANPUR
4	BAYTOO	BANDIKUI	BAP	KISHANGARH	SANKRA	SAM
5	RAJAKHERA	CHHABRA	SHEO	BARMER	PHALODI	BUHANA
6	CHHIPABAROD	KOTKASIM	BIKANER	JHOTWARA	CHAKSU	PADAMPUR
7	CHHOTI SADRI	NOKHA	LUNKARANSAR	JHALRAPATAN	KOTRA	BEHROR
8	SHEO	BAYANA	NOKHA	PHALODI	KAMAN	TODABHIM and
9	DHORIMANNA	BARI SADRI	SANKRA	CHITTAURGARH	SHAHPURA	NIMRANA*
10	CHAKSU	NAGAR PAHARI	PHALODI	BALOTRA	JHOTWARA	BARI*
11	BARMER	RAMGARH	CHOHTAN	NAGAUR	SINDHARI	SURAJGARH*
12	PIRAWA and	KAPASAN	SARDARSHAHAR	SHAHPURA	NAGAR PAHARI	SHEO
13	JHALRAPATAN*	BIKANER	SURATGARH	SAWAI MADHOPUR	SAPOTRA	RAISINGHNAGAR
14	ARNOD	MANDOR	BARMER	BARAN	BASERI	CHIRAWA
15	BHAINSRORGARH and	SIKRAI	BHAINSRORGARH	BASSI	DEOLI	HINDAUN
16	BAKANI*	TIJARA	CHHABRA	MANDOR	ANANDPURI	RUPBAS
17	KUSHALGARH	LACHHMANGARH	BALOTRA	PARBATSAR	PARBATSAR	BAYANA
18	DAG	BAP	SHERGARH	SARDARSHAHAR	DHAULPUR	MANDAWAR and
19	DEOGARH	LALSOT	MANOHARTHANA	UMREN	BAP	JHUNJHUNUN*
20	SINDHARI and	DEEG	KISHANGANJ	RAMGARH	AMBER	KOTKASIM
21	KISHANGARH BAS*	BHINMAL	MANDOR	ANUPGARH	JHALRAPATAN	HANUMANGARH and
22	SHAHBAD	ANUPGARH	BAYTOO	DHAULPUR	KISHANGARH	NAWALGARH*
23	TIJARA	KOLAYAT	DHORIMANNA	KHETRI	PEEPALKHOONT	RAJAKHERA and
24	KOTRA	SEWAR	DUNGARGARH	NAGAR PAHARI	HANUMANGARH	BASERI*
25	BHADESAR	KISHANGARH BAS	ANUPGARH	SIKRAI	RAMGARH	DHOND
26	DHAULPUR and	BARAN	NOHAR	BONLI	TODABHIM	KOTPUTLI
27	ANUPGARH*	JHALRAPATAN	MUNDWA	PRATAPGARH	ASIND	LACHHMANGARH
28	KOTKASIM	BHADESAR	SHAHBAD	LALSOT	KHETRI	MAHWA and
29	LALSOT	RANIWARA	SINDHARI	KOTPUTLI	BARMER	DHAULPUR*
30	NAGAR PAHARI	AMBER	PALI	PALI	KOTKASIM	PIPRALI
31	KESHORAIPATAN	HANUMANGARH	OSIAN	KARAULI	BAYTOO	NADOTI and
32	SIKRAI	BANSURE	SANCHORE	HANUMANGARH	BONLI	SIROHI*
33	BEGUN	KISHANGANJ	BHINMAL	RAJAKHERA	SAM	KHETRI*
34	JAWAJA	SRI MADHOPUR	SUJANGARH	KAMAN	NAGAUR	BHADRA*
35	PRATAPGARH and	BASERI	KAPASAN	SAPOTRA	SARDARSHAHAR	FATEHPUR
36	BASERI*	UMREN	BARI SADRI	DUDU	UMREN	ALSISAR and
37	SURATGARH	CHHIPABAROD	NAGAUR	PINDWARA	MANDOR	KARAULI*
38	NAINWA and	CHAKSU	ROHAT	BASERI	TALERA	KUMHER and
39	DHARIAWAD*	NADBAI	TALERA	NADBAI	BAMANWAS	WEIR*
40	TALERA	PHALODI	UNIARA	SINDHARI	RAJAKHERA	DEEG
41	PHAGI	TALERA	JAYAL	HINDAUN	JAISALMER	JAISALMER
42	CHITTAURGARH	HINDAUN	JHALRAPATAN	TODABHIM	DUDU	RAJGARH
43	RAISINGHNAGAR	SHERGARH	SIWANA	KATHUMAR	SAMBHAR	GANGAPUR and
44	AMET	GOVINDGARH	DEOGARH	RUPBAS	SADULSHAHAR	NADBAI*
45	KISHANGANJ	DHAULPUR	RAJGARH	BAYTOO	GHATOL	SIKRAI*
46	BAP	BAKANI	CHHOTI SADRI	SAMBHAR	KOTPUTLI	ANUPGARH*
47	BARAN	NIMRANA	PHAGI	THANAGAZI	PINDWARA	DANTA RAMGARH
48	BARI SADRI	CHOHTAN	BALESAR	HINDOLI	BALOTRA	KHANDAR and
49	NOHAR and	CHHOTI SADRI	CHHIPABAROD	BANDIKUI	PHAGI	SANKRA*
50	BAYANA, KAMAN* and RAJGARH*	MAHWA	LADPURA	TALERA	NADBAI	NAGAR PAHARI*

(contd.)

Note:* PS having same rank as the preceding PS.

BOX 18.16: ACTION PLAN *(A) STATE LEVEL* (Contd.)

Top Priority should be given for the Improvement in Human Development Status of the following Bottom 50 PSs

Rank	Criteria (2001) / Name of PSs					
	FLR	%age of Rural Pop. Served by Education Amenities	%age of Rural Pop. Served by Drinking Water Amenities	%age of Rural Pop. Served by Pucca Road Amenities	%age of Rural Pop. Served by Power Amenities	%age of Rural Pop. Served by Post Office Amenities
	8	9	10	11	12	13
1	KOTRA	ANUPGARH	SARDARSHAHAR	MANOHARTHANA	KOTRA	KUSHALGARH
2	PEEPALKHOONT	SURATGARH	BAP	CHHABRA	BAYTOO	SAJJANGARH
3	KUSHALGARH	HANUMANGARH	JAISALMER	DAG	SAM	CHHABRA
4	DHARIAWAD	BAKANI	JAYAL	PIRAWA	PEEPALKHOONT	ANUPGARH
5	SHERGARH	NOHAR	KOLAYAT	BAYTOO	BARMER	BHAINSRORGARH
6	BALESAR	BHAINSRORGARH	NOHAR	BAKANI	SHEO	BAYTOO
7	BHINMAL	BEGUN	BIKANER	KUSHALGARH	SANKRA	MANOHARTHANA
8	KHANDAR	BAP	CHURU	KOTRA	SURATGARH	KOTRA
9	SAJJANGARH	BARMER	LUNKARANSAR	PEEPALKHOONT	SINDHARI	DEOGARH
10	OSIAN	BAYTOO	BARMER	CHAKSU	BARI	KISHANGANJ
11	BHINAY	RAISINGHNAGAR	MAKRANA	JHALRAPATAN	KUSHALGARH	TIJARA
12	JASWANTPURA	KHANPUR	NAGAUR	SHEO	JAISALMER	SURATGARH
13	TONK	MANOHARTHANA	SURATGARH	JHADOL	BASERI	JHALRAPATAN
14	KOTRI	KOTRA	SADULSHAHAR	DEOGARH	BAGIDORA	BAKANI
15	UNIARA	GANGANAGAR and	SHEO	KAPASAN	SAJJANGARH	TALWARA and
16	ASIND	BHADRA*	BALOTRA	SAJJANGARH	KHERWARA	CHAKSU*
17	GHATOL	CHAKSU	TARANAGAR	CHHIPABAROD	ANUPGARH	KHERWARA
18	SAYLA	CHHABRA and	SINDHARI	SINDHARI	BIKANER	CHECHAT
19	SAM	PADAMPUR*	SAM	KHANPUR	NOHAR	PEEPALKHOONT
20	DEOLI	BARI SADRI and	ANUPGARH	BEGUN	SAPOTRA	SHAHBAD and
21	BHOPALGARH	SADULSHAHAR*	SANKRA	SANKRA	JHADOL	BHADESAR*
22	BAKANI	CHHIPABAROD and	RAJGARH	RAIPUR	CHOHTAN	RAISINGHNAGAR
23	BAGIDORA	UNIARA*	CHOHTAN	SHAHPURA and	MANOHARTHANA	BASERI
24	MUNDWA	KISHANGANJ	BHINMAL	AMET*	ANANDPURI	JHADOL
25	KOLAYAT	ARNOD	BHADRA	ARNOD and	BALOTRA and	RAMGARH
26	RAIPUR	PRATAPGARH and	SANCHORE	BARI SADRI*	DHORIMANNA*	ANANDPURI
27	ANANDPURI	BHINDAR*	ALSISAR	KOTRI	SHERGARH	TALERA
28	SHAHPURA	BALESAR	DEGANA	BARMER	KHANDAR	LADPURA
29	RASHMI	SAM	DUNGARGARH	JAHAZPUR and	KOLAYAT	BEGUN
30	SAWAI MADHOPUR	JAHAZPUR and	SHERGARH	CHHOTI SADRI*	BAP	CHHIPABAROD
31	KAPASAN	MANDALGARH*	SURAJGARH	SHAHBAD and	ARNOD	JAWAJA
32	BAP	SHERGARH*	SUJANGARH	BARI*	DHAULPUR and	BAGIDORA
33	BARI SADRI	CHHOTI SADRI	KUCHAMAN	DHORIMANNA	PRATAPGARH*	AMET and
34	MANDAL	BHADESAR and	DHORIMANNA	UNIARA	SALUMBAR	DHARIAWAD*
35	SIMALWARA	BARI*	BAYTOO	KESHORAIPATAN	SARADA	PADAMPUR
36	THANAGAZI	JHALRAPATAN	KOTRA	DUNGLA and	GHATOL and	BARMER
37	KEKRI	RAJGARH and	RAISINGHNAGAR	S.M*	DEOLI*	SINDHARI and
38	MANOHARTHANA	SHEO*	RATANGARH and	SALUMBAR	ABU ROAD	JHOTWARA*
39	SANCHORE	SHAHBAD and	MANDOR*	NAINWA and	KARAULI	LALSOT
40	ABU ROAD	BIKANER*	BAMANWAS	GANGRAR*	DAG	BARI
41	KAMAN and	LUNKARANSAR*	KAMAN and	ANANDPURI	TALWARA	KAPASAN
42	MANDALGARH*	SANGANER*	BUHANA*	PRATAPGARH	BAMANWAS	CHHOTI SADRI
43	JAITARAN	TIJARA and	DIDWANA	KUMBHALGARH	SANCHORE and	RAJAKHERA
44	SUWANA	MAHWA*	PALI	DEOLI	BAKANI*	SALUMBAR
45	MANDOR	KARANPUR*	RIYAN	BHADESAR and	RAISINGHNAGAR	KOTKASIM and
46	PHALODI	LALSOT	PADAMPUR	FATEHPUR*	SHAHBAD	KUMBHALGARH*
47	MALPURA	DAG and	SUMERPUR	SANGOD	DHARIAWAD	DHAULPUR
48	SAHARA and	ITAWA*	JHOTWARA	SHERGARH	TONK	SHEO
49	TALWARA*	DEOGARH	LUNI	DHARIAWAD	SIMALWARA	BIKANER
50	DAG	KHERWARA, DEO-GARH and CHITT.	JHUNJHUNUN and KARANPUR	BONLI	S.M	DAG

(contd.)

Note:* PS having same rank as the preceding PS

BOX 18.16: ACTION PLAN *(A) STATE LEVEL* (Contd.)

Top Priority should be given for the Improvement in Human Development Status of the following Bottom 50 PSs

Rank	Criteria (2001) / Name of PSs				Human Development INdices	
	%age of Rural Pop. Served by Agri. Amenities	%age of Rural Pop. Served by Transport Communications Amenities	%age of Rural Pop. Served by Telephone Amenities	%age of Rural Pop. Served by Bank Amenities	HSI	EDI
	14	15	16	17	18	19
1	DUNGARPUR	CHHABRA	KOTRA	RAJAKHERA	SAM	KOTRA
2	KUSHALGARH	RAJAKHERA	BHAINSRORGARH	KUSHALGARH and	BARMER	PEEPALKHOONT
3	GOGUNDA	MAHWA	ANANDPURI	CHHABRA*	SHEO	KUSHALGARH
4	BARI	KAMAN	KUSHALGARH	BARMER and	BAYTOO	DHARIAWAD
5	RAJAKHERA	MANOHARTHANA	SAJJANGARH	MANOHARTHANA*	KOTRA	SAJJANGARH
6	KHERWARA	KUSHALGARH	PEEPALKHOONT	RAISINGHNAGAR	MANOHARTHANA	JASWANTPURA
7	KAMAN	NAGAR PAHARI	ARNOD	KHERWARA	SURATGARH	BHINMAL
8	JAWAJA	BAKANI	PRATAPGARH	BARI	CHHABRA	KOTRI
9	KOTRA	LADPURA	BAYANA	JHUNJHUNUN	SANKRA	GHATOL
10	WEIR	BARI	KARAULI	RASHMI	BAKANI	SHERGARH
11	BARGAON	SEWAR and	SAPOTRA	ANANDPURI	JAISALMER	ANANDPURI
12	KARAULI	TIJARA*	MANOHARTHANA	KARANPUR	BAP	BALESAR
13	DHARIAWAD	TONK	KAMAN	SINDHARI	ANUPGARH	BAGIDORA
14	ANANDPURI	DHAULPUR	CHAKSU	BUHANA	SINDHARI	BHINAY
15	SALUMBAR	JHALRAPATAN	KESHORAIPATAN	SURATGARH	KUSHALGARH and	ASIND
16	BAKANI	KUMHER	BARI	SAJJANGARH and	CHAKSU*	KOLAYAT and
17	SAJJANGARH	UMREN	JHADOL	DHARIAWAD*	BASERI	KHANDAR*
18	BAYANA	KISHANGARH BAS	BAKANI	KOTRA	CHHIPABAROD	SIMALWARA
19	PEEPALKHOONT	CHHIPABAROD	NADOTI	BAYTOO	PEEPALKHOONT	SAYLA
20	NIMRANA	DEEG	CHHABRA	BHAINSRORGARH	DAG	BAKANI
21	JHADOL	SHAHBAD	JAMWA RAMGARH	DHORIMANNA and	KOLAYAT	RAIPUR
22	PRATAPGARH	RENI and	KOLAYAT	ANUPGARH*	NOHAR and	SHAHPURA
23	MANOHARTHANA	PIRAWA*	SHAHBAD	JHADOL*	RAJAKHERA*	MANDOR
24	BHINDER	CHAKSU	GHATOL	SURAJGARH	SHAHBAD	MANDAL
25	SAM and	BARAN	SALUMBAR	MAHWA and	BHAINSRORGARH	BAP
26	KUMBHALGARH*	PEEPALKHOONT	BARMER and	FATEHPUR*	BARI	RASHMI
27	NADBAI and	WEIR	DHAULPUR*	PRATAPGARH	CHOHTAN	TONK
28	BHIM*	RAJGARH and	RAJAKHERA*	SHEO	ARNOD	MANDALGARH
29	LACHHMANGARH	DAG*	BARI SADRI	TODABHIM	BIKANER	ABU ROAD
30	RAJGARH and	SIKRAI	BAP	CHOHTAN and	DHAULPUR	SAM
31	BAYTOO*	BANDIKUI	TALERA and	DUNGARPUR*	JHALRAPATAN	SAHARA and
32	BICHHIWARA and	LALSOT	DAG*	GOGUNDA	DHORIMANNA	MUNDWA*
33	AMET*	ANANDPURI	SIKRAI	KAMAN	UNIARA	BARI SADRI and
34	BALESAR	TALERA	BAGIDORA	SARDARSHAHAR	KAPASAN	DEOLI*
35	SARADA	RAMGARH	LALSOT	KHANDAR	SAJJANGARH	KAPASAN
36	BARMER and	JAWAJA and	MUNDWA	BARAN	SHERGARH	ASPUR and
37	SIMALWARA*	KATHUMAR*	BHADESAR	SALUMBAR	LALSOT	UNIARA*
38	ASPUR	SULTANPUR	NAINWA	BALESAR	KHANDAR	JALOR*
39	CHECHAT	BAYANA and	BASERI	AMET	BAYANA	BHOPALGARH*
40	KOTPUTLI	HINDOLI*	CHHIPABAROD	KAPASAN and	NAINWA	TALWARA
41	KISHANGARH BAS	KHANPUR	BIKANER and	BICHHIWARA*	CHHOTI SADRI	SUWANA and
42	BANSURE	JAHAZPUR	NIMBAHERA*	SANKRA and	KESHORAIPATAN	SANCHORE*
43	TIJARA	KOTKASIM and	BICHHIWARA*	NAGAUR*	KAMAN	BICHHIWARA and
44	BASERI	KISHANGANJ*	DHARIAWAD*	HINDAUN	SAPOTRA	DAG*
45	GHATOL and	CHHOTI SADRI	SIMALWARA	CHHOTI SADRI	PIRAWA	KEKRI
46	DEOGARH*	BASERI and	SHEO and	JHOTWARA and	ANANDPURI	MALPURA and
47	BAGIDORA and	KOTRA*	KHERWARA*	KUMBHALGARH*	SARDARSHAHAR	JAITARAN*
48	SHAHBAD*	UNIARA	HINDOLI	CHHIPABAROD and	PRATAPGARH	BHAINSRORGARH
49	LADPURA and	SAJJANGARH	BAMANWAS	JAHAZPUR*	TIJARA	DUNGARPUR
50	SHEO*	NIWAI	SHERGARH and KUMBHALGARH*	KARAULI*	BEGUN	KUMBHALGARH

(contd.)

Note:* PS having same rank as the preceding PS.

BOX 18.16: ACTION PLAN *(A) STATE LEVEL* (Contd.)

Top Priority should be given for the Improvement in Human Development Status of the following Bottom 50 PSs

Rank	Human Development Indices					
	GEDI	INI#	GINI#	HPI	GEM	HDI
	20	21	22	23	24	25
1	KOTRA	ASPUR	SIWANA	PEEPALKHOONT	SHEO	PEEPALKHOONT
2	PEEPALKHOONT	SIWANA	ASPUR	SAJJANGARH	CHOHTAN	KOTRA
3	KUSHALGARH	BICHHIWARA	SHEO	KOTRA	SAM	SHEO
4	DHARIAWAD	SHEO	BICHHIWARA	KUSHALGARH	RANIWARA	KUSHALGARH
5	BHINMAL	SAGWARA	SAGWARA	BALESAR	BASERI	BARMER
6	SHERGARH	DUNGARPUR	DUNGARPUR	BAGIDORA	DHORIMANNA	SIMALWARA
7	SAJJANGARH	SIMALWARA	SIMALWARA	ANANDPURI	SAPOTRA	SAM
8	JASWANTPURA	BARMER	BARMER	GHATOL	TODABHIM	ASPUR
9	BALESAR	BALOTRA	KUCHAMAN	DHARIAWAD	NEEM KA THANA	SAJJANGARH
10	GHATOL	DHORIMANNA	BALOTRA	DUNGARPUR	KHANDELA	BICHHIWARA
11	BHINAY and	SINDHARI	JALOR	MANOHARTHANA	LADNU	DAG
12	KHANDAR*	RANIWARA	DHORIMANNA	ARNOD	ANANDPURI	DUNGARPUR
13	KOTRI	SAYLA	MAKRANA	PRATAPGARH	BICHHIWARA	BAYTOO
14	ASIND	KUCHAMAN	SINDHARI	JHADOL	TODARAISINGH	GHATOL
15	TONK	CHOHTAN	DHAULPUR	BAKANI	BAKANI	CHOHTAN
16	SAYLA and	BAYTTOO	DAG	BHAINSRORGARH	KATHUMAR	SANCHORE
17	MANDOR*	TALWARA	RAJAKHERA	SIMALWARA	KAMAN	JAISALMER
18	ANANDPURI	DHAULPUR	RANIWARA	BARI SADRI	ASPUR	BAGIDORA
19	BAGIDORA	SANCHORE	CHOHTAN	SURATGARH	BONLI	ANANDPURI
20	RAIPUR	RAJAKHERA	SAYLA	KHERWARA	DIDWANA	MANOHARTHANA
21	SIMALWARA and	JALOR	DIDWANA	CHHOTI SADRI	KARAULI	TALWARA
22	BAKANI*	KHANPUR	JAISALMER	ANUPGARH	DHOND	BHINMAL
23	UNIARA	DIDWANA	TALWARA	JAHAZPUR	NADOTI	BALOTRA
24	MANDAL and	MAKRANA	BAYTOO	SHAHBAD	LACHHMANGARH	DHARIAWAD
25	KOLAYAT*	JASWANTPURA	GARHI	BEGUN	RENI and	BAKANI
26	SHAHPURA and	SRI MADHOPUR	KHANPUR	GANGRAR	SRI MADHOPUR*	SIWANA
27	BHOPALGARH*	GHATOL	JASWANTPURA	TALWARA	SINDHARI	JASWANTPURA
28	DEOLI*	BHINMAL	PARBATSAR	BHADESAR	KOTKASIM	SINDHARI
29	RASHMI	DAG	SRI MADHOPUR	DUNGLA	DEEG	RAJAKHERA
30	BAP and	GARHI	SANCHORE	HANUMANGARH	RATANGARH	SAYLA
31	MUNDWA*	PEEPALKHOONT	NEEM KA THANA	BICHHIWARA	DESURI	RANIWARA
32	BARI SADRI	LADHU	RAJSAMAND	SAM	RANI STATION	SAGWARA
33	SAM	KUSHALGARH	LADNU	UNIARA	BARMER	DHAULPUR
34	KAPASAN	HINDAUN	PHALODI	DEOGARH	SANCHORE	PHALODI
35	MANDALGARH	BASERI	BASERI	CHITTAURGARH	RUPBAS and	UNIARA
36	SAHARA	NAWALGARH	GHATOL	CHHABRA	JASWANTPURA*	MUNDWA
37	ABU ROAD	SARDARSHAHAR	NAWALGARH	KHANDAR	ARNOD and	BARI
38	KEKRI	NEEM KA THANA	SAM	KISHANGANJ	UDAIPURWATI*	SHERGARH
39	TALWARA and	MERTA	PEEPALKHOONT	KAPASAN	DEGANA	NAGAUR
40	SANCHORE*	BARI	BHINMAL	CHAKSU	RAJSAMAND	BASERI
41	SUWANA and	PHALODI	MERTA	MANDALGARH	JAISALMER	KOTRI
42	ASPUR*	SAJJANGARH	KHAMNOR	CHHIPABAROD	BAYTOO	SANKRA
43	JALOR	SUJANGARH	KUSHALGARH	SALUMBAR	HINDAUN	JALOR
44	SAWAI MADHOPUR	PARBATSAR	HINDAUN	DAG	SIMALWARA	KHANDAR
45	MALPURA	CHURU	SARDARSHAHAR	KOTRI	KHARCHI/MAR., JUN.	BALESAR
46	JAITARAN	JAYAL	DANTA RAMGARH	JHALRAPATAN	MUNDWA	MANDALGARH
47	KAMAN	NAGAUR	SEWAR	DEOLI	DAUSA	KAMAN
48	THANAGAZI	BAGIDORA	BARI	RAISINGHNAGAR	SIWANA	TIJARA
49	DUNGARPUR	MUNDWA	AMET	LALSOT	NAGAUR	JAYAL
50	BICHHIWARA and DAG*	DANTA RAMGARH	GIRWA	ASIND	BAYANA	DHORIMANNA

Note: *PS having same rank as the preceding PS. # For ther year 1998-99

Source: 1. Hemlata Joshi. 2005. *'Economic Development Index and Health Status Index-Rajasthan* (Spatio-Temporal and Gender Appraisal at Panchayat Samiti / Block Level), Published Reaserch Reports, IDSJ.

2. Annex 4.1, 4.9, 4.11, 4.13, 4.15, 4.17, 4.19, 4.21, 6.2 to 6.6, 8.3, 10.3, 12.2, 15.2,17.3 and K-5

BOX 18.16: ACTION PLAN *(B) DISTRICT LEVEL*

Top Priority should be given for the Improvement in Human Development Status of the Worst PSs

S.No	Human Development Indices, 2001/PSs						
	HSI	EDI	GEDI	INI	GINI	GEM	HDI
1	2	3	4	5	6	7	8
				(1) AJMER DISTRICT			
1(Worst)	ARAIN	BHINAY#	BHINAY	JAWAJA	SRINAGAR	BHINAY	BHINAY
2	BHINAY	KEKRI	KEKRI	PISANGAN	JAWAJA	SRINAGAR	ARAIN
3	MASOODA	ARAIN	ARAIN	KISHANGARH	PISANGAN	KISHANGARH*	MASOODA
4	SRINAGAR	SRINAGAR	SRINAGAR	SRINAGAR	KISHANGARH	ARAIN*	PISANGAN
5	KISHANGARH	PISANGAN	PISANGAN	MASOODA	MASOODA	JAWAJA	KEKRI
6	JAWAJA	KISHANGARH	MASOODA	KEKRI	KEKRI	KEKRI	SRINAGAR
7	KEKRI	MASOODA	KISHANGARH	BHINAY	BHINAY	PISANGAN	KISHANGARH
8 (Best)	PISANGAN	JAWAJA##	JAWAJA	ARAIN##	ARAIN	MASOODA	JAWAJA
				(2) ALWAR			
1 (Worst)	TIJARA#	THANAGAZI#	THANAGAZI	RAMGARH#	RAMGARH	KATHUMAR	TIJARA
2	KISHANGARH-BAS	TIJARA	UMREN	TIJARA	TIJARA	RENI	RAMGARH
3	RAJGARH	UMREN	RAMGARH	UMREN	UMREN	KOTKASIM	THANAGAZI
4	RAMGARH	RAMGARH	TIJARA	NIMRANA	NIMRANA	TIJARA	UMREN
5	KOTKASIM	RAJGARH	RAJGARH	MANDAWAR	BANSURE	NIMRANA	KISHANGARH-BAS
6	KATHUMAR	LACHHMAN-GARH	LACHHMAN-GARH	KOTKASIM	MANDAWAR	RAMGARH	RAJGARH
7	LACHHMAN-GARH	KISHANGARH BAS	KISHANGARH BAS	BANSURE	KOTKASIM	RAJGARH	BANSURE
8	THANAGAZI	RENI	RENI	KISHANGARH-BAS	KISHANGARH-BAS	MANDAWAR	LACHHMAN-GARH
9	UMREN	KATHUMAR	KATHUMAR	THANAGAZI	THANAGAZI	BANSURE	KATHUMAR
10	BANSURE	BANSURE	BANSURE	KATHUMAR	LACHHMAN-GARH	BEHROR	NIMRANA
11	RENI	NIMRANA	NIMRANA	LACHHMAN-GARH	KATHUMAR	THANAGAZI	RENI
12	MANDAWAR	MANDAWAR	MANDAWAR	BEHROR	RAJGARH	LACHHMAN-GARH	KOTKASIM
13	NIMRANA	KOTKASIM	KOTKASIM	RAJGARH	BEHROR	KISHANGARH-BAS	MANDAWAR
14 (Best)	BEHROR##	BEHROR	BEHROR	RENI##	RENI	UMREN	BEHROR
				(3) BANSWARA			
1 (Worst)	KUSHALGARH	PEEPAL-KHOONT#	PEEPALKHOONT	TALWARA#	TALWARA	ANANDPURI	PEEPALKHOONT
2	PEEPAL-KHOONT	KUSHALGARH	KUSHALGARH	GHATOL	GARHI	PEEPALKHOONT	KUSHALGARH
3	SAJJANGARH	SAJJANGARH	SAJJANGARH	GARHI	GHATOL	SAJJANGARH	SAJJANGARH
4	ANANDPURI	GHATOL	GHATOL	PEEPALKHOONT	PEEPALKHOONT	KUSHALGARH	GHATOL
5	BAGIDORA	ANANDPURI	ANANDPURI	KUSHALGARH	KUSHALGARH	GHATOL	BAGIDORA
6	GHATOL	BAGIDORA	BAGIDORA	SAJJANGARH	SAJJANGARH	BAGIDORA	ANANDPURI
7	TALWARA	TALWARA	TALWARA	BAGIDORA	BAGIDORA	TALWARA	TALWARA
8 (Best))	GARHI##	GARHI	GARHI	ANANDPURI##	ANANDPURI	GARHI	GARHI
				(4) BARAN			
1 (Worst)	CHHABRA#	CHHIPA-BAROD#	CHHIPABAROD	ANTA#	ANTA	ATRU	CHHABRA
2	CHHIPABAROD	CHHABRA	CHHABRA	BARAN	BARAN	CHHABRA	SHAHBAD
3	SHAHBAD	SHAHBAD	SHAHBAD	SHAHBAD	ATRU	ANTA	CHHIPABAROD
4	KISHANGANJ	KISHANGANJ	KISHANGANJ	ATRU	SHAHBAD	SHAHBAD	KISHANGANJ
5	ANTA	ATRU	ATRU	KISHANGANJ	KISHANGANJ	KISHANGANJ	ANTA
6	ATRU	ANTA	ANTA	CHHABRA	CHHABRA	BARAN	ATRU
7 (Best)	BARAN##	BARAN	BARAN	CHHIPA-BAROD##	CHHIPABAROD	CHHIPABAROD	BARAN
				(5) BARMER			
1 (Worst)	BARMER	CHOHTAN#	CHOHTAN	SIWANA#	SIWANA	SHEO#	SHEO
2	SHEO	BARMER	BARMER	SHEO	SHEO	CHOHTAN	BARMER
3	BAYTOO	BALOTRA	BALOTRA	BARMER	BARMER	DHORIMANNA	BAYTOO
4	SINDHARI	SHEO	SHEO	BALOTRA	BALOTRA	SINDHARI	CHOHTAN
5	CHOHTAN	BAYTOO	BAYTOO	DHORIMANNA	DHORIMANNA	BARMER	BALOTRA
6	DHORIMANNA	SIWANA	SIWANA	SINDHARI	SINDHARI	BAYTOO	SIWANA
7	BALOTRA	SINDHARI	SINDHARI	CHOHTAN	CHOHTAN	SIWANA	SINDHARI
8 (Best)	SIWANA	DHORI-MANNA##	DHORIMANNA	BAYTOO##	BAYTOO	BALOTRA	DHORIMANNA

contd.

Note : # PS/PSs having worst position in two or more than two human development indices in their respective districts.
PS/PSs having best position in two or more than two human development indices in their respective districts.

(contd.)

S.No	Human Development Indices, 2001/PSs						
	HSI	**EDI**	**GEDI**	**INI**	**GINI**	**GEM**	**HDI**
1	**2**	**3**	**4**	**5**	**6**	**7**	**8**
				(6) BHARATPUR			
1(**Worst**)	BAYANA	KAMAN#	KAMAN	RUPBAS	SEWAR	KAMAN	KAMAN
2	KAMAN	BAYANA	BAYANA	SEWAR	RUPBAS	DEEG	BAYANA
3	NAGAR PAHARI	DEEG	DEEG	NAGAR PAHARI	BAYANA	RUPBAS	NAGAR PAHARI
4	WEIR	NAGAR PAHARI	NAGAR PAHARI	BAYANA	NAGAR PAHARI	BAYANA	WEIR
5	RUPBAS	WEIR	WEIR	WEIR	WEIR	KUMHER	RUPBAS
6	SEWAR	KUMHER	KUMHER	NADBAI	NADBAI	WEIR	DEEG
7	DEEG	SEWAR	SEWAR	KAMAN	KUMHER	NAGAR PAHARI	SEWAR
8	NADBAI	RUPBAS	RUPBAS	KUMHER	KAMAN	NADBAI	NADBAI
9 (**Best**)	KUMHER##	NADBAI##	NADBAI	DEEG##	DEEG	SEWAR	KUMHER
				(7) BHILWARA			
1 (**Worst**)	KOTRI#	KOTRI	KOTRI	JAHAZPUR#	JAHAZPUR	BANERA	KOTRI
2	MANDALGARH	ASIND	ASIND	RAIPUR	RAIPUR	KOTRI	MANDALGARH
3	JAHAZPUR	RAIPUR	RAIPUR	MANDAL	HURDA	JAHAZPUR	JAHAZPUR
4	SHAHPURA	SHAHPURA	MANDAL	HURDA	MANDAL	SUWANA	SHAHPURA
5	ASIND	MANDAL	SHAHPURA	MANDALGARH	MANDALGARH	ASIND*	RAIPUR
6	MANDAL	MANDALGARH	MANDALGARH	SUWANA	SUWANA	RAIPUR*	MANDAL
7	RAIPUR	SAHARA	SAHARA	SHAHPURA	SHAHPURA	SAHARA	ASIND
8	SUWANA	SUWANA	SUWANA	ASIND	KOTRI	HURDA	SUWANA
9	HURDA	JAHAZPUR	JAHAZPUR	KOTRI	BANERA	SHAHPURA	HURDA
10	SAHARA	BANERA	BANERA	BANERA	ASIND	MANDAL	SAHARA
11 (**Best**)	BANERA##	HURDA##	HURDA	SAHARA##	SAHARA	MANDALGARH	BANERA
				(8) BIKANER			
1 (**Worst**)	KOLAYAT#	KOLAYAT	KOLAYAT	DUNGARGARH#	DUNGARGARH	NOKHA	KOLAYAT
2	BIKANER	LUNKARANSAR	NOKHA	BIKANER#	BIKANER	BIKANER	BIKANER
3	LUNKARANSAR	BIKANER	LUNKARANSAR	KOLAYAT	KOLAYAT	DUNGARGARH	LUNKARANSAR
4	NOKHA	NOKHA	BIKANER	LUNKARANSAR	LUNKARANSAR	LUNKARANSAR	DUNGARGARH
5 (**Best**)	DUNGAR-GARH##	DUNGARGARH	DUNGARGARH	NOKHA	NOKHA	KOLAYAT	NOKHA
				(9) BUNDI			
1 (**Worst**)	NAINWA#	HINDOLI#	HINDOLI	TALERA#	TALERA	HINDOLI	NAINWA
2	KESHORAI-PATAN	NAINWA	NAINWA	KESHORAI-PATAN	KESHORAI-PATAN	NAINWA	HINDOLI
3	TALERA	TALERA	TALERA	NAINWA	NAINWA	KESHORAI-PATAN	TALERA
4 (**Best**)	HINDOLI#	KESHORAI-PATAN##	KESHORAI-PATAN	HINDOLI	HINDOLI	TALERA	KESHORAIPATAN
				(10) CHITTAURGARH			
1 (**Worst**)	BHAINSROR-GARH	RASHMI#	RASHMI	ARNOD#	ARNOD	ARNOD	ARNOD
2	ARNOD	BARI SADRI	BARI SADRI	PRATAPGARH	BHAINSROR-GARH	RASHMI	BHAINSROR-GARH
3	KAPASAN	KAPASAN	KAPASAN	BHAINSROR-GARH	PRATAPGARH	GANGRAR	PRATAPGARH
4	CHHOTI SADRI	BHAINSROR-GARH	BHAINSROR-GARH	NIMBAHERA	CHITTAUR-GARH	BEGUN	KAPASAN
5	PRATAPGARH	GANGRAR	GANGRAR	CHITTAURGARH	NIMBAHERA	BARI SADRI	BARI SADRI
6	BEGUN	BHADESAR	BHADESAR	BHOPALSAGAR	BHOPALSAGAR	CHHOTI SADRI	BHADESAR
7	BHADESAR	ARNOD	DUNGLA	BHADESAR	GANGRAR	BHOPALSAGAR	BEGUN
8	BARI SADRI	DUNGLA	ARNOD	BEGUN	BHADESAR	PRATAPGARH	CHITTAURGARH
9	CHITTAUR-GARH	BEGUN	BEGUN	DUNGLA	BEGUN	CHITTAURGARH	GANGRAR
10	GANGRAR	CHITTAUR-GARH	CHITTAUR-GARH	RASHMI	RASHMI	DUNGLA	CHHOTI SADRI
11	BHOPALSAGAR	BHOPALSAGAR	BHOPALSAGAR	CHHOTI SADRI	DUNGLA	KAPASAN*	RASHMI
12	NIMBAHERA	CHHOTI SADRI	CHHOTI SADRI	BARI SADRI*	CHHOTI SADRI	NIMBAHERA*	BHOPALSAGAR
13	DUNGLA	PRATAPGARH	NIMBAHERA	GANGRAR*	BARI SADRI	BHADESAR	DUNGLA
14 (**Best**)	RASHMI	NIMBAHERA##	PRATAPGARH	KAPASAN##	KAPASAN	BHAINSROR-GARH	NIMBAHERA
				(11) CHURU			
1 (**Worst**)	SARDAR-SHAHAR#	DUNGAR-GARH#	DUNGARGARH	SARDAR-SHAHAR#	SARDAR-SHAHAR#	RATANGARH	SARDARSHAHAR
2	RAJGARH	SARDAR-SHAHAR	SARDAR-SHAHAR	SUJANGARH	SUJANGARH	SARDAR-SHAHAR	SUJANGARH
3	TARANAGAR	SUJANGARH	SUJANGARH	CHURU	CHURU	TARANAGAR	CHURU
4	SUJANGARH	RATANGARH	RATANGARH	RATANGARH	RATANGARH	SUJANGARH	RAJGARH
		CHURU	CHURU	RAJGARH	RAJGARH	RAJGARH	RATANGARH

contd.

Note : # PS/PSs having worst position in two or more than two human development indices in their respective districts.
PS/PSs having best position in two or more than two human development indices in their respective districts.
* Dungarh PS shifted from Churu to Bikaner District on 1st April 2001

(contd.)

S.No	HSI	EDI	GEDI	INI	GINI	GEM	HDI
	Human Development Indices, 2001/PSs						
1	2	3	4	5	6	7	8
5	CHURU	RAJGARH	RAJGARH	TARANAGAR	TARANAGAR	CHURU	
6 **(Best)**	RATANGARH	TARANAGAR##	TARANAGAR				TARANAGAR
				(12) DAUSA			
1 **(Worst)**	LALSOT#	LALSOT	LALSOT	BANDIKUI#	BANDIKUI	DAUSA	LALSOT
2	MAHWA	DAUSA	DAUSA	LALSOT	LALSOT	MAHWA	DAUSA
3	SIKRAI	SIKRAI	SIKRAI	SIKRAI	MAHWA	BANDIKUI	BANDIKUI
4	DAUSA	MAHWA	MAHWA	DAUSA	SIKRAI	LALSOT	SIKRAI
5 **(Best)**	BANDIKUI##	BANDIKUI	BANDIKUI	MAHWA##	DAUSA	SIKRAI	MAHWA
				(13) DHAULPUR			
1 **(Worst)**	BASERI#	BARI#	BARI	DHAULPUR#	DHAULPUR	BASERI	RAJAKHERA
2	RAJAKHERA	RAJAKHERA	RAJAKHERA	RAJAKHERA	RAJAKHERA	RAJAKHERA	DHAULPUR
3	BARI	DHAULPUR	DHAULPUR	BASERI	BASERI	DHAULPUR	BARI
4 **(Best)**	DHAULPUR	BASERI##	BASERI	BARI##	BARI	BARI	BASERI
				(14) DUNGARPUR			
1 **(Worst)**	SIMALWARA#	SIMALWARA	SIMALWARA	ASPUR#	ASPUR	BICHHIWARA	SIMALWARA
2	DUNGARPUR	ASPUR	ASPUR	BICHHIWARA	BICHHIWARA	ASPUR	ASPUR
3	BICHHIWARA	BICHHIWARA	DUNGARPUR	SAGWARA	SAGWARA	SIMALWARA	BICHHIWARA
4	ASPUR	DUNGARPUR	BICHHIWARA	DUNGARPUR	DUNGARPUR	SAGWARA	DUNGARPUR
5 **(Best)**	SAGWARA##	SAGWARA	SAGWARA	SIMALWARA##	SIMALWARA	DUNGARPUR	SAGWARA
				(15) GANGANAGAR			
1 **(Worst)**	SURATGARH#	SURATGARH	SURATGARH	ANUPGARH#	PADAMPUR#	PADAMPUR	ANUPGARH
2	ANUPGARH	ANUPGARH	ANUPGARH	PADAMPUR	ANUPGARH	RAISINGH-NAGAR	SURATGARH
3	RAISINGH-NAGAR	KARANPUR	KARANPUR	GANGANAGAR	GANGANAGAR	ANUPGARH	PADAMPUR
4	SADUL-SHAHAR	SADUL-SHAHAR	SADUL-SHAHAR	RAISINGH-NAGAR	RAISINGH-NAGAR	SADUL-SHAHAR	RAISINGH-NAGAR
5	KARANPUR	PADAMPUR	PADAMPUR	KARANPUR	KARANPUR*	KARANPUR	GANGANAGAR
6	PADAMPUR	GANGANAGAR	GANGANAGAR	SURATGARH	SURATGARH*	SURATGARH	KARANPUR
7 **(Best)**	GANGA-NAGAR##	RAISINGH-NAGAR##	RAISINGH-NAGAR	SADUL-SHAHAR##	SADULSHAHAR	GANGANAGAR	SADULSHAHAR
				(16) HANUMANGARH			
1 **(Worst)**	NOHAR#	HANUMAN-GARH#	HANUMAN-GARH	HANUMAN-GARH	HANUMAN-GARH	NOHAR	HANUMANGARH
2	HANUMAN-GARH	NOHAR	NOHAR	NOHAR	NOHAR	BHADRA	NOHAR
3 **(Best)**	BHADRA##	BHADRA	BHADRA	BHADRA	BHADRA	HANUMANGARH	BHADRA
				(17) JAIPUR			
1 **(Worst)**	CHAKSU#	CHAKSU	CHAKSU	VIRATNAGAR	GOVINDGARH	PHAGI	CHAKSU
2	PHAGI	DUDU	DUDU	SHAHPURA	SHAHPURA	VIRATNAGAR	DUDU
3	SANGANER	BASSI	BASSI	GOVINDGARH	SAMBHAR	CHAKSU	BASSI
4	DUDU	AMBER	AMBER	SAMBHAR	VIRATNAGAR	SAMBHAR	AMBER
5	JHOTWARA	PHAGI	PHAGI	KOTPUTLI	KOTPUTLI	GOVINDGARH	SHAHPURA
6	BASSI	SANGANER	SANGANER	BASSI	BASSI	SHAHPURA	VIRATNAGAR
7	AMBER	JAMWA RAM-GARH	JAMWA RAM-GARH	JAMWA RAM-GARH	AMBER	JAMWA RAM-GARH	PHAGI
8	JAMWA RAM-GARH	SHAHPURA	SHAHPURA	DUDU	DUDU	BASSI	JAMWA RAMGARH
9	KOTPUTLI	GOVINDGARH	GOVINDGARH	AMBER	JAMWA RAM-GARH	KOTPUTLI	GOVINDGARH
10	VIRATNAGAR	JHOTWARA	JHOTWARA	PHAGI	PHAGI	DUDU	SAMBHAR
11	SAMBHAR	SAMBHAR	SAMBHAR	CHAKSU	CHAKSU	AMBER	KOTPUTLI
12	SHAHPURA	VIRATNAGAR	VIRATNAGAR	JHOTWARA	JHOTWARA	JHOTWARA	SANGANER
13 **(Best)**	GOVINDGARH	KOTPUTLI##	KOTPUTLI	SANGANER##	SANGANER	SANGANER	JHOTWARA
				(18) JAISALMER			
1 **(Worst)**	SAM#	SAM	SAM	JAISALMER#	JAISALMER	SAM	SAM
2	SANKRA	JAISALMER	JAISALMER	SAM	SAM	JAISALMER	JAISALMER
3 **(Best)**	JAISALMER	SANKRA##	SANKRA	SANKRA	SANKRA	SANKRA	SANKRA
				(19) JALOR			
1 **(Worst)**	SANCHORE#	JASWANTPURA	BHINMAL	RANIWARA#	JALOR	RANIWARA	SANCHORE
2	BHINMAL	BHINMAL	JASWANTPURA	SAYLA	RANIWARA	SANCHORE	BHINMAL
3	RANIWARA	SAYLA	SAYLA	SANCHORE	SAYLA	JASWANTPURA	JASWANTPURA
4	JASWANTPURA	JALOR	SANCHORE	JALOR	JASWANTPURA	AHORE	SAYLA
5	SAYLA	SANCHORE	JALOR	JASWANTPURA	SANCHORE	BHINMAL	RANIWARA
6	JALOR	RANIWARA	RANIWARA	BHINMAL	BHINMAL	SAYLA	JALOR
7 **(Best)**	AHORE##	AHORE	AHORE	AHORE	AHORE	JALOR	AHORE

contd.

Note : # PS/PSs having worst position in two or more than two human development indices in their respective districts.
PS/PSs having best position in two or more than two human development indices in their respective districts.

(contd.)

S.No	Human Development Indices, 2001/PSs						
	HSI	**EDI**	**GEDI**	**INI**	**GINI**	**GEM**	**HDI**
1	**2**	**3**	**4**	**5**	**6**	**7**	**8**
				(20) JHALAWAR			
1 **(Worst)**	MANOHARTHANA		BAKANI#	BAKANI	KHANPUR	DAG#	BAKANI DAG
2	BAKANI	DAG	DAG	DAG	KHANPUR	DAG	MANOHAR-THANA
3	DAG	MANOHAR-THANA	MANOHAR-THANA	JHALRAPATAN	JHALRAPATAN	PIRAWA	BAKANI
4	JHALRAPATAN	JHALRAPATAN	JHALRAPATAN	PIRAWA	PIRAWA	KHANPUR	JHALRAPATAN
5	PIRAWA	KHANPUR	KHANPUR	MANOHAR-THANA	MANOHAR-THANA	MANOHAR-THANA	KHANPUR
6 **(Best)**	KHANPUR	PIRAWA##	PIRAWA	BAKANI##	BAKANI	JHALRAPATAN	PIRAWA
				(21) JHUNJHUNUN			
1 **(Worst)**	SURAJGARH	KHETRI#	KHETRI	NAWALGARH#	NAWALGARH	UDAIPURWATI	NAWALGARH
2	ALSISAR	NAWALGARH	NAWALGARH	KHETRI	UDAIPURWATI	ALSISAR	KHETRI
3	JHUNJHUNUN	SURAJGARH	SURAJGARH	UDAIPURWATI	KHETRI	BUHANA*	SURAJGARH
4	BUHANA	ALSISAR	ALSISAR	CHIRAWA	CHIRAWA	KHETRI*	ALSISAR
5	NAWALGARH	CHIRAWA	CHIRAWA	ALSISAR	ALSISAR	JHUNJHUNUN	CHIRAWA
6	CHIRAWA	JHUNJHUNUN	JHUNJHUNUN	SURAJGARH	SURAJGARH	SURAJGARH	JHUNJHUNUN
7	KHETRI	BUHANA	BUHANA	JHUNJHUNUN	JHUNJHUNUN	CHIRAWA	UDAIPURWATI
8 **(Best)**	UDAIPUR-WATI##	UDAIPURWATI	UDAIPURWATI	BUHANA##	BUHANA	NAWALGARH	BUHANA
				(22) JODHPUR			
1 **(Worst)**	BAP	SHERGARH#	SHERGARH	PHALODI#	PHALODI	SHERGARH	PHALODI
2	SHERGARH	BALESAR	BALESAR	MANDOR	MANDOR	PHALODI	SHERGARH
3	BALESAR	MANDOR	MANDOR	OSIAN	BALESAR	BALESAR	BALESAR
4	PHALODI	BAP	BHOPALGARH	BALESAR	SHERGARH	BAP	MANDOR
5	MANDOR	BHOPALGARH	BAP	SHERGARH	OSIAN	BHOPALGARH	BAP
6	OSIAN	OSIAN	OSIAN	LUNI	LUNI	MANDOR	OSIAN
7	LUNI	PHALODI	PHALODI	BHOPALGARH	BHOPALGARH	LUNI	BHOPALGARH
8	BHOPALGARH	BILARA	BILARA	BILARA	BILARA	BILARA	LUNI
9 **(Best)**	BILARA##	LUNI##	LUNI	BAP##	BAP	OSIAN	BILARA
				(23) KARAULI			
1 **(Worst)**	SAPOTRA#	KARAULI#	KARAULI	HINDAUN#	HINDAUN	SAPOTRA	KARAULI
2	KARAULI	SAPOTRA	SAPOTRA	TODABHIM	KARAULI	TODABHIM	SAPOTRA
3	NADOTI	TODABHIM	TODABHIM	KARAULI	TODABHIM	KARAULI	TODABHIM
4	TODABHIM	NADOTI	NADOTI	SAPOTRA	SAPOTRA	NADOTI	NADOTI
5 **(Best)**	HINDAUN##	HINDAUN	HINDAUN	NADOTI##	NADOTI	HINDAUN	HINDAUN
				(24) KOTA			
1 **(Worst)**	ITAWA#	ITAWA	ITAWA	LADPURA#	LADPURA	ITAWA	ITAWA
2	SANGOD	LADPURA	LADPURA	SULTANPUR	SULTANPUR	SANGOD	LADPURA
3	CHECHAT	CHECHAT	CHECHAT	ITAWA	ITAWA	LADPURA	SULTANPUR
4	LADPURA	SANGOD	SANGOD	SANGOD	SANGOD	SULTANPUR	SANGOD
5 **(Best)**	SULTANPUR##	SULTANPUR	SULTANPUR	CHECHAT##	CHECHAT	CHECHAT	CHECHAT
				(25) NAGAUR			
1 **(Worst)**	NAGAUR	MUNDWA#	MUNDWA	KUCHAMAN#	KUCHAMAN	LADNU	MUNDWA
2	KUCHAMAN	NAGAUR	NAGAUR	DIDWANA	MAKRANA	DIDWANA	NAGAUR
3	JAYAL	JAYAL	JAYAL	MAKRANA	DIDWANA	DEGANA	JAYAL
4	MUNDWA	RIYAN	RIYAN	LADNU	PARBATSAR	MUNDWA	KUCHAMAN
5	MAKRANA	DEGANA	DEGANA	MERTA	LADNU	NAGAUR	MERTA
6	DEGANA	MERTA	MERTA	PARBATSAR	MERTA	MAKRANA	DEGANA
7	RIYAN	PARBATSAR	PARBATSAR	JAYAL	NAGAUR	MERTA	RIYAN
8	MERTA	LADNU	LADNU	NAGAUR	MUNDWA	RIYAN	MAKRANA
9	PARBATSAR	MAKRANA	MAKRANA	MUNDWA	JAYAL	KUCHAMAN	PARBATSAR
10	DIDWANA	KUCHAMAN	KUCHAMAN	DEGANA	RIYAN	JAYAL	DIDWANA
11 **(Best)**	LADNU##	DIDWANA##	DIDWANA	RIYAN	DEGANA	PARBATSAR	LADNU
				(26) PALI			
1 **(Worst)**	ROHAT	JAITARAN#	JAITARAN	DESURI#	SUMERPUR	DESURI	JAITARAN
2	PALI	PALI	PALI	RAIPUR	DESURI	RANI STATION	RAIPUR
3	RAIPUR	RAIPUR	RAIPUR	SUMERPUR	RAIPUR	MARWAR JUN.	ROHAT
4	JAITARAN	MARWAR JUN.	MARWAR JUN.	BALI	BALI	ROHAT	DESURI
5	MARWAR JUN.	ROHAT	ROHAT	JAITARAN	JAITARAN	SOJAT	MARWAR JUN.
6	SOJAT	DESURI	SOJAT	MARWAR JUN.	RANI STATION	PALI	BALI
7	DESURI	BALI	DESURI	RANI STATION*	MARWAR JUN.	JAITARAN	PALI
8	BALI	SOJAT	BALI	ROHAT*	ROHAT	RAIPUR	SUMERPUR
9	SUMERPUR	SUMERPUR	SUMERPUR	SOJAT	SOJAT	SUMERPUR	SOJAT
10 **(Best)**	RANI STATION##	RANI STATION	RANI STATION	PALI##	PALI	BALI	RANI STATION

contd.

Note : # PS/PSs having worst position in two or more than two human development indices in their respective districts.
PS/PSs having best position in two or more than two human development indices in their respective districts.

(contd.)

S.No	Human Development Indices, 2001/PSs						
	HSI	**EDI**	**GEDI**	**INI**	**GINI**	**GEM**	**HDI**
1	**2**	**3**	**4**	**5**	**6**	**7**	**8**
				(27) RAJSAMAND			
1 **(Worst)**	DEOGARH#	KUMBHAL-GARH#	KUMBHALGARH	KHAMNOR	RAJSAMAND#	RAJSAMAND	DEOGARH
2	AMET	AMET	AMET	RAJSAMAND	KHAMNOR	KHAMNOR	KHAMNOR
3	KUMBHAL-GARH	DEOGARH	DEOGARH	BHIM	AMET	DEOGARH	AMET
4	RAJSAMAND	KHAMNOR	KHAMNOR	DEOGARH	BHIM	BHIM	RAJSAMAND
5	BHIM	BHIM	BHIM	AMET	DEOGARH	RAILMAGRA	BHIM
6	KHAMNOR	RAILMAGRA	RAJSAMAND	KUMBHALGARH	RAILMAGRA	AMET	KUMBHALGARH
7 **(Best)**	RAILMAGRA##	RAJSAMAND	RAILMAGRA	RAILMAGRA	KUMBHAL-GARH##	KUMBHALGARH	RAILMAGRA
				(28) SAWAI MADHOPUR			
1 **(Worst)**	KHANDAR#	KHANDAR	KHANDAR	GANGAPUR#	GANGAPUR	BONLI	KHANDAR
2	BAMANWAS	SAWAI MADHOPUR	SAWAI MADHOPUR	SAWAI MADHOPUR	SAWAI MADHOPUR	BAMANWAS	SAWAI MADHOPUR
3	BONLI	BONLI	BONLI	BAMANWAS	BAMANWAS	KHANDAR	BONLI
4	SAWAI-MADHOPUR	GANGAPUR	GANGAPUR	BONLI	BONLI	GANGAPUR	BAMANWAS
5 **(Best)**	GANGAPUR##	BAMANWAS##	BAMANWAS	KHANDAR##	KHANDAR	SAWAI-MADHOPUR	GANGAPUR
				(29) SIKAR			
1 **(Worst)**	LACHHMAN-GARH	SRI MADHOPUR#	SRI MADHOPUR	SRI MADHOPUR	SRI MADHOPUR	NEEM KA THANA#	NEEM KA THANA
2	NEEM KA THANA	NEEM KA THANA	NEEM KA THANA	NEEM KA THANA	NEEM KA THANA	KHANDELA	SRI MADHOPUR
3	FATEHPUR	DHOND	DHOND	DANTA RAMGARH	DANTA RAMGARH	DHOND	DANTA RAMGARH
4	DANTA RAMGARH	PIPRALI	PIPRALI	DHOND	DHOND	LACHHMAN-GARH	DHOND
5	KHANDELA	DANTA RAMGARH	DANTA RAMGARH	KHANDELA	KHANDELA	SRI MADHOPUR	PIPRALI
6	SRI MADHOPUR	KHANDELA	KHANDELA	PIPRALI	PIPRALI	DANTA RAMGARH	KHANDELA
7	PIPRALI	LACHHMAN-GARH	LACHHMAN-GARH	LACHHMAN-GARH	LACHHMAN-GARH	PIPRALI	LACHHMAN-GARH
8 **(Best)**	DHOND	FATEHPUR##	FATEHPUR	FATEHPUR	FATEHPUR	FATEHPUR	FATEHPUR
				(30) SIROHI			
1 **(Worst)**	ABU ROAD#	ABU ROAD	ABU ROAD	ABU ROAD	SHEOGANJ#	SHEOGANJ	ABU ROAD
2	REODAR	REODAR	REODAR	SHEOGANJ	ABU ROAD	SIROHI	REODAR
3	PINDWARA	SIROHI	SIROHI	SIROHI	SIROHI	REODAR	SHEOGANJ
4	SHEOGANJ	SHEOGANJ	SHEOGANJ	PINDWARA	PINDWARA	ABU ROAD	PINDWARA
5 **(Best)**	SIROHI##	PINDWARA##	PINDWARA	REODAR##	REODAR	PINDWARA	SIROHI
				(31) TONK			
1 **(Worst)**	UNIARA#	TONK#	TONK	UNIARA	UNIARA	TODARAISINGH	UNIARA
2	DEOLI	DEOLI	UNIARA	DEOLI	MALPURA	MALPURA	DEOLI
3	NIWAI	UNIARA	DEOLI	TONK	DEOLI	NIWAI	TONK
4	TONK	MALPURA	MALPURA	MALPURA	TONK	TONK	MALPURA
5	MALPURA	NIWAI	NIWAI	NIWAI	NIWAI	DEOLI	NIWAI
6 **(Best)**	TODARAI-SINGH##	TODARAISINGH	TODARAISINGH	TODARAISINGH	TODARAISINGH	UNIARA	TODARAISINGH
				(32) UDAIPUR			
1 **(Worst)**	KOTRA#	KOTRA	KOTRA	KHERWARA	GIRWA	DHARIAWAD	KOTRA
2	DHARIAWAD	DHARIAWAD	DHARIAWAD	GIRWA	SARADA	SARADA	DHARIAWAD
3	JHADOL	GOGUNDA	GOGUNDA	KOTRA	KHERWARA	GOGUNDA	GOGUNDA
4	KHERWARA	MAVLI	MAVLI	SARADA	MAVLI	JHADOL	KHERWARA
5	GOGUNDA	SARADA	KHERWARA	DHARIAWAD	KOTRA	KOTRA	JHADOL
6	SALUMBAR	KHERWARA	SARADA	GOGUNDA	GOGUNDA	SALUMBAR	SARADA
7	BHINDER	SALUMBAR	GIRWA	JHADOL	JHADOL	KHERWARA	GIRWA
8	BARGAON	GIRWA	SALUMBAR	MAVLI	DHARIAWAD	BHINDER	MAVLI
9	GIRWA	JHADOL	JHADOL	SALUMBAR	BHINDER	GIRWA	SALUMBAR
10	SARADA	BHINDER	BHINDER	BHINDER	SALUMBAR	MAVLI	BHINDER
11 **(Best)**	MAVLI	BARGAON##	BARGAON	BARGAON	BARGAON	BARGAON	BARGAON

Note : # PS/PSs having worst position in two or more than two human development indices in their respective districts.
PS/PSs having best position in two or more than two human development indices in their respective districts.

Source: Annex 6.1, 8.1, 10.1, 12.1, 14.1, 15.1 and 17.1

ANNEXURES

PANCHAYAT SAMITI-WISE AREA, INHABITED VILLAGES AND POPULATION CHARACTERISTICS: RAJASTHAN (1991)

P. Code	*Panchayat Samiti (Concerning Tehsil)*	*Total Rural Area (in sq. km)*	*Total No. of Inhabited Village*	*Total Rural Population*				*Density Per sq. km*	*Sex Ratio*	*Literacy Rate %*		
				Persons	*Male*	*Female*						
						No.	*%*			*Person*	*Male*	*Female*
1	*2*	*3*	*4*	*5*	*6*	*7*	*8*	*9*	*10*	*11*	*12*	*13*
1	ARAIN (Sarwar)	1201.8	122	109697	56513	53184	48.5	91	941	29.11	45.52	11.69
2	BHINAY (Bhinay)	1216.1	120	125267	64675	60592	48.4	103	937	32.67	50.89	13.27
3	JAWAJA* (Beawar)	662.0	193	120052	60437	59615	49.7	181	986	39.37	66.95	12.26
4	KEKRI* (Kekri)	993.4	94	115023	59192	55831	48.5	116	943	40.52	59.94	19.92
5	KISHANGARH (Kishangarh)	1106.9	110	122109	63837	58272	47.7	110	913	30.83	47.35	12.73
6	MASOODA* (Masooda)	875.1	137	127381	66365	61016	47.9	146	919	35.22	56.50	12.08
7	PISANGAN (Pisangan)	1203.5	114	173720	90279	83441	48.0	144	924	38.38	59.00	16.22
8	SRINAGAR (Ajmer)	897.7	95	132383	68796	63587	48.0	147	924	33.41	52.53	12.78
	AJMER DISTRICT	**8156.5**	**985**	**1025632**	**530094**	**495538**	**48.3**	**126**	**935**	**35.10**	**54.97**	**13.96**
9	BANSURE* (Bansure)	664.4	131	163582	86949	76633	46.8	246	881	33.66	51.94	12.73
10	BEHROR (Behror)	336.6	90	115045	59515	55530	48.3	342	933	51.65	73.33	28.57
11	KATHUMAR (Kathumar)	565.0	158	169565	92297	77268	45.6	300	837	35.58	55.48	11.44
12	KISHANGARH BAS (Kishangarh Bas)	505.4	135	136088	71565	64523	47.4	269	902	38.22	55.47	18.94
13	KOTKASIM* (Kotkasim)	344.4	115	95361	50302	45059	47.3	277	896	49.01	69.28	26.32
14	LACHHMANGARH (Lachmangarh)	618.9	184	176309	93697	82612	46.9	285	882	33.82	52.71	12.17
15	MANDAWAR* (Mandawar)	577.3	142	162010	84527	77483	47.8	281	917	48.19	69.17	25.29
16	NIMRANA (Behror)	378.3	85	120331	61905	58426	48.6	318	944	53.72	74.52	31.95
17	RAJGARH (Rajgarh)	1009.2	136	112540	59807	52733	46.9	112	882	35.15	55.08	12.21
18	RAMGARH (Ramgarh)	617.0	171	161672	86058	75614	46.8	262	879	33.90	50.73	14.38
19	RENI (Rajgarh)	392.0	102	105755	56388	49367	46.7	270	875	34.19	54.05	11.20
20	THANAGAZI* (Thanagazi)	1060.3	148	144119	76286	67833	47.1	136	889	28.09	44.79	8.93
21	TIJARA* (Tijara)	643.5	199	151193	80149	71044	47.0	235	886	33.41	50.17	14.27
22	UMREN (Alwar)	848.3	150	162723	87156	75567	46.4	192	867	32.40	49.93	11.92
	ALWAR	**8560.6**	**1946**	**1976293**	**1046601**	**929692**	**47.0**	**231**	**888**	**38.02**	**56.76**	**16.73**
23	ANANDPURI (Bagidora)	341.8	123	84905	43249	41656	49.1	248	963	21.16	34.56	7.08
24	BAGIDORA (Bagidora)	515.6	137	137270	69642	67628	49.3	266	971	23.93	36.80	10.60
25	GARHI* (Garhi)	704.1	163	188399	95494	92905	49.3	268	973	31.92	47.38	16.14
26	GHATOL (Ghatol)	783.3	218	175991	88626	87365	49.6	225	986	21.47	34.73	8.10
27	KUSHALGARH (Kushalgarh)	640.9	208	101900	51818	50082	49.1	159	966	12.56	20.85	3.91
28	PEEPALKHOONT (Banswara)	912.8	186	110617	56255	54362	49.1	121	966	11.23	19.17	2.95
29	SAJJANGARH (Kushalgarh)	402.5	182	103172	52713	50459	48.9	256	957	17.44	27.77	6.61
30	TALWARA (Banswara)	750.4	214	164157	82571	81586	49.7	219	988	21.94	34.89	8.87
	BANSWARA	**5051.4**	**1431**	**1066411**	**540368**	**526043**	**49.3**	**211**	**973**	**21.46**	**33.70**	**8.87**
31	ANTA (Mangrol & Anta)	932.2	147	123431	64669	58762	47.6	132	909	39.47	60.03	16.80
32	ATRU* (Atru)	859.5	135	107431	56737	50694	47.2	125	893	38.37	58.33	15.78
33	BARAN* (Baran)	612.6	98	80869	42465	38404	47.5	132	904	39.04	60.17	15.68
34	CHHABRA* (Chhabra)	783.7	172	102555	43316	38276	46.9	131	884	24.62	40.62	6.36
35	CHHIPABAROD* (Chhipabarod)	824.4	183	81592	53842	48713	47.5	99	905	25.99	42.87	7.12
36	KISHANGANJ* (Kishanganj)	1450.6	176	108345	56975	51370	47.4	75	902	25.63	38.63	11.10
37	SHAHBAD* (Shahbad)	1468.2	159	83028	44244	38784	46.7	57	877	27.84	42.41	10.92
	BARAN #	**6931.2**	**1070**	**687251**	**362248**	**325003**	**47.3**	**99**	**897**	**31.93**	**49.45**	**12.25**
38	BALOTRA* (Panchpadra)	3885.1	189	192132	100111	92021	47.9	49	919	23.31	38.30	6.93
39	BARMER (Ramsar)	3813.3	265	171158	92170	78988	46.1	45	857	19.38	32.98	3.42
40	BAYTOO (Baytoo)	3228.0	248	151787	79062	72725	47.9	47	920	20.22	34.57	4.70
41	CHOHTAN (Chohtan)	3266.5	167	171105	91349	79756	46.6	52	873	12.38	21.16	2.23
42	DHORIMANNA (Gudha Malani)	2668.3	252	181025	94679	86346	47.7	68	912	16.76	29.18	3.04
43	SHEO* (Sheo)	6616.4	167	121551	66572	54979	45.2	18	826	19.34	32.56	3.32
44	SINDHARI (Gudha Malani)	3115.7	240	167810	87661	80149	47.8	54	914	17.07	30.05	2.89
45	SIWANA* (Siwana)	1982.2	97	134488	69393	65095	48.4	68	938	22.59	37.31	7.06
	BARMER	**28575.5**	**1625**	**1291056**	**680997**	**610059**	**47.3**	**45**	**896**	**18.79**	**31.83**	**4.20**

P. Code	Panchayat Samiti (Concerning Tehsil)	Total Rural Area (in sq. km)	Total No. of Inhabited Village	Total Rural Population				Density Per sq. km	Sex Ratio	Literacy Rate %		
				Persons	Male	Female						
						No.	%			Person	Male	Female
1	2	3	4	5	6	7	8	9	10	11	12	13
46	BAYANA* (Bayana)	799.7	159	151810	84944	66866	44.0	190	787	34.98	54.48	9.71
47	DEEG* (Deeg)	490.4	120	125627	69105	56522	45.0	256	818	37.46	57.83	12.00
48	KAMAN (Kaman)	556.5	187	154287	82777	71510	46.3	277	864	24.27	39.80	6.06
49	KUMHER* (Kumher)	440.2	111	129059	70678	58381	45.2	293	826	45.21	68.60	16.38
50	NADBAI* (Nadbai)	431.8	114	127668	70162	57506	45.0	296	820	43.44	67.13	14.21
51	NAGAR PAHARI (Nagar)	621.8	217	181672	98229	83443	45.9	292	849	30.75	48.33	9.75
52	RUPBAS* (Rupbas)	539.0	141	166569	91623	74946	45.0	309	818	43.38	64.65	16.96
53	SEWAR* (Bharatpur)	458.1	154	133563	73266	60297	45.1	292	823	42.56	65.26	14.38
54	WEIR* (Weir)	576.1	142	160526	87988	72538	45.2	279	824	41.10	63.19	13.85
	BHARATPUR	**4913.6**	**1345**	**1330781**	**728772**	**602009**	**45.2**	**271**	**826**	**37.84**	**58.43**	**12.48**
55	ASIND* (Asind)	1110.2	203	156028	78451	77577	49.7	141	989	24.38	40.33	8.41
56	BANERA* (Banera)	676.5	82	88063	45076	42987	48.8	130	954	25.69	40.39	10.15
57	HURDA* (Hurda)	617.3	68	72959	37811	35148	48.2	118	930	34.28	48.87	18.51
58	JAHAZPUR* (Jahazpur)	1033.3	181	132876	69362	63514	47.8	129	916	25.83	41.25	8.83
59	KOTRI* (Kotri)	950.1	146	121812	63084	58728	48.2	128	931	23.60	33.19	13.21
60	MANDAL* (Mandal)	1155.2	158	146986	73635	73351	49.9	127	996	23.39	37.76	9.05
61	MANDALGARH (Mandalgarh)	1392.4	270	156392	82265	74127	47.4	112	901	22.12	33.80	8.99
62	RAIPUR* (Raipur)	515.4	86	71377	35377	36000	50.4	138	1018	24.89	40.45	9.79
63	SAHARA* (Sahara)	633.2	91	85124	41743	43381	51.0	134	1039	24.97	40.65	10.14
64	SHAHPURA* (Sahahpura)	1127.3	149	120640	62144	58496	48.5	107	941	21.15	33.74	7.73
65	SUWANA* (Bhilwara)	832.3	131	129727	66211	63516	49.0	156	959	24.22	38.54	9.30
	BHILWARA	**10043.2**	**1565**	**1281984**	**655159**	**626825**	**48.9**	**128**	**957**	**24.48**	**38.36**	**9.96**
66	BIKANER (Bikaner)	8944.7	155	232046	124026	108020	46.6	26	871	25.46	38.75	10.03
67	DUNGARGARH* (Dungargarh)	3002.8	90	133598	69106	64492	48.3	44	933	22.90	36.82	8.03
68	KOLAYAT* (Kolayat)	7318.6	169	132657	70699	61958	46.7	18	876	22.80	35.05	8.66
69	LUNKARANSAR (Lunkaransar)	6214.0	130	156382	82141	74241	47.5	25	904	24.93	38.04	10.30
70	NOKHA* (Nokha)	3767.7	126	208913	108483	100430	48.1	55	926	22.69	37.60	6.59
	BIKANER**	**26245.0**	**580**	**729998**	**385349**	**344649**	**47.2**	**28**	**894**	**24.07**	**37.59**	**8.84**
71	HINDOLI* (Hindoli)	1339.0	174	151669	80188	71481	47.1	113	891	22.16	34.77	7.86
72	KESHORAIPATAN (Indragarh)	1287.2	216	149166	78619	70547	47.3	116	897	30.93	48.76	10.94
73	NAINWA* (Nainwa)	1140.0	175	121652	64536	57116	47.0	107	885	23.57	37.55	7.67
74	TALERA* (Bundi)	1882.6	261	214017	113956	100061	46.8	114	878	26.74	40.95	10.40
	BUNDI	**5648.8**	**826**	**636504**	**337299**	**299205**	**47.0**	**113**	**887**	**26.02**	**40.65**	**9.39**
75	ARNOD* (Arnod)	701.5	171	91408	46438	44970	49.2	130	968	27.32	41.36	12.77
76	BARI SADRI* (Bari Sadri)	474.5	144	76910	38859	38051	49.5	162	979	26.99	44.32	9.48
77	BEGUN (Begun)	957.5	219	85822	44048	41774	48.7	90	948	27.05	44.40	8.63
78	BHADESAR* (Bhadesar)	540.5	161	89539	45817	43722	48.8	166	954	26.33	42.22	9.78
79	BHAINSRORGARH (Rawatbhata)	1369.8	150	63941	33825	30116	47.1	47	890	25.05	38.95	9.27
80	BHOPALSAGAR (Kapasan)	398.2	83	64086	32533	31553	49.2	161	970	29.43	46.66	11.83
81	CHHOTI SADRI * (Chhoti Sadri)	691.9	141	84902	43383	41519	48.9	123	957	31.63	50.39	12.03
82	CHITTAURGARH* (Chittaurgarh)	814.0	218	135718	69237	66481	49.0	167	960	28.09	44.43	11.15
83	DUNGLA* (Dungla)	493.6	102	77050	38964	38086	49.4	156	977	27.36	44.65	9.84
84	GANGRAR* (Gangrar)	555.6	127	75031	38738	36293	48.4	135	937	25.99	40.88	9.99
85	KAPASAN (Kapasan)	482.6	107	72870	36814	36056	49.5	151	979	23.17	38.96	7.06
86	NIMBAHERA* (Nimbahera)	812.7	150	110286	56298	53988	49.0	136	959	33.56	54.03	12.20
87	PRATAPGARH* (Pratapgarh)	1427.9	320	159206	81501	77705	48.8	111	953	27.25	42.82	10.90
88	RASHMI* (Rashmi)	449.7	79	65794	32854	32940	50.1	146	1003	27.40	44.08	10.98
	CHITTAURGARH	**10170.0**	**2172**	**1252563**	**639309**	**613254**	**49.0**	**123**	**959**	**27.80**	**44.37**	**10.55**
89	CHURU* (Churu)	1559.6	101	123292	62987	60305	48.9	79	957	30.01	48.98	10.63
90	RAJGARH* (Rajgarh)	2197.3	205	221371	113925	107446	48.5	101	943	34.23	53.66	13.74
91	RATANGARH* (Ratangarh)	1642.3	96	125447	64764	60683	48.4	76	937	26.54	43.37	8.85
92	SARDARSHAHAR* (Sardarshahar)	3814.4	170	174959	90422	84537	48.3	46	935	22.38	37.70	6.13
93	SUJANGARH* (Sujangarh)	2596.0	153	194402	100128	94274	48.5	75	942	23.38	38.42	7.52
94	TARANAGAR* (Taranagar)	1782.9	111	124103	63704	60399	48.7	70	948	26.96	44.05	9.04
	CHURU***	**16595.3**	**926**	**1097172**	**565036**	**532136**	**48.5**	**66**	**942**	**26.89**	**43.60**	**9.31**
95	BANDIKUI* (Baswa)	600.8	207	186479	98697	87782	47.1	310	889	37.27	58.72	12.89
96	DAUSA* (Dausa)	907.9	221	207958	110174	97784	47.0	229	888	33.42	54.21	9.78
97	LALSOT* (Lalsot)	854.0	293	187439	98885	88554	47.2	219	896	29.82	47.84	9.42
98	MAHWA* (Mahwa)	473.5	150	146684	79109	67575	46.1	310	854	39.26	60.73	13.92
99	SIKRAI* (Sikrai)	502.7	138	160624	84813	75811	47.2	320	894	30.67	49.82	9.05
	DAUSA #	**3338.9**	**1009**	**889184**	**471678**	**417506**	**47.0**	**266**	**885**	**33.96**	**54.15**	**10.90**
100	BARI* (Bari)	794.0	126	117351	66556	50795	43.3	148	763	26.24	40.73	6.68
101	BASERI* (Baseri)	1001.4	122	151187	84489	66698	44.1	151	789	31.56	46.56	11.99
102	DHAULPUR (Sepau)	577.3	156	201089	111852	89237	44.4	348	798	33.84	51.18	11.53
103	RAJAKHERA (Rajakhera)	572.0	147	151027	84595	66432	44.0	264	785	30.46	47.47	8.02
	DHAULPUR	**2944.7**	**551**	**620654**	**347492**	**273162**	**44.0**	**211**	**786**	**31.01**	**47.13**	**9.89**

P. Code	Panchayat Samiti (Concerning Tehsil)	Total Rural Area (in sq. km)	Total No. of Inhabited Village	Total Rural Population				Density Per sq. km	Sex Ratio	Literacy Rate %		
				Persons	Male	Female No.	Female %			Person	Male	Female
1	2	3	4	5	6	7	8	9	10	11	12	13
104	ASPUR* (Aspur)	691.7	142	146507	71377	75130	51.3	212	1053	27.27	42.65	12.88
105	BICHHIWARA (Dungarpur)	745.9	174	180805	91481	89324	49.4	242	976	25.05	40.11	9.65
106	DUNGARPUR (Dungarpur)	575.1	158	133212	65893	67319	50.5	232	1022	26.54	43.35	10.29
107	SAGWARA (Sagwara)	611.8	153	160585	79459	81126	50.5	262	1021	32.98	49.94	16.57
108	SIMALWARA (Simalwara)	913.6	219	189623	96478	93145	49.1	208	965	23.87	36.87	10.32
	DUNGARPUR	**3538.1**	**846**	**810732**	**404688**	**406044**	**50.1**	**229**	**1003**	**27.01**	**42.26**	**11.92**
109	ANUPGARH (Garsana)	3543.7	1065	294097	157267	136830	46.5	83	870	32.05	44.63	17.46
110	GANGANAGAR (Ganganagar)	854.9	241	162395	87416	74979	46.2	190	858	44.63	58.33	28.49
111	KARANPUR* (Karanpur)	810.5	200	92181	48390	43791	47.5	114	905	40.12	51.29	27.83
112	PADAMPUR* (Padampur)	842.5	236	105870	55562	50308	47.5	126	905	42.88	56.17	28.31
113	RAISINGHNAGAR* (Raisinghnagar)	1315.4	353	128836	67266	61570	47.8	98	915	38.12	51.74	23.31
114	SADULSHAHAR (Sadulshahar)	1484.5	377	208380	111888	96492	46.3	140	862	39.65	54.05	22.83
115	SURATGARH* (Suratgarh)	3791.5	680	274376	148174	126202	46.0	72	852	33.55	48.03	16.32
	GANGANAGAR	**12643.0**	**3152**	**1266135**	**675963**	**590172**	**46.6**	**100**	**873**	**37.40**	**50.89**	**21.86**
116	BHADRA* (Bhadra)	1713.1	190	180760	94908	85852	47.5	106	905	37.37	56.07	16.76
117	HANUMANGARH (Hanumangarh)	2035.0	621	333914	176677	157237	47.1	164	890	33.33	46.42	18.58
118	NOHAR (Rawatsar)	4304.9	475	289856	151940	137916	47.6	67	908	30.25	46.86	12.06
	HANUMANGARH ##	**8053.0**	**1286**	**804530**	**423525**	**381005**	**47.4**	**100**	**900**	**33.14**	**48.75**	**15.81**
119	AMBER* (Amber)	839.4	194	205355	107576	97779	47.6	245	909	35.39	57.15	11.14
120	BASSI* (Bassi)	630.9	209	159749	83949	75800	47.4	253	903	33.47	54.76	9.72
121	CHAKSU* (Chaksu)	766.8	258	125703	65878	59825	47.6	164	908	29.14	48.24	7.99
122	DUDU (Dudu)	1855.2	210	210655	110037	100618	47.8	114	914	32.67	50.90	12.58
123	GOVINDGARH* (Chomu)	666.0	95	210430	109896	100534	47.8	316	915	40.89	63.88	15.66
124	JAMWA RAMGARH* (Jamwa Ramgarh)	1011.5	231	190822	100252	90570	47.5	189	903	31.75	51.86	9.24
125	JHOTWARA* (Jaipur)	385.0	102	103076	54701	48375	46.9	268	884	39.23	59.78	15.60
126	KOTPUTLI (Kotputli)	663.3	119	177608	92951	84657	47.7	268	911	36.09	56.35	13.91
127	PHAGI* (Phagi)	1113.3	168	130453	68466	61987	47.5	117	905	29.46	46.06	10.94
128	SAMBHAR (Phulara)	832.4	143	162221	84051	78170	48.2	195	930	36.39	58.39	12.62
129	SANGANER* (Sanganer)	583.9	205	153893	81279	72614	47.2	264	893	38.46	59.44	14.63
130	SHAHPURA (Shahpura)	408.0	79	128177	67148	61029	47.6	314	909	37.92	59.56	13.89
131	VIRATNAGAR (Viratnagar)	649.1	118	155270	81683	73587	47.4	239	901	34.36	53.91	12.45
	JAIPUR	**10404.8**	**2131**	**2113412**	**1107867**	**1005545**	**47.6**	**203**	**908**	**35.05**	**55.52**	**12.32**
132	JAISALMER (Jaisalmer)	12849.5	137	80310	45121	35189	43.8	6	780	26.86	42.53	6.38
133	SAM (Jaisalmer)	21111.0	251	94930	52919	42011	44.3	4	794	21.21	35.15	3.48
134	SANKRA (Pokaran)	5486.6	130	115677	62258	53419	46.2	21	858	22.02	36.88	4.58
	JAISALMER	**39447.1**	**518**	**290917**	**160298**	**130619**	**44.9**	**7**	**815**	**23.10**	**37.92**	**4.71**
135	AHORE (Ahore)	1596.5	108	150191	75636	74555	49.6	94	986	28.44	46.36	10.89
136	BHINMAL (Bagora)	1337.7	79	146196	75699	70497	48.2	109	931	17.50	30.92	3.20
137	JALOR (Jalor)	1054.8	66	107936	54808	53128	49.2	102	969	26.03	42.43	9.38
138	JASWANTPURA (Bhinmal)	1068.8	72	106325	54181	52144	49.0	99	962	20.73	35.53	5.49
139	RANIWARA* (Raniwara)	984.0	83	123125	64108	59017	47.9	125	921	20.23	34.38	4.82
140	SANCHORE* (Sanchore)	3008.5	180	260312	135290	125022	48.0	87	924	19.17	34.17	2.99
141	SAYLA (Sayla)	1459.4	77	165270	84509	80761	48.9	113	956	19.79	32.72	6.36
	JALOR	**10509.7**	**665**	**1059355**	**544231**	**515124**	**48.6**	**101**	**947**	**21.36**	**36.20**	**5.85**
142	BAKANI (Jhalrapatan)	885.5	282	129817	67593	62224	47.9	147	921	23.37	36.64	8.79
143	DAG (Gangdhar)	1130.5	220	138701	71529	67172	48.4	123	939	21.07	32.82	8.43
144	JHALRAPATAN (Jhalrapatan)	1329.2	282	162994	84932	78062	47.9	123	919	29.35	46.88	10.25
145	KHANPUR* (Khanpur)	940.1	190	118513	62502	56011	47.3	126	896	38.97	60.50	14.91
146	MANOHARTHANA (Manoharthana)	922.7	274	126037	65774	60263	47.8	137	916	15.92	27.47	3.18
147	PIRAWA* (Pirwa)	1001.1	200	129946	67323	62623	48.2	130	930	29.63	47.51	10.29
	JHALAWAR	**6209.1**	**1448**	**806008**	**419653**	**386355**	**47.9**	**130**	**921**	**26.32**	**41.89**	**9.29**
148	ALSISAR (Jhunjhunun)	747.0	113	112705	56906	55799	49.5	151	981	43.12	64.58	21.57
149	BUHANA* (Buhana)	653.5	122	172845	89282	83563	48.3	264	936	48.66	70.82	25.30
150	CHIRAWA (Chirawa)	489.0	82	124621	63972	60649	48.7	255	948	45.37	66.63	23.33
151	JHUNJHUNUN (Jhunjhunun)	820.5	156	157320	80014	77306	49.1	192	966	48.20	70.89	25.25
152	KHETRI* (Khetri)	796.2	80	179811	94715	85096	47.3	226	898	42.00	62.62	18.90
153	NAWALGARH* (Nawalgarh)	665.2	70	181313	92535	88778	49.0	273	959	45.31	68.13	21.94
154	SURAJGARH (Chirawa)	781.4	120	141222	73678	67544	47.8	181	917	43.34	63.31	21.70
155	UDAIPURWATI* (Udaipurwati)	831.0	81	187540	96238	91302	48.7	226	949	41.25	62.73	18.91
	JHUNJHUNUN	**5783.8**	**824**	**1257377**	**647340**	**610037**	**48.5**	**217**	**942**	**44.65**	**66.23**	**22.04**
156	BALESAR (Shergarh)	1854.1	68	127529	66288	61241	43.6	69	924	24.98	39.76	4.92
157	BAP (Phalodi)	4431.2	93	103647	54995	48652	46.9	23	885	20.30	33.52	5.25
158	BHOPALGARH (Bhopalgarh)	1743.3	84	156516	81088	75428	48.2	90	930	28.40	48.61	6.97
159	BILARA* (Bilara)	1499.4	79	141630	73774	67856	47.9	94	920	30.93	51.44	8.77
160	LUNI (Luni)	1982.5	128	166729	86946	79783	47.9	84	918	30.34	49.53	9.37
161	MANDOR (Jodhpur)	1269.2	105	111928	58734	53194	47.5	88	906	29.99	50.30	7.52

P. Code	Panchayat Samiti (Concerning Tehsil)	Total Rural Area (in sq. km)	Total No. of Inhabited Village	Total Rural Population				Density Per sq. km	Sex Ratio	Literacy Rate %		
				Persons	Male	Female						
						No.	%			Person	Male	Female
1	2	3	4	5	6	7	8	9	10	11	12	13
162	OSIAN (Osian)	4184.5	167	306437	160069	146368	47.8	73	914	24.87	42.14	5.92
163	PHALODI (Phalodi)	3237.9	86	161438	84239	77199	47.8	50	916	23.61	39.79	5.78
164	SHERGARH (Shergarh)	1975.0	50	113079	59679	53400	47.2	57	895	21.74	37.30	4.28
	JODHPUR	**22177.1**	**860**	**1388933**	**725812**	**663121**	**47.4**	**63**	**914**	**26.24**	**43.82**	**6.62**
165	HINDAUN* (Hindaun)	631.5	119	196305	107094	89211	45.4	311	833	35.41	56.62	9.75
166	KARAULI* (Karauli)	1219.7	196	166459	91581	74878	45.0	136	818	25.36	40.08	6.99
167	NADOTI* (Nadoti)	646.0	84	101680	54560	47120	46.3	157	864	35.43	56.58	10.97
168	SAPOTRA (Sapotra)	1962.0	209	182378	99753	82625	45.3	93	828	27.47	41.78	9.74
169	TODABHIM* (Todabhim)	522.5	142	154373	83775	70598	45.7	295	843	35.31	57.58	8.86
	KARAULI ###	**4981.7**	**750**	**801195**	**436763**	**364432**	**45.5**	**161**	**834**	**31.51**	**49.92**	**9.17**
170	CHECHAT* (Ranganjmandi)	770.9	146	120614	64065	56549	46.9	156	883	37.45	56.01	16.30
171	ITAWA* (Pipalda)	887.1	161	127120	67286	59834	47.1	143	889	34.91	53.67	13.78
172	LADPURA* (Ladpura)	1307.5	146	109602	57801	51801	47.3	84	896	37.40	55.71	16.79
173	SANGOD* (Sangod)	1046.2	198	122585	64303	58282	47.5	117	906	40.50	61.41	17.18
174	SULTANPUR* (Digod)	911.8	160	123824	65430	58394	47.2	136	892	41.22	61.77	18.01
	KOTA	**4923.5**	**811**	**603745**	**318885**	**284860**	**47.2**	**123**	**893**	**38.30**	**57.74**	**16.39**
175	DEGANA (Degana)	1457.5	146	154314	78707	75607	49.0	106	961	27.84	45.77	9.40
176	DIDWANA* (Didwana)	1608.1	167	224202	113117	111085	49.5	139	982	30.89	50.91	10.87
177	JAYAL* (Jayal)	2088.2	132	176728	90450	86278	48.8	85	954	24.03	40.22	7.25
178	KUCHAMAN* (Nawa)	1436.1	146	205068	105502	99566	48.6	143	944	30.72	49.19	11.25
179	LADNU* (Ladnu)	1371.2	96	123172	62293	60879	49.4	90	977	32.01	51.52	12.41
180	MAKRANA* (Makrana)	1106.2	120	156267	79940	76327	48.8	141	955	30.79	48.92	11.96
181	MERTA (Merta)	1397.1	96	142563	74295	68268	47.9	102	919	31.24	49.66	11.16
182	MUNDWA (Nagaur)	2184.3	110	152729	79149	73580	48.2	70	930	23.41	39.46	6.30
183	NAGAUR (Nagaur)	2380.6	133	181365	93742	87623	48.3	76	935	24.93	41.73	7.07
184	PARBATSAR* (Parbatsar)	1070.9	108	142838	73565	69273	48.5	133	942	26.32	41.30	10.51
185	RIYAN (Merta)	1239.4	120	142928	73687	69241	48.4	115	940	27.25	44.00	9.50
	NAGAUR	**17339.6**	**1374**	**1802174**	**924447**	**877727**	**48.7**	**104**	**949**	**28.14**	**45.76**	**9.75**
186	BALI* (Bali)	1369.8	89	149232	75114	74118	49.7	109	987	30.57	45.91	15.35
187	DESURI (Desuri)	829.1	76	85369	42543	42826	50.2	103	1007	31.36	49.72	13.59
188	JAITARAN* (Jaitaran)	1289.8	92	134851	69221	65630	48.7	105	948	26.04	43.59	7.75
189	KHARCHI (Marwar Jun.)*	1390.6	137	154855	78087	76768	49.6	111	983	31.01	50.90	11.18
190	PALI (Pali)	1296.6	80	84540	43740	40800	48.3	65	933	27.45	45.23	8.73
191	RAIPUR* (Raipur)	986.5	103	132128	67364	64764	49.0	134	961	28.62	47.96	8.87
192	RANI STATION (Desuri)	762.6	73	94105	46950	47155	50.1	123	1004	33.49	51.85	15.77
193	ROHAT* (Rohat)	1404.4	79	81290	41822	39468	48.6	58	944	27.00	45.67	7.50
194	SOJAT* (Sojat)	1627.0	112	131378	66535	64843	49.4	81	975	32.57	53.97	11.14
195	SUMERPUR* (Sumerpur)	911.9	63	115337	58478	56859	49.3	126	972	32.47	51.00	13.79
	PALI	**11868.3**	**904**	**1163085**	**589854**	**573231**	**49.3**	**98**	**972**	**30.13**	**48.63**	**11.47**
196	AMET* (Amet)	505.4	136	71557	36287	35270	49.3	142	972	22.93	37.72	7.80
197	BHIM* (Bhim)	677.7	109	104066	50892	53174	51.1	154	1045	32.02	56.46	9.56
198	DEOGARH* (Deogarh)	589.1	131	63804	31692	32112	50.3	108	1013	22.72	39.24	6.64
199	KHAMNOR* (Nathdwara)	594.8	132	112075	55637	56438	50.4	188	1014	30.74	48.31	13.66
200	KUMBHALGARH* (Kumbhalgarh)	776.0	161	113501	56953	56548	49.8	146	993	23.33	38.39	8.29
201	RAILMAGRA* (Railmagra)	544.2	90	100294	50490	49804	49.7	184	986	32.57	50.38	14.69
202	RAJSAMAND* (Rajsamand)	569.3	130	108526	54712	53814	49.6	191	984	31.70	49.84	13.34
	RAJSAMAND #	**4256.5**	**889**	**673823**	**336663**	**337160**	**50.0**	**158**	**1001**	**28.51**	**46.35**	**10.94**
203	BAMANWAS* (Bamanwas)	728.8	132	120238	64413	55825	46.4	165	867	32.66	52.32	9.85
204	BONLI (Bonli)	1009.5	157	164512	87397	77115	46.9	163	882	30.45	48.08	10.38
205	GANGAPUR* (Gangapur)	644.7	115	146685	78993	67692	46.1	228	857	35.34	55.97	11.06
206	KHANDAR (Khandar)	1352.3	156	119379	64245	55134	46.2	88	858	24.53	39.23	7.26
207	SAWAI MADHOPUR (S. Madhopur)	1232.4	154	173279	91800	81479	47.0	141	888	31.57	51.47	9.02
	S. MADHOPUR	**4967.7**	**714**	**724093**	**386848**	**337245**	**46.6**	**146**	**872**	**31.09**	**49.71**	**9.59**
208	DANTA RAMGARH (Danta Ramgarh)	1115.7	135	206470	105950	100520	48.7	185	949	38.04	59.84	15.19
209	DHOND (Sikar)	912.3	108	171290	87053	84237	49.2	188	968	38.65	62.18	14.71
210	FATEHPUR (Fatehpur)	1236.9	141	157370	78862	78508	49.9	127	996	37.57	60.75	15.18
211	KHANDELA (Sri Madhopur)	783.8	116	176571	90844	85727	48.6	225	944	39.32	63.08	14.45
212	LACHHMANGARH (Lachhmangarh)	1027.0	136	158995	80062	78933	49.6	155	986	38.50	61.74	15.49
213	NEEM KA THANA* (Neem Ka Thana)	1186.7	143	252849	132085	120764	47.8	213	914	39.02	60.39	15.71
214	PIPRALI (Sikar)	797.7	91	164117	84316	79801	48.6	206	946	39.83	62.88	15.89
215	SRI MADHOPUR (Sri Madhopur)	566.6	61	167731	86598	81133	48.4	296	937	41.43	64.57	16.77
	SIKAR	**7626.7**	**931**	**1455393**	**745770**	**709623**	**48.8**	**191**	**952**	**39.03**	**61.80**	**15.42**
216	ABU ROAD* (Abu Road)	858.1	78	80611	41533	39078	48.5	94	941	18.53	28.89	7.37
217	PINDWARA* (Pindwara)	1138.3	98	128032	65180	62852	49.1	112	964	22.76	34.67	10.60
218	REODAR* (Reodar)	1086.8	122	132122	67862	64260	48.6	122	947	21.26	33.71	8.23

P. Code	Panchayat Samiti (Concerning Tehsil)	Total Rural Area (in sq. km)	Total No. of Inhabited Village	Total Rural Population				Density Per sq. km	Sex Ratio	Literacy Rate %		
				Persons	Male	Female No.	Female %			Person	Male	Female
1	2	3	4	5	6	7	8	9	10	11	12	13
219	SHEOGANJ* (Sheoganj)	892.3	66	79876	40724	39152	49.0	90	961	24.03	39.38	8.36
220	SIROHI* (Sirohi)	1090.4	82	105806	52639	53167	50.2	97	1010	28.22	46.49	10.74
	SIROHI	**5065.9**	**446**	**526447**	**267938**	**258509**	**49.1**	**104**	**965**	**23.05**	**36.57**	**9.23**
221	DEOLI* (Deoli)	1235.3	157	135553	70652	64901	47.9	110	919	30.96	49.15	11.12
222	MALPURA* (Malpura)	1439.1	123	148406	76818	71588	48.2	103	932	27.33	43.37	10.13
223	NIWAI* (Niwai)	1030.1	191	137463	70877	66586	48.4	133	939	29.94	46.34	12.46
224	TODARAISINGH* (Todaraisingh)	985.5	109	90790	46695	44095	48.6	92	944	28.51	47.38	8.71
225	TONK (Tonk)	1415.5	248	168956	88261	80695	47.8	119	914	26.51	44.54	6.70
226	UNIARA* (Uniara)	986.4	191	103418	54127	49291	47.7	105	911	26.65	43.90	7.58
	TONK	**7091.9**	**1019**	**784586**	**407430**	**377156**	**48.1**	**111**	**926**	**28.29**	**45.68**	**9.48**
227	BARGAON (Girwa)	648.0	143	123482	63797	59685	48.3	191	936	32.97	49.92	14.81
228	BHINDER* (Vallabhnagar)	985.1	264	169382	85830	83552	49.3	172	973	29.17	46.86	11.16
229	DHARIAWAD* (Dhariawad)	1177.4	246	156024	79516	76508	49.0	133	962	12.93	20.64	4.90
230	GIRWA (Girwa)	1349.1	159	177158	91243	85915	48.5	131	942	27.20	41.69	11.72
231	GOGUNDA* (Gogunda)	871.8	146	121703	61630	60073	49.4	140	975	23.01	36.84	8.85
232	JHADOL* (Jhadol)	1428.3	256	147044	75228	71816	48.8	103	955	19.81	31.83	7.18
233	KHERWARA* (Kherwara)	1076.7	241	199059	98413	100646	50.6	185	1023	32.11	51.77	13.06
234	KOTRA* (Kotra)	1191.5	302	130449	66743	63706	48.8	109	954	8.67	14.42	2.57
235	MAVLI* (Mavli)	798.9	148	164468	83914	80554	49.0	206	960	31.58	48.60	13.93
236	SALUMBAR* (Salumbar)	921.8	231	161630	80736	80894	50.0	175	1002	22.10	35.89	8.45
237	SARADA* (Sarada)	1078.2	154	171060	85065	85995	50.3	159	1011	26.95	42.62	11.59
	UDAIPUR	**11526.8**	**2290**	**1721459**	**872115**	**849344**	**49.3**	**149**	**974**	**24.74**	**39.04**	**10.08**
	RAJASTHAN	**335589**	**37889**	**3393882**	**17686463**	**16252414**	**47.9**	**101**	**919**	**30.39**	**47.64**	**11.61**

Note: Dungargarh PS shifted from Churu to Bikaner district on 1st April 2001. * Co-terminus Panchayat Samiti (with Tehsil); ** Excluding data of Dungargarh PS; *** Including data of Dungargarh PS.
Came in force from April, 1991; ## Came in force from July 1994; ### Came in force from July 1997.

Source: 1. Computed from data given in Primary Census Abustract, Rajasthan, Series -21, Census of India, 1991.
2. District Census Handbooks (all districts), Rajasthan, 1991.

PANCHAYAT SAMITI-WISE PERCENTAGE OF RURAL POP. SERVED BY BASIC SOCIO-ECONOMIC AMENITIES: RAJASTHAN (1991)

P. Code	*Panchayat Samiti/District*	*%age of Pop. Served by Amenity of*							
		Medical	*Drinking Water*	*Education*	*Post & Telegraph*	*Market/ Hat*	*Commu- nications*	*Approach By Pucca Road*	*Power Supply*
1	*2*	*3*	*4*	*5*	*6*	*7*	*8*	*9*	*10*
1	ARAIN	49.69	100.00	99.06	53.01	—	47.98	33.04	75.23
2	BHINAY	61.21	100.00	99.35	64.12	—	58.74	54.30	83.15
3	JAWAJA	33.60	99.08	93.02	40.24	—	41.93	56.92	61.43
4	KEKRI	66.66	100.00	99.60	72.09	—	29.04	56.23	94.58
5	KISHANGARH	61.56	100.00	96.24	70.48	—	59.56	56.80	92.28
6	MASOODA	53.89	100.00	95.36	57.57	—	54.18	59.51	88.78
7	PISANGAN	66.45	100.00	99.74	71.21	—	51.72	75.18	99.02
8	SRINAGAR	48.26	100.00	99.84	54.55	—	59.60	71.81	94.48
	AJMER DISTRICT	**55.71**	**99.89**	**97.87**	**60.94**	—	**50.74**	**59.29**	**86.98**
9	BANSURE	43.66	100.00	98.03	49.09	6.74	46.67	49.59	99.32
10	BEHROR	51.70	100.00	99.14	61.31	—	45.34	46.41	99.77
11	KATHUMAR	44.10	100.00	98.16	44.71	—	33.55	45.42	67.66
12	KISHANGARH BAS	39.46	100.00	94.84	48.70	5.00	36.76	53.29	99.82
13	KOTKASIM	40.96	100.00	95.15	45.28	—	38.80	44.12	84.95
14	LACHHMANGARH	33.66	100.00	95.38	41.57	—	33.99	47.48	63.11
15	MANDAWAR	44.44	100.00	98.94	48.70	—	46.83	48.61	97.08
16	NIMRANA	49.90	100.00	98.47	61.42	—	39.77	52.25	99.99
17	RAJGARH	47.48	100.00	94.10	52.99	—	34.23	55.58	79.08
18	RAMGARH	36.72	100.00	93.48	41.31	9.68	34.24	52.36	88.68
19	RENI	40.87	100.00	93.94	54.90	—	34.76	42.11	80.84
20	THANAGAZI	54.16	100.00	96.97	49.58	—	52.39	56.25	82.39
21	TIJARA	30.22	100.00	92.70	37.39	—	24.20	38.57	80.50
22	UMREN	40.52	100.00	93.88	49.07	4.90	43.74	43.41	95.59
	ALWAR	**42.28**	**100.00**	**95.97**	**48.27**	**2.10**	**38.97**	**48.23**	**86.60**
23	ANANDPURI	39.46	100.00	96.69	32.92	—	36.27	44.38	48.42
24	BAGIDORA	49.32	100.00	93.58	36.56	—	48.64	59.05	58.17
25	GARHI	57.70	100.00	97.85	47.91	—	58.44	59.48	90.16
26	GHATOL	42.31	100.00	95.51	44.71	8.63	39.34	48.55	68.35
27	KUSHALGARH	16.90	99.75	85.70	7.35	4.70	18.68	21.96	41.36
28	PEEPALKHOONT	44.79	100.00	85.08	27.46	16.13	25.91	36.75	28.32
29	SAJJANGARH	23.46	100.00	85.12	22.56	3.37	22.31	31.53	35.33
30	TALWARA	50.26	100.00	92.30	42.39	0.60	54.48	59.56	63.92
	BANSWARA	**42.93**	**99.98**	**92.25**	**35.42**	**3.97**	**40.98**	**47.78**	**58.70**
31	ANTA	45.34	100.00	95.29	50.07	25.62	37.92	37.02	78.99
32	ATRU	49.63	100.00	91.66	56.57	25.89	40.55	34.85	86.89
33	BARAN	31.62	100.00	99.06	42.22	8.70	27.23	38.47	92.87
34	CHHABRA	24.20	100.00	89.27	25.35	7.41	12.50	13.71	70.79
35	CHHIPABAROD	29.30	100.00	88.85	31.35	13.51	26.72	21.67	46.26
36	KISHANGANJ	37.27	99.90	83.73	35.20	24.98	42.28	33.70	83.90
37	SHAHBAD	29.04	99.45	85.51	36.42	13.58	28.16	34.95	65.45
	BARAN #	**36.10**	**99.92**	**90.50**	**40.26**	**17.96**	**31.46**	**30.78**	**75.89**
38	BALOTRA	34.77	99.68	91.72	61.05	—	79.52	48.60	61.52
39	BARMER	20.21	97.29	83.65	44.92	—	36.34	46.00	21.99
40	BAYTOO	15.49	96.39	74.35	37.35	3.94	38.04	19.60	25.00
41	CHOHTAN	36.45	100.00	90.54	59.00	—	44.91	34.84	28.30
42	DHORIMANNA	20.23	100.00	77.69	37.75	—	35.75	29.64	49.91
43	SHEO	21.26	99.24	91.67	38.22	—	51.52	52.70	33.15
44	SINDHARI	25.07	99.71	79.53	38.31	0.47	44.61	37.19	34.02
45	SIWANA	45.72	100.00	98.01	68.24	3.20	77.92	40.98	90.23
	BARMER	**27.37**	**99.06**	**85.55**	**48.23**	**0.86**	**50.86**	**38.47**	**42.70**
46	BAYANA	44.02	100.00	97.91	58.64	1.54	31.94	43.22	72.19
47	DEEG	33.08	100.00	97.64	45.10	9.30	10.81	53.77	72.50
48	KAMAN	29.99	99.86	92.16	41.58	—	16.43	30.99	54.12
49	KUMHER	58.39	99.43	99.42	58.56	—	31.15	63.22	94.74
50	NADBAI	34.37	100.00	98.55	54.45	4.41	43.18	46.51	87.60

P. Code	Panchayat Samiti/District	%age of Pop. Served by Amenity of							
		Medical	Drinking Water	Education	Post & Telegraph	Market/ Hat	Commu-nications	Approach By Pucca Road	Power Supply
1	2	3	4	5	6	7	8	9	10
51	NAGAR PAHARI	24.36	100.00	93.95	44.77	1.13	27.13	39.78	44.80
52	RUPBAS	42.28	100.00	98.35	47.87	10.62	46.01	53.20	61.63
53	SEWAR	33.86	99.89	98.18	40.48	—	29.20	60.67	85.68
54	WEIR	47.23	100.00	98.86	60.69	7.06	30.76	49.05	99.09
	BHARATPUR	**38.29**	**99.92**	**97.08**	**50.07**	**3.81**	**29.84**	**48.29**	**73.33**
55	ASIND	55.33	100.00	93.89	53.56	—	62.25	43.62	87.27
56	BANERA	74.52	100.00	97.32	58.04	—	58.35	53.29	97.74
57	HURDA	72.82	100.00	99.29	48.91	6.22	75.25	62.07	100.00
58	JAHAZPUR	60.42	100.00	95.72	49.81	1.51	40.85	44.23	87.71
59	KOTRI	51.05	100.00	96.26	49.69	—	53.22	42.57	85.41
60	MANDAL	60.90	100.00	96.74	51.25	—	70.56	46.93	92.72
61	MANDALGARH	51.48	100.00	87.08	45.23	—	43.47	46.04	88.47
62	RAIPUR	58.84	100.00	98.27	55.55	—	73.60	38.20	92.67
63	SAHARA	64.86	100.00	97.82	65.50	—	63.69	47.41	97.50
64	SHAHPURA	54.26	100.00	98.07	50.19	—	56.82	53.29	93.70
65	SUWANA	52.81	100.00	98.14	52.86	—	62.94	61.51	97.57
	BHILWARA	**58.41**	**100.00**	**95.67**	**52.08**	**0.51**	**58.58**	**48.64**	**91.98**
66	BIKANER	62.59	98.42	98.48	53.04	—	64.48	60.00	80.10
67	DUNGARGARH *	61.86	99.18	97.62	73.38	—	65.87	54.62	90.27
68	KOLAYAT	44.43	97.53	94.12	55.51	1.92	65.20	56.99	76.59
69	LUNKARANSAR	44.96	99.81	97.98	51.89	—	56.67	54.02	86.80
70	NOKHA	51.78	99.43	98.50	64.79	—	65.35	52.29	91.41
	BIKANER **	**52.42**	**98.85**	**97.54**	**56.60**	**0.35**	**63.19**	**55.97**	**84.14**
71	HINDOLI	26.47	100.00	96.24	39.42	2.32	37.56	32.55	86.26
72	KESHORAIPATAN	38.22	100.00	93.11	44.40	12.93	36.97	29.43	58.07
73	NAINWA	42.07	100.00	94.52	41.67	17.19	44.81	35.42	85.91
74	TALERA	34.98	100.00	90.99	40.08	18.07	34.60	45.82	79.43
	BUNDI	**35.07**	**100.00**	**93.41**	**41.24**	**12.94**	**37.81**	**36.82**	**68.00**
75	ARNOD	39.79	100.00	89.30	46.66	17.59	37.71	31.82	72.13
76	BARI SADRI	33.53	100.00	86.91	39.08	—	46.57	41.15	79.58
77	BEGUN	34.91	100.00	83.91	33.65	—	42.62	44.37	86.83
78	BHADESAR	36.66	100.00	86.85	42.57	—	49.21	43.04	68.60
79	BHAINSRORGARH	23.52	100.00	81.15	23.76	6.42	52.81	39.55	76.44
80	BHOPALSAGAR	52.38	100.00	94.01	50.34	—	64.52	65.40	98.43
81	CHHOTI SADRI	20.08	100.00	91.21	40.08	—	42.41	32.39	93.32
82	CHITTAURGARH	33.39	100.00	90.65	48.53	—	54.54	45.17	86.91
83	DUNGLA	36.47	100.00	94.79	45.17	—	45.90	33.99	80.62
84	GANGRAR	39.45	100.00	91.41	42.92	1.08	56.69	34.50	83.01
85	KAPASAN	40.30	100.00	93.20	41.34	—	50.33	36.67	98.59
86	NIMBAHERA	25.09	99.88	93.17	45.02	—	47.04	42.87	94.73
87	PRATAPGARH	33.18	100.00	84.47	34.14	0.83	40.11	27.99	57.96
88	RASHMI	57.13	100.00	98.29	56.04	3.45	74.66	54.92	81.47
	CHITTAURGARH	**35.21**	**99.99**	**89.60**	**41.92**	**1.96**	**49.14**	**39.93**	**81.86**
89	CHURU	37.04	98.21	99.24	43.21	—	70.79	41.65	89.99
90	RAJGARH	33.61	95.52	96.82	49.06	—	56.58	41.20	48.25
91	RATANGARH	54.03	99.94	97.66	71.34	—	71.97	33.55	96.21
92	SARDARSHAHAR	33.05	99.67	96.60	49.11	—	66.08	33.71	65.90
93	SUJANGARH	48.32	99.18	97.69	62.75		67.26	31.30	81.40
94	TARANAGAR	54.77	100.00	97.08	63.34	8.02	67.99	47.70	78.86
	CHURU ***	**44.68**	**99.40**	**97.43**	**57.85**	**0.91**	**65.77**	**39.80**	**75.68**
95	BANDIKUI	35.14	100.00	87.60	38.18	1.53	29.68	27.56	96.02
96	DAUSA	41.91	100.00	91.84	50.76	—	48.71	43.96	86.02
97	LALSOT	31.00	100.00	89.73	36.67	4.88	34.05	36.70	70.32
98	MAHWA	39.16	100.00	95.78	50.85	4.40	17.30	43.14	59.28
99	SIKRAI	42.43	100.00	95.87	48.70	5.18	42.06	44.26	70.09
	DAUSA #	**37.83**	**100.00**	**91.88**	**44.79**	**3.01**	**35.25**	**38.91**	**77.52**
100	BARI	36.22	100.00	92.99	41.80	1.90	19.90	35.05	22.36
101	BASERI	48.81	100.00	96.25	52.49	—	40.78	60.56	37.45
102	DHAULPUR	54.95	100.00	99.64	50.93	18.03	21.89	52.65	48.88
103	RAJAKHERA	28.16	100.00	96.21	46.81	5.06	11.05	38.87	72.47
	DHAULPUR	**43.40**	**100.00**	**96.72**	**48.58**	**7.43**	**23.47**	**47.89**	**46.82**
104	ASPUR	49.97	99.97	92.25	52.63	0.66	57.58	51.20	78.67
105	BICHHIWARA	48.60	100.00	97.03	62.22	—	54.76	58.76	78.26
106	DUNGARPUR	40.56	100.00	96.75	43.57	—	47.52	53.17	57.59
107	SAGWARA	64.03	100.00	98.99	56.66	—	68.22	60.25	68.11
108	SIMALWARA	41.42	100.00	93.24	46.63	—	48.10	45.52	61.29
	DUNGARPUR	**48.90**	**99.99**	**96.62**	**52.65**	**0.12**	**55.55**	**53.70**	**65.24**
109	ANUPGARH	23.07	100.00	56.53	27.35	—	54.75	55.68	23.09
110	GANGANAGAR	53.05	100.00	87.95	65.27	—	63.86	71.40	93.11
111	KARANPUR	34.03	100.00	92.46	59.98	—	53.36	56.84	97.91
112	PADAMPUR	40.47	100.00	92.63	47.18	1.34	56.19	51.18	75.74
113	RAISINGHNAGAR	39.53	100.00	82.59	34.69	—	59.22	51.38	62.02

P. Code	Panchayat Samiti/District	%age of Pop. Served by Amenity of							
		Medical	Drinking Water	Education	Post & Telegraph	Market/ Hat	Commu-nications	Approach By Pucca Road	Power Supply
1	2	3	4	5	6	7	8	9	10
114	SADULSHAHAR	51.17	99.73	85.51	56.76	—	70.23	70.57	86.71
115	SURATGARH	41.22	100.00	74.25	34.60	—	63.60	57.34	43.31
	GANGANAGAR	**39.40**	**99.96**	**77.46**	**43.41**	**0.11**	**60.86**	**59.78**	**60.73**
116	BHADRA	58.13	100.00	94.23	65.30	—	67.75	47.44	54.97
117	HANUMANGARH	61.81	100.00	76.20	52.89	—	70.17	75.79	82.33
118	NOHAR	53.42	99.73	88.34	50.06	4.27	57.25	37.22	48.94
	HANUMANGARH ##	**57.96**	**99.9**	**84.62**	**54.66**	**1.54**	**64.97**	**55.52**	**64.15**
119	AMBER	40.10	99.85	92.59	48.81	—	56.63	57.57	98.01
120	BASSI	45.36	100.00	93.16	42.11	—	61.74	61.51	85.38
121	CHAKSU	37.06	99.98	78.13	29.70	—	33.80	28.30	67.92
122	DUDU	45.57	99.73	94.97	54.51	—	47.38	50.46	40.58
123	GOVINDGARH	78.48	100.00	99.34	79.30	—	68.43	67.16	100.00
124	JAMWA RAMGARH	46.40	100.00	94.75	43.82	0.72	51.70	50.93	99.01
125	JHOTWARA	37.02	100.00	94.81	55.62	—	56.78	75.19	99.92
126	KOTPUTLI	47.34	100.00	97.87	62.23	—	46.70	53.49	93.58
127	PHAGI	46.57	99.70	93.40	50.27	—	48.89	46.47	73.50
128	SAMBHAR	46.52	99.86	97.29	49.34	—	56.07	54.29	98.71
129	SANGANER	39.08	100.00	89.88	43.54	4.81	51.91	61.05	99.94
130	SHAHPURA	57.66	99.96	99.96	56.36	—	39.76	69.72	99.54
131	VIRATNAGAR	55.76	99.75	92.62	46.85	—	38.00	58.97	99.18
	JAIPUR	**48.74**	**99.91**	**94.09**	**51.84**	**0.42**	**51.38**	**56.45**	**88.41**
132	JAISALMER	40.03	98.50	94.45	59.47	1.31	58.49	54.67	38.59
133	SAM	30.42	99.91	90.78	48.57	7.25	47.90	30.11	1.51
134	SANKRA	32.92	100.00	94.69	53.05	—	64.28	48.92	19.51
	JAISALMER	**34.07**	**99.56**	**93.35**	**53.36**	**2.73**	**57.34**	**44.37**	**18.90**
135	AHORE	61.62	100.00	98.94	67.49	—	85.53	44.36	98.30
136	BHINMAL	37.27	100.00	98.24	60.49	—	73.55	40.64	88.50
137	JALOR	63.83	100.00	99.66	63.27	—	87.47	64.94	98.77
138	JASWANTPURA	46.36	100.00	98.86	60.58	—	77.22	54.35	97.74
139	RANIWARA	35.35	100.00	99.98	56.69	—	74.22	58.53	99.74
140	SANCHORE	35.96	98.29	98.33	45.48	—	68.06	38.18	60.02
141	SAYLA	62.45	99.92	99.91	70.70	—	90.36	58.32	97.38
	JALOR	**47.69**	**99.57**	**99.04**	**59.24**	**—**	**78.39**	**49.21**	**87.57**
142	BAKANI	37.62	100.00	80.66	39.76	19.97	33.97	38.87	68.18
143	DAG	37.02	100.00	89.62	37.71	14.37	37.38	32.18	46.85
144	JHALRAPATAN	33.21	100.00	85.26	34.38	7.87	33.44	36.92	90.24
145	KHANPUR	39.25	100.00	89.75	34.86	17.06	30.23	33.22	83.13
146	MANOHARTHANA	28.21	100.00	74.31	24.65	8.38	20.80	23.14	40.79
147	PIRAWA	35.14	100.00	96.82	36.42	13.04	23.58	12.43	88.43
	JHALAWAR	**35.00**	**100.00**	**86.08**	**34.71**	**13.20**	**30.17**	**29.77**	**70.15**
148	ALSISAR	54.82	100.00	98.87	59.37	8.83	69.19	54.93	83.48
149	BUHANA	41.81	100.00	99.00	68.75	—	61.11	48.81	92.29
150	CHIRAWA	55.30	99.65	98.43	69.64	—	74.51	66.65	100.00
151	JHUNJHUNUN	46.68	99.68	98.06	52.43	7.85	71.94	70.30	97.59
152	KHETRI	64.87	100.00	98.21	65.33	—	76.23	62.31	94.15
153	NAWALGARH	73.61	100.00	100.00	81.64	13.51	82.12	69.44	100.00
154	SURAJGARH	35.21	98.87	99.67	54.23	—	60.27	49.19	95.91
155	UDAIPURWATI	62.41	100.00	99.38	77.88	—	74.18	83.25	99.11
	JHUNJHUNUN	**55.14**	**99.80**	**98.98**	**67.06**	**3.72**	**71.56**	**63.90**	**95.73**
156	BALESAR	65.93	99.52	99.43	65.29	5.56	76.73	50.89	93.05
157	BAP	26.40	99.79	90.26	49.95	0.49	57.50	20.79	33.77
158	BHOPALGARH	57.94	99.34	98.94	69.95	—	89.94	79.73	93.15
159	BILARA	75.35	100.00	99.73	75.33	—	93.18	77.71	99.59
160	LUNI	54.43	100.00	99.04	60.79	—	84.48	71.73	83.01
161	MANDOR	27.67	98.37	98.81	56.44	—	60.65	64.26	90.45
162	OSIAN	42.29	99.86	90.02	73.83	—	97.07	57.89	82.44
163	PHALODI	36.59	93.03	97.26	57.81	1.36	69.30	50.31	75.41
164	SHERGARH	56.34	95.15	100.00	72.50	35.33	84.37	62.89	77.72
	JODHPUR	**46.93**	**95.64**	**94.73**	**61.27**	**3.56**	**73.04**	**58.04**	**78.62**
165	HINDAUN	49.73	100.00	97.83	50.85	11.12	41.39	55.31	94.97
166	KARAULI	37.77	100.00	91.38	41.94	3.68	26.16	32.14	55.68
167	NADOTI	50.63	100.00	94.53	59.77	17.46	57.40	52.95	89.21
168	SAPOTRA	45.68	99.54	93.49	51.81	9.37	35.10	37.54	57.96
169	TODABHIM	44.80	100.00	96.24	50.48	6.91	25.80	49.57	69.77
	KARAULI ###	**45.49**	**99.90**	**94.78**	**50.28**	**9.17**	**35.82**	**45.05**	**72.80**
170	CHECHAT	48.55	99.89	92.39	46.61	20.61	39.88	49.46	97.92
171	ITAWA	45.23	100.00	91.19	50.02	37.48	43.33	37.61	44.90
172	LADPURA	44.19	100.00	95.43	37.45	8.70	25.09	74.97	86.66
173	SANGOD	38.03	100.00	83.71	42.48	22.16	37.01	38.99	85.45
174	SULTANPUR	42.97	100.00	92.60	48.58	30.13	39.37	36.39	81.21
	KOTA	**43.78**	**99.98**	**90.97**	**45.23**	**24.27**	**37.23**	**46.79**	**78.75**

P. Code	Panchayat Samiti/District	%age of Pop. Served by Amenity of							
		Medical	Drinking Water	Education	Post & Telegraph	Market/ Hat	Commu-nications	Approach By Pucca Road	Power Supply
1	2	3	4	5	6	7	8	9	10
175	DEGANA	47.79	100.00	99.32	49.97	—	74.88	46.16	83.96
176	DIDWANA	43.15	100.00	97.60	59.09	3.36	77.27	4.84	87.87
177	JAYAL	49.20	100.00	97.99	58.95	11.32	72.14	41.60	61.73
178	KUCHAMAN	50.62	99.83	98.26	65.16	—	73.52	28.74	99.58
179	LADNU	53.60	100.00	98.74	65.98	—	82.42	33.19	75.53
180	MAKRANA	47.23	100.00	98.30	71.56	1.99	70.89	19.99	90.66
181	MERTA	60.84	100.00	97.35	60.97	3.17	86.95	63.84	97.96
182	MUNDWA	46.95	100.00	98.76	61.68	—	75.83	47.85	80.57
183	NAGAUR	56.47	100.00	97.38	52.73	3.55	70.18	32.85	68.65
184	PARBATSAR	45.59	99.27	98.03	60.16	3.05	70.02	33.20	98.68
185	RIYAN	51.70	99.58	98.92	61.17	10.75	71.26	58.40	95.87
	NAGAUR	**49.99**	**99.89**	**98.19**	**60.52**	**3.40**	**74.81**	**35.58**	**85.44**
186	BALI	73.69	100.00	99.86	66.52	—	78.23	66.07	93.69
187	DESURI	69.91	100.00	98.10	59.39	14.70	63.88	57.32	96.47
188	JAITARAN	60.77	100.00	97.54	64.99	—	67.83	32.30	94.95
189	KHARCHI/MARWAR JUN.	56.45	100.00	95.37	67.14	7.63	78.51	54.49	91.71
190	PALI	52.13	100.00	99.15	55.72	—	78.93	62.32	97.32
191	RAIPUR	36.11	100.00	95.25	66.87	—	54.34	42.68	77.13
192	RANI STATION	72.90	100.00	99.39	78.51	6.86	81.60	44.43	99.59
193	ROHAT	34.73	100.00	99.17	38.53	—	65.36	36.26	94.98
194	SOJAT	52.75	100.00	99.51	66.37	3.76	75.74	53.56	90.21
195	SUMERPUR	71.11	100.00	98.36	82.52	—	89.47	87.74	100.00
	PALI	**60.65**	**100.00**	**98.05**	**60.05**	**2.00**	**73.89**	**53.95**	**92.96**
196	AMET	41.18	100.00	90.05	40.08	—	64.89	34.17	86.00
197	BHIM	47.94	100.00	95.03	55.52	—	57.60	60.06	80.18
198	DEOGARH	28.25	100.00	80.52	35.37	—	52.87	40.34	73.96
199	KHAMNOR	61.20	100.00	96.90	54.45	—	73.47	48.45	94.22
200	KUMBHALGARH	39.80	100.00	92.88	43.65	—	60.14	42.14	26.08
201	RAILMAGRA	60.35	100.00	97.04	55.84	—	70.88	60.30	100.00
202	RAJSAMAND	45.94	100.00	97.51	58.55	—	79.59	48.26	26.00
	RAJSAMAND #	**47.72**	**100.00**	**93.77**	**50.33**	—	**66.51**	**48.63**	**67.66**
203	BAMANWAS	50.75	100.00	97.30	51.68	10.76	38.19	50.14	77.86
204	BONLI	42.81	99.83	95.86	49.38	28.82	43.95	36.28	88.02
205	GANGAPUR	57.32	100.00	98.87	59.11	7.34	43.46	45.02	90.65
206	KHANDAR	46.80	100.00	89.45	43.45	17.09	55.00	40.69	43.50
207	SAWAI MADHOPUR	47.33	100.00	97.68	56.12	13.64	38.35	35.37	74.47
	SAWAI MADHOPUR	**48.81**	**99.96**	**96.09**	**52.37**	**15.90**	**43.38**	**40.86**	**76.28**
208	DANTA RAMGARH	64.52	100.00	98.34	71.13	0.75	79.79	57.35	94.24
209	DHOND	70.61	99.76	98.47	65.57	—	79.24	52.68	100.00
210	FATEHPUR	47.62	100.00	99.76	64.49	—	67.65	24.68	97.62
211	KHANDELA	57.41	100.00	98.76	68.66	—	61.45	53.51	99.59
212	LACHHMANGARH	47.16	99.73	99.15	57.96	—	66.81	37.38	99.30
213	NEEM KA THANA	61.28	99.34	97.70	64.40	—	53.35	47.73	93.39
214	PIPRALI	61.62	100.00	99.23	78.90	8.18	25.86	68.81	38.37
215	SRI MADHOPUR	52.56	100.00	99.93	76.68	—	71.13	58.77	99.76
	SIKAR	**58.38**	**99.82**	**98.82**	**68.36**	**1.02**	**62.68**	**48.97**	**90.67**
216	ABU ROAD	4.41	100.00	99.71	52.46	—	46.46	73.83	76.11
217	PINDWARA	54.31	99.42	99.13	80.37	—	64.47	68.95	83.82
218	REODAR	38.66	100.00	98.09	49.93	2.66	58.62	64.81	97.24
219	SHEOGANJ	62.27	100.00	98.80	67.83	6.51	68.78	98.01	65.25
220	SIROHI	51.63	100.00	98.84	78.48	—	66.36	66.05	99.68
	SIROHI	**43.40**	**99.86**	**98.85**	**61.31**	**1.66**	**61.28**	**72.48**	**86.38**
221	DEOLI	59.57	100.00	95.39	55.41	—	42.69	37.15	61.79
222	MALPURA	57.64	100.00	97.62	58.59	—	34.12	45.15	82.89
223	NIWAI	40.04	100.00	93.73	43.57	10.31	34.33	29.38	88.31
224	TODARAISINGH	48.57	100.00	91.58	0.44	—	52.54	34.54	49.23
225	TONK	43.08	100.00	91.48	42.64	—	26.38	30.92	62.37
226	UNIARA	38.55	100.00	87.49	45.03	10.70	41.75	33.35	70.80
	TONK	**48.19**	**100.00**	**93.20**	**49.90**	**3.22**	**35.52**	**35.16**	**70.29**
227	BARGAON	44.27	100.00	96.55	58.16	—	56.11	54.57	93.85
228	BHINDER	46.70	100.00	91.20	43.15	—	56.36	54.96	89.10
229	DHARIAWAD	34.79	100.00	86.99	39.40	—	49.07	37.89	65.53
230	GIRWA	61.35	100.00	95.96	64.67	0.59	62.26	61.28	81.16
231	GOGUNDA	36.94	100.00	97.17	47.45	—	54.38	40.13	76.94
232	JHADOL	45.76	100.00	90.58	32.84	—	42.14	33.00	46.34
233	KHERWARA	41.44	100.00	94.95	46.25	—	51.19	36.09	50.08
234	KOTRA	23.73	100.00	72.73	30.62	—	37.04	30.72	29.21
235	MAVLI	58.29	100.00	98.60	55.93	—	67.80	59.18	89.54
236	SALUMBAR	46.31	100.00	84.64	39.58	0.71	48.94	43.91	63.88
237	SARADA	59.24	100.00	95.70	65.45	—	65.67	51.71	75.39
	UDAIPUR	**46.15**	**100.00**	**91.63**	**48.04**	**0.13**	**54.19**	**46.13**	**69.24**
	RAJASTHAN	**46.17**	**99.68**	**93.90**	**52.19**	**3.40**	**53.43**	**48.21**	**77.09**

Note: * Dungargarh PS shifted from Churu to Bikaner district on 1st April 2001 ** Excluding data of Dungargarh PS; *** Including data of Dungargarh PS.
Came in force from April, 1991; ## Came in force from July 1994 ### Came in force from July 1997.

Source: 1. Computed from data given in Primary Census Abustract, Rajasthan, Series-21, Census of India, 1991.
2. District Census Handbooks (all districts), Rajasthan, 1991.

PANCHAYAT SAMITI-WISE PERCENTAGE OF INHABITED VILLAGES HAVING BASIC SOCIO-ECONOMIC AMENITIES: RAJASTHAN (1991)

P. Code	Panchayat Samiti District	%age of Village having Amenity of							
		Medical	Drinking Water	Education	Post & Telegraph	Market/ Hat	Commu-nications	Approach By Pucca Road	Power Supply
1	2	3	4	5	6	7	8	9	10
1	ARAIN	23.77	100.00	94.26	26.23	—	27.05	18.85	59.02
2	BHINAY	39.17	100.00	95.82	39.17	—	38.33	36.67	68.33
3	JAWAJA	19.69	98.45	76.68	21.24	—	29.53	44.56	47.67
4	KEKRI	37.23	100.00	96.81	42.55	—	16.17	39.36	84.04
5	KISHANGARH	32.73	100.00	90.00	38.18	—	43.64	40.91	83.64
6	MASOODA	27.01	100.00	79.56	23.36	—	31.39	37.96	73.72
7	PISANGAN	44.74	100.00	95.61	51.75	—	51.75	58.77	92.11
8	SRINAGAR	32.63	100.00	97.89	34.74	—	46.32	55.79	88.42
	AJMER DISTRICT	**30.86**	**99.70**	**89.24**	**33.10**	**—**	**36.95**	**41.32**	**71.78**
9	BANSURE	19.85	100.00	90.84	33.66	0.76	24.43	25.19	97.71
10	BEHROR	28.89	100.00	90.00	32.22	—	32.22	33.33	96.67
11	KATHUMAR	20.89	100.00	93.04	21.52	—	18.99	31.65	49.37
12	KISHANGARH BAS	20.00	100.00	82.96	25.19	0.74	22.96	40.00	98.52
13	KOTKASIM	20.00	100.00	84.35	20.00	—	22.61	27.83	77.39
14	LACHHMANGARH	13.69	100.00	86.96	19.57	—	19.57	33.15	46.20
15	MANDAWAR	26.06	100.00	95.77	27.46	—	33.80	35.21	94.37
16	NIMRANA	29.41	100.00	94.12	38.82	—	29.41	38.82	98.82
17	RAJGARH	16.18	100.00	76.47	22.06	—	19.85	29.41	62.50
18	RAMGARH	18.13	100.00	81.87	19.30	1.17	17.54	33.92	77.78
19	RENI	15.69	100.00	84.31	25.49	—	15.69	20.59	66.67
20	THANAGAZI	21.62	100.00	77.70	20.95	—	30.41	37.16	49.32
21	TIJARA	13.07	100.00	78.39	17.59	—	17.59	26.63	64.32
22	UMREN	20.00	100.00	77.33	24.00	0.67	26.00	44.00	86.67
	ALWAR	**19.48**	**100.00**	**84.74**	**23.12**	**0.26**	**23.07**	**32.68**	**73.74**
23	ANANDPURI	21.14	100.00	86.18	14.63	—	24.39	28.46	32.52
24	BAGIDORA	26.28	100.00	78.10	14.60	—	27.01	39.42	32.12
25	GARHI	38.04	100.00	87.73	22.70	—	37.42	40.49	74.23
26	GHATOL	16.06	100.00	77.98	16.51	1.38	22.48	30.28	41.74
27	KUSHALGARH	9.62	99.04	67.79	5.29	2.88	13.46	19.23	31.25
28	PEEPALKHOONT	22.58	100.00	55.91	9.68	3.76	14.52	21.51	13.44
29	SAJJANGARH	13.74	100.00	63.74	7.14	1.10	15.93	24.73	23.08
30	TALWARA	24.30	100.00	72.43	19.63	0.47	35.51	39.25	37.85
	BANSWARA	**20.82**	**99.86**	**72.82**	**13.63**	**1.33**	**23.55**	**30.55**	**35.57**
31	ANTA	17.69	100.00	81.63	19.73	4.76	17.01	18.37	59.86
32	ATRU	22.22	100.00	77.04	27.41	6.67	22.96	18.52	72.59
33	BARAN	15.31	100.00	93.88	21.43	2.04	18.37	22.45	86.73
34	CHHABRA	11.05	100.00	68.60	11.05	2.91	12.79	12.21	27.91
35	CHHIPABAROD	12.02	100.00	73.22	11.48	3.83	11.48	12.57	60.66
36	KISHANGANJ	11.93	99.43	56.82	11.36	5.11	18.18	14.20	65.34
37	SHAHBAD	8.80	96.86	58.49	12.58	3.14	9.43	13.84	35.85
	BARAN #	**13.74**	**99.44**	**71.12**	**15.61**	**4.11**	**15.33**	**15.42**	**56.26**
38	BALOTRA	14.81	99.47	73.54	32.80	—	62.43	33.33	41.27
39	BARMER	11.32	95.09	67.17	26.04	—	26.04	32.83	10.57
40	BAYTOO	6.85	94.35	60.08	21.77	1.21	25.00	11.69	15.32
41	CHOHTAN	18.56	100.00	79.64	34.73	—	28.14	23.35	16.17
42	DHORIMANNA	13.10	100.00	68.65	24.21	—	27.38	26.59	41.27
43	SHEO	10.78	98.20	80.84	23.35	—	37.72	38.92	20.36
44	SINDHARI	12.50	99.58	65.83	22.08	0.42	30.00	22.50	20.00
45	SIWANA	30.93	100.00	95.88	44.33	2.06	59.79	24.74	84.54
	BARMER	**13.35**	**98.03**	**71.26**	**27.02**	**0.37**	**34.34**	**26.34**	**27.02**
46	BAYANA	23.90	100.00	86.16	32.70	0.63	23.90	31.45	50.12
47	DEEG	15.00	100.00	85.83	22.50	2.50	6.67	30.00	55.83
48	KAMAN	18.72	99.47	76.47	18.18	—	9.63	19.25	31.55

P. Code	Panchayat Samiti/District	%age of Village having Amenity of							
		Medical	Drinking Water	Education	Post & Telegraph	Market Hat	Commu-nications	Approach By Pucca Road	Power Supply
1	2	3	4	5	6	7	8	9	10
49	KUMHER	32.43	98.20	95.50	27.93	—	18.02	44.14	87.39
50	NADBAI	21.05	100.00	88.60	29.82	2.62	29.82	34.21	79.82
51	NAGAR PAHARI	11.98	100.00	81.57	20.74	0.92	15.67	26.27	28.57
52	RUPBAS	23.40	100.00	95.04	25.53	2.84	34.04	40.43	48.23
53	SEWAR	20.13	98.70	84.42	16.23	—	17.53	40.91	72.73
54	WEIR	26.76	100.00	93.66	35.92	2.82	18.31	33.10	95.77
	BHARATPUR	**20.74**	**99.63**	**86.54**	**24.91**	**1.26**	**18.81**	**32.27**	**58.44**
55	ASIND	26.60	100.00	75.37	23.15	—	39.41	24.63	69.95
56	BANERA	42.68	100.00	90.24	26.83	—	30.49	29.27	90.24
57	HURDA	41.18	100.00	94.12	26.47	7.35	55.88	36.76	100.00
58	JAHAZPUR	30.94	100.00	78.45	19.34	0.55	23.20	23.20	68.51
59	KOTRI	24.66	100.00	87.61	21.92	—	34.25	20.55	80.82
60	MANDAL	27.85	100.00	85.44	22.15	—	50.00	27.22	81.01
61	MANDALGARH	19.63	100.00	59.63	14.44	—	21.48	22.59	72.59
62	RAIPUR	29.07	100.00	90.70	25.58	—	50.00	19.77	77.91
63	SAHARA	31.87	100.00	91.21	34.07	—	39.56	30.77	96.70
64	SHAHPURA	28.19	100.00	93.29	24.83	—	38.93	28.19	83.89
65	SUWANA	24.43	100.00	88.55	23.66	—	45.04	38.93	92.37
	BHILWARA	**27.73**	**100.00**	**81.34**	**22.30**	**0.38**	**36.29**	**26.39**	**79.94**
66	BIKANER	28.39	96.13	87.10	24.52	—	43.23	45.16	71.61
67	DUNGARGARH *	40.00	97.78	97.78	53.33	—	53.33	40.00	77.78
68	KOLAYAT	17.16	96.45	69.82	21.89	0.59	39.64	30.77	46.75
69	LUNKARANSAR	19.23	99.23	89.23	24.62	—	37.69	33.08	76.15
70	NOKHA	27.78	98.41	88.89	38.10	—	46.83	35.71	81.75
	BIKANER **	**22.93**	**97.41**	**82.93**	**26.72**	**0.17**	**41.72**	**36.21**	**67.59**
71	HINDOLI	11.49	100.00	82.76	15.52	0.57	18.39	20.11	73.56
72	KESHORAIPATAN	15.74	100.00	78.70	18.52	3.70	23.61	20.83	43.98
73	NAINWA	14.86	100.00	85.14	16.57	3.43	22.29	17.14	73.14
74	TALERA	16.86	100.00	79.69	17.62	5.36	22.22	29.89	63.60
	BUNDI	**15.01**	**100.00**	**81.23**	**17.19**	**3.51**	**21.79**	**22.76**	**62.59**
75	ARNOD	12.87	100.00	59.06	15.79	4.09	19.88	13.45	43.86
76	BARI SADRI	10.42	100.00	61.11	13.19	—	21.53	18.75	56.94
77	BEGUN	11.87	100.00	54.34	10.05	—	25.11	27.40	67.12
78	BHADESAR	10.56	100.00	63.35	15.53	—	29.19	24.22	57.14
79	BHAINSRORGARH	7.33	100.00	51.33	8.00	2.00	28.67	23.33	64.00
80	BHOPALSAGAR	18.07	100.00	79.52	16.87	—	39.76	40.96	92.77
81	CHHOTI SADRI	6.38	100.00	68.79	15.60	—	30.50	24.11	82.98
82	CHITTAURGARH	7.80	100.00	66.06	16.06	—	26.15	22.48	62.84
83	DUNGLA	12.75	100.00	81.37	18.63	—	28.43	20.59	62.75
84	GANGRAR	12.60	100.00	68.50	14.96	0.79	31.50	14.17	69.29
85	KAPASAN	21.50	100.00	79.44	16.82	—	31.78	22.43	97.20
86	NIMBAHERA	7.33	98.67	73.33	16.00	—	27.33	20.67	80.67
87	PRATAPGARH	13.44	100.00	57.50	12.81	0.63	25.31	16.25	40.63
88	RASHMI	25.32	100.00	89.87	24.05	1.27	48.10	34.18	63.29
	CHITTAURGARH	**11.88**	**99.91**	**65.10**	**14.55**	**0.64**	**27.90**	**21.96**	**63.54**
89	CHURU	24.75	96.04	96.04	27.72	—	60.40	38.61	80.20
90	RAJGARH	19.51	99.02	94.63	30.73	—	47.32	34.63	40.00
91	RATANGARH	34.37	97.92	90.63	48.96	—	57.29	22.92	88.54
92	SARDARSHAHAR	21.18	99.41	90.59	31.76	—	55.88	30.59	59.41
93	SUJANGARH	27.45	93.46	85.62	37.25	—	49.67	22.88	68.63
94	TARANAGAR	23.42	98.20	85.59	32.43	0.90	43.24	26.13	55.86
	CHURU ***	**25.70**	**97.52**	**91.36**	**35.96**	**0.11**	**51.84**	**30.67**	**63.28**
95	BANDIKUI	14.49	100.00	69.08	15.94	0.48	13.53	14.98	90.34
96	DAUSA	15.84	100.00	69.68	19.91	—	25.34	24.43	69.23
97	LALSOT	9.90	100.00	63.14	12.29	0.68	16.72	20.14	50.85
98	MAHWA	15.33	100.00	84.00	22.67	2.00	7.33	25.33	44.00
99	SIKRAI	18.84	100.00	83.33	23.91	0.72	24.64	30.43	53.62
	DAUSA #	**14.17**	**100.00**	**71.66**	**17.84**	**0.59**	**17.64**	**22.20**	**62.34**
100	BARI	23.02	100.00	83.33	25.40	0.79	14.29	33.33	16.67
101	BASERI	22.95	100.00	81.15	22.95	—	22.95	36.07	20.49
102	DHAULPUR	40.38	100.00	96.15	26.92	5.77	10.26	42.95	33.97
103	RAJAKHERA	15.65	100.00	89.80	29.93	1.36	7.48	33.33	65.31
	DHAULPUR	**25.95**	**100.00**	**88.20**	**26.50**	**2.18**	**13.25**	**36.66**	**35.39**
104	ASPUR	30.28	99.30	88.03	30.28	0.70	35.92	30.28	59.15
105	BICHHIWARA	24.71	100.00	86.78	28.16	0.00	35.06	40.80	66.09
106	DUNGARPUR	27.85	100.00	87.34	27.22	0.00	36.71	46.20	45.57
107	SAGWARA	32.68	100.00	92.16	25.49	0.00	41.83	36.60	63.40
108	SIMALWARA	17.35	100.00	77.17	21.92	0.00	26.03	29.22	51.60
	DUNGARPUR	**25.77**	**99.88**	**85.58**	**26.24**	**0.12**	**34.40**	**36.29**	**56.86**

P. Code	*Panchayat Samiti/District*	*%age of Village having Amenity of*							
		Medical	*Drinking Water*	*Education*	*Post & Telegraph*	*Market Hat*	*Communications*	*Approach By Pucca Road*	*Power Supply*
1	*2*	*3*	*4*	*5*	*6*	*7*	*8*	*9*	*10*
109	ANUPGARH	7.61	100.00	27.89	8.45	—	36.15	11.64	11.64
110	GANGANAGAR	26.97	100.00	60.17	39.42	—	42.74	54.36	87.55
111	KARANPUR	14.50	100.00	74.00	39.00	—	37.00	40.00	87.00
112	PADAMPUR	18.64	100.00	71.19	22.46	0.42	41.95	36.86	62.29
113	RAISINGHNAGAR	21.81	100.00	56.94	17.85	—	45.33	41.08	47.03
114	SADULSHAHAR	14.85	99.47	34.22	15.38	—	35.54	39.79	43.24
115	SURATGARH	13.68	100.00	30.44	9.41	—	33.09	36.18	20.00
	GANGANAGAR	**14.12**	**99.94**	**41.09**	**15.89**	**0.03**	**37.44**	**30.55**	**35.56**
116	BHADRA	19.47	100.00	52.63	21.05	—	35.79	28.42	28.42
117	HANUMANGARH	15.30	100.00	25.76	14.01	—	31.24	47.34	57.00
118	NOHAR	17.68	99.37	42.53	13.68	0.84	28.63	22.53	17.05
	HANUMANGARH ##	**16.80**	**99.77**	**35.93**	**14.93**	**0.31**	**30.95**	**35.46**	**38.02**
119	AMBER	21.13	99.48	75.26	21.65	—	35.57	35.05	97.42
120	BASSI	24.40	100.00	78.95	17.22	—	38.76	44.50	72.73
121	CHAKSU	17.83	99.61	53.10	9.30	—	14.73	13.57	56.59
122	DUDU	18.10	99.52	81.43	22.86	—	25.24	27.14	66.67
123	GOVINDGARH	47.37	100.00	92.63	46.32	—	40.00	41.05	100.00
124	JAMWA RAMGARH	21.65	100.00	84.42	17.75	0.43	31.17	31.60	95.67
125	JHOTWARA	16.67	100.00	76.47	28.43	—	41.18	50.98	99.02
126	KOTPUTLI	31.09	100.00	94.96	37.82	—	35.29	44.45	87.39
127	PHAGI	18.45	98.81	80.36	20.24	—	23.21	22.62	55.95
128	SAMBHAR	23.08	98.60	87.21	24.48	—	37.76	36.36	97.20
129	SANGANER	16.10	100.00	65.37	20.00	0.98	30.73	36.10	98.05
130	SHAHPURA	39.24	98.73	98.73	31.65	—	22.78	49.37	98.73
131	VIRATNAGAR	26.27	99.15	89.83	21.19	—	24.58	45.76	95.76
	JAIPUR	**22.71**	**99.58**	**78.40**	**22.01**	**0.14**	**29.94**	**34.11**	**83.20**
132	JAISALMER	16.06	95.62	78.83	31.39	1.46	38.69	35.04	22.63
133	SAM	9.96	99.60	58.17	19.92	3.19	24.70	15.94	0.40
134	SANKRA	21.54	100.00	88.46	36.15	—	51.54	34.62	10.00
	JAISALMER	**14.48**	**98.65**	**71.24**	**27.03**	**1.93**	**35.14**	**25.68**	**8.69**
135	AHORE	32.41	100.00	92.59	36.11	—	65.74	25.00	91.67
136	BHINMAL	21.52	100.00	93.67	41.77	—	65.82	31.65	81.01
137	JALOR	45.45	100.00	96.97	39.39	—	72.73	48.48	95.45
138	JASWANTPURA	27.78	100.00	94.44	34.72	—	63.89	41.67	94.44
139	RANIWARA	19.28	100.00	98.80	34.94	—	60.24	42.17	97.59
140	SANCHORE	22.78	97.78	92.22	26.11	—	54.44	28.89	50.56
141	SAYLA	38.96	98.70	98.70	42.86	—	77.92	44.16	93.51
	JALOR	**28.42**	**99.25**	**94.74**	**34.89**	**—**	**63.91**	**35.34**	**80.90**
142	BAKANI	13.48	100.00	50.35	12.06	3.19	14.54	20.57	46.45
143	DAG	15.45	100.00	74.55	13.64	3.64	20.91	15.45	33.18
144	JHALRAPATAN	14.54	100.00	63.12	13.83	2.13	18.09	25.18	76.60
145	KHANPUR	14.21	100.00	69.47	12.11	3.16	12.63	17.37	63.68
146	MANOHARTHANA	14.60	100.00	50.36	10.22	2.92	12.77	15.69	26.64
147	PIRAWA	17.00	100.00	87.50	17.50	4.00	13.00	8.50	79.00
	JHALAWAR	**14.78**	**100.00**	**64.16**	**13.05**	**3.11**	**15.40**	**17.68**	**53.31**
148	ALSISAR	23.01	100.00	96.46	28.32	0.88	51.33	31.86	70.80
149	BUHANA	24.59	100.00	96.72	42.62	—	45.90	34.43	90.98
150	CHIRAWA	30.49	98.78	95.12	41.46	—	53.66	43.90	100.00
151	JHUNJHUNUN	24.36	99.36	91.67	31.41	5.13	58.97	56.41	94.87
152	KHETRI	41.25	100.00	95.00	42.50	—	55.00	42.50	88.75
153	NAWALGARH	54.29	100.00	100.00	55.71	2.86	70.00	48.57	100.00
154	SURAJGARH	23.33	97.50	98.33	34.17	—	45.83	39.17	96.67
155	UDAIPURWATI	37.04	100.00	97.53	55.56	—	58.02	60.49	96.30
	JHUNJHUNUN	**30.10**	**99.39**	**96.00**	**39.56**	**1.33**	**54.00**	**44.42**	**91.75**
156	BALESAR	42.65	100.00	97.06	45.59	1.47	57.35	35.29	85.29
157	BAP	16.13	98.92	80.65	27.96	1.08	45.16	25.81	29.03
158	BHOPALGARH	32.14	100.00	97.62	41.67	—	79.76	63.10	90.48
159	BILARA	48.10	100.00	97.47	49.37	—	60.76	59.49	98.73
160	LUNI	26.56	100.00	94.58	30.47	—	64.84	48.44	64.06
161	MANDOR	15.24	99.05	97.14	34.29	—	49.52	46.67	79.05
162	OSIAN	25.75	98.80	92.81	42.51	—	65.27	45.51	73.05
163	PHALODI	25.58	97.67	91.86	39.53	1.16	56.98	41.86	66.28
164	SHERGARH	46.00	96.00	100.00	56.00	28.00	72.00	48.00	70.00
	JODHPUR	**28.72**	**99.07**	**93.84**	**39.42**	**1.98**	**61.05**	**45.93**	**71.86**
165	HINDAUN	31.93	100.00	97.48	30.25	4.20	28.57	42.02	92.44
166	KARAULI	19.39	100.00	76.53	22.45	1.02	16.33	20.92	41.84
167	NADOTI	27.38	100.00	83.33	34.52	4.76	39.29	38.10	76.19
168	SAPOTRA	18.66	99.04	71.29	23.92	1.91	17.70	21.53	42.11

P. Code	Panchayat Samiti/District	%age of Village having Amenity of							
		Medical	Drinking Water	Education	Post & Telegraph	Market Hat	Commu-nications	Approach By Pucca Road	Power Supply
1	2	3	4	5	6	7	8	9	10
169	TODABHIM	26.76	100.00	86.62	28.87	2.82	19.01	36.62	57.75
	KARAULI ###	**23.47**	**99.73**	**81.07**	**26.67**	**2.53**	**21.73**	**29.33**	**56.80**
170	CHECHAT	19.86	99.31	73.97	17.12	3.42	21.92	30.82	93.15
171	ITAWA	16.15	100.00	70.19	17.39	9.32	20.50	16.77	21.12
172	LADPURA	18.49	100.00	78.08	13.70	2.05	17.12	60.96	73.29
173	SANGOD	13.64	100.00	62.12	16.16	5.05	19.70	22.22	74.75
174	SULTANPUR	16.87	100.00	75.63	20.62	6.87	17.50	18.12	63.12
	KOTA	**16.77**	**99.88**	**70.16**	**17.02**	**5.43**	**19.36**	**28.85**	**64.86**
175	DEGANA	24.66	100.00	95.21	26.03	—	59.59	31.51	73.29
176	DIDWANA	22.75	100.00	95.21	34.73	0.60	62.87	32.34	77.84
177	JAYAL	23.48	100.00	92.42	28.79	3.03	45.45	17.42	43.18
178	KUCHAMAN	29.45	98.63	93.15	39.04	—	57.53	21.23	97.26
179	LADNU	30.21	100.00	90.63	39.58	—	68.75	30.21	62.50
180	MAKRANA	20.83	100.00	90.83	41.67	0.83	57.50	8.33	85.00
181	MERTA	26.04	100.00	85.42	30.21	2.08	60.42	33.33	90.63
182	MUNDWA	24.55	100.00	91.82	32.73	—	58.18	32.73	70.00
183	NAGAUR	28.57	100.00	91.73	24.81	0.75	55.64	30.83	50.38
184	PARBATSAR	27.78	99.07	95.37	34.26	1.85	51.85	21.30	97.22
185	RIYAN	25.83	99.17	91.67	32.50	4.17	46.67	35.83	89.17
	NAGAUR	**25.69**	**99.71**	**92.43**	**32.97**	**1.16**	**56.70**	**26.78**	**75.76**
186	BALI	41.57	100.00	97.75	39.33	2.25	58.43	47.19	86.52
187	DESURI	39.47	100.00	86.84	30.26	6.58	43.42	34.21	88.16
188	JAITARAN	33.70	100.00	90.22	36.96	—	48.91	17.39	86.96
189	KHARCHI/MARWAR JUN.	26.28	100.00	89.05	36.50	2.19	54.01	32.85	78.83
190	PALI	26.25	100.00	95.00	32.50	—	67.50	42.50	90.00
191	RAIPUR	27.18	100.00	82.52	34.95	—	32.04	24.27	60.19
192	RANI STATION	43.84	100.00	93.15	52.05	2.74	65.75	26.03	94.52
193	ROHAT	18.99	100.00	97.47	22.78	—	55.70	26.58	88.61
194	SOJAT	31.25	100.00	96.43	39.29	0.89	58.04	33.04	82.14
195	SUMERPUR	46.03	100.00	95.24	60.32	—	79.37	74.60	100.00
	PALI	**32.52**	**100.00**	**92.04**	**37.83**	**1.22**	**55.09**	**34.51**	**84.07**
196	AMET	19.12	100.00	68.38	17.65	—	53.68	25.00	70.59
197	BHIM	22.02	100.00	82.57	27.52	—	45.87	45.87	58.72
198	DEOGARH	11.45	100.00	59.54	17.56	—	36.64	24.43	55.73
199	KHAMNOR	33.33	100.00	78.03	26.52	—	50.00	30.30	89.39
200	KUMBHALGARH	21.12	100.00	84.47	24.22	—	43.48	29.81	62.11
201	RAILMAGRA	28.89	100.00	92.22	26.67	—	53.33	41.11	100.00
202	RAJSAMAND	20.00	100.00	90.00	32.31	—	50.77	30.00	78.46
	RAJSAMAND #	**21.93**	**100.00**	**78.74**	**24.41**	**—**	**47.36**	**31.50**	**72.33**
203	BAMANWAS	19.70	100.00	80.30	25.76	2.27	20.45	27.27	56.09
204	BONLI	17.83	99.36	84.07	21.02	8.28	21.66	15.92	77.07
205	GANGAPUR	31.30	100.00	91.30	31.30	1.74	26.96	33.91	81.74
206	KHANDAR	17.95	100.00	66.67	18.59	3.85	28.85	21.79	33.97
207	SAWAI MADHOPUR	20.13	100.00	88.96	32.47	2.60	17.53	15.58	55.19
	SAWAI MADHOPUR	**20.87**	**99.86**	**81.79**	**25.49**	**3.92**	**22.97**	**22.13**	**60.36**
208	DANTA RAMGARH	37.04	100.00	88.89	43.70	0.74	60.74	35.56	92.59
209	DHOND	50.93	99.07	97.22	43.52	—	69.44	38.89	100.00
210	FATEHPUR	29.79	100.00	99.29	46.10	—	58.16	22.70	95.74
211	KHANDELA	31.90	100.00	88.79	43.97	—	43.97	38.79	94.83
212	LACHHMANGARH	26.47	99.26	97.79	38.24	—	58.82	27.21	98.53
213	NEEM KA THANA	41.26	99.30	89.51	40.56	—	36.36	34.27	86.01
214	PIPRALI	31.87	100.00	90.11	51.65	4.40	49.45	45.05	82.42
215	SRI MADHOPUR	39.34	100.00	98.36	52.46	—	47.54	39.34	98.36
	SIKAR	**35.66**	**99.68**	**93.56**	**44.15**	**0.54**	**53.28**	**34.16**	**93.45**
216	ABU ROAD	23.08	100.00	96.15	28.21	—	32.05	56.41	61.54
217	PINDWARA	29.59	98.98	88.78	26.53	—	43.88	47.96	65.31
218	REODAR	17.21	100.00	90.16	22.95	0.82	37.70	39.34	90.98
219	SHEOGANJ	30.30	100.00	92.42	34.85	3.03	45.45	42.42	89.39
220	SIROHI	25.61	100.00	86.59	48.78	—	46.34	41.46	97.56
	SIROHI	**24.44**	**99.78**	**90.58**	**31.17**	**0.67**	**40.81**	**45.07**	**81.17**
221	DEOLI	28.66	100.00	76.43	21.02	—	20.38	18.47	32.48
222	MALPURA	30.89	100.00	85.37	24.39	—	27.64	20.33	68.29
223	NIWAI	12.57	100.00	74.87	15.18	2.09	15.18	12.57	69.63
224	TODARAISINGH	23.85	100.00	73.39	22.02	—	18.35	15.60	33.03
225	TONK	18.15	100.00	69.76	16.94	—	10.89	21.37	39.92
226	UNIARA	13.09	100.00	59.69	14.14	1.57	18.32	17.80	40.84
	TONK	**19.92**	**100.00**	**72.13**	**18.16**	**0.69**	**17.37**	**17.86**	**47.20**

P. Code	Panchayat Samiti/District	%age of Village having Amenity of							
		Medical	Drinking Water	Education	Post & Telegraph	Market/ Hat	Commu-nications	Approach By Pucca Road	Power Supply
1	2	3	4	5	6	7	8	9	10
227	BARGAON	20.98	100.00	77.62	23.78	—	38.46	32.17	83.92
228	BHINDER	14.77	100.00	64.02	14.77	—	31.82	29.92	32.58
229	DHARIAWAD	10.98	100.00	58.94	13.41	—	30.08	28.05	43.09
230	GIRWA	27.67	100.00	78.62	29.56	0.63	33.96	35.85	62.26
231	GOGUNDA	18.49	100.00	89.73	25.34	—	40.41	30.14	68.49
232	JHADOL	23.83	100.00	69.53	11.72	—	27.73	16.41	31.25
233	KHERWARA	21.99	100.00	81.33	25.73	—	38.59	24.90	36.51
234	KOTRA	7.62	100.00	44.04	12.25	—	22.19	17.55	18.87
235	MAVLI	33.11	100.00	91.89	28.38	—	47.97	39.19	77.03
236	SALUMBAR	23.38	100.00	66.67	15.58	0.43	30.74	23.81	47.62
237	SARADA	31.12	100.00	83.12	32.52	—	49.35	37.01	59.09
	UDAIPUR	**19.87**	**100.00**	**70.13**	**19.39**	**0.09**	**34.19**	**27.47**	**47.55**
	RAJASTHAN	**20.68**	**99.63**	**74.97**	**23.37**	**1.02**	**33.20**	**29.66**	**59.78**

Note: * Dungargarh PS shifted from Churu to Bikaner district on 1st April 2001
** Excluding data of Dungargarh PS;
*** Including data of Dungargarh PS.
# Came in force from April, 1991;
Came in force from July 1994
Came in force from July 1997.

Source: 1. Computed from data given in Primary Census Abustract, Rajasthan, Series -21, Census of India, 1991.
2. District Census Handbooks (all districts), Rajasthan, 1991.

PANCHAYAT SAMITI-WISE NO. OF MEDICAL INSTITUTIONS: RAJASTHAN, 1991

P. Code	Panchayat Samiti/District	No. of Medical Institutions								Community Health Workers	Pop. Served Per Medical Institution $	Area Served Per Medical Institution (sq. km) $
		Dispensary	Hospital	MCWC	PHC	FPC	SHC	Others	Total No. of Medical Institutions $			
1	2	3	4	5	6	7	8	9	10	11	12	13
1	ARAIN	5	7	1	8	2	13	4	34	16	3226	35.35
2	BHINAY	20	6	3	9	1	21	10	59	29	2123	20.61
3	JAWAJA	5	7	5	9	1	15	1	41	17	2928	16.15
4	KEKRI	23	9	2	5	3	16	4	55	18	2091	18.06
5	KISHANGARH	19	10	4	14	1	15	14	62	8	1970	17.85
6	MASOODA	14	4	4	3	1	14	5	39	22	3266	22.44
7	PISANGAN	27	12	6	8	2	25	9	78	17	2227	15.43
8	SRINAGAR	9	4	5	6	2	11	7	35	12	3782	25.65
	AJMER DISTRICT	**122**	**59**	**30**	**62**	**13**	**130**	**54**	**403**	**139**	**2545**	**20.24**
9	BANSURE	21	1	6	4	1	4	17	36	8	4544	18.46
10	BEHROR	13	11	4	5	1	6	30	39	5	2950	8.63
11	KATHUMAR	15	6	8	8	3	7	9	44	6	3854	12.84
12	KISHANGARH BAS	8	0	1	2	0	7	37	18	14	7560	28.08
13	KOTKASIM	13	5	0	2	1	6	40	26	21	3668	13.25
14	LACHHMANGARH	12	6	2	8	0	5	27	33	10	5343	18.75
15	MANDAWAR	18	6	1	2	0	12	14	39	4	4154	14.80
16	NIMRANA	12	7	0	1	1	8	18	28	2	4298	13.51
17	RAJGARH	16	5	1	2	1	14	7	38	9	2962	26.56
18	RAMGARH	11	2	3	8	2	11	44	35	18	4619	17.63
19	RENI	10	3	1	4	2	6	15	24	2	4406	16.33
20	THANAGAZI	18	4	3	6	5	9	18	40	8	3603	26.51
21	TIJARA	16	0	1	5	0	6	23	28	4	5400	22.98
22	UMREN	12	8	1	3	2	9	22	33	5	4931	25.71
	ALWAR	**195**	**64**	**32**	**60**	**19**	**110**	**321**	**461**	**116**	**4287**	**18.57**
23	ANANDPURI	5	1	1	7	0	20	1	34	4	2497	10.05
24	BAGIDORA	10	20	6	11	2	15	8	62	8	2214	8.32
25	GARHI	25	6	26	22	1	25	1	104	7	1812	6.77
26	GHATOL	25	5	4	12	1	20	4	66	3	2667	11.87
27	KUSHALGARH	14	1	0	9	0	8	0	32	6	3184	20.03
28	PEEPALKHOONT	8	4	0	10	2	11	0	33	28	3352	27.66
29	SAJJANGARH	7	2	2	7	1	10	4	28	12	3685	14.38
30	TALWARA	16	6	10	17	4	23	3	72	5	2280	10.42
	BANSWARA	**110**	**45**	**49**	**95**	**11**	**132**	**21**	**431**	**73**	**2474**	**11.72**
31	ANTA	13	6	5	7	1	9	17	40	10	3086	23.31
32	ATRU	14	13	12	6	2	14	15	59	15	1821	14.57
33	BARAN	4	9	2	4	1	7	4	26	3	3110	23.56
34	CHHABRA	13	4	1	3	1	8	7	29	8	3536	27.02
35	CHHIPABAROD	7	5	2	7	1	8	8	29	6	2814	28.43
36	KISHANGANJ	11	6	3	11	2	8	13	39	6	2778	37.19
37	SHAHBAD	8	5	3	2	1	3	22	21	2	3954	69.91
	BARAN #	**70**	**48**	**28**	**40**	**9**	**57**	**86**	**243**	**50**	**2828**	**28.52**
38	BALOTRA	11	7	1	7	1	14	3	40	3	4803	97.13
39	BARMER	9	2	3	7	0	14	0	35	4	4890	108.95
40	BAYTOO	7	0	0	6	0	12	0	25	4	6071	129.12
41	CHOHTAN	11	4	0	5	1	10	0	30	11	5704	108.88
42	DHORIMANNA	9	4	3	10	0	16	2	42	6	4310	63.53
43	SHEO	10	1	1	3	0	5	0	20	9	6078	330.82
44	SINDHARI	11	3	1	7	0	17	5	39	0	4303	79.89
45	SIWANA	11	9	2	12	2	11	4	45	3	2989	44.05
	BARMER	**79**	**30**	**11**	**57**	**4**	**99**	**14**	**276**	**40**	**4678**	**103.53**

P. Code	Panchayat Samiti/District	No. of Medical Institutions								Community Health Workers	Pop. Served Per Medical Institution $	Area Served Per Medical Institution (sq. km) $
		Dispensary	Hospital	MCWC	PHC	FPC	SHC	Others	Total No. of Medical Institutions $			
1	2	3	4	5	6	7	8	9	10	11	12	13
46	BAYANA	11	5	1	0	1	15	17	32	8	4744	24.99
47	DEEG	10	2	3	3	0	5	8	23	14	5462	21.32
48	KAMAN	6	6	0	1	0	4	10	17	25	9076	32.74
49	KUMHER	16	3	5	5	1	6	21	35	13	3687	12.58
50	NADBAI	14	4	1	1	0	4	9	24	3	5320	17.99
51	NAGAR PAHARI	13	5	11	8	4	8	29	45	16	4037	13.82
52	RUPBAS	20	12	12	8	2	9	47	61	9	2731	8.84
53	SEWAR	7	8	0	5	0	6	24	26	5	5137	17.62
54	WEIR	29	17	4	3	0	5	6	58	9	2768	9.93
	BHARATPUR	**126**	**62**	**37**	**34**	**8**	**62**	**171**	**321**	**102**	**4146**	**15.31**
55	ASIND	18	3	1	7	4	13	5	42	7	3715	26.43
56	BANERA	15	1	4	6	1	23	1	49	11	1797	13.81
57	HURDA	22	5	1	9	0	20	1	57	31	1280	10.83
58	JAHAZPUR	25	2	2	13	2	22	4	64	15	2076	16.15
59	KOTRI	15	11	4	18	1	11	0	59	6	2065	16.10
60	MANDAL	20	8	6	15	1	23	8	72	10	2041	16.04
61	MANDALGARH	34	12	8	15	2	31	2	100	11	1564	13.92
62	RAIPUR	7	8	4	10	3	9	2	38	0	1878	13.56
63	SAHARA	12	9	1	6	2	16	0	44	1	1935	14.39
64	SHAHPURA	24	1	2	6	1	23	2	56	2	2154	20.13
65	SUWANA	13	4	2	9	3	14	3	42	2	3089	19.82
	BHILWARA	**205**	**64**	**35**	**114**	**20**	**205**	**28**	**623**	**96**	**2058**	**16.12**
66	BIKANER	24	7	0	4	2	16	9	51	3	4550	175.39
67	DUNGARGARH *	14	2	1	2	1	9	0	28	2	4771	107.24
68	KOLAYAT	13	8	1	10	2	7	9	39	2	3401	187.66
69	LUNKARANSAR	19	9	0	1	2	8	33	37	15	4227	167.95
70	NOKHA	18	10	1	4	2	10	4	43	7	4858	87.62
	BIKANER **	**88**	**36**	**3**	**21**	**9**	**50**	**55**	**198**	**29**	**3687**	**147.72**
71	HINDOLI	9	11	3	9	2	12	13	44	4	3447	30.43
72	KESHORAIPATAN	15	13	3	4	1	8	20	43	13	3469	29.93
73	NAINWA	18	6	3	3	2	13	9	43	9	2829	26.51
74	TALERA	21	12	2	13	1	9	31	57	16	3755	33.03
	BUNDI	**63**	**42**	**11**	**29**	**6**	**42**	**73**	**187**	**42**	**3404**	**30.21**
75	ARNOD	11	10	5	9	1	8	4	43	3	2126	16.31
76	BARI SADRI	8	9	1	0	1	8	3	26	10	2958	18.25
77	BEGUN	12	7	6	4	2	14	4	43	11	1996	22.27
78	BHADESAR	8	5	0	6	0	7	1	26	1	3444	20.79
79	BHAINSRORGARH	1	4	0	3	1	8	1	16	1	3996	85.61
80	BHOPALSAGAR	10	9	0	7	2	11	2	37	2	1732	10.76
81	CHHOTI SADRI	4	3	6	2	0	3	1	18	5	4717	38.44
82	CHITTAURGARH	8	4	0	4	1	7	6	23	3	5901	35.39
83	DUNGLA	7	5	0	1	1	8	1	21	3	3669	23.50
84	GANGRAR	9	4	1	1	0	11	1	26	3	2886	21.37
85	KAPASAN	4	2	2	6	1	15	1	29	9	2513	16.64
86	NIMBAHERA	3	5	0	5	0	3	3	16	2	6893	50.79
87	PRATAPGARH	13	3	8	17	1	17	10	58	2	2745	24.62
88	RASHMI	10	2	2	10	2	13	0	37	4	1778	12.15
	CHITTAURGARH	**108**	**72**	**31**	**75**	**13**	**133**	**38**	**419**	**59**	**2989**	**24.27**
89	CHURU	19	7	1	1	0	21	3	49	2	2516	31.83
90	RAJGARH	20	7	2	7	1	16	15	52	10	4257	42.26
91	RATANGARH	14	3	0	5	1	14	4	36	8	3485	45.62
92	SARDARSHAHAR	18	2	0	3	1	2	3	25	17	6998	152.58
93	SUJANGARH	23	7	1	8	1	17	8	56	3	3471	46.36
94	TARANAGAR	15	5	1	5	1	7	6	33	20	3761	54.03
	CHURU ***	**109**	**31**	**5**	**29**	**5**	**77**	**39**	**251**	**60**	**4371**	**54.15**
95	BANDIKUI	19	0	2	3	1	7	6	31	8	6015	19.38
96	DAUSA	21	4	3	6	0	6	13	40	10	5199	22.70
97	LALSOT	15	1	2	1	1	11	4	30	12	6248	28.47
98	MAHWA	21	10	8	9	0	11	11	59	7	2486	8.03
99	SIKRAI	19	3	4	5	2	7	21	38	10	4227	13.23
	DAUSA #	**95**	**18**	**19**	**24**	**4**	**42**	**55**	**198**	**47**	**4491**	**16.86**
100	BARI	10	9	1	1	0	13	3	34	5	3452	23.35
101	BASERI	9	5	3	5	0	8	14	30	11	5040	33.38
102	DHAULPUR	18	10	8	3	1	9	47	48	34	4189	12.03
103	RAJAKHERA	7	2	0	8	1	6	9	23	10	6566	24.87
	DHAULPUR	**44**	**26**	**12**	**17**	**2**	**36**	**73**	**135**	**60**	**4597**	**21.81**

P. Code	Panchayat Samiti/District	No. of Medical Institutions: Dispensary	Hospital	MCWC	PHC	FPC	SHC	Others	Total No. of Medical Institutions $	Community Health Workers	Pop. Served Per Medical Institution $	Area Served Per Medical Institution (sq. km) $
1	2	3	4	5	6	7	8	9	10	11	12	13
104	ASPUR	22	8	27	14	1	17	0	88	4	1665	7.86
105	BICHHIWARA	17	12	11	15	2	13	1	68	8	2659	10.97
106	DUNGARPUR	12	8	8	9	0	25	1	62	6	2149	9.28
107	SAGWARA	28	12	3	8	1	23	4	74	4	2170	8.27
108	SIMALWARA	22	4	3	6	1	16	7	51	5	3718	17.91
	DUNGARPUR	**101**	**44**	**52**	**52**	**5**	**94**	**13**	**343**	**27**	**2364**	**10.32**
109	ANUPGARH	12	2	0	8	1	6	110	28	15	10503	126.56
110	GANGANAGAR	10	4	2	11	2	9	116	36	21	4511	23.75
111	KARANPUR	3	2	0	2	0	5	30	12	6	7682	67.54
112	PADAMPUR	19	2	0	8	3	3	47	32	11	3308	26.33
113	RAISINGHNAGAR	12	4	28	3	1	13	59	60	52	2147	21.92
114	SADULSHAHAR	15	7	2	7	2	11	112	42	25	4961	35.35
115	SURATGARH	33	6	0	9	0	11	129	59	12	4650	64.26
	GANGANAGAR	**104**	**27**	**32**	**48**	**9**	**58**	**603**	**269**	**142**	**4707**	**47.00**
116	BHADRA	25	7	2	1	1	5	38	40	13	4519	42.83
117	HANUMANGARH	25	5	1	8	2	15	170	54	46	6184	37.69
118	NOHAR	35	15	0	2	0	3	100	55	5	5270	78.27
	HANUMANGARH ##	**85**	**27**	**3**	**11**	**3**	**23**	**308**	**149**	**64**	**5400**	**54.05**
119	AMBER	12	1	2	8	3	10	14	33	19	6223	25.44
120	BASSI	13	5	4	2	0	15	23	39	38	4096	16.18
121	CHAKSU	15	0	5	2	1	22	15	44	21	2857	17.43
122	DUDU	24	4	5	4	1	13	34	50	16	4213	37.10
123	GOVINDGARH	34	5	5	3	3	14	22	61	29	3450	10.92
124	JAMWA RAMGARH	30	2	1	11	1	7	16	51	19	3742	19.83
125	JHOTWARA	10	1	1	3	1	7	8	22	5	4685	17.50
126	KOTPUTLI	27	6	0	6	3	11	22	50	6	3552	13.27
127	PHAGI	15	2	3	3	1	12	5	35	15	3727	31.81
128	SAMBHAR	28	1	3	5	1	15	6	52	12	3120	16.01
129	SANGANER	17	3	8	3	2	10	26	41	8	3753	14.24
130	SHAHPURA	25	7	1	4	2	8	1	45	3	2848	9.07
131	VIRATNAGAR	19	4	2	6	1	5	15	36	25	4313	18.03
	JAIPUR	**269**	**41**	**40**	**60**	**20**	**149**	**207**	**559**	**216**	**3781**	**18.61**
132	JAISALMER	8	2	0	9	2	11	0	30	6	2677	428.32
133	SAM	9	2	2	9	0	14	2	36	0	2637	586.42
134	SANKRA	15	9	0	9	0	12	0	45	8	2571	121.92
	JAISALMER	**32**	**13**	**2**	**27**	**2**	**37**	**2**	**111**	**14**	**2621**	**355.38**
135	AHORE	12	9	4	7	3	22	9	54	15	2781	29.56
136	BHINMAL	4	2	1	5	0	11	0	23	6	6356	58.16
137	JALOR	11	7	1	11	1	17	7	47	1	2297	22.44
138	JASWANTPURA	9	10	0	4	1	14	4	37	4	2874	28.89
139	RANIWARA	6	3	1	3	0	3	3	16	10	7695	61.50
140	SANCHORE	7	5	0	10	1	25	3	47	9	5539	64.01
141	SAYLA	12	5	2	8	0	22	1	49	4	3373	29.78
	JALOR	**61**	**41**	**9**	**48**	**6**	**114**	**27**	**273**	**49**	**3880**	**38.50**
142	BAKANI	7	6	2	5	4	11	8	31	35	4188	28.56
143	DAG	17	16	4	7	1	20	9	64	10	2167	17.66
144	JHALRAPATAN	17	11	6	8	1	15	14	57	14	2860	23.32
145	KHANPUR	10	7	0	3	1	9	7	29	11	4087	32.42
146	MANOHARTHANA	8	7	4	4	0	12	30	35	28	3601	26.36
147	PIRAWA	13	15	0	8	2	14	7	50	4	2599	20.02
	JHALAWAR	**72**	**62**	**16**	**35**	**9**	**81**	**75**	**266**	**102**	**3030**	**23.34**
148	ALSISAR	14	9	4	5	4	6	5	38	2	2966	19.66
149	BUHANA	18	4	0	7	2	5	12	34	3	5084	19.22
150	CHIRAWA	20	3	2	5	1	4	6	34	9	3665	14.38
151	JHUNJHUNUN	27	10	0	4	3	9	10	50	10	3146	16.41
152	KHETRI	17	13	1	3	2	14	23	48	9	3746	16.59
153	NAWALGARH	19	6	7	6	3	10	15	48	25	3777	13.86
154	SURAJGARH	9	3	8	6	1	2	7	28	5	5044	27.91
155	UDAIPURWATI	19	9	3	7	2	3	19	41	14	4574	20.27
	JHUNJHUNUN	**143**	**57**	**25**	**43**	**18**	**53**	**97**	**321**	**77**	**3917**	**18.02**
156	BALESAR	9	10	3	9	2	10	1	41	10	3110	45.22
157	BAP	2	3	0	3	0	5	0	13	5	7973	340.86
158	BHOPALGARH	9	5	1	7	7	14	0	36	5	4348	48.43
159	BILARA	13	7	0	7	2	24	2	51	9	2777	29.40

P. Code	Panchayat Samiti/District	No. of Medical Institutions: Dispensary	Hospital	MCWC	PHC	FPC	SHC	Others	Total No. of Medical Institutions $	Community Health Workers	Pop. Served Per Medical Institution $	Area Served Per Medical Institution (sq. km) $
1	2	3	4	5	6	7	8	9	10	11	12	13
160	LUNI	7	7	6	10	5	15	3	45	7	3705	44.06
161	MANDOR	3	0	1	6	0	8	3	18	1	6218	70.51
162	OSIAN	21	9	3	12	4	13	8	58	7	5283	72.15
163	PHALODI	13	7	8	8	5	11	6	47	3	3435	68.89
164	SHERGARH	20	4	0	7	1	9	6	40	0	2827	49.38
	JODHPUR	**97**	**52**	**22**	**69**	**26**	**109**	**29**	**349**	**47**	**3980**	**63.54**
165	HINDAUN	11	5	8	4	1	6	16	34	24	5774	18.57
166	KARAULI	13	7	3	3	0	18	10	44	14	3783	27.72
167	NADOTI	14	4	6	4	1	8	5	36	4	2824	17.94
168	SAPOTRA	15	6	3	8	3	11	12	43	25	4241	45.63
169	TODABHIM	15	5	2	4	2	16	16	42	10	3676	12.44
	KARAULI ###	**68**	**27**	**22**	**23**	**7**	**59**	**59**	**199**	**77**	**4026**	**25.03**
170	CHECHAT	8	9	4	8	0	10	21	39	13	3093	19.77
171	ITAWA	16	13	3	6	1	9	11	47	13	2705	18.87
172	LADPURA	8	4	2	0	1	17	10	31	5	3536	42.18
173	SANGOD	14	8	0	2	0	10	20	34	4	3605	30.77
174	SULTANPUR	10	7	2	7	3	10	28	36	15	3440	25.33
	KOTA	**56**	**41**	**11**	**23**	**5**	**56**	**90**	**187**	**50**	**3229**	**26.33**
175	DEGANA	8	5	9	8	1	26	2	56	2	2756	26.03
176	DIDWANA	15	13	4	6	4	19	7	57	5	3933	28.21
177	JAYAL	14	8	1	5	5	25	2	53	4	3334	39.40
178	KUCHAMAN	16	18	0	5	1	21	11	60	8	3418	23.94
179	LADNU	10	6	0	9	0	15	6	40	3	3079	34.28
180	MAKRANA	11	5	0	9	1	15	2	40	3	3907	27.66
181	MERTA	12	6	1	10	1	14	0	43	3	3315	32.49
182	MUNDWA	10	2	2	1	0	19	4	34	4	4492	64.24
183	NAGAUR	13	5	0	5	2	18	6	41	19	4424	58.06
184	PARBATSAR	14	8	1	9	1	11	5	43	6	3322	24.90
185	RIYAN	14	5	3	4	6	11	6	37	15	3863	33.50
	NAGAUR	**137**	**81**	**21**	**71**	**22**	**194**	**51**	**504**	**72**	**3576**	**34.40**
186	BALI	24	17	0	3	1	15	8	59	0	2529	23.22
187	DESURI	17	15	2	2	4	18	5	54	2	1581	15.35
188	JAITARAN	10	9	3	7	3	14	8	43	3	3136	30.00
189	KHARCHI/MARWAR JUN.	12	15	2	12	2	18	9	59	3	2625	23.57
190	PALI	6	5	0	4	1	14	0	29	4	2915	44.71
191	RAIPUR	13	8	10	6	1	16	0	53	15	2493	18.61
192	RANI STATION	15	5	6	4	2	22	8	52	12	1810	14.67
193	ROHAT	4	3	3	1	2	9	1	20	1	4065	70.22
194	SOJAT	7	11	4	5	3	16	1	43	1	3055	37.84
195	SUMERPUR	10	9	4	7	2	13	6	43	6	2682	21.21
	PALI	**118**	**97**	**34**	**51**	**21**	**155**	**46**	**455**	**47**	**2556**	**26.08**
196	AMET	7	0	0	4	2	20	1	31	8	2308	16.30
197	BHIM	11	6	7	6	2	10	6	40	4	2602	16.94
198	DEOGARH	3	2	0	1	0	7	0	13	3	4908	45.32
199	KHAMNOR	12	4	9	7	1	27	0	59	19	1900	10.08
200	KUMBHALGARH	13	1	14	7	2	11	6	46	4	2467	16.87
201	RAILMAGRA	15	4	2	8	1	6	2	35	1	2866	15.55
202	RAJSAMAND	19	2	5	2	1	16	0	44	3	2467	12.94
	RAJSAMAND #	**80**	**19**	**37**	**35**	**9**	**97**	**15**	**268**	**42**	**2514**	**15.88**
203	BAMANWAS	12	6	2	6	1	7	13	33	11	3644	22.08
204	BONLI	15	10	2	6	5	7	8	40	2	4113	25.24
205	GANGAPUR	23	9	10	2	0	10	14	54	13	2716	11.94
206	KHANDAR	19	4	8	2	2	9	7	42	12	2842	32.20
207	SAWAI MADHOPUR	25	12	1	5	4	16	11	59	2	2937	20.89
	SAWAI MADHOPUR	**94**	**41**	**23**	**21**	**12**	**49**	**53**	**228**	**40**	**3176**	**21.79**
208	DANTA RAMGARH	26	13	5	18	4	19	22	81	10	2549	13.77
209	DHOND	23	2	0	16	3	24	12	65	5	2635	14.04
210	FATEHPUR	13	9	0	6	1	12	12	40	7	3934	30.92
211	KHANDELA	8	7	0	3	2	14	14	32	18	5518	24.49
212	LACHHMANGARH	16	4	0	4	0	21	7	45	8	3533	22.82
213	NEEM KA THANA	19	12	3	10	3	21	31	65	26	3890	18.26
214	PIPRALI	13	3	2	5	1	19	3	42	6	3908	18.99
215	SRI MADHOPUR	15	7	3	4	2	8	9	37	7	4533	15.31
	SIKAR	**133**	**57**	**13**	**66**	**16**	**138**	**110**	**407**	**87**	**3576**	**18.74**

P. Code	Panchayat Samiti/District	No. of Medical Institutions								Community Health Workers	Pop. Served Per Medical Institution $	Area Served Per Medical Institution (sq. km) $
		Dispensary	Hospital	MCWC	PHC	FPC	SHC	Others	Total No. of Medical Institutions $			
1	2	3	4	5	6	7	8	9	10	11	12	13
216	ABU ROAD	7	6	2	2	0	6	4	23	3	3505	37.31
217	PINDWARA	5	8	10	4	1	19	3	46	1	2783	24.75
218	REODAR	12	4	3	17	4	2	5	38	2	3477	28.60
219	SHEOGANJ	2	6	0	4	0	14	6	26	2	3072	34.32
220	SIROHI	11	3	2	2	0	12	4	30	11	3527	36.35
	SIROHI	**37**	**27**	**17**	**29**	**5**	**53**	**22**	**163**	**19**	**3230**	**31.08**
221	DEOLI	19	10	1	9	1	13	4	52	47	2607	23.76
222	MALPURA	18	2	6	5	1	11	3	42	28	3533	34.26
223	NIWAI	17	0	1	4	0	13	9	35	12	3928	29.43
224	TODARAISINGH	10	0	0	2	2	9	0	21	25	4323	46.93
225	TONK	16	4	1	13	4	18	9	52	17	3249	27.22
226	UNIARA	8	2	0	3	1	15	10	28	22	3694	35.23
	TONK	**88**	**18**	**9**	**36**	**9**	**79**	**35**	**230**	**151**	**3411**	**30.83**
227	BARGAON	15	2	5	4	1	9	8	35	4	3528	18.51
228	BHINDER	20	11	9	11	5	13	0	64	3	2647	15.39
229	DHARIAWAD	14	0	12	4	0	9	3	39	3	4001	30.19
230	GIRWA	18	5	7	7	2	18	7	55	15	3221	24.53
231	GOGUNDA	11	8	13	7	1	10	4	49	3	2484	17.79
232	JHADOL	23	6	4	21	1	25	7	79	14	1861	18.08
233	KHERWARA	15	10	11	19	7	24	12	79	11	2520	13.63
234	KOTRA	10	4	0	5	1	13	1	32	1	4077	37.23
235	MAVLI	19	6	9	8	3	22	2	64	10	2570	12.48
236	SALUMBAR	17	3	10	10	1	16	10	56	23	2886	16.46
237	SARADA	26	9	11	15	1	10	4	71	16	2409	15.19
	UDAIPUR	**188**	**64**	**91**	**111**	**23**	**169**	**58**	**623**	**103**	**2763**	**18.50**
	RAJASTHAN	**3377**	**1433**	**782**	**1516**	**350**	**2942**	**2928**	**10050**	**2339**	**3377**	**33.39**

Note: $ Include dispensary, hospital, MCWC, PHC and SHC, * Dungargarh PS shifted from Churu to Bikaner district on 1st April 2001,
** Excluding data of Dungargarh PS; *** Including data of Dungargarh PS.
# Came in force from April, 1991; ## Came in force from July 1994
Came in force from July 1997.

Source: 1. Computed from data given in Primary Census Abustract, Rajasthan, Series -21, Census of India, 1991.
2. District Census Handbooks (all districts), Rajasthan, 1991.
3. General Annex-I, Col. 3 & 5.

PANCHAYAT SAMITI-WISE NO. OF EDUCATIONAL INSTITUTIONS AND POP./AREA SERVED PER INSTITUTION (1991)

Panchayat Samities		*Educational Institutes (Number)*						*Pop. Served Per Institution (No.)*				*Area Served Per Institution (sq. km)*			
P. Code	*Name*	*Primary Schools*	*Upper Primary*	*Sec. Schools*	*Senior Sec. Schools*	*Adult Lit. Cent.*	*Colle-ges*	*Pr. School*	*UPS*	*SS*	*SSS*	*Pr. Schools*	*UPS*	*SS*	*SSS*
1	*2*	*3*	*4*	*5*	*6*	*7*	*8*	*9*	*10*	*11*	*12*	*13*	*14*	*15*	*16*
1	ARAIN	119	25	8	2	160	—	922	4388	14	55	10.1	48.1	150.2	600.9
2	BHINAY	121	42	12	2	125	—	1035	2983	10	63	10.1	29.0	101.3	608.1
3	JAWAJA	169	50	16	4	82	—	710	2401	8	30	3.9	13.2	41.4	165.5
4	KEKRI	117	43	18	3	47	—	983	2675	6	38	8.5	23.1	55.2	331.1
5	KISHANGARH	117	37	12	4	72	—	1044	3300	10	31	9.5	29.9	92.2	276.7
6	MASOODA	121	40	13	2	95	—	1053	3185	10	64	7.2	21.9	67.3	437.6
7	PISANGAN	172	58	23	7	65	1	1010	2995	8	25	7.0	20.8	52.3	171.9
8	SRINAGAR	102	41	9	2	67	—	1298	3229	15	66	8.8	21.9	99.7	448.9
	AJMER DISTRICT	**1038**	**336**	**111**	**26**	**713**	**1**	**988**	**305**	**9**	**39**	**7.9**	**24.3**	**73.5**	**313.7**
9	BANSURE	140	33	11	2	46	—	1168	4957	15	82	4.8	20.1	60.4	332.2
10	BEHROR	100	35	11	2	47	—	1150	3287	11	58	3.4	9.6	30.6	168.3
11	KATHUMAR	141	36	12	1	102	—	1203	4710	14	170	4.0	15.7	47.1	565.0
12	KISHANGARH BAS	117	33	9	2	5	—	1163	4124	15	68	4.3	15.3	56.2	252.7
13	KOTKASIM	108	38	11	4	2	—	883	2510	9	24	3.2	9.1	31.3	86.1
14	LACHHMANGARH	172	48	13	4	37	1	1025	3673	14	44	3.6	12.9	47.6	154.7
15	MANDAWAR	137	50	13	3	31	—	1183	3240	13	54	4.2	11.6	44.4	192.4
16	NIMRANA	87	43	14	3	13	—	1383	2798	9	40	4.4	8.8	27.0	126.1
17	RAJGARH	109	31	9	1	23	—	1032	3630	13	113	9.3	32.6	112.1	1009.2
18	RAMGARH	132	33	8	2	47	—	1225	4899	20	81	4.7	18.7	77.1	308.5
19	RENI	105	27	9	2	1	—	1007	3917	12	53	3.7	14.5	43.6	196.0
20	THANAGAZI	136	37	12	3	52	—	1060	3895	12	48	7.8	28.7	88.4	353.4
21	TIJARA	150	33	7	1	36	—	1008	4582	22	151	4.3	19.5	91.9	643.5
22	UMREN	138	24	11	3	46	—	1179	6780	15	54	6.2	35.4	77.1	282.8
	ALWAR	**1772**	**501**	**150**	**33**	**488**	**1**	**1115**	**394**	**13**	**60**	**4.8**	**17.1**	**57.1**	**259.4**
23	ANANDPURI	95	22	5	1	60	—	894	3859	17	85	3.6	15.5	68.4	341.8
24	BAGIDORA	121	29	11	4	67	—	1134	4733	13	34	4.3	17.8	46.9	128.9
25	GARHI	147	68	24	3	13	—	1282	2771	8	63	4.8	10.4	29.3	234.7
26	GHATOL	182	48	15	3	99	—	967	3666	12	59	4.3	16.3	52.2	261.1
27	KUSHALGARH	130	20	3	—	70	—	784	5095	34	—	4.9	32.1	213.6	—
28	PEEPALKHOONT	110	14	—	4	34	—	1006	7901	—	28	8.3	65.2	—	228.2
29	SAJJANGARH	106	20	9	1	74	—	973	5159	12	103	3.8	20.1	44.7	402.5
30	TALWARA	182	40	11	1	73	—	902	4104	15	164	4.1	18.8	68.2	750.4
	BANSWARA	**1073**	**261**	**78**	**17**	**490**	**0**	**994**	**409**	**14**	**63**	**4.7**	**19.4**	**64.8**	**297.1**
31	ANTA	119	28	11	2	54	—	1037	4408	11	62	7.8	33.3	84.8	466.1
32	ATRU	104	22	12	2	11	—	1033	4883	9	54	8.3	39.1	71.6	429.8
33	BARAN	90	25	7	—	23	—	899	3235	12	—	6.8	24.5	87.5	—
34	CHHABRA	126	20	5	—	2	—	648	4080	16	—	6.2	39.2	156.7	—
35	CHHIPABAROD	120	18	3	—	1	—	855	5698	34	—	6.9	45.8	274.8	—
36	KISHANGANJ	97	22	8	2	2	—	1117	4925	14	54	15.0	65.9	181.3	725.3
37	SHAHBAD	90	12	6	1	2	—	923	6919	14	83	16.3	122.4	244.7	1468.2
	BARAN	**746**	**147**	**52**	**7**	**95**	**0**	**921**	**468**	**13**	**98**	**9.3**	**47.2**	**133.3**	**990.2**
38	BALOTRA	138	41	10	1	91	—	1392	4686	19	192	28.2	94.8	388.5	3885.1
39	BARMER	186	36	10	—	80	—	920	4754	17	—	20.5	105.9	381.3	—
40	BAYTOO	146	41	8	1	39	—	1040	3702	19	152	22.1	78.7	403.5	3228.0
41	CHOHTAN	143	23	5	1	39	—	1197	7439	34	171	22.8	142.0	653.3	3266.5
42	DHORIMANNA	167	39	7	4	66	—	1084	4642	26	45	16.0	68.4	381.2	667.1
43	SHEO	141	25	6	1	43	—	862	4862	20	122	46.9	264.7	1102.7	6616.4
44	SINDHARI	170	36	10	1	37	—	987	4661	17	168	18.3	86.6	311.6	3115.7
45	SIWANA	102	32	6	—	87	—	1319	4203	22	—	19.4	61.9	330.4	—
	BARMER	**1193**	**273**	**62**	**9**	**482**	**0**	**1082**	**473**	**21**	**143**	**24.0**	**104.7**	**460.9**	**3175.1**
46	BAYANA	155	48	14	—	33	—	979	3163	11	—	5.2	16.7	57.1	—
47	DEEG	111	34	13	1	48	—	1132	3695	10	126	4.4	14.4	37.7	490.4
48	KAMAN	142	30	10	—	19	—	1087	5143	15	—	3.9	18.6	55.7	—
49	KUMHER	121	37	15	3	26	—	1067	3488	9	43	3.6	11.9	29.4	146.7
50	NADBAI	106	41	12	2	81	—	1204	3114	11	64	4.1	10.5	36.0	215.9
51	NAGAR PAHARI	183	50	20	5	23	—	993	3633	9	36	3.4	12.4	31.1	124.4
52	RUPBAS	150	55	21	4	54	—	1110	3029	8	42	3.6	9.8	25.7	134.8
53	SEWAR	138	49	13	—	75	—	968	2726	10	—	3.3	9.4	35.2	—
54	WEIR	152	53	15	2	55	—	1056	3029	11	80	3.8	10.9	38.4	288.1
	BHARATPUR	**1258**	**397**	**133**	**17**	**414**	**0**	**1058**	**335**	**10**	**78**	**3.9**	**12.4**	**36.9**	**289.0**

Panchayat Samities		Educational Institutes (Number)						Pop. Served Per Institution (No.)				Area Served Per Institution (sq. km)			
P. Code	Name	Primary Schools	Upper Primary	Sec. Schools	Senior Sec. Schools	Adult Lit. Cent.	Colleges	Pr. School	UPS	SS	SSS	Pr. Schools	UPS	SS	SSS
1	2	3	4	5	6	7	8	9	10	11	12	13	14	15	16
55	ASIND	157	55	14	3	58	—	994	2837	11	52	7.1	20.2	79.3	370.1
56	BANERA	81	34	8	2	102	—	1087	2590	11	44	8.4	19.9	84.6	338.3
57	HURDA	74	19	8	1	31	1	986	3840	9	73	8.3	32.5	77.2	617.3
58	JAHAZPUR	136	44	14	3	66	1	977	3020	10	44	7.6	23.5	73.8	344.4
59	KOTRI	121	48	25	9	5	3	1007	2538	5	14	7.9	19.8	38.0	105.6
60	MANDAL	155	42	14	3	94	—	948	3500	11	49	7.5	27.5	82.5	385.1
61	MANDALGARH	156	42	12	2	67	—	1003	3724	13	78	8.9	33.2	116.0	696.2
62	RAIPUR	80	24	9	1	54	—	892	2974	8	71	6.4	21.5	57.3	515.4
63	SAHARA	90	38	11	4	43	3	946	2240	8	21	7.0	16.7	57.6	158.3
64	SHAHPURA	146	41	13	3	126	1	826	2942	9	40	7.7	27.5	86.7	375.8
65	SUWANA	123	36	15	1	16	—	1055	3604	9	130	6.8	23.1	55.5	832.3
	BHILWARA	**1319**	**423**	**143**	**32**	**662**	**9**	**972**	**303**	**9**	**40**	**7.6**	**23.7**	**70.2**	**313.9**
66	BIKANER	177	35	15	1	103	—	1311	6630	16	232	50.5	255.6	596.3	8944.7
67	DUNGARGARH *	96	40	13	—	81	—	1392	3340	10	—	31.3	75.1	231.0	—
68	KOLAYAT	133	24	9	1	108	—	997	5527	15	133	55.0	304.9	813.2	7318.6
69	LUNKARANSAR	149	29	8	2	129	—	1050	5392	20	78	41.7	214.3	776.8	3107.0
70	NOKHA	154	44	15	1	65	—	1357	4748	14	209	24.5	85.6	251.2	3767.7
	BIKANER **	**613**	**132**	**47**	**5**	**405**	**0**	**1191**	**553**	**16**	**146**	**42.8**	**198.8**	**558.4**	**5249.0**
71	HINDOLI	146	31	12	2	130	—	1039	4893	13	76	9.2	43.2	111.6	669.5
72	KESHORAIPATAN	174	46	9	1	88	—	857	3243	17	149	7.4	28.0	143.0	1287.2
73	NAINWA	148	37	12	2	131	—	822	3288	10	61	7.7	30.8	95.0	570.0
74	TALERA	205	51	18	3	66	1	1044	4196	12	71	9.2	36.9	104.6	627.5
	BUNDI	**673**	**165**	**51**	**8**	**415**	**1**	**946**	**386**	**12**	**80**	**8.4**	**34.2**	**110.8**	**706.1**
75	ARNOD	102	22	4	1	52	—	896	4155	23	91	6.9	31.9	175.4	701.5
76	BARI SADRI	81	20	5	2	26	—	950	3846	15	39	5.9	23.7	94.9	237.3
77	BEGUN	111	23	7	1	70	—	773	3731	12	86	8.6	41.6	136.8	957.5
78	BHADESAR	99	20	7	3	19	—	904	4477	13	30	5.5	27.0	77.2	180.2
79	BHAINSRORGARH	77	16	6	1	1	—	830	3997	11	64	17.8	85.6	228.3	1369.8
80	BHOPALSAGAR	83	22	6	—	1	—	772	2913	11	—	4.8	18.1	66.4	—
81	CHHOTI SADRI	97	22	2	—	24	—	875	3859	43	—	7.1	31.5	346.0	—
82	CHITTAURGARH	148	32	9	2	14	—	917	4241	15	68	5.5	25.4	90.4	407.0
83	DUNGLA	78	20	6	2	16	—	988	3853	13	39	6.3	24.7	82.3	246.8
84	GANGRAR	88	26	7	1	14	—	853	2886	11	75	6.3	21.4	79.4	555.6
85	KAPASAN	74	19	8	2	—	—	985	3835	9	36	6.5	25.4	60.3	241.3
86	NIMBAHERA	106	25	9	1	20	—	1040	4411	12	110	7.7	32.5	90.3	812.7
87	PRATAPGARH	169	35	10	—	77	—	942	4549	16	—	8.5	40.8	142.8	—
88	RASHMI	68	24	6	2	56	—	968	2741	11	33	6.6	18.7	75.0	224.9
	CHITTAURGARH	**1381**	**326**	**92**	**18**	**390**	**0**	**907**	**384**	**14**	**70**	**7.4**	**31.2**	**110.5**	**565.0**
89	CHURU	98	38	11	1	23	—	1258	3245	11	123	15.9	41.0	141.8	1559.6
90	RAJGARH	191	70	21	4	62	—	1159	3162	11	55	11.5	31.4	104.6	549.3
91	RATANGARH	89	33	9	—	97	—	1410	3801	14	—	18.5	49.8	182.5	—
92	SARDARSHAHAR	146	51	12	—	104	—	1198	3431	15	—	26.1	74.8	317.9	—
93	SUJANGARH	142	51	10	2	79	—	1369	3812	19	97	18.3	50.9	259.6	1298.0
94	TARANAGAR	99	32	10	1	45	—	1254	3878	12	124	18.0	55.7	178.3	1782.9
	CHURU ***	**861**	**315**	**86**	**8**	**491**	**0**	**1274**	**348**	**13**	**137**	**19.3**	**52.7**	**193.0**	**2074.4**
95	BANDIKUI	148	47	14	—	44	1	1260	3968	13	—	4.1	12.8	42.9	—
96	DAUSA	163	57	20	2	38	3	1276	3648	10	104	5.6	15.9	45.4	454.0
97	LALSOT	184	51	17	2	42	1	1019	3675	11	94	4.6	16.8	50.2	427.0
98	MAHWA	132	42	10	4	17	—	1111	3492	15	37	3.6	11.3	47.4	118.4
99	SIKRAI	118	43	11	4	63	—	1361	3735	15	40	4.3	11.7	45.7	125.7
	DAUSA	**745**	**240**	**72**	**12**	**204**	**5**	**1194**	**370**	**12**	**74**	**4.5**	**13.9**	**46.4**	**278.2**
100	BARI	116	20	4	1	55	—	1012	5868	29	117	6.8	39.7	198.5	794.0
101	BASERI	135	41	12	2	45	—	1120	3687	13	76	7.4	24.4	83.5	500.7
102	DHAULPUR	180	51	15	5	72	—	1117	3943	13	40	3.2	11.3	38.5	115.5
103	RAJAKHERA	147	32	8	—	39	—	1027	4720	19	—	3.9	17.9	71.5	—
	DHAULPUR	**578**	**144**	**39**	**8**	**211**	**0**	**1074**	**431**	**16**	**78**	**5.1**	**20.5**	**75.5**	**368.1**
104	ASPUR	129	38	10	2	76	—	1136	3855	15	73	5.4	18.2	69.2	345.9
105	BICHHIWARA	148	43	11	1	158	—	1222	4205	16	181	5.0	17.4	67.8	745.9
106	DUNGARPUR	145	47	9	1	93	—	919	2834	15	133	4.0	12.2	63.9	575.1
107	SAGWARA	153	50	15	3	87	—	1050	3212	11	54	4.0	12.2	40.8	203.9
108	SIMALWARA	196	46	14	1	100	—	967	4122	14	190	4.7	19.9	65.3	913.6
	DUNGARPUR	**771**	**224**	**59**	**8**	**514**	**0**	**1052**	**362**	**14**	**101**	**4.6**	**15.8**	**60.0**	**442.3**
109	ANUPGARH	293	36	6	—	86	—	1004	8169	49	—	12.1	98.4	590.6	—
110	GANGANAGAR	160	70	17	5	25	—	1015	2320	10	33	5.3	12.2	50.3	171.0
111	KARANPUR	148	43	9	1	56	1	623	2144	10	92	5.5	18.9	90.1	810.5
112	PADAMPUR	170	41	11	1	9	—	623	2582	10	106	5.0	20.6	76.6	842.5
113	RAISINGHNAGAR	196	44	8	2	22	1	657	2928	16	64	6.7	29.9	164.4	657.7
114	SADULSHAHAR	140	64	21	7	27	—	1488	3256	10	30	10.6	23.2	70.7	212.1
115	SURATGARH	213	58	20	—	7	—	1288	4731	14	—	17.8	65.4	189.6	—
	GANGANAGAR	**1320**	**356**	**92**	**16**	**232**	**2**	**959**	**356**	**14**	**79**	**9.6**	**35.5**	**137.4**	**790.2**
116	BHADRA	116	57	17	5	43	—	1558	3171	11	36	14.8	30.1	100.8	342.6
117	HANUMANGARH	171	87	25	5	80	1	1953	3838	13	67	11.9	23.4	81.4	407.0
118	NOHAR	213	77	20	4	14	—	1361	3764	15	73	20.2	55.9	215.3	1076.2
	HANUMANGARH	**500**	**221**	**62**	**14**	**137**	**1**	**1609**	**364**	**13**	**57**	**16.1**	**36.4**	**129.9**	**575.2**

Panchayat Samities		*Educational Institutes (Number)*						*Pop. Served Per Institution (No.)*				*Area Served Per Institution (sq. km)*			
P. Code	*Name*	*Primary Schools*	*Upper Primary*	*Sec. Schools*	*Senior Sec. Schools*	*Adult Lit. Cent.*	*Colle-ges*	*Pr. School*	*UPS*	*SS*	*SSS*	*Pr. Schools*	*UPS*	*SS*	*SSS*
1	*2*	*3*	*4*	*5*	*6*	*7*	*8*	*9*	*10*	*11*	*12*	*13*	*14*	*15*	*16*
119	AMBER	153	52	15	2	15	—	1342	3949	14	103	5.5	16.1	56.0	419.7
120	BASSI	173	46	11	3	19	—	923	3473	15	53	3.7	13.7	57.4	210.3
121	CHAKSU	145	35	14	1	5	—	867	3592	9	126	5.3	21.9	54.8	766.8
122	DUDU	182	52	19	3	92	—	1157	4051	11	70	10.2	35.7	97.6	618.4
123	GOVINDGARH	142	53	18	4	6	2	1482	3970	12	53	4.7	12.6	37.0	166.5
124	JAMWA RAMGARH	194	64	20	3	15	—	984	2982	10	64	5.2	15.8	50.6	337.2
125	JHOTWARA	90	23	10	2	1	1	1145	4482	10	52	4.3	16.7	38.5	192.5
126	KOTPUTLI	145	47	11	2	36	—	1225	3779	16	89	4.6	14.1	60.3	331.7
127	PHAGI	134	33	12	1	49	—	974	3953	11	131	8.3	33.7	92.8	1113.3
128	SAMBHAR	148	41	13	1	11	—	1096	3957	13	162	5.6	20.3	64.0	832.4
129	SANGANER	139	36	11	2	7	1	1107	4275	14	77	4.2	16.2	53.1	292.0
130	SHAHPURA	95	51	13	3	10	—	1349	2513	10	43	4.3	8.0	31.4	136.0
131	VIRATNAGAR	122	48	16	1	1	—	1273	3235	10	155	5.3	13.5	40.6	649.1
	JAIPUR	**1862**	**581**	**183**	**28**	**267**	**4**	**1135**	**364**	**12**	**75**	**5.6**	**17.9**	**56.9**	**371.6**
132	JAISALMER	107	27	6	1	101	—	751	2974	13	80	120.1	475.9	2141.6	12849.5
133	SAM	149	19	5	1	80	—	637	4996	19	95	141.7	1111.1	4222.2	21111.0
134	SANKRA	121	25	10	—	162	—	956	4627	12	—	45.3	219.5	548.7	—
	JAISALMER	**377**	**71**	**21**	**2**	**343**	**0**	**772**	**410**	**14**	**145**	**104.6**	**555.6**	**1878.4**	**19723.6**
135	AHORE	112	34	9	2	131	—	1341	4417	17	75	14.3	47.0	177.4	798.3
136	BHINMAL	93	30	6	1	2	—	1572	4873	24	146	14.4	44.6	223.0	1337.7
137	JALOR	72	26	6	1	29	—	1499	4151	18	108	14.7	40.6	175.8	1054.8
138	JASWANTPURA	71	22	5	2	39	—	1498	4833	21	53	15.1	48.6	213.8	534.4
139	RANIWARA	82	22	5	1	18	—	1502	5597	25	123	12.0	44.7	196.8	984.0
140	SANCHORE	198	44	11	2	18	—	1315	5916	24	130	15.2	68.4	273.5	1504.3
141	SAYLA	91	32	11	1	18	—	1816	5165	15	165	16.0	45.6	132.7	1459.4
	JALOR	**719**	**210**	**53**	**10**	**255**	**0**	**1473**	**504**	**20**	**106**	**14.6**	**50.1**	**198.3**	**1051.0**
142	BAKANI	126	21	7	1	121	—	1030	6182	19	130	7.0	42.2	126.5	885.5
143	DAG	155	17	8	2	62	—	895	8159	17	69	7.3	66.5	141.3	565.3
144	JHALRAPATAN	165	35	8	—	64	1	988	4657	20	—	8.1	38.0	166.2	—
145	KHANPUR	125	36	8	—	41	—	948	3292	15	—	7.5	26.1	117.5	—
146	MANOHARTHANA	128	23	3	—	68	—	985	5480	42	—	7.2	40.1	307.6	—
147	PIRAWA	162	34	10	2	73	1	802	3822	13	65	6.2	29.4	100.1	500.6
	JHALAWAR	**861**	**166**	**44**	**5**	**429**	**2**	**936**	**486**	**18**	**161**	**7.2**	**37.4**	**141.1**	**1241.8**
148	ALSISAR	125	40	14	5	40	—	902	2818	8	23	6.0	18.7	53.4	149.4
149	BUHANA	150	75	21	4	2	1	1152	2305	8	43	4.4	8.7	31.1	163.4
150	CHIRAWA	95	34	13	4	68	1	1312	3665	10	31	5.2	14.4	37.6	122.3
151	JHUNJHUNUN	166	65	23	2	90	—	948	2420	7	79	4.9	12.6	35.7	410.3
152	KHETRI	121	36	13	3	29	—	1486	4995	14	60	6.6	22.1	61.3	265.4
153	NAWALGARH	141	45	22	2	13	1	1286	4029	8	91	4.7	14.8	30.2	332.6
154	SURAJGARH	130	41	14	3	70	—	1086	3444	10	47	6.0	19.1	55.8	260.5
155	UDAIPURWATI	147	48	19	4	52	1	1276	3907	10	47	5.7	17.3	43.7	207.8
	JHUNJHUNUN	**1075**	**384**	**139**	**27**	**364**	**4**	**1170**	**327**	**9**	**47**	**5.4**	**15.1**	**41.6**	**214.2**
156	BALESAR	102	36	7	1	28	—	1152	3265	17	118	18.2	51.5	264.9	1854.1
157	BAP	87	25	7	2	2	—	1191	4146	15	52	50.9	177.3	633.0	2215.6
158	BHOPALGARH	129	43	13	2	17	—	1213	3640	12	78	13.5	40.5	134.1	871.7
159	BILARA	105	39	12	2	137	—	1349	3632	12	71	14.3	38.5	125.0	749.7
160	LUNI	160	47	13	4	158	—	1042	3547	13	42	12.4	42.2	152.5	495.6
161	MANDOR	103	35	7	2	38	—	1087	3198	16	56	12.3	36.3	181.3	634.6
162	OSIAN	230	78	24	6	62	—	1332	3929	13	51	18.2	53.7	174.4	697.4
163	PHALODI	116	46	11	3	9	1	1392	3510	15	54	27.9	70.4	294.4	1079.3
164	SHERGARH	83	28	9	2	83	—	1362	4039	13	57	23.8	70.5	219.4	987.5
	JODHPUR	**1115**	**377**	**103**	**24**	**534**	**1**	**1237**	**366**	**13**	**57**	**19.9**	**58.8**	**215.3**	**924.1**
165	HINDAUN	131	48	18	2	19	—	1499	4090	11	98	4.8	13.2	35.1	315.8
166	KARAULI	157	42	13	1	28	—	1060	3963	13	167	7.8	29.0	93.8	1219.7
167	NADOTI	87	30	12	3	42	—	1169	3389	9	34	7.4	21.5	53.8	215.3
168	SAPOTRA	176	42	18	3	55	—	1036	4342	10	61	11.2	46.7	109.0	654.0
169	TODABHIM	131	44	16	2	20	—	1178	3508	10	77	4.0	11.9	32.7	261.3
	KARAULI	**682**	**206**	**77**	**11**	**164**	**0**	**1175**	**389**	**10**	**73**	**7.3**	**24.2**	**64.7**	**452.9**
170	CHECHAT	108	22	7	3	16	1	1117	5482	17	40	7.1	35.0	110.1	257.0
171	ITAWA	109	31	11	1	65	—	1166	4101	12	127	8.1	28.6	80.7	887.1
172	LADPURA	107	30	5	—	22	—	1024	3653	22	—	12.2	43.6	261.5	—
173	SANGOD	120	34	8	—	16	—	1022	3605	15	—	8.7	30.8	130.8	—
174	SULTANPUR	119	31	13	1	31	—	1041	3994	10	124	7.7	29.4	70.1	911.8
	KOTA	**563**	**148**	**44**	**5**	**150**	**1**	**1072**	**408**	**14**	**121**	**8.7**	**33.3**	**111.9**	**984.7**
175	DEGANA	139	40	12	4	35	—	1110	3358	13	39	10.5	36.4	121.5	364.4
176	DIDWANA	165	48	20	2	56	—	1359	4671	11	112	9.8	33.5	80.4	804.1
177	JAYAL	130	36	13	1	8	—	1359	4909	14	177	16.1	58.0	160.6	2088.2
178	KUCHAMAN	146	45	16	3	9	—	1405	4557	13	68	9.8	31.9	89.8	478.7
179	LADNU	95	34	9	2	15	1	1297	3623	14	62	14.4	40.3	152.4	685.6
180	MAKRANA	112	38	10	1	5	—	1395	4112	16	156	9.9	29.1	110.6	1106.2
181	MERTA	93	31	9	1	45	—	1533	4599	16	143	15.0	45.1	155.2	1397.1
182	MUNDWA	123	33	13	—	49	—	1242	4628	12	—	17.8	66.2	168.0	—
183	NAGAUR	146	36	12	—	37	—	1242	5038	15	—	16.3	66.1	198.4	—
184	PARBATSAR	111	37	11	2	18	—	1287	3860	13	71	9.7	28.9	97.4	535.5

Panchayat Samities		Educational Institutes (Number)						Pop. Served Per Institution (No.)				Area Served Per Institution (sq. km)			
P. Code	Name	Primary Schools	Upper Primary	Sec. Schools	Senior Sec. Schools	Adult Lit. Cent.	Colleges	Pr. School	UPS	SS	SSS	Pr. Schools	UPS	SS	SSS
1	2	3	4	5	6	7	8	9	10	11	12	13	14	15	16
185	RIYAN	118	34	12	—	49	—	1211	4204	12	—	10.5	36.5	103.3	—
	NAGAUR	**1378**	**412**	**137**	**16**	**326**	**1**	**1308**	**437**	**13**	**113**	**12.6**	**42.1**	**126.6**	**1083.7**
186	BALI	89	31	14	4	26	—	1677	4814	11	37	15.4	44.2	97.8	342.5
187	DESURI	69	23	8	2	6	—	1237	3712	11	43	12.0	36.1	103.6	414.6
188	JAITARAN	89	37	7	1	47	—	1515	3645	19	135	14.5	34.9	184.3	1289.8
189	KHARCHI / MARWAR JUN.	122	38	15	3	69	—	1269	4075	10	52	11.4	36.6	92.7	463.5
190	PALI	75	25	5	—	9	—	1127	3382	17	—	17.3	51.9	259.3	—
191	RAIPUR	98	31	10	1	125	—	1348	4262	13	132	10.1	31.8	98.7	986.5
192	RANI STATION	77	31	10	3	66	—	1222	3036	9	31	9.9	24.6	76.3	254.2
193	ROHAT	73	17	3	1	8	—	1114	4782	27	81	19.2	82.6	468.1	1404.4
194	SOJAT	106	41	13	3	76	—	1239	3204	10	44	15.4	39.7	125.2	542.3
195	SUMERPUR	55	30	10	—	13	—	2097	3845	12	—	16.6	30.4	91.2	—
	PALI	**853**	**304**	**95**	**18**	**445**	**0**	**1364**	**383**	**12**	**65**	**13.9**	**39.0**	**124.9**	**659.4**
196	AMET	93	20	4	1	—	—	769	3578	18	72	5.4	25.3	126.4	505.4
197	BHIM	114	31	11	1	34	—	913	3357	10	104	5.9	21.9	61.6	677.7
198	DEOGARH	74	15	6	—	18	—	862	4254	11	—	8.0	39.3	98.2	—
199	KHAMNOR	115	47	13	1	73	—	975	2385	9	112	5.2	12.7	45.8	594.8
200	KUMBHALGARH	148	37	13	2	84	—	767	3068	9	57	5.2	21.0	59.7	388.0
201	RAILMAGRA	78	34	8	4	67	—	1286	2950	13	25	7.0	16.0	68.0	136.1
202	RAJSAMAND	124	34	12	—	4	—	875	3192	9	—	4.6	16.7	47.4	—
	RAJSAMAND	**746**	**218**	**67**	**9**	**280**	**0**	**903**	**309**	**10**	**75**	**5.7**	**19.5**	**63.5**	**472.9**
203	BAMANWAS	135	33	10	1	16	—	891	3644	12	120	5.4	22.1	72.9	728.8
204	BONLI	132	51	13	1	3	—	1246	3226	13	165	7.7	19.8	77.7	1009.5
205	GANGAPUR	123	47	19	1	63	1	1193	3121	8	147	5.2	13.7	33.9	644.7
206	KHANDAR	111	28	7	1	3	—	1075	4264	17	119	12.2	48.3	193.2	1352.3
207	SAWAI MADHOPUR	145	52	18	3	90	—	1195	3332	10	58	8.5	23.7	68.5	410.8
	SAWAI MADHOPUR	**646**	**211**	**67**	**7**	**175**	**1**	**1121**	**343**	**11**	**103**	**7.7**	**23.5**	**74.1**	**709.7**
208	DANTA RAMGARH	192	65	22	4	80	—	1075	3176	9	52	5.8	17.2	50.7	278.9
209	DHOND	124	53	17	5	12	—	1381	3232	10	34	7.4	17.2	53.7	182.5
210	FATEHPUR	140	62	16	—	88	—	1124	2538	10	—	8.8	20.0	77.3	—
211	KHANDELA	126	50	17	—	28	—	1401	3531	10	—	6.2	15.7	46.1	—
212	LACHHMANGARH	146	53	15	3	63	—	1089	3000	11	53	7.0	19.4	68.5	342.3
213	NEEM KA THANA	183	64	24	3	23	—	1382	3951	11	84	6.5	18.5	49.5	395.6
214	PIPRALI	117	43	15	2	149	—	1403	3817	11	82	6.8	18.6	53.2	398.9
215	SRI MADHOPUR	104	38	11	1	57	—	1613	4414	15	168	5.5	14.9	51.5	566.6
	SIKAR	**1132**	**428**	**137**	**18**	**500**	**0**	**1286**	**340**	**11**	**81**	**6.7**	**17.8**	**55.7**	**423.7**
216	ABU ROAD	76	17	8	—	39	—	1061	4742	10	—	11.3	50.5	107.3	—
217	PINDWARA	82	24	18	2	39	1	1561	5335	7	64	13.9	47.4	63.2	569.2
218	REODAR	112	30	8	—	68	—	1180	4404	17	—	9.7	36.2	135.9	—
219	SHEOGANJ	64	21	5	—	51	—	1248	3804	16	—	13.9	42.5	178.5	—
220	SIROHI	71	29	13	2	50	—	1490	3648	8	53	15.4	37.6	83.9	545.2
	SIROHI	**405**	**121**	**52**	**4**	**247**	**1**	**1300**	**435**	**10**	**132**	**12.5**	**41.9**	**97.4**	**1266.5**
221	DEOLI	120	39	13	1	81	—	1130	3476	10	136	10.3	31.7	95.0	1235.3
222	MALPURA	132	40	10	3	34	1	1124	3710	15	50	10.9	36.0	143.9	479.7
223	NIWAI	153	35	8	1	48	—	898	3928	17	138	6.7	29.4	128.8	1030.1
224	TODARAISINGH	87	28	10	1	56	—	1044	3243	9	91	11.3	35.2	98.6	985.5
225	TONK	172	49	22	—	48		982	3418	8	—	8.2	28.9	64.3	—
226	UNIARA	106	30	9	2	41	—	976	3447	12	52	9.3	32.9	109.6	493.2
	TONK	**770**	**221**	**72**	**8**	**308**	**1**	**1019**	**355**	**11**	**98**	**9.2**	**32.1**	**98.5**	**886.5**
227	BARGAON	125	43	15	4	34	—	988	2872	8	31	5.2	15.1	43.2	162.0
228	BHINDER	176	50	19	2	9	—	962	3388	9	85	5.6	19.7	51.9	492.6
229	DHARIAWAD	145	29	8	—	28	—	1076	5380	20	—	8.1	40.6	147.2	—
230	GIRWA	161	44	12	3	9	—	1100	4026	15	59	8.4	30.7	112.4	449.7
231	GOGUNDA	116	35	7	1	54	—	1049	3477	17	122	7.5	24.9	124.5	871.8
232	JHADOL	153	29	10	2	80	—	961	5070	15	74	9.3	49.3	142.8	714.2
233	KHERWARA	206	53	19	4	5	—	966	3756	11	50	5.2	20.3	56.7	269.2
234	KOTRA	126	19	4	1	46	—	1035	6866	33	130	9.5	62.7	297.9	1191.5
235	MAVLI	156	48	16	6	41	—	1054	3426	10	27	5.1	16.6	49.9	133.2
236	SALUMBAR	132	42	13	2	13	—	1224	3848	12	81	7.0	22.0	70.9	460.9
237	SARADA	146	55	17	3	53	—	1172	3110	10	57	7.4	19.6	63.4	359.4
	UDAIPUR	1642	447	140	28	372	0	1048	385	12	61	7.0	25.8	82.3	411.7
	RAJASTHAN (RURAL)	**30667**	**8966**	**2760**	**458**	**11502**	**36**	**1106**	**3784**	**12**	**74**	**10.9**	**37.4**	**121.6**	**732.7**

Note: * Dungargarh PS shifted from Churu to Bikaner district on 1st April 2001
** Excluding data of Dungargarh PS;
*** Including data of Dungargarh PS.
# Came in force from April, 1991; ## Came in force from July 1994
Came in force from July 1997.
Source: Hemlata Joshi. 2003. '*Educational Development Index-Rajasthan* (Spatio-Temporal Appraisal at Panchayat Samiti/Block Level), Published Research Report, IDSJ, University Book House, Jaipur.

PANCHAYAT SAMITI-WISE WORKING/ WORK PARTICIPATION

P. Code	Panchayat Samiti	Working Population											(000 No.)
		Main Workers			Marginal Workers			Total Workers					
		Person	Male	Female	Person	Male	Female	Person	% Share in District	Male	% Share in District	Female	% Share in District
1	2	3	4	5	6	7	8	9		10		11	
1	ARAIN	51.0	31.8	19.2	6.2	0.6	5.6	57.2	(11.9)	32.4	(11.6)	24.8	(12.3)
2	BHINAY	54.1	35.9	18.2	9.2	0.3	8.9	63.3	(13.1)	36.2	(12.9)	27.1	(13.5)
3	JAWAJA	39.9	26.8	13.1	9.2	0.7	8.4	49.1	(10.2)	27.6	(9.8)	21.5	(10.7)
4	KEKRI	47.3	31.6	15.7	7.8	0.3	7.4	55.1	(11.4)	31.9	(11.4)	23.2	(11.5)
5	KISHANGARH	46.8	33.2	13.6	8.9	0.7	8.3	55.8	(11.6)	33.9	(12.1)	21.9	(10.9)
6	MASOODA	53.4	34.4	19.0	5.6	0.4	5.1	59.0	(12.3)	34.8	(12.4)	24.2	(12.0)
7	PISANGAN	73.7	46.4	27.2	6.2	0.5	5.6	79.8	(16.6)	47.0	(16.8)	32.8	(16.4)
8	SRINAGAR	54.7	35.8	18.9	7.5	0.7	6.8	62.1	(12.9)	36.5	(13.0)	25.6	(12.8)
	AJMER DISTRICT	**420.9**	**275.9**	**144.9**	**60.6**	**4.2**	**56.1**	**481.4**	**(100.0)**	**280.3**	**(100.0)**	**201.1**	**(100.0)**
9	BANSURE	45.9	40.4	5.5	21.9	1.6	20.3	67.9	(8.1)	42.1	(8.4)	25.8	(7.7)
10	BEHROR	34.8	25.7	9.1	16.5	1.4	15.1	51.3	(6.2)	27.2	(5.4)	24.1	(7.2)
11	KATHUMAR	54.2	43.1	11.1	20.8	1.5	19.3	75.0	(9.0)	44.6	(8.9)	30.4	(9.1)
12	KISHANGARH BAS	38.5	33.1	5.4	14.7	0.5	14.1	53.1	(6.4)	33.6	(6.7)	19.5	(5.8)
13	KOTKASIM	24.1	21.9	2.1	12.4	0.3	12.1	36.5	(4.4)	22.2	(4.4)	14.3	(4.3)
14	LACHHMANGARH	54.2	43.6	10.6	25.4	1.8	23.6	79.7	(9.6)	45.5	(9.1)	34.2	(10.2)
15	MANDAWAR	42.9	37.0	5.9	18.4	1.5	16.8	61.2	(7.3)	38.5	(7.7)	22.7	(6.8)
16	NIMRANA	31.1	26.0	5.1	12.6	0.7	11.9	43.7	(5.2)	26.7	(5.3)	17.0	(5.1)
17	RAJGARH	47.3	29.5	17.9	7.0	0.6	6.4	54.3	(6.5)	30.1	(6.0)	24.2	(7.3)
18	RAMGARH	47.7	41.3	6.4	15.1	0.7	14.4	62.8	(7.5)	42.0	(8.4)	20.8	(6.2)
19	RENI	44.4	27.1	17.4	8.6	1.5	7.1	53.1	(6.4)	28.6	(5.7)	24.5	(7.3)
20	THANAGAZI	47.9	37.4	10.5	15.7	0.9	14.9	63.6	(7.6)	38.3	(7.7)	25.3	(7.6)
21	TIJARA	39.2	37.6	1.6	26.5	1.1	25.4	65.7	(7.9)	38.7	(7.7)	27.0	(8.1)
22	UMREN	54.7	40.8	13.9	11.2	0.8	10.4	65.9	(7.9)	41.6	(8.3)	24.3	(7.3)
	ALWAR	**606.9**	**484.5**	**122.5**	**226.8**	**14.9**	**211.8**	**833.8**	**(100.0)**	**499.7**	**(100.0)**	**334.1**	**(100.0)**
23	ANANDPURI	28.5	22.3	6.1	15.5	0.7	14.8	43.9	(8.6)	23.0	(8.1)	20.9	(9.2)
24	BAGIDORA	46.9	36.0	10.9	22.8	1.0	21.8	69.7	(13.6)	37.0	(13.1)	32.7	(14.3)
25	GARHI	62.5	47.8	14.7	23.1	1.2	21.9	85.6	(16.8)	49.0	(17.3)	36.6	(16.0)
26	GHATOL	58.1	45.6	12.5	24.4	0.9	23.5	82.4	(16.1)	46.5	(16.4)	35.9	(15.8)
27	KUSHALGARH	33.1	26.6	6.4	18.1	0.8	17.3	51.1	(10.0)	27.4	(9.7)	23.7	(10.4)
28	PEEPALKHOONT	40.2	29.5	10.7	15.1	1.0	14.1	55.3	(10.8)	30.5	(10.8)	24.8	(10.9)
29	SAJJANGARH	34.5	27.3	7.2	17.5	0.8	16.7	52.0	(10.2)	28.1	(9.9)	23.9	(10.5)
30	TALWARA	48.0	40.9	7.1	23.3	0.8	22.5	71.3	(13.9)	41.7	(14.7)	29.6	(13.0)
	BANSWARA	**351.8**	**276**	**75.6**	**159.8**	**7.2**	**152.6**	**511.3**	**(100.0)**	**283.2**	**(100.0)**	**228.1**	**(100.0)**
31	ANTA	36.7	31.6	5.2	7.4	0.4	6.9	44.1	(15.5)	32.0	(17.3)	12.1	(12.2)
32	ATRU	33.4	27.7	5.7	8.3	0.4	8.0	41.8	(14.7)	28.1	(15.2)	13.7	(13.8)
33	BARAN	25.7	20.8	4.9	5.9	0.3	5.6	31.6	(11.1)	21.1	(11.4)	10.5	(10.6)
34	CHHABRA	28.1	21.9	6.2	8.3	0.5	7.8	36.4	(12.8)	22.4	(12.1)	14.0	(14.1)
35	CHHIPABAROD	41.4	28.1	13.3	9.2	0.6	8.6	50.6	(17.8)	28.7	(15.5)	21.9	(22.1)
36	KISHANGANJ	38.9	29.1	9.8	5.3	0.3	5.0	44.3	(15.6)	29.5	(16.0)	14.8	(14.9)
37	SHAHBAD	29.9	22.8	7.2	5.3	0.3	5.0	35.3	(12.4)	23.1	(12.5)	12.2	(12.3)
	BARAN	**234.1**	**182**	**52.3**	**49.7**	**2.8**	**46.9**	**284.1**	**(100.0)**	**184.9**	**(100.0)**	**99.2**	**(100.0)**
38	BALOTRA	63.4	49.9	13.5	24.9	1.4	23.5	88.3	(14.8)	51.3	(14.5)	37.0	(15.3)
39	BARMER	53.6	46.3	7.3	24.1	1.6	22.4	77.6	(13.0)	47.9	(13.5)	29.7	(12.3)
40	BAYTOO	52.2	38.9	13.3	23.8	2.0	21.8	76.0	(12.7)	40.9	(11.5)	35.1	(14.5)
41	CHOHTAN	65.4	49.6	15.8	16.2	1.1	15.1	81.6	(13.7)	50.7	(14.3)	30.9	(12.8)
42	DHORIMANNA	64.4	48.3	16.0	21.2	1.1	20.0	85.5	(14.3)	49.5	(13.9)	36.0	(14.9)
43	SHEO	40.9	33.8	7.1	9.9	0.5	9.4	50.8	(8.5)	34.3	(9.7)	16.5	(6.8)
44	SINDHARI	61.5	44.8	16.7	20.5	1.5	19.0	82.0	(13.7)	46.3	(13.0)	35.7	(14.8)
45	SIWANA	42.2	33.3	8.9	12.6	0.7	12.0	54.9	(9.2)	34.0	(9.6)	20.9	(8.6)
	BARMER	**443.6**	**344.9**	**98.6**	**153.2**	**9.9**	**143.2**	**596.7**	**(100.0)**	**354.9**	**(100.0)**	**241.8**	**(100.0)**
46	BAYANA	42.6	40.0	2.7	11.5	0.4	11.1	54.1	(11.1)	40.3	(12.0)	13.8	(9.1)
47	DEEG	32.9	31.3	1.6	19.0	0.3	18.6	51.9	(10.7)	31.6	(9.4)	20.3	(13.5)
48	KAMAN	44.5	39.6	4.9	18.9	0.4	18.5	63.4	(13.0)	40.0	(11.9)	23.4	(15.6)
49	KUMHER	34.2	31.2	3.0	14.3	0.4	13.9	48.4	(9.9)	31.5	(9.4)	16.9	(11.2)
50	NADBAI	34.5	31.2	3.3	12.0	0.3	11.8	46.6	(9.6)	31.5	(9.4)	15.1	(10.0)
51	NAGAR PAHARI	50.0	45.3	4.7	15.7	0.3	15.5	65.8	(13.5)	45.6	(13.6)	20.2	(13.4)
52	RUPBAS	44.7	41.7	3.0	8.2	0.6	7.6	52.9	(10.9)	42.3	(12.6)	10.6	(7.0)
53	SEWAR	36.3	32.7	3.6	9.8	0.5	9.3	46.1	(9.5)	33.2	(9.9)	12.9	(8.5)
54	WEIR	44.6	39.1	5.5	12.8	0.5	12.3	57.4	(11.8)	39.6	(11.8)	17.8	(11.8)
	BHARATPUR	**364.3**	**332.1**	**32.3**	**122.2**	**3.7**	**118.6**	**486.6**	**(100.0)**	**335.6**	**(100.0)**	**151.0**	**(100.0)**

NON-WORKING POPULATION AND RATE BY SEX (1991)

P. Code	*Panchayat Samiti*	*% Share to Total Workers*		*Non Workers (000 No.)*			*Work Participation Rate*		
		Male	*Female*	*Person*	*Male*	*Female*	*Person*	*Male*	*Female*
1	*2*	*12*	*13*	*14*	*15*	*16*	*17*	*18*	*19*
1	ARAIN	56.6	43.4	52.5	24.1	28.4	52.1	57.3	46.6
2	BHINAY	54.6	42.8	62.0	28.5	33.5	50.5	56.0	44.7
3	JAWAJA	56.2	43.8	71.0	32.9	38.2	40.9	45.5	36.1
4	KEKRI	57.9	42.1	59.9	27.3	32.6	47.9	53.9	41.6
5	KISHANGARH	60.8	39.2	66.3	29.9	36.4	45.7	53.1	37.6
6	MASOODA	59.0	41.0	68.4	31.5	36.8	46.3	52.4	39.7
7	PISANGAN	58.9	41.1	93.9	43.3	50.6	45.9	52.1	39.3
8	SRINAGAR	58.8	41.2	70.2	32.3	37.9	46.9	53.1	40.4
	AJMER DISTRICT	**58.2**	**41.8**	**544.2**	**249.8**	**294.4**	**46.9**	**52.9**	**40.6**
9	BANSURE	62.0	38.0	95.7	44.9	50.8	41.5	48.4	33.7
10	BEHROR	53.0	47.0	63.8	32.4	31.4	44.6	45.5	43.4
11	KATHUMAR	59.5	40.5	94.6	47.7	46.9	44.2	48.3	39.3
12	KISHANGARH BAS	63.3	36.7	83.0	37.9	45.0	39.0	47.0	30.2
13	KOTKASIM	60.8	39.2	58.9	28.1	30.8	38.3	44.1	31.7
14	LACHHMANGARH	57.1	42.9	96.6	48.2	48.4	45.2	48.6	41.4
15	MANDAWAR	62.9	37.1	100.8	46.0	54.7	37.8	45.5	29.3
16	NIMRANA	61.1	38.9	76.6	35.2	41.4	36.3	43.1	29.1
17	RAJGARH	55.4	44.6	58.2	29.7	28.5	48.2	50.3	46.1
18	RAMGARH	66.9	33.1	98.8	44.0	54.8	38.8	48.8	27.5
19	RENI	53.9	46.1	52.7	27.8	24.9	50.2	50.7	49.6
20	THANAGAZI	60.2	39.8	80.5	38.0	42.5	44.1	50.2	37.4
21	TIJARA	58.9	41.1	85.5	41.4	44.0	43.5	48.3	38.0
22	UMREN	63.1	36.9	96.8	45.6	51.2	40.5	47.7	32.2
	ALWAR	**59.9**	**40.1**	**1142.5**	**546.9**	**595.3**	**42.2**	**47.7**	**36.0**
23	ANANDPURI	52.4	47.6	41.0	20.3	20.7	51.7	53.2	50.4
24	BAGIDORA	53.1	46.9	67.6	32.7	34.9	50.8	53.1	48.4
25	GARHI	57.2	42.8	102.7	46.5	56.2	45.4	51.3	39.4
26	GHATOL	56.4	43.6	93.7	42.1	51.5	46.8	52.5	41.2
27	KUSHALGARH	53.6	46.4	50.8	24.4	26.4	50.1	52.9	47.3
28	PEEPALKHOONT	55.2	44.8	55.3	25.8	29.5	50.0	54.2	45.6
29	SAJJANGARH	54.0	46.0	51.2	24.6	26.6	50.4	53.3	47.4
30	TALWARA	58.5	41.5	92.8	40.9	51.9	43.4	50.5	36.3
	BANSWARA	**55.4**	**44.6**	**555.1**	**257.3**	**297.7**	**47.9**	**52.4**	**43.4**
31	ANTA	72.6	27.4	79.4	32.7	46.7	35.7	49.5	20.6
32	ATRU	67.2	32.8	65.7	28.7	37.0	38.9	49.5	27.0
33	BARAN	66.8	33.2	49.2	21.3	27.9	39.1	49.7	27.3
34	CHHABRA	61.5	38.5	45.1	20.9	24.2	44.6	51.7	36.6
35	CHHIPABAROD	56.7	43.3	52.0	25.2	26.8	49.3	53.3	45.0
36	KISHANGANJ	66.6	33.4	64.1	27.5	36.6	40.9	51.8	28.8
37	SHAHBAD	65.4	34.6	47.8	21.2	26.6	42.5	52.2	31.5
	BARAN	**65.1**	**34.9**	**403.3**	**177.5**	**225.8**	**41.3**	**51.0**	**30.5**
38	BALOTRA	58.1	41.9	103.9	48.8	55.0	46.0	51.2	40.2
39	BARMER	61.7	38.3	93.5	44.2	49.3	45.3	52.0	37.6
40	BAYTOO	53.8	46.2	75.8	38.2	37.6	50.1	51.6	48.3
41	CHOHTAN	62.1	37.9	89.5	40.6	48.9	47.7	55.5	38.7
42	DHORIMANNA	57.9	41.1	95.5	45.2	50.3	47.2	52.3	41.7
43	SHEO	67.5	32.5	70.8	32.3	38.5	41.8	51.5	30.0
44	SINDHARI	56.5	43.5	85.8	41.3	44.5	48.9	52.8	44.5
45	SIWANA	61.9	38.1	79.6	35.4	44.2	40.8	49.0	32.1
	BARMER	**59.5**	**40.5**	**694.4**	**326**	**368.3**	**46.2**	**52.1**	**39.6**
46	BAYANA	74.5	25.5	97.7	44.6	53.1	35.6	47.4	20.6
47	DEEG	60.9	39.1	73.7	37.5	36.3	41.3	45.7	35.9
48	KAMAN	63.1	36.9	90.8	42.8	48.0	41.1	48.3	32.9
49	KUMHER	65.1	34.9	80.6	39.1	41.5	37.5	44.6	28.9
50	NADBAI	67.6	32.4	81.1	38.7	42.4	36.5	44.9	26.3
51	NAGAR PAHARI	69.3	30.7	115.9	52.7	63.2	36.2	46.4	24.2
52	RUPBAS	80.0	20.0	113.7	49.3	64.4	31.8	46.2	14.1
53	SEWAR	72.0	28.0	87.5	40.1	47.4	34.5	45.3	21.4
54	WEIR	69.0	31.0	103.1	48.4	54.7	35.8	45.0	24.5
	BHARATPUR	**69.0**	**31.0**	**844.1**	**393.2**	**451**	**36.6**	**46.1**	**25.1**

P. Code	Panchayat Samiti	Working Population											(000 No.)
		Main Workers			Marginal Workers			Total Workers					
		Person	Male	Female	Person	Male	Female	Person	% Share in District	Male	% Share in District	Female	% Share in District
1	2	3	4	5	6	7	8	9		10		11	
55	ASIND	67.2	43.5	23.6	12.0	0.6	11.4	79.2	(12.3)	44.1	(11.7)	35.1	(13.2)
56	BANERA	39.0	26.2	12.8	5.9	0.3	5.6	45.0	(7.0)	26.6	(7.1)	18.4	(6.9)
57	HURDA	32.5	21.5	11.1	2.9	0.2	2.8	35.5	(5.5)	21.6	(5.7)	13.9	(5.2)
58	JAHAZPUR	51.5	36.2	15.3	9.2	0.6	8.7	60.7	(9.4)	36.8	(9.8)	23.9	(9.0)
59	KOTRI	55.4	36.4	19.0	6.5	0.3	6.2	62.0	(9.6)	36.7	(9.8)	25.3	(9.5)
60	MANDAL	62.8	42.0	20.8	13.5	0.6	12.8	76.3	(11.9)	42.6	(11.3)	33.7	(12.6)
61	MANDALGARH	69.7	48.1	21.6	10.2	0.5	9.7	80.0	(12.4)	48.7	(12.9)	31.3	(11.7)
62	RAIPUR	26.5	19.6	6.8	5.6	0.1	5.5	32.1	(5.0)	19.8	(5.3)	12.3	(4.6)
63	SAHARA	37.9	23.9	14.0	7.3	0.4	6.9	45.2	(7.0)	24.3	(6.5)	20.9	(7.8)
64	SHAHPURA	49.1	35.1	14.1	11.7	0.5	11.2	60.8	(9.5)	35.6	(9.5)	25.2	(9.4)
65	SUWANA	55.9	39.3	16.6	10.8	0.4	10.3	66.6	(10.4)	39.7	(10.5)	26.9	(10.1)
	BHILWARA	**547.5**	**371.8**	**175.7**	**95.6**	**4.5**	**91.1**	**643.4**	**(100.0)**	**376.5**	**(100.1)**	**266.9**	**(100.0)**
66	BIKANER	77.6	62.9	14.6	19.3	1.5	17.8	96.9	(31.9)	64.5	(32.6)	32.4	(30.4)
67	DUNGARGARH *	51.6	34.6	17.0	13.1	0.8	12.3	64.6	(13.4)	35.3	(12.9)	29.3	(14.1)
68	KOLAYAT	42.9	36.0	6.9	11.6	0.8	10.8	54.5	(17.9)	36.8	(18.6)	17.7	(16.6)
69	LUNKARANSAR	50.8	41.3	9.5	11.3	0.8	10.5	62.1	(20.4)	42.1	(21.3)	20.0	(18.8)
70	NOKHA	63.6	52.8	10.8	27.1	1.3	25.8	90.7	(29.8)	54.2	(27.4)	36.5	(34.2)
	BIKANER **	**234.9**	**193**	**41.8**	**69.3**	**4.4**	**64.9**	**304.2**	**(100.0)**	**197.6**	**(100.0)**	**106.6**	**(100.0)**
71	HINDOLI	57.1	42.8	14.2	11.7	0.4	11.3	68.7	(25.3)	43.2	(24.1)	25.5	(27.4)
72	KESHORAIPATAN	50.3	40.6	9.7	10.9	0.4	10.5	61.2	(22.5)	41.0	(22.9)	20.2	(21.7)
73	NAINWA	43.4	33.3	10.1	11.3	0.8	10.5	54.7	(20.1)	34.1	(19.1)	20.6	(22.2)
74	TALERA	77.5	59.9	17.6	10.0	0.8	9.1	87.4	(32.1)	60.7	(33.9)	26.7	(28.7)
	BUNDI	**228.3**	**176.6**	**51.6**	**43.9**	**2.4**	**41.4**	**272**	**(100.0)**	**179.0**	**(100.0)**	**93.0**	**(100.0)**
75	ARNOD	38.5	24.4	14.1	5.8	0.2	5.7	44.4	(6.8)	24.6	(6.7)	19.8	(6.8)
76	BARI SADRI	33.7	21.8	11.9	7.8	0.4	7.5	41.6	(6.3)	22.2	(6.1)	19.4	(6.7)
77	BEGUN	42.1	26.2	15.8	3.7	0.1	3.6	45.8	(7.0)	26.3	(7.2)	19.5	(6.7)
78	BHADESAR	39.0	26.8	12.2	9.9	0.3	9.5	48.9	(7.4)	27.1	(7.4)	21.8	(7.5)
79	BHAINSRORGARH	27.9	18.7	9.1	4.0	0.3	3.7	31.8	(4.8)	19.0	(5.2)	12.8	(4.4)
80	BHOPALSAGAR	29.3	18.6	10.7	3.7	0.2	3.6	33.0	(5.0)	18.8	(5.1)	14.2	(4.9)
81	CHHOTI SADRI	36.5	24.1	12.4	9.5	0.6	9.0	46.0	(7.0)	24.7	(6.7)	21.3	(7.4)
82	CHITTAURGARH	58.5	39.2	19.3	14.0	0.8	13.2	72.5	(11.0)	40.0	(10.9)	32.5	(11.2)
83	DUNGLA	31.3	21.9	9.5	9.2	0.2	9.0	40.5	(6.2)	22.1	(6.0)	18.4	(6.4)
84	GANGRAR	36.4	23.3	13.1	5.1	0.3	4.8	41.5	(6.3)	23.6	(6.4)	17.9	(6.2)
85	KAPASAN	32.5	22.2	10.3	8.4	0.2	8.2	40.9	(6.2)	22.4	(6.1)	18.5	(6.4)
86	NIMBAHERA	48.1	31.8	16.3	9.4	0.4	9.1	57.5	(8.8)	32.1	(8.8)	25.4	(8.7)
87	PRATAPGARH	62.4	43.2	19.3	15.5	0.9	14.6	77.9	(11.9)	44.1	(12.0)	33.8	(11.6)
88	RASHMI	31.1	19.0	12.1	3.7	0.1	3.6	35.1	(5.3)	19.1	(5.2)	16.0	(5.5)
	CHITTAURGARH	**547.3**	**361.2**	**186.1**	**109.7**	**5**	**105.1**	**657.4**	**(100.0)**	**366.1**	**(100.0)**	**291.3**	**(100.0)**
89	CHURU	36.8	28.8	8.0	13.6	0.5	13.1	50.4	(10.5)	29.2	(10.7)	21.2	(10.1)
90	RAJGARH	70.9	51.0	19.9	28.2	1.7	26.4	99.1	(20.6)	52.7	(19.2)	46.4	(22.2)
91	RATANGARH	41.5	30.9	10.6	12.6	0.7	11.9	54.1	(11.2)	31.6	(11.5)	22.5	(10.8)
92	SARDARSHAHAR	52.3	44.1	8.2	19.2	0.8	18.5	71.5	(14.8)	44.9	(16.4)	26.6	(12.8)
93	SUJANGARH	64.4	47.8	16.6	19.5	1.2	18.3	83.9	(17.4)	49.0	(17.9)	34.9	(16.8)
94	TARANAGAR	37.7	30.1	7.6	21.0	1.1	20.0	58.7	(12.2)	31.2	(11.4)	27.5	(13.2)
	CHURU ***	**355.2**	**267.3**	**87.9**	**127.2**	**6.8**	**120.5**	**482.3**	**(100.1)**	**273.9**	**(100.0)**	**208.4**	**(100.0)**
95	BANDIKUI	52.3	44.2	8.1	17.2	0.8	16.4	69.4	(20.0)	44.9	(20.4)	24.5	(19.4)
96	DAUSA	69.5	51.6	17.8	14.6	0.5	14.0	84.0	(24.3)	52.2	(23.7)	31.8	(25.3)
97	LALSOT	64.3	47.1	17.3	7.9	0.5	7.4	72.2	(20.8)	47.5	(21.6)	24.7	(19.6)
98	MAHWA	41.5	35.4	6.1	14.1	0.4	13.7	55.6	(16.1)	35.8	(16.3)	19.8	(15.7)
99	SIKRAI	50.9	39.3	11.6	14.2	0.6	13.6	65.1	(18.8)	39.9	(18.1)	25.2	(20.0)
	DAUSA	**278.5**	**217.6**	**60.9**	**68**	**2.8**	**65.1**	**346.3**	**(100.0)**	**220.3**	**(100.1)**	**126.0**	**(100.0)**
100	BARI	33.2	32.0	1.1	4.8	0.3	4.5	38.0	(20.1)	32.4	(19.2)	5.6	(27.2)
101	BASERI	42.3	40.7	1.7	7.4	0.1	7.3	49.7	(26.2)	40.8	(24.2)	8.9	(43.7)
102	DHAULPUR	56.0	53.7	2.3	2.3	0.4	1.9	58.3	(30.8)	54.1	(32.1)	4.2	(20.4)
103	RAJAKHERA	42.3	41.3	1.0	1.1	0.2	0.9	43.3	(22.9)	41.5	(24.6)	1.8	(8.7)
	DHAULPUR	**173.8**	**167.7**	**6.1**	**15.6**	**1**	**14.6**	**189.3**	**(100.0)**	**168.8**	**(100.1)**	**20.5**	**(100.0)**
104	ASPUR	43.1	36.0	7.1	17.1	0.7	16.4	60.2	(16.2)	36.8	(17.6)	23.4	(14.3)
105	BICHHIWARA	52.7	45.7	7.0	31.3	1.0	30.3	84.1	(22.6)	46.7	(22.3)	37.4	(22.9)
106	DUNGARPUR	41.6	33.1	8.5	21.9	0.9	21.0	63.5	(17.1)	34.1	(16.3)	29.4	(18.1)
107	SAGWARA	50.3	39.6	10.7	20.8	0.9	19.9	71.1	(19.1)	40.5	(19.3)	30.6	(18.8)
108	SIMALWARA	59.8	49.8	10.0	33.9	1.6	32.3	93.7	(25.2)	51.4	(24.5)	42.3	(25.9)
	DUNGARPUR	**247.5**	**204.2**	**43.3**	**125**	**5.1**	**119.9**	**372.6**	**(100.2)**	**209.5**	**(100.0)**	**163.1**	**(100.0)**
109	ANUPGARH	93.0	85.4	7.5	22.2	0.6	21.6	115.2	(23.2)	86.0	(23.2)	29.2	(23.2)
110	GANGANAGAR	51.8	48.3	3.5	8.7	0.3	8.4	60.4	(12.2)	48.5	(13.1)	11.9	(9.5)
111	KARANPUR	29.1	27.5	1.6	17.9	1.0	16.9	46.9	(9.4)	28.5	(7.7)	18.4	(14.6)
112	PADAMPUR	29.9	28.9	0.9	6.2	0.2	6.0	36.1	(7.3)	29.2	(7.9)	6.9	(5.5)
113	RAISINGHNAGAR	39.7	35.8	4.0	19.3	1.2	18.2	59.1	(11.9)	36.9	(9.9)	22.2	(17.6)
114	SADULSHAHAR	64.6	61.7	3.0	11.7	0.4	11.2	76.3	(15.4)	62.1	(16.7)	14.2	(11.3)
115	SURATGARH	85.4	79.0	6.4	17.4	0.6	16.7	102.8	(20.7)	79.7	(21.5)	23.1	(18.3)
	GANGANAGAR	**393.5**	**366.6**	**26.9**	**103.4**	**4.3**	**99**	**496.8**	**(100.0)**	**370.9**	**(100.0)**	**125.9**	**(100.0)**
116	BHADRA	57.2	45.6	11.5	22.3	0.4	21.9	79.5	(24.6)	46.0	(21.4)	33.5	(31.0)
117	HANUMANGARH	99.9	93.5	6.4	20.5	0.7	19.9	120.5	(37.2)	94.2	(43.8)	26.3	(24.3)

P. Code	Panchayat Samiti	% Share to Total Workers		Non Workers (000 No.)			Work Participation Rate		
		Male	Female	Person	Male	Female	Person	Male	Female
1	2	12	13	14	15	16	17	18	19
55	ASIND	55.7	44.3	76.8	34.3	42.5	50.8	56.2	45.2
56	BANERA	59.1	40.9	43.1	18.5	24.6	51.1	59.0	42.8
57	HURDA	60.8	39.2	37.5	16.2	21.3	48.7	57.1	39.5
58	JAHAZPUR	60.6	39.4	72.2	32.6	39.6	45.7	52.9	37.6
59	KOTRI	59.2	40.8	59.8	26.3	33.5	50.9	58.2	43.1
60	MANDAL	55.8	44.2	70.7	31.0	39.7	51.9	57.9	45.9
61	MANDALGARH	60.9	39.1	76.4	33.6	42.8	51.2	59.1	42.2
62	RAIPUR	61.7	38.3	39.3	15.6	23.7	45.0	56.0	34.2
63	SAHARA	53.8	46.2	39.9	17.4	22.5	53.1	58.2	48.2
64	SHAHPURA	58.6	41.4	59.8	26.6	33.3	50.4	57.3	43.1
65	SUWANA	59.6	40.4	63.1	26.5	36.6	51.3	60.0	42.4
	BHILWARA	**58.5**	**41.5**	**638.6**	**278.6**	**360.1**	**50.2**	**57.4**	**42.6**
66	BIKANER	66.6	33.3	135.1	59.5	75.6	41.8	52.0	30.0
67	DUNGARGARH *	54.6	45.4	69.0	33.8	35.2	48.4	51.1	45.4
68	KOLAYAT	67.5	32.5	78.2	33.9	44.3	41.1	52.1	28.6
69	LUNKARANSAR	67.8	32.2	94.3	40.0	54.3	39.7	51.3	26.9
70	NOKHA	59.8	40.2	118.2	54.3	63.9	43.4	49.9	36.3
	BIKANER **	**65.0**	**35.0**	**425.8**	**187.7**	**238.1**	**41.7**	**51.3**	**30.9**
71	HINDOLI	62.9	37.1	82.9	37.0	46.0	45.3	53.9	35.7
72	KESHORAIPATAN	67.0	33.0	88.0	37.6	50.4	41.0	52.2	28.6
73	NAINWA	62.3	37.7	66.9	30.5	36.5	45.0	52.8	36.1
74	TALERA	69.5	30.5	126.6	53.2	73.4	40.8	53.3	26.7
	BUNDI	**65.8**	**34.2**	**364.4**	**158.3**	**206.3**	**42.7**	**53.1**	**31.1**
75	ARNOD	55.4	44.6	47.0	21.8	25.2	48.6	53.0	44.0
76	BARI SADRI	53.4	46.6	35.4	16.7	18.7	54.1	57.1	51.0
77	BEGUN	57.4	42.6	40.0	17.7	22.3	53.4	59.7	46.7
78	BHADESAR	54.4	44.6	40.7	18.7	21.9	54.6	59.1	49.9
79	BHAINSRORGARH	59.7	40.3	32.1	14.8	17.3	49.7	56.2	42.5
80	BHOPALSAGAR	57.0	43.0	31.1	13.8	17.3	51.5	57.8	45.0
81	CHHOTI SADRI	53.7	46.3	38.9	18.7	20.2	54.2	56.9	51.5
82	CHITTAURGARH	55.2	44.8	63.2	29.2	34.0	53.4	57.8	48.9
83	DUNGLA	54.6	45.4	36.5	16.9	19.6	52.6	56.7	48.6
84	GANGRAR	56.9	43.1	33.6	15.2	18.4	55.3	60.9	49.3
85	KAPASAN	54.8	45.2	32.0	14.4	17.6	56.1	60.8	51.3
86	NIMBAHERA	55.8	44.2	52.8	24.2	28.6	52.1	57.0	47.0
87	PRATAPGARH	56.6	43 4	81.3	37.4	43.9	48.9	54.1	43.5
88	RASHMI	54.4	45.6	30.7	13.8	17.0	53.3	58.1	48.6
	CHITTAURGARH	**55.7**	**44.3**	**595.3**	**273.3**	**322**	**52.5**	**57.3**	**47.5**
89	CHURU	57.9	42.1	72.9	33.8	39.2	40.9	46.4	35.0
90	RAJGARH	53.2	46.8	122.3	61.2	61.1	44.8	46.3	43.1
91	RATANGARH	58.4	41.6	71.4	33.2	38.2	43.1	48.8	37.1
92	SARDARSHAHAR	62.8	37.2	103.5	45.5	57.9	40.9	49.7	31.5
93	SUJANGARH	58.4	41.6	110.5	51.2	59.4	43.2	48.9	37.0
94	TARANAGAR	53.2	46.8	65.4	32.5	32.9	47.3	49.0	45.5
	CHURU ***	**56.8**	**43.2**	**615**	**291.2**	**323.9**	**44.0**	**48.5**	**39.1**
95	BANDIKUI	64.7	35.3	117.0	53.8	63.3	37.2	45.5	27.9
96	DAUSA	62.1	37.9	123.9	58.0	65.9	40.4	47.4	32.6
97	LALSOT	65.8	34.2	115.2	51.4	63.8	38.5	48.0	27.9
98	MAHWA	64.4	35.6	91.1	43.3	47.8	37.9	45.3	29.3
99	SIKRAI	61.3	38.7	95.5	44.9	50.6	40.5	47.0	33.2
	DAUSA	**63.6**	**36.4**	**542.7**	**251.4**	**291.4**	**38.9**	**46.7**	**30.2**
100	BARI	85.3	14.7	79.4	34.2	45.2	32.4	48.7	11.0
101	BASERI	82.1	17.9	101.4	43.7	57.7	32.9	48.3	13.5
102	DHAULPUR	92.8	7.2	142.8	57.7	85.0	29.0	48.4	4.7
103	RAJAKHERA	95.8	4.2	107.7	43.1	64.6	28.7	49.1	2.7
	DHAULPUR	**89.2**	**10.8**	**431.3**	**178.7**	**252.5**	**30.5**	**48.6**	**7.5**
104	ASPUR	61.1	38.9	86.3	34.6	51.7	41.1	51.6	31.1
105	BICHHIWARA	55.5	44.5	96.7	44.8	52.0	46.5	51.0	41.9
106	DUNGARPUR	53.7	46.3	69.7	31.8	37.9	47.7	51.8	43.8
107	SAGWARA	57.0	43.0	89.5	39.0	50.5	44.3	51.0	37.7
108	SIMALWARA	54.9	45.1	96.0	45.1	50.9	49.4	53.3	45.4
	DUNGARPUR	**56.2**	**43.8**	**438.2**	**195.3**	**243**	**46.0**	**51.8**	**40.2**
109	ANUPGARH	74.7	25.3	178.9	71.2	107.7	39.2	54.7	21.3
110	GANGANAGAR	80.3	19.7	102.0	38.9	63.1	37.2	55.5	15.9
111	KARANPUR	60.8	39.2	45.2	19.9	25.3	50.9	58.9	42.0
112	PADAMPUR	80.9	19.1	69.8	26.4	43.4	34.1	52.6	13.7
113	RAISINGHNAGAR	62.4	37.6	69.8	30.3	39.4	45.9	54.9	36.1
114	SADULSHAHAR	81.4	18.6	132.1	49.8	82.3	36.6	55.5	14.7
115	SURATGARH	77.5	22.5	171.6	68.5	103.1	37.5	53.8	18.3
	GANGANAGAR	**74.7**	**25.3**	**769.4**	**305**	**464.3**	**39.2**	**54.9**	**21.3**
116	BHADRA	57.9	42.1	101.3	48.9	52.4	44.0	48.5	39.0
117	HANUMANGARH	78.2	21.8	213.4	82.5	130.9	36.1	53.3	16.7

P. Code	Panchayat Samiti	Working Population: Main Workers Person	Main Workers Male	Main Workers Female	Marginal Workers Person	Marginal Workers Male	Marginal Workers Female	Total Workers Person	% Share in District	Total Workers Male	% Share in District	Total Workers Female	% Share in District (000 No.)
1	2	3	4	5	6	7	8	9		10		11	
118	NOHAR	86.4	74.2	12.2	37.2	0.9	36.3	123.5	(38.2)	75.1	(34.9)	48.4	(44.7)
	HANUMANGARH	**243.5**	**213.3**	**30.1**	**80**	**2**	**78.1**	**323.5**	**(100.0)**	**215.3**	**(100.1)**	**108.2**	**(100.0)**
119	AMBER	67.2	48.8	18.4	14.6	0.7	13.9	81.8	(10.3)	49.5	(9.6)	32.3	(11.4)
120	BASSI	61.5	39.5	22.0	6.4	0.5	5.9	67.9	(8.5)	40.1	(7.8)	27.8	(9.8)
121	CHAKSU	51.7	33.1	18.6	7.8	0.7	7.1	59.5	(7.5)	33.8	(6.6)	25.7	(9.1)
122	DUDU	68.9	52.8	16.2	14.4	0.6	13.8	83.3	(10.5)	53.4	(10.4)	29.9	(10.6)
123	GOVINDGARH	55.9	46.9	8.9	11.9	0.6	11.3	67.7	(8.5)	47.5	(9.2)	20.2	(7.1)
124	JAMWA RAMGARH	62.0	46.6	15.4	13.9	0.7	13.2	75.9	(9.5)	47.4	(9.2)	28.5	(10.1)
125	JHOTWARA	31.9	24.8	7.1	3.1	0.2	2.9	35.0	(4.4)	25.0	(4.9)	10.0	(3.5)
126	KOTPUTLI	48.6	40.1	8.5	12.9	0.7	12.3	61.6	(7.7)	40.8	(7.9)	20.8	(7.3)
127	PHAGI	46.4	34.1	12.3	10.0	0.7	9.4	56.5	(7.1)	34.8	(6.8)	21.7	(7.7)
128	SAMBHAR	44.6	37.3	7.3	10.0	0.3	9.7	54.6	(6.9)	37.6	(7.3)	17.0	(6.0)
129	SANGANER	50.9	38.4	12.5	8.4	0.4	8.0	59.3	(7.4)	38.8	(7.6)	20.5	(7.3)
130	SHAHPURA	33.9	28.2	5.7	9.9	0.3	9.6	43.8	(5.5)	28.5	(5.5)	15.3	(5.4)
131	VIRATNAGAR	41.9	36.3	5.6	8.0	0.3	7.8	50.0	(6.3)	36.6	(7.1)	13.4	(4.7)
	JAIPUR	**665.4**	**506.9**	**158.5**	**131.3**	**6.7**	**124.9**	**796.9**	**(100.1)**	**513.8**	**(100.0)**	**283.1**	**(100.0)**
132	JAISALMER	25.0	22.3	2.7	3.4	0.5	2.9	28.4	(25.6)	22.8	(28.3)	5.6	(18.5)
133	SAM	28.3	25.7	2.6	5.7	1.4	4.3	34.0	(30.6)	27.1	(33.6)	6.9	(22.8)
134	SANKRA	32.7	29.4	3.3	15.9	1.4	14.4	48.6	(43.8)	30.8	(38.2)	17.8	(58.7)
	JAISALMER	**86**	**77.4**	**8.6**	**25**	**3.3**	**21.6**	**111**	**(100.0)**	**80.7**	**(100.1)**	**30.3**	**(100.0)**
135	AHORE	57.7	38.0	19.7	17.8	3.3	14.5	75.5	(16.9)	41.3	(14.9)	34.2	(20.0)
136	BHINMAL	45.3	37.3	8.0	16.3	0.4	15.9	61.6	(13.8)	37.7	(13.6)	23.9	(14.0)
137	JALOR	33.1	26.2	6.9	9.3	0.8	8.5	42.3	(9.5)	26.9	(9.7)	15.4	(9.0)
138	JASWANTPURA	33.0	26.2	6.8	10.3	0.9	9.5	43.3	(9.7)	27.0	(9.8)	16.3	(9.6)
139	RANIWARA	40.7	32.4	8.3	9.1	0.3	8.8	49.8	(11.1)	32.7	(11.8)	17.1	(10.0)
140	SANCHORE	83.3	67.7	15.7	26.4	0.9	25.6	109.8	(24.6)	68.6	(24.8)	41.2	(24.2)
141	SAYLA	50.7	41.8	8.9	14.1	0.5	13.6	64.8	(14.5)	42.4	(15.3)	22.4	(13.2)
	JALOR	**343.8**	**269.6**	**74.3**	**103.3**	**7.1**	**96.4**	**447.1**	**(100.1)**	**276.6**	**(100.0)**	**170.5**	**(100.0)**
142	BAKANI	55.7	37.7	18.0	10.8	0.5	10.3	66.5	(17.7)	38.2	(16.4)	28.3	(19.9)
143	DAG	50.8	41.3	9.5	3.8	0.3	3.5	54.6	(14.5)	41.7	(17.9)	12.9	(9.1)
144	JHALRAPATAN	69.0	46.7	22.3	7.3	0.5	6.8	76.4	(20.4)	47.2	(20.2)	29.2	(20.5)
145	KHANPUR	41.9	30.9	11.0	6.3	0.2	6.1	48.2	(12.8)	31.2	(13.3)	17.0	(12.0)
146	MANOHARTHANA	51.7	35.9	15.8	13.7	0.5	13.1	65.4	(17.4)	36.5	(15.7)	28.9	(20.3)
147	PIRAWA	55.9	38.2	17.7	8.2	0.4	7.9	64.2	(17.1)	38.6	(16.6)	25.6	(18.0)
	JHALAWAR	**325**	**230.7**	**94.3**	**50.1**	**2.4**	**47.7**	**375.3**	**(100.0)**	**233.4**	**(100.1)**	**141.9**	**(100.0)**
148	ALSISAR	31.6	23.9	7.6	10.8	0.6	10.2	42.4	(9.4)	24.6	(8.7)	17.8	(10.5)
149	BUHANA	43.3	36.4	7.0	25.8	2.9	22.9	69.1	(15.3)	39.2	(13.9)	29.9	(17.6)
150	CHIRAWA	29.9	27.2	2.6	13.1	1.3	11.8	43.0	(9.5)	28.6	(10.2)	14.4	(8.5)
151	JHUNJHUNUN	38.9	32.5	6.3	20.5	1.0	19.4	59.4	(13.2)	33.6	(12.0)	25.8	(15.2)
152	KHETRI	43.2	39.9	3.3	16.9	0.9	16.0	60.1	(13.3)	40.8	(14.5)	19.3	(11.4)
153	NAWALGARH	42.0	38.0	4.0	14.0	0.7	13.3	56.1	(12.4)	38.8	(13.8)	17.3	(10.2)
154	SURAJGARH	40.0	32.3	7.7	14.4	1.3	13.1	54.4	(12.1)	33.6	(12.0)	20.8	(12.2)
155	UDAIPURWATI	44.7	39.8	4.9	21.9	2.2	19.7	66.7	(14.8)	42.1	(14.9)	24.6	(14.5)
	JHUNJHUNUN	**313.6**	**270**	**43.4**	**137.4**	**10.9**	**126.4**	**451.2**	**(100.0)**	**281.3**	**(100.0)**	**169.9**	**(100.0)**
156	BALESAR	35.3	29.8	5.4	14.8	1.2	13.6	50.1	(8.8)	31.1	(8.9)	19.0	(8.7)
157	BAP	31.4	26.4	5.0	8.0	0.5	7.6	39.4	(6.9)	26.8	(7.7)	12.6	(5.8)
158	BHOPALGARH	52.1	38.1	14.0	18.6	1.3	17.3	70.7	(12.4)	39.4	(11.3)	31.3	(14.3)
159	BILARA	51.9	35.3	16.6	11.6	0.8	10.8	63.5	(11.2)	36.1	(10.3)	27.4	(12.5)
160	LUNI	58.4	42.0	16.4	11.3	0.6	10.7	69.7	(12.3)	42.7	(12.2)	27.0	(12.4)
161	MANDOR	36.1	27.9	8.2	7.9	0.5	7.4	44.0	(7.7)	28.4	(8.1)	15.6	(7.1)
162	OSIAN	98.8	75.4	23.4	19.9	1.0	18.9	118.7	(20.9)	76.4	(21.8)	42.3	(19.4)
163	PHALODI	46.6	39.2	7.4	17.2	0.8	16.4	63.8	(11.2)	40.0	(11.4)	23.8	(10.9)
164	SHERGARH	36.8	28.6	8.2	11.8	0.8	11.0	48.6	(8.5)	29.4	(8.4)	19.2	(8.8)
	JODHPUR	**447.4**	**342.7**	**104.6**	**121.1**	**7.5**	**113.7**	**568.5**	**(100.0)**	**350.3**	**(100.1)**	**218.2**	**(100.0)**
165	HINDAUN	55.8	48.2	7.7	15.9	0.5	15.4	71.7	(23.0)	48.7	(23.6)	23.0	(21.8)
166	KARAULI	53.0	44.7	8.3	14.2	0.7	13.5	67.2	(21.5)	45.4	(22.0)	21.8	(20.6)
167	NADOTI	29.1	24.2	4.9	11.1	0.5	10.6	40.3	(12.9)	24.7	(12.0)	15.6	(14.8)
168	SAPOTRA	59.2	49.2	10.0	16.1	1.2	14.9	75.2	(24.1)	50.4	(24.4)	24.8	(23.5)
169	TODABHIM	48.1	36.8	11.3	9.4	0.3	9.1	57.5	(18.4)	37.1	(18.0)	20.4	(19.3)
	KARAULI	**245.2**	**203.1**	**42.2**	**66.7**	**3.2**	**63.5**	**311.9**	**(100.0)**	**206.3**	**(100.0)**	**105.6**	**(100.0)**
170	CHECHAT	45.1	33.8	11.3	5.4	0.3	5.1	50.5	(21.2)	34.1	(21.2)	16.4	(21.2)
171	ITAWA	38.3	33.1	5.3	11.0	0.5	10.5	49.4	(20.7)	33.6	(20.9)	15.8	(20.4)
172	LADPURA	35.2	28.5	6.7	5.9	0.2	5.7	41.1	(17.3)	28.7	(17.9)	12.4	(16.0)
173	SANGOD	38.6	31.4	7.2	13.5	0.7	12.8	52.1	(21.9)	32.1	(20.0)	20.0	(25.8)
174	SULTANPUR	38.6	31.9	6.8	6.4	0.3	6.1	45.0	(18.9)	32.2	(20.0)	12.8	(16.5)
	KOTA	**195.8**	**158.7**	**37.3**	**42.2**	**2**	**40.2**	**238.1**	**(100.0)**	**160.7**	**(100.0)**	**77.4**	**(100.0)**
175	DEGANA	56.5	38.4	18.1	12.1	0.7	11.4	68.6	(9.0)	39.1	(8.7)	29.5	(9.6)
176	DIDWANA	73.1	51.0	22.1	14.1	0.9	13.3	87.3	(11.5)	51.9	(11.5)	35.4	(11.5)
177	JAYAL	65.7	43.4	22.3	11.3	0.6	10.6	77.0	(10.1)	44.0	(9.8)	33.0	(10.7)
178	KUCHAMAN	64.8	49.7	15.2	12.9	0.7	12.1	77.7	(10.2)	50.4	(11.2)	27.3	(8.8)
179	LADNU	40.3	28.4	11.9	10.5	0.7	9.8	50.9	(6.7)	29.1	(6.5)	21.8	(7.1)
180	MAKRANA	50.6	38.2	12.4	11.0	0.7	10.4	61.6	(8.1)	38.9	(8.6)	22.7	(7.4)

P. Code	Panchayat Samiti	% Share to Total Workers		Non Workers (000 No.)			Work Participation Rate		
		Male	Female	Person	Male	Female	Person	Male	Female
1	2	12	13	14	15	16	17	18	19
118	NOHAR	60.8	39.2	166.3	76.9	89.5	42.6	49.4	35.1
	HANUMANGARH	**66.6**	**33.4**	**481**	**208.3**	**272.8**	**40.2**	**50.8**	**28.4**
119	AMBER	60.5	39.5	123.6	58.1	65.5	39.8	46.0	33.0
120	BASSI	59.1	40.9	91.9	43.9	48.0	42.5	47.6	36.7
121	CHAKSU	56.8	43.2	66.2	32.0	34.1	47.3	51.3	43.0
122	DUDU	64.1	35.9	127.4	56.7	70.7	39.5	48.5	29.7
123	GOVINDGARH	70.2	29.8	142.7	62.4	80.3	32.2	43.2	20.1
124	JAMWA RAMGARH	62.5	37.5	114.9	52.9	62.0	39.8	47.3	31.5
125	JHOTWARA	71.4	28.6	68.1	29.7	38.4	34.0	45.7	20.7
126	KOTPUTLI	66.2	33.8	116.0	52.2	63.9	34.7	43.9	24.6
127	PHAGI	61.6	38.4	74.0	33.7	40.3	43.3	50.8	35.0
128	SAMBHAR	68.9	31.1	107.6	46.5	61.2	33.7	44.7	21.7
129	SANGANER	65.4	34.6	94.6	42.5	52.0	38.5	47.7	28.4
130	SHAHPURA	65.1	34.9	84.4	38.6	45.8	34.2	42.4	25.1
131	VIRATNAGAR	73.2	26.8	105.3	45.1	60.2	32.2	44.8	18.2
	JAIPUR	**64.5**	**35.5**	**1316.7**	**594.3**	**722.4**	**37.7**	**46.4**	**28.2**
132	JAISALMER	80.3	19.7	51.9	22.3	29.6	35.4	50.5	15.9
133	SAM	79.7	20.3	60.9	25.8	35.1	35.8	51.2	16.4
134	SANKRA	63.4	36.6	67.1	31.4	35.7	42.0	49.5	33.3
	JAISALMER	**72.7**	**27.3**	**179.9**	**79.5**	**100.4**	**38.2**	**50.3**	**23.2**
135	AHORE	54.7	45.3	74.7	34.4	40.3	50.3	54.6	45.9
136	BHINMAL	61.2	38.8	84.6	38.0	46.6	42.1	49.8	33.9
137	JALOR	63.6	36.4	65.6	27.9	37.7	39.2	49.1	29.0
138	JASWANTPURA	62.4	37.6	63.0	27.2	35.8	40.7	49.8	31.3
139	RANIWARA	65.7	34.3	73.3	31.4	41.9	40.4	51.0	29.0
140	SANCHORE	62.5	37.5	150.6	66.8	83.8	42.2	50.6	33.0
141	SAYLA	65.4	34.6	100.4	42.1	58.3	39.2	50.2	27.9
	JALOR	**61.9**	**38.1**	**612.2**	**267.8**	**344.4**	**42.2**	**50.8**	**33.1**
142	BAKANI	57.4	42.6	63.3	29.4	33.9	51.2	56.5	45.5
143	DAG	76.4	23.6	84.1	29.9	54.2	39.4	58.3	19.4
144	JHALRAPATAN	61.8	38.2	86.6	37.7	48.9	46.9	55.6	37.3
145	KHANPUR	64.7	35.3	70.3	31.4	38.9	40.7	49.8	30.5
146	MANOHARTHANA	55.8	44.2	60.7	29.3	31.3	51.9	55.5	48.0
147	PIRAWA	60.1	39.9	65.8	28.8	37.0	49.4	57.3	40.9
	JHALAWAR	**62.2**	**37.8**	**430.8**	**186.5**	**244.2**	**46.6**	**55.6**	**36.8**
148	ALSISAR	58.0	42.0	70.3	32.4	38.0	37.6	43.1	31.9
149	BUHANA	56.7	43.3	103.7	50.0	53.7	40.0	43.9	35.8
150	CHIRAWA	66.5	33.5	81.6	35.4	46.2	34.5	44.7	23.9
151	JHUNJHUNUN	56.6	43.4	98.0	46.4	51.5	37.8	42.0	33.4
152	KHETRI	67.9	32.1	119.7	53.9	65.8	33.4	43.1	22.7
153	NAWALGARH	69.2	30.8	125.2	53.8	71.5	30.9	41.9	19.5
154	SURAJGARH	61.8	38.2	86.8	40.1	46.7	38.5	45.6	30.8
155	UDAIPURWATI	63.1	36.9	120.9	54.2	66.7	35.6	43.6	26.9
	JHUNJHUNUN	**62.3**	**37.7**	**806.2**	**366.2**	**440.1**	**35.9**	**43.4**	**27.9**
156	BALESAR	61.1	37.9	77.4	35.2	42.3	39.3	46.9	31.0
157	BAP	68.0	32.0	64.2	28.2	36.1	38.0	48.7	25.9
158	BHOPALGARH	55.7	44.3	85.8	41.7	44.1	45.2	48.6	41.5
159	BILARA	56.9	43.1	78.1	37.7	40.4	44.8	48.9	40.4
160	LUNI	61.3	38.7	97.0	44.3	52.7	41.8	49.0	33.8
161	MANDOR	64.5	35.5	68.0	30.4	37.6	39.3	48.4	29.3
162	OSIAN	64.4	35.6	187.7	83.7	104.1	38.7	47.7	28.9
163	PHALODI	62.7	37.3	97.6	44.3	53.3	39.5	47.5	31.0
164	SHERGARH	60.5	39.5	64.5	30.3	34.1	43.0	49.3	36.1
	JODHPUR	**61.6**	**38.4**	**820.3**	**375.8**	**444.7**	**40.9**	**48.2**	**32.9**
165	HINDAUN	67.9	32.1	124.6	58.4	66.2	36.5	45.5	25.8
166	KARAULI	67.6	32.4	99.3	46.2	53.1	40.4	49.6	29.1
167	NADOTI	61.3	38.7	61.4	29.9	31.6	39.6	45.3	33.1
168	SAPOTRA	67.0	33.0	107.2	49.4	57.8	41.2	50.5	30.0
169	TODABHIM	64.5	35.5	96.9	46.7	50.2	37.2	44.3	28.9
	KARAULI	**66.1**	**33.9**	**489.4**	**230.6**	**258.9**	**38.9**	**47.2**	**29.0**
170	CHECHAT	67.5	32.5	70.1	30.0	40.1	41.9	53.2	29.0
171	ITAWA	68.0	32.0	77.8	33.7	44.0	38.9	49.9	26.4
172	LADPURA	69.8	30.2	68.5	29.1	39.4	37.5	49.7	23.9
173	SANGOD	61.6	38.4	70.5	32.2	38.3	42.5	49.9	34.3
174	SULTANPUR	71.6	28.4	78.8	33.2	45.6	36.3	49.2	21.9
	KOTA	**67.5**	**32.5**	**365.7**	**158.2**	**207.4**	**39.4**	**50.4**	**27.2**
175	DEGANA	57.0	43.0	85.7	39.6	46.1	44.5	49.7	39.0
176	DIDWANA	59.5	40.5	136.9	61.2	75.7	38.9	45.9	31.9
177	JAYAL	57.1	42.9	99.7	46.4	53.3	43.6	48.6	38.2
178	KUCHAMAN	64.9	35.1	127.4	55.1	72.3	37.9	47.8	27.4
179	LADNU	57.2	42.8	72.3	33.2	39.1	41.3	46.7	35.8
180	MAKRANA	63.1	3.9	94.7	41.1	53.6	39.4	48.7	29.7

P. Code	Panchayat Samiti	Working Population											(000 No.)
		Main Workers			Marginal Workers			Total Workers					
		Person	Male	Female	Person	Male	Female	Person	% Share in District	Male	% Share in District	Female	% Share in District
1	2	3	4	5	6	7	8	9		10		11	
181	MERTA	54.8	36.8	18.0	7.0	0.6	6.4	61.8	(8.1)	37.4	(8.3)	24.4	(7.9)
182	MUNDWA	55.2	39.0	16.2	13.9	0.9	13.0	69.1	(9.1)	40.0	(8.9)	29.1	(9.4)
183	NAGAUR	61.0	44.1	16.8	14.5	1.3	13.2	75.5	(9.9)	45.4	(10.1)	30.1	(9.8)
184	PARBATSAR	49.3	36.5	12.8	14.1	0.8	13.3	63.4	(8.3)	37.3	(8.3)	26.1	(8.5)
185	RIYAN	57.3	37.2	20.1	9.7	0.5	9.2	67.0	(8.8)	37.7	(8.4)	29.3	(9.5)
	NAGAUR	**628.6**	**442.7**	**185.9**	**131.1**	**8.4**	**122.7**	**759.9**	**(100.0)**	**451.2**	**(100.3)**	**308.7**	**(100.0)**
186	BALI	45.3	36.3	8.9	11.5	0.5	11.0	56.8	(12.1)	36.9	(12.9)	19.9	(10.8)
187	DESURI	25.6	20.1	5.5	5.1	0.1	5.0	30.7	(6.5)	20.2	(7.1)	10.5	(5.7)
188	JAITARAN	47.8	33.6	14.3	10.7	0.5	10.2	58.5	(12.5)	34.1	(12.0)	24.4	(13.2)
189	KHARCHI / MARWAR JUN.	46.3	35.6	10.8	15.5	0.7	14.8	61.8	(13.2)	36.2	(12.7)	25.6	(13.9)
190	PALI	27.5	22.0	5.5	8.2	0.4	7.9.	35.8	(7.6)	22.4	(7.9)	13.4	(7.3)
191	RAIPUR	45.8	31.5	14.3	8.6	0.4	8.2	54.4	(11.6)	31.9	(11.2)	22.5	(12.2)
192	RANI STATION	29.8	21.5	8.3	6.1	0.5	5.6	35.8	(7.6)	22.0	(7.7)	13.8	(7.5)
193	ROHAT	29.5	20.5	9.0	6.3	0.4	5.9	35.8	(7.6)	20.9	(7.3)	14.9	(8.1)
194	SOJAT	46.4	32.1	14.3	11.6	0.4	11.2	58.0	(12.4)	32.5	(11.4)	25.5	(13.8)
195	SUMERPUR	33.7	28.1	5.6	8.3	0.2	8.0	41.9	(8.9)	28.3	(9.9)	13.6	(7.4)
	PALI	**377.7**	**281.3**	**96.5**	**91.9**	**4.1**	**87.8**	**469.5**	**(100.0)**	**285.4**	**(100.1)**	**184.1**	**(100.0)**
196	AMET	26.5	20.4	6.1	5.3	0.3	5.0	31.8	(10.7)	20.7	(11.4)	11.1	(9.5)
197	BHIM	34.1	22.1	12.0	10.2	0.4	9.7	44.3	(14.8)	22.6	(12.4)	21.7	(18.5)
198	DEOGARH	21.2	16.5	4.6	5.6	0.2	5.4	26.8	(9.0)	16.8	(9.2)	10.0	(8.5)
199	KHAMNOR	36.3	30.0	6.4	14.8	0.9	13.9	51.2	(17.2)	30.9	(17.1)	20.3	(17.4)
200	KUMBHALGARH	44.0	32.3	11.7	10.1	0.4	9.7	54.1	(18.1)	32.7	(18.0)	21.4	(18.3)
201	RAILMAGRA	37.8	27.6	10.2	8.9	0.4	8.4	46.7	(15.6)	28.1	(15.5)	18.6	(15.9)
202	RAJSAMAND	37.1	29.4	7.7	6.5	0.3	6.3	43.6	(14.6)	29.7	(16.4)	13.9	(11.9)
	RAJSAMAND	**237**	**178.3**	**58.7**	**61.4**	**2.9**	**58.4**	**298.5**	**(100.0)**	**181.5**	**(100.0)**	**117.0**	**(100.0)**
203	BAMANWAS	36.9	30.4	6.6	13.6	0.5	13.2	50.6	(16.4)	30.8	(16.3)	19.8	(16.7)
204	BONLI	54.4	43.2	11.2	21.6	1.1	20.6	76.1	(24.7)	44.3	(23.4)	31.8	(26.8)
205	GANGAPUR	42.7	35.9	6.8	13.5	0.7	12.8	56.2	(18.3)	36.6	(19.4)	19.6	(16.5)
206	KHANDAR	39.6	32.8	6.8	12.8	0.4	12.4	52.4	(17.0)	33.1	(17.5)	19.3	(16.3)
207	SAWAI MADHOPUR	57.4	43.6	13.8	15.1	0.7	14.4	72.5	(23.6)	44.3	(23.4)	28.2	(23.8)
	SAWAI MADHOPUR	**231**	**185.9**	**45.2**	**76.6**	**3.4**	**73.4**	**307.8**	**(100.0)**	**189.1**	**(100.0)**	**118.7**	**(100.0)**
208	DANTA RAMGARH	54.3	46.4	8.0	11.7	0.6	11.1	66.0	(13.5)	47.0	(14.6)	19.0	(11.4)
209	DHOND	44.9	37.9	7.0	13.0	0.8	12.2	57.9	(11.8)	38.7	(12.0)	19.2	(11.5)
210	FATEHPUR	43.7	33.8	9.9	21.2	1.5	19.6	64.9	(13.3)	35.4	(11.0)	29.5	(17.7)
211	KHANDELA	44.7	36.6	8.0	14.6	0.8	13.8	59.3	(12.1)	37.5	(11.6)	21.8	(13.1)
212	LACHHMANGARH	42.4	34.6	7.8	19.8	1.3	18.5	62.2	(12.7)	35.9	(11.1)	26.3	(15.8)
213	NEEM KA THANA	60.3	54.1	6.2	14.6	0.7	13.9	74.3	(15.2)	54.8	(17.0)	19.5	(11.7)
214	PIPRALI	41.1	36.5	4.5	14.4	0.7	13.7	55.5	(11.3)	37.2	(11.5)	18.3	(11.0)
215	SRI MADHOPUR	42.0	35.7	6.4	6.3	0.3	6.0	48.4	(9.9)	36.0	(11.1)	12.4	(7.4)
	SIKAR	**373.4**	**315.6**	**57.8**	**115.6**	**6.7**	**108.8**	**488.5**	**(100.0)**	**322.5**	**(100.0)**	**166.0**	**(100.0)**
216	ABU ROAD	25.4	22.0	3.4	7.7	0.4	7.3	33.1	(15.4)	22.4	(16.4)	10.7	(13.7)
217	PINDWARA	41.1	33.3	7.9	16.0	1.0	15.0	57.1	(26.6)	34.3	(25.1)	22.8	(29.3)
218	REODAR	46.2	34.1	12.0	9.3	0.8	8.6	55.5	(25.9)	34.9	(25.6)	20.6	(26.4)
219	SHEOGANJ	25.4	19.9	5.5	4.8	0.2	4.6	30.2	(14.1)	20.2	(14.8)	10.0	(12.8)
220	SIROHI	31.4	24.1	7.3	7.3	0.7	6.6	38.7	(18.0)	24.8	(18.2)	13.9	(17.8)
	SIROHI	**169.5**	**133.4**	**36.1**	**45.1**	**3.1**	**42.1**	**214.6**	**(100.0)**	**136.6**	**(100.1)**	**78.0**	**(100.0)**
221	DEOLI	52.4	36.0	16.4	8.5	0.4	8.0	60.9	(17.5)	36.5	(17.5)	24.4	(17.6)
222	MALPURA	55.7	39.5	16.2	8.9	0.3	8.6	64.6	(18.6)	39.9	(19.1)	24.7	(17.9)
223	NIWAI	51.4	35.2	16.2	10.0	0.5	9.6	61.4	(17.7)	35.7	(17.1)	25.7	(18.6)
224	TODARAISINGH	36.5	25.2	11.3	6.2	0.2	6.0	42.7	(12.3)	25.4	(12.2)	17.3	(12.5)
225	TONK	64.5	43.7	20.8	9.3	0.7	8.6	73.8	(21.2)	44.4	(21.2)	29.4	(21.2)
226	UNIARA	35.3	26.7	8.5	8.7	0.4	8.2	44.0	(12.7)	27.2	(13.0)	16.8	(12.1)
	TONK	**295.8**	**206.3**	**89.4**	**51.6**	**2.5**	**49**	**347.4**	**(100.0)**	**209.1**	**(100.1)**	**138.3**	**(100.0)**
227	BARGAON	43.9	35.4	8.6	14.5	0.6	13.9	58.4	(7.3)	36.0	(7.6)	22.4	(6.8)
228	BHINDER	62.6	47.1	15.5	22.1	0.7	21.3	84.7	(10.6)	47.9	(10.2)	36.8	(11.2)
229	DHARIAWAD	51.5	43.2	8.3	22.5	0.6	22.0	74.0	(9.2)	43.8	(9.3)	30.2	(9.2)
230	GIRWA	57.5	48.4	9.1	20.0	1.0	18.9	77.5	(9.7)	49.5	(10.5)	28.0	(8.5)
231	GOGUNDA	45.0	33.5	11.5	9.9	0.5	9.4	54.9	(6.9)	33.9	(7.2)	21.0	(6.4)
232	JHADOL	49.3	39.9	9.4	22.6	0.8	21.8	71.8	(9.0)	40.7	(8.6)	31.1	(9.5)
233	KHERWARA	54.5	45.2	9.2	31.5	1.5	30.0	85.9	(10.7)	46.8	(9.9)	39.1	(11.9)
234	KOTRA	46.2	35.6	10.6	17.9	0.8	17.0	64.0	(8.0)	36.4	(7.7)	27.6	(8.4)
235	MAVLI	58.1	45.1	13.0	16.0	0.4	15.6	74.1	(9.3)	45.5	(9.7)	28.6	(8.7)
236	SALUMBAR	53.1	44.5	8.6	26.7	1.7	25.0	79.8	(10.0)	46.1	(9.8)	33.7	(10.2)
237	SARADA	50.2	43.5	6.7	25.0	1.4	23.6	75.2	(9.4)	44.9	(9.5)	30.3	(9.2)
	UDAIPUR	**571.9**	**461.4**	**110.5**	**228.7**	**10**	**218.5**	**800.3**	**(100.1)**	**471.5**	**(100.0)**	**328.8**	**(100.0)**
	RAJASTHAN (RURAL)	**11179.1**	**8698.7**	**2480.3**	**3089.1**	**165.5**	**2923.7**	**14268.2**		**8864.2**		**5404.0**	

* Dungargarh PS Shifted from Churu to Bikaner District on 1st April 2001,
** Excluding Data of Dungarpur PS,
*** Including Data of Dungarpur PS.
Source: Computed from data given in Primary Census Abstract, Rajasthan, Series-21, Census of India, 1991.

P. Code	Panchayat Samiti	% Share to Total Workers		Non Workers (000 No.)			Work Participation Rate		
		Male	Female	Person	Male	Female	Person	Male	Female
1	2	12	13	14	15	16	17	18	19
181	MERTA	60.5	39.5	80.8	36.9	43.9	43.3	50.3	35.7
182	MUNDWA	57.9	42.1	83.7	39.2	44.5	45.2	50.5	39.5
183	NAGAUR	60.1	39.9	105.9	48.3	57.6	41.6	48.4	34.4
184	PARBATSAR	58.8	41.2	79.5	36.3	43.2	44.4	50.7	37.7
185	RIYAN	56.3	43.7	75.9	36.0	39.9	46.9	51.2	42.3
	NAGAUR	**59.4**	**40.6**	**1042.5**	**473.3**	**569.2**	**42.2**	**48.8**	**35.2**
186	BALI	65.0	35.0	92.5	38.3	54.2	38.1	49.0	26.8
187	DESURI	65.8	34.2	54.7	22.3	31.4	36.0	47.5	24.5
188	JAITARAN	58.3	41.7	76.3	35.1	41.2	43.4	49.3	37.2
189	KHARCHI / MARWAR JUN.	58.6	41.4	93.0	41.9	51.1	39.9	46.4	33.3
190	PALI	62.6	37.4	48.8	21.4	27.4	42.3	51.2	32.8
191	RAIPUR	58.6	41.4	77.7	35.5	42.3	41.2	47.4	34.7
192	RANI STATION	61.5	38.5	58.3	25.0	33.3	38.0	46.9	29.5
193	ROHAT	58.4	41.6	45.5	20.9	24.6	44.0	50.0	37.8
194	SOJAT	56.0	44.0	73.4	34.0	39.4	44.1	48.8	39.3
195	SUMERPUR	67.5	32.5	73.4	30.2	43.2	36.3	48.4	23.9
	PALI	**60.8**	**39.2**	**693.6**	**304.6**	**388.1**	**40.4**	**48.4**	**32.1**
196	AMET	65.1	34.9	39.8	15.6	24.1	44.4	57.0	31.5
197	BHIM	51.0	49.0	59.8	28.4	31.4	42.6	44.2	40.8
198	DEOGARH	62.7	37.3	37.1	15.0	22.1	42.0	52.7	31.1
199	KHAMNOR	60.4	39.6	60.9	24.8	36.2	45.7	55.5	36.0
200	KUMBHALGARH	60.4	39.6	59.4	24.3	35.1	47.7	57.4	37.8
201	RAILMAGRA	60.2	39.8	53.6	22.5	31.2	46.6	55.5	37.3
202	RAJSAMAND	68.1	31.9	64.9	25.0	39.9	40.2	54.3	25.8
	RAJSAMAND	**60.8**	**39.2**	**375.5**	**155.6**	**220**	**44.3**	**53.8**	**34.7**
203	BAMANWAS	60.9	39.1	69.7	33.6	36.1	42.1	47.8	35.5
204	BONLI	58.2	41.8	88.4	43.1	45.3	46.3	50.7	41.2
205	GANGAPUR	65.1	34.9	90.5	42.4	48.1	38.3	46.3	29.0
206	KHANDAR	63.2	36.8	67.0	31.1	35.9	43.9	51.5	35.0
207	SAWAI MADHOPUR	61.1	38.9	100.8	47.5	53.3	41.8	48.3	34.6
	SAWAI MADHOPUR	**61.4**	**38.6**	**416.4**	**197.7**	**218.7**	**42.5**	**48.9**	**35.2**
208	DANTA RAMGARH	71.2	28.8	140.4	59.0	81.5	32.0	44.4	18.9
209	DHOND	66.8	32.2	113.4	48.4	65.0	33.8	44.5	22.8
210	FATEHPU	54.5	45.5	92.5	43.5	49.0	41.2	44.8	37.6
211	KHANDELA	63.2	36.8	117.3	53.4	63.9	33.6	41.2	25.4
212	LACHHMANGARH	57.7	42.3	96.8	44.2	52.6	39.1	44.8	33.3
213	NEEM KA THANA	73.8	26.2	178.5	77.3	101.2	29.4	41.5	16.1
214	PIPRALI	67.0	33.0	108.6	47.1	61.5	33.8	44.1	22.9
215	SRI MADHOPUR	74.4	25.6	119.4	50.7	68.7	28.9	41.5	15.3
	SIKAR	**66.0**	**34.0**	**966.9**	**423.6**	**543.4**	**33.6**	**43.2**	**23.4**
216	ABU ROAD	67.7	32.3	47.5	19.2	28.4	41.1	53.9	27.4
217	PINDWARA	60.1	39.9	70.9	30.9	40.0	44.6	52.6	36.4
218	REODAR	62.9	37.1	76.6	33.0	43.7	42.0	51.4	32.1
219	SHEOGANJ	66.9	33.1	49.7	20.6	29.1	37.8	49.6	25.5
220	SIROHI	64.1	35.9	67.1	27.8	39.3	36.6	47.1	26.1
	SIROHI	**63.7**	**36.3**	**311.8**	**131.5**	**180.5**	**40.8**	**51.0**	**30.2**
221	DEOLI	59.9	40.1	74.7	34.1	40.5	44.9	51.7	37.6
222	MALPURA	61.8	38.2	83.8	37.0	46.8	43.5	51.9	34.6
223	NIWAI	58.1	41.9	76.0	35.2	40.9	44.7	50.4	38.6
224	TODARAISINGH	59.5	40.5	48.1	21.3	26.8	47.0	54.4	39.2
225	TONK	60.2	39.8	95.2	43.8	51.4	43.7	50.3	36.3
226	UNIARA	61.8	38.2	59.4	26.9	32.5	42.5	50.3	34.1
	TONK	**60.2**	**39.8**	**437.2**	**198.3**	**238.9**	**44.3**	**51.3**	**36.7**
227	BARGAON	61.6	38.4	65.0	27.8	37.2	47.3	56.4	37.5
228	BHINDER	56.6	43.4	84.7	38.0	46.7	50.0	55.8	44.0
229	DHARIAWAD	59.2	40.8	82.0	35.7	46.3	47.4	55.1	39.5
230	GIRWA	63.9	36.1	99.7	41.8	57.9	43.7	54.3	32.7
231	GOGUNDA	61.7	38.3	66.8	27.7	39.1	45.1	55.0	35.0
232	JHADOL	57.7	43.3	75.2	34.5	40.7	48.8	54.1	43.3
233	KHERWARA	54.5	45.5	113.1	51.7	61.5	43.2	47.6	38.9
234	KOTRA	56.9	43.1	66.4	30.3	36.1	49.1	54.5	43.3
235	MAVLI	61.4	38.6	90.3	38.4	51.9	45.1	54.2	35.6
236	SALUMBAR	57.8	42.2	81.8	34.6	47.2	49.4	57.1	41.7
237	SARADA	59.7	40.3	95.8	40.1	55.7	44.0	52.8	35.2
	UDAIPUR	**58.9**	**41.1**	**920.8**	**400.6**	**520.3**	**46.5**	**54.1**	**38.7**
	RAJASTHAN (RURAL)	**62.1**	**37.9**	**19670.8**	**8822.2**	**10848.4**	**42.0**	**50.1**	**33.3**

* Dungargarh PS Shifted from Churu to Bikaner District on 1st April 2001,
** Excluding Data of Dungarpur PS.
*** Including Data of Dungarpur PS.
Source: Computed from data given in Primary Census Abstract, Rajasthan, Series-21, Census of India, 1991.

PANCHAYAT SAMITI-WISE PANCHAYATS AND POPULATION

P. Code	Panchayat Samiti (Concerning Tehsil)	Total No. of Villages	Total No. of Gram Panchayats	Total Population					% share of District Rural Pop.
				Person	Male		Female		
					No.	%	No.	%	
1	2	3	4	5	6	7	8	9	10
1	ARAIN (Sarwar)	129	30	133386	68020	(51.0)	65366	(49.0)	(10.2)
2	BHINAY (Bhinay)	128	35	155111	79164	(51.0)	75947	(49.0)	(10.2)
3	JAWAJA* (Beawar)	200	35	157901	79620	(50.4)	78281	(49.6)	(12.1)
4	KEKRI* (Kekri)	100	31	140921	72021	(51.1)	68900	(48.9)	(10.8)
5	KISHANGARH (Kishangarh)	114	31	153474	79324	(51.7)	74150	(48.3)	(11.7)
6	MASOODA* (Masooda)	143	32	159600	81668	(51.2)	77932	(48.8)	(12.2)
7	PISANGAN (Pisangan)	128	45	236459	121687	(51.5)	114772	(48.5)	(18.1)
8	SRINAGAR (Ajmer)	96	37	170142	88399	(52.0)	81743	(48.0)	(13.0)
	AJMER DISTRICT	**1038**	**276**	**1306994**	**669903**	**(51.3)**	**637091**	**(48.7)**	**(100.0)**
9	BANSURE* (Bansure)	132	36	214351	112580	(52.5)	101771	(47.5)	(8.4)
10	BEHROR (Behror)	90	29	139503	72777	(52.2)	66726	(47.8)	(5.5)
11	KATHUMAR (Kathumar)	160	41	211689	113325	(53.5)	98364	(46.5)	(8.3)
12	KISHANGARH BAS (Kishangarh Bas)	140	29	167495	87756	(52.4)	79739	(47.6)	(6.5)
13	KOTKASIM* (Kotkasim)	116	24	117687	61712	(52.4)	55975	(47.6)	(4.6)
14	LACHHMANGARH (Lachmangarh)	186	44	225836	119382	(52.9)	106454	(47.1)	(8.8)
15	MANDAWAR* (Mandawar)	142	40	197582	103015	(52.1)	94567	(47.9)	(7.7)
16	NIMRANA (Behror)	87	33	143329	74428	(51.9)	68901	(48.1)	(5.6)
17	RAJGARH (Rajgarh)	147	30	144726	76591	(52.9)	68135	(47.1)	(5.7)
18	RAMGARH (Ramgarh)	173	37	220219	116180	(52.8)	104039	(47.2)	(8.6)
19	RENI (Rajgarh)	102	26	136491	72533	(53.1)	63958	(46.9)	(5.3)
20	THANAGAZI* (Thanagazi)	159	35	189977	99870	(52.6)	90107	(47.4)	(7.4)
21	TIJARA* (Tijara)	205	38	226974	121997	(53.7)	104977	(46.3)	(8.9)
22	UMREN (Alwar)	155	36	221794	117622	(53.0)	104172	(47.0)	(8.7)
	ALWAR	**1994**	**478**	**2557653**	**1349768**	**(52.8)**	**1207885**	**(47.2)**	**(100.0)**
23	ANANDPURI (Bagidora)	129	26	111206	56613	(50.9)	54593	(49.1)	(8.0)
24	BAGIDORA (Bagidora)	165	41	176729	89141	(50.4)	87588	(49.6)	(12.7)
25	GARHI* (Garhi)	170	55	237521	120212	(50.6)	117309	(49.4)	(17.0)
26	GHATOL (Ghatol)	223	53	230344	115822	(50.3)	114522	(49.7)	(16.5)
27	KUSHALGARH (Kushalgarh)	210	29	138970	69946	(50.3)	69024	(49.7)	(10.0)
28	PEEPALKHOONT (Banswara)	197	36	151273	76900	(50.8)	74373	(49.2)	(10.8)
29	SAJJANGARH (Kushalgarh)	187	30	134456	68165	(50.7)	66291	(49.3)	(9.6)
30	TALWARA (Banswara)	223	55	213727	108311	(50.7)	105416	(49.3)	(15.3)
	BANSWARA	**1504**	**325**	**1394226**	**705110**	**(50.6)**	**689116**	**(49.4)**	**(100.0)**
31	ANTA (Mangrol & Anta)	156	38	148759	77618	(52.2)	71141	(47.8)	(17.5)
32	ATRU* (Atru)	138	34	127043	66673	(52.5)	60370	(47.5)	(15.0)
33	BARAN* (Baran)	102	27	103142	54173	(52.5)	48969	(47.5)	(12.1)
34	CHHABRA* (Chhabra)	192	27	99472	52510	(52.8)	46962	(47.2)	(11.7)
35	CHHIPABAROD* (Chhipabarod)	180	30	127858	66733	(52.2)	61125	(47.8)	(15.0)
36	KISHANGANJ* (Kishanganj)	203	32	135218	70458	(52.1)	64760	(47.9)	(15.9)
37	SHAHBAD* (Shahbad)	236	27	108146	57040	(52.7)	51106	(47.3)	(12.7)
	BARAN #	**1207**	**215**	**849638**	**445205**	**(52.4)**	**404433**	**(47.6)**	**(100.0)**
38	BALOTRA* (Panchpadra)	233	54	265596	138016	(52.0)	127580	(48.0)	(14.6)
39	BARMER (Ramsar)	309	50	238075	128483	(54.0)	109592	(46.0)	(13.1)
40	BAYTOO (Baytoo)	323	47	210345	110447	(52.5)	99898	(47.5)	(11.6)
41	CHOHTAN (Chohtan)	189	51	225754	120580	(53.4)	105174	(46.6)	(12.4)
42	DHORIMANNA (Gudha Malani)	261	47	250929	131262	(52.3)	119667	(47.7)	(13.8)
43	SHEO* (Sheo)	251	45	178539	96930	(54.3)	81609	(45.7)	(9.8)
44	SINDHARI (Gudha Malani)	259	46	236545	122971	(52.0)	113574	(48.0)	(13.0)
45	SIWANA* (Siwana)	116	40	213648	111155	(52.0)	102493	(48.0)	(11.7)
	BARMER	**1941**	**380**	**1819431**	**959844**	**(52.8)**	**859587**	**(47.2)**	**(100.0)**
46	BAYANA* (Bayana)	177	45	191632	106038	(55.3)	85594	(44.7)	(11.3)
47	DEEG* (Deeg)	132	36	154862	83742	(54.1)	71120	(45.9)	(9.2)
48	KAMAN (Kaman)	209	44	212139	112682	(53.1)	99457	(46.9)	(12.5)
49	KUMHER* (Kumher)	124	36	155122	83545	(53.9)	71577	(46.1)	(9.2)
50	NADBAI* (Nadbai)	117	37	161111	87568	(54.4)	73543	(45.6)	(9.5)
51	NAGAR PAHARI (Nagar)	227	49	236329	126007	(53.3)	110322	(46.7)	(14.0)
52	RUPBAS* (Rupbas)	158	45	211147	114581	(54.3)	96566	(45.7)	(12.5)

NO. OF VILLAGES, GRAM CHARACTERISTICS: RAJASTHAN, (2001)

Population 0-6					% of 0-6 Pop. To Total Pop.	Sex-Ratio		Literacy Rate (%)[a]		
Person	Male		Female			Total Population	0-6 Population	Persons	Male	Female
	No.	%	No.	%						
11	12	13	14	15	16	17	18	19	20	21
24479	12553	(51.3)	11926	(48.7)	18.4	961	950	46.52	64.11	28.30
29934	15380	(51.4)	14554	(48.6)	19.3	959	946	42.66	63.33	21.23
33339	17449	(52.3)	15890	(47.7)	21.1	983	911	74.41	90.89	58.02
25678	13279	(51.7)	12399	(48.3)	18.2	957	934	47.14	67.95	25.57
29018	15060	(51.9)	13958	(48.1)	18.9	935	927	53.12	71.19	33.86
32896	16868	(51.3)	16028	(48.7)	20.6	954	950	54.63	76.35	31.93
46195	24025	(52.0)	22170	(48.0)	19.5	943	923	52.88	73.05	31.64
33894	17765	(52.4)	16129	(47.6)	19.9	925	908	52.25	72.58	30.31
255433	**132379**	**(51.8)**	**123054**	**(48.2)**	**19.5**	**951**	**930**	**53.09**	**72.60**	**32.72**
42987	22638	(52.7)	20349	(47.3)	20.1	904	899	58.15	75.04	39.51
23586	12806	(54.3)	10780	(45.7)	16.9	917	842	93.19	89.75	72.18
42290	22360	(52.9)	19930	(47.1)	20.0	868	891	57.35	75.12	36.76
36092	18844	(52.2)	17248	(47.8)	21.5	909	915	55.90	73.76	36.23
21563	11593	(53.8)	9970	(46.2)	18.3	907	860	69.69	85.26	52.73
47777	25133	(52.6)	22644	(47.4)	21.2	892	901	56.40	75.92	34.48
35992	19366	(53.8)	16626	(46.2)	18.2	918	859	69.29	85.07	52.37
24332	13158	(54.1)	11174	(45.9)	17.0	926	849	56.84	67.56	45.39
28264	14883	(52.7)	13381	(47.3)	19.5	890	899	54.94	74.69	32.72
48269	25284	(52.4)	22985	(47.6)	21.9	895	909	53.82	72.75	32.60
27459	14479	(52.7)	12980	(47.3)	20.1	882	896	57.24	76.55	35.18
40560	21167	(52.2)	19393	(47.8)	21.3	902	916	48.07	67.80	26.20
52773	27732	(52.5)	25041	(47.5)	23.3	860	903	53.14	70.37	32.81
45668	23918	(52.4)	21750	(47.6)	20.6	886	909	53.52	72.10	32.40
517612	**273361**	**(52.8)**	**244251**	**(47.2)**	**20.2**	**895**	**894**	**58.88**	**76.54**	**39.16**
23993	12058	(50.3)	11935	(49.7)	21.6	964	990	40.52	56.38	24.02
38799	19715	(50.8)	19084	(49.2)	22.0	983	968	41.04	57.82	24.03
45631	23510	(51.5)	22121	(48.5)	19.2	976	941	51.98	69.25	34.71
48828	24996	(51.2)	23832	(48.8)	21.2	989	953	39.95	58.32	21.70
32889	16384	(49.8)	16505	(50.2)	23.7	987	1007	33.61	48.80	18.10
34649	17441	(50.3)	17208	(49.7)	22.9	967	987	25.77	39.20	11.87
31212	15742	(50.4)	15470	(49.6)	23.2	973	983	37.51	53.39	21.12
44433	22726	(51.1)	21707	(48.9)	20.8	973	955	45.59	64.20	26.47
300434	**152572**	**(50.8)**	**147862**	**(49.2)**	**21.5**	**977**	**969**	**40.78**	**57.49**	**23.78**
26177	13730	(52.5)	12447	(47.5)	17.6	917	907	63.46	80.37	45.01
21897	11434	(52.2)	10463	(47.8)	17.2	905	915	63.42	81.14	43.82
17668	9249	(52.3)	8419	(47.7)	17.1	904	910	65.52	82.67	46.45
19789	10313	(52.1)	9476	(47.9)	19.9	894	919	53.62	72.10	32.77
25028	13069	(52.2)	11959	(47.8)	19.6	916	915	48.83	68.27	27.71
26838	13734	(51.2)	13104	(48.8)	19.8	919	954	52.88	68.36	35.83
22416	11680	(52.1)	10736	(47.9)	20.7	896	919	52.99	69.80	34.03
159813	**83209**	**(52.1)**	**76604**	**(47.9)**	**18.8**	**908**	**921**	**57.43**	**74.81**	**38.21**
60026	31002	(51.6)	29024	(48.4)	22.6	924	936	55.13	71.90	36.97
53302	27757	(52.1)	25545	(47.9)	22.4	853	920	54.85	70.15	36.53
47344	24726	(52.2)	22618	(47.8)	22.5	904	915	58.26	72.32	42.93
51713	26750	(51.7)	24963	(48.3)	22.9	872	933	50.66	63.92	35.17
58600	30150	(51.5)	28450	(48.5)	23.4	912	944	67.75	77.73	56.72
42110	22756	(54.0)	19354	(46.0)	23.6	842	851	57.63	72.64	39.80
53974	28060	(52.0)	25914	(48.0)	22.8	924	924	60.88	74.24	46.42
44554	23171	(52.0)	21383	(48.0)	20.9	922	923	59.54	74.35	43.56
411623	**214372**	**(52.1)**	**197251**	**(47.9)**	**22.6**	**896**	**920**	**58.14**	**72.15**	**42.43**
39961	21502	(53.8)	18459	(46.2)	20.9	807	858	57.27	76.01	33.74
31674	16856	(53.2)	14818	(46.8)	20.5	849	879	58.54	77.36	36.34
53276	27910	(52.4)	25366	(47.6)	25.1	883	909	47.68	66.52	26.20
30113	16037	(53.3)	14076	(46.7)	19.4	857	878	67.52	85.82	46.09
30836	16352	(53.0)	14484	(47.0)	19.1	840	886	68.76	87.36	46.83
52408	27722	(52.9)	24686	(47.1)	22.2	876	890	58.96	77.22	38.12
45376	24417	(53.8)	20959	(46.2)	21.5	843	858	67.72	84.97	47.27

a For final updated data of Literacy, please see Annex KI.

P. Code	Panchayat Samiti (Concerning Tehsil)	Total No. of Villages	Total No. of Gram Panchayats	Total Population					% share of District Rural Pop.
				Person	Male		Female		
					No.	%	No.	%	
1	2	3	4	5	6	7	8	9	10
53	SEWAR* (Bharatpur)	177	33	167641	90380	(53.9)	77261	(46.1)	(9.9)
54	WEIR* (Weir)	151	46	202199	109491	(54.2)	92708	(45.8)	(11.9)
	BHARATPUR	**1472**	**371**	**1692182**	**914034**	**(54.0)**	**778148**	**(46.0)**	**(100.0)**
55	ASIND* (Asind)	204	44	192346	95304	(49.5)	97042	(50.5)	(12.0)
56	BANERA* (Banera)	85	26	106222	53578	(50.4)	52644	(49.6)	(6.6)
57	HURDA* (Hurda)	72	20	91088	46735	(51.3)	44353	(48.7)	(5.7)
58	JAHAZPUR* (Jahazpur)	230	37	167782	86965	(51.8)	80817	(48.2)	(10.5)
59	KOTRI* (Kotri)	175	33	148702	76073	(51.2)	72629	(48.8)	(9.3)
60	MANDAL* (Mandal)	191	46	197500	97168	(49.2)	100332	(50.8)	(12.4)
61	MANDALGARH (Mandalgarh)	299	50	199935	103648	(51.8)	96287	(48.2)	(12.5)
62	RAIPUR* (Raipur)	92	22	84354	41301	(49.0)	43053	(51.0)	(5.3)
63	SAHARA* (Sahara)	104	28	98050	47375	(48.3)	50675	(51.7)	(6.1)
64	SHAHPURA* (Sahahpura)	155	38	148955	76354	(51.3)	72601	(48.7)	(9.3)
65	SUWANA* (Bhilwara)	138	34	164004	83478	(50.9)	80526	(49.1)	(10.3)
	BHILWARA	**1745**	**378**	**1598938**	**807979**	**(50.5)**	**790959**	**(49.5)**	**(100.0)**
66	BIKANER (Bikaner)	244	63	374802	198540	(53.0)	176262	(47.0)	(34.7)
67	DUNGARGARH* (Dungargarh) #	97	30	182819	93917	(51.4)	88902	(48.6)	(16.9)
68	KOLAYAT* (Kolayat)	221	37	207749	110666	(53.3)	97083	(46.7)	(19.2)
69	LUNKARANSAR (Lunkaransar)	176	36	217341	113669	(52.3)	103672	(47.7)	(20.1)
70	NOKHA* (Nokha)	137	53	279343	146029	(52.3)	133314	(47.7)	(25.9)
	BIKANER ##	**778**	**189**	**1079235**	**568904**	**(52.7)**	**510331**	**(47.3)**	**(100.0)**
71	HINDOLI* (Hindoli)	174	41	189290	99580	(52.6)	89710	(47.4)	(24.2)
72	KESHORAIPATAN (Indragarh)	227	46	178625	93289	(52.2)	85336	(47.8)	(22.8)
73	NAINWA* (Nainwa)	181	33	156227	81783	(52.3)	74444	(47.7)	(20.0)
74	TALERA* (Bundi)	267	61	258916	135831	(52.5)	123085	(47.5)	(33.1)
	BUNDI	**849**	**181**	**783058**	**410483**	**(52.4)**	**372575**	**(47.6)**	**(100.0)**
75	ARNOD* (Arnod)	179	30	119837	60826	(50.8)	59011	(49.2)	(7.9)
76	BARI SADRI* (Bari Sadri)	153	23	88841	44432	(50.0)	44409	(50.0)	(5.9)
77	BEGUN (Begun)	254	31	102011	51917	(50.9)	50094	(49.1)	(6.7)
78	BHADESAR* (Bhadesar)	168	25	107393	54257	(50.5)	53136	(49.5)	(7.1)
79	BHAINSRORGARH (Rawatbhata)	212	23	80379	42227	(52.5)	38152	(47.5)	(5.3)
80	BHOPALSAGAR (Kapasan)	85	19	72675	36291	(49.9)	36384	(50.1)	(4.8)
81	CHHOTI SADRI * (Chhoti Sadri)	151	24	100067	50890	(50.9)	49177	(49.1)	(6.6)
82	CHITTAURGARH* (Chittaurgarh)	229	39	167960	85545	(50.9)	82415	(49.1)	(11.1)
83	DUNGLA* (Dungla)	108	26	89975	44919	(49.9)	45056	(50.1)	(5.9)
84	GANGRAR* (Gangrar)	128	21	88640	44978	(50.7)	43662	(49.3)	(5.9)
85	KAPASAN (Kapasan)	111	23	84531	42429	(50.2)	42102	(49.8)	(5.6)
86	NIMBAHERA* (Nimbahera)	170	35	135391	68774	(50.8)	66617	(49.2)	(8.9)
87	PRATAPGARH* (Pratapgarh)	358	49	201229	102788	(51.1)	98441	(48.9)	(13.3)
88	RASHMI* (Rashmi)	89	23	75326	37282	(49.5)	38044	(50.5)	(5.0)
	CHITTAURGARH	**2395**	**391**	**1514255**	**767555**	**(50.7)**	**746700**	**(49.3)**	**(100.0)**
89	CHURU* (Churu)	106	35	152178	77677	(51.0)	74501	(49.0)	(11.0)
90	RAJGARH* (Rajgarh)	215	55	267403	138313	(51.7)	129090	(48.3)	(19.3)
91	RATANGARH* (Ratangarh)	101	32	158090	80065	(50.6)	78025	(49.4)	(11.4)
92	SARDARSHAHAR* (Sardarshahar)	184	48	222979	114186	(51.2)	108793	(48.8)	(16.1)
93	SUJANGARH* (Sujangarh)	155	51	253207	128683	(50.8)	124524	(49.2)	(18.2)
94	TARANAGAR* (Taranagar)	121	28	151006	77840	(51.5)	73166	(48.5)	(10.9)
	CHURU ###	**979**	**279**	**1387682**	**710681**	**(51.2)**	**677001**	**(48.8)**	**(100.0)**
95	BANDIKUI* (Baswa)	213	44	267016	140609	(52.7)	126407	(47.3)	(22.6)
96	DAUSA* (Dausa)	233	52	271907	142567	(52.4)	129340	(47.6)	(23.0)
97	LALSOT* (Lalsot)	321	47	251370	131209	(52.2)	120161	(47.8)	(21.3)
98	MAHWA* (Mahwa)	152	41	179173	95701	(53.4)	83472	(46.6)	(15.2)
99	SIKRAI* (Sikrai)	139	41	211779	111505	(52.7)	100274	(47.3)	(17.9)
	DAUSA #	**1058**	**225**	**1181245**	**621591**	**(52.6)**	**559654**	**(47.4)**	**(100.0)**
100	BARI* (Bari)	171	31	150595	83853	(55.7)	66742	(44.3)	(18.7)
101	BASERI* (Baseri)	196	35	201777	110589	(54.8)	91188	(45.2)	(25.0)
102	DHAULPUR (Sepau)	232	48	262456	142925	(54.5)	119531	(45.5)	(32.5)
103	RAJAKHERA (Rajakhera)	203	39	191812	105639	(55.1)	86173	(44.9)	(23.8)
	DHAULPUR	**802**	**153**	**806640**	**443006**	**(54.9)**	**363634**	**(45.1)**	**(100.0)**
104	ASPUR* (Aspur)	146	49	184508	89104	(48.3)	95404	(51.7)	(18.0)
105	BICHHIWARA (Dungarpur)	175	48	236114	118009	(50.0)	118105	(50.0)	(23.0)
106	DUNGARPUR (Dungarpur)	159	36	172385	84844	(49.2)	87541	(50.8)	(16.8)
107	SAGWARA (Sagwara)	158	46	192681	92915	(48.2)	99766	(51.8)	(18.8)
108	SIMALWARA (Simalwara)	220	58	241099	120792	(50.1)	120307	(49.9)	(23.5)
	DUNGARPUR	**858**	**237**	**1026787**	**505664**	**(49.2)**	**521123**	**(50.8)**	**(100.0)**
109	ANUPGARH (Garsana)	1131	88	417746	220600	(52.8)	197146	(47.2)	(31.3)
110	GANGANAGAR (Ganganagar)	273	44	176517	93595	(53.0)	82922	(47.0)	(13.2)
111	KARANPUR* (Karanpur)	237	35	103094	54341	(52.7)	48753	(47.3)	(7.7)
112	PADAMPUR* (Padampur)	247	36	121362	63657	(52.5)	57705	(47.5)	(9.1)
113	RAISINGHNAGAR* (Raisinghnagar)	407	47	157334	82247	(52.3)	75087	(47.7)	(11.8)
114	SADULSHAHAR (Sadulshahar)	252	32	146629	79236	(54.0)	67393	(46.0)	(11.0)

Population 0-6					% of 0-6 Pop. To Total Pop.	Sex-Ratio		Literacy Rate (%)[a]		
Person	Male		Female			Total Population	0-6 Population	Persons	Male	Female
	No.	%	No.	%						
11	12	13	14	15	16	17	18	19	20	21
34807	18408	(52.9)	16399	(47.1)	20.8	855	891	67.89	85.91	46.66
40695	21666	(53.2)	19029	(46.8)	20.1	847	878	61.68	81.32	38.31
359146	**190870**	**(53.1)**	**168276**	**(46.9)**	**21.2**	**851**	**882**	**61.44**	**79.95**	**39.62**
38828	19773	(50.9)	19055	(49.1)	20.2	1018	964	41.93	61.57	22.93
19163	9602	(50.1)	9561	(49.9)	18.0	983	996	50.12	68.03	31.87
17024	8822	(51.8)	8202	(48.2)	18.7	949	930	51.88	70.79	32.11
30576	15884	(51.9)	14692	(48.1)	18.2	929	925	49.11	67.31	29.67
26205	13371	(51.0)	12834	(49.0)	17.6	955	960	39.48	55.71	22.53
36170	18368	(50.8)	17802	(49.2)	18.3	1033	969	43.19	62.75	24.62
37172	18866	(50.8)	18306	(49.2)	18.6	929	970	43.50	59.68	25.94
14690	7476	(50.9)	7214	(49.1)	17.4	1042	965	42.58	62.19	24.21
16559	8412	(50.8)	8147	(49.2)	16.9	1070	968	44.13	63.56	26.44
28732	14652	(51.0)	14080	(49.0)	19.3	951	961	42.82	60.13	24.59
29578	15221	(51.5)	14357	(48.5)	18.0	965	943	45.87	64.76	26.41
294697	**150447**	**(51.1)**	**144250**	**(48.9)**	**18.4**	**979**	**959**	**44.59**	**62.85**	**26.09**
79253	41309	(52.1)	37944	(47.9)	21.1	888	919	47.02	61.80	30.23
43153	22330	(51.7)	20823	(48.3)	23.6	947	933	58.36	74.16	41.71
47328	24860	(52.5)	22468	(47.5)	22.8	877	904	41.34	55.85	24.64
45981	23935	(52.1)	22046	(47.9)	21.2	912	921	46.62	61.41	30.34
65246	33836	(51.9)	31410	(48.1)	23.4	913	928	48.90	67.14	28.78
237808	**123940**	**(52.1)**	**113868**	**(47.9)**	**22.0**	**897**	**919**	**46.33**	**61.92**	**28.83**
36915	19315	(52.3)	17600	(47.7)	19.5	901	911	46.91	64.29	27.60
32106	16650	(51.9)	15456	(48.1)	18.0	915	928	56.21	73.90	36.89
29494	15476	(52.5)	14018	(47.5)	18.9	910	906	51.00	70.39	29.68
48941	25502	(52.1)	23439	(47.9)	18.9	906	919	52.11	68.15	34.39
147456	**76943**	**(52.2)**	**70513**	**(47.8)**	**18.8**	**908**	**916**	**51.59**	**68.99**	**32.41**
25560	13043	(51.0)	12517	(49.0)	21.3	970	960	47.08	63.98	29.72
15112	7767	(51.4)	7345	(48.6)	17.0	999	946	45.01	65.16	25.13
17548	8994	(51.3)	8554	(48.7)	17.2	965	951	48.87	68.32	28.76
18203	9376	(51.5)	8827	(48.5)	16.9	979	941	47.53	66.53	28.33
15574	8146	(52.3)	7428	(47.7)	19.4	903	912	46.37	63.07	27.93
11283	5855	(51.9)	5428	(48.1)	15.5	1003	927	51.10	70.20	32.38
17630	9107	(51.7)	8523	(48.3)	17.6	966	936	51.83	71.27	31.89
28749	14884	(51.8)	13865	(48.2)	17.1	963	932	50.36	68.66	31.58
14923	7782	(52.1)	7141	(47.9)	16.6	1003	918	47.93	67.60	28.62
15113	7884	(52.2)	7229	(47.8)	17.0	971	917	47.18	65.83	28.23
12882	6610	(51.3)	6272	(48.7)	15.2	992	949	45.25	65.23	25.30
23140	12154	(52.5)	10986	(47.5)	17.1	969	904	54.36	75.94	32.44
39889	20547	(51.5)	19342	(48.5)	19.8	958	941	52.53	68.97	35.45
12246	6295	(51.4)	5951	(48.6)	16.3	1020	945	43.97	64.01	24.64
267852	**138444**	**(51.7)**	**129408**	**(48.3)**	**17.7**	**973**	**935**	**49.11**	**67.91**	**29.98**
30213	15969	(52.9)	14244	(47.1)	19.9	959	892	66.67	80.19	52.87
48536	25780	(53.1)	22756	(46.9)	18.2	933	883	71.99	83.55	59.75
33556	17672	(52.7)	15884	(47.3)	21.2	975	899	65.28	78.74	51.80
49073	25335	(51.6)	23738	(48.4)	22.0	953	937	59.70	75.12	43.60
54856	28528	(52.0)	26328	(48.0)	21.7	968	923	62.65	76.27	48.74
28989	15132	(52.2)	13857	(47.8)	19.2	940	916	72.11	82.01	61.68
288376	**150746**	**(52.3)**	**137630**	**(47.7)**	**20.8**	**953**	**913**	**65.29**	**78.63**	**51.45**
52574	27671	(52.6)	24903	(47.4)	19.7	899	900	66.22	82.23	48.43
56352	29052	(51.6)	27300	(48.4)	20.7	907	940	58.37	78.31	36.15
53956	27977	(51.9)	25979	(48.1)	21.5	916	929	54.24	74.39	32.30
35823	19151	(53.5)	16672	(46.5)	20.0	872	871	65.00	82.35	45.15
43293	22954	(53.0)	20339	(47.0)	20.4	899	886	62.37	79.28	43.63
241998	**126805**	**(52.4)**	**115193**	**(47.6)**	**20.5**	**900**	**908**	**61.02**	**79.19**	**40.83**
35668	19288	(54.1)	16380	(45.9)	23.7	796	849	56.87	72.55	36.84
46117	24739	(53.6)	21378	(46.4)	22.9	825	864	61.87	77.41	42.82
61229	32728	(53.5)	28501	(46.5)	23.3	836	871	59.46	76.28	39.12
43679	23432	(53.6)	20247	(46.4)	22.8	816	864	57.95	73.92	38.01
186693	**100187**	**(53.7)**	**86506**	**(46.3)**	**23.1**	**821**	**863**	**59.22**	**75.29**	**39.37**
37060	19225	(51.9)	17835	(48.1)	20.1	1071	928	44.21	62.74	27.61
53041	26816	(50.6)	26225	(49.4)	22.5	1001	978	45.94	64.15	27.92
38452	19680	(51.2)	18772	(48.8)	22.3	1032	954	46.67	66.79	27.56
37047	19061	(51.5)	17986	(48.5)	19.2	1074	944	50.91	70.13	33.61
54560	27590	(50.6)	26970	(49.4)	22.6	996	978	41.52	58.49	24.64
220160	**112372**	**(51.0)**	**107788**	**(49.0)**	**21.4**	**1031**	**959**	**45.69**	**64.12**	**28.19**
77613	41149	(53.0)	36464	(47.0)	18.6	894	886	58.42	70.77	44.63
27938	15326	(54.9)	12612	(45.1)	15.8	886	823	64.42	75.93	51.58
16453	8986	(54.6)	7467	(45.4)	16.0	897	831	61.49	71.96	49.94
19848	10783	(54.3)	9065	(45.7)	16.4	906	841	63.03	74.49	50.58
26965	14551	(54.0)	12414	(46.0)	17.1	913	853	65.34	76.66	53.13
22830	12585	(55.1)	10245	(44.9)	15.6	851	814	62.41	74.60	48.16

a For final updated data of Literacy, please see Annex K1.

P. Code	Panchayat Samiti (Concerning Tehsil)	Total No. of Villages	Total No. of Gram Panchayats	Total Population						% share of District Rural Pop.
				Person	Male		Female			
					No.	%	No.	%		
1	2	3	4	5	6	7	8	9		10
115	SURATGARH* (Suratgarh)	467	38	213384	116034	(54.4)	97350	(45.6)		(16.0)
	GANGANAGAR	**3014**	**320**	**1336066**	**709710**	**(53.1)**	**626356**	**(46.9)**		**(100.0)**
116	BHADRA* (Bhadra)	215	49	220582	116205	(52.7)	104377	(47.3)		(18.2)
117	HANUMANGARH (Hanumangarh)	1152	121	628123	331517	(52.8)	296606	(47.2)		(51.7)
118	NOHAR (Rawatsar)	538	81	365762	192199	(52.5)	173563	(47.5)		(30.1)
	HANUMANGARH ##	**1905**	**251**	**1214467**	**639921**	**(52.7)**	**574546**	**(47.3)**		**(100.0)**
119	AMBER* (Amber)	196	48	262029	137463	(52.5)	124566	(47.5)		(9.9)
120	BASSI* (Bassi)	215	39	229639	120214	(52.3)	109425	(47.7)		(8.6)
121	CHAKSU* (Chaksu)	287	35	161140	84148	(52.2)	76992	(47.8)		(6.1)
122	DUDU (Dudu)	229	56	272517	141434	(51.9)	131083	(48.1)		(10.2)
123	GOVINDGARH* (Chomu)	100	42	275780	143709	(52.1)	132071	(47.9)		(10.4)
124	JAMWA RAMGARH* (Jamwa Ramgarh)	241	43	250132	131112	(52.4)	119020	(47.6)		(9.4)
125	JHOTWARA* (Jaipur)	73	16	88946	46444	(52.2)	42502	(47.8)		(3.3)
126	KOTPUTLI (Kotputli)	121	42	228470	119860	(52.5)	108610	(47.5)		(8.6)
127	PHAGI* (Phagi)	171	31	161610	84238	(52.1)	77372	(47.9)		(6.1)
128	SAMBHAR (Phulara)	144	44	209528	108372	(51.7)	101156	(48.3)		(7.9)
129	SANGANER* (Sanganer)	147	25	131301	68604	(52.2)	62697	(47.8)		(4.9)
130	SHAHPURA (Shahpura)	86	30	181498	95431	(52.6)	86067	(47.4)		(6.8)
131	VIRATNAGAR (Viratnagar)	121	37	206414	108138	(52.4)	98276	(47.6)		(7.8)
	JAIPUR	**2131**	**488**	**2659004**	**1389167**	**(52.2)**	**1269837**	**(47.8)**		**(100.0)**
132	JAISALMER (Jaisalmer)	155	40	127798	70574	(55.2)	57224	(44.8)		(29.6)
133	SAM (Jaisalmer)	303	49	138679	77603	(56.0)	61076	(44.0)		(32.1)
134	SANKRA (Pokaran)	179	39	165376	88132	(53.3)	77244	(46.7)		(38.3)
	JAISALMER	**637**	**128**	**431853**	**236309**	**(54.7)**	**195544**	**(45.3)**		**(100.0)**
135	AHORE (Ahore)	113	41	177342	87839	(49.5)	89503	(50.5)		(13.2)
136	BHINMAL (Bagora)	81	35	184751	93570	(50.6)	91181	(49.4)		(13.8)
137	JALOR (Jalor)	69	28	131827	66029	(50.1)	65798	(49.9)		(9.8)
138	JASWANTPURA (Bhinmal)	75	29	128410	64363	(50.1)	64047	(49.9)		(9.6)
139	RANIWARA* (Raniwara)	85	30	163349	84512	(51.7)	78837	(48.3)		(12.2)
140	SANCHORE* (Sanchore)	206	63	342120	176546	(51.6)	165574	(48.4)		(25.6)
141	SAYLA (Sayla)	77	38	211147	106778	(50.6)	104369	(49.4)		(15.8)
	JALOR	**706**	**264**	**1338946**	**679637**	**(50.8)**	**659309**	**(49.2)**		**(100.0)**
142	BAKANI (Jhalrapatan)	326	42	152329	79045	(51.9)	73284	(48.1)		(15.1)
143	DAG (Gangdhar)	231	40	167192	85787	(51.3)	81405	(48.7)		(16.5)
144	JHALRAPATAN (Jhalrapatan)	316	48	205868	106879	(51.9)	98989	(48.1)		(20.3)
145	KHANPUR* (Khanpur)	207	39	153370	80141	(52.3)	73229	(47.7)		(15.2)
146	MANOHARTHANA (Manoharthana)	302	40	161425	83901	(52.0)	77524	(48.0)		(15.9)
147	PIRAWA* (Pirwa)	218	44	171897	88672	(51.6)	83225	(48.4)		(17.0)
	JHALAWAR	**1600**	**253**	**1012081**	**524425**	**(51.8)**	**487656**	**(48.2)**		**(100.0)**
148	ALSISAR (Jhunjhunun)	125	34	141416	71082	(50.3)	70334	(49.7)		(9.3)
149	BUHANA* (Buhana)	126	42	204411	105164	(51.4)	99247	(48.6)		(13.5)
150	CHIRAWA (Chirawa)	84	29	152843	78052	(51.1)	74791	(48.9)		(10.1)
151	JHUNJHUNUN (Jhunjhunun)	145	36	176693	89388	(50.6)	87305	(49.4)		(11.6)
152	KHETRI* (Khetri)	86	38	214474	110570	(51.6)	103904	(48.4)		(14.1)
153	NAWALGARH* (Nawalgarh)	90	35	217636	110563	(50.8)	107073	(49.2)		(14.3)
154	SURAJGARH (Chirawa)	122	37	175820	91102	(51.8)	84718	(48.2)		(11.6)
155	UDAIPURWATI* (Udaipurwati)	81	37	235280	119855	(50.9)	115425	(49.1)		(15.5)
	JHUNJHUNUN	**859**	**288**	**1518573**	**775776**	**(51.1)**	**742797**	**(48.9)**		**(100.0)**
156	BALESAR (Shergarh)	125	33	174179	90994	(52.2)	83185	(47.8)		(9.1)
157	BAP (Phalodi)	125	32	157290	82819	(52.7)	74471	(47.3)		(8.2)
158	BHOPALGARH (Bhopalgarh)	86	36	202321	104132	(51.5)	98189	(48.5)		(10.6)
159	BILARA* (Bilara)	90	38	180550	93477	(51.8)	87073	(48.2)		(9.5)
160	LUNI (Luni)	137	39	229097	118808	(51.9)	110289	(48.1)		(12.0)
161	MANDOR (Jodhpur)	107	25	151257	79220	(52.4)	72037	(47.6)		(7.9)
162	OSIAN (Osian)	175	67	422181	219499	(52.0)	202682	(48.0)		(22.1)
163	PHALODI (Phalodi)	111	37	229892	120126	(52.3)	109766	(47.7)		(12.0)
164	SHERGARH (Shergarh)	107	32	162656	85097	(52.3)	77559	(47.7)		(8.5)
	JODHPUR	**1063**	**339**	**1909423**	**994172**	**(52.1)**	**915251**	**(47.9)**		**(100.0)**
165	HINDAUN* (Hindaun)	127	51	262403	142377	(54.3)	120026	(45.7)		(25.3)
166	KARAULI* (Karauli)	203	45	222621	121045	(54.4)	101576	(45.6)		(21.5)
167	NADOTI* (Nadoti)	95	29	126089	66752	(52.9)	59337	(47.1)		(12.2)
168	SAPOTRA (Sapotra)	224	55	232513	125743	(54.1)	106770	(45.9)		(22.4)
169	TODABHIM* (Todabhim)	149	44	194094	104458	(53.8)	89636	(46.2)		(18.7)
	KARAULI ###	**798**	**224**	**1037720**	**560375**	**(54.0)**	**477345**	**(46.0)**		**(100.0)**
170	CHECHAT* (Ranganjmandi)	159	36	132073	69342	(52.5)	62731	(47.5)		(18.1)
171	ITAWA* (Pipalda)	169	30	155646	81675	(52.5)	73971	(47.5)		(21.3)
172	LADPURA* (Ladpura)	182	27	144691	76045	(52.6)	68646	(47.4)		(19.8)
173	SANGOD* (Sangod)	211	36	146951	76707	(52.2)	70244	(47.8)		(20.1)
174	SULTANPUR* (Digod)	171	33	150587	78726	(52.3)	71861	(47.7)		(20.6)
	KOTA	**892**	**162**	**729948**	**382495**	**(52.4)**	**347453**	**(47.6)**		**(100.0)**

Population 0-6					% of 0-6 Pop. To Total Pop.	Sex-Ratio		Literacy Rate (%)[a]		
Person	Male		Female			Total Population	0-6 Population	Persons	Male	Female
	No.	%	No.	%						
11	12	13	14	15	16	17	18	19	20	21
39489	20842	(52.8)	18647	(47.2)	18.5	839	895	53.58	64.65	40.06
231136	**124222**	**(53.7)**	**106914**	**(46.3)**	**17.3**	**883**	**861**	**60.39**	**72.00**	**47.27**
37137	19813	(53.4)	17324	(46.6)	16.8	898	874	67.65	81.01	52.87
106323	57123	(53.7)	49200	(46.3)	16.9	895	861	61.65	73.36	48.67
65983	34726	(52.6)	31257	(47.4)	18.0	903	900	64.67	77.41	50.61
209443	**111662**	**(53.3)**	**97781**	**(46.7)**	**17.2**	**898**	**876**	**63.65**	**75.97**	**50.01**
51383	26817	(52.2)	24566	(47.8)	19.6	906	916	59.82	79.52	38.11
46413	24254	(52.3)	22159	(47.7)	20.2	910	914	59.07	79.19	36.96
32849	17238	(52.5)	15611	(47.5)	20.4	915	906	51.93	72.40	29.66
51059	26708	(52.3)	24351	(47.7)	18.7	927	912	56.31	74.53	36.78
54182	28445	(52.5)	25737	(47.5)	19.6	919	905	66.24	83.67	47.39
50781	26434	(52.1)	24347	(47.9)	20.3	908	921	62.87	80.05	43.93
16783	8659	(51.6)	8124	(48.4)	18.9	915	938	66.68	82.09	49.73
45568	24418	(53.6)	21150	(46.4)	19.9	906	866	72.22	83.73	59.70
30415	15830	(52.0)	14585	(48.0)	18.8	918	921	60.92	76.65	43.83
38992	20236	(51.9)	18756	(48.1)	18.6	933	927	66.88	82.36	50.35
24558	12887	(52.5)	11671	(47.5)	18.7	914	906	62.86	80.70	43.38
34932	18350	(52.5)	16582	(47.5)	19.2	902	904	65.03	81.56	46.69
42440	22068	(52.0)	20372	(48.0)	20.6	909	923	68.38	82.53	52.78
520355	**272344**	**(52.3)**	**248011**	**(47.7)**	**19.6**	**914**	**911**	**62.96**	**79.96**	**44.42**
28527	15174	(53.2)	13353	(46.8)	22.3	811	880	47.32	63.21	27.72
31344	17067	(54.5)	14277	(45.5)	22.6	787	837	44.96	61.20	23.98
39043	20661	(52.9)	18382	(47.1)	23.6	876	890	48.55	64.68	30.03
98914	**52902**	**(53.5)**	**46012**	**(46.5)**	**22.9**	**827**	**870**	**47.02**	**63.09**	**27.45**
35199	18348	(52.1)	16851	(47.9)	19.8	1019	918	51.84	69.25	35.28
41857	21706	(51.9)	20151	(48.1)	22.7	974	928	40.07	60.49	19.50
26638	13794	(51.8)	12844	(48.2)	20.2	997	931	44.38	62.01	27.19
26847	14049	(52.3)	12798	(47.7)	20.9	995	911	39.16	58.16	20.68
36158	18975	(52.5)	17183	(47.5)	22.1	933	906	47.43	65.32	28.45
77502	40252	(51.9)	37250	(48.1)	22.7	938	925	46.00	64.81	26.09
46473	24101	(51.9)	22372	(48.1)	22.0	977	928	42.62	62.00	23.10
290674	**151225**	**(52.0)**	**139449**	**(48.0)**	**21.7**	**970**	**922**	**44.81**	**63.52**	**25.88**
28869	14934	(51.7)	13935	(48.3)	19.0	927	933	42.47	59.79	23.85
28177	14393	(51.1)	13784	(48.9)	16.9	949	958	46.08	63.62	27.58
36960	19169	(51.9)	17791	(48.1)	18.0	926	928	57.17	75.26	37.66
26359	13625	(51.7)	12734	(48.3)	17.2	914	935	66.17	83.50	47.17
33437	17148	(51.3)	16289	(48.7)	20.7	924	950	47.47	65.25	28.18
29352	15081	(51.4)	14271	(48.6)	17.1	939	946	65.33	80.68	49.01
183154	**94350**	**(51.5)**	**88804**	**(48.5)**	**18.1**	**930**	**941**	**54.13**	**71.46**	**35.51**
25485	13578	(53.3)	11907	(46.7)	18.0	989	877	73.89	86.24	61.72
33862	18406	(54.4)	15456	(45.6)	16.6	944	840	77.41	89.92	64.48
27065	14602	(54.0)	12463	(46.0)	17.7	958	854	74.51	87.45	61.32
29638	15939	(53.8)	13699	(46.2)	16.8	977	859	76.66	90.33	63.03
40381	21547	(53.4)	18834	(46.6)	18.8	940	874	65.85	80.46	50.40
37720	20265	(53.7)	17455	(46.3)	17.3	968	861	69.68	85.44	53.78
30828	16670	(54.1)	14158	(45.9)	17.5	930	849	70.67	84.62	55.94
44407	23410	(52.7)	20997	(47.3)	18.9	963	897	77.66	87.17	67.95
269386	**144417**	**(53.6)**	**124969**	**(46.4)**	**17.7**	**957**	**865**	**73.24**	**86.36**	**59.80**
39269	20445	(52.1)	18824	(47.9)	22.5	914	921	43.04	64.29	19.80
37045	19337	(52.2)	17708	(47.8)	23.6	899	916	43.36	60.38	24.67
38908	20287	(52.1)	18621	(47.9)	19.2	943	918	46.27	68.00	23.41
33862	17620	(52.0)	16242	(48.0)	18.8	931	922	50.45	71.35	28.18
47331	24493	(51.7)	22838	(48.3)	20.7	928	932	54.82	74.05	34.07
30591	16051	(52.5)	14540	(47.5)	20.2	909	906	44.30	64.87	22.08
92610	48055	(51.9)	44555	(48.1)	21.9	923	927	47.50	65.60	27.45
53415	27750	(52.0)	25665	(48.0)	23.2	914	925	47.50	65.60	27.45
37650	19148	(50.9)	18502	(49.1)	23.1	911	966	41.70	61.61	19.48
410681	**213186**	**(51.9)**	**197495**	**(48.1)**	**21.5**	**921**	**926**	**46.88**	**66.94**	**25.10**
56362	30366	(53.9)	25996	(46.1)	21.5	843	856	73.89	87.51	57.83
49330	26279	(53.3)	23051	(46.7)	22.2	839	877	57.54	75.48	35.89
24708	13187	(53.4)	11521	(46.6)	19.6	889	874	65.04	81.93	46.14
47756	25157	(52.7)	22599	(47.3)	20.5	849	898	58.30	75.34	37.87
38981	21080	(54.1)	17901	(45.9)	20.1	858	849	62.29	81.97	39.72
217137	**116069**	**(53.5)**	**101068**	**(46.5)**	**20.9**	**852**	**871**	**63.62**	**80.45**	**43.84**
25827	13363	(51.7)	12464	(48.3)	19.6	905	933	68.60	83.19	52.35
26315	13550	(51.5)	12765	(48.5)	16.9	906	942	62.48	78.59	44.58
25715	13394	(52.1)	12321	(47.9)	17.8	903	920	66.01	81.53	49.08
26270	13786	(52.5)	12484	(47.5)	17.9	916	906	69.82	85.11	53.14
25682	13458	(52.4)	12224	(47.6)	17.1	913	908	70.14	84.67	54.27
129809	**67551**	**(52.0)**	**62258**	**(48.0)**	**17.8**	**908**	**922**	**67.34**	**82.56**	**50.60**

a For final updated data of Literacy, please see Annex K1.

P. Code	Panchayat Samiti (Concerning Tehsil)	Total No. of Villages	Total No. of Gram Panchayats	Total Population					% share of District Rural Pop.
				Person	Male		Female		
					No.	%	No.	%	
1	2	3	4	5	6	7	8	9	10
175	DEGANA (Degana)	152	43	190085	96026	(50.5)	94059	(49.5)	(8.3)
176	DIDWANA* (Didwana)	172	57	285031	143568	(50.4)	141463	(49.6)	(12.4)
177	JAYAL* (Jayal)	137	45	224944	114881	(51.1)	110063	(48.9)	(9.8)
178	KUCHAMAN* (Nawa)	193	55	268146	138687	(51.7)	129459	(48.3)	(11.7)
179	LADNU* (Ladnu)	98	32	158026	79851	(50.5)	78175	(49.5)	(6.9)
180	MAKRANA* (Makrana)	119	36	199671	102034	(51.1)	97637	(48.9)	(8.7)
181	MERTA (Merta)	115	34	183429	95317	(52.0)	88112	(48.0)	(8.0)
182	MUNDWA (Nagaur)	122	39	197532	101466	(51.4)	96066	(48.6)	(8.6)
183	NAGAUR (Nagaur)	154	47	224815	115606	(51.4)	109209	(48.6)	(9.8)
184	PARBATSAR* (Parbatsar)	110	35	186413	96084	(51.5)	90329	(48.5)	(8.1)
185	RIYAN (Merta)	128	38	179629	92456	(51.5)	87173	(48.5)	(7.8)
	NAGAUR	**1500**	**461**	**2297721**	**1175976**	**(51.2)**	**1121745**	**(48.8)**	**(100.0)**
186	BALI* (Bali)	91	39	183802	91349	(49.7)	92453	(50.3)	(12.9)
187	DESURI (Desuri)	78	24	102245	49781	(48.7)	52464	(51.3)	(7.2)
188	JAITARAN* (Jaitaran)	108	33	186938	94992	(50.8)	91946	(49.2)	(13.1)
189	MARWAR JUNCTION (Marwar Jun.)	142	47	181445	90229	(49.7)	91216	(50.3)	(12.7)
190	PALI (Pali)	82	23	89939	45446	(50.5)	44493	(49.5)	(6.3)
191	RAIPUR* (Raipur)	113	35	182004	91683	(50.4)	90321	(49.6)	(12.7)
192	RANI STATION (Desuri)	76	29	106504	52220	(49.0)	54284	(51.0)	(7.5)
193	ROHAT* (Rohat)	79	23	102599	52215	(50.9)	50384	(49.1)	(7.2)
194	SOJAT* (Sojat)	115	38	155889	77614	(49.8)	78275	(50.2)	(10.9)
195	SUMERPUR* (Sumerpur)	65	29	137999	69169	(50.1)	68830	(49.9)	(9.7)
	PALI	**949**	**320**	**1429364**	**714698**	**(50.0)**	**714666**	**(50.0)**	**(100.0)**
196	AMET* (Amet)	137	20	88162	44077	(50.0)	44085	(50.0)	(10.3)
197	BHIM* (Bhim)	133	30	137578	67968	(49.4)	69610	(50.6)	(16.0)
198	DEOGARH* (Deogarh)	134	19	77865	38126	(49.0)	39739	(51.0)	(9.1)
199	KHAMNOR* (Nathdwara)	190	41	172395	85988	(49.9)	86407	(50.1)	(20.1)
200	KUMBHALGARH* (Kumbhalgarh)	164	37	131346	64616	(49.2)	66730	(50.8)	(15.3)
201	RAILMAGRA* (Railmagra)	94	29	110435	54685	(49.5)	55750	(50.5)	(12.9)
202	RAJSAMAND* (Rajsamand)	135	29	140520	71170	(50.6)	69350	(49.4)	(16.4)
	RAJSAMAND #	**987**	**205**	**858301**	**426630**	**(49.7)**	**431671**	**(50.3)**	**(100.0)**
203	BAMANWAS* (Bamanwas)	150	36	149429	79388	(53.1)	70041	(46.9)	(16.5)
204	BONLI (Bonli)	180	41	209833	110159	(52.5)	99674	(47.5)	(23.2)
205	GANGAPUR* (Gangapur)	122	38	179209	95561	(53.3)	83648	(46.7)	(19.8)
206	KHANDAR (Khandar)	180	35	150136	80241	(53.4)	69895	(46.6)	(16.6)
207	SAWAI MADHOPUR (S. Madhopur)	162	47	215810	113367	(52.5)	102443	(47.5)	(23.9)
	S. MADHOPUR	**794**	**197**	**904417**	**478716**	**(52.9)**	**425701**	**(47.1)**	**(100.0)**
208	DANTA RAMGARH (Danta Ramgarh)	157	45	262183	133320	(50.8)	128863	(49.2)	(14.4)
209	DHOND (Sikar)	109	43	209919	107068	(51.0)	102851	(49.0)	(11.6)
210	FATEHPUR (Fatehpur)	143	35	193473	97033	(50.2)	96440	(49.8)	(10.7)
211	KHANDELA (Sri Madhopur)	131	40	218560	111201	(50.9)	107359	(49.1)	(12.0)
212	LACHHMANGARH (Lachhmangarh)	140	37	197022	99917	(50.7)	97105	(49.3)	(10.9)
213	NEEM KA THANA* (Neem Ka Thana)	151	59	317049	164771	(52.0)	152278	(48.0)	(17.5)
214	PIPRALI (Sikar)	95	36	206064	105679	(51.3)	100385	(48.7)	(11.4)
215	SRI MADHOPUR (Sri Madhopur)	66	34	210980	108206	(51.3)	102774	(48.7)	(11.6)
	SIKAR	**992**	**329**	**1815250**	**927195**	**(51.1)**	**888055**	**(48.9)**	**(100.0)**
216	ABU ROAD* (Abu Road)	81	25	114818	59326	(51.7)	55492	(48.3)	(16.4)
217	PINDWARA* (Pindwara)	100	34	184803	94576	(51.2)	90227	(48.8)	(26.4)
218	REODAR* (Reodar)	126	37	175344	90145	(51.4)	85199	(48.6)	(25.0)
219	SHEOGANJ* (Sheoganj)	70	24	99663	50744	(50.9)	48919	(49.1)	(14.2)
220	SIROHI* (Sirohi)	85	31	125589	62387	(49.7)	63202	(50.3)	(17.9)
	SIROHI	**462**	**151**	**700217**	**357178**	**(51.0)**	**343039**	**(49.0)**	**(100.0)**
221	DEOLI* (Deoli)	171	40	169271	87592	(51.7)	81679	(48.3)	(17.7)
222	MALPURA* (Malpura)	138	36	176932	91000	(51.4)	85932	(48.6)	(18.5)
223	NIWAI* (Niwai)	201	41	165298	86153	(52.1)	79145	(47.9)	(17.2)
224	TODARAISINGH* (Todaraisingh)	118	31	110131	56442	(51.2)	53689	(48.8)	(11.5)
225	TONK (Tonk)	253	50	204362	105759	(51.8)	98603	(48.2)	(21.3)
226	UNIARA* (Uniara)	212	33	132509	69146	(52.2)	63363	(47.8)	(13.8)
	TONK	**1093**	**231**	**958503**	**496092**	**(51.8)**	**462411**	**(48.2)**	**(100.0)**
227	BARGAON (Girwa)	107	25	123802	63731	(51.5)	60071	(48.5)	(5.8)
228	BHINDER* (Vallabhnagar)	284	52	201832	101768	(50.4)	100064	(49.6)	(9.4)
229	DHARIAWAD* (Dhariawad)	250	49	203605	102067	(50.1)	101538	(49.9)	(9.5)
230	GIRWA (Girwa)	180	48	227623	116133	(51.0)	111490	(49.0)	(10.6)
231	GOGUNDA* (Gogunda)	148	40	151575	76505	(50.5)	75070	(49.5)	(7.1)
232	JHADOL* (Jhadol)	258	45	193810	97984	(50.6)	95826	(49.4)	(9.0)
233	KHERWARA* (Kherwara)	252	62	254301	126949	(49.9)	127352	(50.1)	(11.9)
234	KOTRA* (Kotra)	304	36	183504	92736	(50.5)	90768	(49.5)	(8.6)
235	MAVLI* (Mavli)	149	47	194148	98325	(50.6)	95823	(49.4)	(9.1)
236	SALUMBAR* (Salumbar)	234	48	196614	97075	(49.4)	99539	(50.6)	(9.2)
237	SARADA* (Sarada)	185	46	212181	105168	(49.6)	107013	(50.4)	(9.9)
	UDAIPUR	**2351**	**498**	**2142995**	**1078441**	**(50.3)**	**1064554**	**(49.7)**	**(100.0)**
	RAJASTHAN RURAL	**41353**	**9187**	**43292813**	**22426640**	**(51.8)**	**20866173**	**(48.2)**	

Note: Dungargarh PS shifted from Churu to Bikaner district on 1st April 2001. * Co-terminus Panchayat Samiti (with Tehsil); ** Excluding data of Dungargarh PS;
*** Including data of Dungargarh PS. # Came in force from April, 1991; ## Came in force from July 1994; ### Came in force from July 1997.

Source: Computed from data received from Directorate of Census Operations, Jaipur.

Population 0-6					% of 0-6 Pop. To Total Pop.	Sex-Ratio		Literacy Rate (%)[a]		
Person	Male		Female			Total Population	0-6 Population	Persons	Male	Female
	No.	%	No.	%						
11	12	13	14	15	16	17	18	19	20	21
34928	18220	(52.2)	16708	(47.8)	18.4	980	917	53.58	71.80	35.32
55958	29147	(52.1)	26811	(47.9)	19.6	985	920	63.62	80.84	46.46
44400	23050	(51.9)	21350	(48.1)	19.7	958	926	51.12	69.46	32.19
49720	26143	(52.6)	23577	(47.4)	18.5	933	902	62.54	78.68	45.52
29895	15355	(51.4)	14540	(48.6)	18.9	979	947	60.68	78.72	42.38
37280	19482	(52.3)	17798	(47.7)	18.7	957	914	61.81	78.17	44.92
33003	17432	(52.8)	15571	(47.2)	18.0	924	893	54.85	73.90	34.44
39345	20463	(52.0)	18882	(48.0)	19.9	947	923	45.01	64.73	24.44
49544	25728	(51.9)	23816	(48.1)	22.0	945	926	49.84	68.04	30.80
34565	18165	(52.6)	16400	(47.4)	18.5	940	903	55.92	72.16	39.08
31763	16729	(52.7)	15034	(47.3)	17.7	943	899	51.92	70.66	32.30
440401	**229914**	**(52.2)**	**210487**	**(47.8)**	**19.2**	**954**	**916**	**55.92**	**73.66**	**37.58**
35840	18426	(51.4)	17414	(48.6)	19.5	1012	945	50.34	66.60	34.53
19174	10014	(52.2)	9160	(47.8)	18.8	1054	915	50.35	67.75	34.37
34714	18064	(52.0)	16650	(48.0)	18.6	968	922	46.77	66.52	26.68
33182	17140	(51.7)	16042	(48.3)	18.3	1011	936	49.99	69.86	30.73
17063	8867	(52.0)	8196	(48.0)	19.0	979	924	48.79	68.19	29.38
37212	19163	(51.5)	18049	(48.5)	20.4	985	942	50.37	71.03	29.66
18788	9786	(52.1)	9002	(47.9)	17.6	1040	920	52.73	70.23	36.43
21217	11087	(52.3)	10130	(47.7)	20.7	965	914	51.24	71.31	30.91
28933	14985	(51.8)	13948	(48.2)	18.6	1009	931	52.02	72.78	31.78
25646	13477	(52.6)	12169	(47.4)	18.6	995	903	52.69	70.41	35.36
271769	**141009**	**(51.9)**	**130760**	**(48.1)**	**19.0**	**1000**	**927**	**50.39**	**69.39**	**31.76**
16073	8191	(51.0)	7882	(49.0)	18.2	1000	962	49.11	67.53	30.90
29947	15382	(51.4)	14565	(48.6)	21.8	1024	947	56.50	80.98	33.15
15965	8274	(51.8)	7691	(48.2)	20.5	1042	930	49.46	68.85	31.44
30587	15994	(52.3)	14593	(47.7)	17.7	1005	912	50.41	67.01	34.30
25195	12960	(51.4)	12235	(48.6)	19.2	1033	944	46.45	65.71	28.21
17427	8963	(51.4)	8464	(48.6)	15.8	1019	944	54.97	73.83	36.75
25754	13230	(51.4)	12524	(48.6)	18.3	974	947	55.23	73.85	36.25
160948	**82994**	**(51.6)**	**77954**	**(48.4)**	**18.8**	**1012**	**939**	**51.93**	**71.23**	**33.22**
26550	13837	(52.1)	12713	(47.9)	17.8	882	919	60.11	78.76	38.71
40703	21300	(52.3)	19403	(47.7)	19.4	905	911	53.18	73.47	30.75
36353	19278	(53.0)	17075	(47.0)	20.3	875	886	58.27	79.12	34.37
28601	15136	(52.9)	13465	(47.1)	19.1	871	890	43.38	63.15	20.53
39675	20864	(52.6)	18811	(47.4)	18.4	904	902	50.83	74.54	24.74
171882	**90415**	**(52.6)**	**81467**	**(47.4)**	**19.0**	**889**	**901**	**53.24**	**74.13**	**29.69**
48280	25569	(53.0)	22711	(47.0)	18.4	967	888	70.18	84.44	55.74
37786	20259	(53.6)	17527	(46.4)	18.0	961	865	68.64	84.56	52.47
35401	18878	(53.3)	16523	(46.7)	18.3	994	875	74.52	87.10	62.22
42565	22496	(52.9)	20069	(47.1)	19.5	965	892	72.93	86.00	59.38
35575	19053	(53.6)	16522	(46.4)	18.1	972	867	74.49	87.39	61.57
60644	32007	(52.8)	28637	(47.2)	19.1	924	895	67.60	82.66	51.47
37506	20028	(53.4)	17478	(46.6)	18.2	950	873	70.10	85.53	54.18
39581	20927	(52.9)	18654	(47.1)	18.8	950	891	66.77	81.98	51.28
337338	**179217**	**(53.1)**	**158121**	**(46.9)**	**18.6**	**958**	**882**	**70.39**	**84.74**	**55.70**
27161	13788	(50.8)	13373	(49.2)	23.7	935	970	43.55	59.43	26.41
39139	20115	(51.4)	19024	(48.6)	21.2	954	946	52.73	69.02	35.65
36282	18689	(51.5)	17593	(48.5)	20.7	945	941	48.32	65.46	30.24
18871	9939	(52.7)	8932	(47.3)	18.9	964	899	49.51	66.05	32.75
23998	12807	(53.4)	11191	(46.6)	19.1	1013	874	48.75	67.91	30.51
145451	**75338**	**(51.8)**	**70113**	**(48.2)**	**20.8**	**960**	**931**	**48.97**	**65.94**	**31.47**
31077	16087	(51.8)	14990	(48.2)	18.4	932	932	45.81	66.75	23.45
32579	16724	(51.3)	15855	(48.7)	18.4	944	948	46.92	66.24	26.49
32660	17010	(52.1)	15650	(47.9)	19.8	919	920	50.97	71.02	29.16
19888	10273	(51.7)	9615	(48.3)	18.1	951	936	52.88	72.17	32.67
38964	20157	(51.7)	18807	(48.3)	19.1	932	933	45.48	67.42	21.93
25255	13288	(52.6)	11967	(47.4)	19.1	916	901	46.71	69.09	22.56
180423	**93539**	**(51.8)**	**86884**	**(48.2)**	**18.8**	**932**	**929**	**47.77**	**68.48**	**25.62**
22329	11584	(51.9)	10745	(48.1)	18.0	943	928	66.51	81.50	50.66
33962	17606	(51.8)	16356	(48.2)	16.8	983	929	60.82	77.09	44.49
45558	23098	(50.7)	22460	(49.3)	22.4	995	972	35.22	52.30	18.21
44331	22683	(51.2)	21648	(48.8)	19.5	960	954	57.93	74.74	40.48
30258	15394	(50.9)	14864	(49.1)	20.0	981	966	50.12	67.74	32.32
41804	21003	(50.2)	20801	(49.8)	21.6	978	990	59.26	74.73	43.43
54205	27615	(50.9)	26590	(49.1)	21.3	1003	963	55.78	75.68	36.17
44344	22215	(50.1)	22129	(49.9)	24.2	979	996	24.52	37.55	11.14
31824	16562	(52.0)	15262	(48.0)	16.4	975	922	53.72	71.80	35.43
38474	19818	(51.5)	18656	(48.5)	19.6	1025	941	57.38	74.16	41.44
42298	21698	(51.3)	20600	(48.7)	19.9	1018	949	55.34	74.55	36.82
429387	**219276**	**(51.1)**	**210111**	**(48.9)**	**20.0**	**987**	**958**	**52.52**	**69.52**	**35.46**
8587389	**4486277**	**(52.2)**	**4101112**	**(47.8)**	**19.8**	**930**	**914**	**55.92**	**72.96**	**37.74**

a For final updated data of Literacy, please see Annex K1.

PANCHAYAT SAMITI-WISE PERCENTAGE OF RURAL POPULATION SERVED BY BASIC SOCIO-ECONOMIC AMENITIES: RAJASTHAN (2001)

P. Code	Panchayat Samiti	Total Population	Type of Amenity Available									
			Medical	Improved Drinking Water#	Edu-cation	Power Supply	Approach by Pucca Road	Post Office##	Tele-phone	Transport Communi-cations###	Banks	Ag. Credit Societies
1	2	3	4	5	6	7	8	9	10	11	12	13
1	ARAIN	133386	57	99.6	99.8	96.9	64.1	57.9	94.8	53	26.3	25.3
2	BHINAY	155111	57.9	99.2	100	97.3	71.9	61	75.5	62.7	27.4	35.3
3	JAWAJA	157901	41.9	100	97.1	96.1	86.9	36.2	67.9	40.7	12.5	8.7
4	KEKRI	140921	73.1	100	99.8	97.8	82.5	68.4	89.2	63.2	24.8	32.6
5	KISHANGARH	153474	68.4	99.6	99.9	99.3	80.2	61.3	87.1	73.3	29	28.5
6	MASOODA	159600	52.5	100	98.3	99.4	80.2	63.3	78.4	63.7	17.2	35.3
7	PISANGAN	236459	72.4	100	100	98.2	86.3	58.7	87.3	77.9	21.8	31.3
8	SRINAGAR	170142	61.9	100	99.9	97.6	89.6	53.4	88.3	72.7	21.4	19.2
	AJMER DISTRICT	**1306994**	**61.2**	**99.8**	**99.4**	**97.9**	**81**	**57.4**	**83.5**	**64.5**	**22.4**	**27.2**
9	BANSURE	214351	50.9	99.9	99.9	100	76.5	50.1	63.6	68.3	19.4	17.3
10	BEHROR	139503	67.3	99.9	99.3	99.9	81.5	56.7	78.4	70.3	24.1	24.1
11	KATHUMAR	211689	51.4	98.1	100	98.6	82.6	53.7	72.4	40.7	20.9	29.3
12	KISHANGARH BAS	167495	36.2	99.6	98.5	98.2	73.3	42	78.3	35.1	12.6	17.1
13	KOTKASIM	117687	40.3	100	99.6	98.9	72.6	39.2	58.6	42.9	24.4	32.4
14	LACHHMANGARH	225836	54.2	100	99.5	98.3	75	44	70.2	48.9	15.6	43.1
15	MANDAWAR	197582	52.1	100	99.5	98.1	76.3	50.4	72.6	53.9	16	30.3
16	NIMRANA	143329	68	99.8	100	100	88.3	60	57	65.9	22.8	12.3
17	RAJGARH	144726	46.1	95.9	95.9	95	86.8	52.6	53.6	38.3	13.7	14.3
18	RAMGARH	220219	46.4	100	98.4	99.7	81.3	34.1	68.7	40.3	17.9	30.9
19	RENI	136491	58.6	98.6	98.8	100	82.1	54.6	64.7	36.7	26.3	31.6
20	THANAGAZI	189977	61	99.7	98.3	95.5	83.9	55.1	77.5	63.4	22.4	29.7
21	TIJARA	226974	36.6	99.9	96.2	97.9	79.5	28.2	56.3	31.5	15.7	17.8
22	UMREN	221794	54.7	99	97.3	98.4	87.4	46.8	78.4	34.6	16.4	38.1
	ALWAR	**2557653**	**51.3**	**99.4**	**98.6**	**98.5**	**80.5**	**46.9**	**68.4**	**47.5**	**18.7**	**26.9**
23	ANANDPURI	111206	48.1	97.7	98.2	75.4	59.1	34.5	13	39.3	7.1	10.9
24	BAGIDORA	176729	51.5	97.9	99.2	64.6	62.9	36.7	43.9	51.2	20.4	18.9
25	GARHI	237521	68.9	100	99.9	97	80.4	55.3	59.6	69.1	26.3	28.2
26	GHATOL	230344	54	99.9	99.4	84.4	68.4	45.4	40.9	54.9	18.1	18.4
27	KUSHALGARH	138970	34.7	98.2	99	57.8	46.5	11.4	21.1	26.2	3.8	4.6
28	PEEPALKHOONT	151273	61.5	98.9	97	41	47.2	32.5	23.5	38.1	12.9	12.2
29	SAJJANGARH	134456	46.6	100	98.9	66.9	53	17.1	22.6	43.9	8.1	11.5
30	TALWARA	213727	55.9	98.3	98.6	85.8	72.5	31.1	49.4	67.1	17.7	22.2
	BANSWARA	**1394226**	**54.2**	**99**	**98.9**	**74.5**	**63.7**	**35.4**	**37.9**	**51.7**	**15.9**	**17.4**
31	ANTA	148759	48.9	100	99	97.3	69.4	52.1	57.7	53.2	31.4	41.1
32	ATRU	127043	49.1	100	99.1	99.6	66.9	56.3	71.4	48.5	25.2	33.6
33	BARAN	103142	45.4	100	99.7	100	77.3	45.4	60.7	38	11.1	42
34	CHHABRA	99472	14.8	96.4	93.7	93.8	36.4	20.9	36.9	13.1	3.8	21.2
35	CHHIPABAROD	127858	28.8	98.1	94.3	91.8	53.5	35.2	46.7	35.3	12.4	28.9
36	KISHANGANJ	135218	44.9	99.7	94.6	94.3	62	28.1	52.8	42.9	23	25.4
37	SHAHBAD	108146	36.3	99.4	96.1	86.4	57.4	33	37.9	36	14.7	18.9
	BARAN	**849638**	**39.3**	**99.2**	**96.7**	**94.9**	**61**	**39.5**	**52.7**	**39.4**	**18.5**	**30.6**
38	BALOTRA	265596	54.1	82	97.1	77.7	69.6	60	76	85	22.2	26.3
39	BARMER	238075	31.4	77	92.1	51.5	56.9	37.7	41.6	64.5	4.7	16.1
40	BAYTOO	210345	27.4	91.2	92.3	35	44.2	25.4	49.3	52.6	8.6	14.3
41	CHOHTAN	225754	47.1	85.3	99.1	73.1	68.3	55.4	54.1	76.1	10.2	29.8
42	DHORIMANNA	250929	30.8	90.9	97.8	77.7	57.6	41.1	58.8	60.6	8.9	21
43	SHEO	178539	30.3	81	95.9	54.3	50.9	39.6	48.1	60.1	9.6	19.1
44	SINDHARI	236545	36.2	83.4	99.6	56.9	53.9	37.8	57.9	68.5	7.6	19.6
45	SIWANA	213648	70.3	97.7	99.4	98	75.2	71.8	82.5	84.5	27.7	47
	BARMER	**1819431**	**41.2**	**86**	**96.7**	**66.1**	**59.9**	**46.4**	**59**	**69.5**	**12.5**	**24.1**
46	BAYANA	191632	46.1	98.9	99.2	91	76.2	42	27.8	42.3	13.8	11.9
47	DEEG	154862	67	100	100	97.4	81.2	61.6	72.7	35.6	15.3	66.8
48	KAMAN	212139	46.1	93.4	99.4	88.4	71.7	40.4	29.9	22.8	10.5	8.2
49	KUMHER	155122	75.5	99.9	99.9	98.9	85.9	55.2	79.4	33.5	31	59.9
50	NADBAI	161111	76.2	100	99.7	99.1	79.1	62.3	82.3	49	21.3	14

P. Code	*Panchayat Samiti*	*Total Population*	*Type of Amenity Available*									
			Medical	*Improved Drinking Water#*	*Edu-cation*	*Power Supply*	*Approach by Pucca Road*	*Post Office##*	*Tele-phone*	*Transport Communi-cations###*	*Banks*	*Ag. Credit Societies*
1	*2*	*3*	*4*	*5*	*6*	*7*	*8*	*9*	*10*	*11*	*12*	*13*
51	NAGAR PAHARI	236329	41.2	98.8	99.7	93.9	71.6	44.8	55.4	27.9	19.2	25.1
52	RUPBAS	211147	55.6	99.8	99.8	92.8	76	48	60.5	52.3	16.7	35.8
53	SEWAR	167641	54.1	98.9	99.1	99.8	94	48.6	72.2	30.5	20.5	46.3
54	WEIR	202199	52.8	99.6	99.6	99.1	63.8	58.2	62.6	38.2	18.5	9.6
	BHARATPUR	**1692182**	**55.7**	**98.7**	**99.6**	**95.2**	**76.9**	**50.5**	**58.6**	**36.6**	**18.1**	**29**
55	ASIND	192346	52.8	99.3	98.7	97.3	64.5	50	71.9	66	20	33.8
56	BANERA	106222	76.7	99.8	99.9	100	72.1	60.2	89.5	65	24.2	39.1
57	HURDA	91088	70.7	98.9	98.7	98.9	79.7	61.6	92	78.3	35.1	51.4
58	JAHAZPUR	167782	56.1	98.7	95.3	95.1	57	42.7	57.7	42.7	12.4	29.9
59	KOTRI	148702	49	99	98	93.4	56.7	45.1	54.4	55.8	14.3	32.2
60	MANDAL	197500	52.7	99.8	99	95	72.4	50.1	67.6	69.7	20.7	37.8
61	MANDALGARH	199935	50.5	99.6	95.3	96	66	45.7	63.4	53.9	24.8	35.3
62	RAIPUR	84354	57	98.4	99.5	99.9	56.1	50.9	82.2	76.8	20.6	37.7
63	SAHARA	98050	63.9	99.2	99.7	100	74.3	61.4	91.8	72	20.6	39.8
64	SHAHPURA	148955	55.1	97	99.4	95.2	56.3	46.1	62.1	54.2	14.2	32.3
65	SUWANA	164004	59.1	100	99.7	99.6	78.8	48.4	76.8	67.2	27.1	38.3
	BHILWARA	**1598938**	**56.9**	**99.1**	**98.2**	**96.9**	**66.4**	**49.8**	**70.8**	**62.1**	**20.8**	**36.2**
66	BIKANER	374802	47.7	74.3	96.1	71.9	90	40	47.1	76.9	31.3	31
67	DUNGARGARH *	182819	80.7	88.3	99.9	99.7	79.3	77.3	82.5	83.9	29.5	32.8
68	KOLAYAT	207749	49.2	73.2	98.1	80.1	79	51	37.6	80.7	25.4	29.9
69	LUNKARANSAR	217341	53.7	76.2	96.1	89.6	81.2	47.1	51.3	70.2	29	27.5
70	NOKHA	279343	53.9	95.7	98	97.9	79.5	71.4	57.3	87.2	30.8	39.7
	BIKANER **	**1079235**	**50.8**	**80**	**97**	**83.8**	**83.4**	**51.7**	**48.8**	**79**	**29.6**	**32.3**
71	HINDOLI	189290	52.7	98.7	97.5	94.7	66	45.6	48.6	42.3	16	21.8
72	KESHORAIPATAN	178625	41.3	97.4	98.2	91.4	57.9	43.4	30.4	45.9	14.1	37.1
73	NAINWA	156227	43.3	97.5	98.8	97	58.8	44.9	44.8	48.5	20.1	41.5
74	TALERA	258916	43.4	99.6	99.1	93.4	69.7	34.7	43.3	39.6	22.1	19.5
	BUNDI	**783058**	**45.1**	**98.5**	**98.4**	**94**	**63.9**	**41.4**	**41.9**	**43.5**	**18.4**	**28.5**
75	ARNOD	119837	33.8	97.8	94.7	81.6	56.6	50	23.8	45.8	15.4	19.2
76	BARI SADRI	88841	45.7	99.9	94.1	99.2	56.6	41.3	41.8	57.7	22.6	34.8
77	BEGUN	102011	41.6	100	91.4	97.1	55.4	34.9	50.2	52	15.3	23.3
78	BHADESAR	107393	37.3	100	95.5	100	60.3	33	44.5	48.8	21.9	26
79	BHAINSRORGARH	80379	34.1	99.6	88.8	92.3	62.5	24.1	12.1	61.9	8.8	20.4
80	BHOPALSAGAR	72675	50	99.7	99.5	99.2	62.4	47.2	70.8	76.2	36.9	45.9
81	CHHOTI SADRI	100067	30.2	99.8	95.4	99.9	57	38.8	60.8	43	12.1	35.4
82	CHITTAURGARH	167960	43.6	99.5	96.6	98.6	66.5	48.2	73.8	66.4	20.8	38.6
83	DUNGLA	89975	61.9	100	98.9	99.8	58.3	51	69.8	58.4	18	36.1
84	GANGRAR	88640	46.9	100	97.1	99.7	58.8	45.6	72.5	60.1	20.7	28.4
85	KAPASAN	84531	24.3	100	97.3	98.8	52.8	38.6	51.1	63.3	11.6	26.7
86	NIMBAHERA	135391	48.4	100	99.1	99.9	75.8	50.4	47.1	61.4	13.8	44.7
87	PRATAPGARH	201229	42.2	99.2	94.8	82.6	59.8	40.5	24.2	54	9.5	12.5
88	RASHMI	75326	65.2	100	98.1	99.8	78.2	62.9	77.3	80.6	7	48.6
	CHITTAURGARH	**1514255**	**42.8**	**99.6**	**95.8**	**95.3**	**61.7**	**43.4**	**49.6**	**58.3**	**16.2**	**30.3**
89	CHURU	152178	76.4	75.9	98.5	100	89.5	61.4	71.8	69.1	20.5	35.6
90	RAJGARH	267403	55	85.2	99.7	90	74	49.7	63.3	71.3	14.7	27.5
91	RATANGARH	158090	85.9	93	99.1	99.9	90.9	59.4	98	80.6	28.2	36.9
92	SARDARSHAHAR	222979	47.6	52.5	98.3	94.4	62.6	49	54.2	80.9	10.8	25.8
93	SUJANGARH	253207	66.9	89.6	98.5	99.8	69.4	59.3	55.4	82.3	19.4	23.1
94	TARANAGAR	151006	68	82.4	99.8	97.1	73.5	60.3	71.8	73.5	32.6	50.1
	CHURU ***	**1387682**	**66.6**	**80.8**	**99.1**	**96.8**	**75.6**	**58.5**	**68.7**	**77.6**	**21**	**31.5**
95	BANDIKUI	267016	51	98.9	98.9	100	75.9	41.3	50.3	38.8	21.3	20.6
96	DAUSA	271907	52.7	98.6	97.1	96.8	75.2	51.3	66.3	52.8	24.7	25.8
97	LALSOT	251370	40.5	99.7	96.3	90.2	65	38	44.1	38.9	20.4	21.5
98	MAHWA	179173	47.8	99.9	96.2	94.7	70.4	46.6	63.3	20.5	9.4	22.2
99	SIKRAI	211779	41.4	100	99	95.2	83.2	47.2	43.4	38.5	24.8	27.3
	DAUSA	**1181245**	**47**	**99.3**	**97.5**	**95.5**	**73.9**	**44.8**	**53.4**	**39.2**	**20.7**	**23.4**
100	BARI	150595	61.1	96.5	95.5	57.2	57.4	38.1	30.6	30.2	6	6.7
101	BASERI	201777	42.2	98.1	97.4	63.6	70.2	33.3	45.4	43.1	12.8	18.2
102	DHAULPUR	262456	37.9	99	97.8	82.3	73.6	39.4	41.6	32.9	14.8	21.1
103	RAJAKHERA	191812	28.1	98.3	97.6	94.1	72.1	38.9	41.6	19.8	3.3	7.3
	DHAULPUR	**806640**	**41**	**98.1**	**97.2**	**75.7**	**69.4**	**37.5**	**40.5**	**31.8**	**9.9**	**14.4**
104	ASPUR	184508	67.5	100	99.2	92.6	78.2	53.8	57.4	71	22.4	16.4
105	BICHHIWARA	236114	68.4	99.4	99.8	98.7	67.8	61.1	47.1	61	11.6	14.4
106	DUNGARPUR	172385	60.5	97.1	100	93.6	66.8	47.3	53.2	54.5	10.2	2.1
107	SAGWARA	192681	72.9	100	99.8	92.5	78.2	62.7	67	76.3	28	21.6
108	SIMALWARA	241099	58.5	99.7	99.6	87.8	72.4	49.1	47.4	55.8	17	16.1
	DUNGARPUR	**1026787**	**65.4**	**99.3**	**99.7**	**93**	**72.5**	**55**	**53.8**	**63.4**	**17.6**	**14.4**
109	ANUPGARH	417746	37.9	83.9	78.1	69	76.6	22.8	54.3	63.5	8.9	32.1
110	GANGANAGAR	176517	63.9	98.6	93.2	99.5	94.8	57.7	91.9	83	33.9	47.8
111	KARANPUR	103094	54.3	94.8	96.2	98.5	91.1	44.9	86.4	81.3	7.2	24.3
112	PADAMPUR	121362	59.6	94.2	93.7	97.8	77	37.6	81.9	65.6	17.6	33.4

P. Code	Panchayat Samiti	Total Population	Type of Amenity Available									
			Medical	Improved Drinking Water#	Edu-cation	Power Supply	Approach by Pucca Road	Post Office##	Tele-phone	Transport Communi-cations###	Banks	Ag. Credit Societies
1	2	3	4	5	6	7	8	9	10	11	12	13
113	RAISINGHNAGAR	157334	44.7	92.8	92.3	86.3	70.1	33.2	74.1	73.7	5.4	32.4
114	SADULSHAHAR	146629	77.2	79.5	94.1	98.7	92.2	51.0	92.2	82.1	25.8	48.4
115	SURATGARH	213384	42.4	78.7	78.9	56.5	71.8	29.0	57.3	72.1	8.0	33.1
	GANGANAGAR	**1336066**	**50.4**	**87.4**	**86.5**	**81.2**	**80.3**	**35.8**	**71.2**	**72.3**	**14.2**	**35.7**
116	BHADRA	220582	76.3	85.6	93.2	97.3	89.5	66.9	76.6	87.6	25.6	63.0
117	HANUMANGARH	628123	61.8	94.9	85.5	95.1	91.0	53.5	74.3	79.2	23.4	43.8
118	NOHAR	365762	45.8	73.5	87.9	72.0	72.1	47.7	64.1	74.8	18.6	35.1
	HANUMANGARH	**1214467**	**59.6**	**86.8**	**87.6**	**88.6**	**85.1**	**54.2**	**71.7**	**79.4**	**22.4**	**44.7**
119	AMBER	262029	59.0	100.0	98.5	99.6	74.5	43.2	58.8	63.8	20.9	21.9
120	BASSI	229639	56.3	99.9	98.3	99.7	82.4	44.5	55.7	68.4	19.5	31.8
121	CHAKSU	161140	31.4	99.0	93.5	88.4	50.1	31.1	30.0	37.5	16.2	22.7
122	DUDU	272517	58.0	97.1	98.5	94.9	78.2	58.3	68.6	65.2	21.5	35.0
123	GOVINDGARH	275780	79.4	100.0	99.5	99.5	90.1	72.8	79.9	79.5	33.0	59.1
124	JAMWA RAMGARH	250132	56.2	99.7	96.9	100.0	79.7	41.3	37.0	72.8	18.2	20.1
125	JHOTWARA	88946	51.7	94.4	98.1	99.4	83.2	37.8	81.7	69.6	12.3	26.3
126	KOTPUTLI	228470	46.9	100.0	100.0	96.2	85.2	52.6	74.4	54.8	12.8	17.0
127	PHAGI	161610	43.5	99.7	99.1	96.6	64.3	40.6	50.0	55.4	17.9	39.2
128	SAMBHAR	209528	63.6	95.6	99.7	99.9	75.1	52.9	77.4	69.0	16.9	31.2
129	SANGANER	131301	53.0	99.5	96.1	100.0	75.3	42.6	75.8	74.7	15.7	26.3
130	SHAHPURA	181498	72.6	100.0	100.0	99.5	88.1	64.3	71.3	58.1	22.2	37.2
131	VIRATNAGAR	206414	56.7	99.7	99.5	100.0	86.0	57.5	53.9	58.3	22.6	23.0
	JAIPUR	**2659004**	**57.4**	**99.0**	**98.4**	**98.1**	**78.7**	**50.8**	**62.3**	**64.3**	**20.0**	**30.7**
132	JAISALMER	127798	57.8	70.8	97.7	62.9	80.3	57.4	64.9	79.2	20.5	32
133	SAM	138679	47.3	83.5	95.1	39.5	65.0	48.5	66.1	75.5	14.2	13.8
134	SANKRA	165376	49.5	84.1	97.9	55.2	55.9	43.4	70.8	74.6	11.8	26.3
	JAISALMER	**431853**	**51.3**	**80.0**	**97.0**	**52.4**	**66.0**	**49.2**	**67.5**	**76.2**	**15.1**	**24.0**
135	AHORE	177342	83.2	98.8	99.6	99.5	80.6	71.9	84.3	90.9	28.5	56.6
136	BHINMAL	184751	63.8	85.4	100.0	93.7	79.5	62.9	82.6	90.1	17.6	32.3
137	JALOR	131827	73.2	99.8	100.0	99.7	91.8	66.7	81.3	82.8	26.1	43.7
138	JASWANTPURA	128410	70.1	98.5	99.9	100.0	84.0	61.8	81.7	85.6	20.9	25.8
139	RANIWARA	163349	71.0	95.3	100.0	99.7	78.6	61.7	63.5	78.4	17.9	25.0
140	SANCHORE	342120	48.4	85.9	99.3	86.0	72.0	45.0	53.8	73.6	14.2	32.5
141	SAYLA	211147	77.8	99.2	99.8	98.3	87.9	61.9	92.7	95.0	22.5	62.9
	JALOR	**1338946**	**67.1**	**93.4**	**99.7**	**95.1**	**80.6**	**59.5**	**74.5**	**84.2**	**20.2**	**40.0**
142	BAKANI	152329	34.1	97.8	87.0	86.0	46.1	30.7	33.2	29.8	16.3	11.2
143	DAG	167192	34.9	98.6	96.3	85.1	40.9	40.1	43.3	38.3	17	23.5
144	JHALRAPATAN	205868	33.2	97.9	95.6	96.7	50.7	30.5	58.0	33.2	14.8	26.2
145	KHANPUR	153370	46.9	99.4	92.6	97.6	54.2	44.4	60.7	42.6	19.1	24.7
146	MANOHARTHANA	161425	21.1	98.1	92.8	74.3	31.1	26.1	29.5	24.1	4.7	12.9
147	PIRAWA	171897	33.2	99.7	97.3	99.9	44.0	49.6	51.4	36.7	18.8	29.6
	JHALAWAR	**1012081**	**33.8**	**98.6**	**93.8**	**90.3**	**44.7**	**36.8**	**46.6**	**34.1**	**15.1**	**21.7**
148	ALSISAR	141416	58.6	86.2	98.7	98.7	77.5	62.0	77.3	77.8	27.2	44.5
149	BUHANA	204411	69.4	93.4	99.8	98.8	80.1	62.9	63.1	71.0	7.9	25.3
150	CHIRAWA	152843	66.8	98.6	100.0	100.0	90.1	69.3	93.4	87.0	23.4	51.8
151	JHUNJHUNUN	176693	62.1	94.8	99.9	99.9	79.5	56.8	92.1	79.6	6.1	25.3
152	KHETRI	214474	78.8	99.2	100.0	99.7	85.3	71.8	69.6	75.1	13.0	29.5
153	NAWALGARH	217636	66.1	100.0	100.0	100.0	88.9	72.4	96.3	87.5	15.5	52.9
154	SURAJGARH	175820	47.8	88.8	100.0	100.0	75.8	59.2	83.6	71.5	9.3	28.8
155	UDAIPURWATI	235280	80.1	99.8	100.0	99.1	89.9	77.0	84.1	88.3	17.6	25.6
	JHUNJHUNUN	**1518573**	**67.3**	**95.6**	**99.8**	**99.5**	**83.8**	**67.1**	**82.2**	**79.9**	**14.5**	**34.8**
156	BALESAR	174179	62.9	97.5	95.0	90.8	69.9	47.7	54.6	69.7	11.3	15.3
157	BAP	157290	45.0	66.4	91.7	81.4	69.6	45.3	42.5	74.7	17.2	33.0
158	BHOPALGARH	202321	77.1	95.7	100.0	99.4	93.2	72.0	84.2	98.4	29.5	37.2
159	BILARA	180550	86.1	99.4	99.5	100.0	89.9	62.4	87.8	84.7	28.9	51.2
160	LUNI	229097	78.7	94.5	99.7	95.1	84.7	57.0	86.8	83.7	18.5	37.7
161	MANDOR	151257	55.9	93.0	99.2	98.3	77.7	52.2	82.7	79.3	22.5	35.0
162	OSIAN	422181	71.6	99.1	99.7	99.1	84.5	64.4	73.1	89.7	20.2	38.7
163	PHALODI	229892	54.8	95.6	98.4	90.1	76.2	55.0	56.6	74.9	20.9	39.0
164	SHERGARH	162656	58.0	88.7	95.3	79.5	61.2	51.5	49.1	57.0	12.9	23.9
	JODHPUR	**1909423**	**67.0**	**93.6**	**98.0**	**93.7**	**79.9**	**57.8**	**69.8**	**81.0**	**20.4**	**35.5**
165	HINDAUN	262403	64.8	100.0	99.0	99.7	88.4	56.4	79.1	53.5	12.0	29.6
166	KARAULI	222621	55.1	95.8	98.7	84.6	71.0	56.1	28.9	53.6	12.4	10.0
167	NADOTI	126089	59.6	97.7	99.2	91.0	75.1	53.9	36.1	61.8	26.8	49.6
168	SAPOTRA	232513	57.8	96.9	98.0	72.1	69.7	52.1	29.4	49.7	18.4	20.8
169	TODABHIM	194094	63.3	98.2	99.3	91.8	82.8	60.2	57.4	47.0	10.0	33.0
	KARAULI	**1037720**	**60.2**	**97.8**	**98.8**	**87.8**	**77.8**	**55.8**	**47.9**	**52.5**	**14.9**	**26.5**
170	CHECHAT	132073	56.3	99.3	98.4	99.9	74.7	32.2	69.4	46.4	19.2	16.9
171	ITAWA	155646	53.4	99.8	96.3	90.3	64.7	52.8	55.6	51.6	29.5	46.9
172	LADPURA	144691	58.1	99.5	97.9	98.5	91.6	34.7	78.5	30.0	16.7	19.1
173	SANGOD	146951	46.3	100.0	97.6	99.3	60.6	44.5	57.1	44.5	20.4	33.3
174	SULTANPUR	150587	64.8	100.0	98.4	97.6	73.0	48.8	54.2	40.7	32.2	48.1
	KOTA	**729948**	**55.8**	**99.7**	**97.7**	**97.0**	**72.8**	**43.0**	**62.7**	**42.7**	**23.8**	**33.5**

P. Code	Panchayat Samiti	Total Population	Type of Amenity Available									
			Medical	Improved Drinking Water#	Edu-cation	Power Supply	Approach by Pucca Road	Post Office##	Tele-phone	Transport Communi-cations###	Banks	Ag. Credit Societies
1	2	3	4	5	6	7	8	9	10	11	12	13
175	DEGANA	190085	65.0	86.7	99.9	99.9	70.3	56.9	76.8	88.3	17.3	33.3
176	DIDWANA	285031	61.0	93.7	99.6	99.4	77.3	64.2	65.8	80.0	20.3	26.3
177	JAYAL	224944	68.6	73.0	99.5	97.4	72.7	63.8	85.5	85.9	17.3	53.1
178	KUCHAMAN	268146	54.5	89.9	98.9	100.0	66.0	56.3	59.9	69.8	18.7	27.0
179	LADNU	158026	73.4	99.7	99.0	98.1	77.0	65.1	61.8	93.9	23.4	51.3
180	MAKRANA	199671	66.1	77.5	99.8	99.3	67.0	64.8	82.0	84.1	24.9	34.4
181	MERTA	183429	72.4	95.1	98.7	100.0	89.8	71.5	79.4	90.5	36.7	53.0
182	MUNDWA	197532	66.5	96.3	98.7	96.4	73.6	56.1	44.3	85.2	19.4	39.2
183	NAGAUR	224815	62.1	78.3	99.0	91.9	71.3	50.9	64.0	76.3	11.8	22.0
184	PARBATSAR	186413	65.6	96.7	99.8	100.0	77.4	67.7	73.5	83.5	22.2	32.2
185	RIYAN	179629	68.6	94.1	98.7	99.2	84.3	64.7	61.4	81.4	27.4	41.8
	NAGAUR	**2297721**	**65.1**	**88.8**	**99.2**	**98.3**	**74.7**	**61.7**	**68.4**	**82.7**	**21.3**	**36.5**
186	BALI	183802	82.7	100.0	99.9	96.5	95.1	71.5	95.9	90.6	34.1	49.3
187	DESURI	102245	72.1	98.3	99.3	99.2	80.8	65.9	89.9	86.3	39.6	39.4
188	JAITARAN	186938	77.7	97.7	99.9	97.8	80.1	69.4	80.1	69.8	38.5	49.2
189	MARWAR JUNCTION	181445	71.0	97.9	99.2	97.6	81.7	64.5	94.1	82.4	32.6	47.6
190	PALI	89939	66.0	94.0	98.9	99.6	83.3	55.9	93.7	88.5	41.2	47.5
191	RAIPUR	182004	72.8	100.0	99.3	94.7	80.5	71.4	83.9	73.1	34.6	46.8
192	RANI STATION	106504	82.1	100.0	99.9	99.9	86.8	77.9	96.6	94.5	39.9	42.9
193	ROHAT	102599	53.1	96.1	99.9	99.8	73.6	42.1	78.1	83.1	22.7	35.6
194	SOJAT	155889	72.6	95.5	100.0	98.8	81.3	61.8	94.0	88.7	29.2	51.1
195	SUMERPUR	137999	82.1	94.3	99.1	100.0	99.8	74.8	97.7	91.4	29.7	50.6
	PALI	**1429364**	**74.2**	**97.6**	**99.6**	**98.0**	**84.6**	**66.6**	**90.2**	**83.8**	**34.0**	**46.8**
196	AMET	88162	44.8	100.0	97.4	100.0	56.3	37.5	69.7	77.8	11.4	14.4
197	BHIM	137578	48.3	99.0	99.7	95.0	76.0	46.8	58.7	66.0	14.1	14.0
198	DEOGARH	77865	35.2	100.0	96.6	99.1	52.3	27.1	69.3	60.7	13.8	18.4
199	KHAMNOR	172395	56.2	99.7	98.3	98.8	78.6	44.2	74.0	75.1	13.3	27.0
200	KUMBHALGARH	131346	47.8	99.2	98.5	99.1	59.9	39.2	49.1	66.9	12.3	13.8
201	RAILMAGRA	110435	71.0	99.8	99.6	100.0	84.3	53.6	74.3	78.3	23.5	34.1
202	RAJSAMAND	140520	51.3	100.0	98.9	100.0	73.6	52.6	92.4	70.4	20.5	28.0
	RAJSAMAND	**858301**	**51.7**	**99.6**	**98.6**	**98.7**	**70.6**	**44.2**	**69.9**	**71.0**	**15.6**	**21.9**
203	BAMANWAS	149429	57.3	93.2	98.9	85.9	63.7	60.7	49.0	51.0	17.0	39.6
204	BONLI	209833	54.0	98.5	98.7	93.8	61.9	53.4	73.3	48.5	27.6	42.2
205	GANGAPUR	179209	71.1	98.3	99.5	98.1	75.1	55.3	55.5	56.1	24.1	38.5
206	KHANDAR	150136	55.5	99.3	97.7	79.8	69.3	46.1	52.9	56.7	11.0	30.1
207	SAWAI MADHOPUR	215810	64.5	100.0	99.4	88.2	58.3	58.0	80.7	47.2	29.7	44.9
	SAWAI MADHOPUR	**904417**	**60.7**	**98.1**	**98.9**	**89.7**	**65.2**	**54.9**	**64.1**	**51.5**	**22.9**	**39.7**
208	DANTA RAMGARH	262183	72.0	98.9	99.7	100.0	76.5	67.5	87.9	82.0	27.6	41.1
209	DHOND	209919	78.2	99.3	100.0	100.0	84.0	73.4	91.5	93.4	20.7	22.6
210	FATEHPUR	193473	63.4	100.0	99.6	100.0	60.3	63.9	91.7	81.4	9.4	22.5
211	KHANDELA	218560	74.5	99.3	99.4	99.9	71.5	69.4	73.3	76.3	19.6	33.7
212	LACHHMANGARH	197022	56.5	99.1	99.7	99.8	62.1	62.5	85.2	87.4	16.9	14.2
213	NEEM KA THANA	317049	71.6	100.0	99.0	98.2	75.0	61.0	81.4	56.6	23.4	32.9
214	PIPRALI	206064	76.6	99.4	99.9	99.8	88.0	72.3	89.9	82.6	33.3	36.4
215	SRI MADHOPUR	210980	70.9	99.5	100.0	100.0	90.4	75.7	89.3	77.6	26.3	45.4
	SIKAR	**1815250**	**70.7**	**99.4**	**99.6**	**99.6**	**76.1**	**67.9**	**85.9**	**78.3**	**22.5**	**31.7**
216	ABU ROAD	114818	49.7	98.6	100.0	84.5	80.9	64.0	64.2	58.0	16.1	26.7
217	PINDWARA	184803	76.1	99.0	99.4	89.0	85.0	66.5	75.2	59.1	23.2	26.0
218	REODAR	175344	66.2	99.9	99.0	99.8	77.7	61.3	80.2	66.0	22.0	37.4
219	SHEOGANJ	99663	74.5	96.9	99.8	98.6	87.5	73.8	86.5	73.5	30.4	36.6
220	SIROHI	125589	88.1	99.6	99.4	99.7	88.1	78.3	94.0	93.6	37.1	33.6
	SIROHI	**700217**	**71.2**	**99.0**	**99.5**	**94.3**	**83.4**	**68.0**	**79.8**	**68.9**	**25.2**	**31.8**
221	DEOLI	169271	58.2	99.7	97.3	84.4	60.1	55.3	66.3	44.7	23.8	37.2
222	MALPURA	176932	51.9	99.5	99.8	95.1	76.3	54.8	63.1	56.6	32.4	31.8
223	NIWAI	165298	47.3	98.6	97.0	95.9	66.1	47.7	69.9	44.0	20.0	30.5
224	TODARAISINGH	110131	56.7	99.8	98.5	97.0	65.9	54.0	57.1	44.8	12.6	43.1
225	TONK	204362	59.2	98.8	97.8	87.6	71.2	44.4	54.3	32.8	16.7	33.2
226	UNIARA	132509	48.1	98.2	94.3	94.5	57.8	48.3	54.7	43.7	21.6	41.3
	TONK	**958503**	**53.8**	**99.1**	**97.5**	**91.9**	**66.8**	**50.5**	**61.1**	**44.1**	**21.7**	**35.4**
227	BARGAON	123802	46.9	99.3	97.7	97.2	74.7	54.0	61.6	66.2	27.1	9.7
228	BHINDER	201832	54.1	100.0	94.8	98.5	63.5	42.1	60.0	57.2	19.3	13.2
229	DHARIAWAD	203605	43.3	97.8	97.1	86.9	61.6	37.5	47.1	56.7	8.1	10.2
230	GIRWA	227623	64.0	98.0	98.9	91.9	76.3	46.5	62.2	69.4	20.2	21.7
231	GOGUNDA	151575	49.7	97.6	99.5	89.2	64.1	47.1	58.5	63.2	10.4	6.1
232	JHADOL	193810	48.2	98.4	97.2	72.3	51.5	33.5	32.1	56.4	8.9	12.4
233	KHERWARA	254301	48.8	98.7	96.6	68.9	67.3	31.2	48.1	46.9	5.5	7.4
234	KOTRA	183504	36.7	92.4	93.1	33.3	46.8	26.7	11.2	43.1	8.4	9.5
235	MAVLI	194148	69.8	100.0	98.7	100.0	75.1	47.6	91.0	69.3	21.7	21.1
236	SALUMBAR	196614	50.9	99.6	97.7	82.6	58.5	39.0	41.0	61.7	11.2	11.1
237	SARADA	212181	60.6	100.0	98.9	83.1	75.7	53.3	52.7	66.7	18.5	15.6
	UDAIPUR	**2142995**	**52.5**	**98.4**	**97.3**	**81.7**	**65.1**	**41.1**	**51.2**	**59.3**	**14**	**12.8**
	RAJASTHAN RURAL	**43292813**	**56.64**	**95.39**	**97.65**	**91.57**	**73.48**	**51.32**	**63.99**	**63.15**	**19.30**	**29.90**

Note: * Dungargarh PS shifted from Churu to Bikaner district on 1st April 2001 ** Excluding data of Dungargarh PS; *** Including data of Dungargarh PS.
Improved Drinking Water (See Terminology), ## Post office includes Post office, telegraph office and Post and telegraph office.,
Transport Communication includes bus service, rail facility and navigable waterways. *Source*: Directorate of Census Operation, Jaipur.

PANCHAYAT SAMITI-WISE PERCENTAGE OF INHABITED VILLAGES HAVING BASIC SOCIO-ECONOMIC AMENITIES: RAJASTHAN (2001)

P. Code	*Panchayat Samiti*	*Total No. of Inhabited Villages*	*Percentage of Villages Having Amenity of*									
			Medical	*Improved Drinking Water#*	*Edu-cation*	*Power Supply*	*Approach by Pucca Road*	*Post Office##*	*Tele-phone*	*Transport Communi-cations###*	*Banks*	*Ag. Credit Societies*
1	*2*	*3*	*4*	*5*	*6*	*7*	*8*	*9*	*10*	*11*	*12*	*13*
1	ARAIN	125	30.4	98.4	96.0	92.8	40.8	30.4	89.6	30.4	10.4	11.2
2	BHINAY	128	32.0	99.2	100.0	93.0	53.9	34.4	71.9	43.8	8.6	14.1
3	JAWAJA	199	25.6	100.0	86.9	93.0	68.8	19.1	57.8	31.7	4.0	4.0
4	KEKRI	99	47.5	100.0	98.0	91.9	65.7	39.4	85.9	39.4	7.1	15.2
5	KISHANGARH	111	37.8	99.1	98.2	96.4	63.1	32.4	72.1	54.1	9.9	12.6
6	MASOODA	139	23.0	100.0	90.6	97.8	56.1	26.6	63.3	43.2	4.3	10.8
7	PISANGAN	128	47.7	100.0	97.7	93.0	69.5	39.1	79.7	60.9	8.6	15.6
8	SRINAGAR	96	41.7	100.0	97.9	96.9	76.0	36.5	74.0	59.4	9.4	10.4
	AJMER DISTRICT	**1025**	**34.3**	**99.6**	**94.8**	**94.2**	**61.7**	**30.9**	**72.7**	**44.0**	**7.4**	**11.1**
9	BANSURE	131	29.8	98.5	99.2	100.0	57.3	26.0	45.0	46.6	5.3	6.1
10	BEHROR	90	40.0	97.8	91.1	98.9	67.8	28.9	60.0	53.3	7.8	10.0
11	KATHUMAR	158	30.4	95.6	98.7	95.6	69.6	28.5	58.2	29.7	7.6	14.6
12	KISHANGARH BAS	135	19.3	97.0	91.9	97.0	57.0	23.0	65.9	23.7	4.4	9.6
13	KOTKASIM	115	19.1	100.0	97.4	99.1	53.9	18.3	40.0	26.1	7.0	15.7
14	LACHHMANGARH	184	31.0	100.0	97.8	95.7	56.0	20.7	51.6	32.1	3.3	25.0
15	MANDAWAR	142	35.2	100.0	97.9	97.2	60.6	30.3	59.2	41.5	7.0	19.0
16	NIMRANA	85	48.2	97.6	98.8	98.8	72.9	41.2	41.2	51.8	11.8	10.6
17	RAJGARH	140	19.3	90.7	82.9	85.0	68.6	21.4	28.6	24.3	4.3	4.3
18	RAMGARH	173	24.9	98.8	93.6	97.7	64.7	13.9	45.1	22.0	4.6	13.3
19	RENI	102	31.4	97.1	95.1	100.0	64.7	28.4	41.2	18.6	7.8	16.7
20	THANAGAZI	148	29.1	96.6	82.4	75.7	62.2	23.0	50.7	38.5	4.7	6.8
21	TIJARA	202	20.8	98.5	90.1	94.6	67.3	13.9	36.6	21.8	5.4	6.9
22	UMREN	149	31.5	96.0	86.6	91.3	71.1	22.1	59.1	21.5	5.4	20.1
	ALWAR	**1954**	**28.3**	**97.5**	**92.9**	**94.3**	**63.7**	**23.1**	**48.7**	**30.9**	**5.8**	**12.9**
23	ANANDPURI	129	27.1	96.9	90.7	62.8	45.0	16.3	10.1	27.9	3.1	4.7
24	BAGIDORA	165	30.3	97.6	96.4	50.9	47.9	17.0	22.4	33.9	7.9	7.9
25	GARHI	168	48.8	99.4	97.6	91.1	61.3	28.0	41.1	48.8	10.1	11.3
26	GHATOL	220	25.0	99.5	91.4	68.6	45.9	19.1	25.5	36.4	5.5	5.9
27	KUSHALGARH	209	25.4	98.1	94.3	50.7	41.6	9.6	19.6	22.0	3.3	2.9
28	PEEPALKHOONT	187	32.6	95.7	85.0	24.1	26.2	10.7	12.3	21.4	3.7	3.2
29	SAJJANGARH	185	28.6	100.0	93.0	52.4	44.9	7.6	13.0	35.1	3.8	5.9
30	TALWARA	213	28.6	97.7	90.1	68.5	55.9	13.1	31.0	45.5	5.2	8.5
	BANSWARA	**1476**	**30.5**	**98.2**	**92.2**	**58.5**	**46.0**	**14.9**	**22.3**	**34.0**	**5.3**	**6.2**
31	ANTA	148	19.6	99.3	92.6	92.6	44.6	20.9	41.2	33.8	10.1	16.2
32	ATRU	136	25.7	100.0	94.1	98.5	42.6	27.9	59.6	28.7	5.1	16.9
33	BARAN	99	26.3	99.0	97.0	99.0	56.6	25.3	50.5	25.3	3.0	25.3
34	CHHABRA	186	7.5	94.6	80.1	87.6	25.8	10.8	24.7	9.7	1.6	8.6
35	CHHIPABAROD	173	11.0	96.0	78.6	83.8	34.1	15.6	27.2	18.5	2.9	10.4
36	KISHANGANJ	180	18.9	98.3	81.7	84.4	38.3	8.9	30.0	18.3	3.9	8.9
37	SHAHBAD	167	12.6	93.4	82.0	63.5	29.3	13.2	21.6	14.4	4.8	4.2
	BARAN	**1089**	**16.3**	**97.0**	**85.4**	**85.9**	**37.2**	**16.4**	**34.4**	**20.3**	**4.4**	**11.8**
38	BALOTRA	231	26.8	72.7	88.7	62.8	46.8	32.0	62.3	66.7	6.1	8.7
39	BARMER	307	19.9	70.4	90.2	35.8	47.9	23.1	28.3	51.8	2.0	11.4
40	BAYTOO	323	18.0	87.3	87.0	26.9	36.2	16.1	40.9	43.3	2.8	8.7
41	CHOHTAN	187	27.3	74.3	96.3	55.1	53.5	32.1	36.4	61.5	3.2	14.4
42	DHORIMANNA	261	21.5	89.3	95.8	69.7	47.1	28.0	50.2	49.4	3.8	12.3
43	SHEO	250	17.2	74.4	91.2	42.0	36.8	24.0	35.2	48.8	2.4	8.8
44	SINDHARI	259	21.2	79.5	98.5	41.7	40.5	22.0	48.3	55.6	3.5	9.7
45	SIWANA	115	40.9	95.7	97.4	93.9	51.3	40.0	62.6	65.2	7.8	20.0
	BARMER	**1933**	**22.4**	**79.7**	**92.5**	**49.0**	**44.0**	**25.5**	**43.8**	**53.7**	**3.6**	**11.0**
46	BAYANA	161	29.8	96.3	91.9	84.5	61.5	21.7	21.7	28.0	5.6	6.2
47	DEEG	119	45.4	99.2	97.5	90.8	60.5	31.1	61.3	21.0	4.2	53.8
48	KAMAN	194	27.3	90.2	95.9	78.9	54.6	19.1	18.0	12.9	2.6	5.2
49	KUMHER	117	54.7	99.1	98.3	97.4	74.4	28.2	61.5	17.9	14.5	37.6
50	NADBAI	114	57.0	100.0	94.7	97.4	57.9	37.7	76.3	33.3	11.4	7.0
51	NAGAR PAHARI	216	24.5	97.7	97.2	90.7	52.3	24.1	39.8	16.2	5.1	10.6
52	RUPBAS	142	38.7	98.6	97.9	87.3	60.6	26.1	47.9	39.4	3.5	21.1

P. Code	Panchayat Samiti	Total No. of Inhabited Villages	Percentage of Villages Having Amenity of									
			Medical	Improved Drinking Water#	Edu-cation	Power Supply	Approach by Pucca Road	Post Office##	Tele-phone	Transport Communi-cations###	Banks	Ag. Credit Societies
1	2	3	4	5	6	7	8	9	10	11	12	13
53	SEWAR	157	29.3	96.2	89.2	98.1	80.3	22.3	61.1	24.8	7.6	28.7
54	WEIR	146	29.5	98.6	94.5	97.9	47.3	34.2	47.9	24.7	5.5	5.5
	BHARATPUR	**1366**	**35.2**	**96.9**	**95.2**	**90.7**	**60.3**	**26.3**	**45.5**	**23.4**	**6.2**	**17.7**
55	ASIND	204	25.0	98.5	91.7	92.6	39.7	22.1	53.4	45.1	4.9	11.3
56	BANERA	83	47.0	97.6	94.0	100.0	45.8	28.9	74.7	42.2	4.8	15.7
57	HURDA	70	41.4	98.6	95.7	98.6	58.6	30.0	84.3	58.6	11.4	24.3
58	JAHAZPUR	217	27.6	97.2	84.8	88.0	35.5	15.7	40.1	24.4	3.2	10.1
59	KOTRI	175	22.9	98.9	93.7	85.1	32.0	17.1	35.4	29.7	2.3	12.0
60	MANDAL	188	22.9	98.9	93.1	88.8	46.8	18.6	44.7	44.7	5.9	11.2
61	MANDALGARH	281	23.8	97.5	76.9	88.6	37.7	14.9	36.3	28.5	6.0	11.4
62	RAIPUR	89	30.3	97.8	97.8	98.9	28.1	25.8	60.7	55.1	5.6	14.6
63	SAHARA	99	31.3	99.0	96.0	100.0	51.5	27.3	75.8	50.5	4.0	14.1
64	SHAHPURA	151	29.8	96.0	94.7	90.7	36.4	24.5	45.0	36.4	3.3	13.2
65	SUWANA	136	30.1	100.0	97.1	98.5	57.4	22.1	58.8	51.5	8.1	15.4
	BHILWARA	**1693**	**27.9**	**98.1**	**90.3**	**91.8**	**41.1**	**20.6**	**49.7**	**39.0**	**5.1**	**12.8**
66	BIKANER	219	22.8	70.3	86.8	61.2	74.9	18.7	32.0	61.6	11.9	16.9
67	DUNGARGARH *	92	60.9	83.7	97.8	98.9	60.9	54.3	77.2	71.7	13.0	16.3
68	KOLAYAT	196	19.4	52.0	77.0	54.1	50.5	18.4	20.4	53.1	8.2	10.7
69	LUNKARANSAR	160	28.1	66.3	91.3	75.0	62.5	21.9	35.6	56.3	9.4	8.1
70	NOKHA	137	29.2	89.8	91.2	91.2	60.6	43.1	43.1	72.3	13.1	19.0
	BIKANER **	**712**	**24.3**	**68.1**	**86.0**	**68.1**	**62.6**	**24.0**	**31.7**	**60.1**	**10.5**	**13.6**
71	HINDOLI	174	28.7	98.9	93.7	90.2	51.1	23.0	31.0	24.1	4.0	7.5
72	KESHORAIPATAN	223	19.3	95.1	90.1	81.6	39.0	18.8	17.0	29.6	4.0	15.7
73	NAINWA	180	17.8	95.0	93.9	93.3	33.9	18.3	26.7	26.1	4.4	16.1
74	TALERA	262	20.2	99.6	94.7	86.6	50.8	15.6	29.0	24.8	6.5	8.4
	BUNDI	**839**	**21.2**	**97.3**	**93.1**	**87.5**	**44.1**	**18.6**	**25.7**	**26.2**	**4.9**	**11.8**
75	ARNOD	178	12.4	97.2	75.8	64.0	33.1	19.7	9.0	27.0	3.4	5.1
76	BARI SADRI	143	18.9	99.3	76.2	97.9	37.1	14.0	15.4	37.1	3.5	9.8
77	BEGUN	222	16.7	98.6	69.8	87.8	37.8	14.0	29.3	34.2	3.2	7.2
78	BHADESAR	163	11.7	100.0	81.6	100.0	37.4	9.2	19.0	28.8	3.7	11.7
79	BHAINSRORGARH	154	15.6	97.4	70.1	85.1	38.3	9.1	1.9	39.0	1.9	6.5
80	BHOPALSAGAR	83	19.3	98.8	92.8	97.6	43.4	16.9	45.8	53.0	8.4	20.5
81	CHHOTI SADRI	141	11.3	97.2	83.7	97.2	36.2	15.6	36.2	31.2	3.5	13.5
82	CHITTAURGARH	218	15.6	99.1	80.3	91.7	39.0	15.1	45.9	39.0	2.8	11.0
83	DUNGLA	102	33.3	100.0	93.1	99.0	32.4	20.6	50.0	35.3	4.9	13.7
84	GANGRAR	127	19.7	100.0	83.5	96.9	36.2	17.3	49.6	33.9	3.1	7.1
85	KAPASAN	107	10.3	100.0	90.7	97.2	39.3	17.8	29.0	47.7	2.8	10.3
86	NIMBAHERA	152	21.1	99.3	89.5	98.0	53.9	19.1	26.3	38.8	2.6	16.4
87	PRATAPGARH	330	18.8	97.6	80.3	70.0	40.3	17.0	12.4	33.9	3.9	4.8
88	RASHMI	81	30.9	98.8	86.4	97.5	46.9	27.2	49.4	53.1	2.5	18.5
	CHITTAURGARH	**2201**	**17.4**	**98.6**	**80.8**	**88.5**	**39.2**	**16.0**	**26.9**	**36.4**	**3.5**	**9.9**
89	CHURU	105	61.9	70.5	98.1	100.0	80.0	42.9	61.0	60.0	9.5	24.8
90	RAJGARH	213	35.7	80.8	98.1	84.0	59.2	29.6	54.5	59.2	5.2	16.9
91	RATANGARH	101	65.3	87.1	95.0	97.0	77.2	39.6	93.1	69.3	11.9	21.8
92	SARDARSHAHAR	170	34.7	47.1	97.1	91.2	51.2	32.4	42.4	70.6	5.3	17.1
93	SUJANGARH	155	41.3	86.5	92.9	98.7	56.8	37.4	44.5	69.0	7.7	12.9
94	TARANAGAR	110	33.6	67.3	92.7	88.2	49.1	36.4	44.5	46.4	9.1	23.6
	CHURU ***	**946**	**44.7**	**73.9**	**96.1**	**92.8**	**60.6**	**37.1**	**56.6**	**63.7**	**8.0**	**18.4**
95	BANDIKUI	211	25.1	98.6	92.4	99.5	57.8	19.4	30.8	22.7	5.7	8.5
96	DAUSA	223	22.4	97.8	84.3	91.9	51.6	21.5	39.0	26.9	5.8	7.2
97	LALSOT	300	14.3	97.3	77.0	80.7	39.7	15.0	19.3	17.3	4.0	5.7
98	MAHWA	152	29.6	98.7	88.2	88.8	46.7	21.7	45.4	9.9	3.3	11.2
99	SIKRAI	139	18.7	99.3	92.8	91.4	64.7	24.5	24.5	21.6	6.5	12.2
	DAUSA	**1025**	**21.2**	**98.1**	**85.6**	**89.7**	**50.4**	**19.6**	**30.5**	**20.0**	**5.0**	**8.3**
100	BARI	168	51.8	92.3	89.3	46.4	49.4	24.4	19.0	23.8	3.0	4.2
101	BASERI	190	18.4	95.8	91.1	48.9	51.6	14.7	25.3	26.3	4.7	8.4
102	DHAULPUR	229	22.3	97.8	95.2	75.1	59.4	21.8	29.3	19.7	3.9	10.0
103	RAJAKHERA	199	17.1	98.5	94.0	89.4	63.3	24.6	33.2	17.1	2.0	3.5
	DHAULPUR	**786**	**26.3**	**96.3**	**92.6**	**66.3**	**56.4**	**21.4**	**27.1**	**21.5**	**3.4**	**6.7**
104	ASPUR	143	48.3	100.0	95.8	82.5	62.2	33.6	40.6	54.5	8.4	6.3
105	BICHHIWARA	175	44.0	98.9	97.7	96.6	50.9	32.6	27.4	41.7	5.7	5.7
106	DUNGARPUR	159	46.5	95.6	99.4	91.2	59.7	28.9	40.9	45.9	5.0	2.5
107	SAGWARA	157	49.0	99.4	97.5	82.2	57.3	33.8	42.7	52.9	8.9	8.3
108	SIMALWARA	220	32.3	99.5	96.8	75.5	49.1	23.6	29.1	40.5	4.5	4.1
	DUNGARPUR	**854**	**43.1**	**98.7**	**97.4**	**85.1**	**55.2**	**30.0**	**35.4**	**46.4**	**6.3**	**5.3**
109	ANUPGARH	1090	16.8	72.7	49.4	48.5	59.7	7.3	29.9	49.4	1.2	15.5
110	GANGANAGAR	257	31.1	90.7	69.3	94.2	82.1	23.7	73.5	59.1	8.6	19.8
111	KARANPUR	207	26.6	88.4	82.6	92.8	83.1	22.7	74.9	69.1	2.4	14.5
112	PADAMPUR	239	38.9	90.0	79.5	92.9	64.9	15.9	70.3	54.0	5.4	16.3
113	RAISINGHNAGAR	367	26.4	88.3	72.2	73.0	56.9	16.3	55.6	58.3	1.6	18.0
114	SADULSHAHAR	237	27.0	33.6	49.4	86.5	69.6	12.7	51.9	54.9	3.8	16.5
115	SURATGARH	433	18.9	69.5	49.0	38.1	57.5	9.7	30.3	51.7	3.2	14.5
	GANGANAGAR	**2830**	**23.1**	**76.9**	**59.1**	**64.4**	**64.0**	**12.7**	**45.8**	**54.1**	**2.9**	**16.1**

P. Code	Panchayat Samiti	Total No. of Inhabited Villages	Percentage of Villages Having Amenity of									
			Medical	Improved Drinking Water#	Education	Power Supply	Approach by Pucca Road	Post Office##	Telephone	Transport Communications###	Banks	Ag. Credit Societies
1	2	3	4	5	6	7	8	9	10	11	12	13
116	BHADRA	198	35.9	87.9	58.1	71.7	63.1	23.7	39.4	53.5	7.6	27.8
117	HANUMANGARH	1074	18.9	84.6	36.6	80.0	64.5	11.0	35.8	39.9	3.6	8.2
118	NOHAR	501	16.2	67.9	50.5	43.9	50.3	15.6	37.1	49.3	3.8	11.0
	HANUMANGARH	**1773**	**20.0**	**80.3**	**42.9**	**68.9**	**60.3**	**13.7**	**36.6**	**44.0**	**4.1**	**11.2**
119	AMBER	192	37.5	100.0	91.7	99.5	53.6	21.4	44.3	45.8	6.8	7.8
120	BASSI	210	31.9	99.5	91.9	98.6	68.1	17.6	31.4	44.3	4.3	8.6
121	CHAKSU	267	10.1	96.3	74.2	78.3	30.3	10.9	15.4	18.4	3.4	5.6
122	DUDU	219	25.6	92.7	90.4	89.0	52.5	23.7	47.5	36.1	5.0	15.5
123	GOVINDGARH	100	49.0	100.0	93.0	99.0	72.0	44.0	62.0	58.0	11.0	30.0
124	JAMWA RAMGARH	233	35.6	98.3	88.0	99.1	62.7	17.6	21.0	53.6	7.3	8.6
125	JHOTWARA	73	26.0	90.4	90.4	98.6	68.5	15.1	63.0	52.1	2.7	9.6
126	KOTPUTLI	121	32.2	100.0	100.0	92.6	77.7	33.9	66.1	47.1	5.0	11.6
127	PHAGI	169	18.9	97.6	94.1	92.3	40.8	14.8	29.6	30.2	3.6	16.6
128	SAMBHAR	144	41.0	91.0	96.5	99.3	53.5	29.2	62.5	49.3	4.9	16.0
129	SANGANER	143	23.8	96.5	83.2	100.0	54.5	16.8	53.8	50.3	4.2	7.7
130	SHAHPURA	86	47.7	100.0	98.8	98.8	73.3	37.2	55.8	40.7	9.3	17.4
131	VIRATNAGAR	120	36.7	95.8	93.3	99.2	67.5	27.5	28.3	35.0	5.0	7.5
	JAIPUR	**2077**	**29.9**	**96.9**	**89.7**	**94.5**	**56.4**	**21.8**	**40.1**	**41.3**	**5.3**	**11.5**
132	JAISALMER	143	30.1	61.5	88.1	49.7	60.8	28.0	44.8	56.6	7.0	14.0
133	SAM	281	17.1	64.4	66.2	14.6	46.3	18.5	39.1	44.5	2.8	4.3
134	SANKRA	176	30.1	79.5	94.9	40.3	40.9	25.6	60.8	60.2	5.7	14.2
	JAISALMER	**600**	**24.0**	**68.2**	**79.8**	**30.5**	**48.2**	**22.8**	**46.8**	**52.0**	**4.7**	**9.5**
135	AHORE	110	57.3	95.5	95.5	96.4	58.2	42.7	68.2	75.5	10.0	31.8
136	BHINMAL	80	47.5	82.5	100.0	87.5	68.8	45.0	73.8	80.0	10.0	25.0
137	JALOR	68	60.3	98.5	100.0	98.5	77.9	41.2	80.9	73.5	8.8	22.1
138	JASWANTPURA	74	48.6	95.9	97.3	100.0	66.2	36.5	64.9	71.6	6.8	14.9
139	RANIWARA	84	51.2	94.0	97.6	97.6	61.9	39.3	48.8	61.9	4.8	10.7
140	SANCHORE	204	33.8	82.8	96.6	75.5	55.4	26.5	40.7	59.3	6.9	21.6
141	SAYLA	77	55.8	97.4	97.4	96.1	74.0	41.6	84.4	87.0	10.4	40.3
	JALOR	**697**	**47.8**	**90.7**	**97.4**	**90.0**	**63.6**	**36.9**	**61.1**	**70.3**	**8.0**	**23.7**
142	BAKANI	289	14.9	96.2	63.3	70.2	24.6	9.7	17.6	14.9	3.1	3.8
143	DAG	221	15.4	99.1	86.4	73.8	23.1	17.2	24.0	20.4	3.6	10.9
144	JHALRAPATAN	285	15.1	96.8	83.5	91.6	37.9	14.4	43.2	18.2	4.2	10.9
145	KHANPUR	193	18.7	98.4	79.3	93.3	27.5	15.5	47.7	16.6	3.1	6.7
146	MANOHARTHANA	284	10.9	96.5	79.9	61.6	21.8	10.6	16.2	14.8	1.4	4.2
147	PIRAWA	205	13.2	98.0	88.8	99.5	23.4	22.0	29.8	20.0	4.4	11.7
	JHALAWAR	**1477**	**14.5**	**97.4**	**79.5**	**80.3**	**26.6**	**14.4**	**28.8**	**17.3**	**3.2**	**7.8**
148	ALSISAR	124	32.3	75.0	96.0	97.6	56.5	31.5	64.5	59.7	6.5	18.5
149	BUHANA	126	50.0	88.1	99.2	99.2	66.7	42.9	50.8	61.1	2.4	14.3
150	CHIRAWA	84	42.9	96.4	98.8	100.0	73.8	39.3	86.9	72.6	4.8	31.0
151	JHUNJHUNUN	145	40.7	93.1	97.9	99.3	65.5	33.1	87.6	68.3	2.1	10.3
152	KHETRI	85	56.5	97.6	100.0	98.8	70.6	54.1	52.9	64.7	4.7	17.6
153	NAWALGARH	88	45.5	100.0	100.0	100.0	76.1	51.1	90.9	79.5	6.8	33.0
154	SURAJGARH	122	32.8	82.0	100.0	100.0	64.8	39.3	78.7	58.2	4.1	16.4
155	UDAIPURWATI	81	64.2	98.8	100.0	98.8	76.5	53.1	75.3	75.3	7.4	17.3
	JHUNJHUNUN	**855**	**44.2**	**90.2**	**98.8**	**99.2**	**67.7**	**41.6**	**73.2**	**66.4**	**4.6**	**18.7**
156	BALESAR	125	38.4	92.0	86.4	79.2	52.8	29.6	47.2	55.2	4.0	8.0
157	BAP	125	24.8	52.8	82.4	68.8	54.4	26.4	29.6	56.0	6.4	22.4
158	BHOPALGARH	86	52.3	93.0	100.0	97.7	81.4	46.5	69.8	93.0	10.5	18.6
159	BILARA	89	69.7	98.9	97.8	100.0	78.7	37.1	75.3	73.0	10.1	33.7
160	LUNI	135	51.9	89.6	94.8	88.9	59.3	30.4	74.8	65.2	5.9	15.6
161	MANDOR	105	35.2	91.4	99.0	97.1	61.9	27.6	71.4	64.8	6.7	22.9
162	OSIAN	175	52.6	96.6	96.6	96.6	70.3	42.3	60.6	79.4	8.0	21.7
163	PHALODI	111	36.0	88.3	93.7	83.8	59.5	34.2	45.0	60.4	10.8	23.4
164	SHERGARH	107	34.6	82.2	89.7	65.4	42.1	27.1	30.8	37.4	4.7	10.3
	JODHPUR	**1058**	**43.7**	**87.1**	**93.1**	**86.2**	**61.7**	**33.5**	**55.6**	**64.8**	**7.3**	**19.3**
165	HINDAUN	121	50.4	100.0	99.2	99.2	81.8	37.2	71.1	43.0	4.1	20.7
166	KARAULI	195	35.4	92.8	93.8	69.2	52.3	28.7	14.4	40.0	4.1	4.6
167	NADOTI	85	35.3	94.1	95.3	78.8	55.3	30.6	18.8	40.0	9.4	30.6
168	SAPOTRA	210	31.0	93.3	87.6	51.9	48.1	24.3	14.3	28.1	4.8	8.6
169	TODABHIM	144	41.7	96.5	95.1	87.5	69.4	34.7	48.6	30.6	4.2	18.1
	KARAULI	**755**	**37.7**	**95.0**	**93.4**	**73.8**	**59.5**	**30.2**	**30.5**	**35.4**	**4.9**	**13.8**
170	CHECHAT	144	31.3	95.8	90.3	97.9	57.6	16.7	50.0	27.8	4.2	8.3
171	ITAWA	163	20.2	98.2	84.0	71.2	33.7	18.4	27.0	22.7	4.3	17.2
172	LADPURA	145	29.7	99.3	89.0	94.5	80.0	19.3	59.3	22.1	6.9	11.7
173	SANGOD	197	22.3	99.5	88.8	98.0	41.6	17.8	41.6	26.4	4.1	13.2
174	SULTANPUR	163	36.8	99.4	91.4	92.0	49.1	18.4	36.2	19.6	7.4	18.4
	KOTA	**812**	**27.7**	**98.5**	**88.7**	**90.8**	**51.2**	**18.1**	**42.2**	**23.8**	**5.3**	**13.9**
175	DEGANA	148	39.9	76.4	97.3	98.6	52.7	35.1	62.8	79.1	7.4	23.0
176	DIDWANA	170	38.2	90.0	98.2	97.6	58.2	41.8	46.5	66.5	7.1	17.1
177	JAYAL	136	39.7	65.4	97.1	93.4	47.8	34.6	76.5	69.9	5.1	30.9
178	KUCHAMAN	193	32.1	81.3	96.9	100.0	48.2	29.5	42.5	50.8	5.7	12.4
179	LADNU	97	45.4	95.9	92.8	93.8	61.9	39.2	44.3	86.6	6.2	32.0
180	MAKRANA	119	44.5	72.3	96.6	97.5	46.2	40.3	64.7	70.6	8.4	14.3

P. Code	Panchayat Samiti	Total No. of Inhabited Villages	Percentage of Villages Having Amenity of									
			Medical	Improved Drinking Water#	Edu-cation	Power Supply	Approach by Pucca Road	Post Office##	Tele-phone	Transport Communi-cations###	Banks	Ag. Credit Societies
1	2	3	4	5	6	7	8	9	10	11	12	13
181	MERTA	111	35.1	91.9	92.8	98.2	68.5	32.4	56.8	64.0	9.9	21.6
182	MUNDWA	121	38.8	94.2	94.2	93.4	54.5	33.1	31.4	71.9	7.4	28.1
183	NAGAUR	150	39.3	70.0	94.7	84.7	55.3	28.7	53.3	68.7	4.7	14.7
184	PARBATSAR	110	45.5	98.2	98.2	100.0	60.9	41.8	59.1	67.3	7.3	13.6
185	RIYAN	125	38.4	88.0	93.6	96.8	68.0	35.2	38.4	60.8	6.4	25.6
	NAGAUR	**1480**	**39.2**	**83.1**	**95.9**	**95.9**	**55.9**	**35.3**	**52.2**	**67.7**	**6.8**	**20.5**
186	BALI	91	57.1	98.9	96.7	92.3	87.9	42.9	89.0	79.1	9.9	19.8
187	DESURI	78	43.6	98.7	93.6	94.9	56.4	34.6	76.9	70.5	10.3	12.8
188	JAITARAN	103	52.4	91.3	96.1	90.3	59.2	35.9	59.2	47.6	12.6	22.3
189	MARWAR JUNCTION	142	42.3	96.5	96.5	93.7	57.0	35.9	84.5	59.9	12.7	21.8
190	PALI	80	40.0	92.5	96.3	97.5	67.5	28.8	87.5	78.8	17.5	27.5
191	RAIPUR	109	45.0	100.0	95.4	88.1	56.9	36.7	60.6	47.7	10.1	18.3
192	RANI STATION	76	59.2	100.0	98.7	98.7	69.7	50.0	88.2	89.5	15.8	19.7
193	ROHAT	79	35.4	93.7	98.7	98.7	60.8	25.3	72.2	72.2	10.1	20.3
194	SOJAT	115	50.4	91.3	100.0	95.7	60.9	34.8	85.2	77.4	12.2	27.8
195	SUMERPUR	63	61.9	92.1	98.4	100.0	98.4	50.8	93.7	84.1	12.7	30.2
	PALI	**936**	**48.2**	**95.5**	**97.0**	**94.4**	**65.7**	**37.1**	**79.0**	**68.7**	**12.3**	**22.0**
196	AMET	136	20.6	100.0	89.7	100.0	42.6	16.2	58.8	66.2	2.9	3.7
197	BHIM	132	27.3	98.5	97.0	90.2	65.9	25.0	41.7	51.5	4.5	4.5
198	DEOGARH	131	15.3	100.0	90.8	96.9	34.4	11.5	59.5	45.0	3.1	5.3
199	KHAMNOR	187	29.9	98.9	84.5	96.8	54.5	19.8	53.5	49.7	3.7	11.8
200	KUMBHALGARH	164	26.2	98.8	92.7	98.8	42.1	21.3	33.5	51.2	3.0	6.1
201	RAILMAGRA	91	39.6	98.9	96.7	100.0	63.7	26.4	61.5	60.4	5.5	14.3
202	RAJSAMAND	132	24.2	99.2	92.4	99.2	51.5	24.2	84.8	52.3	5.3	9.8
	RAJSAMAND	**973**	**25.8**	**99.2**	**91.4**	**97.3**	**50.1**	**20.3**	**55.1**	**53.2**	**3.9**	**7.8**
203	BAMANWAS	136	29.4	88.2	87.5	73.5	43.4	30.9	32.4	31.6	6.6	17.6
204	BONLI	159	27.0	95.6	91.8	86.8	40.3	24.5	55.3	25.8	6.3	16.4
205	GANGAPUR	113	46.9	94.7	94.7	93.8	54.0	29.2	42.5	36.3	10.6	19.5
206	KHANDAR	155	30.3	96.1	87.1	62.6	47.1	20.6	31.6	37.4	3.9	10.3
207	SAWAI MADHOPUR	156	35.9	98.7	94.9	78.8	34.6	28.8	64.7	23.7	8.3	19.2
	SAWAI MADHOPUR	**719**	**33.2**	**94.9**	**91.1**	**78.4**	**43.3**	**26.6**	**45.9**	**30.6**	**7.0**	**16.4**
208	DANTA RAMGARH	157	45.9	96.8	94.3	99.4	59.9	40.8	73.2	65.0	9.6	23.6
209	DHOND	109	61.5	99.1	100.0	100.0	73.4	52.3	87.2	89.0	10.1	14.7
210	FATEHPUR	143	44.1	100.0	97.9	100.0	49.7	44.8	85.3	73.4	4.2	15.4
211	KHANDELA	126	50.8	98.4	91.3	96.0	54.8	46.8	54.8	58.7	6.3	15.9
212	LACHHMANGARH	140	33.6	98.6	98.6	99.3	47.1	40.7	78.6	75.0	5.7	7.1
213	NEEM KA THANA	151	49.0	98.0	93.4	91.4	53.6	39.1	61.6	39.1	9.9	14.6
214	PIPRALI	94	50.0	96.8	96.8	98.9	73.4	44.7	71.3	59.6	10.6	16.0
215	SRI MADHOPUR	66	54.5	97.0	98.5	100.0	77.3	59.1	80.3	63.6	13.6	22.7
	SIKAR	**986**	**47.7**	**98.2**	**96.0**	**97.9**	**58.9**	**44.7**	**73.4**	**64.9**	**8.3**	**15.9**
216	ABU ROAD	78	34.6	94.9	98.7	73.1	65.4	38.5	48.7	41.0	9.0	14.1
217	PINDWARA	99	45.5	96.0	91.9	74.7	65.7	31.3	55.6	40.4	7.1	10.1
218	REODAR	126	35.7	97.6	91.3	97.6	54.8	31.0	64.3	45.2	5.6	16.7
219	SHEOGANJ	69	49.3	91.3	94.2	92.8	66.7	42.0	66.7	53.6	10.1	13.0
220	SIROHI	83	60.2	95.2	91.6	97.6	65.1	45.8	78.3	73.5	13.3	15.7
	SIROHI	**455**	**44.2**	**95.4**	**93.2**	**87.7**	**62.6**	**36.7**	**62.6**	**49.9**	**8.6**	**14.1**
221	DEOLI	165	27.3	98.8	84.8	64.2	32.1	21.2	46.1	21.8	4.8	12.7
222	MALPURA	130	24.6	96.9	97.7	84.6	49.2	23.1	38.5	33.8	9.2	13.1
223	NIWAI	191	20.9	96.3	86.9	89.5	41.9	17.3	46.1	19.9	4.7	13.6
224	TODARAISINGH	112	26.8	98.2	86.6	86.6	36.6	25.0	44.6	19.6	3.6	19.6
225	TONK	238	28.2	97.9	89.9	74.4	49.6	16.8	32.8	15.1	4.2	11.8
226	UNIARA	196	16.3	94.4	80.6	80.1	32.7	14.8	28.1	19.9	3.1	11.7
	TONK	**1032**	**23.8**	**97.0**	**87.4**	**79.3**	**40.7**	**18.9**	**38.5**	**20.8**	**4.7**	**13.3**
227	BARGAON	107	29.9	99.1	92.5	92.5	53.3	26.2	41.1	45.8	8.4	1.9
228	BHINDER	279	22.2	100.0	79.6	95.0	38.4	14.3	31.5	38.7	3.6	4.3
229	DHARIAWAD	249	18.1	98.0	86.3	71.9	44.6	14.5	25.3	38.6	2.0	2.4
230	GIRWA	179	32.4	96.6	92.7	86.0	51.4	23.5	45.3	48.6	6.7	6.7
231	GOGUNDA	147	31.3	95.9	96.6	85.0	47.6	27.9	40.8	50.3	4.1	4.1
232	JHADOL	258	25.6	97.7	86.4	55.4	31.4	14.7	15.1	40.3	2.7	3.9
233	KHERWARA	250	30.8	98.0	89.6	63.6	48.0	18.8	35.6	35.6	2.8	4.0
234	KOTRA	302	14.2	84.8	76.8	21.5	29.1	9.3	5.3	26.2	2.6	2.6
235	MAVLI	149	41.6	100.0	94.6	100.0	51.7	22.8	81.2	49.0	6.0	9.4
236	SALUMBAR	234	27.8	99.1	91.9	73.9	37.2	19.2	24.4	42.7	3.8	3.8
237	SARADA	185	34.1	99.5	94.1	75.1	56.8	28.1	37.8	51.9	7.0	5.9
	UDAIPUR	**2339**	**26.5**	**96.7**	**87.8**	**70.5**	**42.5**	**18.4**	**31.1**	**40.8**	**4.1**	**4.3**
	RAJASTHAN	**39753**	**29.2**	**91.7**	**86.3**	**81.2**	**52.3**	**23.3**	**43.6**	**42.7**	**5.3**	**12.6**

Note: * Dungargarh PS shifted from Churu to Bikaner district on 1st April 2001.
** Excluding data of Dungargarh PS; *** Including data of Dungargarh PS.
# Improved Drinking Water (See Terminology), ## Post office includes Post office, telegraph office and Post and telegraph office.,
Transport Communication includes bus service, rail facility and navigable waterways.
Source: Directorate of Census Operation, Jaipur.

PANCHAYAT SAMITI-WISE NO. OF MEDICAL INSTITUTIONS AND POPULATION/AREA SERVED PER INSTITUTION: RAJASTHAN, 2001

P. Code	Panchayat Samiti	Medical Institutions								Total No. Medical Institutions#	Total Rural Population (2001)	Population Served Per Medical Institution#	Area Served Per Medical Institution (sq. kms.)#
		Hospital	Dispensary	PHC	SHC	MCWC	FWC	Community Health Workers	Other Instituions				
1	2	3	4	5	6	7	8	9	10	11	12	13	14
1	ARAIN	0	9	9	27	5	1	9	11	50	133386	2668	24.04
2	BHINAY	0	17	12	29	3	5	7	7	61	155111	2543	19.94
3	JAWAJA	0	6	6	39	9	3	9	13	60	157901	2632	11.03
4	KEKRI	0	18	10	28	1	5	18	9	57	140921	2472	17.43
5	KISHANGARH	0	20	9	28	0	0	9	18	57	153474	2693	19.42
6	MASOODA	1	19	8	23	1	1	3	11	52	159600	3069	16.83
7	PISANGAN	0	19	17	38	7	2	31	20	81	236459	2919	14.86
8	SRINAGAR	0	13	9	23	5	0	10	13	50	170142	3403	17.95
	AJMER DISTRICT	**1**	**121**	**80**	**235**	**31**	**17**	**96**	**102**	**468**	**1306994**	**2793**	**17.43**
9	BANSURE	0	24	6	12	5	5	12	24	47	214351	4561	14.14
10	BEHROR	1	18	8	11	1	2	22	18	39	139503	3577	8.63
11	KATHUMAR	4	21	8	12	7	3	32	7	52	211689	4071	10.87
12	KISHANGARH BAS	0	7	8	15	5	1	8	9	35	167495	4786	14.44
13	KOTKASIM	0	7	4	4	2	0	13	14	17	117687	6923	20.26
14	LACHHMANGARH	0	10	14	17	3	2	30	31	44	225836	5133	14.07
15	MANDAWAR	0	30	14	16	5	2	26	51	65	197582	3040	8.88
16	NIMRANA	0	17	8	8	1	2	22	36	34	143329	4216	11.13
17	RAJGARH	0	14	6	12	3	2	22	20	35	144726	4135	28.83
18	RAMGARH	0	11	7	14	4	1	29	40	36	220219	6117	17.14
19	RENI	0	17	11	16	1	1	15	11	45	136491	3033	8.71
20	THANAGAZI	0	21	8	18	7	3	31	23	54	189977	3518	19.64
21	TIJARA	0	22	5	14	3	1	12	43	44	226974	5159	14.63
22	UMREN	0	13	7	29	1	2	29	29	50	221794	4436	16.97
	ALWAR	**5**	**232**	**114**	**198**	**48**	**27**	**303**	**356**	**597**	**2557653**	**4284**	**14.34**
23	ANANDPURI	1	9	9	25	4	0	10	1	48	111206	2317	7.12
24	BAGIDORA	0	6	15	35	6	1	17	15	62	176729	2850	8.32
25	GARHI	0	29	20	55	7	2	29	12	111	237521	2140	6.34
26	GHATOL	0	26	14	36	10	4	14	4	86	230344	2678	9.11
27	KUSHALGARH	0	10	15	25	19	1	18	20	69	138970	2014	9.29
28	PEEPALKHOONT	1	11	19	25	17	6	27	8	73	151273	2072	12.5
29	SAJJANGARH	0	11	17	22	7	2	26	7	57	134456	2359	7.06
30	TALWARA	2	20	29	32	7	6	21	19	90	213727	2375	8.34
	BANSWARA	**4**	**122**	**138**	**255**	**77**	**22**	**162**	**86**	**596**	**1394226**	**2339**	**8.48**
31	ANTA	0	13	13	9	7	3	20	27	42	148759	3542	22.2
32	ATRU	1	15	5	17	0	3	14	32	38	127043	3343	22.62
33	BARAN	0	5	5	12	0	0	11	7	22	103142	4688	27.85
34	CHHABRA	0	4	1	6	3	0	3	2	14	99472	7105	55.98
35	CHHIPABAROD	0	14	3	11	1	0	5	12	29	127858	4409	28.43
36	KISHANGANJ	0	8	7	14	1	3	16	27	30	135218	4507	48.35
37	SHAHBAD	0	4	11	14	11	3	10	28	40	108146	2704	36.71
	BARAN	**1**	**63**	**45**	**83**	**23**	**12**	**79**	**135**	**215**	**849638**	**3952**	**32.24**
38	BALOTRA	0	8	16	42	4	3	8	1	70	265596	3794	55.5
39	BARMER	0	7	10	48	0	2	10	0	65	238075	3663	58.67
40	BAYTOO	0	8	16	45	0	2	12	0	69	210345	3048	46.78
41	CHOHTAN	0	7	18	28	1	1	22	1	54	225754	4181	60.49
42	DHORIMANNA	0	13	8	38	2	1	15	6	61	250929	4114	43.74
43	SHEO	0	10	6	31	0	0	11	0	47	178539	3799	140.77
44	SINDHARI	0	17	23	36	10	6	13	8	86	236545	2751	36.23
45	SIWANA	0	16	19	28	3	3	15	9	66	213648	3237	30.03
	BARMER	**0**	**86**	**116**	**296**	**20**	**18**	**106**	**25**	**518**	**1819431**	**3512**	**55.17**
46	BAYANA	0	11	3	16	0	1	27	11	30	191632	6388	26.66
47	DEEG	0	6	6	17	2	1	42	11	31	154862	4996	15.82
48	KAMAN	0	7	7	13	1	0	37	10	28	212139	7576	19.88
49	KUMHER	0	13	14	17	8	3	46	34	52	155122	2983	8.47
50	NADBAI	0	12	4	20	1	1	50	14	37	161111	4354	11.67
51	NAGAR PAHARI	0	9	11	15	3	4	43	40	38	236329	6219	16.36
52	RUPBAS	1	26	13	17	8	3	41	36	65	211147	3248	8.29
53	SEWAR	0	14	9	9	3	2	23	25	35	167641	4790	13.09
54	WEIR	1	33	11	6	1	0	22	14	52	202199	3888	11.08
.	**BHARATPUR**	**2**	**131**	**78**	**130**	**27**	**15**	**331**	**195**	**368**	**1692182**	**4598**	**13.35**

P. Code	Panchayat Samiti	Medical Institutions								Total No. Medical Institutions#	Total Rural Population (2001)	Population Served Per Medical Institution#	Area Served Per Medical Institution (sq. kms.)#
		Hospital	Dispensary	PHC	SHC	MCWC	FWC	Community Health Workers	Other Instituions				
1	2	3	4	5	6	7	8	9	10	11	12	13	14
55	ASIND	0	25	16	34	9	2	28	6	84	192346	2290	13.22
56	BANERA	0	13	6	34	2	0	9	3	55	106222	1931	12.3
57	HURDA	1	11	7	21	0	0	5	1	40	91088	2277	15.43
58	JAHAZPUR	0	24	15	30	12	3	30	4	81	167782	2071	12.76
59	KOTRI	0	10	15	19	5	2	14	6	49	148702	3035	19.39
60	MANDAL	0	17	10	27	3	4	17	0	57	197500	3465	20.27
61	MANDALGARH	2	23	29	41	14	8	13	9	109	199935	1834	12.77
62	RAIPUR	2	6	11	19	5	3	8	3	43	84354	1962	11.99
63	SAHARA	0	14	11	21	3	1	4	1	49	98050	2001	12.92
64	SHAHPURA	0	21	8	33	0	0	4	1	62	148955	2403	18.18
65	SUWANA	1	18	11	28	5	2	14	2	63	164004	2603	13.21
	BHILWARA	**6**	**182**	**139**	**307**	**58**	**25**	**146**	**36**	**692**	**1598938**	**2311**	**14.51**
66	BIKANER	0	17	21	24	2	7	18	13	64	374802	5856	139.76
67	DUNGARGARH *	0	18	15	35	3	3	20	7	71	182819	2575	42.29
68	KOLAYAT	0	11	8	23	1	3	12	18	43	207749	4831	170.2
69	LUNKARANSAR	0	15	12	22	5	4	12	25	54	217341	4025	115.07
70	NOKHA	0	10	5	25	3	0	7	2	43	279343	6496	87.62
	BIKANER **	**0**	**53**	**46**	**94**	**11**	**14**	**49**	**58**	**204**	**1079235**	**5290**	**143.37**
71	HINDOLI	2	11	18	21	8	4	28	20	60	189290	3155	22.32
72	KESHORAIPATAN	0	16	14	22	7	4	15	30	59	178625	3028	21.82
73	NAINWA	0	17	3	25	9	6	8	21	54	156227	2893	21.11
74	TALERA	0	16	13	27	4	2	18	35	60	258916	4315	31.38
	BUNDI	**2**	**60**	**48**	**95**	**28**	**16**	**69**	**106**	**233**	**783058**	**3361**	**24.24**
75	ARNOD	0	10	10	6	4	1	7	1	30	119837	3995	23.38
76	BARI SADRI	0	5	4	5	0	0	24	2	14	88841	6346	33.89
77	BEGUN	0	13	16	21	13	1	9	3	63	102011	1619	15.2
78	BHADESAR	0	6	5	11	1	3	8	4	23	107393	4669	23.5
79	BHAINSRORGARH	0	10	2	11	1	2	17	6	24	80379	3349	57.08
80	BHOPALSAGAR	0	5	9	11	3	1	0	0	28	72675	2596	14.22
81	CHHOTI SADRI	0	6	6	7	5	1	8	8	24	100067	4169	28.83
82	CHITTAURGARH	0	14	9	25	4	0	6	3	52	167960	3230	15.65
83	DUNGLA	0	7	5	18	4	1	21	5	34	89975	2646	14.52
84	GANGRAR	0	9	3	16	1	0	11	0	29	88640	3057	19.16
85	KAPASAN	0	6	3	5	0	0	1	0	14	84531	6038	34.47
86	NIMBAHERA	0	10	12	16	0	1	21	5	38	135391	3563	21.39
87	PRATAPGARH	0	16	15	37	12	5	20	5	80	201229	2515	17.85
88	RASHMI	0	15	6	16	1	1	8	1	38	75326	1982	11.83
	CHITTAURGARH	**0**	**132**	**105**	**205**	**49**	**17**	**161**	**43**	**491**	**1514255**	**3084**	**20.71**
89	CHURU	0	21	15	45	0	2	15	2	81	152178	1879	19.25
90	RAJGARH	0	22	15	44	4	6	59	46	85	267403	3146	25.85
91	RATANGARH	0	23	13	46	4	3	16	1	86	158090	1838	19.1
92	SARDARSHAHAR	0	28	7	29	0	2	20	14	64	222979	3484	59.6
93	SUJANGARH	0	16	15	39	5	1	13	6	75	253207	3376	34.61
94	TARANAGAR	2	29	10	27	1	0	8	6	69	151006	2188	25.84
	CHURU ***	**2**	**157**	**90**	**265**	**17**	**17**	**151**	**82**	**531**	**1387682**	**2613**	**25.6**
95	BANDIKUI	0	10	8	12	7	2	35	32	37	267016	7217	16.24
96	DAUSA	0	18	14	28	12	3	12	59	72	271907	3776	12.61
97	LALSOT	0	15	8	25	2	2	13	43	50	251370	5027	17.08
98	MAHWA	0	12	11	11	9	3	27	7	43	179173	4167	11.01
99	SIKRAI	0	10	8	14	6	3	26	16	38	211779	5573	13.23
	DAUSA	**0**	**65**	**49**	**90**	**36**	**13**	**113**	**157**	**240**	**1181245**	**4922**	**13.91**
100	BARI	0	11	17	22	6	1	72	3	56	150595	2689	14.18
101	BASERI	2	14	6	15	8	2	20	9	45	201777	4484	22.25
102	DHAULPUR	2	19	16	15	10	4	24	25	62	262456	4233	9.31
103	RAJAKHERA	0	6	7	11	1	3	20	3	25	191812	7672	22.88
	DHAULPUR	**4**	**50**	**46**	**63**	**25**	**10**	**136**	**40**	**188**	**806640**	**4291**	**15.66**
104	ASPUR	1	23	25	49	39	4	10	6	137	184508	1347	5.05
105	BICHHIWARA	2	15	15	54	11	4	21	4	97	236114	2434	7.69
106	DUNGARPUR	1	16	22	50	6	6	18	3	95	172385	1815	6.05
107	SAGWARA	3	30	16	57	7	1	25	5	113	192681	1705	5.41
108	SIMALWARA	1	31	13	51	11	3	38	7	107	241099	2253	8.54
	DUNGARPUR	**8**	**115**	**91**	**261**	**74**	**18**	**112**	**25**	**549**	**1026787**	**1870**	**6.44**
109	ANUPGARH	2	25	13	41	5	7	81	288	86	417746	4858	41.21
110	GANGANAGAR	0	18	12	36	3	5	32	68	69	176517	2558	12.39
111	KARANPUR	1	6	4	34	1	0	20	47	46	103094	2241	17.62
112	PADAMPUR	1	15	6	20	3	4	51	105	45	121362	2697	18.72
113	RAISINGHNAGAR	0	19	6	27	0	2	70	80	52	157334	3026	25.3
114	SADULSHAHAR	1	13	13	32	8	1	23	57	67	146629	2188	22.16
115	SURATGARH	2	29	10	19	4	4	24	76	64	213384	3334	59.24
	GANGANAGAR	**7**	**125**	**64**	**209**	**24**	**23**	**301**	**721**	**429**	**1336066**	**3114**	**29.47**
116	BHADRA	0	30	10	21	4	4	42	58	65	220582	3394	26.36
117	HANUMANGARH	0	47	29	53	8	7	128	335	137	628123	4585	14.85
118	NOHAR	4	44	17	40	2	4	28	71	107	365762	3418	40.23
	HANUMANGARH	**4**	**121**	**56**	**114**	**14**	**15**	**198**	**464**	**309**	**1214467**	**3930**	**26.06**

P. Code	Panchayat Samiti	Medical Institutions								Total No. Medical Institutions#	Total Rural Population (2001)	Population Served Per Medical Institution#	Area Served Per Medical Institution (sq. kms.)#
		Hospi-tal	Dispen-sary	PHC	SHC	MCWC	FWC	Community Health Workers	Other Instituions				
1	2	3	4	5	6	7	8	9	10	11	12	13	14
119	AMBER	0	11	10	28	8	7	39	47	57	262029	4597	14.73
120	BASSI	0	17	14	26	12	4	50	38	69	229639	3328	9.14
121	CHAKSU	0	14	4	13	6	2	2	6	37	161140	4355	20.72
122	DUDU	2	25	17	22	18	2	24	22	84	272517	3244	22.09
123	GOVINDGARH	0	22	10	23	10	5	27	24	65	275780	4243	10.25
124	JAMWA RAMGARH	0	30	17	23	0	3	52	30	70	250132	3573	14.45
125	JHOTWARA	0	13	3	8	7	1	4	13	31	88946	2869	12.42
126	KOTPUTLI	0	28	12	15	6	2	14	15	61	228470	3745	10.87
127	PHAGI	0	14	7	15	3	2	19	9	39	161610	4144	28.55
128	SAMBHAR	0	21	9	25	8	1	33	19	63	209528	3326	13.21
129	SANGANER	0	16	4	20	11	0	10	13	51	131301	2575	11.45
130	SHAHPURA	0	33	4	21	6	5	9	18	64	181498	2836	6.38
131	VIRATNAGAR	0	19	7	24	1	1	10	23	51	206414	4047	12.73
	JAIPUR	**2**	**263**	**118**	**263**	**96**	**35**	**293**	**277**	**742**	**2659004**	**3584**	**14.02**
132	JAISALMER	0	10	14	34	2	0	12	2	60	127798	2130	214.16
133	SAM	0	10	8	44	1	1	16	2	63	138679	2201	335.1
134	SANKRA	1	18	12	31	2	3	27	7	64	165376	2584	85.73
	JAISALMER	**1**	**38**	**34**	**109**	**5**	**4**	**55**	**11**	**187**	**431853**	**2309**	**210.95**
135	AHORE	0	13	7	52	1	2	6	6	73	177342	2429	21.87
136	BHINMAL	0	6	9	22	1	1	8	1	38	184751	4862	35.2
137	JALOR	0	12	8	32	3	1	7	5	55	131827	2397	19.18
138	JASWANTPURA	0	12	11	27	0	2	5	2	50	128410	2568	21.38
139	RANIWARA	0	3	7	25	0	2	19	15	35	163349	4667	28.11
140	SANCHORE	0	13	19	51	2	1	10	5	85	342120	4025	35.39
141	SAYLA	0	13	13	26	1	2	12	9	53	211147	3984	27.54
	JALOR	**0**	**72**	**74**	**235**	**8**	**11**	**67**	**43**	**389**	**1338946**	**3442**	**27.02**
142	BAKANI	0	7	6	20	3	1	32	33	36	152329	4231	24.6
143	DAG	0	11	6	27	1	1	8	9	45	167192	3715	25.12
144	JHALRAPATAN	0	13	14	15	2	2	10	10	44	205868	4679	30.21
145	KHANPUR	0	16	7	23	9	3	13	12	55	153370	2789	17.09
146	MANOHARTHANA	0	5	1	13	0	1	16	12	19	161425	8496	48.56
147	PIRAWA	0	7	11	16	9	1	9	8	43	171897	3998	23.28
	JHALAWAR	**0**	**59**	**45**	**114**	**24**	**9**	**88**	**84**	**242**	**1012081**	**4182**	**25.66**
148	ALSISAR	1	17	7	23	17	6	12	6	65	141416	2176	11.49
149	BUHANA	0	31	18	40	7	9	5	31	96	204411	2129	6.81
150	CHIRAWA	1	17	12	21	1	2	16	20	52	152843	2939	9.4
151	JHUNJHUNUN	0	28	7	45	4	0	9	9	84	176693	2103	9.77
152	KHETRI	0	16	22	26	2	4	18	24	66	214474	3250	12.06
153	NAWALGARH	0	14	19	31	8	7	21	29	72	217636	3023	9.24
154	SURAJGARH	0	7	10	21	12	1	4	2	50	175820	3516	15.63
155	UDAIPURWATI	0	16	16	34	20	7	38	30	86	235280	2736	9.66
	JHUNJHUNUN	**2**	**146**	**111**	**241**	**71**	**36**	**123**	**151**	**571**	**1518573**	**2659**	**10.13**
156	BALESAR	0	13	13	32	7	4	16	2	65	174179	2680	28.52
157	BAP	0	3	7	21	0	1	5	0	31	157290	5074	142.94
158	BHOPALGARH	0	12	11	36	4	5	13	4	63	202321	3211	27.67
159	BILARA	1	10	27	41	3	2	11	1	82	180550	2202	18.29
160	LUNI	0	13	14	43	0	3	19	16	70	229097	3273	28.32
161	MANDOR	0	9	3	14	1	4	9	17	27	151257	5602	47.01
162	OSIAN	0	23	20	70	4	3	38	15	117	422181	3608	35.76
163	PHALODI	0	13	10	27	3	1	6	4	53	229892	4338	61.09
164	SHERGARH	0	9	8	21	0	4	17	5	38	162656	4280	51.97
	JODHPUR	**1**	**105**	**113**	**305**	**22**	**27**	**134**	**64**	**546**	**1909423**	**3497**	**40.62**
165	HINDAUN	2	19	11	16	13	2	42	40	61	262403	4302	10.35
166	KARAULI	0	17	11	27	4	3	45	21	59	222621	3773	20.67
167	NADOTI	0	16	7	11	10	4	12	28	44	126089	2866	14.68
168	SAPOTRA	2	20	12	37	9	6	53	36	80	232513	2906	24.53
169	TODABHIM	1	17	9	18	22	6	32	26	67	194094	2897	7.8
	KARAULI	**5**	**89**	**50**	**109**	**58**	**21**	**184**	**151**	**311**	**1037720**	**3337**	**16.02**
170	CHECHAT	0	11	2	16	5	6	25	34	34	132073	3885	22.67
171	ITAWA	1	20	5	11	6	1	22	28	43	155646	3620	20.63
172	LADPURA	0	10	8	23	5	2	15	39	46	144691	3145	28.42
173	SANGOD	0	14	8	31	4	0	9	18	57	146951	2578	18.35
174	SULTANPUR	0	5	8	30	1	2	38	58	44	150587	3422	20.72
	KOTA	**1**	**60**	**31**	**111**	**21**	**11**	**109**	**177**	**224**	**729948**	**3259**	**21.98**
175	DEGANA	3	15	12	48	12	5	16	12	90	190085	2112	16.19
176	DIDWANA	1	16	10	54	1	3	15	11	82	285031	3476	19.61
177	JAYAL	0	15	11	40	3	3	30	4	69	224944	3260	30.26
178	KUCHAMAN	1	27	17	35	6	7	27	12	86	268146	3118	16.7
179	LADNU	0	11	20	25	14	3	5	9	70	158026	2258	19.59
180	MAKRANA	0	10	13	30	6	4	33	10	59	199671	3384	18.75
181	MERTA	0	12	12	29	4	6	11	3	57	183429	3218	24.51
182	MUNDWA	1	10	14	31	1	0	11	4	57	197532	3465	38.32
183	NAGAUR	0	15	8	51	0	1	16	6	74	224815	3038	32.17
184	PARBATSAR	0	20	22	22	4	2	22	10	68	186413	2741	15.75
185	RIYAN	1	19	14	32	7	5	16	7	73	179629	2461	16.98
	NAGAUR	**7**	**170**	**153**	**397**	**58**	**39**	**202**	**88**	**785**	**2297721**	**2927**	**22.09**

P. Code	Panchayat Samiti	Medical Institutions								Total No. Medical Institutions#	Total Rural Population (2001)	Population Served Per Medical Institution#	Area Served Per Medical Institution (sq. kms.)#
		Hospital	Dispensary	PHC	SHC	MCWC	FWC	Community Health Workers	Other Instituions				
1	2	3	4	5	6	7	8	9	10	11	12	13	14
186	BALI	1	25	10	40	4	4	17	28	80	183802	2298	17.12
187	DESURI	6	13	12	20	3	4	20	11	54	102245	1893	15.35
188	JAITARAN	1	10	19	36	3	2	12	9	69	186938	2709	18.69
189	MARWAR JUNCTION	2	16	19	39	2	6	22	17	78	181445	2326	17.83
190	PALI	1	7	6	22	0	2	9	2	36	89939	2498	36.02
191	RAIPUR	1	17	8	24	7	6	31	11	57	182004	3193	17.31
192	RANI STATION	7	24	5	33	4	1	18	14	73	106504	1459	10.45
193	ROHAT	1	8	14	17	4	2	2	4	44	102599	2332	31.92
194	SOJAT	2	9	35	46	11	12	16	2	103	155889	1513	15.8
195	SUMERPUR	0	8	19	26	4	4	10	14	57	137999	2421	16.00
	PALI	**22**	**137**	**147**	**303**	**42**	**43**	**157**	**112**	**651**	**1429364**	**2196**	**18.23**
196	AMET	0	7	4	23	0	2	3	3	34	88162	2593	14.86
197	BHIM	0	8	13	23	8	8	4	7	52	137578	2646	13.03
198	DEOGARH	0	4	4	12	0	3	9	0	20	77865	3893	29.46
199	KHAMNOR	0	25	17	32	12	5	26	6	86	172395	2005	6.92
200	KUMBHALGARH	1	15	22	33	20	14	28	2	91	131346	1443	8.53
201	RAILMAGRA	0	21	13	32	6	3	10	3	72	110435	1534	7.56
202	RAJSAMAND	0	15	7	22	2	3	4	14	46	140520	3055	12.38
	RAJSAMAND	**1**	**95**	**80**	**177**	**48**	**38**	**84**	**35**	**401**	**858301**	**2140**	**10.61**
203	BAMANWAS	1	21	10	16	2	2	32	19	50	149429	2989	14.58
204	BONLI	0	20	10	21	12	5	11	16	63	209833	3331	16.02
205	GANGAPUR	0	18	6	16	12	7	37	17	52	179209	3446	12.40
206	KHANDAR	0	21	7	21	2	3	38	14	51	150136	2944	26.52
207	SAWAI MADHOPUR	0	21	15	36	7	6	19	19	79	215810	2732	15.60
	SAWAI MADHOPUR	**1**	**101**	**48**	**110**	**35**	**23**	**137**	**85**	**295**	**904417**	**3066**	**16.84**
208	DANTA RAMGARH	3	30	29	46	13	2	26	22	121	262183	2167	9.22
209	DHOND	0	29	14	45	9	5	18	11	97	209919	2164	9.41
210	FATEHPUR	1	21	12	46	4	0	10	27	84	193473	2303	14.73
211	KHANDELA	2	13	28	37	0	3	20	21	80	218560	2732	9.80
212	LACHHMANGARH	0	18	10	31	0	5	7	11	59	197022	3339	17.41
213	NEEM KA THANA	1	30	12	50	8	4	44	53	101	317049	3139	11.75
214	PIPRALI	1	16	21	36	11	5	15	18	85	206064	2424	9.38
215	SRI MADHOPUR	0	12	10	22	3	0	14	21	47	210980	4489	12.06
	SIKAR	**8**	**169**	**136**	**313**	**48**	**24**	**154**	**184**	**674**	**1815250**	**2693**	**11.32**
216	ABU ROAD	0	9	5	16	3	2	4	3	33	114818	3479	26.00
217	PINDWARA	0	13	9	34	2	4	16	11	58	184803	3186	19.63
218	REODAR	1	11	16	29	18	7	24	13	75	175344	2338	14.49
219	SHEOGANJ	0	8	16	21	10	4	9	5	55	99663	1812	16.22
220	SIROHI	1	19	16	39	22	7	27	4	97	125589	1295	11.24
	SIROHI	**2**	**60**	**62**	**139**	**55**	**24**	**80**	**36**	**318**	**700217**	**2202**	**15.93**
221	DEOLI	1	18	14	20	2	2	21	14	55	169271	3078	22.46
222	MALPURA	0	26	11	13	1	2	15	21	51	176932	3469	28.22
223	NIWAI	0	30	6	19	6	2	17	13	61	165298	2710	16.89
224	TODARAISINGH	0	13	12	13	1	1	12	4	39	110131	2824	25.27
225	TONK	0	21	28	43	2	4	18	6	94	204362	2174	15.06
226	UNIARA	0	12	7	13	0	1	28	5	32	132509	4141	30.83
	TONK	**1**	**120**	**78**	**121**	**12**	**12**	**111**	**63**	**332**	**958503**	**2887**	**21.36**
227	BARGAON	2	15	10	14	11	5	10	12	52	123802	2381	12.46
228	BHINDER	0	21	12	33	22	2	10	6	88	201832	2294	11.19
229	DHARIAWAD	0	14	10	33	16	3	17	7	73	203605	2789	16.13
230	GIRWA	0	19	22	37	17	8	24	16	95	227623	2396	14.20
231	GOGUNDA	1	11	8	26	19	1	21	10	65	151575	2332	13.41
232	JHADOL	3	18	16	45	25	2	33	11	107	193810	1811	13.35
233	KHERWARA	0	13	23	48	12	6	23	2	96	254301	2649	11.22
234	KOTRA	1	12	10	36	1	3	5	7	60	183504	3058	19.86
235	MAVLI	0	22	12	43	5	3	15	8	82	194148	2368	9.74
236	SALUMBAR	0	29	14	47	16	3	9	4	106	196614	1855	8.70
237	SARADA	2	33	24	44	8	3	30	6	111	212181	1912	9.71
	UDAIPUR	**9**	**207**	**161**	**406**	**152**	**39**	**197**	**89**	**935**	**2142995**	**2292**	**12.33**
	RAJASTHAN	**109**	**3706**	**2746**	**6353**	**1317**	**675**	**4688**	**4281**	**14231**	**43292813**	**3042**	**23.58**

Note: # Include dispensary, hospital, MCWC, PHC and SHC, * Dungargarh PS shifted from Churu to Bikaner district on 1st April 2001.
** Excluding data of Dungargarh PS; *** Including data of Dungargarh PS.
Source: Directorate of Census Operation, Jaipur.

PANCHAYAT SAMITI-WISE NO. OF DOCTORS, BEDS AND PATIENTS TREATED (2001)

P. Code	Panchayat Samiti	No. of Doctors			No. of Beds	Patients Treated		Population Served Per Doctor	Population Served Per Bed
		Male	Female	Total		Allopathy	Ayurvedic, Homeopathic and Unani		
1	2	3	4	5	6	7	8	9	10
1	ARAIN	10	1	11	66	53120	56150	12126	2021
2	BHINAY	12	—	12	66	74003	230910	12926	2350
3	JAWAJA	15	—	15	78	75693	75008	10527	2024
4	KEKRI	16	3	19	112	97805	190710	7417	1258
5	KISHANGARH	6	—	6	30	6712	225450	25579	5116
6	MASOODA	8	2	10	62	83959	150801	15960	2574
7	PISANGAN	15	3	18	120	96508	200350	13137	1970
8	SRINAGAR	3	—	3	26	88865	101739	56714	6544
	AJMER DISTRICT	**85**	**9**	**94**	**560**	**449542**	**944058**	**13904**	**2334**
9	BANSURE	10	2	12	80	75472	155447	17863	2679
10	BEHROR	18	2	20	130	49342	182287	6975	1073
11	KATHUMAR	13	—	13	66	34758	94193	16284	3207
12	KISHANGARH BAS	9	1	10	74	60152	93265	16750	2263
13	KOTKASIM	5	—	5	48	43259	71846	23537	2452
14	LACHHMANGARH	10	4	14	110	114891	112207	16131	2053
15	MANDAWAR	11	2	13	84	62328	167177	15199	2352
16	NIMRANA	9	1	10	60	26737	134552	14333	2389
17	RAJGARH	16	2	18	86	57346	135245	8040	1683
18	RAMGARH	9	—	9	54	67626	126627	24469	4078
19	RENI	8	—	8	54	47535	126516	17061	2528
20	THANAGAZI	10	4	14	60	51081	143973	13570	3166
21	TIJARA	13	—	13	88	98184	149850	17460	2579
22	UMREN	7	3	10	54	54112	170143	22179	4107
	ALWAR	**148**	**21**	**169**	**1048**	**842823**	**1863328**	**15134**	**2441**
23	ANANDPURI	4	—	4	48	20869	55487	27802	2317
24	BAGIDORA	8	1	9	72	59079	116070	19637	2455
25	GARHI	13	5	18	128	111458	351766	13196	1856
26	GHATOL	10	1	11	102	68611	229340	20940	2258
27	KUSHALGARH	8	1	9	74	56448	59587	15441	1878
28	PEEPALKHOONT	6	—	6	60	34948	74134	25212	2521
29	SAJJANGARH	8	1	9	48	45397	67322	14940	2801
30	TALWARA	9	2	11	72	55490	328481	19430	2968
	BANSWARA	**66**	**11**	**77**	**604**	**452300**	**1282187**	**18107**	**2308**
31	ANTA	20	3	23	120	NA	96166	6468	1240
32	ATRU	7	1	8	54	NA	96875	15880	2353
33	BARAN	5	1	6	24	NA	94603	17190	4298
34	CHHABRA	12	1	13	68	NA	30790	7652	1463
35	CHHIPABAROD	6	2	8	48	NA	97621	15982	2664
36	KISHANGANJ	6	2	8	54	NA	68512	16902	2504
37	SHAHBAD	9	3	12	92	NA	43592	9012	1176
	BARAN #	**65**	**13**	**78**	**460**	**NA**	**431993**	**10893**	**1847**
38	BALOTRA	10	3	13	60	NA	NA	20430	4427
39	BARMER	10	—	10	48	NA	NA	23808	4960
40	BAYTOO	8	1	9	66	NA	NA	23372	3187
41	CHOHTAN	13	—	13	78	NA	NA	17366	2894
42	DHORIMANNA	16	1	17	122	NA	NA	14761	2057
43	SHEO	10	—	10	60	NA	NA	17854	2976
44	SINDHARI	7	1	8	72	NA	NA	29568	3285
45	SIWANA	12	3	15	96	NA	NA	14243	2226
	BARMER	**86**	**9**	**95**	**602**	**NA**	**NA**	**19152**	**3022**
46	BAYANA	12	1	13	80	74460	148410	14741	2395
47	DEEG	11	—	11	80	52169	133125	14078	1936
48	KAMAN	7	—	7	60	15252	85258	30306	3536
49	KUMHER	11	—	11	60	41134	138151	14102	2585
50	NADBAI	7	1	8	48	29266	132045	20139	3356
51	NAGAR PAHARI	7	1	8	60	43120	118443	29541	3939
52	RUPBAS	10	1	11	66	22790	264482	19195	3199
53	SEWAR	2	2	4	24	9529	265951	41910	6985
54	WEIR	19	1	20	108	11847	607050	10110	1872
	BHARATPUR	**86**	**7**	**93**	**586**	**299567**	**1892915**	**18196**	**2888**

P. Code	Panchayat Samiti	No. of Doctors			No. of Beds	Patients Treated		Population Served Per Doctor	Population Served Per Bed
		Male	Female	Total		Allopathy	Ayurvedic, Homeopathic and Unani		
1	2	3	4	5	6	7	8	9	10
55	ASIND	5	3	8	66	NA	NA	24043	2914
56	BANERA	7	1	8	48	NA	NA	13278	2213
57	HURDA	6	4	10	79	NA	NA	9109	1153
58	JAHAZPUR	16	5	21	147	NA	NA	7990	1141
59	KOTRI	8	2	10	84	NA	NA	14870	1770
60	MANDAL	7	4	11	66	NA	NA	17955	2992
61	MANDALGARH	8	6	14	131	NA	NA	14281	1526
62	RAIPUR	5	3	8	54	NA	NA	10544	1562
63	SAHARA	7	2	9	110	NA	NA	10894	891
64	SHAHPURA	3	2	5	34	NA	NA	29791	4381
65	SUWANA	9	2	11	54	NA	NA	14909	3037
	BHILWARA	**81**	**34**	**115**	**873**	**NA**	**NA**	**13904**	**1832**
66	BIKANER	18	4	22	146	NA	NA	17036	2567
67	DUNGARGARH *	12	3	15	78	NA	NA	12188	2344
68	KOLAYAT	6	5	11	76	NA	NA	18886	2734
69	LUNKARANSAR	10	3	13	78	NA	NA	16719	2786
70	NOKHA	15	1	16	104	NA	NA	17459	2686
	BIKANER **	**61**	**16**	**77**	**482**	**NA**	**NA**	**14016**	**2239**
71	HINDOLI	10	—	10	60	35450	99932	18929	3155
72	KESHORAIPATAN	17	2	19	84	30035	107853	9401	2126
73	NAINWA	11	1	12	92	49320	152998	13019	1698
74	TALERA	10	2	12	84	161109	129522	21576	3082
	BUNDI	**48**	**5**	**53**	**320**	**275914**	**490305**	**14775**	**2447**
75	ARNOD	8	—	8	54	19762	78094	14980	2219
76	BARI SADRI	6	1	7	74	20521	87016	12692	1201
77	BEGUN	13	—	13	92	29386	85017	7847	1109
78	BHADESAR	3	4	7	48	30257	122937	15342	2237
79	BHAINSRORGARH	3	2	5	48	13967	58964	16076	1675
80	BHOPALSAGAR	4	1	5	48	39265	77432	14535	1514
81	CHHOTI SADRI	6	1	7	42	6479	60913	14295	2383
82	CHITTAURGARH	8	2	10	36	52399	88530	16796	4666
83	DUNGLA	4	2	6	42	29897	69592	14996	2142
84	GANGRAR	6	—	6	42	28062	147131	14773	2110
85	KAPASAN	6	2	8	68	16849	57286	10566	1243
86	NIMBAHERA	14	3	17	80	25486	70521	7964	1692
87	PRATAPGARH	8	2	10	52	40493	197843	20123	3870
88	RASHMI	4	—	4	42	25329	98634	18832	1793
	CHITTAURGARH	**93**	**20**	**113**	**768**	**378152**	**1299910**	**13400**	**1972**
89	CHURU	14	5	19	96	40311	250436	8009	1585
90	RAJGARH	21	3	24	140	64911	142879	11142	1910
91	RATANGARH	19	1	20	90	49273	209284	7905	1757
92	SARDARSHAHAR	8	2	10	54	41679	145184	22298	4129
93	SUJANGARH	16	3	19	114	72358	260448	13327	2221
94	TARANAGAR	13	2	15	72	38084	151006	10067	2097
	CHURU ***	**91**	**16**	**107**	**566**	**306616**	**1271446**	**12969**	**2452**
95	BANDIKUI	13	1	14	86	148259	98554	19073	3105
96	DAUSA	26	1	27	166	126497	124618	10071	1638
97	LALSOT	11	2	13	66	105794	103435	19336	3809
98	MAHWA	16	2	18	96	105125	122413	9954	1866
99	SIKRAI	8	3	11	54	71668	122852	19253	3922
	DAUSA #	**74**	**9**	**83**	**468**	**409084**	**473318**	**14232**	**2524**
100	BARI	7	3	10	68	NA	NA	15060	2215
101	BASERI	7	—	7	60	NA	NA	28825	3363
102	DHAULPUR	9	1	10	66	NA	NA	26246	3977
103	RAJAKHERA	8	1	9	54	NA	NA	21312	3552
	DHAULPUR	**31**	**5**	**36**	**248**	**NA**	**NA**	**22407**	**3253**
104	ASPUR	14	1	15	96	47326	206140	12301	1922
105	BICHHIWARA	13	—	13	78	29611	183133	18163	3027
106	DUNGARPUR	7	4	11	66	23678	174945	15671	2612
107	SAGWARA	21	4	25	147	21452	473209	7707	1311
108	SIMALWARA	19	1	20	128	67332	259680	12055	1884
	DUNGARPUR	**74**	**10**	**84**	**515**	**189399**	**1297107**	**12224**	**1994**
109	ANUPGARH	17	6	23	104	NA	NA	18163	4017
110	GANGANAGAR	6	5	11	60	NA	NA	16047	2942
111	KARANPUR	9	2	11	68	NA	NA	9372	1516
112	PADAMPUR	9	1	10	66	NA	NA	12136	1839
113	RAISINGHNAGAR	11	3	14	80	NA	NA	11238	1967
114	SADULSHAHAR	5	2	7	66	NA	NA	20947	2222
115	SURATGARH	8	4	12	80	NA	NA	17782	2667
	GANGANAGAR	**65**	**23**	**88**	**524**	**NA**	**NA**	**15183**	**2550**
116	BHADRA	14	1	15	78	74870	149291	14705	2828
117	HANUMANGARH	20	5	25	176	123001	226027	25125	3569
118	NOHAR	23	2	25	158	93375	199776	14630	2315
	HANUMANGARH ##	**57**	**8**	**65**	**412**	**291246**	**575094**	**18684**	**2948**

P. Code	Panchayat Samiti	No. of Doctors			No. of Beds	Patients Treated		Population Served Per Doctor	Population Served Per Bed
		Male	Female	Total		Allopathy	Ayurvedic, Homeopathic and Unani		
1	2	3	4	5	6	7	8	9	10
119	AMBER	6	4	10	104	NA	NA	26203	2520
120	BASSI	11	2	13	54	NA	NA	17665	4253
121	CHAKSU	5	—	5	54	NA	NA	32228	2984
122	DUDU	10	3	13	78	NA	NA	20963	3494
123	GOVINDGARH	10	4	14	90	NA	NA	19699	3064
124	JAMWA RAMGARH	16	3	19	116	NA	NA	13165	2156
125	JHOTWARA	2	1	3	18	NA	NA	29649	4941
126	KOTPUTLI	7	4	11	60	NA	NA	20770	3808
127	PHAGI	8	—	8	54	NA	NA	20201	2993
128	SAMBHAR	8	2	10	66	NA	NA	20953	3175
129	SANGANER	2	5	7	66	NA	NA	18757	1989
130	SHAHPURA	6	4	10	64	NA	NA	18150	2836
131	VIRATNAGAR	9	2	11	116	NA	NA	18765	1779
	JAIPUR	**100**	**34**	**134**	**940**	**NA**	**NA**	**19843**	**2829**
132	JAISALMER	6	—	6	24	55371	36984	21300	5325
133	SAM	6	—	6	60	21811	34891	23113	2311
134	SANKRA	4	1	5	80	35825	58081	33075	2067
	JAISALMER	**16**	**1**	**17**	**164**	**113007**	**129956**	**25403**	**2633**
135	AHORE	10	1	11	66	47566	114805	16122	2687
136	BHINMAL	11	3	14	116	41103	44693	13197	1593
137	JALOR	7	2	9	49	23777	72118	14647	2690
138	JASWANTPURA	9	1	10	66	20361	71643	12841	1946
139	RANIWARA	12	—	12	72	28750	21552	13612	2269
140	SANCHORE	16	3	19	136	34326	43494	18006	2516
141	SAYLA	10	2	12	72	49180	60489	17596	2933
	JALOR	**75**	**12**	**87**	**577**	**245063**	**428794**	**15390**	**2321**
142	BAKANI	8	—	8	60	38929	58124	19041	2539
143	DAG	22	2	24	104	50048	132464	6966	1608
144	JHALRAPATAN	7	1	8	42	72981	103127	25734	4902
145	KHANPUR	8	2	10	60	90863	115614	15337	2556
146	MANOHARTHANA	11	2	13	92	45382	96923	12417	1755
147	PIRAWA	11	2	13	72	67209	146570	13223	2387
	JHALAWAR	**67**	**9**	**76**	**430**	**365412**	**652822**	**13317**	**2354**
148	ALSISAR	9	1	10	60	242898	140992	14142	2357
149	BUHANA	14	1	15	84	262255	154973	13627	2433
150	CHIRAWA	10	1	11	72	257191	135197	13895	2123
151	JHUNJHUNUN	11	1	12	96	296060	260742	14724	1841
152	KHETRI	8	1	9	54	244963	155076	23830	3972
153	NAWALGARH	21	5	26	116	268945	125570	8371	1876
154	SURAJGARH	12	1	13	78	260311	146934	13525	2254
155	UDAIPURWATI	18	2	20	96	247072	127458	11764	2451
	JHUNJHUNUN	**103**	**13**	**116**	**656**	**2079695**	**1246942**	**13091**	**2315**
156	BALESAR	9	—	9	80	20109	16255	19353	2177
157	BAP	4	2	6	60	23068	20623	26215	2622
158	BHOPALGARH	9	3	12	78	39622	37254	16860	2594
159	BILARA	23	11	34	164	43773	61103	5310	1101
160	LUNI	14	2	16	102	1804	34537	14319	2246
161	MANDOR	6	1	7	36	63275	36563	21608	4202
162	OSIAN	17	5	22	144	38883	82519	19190	2932
163	PHALODI	6	1	7	48	97688	50653	32842	4789
164	SHERGARH	9	1	10	60	8225	39452	16266	2711
	JODHPUR	**84**	**24**	**108**	**632**	**253648**	**304827**	**17680**	**3021**
165	HINDAUN	14	1	15	80	54182	156215	17494	3280
166	KARAULI	15	—	15	60	49466	120000	14841	3710
167	NADOTI	10	—	10	48	44570	97252	12609	2627
168	SAPOTRA	8	—	8	66	55823	91212	29064	3523
169	TODABHIM	8	—	8	60	44030	94000	24262	3235
	KARAULI ###	**55**	**1**	**56**	**314**	**248071**	**558679**	**18531**	**3305**
170	CHECHAT	9	5	14	104	97280	75908	9434	1270
171	ITAWA	11	1	12	60	87306	97821	12971	2594
172	LADPURA	18	10	28	170	124807	44630	5168	851
173	SANGOD	9	2	11	60	119215	145909	13359	2449
174	SULTANPUR	9	4	13	72	153425	78735	11584	2091
	KOTA	**56**	**22**	**78**	**466**	**582033**	**443003**	**9358**	**1566**
175	DEGANA	13	2	15	72	71161	16307	12672	2640
176	DIDWANA	17	2	19	114	50075	82781	15002	2500
177	JAYAL	9	5	14	84	47715	99743	16067	2678
178	KUCHAMAN	20	4	24	119	72921	170471	11173	2253
179	LADNU	10	—	10	63	32897	91897	15803	2508
180	MAKRANA	16	3	19	81	40979	102655	10509	2465
181	MERTA	13	2	15	101	75832	99886	12229	1816
182	MUNDWA	12	2	14	81	50042	83328	14109	2439
183	NAGAUR	9	1	10	51	59181	127904	22482	4408
184	PARBATSAR	5	2	7	45	41902	148421	26630	4143

P. Code	Panchayat Samiti	No. of Doctors: Male	No. of Doctors: Female	No. of Doctors: Total	No. of Beds	Patients Treated: Allopathy	Patients Treated: Ayurvedic, Homeopathic and Unani	Population Served Per Doctor	Population Served Per Bed
1	2	3	4	5	6	7	8	9	10
185	RIYAN	12	2	14	72	60698	105507	12831	2495
	NAGAUR	**136**	**25**	**161**	**883**	**482167**	**1029812**	**14272**	**2602**
186	BALI	17	5	22	120	NA	NA	8355	1532
187	DESURI	14	1	15	86	NA	NA	6816	1189
188	JAITARAN	20	4	24	128	NA	NA	7789	1460
189	MARWAR JUNCTION	16	1	17	84	NA	NA	10673	2160
190	PALI	6	—	6	24	NA	NA	14990	3747
191	RAIPUR	13	1	14	84	NA	NA	13000	2167
192	RANI STATION	11	—	11	54	NA	NA	9682	1972
193	ROHAT	8	1	9	48	NA	NA	11400	2137
194	SOJAT	13	2	15	78	NA	NA	10393	1999
195	SUMERPUR	14	2	16	84	NA	NA	8625	1643
	PALI	**132**	**17**	**149**	**790**	**NA**	**NA**	**9593**	**1809**
196	AMET	6	1	7	48	14632	163331	12595	1837
197	BHIM	11	2	13	74	44062	126270	10583	1859
198	DEOGARH	15	1	16	54	19369	252000	4867	1442
199	KHAMNOR	23	4	27	90	62525	161103	6385	1916
200	KUMBHALGARH	10	1	11	72	45917	168331	11941	1824
201	RAILMAGRA	11	1	12	60	42848	99673	9203	1841
202	RAJSAMAND	24	—	24	141	52508	108053	5855	997
	RAJSAMAND #	**100**	**10**	**110**	**539**	**267229**	**915430**	**7803**	**1592**
203	BAMANWAS	6	1	7	54	45053	103362	21347	2767
204	BONLI	9	—	9	54	71858	139057	23315	3886
205	GANGAPUR	11	2	13	74	50750	192346	13785	2422
206	KHANDAR	8	2	10	54	77251	124884	15014	2780
207	SAWAI MADHOPUR	3	1	4	50	44122	239235	53953	4316
	SAWAI MADHOPUR	**37**	**6**	**43**	**286**	**289034**	**798884**	**21033**	**3162**
208	DANTA RAMGARH	21	5	26	156	NA	NA	10084	1681
209	DHOND	13	—	13	84	NA	NA	16148	2499
210	FATEHPUR	22	6	28	128	NA	NA	6910	1512
211	KHANDELA	14	—	14	90	NA	NA	15611	2428
212	LACHHMANGARH	13	—	13	72	NA	NA	15156	2736
213	NEEM KA THANA	28	—	28	176	NA	NA	11323	1801
214	PIPRALI	13	1	14	78	NA	NA	14719	2642
215	SRI MADHOPUR	25	2	27	128	NA	NA	7814	1648
	SIKAR	**149**	**14**	**163**	**912**	**NA**	**NA**	**11137**	**1990**
216	ABU ROAD	11	2	13	98	11710	115015	8832	1172
217	PINDWARA	7	2	9	54	46325	76791	20534	3422
218	REODAR	9	1	10	67	74783	90735	17534	2617
219	SHEOGANJ	9	1	10	48	38299	89446	9966	2076
220	SIROHI	11	1	12	72	75324	116568	10466	1744
	SIROHI	**47**	**7**	**54**	**339**	**188406**	**296749**	**12967**	**2066**
221	DEOLI	5	1	6	66	56722	103573	28212	2565
222	MALPURA	13	2	15	92	61408	122367	11795	1923
223	NIWAI	11	2	13	86	39525	119636	12715	1922
224	TODARAISINGH	10	—	10	54	21974	59342	11013	2039
225	TONK	15	2	17	138	94735	144132	12021	1481
226	UNIARA	6	3	9	48	21968	63522	14723	2761
	TONK	**60**	**10**	**70**	**484**	**296332**	**612572**	**13693**	**1980**
227	BARGAON	5	2	7	48	NA	NA	17686	2579
228	BHINDER	12	6	18	160	NA	NA	11213	1261
229	DHARIAWAD	12	2	14	102	NA	NA	14543	1996
230	GIRWA	14	5	19	90	NA	NA	11980	2529
231	GOGUNDA	9	1	10	54	NA	NA	15158	2807
232	JHADOL	11	3	14	98	NA	NA	13844	1978
233	KHERWARA	11	3	14	108	NA	NA	18164	2355
234	KOTRA	4	2	6	66	NA	NA	30584	2780
235	MAVLI	12	4	16	108	NA	NA	12134	1798
236	SALUMBAR	12	2	14	92	NA	NA	14044	2137
237	SARADA	13	3	16	108	NA	NA	13261	1965
	UDAIPUR	**115**	**33**	**148**	**1034**	**NA**	**NA**	**14480**	**2073**
	RAJASTHAN	**2543**	**454**	**2997**	**18482**	**9304740**	**19240131**	**14445**	**2342**

Note: * Dungargarh PS shifted from Churu to Bikaner district on 1st April 2001; ** Excluding data of Dungargarh PS; *** Including data of Dungargarh PS.
Came in force from April, 1991; ## Came in force from July 1994; ### Came in force from July 1997.

Source: 1. Data related to No. of doctors and beds are compiled from DMHS, GoR, Jaipur.
2. Data related to patients treated are compiled from District Statistical Abstract, 2002 (All Districts), DES, Jaipur.

PANCHAYAT SAMITI-WISE NO. OF REGISTERED BIRTHS AND DEATHS AND PROGRESS OF FWP: RAJASTHAN, 2001

P. Code	Panchayat Samiti	Births			Deaths			Child Deaths			Progress of Family Welfare (Nos.)				
		M	F	T	M	F	T	M	F	T	Sterili zation	I.U.D.	C.C. Users	Oral Pill Users	Total Acce-pted
1	2	3	4	5	6	7	8	9	10	11	12	13	14	15	16
1	ARAIN	338	264	602	415	259	674	7	2	9	624	640	2100	2348	5712
2	BHINAY	731	776	1507	416	319	735	12	9	21	517	756	2413	2416	6102
3	JAWAJA	899	729	1628	524	314	838	10	10	20	550	675	3378	3410	8013
4	KEKRI	531	466	997	441	287	728	6	5	11	768	714	2957	2976	7415
5	KISHANGARH	664	450	1114	747	259	1006	2	1	3	857	672	2785	2557	6871
6	MASOODA	767	677	1444	663	349	1012	17	25	42	522	566	2167	2336	5591
7	PISANGAN	1049	830	1879	912	551	1463	11	9	20	1002	868	3289	3326	8485
8	SRINAGAR	573	451	1024	553	287	840	5	5	10	711	389	1571	1581	4252
	AJMER	**5552**	**4643**	**10195**	**4671**	**2625**	**7296**	**70**	**66**	**136**	**5551**	**5280**	**20660**	**20950**	**52441**
9	BANSURE	NA	NA	1604	NA	NA	894	NA	NA	6	1387	536	1822	1205	4950
10	BEHROR	NA	NA	1159	NA	NA	731	NA	NA	11	845	495	994	582	2916
11	KATHUMAR	NA	NA	747	NA	NA	726	NA	NA	4	1058	442	1150	852	3502
12	KISHANGARH BAS	NA	NA	1069	NA	NA	607	NA	NA	14	647	456	1240	735	3078
13	KOTKASIM	NA	NA	1297	NA	NA	577	NA	NA	2	712	454	855	581	2602
14	LACHHMANGARH	NA	NA	1226	NA	NA	1077	NA	NA	9	1105	645	2050	972	4772
15	MANDAWAR	NA	NA	1388	NA	NA	885	NA	NA	11	840	716	1945	1119	4620
16	NIMRANA	NA	NA	1586	NA	NA	761	NA	NA	2	705	431	943	629	2708
17	RAJGARH	NA	NA	444	NA	NA	476	NA	NA	0	716	312	1406	926	3360
18	RAMGARH	NA	NA	1300	NA	NA	745	NA	NA	6	701	446	1846	845	3838
19	RENI	NA	NA	1208	NA	NA	684	NA	NA	4	722	301	1477	866	3366
20	THANAGAZI	NA	NA	616	NA	NA	395	NA	NA	3	1164	620	979	1011	3774
21	TIJARA	NA	NA	1391	NA	NA	808	NA	NA	1	816	640	1734	1261	4451
22	UMREN	NA	NA	1688	NA	NA	604	NA	NA	3	718	516	1735	988	3957
	ALWAR	**NA**	**NA**	**16723**	**NA**	**NA**	**9970**	**NA**	**NA**	**76**	**12136**	**7010**	**20176**	**12572**	**51894**
23	ANANDPURI	771	482	1253	458	308	766	27	23	50	183	622	482	627	1914
24	BAGIDORA	1176	1143	2319	482	354	836	20	15	35	687	929	999	1506	4121
25	GARHI	860	858	1718	423	339	762	4	7	11	1228	1911	1956	2005	7100
26	GHATOL	1079	2472	3551	1535	502	2037	22	19	41	739	1804	1212	1376	5131
27	KUSHALGARH	877	664	1541	558	378	936	23	26	49	370	672	805	1164	3011
28	PEEPALKHOONT	484	519	1003	265	197	462	20	11	31	464	1029	1218	1290	4001
29	SAJJANGARH	802	869	1671	289	185	474	9	14	23	356	1216	418	763	2753
30	TALWARA	1075	885	1960	504	391	895	38	29	67	1208	1198	935	1057	4398
	BANSWARA	**7124**	**7892**	**15016**	**4514**	**2654**	**7168**	**163**	**144**	**307**	**5235**	**9381**	**8025**	**9788**	**32429**
31	ANTA	275	267	542	139	115	254	1	1	2	1337	1262	3115	2599	8313
32	ATRU	160	157	317	141	99	240	0	0	0	804	469	1225	995	3493
33	BARAN	201	86	287	118	103	221	1	0	1	1525	729	3021	2463	7738
34	CHHABRA	167	124	291	48	66	114	0	0	0	820	789	1829	1383	4821
35	CHHIPABAROD	924	794	1718	263	226	489	5	2	7	875	665	2414	1738	5692
36	KISHANGANJ	247	215	462	88	51	139	0	0	0	848	856	1627	1586	4917
37	SHAHBAD	216	212	428	81	76	157	1	2	3	879	920	1463	1261	4523
	BARAN	**2190**	**1855**	**4045**	**878**	**736**	**1614**	**8**	**5**	**13**	**7088**	**5690**	**14694**	**12025**	**39497**
38	BALOTRA	533	437	970	318	242	560	0	4	4	1094	963	7755	6455	16267
39	BARMER	1742	1548	3290	213	35	248	0	0	0	488	808	5321	4905	11522
40	BAYTOO	855	846	1701	256	198	454	2	3	5	429	616	3714	3434	8193
41	CHOHTAN	2158	1610	3768	455	209	664	15	15	30	256	438	3521	3776	7991
42	DHORIMANNA	946	680	1626	295	152	447	0	0	0	649	379	3825	3625	8478
43	SHEO	380	311	691	173	49	222	1	0	1	277	440	4350	4215	9282
44	SINDHARI	933	833	1766	386	191	577	0	0	0	419	758	7763	5449	14389
45	SIWANA	1153	748	1901	392	314	706	0	0	0	897	650	3999	3564	8950
	BARMER	**8700**	**7013**	**15713**	**2488**	**1390**	**3878**	**18**	**22**	**40**	**4509**	**5052**	**40248**	**35423**	**85072**
46	BAYANA	533	409	942	601	262	863	1	3	4	822	690	2373	1597	5482
47	DEEG	1248	982	2230	720	363	1083	21	20	41	1040	627	1427	1095	4189
48	KAMAN	1316	1070	2386	597	338	935	14	9	23	687	889	1736	1404	4716
49	KUMHER	564	490	1054	382	227	609	3	1	4	877	471	1423	1081	3852
50	NADBAI	711	682	1393	569	258	827	5	5	10	1004	669	1476	1229	4378
51	NAGAR PAHARI	902	804	1706	305	181	486	8	10	18	1023	745	1943	1483	5194
52	RUPBAS	913	817	1730	682	277	959	16	10	26	924	618	1888	1401	4831
53	SEWAR	401	329	730	410	216	626	5	2	7	744	576	1781	1345	4446

P. Code	Panchayat Samiti	Births			Deaths			Child Deaths			Progress of Family Welfare (Nos.)				
		M	F	T	M	F	T	M	F	T	Sterilization	I.U.D.	C.C. Users	Oral Pill Users	Total Accepted
1	2	3	4	5	6	7	8	9	10	11	12	13	14	15	16
54	WEIR	564	384	948	665	238	903	5	0	5	1214	694	1457	1222	4587
	BHARATPUR	**7152**	**5967**	**13119**	**4931**	**2360**	**7291**	**78**	**60**	**138**	**8335**	**5979**	**15504**	**11857**	**41675**
55	ASIND	988	1002	1990	672	326	998	0	0	0	505	1286	3434	3025	8250
56	BANERA	883	663	1546	396	383	779	23	30	53	474	715	1760	1734	4683
57	HURDA	533	396	929	588	247	835	18	24	42	318	605	1538	1378	3839
58	JAHAZPUR	509	547	1056	822	294	1116	2	2	4	943	994	2367	2444	6748
59	KOTRI	420	408	828	400	139	539	5	4	9	673	854	3066	2315	6908
60	MANDAL	564	384	948	818	370	1188	6	4	10	602	1210	2560	3098	7470
61	MANDALGARH	598	340	938	438	256	694	5	3	8	1218	1288	3108	3302	8916
62	RAIPUR	481	467	948	349	164	513	4	0	4	232	484	1184	1074	2974
63	SAHARA	465	373	838	303	196	499	9	6	15	371	588	1428	1856	4243
64	SHAHPURA	731	578	1309	480	246	726	10	8	18	665	1022	2231	2117	6035
65	SUWANA	400	360	760	670	121	791	5	3	8	819	953	2857	2984	7613
	BHILWARA	**6572**	**5518**	**12090**	**5936**	**2742**	**8678**	**87**	**84**	**171**	**6820**	**9999**	**25533**	**25327**	**67679**
66	BIKANER	1662	1367	3029	845	701	1546	3	4	7	1262	1545	4674	5102	12583
67	DUNGARGARH *	503	433	936	524	334	858	8	10	18	756	794	4803	4490	10843
68	KOLAYAT	969	771	1740	747	386	1133	2	3	5	720	871	2701	2533	6825
69	LUNKARANSAR	1701	1335	3036	951	536	1487	2	2	4	978	486	2391	2266	6121
70	NOKHA	1382	1302	2684	745	415	1160	5	1	6	816	1678	4443	4238	11175
	BIKANER **	**5714**	**4775**	**10489**	**3288**	**2038**	**5326**	**12**	**10**	**22**	**3776**	**4580**	**14209**	**14139**	**36704**
71	HINDOLI	1178	949	2127	456	233	689	6	2	8	1035	871	1525	1869	5300
72	KESHORAIPATAN	926	646	1572	632	366	998	—	—	—	1231	1082	1926	2190	6429
73	NAINWA	370	252	622	241	89	330	7	5	12	819	818	1462	1425	4524
74	TALERA	747	608	1355	585	355	940	4	5	9	1869	1489	2340	2764	8432
	BUNDI	**3221**	**2455**	**5676**	**1914**	**1043**	**2957**	**17**	**12**	**29**	**4954**	**4260**	**7253**	**8248**	**24685**
75	ARNOD	406	342	748	357	221	578	7	6	13	490	572	533	664	2259
76	BARI SADRI	309	255	564	320	236	556	2	3	5	277	563	293	406	1539
77	BEGUN	470	405	875	336	253	589	13	15	28	483	742	652	777	2654
78	BHADESAR	435	371	806	347	267	614	2	3	5	381	446	440	489	1756
79	BHAINSRORGARH	605	534	1139	246	179	425	16	11	27	415	355	403	536	1709
80	BHOPALSAGAR	346	302	648	245	179	424	6	8	14	239	339	292	388	1258
81	CHHOTI SADRI	533	457	990	284	199	483	3	5	8	357	236	318	375	1286
82	CHITTAURGARH	880	720	1600	507	364	871	16	8	24	605	730	623	805	2763
83	DUNGLA	367	285	652	215	172	387	3	9	12	680	1343	800	1067	3890
84	GANGRAR	507	444	951	303	232	535	9	5	14	356	474	458	442	1730
85	KAPASAN	390	325	715	301	238	539	6	10	16	256	661	452	603	1972
86	NIMBAHERA	535	443	978	394	307	701	12	9	21	633	640	827	755	2855
87	PRATAPGARH	780	602	1382	463	369	832	5	2	7	768	958	1313	1367	4406
88	RASHMI	425	347	772	265	204	469	7	11	18	760	1532	1222	1563	5077
	CHITTAURGARH	**6988**	**5832**	**12820**	**4583**	**3420**	**8003**	**107**	**105**	**212**	**6700**	**9591**	**8626**	**10237**	**35154**
89	CHURU	312	333	645	247	125	372	0	0	0	1385	1049	6185	6009	13333
90	RAJGARH	1634	1229	2863	926	723	1649	0	0	0	1349	1240	4891	15060	11191
91	RATANGARH	463	407	870	435	328	763	0	1	1	1098	1269	3902	4163	9334
92	SARDARSHAHAR	1930	1594	3524	591	437	1028	95	100	195	1452	1087	7516	6964	15567
93	SUJANGARH	1106	806	1912	987	830	1817	0	0	0	1697	1413	6956	6258	14627
94	TARANAGAR	623	447	1070	369	196	565	15	10	25	994	849	3605	4277	8731
	CHURU ***	**6571**	**5249**	**11820**	**4079**	**2973**	**7052**	**118**	**111**	**221**	**8731**	**7701**	**37858**	**38241**	**83626**
95	BANDIKUI	689	484	1173	554	209	763	6	5	11	1517	761	2236	1418	5922
96	DAUSA	555	462	1017	482	286	768	0	0	0	1802	1080	2547	1783	7212
97	LALSOT	947	801	1748	454	216	670	5	3	8	1332	878	3103	1997	7310
98	MAHWA	897	749	1646	449	141	590	2	1	3	1066	931	1984	1586	5567
99	SIKRAI	766	549	1315	443	239	682	17	8	25	1267	736	1941	1046	4990
	DAUSA	**3854**	**3045**	**6899**	**2382**	**1091**	**3473**	**30**	**17**	**47**	**6984**	**4386**	**11811**	**7830**	**31001**
100	BARI	989	906	1895	394	336	730	6	11	17	363	468	1645	902	3378
101	BASERI	434	230	664	515	154	669	0	1	1	538	391	2077	1098	4104
102	DHAULPUR	598	433	1031	496	284	780	7	4	11	746	484	1892	1262	4384
103	RAJAKHERA	466	290	756	162	140	302	13	20	33	556	413	1957	1278	4204
	DHAULPUR	**2487**	**1859**	**4346**	**1567**	**914**	**2481**	**26**	**36**	**62**	**2203**	**1756**	**7571**	**4540**	**16070**
104	ASPUR	2324	1674	3998	809	649	1458	26	48	74	530	1453	1631	1967	5581
105	BICHHIWARA	2843	2539	5382	982	650	1632	30	17	47	440	1903	2243	2627	7213
106	DUNGARPUR	1785	1548	3333	973	593	1566	60	39	99	348	1104	1366	1619	4437
107	SAGWARA	1690	1604	3294	708	645	1353	1	0	1	714	1704	1989	2108	6515
108	SIMALWARA	1687	1442	3129	695	475	1170	18	11	29	541	1492	1827	2037	5897
	DUNGARPUR	**10329**	**8807**	**19136**	**4167**	**3012**	**7179**	**135**	**115**	**250**	**2573**	**7656**	**9056**	**10358**	**29643**
109	ANUPGARH	650	345	995	930	286	1216	4	3	7	2707	2103	11193	7531	23534
110	GANGANAGAR	289	197	486	399	217	616	0	0	0	796	668	3316	1399	6179
111	KARANPUR	604	422	1026	458	226	684	0	0	0	711	645	1668	1209	4233
112	PADAMPUR	339	213	552	441	172	613	0	0	0	837	757	3985	2051	7630
113	RAISINGHNAGAR	175	143	318	282	164	446	0	0	0	865	664	3783	1816	7128
114	SADULSHAHAR	754	541	1295	495	282	777	8	8	16	816	688	2308	1018	4830
115	SURATGARH	282	315	597	438	213	651	1		1	1514	820	2190	1733	6257
	GANGANAGAR	**3093**	**2176**	**5269**	**3443**	**1560**	**5003**	**13**	**11**	**24**	**8246**	**6345**	**28443**	**16757**	**59791**

P. Code	Panchayat Samiti	Births			Deaths			Child Deaths			Progress of Family Welfare (Nos.)				
		M	F	T	M	F	T	M	F	T	Sterilization	I.U.D.	C.C. Users	Oral Pill Users	Total Accepted
1	2	3	4	5	6	7	8	9	10	11	12	13	14	15	16
116	BHADRA	606	455	1061	919	342	1261	2	0	2	1515	1266	3795	2448	9024
117	HANUMANGARH	1358	977	2335	2083	1128	3211	0	0	0	3545	2036	5016	4946	15543
118	NOHAR	583	528	1111	985	413	1398	4	0	4	4497	2205	8725	7370	22797
	HANUMANGARH	**2547**	**1960**	**4507**	**3987**	**1883**	**5870**	**6**	**0**	**6**	**9557**	**5507**	**17536**	**14764**	**47364**
119	AMBER	1631	1099	2730	289	115	404	9	3	12	1640	317	2188	2050	6195
120	BASSI	683	576	1259	585	268	853	7	3	10	710	638	1519	2083	4950
121	CHAKSU	408	344	752	532	165	697	9	5	14	832	216	1113	1082	3243
122	DUDU	346	302	648	499	214	713	3	4	7	1380	647	2177	1937	6141
123	GOVINDGARH	537	791	1328	759	308	1067	6	8	14	1623	720	2702	2713	7758
124	JAMWA RAMGARH	373	234	607	1044	321	1365	5	4	9	1111	223	1415	1170	3919
125	JHOTWARA	377	325	702	205	97	302	4	7	11	883	174	492	453	2002
126	KOTPUTLI	564	251	815	667	244	911	0	0	0	4338	1614	4649	3942	14543
127	PHAGI	462	378	840	413	182	595	6	3	9	998	379	1394	1548	4319
128	SAMBHAR	462	435	897	640	262	902	3	3	6	1950	762	2544	2106	7362
129	SANGANER	290	334	624	327	73	400	1	3	4	1403	352	1872	1593	5220
130	SHAHPURA	254	211	465	404	120	524	0	2	2	1765	556	1512	1385	5218
131	VIRATNAGAR	370	302	672	397	203	600	8	1	9	1155	541	1377	1113	4186
	JAIPUR	**6757**	**5582**	**12339**	**6761**	**2572**	**9333**	**61**	**46**	**107**	**19788**	**7139**	**24954**	**23175**	**75056**
132	JAISALMER	3049	2341	5390	212	134	346	NA	NA	NA	350	516	1364	1706	3936
133	SAM	631	291	922	72	36	108	NA	NA	NA	300	667	1759	1568	4294
134	SANKRA	556	451	1007	230	181	411	NA	NA	NA	334	600	1927	2155	5016
	JAISALMER	**4236**	**3083**	**7319**	**514**	**351**	**865**	**NA**	**NA**	**NA**	**984**	**1783**	**5050**	**5429**	**13246**
135	AHORE	4115	3060	7175	691	448	1139	8	24	32	522	1686	1553	1593	5354
136	BHINMAL	3725	2170	5895	820	409	1229	22	10	32	980	1166	2021	1824	5991
137	JALOR	2237	2019	4256	604	563	1167	68	72	140	502	1090	1143	1195	3930
138	JASWANTPURA	3594	1902	5496	1198	602	1800	22	31	53	652	1012	1033	1067	3764
139	RANIWARA	3728	2644	6372	838	548	1386	8	5	13	944	881	1240	1386	4451
140	SANCHORE	6091	3098	9189	1370	712	2082	43	11	54	1394	2054	3124	3063	9635
141	SAYLA	3772	3314	7086	1119	679	1798	78	101	179	718	1610	2195	2176	6699
	JALOR	**27262**	**18207**	**45469**	**6640**	**3961**	**10601**	**249**	**254**	**503**	**5712**	**9499**	**12309**	**12304**	**39824**
142	BAKANI	409	315	724	203	122	325	6	3	9	799	799	4981	2375	8954
143	DAG	668	584	1252	278	224	502	4	2	6	1106	598	3139	2136	6979
144	JHALRAPATAN	1165	1048	2213	456	388	844	11	9	20	1283	906	5906	2554	10649
145	KHANPUR	1256	1131	2387	127	86	213	3	2	5	817	726	3704	2612	7859
146	MANOHARTHANA	817	756	1573	326	200	526	15	13	28	821	668	5098	3024	9611
147	PIRAWA	1160	945	2105	450	308	758	28	22	50	1057	725	4440	1380	7602
	JHALAWAR	**5475**	**4779**	**10254**	**1840**	**1328**	**3168**	**67**	**51**	**118**	**5883**	**4422**	**27268**	**14081**	**51654**
148	ALSISAR	NA	NA	NA	NA	NA	NA	NA	NA	NA	848	722	770	739	2379
149	BUHANA	NA	NA	NA	NA	NA	NA	NA	NA	NA	1060	644	906	878	3488
150	CHIRAWA	NA	NA	NA	NA	NA	NA	NA	NA	NA	1020	818	749	822	3409
151	JHUNJHUNUN	NA	NA	NA	NA	NA	NA	NA	NA	NA	898	817	1084	831	3630
152	KHETRI	NA	NA	NA	NA	NA	NA	NA	NA	NA	1098	542	862	924	3426
153	NAWALGARH	NA	NA	NA	NA	NA	NA	NA	NA	NA	911	853	920	823	3507
154	SURAJGARH	NA	NA	NA	NA	NA	NA	NA	NA	NA	746	780	828	766	3120
155	UDAIPURWATI	NA	NA	NA	NA	NA	NA	NA	NA	NA	1020	918	980	981	3899
	JHUNJHUNUN	**3113**	**2356**	**5469**	**1374**	**903**	**2277**	**2**	**0**	**2**	**7601**	**6094**	**7099**	**6764**	**26858**
156	BALESAR	1852	1551	3403	1034	299	1333	17	13	30	366	573	963	885	2787
157	BAP	1448	1041	2489	502	221	723	2	1	3	152	347	717	652	1868
158	BHOPALGARH	730	627	1357	432	241	673	0	0	0	867	1091	1074	1090	4122
159	BILARA	1799	1336	3135	685	441	1126	65	48	113	882	1025	1128	1173	4208
160	LUNI	1046	835	1881	529	337	866	10	14	24	1125	1008	1485	1587	5205
161	MANDOR	1236	984	2220	387	221	608	4	1	5	859	619	1111	1041	3630
162	OSIAN	3050	2483	5533	733	356	1089	32	25	57	1383	1493	2385	2450	7711
163	PHALODI	455	373	828	189	140	329	6	6	12	467	760	933	988	3148
164	SHERGARH	1641	1429	3070	352	216	568	1	1	2	309	731	1058	1034	3132
	JODHPUR	**13257**	**10659**	**23916**	**4843**	**2472**	**7315**	**137**	**109**	**246**	**6410**	**7647**	**10854**	**10900**	**35811**
165	HINDAUN	85	78	163	461	165	626	2	2	4	1758	1255	7538	5510	16061
166	KARAULI	537	493	1030	393	119	512	3	0	3	1412	798	7367	5417	14994
167	NADOTI	400	610	1010	345	156	501	0	0	0	759	658	3821	3362	8600
168	SAPOTRA	296	207	503	389	131	520	0	0	0	1360	873	5787	4598	12618
169	TODABHIM	596	392	988	337	182	519	6	10	16	1158	708	4880	4007	10753
	KARAULI	**1914**	**1780**	**3694**	**1925**	**753**	**2678**	**11**	**12**	**23**	**6447**	**4292**	**29393**	**22894**	**63026**
170	CHECHAT	552	507	1059	393	217	610	4	4	8	1180	1002	1824	1687	5693
171	ITAWA	245	261	506	426	185	611	0	0	0	941	706	1138	1145	3930
172	LADPURA	778	792	1570	392	364	756	0	0	0	859	584	1190	1246	3879
173	SANGOD	555	511	1066	236	218	454	3	2	5	1142	893	1409	1266	4710
174	SULTANPUR	595	545	1140	383	173	556	2	5	7	996	694	1151	1047	3888
	KOTA	**2725**	**2616**	**5341**	**1830**	**1157**	**2987**	**9**	**11**	**20**	**5118**	**3879**	**6712**	**6391**	**22100**
175	DEGANA	904	831	1735	418	340	758	6	3	9	1239	1118	2829	2570	7756
176	DIDWANA	862	738	1600	779	650	1429	0	0	0	1318	1528	4945	5035	12826
177	JAYAL	851	824	1675	308	273	581	5	1	6	862	930	3129	2869	7790
178	KUCHAMAN	1057	1046	2103	878	866	1744	4	3	7	973	734	2724	2545	6976

P. Code	Panchayat Samiti	Births			Deaths			Child Deaths			Progress of Family Welfare (Nos.)				
		M	F	T	M	F	T	M	F	T	Sterilization	I.U.D.	C.C. Users	Oral Pill Users	Total Accepted
1	2	3	4	5	6	7	8	9	10	11	12	13	14	15	16
179	LADNU	529	441	970	292	279	571	0	0	0	738	811	3295	2931	7775
180	MAKRANA	1797	1093	2890	535	466	1001	37	19	56	903	1017	2455	2096	6471
181	MERTA	357	310	667	478	412	890	0	0	0	996	941	2875	2663	7475
182	MUNDWA	822	655	1477	407	337	744	4	4	8	631	921	2544	2492	6588
183	NAGAUR	778	773	1551	477	503	980	0	3	3	824	1387	3788	4507	10506
184	PARBATSAR	383	332	715	448	400	848	0	0	0	915	1023	2958	2895	7791
185	RIYAN	931	722	1653	681	511	1192	1	1	2	1113	1118	2603	2577	7411
	NAGAUR	**9271**	**7765**	**17036**	**5701**	**5037**	**10738**	**57**	**34**	**91**	**10512**	**11528**	**34145**	**33180**	**89365**
186	BALI	321	242	563	191	124	315	4	3	7	642	702	1174	1285	3803
187	DESURI	580	405	985	171	147	318	0	2	2	592	593	287	339	1811
188	JAITARAN	622	600	1222	233	206	439	5	3	8	1034	698	413	518	2663
189	MARWAR JUNCTION	440	328	768	262	102	364	1	0	1	662	615	796	865	2938
190	PALI	528	299	827	161	90	251	0	0	0	481	569	462	595	2107
191	RAIPUR	348	293	641	222	131	353	0	0	0	672	1275	742	881	3507
192	RANI STATION	1892	1768	3660	695	640	1335	20	15	35	660	1090	784	1002	3536
193	ROHAT	182	1141	1323	101	113	214	5	4	9	453	521	400	461	1835
194	SOJAT	291	260	551	210	173	383	6	6	12	800	754	618	762	2934
195	SUMERPUR	314	255	569	145	121	266	0	0	0	482	656	429	699	2266
	PALI	**5518**	**5591**	**11109**	**2391**	**1847**	**4238**	**41**	**33**	**74**	**6478**	**7473**	**6105**	**7407**	**27400**
196	AMET	514	383	897	270	189	459	0	0	0	453	881	700	874	2908
197	BHIM	889	728	1617	476	349	825	21	31	52	417	896	802	771	2886
198	DEOGARH	241	190	431	227	98	325	5	2	7	328	687	764	816	2595
199	KHAMNOR	768	663	1431	517	242	759	46	38	84	665	1165	2081	2149	6060
200	KUMBHALGARH	341	253	594	208	111	319	8	6	14	302	900	1153	1407	3762
201	RAILMAGRA	428	351	779	410	190	600	7	5	12	538	869	1358	1426	4191
202	RAJSAMAND	450	392	842	348	160	508	0	0	0	717	1107	1665	1733	5222
	RAJSAMAND	**3631**	**2960**	**6591**	**2456**	**1339**	**3795**	**87**	**82**	**169**	**3420**	**6505**	**8523**	**9176**	**27624**
203	BAMANWAS	329	275	604	150	102	252	2	0	2	802	612	3434	2387	7235
204	BONLI	690	693	1383	400	384	784	10	12	22	1093	735	4586	4019	10433
205	GANGAPUR	718	510	1228	634	384	1018	0	0	0	1459	883	4788	3727	10857
206	KHANDAR	731	680	1411	368	194	562	18	18	36	986	595	3356	2589	7526
207	SAWAI MADHOPUR	915	737	1652	657	363	1020	6	4	10	1934	1580	8188	5470	17172
	SAWAI MADHOPUR	**3383**	**2895**	**6278**	**2209**	**1427**	**3636**	**36**	**34**	**70**	**6274**	**4405**	**24352**	**18192**	**53223**
208	DANTA RAMGARH	882	648	1530	575	303	878	3	2	5	1417	1059	1663	1274	5413
209	DHOND	1394	1331	2725	549	440	989	0	0	0	1186	1222	1148	1098	4654
210	FATEHPUR	891	779	1670	447	328	775	0	0	0	703	916	1588	1495	4702
211	KHANDELA	751	508	1259	634	301	935	1	0	1	1036	616	1427	1259	4338
212	LACHHMANGARH	1031	640	1671	580	291	871	0	1	1	661	967	1679	1574	4881
213	NEEM KA THANA	1235	838	2073	880	388	1268	0	0	0	2253	1146	2193	1590	7182
214	PIPRALI	698	604	1302	462	325	787	0	0	0	834	519	882	783	3018
215	SRI MADHOPUR	1231	900	2131	664	287	951	0	0	0	1268	630	1457	1167	4522
	SIKAR	**8113**	**6248**	**14361**	**4791**	**2663**	**7454**	**4**	**3**	**7**	**9358**	**7075**	**12037**	**10240**	**38710**
216	ABU ROAD	127	94	221	71	34	105	1	1	2	2855	6353	16656	18127	43991
217	PINDWARA	259	271	530	142	122	264	3	3	6	515	1449	4899	5148	12011
218	REODAR	271	288	559	183	122	305	4	3	7	933	1649	3873	4467	10922
219	SHEOGANJ	148	120	268	77	55	132	0	0	0	483	1023	2348	2675	6529
220	SIROHI	258	207	465	117	105	222	3	5	8	723	1366	2943	3104	8136
	SIROHI	**1063**	**980**	**2043**	**590**	**438**	**1028**	**11**	**12**	**23**	**5509**	**11840**	**30719**	**33521**	**81589**
221	DEOLI	672	686	1358	701	342	1043	5	3	8	1200	853	4049	4636	10738
222	MALPURA	456	377	833	273	194	467	3	3	6	1418	1043	3595	3252	9308
223	NIWAI	595	480	1075	516	369	885	0	0	0	1409	914	5096	4533	11952
224	TODARAISINGH	566	506	1072	390	234	624	3	7	10	796	699	2402	1772	5669
225	TONK	888	742	1630	808	337	1145	7	8	15	1446	1144	4942	4729	12261
226	UNIARA	629	491	1120	314	179	493	10	10	20	552	748	2363	1769	5432
	TONK	**3806**	**3282**	**7088**	**3002**	**1655**	**4657**	**28**	**31**	**59**	**6821**	**5401**	**22447**	**20691**	**55360**
227	BARGAON	269	249	518	490	185	681	3	5	8	1011	1258	3369	3416	9054
228	BHINDER	820	839	1659	860	336	1196	11	6	17	778	1125	1524	1483	4910
229	DHARIAWAD	933	799	1732	756	490	1246	23	16	39	494	1328	1597	1453	4872
230	GIRWA	148	139	287	716	120	836	2	1	3	2082	1660	1173	2034	6949
231	GOGUNDA	645	631	1276	575	169	744	2	0	2	160	458	1405	1622	3645
232	JHADOL	238	225	463	360	166	526	2	1	3	521	611	1314	1342	3788
233	KHERWARA	547	553	1100	614	352	966	9	3	12	515	1655	3177	3498	8845
234	KOTRA	434	486	920	819	209	1028	22	29	51	46	701	2398	1479	4624
235	MAVLI	397	387	784	589	195	784	13	8	21	606	1368	2644	2034	6652
236	SALUMBAR	750	643	1393	414	311	725	12	17	29	527	1749	2137	1805	6218
237	SARADA	361	300	661	327	235	562	31	32	63	461	1494	2058	2384	6397
	UDAIPUR	**5542**	**5251**	**10793**	**6520**	**2768**	**9294**	**130**	**118**	**248**	**7201**	**13407**	**22796**	**22550**	**65954**
	RAJASTHAN	**187160**	**153080**	**356963**	**106215**	**61112**	**177303**	**1818**	**1628**	**3514**	**216914**	**212562**	**571896**	**518931**	**1501525**

Note. * Dungargarh PS shifted from Churu to Bikaner district on 1st April 2001

** Excluding data of Dungargarh PS; *** Including data of Dungargarh PS

Source: 1. District Statistical Abstract (All Districts), 2002, DES, Jaipur.

2. Department of Medical & Family Welfare, Raj., Jaipur.

PANCHAYAT SAMITI-WISE INSTITUTIONS AND TEACHERS:

P. Code	Panchayat Samities Name	Educational Institutions, 2000											
		Primary Schools					Upper Primary Schools				Secondary Schools		
		Govt.	S.K.	RGSJP	Private	Total	Govt.	S.K.	Private	Total	Govt.	Private	Total
1	2	3	4	5	6	7	8	9	10	11	12	13	14
1	ARAIN	71	29	20	6	126	39	1	1	41	12	—	12
2	BHINAY	117	—	14	7	138	44	—	1	45	12	—	12
3	JAWAJA	159	14	37	11	221	44	—	1	45	16	1	17
4	KEKRI	76	18	25	17	136	37	—	3	40	15	—	15
5	KISHANGARH	94	11	32	18	155	41	—	3	44	12	—	12
6	MASOODA	100	26	37	16	179	38	—	6	44	14	—	14
7	PISANGAN	141	15	28	23	207	53	—	5	58	20	2	22
8	SRINAGAR	89	—	17	26	132	40	—	8	48	9	2	11
	AJMER	**847**	**113**	**210**	**124**	**1294**	**336**	**1**	**28**	**365**	**110**	**5**	**115**
9	BANSURE	142	—	71	35	248	65	—	39	104	12	1	13
10	BEHROR	94	—	12	39	145	36	—	28	64	15	1	16
11	KATHUMAR	137	—	33	31	201	42	—	49	91	14	3	17
12	KISHANGARH BAS	104	—	32	27	163	32	—	33	65	9	1	10
13	KOTKASIM	84	—	10	20	114	32	—	25	57	10	2	12
14	LACHHMANGARH	158	—	50	32	240	58	—	27	85	14	—	14
15	MANDAWAR	111	—	12	41	164	57	—	39	96	22	2	24
16	NIMRANA	81	—	2	45	128	50	—	26	76	16	1	17
17	RAJGARH	96	—	41	29	166	43	—	28	71	10	2	12
18	RAMGARH	129	—	63	35	227	42	—	27	69	10	—	10
19	RENI	99	—	34	27	160	33	—	14	47	11	—	11
20	THANAGAZI	115	13	52	44	224	40	—	12	52	13	—	13
21	TIJARA	146	—	30	34	210	42	—	33	75	14	1	15
22	UMREN	123	4	46	44	217	44	—	43	87	14	1	15
	ALWAR	**1619**	**17**	**488**	**483**	**2607**	**616**	**—**	**423**	**1039**	**184**	**15**	**199**
23	ANANDPURI	73	21	25	44	163	33	1	1	35	3	1	4
24	BAGIDORA	109	16	42	20	187	41	—	3	44	7	—	7
25	GARHI	161	38	68	31	298	83	—	5	88	25	1	26
26	GHATOL	153	34	92	29	308	63	1	3	67	15	—	15
27	KUSHALGARH	149	15	53	9	226	27	—	3	30	5	—	5
28	PEEPALKHOONT	126	36	53	12	227	34	—	—	34	4	—	4
29	SAJJANGARH	128	13	49	16	206	32	—	3	35	5	1	6
30	TALWARA	179	29	72	13	293	71	1	—	72	13	—	13
	BANSWARA	**1078**	**202**	**454**	**174**	**1908**	**384**	**3**	**18**	**405**	**77**	**3**	**80**
31	ANTA	91	17	15	29	152	37	—	13	50	12	1	13
32	ATRU	98	11	5	23	137	32	1	11	44	13	2	15
33	BARAN	75	6	9	33	123	30	—	6	36	8	—	8
34	CHHABRA	104	25	23	4	156	24	1	1	26	7	—	7
35	CHHIPABAROD	112	4	31	13	160	30	—	8	38	3	—	3
36	KISHANGANJ	111	29	26	18	184	36	—	6	42	12	—	12
37	SHAHBAD	58	62	15	11	146	27	7	8	42	6	—	6
	BARAN	**649**	**154**	**124**	**131**	**1058**	**216**	**9**	**53**	**278**	**61**	**3**	**64**
38	BALOTRA	182	37	135	21	375	54	2	3	59	12	2	14
39	BARMER	252	22	187	11	472	61	—	—	61	18	—	18
40	BAYTOO	223	37	148	12	420	56	1	3	60	12	—	12
41	CHOHTAN	156	38	138	2	334	58	—	2	60	7	—	7
42	DHORIMANNA	231	9	126	5	371	55	—	—	55	13	—	13
43	SHEO	180	14	128	9	331	41	1	2	44	9	—	9
44	SINDHARI	267	13	118	2	400	50	1	3	54	13	—	13
45	SIWANA	87	30	107	15	239	54	—	5	59	8	1	9
	BARMER	**1578**	**200**	**1087**	**77**	**2942**	**429**	**5**	**18**	**452**	**92**	**3**	**95**
46	BAYANA	125	15	46	25	211	47	1	19	67	15	—	15
47	DEEG	85	9	15	33	142	38	1	21	60	13	—	13
48	KAMAN	130	6	31	13	180	43	—	11	54	12	—	12
49	KUMHER	112	—	5	30	147	36	—	22	58	12	1	13
50	NADBAI	84	—	7	23	114	42	—	41	83	13	1	14
51	NAGAR PAHARI	174	—	36	42	252	50	—	23	73	13	—	13
52	RUPBAS	120	—	15	23	158	52	—	33	85	19	6	25
53	SEWAR	126	—	4	18	148	43	—	25	68	14	1	15
54	WEIR	111	15	30	24	180	61	—	25	86	15	—	15
	BHARATPUR	**1067**	**45**	**189**	**231**	**1532**	**412**	**2**	**220**	**634**	**126**	**9**	**135**

NO. OF EDUCATIONAL RAJASTHAN (2000)

Educational Institutions, 2000				*No. of Working Teachers (Up to 30.11.2002)*				
Sr. Sec. Schools					*Preliminary Education*			
Govt.	*Private*	*Total*	*NFECs*	*Panchayati Raj III Grade*	*II Grade*	*III Grade*	*Physical Education*	*Total*
15	*16*	*17*	*18*	*19*	*20*	*21*	*22*	*23*
3	—	3	389	201	28	203	37	268
6	—	6	256	306	35	206	40	281
7	4	11	156	362	56	455	45	556
7	—	7	228	278	34	260	39	333
5	—	5	177	244	43	333	42	418
5	—	5	188	301	42	257	27	326
9	—	9	256	518	50	361	51	462
4	—	4	164	268	36	270	30	336
46	**4**	**50**	**1814**	**2478**	**324**	**2345**	**311**	**2980**
5	—	5	48	337	36	208	42	286
9	—	9	47	289	40	225	41	306
3	—	3	73	388	41	238	45	324
5	—	5	83	305	31	236	31	298
7	1	8	70	231	25	146	31	202
7	—	7	64	418	47	257	44	348
9	—	9	47	328	38	276	59	373
9	—	9	67	226	36	239	36	311
3	—	3	70	254	39	243	40	322
4	—	4	97	381	34	243	35	312
4	—	4	49	265	36	153	29	218
7	—	7	73	297	24	182	29	235
3	—	3	135	390	35	226	37	298
4	—	4	78	380	28	229	25	282
79	**1**	**80**	**1001**	**4489**	**490**	**3101**	**524**	**4115**
5	—	5	97	217	30	138	27	195
7	—	7	133	364	40	199	38	277
12	—	12	278	497	75	444	74	593
6	—	6	129	417	54	237	47	338
1	—	1	101	268	24	108	14	146
2	2	4	140	273	25	62	17	104
2	—	2	104	312	28	109	24	161
5	1	6	142	503	87	527	81	695
40	**3**	**43**	**1124**	**2851**	**363**	**1824**	**322**	**2509**
4	—	4	38	288	43	244	37	324
4	—	4	81	276	34	154	34	222
2	—	2	52	189	31	246	29	306
—	—	—	91	261	22	99	23	144
3	—	3	102	262	31	133	30	194
3	—	3	232	256	29	143	30	202
6	—	6	168	178	22	83	25	130
22	**—**	**22**	**764**	**1710**	**212**	**1102**	**208**	**1522**
6	—	6	153	364	56	256	54	366
2	—	2	139	466	57	262	47	366
2	—	2	104	367	51	196	42	289
2	—	2	126	269	32	154	43	229
5	—	5	58	404	52	179	45	276
3	—	3	94	259	29	150	24	203
4	—	4	102	368	44	203	49	296
8	—	8	91	228	50	191	42	283
32	**—**	**32**	**867**	**2725**	**371**	**1591**	**346**	**2308**
5	—	5	80	380	47	258	50	355
3	—	3	105	276	39	267	37	343
1	—	1	116	319	45	246	43	334
6	—	6	99	341	42	265	38	345
1	—	1	79	240	42	271	43	356
6	—	6	89	414	46	254	51	351
6	—	6	47	355	52	259	50	361
5	—	5	48	349	47	266	42	355
5	—	5	59	351	54	328	58	440
38	—	38	722	**3025**	**414**	**2414**	**412**	**3240**

P. Code	Panchayat Samities Name	Educational Institutions, 2000											
		Primary Schools					Upper Primary Schools				Secondary Schools		
		Govt.	S.K.	RGSJP	Private	Total	Govt.	S.K.	Private	Total	Govt.	Private	Total
1	2	3	4	5	6	7	8	9	10	11	12	13	14
55	ASIND	138	7	65	14	224	58	—	1	59	14	—	14
56	BANERA	71	12	28	7	118	29	—	1	30	8	—	8
57	HURDA	80	14	39	11	144	25	—	1	26	7	—	7
58	JAHAZPUR	112	20	47	12	191	53	—	4	57	13	—	13
59	KOTRI	109	13	56	12	190	40	—	2	42	16	—	16
60	MANDAL	151	16	72	16	255	45	—	2	47	17	—	17
61	MANDALGARH	145	14	58	15	232	52	2	7	61	14	—	14
62	RAIPUR	66	7	39	5	117	32	—	—	32	9	—	9
63	SAHARA	80	14	27	3	124	30	—	1	31	10	—	10
64	SHAHPURA	131	—	41	6	178	44	—	—	44	14	—	14
65	SUWANA	112	—	37	17	166	44	—	2	46	15	—	15
	BHILWARA	**1195**	**117**	**509**	**118**	**1939**	**452**	**2**	**21**	**475**	**137**	**—**	**137**
66	BIKANER	142	80	63	63	348	59	1	36	96	20	3	23
67	DUNGARGARH *	76	—	38	28	142	39	—	2	41	14	—	14
68	KOLAYAT	150	36	53	31	270	44	—	13	57	11	—	11
69	LUNKARANSAR	100	44	40	31	215	58	3	17	78	6	4	10
70	NOKHA	145	—	65	49	259	53	—	6	59	19	—	19
	BIKANER**	**537**	**160**	**221**	**174**	**1092**	**214**	**4**	**72**	**290**	**56**	**7**	**63**
71	HINDOLI	140	9	58	44	251	39	1	6	46	10	—	10
72	KESHORAIPATAN	152	—	32	36	220	48	—	6	54	16	—	16
73	NAINWA	135	8	29	15	187	39	—	8	47	10	—	10
74	TALERA	184	7	65	65	321	63	—	16	79	17	—	17
	BUNDI	**611**	**24**	**184**	**160**	**979**	**189**	**1**	**36**	**226**	**53**	**—**	**53**
75	ARNOD	108	19	37	4	168	26	—	—	26	7	—	7
76	BARI SADRI	75	24	21	9	129	25	—	2	27	7	—	7
77	BEGUN	99	—	44	10	153	32	—	2	34	8	—	8
78	BHADESAR	89	19	28	9	145	30	—	2	32	5	—	5
79	BHAINSRORGARH	76	12	27	7	122	22	—	—	22	5	—	5
80	BHOPALSAGAR	63	—	22	8	93	22	—	—	22	7	—	7
81	CHHOTI SADRI	87	—	32	5	124	26	—	—	26	9	—	9
82	CHITTAURGARH	121	—	41	18	180	49	—	3	52	6	—	6
83	DUNGLA	72	6	26	10	114	25	—	2	27	7	—	7
84	GANGRAR	92	—	14	13	119	27	—	2	29	8	1	9
85	KAPASAN	73	—	23	4	100	23	—	—	23	7	—	7
86	NIMBAHERA	108	—	22	15	145	36	—	1	37	9	—	9
87	PRATAPGARH	218	29	37	17	301	69	—	—	69	13	—	13
88	RASHMI	55	7	20	15	97	22	—	—	22	9	—	9
	CHITTAURGARH	**1336**	**116**	**394**	**144**	**1990**	**434**	**—**	**14**	**448**	**107**	**1**	**108**
89	CHURU	86	—	15	25	126	53	—	12	65	20	—	20
90	RAJGARH	185	4	12	38	239	60	—	44	104	29	2	31
91	RATANGARH	92	10	12	11	125	49	—	5	54	16	—	16
92	SARDARSHAHAR	111	12	25	23	171	57	—	6	63	16	1	17
93	SUJANGARH	111	36	70	36	253	62	1	4	67	17	1	18
94	TARANAGAR	85	6	9	19	119	35	—	16	51	15	3	18
	CHURU ***	**746**	**68**	**181**	**180**	**1175**	**355**	**1**	**89**	**445**	**127**	**7**	**134**
95	BANDIKUI	153	21	65	69	308	56	1	81	138	18	11	29
96	DAUSA	154	16	64	48	282	52	—	48	100	18	3	21
97	LALSOT	183	26	86	42	337	66	1	26	93	16	6	22
98	MAHWA	109	—	73	30	212	49	—	56	105	9	11	20
99	SIKRAI	79	34	61	35	209	54	1	37	92	13	4	17
	DAUSA	**678**	**97**	**349**	**224**	**1348**	**277**	**3**	**248**	**528**	**74**	**35**	**109**
100	BARI	111	20	43	12	186	38	—	5	43	7	1	8
101	BASERI	140	23	77	16	256	35	1	10	46	14	1	15
102	DHAULPUR	165	27	35	33	260	64	—	15	79	20	—	20
103	RAJAKHERA	130	18	38	11	197	49	—	5	54	11	—	11
	DHAULPUR	**546**	**88**	**193**	**72**	**899**	**186**	**1**	**35**	**222**	**52**	**2**	**54**
104	ASPUR	149	3	68	28	248	50	—	5	55	12	—	12
105	BICHHIWARA	167	32	80	27	306	61	—	2	63	14	—	14
106	DUNGARPUR	160	—	55	22	237	58	—	—	58	9	1	10
107	SAGWARA	147	11	100	39	297	55	—	3	58	21	—	21
108	SIMALWARA	222	4	91	16	333	58	2	6	66	13	—	13
	DUNGARPUR	**845**	**50**	**394**	**132**	**1421**	**282**	**2**	**16**	**300**	**69**	**1**	**70**
109	ANUPGARH	365	8	140	50	563	102	—	96	198	5	12	17
110	GANGANAGAR	132	—	23	22	177	55	—	38	93	19	1	20
111	KARANPUR	135	—	5	7	147	50	—	6	56	14	—	14
112	PADAMPUR	154	—	16	15	185	38	—	23	61	13	—	13
113	RAISINGHNAGAR	184	8	30	11	233	60	—	21	81	11	6	17
114	SADULSHAHAR	76	—	11	28	115	43	—	29	72	13	1	14
115	SURATGARH	105	12	97	44	258	48	—	17	65	10	2	12
	GANGANAGAR	**1151**	**28**	**322**	**177**	**1678**	**396**	**—**	**230**	**626**	**85**	**22**	**107**
116	BHADRA	107	—	46	39	192	61	—	55	116	21	3	24
117	HANUMANGARH	260	—	122	141	523	143	—	109	252	51	11	62
118	NOHAR	197	—	72	68	337	89	—	90	179	31	2	33
	HANUMANGARH	**564**	**—**	**240**	**248**	**1052**	**293**	**—**	**254**	**547**	**103**	**16**	**119**

Educational Institutions, 2000				*No. of Working Teachers (Up to 30.11.2002)*				
Sr. Sec. Schools					*Preliminary Education*			
Govt.	*Private*	*Total*	*NFECs*	*Panchayati Raj III Grade*	*II Grade*	*III Grade*	*Physical Education*	*Total*
15	*16*	*17*	*18*	*19*	*20*	*21*	*22*	*23*
7	—	7	120	303	58	254	51	363
2	—	2	110	189	23	119	29	171
3	2	5	82	194	26	134	23	183
3	—	3	154	284	52	315	54	421
4	—	4	241	248	33	156	33	222
4	1	5	110	329	41	232	45	318
5	—	5	129	318	48	212	50	310
2	—	2	107	110	20	84	24	128
3	—	3	78	168	33	163	33	229
4	—	4	142	288	46	235	39	320
5	—	5	144	271	43	217	42	302
42	**3**	**45**	**1417**	**2702**	**423**	**2121**	**423**	**2967**
5	—	5	193	470	66	385	60	511
3	—	3	148	219	19	175	41	235
3	—	3	105	307	29	218	41	288
5	—	5	206	231	38	224	49	311
3	—	3	106	339	43	278	50	371
16	—	**16**	**610**	**1347**	**176**	**1105**	**200**	**1481**
6	—	6	127	284	40	172	29	241
1	—	1	273	408	60	336	45	441
4	—	4	118	321	42	183	37	262
6	—	6	220	511	61	384	53	498
17	—	**17**	**738**	**1524**	**203**	**1075**	**164**	**1442**
3	—	3	110	223	23	98	6	127
3	—	3	104	131	36	115	27	178
1	—	1	91	204	40	106	28	174
5	—	5	129	223	25	78	30	133
4	—	4	49	198	20	106	18	144
2	—	2	39	147	18	68	17	103
—	—	—	78	187	30	124	15	169
6	1	7	95	348	59	362	48	469
4	—	4	62	143	25	80	25	130
5	—	5	101	180	25	98	26	149
—	1	1	45	154	29	151	23	203
3	—	3	150	267	37	197	27	261
4	—	4	211	455	58	253	24	335
3	—	3	100	155	24	93	19	136
43	**2**	**45**	**1364**	**3015**	**449**	**1929**	**333**	**2711**
4	—	4	134	255	60	377	55	492
11	2	13	129	492	72	445	57	574
5	—	5	90	252	47	280	50	377
3	—	3	192	222	54	247	39	340
4	1	5	138	280	54	344	57	455
2	—	2	173	234	34	205	35	274
32	**3**	**35**	**1004**	**1954**	**340**	**2073**	**334**	**2747**
4	5	9	119	367	53	285	53	391
7	—	7	162	416	49	344	51	444
6	—	6	162	416	43	299	58	400
7	1	8	57	334	43	219	48	310
6	1	7	47	257	50	246	48	344
30	**7**	**37**	**547**	**1790**	**238**	**1393**	**258**	**1889**
1	—	1	157	251	35	190	37	262
3	—	3	109	305	34	142	33	209
6	—	6	138	453	64	368	65	497
2	—	2	12	296	46	196	43	285
12	—	**12**	**416**	**1305**	**179**	**896**	**178**	**1253**
7	—	7	104	409	42	207	39	288
4	—	4	108	528	54	312	49	415
6	—	6	127	447	53	391	56	500
6	2	8	173	408	59	379	52	490
9	2	11	159	600	60	283	55	398
32	**4**	**36**	**671**	**2392**	**268**	**1572**	**251**	**2091**
6	1	7	334	580	58	324	59	441
2	—	2	97	342	77	407	67	551
2	—	2	104	307	44	189	47	280
4	—	4	100	336	26	140	33	199
1	1	2	131	367	47	199	53	299
5	2	7	104	180	39	175	39	253
2	—	2	168	229	26	162	31	219
22	**4**	**26**	**1038**	**2341**	**317**	**1596**	**329**	**2242**
9	—	9	103	282	53	271	53	377
15	2	17	234	739	124	674	139	937
5	2	7	51	454	57	326	60	443
29	**4**	**33**	**388**	**1475**	**234**	**1271**	**252**	**1757**

P. Code	Panchayat Samities Name	Educational Institutions, 2000											
		Primary Schools					Upper Primary Schools				Secondary Schools		
		Govt.	S.K.	RGSJP	Private	Total	Govt.	S.K.	Private	Total	Govt.	Private	Total
1	2	3	4	5	6	7	8	9	10	11	12	13	14
119	AMBER	174	—	79	53	306	69	—	56	125	18	3	21
120	BASSI	180	—	44	30	254	45	—	26	71	13	1	14
121	CHAKSU	164	11	49	27	251	40	—	9	49	14	—	14
122	DUDU	186	27	70	47	330	68	1	15	84	17	1	18
123	GOVINDGARH	129	—	52	53	234	58	—	43	101	20	8	28
124	JAMWA RAMGARH	168	—	73	46	287	73	—	22	95	16	3	19
125	JHOTWARA	74	—	21	37	132	14	—	22	36	7	6	13
126	KOTPUTLI	120	24	42	55	241	47	—	22	69	15	1	16
127	PHAGI	131	5	37	26	199	40	1	9	50	15	—	15
128	SAMBHAR	142	12	76	26	256	47	—	34	81	17	6	23
129	SANGANER	184	—	54	68	306	33	3	28	64	6	1	7
130	SHAHPURA	96	—	48	36	180	55	—	24	79	20	—	20
131	VIRATNAGAR	129	—	52	59	240	50	—	12	62	15	—	15
	JAIPUR	**1877**	**79**	**697**	**563**	**3216**	**639**	**5**	**322**	**966**	**193**	**30**	**223**
132	JAISALMER	131	—	35	6	172	43	—	3	46	10	—	10
133	SAM	171	2	96	3	272	43	—	—	43	10	—	10
134	SANKRA	189	27	70	7	293	44	1	1	46	10	—	10
	JAISALMER	**491**	**29**	**201**	**16**	**737**	**130**	**1**	**4**	**135**	**30**	**—**	**30**
135	AHORE	88	5	25	18	136	46	2	4	52	18	—	18
136	BHINMAL	75	18	41	15	149	35	—	—	35	10	—	10
137	JALOR	48	16	23	15	102	30	—	3	33	10	—	10
138	JASWANTPURA	58	8	30	19	115	27	—	2	29	7	—	7
139	RANIWARA	75	16	62	18	171	35	—	—	35	6	—	6
140	SANCHORE	224	—	148	6	378	70	—	1	71	15	—	15
141	SAYLA	68	7	41	32	148	32	—	2	34	10	—	10
	JALOR	**636**	**70**	**370**	**123**	**1199**	**275**	**2**	**12**	**289**	**76**	**—**	**76**
142	BAKANI	137	15	46	12	210	36	1	4	41	5	—	5
143	DAG	144	13	34	10	201	39	1	2	42	7	—	7
144	JHALRAPATAN	181	28	29	20	258	51	3	2	56	12	—	12
145	KHANPUR	119	9	28	17	173	39	—	13	52	8	—	8
146	MANOHARTHANA	171	18	45	7	241	37	1	1	39	5	—	5
147	PIRAWA	139	10	13	19	181	49	—	1	50	13	—	13
	JHALAWAR	**891**	**93**	**195**	**85**	**1264**	**251**	**6**	**23**	**280**	**50**	**—**	**50**
148	ALSISAR	121	—	22	30	173	40	—	37	77	12	6	18
149	BUHANA	116	—	45	41	202	50	—	71	121	28	4	32
150	CHIRAWA	105	—	26	36	167	30	—	47	77	16	5	21
151	JHUNJHUNUN	134	—	32	45	211	53	—	56	109	19	7	26
152	KHETRI	151	2	48	40	241	44	—	65	109	20	2	22
153	NAWALGARH	132	—	51	45	228	48	—	49	97	22	9	31
154	SURAJGARH	133	—	12	31	176	43	—	48	91	23	1	24
155	UDAIPURWATI	148	—	63	35	246	62	—	75	137	20	11	31
	JHUNJHUNUN	**1040**	**2**	**299**	**303**	**1644**	**370**	**—**	**448**	**818**	**160**	**45**	**205**
156	BALESAR	97	7	67	13	184	35	—	3	38	7	—	7
157	BAP	98	12	62	9	181	42	—	1	43	5	—	5
158	BHOPALGARH	143	7	60	36	246	62	—	11	73	19	1	20
159	BILARA	100	—	54	38	192	42	—	6	48	19	—	19
160	LUNI	144	14	53	43	254	58	—	9	67	18	1	19
161	MANDOR	96	5	40	19	160	46	—	8	54	13	2	15
162	OSIAN	312	29	166	78	585	152	2	16	170	63	3	66
163	PHALODI	177	62	65	4	308	70	—	4	74	14	1	15
164	SHERGARH	86	33	60	12	191	33	—	1	34	10	—	10
	JODHPUR	**1253**	**169**	**627**	**252**	**2301**	**540**	**2**	**59**	**601**	**168**	**8**	**176**
165	HINDAUN	121	19	90	47	277	59	1	30	90	19	3	22
166	KARAULI	144	34	106	30	314	51	1	15	67	12	—	12
167	NADOTI	67	11	36	16	130	31	—	29	60	11	1	12
168	SAPOTRA	137	19	123	27	306	52	4	21	77	18	1	19
169	TODABHIM	117	2	49	47	215	34	—	28	62	20	2	22
	KARAULI	**586**	**85**	**404**	**167**	**1242**	**227**	**6**	**123**	**356**	**80**	**7**	**87**
170	CHECHAT	106	—	25	35	166	31	—	13	44	14	—	14
171	ITAWA	95	14	25	46	180	38	—	21	59	10	2	12
172	LADPURA	95	—	27	27	149	38	—	26	64	10	1	11
173	SANGOD	118	12	28	31	189	40	—	10	50	11	2	13
174	SULTANPUR	120	—	36	37	193	37	—	24	61	12	3	15
	KOTA	**534**	**26**	**141**	**176**	**877**	**184**	**—**	**94**	**278**	**57**	**8**	**65**
175	DEGANA	127	—	36	37	200	49	—	9	58	15	—	15
176	DIDWANA	159	—	57	72	288	57	—	22	79	20	3	23
177	JAYAL	106	—	69	39	214	46	—	19	65	14	2	16
178	KUCHAMAN	127	44	117	39	327	59	3	30	92	16	—	16
179	LADNU	77	—	33	25	135	35	—	11	46	10	—	10
180	MAKRANA	106	—	40	47	193	58	1	11	70	15	2	17
181	MERTA	87	9	38	26	160	48	—	12	60	15	—	15
182	MUNDWA	115	—	71	31	217	31	—	8	39	17		17
183	NAGAUR	122	48	122	26	318	59	1	3	63	18	2	20
184	PARBATSAR	107	8	41	39	195	42	—	10	52	16	—	16
185	RIYAN	96	—	38	28	162	43	—	11	54	13	1	14
	NAGAUR	**1229**	**109**	**662**	**409**	**2409**	**527**	**5**	**146**	**678**	**169**	**10**	**179**

Educational Institutions, 2000				*No. of Working Teachers (Up to 30.11.2002)*				
Sr. Sec. Schools					*Preliminary Education*			
Govt.	*Private*	*Total*	*NFECs*	*Panchayati Raj III Grade*	*II Grade*	*III Grade*	*Physical Education*	*Total*
15	*16*	*17*	*18*	*19*	*20*	*21*	*22*	*23*
6	2	8	118	369	56	255	45	356
4	—	4	57	424	40	246	39	325
3	—	3	121	392	39	228	15	282
9	1	10	235	426	43	263	35	341
11	1	12	115	380	57	353	44	454
9	—	9	102	377	53	256	50	359
2	—	2	49	178	23	395	18	436
6	1	7	126	347	47	231	49	327
6	—	6	132	312	25	144	12	181
4	—	4	120	365	49	279	48	376
4	—	4	102	250	41	540	42	623
8	—	8	129	229	40	261	43	344
9	—	9	57	306	41	166	44	251
81	**5**	**86**	**1463**	**4355**	**554**	**3617**	**484**	**4655**
2	—	2	103	251	50	257	45	352
2	1	3	73	223	37	150	18	205
5	—	5	107	287	56	260	38	354
9	**1**	**10**	**283**	**761**	**143**	**667**	**101**	**911**
5	—	5	96	191	46	244	32	322
2	—	2	41	155	33	176	30	239
3	—	3	91	146	39	277	21	337
4	—	4	69	65	20	101	19	140
3	—	3	136	167	33	130	29	192
4	—	4	123	491	72	324	—	396
3	—	3	85	119	30	127	32	189
24	**—**	**24**	**641**	**1334**	**273**	**1379**	**163**	**1815**
5	—	5	121	323	37	148	25	210
5	—	5	94	233	48	113	42	203
3	1	4	103	495	76	487	58	621
6	—	6	68	320	38	220	37	295
3	—	3	150	301	27	159	25	211
2	—	2	77	349	52	167	18	237
24	**1**	**25**	**613**	**2021**	**278**	**1294**	**205**	**1777**
6	1	7	86	302	33	177	42	252
11	—	11	47	320	47	246	48	341
10	1	11	67	294	34	194	42	270
11	3	14	35	382	59	326	58	443
8	2	10	38	435	31	249	47	327
9	1	10	30	379	45	275	55	375
7	—	7	37	357	46	228	44	318
7	2	9	43	396	50	279	65	394
69	**10**	**79**	**383**	**2865**	**345**	**1974**	**401**	**2720**
2	—	2	29	243	33	132	21	186
1	—	1	87	207	31	98	36	165
6	—	6	188	299	47	184	—	231
4	—	4	129	240	68	337	51	456
10	—	10	180	349	52	335	41	428
6	1	7	94	268	48	250	40	338
11	—	11	125	512	76	307	52	435
6	—	6	174	425	43	277	47	367
3	—	3	98	201	24	114	—	138
49	**1**	**50**	**1104**	**2744**	**422**	**2034**	**288**	**2744**
6	1	7	59	386	72	364	59	495
4	—	4	119	393	62	281	65	408
2	—	2	66	200	29	127	28	184
6	—	6	195	343	43	178	41	262
6	—	6	84	369	45	226	41	312
24	**1**	**25**	**523**	**1691**	**251**	**1176**	**234**	**1661**
4	—	4	119	311	27	155	20	202
4	—	4	106	271	27	145	27	199
2	—	2	53	273	31	265	29	325
3	—	3	106	316	34	213	29	276
5	—	5	118	315	27	193	31	251
18	**—**	**18**	**502**	**1486**	**146**	**971**	**136**	**1253**
7	—	7	46	347	44	230	38	312
8	1	9	71	438	70	306	46	422
4	—	4	123	288	34	196	37	267
6	—	6	73	410	68	352	49	469
4	1	5	69	236	39	210	31	280
3	—	3	127	250	51	237	28	316
2	—	2	18	273	43	229	32	304
4	—	4	67	230	32	168	24	224
13	—	13	107	354	52	297	33	382
4	—	4	137	270	46	200	28	274
5	—	5	39	281	46	217	38	301
60	**2**	**62**	**877**	**3377**	**525**	**2642**	**384**	**3551**

P. Code	Panchayat Samities Name	Educational Institutions, 2000											
		Primary Schools					Upper Primary Schools				Secondary Schools		
		Govt.	S.K.	RGSJP	Private	Total	Govt.	S.K.	Private	Total	Govt.	Private	Total
1	2	3	4	5	6	7	8	9	10	11	12	13	14
186	BALI	88	35	26	24	173	51	—	—	51	16	—	16
187	DESURI	74	—	5	6	85	32	—	3	35	8	—	8
188	JAITARAN	102	—	40	19	161	43	—	5	48	13	—	13
189	MARWAR JUN.	129	3	30	21	183	49	—	5	54	13	1	14
190	PALI	74	—	23	10	107	25	—	—	25	6	—	6
191	RAIPUR	123	34	38	15	210	39	—	7	46	13	—	13
192	RANI STATION	54	—	9	18	81	33	—	1	34	9	1	10
193	ROHAT	78	—	11	3	92	21	—	—	21	7	—	7
194	SOJAT	99	—	25	18	142	45	—	2	47	18	—	18
195	SUMERPUR	48	—	21	17	86	34	—	2	36	13	—	13
	PALI	**869**	**72**	**228**	**151**	**1320**	**372**	—	**25**	**397**	**116**	**2**	**118**
196	AMET	93	—	39	8	140	24	—	1	25	10	—	10
197	BHIM	130	15	105	11	261	50	—	1	51	9	—	9
198	DEOGARH	85	10	24	1	120	20	—	—	20	6	—	6
199	KHAMNOR	143	12	142	20	317	59	1	2	62	18	—	18
200	KUMBHALGARH	100	47	51	6	204	43	1	—	44	9	—	9
201	RAILMAGRA	82	1	29	16	128	34	—	2	36	12	—	12
202	RAJSAMAND	118	—	55	17	190	28	—	8	36	11	2	13
	RAJSAMAND	**751**	**85**	**445**	**79**	**1360**	**258**	**2**	**14**	**274**	**75**	**2**	**77**
203	BAMANWAS	145	—	50	31	226	30	—	21	51	13	—	13
204	BONLI	108	15	40	53	216	47	—	23	70	15	2	17
205	GANGAPUR	119	4	42	30	195	45	—	24	69	20	1	21
206	KHANDAR	93	24	49	21	187	38	—	10	48	8	—	8
207	S.M.	119	—	38	53	210	52	—	27	79	13	2	15
	SAWAI MADHOPUR	**584**	**43**	**219**	**188**	**1034**	**212**	—	**105**	**317**	**69**	**5**	**74**
208	DANTA RAMGARH	178	—	86	38	302	53	—	52	105	22	4	26
209	DHOND	150	—	58	39	247	43	—	43	86	28	5	33
210	FATEHPUR	109	—	29	31	169	53	—	12	65	20	1	21
211	KHANDELA	128	—	72	41	241	51	—	46	97	20	1	21
212	LACHHMANGARH	135	—	52	34	221	41	—	38	79	19	2	21
213	NEEM KA THANA	168	23	75	69	335	64	2	31	97	24	4	28
214	PIPRALI	92	—	68	37	197	48	—	57	105	16	6	22
215	SRI MADHOPUR	103	—	64	37	204	37	—	39	76	22	2	24
	SIKAR	**1063**	**23**	**504**	**326**	**1916**	**390**	**2**	**318**	**710**	**171**	**25**	**196**
216	ABU ROAD	41	33	50	2	126	24	—	—	24	10	—	10
217	PINDWARA	70	16	73	16	175	29	—	2	31	15	—	15
218	REODAR	94	8	43	5	150	39	—	—	39	10	—	10
219	SHEOGANJ	46	7	15	8	76	26	—	—	26	7	—	7
220	SIROHI	64	—	25	23	112	29	—	—	29	13	—	13
	SIROHI	**315**	**64**	**206**	**54**	**639**	**147**	—	**2**	**149**	**55**	—	**55**
221	DEOLI	118	—	29	16	163	40	1	7	48	12	2	14
222	MALPURA	117	22	41	35	215	41	—	7	48	10	—	10
223	NIWAI	142	11	68	32	253	47	—	8	55	14	—	14
224	TODARAISINGH	82	7	14	15	118	39	—	3	42	10	—	10
225	TONK	156	17	45	35	253	53	—	9	62	16	1	17
226	UNIARA	105	—	60	27	192	37	—	7	44	7	—	7
	TONK	**720**	**57**	**257**	**160**	**1194**	**257**	**1**	**41**	**299**	**69**	**3**	**72**
227	BARGAON	81	—	50	25	156	22	—	8	30	17	1	18
228	BHINDER	129	34	65	25	253	57	1	1	59	15	—	15
229	DHARIAWAD	164	13	83	10	270	55	—	4	59	5	—	5
230	GIRWA	173	15	76	23	287	55	—	6	61	15	1	16
231	GOGUNDA	106	16	64	9	195	49	—	5	54	16	—	16
232	JHADOL	185	58	58	16	317	41	1	1	43	13	—	13
233	KHERWARA	205	—	141	28	374	66	—	8	74	17	—	17
234	KOTRA	162	33	51	7	253	36	1	—	37	5	—	5
235	MAVLI	149	1	81	36	267	50	—	7	57	15	—	15
236	SALUMBAR	154	32	98	27	311	59	1	—	60	13	—	13
237	SARADA	141	30	82	17	270	51	1	4	56	17	1	18
	UDAIPUR	**1649**	**232**	**849**	**223**	**2953**	**541**	**5**	**44**	**590**	**148**	**3**	**151**
	RAJASTHAN	**29535**	**2717**	**11843**	**6124**	**50219**	**10791**	**71**	**3555**	**14417**	**3199**	**277**	**3476**

Educational Institutions, 2000				*No. of Working Teachers (Up to 30.11.2002)*				
Sr. Sec. Schools					*Preliminary Education*			
Govt.	*Private*	*Total*	*NFECs*	*Panchayati Raj III Grade*	*II Grade*	*III Grade*	*Physical Education*	*Total*
15	*16*	*17*	*18*	*19*	*20*	*21*	*22*	*23*
9	—	9	119	294	45	308	49	402
4	—	4	29	184	30	188	21	239
4	—	4	47	251	51	284	41	376
5	3	8	60	312	42	245	41	328
3	—	3	31	205	45	344	35	424
3	1	4	96	292	41	223	33	297
10	1	11	47	168	25	168	25	218
1	—	1	86	163	20	94	20	134
4	—	4	69	316	48	286	41	375
2	—	2	36	171	34	198	28	260
45	**5**	**50**	**620**	**2356**	**381**	**2338**	**334**	**3053**
1	—	1	66	143	24	98	12	134
14	—	14	89	234	38	156	35	229
1	—	1	110	141	25	113	14	152
5	—	5	55	308	58	298	49	405
5	1	6	137	189	33	91	31	155
6	—	6	34	189	35	183	34	252
5	1	6	45	275	37	251	32	320
37	**2**	**39**	**536**	**1479**	**250**	**1190**	**207**	**1647**
4	—	4	127	273	28	127	25	180
6	—	6	124	295	42	184	38	264
2	—	2	107	309	53	276	43	372
4	—	4	68	222	35	138	33	206
7	—	7	120	305	60	374	45	479
23	**—**	**23**	**546**	**1404**	**218**	**1099**	**184**	**1501**
9	—	9	72	463	37	217	50	304
3	—	3	35	420	38	186	42	266
11	—	11	63	278	55	282	52	389
3	—	3	26	376	44	245	51	340
6	—	6	67	344	42	243	43	328
9	—	9	53	521	61	319	63	443
8	—	8	42	337	48	225	50	323
3	—	3	41	332	33	246	44	323
52	**—**	**52**	**399**	**3071**	**358**	**1963**	**395**	**2716**
—	—	—	121	142	33	237	21	291
4	1	5	118	254	38	192	30	260
4	—	4	105	255	29	138	18	185
3	—	3	81	140	29	174	24	227
3	—	3	77	210	34	241	28	303
14	**1**	**15**	**502**	**1001**	**163**	**982**	**121**	**1266**
5	—	5	9	339	45	236	37	318
6	—	6	134	337	44	258	45	347
3	—	3	111	263	48	226	46	320
4	—	4	37	252	36	181	39	256
5	—	5	36	414	65	409	59	533
3	—	3	156	287	39	140	31	210
26	**—**	**26**	**483**	**1892**	**277**	**1450**	**257**	**1984**
2	1	3	32	308	19	133	19	171
4	—	4	180	407	58	322	58	438
6	—	6	121	333	40	110	41	191
6	—	6	89	459	50	358	45	453
5	—	5	142	274	36	152	25	213
7	—	7	257	449	34	150	28	212
9	2	11	106	546	65	326	62	453
2	—	2	172	279	17	52	11	80
7	1	8	58	392	51	283	41	375
5	—	5	91	376	56	227	51	334
10	—	10	117	409	50	205	45	300
63	**4**	**67**	**1365**	**4232**	**476**	**2318**	**426**	**3220**
1150	**68**	**1218**	**25325**	**73192**	**10061**	**54502**	**9165**	**73728**

Note: * Dungargarh PS shifted from Churu to Bikaner district on 1st April 2001
** Excluding data of Dungargarh ps; *** Including data of Dungargarh PS.
Source: 1. Hemlata Joshi. 2005. *'Economic Development Index, Rajasthan* (Spatio-Temporal & Gender Appraisal at Panchayat Samiti / Block Level), Published Research Report, IDSJ, University Book House, Jaipur.

PANCHAYAT SAMITI-WISE NO. OF SARPANCHS, PS MEMBERS AND CO-OPERATIVE SOCIETIES, 2001

P. Code	Panchayat Samiti	No. of Sarpanchs (2000)			Panchayat Samiti Members (2000)			Co-operative Societies	
		Total	Male	Female (%)	Total	Male	Female (%)	Numbers	Members
1	2	3	4	5	6	7	8	9	10
1	ARAIN	30	20	10 (33.3)	17	10	7 (41.2)	67	23172
2	BHINAY	35	23	12 (34.3)	19	11	8 (42.1)	90	22380
3	JAWAJA	35	22	13 (37.1)	19	11	8 (42.1)	41	21268
4	KEKRI	31	21	10 (32.3)	19	13	6 (31.6)	71	20644
5	KISHANGARH	31	21	10 (32.3)	19	13	6 (31.6)	72	29512
6	MASOODA	32	21	11 (34.4)	19	10	9 (47.4)	119	25050
7	PISANGAN	45	29	16 (35.6)	27	18	9 (33.3)	135	41928
8	SRINAGAR	37	25	12 (32.4)	20	14	6 (30.0)	72	18296
	AJMER	**276**	**182**	**94 (34.1)**	**159**	**100**	**59 (37.1)**	**667**	**202250**
9	BANSURE	37	25	12 (32.4)	25	16	9 (36.0)	22	21236
10	BEHROR	29	18	11 (37.9)	19	12	7 (36.8)	25	14196
11	KATHUMAR	39	23	16 (41.0)	25	14	11 (44.0)	98	28726
12	KISHANGARH BAS	28	17	11 (39.3)	21	12	9 (42.9)	76	28708
13	KOTKASIM	22	14	8 (36.4)	15	10	5 (33.3)	27	16853
14	LACHHMANGARH	44	29	15 (34.1)	27	18	9 (33.3)	153	37434
15	MANDAWAR	38	25	13 (34.2)	25	17	8 (32.0)	38	23646
16	NIMRANA	32	22	10 (31.3)	19	13	6 (31.6)	17	14217
17	RAJGARH	29	19	10 (34.5)	17	11	6 (35.3)	91	17520
18	RAMGARH	37	23	14 (37.8)	25	14	11 (44.0)	135	24467
19	RENI	26	16	10 (38.5)	17	11	6 (35.3)	66	19930
20	THANAGAZI	35	23	12 (34.3)	21	13	8 (38.1)	56	18115
21	TIJARA	38	22	16 (42.1)	25	16	9 (36.0)	83	28115
22	UMREN	36	22	14 (38.9)	25	17	8 (32.0)	136	23030
	ALWAR	**470**	**298**	**172 (36.6)**	**306**	**194**	**112 (36.6)**	**1023**	**316193**
23	ANANDPURI	26	16	10 (38.5)	15	9	6 (40.0)	10	20095
24	BAGIDORA	39	21	18 (46.2)	21	13	8 (38.1)	40	24652
25	GARHI	52	33	19 (36.5)	29	18	11 (37.9)	73	32596
26	GHATOL	53	33	20 (37.7)	27	16	11 (40.7)	36	25528
27	KUSHALGARH	29	17	12 (41.4)	17	11	6 (35.3)	15	17238
28	PEEPALKHOONT	36	23	13 (36.1)	17	11	6 (35.3)	24	21019
29	SAJJANGARH	30	15	15 (50.0)	17	11	6 (35.3)	29	18934
30	TALWARA	55	36	19 (34.5)	25	17	8 (32.0)	75	27869
	BANSWARA	**320**	**194**	**126 (39.4)**	**168**	**106**	**62 (36.9)**	**1801**	**187931**
31	ANTA	38	24	14 (36.8)	19	13	6 (31.6)	77	31881
32	ATRU	34	23	11 (32.4)	17	11	6 (35.3)	42	21753
33	BARAN	26	17	9 (34.6)	15	10	5 (33.3)	37	24877
34	CHHABRA	27	17	10 (37.0)	15	8	7 (46.7)	21	16405
35	CHHIPABAROD	30	20	10 (33.3)	19	13	6 (31.6)	26	24491
36	KISHANGANJ	31	20	11 (35.5)	17	10	7 (41.2)	47	22140
37	SHAHBAD	27	18	9 (33.3)	15	10	5 (33.3)	27	16746
	BARAN	**213**	**139**	**74 (34.7)**	**117**	**75**	**42 (35.9)**	**277**	**158293**
38	BALOTRA	54	34	20 (37.0)	29	15	14 (48.3)	77	23144
39	BARMER	50	32	18 (36.0)	25	17	8 (32.0)	77	29280
40	BAYTOO	47	29	18 (38.3)	23	12	11 (47.8)	59	25447
41	CHOHTAN	50	31	19 (38.0)	25	16	9 (36.0)	46	30109
42	DHORIMANNA	47	30	17 (36.2)	27	18	9 (33.3)	66	31129
43	SHEO	45	29	16 (35.6)	19	12	7 (36.8)	42	30225
44	SINDHARI	46	27	19 (41.3)	25	17	8 (32.0)	47	28613
45	SIWANA	40	27	13 (32.5)	25	17	8 (32.0)	38	24001
	BARMER	**379**	**239**	**140 (36.9)**	**198**	**124**	**74 (37.4)**	**452**	**221948**
46	BAYANA	44	26	18 (40.9)	23	14	9 (39.1)	63	19669
47	DEEG	35	20	15 (42.9)	18	12	6 (33.3)	59	26372
48	KAMAN	44	26	18 (40.9)	23	14	9 (39.1)	78	21291
49	KUMHER	35	20	15 (42.9)	19	9	10 (52.6)	92	40068
50	NADBAI	37	24	13 (35.1)	19	12	7 (36.8)	72	23517
51	NAGAR PAHARI	49	33	16 (32.7)	27	17	10 (37.0)	90	23951
52	RUPBAS	45	29	16 (35.6)	24	16	8 (33.3)	58	24182
53	SEWAR	33	20	13 (39.4)	21	14	7 (33.3)	62	28127
54	WEIR	45	24	21 (46.7)	25	12	13 (52.0)	81	25006
	BHARATPUR	**367**	**222**	**145 (39.5)**	**199**	**120**	**79 (39.7)**	**655**	**232183**

P. Code	Panchayat Samiti	No. of Sarpanchs (2000)			Panchayat Samiti Members (2000)			Co-operative Societies	
		Total	Male	Female (%)	Total	Male	Female (%)	Numbers	Members
1	2	3	4	5	6	7	8	9	10
55	ASIND	44	27	17 (38.6)	23	15	8 (34.8)	121	26653
56	BANERA	26	18	8 (30.8)	15	10	5 (33.3)	66	15747
57	HURDA	20	12	8 (40.0)	15	10	5 (33.3)	75	27159
58	JAHAZPUR	37	23	14 (37.8)	21	13	8 (38.1)	42	28719
59	KOTRI	33	22	11 (33.3)	19	13	6 (31.6)	51	19034
60	MANDAL	46	32	14 (30.4)	25	15	10 (40.0)	112	29138
61	MANDALGARH	50	32	18 (36.0)	25	16	9 (36.0)	86	30470
62	RAIPUR	22	15	7 (31.8)	15	10	5 (33.3)	34	13520
63	SAHARA	28	19	9 (32.1)	15	8	7 (46.7)	70	23075
64	SHAHPURA	38	26	12 (31.6)	19	13	6 (31.6)	73	20150
65	SUWANA	34	24	10 (29.4)	19	11	8 (42.1)	60	26209
	BHILWARA	**378**	**250**	**128 (33.9)**	**211**	**134**	**77 (36.5)**	**790**	**261274**
66	BIKANER	62	41	21 (33.9)	35	23	12 (34.3)	288	59428
67	DUNGARGARH *	30	20	10 (33.3)	21	13	8 (38.1)	115	34598
68	KOLAYAT	37	25	12 (32.4)	21	13	8 (38.1)	219	37588
69	LUNKARANSAR	36	24	12 (33.3)	23	13	10 (43.5)	250	24974
70	NOKHA	53	35	18 (34.0)	31	21	10 (32.3)	145	38269
	BIKANER **	**188**	**125**	**63 (33.5)**	**110**	**70**	**40 (36.6)**	**902**	**160259**
71	HINDOLI	41	26	15 (36.6)	23	15	8 (34.8)	69	16226
72	KESHORAIPATAN	46	31	15 (32.6)	23	13	10 (43.5)	116	45950
73	NAINWA	33	22	11 (33.3)	19	13	6 (31.6)	37	10950
74	TALERA	61	41	20 (32.8)	31	21	10 (32.3)	110	42500
	BUNDI	**181**	**120**	**61 (33.7)**	**96**	**62**	**34 (35.4)**	**332**	**115626**
75	ARNOD	29	17	12 (41.4)	15	10	5 (33.3)	35	18248
76	BARI SADRI	23	15	8 (34.8)	15	10	5 (33.3)	39	13631
77	BEGUN	31	21	10 (32.3)	15	9	6 (40.0)	41	22027
78	BHADESAR	25	16	9 (36.0)	15	10	5 (33.3)	45	12981
79	BHAINSRORGARH	22	13	9 (40.9)	15	10	5 (33.3)	31	13230
80	BHOPALSAGAR	19	13	6 (31.6)	15	10	5 (33.3)	29	10331
81	CHHOTI SADRI	24	16	8 (33.3)	15	10	5 (33.3)	39	18813
82	CHITTAURGARH	39	25	14 (35.9)	21	14	7 (33.3)	60	23516
83	DUNGLA	26	17	9 (34.6)	15	9	6 (40.0)	37	14772
84	GANGRAR	21	13	8 (38.1)	15	9	6 (40.0)	44	15138
85	KAPASAN	23	15	8 (34.8)	15	10	5 (33.3)	82	19692
86	NIMBAHERA	35	22	13 (37.1)	17	11	6 (35.3)	40	24488
87	PRATAPGARH	48	31	17 (35.4)	23	16	7 (30.4)	76	29844
88	RASHMI	23	12	11 (47.8)	15	10	5 (33.3)	51	15027
	CHITTAURGARH	**388**	**246**	**142 (36.6)**	**226**	**148**	**78 (34.5)**	**649**	**251738**
89	CHURU	35	22	13 (37.1)	19	11	8 (42.1)	58	24551
90	RAJGARH	55	37	18 (32.7)	33	18	15 (45.5)	65	43260
91	RATANGARH	31	19	12 (38.7)	19	13	6 (31.6)	52	23267
92	SARDARSHAHAR	48	32	16 (33.3)	25	17	8 (32.0)	155	41065
93	SUJANGARH	51	34	17 (33.3)	29	18	11 (37.9)	69	30812
94	TARANAGAR	28	19	9 (32.1)	19	12	7 (36.8)	26	24403
	CHURU ***	**278**	**183**	**95 (34.3)**	**165**	**102**	**63 (38.2)**	**540**	**221956**
95	BANDIKUI	39	21	18 (46.2)	26	17	9 (34.6)	50	23614
96	DAUSA	51	29	22 (43.1)	30	21	9 (30.0)	94	37642
97	LALSOT	47	25	22 (46.8)	27	13	14 (51.9)	57	23681
98	MAHWA	41	26	15 (36.6)	23	15	8 (34.8)	65	23431
99	SIKRAI	41	26	15 (36.6)	25	16	9 (36.0)	60	19184
	DAUSA	**219**	**127**	**92 (42.0)**	**131**	**82**	**49 (37.4)**	**326**	**127572**
100	BARI	31	20	11 (35.5)	19	13	6 (31.6)	54	13880
101	BASERI	35	21	14 (40.0)	23	15	8 (34.8)	53	12926
102	DHAULPUR	48	32	16 (33.3)	29	17	12 (41.4)	75	18133
103	RAJAKHERA	41	28	13 (31.7)	23	13	10 (43.5)	62	12041
	DHAULPUR	**155**	**101**	**54 (34.8)**	**94**	**58**	**36 (38.3)**	**244**	**56980**
104	ASPUR	48	32	16 (33.3)	23	15	8 (34.8)	28	31077
105	BICHHIWARA	48	31	17 (35.4)	27	18	9 (33.3)	45	30025
106	DUNGARPUR	36	25	11 (30.6)	21	14	7 (33.3)	44	23203
107	SAGWARA	42	27	15 (35.7)	25	17	8 (32.0)	54	34937
108	SIMALWARA	58	39	19 (32.8)	29	19	10 (34.5)	65	33126
	DUNGARPUR	**232**	**154**	**78 (33.6)**	**125**	**83**	**42 (33.6)**	**236**	**152368**
109	ANUPGARH	87	55	32 (36.8)	41	22	19 (46.3)	238	69161
110	GANGANAGAR	43	27	16 (37.2)	25	14	11 (44.0)	189	118079
111	KARANPUR	35	24	11 (31.4)	15	10	5 (33.3)	66	47667
112	PADAMPUR	36	24	12 (33.3)	17	11	6 (35.3)	41	47961
113	RAISINGHNAGAR	45	30	15 (33.3)	19	13	6 (31.6)	45	41500
114	SADULSHAHAR	32	21	11 (34.4)	19	13	6 (31.6)	95	71215
115	SURATGARH	38	25	13 (34.2)	23	15	8 (34.8)	362	112968
	GANGANAGAR	**316**	**206**	**110 (34.8)**	**159**	**98**	**61 (38.4)**	**1036**	**508551**
116	BHADRA	48	28	20 (41.7)	27	17	10 (37.0)	41	62617
117	HANUMANGARH	120	80	40 (33.3)	72	42	30 (41.7)	143	74963
118	NOHAR	81	54	27 (33.3)	41	26	15 (36.6)	88	65668
	HANUMANGARH	**249**	**162**	**87 (34.9)**	**140**	**85**	**55 (39.3)**	**272**	**203248**

P. Code	Panchayat Samiti	No. of Sarpanchs (2000)			Panchayat Samiti Members (2000)			Co-operative Societies	
		Total	Male	Female (%)	Total	Male	Female (%)	Numbers	Members
1	2	3	4	5	6	7	8	9	10
119	AMBER	46	30	16 (34.8)	29	19	10 (34.5)	140	25730
120	BASSI	38	26	12 (31.6)	25	16	9 (36.0)	109	21345
121	CHAKSU	34	22	12 (35.3)	19	13	6 (31.6)	102	30434
122	DUDU	55	36	19 (34.5)	33	22	11 (33.3)	148	43912
123	GOVINDGARH	41	27	14 (34.1)	31	21	10 (32.3)	143	34732
124	JAMWA RAMGARH	43	29	14 (32.6)	29	18	11 (37.9)	79	34878
125	JHOTWARA	16	11	5 (31.3)	15	10	5 (33.3)	115	25355
126	KOTPUTLI	42	26	16 (38.1)	27	18	9 (33.3)	63	50049
127	PHAGI	31	21	10 (32.3)	21	14	7 (33.3)	118	33411
128	SAMBHAR	44	29	15 (34.1)	25	17	8 (32.0)	92	41130
129	SANGANER	25	17	8 (32.0)	15	9	6 (40.0)	145	21940
130	SHAHPURA	29	20	9 (31.0)	23	14	8 (34.8)	74	28008
131	VIRATNAGAR	37	25	12 (32.4)	22	15	7 (31.8)	68	21811
	JAIPUR	**481**	**319**	**162 (33.7)**	**314**	**206**	**107 (34.1)**	**1396**	**412735**
132	JAISALMER	40	27	13 (32.5)	15	10	5 (33.3)	99	20201
133	SAM	49	33	16 (32.7)	15	10	5 (33.3)	55	15985
134	SANKRA	39	26	13 (33.3)	19	9	10 (52.6)	61	18371
	JAISALMER	**128**	**86**	**42 (32.8)**	**49**	**29**	**20 (40.8)**	**215**	**54557**
135	AHORE	41	26	15 (36.6)	23	15	8 (34.8)	76	24788
136	BHINMAL	35	23	12 (34.3)	23	15	8 (34.8)	55	22372
137	JALOR	28	18	10 (35.7)	17	11	6 (35.3)	55	19229
138	JASWANTPURA	29	19	10 (34.5)	17	11	6 (35.3)	43	18185
139	RANIWARA	30	20	10 (33.3)	19	11	8 (42.1)	69	21186
140	SANCHORE	63	40	23 (36.5)	37	24	13 (35.1)	106	54935
141	SAYLA	37	25	12 (32.4)	25	15	10 (40.0)	57	23161
	JALOR	**263**	**171**	**92 (35.0)**	**161**	**102**	**59 (36.6)**	**461**	**183856**
142	BAKANI	41	28	13 (31.7)	19	12	7 (36.8)	39	19041
143	DAG	40	27	13 (32.5)	21	13	8 (38.1)	42	23101
144	JHALRAPATAN	48	31	17 (35.4)	25	17	8 (32.0)	55	29537
145	KHANPUR	38	25	13 (34.2)	19	13	6 (31.6)	48	21010
146	MANOHARTHANA	39	25	14 (35.9)	21	14	7 (33.3)	49	19263
147	PIRAWA	42	27	15 (35.7)	21	14	7 (33.3)	61	24911
	JHALAWAR	**248**	**163**	**85 (34.3)**	**126**	**83**	**43 (34.1)**	**294**	**136863**
148	ALSISAR	33	21	12 (36.4)	19	13	6 (31.6)	41	39089
149	BUHANA	41	26	15 (36.6)	25	13	12 (48.0)	35	26624
150	CHIRAWA	29	19	10 (34.5)	19	12	7 (36.8)	62	45147
151	JHUNJHUNUN	37	23	14 (37.8)	23	15	8 (34.8)	76	42505
152	KHETRI	36	23	13 (36.1)	28	19	9 (32.1)	37	25257
153	NAWALGARH	35	22	13 (37.1)	27	17	10 (37.0)	66	40242
154	SURAJGARH	37	24	13 (35.1)	21	14	7 (33.3)	52	30187
155	UDAIPURWATI	37	25	12 (32.4)	26	15	11 (42.3)	37	36649
	JHUNJHUNUN	**211**	**136**	**75 (35.5)**	**188**	**118**	**70 (37.2)**	**406**	**285700**
156	BALESAR	33	21	12 (36.4)	19	12	7 (36.8)	33	13042
157	BAP	31	20	11 (35.5)	17	11	6 (35.3)	53	21572
158	BHOPALGARH	36	24	12 (33.3)	23	15	8 (34.8)	88	38151
159	BILARA	37	23	14 (37.8)	21	14	7 (33.3)	152	67618
160	LUNI	39	27	12 (30.8)	25	17	8 (32.0)	114	27798
161	MANDOR	25	16	9 (36.0)	17	10	7 (41.2)	79	24207
162	OSIAN	67	44	23 (34.3)	43	27	16 (37.2)	121	41681
163	PHALODI	37	24	13 (35.1)	25	14	11 (44.0)	137	30577
164	SHERGARH	32	20	12 (37.5)	17	11	6 (35.3)	26	11900
	JODHPUR	**337**	**219**	**118 (35.0)**	**207**	**131**	**76 (36.7)**	**803**	**276546**
165	HINDAUN	51	32	19 (37.3)	29	17	12 (41.4)	68	27115
166	KARAULI	45	29	16 (35.6)	25	17	8 (32.0)	52	61822
167	NADOTI	29	20	9 (31.0)	17	11	6 (35.3)	37	15616
168	SAPOTRA	55	38	17 (30.9)	27	18	9 (33.3)	42	17425
169	TODABHIM	43	23	20 (46.5)	23	12	11 (47.8)	63	22585
	KARAULI	**223**	**142**	**81 (36.3)**	**121**	**75**	**46 (38.0)**	**262**	**144563**
170	CHECHAT	26	13	13 (50.0)	23	14	9 (39.1)	40	19016
171	ITAWA	30	20	10 (33.3)	19	12	7 (36.8)	59	29857
172	LADPURA	27	18	9 (33.3)	17	11	6 (35.3)	79	26444
173	SANGOD	35	22	13 (37.1)	19	13	6 (31.6)	66	42781
174	SULTANPUR	33	22	11 (33.3)	19	12	7 (36.8)	87	41785
	KOTA	**125**	**82**	**43 (34.4)**	**97**	**62**	**35 (36.1)**	**331**	**159883**
175	DEGANA	43	30	13 (30.2)	25	17	8 (32.0)	70	28752
176	DIDWANA	57	38	19 (33.3)	33	22	11 (33.3)	53	27801
177	JAYAL	45	30	15 (33.3)	27	16	11 (40.7)	55	36408
178	KUCHAMAN	52	32	20 (38.5)	31	19	12 (38.7)	40	24501
179	LADNU	32	19	13 (40.6)	19	13	6 (31.6)	28	22180
180	MAKRANA	36	17	19 (52.8)	25	17	8 (32.0)	38	20805
181	MERTA	32	21	11 (34.4)	21	14	7 (33.3)	66	26266
182	MUNDWA	38	24	14 (36.8)	23	15	8 (34.8)	70	28958
183	NAGAUR	50	34	16 (32.0)	27	18	9 (33.3)	84	32799
184	PARBATSAR	32	20	12 (37.5)	21	13	8 (38.1)	32	18856
185	RIYAN	39	26	13 (33.3)	21	14	7 (33.3)	60	26834
	NAGAUR	**456**	**291**	**165 (36.2)**	**273**	**178**	**95 (34.8)**	**596**	**294160**

P. Code	Panchayat Samiti	No. of Sarpanchs (2000)			Panchayat Samiti Members (2000)			Co-operative Societies	
		Total	Male	Female (%)	Total	Male	Female (%)	Numbers	Members
1	2	3	4	5	6	7	8	9	10
186	BALI	39	25	14 (35.9)	23	14	9 (39.1)	95	25209
187	DESURI	24	16	8 (33.3)	15	9	6 (40.0)	52	19649
188	JAITARAN	32	21	11 (34.4)	23	15	8 (34.8)	79	35395
189	MARWAR JUN.	46	31	15 (32.6)	25	16	9 (36.0)	70	28773
190	PALI	23	15	8 (34.8)	15	10	5 (33.3)	83	21522
191	RAIPUR	35	19	16 (45.7)	21	12	9 (42.9)	66	32756
192	RANI STATION	29	19	10 (34.5)	15	10	5 (33.3)	40	22964
193	ROHAT	23	15	8 (34.8)	15	10	5 (33.3)	55	23444
194	SOJAT	37	24	13 (35.1)	21	14	7 (33.3)	81	35362
195	SUMERPUR	28	17	11 (39.3)	19	12	7 (36.8)	39	21664
	PALI	**316**	**202**	**114 (36.1)**	**192**	**122**	**70 (36.5)**	**660**	**266738**
196	AMET	20	13	7 (35.0)	15	10	5 (33.3)	19	13868
197	BHIM	29	19	10 (34.5)	17	11	6 (35.3)	10	13686
198	DEOGARH	18	11	7 (38.9)	15	9	6 (40.0)	13	10583
199	KHAMNOR	40	26	14 (35.0)	21	14	7 (33.3)	34	15051
200	KUMBHALGARH	37	25	12 (32.4)	17	11	6 (35.3)	33	17918
201	RAILMAGRA	29	18	11 (37.9)	17	11	6 (35.3)	75	24038
202	RAJSAMAND	29	19	10 (34.5)	17	11	6 (35.3)	40	17445
	RAJSAMAND	**202**	**131**	**71 (35.1)**	**119**	**77**	**42 (35.3)**	**224**	**112589**
203	BAMANWAS	35	22	13 (37.1)	19	9	10 (52.6)	43	16985
204	BONLI	41	27	14 (34.1)	23	16	7 (30.4)	53	19761
205	GANGAPUR	38	25	13 (34.2)	23	15	8 (34.8)	70	24478
206	KHANDAR	35	23	12 (34.3)	19	13	6 (31.6)	50	13714
207	SAWAI MADHOPUR	45	27	18 (40.0)	25	15	10 (40.0)	72	23655
	SAWAI MADHOPUR	**194**	**124**	**70 (36.1)**	**109**	**68**	**41 (37.6)**	**288**	**98593**
208	DANTA RAMGARH	45	29	16 (35.6)	31	21	10 (32.3)	70	39386
209	DHOND	43	29	14 (32.6)	25	17	8 (32.0)	74	39748
210	FATEHPUR	35	23	12 (34.3)	23	15	8 (34.8)	41	34694
211	KHANDELA	39	24	15 (38.5)	27	16	11 (40.7)	30	42982
212	LACHHMANGARH	37	23	14 (37.8)	23	12	11 (47.8)	38	32331
213	NEEM KA THANA	59	38	21 (35.6)	37	25	12 (32.4)	42	31881
214	PIPRALI	36	23	13 (36.1)	25	15	10 (40.0)	43	32629
215	SRI MADHOPUR	34	22	12 (35.3)	25	15	10 (40.0)	57	33428
	SIKAR	**328**	**211**	**117 (35.7)**	**216**	**136**	**80 (37.0)**	**395**	**287079**
216	ABU ROAD	25	17	8 (32.0)	15	8	7 (46.7)	12	14807
217	PINDWARA	34	23	11 (32.4)	21	13	8 (38.1)	22	19883
218	REODAR	37	24	13 (35.1)	21	14	7 (33.3)	49	24779
219	SHEOGANJ	24	16	8 (33.3)	15	10	5 (33.3)	25	16681
220	SIROHI	31	20	11 (35.5)	17	11	6 (35.3)	23	18766
	SIROHI	**151**	**100**	**51 (33.8)**	**89**	**56**	**33 (37.1)**	**131**	**94916**
221	DEOLI	39	26	13 (33.3)	21	13	8 (38.1)	48	20154
222	MALPURA	36	24	12 (33.3)	23	15	8 (34.8)	105	25453
223	NIWAI	41	27	14 (34.1)	21	14	7 (33.3)	47	28364
224	TODARAISINGH	31	21	10 (32.3)	15	10	5 (33.3)	46	17298
225	TONK	50	32	18 (36.0)	25	15	10 (40.0)	84	32645
226	UNIARA	33	22	11 (33.3)	17	10	7 (41.2)	44	25176
	TONK	**230**	**152**	**78 (33.9)**	**122**	**77**	**45 (36.9)**	**374**	**149090**
227	BARGAON	25	15	10 (40.0)	15	10	5 (33.3)	21	12283
228	BHINDER	51	35	16 (31.4)	25	17	8 (32.0)	60	33949
229	DHARIAWAD	48	30	18 (37.5)	25	16	9 (36.0)	22	23039
230	GIRWA	47	30	17 (36.2)	27	16	11 (40.7)	71	31863
231	GOGUNDA	40	27	13 (32.5)	19	13	6 (31.6)	35	22180
232	JHADOL	45	30	15 (33.3)	23	15	8 (34.8)	39	19054
233	KHERWARA	62	39	23 (37.1)	29	18	11 (37.9)	24	21395
234	KOTRA	36	24	12 (33.3)	21	14	7 (33.3)	21	26199
235	MAVLI	47	29	18 (38.3)	25	17	8 (32.0)	94	22594
236	SALUMBAR	48	31	17 (35.4)	25	17	8 (32.0)	49	21681
237	SARADA	46	32	14 (30.4)	24	17	7 (29.2)	58	24206
	UDAIPUR	**495**	**322**	**173 (34.9)**	**258**	**170**	**88 (34.1)**	**494**	**258443**
	RAJASTHAN (RURAL)	**8997**	**5799**	**3198 (35.5)**	**5245**	**3331**	**1913 (36.5)**	**17532**	**6594681**

Note: * Dungargarh PS shifted from Churu to Bikaner district on 1st April 2001
** Excluding data of Dungargarh ps; *** Including data of Dungargarh PS

Source: 1. Election Directorate, GoR, Jaipur; 2. Cooperative Department, GoR, Jaipur.

GENERAL ANNEX-XV

PANCHAYAT SAMITI-WISE DETAILS OF BPL FAMILIES

P. Code	Panchayat Samities	Total Rural Families	No. of Families Below Poverty Line	%age of BPL Families to Total Families	Selected Families				Details of Families as Per Occupation							Out of Total Families				
					S.C.	S.T.	Back Ward	Others	Agriculture Worker	Other Rural Worker	Small Farmer Agriculture	Marginal Farmer	Under Non Agriculture	Rural Artisians	Others	Widow	Handicaped	Selling Land Allotte	Small Scale	Bonded Labour
1	2	3	4	5	6	7	8	9	10	11	12	13	14	15	16	17	18	19	20	21
1	ARAIN	22721	8397	37	2832	545	3298	1722	3400	1665	880	914	556	75	907	449	311	4	175	—
2	BHINAY	30069	10634	35	3309	1035	4906	1384	7969	2023	366	20	164	92	—	569	8	—	299	—
3	JAWAJA	30799	10623	34	1311	169	8816	327	3390	3167	184	1708	709	92	1373	1064	155	—	63	—
4	KEKRI	29699	7386	25	2664	1151	2994	597	3327	1557	1103	384	401	106	508	342	7	101	128	—
5	KISHANGARH	31737	3709	12	715	179	1694	1121	1622	1242	274	1	164	21	385	16	—	—	374	—
6	MASOODA	29848	10252	34	1710	745	6608	1189	1604	1284	1269	5317	348	81	349	1005	51	1	215	—
7	PISANGAN	39097	6814	17	1632	79	3885	1218	2767	2329	177	471	291	95	684	249	3	26	799	—
8	SRINAGAR	23494	5117	22	1891	100	1601	1525	2050	1937	126	271	145	42	546	435	55	343	215	—
	AJMER DISTRICT	**237514**	**62932**	**26**	**16064**	**4003**	**33782**	**9083**	**26129**	**15204**	**4379**	**9086**	**2778**	**604**	**4752**	**4129**	**590**	**475**	**2268**	**—**
9	BANSURE	26495	7108	27	2473	474	2997	1164	1068	877	984	2688	718	459	314	361	16	—	47	—
10	BEHROR	20975	1520	7	691	38	562	229	448	614	39	218	61	92	48	560	187	—	43	—
11	KATHUMAR	30306	7342	24	2976	859	1820	1687	2710	—	2014	2461	74	83	—	293	42	—	180	—
12	KISHANGARH BAS	24354	4831	20	1855	12	924	2040	1458	1425	442	937	242	46	281	384	2	—	1148	3
13	KOTKASIM	17334	2956	17	1550	31	857	518	824	720	155	1018	35	109	95	256	3	—	71	—
14	LACHHMANGARH	32335	8272	26	2900	544	1603	3226	1189	889	2100	3456	142	147	349	486	7	—	283	—
15	MANDAWAR	27394	4744	17	2107	225	1247	1165	643	520	194	2074	503	375	435	215	—	—	124	—
16	NIMRANA	22127	2502	11	1104	52	854	492	262	241	107	746	146	157	843	279	1	—	44	—
17	RAJGARH	22349	5016	22	1382	1318	1639	677	2000	1108	601	911	185	89	122	223	16	—	—	—
18	RAMGARH	32372	11068	34	2945	284	2106	5733	2720	2204	2020	2307	489	165	1155	487	32	307	630	—
19	RENI	20579	3759	18	1022	866	1069	902	1066	249	1203	884	84	124	144	191	13	15	19	—
20	THANAGAZI	22722	6742	30	1782	1307	2433	1220	1428	2127	338	1356	422	145	934	699	22	13	77	—
21	TIJARA	29886	6015	20	1796	19	1078	3122	1722	1675	513	1353	264	203	285	313	11	—	3490	—
22	UMREN	29399	7036	24	2585	474	1931	2046	2842	1974	403	552	227	87	244	356	6	—	1332	17
	ALWAR	**358627**	**78911**	**22**	**27168**	**6503**	**21120**	**24120**	**20395**	**14623**	**11110**	**20961**	**3592**	**2281**	**5949**	**5013**	**350**	**335**	**7193**	**20**
23	ANANDPURI	18311	14799	81	387	14174	95	143	1046	611	4419	8140	367	1	215	187	82	—	—	—
24	BAGIDORA	29480	24089	82	1555	20261	1088	1185	2719	1303	8604	9611	1064	116	672	444	237	664	89	—
25	GARHI	42254	22114	52	2037	16521	1414	2142	5627	2239	4016	7547	1456	255	974	718	179	467	414	—
26	GHATOL	38966	29010	74	1712	25259	852	1187	9301	1404	4962	12000	748	109	486	633	68	—	96	—
27	KUSHALGARH	20514	15435	75	253	14781	134	267	5438	3044	4090	2449	350	33	31	107	2	10197	—	—
28	PEEPALKHOONT	25013	22428	90	1097	21002	149	180	2391	906	5779	9876	3392	12	72	286	6	—	—	—
29	SAJJANGARH	22524	19007	84	764	17662	409	172	4715	1247	2881	7272	734	162	1996	354	151	40	49	—
30	TALWARA	35595	22910	64	1070	19582	773	1485	8375	2071	2990	7594	828	62	990	707	192	90	65	—
	BANSWARA	**232657**	**169792**	**73**	**8875**	**149242**	**4914**	**6761**	**39612**	**12825**	**37741**	**64489**	**8939**	**750**	**5436**	**3436**	**917**	**11458**	**713**	**—**
31	ANTA	23401	5928	25	2208	668	2502	550	2210	1211	551	1385	246	62	263	206	52	81	273	—
32	ATRU	21635	7463	34	2898	1303	2442	820	2036	1901	878	1164	678	171	635	290	90	82	210	—
33	BARAN	14866	3349	23	1487	388	1305	169	2248	—	260	841	—	—	—	129	6	27	66	5
34	CHHABRA	17140	5534	32	1483	1421	2195	435	1832	870	686	1796	100	48	202	191	12	4	126	—
35	CHHIPABAROD	23967	9245	39	2289	2322	3987	645	3053	1987	1246	1555	344	122	936	168	4	119	250	—
36	KISHANGANJ	22309	7760	35	1283	3564	2085	828	2634	1910	750	2022	272	74	98	221	181	18	125	9
37	SHAHBAD	16854	6407	38	1286	3511	1289	321	1407	1673	878	1734	304	62	349	177	15	884	37	122
	BARAN	**140172**	**45684**	**33**	**12934**	**13177**	**15805**	**3768**	**15420**	**9552**	**5249**	**10497**	**1944**	**539**	**2483**	**1382**	**360**	**1215**	**1087**	**136**

38	BALOTRA	39601	10158	26	2284	1811	2701	3362	1122	681	1383	6946	—	17	9	636	—	2	1109	—
39	BARMER	34734	7526	22	1792	789	1264	3681	559	250	1738	4491	165	28	295	390	4	132	957	—
40	BAYTOO	31571	11135	35	2402	769	1988	5976	271	138	3759	6582	101	13	271	537	40	13	309	—
41	CHOHTAN	39360	14875	38	5003	2057	1858	5957	1086	323	4688	6742	989	—	1047	565	6	7	2816	—
42	DHORIMANNA	33878	8828	26	2235	856	1789	3948	1007	96	1142	6546	13	12	12	299	114	99	188	—
43	SHEO	27783	7042	25	1685	302	1671	3384	336	555	2348	3011	26	254	512	327	18	187	1044	—
44	SINDHARI	34395	10988	32	2373	713	2659	5243	1276	750	3698	4489	208	111	457	407	31	51	123	8
45	SIWANA	32428	8051	25	2308	1753	2815	1175	2814	1781	1013	995	423	178	847	610	48	66	389	—
	BARMER	**273750**	**78603**	**29**	**23082**	**9050**	**16745**	**32726**	**8471**	**4574**	**19768**	**39802**	**1925**	**613**	**3450**	**3771**	**261**	**557**	**6935**	**8**
46	BAYANA	29646	2745	9	1224	59	1135	327	1161	655	86	501	201	27	114	232	1	—	—	—
47	DEEG	23108	4112	18	1543	60	1103	1406	1767	1409	418	174	104	237	3	169	—	—	—	—
48	KAMAN	30757	7865	26	1592	13	1103	5157	1762	1823	426	2826	95	158	775	517	19	—	3252	—
49	KUMHER	24040	3465	14	1549	103	881	932	1202	1334	271	145	181	91	241	243	—	—	—	—
50	NADBAI	24218	3328	14	1618	103	808	799	1514	781	322	70	228	84	329	201	19	4	18	—
51	NAGAR PAHARI	31879	6148	19	1732	267	1449	2700	1896	1782	486	1004	328	149	503	480	71	33	1189	3
52	RUPBAS	30956	7490	24	2838	93	2929	1630	1636	2030	496	2464	341	49	474	626	—	—	—	—
53	SEWAR	24901	3688	15	1783	50	1063	792	1320	1430	47	151	183	56	501	197	—	—	28	—
54	WEIR	29752	7028	24	3321	579	1934	1194	2899	962	765	1997	205	83	117	336	83	—	34	—
	BHARATPUR	**249257**	**45869**	**18**	**17200**	**1327**	**12405**	**14937**	**15157**	**12206**	**3317**	**9332**	**1866**	**934**	**3057**	**3001**	**193**	**37**	**4521**	**3**
55	ASIND	35951	9403	26	1938	1702	5049	714	3375	2151	2723	3263	402	94	558	398	23	1341	77	—
56	BANERA	19599	6851	35	1866	1026	2968	991	2208	1994	2547	2133	215	60	606	199	3	538	393	222
57	HURDA	15739	3951	25	1064	799	1614	474	1289	819	890	1161	83	45	146	107	—	122	26	8
58	JAHAZPUR	34217	20201	59	4857	7541	6329	1474	4563	3186	5753	6478	528	173	801	238	—	1604	72	700
59	KOTRI	28187	10484	37	2818	1109	4765	1792	2497	1221	3612	3606	206	65	519	151	4	50	310	103
60	MANDAL	36592	9535	26	2408	1566	4505	1056	2970	2095	3201	2662	550	98	829	806	—	16	66	10
61	MANDALGARH	35508	12973	37	3208	2984	5352	1429	3253	1941	2493	4353	506	113	1085	242	—	764	23	2
62	RAIPUR	17938	3674	20	955	989	1392	338	1252	928	1251	1104	158	38	250	167	1	607	20	349
63	SAHARA	18944	6780	36	1971	1105	2776	928	3277	1509	1960	2194	191	93	536	379	11	618	128	—
64	SHAHPURA	28576	12419	43	3653	1895	5575	1296	1319	1803	4949	3762	165	82	441	559	—	13	283	64
65	SUWANA	30200	8392	28	2515	1011	3700	1166	2919	1705	1770	2364	254	69	847	487	4	120	52	6
	BHILWARA	**301451**	**104663**	**35**	**27253**	**21727**	**44025**	**11658**	**28922**	**19352**	**31149**	**33080**	**3258**	**920**	**6618**	**3733**	**46**	**5793**	**1450**	**1464**
66	BIKANER	55564	20437	37	7231	529	2824	9853	4624	2396	2878	6151	1604	1474	1310	570	124	851	720	—
67	DUNGARGARH *	25737	7061	27	3447	—	1056	2558	2070	544	1952	1768	192	26	509	252	58	8	61	—
68	KOLAYAT	28353	9277	33	3113	72	2265	3827	1260	663	2825	3247	830	374	78	391	78	46	529	—
69	LUNKARANSAR	28819	8647	30	2692	19	2258	3678	1324	1119	2233	3447	15	232	277	183	16	—	752	—
70	NOKHA	38769	17450	45	6390	1	3407	7652	7910	1140	1153	6041	165	657	384	458	7	—	—	—
	BIKANER **	**151505**	**55811**	**37**	**19426**	**621**	**10754**	**25010**	**15118**	**5318**	**9089**	**18886**	**2614**	**2737**	**2049**	**1602**	**225**	**897**	**2001**	—
71	HINDOLI	30107	10217	34	2846	2170	4088	1113	347	3360	1167	4319	322	185	517	218	21	17	305	—
72	KESHORAIPATAN	28260	9606	34	2842	2008	4039	717	2202	1825	1409	1218	1782	868	302	96	73	—	69	—
73	NAINWA	24973	7324	29	2138	1297	3035	854	1831	927	1722	1880	347	228	389	157	32	28	19	—
74	TALERA	38598	16771	43	5132	4518	5853	1268	5198	2762	2541	4227	789	359	895	675	310	301	269	—
	BUNDI	**121938**	**43918**	**36**	**12958**	**9993**	**17015**	**3952**	**9578**	**8874**	**6839**	**11644**	**3240**	**1640**	**2103**	**1146**	**436**	**346**	**662**	—
75	ARNOD	20399	12758	63	809	9924	860	1165	2669	314	3979	5796	—	—	—	—	—	—	—	—
76	BARI SADRI	17973	8548	48	1467	2914	2751	1416	1174	678	3004	2577	528	150	437	505	—	—	105	—
77	BEGUN	19086	7796	41	2114	1695	3391	596	1884	984	982	3347	231	39	329	415	149	329	199	5
78	BHADESAR	16130	7827	49	2333	1123	2659	1712	3190	683	1192	1848	408	113	393	308	80	—	248	—
79	BHAINSRORGARH	16765	8157	49	1734	3421	1978	1024	2126	1331	965	1436	1555	229	515	338	131	27	78	—
80	BHOPALSAGAR	12835	5030	39	1226	1366	1865	573	880	590	1223	2246	14	273	4	183	10	—	41	—
81	CHHOTI SADRI	15886	7611	48	1427	3651	1442	1091	3814	1453	951	498	501	51	343	282	—	1486	57	5450
82	CHITTAURGARH	30220	13462	45	3288	3031	4528	2615	3828	2034	2161	4040	572	128	699	571	87	—	249	—
83	DUNGLA	15807	8561	54	2235	2188	2619	1519	1741	477	2532	1843	1805	21	142	412	5	—	92	—
84	GANGRAR	14172	7243	51	1881	898	2980	1484	430	410	2429	3311	245	79	339	293	25	—	33	—
85	KAPASAN	18170	8578	47	2512	1730	2363	2003	1945	1179	1493	2843	455	293	370	224	46	—	150	—
86	NIMBAHERA	25703	11057	43	2710	2453	4088	1796	2120	1885	1942	4144	357	222	387	558	130	19	62	4
87	PRATAPGARH	33737	19880	59	2278	12776	2678	2148	7282	4863	3847	3270	276	150	192	95	3	—	45	—
88	RASHMI	14301	6745	47	2397	856	2448	1034	1575	544	1320	2791	236	163	116	331	17	65	198	—
	CHITTAURGARH	**271184**	**133253**	**49**	**28411**	**48016**	**36650**	**20176**	**34658**	**17225**	**28020**	**39990**	**7183**	**1911**	**4266**	**4515**	**683**	**1926**	**1557**	**5459**
89	CHURU	26461	7478	28	3460	56	1454	2498	2747	1033	1272	1879	177	73	297	430	81	2	365	—
90	RAJGARH	44326	11601	26	5680	119	2119	3683	6408	38	1232	2426	669	828	—	499	13	—	80	5
91	RATANGARH	27066	6131	23	3017	48	853	2215	1918	1114	899	1422	238	100	440	438	121	3	83	—
92	SARDARSHAHAR	35117	10351	29	4393	55	2187	3706	2565	731	3131	3354	107	164	299	499	398	149	145	11
93	SUJANGARH	41345	13456	33	7245	33	1878	4300	3453	2086	3351	3508	446	107	505	722	129	200	241	142

P. Code	Panchayat Samities	Total Rural Families	No. of Families Below Poverty Line	%age of BPL Families to Total Families	Selected Families				Details of Families as Per Occupation							Out of Total Families				
					S.C.	S.T.	Back Ward	Others	Agriculture Worker	Other Rural Worker	Small Farmer Agriculture	Marginal Farmer	Under Non Agriculture	Rural Artisians	Others	Widow	Handicaped	Selling Land Allotte	Small Scale	Bonded Labour
1	2	3	4	5	6	7	8	9	10	11	12	13	14	15	16	17	18	19	20	21
94	TARANAGAR	24209	8113	34	3404	71	1952	2686	2860	706	1731	2052	358	45	361	431	129	—	346	—
	CHURU ***	**224261**	**64191**	**29**	**30646**	**402**	**11499**	**21644**	**22021**	**6252**	**13568**	**16409**	**2187**	**1343**	**2411**	**3271**	**929**	**362**	**1321**	**158**
95	BANDIKUI	39407	8098	21	2366	1563	3327	842	2066	2312	1004	2011	318	255	132	364	—	132	90	—
96	DAUSA	40381	9727	24	3208	2714	2865	940	3372	1519	1771	2765	124	176	—	691	—	343	88	—
97	LALSOT	33036	9773	30	3018	3098	2535	1122	2407	1912	1939	2721	485	201	108	452	—	1335	147	—
98	MAHWA	28768	5217	18	1876	690	1845	806	1598	1365	306	1142	226	101	479	265	—	472	265	—
99	SIKRAI	30993	7530	24	2515	1753	2444	818	2360	1551	724	1945	449	165	336	613	—	179	116	—
	DAUSA	**172585**	**40345**	**23**	**12983**	**9818**	**13016**	**4528**	**11803**	**8659**	**5744**	**10584**	**1602**	**898**	**1055**	**2385**	**—**	**2741**	**706**	**—**
100	BARI	17127	5956	35	2124	451	2440	941	3051	1148	555	754	257	52	139	292	5	193	42	5427
101	BASERI	22479	8165	36	2412	1364	2423	1966	2460	1564	261	763	956	93	2068	494	—	—	15	—
102	DHAULPUR	28307	8790	31	2732	—	4869	1189	4201	2051	354	1874	76	64	170	425	—	1974	223	439
103	RAJAKHERA	21147	8136	38	2429	—	4167	1540	2003	2487	1410	1760	359	23	94	270	5	21	23	1975
	DHAULPUR	**89060**	**31047**	**35**	**9697**	**1815**	**13899**	**5636**	**11715**	**7250**	**2580**	**5151**	**1648**	**232**	**2471**	**1481**	**10**	**2188**	**303**	**7840**
104	ASPUR	34920	22143	63	1766	14279	2190	3908	5320	3568	3562	5759	2237	374	1323	824	572	319	54	1467
105	BICHHIWARA	39911	28894	72	1805	25242	933	914	9784	3342	3789	7499	3065	122	1293	1386	939	3406	21	416
106	DUNGARPUR	31085	24797	80	753	22272	669	1103	8426	3213	1657	7927	2550	277	747	647	23	—	—	—
107	SAGWARA	34160	24022	70	1627	17549	1301	3545	9081	1184	220	11985	691	645	216	851	104	41	3	36
108	SIMALWARA	42824	30603	71	1298	27115	1287	903	13989	2872	9567	3366	353	444	12	429	43	7523	88	19
	DUNGARPUR	**182900**	**130459**	**71**	**7249**	**106457**	**6380**	**10373**	**46600**	**14179**	**18795**	**36536**	**8896**	**1862**	**3591**	**4137**	**1681**	**11289**	**166**	**1938**
109	ANUPGARH	52955	9243	17	6108	16	1693	1426	5674	2266	151	490	135	115	412	484	15	101	63	1
110	GANGANAGAR	28073	6195	22	3920	22	992	1261	4471	1011	200	112	113	120	168	426	32	—	—	—
111	KARANPUR	19280	6123	32	3924	—	1276	923	3858	890	672	9	194	134	366	120	65	57	3	—
112	PADAMPUR	19062	3406	18	2244	10	785	367	2038	663	94	339	46	88	138	331	54	—	6	885
113	RAISINGHNAGAR	21380	3858	18	2855	—	587	416	1091	815	504	371	438	97	542	190	15	—	—	—
114	SADULSHAHAR	21503	5400	25	3600	—	1318	482	3677	517	12	781	85	80	248	237	7	3	115	—
115	SURATGARH	27214	6056	22	3372	15	1407	1262	4224	835	558	3	121	85	230	182	38	146	8	31
	GANGANAGAR	**189467**	**40281**	**21**	**26023**	**63**	**8058**	**6137**	**25033**	**6997**	**2191**	**2105**	**1132**	**719**	**2104**	**1970**	**226**	**307**	**195**	**917**
116	BHADRA	34254	7445	22	3601	36	1759	2049	1655	296	2853	2464	65	81	31	262	36	1	126	—
117	HANUMANGARH	84225	19750	23	11573	88	4021	4068	15791	2010	1088	27	300	143	391	897	26	—	18	—
118	NOHAR	54659	10683	20	4925	27	2891	2840	5849	1203	1963	981	231	146	310	436	99	5	586	1
	HANUMANGARH	**173138**	**37878**	**22**	**20099**	**151**	**8671**	**8957**	**23295**	**3509**	**5904**	**3472**	**596**	**370**	**732**	**1595**	**161**	**6**	**730**	**1**
119	AMBER	32100	5769	18	1660	1042	1683	1384	1435	2455	423	380	312	151	613	176	70	535	4012	4
120	BASSI	33100	5939	18	1899	2052	1239	649	1060	2158	766	789	278	77	611	3	1	2	1	1
121	CHAKSU	25600	5504	22	1793	1303	1410	998	3437	997	158	158	403	55	296	—	4	—	—	—
122	DUDU	45600	3778	8	1350	181	1528	719	962	1591	127	131	189	136	642	3	1	1	—	—
123	GOVINDGARH	42500	5479	13	1260	649	2368	1202	1584	2148	563	556	263	53	312	147	15	1559	195	—
124	JAMWA RAMGARH	42900	3676	9	1099	1083	906	588	1321	1391	177	172	295	63	257	20	—	—	—	—
125	JHOTWARA	15900	950	6	420	82	256	192	261	376	88	88	24	31	82	4	9	10	5	—
126	KOTPUTLI	34900	5525	16	1625	651	2022	1227	1445	2515	—	—	—	84	1481	—	7	116	—	—
127	PHAGI	21700	4420	20	1556	264	1729	871	1378	1778	275	231	195	206	357	106	11	35	12	—
128	SAMBHAR	22000	3389	15	1923	260	883	1323	1670	1484	393	101	110	27	604	16	6	123	511	2
129	SANGANER	26600	3564	13	1133	674	817	940	1032	1764	90	89	73	145	371	367	2	2	3	—
130	SHAHPURA	27200	6980	26	1236	440	3330	1974	1393	2721	—	—	—	149	2717	1	—	1	—	—
131	VIRATNAGAR	26700	6658	25	1717	640	2937	1364	1543	3105	515	590	248	151	506	273	8	49	364	—
	JAIPUR	**396800**	**61631**	**16**	**18671**	**9321**	**21108**	**13431**	**18521**	**24483**	**3575**	**3285**	**2390**	**1328**	**8849**	**1116**	**134**	**2433**	**5103**	**7**
132	JAISALMER	19623	3382	17	631	428	820	1503	755	1512	79	82	514	28	412	372	40	23	720	—
133	SAM	26591	6584	25	1085	374	1011	4114	1577	3841	179	190	383	57	357	446	31	151	2237	—
134	SANKRA	26003	8891	34	1616	805	1536	4934	4862	1384	977	749	344	63	512	578	89	599	2625	—
	JAISALMER	**72217**	**18857**	**26**	**3332**	**1607**	**3367**	**10551**	**7194**	**6737**	**1235**	**1021**	**1241**	**148**	**1281**	**1396**	**160**	**773**	**5582**	**—**
135	AHORE	28356	6394	23	2630	1589	1723	452	2159	2358	480	317	291	65	724	558	29	598	29	—
136	BHINMAL	23304	6972	30	1785	1472	2221	1494	2681	1189	1378	849	397	141	337	262	3	141	506	—
137	JALOR	19304	4146	21	1849	910	869	518	1017	1416	740	446	211	92	224	183	4	19	8	—
138	JASWANTPURA	18665	5511	30	2172	1139	1515	685	1266	755	1181	1566	257	250	236	252	—	13	69	—
139	RANIWARA	20398	8822	43	2901	2154	2472	1295	2171	242	2068	3896	125	58	262	201	19	—	233	—

140	SANCHORE	41364	27282	66	7590	1963	9082	8647	5255	2765	10676	5244	1186	793	1363	500	196	166	508	—
141	SAYLA	27667	8023	29	2962	1437	2342	1282	2308	2650	934	1008	610	234	279	460	102	22	372	—
	JALOR	**179085**	**67150**	**37**	**21889**	**10664**	**20224**	**14373**	**16857**	**11375**	**17457**	**13326**	**3077**	**1633**	**3425**	**2416**	**353**	**959**	**1725**	**—**
142	BAKANI	28303	9921	35	2035	1688	3857	2341	3555	1328	1226	2742	334	218	518	535	30	—	269	—
143	DAG	28338	6900	24	3209	18	1256	2417	2398	27	1334	3105	18	18	—	467	2	—	194	—
144	JHALRAPATAN	30569	8605	28	2738	2160	2494	1213	3151	2234	1296	1648	121	57	98	517	3	—	151	—
145	KHANPUR	24200	8962	37	2951	1350	3726	935	4794	1968	297	623	594	105	581	340	1	1	465	—
146	MANOHARTHANA	27921	13177	47	2044	3738	4736	2659	3553	2206	2284	5113	5	11	5	481	4	—	608	—
147	PIRAWA	26872	7625	28	3226	717	2002	1680	2510	844	1754	2249	118	70	80	347	109	9	79	1
	JHALAWAR	**166203**	**55190**	**33**	**16203**	**9671**	**18071**	**11245**	**19961**	**8607**	**8191**	**15480**	**1190**	**479**	**1282**	**2687**	**149**	**10**	**1766**	**1**
148	ALSISAR	22879	2556	11	1274	117	473	692	1455	462	124	134	93	37	251	87	11	—	143	—
149	BUHANA	30983	2284	7	1036	6	673	569	427	800	242	684	—	119	12	327	—	—	30	—
150	CHIRAWA	22563	1848	8	869	61	476	442	651	401	196	491	42	34	33	145	11	—	96	—
151	JHUNJHUNUN	30274	3596	12	1832	124	789	851	1590	1737	56	88	17	52	56	249	4	—	224	—
152	KHETRI	36018	4829	13	1486	271	1983	1089	1205	1286	322	914	141	139	822	554	50	79	142	13
153	NAWALGARH	35856	3998	11	1392	219	1182	1205	1222	1297	456	512	105	136	270	329	20	—	49	—
154	SURAJGARH	25564	2687	11	1705	36	356	590	1169	255	354	843	21	6	39	212	3	—	11	—
155	UDAIPURWATI	34264	3404	10	1081	200	1498	625	873	767	316	1152	52	18	226	289	4	—	29	—
	JHUNJHUNUN	**238401**	**25202**	**11**	**10675**	**1034**	**7430**	**6063**	**8592**	**7005**	**2066**	**4818**	**471**	**541**	**1709**	**2190**	**103**	**79**	**724**	**13**
156	BALESAR	4051	3671	91	997	429	947	1298	790	523	1123	910	162	75	88	393	87	—	92	—
157	BAP	21796	3178	15	734	225	443	1776	920	816	641	439	165	28	169	192	18	88	—	—
158	BHOPALGARH	33770	2026	6	897	72	553	504	—	—	649	597	—	—	798	98	—	—	111	2
159	BILARA	29010	1651	6	804	—	467	380	493	408	177	167	84	22	300	110	13	45	—	84
160	LUNI	33700	3981	12	1170	458	1269	1084	—	1114	1204	1082	224	82	275	—	—	—	—	—
161	MANDOR	22939	2618	11	714	322	639	943	562	247	805	632	103	1	268	269	33	6	47	—
162	OSIAN	55193	6746	12	2159	868	1387	2332	1651	875	1818	1409	251	93	631	559	141	22	52	—
163	PHALODI	32592	6366	20	1847	556	813	3150	2388	1178	1014	1040	338	160	248	457	72	75	755	—
164	SHERGARH	22429	4507	20	1170	647	1078	1612	401	399	1945	1505	98	35	124	127	3	0	2	—
	JODHPUR	**255480**	**34744**	**14**	**10492**	**3577**	**7596**	**13079**	**7205**	**5560**	**9376**	**7781**	**1425**	**496**	**2901**	**2205**	**367**	**236**	**1059**	**86**
165	HINDAUN	40374	13619	34	5592	1882	2782	3363	3216	3758	2246	2732	631	155	881	143	—	1425	444	—
166	KARAULI	26351	13878	53	3758	3006	4835	2279	2447	2369	2307	4351	1478	103	823	27	1	1	308	—
167	NADOTI	17987	7282	40	1928	1275	3132	947	1656	2048	1604	1455	60	71	388	2	—	782	102	—
168	SAPOTRA	36195	19612	54	5215	6889	4455	3053	2989	3376	5274	5883	964	137	989	404	—	1874	439	—
169	TODABHIM	27566	6208	23	2027	1655	1702	824	3216	1559	654	1246	191	101	235	13	—	141	0	—
	KARAULI	**148473**	**60599**	**41**	**18520**	**14707**	**16906**	**10466**	**12530**	**13110**	**12085**	**15667**	**3324**	**567**	**3316**	**589**	**1**	**4223**	**1293**	**—**
170	CHECHAT	27768	7873	28	3205	1004	2575	1089	1257	4789	293	156	487	67	824	55	1	5	449	32
171	ITAWA	22868	7260	32	2626	679	3312	643	1534	2469	989	904	174	188	1002	55	5	2	308	9
172	LADPURA	22056	8148	37	1957	1629	3572	990	2174	4027	257	185	384	77	1044	171	7	70	260	1
173	SANGOD	22435	6935	31	2525	747	3144	519	2943	1958	630	430	453	144	377	89	2	41	242	2
174	SULTANPUR	22807	7651	34	2821	862	3079	889	3037	2978	208	406	152	104	766	115	5	23	546	1
	KOTA	**117934**	**37867**	**32**	**13134**	**4921**	**15682**	**4130**	**10945**	**16221**	**2377**	**2081**	**1650**	**580**	**4013**	**485**	**20**	**141**	**1805**	**45**
175	DEGANA	33784	8082	24	3840	—	2023	2165	1210	4	3139	3226	265	206	5	206	1	—	—	—
176	DIDWANA	40396	6098	15	3011	—	1203	1884	1642	1541	78	1203	812	435	557	498	2	—	522	—
177	JAYAL	32930	4943	15	2846	—	1120	853	519	275	550	3285	205	49	170	227	2	11	146	—
178	KUCHAMAN	36525	6436	18	3070	220	2002	1576	1808	2620	243	804	147	180	637	369	6	—	16	101
179	LADNU	22497	3336	15	2148	3	680	881	562	304	287	1905	114	23	120	182	9	—	24	—
180	MAKRANA	29429	4204	14	2055	—	810	1329	1270	1112	240	817	458	29	273	162	3	—	92	—
181	MERTA	27766	2963	11	1458	7	852	636	634	297	173	1613	147	98	133	138	1	—	145	9
182	MUNDWA	28455	4871	17	2162	—	1030	1680	1192	475	725	1908	118	190	148	182	2	—	68	—
183	NAGAUR	34007	6280	18	3058	24	1109	2023	1008	143	1357	3318	103	188	2097	242	30	5	101	—
184	PARBATSAR	25309	4350	17	1942	23	1305	1103	1406	1086	370	616	139	130	429	296	37	—	234	—
185	RIYAN	28727	4594	16	2230	20	1463	928	1610	500	59	2176	76	43	130	299	0	—	240	—
	NAGAUR	**339825**	**56157**	**17**	**27820**	**297**	**13597**	**15058**	**12861**	**8357**	**7221**	**20871**	**2584**	**1571**	**4699**	**2801**	**93**	**16**	**1588**	**110**
186	BALI	34938	10907	31	2422	6261	1515	709	6036	2612	407	409	510	35	898	575	5	—	—	—
187	DESURI	19270	2557	13	1020	464	717	366	478	945	366	495	63	9	201	291	33	—	72	—
188	JAITARAN	33581	9618	29	4166	0	3847	1605	2047	1824	1536	3060	416	219	516	638	179	118	497	8
189	MARWAR JUN.	35508	7123	20	2819	428	3043	833	2264	2526	407	510	373	209	834	892	118	15	123	23
190	PALI	17795	5141	29	1873	700	2118	450	935	1978	612	774	458	89	295	331	19	8	49	—
191	RAIPUR	35539	9118	26	2346	41	5853	878	3078	4126	747	263	415	155	334	888	12	875	222	129
192	RANI STATION	20889	2543	12	1233	293	651	366	761	731	283	223	149	58	338	326	40	1	53	—
193	ROHAT	15833	5304	33	1917	603	2037	747	2028	1254	698	900	77	56	291	213	4	109	172	—
194	SOJAT	29333	6379	22	2494	134	2735	1016	1737	1612	944	1231	456	77	322	56	22	22	20	—

P. Code	Panchayat Samities	Total Rural Families	No. of Families Below Poverty Line	%age of BPL Families to Total Families	Selected Families: S.C.	S.T.	Back Ward	Others
1	2	3	4	5	6	7	8	9
195	SUMERPUR	25594	5724	22	2153	1515	1463	593
	PALI	**268280**	**64414**	**24**	**22443**	**10439**	**23979**	**7553**
196	AMET	13922	3724	27	918	843	1248	715
197	BHIM	26625	13810	52	1953	486	11142	229
198	DEOGARH	15438	6139	40	1448	647	3609	435
199	KHAMNOR	32122	13307	41	1879	5658	2938	2832
200	KUMBHALGARH	26156	10544	40	1443	5001	1632	2460
201	RAILMAGRA	24481	5356	22	1486	1114	1989	767
202	RAJSAMAND	23318	5081	22	910	1606	1497	1068
	RAJSAMAND	**162062**	**57961**	**36**	**10037**	**15355**	**24055**	**8514**
203	BAMANWAS	21187	8479	40	2357	2026	3240	856
204	BONLI	32323	8953	28	2742	1606	3291	1314
205	GANGAPUR	24637	12828	52	3799	1921	4624	2484
206	KHANDAR	26631	10712	40	4175	687	4386	1464
207	SAWAI MADHOPUR	33558	10868	32	2233	3426	3461	1748
	SAWAI MADHOPUR	**138336**	**51840**	**37**	**15306**	**9666**	**19002**	**7866**
208	DANTA RAMGARH	35851	3443	10	1757	155	656	875
209	DHOND	28563	3017	11	1564	66	470	917
210	FATEHPUR	28621	3734	13	2008	61	515	1150
211	KHANDELA	31856	4453	14	1486	498	1311	1158
212	LACHHMANGARH	27946	2708	10	1547	39	444	678
213	NEEM KA THANA	42892	4302	10	1530	453	1513	806
214	PIPRALI	26709	2887	11	1166	88	748	885
215	SRI MADHOPUR	26493	3916	15	1223	276	1280	1137
	SIKAR	**248931**	**28460**	**11**	**12281**	**1636**	**6937**	**7606**
216	ABU ROAD	16687	8285	50	469	6698	617	499
217	PINDWARA	30282	12316	41	2163	7705	1766	682
218	REODAR	28601	9494	33	4826	2026	2057	585
219	SHEOGANJ	18262	3211	18	1274	985	819	133
220	SIROHI	22433	2756	12	1444	526	635	151
	SIROHI	**116265**	**36060**	**31**	**10176**	**17940**	**5894**	**2050**
221	DEOLI	32691	16402	50	4517	4645	5224	2016
222	MALPURA	29953	9283	31	3052	560	3806	2065
223	NIWAI	28082	6269	22	2141	960	2180	980
224	TODARAISINGH	18307	2721	15	876	309	1248	289
225	TONK	34948	9621	28	3134	1422	3452	1613
226	UNIARA	25654	10580	41	2596	2961	3886	1337
	TONK	**166625**	**54876**	**33**	**16316**	**10857**	**19404**	**8299**
227	BARGAON	19101	8678	45	578	5257	624	2219
228	BHINDER	37058	17061	46	2336	5344	5391	4900
229	DHARIAWAD	35663	23787	67	1209	19659	1245	1675
230	GIRWA	39016	14747	38	869	10723	886	2269
231	GOGUNDA	29001	16050	55	1077	9234	3245	2494
232	JHADOL	36492	26290	72	642	20400	1763	3485
233	KHERWARA	47700	36204	76	1645	30319	2283	1957
234	KOTRA	26677	17603	66	274	16277	354	690
235	MAVLI	36050	13094	36	2012	5156	3035	2891
236	SALUMBAR	36136	22741	63	1448	15232	1666	3395
237	SARADA	42291	25860	61	1490	18939	1927	3505
	UDAIPUR	**384185**	**222915**	**58**	**13578**	**157539**	**22409**	**29388**
	RAJASTHAN	**6768568**	**2097560**	**31**	**537941**	**661596**	**520399**	**379138**

P. Code	Panchayat Samities	Details of Families as Per Occupation: Agriculture Worker	Other Rural Worker	Small Farmer Agriculture	Marginal Farmer	Under Non Agriculture	Rural Artisians	Others	Out of Total Families: Widow	Handicaped	Selling Land Allotte	Small Scale	Bonded Labour
1	2	10	11	12	13	14	15	16	17	18	19	20	21
195	SUMERPUR	760	1709	845	1336	295	77	702	—	—	—	—	—
	PALI	**20124**	**19317**	**6845**	**9201**	**3212**	**984**	**4731**	**4210**	**432**	**1178**	**1208**	**160**
196	AMET	951	442	669	1383	142	34	103	66	3	—	6	—
197	BHIM	3894	1781	961	6020	649	239	266	1085	94	—	45	—
198	DEOGARH	2850	1038	208	1244	245	110	444	38	34	—	43	1
199	KHAMNOR	2380	1742	1390	5054	748	280	1677	648	45	—	23	—
200	KUMBHALGARH	2863	1806	2248	2822	326	83	396	498	68	25	31	—
201	RAILMAGRA	2253	1233	267	827	398	95	398	217	3	—	113	—
202	RAJSAMAND	427	635	777	2049	731	148	314	242	15	2	36	—
	RAJSAMAND	**15618**	**8677**	**6520**	**19399**	**3239**	**989**	**3598**	**2794**	**262**	**27**	**297**	**1**
203	BAMANWAS	735	739	2646	3151	153	93	962	349	1	—	195	—
204	BONLI	1840	1866	1991	1806	425	331	694	353	30	117	797	—
205	GANGAPUR	3496	2813	2979	2049	458	163	870	484	91	—	940	—
206	KHANDAR	1789	1535	3327	2843	407	135	676	345	103	—	319	—
207	SAWAI MADHOPUR	2565	1837	2476	2216	618	321	835	590	118	—	386	—
	SAWAI MADHOPUR	**10425**	**8790**	**13419**	**12065**	**2061**	**1043**	**4037**	**2121**	**343**	**117**	**2637**	**—**
208	DANTA RAMGARH	811	1142	423	552	187	87	241	434	46	19	88	—
209	DHOND	1267	365	361	743	126	46	109	212	21	—	41	—
210	FATEHPUR	1193	305	1101	946	87	19	83	284	—	—	285	—
211	KHANDELA	522	476	557	1689	174	80	955	328	21	—	33	—
212	LACHHMANGARH	538	307	743	986	66	24	44	214	—	—	90	—
213	NEEM KA THANA	900	1476	279	892	161	85	509	438	16	—	48	—
214	PIPRALI	1015	406	436	896	29	25	80	157	—	—	38	—
215	SRI MADHOPUR	1021	954	331	1018	312	56	224	261	1	—	23	—
	SIKAR	**7267**	**5431**	**4231**	**7722**	**1142**	**422**	**2245**	**2328**	**105**	**19**	**646**	**—**
216	ABU ROAD	2435	1190	1182	2840	406	16	214	20	2	152	90	—
217	PINDWARA	1759	2314	1454	5438	344	53	954	156	9	89	102	—
218	REODAR	1647	2209	1519	3158	237	122	602	238	5	167	171	—
219	SHEOGANJ	879	555	570	776	71	89	271	74	4	45	26	—
220	SIROHI	584	664	303	894	84	18	209	217	—	226	30	—
	SIROHI	**7304**	**6932**	**5028**	**13106**	**1142**	**298**	**2250**	**705**	**20**	**679**	**419**	**—**
221	DEOLI	3230	2850	3486	4551	565	424	1286	291	152	9	111	—
222	MALPURA	2397	1905	1861	1953	426	251	490	227	82	12	248	—
223	NIWAI	747	916	1769	1636	377	98	727	378	101	39	125	—
224	TODARAISINGH	749	500	475	557	122	88	142	130	49	—	16	—
225	TONK	1890	1649	1952	2390	904	239	608	540	238	—	572	—
226	UNIARA	2091	1976	2504	2574	522	216	707	242	7	47	359	—
	TONK	**11102**	**9884**	**12046**	**13651**	**2916**	**1315**	**3962**	**1808**	**629**	**107**	**1431**	**—**
227	BARGAON	1243	4033	668	984	618	104	1028	190	4	—	14	—
228	BHINDER	3693	2765	3789	3945	905	369	2495	1092	192	261	15	—
229	DHARIAWAD	5969	2755	4265	7817	1115	609	1258	474	145	155	—	—
230	GIRWA	4418	4066	951	2739	1180	219	1174	826	302	—	74	—
231	GOGUNDA	4414	3969	3855	2287	1049	402	74	709	258	—	44	—
232	JHADOL	8150	1197	4784	11379	316	90	375	65	5	—	55	—
233	KHERWARA	3293	3707	2469	21966	2505	1204	980	931	17	—	261	—
234	KOTRA	5668	732	4158	6663	176	146	60	228	69	—	202	—
235	MAVLI	4846	2512	3419	823	660	208	626	501	3	—	—	—
236	SALUMBAR	3890	3904	5915	7855	770	401	205	480	50	—	45	—
237	SARADA	5258	4919	4309	6189	3269	402	1514	950	527	43	157	—
	UDAIPUR	**50842**	**34459**	**38482**	**72546**	**12563**	**4233**	**9790**	**6445**	**1571**	**459**	**868**	**—**
	RAJASTHAN	**591275**	**361544**	**355597**	**564044**	**97027**	**34980**	**114615**	**82863**	**11810**	**51388**	**59959**	**18367**

Note: 1. * Dungargarh PS Shifted from Churu to Bikaner District on 1st April 2001 ** Excluding data of Dungargarh PS; *** Including data of Dungargarh PS.

Source: BPL Census Survey, 1997, Planning Deptt., GoR, Jaipur.

TEHSIL-WISE POPULATION AND LITERACY SCENARIO: RAJASTHAN (2001)

District/ Tehsil	*Population in "000 No.*			*Child population in the age-group 0-6 in "000 No.*			*Literates in "000 No.*			*Literacy Rate (%)*		
	Person	*Male*	*Female*	*Person*	*Male*	*Female*	*Person*	*Male*	*Female*	*Person*	*Male*	*Female*
1	*2*	*3*	*4*	*5*	*6*	*7*	*8*	*9*	*10*	*11*	*12*	**13**
Ajmer District	**2181 (60)**	**1129 (59)**	**1052 (61)**	**365 (69)**	**190 (68)**	**175 (69)**	**1181 (47)**	**751 (52)**	**430 (39)**	**65.06**	**79.96**	**49.10**
Ajmer	690 (27)	360 (27)	329 (27)	96 (37)	50 (37)	46 (37)	455 (18)	269 (22)	187 (13)	76.64	86.54	65.80
Beawar	284 (56)	145 (55)	139 (56)	50 (65)	26 (65)	24 (65)	183 (51)	109 (52)	74 (49)	78.27	91.54	64.54
Bhinay	108 (100)	55 (100)	53 (100)	21 (100)	11 (100)	10 (100)	39 (100)	29 (100)	10 (100)	44.73	65.91	22.87
Kekri	175 (80)	90 (80)	85 (81)	31 (83)	16 (83)	15 (83)	76 (72)	53 (75)	23 (63)	52.52	71.86	32.39
Kishangarh	335 (65)	174 (65)	161 (66)	58 (69)	30 (68)	28 (69)	164 (56)	107 (59)	56 (50)	59.11	74.74	42.30
Masuda	187 (85)	96 (85)	91 (85)	36 (89)	19 (89)	18 (89)	89 (78)	61 (82)	28 (71)	58.75	78.60	37.86
Nasirabad	162 (70)	86 (67)	76 (72)	29 (78)	15 (78)	14 (78)	82 (55)	57 (58)	25 (47)	61.56	79.31	41.05
Peesangan	109 (100)	56 (100)	53 (100)	20 (100)	11 (100)	10 (100)	46 (100)	32 (100)	14 (100)	51.83	71.04	31.72
Sarwar	131 (88)	67 (88)	64 (88)	24 (88)	12 (87)	12 (88)	48 (84)	35 (85)	14 (81)	45.04	63.52	25.80
Alwar	**2991 (85)**	**1585 (85)**	**1406 (86)**	**569 (89)**	**301 (89)**	**268 (89)**	**1513 (80)**	**1013 (82)**	**500 (76)**	**62.48**	**78.91**	**43.95**
Alwar	568 (53)	304 (53)	265 (54)	96 (64)	51 (63)	45 (65)	326 (40)	209 (45)	117 (32)	68.97	82.74	53.14
Bansur	214 (100)	112 (100)	102 (100)	42 (100)	22 (100)	20 (100)	100 (100)	68 (100)	32 (100)	58.15	75.04	39.51
Behror	306 (93)	160 (92)	146 (93)	50 (93)	27 (93)	23 (93)	191 (92)	118 (92)	73 (91)	74.68	89.27	59.03
Kathumar	206 (92)	110 (92)	96 (92)	40 (94)	21 (94)	19 (95)	102 (89)	71 (91)	32 (85)	61.45	79.01	41.12
Kishangarh Bas	162 (74)	85 (74)	77 (75)	32 (79)	17 (79)	15 (80)	80 (66)	53 (69)	27 (60)	61.96	77.52	44.72
Kotkasim	118 (100)	62 (100)	56 (100)	21 (100)	11 (100)	10 (100)	67 (100)	43 (100)	24 (100)	69.69	85.26	52.73
Lachhmangarh	242 (96)	128 (96)	114 (96)	49 (96)	26 (96)	23 (96)	107 (94)	76 (95)	32 (92)	55.92	74.48	34.94
Mandawar	197 (100)	103 (100)	95 (100)	35 (100)	19 (100)	16 (100)	112 (100)	71 (100)	41 (100)	69.29	85.07	52.37
Rajgarh	306 (92)	162 (92)	144 (92)	58 (93)	31 (93)	28 (93)	143 (89)	101 (90)	42 (86)	57.83	76.95	36.14
Ramgarh	202 (100)	106 (100)	96 (100)	44 (100)	23 (100)	21 (100)	83 (100)	59 (100)	24 (100)	52.67	71.41	31.96
Thanagazi	190 (100)	100 (100)	90 (100)	40 (100)	21 (100)	19 (100)	72 (100)	53 (100)	19 (100)	48.07	67.80	26.20
Tijara	281 (81)	154 (79)	127 (83)	61 (85)	32 (84)	29 (85)	128 (73)	90 (74)	38 (70)	58.43	74.47	38.50
Banswara	**1500 (93)**	**758 (93)**	**742 (93)**	**312 (95)**	**158 (95)**	**154 (96)**	**525 (85)**	**361 (88)**	**164 (79)**	**44.22**	**60.24**	**27.86**
Bagidora	288 (100)	146 (100)	142 (100)	62 (100)	32 (100)	31 (100)	92 (100)	65 (100)	27 (100)	40.84	57.27	24.03
Banswara	371 (76)	189 (76)	182 (77)	71 (84)	36 (83)	35 (85)	157 (59)	103 (65)	54 (48)	52.31	67.25	36.74
Garhi	247 (96)	124 (96)	123 (96)	46 (97)	24 (97)	23 (97)	107 (93)	70 (95)	37 (91)	53.24	70.15	36.34
Gatol	311 (100)	156 (100)	155 (100)	68 (100)	35 (100)	33 (100)	87 (100)	64 (100)	23 (100)	35.92	52.83	18.98
Kushalgarh	283 (96)	143 (96)	140 (97)	65 (98)	32 (98)	32 (98)	82 (91)	59 (93)	24 (86)	37.53	52.79	21.84
Baran	**1023 (83)**	**536 (83)**	**487 (83)**	**186 (84)**	**97 (84)**	**89 (85)**	**505 (79)**	**337 (81)**	**168 (75)**	**60.37**	**76.86**	**42.18**
Antah	104 (74)	54 (74)	49 (74)	18 (74)	9 (74)	9 (74)	57 (72)	37 (73)	20 (69)	66.75	82.57	49.34
Atru	134 (95)	70 (95)	64 (94)	23 (95)	12 (95)	11 (95)	71 (94)	48 (94)	24 (93)	63.71	81.30	44.29
Baran	181 (57)	95 (57)	86 (57)	30 (58)	16 (58)	14 (58)	108 (52)	68 (55)	40 (47)	71.00	85.33	55.17
Chhabra	122 (81)	65 (81)	58 (81)	23 (84)	12 (83)	11 (84)	57 (76)	39 (78)	18 (70)	57.25	74.36	37.98
Chhipabarod	144 (89)	75 (89)	69 (89)	28 (90)	14 (90)	13 (90)	60 (84)	43 (86)	18 (78)	51.78	70.53	31.48
Kishanganj	135 (100)	71 (100)	65 (100)	26 (100)	14 (100)	13 (100)	58 (100)	39 (100)	19 (100)	52.88	68.36	35.83
Mangrol	94 (77)	49 (77)	45 (76)	16 (76)	9 (76)	8 (76)	49 (76)	32 (76)	17 (75)	63.28	80.09	45.19
Shahbad	108 (100)	57 (100)	51 (100)	22 (100)	11 (100)	10 (100)	46 (100)	32 (100)	14 (100)	52.99	69.80	34.03
Barmer	**1964 (93)**	**1036 (92)**	**928 (93)**	**432 (95)**	**225 (94)**	**207 (95)**	**914 (90)**	**597 (90)**	**316 (89)**	**59.65**	**73.64**	**43.91**
Barmer	287 (71)	154 (71)	132 (71)	57 (77)	30 (77)	27 (78)	154 (64)	101 (65)	53 (62)	67.06	80.94	50.70
Baytoo	193 (100)	100 (100)	92 (100)	43 (100)	23 (100)	21 (100)	85 (100)	55 (100)	30 (100)	56.71	70.91	41.28
Chohtan	344 (100)	183 (100)	161 (100)	79 (100)	41 (100)	38 (100)	140 (100)	93 (100)	46 (100)	52.57	65.62	37.50
Gudha Malani	341 (100)	178 (100)	164 (100)	78 (100)	40 (100)	38 (100)	172 (100)	106 (100)	67 (100)	65.50	77.05	52.90
Pachpadra	327 (81)	171 (81)	156 (82)	70 (85)	36 (85)	34 (85)	152 (75)	101 (76)	51 (72)	59.12	75.27	41.36
Ramsar	80 (100)	43 (100)	37 (100)	18 (100)	9 (100)	9 (100)	32 (100)	22 (100)	10 (100)	51.76	66.71	34.33
Sheo	178 (100)	97 (100)	82 (100)	42 (100)	23 (100)	19 (100)	79 (100)	54 (100)	25 (100)	57.63	72.64	39.80
Siwana	213 (100)	111 (100)	103 (100)	44 (100)	23 (100)	21 (100)	101 (100)	65 (100)	35 (100)	59.54	74.35	43.56
Bharatpur	**2098 (81)**	**1130 (81)**	**968 (80)**	**419 (84)**	**224 (84)**	**196 (84)**	**1078 (76)**	**738 (78)**	**341 (71)**	**64.24**	**81.39**	**44.12**
Bayana	225 (85)	124 (85)	101 (85)	45 (88)	24 (87)	21 (88)	109 (80)	78 (83)	31 (74)	60.22	78.03	38.17
Bharatpur	373 (45)	200 (45)	172 (45)	65 (52)	35 (51)	31 (52)	226 (40)	144 (43)	82 (35)	73.56	87.17	57.67
Deeg	195 (79)	105 (79)	90 (79)	38 (82)	20 (82)	18 (82)	97 (74)	67 (77)	30 (69)	61.71	79.12	41.24
Kaman	158 (80)	84 (80)	73 (81)	36 (85)	19 (84)	17 (85)	62 (72)	45 (75)	17 (64)	51.11	68.95	30.44
Kumher	174 (88)	94 (88)	80 (88)	33 (88)	18 (88)	15 (89)	95 (89)	65 (89)	30 (88)	67.33	85.18	46.45
Nadbai	183 (88)	99 (88)	84 (88)	35 (90)	19 (90)	16 (90)	103 (86)	70 (88)	33 (84)	69.67	87.49	48.70
Nagar	195 (89)	104 (89)	91 (89)	41 (91)	22 (90)	19 (91)	92 (87)	64 (88)	28 (84)	59.86	77.66	39.45
Pahari	147 (100)	77 (100)	70 (100)	36 (100)	19 (100)	17 (100)	60 (100)	43 (100)	18 (100)	54.22	72.80	33.43
Rupbas	211 (100)	114 (100)	97 (100)	45 (100)	24 (100)	21 (100)	113 (100)	77 (100)	36 (100)	67.72	84.97	47.27
Weir	237 (85)	128 (86)	110 (85)	46 (87)	24 (87)	22 (86)	121 (83)	85 (84)	36 (78)	63.36	82.35	41.13
Bhilwara	**2010 (79)**	**1023 (79)**	**986 (80)**	**355 (82)**	**182 (82)**	**173 (82)**	**845 (69)**	**573 (72)**	**272 (62)**	**51.09**	**68.12**	**33.47**
Asind	206 (93)	102 (93)	104 (93)	41 (94)	21 (94)	20 (94)	72 (89)	51 (91)	21 (87)	43.56	62.95	24.70

Figures in brackets show percentage of rural population to total population

District/ Tehsil	*Population in "000 No.*			*Child population in the age-group 0-6 in "000 No.*			*Literates in "000 No.*			*Literacy Rate (%)*		
	Person	*Male*	*Female*	*Person*	*Male*	*Female*	*Person*	*Male*	*Female*	*Person*	*Male*	*Female*
1	*2*	*3*	*4*	*5*	*6*	*7*	*8*	*9*	*10*	*11*	*12*	**13**
Banera	106 (100)	53 (100)	53 (100)	19 (100)	10 (100)	10 (100)	44 (100)	30 (100)	14 (100)	50.12	68.03	31.87
Beejoliya	81 (85)	42 (85)	39 (85)	15 (88)	8 (87)	7 (88)	33 (76)	23 (79)	10 (68)	50.28	66.77	32.19
Bhilwara	444 (37)	232 (36)	212 (38)	72 (40)	37 (40)	34 (41)	245 (25)	155 (29)	90 (20)	65.79	79.49	50.76
Hurda	115 (79)	60 (78)	56 (80)	20 (82)	11 (81)	10 (82)	56 (69)	37 (72)	18 (64)	58.63	75.98	39.96
Jahazpur	186 (90)	96 (90)	90 (90)	33 (91)	17 (91)	16 (91)	78 (86)	55 (87)	24 (83)	51.28	69.30	32.07
Kotri	146 (100)	75 (100)	71 (100)	26 (100)	13 (100)	13 (100)	48 (100)	34 (100)	13 (100)	39.48	55.71	22.53
Mandal	197 (100)	97 (100)	101 (100)	36 (100)	18 (100)	18 (100)	70 (100)	49 (100)	20 (100)	43.19	62.75	24.62
Mandalgarh	152 (87)	78 (87)	73 (87)	26 (89)	13 (88)	13 (89)	56 (82)	39 (83)	17 (79)	44.71	60.19	28.10
Raipur	84 (100)	41 (100)	43 (100)	15 (100)	7 (100)	7 (100)	30 (100)	21 (100)	9 (100)	42.58	62.19	24.21
Sahara	115 (85)	56 (84)	59 (86)	19 (86)	10 (85)	9 (87)	46 (78)	31 (79)	15 (75)	48.01	67.28	30.08
Shahpura	176 (84)	90 (84)	86 (84)	33 (87)	17 (87)	16 (87)	68 (75)	47 (78)	21 (68)	47.70	64.23	30.36
Bikaner	**1674 (64)**	**886 (64)**	**788 (65)**	**320 (73)**	**167 (73)**	**153 (73)**	**779 (50)**	**509 (54)**	**270 (42)**	**57.54**	**70.78**	**42.55**
Bikaner	726 (25)	385 (25)	340 (25)	115 (33)	60 (33)	55 (33)	428 (16)	263 (18)	165 (13)	70.11	80.78	57.96
Chhatargarh	72 (100)	38 (100)	34 (100)	15 (100)	8 (100)	7 (100)	23 (100)	16 (100)	7 (100)	39.67	52.43	25.21
Khajuwala	92 (100)	49 (100)	42 (100)	17 (100)	9 (100)	8 (100)	40 (100)	27 (100)	13 (100)	53.50	67.50	37.20
Kolayat	207 (100)	110 (100)	97 (100)	46 (100)	24 (100)	22 (100)	67 (100)	48 (100)	18 (100)	41.34	55.85	24.64
Lunkaransar	174 (100)	91 (100)	83 (100)	36 (100)	19 (100)	17 (100)	67 (100)	46 (100)	21 (100)	48.42	63.74	31.60
Nokha	329 (85)	172 (85)	157 (85)	74 (88)	38 (87)	36 (88)	134 (78)	93 (81)	41 (72)	52.49	69.70	33.49
Poogal	74 (100)	40 (100)	34 (100)	16 (100)	8 (100)	8 (100)	21 (100)	16 (100)	5 (100)	36.82	50.81	20.44
Bundi	**961 (81)**	**504 (81)**	**457 (81)**	**172 (84)**	**90 (84)**	**82 (85)**	**440 (75)**	**299 (77)**	**142 (69)**	**55.80**	**72.17**	**37.76**
Bundi	351 (74)	185 (73)	167 (74)	61 (79)	32 (78)	29 (79)	170 (65)	111 (68)	59 (59)	58.44	72.78	42.58
Hindoli	189 (100)	99 (100)	90 (100)	36 (100)	19 (100)	17 (100)	72 (100)	52 (100)	20 (100)	46.91	64.29	27.60
Indragarh	112 (71)	58 (71)	54 (71)	19 (75)	10 (75)	9 (75)	57 (64)	38 (67)	19 (59)	61.59	78.57	43.13
Keshoraipatan	138 (72)	72 (72)	66 (72)	24 (72)	13 (72)	11 (73)	68 (68)	46 (69)	23 (64)	59.77	76.46	41.55
Nainwa	171 (91)	90 (91)	82 (91)	31 (92)	16 (92)	15 (92)	74 (88)	53 (89)	21 (84)	52.92	71.84	32.13
Chittaurgarh	**1803 (84)**	**917 (84)**	**886 (84)**	**305 (86)**	**158 (86)**	**147 (86)**	**814 (75)**	**545 (79)**	**269 (69)**	**54.37**	**71.82**	**36.45**
Arnod	120 (100)	61 (100)	59 (100)	25 (100)	13 (100)	12 (100)	45 (100)	31 (100)	14 (100)	47.08	63.98	29.72
Bari Sadri	104 (86)	52 (85)	52 (86)	17 (88)	9 (88)	8 (88)	43 (77)	30 (80)	13 (70)	49.64	68.81	30.57
Begun	119 (84)	61 (84)	58 (84)	20 (84)	10 (84)	10 (85)	53 (77)	37 (79)	17 (71)	53.60	72.28	34.22
Bhadesar	107 (100)	54 (100)	53 (100)	18 (100)	9 (100)	9 (100)	43 (100)	30 (100)	13 (100)	47.53	66.53	28.33
Chhoti Sadri	117 (86)	59 (86)	57 (86)	20 (88)	10 (87)	9 (88)	55 (79)	37 (81)	18 (73)	56.23	74.61	37.35
Chittaurgarh	264 (64)	136 (63)	128 (64)	42 (67)	22 (67)	20 (67)	138 (51)	88 (55)	50 (44)	62.01	77.12	46.08
Dungla	90 (100)	45 (100)	45 (100)	15 (100)	8 (100)	7 (100)	36 (100)	25 (100)	11 (100)	47.93	67.60	28.62
Gangrar	89 (100)	45 (100)	44 (100)	15 (100)	8 (100)	7 (100)	35 (100)	24 (100)	10 (100)	47.18	65.83	28.23
Kapasan	176 (89)	88 (89)	88 (90)	26 (89)	14 (89)	13 (90)	76 (84)	52 (86)	24 (80)	50.78	69.83	31.85
Nimbahera	189 (72)	96 (71)	92 (72)	31 (73)	16 (73)	15 (74)	97 (63)	64 (67)	33 (55)	61.54	79.94	42.65
Pratapgarh	237 (85)	121 (85)	115 (85)	44 (89)	23 (88)	21 (90)	111 (77)	72 (79)	40 (71)	57.75	72.83	42.00
Rashmi	75 (100)	37 (100)	38 (100)	12 (100)	6 (100)	6 (100)	28 (100)	20 (100)	8 (100)	43.97	64.01	24.64
Rawatbhata	117 (70)	61 (70)	56 (71)	21 (76)	11 (76)	10 (76)	56 (55)	36 (60)	19 (45)	57.86	71.85	42.40
Churu	**1923 (72)**	**987 (72)**	**936 (72)**	**377 (75)**	**197 (75)**	**180 (75)**	**1036 (70)**	**628 (70)**	**407 (68)**	**66.97**	**79.52**	**53.87**
Churu	265 (57)	136 (57)	129 (58)	49 (61)	26 (62)	23 (61)	152 (54)	92 (54)	59 (54)	70.04	83.26	56.21
Dungargarh	227 (80)	117 (80)	111 (80)	50 (85)	26 (85)	24 (84)	109 (75)	69 (77)	40 (71)	61.57	76.13	46.22
Rajgarh	319 (84)	165 (84)	154 (84)	56 (85)	30 (84)	26 (85)	191 (83)	114 (83)	77 (83)	72.73	84.22	60.52
Ratangarh	244 (65)	124 (64)	120 (65)	48 (68)	25 (68)	23 (68)	132 (62)	80 (62)	53 (61)	67.56	80.79	54.12
Sardarshahar	304 (73)	156 (73)	148 (74)	62 (78)	32 (77)	30 (78)	145 (72)	89 (75)	56 (66)	60.17	71.91	47.79
Sujangarh	385 (66)	196 (66)	189 (66)	78 (70)	41 (70)	37 (70)	202 (62)	123 (62)	79 (61)	65.77	78.83	52.34
Taranagar	178 (85)	92 (85)	86 (85)	33 (85)	18 (85)	16 (86)	104 (85)	61 (85)	43 (86)	71.68	81.99	60.82
Dausa	**1317 (90)**	**693 (90)**	**623 (90)**	**260 (91)**	**137 (91)**	**123 (92)**	**663 (87)**	**447 (88)**	**216 (84)**	**62.75**	**80.37**	**43.15**
Baswa	283 (94)	149 (94)	134 (94)	54 (96)	28 (96)	26 (96)	155 (92)	100 (93)	54 (91)	67.35	83.03	49.89
Dausa	333 (82)	175 (81)	158 (82)	65 (85)	34 (85)	31 (86)	167 (76)	114 (78)	52 (71)	62.10	80.60	41.39
Lalsot	280 (90)	146 (90)	134 (90)	58 (91)	31 (91)	28 (91)	124 (87)	87 (88)	37 (83)	56.07	75.73	34.73
Mahwa	209 (86)	111 (86)	97 (86)	41 (87)	22 (87)	19 (87)	112 (83)	75 (84)	37 (81)	66.71	83.44	47.59
Sikrai	212 (100)	111 (100)	100 (100)	42 (100)	23 (100)	20 (100)	105 (100)	70 (100)	35 (100)	62.37	79.28	43.63
Dhaulpur	**983 (82)**	**538 (82)**	**445 (82)**	**215 (85)**	**116 (85)**	**99 (85)**	**466 (79)**	**320 (81)**	**146 (75)**	**60.77**	**75.85**	**42.36**
Bari	201 (75)	111 (75)	90 (74)	45 (78)	24 (78)	21 (78)	92 (72)	63 (74)	28 (66)	58.77	73.36	40.58
Baseri	202 (100)	110 (100)	91 (100)	45 (100)	24 (100)	21 (100)	97 (100)	67 (100)	30 (100)	61.87	77.41	42.82
Dhaulpur	285 (66)	155 (66)	130 (65)	60 (71)	32 (71)	28 (72)	140 (59)	94 (63)	46 (52)	62.41	76.69	45.31
Rajakhera	138 (79)	76 (80)	62 (79)	30 (81)	16 (81)	14 (81)	64 (78)	44 (79)	19 (76)	58.61	73.56	39.93
Sepau	157 (100)	85 (100)	72 (100)	35 (100)	19 (100)	16 (100)	74 (100)	52 (100)	23 (100)	60.82	77.62	40.65
Dungarpur	**1107 (93)**	**546 (92)**	**561 (93)**	**230 (95)**	**117 (95)**	**113 (95)**	**424 (87)**	**284 (89)**	**140 (84)**	**48.32**	**66.19**	**31.22**
Aspur	184 (100)	89 (100)	96 (100)	36 (100)	19 (100)	18 (100)	65 (100)	44 (100)	22 (100)	44.21	62.74	27.61
Dungarpur	392 (89)	196 (88)	196 (90)	82 (93)	42 (93)	40 (94)	161 (80)	107 (82)	53 (74)	51.83	69.66	34.14
Sagwara	288 (87)	140 (87)	148 (87)	55 (89)	28 (89)	27 (89)	121 (82)	78 (84)	43 (79)	52.12	69.84	35.79
Simalwara	243 (100)	122 (100)	122 (100)	56 (100)	28 (100)	28 (100)	77 (100)	55 (100)	22 (100)	41.06	58.67	23.49
Ganganagar	**1788 (75)**	**955 (74)**	**833 (75)**	**291 (78)**	**157 (77)**	**134 (78)**	**971 (69)**	**602 (70)**	**369 (67)**	**64.84**	**75.49**	**52.69**
Anupgarh	174 (83)	92 (83)	82 (84)	31 (85)	17 (84)	15 (86)	86 (79)	54 (80)	32 (77)	59.90	71.13	47.38
Ganganagar	424 (47)	229 (47)	196 (48)	61 (51)	34 (51)	28 (51)	264 (41)	160 (42)	105 (39)	72.83	81.97	62.23
Gharsana	176 (94)	93 (94)	83 (94)	32 (94)	17 (94)	15 (95)	84 (92)	55 (93)	30 (91)	58.70	71.69	44.09
Karanpur	137 (75)	72 (75)	65 (75)	21 (76)	12 (76)	10 (77)	75 (71)	45 (72)	29 (70)	64.60	74.73	53.41
Padampur	148 (82)	78 (82)	70 (82)	23 (83)	13 (83)	11 (83)	81 (79)	49 (80)	32 (77)	65.30	75.96	53.66
Raisinghnagar	185 (85)	97 (85)	88 (85)	30 (87)	16 (87)	14 (87)	104 (82)	63 (82)	41 (81)	67.48	78.32	55.63
Sadulshahar	144 (85)	78 (85)	66 (84)	22 (85)	12 (85)	10 (86)	79 (83)	51 (84)	29 (81)	64.80	76.74	50.77
Suratgarh	275 (78)	149 (78)	125 (78)	48 (81)	25 (80)	22 (81)	132 (71)	85 (73)	47 (68)	58.01	68.53	45.34
Vijainagar	126 (86)	67 (86)	59 (86)	22 (87)	12 (87)	10 (88)	65 (83)	41 (84)	25 (82)	63.01	74.13	50.48

Figures in brackets show percentage of rural population to total population

District/ Tehsil	Population in "000 No.			Child population in the age-group 0-6 in "000 No.			Literates in "000 No.			Literacy Rate (%)		
	Person	Male	Female	Person	Male	Female	Person	Male	Female	Person	Male	Female
1	2	3	4	5	6	7	8	9	10	11	12	13
Hanumangarh	**1517 (80)**	**801 (80)**	**717 (80)**	**250 (82)**	**133 (82)**	**117 (82)**	**833 (77)**	**517 (78)**	**316 (76)**	**65.72**	**77.41**	**52.71**
Bhadra	256 (86)	135 (86)	121 (86)	42 (87)	22 (87)	19 (87)	147 (85)	92 (86)	55 (84)	68.50	81.53	54.09
Hanumangarh	363 (64)	193 (64)	170 (65)	58 (68)	31 (67)	27 (68)	202 (58)	124 (60)	78 (56)	66.03	76.63	54.06
Nohar	267 (84)	141 (84)	127 (84)	45 (85)	24 (85)	21 (84)	150 (83)	93 (83)	57 (82)	67.40	79.54	53.94
Pilibanga	179 (81)	94 (81)	84 (81)	29 (82)	16 (82)	14 (82)	95 (80)	59 (80)	36 (79)	63.76	75.66	50.56
Rawatsar	169 (83)	89 (83)	81 (83)	31 (85)	16 (85)	15 (85)	86 (82)	55 (82)	32 (82)	62.64	75.34	48.62
Sangaria	142 (76)	75 (75)	67 (76)	21 (79)	11 (79)	10 (80)	78 (69)	47 (71)	30 (67)	64.45	74.72	53.10
Tibi	141 (100)	74 (100)	67 (100)	24 (100)	13 (100)	11 (100)	75 (100)	46 (100)	29 (100)	64.06	75.37	51.58
Jaipur	**5252 (51)**	**2769 (50)**	**2483 (51)**	**897 (57)**	**473 (57)**	**424 (57)**	**3076 (44)**	**1919 (47)**	**1157 (39)**	**70.63**	**83.58**	**56.18**
Amber	262 (100)	137 (100)	125 (100)	51 (100)	26 (100)	24 (100)	126 (100)	88 (100)	38 (100)	59.82	79.52	38.11
Bassi	230 (100)	120 (100)	110 (100)	47 (100)	24 (100)	22 (100)	108 (100)	76 (100)	32 (100)	59.07	79.19	36.96
Chaksu	190 (85)	99 (85)	91 (85)	38 (86)	20 (85)	18 (86)	82 (81)	59 (83)	24 (77)	54.06	73.96	32.38
Chomu	326 (84)	170 (84)	156 (85)	61 (86)	32 (86)	29 (86)	179 (82)	117 (83)	63 (81)	67.68	84.68	49.24
Dudu	175 (100)	90 (100)	84 (100)	32 (100)	17 (100)	15 (100)	76 (100)	53 (100)	22 (100)	53.12	72.28	32.64
Jaipur	2413 (4)	1286 (4)	1127 (4)	357 (5)	189 (4)	167 (5)	1609 (3)	952 (3)	657 (3)	78.23	86.79	68.44
Jamwa Ramgarh	250 (100)	131 (100)	119 (100)	50 (100)	26 (100)	24 (100)	126 (100)	84 (100)	42 (100)	62.87	80.05	43.93
Kotputli	340 (88)	178 (88)	162 (88)	65 (90)	35 (90)	30 (90)	200 (87)	122 (87)	78 (86)	72.79	85.05	59.41
Phagi	162 (100)	84 (100)	77 (100)	30 (100)	16 (100)	14 (100)	80 (100)	53 (100)	28 (100)	60.92	76.65	43.83
Phulera	389 (79)	202 (79)	188 (79)	68 (82)	36 (82)	33 (82)	217 (76)	138 (77)	80 (74)	67.72	82.99	51.34
Sanganer	153 (86)	80 (86)	73 (86)	27 (86)	14 (86)	13 (85)	79 (85)	53 (86)	26 (85)	63.01	80.64	43.74
Shahpura	226 (88)	119 (88)	107 (88)	42 (88)	22 (88)	20 (89)	121 (87)	80 (87)	42 (86)	66.05	82.40	47.94
Viratnagar	136 (87)	71 (87)	64 (87)	28 (88)	14 (87)	13 (88)	72 (88)	46 (87)	26 (89)	66.36	80.72	50.40
Jaisalmer	**508 (85)**	**279 (84)**	**229 (85)**	**111 (88)**	**59 (88)**	**51 (88)**	**204 (77)**	**147 (78)**	**57 (72)**	**51.40**	**66.89**	**32.25**
Fatehgarh	74 (100)	41 (100)	33 (100)	17 (100)	10 (100)	8 (100)	27 (100)	20 (100)	7 (100)	47.99	64.40	27.86
Jaisalmer	205 (72)	115 (71)	89 (72)	41 (77)	22 (77)	19 (77)	91 (59)	65 (62)	25 (51)	55.29	69.95	35.96
Pokaran	229 (92)	123 (91)	106 (92)	52 (93)	28 (93)	25 (93)	87 (88)	62 (88)	25 (86)	48.89	64.71	30.41
Jalor	**1448 (92)**	**736 (92)**	**712 (93)**	**307 (94)**	**159 (93)**	**147 (94)**	**531 (89)**	**375 (89)**	**156 (87)**	**46.51**	**65.10**	**27.53**
Ahore	208 (100)	102 (100)	105 (100)	41 (100)	21 (100)	20 (100)	87 (100)	56 (100)	30 (100)	52.01	69.51	35.45
Bagora	131 (100)	67 (100)	64 (100)	30 (100)	15 (100)	14 (100)	40 (100)	30 (100)	10 (100)	39.57	58.93	19.77
Bhinmal	222 (82)	111 (81)	110 (83)	45 (84)	24 (84)	22 (84)	78 (74)	56 (76)	22 (69)	44.18	64.08	24.37
Jalor	219 (80)	112 (79)	108 (81)	43 (83)	22 (83)	20 (83)	87 (69)	60 (71)	26 (64)	49.01	67.31	30.30
Raniwara	163 (100)	84 (100)	79 (100)	36 (100)	19 (100)	17 (100)	60 (100)	43 (100)	18 (100)	47.43	65.32	28.45
Sanchore	368 (93)	190 (93)	178 (93)	82 (94)	42 (94)	39 (94)	135 (91)	97 (91)	38 (90)	46.99	65.72	27.09
Sayla	138 (100)	70 (100)	68 (100)	31 (100)	16 (100)	15 (100)	45 (100)	33 (100)	12 (100)	41.76	60.37	22.86
Jhalawar	**1180 (86)**	**612 (86)**	**568 (86)**	**208 (88)**	**108 (87)**	**100 (88)**	**564 (80)**	**375 (82)**	**189 (75)**	**57.98**	**74.29**	**40.39**
Aklera	142 (87)	74 (87)	68 (87)	28 (89)	14 (89)	13 (89)	55 (80)	39 (82)	17 (74)	48.37	64.80	30.37
Gangdhar	142 (94)	73 (94)	69 (95)	24 (95)	12 (95)	11 (95)	57 (91)	39 (92)	17 (87)	47.63	64.59	29.74
Jhalrapatan	291 (70)	151 (70)	140 (71)	51 (75)	27 (74)	24 (75)	147 (59)	96 (63)	52 (51)	61.32	76.72	44.67
Khanpur	154 (100)	80 (100)	73 (100)	26 (100)	14 (100)	12 (100)	84 (100)	56 (100)	29 (100)	66.17	83.50	47.17
Manohar Thana	116 (92)	60 (92)	56 (92)	24 (93)	12 (93)	12 (94)	43 (86)	31 (89)	12 (80)	46.41	63.99	27.43
Pachpahar	152 (77)	79 (76)	73 (77)	25 (80)	13 (80)	12 (81)	77 (68)	51 (71)	26 (62)	60.27	77.13	42.01
Pirawa	183 (94)	94 (94)	89 (94)	31 (94)	16 (94)	15 (94)	101 (93)	64 (93)	37 (92)	66.18	81.20	50.23
Jhunjhunun	**1913 (79)**	**983 (79)**	**930 (80)**	**327 (80)**	**175 (80)**	**152 (81)**	**1167 (79)**	**700 (78)**	**468 (79)**	**73.61**	**86.61**	**60.10**
Buhana	204 (100)	105 (100)	99 (100)	33 (100)	18 (100)	15 (100)	133 (100)	78 (100)	54 (100)	77.41	89.92	64.48
Chirawa	420 (77)	218 (76)	202 (78)	69 (81)	37 (81)	32 (80)	261 (74)	158 (74)	103 (75)	74.25	87.14	60.55
Jhunjhunun	480 (67)	245 (66)	235 (68)	82 (67)	44 (66)	38 (67)	297 (68)	176 (67)	121 (69)	74.81	87.72	61.64
Khetri	254 (85)	131 (84)	122 (85)	44 (89)	23 (88)	21 (89)	144 (80)	90 (81)	54 (79)	68.67	82.73	53.63
Nawalgarh	292 (75)	149 (74)	143 (75)	50 (74)	27 (74)	23 (74)	168 (75)	104 (75)	64 (75)	69.47	84.81	53.83
Udaipurwati	263 (89)	134 (89)	129 (90)	49 (89)	26 (89)	23 (89)	165 (90)	94 (89)	70 (92)	76.78	86.93	66.34
Jodhpur	**2881 (66)**	**1510 (66)**	**1371 (67)**	**545 (74)**	**284 (74)**	**261 (74)**	**1340 (53)**	**905 (58)**	**435 (42)**	**57.38**	**73.86**	**39.18**
Bhopalgarh	271 (100)	140 (100)	132 (100)	53 (100)	28 (100)	25 (100)	99 (100)	75 (100)	24 (100)	45.34	67.10	22.39
Bilara	251 (72)	130 (72)	121 (72)	45 (73)	24 (73)	22 (73)	113 (65)	80 (68)	33 (60)	54.87	75.13	33.27
Jodhpur	1065 (20)	565 (19)	499 (20)	163 (26)	85 (26)	78 (26)	657 (13)	402 (16)	255 (9)	72.85	83.82	60.38
Luni	172 (100)	88 (100)	83 (100)	35 (100)	18 (100)	17 (100)	73 (100)	51 (100)	21 (100)	53.17	72.92	32.16
Osian	353 (100)	183 (100)	169 (100)	76 (100)	39 (100)	37 (100)	124 (100)	94 (100)	30 (100)	44.66	64.98	22.64
Phalodi	433 (90)	227 (90)	206 (90)	97 (92)	51 (92)	47 (92)	164 (84)	117 (86)	48 (80)	49.03	66.36	29.87
Shergarh	337 (100)	176 (100)	161 (100)	76 (100)	39 (100)	37 (100)	111 (100)	86 (100)	24 (100)	42.39	62.99	19.65
Karauli	**1206 (86)**	**649 (86)**	**557 (86)**	**247 (87)**	**131 (87)**	**115 (87)**	**619 (84)**	**419 (85)**	**201 (82)**	**64.59**	**80.93**	**45.44**
Hindaun	347 (76)	187 (76)	160 (75)	71 (79)	38 (79)	33 (79)	203 (75)	130 (75)	74 (74)	73.93	87.29	58.23
Karauli	289 (77)	156 (77)	133 (77)	61 (80)	32 (80)	29 (79)	135 (74)	95 (76)	41 (69)	59.45	76.32	39.37
Mandrail	61 (100)	33 (100)	28 (100)	13 (100)	7 (100)	6 (100)	27 (100)	20 (100)	7 (100)	55.49	73.77	32.90
Nadoti	123 (100)	65 (100)	58 (100)	24 (100)	13 (100)	11 (100)	65 (100)	43 (100)	22 (100)	65.04	81.93	46.14
Sapotra	171 (100)	92 (100)	79 (100)	34 (100)	18 (100)	16 (100)	81 (100)	57 (100)	25 (100)	59.28	75.90	39.57
Todabhim	215 (90)	115 (90)	100 (90)	43 (91)	23 (91)	20 (91)	108 (89)	75 (90)	33 (88)	62.96	82.46	40.70
Kota	**1569 (47)**	**828 (46)**	**741 (47)**	**245 (52)**	**129 (52)**	**116 (52)**	**985 (41)**	**603 (43)**	**383 (38)**	**74.45**	**86.25**	**61.25**
Digod	150 (100)	79 (100)	72 (100)	25 (100)	13 (100)	12 (100)	88 (100)	55 (100)	32 (100)	70.14	84.67	54.27
Ladpura	869 (17)	460 (16)	408 (17)	123 (21)	65 (22)	58 (21)	587 (13)	349 (14)	238 (12)	78.76	88.29	68.00
Pipalda	156 (100)	82 (100)	74 (100)	26 (100)	13 (100)	12 (100)	81 (100)	54 (100)	27 (100)	62.48	78.59	44.58
Ramganj Mandi	228 (59)	120 (59)	108 (59)	43 (61)	22 (60)	20 (61)	132 (56)	83 (57)	49 (55)	71.22	84.76	56.04
Sangod	166 (89)	87 (89)	79 (89)	29 (89)	15 (89)	14 (89)	97 (88)	61 (88)	35 (87)	70.67	85.76	54.19
Nagaur	**2774 (83)**	**1421 (83)**	**1352 (83)**	**521 (84)**	**271 (84)**	**249 (84)**	**1313 (79)**	**866 (80)**	**446 (77)**	**58.26**	**75.33**	**40.45**
Degana	266 (96)	135 (96)	131 (96)	48 (97)	25 (97)	23 (97)	117 (95)	79 (95)	38 (94)	53.69	71.53	35.57
Didwana	330 (86)	167 (86)	163 (87)	63 (88)	33 (88)	30 (88)	173 (85)	109 (85)	63 (85)	64.60	81.49	47.63
Jayal	225 (100)	115 (100)	110 (100)	44 (100)	23 (100)	21 (100)	93 (100)	64 (100)	29 (100)	51.12	69.46	32.19
Kheenvsar	144 (100)	74 (100)	70 (100)	32 (100)	16 (100)	15 (100)	51 (100)	37 (100)	14 (100)	45.52	64.39	25.80

Figures in brackets show percentage of rural population to total population

District/ Tehsil	Population in "000 No.			Child population in the age-group 0-6 in "000 No.			Literates in "000 No.			Literacy Rate (%)		
	Person	Male	Female	Person	Male	Female	Person	Male	Female	Person	Male	Female
1	2	3	4	5	6	7	8	9	10	11	12	13
Ladnu	215 (73)	109 (73)	106 (74)	39 (75)	20 (74)	19 (75)	112 (70)	72 (71)	41 (67)	63.86	80.59	46.72
Makrana	291 (68)	150 (68)	142 (69)	55 (67)	29 (67)	27 (66)	150 (67)	95 (68)	55 (66)	63.64	78.87	47.63
Merta	337 (88)	175 (88)	162 (88)	58 (89)	31 (89)	27 (88)	157 (85)	108 (86)	49 (81)	56.19	74.77	36.30
Nagaur	429 (65)	221 (65)	208 (65)	84 (67)	44 (67)	41 (68)	189 (57)	128 (60)	61 (51)	54.75	72.28	36.21
Nawa	337 (80)	174 (79)	163 (80)	61 (81)	32 (81)	29 (81)	178 (77)	114 (78)	65 (75)	64.57	80.05	48.16
Parbatsar	200 (93)	103 (93)	97 (93)	37 (94)	19 (94)	18 (94)	93 (91)	61 (91)	32 (91)	57.09	73.21	40.23
Pali	**1819 (79)**	**917 (78)**	**902 (79)**	**331 (81)**	**172 (81)**	**159 (81)**	**817 (72)**	**545 (73)**	**273 (68)**	**54.92**	**73.06**	**36.70**
Bali	223 (82)	111 (82)	112 (83)	42 (85)	21 (85)	20 (85)	98 (76)	63 (77)	35 (75)	54.01	70.10	38.12
Desuri	215 (83)	106 (82)	110 (83)	38 (83)	20 (83)	18 (83)	94 (80)	60 (80)	34 (80)	53.33	70.45	37.27
Jaitaran	206 (91)	105 (90)	101 (91)	38 (91)	19 (91)	18 (91)	82 (87)	58 (88)	24 (84)	48.92	68.37	28.98
Marwar Junction	192 (95)	95 (94)	96 (95)	35 (95)	18 (95)	17 (95)	81 (92)	55 (92)	26 (90)	51.53	71.11	32.42
Pali	307 (39)	159 (38)	148 (40)	52 (43)	27 (43)	25 (43)	164 (29)	106 (31)	58 (26)	64.17	80.05	47.15
Raipur	182 (100)	92 (100)	90 (100)	36 (100)	19 (100)	18 (100)	73 (100)	52 (100)	22 (100)	50.37	71.03	29.66
Rohat	103 (100)	52 (100)	51 (100)	21 (100)	11 (100)	10 (100)	42 (100)	29 (100)	13 (100)	51.24	71.31	30.91
Sojat	206 (76)	104 (75)	102 (76)	37 (77)	19 (77)	18 (78)	96 (69)	65 (71)	32 (65)	56.76	76.30	37.24
Sumerpur	185 (74)	93 (74)	92 (75)	33 (75)	17 (75)	16 (76)	86 (69)	56 (70)	30 (67)	56.73	73.88	39.54
Rajsamand	**986 (87)**	**493 (86)**	**494 (87)**	**177 (89)**	**91 (89)**	**85 (90)**	**452 (80)**	**297 (83)**	**155 (76)**	**55.82**	**74.05**	**37.89**
Amet	105 (84)	53 (84)	52 (84)	18 (86)	9 (86)	9 (87)	47 (76)	31 (79)	16 (71)	53.85	71.31	36.47
Bhim	138 (100)	68 (100)	70 (100)	30 (100)	15 (100)	14 (100)	61 (100)	43 (100)	18 (100)	56.50	80.98	33.15
Deogarh	94 (82)	46 (82)	48 (83)	18 (85)	10 (85)	9 (86)	41 (74)	27 (76)	14 (70)	54.63	73.10	37.15
Kumbhalgarh	131 (100)	64 (100)	67 (100)	25 (100)	13 (100)	12 (100)	49 (100)	34 (100)	15 (100)	46.45	65.71	28.21
Nathdwara	209 (82)	105 (82)	104 (83)	35 (86)	18 (86)	17 (86)	98 (73)	62 (75)	36 (68)	56.49	71.80	41.32
Railmagra	113 (97)	56 (97)	57 (98)	17 (99)	9 (99)	8 (99)	54 (96)	35 (96)	19 (94)	55.96	74.52	37.97
Rajsamand	196 (72)	100 (71)	96 (72)	34 (75)	17 (75)	16 (75)	101 (63)	65 (66)	36 (58)	62.32	78.81	45.15
S. Madhopur	**1116 (81)**	**591 (81)**	**525 (81)**	**203 (83)**	**107 (83)**	**96 (83)**	**523 (75)**	**371 (78)**	**152 (67)**	**57.34**	**76.75**	**35.44**
Bamanwas	149 (100)	79 (100)	70 (100)	26 (100)	14 (100)	13 (100)	74 (100)	52 (100)	22 (100)	60.11	78.76	38.71
Bonli	120 (100)	63 (100)	57 (100)	23 (100)	12 (100)	11 (100)	52 (100)	37 (100)	15 (100)	53.42	72.35	32.35
Chauth Ka Barwara	84 (100)	44 (100)	40 (100)	15 (100)	8 (100)	7 (100)	36 (100)	26 (100)	9 (100)	51.72	73.00	28.27
Gangapur	284 (63)	152 (63)	133 (63)	53 (67)	28 (67)	25 (67)	148 (57)	101 (60)	47 (49)	63.87	81.92	43.21
Khandar	110 (100)	59 (100)	51 (100)	21 (100)	11 (100)	10 (100)	39 (100)	30 (100)	9 (100)	43.59	63.15	20.94
Malarna Doongar	90 (100)	47 (100)	43 (100)	17 (100)	9 (100)	8 (100)	38 (100)	28 (100)	10 (100)	52.85	74.97	28.64
Sawai Madhopur	278 (61)	147 (61)	132 (62)	48 (65)	26 (66)	23 (65)	137 (50)	96 (56)	40 (36)	59.36	79.32	37.15
Sikar	**2287 (79)**	**1172 (79)**	**1115 (80)**	**406 (81)**	**216 (81)**	**190 (81)**	**1339 (78)**	**815 (78)**	**524 (78)**	**71.19**	**85.20**	**56.70**
Danta Ramgarh	358 (93)	182 (93)	176 (93)	64 (93)	34 (93)	30 (93)	208 (93)	126 (93)	82 (93)	70.65	84.89	56.24
Fatehpur	261 (59)	132 (58)	129 (60)	46 (60)	25 (60)	22 (59)	157 (60)	92 (58)	65 (61)	73.13	85.77	60.55
Lachhmangarh	284 (83)	145 (83)	139 (84)	49 (83)	26 (84)	23 (83)	174 (84)	103 (83)	71 (85)	74.29	87.24	61.08
Neem Ka Thana	347 (91)	180 (91)	166 (92)	63 (93)	33 (93)	30 (93)	195 (90)	123 (90)	72 (89)	68.67	83.47	52.73
Sikar	530 (65)	273 (65)	257 (65)	90 (68)	48 (68)	42 (67)	314 (62)	193 (63)	121 (60)	71.21	85.66	56.11
Sri Madhopur	507 (85)	260 (84)	247 (85)	93 (86)	49 (86)	44 (86)	292 (84)	179 (83)	113 (84)	70.53	84.72	55.80
Sirohi	**851 (82)**	**438 (82)**	**413 (83)**	**167 (86)**	**87 (86)**	**80 (87)**	**372 (73)**	**247 (75)**	**125 (69)**	**54.39**	**70.58**	**37.37**
Abu Road	184 (62)	97 (61)	87 (64)	37 (72)	19 (71)	18 (73)	86 (45)	56 (48)	29 (38)	58.21	72.03	42.56
Pindwara	205 (90)	106 (90)	100 (90)	42 (92)	22 (91)	20 (92)	89 (86)	59 (87)	30 (85)	54.77	71.02	37.66
Reodar	175 (100)	90 (100)	85 (100)	36 (100)	19 (100)	18 (100)	67 (100)	47 (100)	20 (100)	48.32	65.46	30.24
Sheoganj	124 (80)	64 (80)	61 (80)	23 (83)	12 (82)	10 (83)	57 (71)	37 (73)	20 (67)	55.54	71.44	39.28
Sirohi	161 (78)	81 (77)	80 (79)	29 (82)	15 (82)	13 (83)	73 (68)	48 (70)	25 (64)	55.19	73.22	37.45
Tonk	**1211 (79)**	**626 (79)**	**586 (79)**	**219 (81)**	**114 (80)**	**105 (81)**	**520 (72)**	**365 (76)**	**155 (62)**	**52.39**	**71.25**	**32.30**
Deoli	189 (89)	98 (89)	91 (90)	33 (91)	17 (91)	16 (91)	78 (82)	56 (85)	21 (74)	49.76	69.48	28.51
Malpura	204 (87)	105 (87)	99 (87)	36 (87)	19 (87)	18 (88)	85 (80)	60 (83)	25 (74)	50.66	69.16	31.08
Niwai	203 (81)	105 (82)	99 (80)	37 (85)	20 (85)	18 (85)	93 (73)	63 (78)	30 (62)	56.30	74.27	37.36
Peeplu	101 (100)	52 (100)	49 (100)	19 (100)	10 (100)	9 (100)	37 (100)	28 (100)	9 (100)	45.05	66.38	22.39
Todaraisingh	131 (84)	67 (84)	64 (84)	23 (84)	12 (83)	11 (85)	60 (80)	41 (81)	19 (77)	55.43	74.53	35.48
Tonk	239 (43)	124 (43)	115 (43)	43 (44)	23 (44)	21 (44)	110 (35)	74 (41)	37 (24)	56.50	72.80	38.99
Uniara	143 (92)	75 (93)	69 (92)	27 (93)	14 (94)	13 (93)	56 (89)	42 (91)	14 (84)	48.29	70.20	24.69
Udaipur	**2632 (81)**	**1335 (81)**	**1297 (82)**	**483 (88)**	**248 (87)**	**234 (88)**	**1274 (71)**	**809 (74)**	**464 (65)**	**59.26**	**74.47**	**43.71**
Dhariawad	214 (95)	107 (95)	107 (95)	47 (97)	24 (97)	23 (97)	63 (89)	45 (91)	17 (83)	37.61	54.34	20.90
Girwa	741 (47)	385 (47)	355 (48)	112 (59)	58 (58)	53 (60)	476 (37)	283 (40)	193 (32)	75.66	86.52	63.93
Gogunda	152 (100)	76 (100)	75 (100)	30 (100)	15 (100)	15 (100)	61 (100)	41 (100)	20 (100)	50.12	67.74	32.32
Jhadol	194 (100)	98 (100)	96 (100)	41 (100)	21 (100)	21 (100)	90 (100)	58 (100)	33 (100)	59.26	74.73	43.43
Kherwara	269 (95)	135 (94)	134 (95)	56 (96)	28 (96)	27 (96)	123 (91)	82 (92)	41 (89)	57.60	76.86	38.53
Kotra	183 (100)	93 (100)	91 (100)	44 (100)	22 (100)	22 (100)	34 (100)	27 (100)	8 (100)	24.52	37.55	11.14
Mavli	214 (91)	108 (91)	105 (91)	34 (92)	18 (92)	16 (92)	99 (88)	66 (89)	33 (86)	55.24	72.91	37.31
Salumbar	212 (93)	105 (92)	107 (93)	40 (95)	21 (95)	19 (95)	103 (88)	64 (89)	39 (86)	59.80	76.02	44.27
Sarada	223 (95)	111 (95)	112 (95)	43 (97)	22 (97)	21 (97)	103 (92)	67 (93)	36 (90)	57.08	75.73	38.97
Vallabhnagar	230 (87)	117 (87)	114 (88)	37 (90)	19 (89)	18 (90)	121 (84)	77 (85)	45 (84)	62.61	78.54	46.47
Rajasthan	**56473 (77)**	**29382 (76)**	**27091 (77)**	**10451 (81)**	**5475 (81)**	**4976 (81)**	**28086 (69)**	**18280 (72)**	**9807 (65)**	**61.03**	**76.46**	**44.34**

Figures in brackets show percentage of rural population to total population

Source: Calculated from Census of India 2001, series-9, Rajasthan, Provisional Population Totals, Paper-2 of 2001

CITY/TOWN-WISE POPULATION AND LITERACY SCENARIO: RAJASTHAN (2001)

Urban Area/City/Town	Civic Status of City/Town	Population in '000 No.			Child Population in the age-group 0-6 in '000 No.			Literates in '000 No.			Literacy Rate (%)		
		Person	Male	Female	Person	Male	Female	Person	Male	Female	Person	Male	Female
1	2	3	4	5	6	7	8	9	10	11	12	13	14
Ajmer	UA	490.1	256.4	233.8	58.1	30.4	27.7	363.2	204.3	158.9	84.1	90.4	77.1
(a) Ajmer	MCL	485.2	253.9	231.3	57.5	30.1	27.4	359.5	202.2	157.3	84.1	90.4	77.1
(b) Kiranipura	CT	4.9	2.5	2.4	0.6	0.3	0.3	3.7	2.1	1.6	83.8	92.2	75.0
Beawar	UA	125.9	65.6	60.4	17.4	9.2	8.2	89.8	52.0	37.7	82.7	92.3	72.4
(a) Beawar	MCL	123.7	64.4	59.3	17.1	9.0	8.1	88.1	51.1	37.0	82.7	92.2	72.3
(i) Naya Nagar	-	2.2	1.2	1.0	0.3	0.2	0.1	1.6	0.9	0.7	86.1	94.6	76.9
Kekri	M	34.1	17.6	16.5	5.2	2.7	2.5	21.4	13.0	8.4	74.0	87.3	59.9
Kishangarh	M	116.2	61.0	55.1	18.2	9.6	8.5	72.3	43.9	28.4	73.8	85.4	61.0
Nasirabad	CB	49.1	28.2	20.9	6.4	3.3	3.1	36.9	23.6	13.3	86.5	94.6	75.1
Pushkar	M	14.8	8.0	6.8	2.1	1.2	1.0	10.3	6.1	4.1	81.0	90.3	70.1
Sarwar	M	16.2	8.4	7.8	3.0	1.6	1.5	7.6	5.1	2.5	57.8	74.7	39.8
Vijainagar	M	27.7	14.4	13.3	3.9	2.0	1.9	19.2	11.2	8.0	80.7	90.4	70.3
Ajmer District		**874.1**	**459.6**	**414.5**	**114.3**	**59.9**	**54.4**	**620.7**	**359.2**	**261.4**	**81.7**	**89.9**	**72.6**
Alwar	UA	265.9	143.2	122.6	34.4	18.8	15.6	194.0	114.9	79.0	83.8	92.3	73.9
(a)Alwar	MCL	260.2	139.1	121.1	33.8	18.4	15.3	189.1	111.2	77.9	83.5	92.1	73.7
(i) Itarana (OG)	-	5.6	4.1	1.5	0.6	0.3	0.3	4.9	3.7	1.1	97.1	99.8	88.8
Behror	M	22.8	12.3	10.6	3.6	2.0	1.7	16.0	9.6	6.4	83.0	92.9	71.6
Bhiwadi	CT	33.8	21.5	12.4	5.7	3.2	2.6	22.8	16.3	6.5	81.1	89.1	66.2
Govindgarh	CT	10.1	5.3	4.8	1.8	0.9	0.8	6.4	3.9	2.5	77.3	89.8	63.5
Khairthal	M	32.0	17.0	15.0	5.3	2.8	2.5	20.7	12.3	8.4	77.3	86.8	66.6
Kherli	M	15.5	8.3	7.2	2.2	1.2	1.0	11.4	6.7	4.7	85.4	94.3	75.2
Kishangarh	CT	9.5	5.0	4.4	1.4	0.8	0.7	6.7	4.0	2.7	83.3	92.6	72.6
Rajgarh	M	25.0	13.4	11.6	4.0	2.2	1.8	16.2	10.3	5.9	77.0	91.5	60.4
Tijara	M	19.9	10.5	9.4	3.6	1.9	1.7	12.4	7.6	4.8	76.1	88.6	62.3
Alwar		**434.5**	**236.4**	**198.0**	**62.0**	**33.7**	**28.2**	**306.5**	**185.5**	**121.0**	**82.3**	**91.5**	**71.2**
Banswara	UA	87.3	45.5	41.8	11.6	6.3	5.3	64.4	36.0	28.3	85.0	92.1	77.5
(a) Banswara	M	85.6	44.5	41.1	11.4	6.2	5.2	63.1	35.3	27.9	85.0	92.0	77.5
(i) Bhawanpura & Thikaria	-	1.6	1.0	0.7	0.2	0.1	0.1	1.2	0.8	0.4	87.3	95.8	75.5
Kushalgarh	M	10.1	5.2	4.9	1.5	0.8	0.7	7.4	4.2	3.2	86.1	94.0	77.7
Partapur	CT	9.9	5.0	5.0	1.4	0.8	0.7	7.0	3.8	3.1	81.5	90.8	72.4
Banswara		**107.3**	**55.6**	**51.7**	**14.5**	**7.8**	**6.7**	**78.7**	**44.0**	**34.7**	**84.8**	**92.1**	**77.0**
Antah	M	26.8	14.1	12.7	4.6	2.4	2.2	16.2	10.0	6.2	73.2	86.1	59.0
Baran	M	78.4	41.0	37.4	12.6	6.6	6.0	51.4	30.5	20.9	78.1	88.8	66.5
Chhabra	M	22.8	12.1	10.7	3.8	2.1	1.8	13.8	8.4	5.4	72.6	83.9	59.9
Chhipabarod	CT	16.0	8.2	7.8	2.8	1.5	1.4	9.9	6.0	3.9	74.8	88.5	60.4
Kherliganj	CT	7.4	3.8	3.5	1.2	0.6	0.5	4.3	2.7	1.6	68.7	84.2	52.2
Mangrol	M	21.8	11.3	10.6	4.0	2.1	1.9	11.8	7.6	4.3	66.4	82.7	49.1
Baran		**173.2**	**90.5**	**82.7**	**29.0**	**15.3**	**13.8**	**107.4**	**65.2**	**42.2**	**74.5**	**86.8**	**61.1**
Balotra	M	61.7	33.1	28.6	10.7	5.6	5.1	38.4	24.3	14.1	75.2	88.4	59.8
Barmer	M	83.5	45.1	38.4	12.9	6.9	6.0	55.5	35.2	20.3	78.6	92.0	62.8
Barmer		**145.2**	**78.2**	**67.1**	**23.6**	**12.5**	**11.1**	**93.9**	**59.5**	**34.4**	**77.2**	**90.5**	**61.5**
Bayana	M	33.5	18.0	15.5	5.6	3.0	2.5	21.3	13.4	7.9	76.3	89.5	61.2
Bharatpur	UA	205.1	110.1	95.0	31.5	16.9	14.6	135.3	82.2	53.1	77.9	88.1	66.1
(a) Bharatpur	MCL	204.5	109.8	94.6	31.5	16.9	14.6	134.7	81.9	52.8	77.9	88.1	66.0
(i) Chak No.1 (OG)	-	0.6	0.3	0.3	0.1	0.0	0.0	0.6	0.3	0.3	99.8	100.0	99.6
Bhusawar	M	17.7	8.9	8.8	3.0	1.6	1.4	11.2	6.7	4.6	76.1	90.9	61.5
Deeg	M	40.8	21.8	19.0	6.8	3.6	3.2	24.9	15.6	9.3	73.2	85.6	58.8
Kaman	M	30.8	16.6	14.2	5.5	3.0	2.5	17.4	11.2	6.2	68.8	82.4	53.0
Kumher	M	20.3	10.9	9.4	3.8	2.1	1.7	10.9	7.1	3.8	65.9	80.3	49.2
Nadbai	M	21.6	11.7	10.0	3.3	1.8	1.5	13.9	8.7	5.2	76.1	88.4	61.9
Nagar	M	21.3	11.5	9.8	3.9	2.1	1.7	12.4	8.0	4.4	70.8	85.1	54.3
Weir	M	17.3	9.2	8.1	3.1	1.6	1.5	9.8	6.6	3.3	69.3	86.1	49.8
Bharatpur		**408.5**	**218.8**	**189.8**	**66.4**	**35.7**	**30.7**	**257.2**	**159.4**	**97.8**	**75.2**	**87.1**	**61.5**
Asind	M	14.1	7.2	6.9	2.5	1.3	1.2	7.6	4.8	2.8	65.1	80.6	49.0
Beejoliya Kalan	CT	12.4	6.4	6.0	1.9	1.0	0.9	7.9	4.7	3.2	75.4	86.8	63.4
Bhilwara	MCL	280.2	148.6	131.5	42.9	22.4	20.5	183.1	110.5	72.6	77.1	87.5	65.4
Gangapur	M	17.0	8.8	8.2	2.7	1.4	1.2	10.1	6.4	3.7	70.0	86.9	52.2
Gulabpura	M	24.3	13.2	11.1	3.7	2.0	1.7	17.1	10.5	6.6	82.9	93.5	70.3
Jahazpur	M	18.8	9.7	9.1	3.0	1.6	1.4	11.1	7.0	4.1	70.1	86.7	52.7
Mandalgarh	M	20.2	10.4	9.8	3.0	1.5	1.4	10.1	6.6	3.5	58.6	74.4	42.1
Shahpura	M	27.7	14.1	13.6	4.3	2.2	2.1	17.0	10.1	6.9	72.7	85.6	59.6
Bhilwara		**414.7**	**218.4**	**196.4**	**63.9**	**33.4**	**30.5**	**263.9**	**160.6**	**103.4**	**75.2**	**86.8**	**62.3**

Urban Area/City/Town	*Civic Status of City/Town*	*Population in '000 No.*			*Child Population in the age-group 0-6 in '000 No.*			*Literates in '000 No.*			*Literacy Rate (%)*		
		Person	*Male*	*Female*	*Person*	*Male*	*Female*	*Person*	*Male*	*Female*	*Person*	*Male*	*Female*
1	*2*	*3*	*4*	*5*	*6*	*7*	*8*	*9*	*10*	*11*	*12*	*13*	*14*
Bikaner	MCL	529.0	282.5	246.6	73.8	38.7	35.1	350.4	209.3	141.0	77.0	85.9	66.7
Deshnoke	M	15.8	8.1	7.7	3.0	1.5	1.4	8.0	4.8	3.2	62.8	74.0	51.0
Nokha	M	49.7	26.1	23.6	9.2	4.8	4.4	29.0	17.7	11.2	71.5	83.2	58.5
Bikaner		**594.5**	**316.6**	**277.9**	**86.0**	**45.0**	**40.9**	**387.4**	**231.9**	**155.5**	**76.2**	**85.4**	**65.6**
Budhpura	CT	4.4	2.4	2.0	0.9	0.5	0.4	1.1	0.8	0.3	31.0	43.6	16.4
Bundi	M	88.3	46.6	41.8	12.2	6.6	5.7	58.8	34.8	24.0	77.2	87.0	66.5
Kaprain	M	17.8	9.3	8.4	3.1	1.7	1.4	9.5	6.2	3.3	65.2	81.7	47.2
Keshoraipatan	M	21.1	11.1	10.1	3.4	1.8	1.6	12.6	7.8	4.8	71.2	84.3	56.9
Lakheri	UA	32.2	16.7	15.5	4.8	2.5	2.3	20.5	12.7	7.8	74.8	89.6	58.9
(a) Lakheri	M	26.9	14.0	12.9	3.9	2.0	1.9	17.2	10.8	6.4	74.5	89.9	57.9
(b) Indragarh	M	5.3	2.7	2.6	0.9	0.5	0.4	3.3	2.0	1.4	75.9	88.0	63.5
Nainwa	M	15.2	7.9	7.2	2.4	1.3	1.1	9.2	5.7	3.4	72.1	86.5	56.5
Bundi		**178.9**	**93.9**	**85.0**	**26.8**	**14.3**	**12.5**	**111.7**	**68.1**	**43.6**	**73.4**	**85.5**	**60.1**
Bari Sadri	M	15.0	7.7	7.3	2.0	1.1	1.0	9.9	5.9	4.0	76.1	89.0	62.5
Begun	M	19.3	10.0	9.3	3.1	1.6	1.5	12.3	7.6	4.8	76.0	90.1	60.9
Chhoti Sadri	M	16.6	8.5	8.1	2.4	1.3	1.1	11.6	6.8	4.8	81.9	94.0	69.3
Chittaurgarh	M	96.0	50.3	45.7	13.9	7.3	6.7	67.2	39.2	28.0	81.9	91.1	71.7
Kapasan	M	18.7	9.6	9.1	2.8	1.5	1.3	11.8	7.2	4.7	74.2	88.7	59.4
Nimbahera	M	53.3	27.5	25.8	8.2	4.4	3.9	35.9	20.8	15.1	79.5	89.7	68.7
Pratapgarh	M	35.4	18.5	17.0	4.8	2.6	2.2	26.1	14.7	11.4	85.3	93.0	77.2
Rawatbhata	M	34.7	18.2	16.4	5.0	2.6	2.4	25.1	14.4	10.7	84.6	92.3	76.0
Chittaurgarh		**289.1**	**150.3**	**138.7**	**42.2**	**22.3**	**19.9**	**200.0**	**116.5**	**83.4**	**81.0**	**91.1**	**70.2**
Bidasar	M	30.1	15.6	14.6	5.7	3.0	2.7	13.6	8.7	4.9	55.8	69.3	41.5
Chhapar	M	17.9	9.0	8.8	3.4	1.8	1.6	9.9	5.9	4.0	68.2	80.4	55.9
Churu	UA	101.9	53.1	48.8	16.8	8.8	8.1	63.4	38.6	24.8	74.5	87.1	60.9
(a)Churu	M	97.6	50.7	46.9	16.2	8.4	7.8	60.4	36.7	23.7	74.2	86.9	60.6
(i) Churu Rural (OG)	_	4.2	2.4	1.8	0.6	0.3	0.3	3.0	1.9	1.1	81.8	91.1	69.3
Dungargarh	M	44.7	22.9	21.8	7.6	3.8	3.8	27.3	15.9	11.4	73.8	83.6	63.3
Rajaldesar	M	22.8	11.7	11.2	4.4	2.3	2.1	11.0	7.0	4.0	59.5	74.2	44.3
Rajgarh	UA	51.6	27.1	24.5	8.6	4.7	4.0	32.9	19.6	13.3	76.5	87.6	64.5
(a) Rajgarh	M	48.1	25.1	22.9	8.1	4.4	3.7	30.7	18.2	12.5	77.0	87.9	65.1
(i) Rajgarh Rural (OG)	_	3.5	1.9	1.6	0.5	0.3	0.2	2.1	1.4	0.8	70.7	83.0	56.1
Ratangarh	M	63.5	32.6	30.9	10.9	5.8	5.2	39.8	23.6	16.3	75.8	87.9	63.2
Ratannagar	M	11.0	5.5	5.5	1.9	1.0	0.9	6.7	4.0	2.7	73.2	87.6	58.7
Sardarshahar	M	81.4	42.4	39.0	14.0	7.4	6.6	41.3	22.3	19.1	61.4	63.7	58.8
Sujangarh	M	83.8	43.0	40.8	14.3	7.5	6.8	54.0	31.6	22.4	77.7	89.1	65.8
Taranagar	M	27.1	14.0	13.1	4.9	2.6	2.3	15.4	9.3	6.1	69.3	81.9	56.1
Churu		**535.7**	**276.8**	**258.9**	**92.7**	**48.6**	**44.0**	**315.2**	**186.4**	**128.9**	**71.2**	**81.7**	**60.0**
Bandikui	M	16.3	8.7	7.6	2.2	1.1	1.0	11.9	7.2	4.8	84.5	95.0	72.5
Dausa	M	61.6	32.8	28.7	9.6	5.2	4.4	40.4	24.9	15.4	77.6	90.1	63.5
Lalsot	M	28.3	14.7	13.6	5.1	2.8	2.4	16.6	10.4	6.2	71.8	87.3	55.3
Mahwa	CT	19.6	10.3	9.2	3.8	2.0	1.8	11.8	7.4	4.4	74.8	88.7	59.1
Mandawar	CT	10.1	5.4	4.7	1.6	0.8	0.7	6.9	4.2	2.7	80.6	92.3	67.3
Dausa		**135.8**	**71.9**	**63.9**	**22.2**	**11.9**	**10.4**	**87.6**	**54.1**	**33.5**	**77.1**	**90.1**	**62.5**
Bari	M	50.5	27.2	23.2	9.9	5.4	4.5	26.0	16.5	9.5	64.2	75.8	50.7
Dhaulpur	UA	97.6	52.4	45.3	17.2	9.4	7.8	56.9	34.6	22.3	70.8	80.5	59.6
(a) Dhaulpur	M	92.1	49.4	42.7	16.2	8.8	7.4	53.9	32.5	21.3	70.9	80.1	60.3
(i) Purani Chawani(OG)	_	3.7	2.0	1.7	0.7	0.4	0.3	2.1	1.4	0.7	71.8	88.3	52.6
(Ii) Tagawali Rural (OG)	_	1.8	1.0	0.8	0.3	0.2	0.1	0.9	0.7	0.3	62.3	83.4	37.7
Rajakhera	M	28.3	15.4	12.9	5.5	3.0	2.6	14.1	9.4	4.7	61.7	75.4	45.2
Dhaulpur		**176.4**	**95.0**	**81.4**	**32.7**	**17.8**	**14.9**	**97.0**	**60.5**	**36.5**	**67.5**	**78.3**	**54.9**
Dungarpur	M	42.5	22.8	19.7	5.4	2.9	2.5	32.5	18.9	13.7	87.7	95.0	79.2
Galiakot	CT	6.6	3.4	3.3	1.2	0.6	0.5	3.7	2.3	1.5	67.8	82.1	53.2
Sagwara	M	31.0	15.3	15.7	5.1	2.7	2.4	18.2	10.3	7.8	70.1	81.8	59.0
Dungarpur		**80.1**	**41.4**	**38.7**	**11.7**	**6.2**	**5.5**	**54.4**	**31.4**	**22.9**	**79.4**	**89.3**	**69.0**
Anupgarh	M	29.5	16.0	13.5	4.6	2.6	2.0	18.1	10.8	7.3	72.5	80.2	63.6
3 STR	CT	10.9	5.9	5.1	1.8	1.0	0.8	6.8	4.1	2.7	74.5	83.1	64.6
Gajsinghpur	M	9.5	5.1	4.4	1.3	0.7	0.6	6.1	3.5	2.6	74.5	81.0	67.1
Ganganagar	UA	222.8	121.9	101.0	30.0	16.6	13.4	156.2	92.6	63.7	81.0	87.9	72.7
(a) Ganganagar	MCL	210.8	115.4	95.4	27.9	15.4	12.5	149.2	88.2	61.0	81.6	88.2	73.6
(i) 2e Village (OG)	_	7.8	4.2	3.6	1.3	0.7	0.6	4.6	2.8	1.8	71.7	82.5	59.2
(ii) 3eVillage (OG)	_	0.6	0.3	0.3	0.1	0.1	0.0	0.3	0.2	0.1	55.9	69.4	39.6
(iii) 5eVillage (OG)	_	1.8	1.0	0.8	0.3	0.2	0.1	1.1	0.7	0.4	72.2	83.4	59.0
(iv) 6eVillage (OG)	_	0.7	0.4	0.3	0.1	0.1	0.0	0.3	0.2	0.1	58.4	69.6	44.0
(v) 7eVillage (OG)	_	1.2	0.6	0.6	0.2	0.1	0.1	0.7	0.4	0.3	72.4	84.4	59.7
Karanpur	M	20.7	11.0	9.7	3.0	1.6	1.4	13.2	7.8	5.4	74.6	83.0	65.1
Kesrisinghpur	M	13.2	6.9	6.2	2.1	1.1	0.9	8.1	4.8	3.3	73.0	83.0	62.1
Padampur	M	17.0	9.0	8.0	2.6	1.5	1.2	10.9	6.2	4.7	76.1	83.4	68.1
Raisinghnagar	M	27.7	15.0	12.7	4.1	2.2	1.9	18.7	11.1	7.6	79.3	87.1	70.1
Sadulshahar	M	22.3	11.9	10.4	3.2	1.8	1.4	13.8	8.3	5.5	72.1	81.8	61.3
Suratgarh	M	58.1	31.1	27.0	8.7	4.7	4.0	36.5	21.8	14.7	74.0	83.0	63.7
Vijainagar	M	17.9	9.6	8.3	2.8	1.6	1.3	11.1	6.6	4.5	73.6	82.6	63.4
1 SGM	CT	2.5	1.3	1.2	0.5	0.3	0.2	1.1	0.7	0.4	52.8	63.6	40,3
Ganganagar		**452.1**	**244.6**	**207.5**	**64.7**	**35.6**	**29.1**	**300.6**	**178.3**	**122.3**	**77.6**	**85.3**	**68.5**
Bhadra	M	35.1	18.5	16.6	5.1	3.0	2.4	21.9	13.2	8.7	73.7	84.8	61.6
Hanumangarh	M	129.7	69.6	60.1	18.7	10.2	8.5	83.9	49.9	34.1	75.6	84.0	66.0

Urban Area/City/Town	*Civic Status of City/Town*	*Population in '000 No.*			*Child Population in the age-group 0-6 in '000 No.*			*Literates in '000 No.*			*Literacy Rate (%)*		
		Person	*Male*	*Female*	*Person*	*Male*	*Female*	*Person*	*Male*	*Female*	*Person*	*Male*	*Female*
1	*2*	*3*	*4*	*5*	*6*	*7*	*8*	*9*	*10*	*11*	*12*	*13*	*14*
Nohar	M	42.3	22.3	20.0	6.9	3.5	3.4	25.9	15.5	10.4	73.2	82.7	62.5
Pilibanga	M	33.6	17.9	15.7	5.2	2.8	2.4	19.4	11.8	7.6	68.2	78.0	57.0
Rawatsar	M	28.4	15.0	13.4	4.7	2.5	2.3	15.6	9.7	5.9	65.8	77.4	52.7
Sangaria	M	34.5	18.4	16.2	4.4	2.4	2.0	24.0	13.9	10.1	79.6	87.1	71.2
Hanumangarh		**303.6**	**161.6**	**142.0**	**45.3**	**24.3**	**21.0**	**190.7**	**114.0**	**76.7**	**73.8**	**83.0**	**63.4**
Bagru	M	22.1	11.6	10.5	4.0	2.1	1.9	11.6	7.6	4.0	63.9	80.3	45.9
Chaksu	M	29.1	15.3	13.9	5.5	2.9	2.6	15.5	10.2	5.3	65.7	82.4	47.3
Chomu	M	50.7	26.6	24.1	8.4	4.4	4.0	31.8	20.0	11.9	75.3	89.9	59.1
Jaipur	M Corp.	2324.3	1239.7	1084.6	340.3	181.0	159.3	1560.4	920.7	639.8	78.7	87.0	69.1
Jobner	M	10.5	5.5	5.0	1.7	0.9	0.8	6.7	4.1	2.6	75.6	89.8	60.5
Kishangarh Renwal	M	27.6	14.2	13.3	4.6	2.4	2.2	16.3	10.3	6.1	71.3	86.9	54.7
Kotputli	M	40.2	21.4	18.8	6.5	3.6	2.9	27.0	16.4	10.6	80.2	92.2	66.7
Phulera	M	21.6	11.3	10.4	2.8	1.4	1.4	15.8	9.3	6.4	83.9	94.8	71.8
Sambhar	M	22.3	11.6	10.7	3.4	1.8	1.6	14.3	8.6	5.6	75.4	87.7	62.0
Shahpura	M	28.2	14.8	13.4	4.9	2.6	2.3	16.2	10.5	5.7	69.8	86.3	51.7
Viratnagar	M	17.2	9.1	8.2	3.4	1.8	1.6	8.6	5.8	2.8	62.7	80.9	42.6
Jaipur		**2593.8**	**1381.0**	**1212.8**	**385.6**	**205.0**	**180.6**	**1724.3**	**1023.5**	**700.8**	**78.1**	**87.0**	**67.9**
Jaisalmer	M	58.3	33.4	24.9	9.3	5.1	4.3	37.1	24.5	12.6	75.7	86.5	60.9
Pokaran	M	19.2	10.5	8.7	3.6	1.9	1.7	10.7	7.1	3.6	68.6	83.2	50.7
Jaisalmer		**77.5**	**43.9**	**33.6**	**12.9**	**7.0**	**5.9**	**47.8**	**31.6**	**16.1**	**74.0**	**85.7**	**58.3**
Bhinmal	M	39.3	20.6	18.6	7.3	3.8	3.5	20.5	13.7	6.8	64.1	81.7	44.6
Jalor	M	44.8	23.9	20.9	7.3	3.9	3.5	26.9	17.3	9.6	71.9	86.4	55.2
Sanchore	M	25.9	13.6	12.3	5.3	2.7	2.5	12.3	8.4	3.9	59.7	77.2	40.3
Jalor		**110.0**	**58.2**	**51.8**	**19.8**	**10.4**	**9.4**	**59.8**	**39.5**	**20.3**	**66.3**	**82.6**	**48.0**
Aklera	M	18.2	9.5	8.6	3.2	1.7	1.5	11.1	6.9	4.3	74.1	87.2	59.7
Bakani	CT	7.9	4.1	3.8	1.3	0.7	0.6	5.2	3.2	2.0	78.3	92.2	63.1
Bhawani Mandi	M	35.7	18.9	16.8	4.9	2.6	2.3	24.6	14.8	9.8	80.0	90.9	67.6
Jhalawar	M	48.0	25.2	22.8	7.0	3.7	3.3	34.2	19.7	14.5	83.3	91.5	74.2
Jhalrapatan	M	30.1	15.7	14.4	4.7	2.5	2.2	20.7	12.1	8.7	81.4	91.2	70.9
Kolvi @ Mandi Rajendra pur	CT	7.9	4.1	3.7	1.2	0.7	0.5	5.4	3.1	2.2	80.4	90.7	69.3
Manohar Thana	CT	9.2	4.8	4.4	1.6	0.9	0.8	5.9	3.5	2.4	77.8	89.2	65.6
Pirawa	M	11.2	5.7	5.4	1.8	1.0	0.9	7.4	4.3	3.1	79.1	89.2	68.6
Jhalawar		**168.2**	**88.2**	**80.0**	**25.7**	**13.6**	**12.1**	**114.5**	**67.6**	**46.9**	**80.3**	**90.6**	**69.1**
Baggar	M	14.6	8.1	6.5	2.1	1.1	1.0	10.3	6.6	3.7	82.1	93.8	67.2
Bissau	M	21.1	10.8	10.4	3.8	2.0	1.7	12.7	7.6	5.1	73.2	86.5	59.7
Chirawa	M	37.2	19.5	17.7	5.7	3.1	2.6	24.5	14.6	9.9	77.8	89.1	65.5
Jhunjhunun	M	100.5	52.8	47.7	17.9	9.9	8.0	60.1	36.3	23.7	72.8	84.7	59.9
Khetri	UA	39.2	20.9	18.3	5.0	2.7	2.3	28.5	17.1	11.4	83.2	94.0	70.8
(a) Khetri	M	17.4	9.1	8.3	2.7	1.4	1.2	11.6	7.0	4.6	78.9	91.5	65.4
(b) Gothra	CT	21.8	11.8	10.0	2.3	1.2	1.0	16.9	10.1	6.8	86.3	95.9	75.1
Mandawa	M	20.7	10.6	10.2	3.8	2.0	1.8	12.0	7.4	4.6	70.7	86.0	55.1
Mukandgarh	M	17.8	9.1	8.7	3.1	1.7	1.5	9.9	6.2	3.7	67.3	82.6	51.4
Nawalgarh	M	56.5	29.2	27.3	9.7	5.2	4.5	32.4	20.0	12.5	69.3	83.1	54.8
Pilani	UA	40.6	22.2	18.4	4.7	2.5	2.3	29.9	18.4	11.5	83.5	93.5	71.2
(a) Pilani	M	26.2	13.6	12.6	3.5	1.9	1.7	18.0	10.8	7.2	79.5	91.9	66.2
(b) Vidyavihar	M	14.4	8.6	5.8	1.2	0.6	0.6	11.9	7.6	4.3	90.2	95.9	81.6
Surajgarh	M	18.9	10.0	8.9	3.1	1.7	1.4	12.2	7.3	4.9	77.3	88.5	65.0
Udaipurwati	M	27.8	14.6	13.3	5.2	2.8	2.4	15.7	10.0	5.7	69.3	85.0	52.3
Jhunjhunun		**394.9**	**207.7**	**187.2**	**64.0**	**34.6**	**29.4**	**248.2**	**151.5**	**96.7**	**75.0**	**87.5**	**61.3**
Bilara	M	38.7	20.0	18.6	6.2	3.2	3.0	22.0	14.6	7.4	67.8	87.1	47.2
Jodhpur	UA	856.0	455.9	400.2	121.1	63.6	57.5	570.0	338.9	231.1	77.6	86.4	67.4
(a) Jodhpur	M Corp.	846.4	450.8	395.6	119.4	62.7	56.7	565.5	335.9	229.6	77.8	86.5	67.7
(i) Mandor Industrial Area (OG)		–	0.3	0.2	0.1	0.1	0.0	0.0	0.1	0.1	0.0	43.7	53.6
33.0													
(ii) Nandri Village (OG)	–	5.5	2.9	2.6	1.0	0.5	0.5	2.9	1.9	1.0	64.4	80.3	46.5
(iii) Pal Village (OG)	–	3.9	2.0	1.8	0.7	0.4	0.3	1.6	1.1	0.5	49.0	66.7	30.2
Phalodi	UA	44.8	23.5	21.3	7.7	4.0	3.7	25.9	16.2	9.7	69.7	82.8	55.0
(a) Phalodi	M	44.8	23.5	21.2	7.7	4.0	3.7	25.9	16.2	9.7	69.7	82.9	55.1
(i) Phalodi Rural (OG)	–	0.1	0.0	0.0	0.0	0.0	0.0	0.0	0.0	0.0	34.4	57.1	16.7
Pipar City	M	32.7	16.9	15.8	5.9	3.1	2.8	17.0	11.2	5.8	63.3	81.2	44.3
Jodhpur		**972.3**	**516.4**	**455.9**	**140.9**	**73.9**	**67.0**	**634.9**	**381.0**	**253.9**	**76.4**	**86.1**	**65.3**
Hindaun	M	84.8	45.5	39.3	15.0	8.0	7.1	51.7	32.5	19.2	74.1	86.7	59.4
Karauli	M	66.2	35.2	31.0	12.3	6.5	5.9	35.3	22.7	12.6	65.6	79.1	50.2
Todabhim	M	20.8	10.9	9.9	3.9	2.0	1.8	11.7	7.7	4.0	69.1	86.9	49.4
Karauli		**171.8**	**91.6**	**80.2**	**31.2**	**16.5**	**14.7**	**98.7**	**62.9**	**35.8**	**70.2**	**83.8**	**54.6**
Chechat	CT	10.3	5.4	4.8	1.7	0.9	0.8	6.4	4.0	2.4	74.7	87.7	60.1
Kaithoon	M	20.4	10.6	9.8	3.4	1.7	1.6	12.7	7.7	4.9	74.5	87.3	60.6
Kota	UA	704.7	374.6	330.2	93.6	49.4	44.2	497.0	291.3	205.7	81.3	89.6	71.9
(a) Kota	M Corp.	695.9	369.9	326.0	92.5	48.8	43.7	490.4	287.4	203.1	81.3	89.5	71.9
(b) Sogariya	CT	8.8	4.7	4.2	1.1	0.6	0.5	6.5	3.9	2.6	84.5	95.9	71.6
Kumbhkot	CT	5.9	3.1	2.7	1.2	0.6	0.6	2.6	1.9	0.7	55.6	77.4	30.3
Modak	CT	6.4	3.4	2.9	1.1	0.6	0.5	4.3	2.7	1.6	82.9	96.1	67.7
Ramganj Mandi	M	31.0	16.3	14.7	4.9	2.6	2.2	21.1	12.2	8.9	80.8	89.5	71.2
Sangod	M	18.6	9.8	8.9	3.1	1.6	1.5	12.0	7.4	4.6	77.3	90.7	62.5
Satalkheri	CT	15.0	8.0	7.0	3.1	1.6	1.5	7.3	5.0	2.3	61.8	77.9	42.7
Suket	CT	17.0	9.0	8.0	3.3	1.8	1.5	10.3	6.3	4.0	75.5	87.5	62.2
Udpura	CT	8.8	4.7	4.1	1.5	0.8	0.7	5.9	3.6	2.3	81.0	90.7	69.4
Kota		**837.9**	**444.8**	**393.1**	**116.9**	**61.6**	**55.3**	**579.6**	**342.2**	**237.4**	**80.4**	**89.3**	**70.3**

Urban Area City/Town	Civic Status of City/Town	Population in '000 No.			Child Population in the age-group 0-6 in '000 No.			Literates in '000 No.			Literacy Rate (%)		
		Person	Male	Female	Person	Male	Female	Person	Male	Female	Person	Male	Female
1	2	3	4	5	6	7	8	9	10	11	12	13	14
Basni Belima	CT	21.6	10.8	10.8	4.4	2.3	2.1	11.7	7.3	4.4	68.1	87.0	49.9
Didwana	M	44.7	23.4	21.3	7.7	4.1	3.7	26.1	16.4	9.7	70.7	84.7	55.3
Goredi Chancha	CT	9.8	5.2	4.6	1.6	0.9	0.7	6.3	3.9	2.4	75.8	89.2	60.6
Kuchaman City	M	50.6	26.2	24.4	8.6	4.4	4.1	29.6	18.4	11.2	70.5	84.5	55.4
Kuchera	M	19.6	10.2	9.4	4.8	2.5	2.3	9.7	6.6	3.0	65.8	87.2	42.8
Ladnu	M	57.0	29.3	27.7	9.9	5.2	4.7	34.2	20.7	13.5	72.5	85.6	58.8
Makrana	UA	91.8	47.8	44.1	18.3	9.4	8.9	49.7	30.8	18.9	67.7	80.4	53.8
(a) Makrana	M	83.3	43.3	39.9	16.7	8.5	8.1	45.5	28.1	17.4	68.3	80.8	54.6
(i) Makrana Village (OG)	_	8.5	4.4	4.1	1.6	0.9	0.8	4.2	2.7	1.5	61.6	76.2	46.1
Merta City	M	40.2	21.2	19.0	6.6	3.4	3.1	24.2	15.2	9.1	72.0	85.4	56.9
Mundwa	M	16.0	8.2	7.8	2.9	1.5	1.4	7.5	4.9	2.6	57.1	73.9	39.7
Nagaur	UA	93.9	49.4	44.5	15.5	8.1	7.4	52.5	32.8	19.7	67.0	79.4	53.1
(a)Nagaur	M	88.3	46.4	41.9	14.6	7.7	7.0	49.4	30.7	18.7	67.0	79.2	53.5
(i) Chenar Village (OG)	_	4.6	2.4	2.2	0.8	0.4	0.4	2.5	1.6	0.8	63.8	81.4	44.2
(ii) Manasar Village (OG)	_	0.9	0.6	0.4	0.1	0.1	0.0	0.7	0.5	0.2	78.5	89.3	59.6
Nawa	M	18.2	9.6	8.6	2.9	1.5	1.4	11.9	7.1	4.8	77.4	87.2	66.5
Parbatsar	M	13.8	7.4	6.4	2.3	1.2	1.1	8.3	5.4	3.0	72.4	86.2	56.3
Nagaur		**477.2**	**248.6**	**228.6**	**85.4**	**44.5**	**40.9**	**271.7**	**169.5**	**102.2**	**69.4**	**83.1**	**54.5**
Bali	M	18.2	9.3	8.9	2.8	1.5	1.3	10.8	6.7	4.1	70.0	85.3	54.4
Falna	M	21.0	10.9	10.1	3.5	1.8	1.7	12.4	7.8	4.7	71.0	85.2	55.6
Jaitaran	M	19.3	10.1	9.2	3.4	1.7	1.6	11.1	7.1	3.9	69.4	85.4	51.8
Marwar Junction	CT	10.5	5.5	5.1	1.7	0.9	0.8	6.8	4.2	2.7	77.3	91.2	62.4
Pali	MCL	187.6	99.3	88.3	29.7	15.5	14.2	115.9	72.7	43.2	73.4	86.7	58.4
Rani	M	12.4	6.4	6.0	2.0	1.0	1.0	7.6	4.7	2.9	73.2	87.2	58.3
Sadri	M	24.4	12.2	12.2	4.4	2.3	2.1	11.0	7.1	3.9	54.8	72.1	38.0
Sojat	M	38.9	20.2	18.6	6.5	3.4	3.1	22.5	14.4	8.1	69.4	85.4	52.1
Sojat Road	CT	11.2	5.8	5.4	1.8	0.9	0.8	7.3	4.4	2.9	77.5	90.7	63.7
Sumerpur	M	31.5	16.5	15.0	5.3	2.8	2.5	18.8	11.7	7.1	71.6	85.3	56.6
Takhatgarh	M	15.8	8.1	7.7	2.8	1.5	1.3	8.0	5.2	2.8	61.9	79.6	43.6
Pali		**390.7**	**204.1**	**186.6**	**63.8**	**33.3**	**30.5**	**232.2**	**145.9**	**86.3**	**71.0**	**85.4**	**55.3**
Amet	M	16.7	8.5	8.1	2.5	1.3	1.2	11.1	6.5	4.6	78.1	90.3	65.6
Dariba	CT	2.8	1.5	1.3	0.2	0.1	0.1	2.4	1.3	1.0	91.7	97.3	85.5
Deogarh	M	16.5	8.4	8.1	2.7	1.4	1.2	10.8	6.4	4.4	77.8	91.3	64.0
Nathdwara	M	37.0	19.3	17.7	4.8	2.5	2.3	26.8	15.4	11.4	83.3	91.8	74.2
Rajsamand	M	55.7	29.0	26.7	8.5	4.4	4.2	37.5	22.3	15.2	79.6	90.5	67.7
Rajsamand		**128.7**	**66.8**	**61.9**	**18.7**	**9.8**	**9.0**	**88.6**	**51.9**	**36.7**	**80.6**	**91.1**	**69.2**
Gangapur City	UA	105.3	56.1	49.2	17.5	9.3	8.2	64.1	40.5	23.6	73.0	86.5	57.7
(a) Gangapur City	M	96.8	51.6	45.2	16.1	8.5	7.6	59.0	37.2	21.8	73.1	86.2	58.0
(b) Mahu Kalan	CT	8.5	4.5	4.1	1.5	0.8	0.7	5.1	3.3	1.8	72.7	90.0	54.1
Sawai Madhopur	UA	102.0	53.9	48.1	15.9	8.4	7.5	65.2	40.4	24.7	75.7	88.7	61.1
(a)Sawai Madhopur	M	97.5	51.5	45.9	15.2	8.0	7.2	62.6	38.7	23.8	76.0	88.9	61.6
(i) Sahunagar Cement Factory (OG)		_	4.5	2.4	2.1	0.7	0.4	0.3	2.6	1.7	0.9	68.2	83.7
Todra	CT	5.2	2.7	2.6	0.9	0.4	0.4	3.0	1.9	1.1	69.5	85.9	52.0
Sawai Madhopur		**212.6**	**112.7**	**99.9**	**34.3**	**18.1**	**16.2**	**132.3**	**82.8**	**49.5**	**74.2**	**87.5**	**59.2**
Fatehpur	M	78.5	40.5	38.0	13.6	7.2	6.4	46.6	28.1	18.5	71.8	84.5	58.5
Khandela	UA	26.0	13.4	12.6	4.7	2.5	2.3	14.8	9.3	5.5	69.9	85.3	53.6
(a) Khandela	M	22.5	11.6	10.9	4.0	2.1	2.0	12.9	8.0	4.9	69.9	84.7	54.2
(i) Dayra Village	_	0.4	0.2	0.2	0.1	0.0	0.0	0.2	0.1	0.0	49.1	65.0	32.0
(ii) Khandela Rural	_	2.3	1.2	1.1	0.5	0.3	0.2	1.3	0.9	0.4	71.5	91.2	50.1
(iii) Mehro ki Dhani	_	0.8	0.4	0.4	0.1	0.1	0.1	0.5	0.3	0.2	76.4	93.2	57.5
Lachhmangarh	M	47.3	24.6	22.7	8.2	4.3	3.9	28.1	17.3	10.7	71.9	85.5	57.2
Losal	M	25.4	12.8	12.6	4.7	2.5	2.2	14.2	8.6	5.5	68.7	84.4	53.1
Neem-Ka-Thana	M	29.5	15.7	13.9	4.7	2.5	2.2	19.8	12.1	7.7	79.7	91.7	66.2
Ramgarh	M	28.4	14.5	14.0	5.0	2.6	2.4	16.7	10.0	6.7	71.5	84.5	58.2
Reengus	M	22.9	12.3	10.6	3.7	1.9	1.7	14.3	9.2	5.1	74.4	88.7	57.7
Sikar	UA	185.5	96.6	88.9	29.1	15.4	13.7	118.8	71.0	47.8	76.0	87.4	63.6
(a)Sikar	MCL	184.9	96.3	88.6	29.0	15.4	13.6	118.4	70.8	47.7	76.0	87.4	63.6
(I) Samrathpura Rural (OG)	_	0.6	0.3	0.3	0.1	0.1	0.0	0.4	0.2	0.2	77.9	87.3	67.5
Sri Madhopur	M	28.5	15.0	13.5	4.5	2.4	2.1	18.8	11.5	7.4	78.6	91.5	64.4
Sikar		**472.0**	**245.3**	**226.7**	**78.3**	**41.4**	**36.9**	**292.2**	**177.2**	**115.0**	**74.2**	**86.9**	**60.6**
Abu Road	UA	47.6	25.4	22.3	7.2	3.8	3.3	32.6	19.5	13.1	80.7	90.5	69.4
(a) Abu Road	M	47.3	25.2	22.1	7.1	3.8	3.3	32.4	19.4	13.0	80.5	90.5	69.2
(I) Santpur (OG)	_	0.3	0.2	0.1	0.0	0.0	0.0	0.3	0.1	0.1	97.8	100.0	95.1
Mount Abu	M	22.0	12.7	9.3	3.1	1.7	1.5	14.8	9.7	5.1	78.5	88.1	64.9
Pindwara	M	20.8	10.9	9.8	3.4	1.9	1.5	12.5	7.9	4.5	72.0	87.5	54.9
Sheoganj	M	24.8	12.9	11.9	3.9	2.1	1.8	16.5	9.9	6.6	78.9	91.9	65.2
Sirohi	M	35.5	18.8	16.8	5.1	2.8	2.3	23.3	14.3	9.0	76.8	89.7	62.6
Sirohi		**150.7**	**80.7**	**70.1**	**22.8**	**12.3**	**10.4**	**99.8**	**61.3**	**38.4**	**78.0**	**89.8**	**64.4**
Banasthali	CT	6.7	2.1	4.6	0.6	0.3	0.3	5.5	1.6	3.9	90.1	93.0	88.9
Deoli	M	20.0	10.8	9.3	3.0	1.6	1.4	14.0	8.3	5.6	82.0	90.7	71.7
Malpura	UA	27.4	14.2	13.2	4.6	2.4	2.2	17.0	10.3	6.7	74.5	87.6	60.5
(a) Malpura	M	27.2	14.1	13.2	4.5	2.4	2.2	16.9	10.3	6.7	74.5	87.7	60.6
(i) Malpura Rural (OG)	_	0.01	0.0	0.0	0.0	0.0	—	0.0	0.0	0.0	81.8	100.0	
(ii) Brijlal Nagar (OG)	_	0.1	0.1	0.0	0.0	0.0	0.0	0.1	0.1	0.0	61.9	70.9	22.2

Urban Area/City/Town	Civic Status of City/Town	Population in '000 No.			Child Population in the age-group 0-6 in '000 No.			Literates in '000 No.			Literacy Rate (%)		
		Person	Male	Female	Person	Male	Female	Person	Male	Female	Person	Male	Female
1	2	3	4	5	6	7	8	9	10	11	12	13	14
Niwai	M	31.4	16.5	14.8	5.0	2.6	2.4	19.9	12.3	7.6	75.6	88.2	61.4
Todaraisingh	M	21.2	10.9	10.3	3.7	2.1	1.7	12.0	7.7	4.3	68.7	86.9	50.0
Tonk	MCL	135.7	70.1	65.5	24.0	12.5	11.5	72.0	43.8	28.1	64.5	76.1	52.1
Uniara	M	10.8	5.6	5.3	1.8	0.9	0.9	6.1	3.9	2.2	67.1	83.5	49.8
Tonk		**253.1**	**130.1**	**123.0**	**42.7**	**22.4**	**20.3**	**146.4**	**87.9**	**58.4**	**69.6**	**81.7**	**56.9**
Bhalariya	CT	6.5	3.5	3.1	0.7	0.4	0.3	5.4	3.0	2.4	92.4	97.2	87.0
Bhinder	M	16.4	8.3	8.1	2.2	1.2	1.0	10.3	6.2	4.2	73.2	87.2	59.2
Dhariawad	CT	10.5	5.4	5.1	1.6	0.8	0.8	7.1	4.1	3.0	80.2	89.8	70.1
Fatehnagar	M	19.6	10.0	9.6	2.8	1.4	1.4	11.8	7.2	4.6	69.9	83.5	55.9
Kanor	M	12.6	6.8	5.8	1.5	0.8	0.7	8.5	5.3	3.1	76.2	88.7	61.5
Kherwara Chhaoni	CT	6.6	3.4	3.2	1.0	0.5	0.4	4.8	2.7	2.0	83.6	93.0	73.7
Newa Talai	CT	4.7	2.5	2.2	0.6	0.3	0.3	3.2	1.9	1.3	79.1	90.7	66.3
Rikhabdeo	CT	8.0	4.2	3.8	1.1	0.6	0.5	6.1	3.4	2.7	89.1	96.4	81.3
Salumbar	M	15.9	8.1	7.7	2.1	1.1	1.0	12.0	6.8	5.3	87.6	96.5	78.3
Udaipur	MCL	389.3	205.3	184.0	46.1	24.6	21.5	301.7	170.1	131.6	87.9	94.1	81.0
Udaipur		**490.1**	**257.5**	**232.6**	**59.8**	**31.8**	**27.9**	**370.9**	**210.7**	**160.3**	**86.2**	**93.4**	**78.3**
Rajasthan		**13205.4**	**6987.2**	**6218.3**	**2000.8**	**1060.7**	**940.1**	**8614.7**	**5161.8**	**3452.8**	**76.9**	**87.1**	**65.4**

CT – Census Town **M** – Municipality **MC** – Municipal Council **UG** – Urban Out-Growth **UA** – Urban Agglomeration

Source: Calculated from the data given in the Census of India 2001, Series-9, Rajasthan, Provisional Population Totals, Paper-2 of 2001

TEHSIL-WISE DISTRIBUTION OF WORKING POPULATION (MAIN + MARGINAL): RAJASTHAN (2001)

S. No.	Tehsil/District	Total Workers (Main+Marginal)									Percentage to Total Workers			
		Persons	Total Male	Female	Rural Persons	Rural Male (%)	Rural Female (%)	Urban Persons	Urban Male	Urban Female	Culti-vators	Agricul-tural Lab-ourers	Workers in house-hold	Other workers
1	2	3	4	5	6	7	8	9	10	11	12	13	14	15
1	Ajmer	210,469	168,874	41,595	66,982	69.63	30.37	143,487	122,234	21,253	12.2	5.2	5.3	77.3
2	Beawar	107,155	68,332	38,823	68,015	54.09	45.91	39,140	31,545	7,595	37.6	7.5	6.0	48.8
3	Bhinay	58,486	30,990	27,496	58,486	52.99	47.01	—	—	—	60.0	8.9	2.7	28.4
4	Kekri	83,045	47,817	35,228	72,470	54.08	45.92	10,575	8,624	1,951	51.6	16.8	3.0	28.6
5	Kishangarh	128,551	86,639	41,912	94,877	59.74	40.26	33,674	29,956	3,718	41.3	10.3	2.8	45.6
6	Masuda	85,653	49,226	36,427	77,268	54.45	45.55	8,385	7,153	1,232	46.0	9.5	3.1	41.4
7	Nasirabad	72,162	47,304	24,858	54,152	56.69	43.31	18,010	16,607	1,403	37.7	9.5	3.2	49.5
8	Peesangan	47,521	28,500	19,021	47,521	59.97	40.03	—	—	—	48.8	19.6	3.7	27.8
9	Sarwar	63,937	35,989	27,948	58,426	54.66	45.34	5,511	4,051	1,460	58.4	16.6	2.1	23.0
	Ajmer District	**856,979**	**563,671**	**293,308**	**598,197**	**57.42**	**42.58**	**258,782**	**220,170**	**38,612**	**37.8**	**10.1**	**3.9**	**48.2**
10	Alwar	234,607	154,338	80,269	158,863	55.14	44.86	75,744	66,738	9,006	44.5	7.9	2.6	45.1
11	Bansur	102,531	57,714	44,817	102,531	56.29	43.71	—	—	—	72.0	6.7	2.0	19.3
12	Behror	163,538	89,397	74,141	155,479	53.54	46.46	8,059	6,159	1,900	64.7	11.4	1.7	22.2
13	Kathumar	105,772	58,755	47,017	101,475	54.05	45.95	4,297	3,904	393	72.5	7.9	1.5	18.1
14	Kishangarh Bas	69,976	41,630	28,346	55,668	55.21	44.79	14,308	10,893	3,415	52.8	12.4	2.2	32.7
15	Kotkasim	60,226	32,785	27,441	60,226	54.44	45.56	—	—	—	66.2	13.3	1.6	18.9
16	Lachhmangarh	139,159	76,050	63,109	135,330	54.17	45.83	3,829	2,740	1,089	81.5	5.2	1.3	12.0
17	Mandawar	121,438	64,832	56,606	121,438	53.39	46.61	—	—	—	70.5	12.8	1.5	15.2
18	Rajgarh	128,253	74,593	53,660	120,625	56.71	43.29	7,628	6,188	1,440	67.8	7.3	2.6	22.4
19	Ramgarh	89,738	50,656	39,082	89,738	56.45	43.55	—	—	—	65.6	13.0	1.5	20.0
20	Thanagazi	93,280	51,321	41,959	93,280	55.02	44.98	—	—	—	58.7	6.1	5.2	30.0
21	Tijara	151,940	91,160	60,780	127,508	56.15	43.85	24,432	19,562	4,870	46.5	6.2	1.4	45.9
	Alwar	**1,460,458**	**843,231**	**617,227**	**1,322,161**	**54.99**	**45.01**	**138,297**	**116,184**	**22,113**	**62.2**	**8.8**	**2.1**	**27.0**
22	Bagidora	145,116	74,658	70,458	145,116	51.45	48.55	—	—	—	85.0	7.2	1.6	6.2
23	Banswara	169,436	96,798	72,638	143,796	52.50	47.50	25,640	21,301	4,339	65.4	8.5	2.0	24.0
24	Garhi	101,217	60,785	40,432	98,304	59.42	40.58	2,913	2,374	539	56.5	18.3	3.6	21.7
25	Ghatol	155,992	80,520	75,472	155,992	51.62	48.38	—	—	—	81.0	11.9	1.1	6.1
26	Kushalgarh	141,476	73,081	68,395	138,446	50.96	49.04	3,030	2,522	508	83.2	9.2	1.2	6.4
	Banswara	**713,237**	**385,842**	**327,395**	**681,654**	**52.76**	**47.24**	**31,583**	**26,197**	**5,386**	**75.1**	**10.5**	**1.8**	**12.7**
27	Antah	41,745	26,290	15,455	33,629	58.53	41.47	8,116	6,607	1,509	43.0	31.7	2.0	23.4
28	Atru	57,370	34,578	22,792	54,188	60.27	39.73	3,182	1,919	1,263	57.1	24.9	1.7	16.3
29	Baran	65,825	45,420	20,405	43,587	61.03	38.97	22,238	18,818	3,420	36.3	18.8	4.1	40.8
30	Chhabra	56,664	32,545	24,119	49,395	54.33	45.67	7,269	5,711	1,558	63.4	18.3	2.6	15.7
31	Chhipabarod	69,249	38,348	30,901	63,763	53.80	46.20	5,486	4,041	1,445	70.8	16.6	2.0	10.6
32	Kishanganj	59,729	34,634	25,095	59,729	57.99	42.01	—	—	—	42.5	40.2	3.4	13.9
33	Mangrol	38,195	23,547	14,648	30,220	60.62	39.38	7,975	5,228	2,747	45.3	27.3	5.5	21.9
34	Shahbad	49,835	28,967	20,868	49,835	58.13	41.87	—	—	—	48.7	35.6	2.3	13.5
	Baran	**438,612**	**264,329**	**174,283**	**384,346**	**57.76**	**42.24**	**54,266**	**42,324**	**11,942**	**51.6**	**26.0**	**2.9**	**19.5**
35	Barmer	126,722	80,867	45,855	102,537	57.45	42.55	24,185	21,959	2,226	60.7	2.0	3.9	33.5
36	Baytoo	97,394	51,636	45,758	97,394	53.02	46.98	—	—	—	76.8	2.1	1.6	19.5
37	Chohtan	172,069	96,512	75,557	172,069	56.09	43.91	—	—	—	84.7	4.0	2.8	8.5
38	Gudha Malani	170,989	91,610	79,379	170,989	53.58	46.42	—	—	—	84.3	2.9	2.1	10.7
39	Pachpadra	144,547	87,009	57,538	126,770	55.99	44.01	17,777	16,025	1,752	60.2	5.8	2.9	31.2
40	Ramsar	37,092	21,513	15,579	37,092	58.00	42.00	—	—	—	82.5	2.2	2.8	12.5
41	Sheo	82,906	49,248	33,658	82,906	59.40	40.60	—	—	—	77.0	3.5	3.2	16.2
42	Siwana	87,596	53,385	34,211	87,596	60.94	39.06	—	—	—	59.6	15.0	3.5	22.0
	Barmer	**919,315**	**531,780**	**387,535**	**877,353**	**56.28**	**43.72**	**41,962**	**37,984**	**3,978**	**73.4**	**4.5**	**2.8**	**19.2**
43	Bayana	95,348	61,060	34,288	86,649	61.28	38.72	8,699	7,958	741	58.4	15.3	2.0	24.4
44	Bharatpur	113,464	89,621	23,843	58,910	70.18	29.82	54,554	48,277	6,277	31.2	9.0	2.7	57.0
45	Deeg	83,398	49,351	34,047	72,237	54.88	45.12	11,161	9,709	1,452	67.4	11.2	1.9	19.5
46	Kaman	72,624	42,447	30,177	63,088	54.92	45.08	9,536	7,796	1,740	68.4	10.2	2.2	19.2
47	Kumher	65,868	42,809	23,059	59,678	63.23	36.77	6,190	5,076	1,114	63.4	14.3	1.7	20.6
48	Nadbai	78,862	46,609	32,253	72,016	57.19	42.81	6,846	5,426	1,420	64.7	15.8	1.4	18.1
49	Nagar	81,358	47,278	34,080	75,300	56.15	43.85	6,058	4,997	1,061	70.8	11.3	1.4	16.5
50	Pahari	57,090	33,989	23,101	57,090	59.54	40.46	—	—	—	73.3	13.5	0.9	12.3
51	Rupbas	92,857	56,396	36,461	92,857	60.73	39.27	—	—	—	60.0	16.3	1.2	22.4
52	Weir	111,644	63,523	48,121	100,524	55.05	44.95	11,120	8,188	2,932	69.6	13.9	1.2	15.3
	Bharatpur	**852,513**	**533,083**	**319,430**	**738,349**	**59.00**	**41.00**	**114,164**	**97,427**	**16,737**	**61.3**	**13.0**	**1.7**	**24.0**

S. No.	Tehsil/District	Total Workers (Main+Marginal)									Percentage to Total Workers			
		Total			Rural			Urban						
		Persons	Male	Female	Persons	Male (%)	Female (%)	Persons	Male	Female	Cultivators	Agricultural Labourers	Workers in household	Other workers
1	2	3	4	5	6	7	8	9	10	11	12	13	14	15
53	Asind	106,874	56,520	50,354	102,018	51.96	48.04	4,856	3,512	1,344	63.2	8.1	2.4	26.3
54	Banera	54,812	30,410	24,402	54,812	55.48	44.52	—	—	—	57.6	11.8	3.2	27.3
55	Beejoliya	38,929	23,468	15,461	34,970	57.70	42.30	3,959	3,291	668	54.0	3.9	1.2	40.9
56	Bhilwara	185,620	129,005	56,615	93,260	54.41	45.59	92,360	78,261	14,099	29.2	4.5	3.5	62.7
57	Hurda	48,319	31,211	17,108	40,771	60.09	39.91	7,548	6,711	837	47.9	8.8	2.5	40.8
58	Jahazpur	85,293	49,177	36,116	78,450	56.90	43.10	6,843	4,537	2,306	67.1	9.2	2.7	21.0
59	Kotri	74,364	42,579	31,785	74,364	57.26	42.74	—	—	—	74.1	4.7	2.0	19.2
60	Mandal	91,674	51,099	40,575	91,674	55.74	44.26	—	—	—	60.2	10.6	2.9	26.3
61	Mandalgarh	75,711	43,678	32,033	67,259	56.89	43.11	8,452	5,415	3,037	75.3	5.0	1.9	17.8
62	Raipur	37,688	22,180	15,508	37,688	58.85	41.15	—	—	—	61.9	8.5	3.0	26.6
63	Sahara	55,377	30,481	24,896	49,862	52.25	47.75	5,515	4,426	1,089	56.1	8.6	3.3	32.0
64	Shahpura	83,499	48,151	35,348	74,361	55.80	44.20	9,138	6,654	2,484	67.1	8.6	2.7	21.5
	Bhilwara	**938,160**	**557,959**	**380,201**	**799,489**	**55.68**	**44.32**	**138,671**	**112,807**	**25,864**	**56.8**	**7.4**	**2.7**	**33.1**
65	Bikaner	233,678	187,167	46,511	76,304	62.61	37.39	157,374	139,392	17,982	22.1	2.7	5.2	70.1
66	Chhatargarh	36,946	20,865	16,081	36,946	56.47	43.53	—	—	—	86.1	5.2	0.9	7.9
67	Dungargarh *	122,863	67,324	55,539	110,104	51.24	48.76	12,759	10,903	1,856	81.6	5.0	1.6	11.8
68	Khajuwala	36,269	25,708	10,561	36,269	70.88	29.12	—	—	—	66.0	14.8	1.3	17.9
69	Kolayat	88,300	56,258	32,042	88,300	63.71	36.29	—	—	—	72.3	6.8	1.8	19.1
70	Lunkaransar	81,772	47,224	34,548	81,772	57.75	42.25	—	—	—	78.1	5.7	1.2	15.0
71	Nokha	148,783	86,371	62,412	135,339	54.85	45.15	13,444	12,136	1,308	72.6	6.2	2.6	18.6
72	Poogal	36,158	21,803	14,355	36,158	60.30	39.70	—	—	—	74.3	8.7	3.1	14.0
	Bikaner **	**661,906**	**445,396**	**216,510**	**491,088**	**59.84**	**40.16**	**170,818**	**151,528**	**19,290**	**55.9**	**5.5**	**3.1**	**35.5**
73	Bundi	151,587	95,789	55,798	123,971	58.64	41.36	27,616	23,090	4,526	49.8	14.5	2.0	33.7
74	Hindoli	113,513	62,096	51,417	113,513	54.70	45.30	—	—	—	69.1	8.7	1.8	20.4
75	Indragarh	47,006	29,725	17,281	38,011	58.40	41.60	8,995	7,525	1,470	51.9	14.9	1.6	31.7
76	Keshoraipatan	64,788	38,223	26,565	51,889	54.86	45.14	12,899	9,755	3,144	53.2	25.5	2.1	19.2
77	Nainwa	80,324	45,655	34,669	75,650	55.51	44.49	4,674	3,662	1,012	65.8	10.6	2.5	21.2
	Bundi	**457,218**	**271,488**	**185,730**	**403,034**	**56.44**	**43.56**	**54,184**	**44,032**	**10,152**	**58.1**	**14.0**	**2.0**	**25.9**
78	Arnod	65,739	34,245	31,494	65,739	52.09	47.91	—	—	—	82.9	10.7	1.3	5.1
79	Bari Sadri	54,783	29,222	25,561	49,669	50.74	49.26	5,114	4,021	1,093	71.4	8.7	1.9	17.9
80	Begun	64,652	35,333	29,319	57,509	52.55	47.45	7,143	5,113	2,030	77.0	4.6	1.6	16.8
81	Bhadesar	61,421	32,479	28,942	61,421	52.88	47.12	—	—	—	71.1	10.4	1.7	16.8
82	Chhoti Sadri	63,785	34,430	29,355	57,815	52.06	47.94	5,970	4,329	1,641	69.4	16.0	1.3	13.3
83	Chittaurgarh	116,958	73,933	43,025	84,662	56.91	43.09	32,296	25,752	6,544	49.2	6.0	2.4	42.4
84	Dungla	51,586	26,243	25,343	51,586	50.87	49.13	—	—	—	74.3	10.1	1.7	14.0
85	Gangrar	45,578	25,813	19,765	45,578	56.63	43.37	—	—	—	71.6	7.6	1.7	19.2
86	Kapasan	91,829	50,909	40,920	85,686	53.88	46.12	6,143	4,744	1,399	63.5	14.0	2.8	19.7
87	Nimbahera	93,988	54,572	39,416	78,129	52.44	47.56	15,859	13,605	2,254	56.3	12.9	1.6	29.2
88	Pratapgarh	125,276	68,333	56,943	113,356	51.94	48.06	11,920	9,460	2,460	73.1	13.7	1.5	11.8
89	Rashmi	43,099	22,374	20,725	43,099	51.91	48.09	—	—	—	73.3	7.3	3.1	16.3
90	Rawatbhata	52,695	33,287	19,408	42,563	57.18	42.82	10,132	8,949	1,183	52.7	12.5	1.2	33.6
	Chittaurgarh	**931,389**	**521,173**	**410,216**	**836,812**	**53.20**	**46.80**	**94,577**	**75,973**	**18,604**	**66.8**	**10.6**	**1.8**	**20.8**
91	Churu	100,802	63,530	37,272	72,517	52.99	47.01	28,285	25,100	3,185	63.4	2.8	3.1	30.7
92	Rajgarh	153,999	83,562	70,437	138,880	51.31	48.69	15,119	12,309	2,810	81.8	3.6	1.0	13.6
93	Ratangarh	108,425	64,111	44,314	84,107	52.41	47.59	24,318	20,033	4,285	66.8	4.9	2.9	25.4
94	Sardarshahar	135,926	79,063	56,863	114,298	52.14	47.86	21,628	19,471	2,157	73.7	3.1	2.2	21.0
95	Sujangarh	153,021	92,839	60,182	116,382	53.51	46.49	36,639	30,562	6,077	61.4	7.4	3.0	28.3
96	Taranagar	80,258	44,382	35,876	71,035	53.50	46.50	9,223	6,381	2,842	81.1	3.9	1.6	13.3
	Churu ***	**855,294**	**494,811**	**360,483**	**707,323**	**52.32**	**47.68**	**147,971**	**124,759**	**23,212**	**72.7**	**4.5**	**2.2**	**20.6**
97	Baswa	122,437	69,075	53,362	118,393	55.23	44.77	4,044	3,685	359	64.9	6.6	2.0	26.6
98	Dausa	137,985	81,297	56,688	121,311	55.31	44.69	16,674	14,204	2,470	63.3	4.4	4.7	27.5
99	Lalsot	117,622	67,162	50,460	109,658	55.36	44.64	7,964	6,450	1,514	71.9	5.4	2.9	19.8
100	Mahwa	75,551	49,977	25,574	67,180	63.68	36.32	8,371	7,200	1,171	60.1	13.5	1.9	24.6
101	Sikrai	90,222	50,406	39,816	90,222	55.87	44.13	—	—	—	74.3	5.8	1.7	18.2
	Dausa	**543,817**	**317,917**	**225,900**	**506,764**	**56.51**	**43.49**	**37,053**	**31,539**	**5,514**	**66.9**	**6.6**	**2.8**	**23.7**
102	Bari	107,365	65,552	41,813	90,898	57.50	42.50	16,467	13,289	3,178	49.6	4.1	1.1	45.2
103	Baseri	94,016	57,891	36,125	94,016	61.58	38.42	—	—	—	49.9	9.4	1.8	39.0
104	Dhaulpur	94,975	71,120	23,855	69,642	70.04	29.96	25,333	22,342	2,991	44.2	7.2	2.9	45.6
105	Rajakhera	65,054	41,357	23,697	52,112	63.11	36.89	12,942	8,470	4,472	48.0	6.7	2.3	43.0
106	Sepau	69,230	43,022	26,208	69,230	62.14	37.86	—			54.5	10.6	1.8	33.1
	Dhaulpur	**430,640**	**278,942**	**151,698**	**375,898**	**62.47**	**37.53**	**54,742**	**44,101**	**10,641**	**49.0**	**7.4**	**2.0**	**41.6**
107	Aspur	85,275	44,749	40,526	85,275	52.48	47.52	—	—	—	58.5	17.5	2.2	21.7
108	Dungarpur	179,142	97,783	81,359	165,942	52.16	47.84	13,200	11,227	1,973	61.8	10.4	1.2	26.6
109	Sagwara	125,414	67,179	58,235	112,977	51.84	48.16	12,437	8,607	3,830	50.2	22.5	3.3	24.1
110	Simalwara	145,726	73,299	72,427	145,726	50.30	49.70	—	—	—	64.5	17.8	1.2	16.4
	Dungarpur	**535,557**	**283,010**	**252,547**	**509,920**	**51.61**	**48.39**	**25,637**	**19,834**	**5,803**	**59.3**	**16.4**	**1.9**	**22.5**
111	Anupgarh	72,964	48,896	24,068	63,800	63.72	36.28	9,164	8,243	921	45.3	25.7	2.0	27.0
112	Ganganagar	148,143	120,974	27,169	77,696	74.02	25.98	70,447	63,462	6,985	19.3	18.9	3.2	58.6
113	Gharsana	72,255	49,028	23,227	69,030	66.79	33.21	3,225	2,925	300	49.5	22.6	1.9	25.9
114	Karanpur	62,588	40,702	21,886	52,286	60.53	39.47	10,302	9,055	1,247	32.4	36.2	1.7	29.7
115	Padampur	56,389	41,497	14,892	48,657	70.85	29.15	7,732	7,024	708	38.2	29.3	1.8	30.6
116	Raisinghnagar	74,641	51,729	22,912	66,230	66.70	33.30	8,411	7,554	857	47.4	25.7	2.1	24.8
117	Sadulshahar	68,425	44,193	24,232	60,772	62.72	37.28	7,653	6,075	1,578	32.8	23.9	2.6	40.7
118	Suratgarh	113,690	80,492	33,198	96,740	67.24	32.76	16,950	15,441	1,509	45.4	12.7	1.5	40.4
119	Vijainagar	50,812	35,357	15,455	45,564	66.80	33.20	5,248	4,919	329	46.4	25.4	1.4	26.8
	Ganganagar	**719,907**	**512,868**	**207,039**	**580,775**	**66.84**	**33.16**	**139,132**	**124,698**	**14,434**	**37.8**	**22.9**	**2.1**	**37.1**

S. No.	Tehsil/District	Total Workers (Main+Marginal)									Percentage to Total Workers			
		Persons	Total Male	Female	Rural Persons	Rural Male (%)	Rural Female (%)	Urban Persons	Urban Male	Urban Female	Cultivators	Agricultural Labourers	Workers in household	Other workers
1	2	3	4	5	6	7	8	9	10	11	12	13	14	15
120	Bhadra	121,161	69,411	51,750	110,863	54.47	45.53	10,298	9,029	1,269	77.8	6.5	1.8	13.9
121	Hanumangarh	129,250	99,410	29,840	91,974	71.33	28.67	37,276	33,807	3,469	38.5	19.5	3.1	38.9
122	Nohar	116,786	70,982	45,804	105,573	57.28	42.72	11,213	10,506	707	76.0	6.6	1.6	15.8
123	Pilibanga	72,056	49,958	22,098	62,126	65.82	34.18	9,930	9,067	863	49.5	23.8	2.0	24.7
124	Rawatsar	73,363	46,044	27,319	65,439	59.35	40.65	7,924	7,209	715	71.5	12.4	1.6	14.5
125	Sangaria	56,119	39,764	16,355	46,076	66.77	33.23	10,043	9,000	1,043	44.4	23.7	1.9	30.1
126	Tibi	59,355	38,956	20,399	59,355	65.63	34.37	—	—	—	54.8	33.2	1.0	10.9
	Hanumangarh	**628,090**	**414,525**	**213,565**	**541,406**	**62.04**	**37.96**	**86,684**	**78,618**	**8,066**	**60.2**	**15.9**	**2.0**	**21.9**
127	Amber	98,885	61,761	37,124	98,885	62.46	37.54	—	—	—	60.7	4.9	3.0	31.5
128	Bassi	96,609	55,817	40,792	96,609	57.78	42.22	—	—	—	58.6	5.4	3.8	32.3
129	Chaksu	83,863	47,801	36,062	74,811	54.65	45.35	9,052	6,917	2,135	65.1	5.3	3.0	26.6
130	Chomu	114,167	74,167	40,000	99,324	62.93	37.07	14,843	11,664	3,179	54.5	3.9	4.3	37.3
131	Dudu	75,649	43,793	31,856	75,649	57.89	42.11	—	—	—	54.4	11.7	2.8	31.0
132	Jaipur	742,680	633,735	108,945	34,524	63.20	36.80	708,156	611,917	96,239	5.7	0.9	5.1	88.3
133	Jamwa Ramgarh	114,181	62,733	51,448	114,181	54.94	45.06	—	—	—	58.8	7.5	4.3	29.3
134	Kotputli	136,770	79,843	56,927	125,981	56.14	43.86	10,789	9,122	1,667	58.1	10.8	2.5	28.6
135	Phagi	69,935	41,164	28,771	69,935	58.86	41.14	—	—	—	60.3	10.2	2.6	26.9
136	Phulera	133,551	91,493	42,058	111,483	65.20	34.80	22,068	18,802	3,266	50.6	5.9	3.6	40.0
137	Sanganer	58,797	37,703	21,094	50,080	64.27	35.73	8,717	5,519	3,198	51.2	7.5	5.8	35.5
138	Shahpura	84,215	52,133	32,082	75,779	60.46	39.54	8,436	6,316	2,120	57.2	3.5	4.6	34.6
139	Viratnagar	53,744	31,766	21,978	48,655	57.26	42.74	5,089	3,906	1,183	58.3	6.3	4.5	30.9
	Jaipur	**1,863,046**	**1,313,909**	**549,137**	**1,1075,896**	**59.46**	**40.54**	**787,150**	**674,163**	**112,987**	**36.7**	**4.5**	**4.2**	**54.6**
140	Fatehgarh	29,912	20,473	9,439	29,912	68.44	31.56	—	—	—	65.8	6.1	1.9	26.2
141	Jaisalmer	79,389	61,093	18,296	60,255	72.21	27.79	19,134	17,582	1,552	19.9	5.7	2.9	71.6
142	Pokaran	102,503	63,125	39,378	96,661	59.94	40.06	5,842	5,190	652	62.5	10.6	2.1	24.8
	Jaisalmer	**211,804**	**144,691**	**67,113**	**186,828**	**65.26**	**34.74**	**24,976**	**22,772**	**2,204**	**47.0**	**8.1**	**2.3**	**42.5**
143	Ahore	90,979	48,714	42,265	90,979	53.54	46.46	—	—	—	44.3	24.4	3.7	27.6
144	Bagora	68,625	34,538	34,087	68,625	50.33	49.67	—	—	—	79.6	6.6	2.8	11.0
145	Bhinmal	88,744	52,351	36,393	76,501	55.67	44.33	12,243	9,764	2,479	48.1	12.9	4.9	34.2
146	Jalor	80,019	52,942	27,077	66,486	63.18	36.82	13,533	10,936	2,597	32.1	21.2	4.6	42.0
147	Raniwara	78,761	41,717	37,044	78,761	52.97	47.03				74.2	8.9	2.2	14.7
148	Sanchore	249,292	131,600	117,692	240,545	51.94	48.06	8,747	6,654	2,093	82.7	4.8	2.6	9.9
149	Sayla	72,175	37,321	34,854	72,175	51.71	48.29	—	—	—	75.7	8.6	2.3	13.3
	Jalor	**728,595**	**399,183**	**329,412**	**694,072**	**53.57**	**46.43**	**34,523**	**27,354**	**7,169**	**66.2**	**11.0**	**3.2**	**19.5**
150	Aklera	69,377	38,896	30,481	64,861	53.68	46.32	4,516	4,077	439	67.2	19.7	1.3	11.7
151	Gangdhar	65,200	42,120	23,080	62,516	63.90	36.10	2,684	2,172	512	55.9	28.3	1.6	14.1
152	Jhalrapatan	126,147	78,413	47,734	101,397	56.32	43.68	24,750	21,310	3,440	52.0	17.6	2.2	28.2
153	Khanpur	71,794	40,998	30,796	71,794	57.11	42.89	—	—	—	59.0	24.2	1.8	15.0
154	Manohar Thana	60,624	31,896	28,728	57,887	51.30	48.70	2,737	2,201	536	77.4	13.7	1.8	7.1
155	Pachpahar	67,140	44,438	22,702	56,214	62.02	37.98	10,926	9,576	1,350	52.8	20.4	1.7	25.0
156	Pirawa	95,566	54,024	41,542	92,017	55.56	44.44	3,549	2,900	649	60.6	26.3	1.7	11.4
	Jhalawar	**555,848**	**330,785**	**225,063**	**506,686**	**56.95**	**43.05**	**49,162**	**42,236**	**6,926**	**59.6**	**21.4**	**1.8**	**17.2**
157	Buhana	100,580	53,807	46,773	100,580	53.50	46.50	—	—	—	72.9	10.1	1.7	15.3
158	Chirawa	166,326	101,730	64,596	141,867	56.78	43.22	24,459	21,171	3,288	66.1	6.5	2.1	25.3
159	Jhunjhunun	170,433	108,050	62,383	130,944	57.06	42.94	39,489	33,339	6,150	53.8	8.2	3.8	34.1
160	Khetri	116,095	66,694	49,401	106,627	54.60	45.40	9,468	8,480	988	60.2	4.5	1.9	33.5
161	Nawalgarh	103,779	66,688	37,091	86,515	58.63	41.37	17,264	15,962	1,302	57.8	7.2	3.3	31.7
162	Udaipurwati	104,608	61,533	43,075	97,246	57.09	42.91	7,362	6,018	1,344	66.5	6.9	2.3	24.4
	Jhunjhunun	**761,821**	**458,502**	**303,319**	**663,779**	**56.27**	**43.73**	**98,042**	**84,970**	**13,072**	**62.3**	**7.2**	**2.6**	**27.9**
163	Bhopalgarh	129,441	69,049	60,392	129,441	53.34	46.66	—	—	—	66.2	14.6	2.0	17.3
164	Bilara	107,515	63,243	44,272	83,067	55.60	44.40	24,448	17,056	7,392	50.7	18.8	3.0	27.5
165	Jodhpur	334,425	277,328	57,097	85,446	62.82	37.18	248,979	223,652	25,327	13.1	3.4	4.4	79.1
166	Luni	74,147	44,223	29,924	74,147	59.64	40.36	—	—	—	69.8	7.6	2.4	20.1
167	Osian	165,080	93,528	71,552	165,080	56.66	43.34	—	—	—	72.3	13.3	1.7	12.6
168	Phalodi	162,370	104,427	57,943	150,922	62.10	37.90	11,448	10,704	744	65.1	10.1	2.4	22.4
169	Shergarh	132,643	82,827	49,816	132,643	62.44	37.56	—	—	—	64.8	11.2	2.2	21.9
	Jodhpur	**1,105,621**	**734,625**	**370,996**	**820,746**	**58.87**	**41.13**	**284,875**	**251,412**	**33,463**	**49.5**	**9.9**	**2.9**	**37.8**
170	Hindaun	136,396	82,762	53,634	113,537	55.37	44.63	22,859	19,896	2,963	51.5	14.3	2.9	31.3
171	Karauli	107,988	70,214	37,774	89,474	61.76	38.24	18,514	14,956	3,558	55.2	6.2	3.2	35.3
172	Mandrail	26,622	16,751	9,871	26,622	62.92	37.08	—	—	—	69.7	5.8	1.3	23.1
173	Nadoti	50,908	28,575	22,333	50,908	56.13	43.87	—	—	—	68.7	12.0	2.1	17.2
174	Sapotra	72,970	43,297	29,673	72,970	59.34	40.66	—	—	—	73.5	7.7	2.0	16.9
175	Todabhim	85,184	48,688	36,496	78,645	56.04	43.96	6,539	4,616	1,923	67.1	12.5	1.9	18.6
	Karauli	**480,068**	**290,287**	**189,781**	**432,156**	**58.04**	**41.96**	**47,912**	**39,468**	**8,444**	**61.3**	**10.4**	**2.5**	**25.8**
176	Digod	61,779	39,061	22,718	61,779	63.23	36.77	—	—	—	45.7	35.4	1.7	17.1
177	Ladpura	261,903	215,854	46,049	55,230	68.00	32.00	206,673	178,299	28,374	9.0	5.8	5.1	80.1
178	Pipalda	59,549	40,000	19,549	59,549	67.17	32.83	—	—	—	51.9	28.2	2.2	17.7
179	Ramganj Mandi	87,727	61,300	26,427	58,182	63.43	36.57	29,545	24,397	5,148	27.9	11.8	2.0	58.4
180	Sangod	70,105	43,052	27,053	64,840	59.55	40.45	5,265	4,443	822	52.6	25.9	2.0	19.5
	Kota	**541,063**	**399,267**	**141,796**	**299,580**	**64.13**	**35.87**	**35.87**	**207,139**	**34,344**	**26.6**	**15.2**	**3.5**	**51.7**
181	Degana	130,617	70,514	60,103	127,730	53.43	46.57	2,887	2,271	616	68.4	12.6	3.0	16.0
182	Didwana	118,235	73,445	44,790	106,629	59.29	40.71	11,606	10,224	1,382	61.7	9.6	3.2	25.5
183	Jayal	113,559	58,638	54,921	113,559	51.64	48.36	—	—	—	74.2	11.6	2.0	12.2
184	Kheenvsar	67,468	36,380	31,088	67,468	53.92	46.08	—	—	—	76.0	8.7	1.8	13.5
185	Ladnu	81,626	50,377	31,249	66,418	55.87	44.13	15,208	13,270	1,938	61.3	8.0	3.2	27.5

S. No.	Tehsil District	Total Workers (Main+Marginal)									Percentage to Total Workers			
		Total			Rural			Urban						
		Persons	Male	Female	Persons	Male (%)	Female (%)	Persons	Male	Female	Cultivators	Agricultural Labourers	Workers in household	Other workers
1	2	3	4	5	6	7	8	9	10	11	12	13	14	15
186	Makrana	96,501	68,553	27,948	75,295	64.10	35.90	21,206	20,290	916	47.0	6.6	2.3	44.1
187	Merta	140,202	85,453	54,749	129,243	58.69	41.31	10,959	9,602	1,357	54.8	20.5	2.3	22.5
188	Nagaur	183,322	110,089	73,233	139,456	53.11	46.89	43,866	36,022	7,844	65.4	7.1	3.1	24.4
189	Nawa	121,069	81,464	39,605	101,899	63.95	36.05	19,170	16,295	2,875	54.4	7.7	3.2	34.7
190	Parbatsar	74,263	48,553	25,710	70,600	64.28	35.72	3,663	3,172	491	54.8	11.4	3.3	30.4
	Nagaur	**1,126,862**	**683,466**	**443,396**	**998,297**	**57.33**	**42.67**	**128,565**	**111,146**	**17,419**	**61.8**	**10.6**	**2.8**	**24.8**
191	Bali	88,621	55,065	33,556	76,332	59.52	40.48	12,289	9,634	2,655	28.5	18.3	5.0	48.2
192	Desuri	82,342	49,432	32,910	69,700	58.04	41.96	12,642	8,978	3,664	34.2	18.4	5.1	42.4
193	Jaitaran	91,198	50,975	40,223	85,016	54.36	45.64	6,182	4,758	1,424	50.0	23.8	3.5	22.7
194	Marwar Junction	79,460	45,874	33,586	76,463	56.61	43.39	2,997	2,591	406	40.6	22.4	5.1	31.9
195	Pali	106,197	77,756	28,441	50,469	57.52	42.48	55,728	48,724	7,004	20.0	11.4	4.7	63.9
196	Raipur	73,930	42,999	30,931	73,930	58.16	41.84	—	—	—	46.6	23.3	2.7	27.3
197	Rohat	46,313	26,278	20,035	46,313	56.74	43.26	—	—	—	52.3	23.5	2.5	21.7
198	Sojat	85,603	50,351	35,252	69,149	54.83	45.17	16,454	12,435	4,019	41.5	23.1	3.8	31.6
199	Sumerpur	67,487	45,580	21,907	52,936	63.06	36.94	14,551	12,198	2,353	22.9	22.3	4.4	50.4
	Pali	**721,151**	**444,310**	**276,841**	**600,308**	**57.47**	**42.53**	**120,843**	**99,318**	**21,525**	**36.4**	**20.2**	**4.2**	**39.2**
200	Amet	38,357	28,083	10,274	33,107	71.87	28.13	5,250	4,289	961	30.2	6.1	3.9	59.8
201	Bhim	57,301	30,819	26,482	57,301	53.78	46.22	—	—	—	51.8	21.4	1.9	24.9
202	Deogarh	44,500	24,675	19,825	39,277	52.41	47.59	5,223	4,090	1,133	53.5	11.3	2.0	33.2
203	Kumbhalgarh	60,629	34,167	26,462	60,629	56.35	43.65	—	—	—	54.6	20.9	2.3	22.3
204	Nathdwara	81,047	54,357	26,690	69,715	63.67	36.33	11,332	9,968	1,364	32.8	10.2	5.0	52.1
205	Railmagra	49,670	30,293	19,377	48,900	60.49	39.51	770	712	58	47.5	13.4	3.5	35.6
206	Rajsamand	70,122	51,354	18,768	54,203	68.42	31.58	15,919	14,271	1,648	23.2	9.4	3.8	63.6
	Rajsamand	**401,626**	**253,748**	**147,878**	**363,132**	**60.70**	**39.30**	**38,494**	**33,330**	**5,164**	**41.0**	**13.4**	**3.3**	**42.3**
207	Bamanwas	64,793	36,840	27,953	64,793	56.86	43.14	—	—	—	72.7	12.2	2.4	12.7
208	Bonli	60,025	32,607	27,418	60,025	54.32	45.68	—	—	—	77.2	5.8	3.0	14.0
209	Chauth Ka Barwara	35,303	21,360	13,943	35,303	60.50	39.50	—	—	—	65.4	9.0	3.4	22.2
210	Gangapur	98,811	65,898	32,913	72,424	58.23	41.77	26,387	23,729	2,658	48.4	9.8	2.6	39.3
211	Khandar	62,195	34,528	27,667	62,195	55.52	44.48	—	—	—	77.8	9.6	1.1	11.5
212	Malarna Doongar	38,721	21,613	17,108	38,721	55.82	44.18	—	—	—	74.6	6.7	2.0	16.7
213	Sawai Madhopur	109,234	69,466	39,768	78,604	55.98	44.02	30,630	25,461	5,169	53.9	6.4	4.0	35.7
	Sawai Madhopur	**469,082**	**282,312**	**186,770**	**412,065**	**56.57**	**43.43**	**57,017**	**49,190**	**7,827**	**64.1**	**8.5**	**2.7**	**24.7**
214	Danta Ramgarh	140,279	82,633	57,646	132,889	58.03	41.97	7,390	5,516	1,874	62.3	5.3	4.1	28.2
215	Fatehpur	105,775	62,581	43,194	79,925	48.55	51.45	25,850	23,777	2,073	57.7	5.5	2.5	34.3
216	Lachhmangarh	138,961	75,929	63,032	127,214	51.23	48.77	11,747	10,761	986	69.3	8.8	2.4	19.5
217	Neem Ka Thana	128,573	80,043	48,530	120,416	60.78	39.22	8,157	6,853	1,304	56.6	4.5	2.8	36.1
218	Sikar	190,312	123,770	66,542	143,456	56.41	43.59	46,856	42,840	4,016	54.4	7.0	3.3	35.3
219	Sri Madhopur	186,368	112,760	73,608	163,529	57.58	42.42	22,839	18,594	4,245	61.9	3.7	2.9	31.5
	Sikar	**890,268**	**537,716**	**352,552**	**767,429**	**55.95**	**44.05**	**122,839**	**108,341**	**14,498**	**60.3**	**5.8**	**3.0**	**30.9**
220	Abu Road	72,114	49,836	22,278	49,680	60.75	39.25	22,434	19,653	2,781	29.2	14.1	1.5	55.2
221	Pindwara	88,681	53,771	34,910	82,248	58.80	41.20	6,433	5,406	1,027	24.3	19.3	2.8	53.6
222	Reodar	81,178	46,761	34,417	81,178	57.60	42.40	—	—	—	53.7	16.1	2.8	27.4
223	Sheoganj	46,302	31,774	14,528	39,168	64.82	35.18	7,134	6,387	747	22.8	26.3	3.8	47.1
224	Sirohi	58,215	37,332	20,883	48,037	59.99	40.01	10,178	8,517	1,661	25.5	16.3	4.0	54.2
	Sirohi	**346,490**	**219,474**	**127,016**	**300,311**	**59.78**	**40.22**	**46,179**	**39,963**	**6,216**	**32.2**	**17.9**	**2.9**	**47.0**
225	Deoli	87,752	50,960	36,792	81,496	55.80	44.20	6,256	5,487	769	58.0	13.0	3.3	25.7
226	Malpura	85,733	51,251	34,482	77,223	57.93	42.07	8,510	6,512	1,998	51.2	15.0	3.4	30.3
227	Niwai	92,209	51,919	40,290	81,350	53.20	46.80	10,859	8,637	2,222	67.5	4:5	1.9	26.0
228	Peeplu	47,103	25,488	21,615	47,103	54.11	45.89	—	—	—	66.4	11.7	2.3	19.6
229	Todaraisingh	60,230	33,875	26,355	53,429	54.02	45.98	6,801	5,013	1,788	61.3	14.8	2.4	21.5
230	Tonk	92,210	58,449	33,761	49,680	54.14	45.86	42,530	31,552	10,978	40.9	8.7	7.7	42.8
231	Uniara	67,868	36,863	31,005	64,287	53.44	46.56	3,581	2,505	1,076	69.7	8.7	3.2	18.5
	Tonk	**533,105**	**308,805**	**224,300**	**454,568**	**54.80**	**45.20**	**78,537**	**59,706**	**18,831**	**58.2**	**10.7**	**3.6**	**27.5**
232	Dhariawad	106,127	57,315	48,812	102,785	53.03	46.97	3,342	2,811	531	75.0	9.7	1.3	14.0
233	Girwa	266,001	199,707	66,294	142,786	66.62	33.38	123,215	104,582	18,633	21.8	4.8	4.0	69.4
234	Gogunda	71,754	41,142	30,612	71,754	57.34	42.66	—	—	—	58.2	16.4	2.2	23.2
235	Jhadol	89,200	51,066	38,134	89,200	57.25	42.75	—	—	—	71.0	15.6	1.1	12.3
236	Kherwara	115,229	63,685	51,544	110,810	54.10	45.90	4,419	3,733	686	68.4	14.0	1.1	16.6
237	Kotra	80,765	45,111	35,654	80,765	55.85	44.15	—	—	—	76.2	14.2	0.7	8.8
238	Mavli	87,565	57,755	29,810	81,126	64.81	35.19	6,439	5,179	1,260	44.1	11.0	3.3	41.6
239	Salumbar	98,493	55,697	42,796	93,531	55.22	44.78	4,962	4,052	910	62.3	10.5	2.7	24.5
240	Sarada	90,377	55,476	34,901	87,422	60.52	39.48	2,955	2,568	387	52.3	12.4	2.3	33.0
241	Vallabhnagar	96,204	61,990	34,214	87,108	63.03	36.97	9,096	7,088	2,008	54.4	13.0	2.9	29.7
	Udaipur	**1,101,715**	**688,944**	**412,771**	**947,287**	**59.00**	**41.00**	**154,428**	**130,013**	**24,415**	**52.9**	**10.9**	**2.4**	**33.8**
	Rajasthan	**23,781,257**	**14,710,049**	**9,071,208**	**19,877,709**	**57.26**	**42.74**	**3,903,548**	**3,328,696**	**574,852**	**55.4**	**10.6**	**2.7**	**31.3**

* Dungargarh tehsil shifted from Churu to Bikaner District On 1st April 2001

** Excluding data of Dungargarh tehsil

*** Including data of Dungargarh tehsil

Source: Census of India 2001, Rajasthan, Paper-3 of 2001, Directorate of Census Operation, Jaipur.

GENERAL ANNEX-XIX

DISTRICT-WISE AREA AND POPULATION CHARACTERISTICS: RAJASTHAN, 1991

S.No.	Districts	Area				Population (000's)	Annual Exponential Growth Rate	Density (Persons Per sq. km.)	Female Sex Ratio (Female Per 1000 Male)	Urban Population (%)	Literacy Rate		Work Participation Rate		Percentage of Workers in Secondary and Tertiary Sectors		Female Mean Age at Marriage
		Total ('000 sq km)	Rural ('000 sq km)	Percentage of Rural Area to Total Area (%)	% share of Total Rural Area of the State						Male	Female	Male	Female	Male	Female	
1	2	3	4	5	6	7	8	9	10	11	12	13	14	15	16	17	18
1	Ajmer	8.48	8.16	96.23	2.42	1729	1.83	204	918	40.70	68.70	34.50	50.40	27.90	50.30	15.30	16.40
2	Alwar	8.38	8.22	98.09	2.44	2297	2.69	274	880	13.90	61.00	22.50	47.80	32.00	31.30	8.10	16.90
3	Banswara	5.04	5.01	99.40	1.49	1156	2.65	229	969	7.70	38.20	13.40	51.90	40.70	15.30	7.70	17.70
4	Baran #	6.96	6.92	99.43	2.05					Included in Kota District							
5	Barmer	28.39	28.33	99.79	8.40	1435	2.49	51	891	10.00	36.60	7.70	51.50	36.40	18.60	4.80	18.10
6	Bharatpur	5.07	4.94	97.44	1.46	1652	2.40	326	832	19.40	62.10	19.60	45.80	21.60	28.40	17.70	17.20
7	Bhilwara	10.46	10.10	96.56	2.99	1593	1.95	152	945	19.50	45.90	16.50	56.10	36.80	28.10	6.10	15.30
8	Bikaner	27.24	27.06	99.34	8.02	1211	3.56	44	885	39.70	54.60	27.00	49.10	20.90	41.10	20.10	16.50
9	Bundi	5.55	5.38	96.94	1.59	770	2.30	139	889	17.40	47.40	16.10	51.70	27.20	23.50	9.30	15.30
10	Chittaurgarh	10.86	10.70	98.53	3.17	1484	1.86	137	950	15.60	50.50	17.20	56.00	41.70	23.40	5.00	15.60
11	Churu	16.83	16.64	98.87	4.93	1543	2.69	92	937	28.90	51.30	17.30	47.20	29.30	27.50	5.20	15.90
12	Dausa#	3.39	3.34	98.53	0.99					Included in Jaipur District							
13	Dhaulpur	3.03	2.97	98.02	0.88	749	2.48	247	795	17.20	50.50	15.20	47.90	6.60	19.70	22.00	16.80
14	Dungarpur	3.77	3.74	99.20	1.11	875	2.47	232	995	7.30	45.70	15.40	51.30	38.00	19.50	9.70	17.50
15	Ganganagar	12.58	12.47	99.13	3.28	2623	2.56	127	877	21.10	55.30	26.40	52.40	19.90	28.70	16.70	17.60
16	Hanumangarh#	8.05	8.05	99.98	2.84					Included in Ganganagar District							
17	Jaipur	10.68	10.40	97.38	3.08	4723	3.18	336	891	39.50	64.80	28.70	46.80	20.00	52.70	18.90	16.40
18	Jaisalmer	38.40	38.27	99.66	11.34	345	3.49	9	807	15.60	45.00	11.30	50.10	20.50	36.70	25.20	17.80
19	Jalor	10.64	10.59	99.53	3.14	1143	2.35	107	942	7.30	39.00	7.80	50.40	31.60	17.90	5.00	18.30
20	Jhalawar	6.22	6.14	98.71	1.82	957	1.98	154	918	15.80	48.20	16.20	54.10	32.30	19.80	5.00	15.70
21	Jhunjhunun	5.93	5.79	97.64	1.72	1582	2.67	267	931	20.50	68.30	25.50	42.70	23.40	35.40	11.00	16.40
22	Jodhpur	22.85	22.64	99.08	6.71	2153	2.56	94	891	35.50	56.70	22.60	47.90	23.60	42.40	12.80	17.50
23	Karauli#	5.48	5.39	98.36	1.48					Included in Sawai Madhopur District							
24	Kota	5.48	4.92	89.78	1.46	2031	2.80	163	887	36.40	64.00	29.50	49.30	21.40	41.00	20.90	16.30
25	Nagaur	17.72	17.45	98.48	5.17	2145	2.75	121	942	16.00	49.30	13.30	48.20	30.70	27.90	4.10	16.40
26	Pali	12.39	12.07	97.42	3.58	1486	1.54	120	956	21.80	54.40	17.00	48.30	27.50	34.40	8.40	17.40
27	Rajsamand#	4.56	4.42	96.93	1.32					Included in Udaipur District							
28	Sawai Madhopur	5.04	4.97	98.61	1.47	1963	2.46	186	854	14.80	54.60	14.60	47.10	28.20	25.60	7.60	16.40
29	Sikar	7.73	7.54	97.54	2.23	1843	2.91	238	946	21.00	64.10	19.90	42.90	19.70	38.10	11.00	16.20
30	Sirohi	5.14	5.06	98.44	1.50	654	1.88	127	949	19.50	46.20	17.00	50.30	25.80	37.40	13.60	18.00
31	Tonk	7.19	7.03	97.77	2.08	975	2.18	136	923	19.50	50.60	15.20	50.20	32.10	29.20	9.90	14.90
32	Udaipur	12.29	11.53	93.82	3.83	2889	2.04	167	965	17.10	49.30	19.00	53.10	33.10	30.40	12.80	16.80
	RAJASTHAN	**342.24**	**337.37**	**98.58**	**100.00**	**44006**	**2.50**	**129**	**910**	**22.90**	**55.00**	**20.40**	**49.30**	**27.40**	**32.70**	**10.50**	**16.70**

Note: - # Came in force after 1991 Census

Source: 1. Computed from data given in Primary Census Abstract, Rajasthan, Series-21, Census of India, 1991.
2. Occasional Paper No. 1 of 1997, District Level Estimates of Fertility and Child Mortality for 1991 and Their Inter-relations with Other Variables

DISTRICT-WISE ESTIMATES OF FERTILITY INDICATORS: RAJASTHAN, 1981 AND 1991

S.No.	Districts	CBR		TFR		TMFR		GFR		GMFR	
		1981	1991	1981	1991	1981	1991	1981	1991	1981	1991
1	2	3	4	5	6	7	8	9	10	11	12
1	Ajmer	39.08	34.99	5.50	4.75	6.10	5.41	167.00	152.00	194.00	178.00
2	Alwar	41.36	35.00	6.40	5.04	6.90	5.73	194.00	164.00	220.00	187.00
3	Banswara	42.39	38.41	6.10	5.13	6.80	6.04	187.00	167.00	223.00	196.00
4	Baran#	Included in Kota District									
5	Barmer	39.75	36.03	6.20	5.57	6.90	6.11	194.00	174.00	225.00	201.00
6	Bharatpur	44.02	34.96	7.00	5.30	7.60	6.03	214.00	169.00	240.00	194.00
7	Bhilwara	37.99	35.23	5.30	4.80	5.60	5.11	162.00	150.00	175.00	164.00
8	Bikaner	41.32	35.36	6.00	4.99	6.40	5.66	188.00	165.00	216.00	189.00
9	Bundi	40.68	35.70	5.90	5.03	6.30	5.35	179.00	160.00	193.00	175.00
10	Chittaurgarh	38.96	33.00	5.40	4.41	5.70	4.77	168.00	139.00	183.00	155.00
11	Churu	42.08	28.53	6.10	4.14	6.60	4.57	193.00	133.00	214.00	148.00
12	Dausa#	Included in Jaipur District									
13	Dhaulpur	44.02	40.38	7.00	6.36	7.60	7.04	214.00	204.00	240.00	229.00
14	Dungarpur	45.12	40.24	6.10	5.16	6.60	5.86	185.00	166.00	216.00	197.00
15	Ganganagar	39.15	32.75	5.70	4.22	6.40	5.11	183.00	150.00	218.00	176.00
16	Hanumangarh#	Included in Ganganagar District									
17	Jaipur	41.62	35.26	6.20	4.88	6.70	5.55	188.00	158.00	212.00	183.00
18	Jaisalmer	41.55	34.01	5.50	5.48	6.10	6.14	173.00	175.00	199.00	202.00
19	Jalore	37.99	34.95	6.50	5.23	7.10	5.95	198.00	165.00	228.00	193.00
20	Jhalawar	40.16	32.62	6.10	4.47	6.40	4.82	184.00	143.00	200.00	158.00
21	Jhunjhunun	39.98	34.48	5.90	4.83	6.30	5.35	179.00	159.00	202.00	179.00
22	Jodhpur	41.46	34.67	6.10	5.05	6.60	5.79	186.00	162.00	216.00	190.00
23	Karauli#	Included in Sawai Madhopur District									
24	Kota	40.14	36.60	6.30	5.00	6.80	5.52	196.00	163.00	219.00	184.00
25	Nagaur	40.14	34.68	6.10	4.78	6.50	5.14	184.00	157.00	201.00	172.00
26	Pali	41.45	33.84	6.00	4.88	6.50	5.55	181.00	153.00	205.00	176.00
27	Rajsamand#	Included in Udaipur District									
28	Sawai Madhopur	43.34	40.01	6.70	5.95	7.10	6.37	200.00	187.00	218.00	206.00
29	Sikar	41.00	37.64	6.20	5.41	6.50	5.81	189.00	174.00	207.00	192.00
30	Sirohi	39.75	33.33	5.80	4.73	6.40	5.46	174.00	148.00	206.00	176.00
31	Tonk	36.18	35.50	6.50	4.99	6.80	5.37	190.00	159.00	209.00	175.00
32	Udaipur	40.65	34.69	5.60	4.62	6.20	5.17	173.00	145.00	199.00	167.00
	RAJASTHAN	**41.01**	**35.75**	**6.10**	**5.01**	**6.50**	**5.59**	**185.00**	**162.00**	**209.00**	**184.00**

Note: # Came in force after 1991 Census
Source: Occasional Paper No. 1 of 1997, District Level Estimates of Fertility and Child Mortality for 1991 and their Inter-relations with Other Variables.

ESTIMATES OF CHILD MORTALITY INDICATORS BY SEX AT DISTRICT LEVEL, RAJASTHAN, 1981 AND 1991

S.No.	*District*	*Year*	*Person*				*Male*				*Female*			
			q(1)	*q(2)*	*q(3)*	*q(5)*	*q(1)*	*q(2)*	*q(3)*	*q(5)*	*q(1)*	*q(2)*	*q(3)*	*q(5)*
1	2	3	4	5	6	7	8	9	10	11	12	13	14	15
1	Ajmer	1991	113	118	126	130	115	122	129	134	111	116	121	124
		1981	174	172	178	202	178	176	176	195	170	169	180	210
2	Alwar	1991	101	106	115	124	99	103	112	119	103	112	119	128
		1981	160	170	181	204	165	172	173	188	154	168	190	221
3	Banswara	1991	92	135	143	148	97	140	144	149	87	130	143	147
		1981	150	165	153	167	170	184	167	172	126	145	138	161
4	Baran#	1991	Included in Kota District											
		1981												
5	Barmer	1991	99	121	138	143	82	124	136	141	102	118	142	147
		1981	115	129	140	157	117	122	134	146	113	136	147	170
6	Bharatpur	1991	78	101	111	126	72	89	97	110	95	114	128	145
		1981	186	199	215	236	175	184	185	199	199	216	249	278
7	Bhilwara	1991	120	125	129	143	121	134	137	144	119	123	127	142
		1981	191	196	206	225	204	204	208	226	176	188	203	224
8	Bikaner	1991	60	69	76	82	60	69	75	81	59	69	76	82
		1981	69	74	78	89	72	75	74	87	66	73	82	92
9	Bundi	1991	82	105	108	120	61	102	109	114	96	106	108	127
		1981	151	165	161	196	143	164	163	185	160	166	159	208
10	Chittaurgarh	1991	99	134	142	149	103	141	148	151	83	127	136	145
		1981	180	197	196	218	192	210	204	217	166	183	187	220
11	Churu	1991	64	75	79	83	59	72	76	79	69	77	82	91
		1981	84	98	111	116	88	95	104	112	79	102	118	121
12	Dausa#	1991	Included in Jaipur District											
		1981												
13	Dhaulpur	1991	107	127	133	150	109	110	125	142	105	147	166	183
		1981	186	199	215	236	175	184	185	199	199	216	249	278
14	Dungarpur	1991	98	129	134	140	97	131	136	141	99	127	131	139
		1981	171	160	160	169	178	171	170	177	163	150	150	161
15	Ganganagar	1991	54	64	68	73	57	60	69	71	50	68	72	74
		1981	107	102	110	119	125	108	110	115	89	95	110	124
16	Hanumangarh#	1991	Included in Ganganagar District											
		1981												
17	Jaipur	1991	67	78	84	94	65	76	81	88	69	81	87	102
		1981	137	144	148	162	144	146	143	151	129	142	154	174
18	Jaisalmer	1991	87	97	111	124	87	96	109	119	86	99	113	134
		1981	112	118	114	134	124	119	103	113	100	117	128	158
19	Jalore	1991	91	112	124	129	90	104	117	125	96	120	132	139
		1981	145	137	142	156	142	135	141	146	149	139	144	167
20	Jhalawar	1991	100	111	118	124	122	113	119	122	88	110	117	128
		1981	140	174	179	196	142	173	180	190	138	175	179	203
21	Jhunjhunun	1991	56	66	67	80	48	63	65	73	66	69	71	88
		1981	108	113	128	138	100	109	121	126	116	117	135	152
22	Jodhpur	1991	72	75	83	86	74	77	79	82	69	71	89	96
		1981	108	111	114	131	108	111	107	120	107	111	122	143
23	Karauli#	1991	Included in Sawai Madhopur District											
		1981												
24	Kota	1991	84	95	99	140	76	90	97	121	91	96	101	124
		1981	141	142	155	178	148	144	152	168	133	141	159	188
25	Nagaur	1991	82	89	96	102	91	92	96	99	71	87	96	105
		1981	99	118	131	147	104	120	123	142	105	126	144	163
26	Pali	1991	111	128	137	156	97	123	124	140	127	136	152	174
		1981	166	168	182	218	161	167	175	208	170	170	189	229
27	Rajsamand#	1991	Included in Udaipur District											
		1981												
28	Sawai Madhopur	1991	79	106	116	122	74	95	97	101	102	122	135	144
		1981	175	189	206	227	185	182	191	203	164	197	222	254
29	Sikar	1991	57	70	74	78	61	62	69	74	51	78	80	83
		1981	106	127	128	145	106	127	116	129	106	127	142	162
30	Sirohi	1991	118	126	129	139	119	130	128	132	117	125	129	147
		1981	160	157	174	186	136	159	170	175	190	155	179	198
31	Tonk	1991	123	127	136	149	109	123	137	146	129	134	136	157
		1981	164	203	217	233	177	218	213	232	152	188	222	233
32	Udaipur	1991	92	113	120	129	71	103	114	122	109	127	139	146
		1981	179	177	173	189	200	191	176	194	156	163	169	184
	RAJASTHAN	**1991**	**87**	**97**	**100**	**110**	**94**	**95**	**98**	**103**	**79**	**99**	**106**	**117**
		1981	**141**	**149**	**157**	**176**	**146**	**151**	**153**	**166**	**135**	**148**	**163**	**186**

Note: # Came in force after 1991 Census
Source: Occasional Paper No. 1 of 1997, District Level Estimates of Fertility and Child Mortality for 1991 and their Inter-relations with Other Variables.

DISTRICT-WISE POPULATION CHARACTERISTICS: RAJASTHAN (2001)

S.No.	*Name of Districts*	*Population, 2001 ('000' Number)*						*Percentage*	*Sex-Ratio*	*Density*	*Literacy Rate*		
		Male	*Female*	*Total*	*(%age share to State Pop.)*	*S.C.*	*S.T.*	*of Rural Pop. to Total Pop.*	*(No. of females per 1000 males)*	*of Pop. per sq. km.*	*Male*	*Female*	*Total*
1	2	3	4	5		6	7	8	9	10	11	12	13
1	Ajmer	1130	1052	2182	(8)	386	53	60	931	257	79.96	49.10	65.06
2	Alwar	1587	1406	2993	(5)	539	240	85	886	357	78.91	43.95	62.48
3	Banswara	761	741	1502	(3)	64	1085	93	974	298	60.24	27.86	44.22
4	Baran	535	487	1022	(2)	181	217	83	909	146	76.86	42.18	60.37
5	Barmer	1038	927	1965	(3)	309	119	93	892	69	73.64	43.91	59.65
6	Bharatpur	1130	968	2098	(4)	456	47	81	854	414	81.39	44.12	64.24
7	Bhilwara	1027	987	2014	(4)	317	181	79	962	192	68.12	33.47	51.09
8	Bikaner	886	788	1674	(3)	334	6	64	890	61	70.78	42.55	57.54
9	Bundi	503	458	963	(3)	174	195	81	907	173	72.17	37.76	55.80
10	Chittaurgarh	918	885	1804	(3)	251	388	84	964	166	71.82	36.45	54.37
11	Churu	988	936	1924	(2)	407	10	72	948	114	79.52	53.87	66.97
12	Dausa	693	623	1317	(2)	279	353	90	899	384	80.37	43.15	62.75
13	Dhaulpur	538	445	983	(2)	198	48	82	827	324	75.85	42.36	60.77
14	Dungarpur	548	560	1108	(2)	46	721	93	1022	294	66.19	31.22	48.32
15	Ganganagar	955	834	1789	(3)	603	15	75	873	224	75.49	52.69	64.84
16	Hanumangarh	801	717	1518	(3)	397	10	80	894	120	77.41	52.71	65.72
17	Jaipur	2768	2483	5251	(9)	778	413	51	897	471	83.58	56.18	70.63
18	Jaisalmer	279	229	508	(1)	74	28	85	821	13	66.89	32.25	51.40
19	Jalor	738	711	1449	(3)	261	127	92	964	136	65.10	27.53	46.51
20	Jhalawar	612	568	1180	(2)	185	142	86	926	190	74.29	40.39	57.98
21	Jhunjhunun	984	930	1914	(3)	309	37	79	946	323	86.61	60.10	73.61
22	Jodhpur	1514	1373	2887	(5)	456	80	66	907	126	73.86	39.18	57.38
23	Karauli	652	558	1210	(2)	280	271	86	855	218	80.93	45.44	64.59
24	Kota	828	741	1569	(3)	301	152	47	896	288	86.25	61.25	74.45
25	Nagaur	1425	1350	2775	(5)	545	6	83	947	157	75.33	40.45	58.26
26	Pali	919	901	1820	(3)	323	106	79	981	147	73.06	36.70	54.92
27	Rajsamand	493	494	987	(2)	123	129	87	1000	256	74.05	37.89	55.82
28	Sawai Madhopur	591	526	1117	(2)	223	241	81	889	248	76.75	35.44	57.34
29	Sikar	1173	1115	2288	(4)	340	63	79	951	296	85.20	56.70	71.19
30	Sirohi	438	413	851	(2)	163	211	82	943	166	70.58	37.37	54.39
31	Tonk	627	585	1212	(2)	233	146	79	934	168	71.25	32.30	52.39
32	Udaipur	1336	1297	2633	(5)	158	1260	81	971	196	74.47	43.71	59.26
	Total	**29420**	**27087**	**56507**		**9694**	**7098**	**77**	**921**	**165**	**76.46**	**44.34**	**61.03**

Source: Primary Census Abstract 'PCA (CD)', Raj. 2001, Directorate of Census Operations, Jaipur.

DISTRICT-WISE NO. OF MEDDICAL INSTITUTIONS AND BEDS (AS ON 31ST DEC. 2004): RAJASTHAN

S.No.	Name of Districts	No. of Medical Institutions (As on 31st Dec. 2004)								No. of Beds.	Average Area Served Per Medical Institution	Average Population Served Per Medical Institution	Average Population Served Per Bed
		Hospitals	Dispensaries	MCWCs	PHCs Rural	PHCs Urban	Aids (Posts) Urban	SHCs	Total				
1	2	3	4	5	6	7	8	9	10	11	12	13	14
1	Ajmer	14 (5)	12	7	48 (5)	2	1	279	363	2100	23	6010	1039
2	Alwar	9 (5)	6	4	83 (12)	2	—	459	563	1548	15	5315	1933
3	Banswara	2	6	1	57 (10)	1	—	334	401	942	13	3745	1594
4	Baran	5 (4)	2	—	36 (4)	—	—	197	240	622	29	4257	1643
5	Barmer	3	3	3	66 (9)	—	—	443	518	916	55	3793	2145
6	Bharatpur	4 (1)	5	3	57 (7)	—	—	362	431	1023	12	4875	2054
7	Bhilwara	8 (5)	7	2	72 (9)	1	1	391	482	1343	22	4178	1499
8	Bikaner	9 (2)	12	4	45 (5)	3	—	297	370	1879	74	4525	891
9	Bundi	4 (2)	4	3	28 (3)	1	1	174	215	497	26	4477	1937
10	Chittaurgarh	5 (2)	6	3	64 (10)	1	—	391	470	1102	23	3837	1637
11	Churu	10 (5)	5	5	59 (3)	4	1	349	433	1082	39	4443	1778
12	Dausa	3 (2)	1	3	32 (4)	—	—	232	271	486	13	4860	2710
13	Dhaulpur	1	3	2	25 (3)	—	—	159	190	404	16	5175	2434
14	Dungarpur	2	5	—	43 (7)	—	—	306	356	691	11	3111	1603
15	Ganganagar	4 (3)	7	1	44 (5)	1	—	348	405	876	27	4418	2043
16	Hanumangarh	3 (2)	2	4	42 (5)	1	—	272	324	654	30	4685	2321
17	Jaipur	28 (8)	41	17	93 (7)	4	2	506	691	5669	16	7599	926
18	Jaisalmer	3 (1)	5	1	16 (2)	—	—	127	152	360	253	3344	1412
19	Jalor	2	2	4	56 (8)	—	—	354	418	767	25	3466	1889
20	Jhalawar	5 (3)	3	3	35 (8)	—	—	228	274	860	23	4308	1372
21	Jhunjhunun	11 (8)	6	10	76 (4)	—	1	423	527	1127	11	3631	1698
22	Jodhpur	15 (3)	15	4	75 (10)	4	5	493	611	3152	37	4934	916
23	Karauli	2 (1)	3	1	27 (4)	—	—	225	258	466	20	4689	2596
24	Kota	9 (5)	11	1	30 (4)	2	—	159	212	1120	26	7399	1400
25	Nagaur	10 (6)	4	7	94 (8)	—	1	600	716	1406	25	3076	1974
26	Pali	9 (6)	5	11	71 (6)	—	—	414	510	1276	24	3569	1427
27	Rajsamand	3 (1)	1	—	40 (6)	—	—	205	249	739	19	3964	1336
28	Sawai Madhopur	2	2	2	26 (4)	1	—	197	230	468	22	4857	2387
29	Sikar	9 (8)	6	9	74 (8)	—	—	490	588	1312	13	3891	1744
30	Sirohi	4 (2)	3	1	26 (4)	—	—	187	221	509	23	3851	1672
31	Tonk	7 (4)	6	2	47 (3)	—	—	246	308	723	23	3934	1676
32	Udaipur	10 (1)	10	—	90 (16)	1	—	540	651	2754	19	4045	956
	Total	**215 (95)**	**209**	**118**	**1677 (203)**	**29**	**13**	**10387**	**12648**	**38873**	**27**	**4468**	**1454**

Note: Figures in brackets show No. of CHCs.
Source: *Pragati Prativedan*, 2004-05, Directorate of Medical & Health, Jaipur.

DISTRICT-WISE TOTAL NO. OF PATIENTS TREATED IN GOVT. HOSPITALS: RAJASTHAN (2003)

S.No.	Name of Districts	Patients Treated in Govt. Hospitals (in '000 No.)			Deaths
		Outdoor	Indoor	Total	
1	2	3	4	5	6
1	Ajmer	1067	90	1157	2915
2	Alwar	1623	65	1688	812
3	Banswara	678	67	745	644
4	Baran	957	42	999	550
5	Barmer	552	25	577	470
6	Bharatpur	948	52	1000	662
7	Bhilwara	1347	81	1428	1392
8	Bikaner	1333	89	1422	2152
9	Bundi	514	35	549	413
10	Chittaurgarh	921	71	992	871
11	Churu	919	35	954	360
12	Dausa	713	24	737	134
13	Dhaulpur	393	27	420	402
14	Dungarpur	428	41	469	504
15	Ganganagar	924	22	946	625
16	Hanumangarh	705	16	721	305
17	Jaipur	3925	261	4186	7381
18	Jaisalmer	429	22	451	166
19	Jalor	579	19	598	169
20	Jhalawar	639	51	690	887
21	Jhunjhunun	984	28	1012	282
22	Jodhpur	1626	102	1728	3741
23	Karauli	482	41	523	342
24	Kota	1494	74	1568	2315
25	Nagaur	1129	30	1159	228
26	Pali	1026	41	1067	596
27	Rajsamand	503	30	533	148
28	Sawai Madhopur	516	44	560	459
29	Sikar	1199	43	1242	501
30	Sirohi	490	19	509	236
31	Tonk	764	34	798	258
32	Udaipur	1523	123	1646	2767
	Total	**31329**	**1743**	**33072**	**33687**

Source. *Pragati Prativedan*, 2004-05, Directorate of Medical & Health, Jaipur.

GENERAL ANNEX-XXV

DISTRICT-WISE DISTRIBUTION OF RURAL AND URBAN WORKING/NON WORKING POPULATION BY SEX (1991)

S. No.	Districts		Total Population (000 No.)			Working Population (000 No.)									Non Workers (000 No.)			%age of Workers and Non Workers to Total Male/Female Pop.											
						Main Workers			Marginal Workers			Total Working Population (Main+Marginal)						Main Workers			Marginal Workers			Total Working Population (Main+Marginal)			Non Workers		
			Persons	Male	Female	P	M	F	P	M	F	P	M	F	P	M	F	P	M	F	P	M	F	P	M	F	P	M	F
1	2		3	4	5	6	7	8	9	10	11	12	13	14	15	16	17	18	19	20	21	22	23	24	25	26	27	28	29
1	Ajmer	T	1729.2	901.4	827.8	618.8	449.2	169.6	66.4	5.2	61.2	685.2	454.4	230.8	1044.0	447.0	597.1	35.78	49.84	20.48	3.84	0.57	7.40	39.62	50.41	27.88	60.38	49.59	72.12
		R	1025.6	530.1	495.5	420.9	275.9	145.0	60.6	4.3	56.2	481.4	280.2	201.2	544.2	249.9	294.3	41.03	52.04	29.26	5.90	0.82	11.34	46.94	52.86	40.60	53.06	47.14	59.40
		U	703.6	371.3	332.3	197.9	173.3	24.6	5.8	0.8	5.0	203.7	174.2	29.6	499.8	197.1	302.7	28.13	46.69	7.39	0.83	0.22	1.51	28.96	46.91	8.90	71.04	53.09	91.10
2	Alwar	T	2296.6	1221.5	1075.0	697.6	568.1	129.5	229.5	15.4	214.2	927.1	583.4	343.7	1369.6	638.1	731.4	30.38	46.51	12.05	9.99	1.26	19.92	40.37	47.76	31.97	59.63	52.24	68.03
		R	1976.3	1046.6	929.7	607.1	484.6	122.5	226.8	15.1	211.8	833.9	499.7	334.3	1142.5	546.9	595.4	30.72	46.30	13.18	11.48	1.44	22.78	42.20	47.74	35.95	57.81	52.26	64.05
		U	320.3	174.9	145.4	90.5	83.5	7.0	2.7	0.3	2.4	93.2	83.8	9.4	227.1	91.2	136.0	28.25	47.73	4.81	0.84	0.17	1.66	29.09	47.89	6.47	70.91	52.11	93.53
3	Banswara	T	1155.6	586.9	568.7	375.6	297.0	78.6	160.5	7.5	153.1	536.1	304.5	231.7	619.5	282.4	337.1	32.50	50.61	13.82	13.89	1.27	26.92	46.39	51.88	40.73	53.61	48.12	59.27
		R	1066.4	540.3	526.1	351.7	276.0	75.8	159.9	7.2	152.7	511.6	283.1	228.4	554.8	257.2	297.6	32.98	51.07	14.40	14.99	1.33	29.02	47.97	52.40	43.42	52.03	47.60	56.58
		U	89.2	46.5	42.7	23.9	21.0	2.8	0.7	0.3	0.4	24.5	21.3	3.2	64.6	25.2	39.5	26.75	45.23	6.61	0.77	0.63	0.93	27.52	45.86	7.54	72.48	54.14	92.46
4	Baran	T	INCLUDED IN KOTA DISTRICT																										
		R																											
		U																											
5	Barmer	T	1435.2	759.1	676.1	481.8	381.0	100.9	155.3	10.2	145.2	637.1	391.1	246.0	798.1	368.0	430.1	33.57	50.19	14.92	10.82	1.34	21.47	44.39	51.52	36.39	55.61	48.48	63.61
		R	1291.1	681.0	610.1	443.5	344.9	98.6	153.1	9.9	143.2	596.6	354.9	241.8	694.4	326.1	368.3	34.35	50.65	16.16	11.86	1.46	23.47	46.21	52.11	39.63	53.79	47.89	60.37
		U	144.2	78.1	66.1	38.3	36.0	2.3	2.2	0.2	2.0	40.5	36.2	4.3	103.7	41.8	61.8	26.58	46.13	3.49	1.51	0.29	2.95	28.09	46.42	6.44	71.91	53.58	93.56
6	Bharatpur	T	1651.6	901.6	750.0	446.7	408.6	38.1	127.7	4.0	123.6	574.4	412.7	161.7	1077.2	488.9	588.3	27.05	45.32	5.08	7.73	0.45	16.48	34.78	45.77	21.56	65.22	54.23	78.44
		R	1330.8	728.8	602.0	364.5	332.1	32.3	122.2	3.5	118.6	486.6	335.7	150.9	844.2	393.1	451.1	27.39	45.57	5.37	9.18	0.49	19.70	36.57	46.06	25.07	63.43	53.94	74.93
		U	320.8	172.8	148.0	82.2	76.5	5.7	5.5	0.5	5.0	87.8	77.0	10.8	233.1	95.8	137.3	25.64	44.28	3.88	1.72	0.28	3.39	27.35	44.56	7.27	72.65	55.44	92.73
7	Bhilwara	T	1593.1	819.2	774.0	643.4	454.7	188.6	101.0	5.0	96.0	744.4	459.7	284.7	848.7	359.4	489.3	40.38	55.51	24.37	6.34	0.61	12.41	46.73	56.12	36.78	53.27	43.88	63.22
		R	1282.0	655.2	626.8	547.6	371.8	175.7	95.7	4.6	91.1	643.3	376.4	266.8	638.7	278.7	360.0	42.71	56.75	28.04	7.47	0.70	14.53	50.18	57.46	42.57	49.82	42.54	57.43
		U	311.1	164.0	147.1	95.8	82.9	12.9	5.3	0.4	4.9	101.1	83.3	17.8	210.0	80.7	129.3	30.79	50.56	8.76	1.71	0.23	3.36	32.50	50.79	12.12	67.50	49.21	87.88
8	Bikaner	T	1211.1	642.6	568.6	361.9	310.3	51.6	72.2	5.2	67.0	434.1	315.4	118.7	777.1	327.1	449.9	29.88	48.29	9.08	5.96	0.80	11.79	35.84	49.09	20.87	64.16	50.91	79.13
		R	730.0	385.3	344.6	234.8	193.1	41.7	69.4	4.5	64.9	304.2	197.6	106.6	425.8	187.8	238.0	32.16	50.10	12.11	9.50	1.17	18.83	41.67	51.27	30.94	58.33	48.73	69.06
		U	481.1	257.2	223.9	127.1	117.2	9.9	2.8	0.7	2.1	129.9	117.9	12.0	351.3	139.3	211.9	26.42	45.57	4.42	0.58	0.26	0.95	27.00	45.83	5.37	73.00	54.17	94.63
9	Bundi	T	770.2	407.8	362.4	263.5	208.2	55.3	45.9	2.7	43.2	309.4	211.0	98.5	460.8	196.9	263.9	34.21	51.06	15.25	5.96	0.66	11.92	40.17	51.73	27.17	59.83	48.27	72.83
		R	636.5	337.3	299.2	228.2	176.6	51.6	43.8	2.4	41.4	272.0	179.0	93.0	364.5	158.3	206.2	35.85	52.36	17.24	6.88	0.71	13.84	42.73	53.07	31.08	57.27	46.93	68.92
		U	133.7	70.5	63.2	35.3	31.6	3.7	2.1	0.3	1.8	37.4	32.0	5.5	96.3	38.6	57.7	26.41	44.85	5.84	1.58	0.46	2.83	27.99	45.31	8.67	72.01	54.69	91.33
10	Chittaurgarh	T	1484.2	761.3	722.9	615.2	420.9	194.3	112.5	5.1	107.4	727.7	426.1	301.7	756.4	335.2	421.3	41.45	55.29	26.87	7.58	0.68	14.85	49.03	55.97	41.73	50.97	44.03	58.27
		R	1252.6	639.3	613.3	547.3	361.2	186.1	109.7	4.9	104.8	657.0	366.0	291.0	595.6	273.3	322.3	43.69	56.49	30.35	8.76	0.76	17.09	52.45	57.25	47.45	47.55	42.75	52.55
		U	231.6	122.0	109.6	67.9	59.8	8.1	2.8	0.3	2.5	70.8	60.1	10.7	160.9	61.9	99.0	29.32	49.02	7.41	1.22	0.23	2.32	30.55	49.25	9.73	69.45	50.74	90.27
11	Churu	T	1543.2	796.7	746.5	463.0	368.7	94.3	132.2	7.5	124.8	595.2	376.2	219.1	948.0	420.6	527.4	30.00	46.27	12.63	8.57	0.94	16.71	38.57	47.21	29.35	61.43	52.79	70.65
		R	1097.2	565.0	532.1	355.1	267.3	87.8	127.1	6.7	120.5	482.2	273.9	208.3	614.9	291.1	323.8	32.37	47.30	16.51	11.59	1.18	22.64	43.95	48.48	39.14	56.05	51.52	60.86
		U	446.0	231.7	214.3	107.9	101.4	6.5	5.1	0.8	4.3	113.0	102.2	10.8	333.0	129.5	203.6	24.18	43.77	3.01	1.15	0.35	2.01	25.33	44.12	5.03	74.67	55.88	94.97
12	Dausa	T	INCLUDED IN JAIPUR DISTRICT																										
		R																											
		U																											
13	Dhaulpur	T	749.5	417.5	332.0	205.9	198.7	7.3	15.8	1.1	14.7	221.7	199.8	21.9	527.8	217.7	310.1	27.43	47.59	2.19	2.10	0.27	4.41	29.58	47.85	6.61	70.42	52.15	93.39
		R	620.7	347.5	273.2	173.8	167.7	6.1	15.6	1.1	14.5	189.4	168.7	20.6	431.3	178.8	252.5	28.00	48.25	2.24	2.51	0.30	5.32	30.51	48.56	7.56	69.49	51.44	92.44
		U	128.8	70.0	58.9	32.2	31.0	1.2	0.2	0.1	0.1	32.3	31.0	1.3	96.5	38.9	57.6	24.95	44.29	1.98	0.15	0.08	0.22	25.10	44.37	2.20	74.90	55.63	97.80
14	Dungarpur	T	874.5	438.3	436.2	264.5	219.5	45.0	126.0	5.4	120.6	390.5	224.9	165.6	484.0	213.4	270.6	30.25	50.09	10.31	14.41	1.23	27.66	44.66	51.32	37.97	55.34	48.68	62.03
		R	810.7	404.7	406.0	247.5	204.2	43.3	125.0	5.2	119.8	372.4	209.4	163.1	438.3	195.3	243.0	30.52	50.45	10.66	15.42	1.28	29.51	45.94	51.73	40.17	54.06	48.27	59.83
		U	63.8	33.6	30.2	17.1	15.4	1.7	1.0	0.2	0.8	18.1	15.6	2.5	45.7	18.1	27.7	26.72	45.69	5.58	1.63	0.60	2.78	28.35	46.29	8.36	71.65	53.71	91.64

T-Total R-Rural U- Urban P-Persons M- Males F-Females

S. No.	Districts		Total Population (000 No.)			Working Population (000 No.)									Non Workers (000 No.)			%age of Workers and Non Workers to Total Male Female Pop.											
						Main Workers			Marginal Workers			Total Working Population (Main+Marginal)						Main Workers			Marginal Workers			Total Working Population (Main+Marginal)			Non Workers		
			Persons	Male	Female	P	M	F	P	M	F	P	M	F	P	M	F	P	M	F	P	M	F	P	M	F	P	M	F
1	2		3	4	5	6	7	8	9	10	11	12	13	14	15	16	17	18	19	20	21	22	23	24	25	26	27	28	29
15	Ganganagar	T	2622.8	1397.1	1225.6	790.8	725.9	64.9	185.9	6.8	179.1	976.8	732.7	244.0	1646.0	664.4	981.6	30.15	51.96	5.30	7.09	0.49	14.61	37.24	52.45	19.91	62.76	47.55	80.09
		R	2070.7	1099.5	971.2	636.9	579.9	57.0	183.4	6.3	177.1	820.4	586.2	234.2	1250.3	513.3	737.0	30.76	52.74	5.87	8.86	0.57	18.24	39.62	53.32	24.11	60.38	46.68	75.89
		U	552.1	297.6	254.5	153.9	146.0	7.9	2.5	0.5	2.0	156.4	146.5	9.9	395.7	151.1	244.6	27.87	49.06	3.09	0.45	0.17	0.79	28.33	49.23	3.87	71.67	50.77	96.13
16	Hanumangarh	T, R, U	INCLUDED IN GANGANAGAR DISTRICT																										
17	Jaipur	T	4722.6	2496.8	2225.8	1420.5	1159.2	261.3	194.6	10.6	184.0	1615.0	1169.7	445.3	3107.5	1327.1	1780.5	30.08	46.43	11.74	4.12	0.42	8.27	34.20	46.85	20.01	65.80	53.15	79.99
		R	2855.9	1500.4	1355.5	902.4	689.2	213.2	185.2	9.0	176.2	1087.6	698.2	389.4	1768.3	802.2	966.1	31.60	45.93	15.73	6.48	0.60	13.00	38.08	46.53	28.73	61.92	53.47	71.27
		U	1866.6	996.4	870.3	518.0	470.0	48.1	9.4	1.6	7.8	527.4	471.5	55.9	1339.2	524.8	814.4	27.75	47.17	5.53	0.50	0.16	0.89	28.25	47.33	6.42	71.75	52.67	93.58
18	Jaisalmer	T	344.5	190.7	153.8	101.6	92.1	9.4	25.4	3.4	22.0	127.0	95.5	31.5	217.6	95.2	122.4	29.48	48.32	6.13	7.37	1.76	14.33	36.85	50.08	20.45	63.15	49.92	79.55
		R	290.9	160.3	130.6	86.0	77.4	8.7	24.9	3.3	21.6	111.0	80.7	30.3	179.9	79.6	100.3	29.58	48.28	6.63	8.57	2.07	16.56	38.15	50.34	23.18	61.85	49.66	76.82
		U	53.6	30.4	23.2	15.5	14.8	0.8	0.5	0.0	0.4	16.0	14.8	1.2	37.6	15.6	22.0	28.97	48.56	3.31	0.85	0.13	1.78	29.81	48.70	5.09	70.19	51.30	94.91
19	Jalor	T	1142.6	588.5	554.1	365.5	289.2	76.3	105.8	7.2	98.6	471.3	296.4	174.9	671.3	292.0	379.2	31.99	49.14	13.77	9.26	1.23	17.79	41.25	50.37	31.56	58.75	49.63	68.44
		R	1059.4	544.2	515.1	343.8	269.5	74.3	103.4	7.1	96.3	447.2	276.6	170.6	612.2	267.7	344.5	32.46	49.52	14.43	9.76	1.30	18.69	42.21	50.82	33.13	57.79	49.18	66.87
		U	83.2	44.2	39.0	21.6	19.7	2.0	2.4	0.2	2.3	24.1	19.9	4.2	59.1	24.4	34.7	26.01	44.51	5.02	2.94	0.38	5.85	28.95	44.90	10.86	71.05	55.10	89.14
20	Jhalawar	T	957.0	498.9	458.0	366.0	267.4	98.6	52.1	2.7	49.4	418.1	270.1	148.0	538.9	228.9	310.0	38.25	53.59	21.53	5.44	0.54	10.78	43.69	54.13	32.32	56.31	45.87	67.68
		R	806.0	419.7	386.4	325.1	230.8	94.3	50.2	2.5	47.8	375.3	233.2	142.1	430.7	186.4	244.3	40.33	54.99	24.41	6.23	0.59	12.36	46.56	55.58	36.77	53.44	44.42	63.23
		U	151.0	79.3	71.7	40.9	36.5	4.3	1.9	0.2	1.6	42.8	36.8	6.0	108.2	42.4	65.7	27.12	46.18	6.04	1.23	0.30	2.26	28.35	46.48	8.31	71.65	53.52	91.69
21	Jhunjhunun	T	1582.4	819.4	763.0	386.3	338.5	47.6	142.6	11.7	131.0	528.9	350.3	178.6	1053.5	469.2	584.4	24.41	41.32	6.24	9.01	1.42	17.17	33.42	42.75	23.41	66.58	57.25	76.59
		R	1257.4	647.3	610.0	313.6	270.1	43.5	137.4	10.9	126.5	451.0	281.1	170.0	806.4	366.3	440.1	24.94	41.73	7.13	10.93	1.69	20.73	35.87	43.42	27.86	64.13	56.58	72.14
		U	325.0	172.1	152.9	72.6	68.5	4.1	5.2	0.7	4.5	77.9	69.2	8.6	247.2	102.9	144.3	22.35	39.81	2.70	1.61	0.42	2.94	23.96	40.23	5.64	76.04	59.77	94.36
22	Jodhpur	T	2153.5	1138.5	1014.9	660.6	538.1	122.5	125.2	7.8	117.3	785.8	545.9	239.9	1367.7	592.6	775.1	30.68	47.26	12.07	5.81	0.69	11.56	36.49	47.95	23.63	63.51	52.05	76.37
		R	1388.9	725.8	663.1	447.4	342.7	104.7	121.2	7.4	113.8	568.6	350.1	218.4	820.4	375.7	444.7	32.21	47.21	15.79	8.72	1.02	17.15	40.93	48.24	32.94	59.07	51.76	67.06
		U	764.6	412.7	351.8	213.2	195.4	17.9	4.0	0.4	3.6	217.2	195.8	21.4	547.3	216.9	330.4	27.89	47.34	5.08	0.52	0.10	1.02	28.41	47.44	6.09	71.59	52.56	93.91
23	Karauli	T, R, U	INCLUDED IN SAWAI MADHOPUR DISTRICT																										
24	Kota	T	2030.8	1076.2	954.6	637.8	525.6	112.3	97.5	5.5	92.0	735.3	531.1	204.2	1295.5	545.1	750.4	31.41	48.84	11.76	4.80	0.51	9.63	36.21	49.35	21.39	63.79	50.65	78.61
		R	1291.0	68[illegible].1	609.9	430.1	340.7	89.4	91.9	4.8	87.1	522.0	345.6	176.5	769.0	335.6	433.4	33.32	50.02	14.66	7.12	0.71	14.28	40.44	50.73	28.94	59.56	49.27	71.06
		U	739.8	395.1	344.8	207.7	184.8	22.9	5.5	0.6	4.9	213.2	185.5	27.8	526.6	209.6	317.0	28.08	46.79	6.63	0.75	0.16	1.42	28.82	46.95	8.05	71.18	53.05	91.95
25	Nagaur	T	2144.8	1104.6	1040.2	717.1	523.6	193.5	135.3	8.9	126.3	852.4	532.6	319.8	1292.4	572.0	720.4	33.43	47.40	18.60	6.31	0.81	12.14	39.74	48.21	30.74	60.26	51.79	69.26
		R	1802.2	924.4	877.7	628.7	442.7	186.[illegible]	131.0	8.5	122.6	759.8	451.1	308.6	1042.4	473.3	569.1	34.89	47.88	21.20	7.27	0.91	13.96	42.16	48.80	35.16	57.84	51.20	64.84
		U	342.6	180.1	162.5	88.4	81.0	7.4	4.2	0.5	3.8	92.6	81.4	11.2	250.0	98.7	151.3	25.79	44.94	4.56	1.24	0.27	2.31	27.03	45.21	6.87	72.97	54.79	93.13
26	Pali	T	1486.4	759.8	726.6	468.7	362.2	106.4	98.2	4.5	93.7	566.9	366.8	200.2	919.5	393.1	526.5	31.53	47.67	14.65	6.61	0.60	12.90	38.14	48.27	27.55	61.86	51.73	72.45
		R	1163.1	589.9	573.2	377.7	281.2	96.5	91.8	4.1	87.7	469.5	285.3	184.3	693.5	304.6	389.0	32.48	47.67	16.84	7.89	0.69	15.30	40.37	48.37	32.14	59.63	51.63	67.86
		U	323.3	170.0	153.4	90.9	81.0	9.9	6.4	0.4	6.0	97.4	81.5	15.9	226.0	88.5	137.5	28.13	47.68	6.46	1.98	0.26	3.90	30.11	47.94	10.36	69.89	52.06	89.64
27	Rajsamand	T, R, U	INCLUDED IN UDAIPUR DISTRICT																										
28	Sawai Madhopur	T	1963.2	1053.8	904.5	592.1	492.0	100.2	161.9	7.2	154.7	754.0	499.2	254.8	1209.2	559.6	649.6	30.16	46.47	11.07	8.25	0.68	17.10	38.41	47.15	28.17	61.59	52.85	71.83
		R	1672.0	902.7	769.3	517.8	424.3	93.5	157.4	6.9	150.5	675.2	431.2	244.0	996.8	471.5	525.2	30.97	47.00	12.15	9.41	0.76	19.57	40.38	47.77	31.72	59.62	52.23	68.28
		U	291.3	155.1	135.2	74.3	67.7	6.7	4.5	0.3	4.2	78.8	68.0	10.8	212.5	88.1	124.4	25.52	43.36	4.93	1.54	0.22	3.07	27.06	43.57	8.00	72.94	56.43	92.00
29	Sikar	T	1842.9	947.2	895.7	462.1	399.0	63.1	121.3	7.5	113.7	583.3	406.5	176.8	1259.6	540.7	718.9	25.07	42.12	7.04	6.58	0.80	12.70	31.65	42.92	19.74	68.35	57.08	80.26
		R	1455.4	745.8	709.6	373.4	315.6	57.8	115.6	6.7	108.9	489.0	322.3	166.7	966.4	423.5	542.9	25.66	42.32	8.15	7.94	0.89	15.35	33.60	43.21	23.50	66.40	56.79	76.50
		U	387.5	201.5	186.1	88.6	83.4	5.3	5.7	0.9	4.8	94.3	84.2	10.1	293.2	117.2	176.0	22.87	41.38	2.83	1.47	0.44	2.59	24.34	41.82	5.41	75.66	58.18	94.59
30	Sirohi	T	654.0	335.5	318.5	204.4	165.6	38.3	46.7	3.3	43.3	251.1	168.9	82.2	403.0	166.6	236.3	31.25	49.34	12.19	7.14	1.00	13.61	38.39	50.34	25.80	61.61	49.66	74.20
		R	526.4	267.9	258.5	169.5	133.4	36.1	45.1	3.1	42.0	214.6	136.5	78.1	311.8	131.4	180.4	32.19	49.78	13.95	8.58	1.16	16.26	40.76	50.94	30.22	59.24	49.06	69.78
		U	127.6	67.6	60.0	34.9	32.2	2.3	1.5	0.2	1.3	36.5	32.4	4.1	91.1	35.2	55.9	27.38	47.60	4.60	1.21	0.35	2.18	28.59	47.95	6.78	71.41	52.05	93.22
31	Tonk	T	975.0	506.9	468.1	349.8	251.7	98.0	55.2	2.9	52.3	405.0	254.6	150.4	570.0	252.3	317.7	35.87	49.66	20.94	5.66	0.57	11.18	41.54	50.23	32.12	58.46	49.77	67.88
		R	784.6	407.4	377.2	295.7	206.3	89.4	51.6	2.6	49.0	347.3	209.0	138.4	437.3	198.5	238.8	37.69	50.65	23.69	6.58	0.64	12.99	44.27	51.29	36.68	55.73	48.71	63.32
		U	190.4	99.5	90.9	54.1	45.4	8.7	3.6	0.3	3.3	57.7	45.7	12.0	132.8	53.8	78.9	28.39	45.61	9.55	1.89	0.28	3.64	30.28	45.89	13.19	69.72	54.11	86.81
32	Udaipur	T	2889.3	1470.0	1419.3	954.0	766.9	187.0	296.6	13.9	282.7	1250.6	780.9	469.7	1638.7	689.2	949.6	33.02	52.17	13.18	10.27	0.95	19.92	43.28	53.12	33.09	56.72	46.88	66.91
		R	2395.3	1208.8	1186.5	808.9	639.7	169.2	290.1	13.0	277.1	1099.0	652.7	446.3	1296.3	556.1	740.2	33.77	52.92	14.26	12.11	1.08	23.35	45.88	54.00	37.61	54.12	46.00	62.39
		U	494.0	261.3	232.8	145.0	127.2	17.3	6.5	0.9	5.6	151.5	128.2	23.4	342.5	133.1	209.4	29.36	48.71	7.64	1.32	0.35	2.41	30.68	49.06	10.05	69.32	50.94	89.95
	RAJASTHAN	T	44006	23043	20963	13915	11182	27[illegible]3	3189	178	3011	17104	11360	5744	26902	11683	15219	31.62	48.53	13.04	7.25	0.77	14.36	38.87	49.30	27.40	61.13	50.70	72.60
		R	33939	17687	16252	11179	8699	2480	3089	16[illegible]	2924	14268	8864	5404	19671	8822	10848	32.94	49.18	15.26	9.10	0.94	17.99	42.04	50.12	33.25	57.96	49.88	66.75
		U	10067	5356	4711	2736	2483	253	100	12	87	2836	2496	340	7231	2860	4371	27.18	46.36	5.36	0.99	0.24	1.86	28.17	46.60	7.22	71.83	53.40	92.78

T-Total R-Rural U- Urban P-Persons M- Males F-Females

Source: Computed from data given in Primary Census Abstract, Rajasthan, Series -21, Census of India, 1991.

GENERAL ANNEX XXVI

DISTRICT-WISE DISTRIBUTION OF RURAL & URBAN WORKING POPULATION : RAJASTHAN (2001)

S. No.	*District Total*	*Total Working Population (Main + Marginal)*			
		Total	*Rural*		*Urban*
			No.	*% Share to Total Working Pop.*	
1	*2*	*3*	*4*		*5*
1	Ajmer	856,979	598,197	69.80	258,782
2	Alwar	1,460,458	1,322,161	90.53	138,297
3	Banswara	713,237	681,654	95.57	31,583
4	Baran	438,612	384,346	87.63	54,266
5	Barmer	919,315	877,353	95.44	41,962
6	Bharatpur	852,513	738,349	86.61	114,164
7	Bhilwara	938,160	799,489	85.22	138,671
8	Bikaner	661,906	491,088	74.19	170,818
9	Bundi	457,218	403,034	88.15	54,184
10	Chittaurgarh	931,389	836,812	89.85	94,577
11	Churu	855,294	707,323	82.70	147,971
12	Dausa	543,817	506,764	93.19	37,053
13	Dhaulpur	430,640	375,898	87.29	54,742
14	Dungarpur	535,557	509,920	95.21	25,637
15	Ganganagar	719,907	580,775	80.67	139,132
16	Hanumangarh	628,090	541,406	86.20	86,684
17	Jaipur	1,863,046	1,075,896	57.75	787,150
18	Jaisalmer	211,804	186,828	88.21	24,976
19	Jalor	728,595	694,072	95.26	34,523
20	Jhalawar	555,848	506,686	91.16	49,162
21	Jhunjhunun	761,821	663,779	87.13	98,042
22	Jodhpur	1,105,621	820,746	74.23	284,875
23	Karauli	480,068	432,156	90.02	47,912
24	Kota	541,063	299,580	55.37	241,483
25	Nagaur	1,126,862	998,297	88.59	128,565
26	Pali	721,151	600,308	83.24	120,843
27	Rajsamand	401,626	363,132	90.42	38,494
28	Sawai Madhopur	469,082	412,065	87.84	57,017
29	Sikar	890,268	767,429	86.20	122,839
30	Sirohi	346,490	300,311	86.67	46,179
31	Tonk	533,105	454,568	85.27	78,537
32	Udaipur	1,101,715	947,287	85.98	154,428
	Rajasthan State	**23,781,257**	**19,877,709**	**83.59**	**3,903,548**

Source: Complied from Census of India 2001, Rajasthan, Paper-3 of 2001, Directorate of Census Operation, Jaipur

GENERAL ANNEX XXVII

DISTRICT-WISE DETAILES OF BPL FAMILIES: RAJASTHAN

S. No.	District	Detailes of BPL Families																	
		Total Rural Families	No. of Familes Below Poverty	Selected Families				Details of Families As Per Occupation						Other	Out of Total Families				
				S.C.	S.T.	Back Ward	Other	Self Employment							Widow	Handi-capped	Ceiling Surplus Land	Minority	Bonded Labour
								Agricultural Worker	Other Rural	Small Farmer	Marginal Farmer	Under Non-Agri.	Rural Artisians						
1	2	3	4	5	6	7	8	9	10	11	12	13	14	15	16	17	18	19	20
1	Ajmer	237514	62932	16064	4003	33782	9083	26129	15204	4379	9086	2778	604	4752	4129	590	475	2268	—
2	Alwar	358627	78911	27168	6503	21120	24120	20395	14623	11110	20961	3592	2281	5949	5013	350	335	7193	20
3	Banswara	232657	169792	8875	149242	4914	6761	39612	12825	37741	64489	8939	750	5436	3436	917	11458	713	—
4	Baran	140172	45684	12934	13177	15805	3768	15420	9552	5249	10497	1944	539	2483	1382	360	1215	1087	136
5	Barmer	273750	78603	20082	9050	16745	32726	8471	4574	19768	39802	1925	613	3450	3771	261	557	6935	8
6	Bharatpur	249257	45869	17200	1327	12405	14937	15157	12206	3317	9332	1866	934	3057	3001	193	37	4521	3
7	Bhilwara	301451	104663	27253	21727	44025	11658	28922	19352	31149	33080	3258	920	6618	3733	46	5793	1450	1464
8	Bikaner	151505	55811	19426	621	10754	25010	15118	5318	9089	18886	2614	2737	2049	1602	225	897	2001	—
9	Bundi	121938	43918	12958	9993	17015	3952	9578	8874	6839	11644	3240	1640	2103	1146	436	346	662	—
10	Chittaurgarh	271184	133253	28411	48016	36650	20176	34658	17225	28020	39990	7183	1911	4266	4515	683	1926	1557	5459
11	Churu	224261	64191	30646	402	11499	21644	22021	6252	13568	16409	2187	1343	2411	3271	929	362	1321	158
12	Dausa	172585	40345	12983	9818	13016	4528	11803	8659	5744	10584	1602	898	1055	2385	—	2741	706	—
13	Dhaulpur	89060	31047	9697	1815	13899	5636	11715	7250	2580	5151	1648	232	2471	1481	10	2188	303	7840
14	Dungarpur	182900	130459	7249	106457	6380	10373	46600	14179	18795	36536	8896	1862	3591	4137	1681	11289	166	1938
15	Ganganagar	189467	40281	26023	63	8058	6137	25033	6997	2191	2105	1132	719	2104	1970	226	307	195	917
16	Hanumangarh	173138	37878	20099	151	8671	8957	23295	3509	5904	3472	596	370	732	1595	161	6	730	1
17	Jaipur	396800	61631	18671	9321	21108	13431	18521	24483	3575	3285	2390	1328	8849	1116	134	2433	5103	7
18	Jaisalmer	72217	18857	3332	1607	3367	10551	7194	6737	1235	1021	1241	148	1281	1396	160	773	5582	—
19	Jalore	179058	67150	21889	10664	20224	14373	16857	11375	17457	13326	3077	1633	3425	2416	353	959	1725	—
20	Jhalawar	166203	55190	16203	9671	18071	11245	19961	8607	8191	15480	1190	479	1282	2687	149	10	1766	1
21	Jhunjhunun	238401	25202	10675	1034	7430	6063	8592	7005	2066	4818	471	541	1709	2190	103	79	724	13
22	Jodhpur	255480	34744	10492	3577	7596	13079	7205	5560	9376	7781	1425	496	2901	2205	367	236	1059	86
23	Karauli	148473	60599	18520	14707	16906	10466	12530	13110	12085	15667	3324	567	3316	589	1	4223	1293	—
24	Kota	117934	37867	13134	4921	15682	4130	10945	16221	2377	2081	1650	580	4013	485	20	141	1805	45
25	Nagaur	339825	56157	27820	297	13597	15058	12861	8357	7221	20871	2584	1571	4699	2801	93	16	1588	110
26	Pali	268280	64414	22443	10439	23979	7553	20124	19317	6845	9201	3212	984	4731	4210	432	1178	1208	160
27	Rajsamand	162062	57961	10037	15355	24055	8514	15618	8677	6520	19399	3239	989	3598	2794	262	27	297	1
28	Sawai Madhopur	138336	51840	15306	9666	19002	7866	10425	8790	13419	12065	2061	1043	4037	2121	343	117	2637	—
29	Sikar	248931	28460	12281	1636	6937	7606	7267	5431	4231	7722	1142	422	2245	2328	105	19	646	—
30	Sirohi	116265	36060	10176	17940	5894	2050	7304	6932	5028	13106	1142	298	2250	705	20	679	419	—
31	Tonk	166625	54876	16316	10857	19404	8299	11102	9884	12046	13651	2916	1315	3962	1808	629	107	1431	—
32	Udaipur	384185	222915	13578	157539	22409	29388	50842	34459	38482	72546	12563	4233	9790	6445	1571	459	868	—
	Total	**6768541**	**2097560**	**537941**	**661596**	**520399**	**379138**	**591275**	**361544**	**355597**	**564044**	**97027**	**34980**	**114615**	**82863**	**11810**	**51388**	**59959**	**18367**

Source: BPL Census Survey, 1997, GcR, Jaipur.

ANNEX-1.1

PANCHAYAT SAMITIES OF RAJASTHAN: CODE NUMBERS

P. Code*	Census Code	PANCHAYAT SAMITIES NAME
		AJMER DISTRICT
1	2102	ARAIN
2	2107	BHINAY
3	2105	JAWAJA
4	2108	KEKRI
5	2101	KISHANGARH
6	2106	MASOODA
7	2104	PISANGAN
8	2103	SRINAGAR
		ALWAR
9	0609	BANSURE
10	0601	BEHROR
11	0614	KATHUMAR
12	0604	KISHANGARH BAS
13	0605	KOTKASIM
14	0613	LACHHMANGARH
15	0603	MANDAWAR
16	0602	NIMRANA
17	0611	RAJGARH
18	0607	RAMGARH
19	0612	RENI
20	0610	THANAGAZI
21	0606	TIJARA
22	0608	UMREN
		BANSWARA
23	2805	ANANDPURI
24	2806	BAGIDORA
25	2804	GARHI
26	2801	GHATOL
27	2808	KUSHALGARH
28	2802	PEEPALKHOONT
29	2807	SAJJANGARH
30	2803	TALWARA
		BARAN
31	3101	ANTA
32	3105	ATRU
33	3102	BARAN
34	3107	CHHABRA
35	3106	CHHIPABAROD
36	3103	KISHANGANJ
37	3104	SHAHBAD
		BARMER
38	1703	BALOTRA
39	1706	BARMER
40	1702	BAYTOO
41	1707	CHOHTAN
42	1708	DHORIMANNA
43	1701	SHEO
44	1705	SINDHARI
45	1704	SIWANA
		BHARATPUR
46	0708	BAYANA
47	0703	DEEG
48	0701	KAMAN
49	0704	KUMHER
50	0706	NADBAI
51	0702	NAGAR PAHARI
52	0709	RUPBAS
53	0705	SEWAR
54	0707	WEIR
		BHILWARA
55	2401	ASIND
56	2404	BANERA
57	2402	HURDA
58	2410	JAHAZPUR
59	2409	KOTRI
60	2405	MANDAL
61	2411	MANDALGARH
62	2406	RAIPUR
63	2407	SAHARA
64	2403	SHAHPURA
65	2408	SUWANA
		BIKANER
66	0301	BIKANER
67	0405	DUNGARGARH #
68	0303	KOLAYAT
69	0302	LUNKARANSAR
70	0304	NOKHA
		BUNDI
71	2301	HINDOLI
72	2303	KESHORAIPATAN
73	2302	NAINWA
74	2304	TALERA
		CHITTAURGARH
75	2914	ARNOD
76	2912	BARI SADRI
77	2903	BEGUN
78	2909	BHADESAR
79	2904	BHAINSRORGARH
80	2907	BHOPALSAGAR
81	2911	CHHOTI SADRI
82	2905	CHITTAURGARH
83	2908	DUNGLA
84	2902	GANGRAR
85	2906	KAPASAN
86	2910	NIMBAHERA
87	2913	PRATAPGARH
88	2901	RASHMI
		CHURU
89	0404	CHURU
90	0402	RAJGARH
91	0406	RATANGARH
92	0403	SARDARSHAHAR
93	0407	SUJANGARH
94	0401	TARANAGAR
		DAUSA
95	1101	BANDIKUI
96	1104	DAUSA
97	1105	LALSOT
98	1102	MAHWA
99	1103	SIKRAI
		DHAULPUR
100	0802	BARI
101	0801	BASERI
102	0803	DHAULPUR
103	0804	RAJAKHERA
		DUNGARPUR
104	2703	ASPUR
105	2701	BICHHIWARA
106	2702	DUNGARPUR
107	2704	SAGWARA
108	2705	SIMALWARA
		GANGANAGAR
109	0106	ANUPGARH
110	0102	GANGANAGAR
111	0101	KARANPUR
112	0104	PADAMPUR
113	0105	RAISINGHNAGAR
114	0103	SADULSHAHAR
115	0107	SURATGARH
		HANUMANGARH
116	0203	BHADRA
117	0201	HANUMANGARH
118	0202	NOHAR
		JAIPUR
119	1206	AMBER
120	1208	BASSI
121	1213	CHAKSU
122	1210	DUDU
123	1204	GOVINDGARH
124	1207	JAMWA RAMGARH
125	1209	JHOTWARA
126	1201	KOTPUTLI
127	1211	PHAGI
128	1205	SAMBHAR
129	1212	SANGANER
130	1203	SHAHPURA
131	1202	VIRATNAGAR
		JAISALMER
132	1601	JAISALMER
133	1602	SAM
134	1603	SANKRA
		JALOR
135	1801	AHORE
136	1804	BHINMAL
137	1802	JALOR
138	1807	JASWANTPURA
139	1806	RANIWARA
140	1805	SANCHORE
141	1803	SAYLA
		JHALAWAR
142	3204	BAKANI
143	3206	DAG
144	3202	JHALRAPATAN
145	3201	KHANPUR
146	3203	MANOHARTHANA
147	3205	PIRAWA
		JHUNJHUNUN
148	0502	ALSISAR
149	0505	BUHANA
150	0503	CHIRAWA
151	0501	JHUNJHUNUN
152	0506	KHETRI
153	0507	NAWALGARH
154	0504	SURAJGARH
155	0508	UDAIPURWATI
		JODHPUR
156	1504	BALESAR
157	1501	BAP
158	1506	BHOPALGARH
159	1509	BILARA
160	1508	LUNI
161	1507	MANDOR
162	1505	OSIAN
163	1502	PHALODI
164	1503	SHERGARH
		KARAULI
165	0903	HINDAUN
166	0904	KARAULI
167	0901	NADOTI
168	0905	SAPOTRA
169	0902	TODABHIM
		KOTA
170	3004	CHECHAT
171	3001	ITAWA
172	3003	LADPURA
173	3005	SANGOD
174	3002	SULTANPUR
		NAGAUR
175	1408	DEGANA
176	1402	DIDWANA
177	1405	JAYAL
178	1403	KUCHAMAN
179	1401	LADNU
180	1404	MAKRANA
181	1409	MERTA
182	1407	MUNDWA
183	1406	NAGAUR
184	1411	PARBATSAR
185	1410	RIYAN
		PALI
186	2009	BALI
187	2010	DESURI
188	2001	JAITARAN
189	2006	KHARCHI / MARWAR JUN.
190	2005	PALI
191	2002	RAIPUR
192	2007	RANI STATION
193	2004	ROHAT
194	2003	SOJAT
195	2008	SUMERPUR
		RAJSAMAND
196	2503	AMET
197	2501	BHIM
198	2502	DEOGARH
199	2505	KHAMNOR
200	2504	KUMBHALGARH
201	2507	RAILMAGRA
202	2506	RAJSAMAND
		SAWAI MADHOPUR
203	1001	BAMANWAS
204	1003	BONLI
205	1002	GANGAPUR
206	1005	KHANDAR
207	1004	SAWAI MADHOPUR
		SIKAR
208	1304	DANTA RAMGARH
209	1303	DHOND
210	1301	FATEHPUR
211	1306	KHANDELA
212	1302	LACHHMANGARH
213	1307	NEEM KA THANA
214	1305	PIPRALI
215	1308	SRI MADHOPUR
		SIROHI
216	1904	ABU ROAD
217	1905	PINDWARA
218	1903	REODAR
219	1901	SHEOGANJ
220	1902	SIROHI
		TONK
221	2205	DEOLI
222	2201	MALPURA
223	2203	NIWAI
224	2204	TODARAISINGH
225	2202	TONK
226	2206	UNIARA
		UDAIPUR
227	2602	BARGAON
228	2604	BHINDER
229	2611	DHARIAWAD
230	2605	GIRWA
231	2601	GOGUNDA
232	2607	JHADOL
233	2608	KHERWARA
234	2606	KOTRA
235	2603	MAVLI
236	2610	SALUMBAR
237	2609	SARADA

*Note:** Panchayat samiti code number used in the research, # Dungargarh PS shifted from Churu to Bikaner district on 1st April 2001.

ANNEX-2.1

RANKING OF PSS BY TOTAL RURAL POPULATION: RAJASTHAN, 2001

(*Descending Order*)

RANK	PANCHAYAT SAMITIES P. CODE	NAME	TOTAL RURAL POP.
1	2	3	4
	VERY HIGH (>=160,000)		
1	117	**HANUMANGARH**	**628123**
2	162	**OSIAN**	**422181**
3	109	**ANUPGARH**	**417746**
4	66	**BIKANER**	**374802**
5	118	**NOHAR**	**365762**
6	140	**SANCHORE**	**342120**
7	213	**NEEM KA THANA**	**317049**
8	176	**DIDWANA**	**285031**
9	70	**NOKHA**	**279343**
10	123	**GOVINDGARH**	**275780**
11	122	**DUDU**	**272517**
12	96	**DAUSA**	**271907**
13	178	**KUCHAMAN**	**268146**
14	90	**RAJGARH**	**267403**
15	95	**BANDIKUI**	**267016**
16	38	**BALOTRA**	**265596**
17	102	**DHAULPUR**	**262456**
18	165	**HINDAUN**	**262403**
19	208	**DANTA RAMGARH**	**262183**
20	119	**AMBER**	**262029**
21	74	**TALERA**	**258916**
22	233	**KHERWARA**	**254301**
23	93	**SUJANGARH**	**253207**
24	97	**LALSOT**	**251370**
25	42	**DHORIMANNA**	**250929**
26	124	**JAMWA RAMGARH**	**250132**
27	168	**SIMALWARA**	**241099**
28	39	**BARMER**	**238075**
29	25	**GARHI**	**237521**
30	44	**SINDHARI**	**236545**
31	7	**PISANGAN**	**236459**
32	51	**NAGAR PAHARI**	**236329**
33	105	**BICHHIWARA**	**236114**
34	155	**UDAIPURWATI**	**235280**
35	168	**SAPOTRA**	**232513**
36	26	**GHATOL**	**230344**
37	163	**PHALODI**	**229892**
38	120	**BASSI**	**229639**
39	160	**LUNI**	**229097**
40	126	**KOTPUTLI**	**228470**
41	230	**GIRWA**	**227623**
42	21	**TIJARA**	**226974**
43	14	**LACHHMANGARH**	**225836**
44	41	**CHOHTAN**	**225754**
45	177	**JAYAL**	**224944**
46	183	**NAGAUR**	**224815**
47	92	**SARDARSHAHAR**	**222979**
48	166	**KARAULI**	**222621**
49	22	**UMREN**	**221794**
50	116	**BHADRA**	**220582**
51	18	**RAMGARH**	**220219**
52	211	**KHANDELA**	**218560**
53	153	**NAWALGARH**	**217636**
54	69	**LUNKARANSAR**	**217341**
55	207	**SAWAI MADHOPUR**	**215810**
56	152	**KHETRI**	**214474**
57	9	**BANSURE**	**214351**
58	30	**TALWARA**	**213727**
59	45	**SIWANA**	**213648**
60	115	**SURATGARH**	**213384**
61	237	**SARADA**	**212181**
62	48	**KAMAN**	**212139**
63	99	**SIKRAI**	**211779**
64	11	**KATHUMAR**	**211689**
65	52	**RUPBAS**	**211147**
65	141	**SAYLA**	**211147**
67	215	**SRI MADHOPUR**	**210980**
68	40	**BAYTOO**	**210345**
69	209	**DHOND**	**209919**
70	204	**BONLI**	**209833**
71	128	**SAMBHAR**	**209528**
72	68	**KOLAYAT**	**207749**
73	131	**VIRATNAGAR**	**206414**
74	214	**PIPRALI**	**206064**
75	144	**JHALRAPATAN**	**205868**
76	149	**BUHANA**	**204411**
77	225	**TONK**	**204362**
78	229	**DHARIAWAD**	**203605**
79	158	**BHOPALGARH**	**202321**
80	54	**WEIR**	**202199**
81	228	**BHINDER**	**201832**

RANK	PANCHAYAT SAMITIES P. CODE	NAME	TOTAL RURAL POP.
1	2	3	4
82	101	**BASERI**	**201777**
83	87	**PRATAPGARH**	**201229**
84	61	**MANDALGARH**	**199935**
85	180	**MAKRANA**	**199671**
86	15	**MANDAWAR**	**197582**
87	182	**MUNDWA**	**197532**
88	60	**MANDAL**	**197500**
89	212	**LACHHMANGARH**	**197022**
90	236	**SALUMBAR**	**196614**
91	235	**MAVLI**	**194148**
92	169	**TODABHIM**	**194094**
93	232	**JHADOL**	**193810**
94	210	**FATEHPUR**	**193473**
95	107	**SAGWARA**	**192681**
96	55	**ASIND**	**192346**
97	103	**RAJAKHERA**	**191812**
98	46	**BAYANA**	**191632**
99	175	**DEGANA**	**190085**
100	20	**THANAGAZI**	**189977**
101	71	**HINDOLI**	**189290**
102	188	**JAITARAN**	**186938**
103	184	**PARBATSAR**	**186413**
104	217	**PINDWARA**	**184803**
105	136	**BHINMAL**	**184751**
106	104	**ASPUR**	**184508**
107	186	**BALI**	**183802**
108	234	**KOTRA**	**183504**
109	181	**MERTA**	**183429**
110	67	**DUNGARGARH**	**182819**
111	191	RAIPUR	182004
112	130	SHAHPURA	181498
113	189	MARWAR JUN.	181445
114	159	BILARA	180550
115	185	RIYAN	179629
116	205	GANGAPUR	179209
117	98	MAHWA	179173
118	72	KESHORAIPATAN	178625
119	43	SHEO	178539
120	135	AHORE	177342
121	222	MALPURA	176932
122	24	BAGIDORA	176729
123	151	JHUNJHUNUN	176693
124	110	GANGANAGAR	176517
125	154	SURAJGARH	175820
126	218	REODAR	175344
127	156	BALESAR	174179
128	199	KHAMNOR	172395
129	106	DUNGARPUR	172385
130	147	PIRAWA	171897
131	8	SRINAGAR	170142
132	221	DEOLI	169271
133	82	CHITTAURGARH	167960
134	58	JAHAZPUR	167782
135	53	SEWAR	167641
136	12	KISHANGARH BAS	167495
137	143	DAG	167192
138	134	SANKRA	165376
139	223	NIWAI	165298
140	65	SUWANA	164004
141	139	RANIWARA	163349
142	164	SHERGARH	162656
143	127	PHAGI	161610
144	146	MANOHARTHANA	161425
145	121	CHAKSU	161140
146	50	NADBAI	161111
	HIGH (140,000-160,000)		
147	6	MASOODA	159600
148	91	RATANGARH	158090
149	179	LADNU	158026
150	3	JAWAJA	157901
151	113	RAISINGHNAGAR	157334
152	157	BAP	157290
153	73	NAINWA	156227
154	194	SOJAT	155889
155	171	ITAWA	155646
156	49	KUMHER	155122
157	2	BHINAY	155111
158	47	DEEG	154862
159	5	KISHANGARH	153474
160	145	KHANPUR	153370
161	150	CHIRAWA	152843
162	142	BAKANI	152329

RANK	PANCHAYAT SAMITIES P. CODE	NAME	TOTAL RURAL POP.
1	2	3	4
163	89	CHURU	152178
164	231	GOGUNDA	151575
165	28	PEEPALKHOONT	151273
166	161	MANDOR	151257
167	94	TARANAGAR	151006
168	100	BARI	150595
169	174	SULTANPUR	150587
170	206	KHANDAR	150136
171	203	BAMANWAS	149429
172	64	SHAHPURA	148955
173	31	ANTA	148759
174	59	KOTRI	148702
175	173	SANGOD	146951
176	114	SADULSHAHAR	146629
177	17	RAJGARH	144726
178	172	LADPURA	144691
179	16	NIMRANA	143329
180	148	ALSISAR	141416
181	4	KEKRI	140921
182	202	RAJSAMAND	140520
	MEDIUM (120,000-140,000)		
183	10	BEHROR	139503
184	27	KUSHALGARH	138970
185	133	SAM	138679
186	195	SUMERPUR	137999
187	197	BHIM	137578
188	19	RENI	136491
189	86	NIMBAHERA	135391
190.	36	KISHANGANJ	135218
191	29	SAJJANGARH	134456
192	1	ARAIN	133386
193	226	UNIARA	132509
194	170	CHECHAT	132073
195	137	JALOR	131827
196	200	KUMBHALGARH	131346
197	129	SANGANER	131301
198	138	JASWANTPURA	128410
199	35	CHHIPABAROD	127858
200	132	JAISALMER	127798
201	32	ATRU	127043
202	167	NADOTI	126089
203	220	SIROHI	125589
204	227	BARGAON	123802
205	112	PADAMPUR	121362
	LOW (100,000-120,000)		
206	75	ARNOD	119837
207	13	KOTKASIM	117687
208	216	ABU ROAD	114818
209	23	ANANDPURI	111206
210	201	RAILMAGRA	110435
211	224	TODARAISINGH	110131
212	37	SHAHBAD	108146
213	78	BHADESAR	107393
214	192	RANI STATION	106504
215	56	BANERA	106222
216	33	BARAN	103142
217	111	KARANPUR	103094
218	193	ROHAT	102599
219	187	DESURI	102245
220	77	BEGUN	102011
221	81	CHHOTI SADRI	100067
	VERY LOW (<100,000)		
222	219	SHEOGANJ	99663
223	34	CHHABRA	99472
224	63	SAHARA	98050
225	57	HURDA	91088
226	83	DUNGLA	89975
227	190	PALI	89939
228	125	JHOTWARA	88946
229	76	BARI SADRI	88841
230	84	GANGRAR	88640
231	196	AMET	88162
232	85	KAPASAN	84531
233	62	RAIPUR	84354
234	79	BHAINSRORGARH	80379
235	198	DEOGARH	77865
236	88	RASHMI	75326
237	80	BHOPALSAGAR	72675
RAJASTHAN		**TOTAL**	**43,292,813**
		AVERAGE	**182,670**
		% AGE OF AAPs	**46.41**

BOLD: Equal/Above Average Panchayat Samities (AAPs)
Source: General Annex VII, Col. 5.

ANNEX-2.2

RANKING OF PSS BY PERCENTAGE OF 0-6 POP. TO TOTAL POPULATION: RAJASTHAN, 2001

(Descending Order)

RANK	P. CODE	PANCHAYAT SAMITIES NAME	%
1	2	3	4
	VERY-HIGH (>=22)		
1	48	**KAMAN**	25.1
2	234	**KOTRA**	24.2
3	216	**ABU ROAD**	23.7
3	100	**BARI**	23.7
3	27	**KUSHALGARH**	23.7
6	157	**BAP**	23.6
6	67	**DUNGARGARH**	23.6
6	134	**SANKRA**	23.6
6	43	**SHEO**	23.6
10	42	**DHORIMANNA**	23.4
10	70	**NOKHA**	23.4
12	102	**DHAULPUR**	23.3
12	21	**TIJARA**	23.3
14	163	**PHALODI**	23.2
14	29	**SAJJANGARH**	23.2
16	164	**SHERGARH**	23.1
17	101	**BASERI**	22.9
17	41	**CHOHTAN**	22.9
17	28	**PEEPALKHOON**	22.9
20	68	**KOLAYAT**	22.8
20	103	**RAJAKHERA**	22.8
20	44	**SINDHARI**	22.8
23	136	**BHINMAL**	22.7
23	140	**SANCHORE**	22.7
25	38	**BALOTRA**	22.6
25	133	**SAM**	22.6
25	108	**SIMALWARA**	22.6
28	156	**BALESAR**	22.5
28	40	**BAYTOO**	22.5
28	105	**BICHHIWARA**	22.5
31	39	**BARMER**	22.4
31	229	**DHARIAWAD**	22.4
33	106	**DUNGARPUR**	22.3
33	132	**JAISALMER**	22.3
35	166	**KARAULI**	22.2
35	51	**NAGAR PAHARI**	22.2
37	139	**RANIWARA**	22.1
38	24	**BAGIDORA**	22.0
38	183	**NAGAUR**	22.0
38	92	**SARDARSHAHAR**	22.0
38	141	**SAYLA**	22.0
	HIGH (20-22)		
42	162	**OSIAN**	21.9
42	18	**RAMGARH**	21.9
44	197	**BHIM**	21.8
45	93	**SUJANGARH**	21.7
46	23	**ANANDPURI**	21.6
46	232	**JHADOL**	21.6
48	165	**HINDAUN**	21.5
48	12	**KISHANGARH BAS**	21.5
48	97	**LALSOT**	21.5
48	52	**RUPBAS**	21.5
52	75	**ARNOD**	21.3
52	233	**KHERWARA**	21.3
52	20	**THANAGAZI**	21.3
55	26	**GHATOL**	21.2
55	212	**LACHHMANGARH**	21.2
55	69	**LUNKARANSAR**	21.2
55	217	**PINDWARA**	21.2
55	91	**RATANGARH**	21.2
60	66	**BIKANER**	21.1
60	3	**JAWAJA**	21.1
62	46	**BAYANA**	20.9
62	138	**JASWANTPURA**	20.9
62	45	**SIWANA**	20.9
65	53	**SEWAR**	20.8
65	30	**TALWARA**	20.8
67	96	**DAUSA**	20.7
67	160	**LUNI**	20.7
67	146	**MANOHARTHANA**	20.7
67	218	**REODAR**	20.7
67	193	**ROHAT**	20.7
67	37	**SHAHBAD**	20.7
73	6	**MASOODA**	20.6
73	22	**UMREN**	20.6
73	131	**VIRATNAGAR**	20.6
76	47	**DEEG**	20.5
76	198	**DEOGARH**	20.5
76	168	**SAPOTRA**	20.5
79	121	**CHAKSU**	20.4
79	191	**RAIPUR**	20.4
79	99	**SIKRAI**	20.4
82	205	**GANGAPUR**	20.3
82	124	**JAMWA RAMGARH**	20.3
84	55	**ASIND**	20.2
84	120	**BASSI**	20.2
84	137	**JALOR**	20.2
84	161	**MANDOR**	20.2
88	104	**ASPUR**	20.1
88	9	**BANSURE**	20.1
88	19	**RENI**	20.1
88	169	**TODABHIM**	20.1
88	54	**WEIR**	20.1
93	231	**GOGUNDA**	20.0
93	11	**KATHUMAR**	20.0
93	98	**MAHWA**	20.0
	MEDIUM (18-20)		
96	34	**CHHABRA**	19.9
96	89	**CHURU**	19.9
96	126	**KOTPUTLI**	19.9
96	182	**MUNDWA**	19.9
96	237	**SARAD**	19.9
96	8	**SRINAGAR**	19.9
102	135	**AHORE**	19.8
102	36	**KISHANGANJ**	19.8
102	223	**NIWAI**	19.8
102	87	**PRATAPGARH**	19.8
106	95	BANDIKUI	19.7
106	177	JAYAL	19.7
108	119	AMBER	19.6
108	170	CHECHAT	19.6
108	35	CHHIPABAROD	19.6
108	176	DIDWANA	19.6
108	123	GOVINDGARH	19.6
108	167	NADOTI	19.6
108	236	SALUMBAR	19.6
115	186	BALI	19.5
115	230	GIRWA	19.5
115	71	HINDOLI	19.5
115	211	KHANDELA	19.5
115	7	PISANGAN	19.5
115	17	RAJGARH	19.5
121	79	BHAINSRORGARH	19.4
121	204	BONLI	19.4
121	49	KUMHER	19.4
124	2	BHINAY	19.3
124	130	SHAHPURA	19.3
126	158	BHOPALGARH	19.2
126	25	GARHI	19.2
126	200	KUMBHALGARH	19.2
126	107	SAGWARA	19.2
126	64	SHAHPURA	19.2
126	94	TARANAGAR	19.2
132	206	KHANDAR	19.1
132	50	NADBAI	19.1
132	213	NEEM KA THANA	19.1
132	220	SIROHI	19.1
132	225	TONK	19.1
132	226	UNIARA	19.1
138	142	BAKANI	19.0
138	190	PALI	19.0
140	125	JHOTWARA	18.9
140	5	KISHANGARH	18.9
140	179	LADNU	18.9
140	73	NAINWA	18.9
140	219	SHEOGANJ	18.9
140	74	TALERA	18.9
140	155	UDAIPURWATI	18.9
147	159	BILARA	18.8
147	187	DESURI	18.8
147	152	KHETRI*	18.8
147	127	PHAGI	18.8
147	215	SRI MADHOPUR	18.8
152	122	DUDU	18.7
152	57	HURDA	18.7
152	180	MAKRANA	18.7
152	129	SANGANER	18.7
156	109	ANUPGARH	18.6
156	188	JAITARAN	18.6
156	61	MANDALGARH	18.6
156	128	SAMBHAR	18.6
156	194	SOJAT	18.6
156	195	SUMERPUR	18.6
162	178	KUCHAMAN	18.5
162	184	PARBATSAR	18.5
162	115	SURATGARH	18.5
165	1	ARAIN	18.4
165	208	DANTA RAMGARH	18.4
165	175	DEGANA	18.4
165	221	DEOLI	18.4
165	222	MALPURA	18.4
165	207	SAWAI MADHOPUR	18.4
171	210	FATEHPUR	18.3
171	189	MARWAR JUN.	18.3
171	13	KOTKASIM	18.3
171	60	MANDAL	18.3
171	202	RAJSAMAND	18.3
176	196	AMET	18.2
176	58	JAHAZPUR	18.2
176	4	KEKRI*	18.2
176	15	MANDAWAR	18.2
176	214	PIPRALI	18.2
176	90	RAJGARH	18.2
182	14	LACHHMANGARH	18.1
182	224	TODARAISINGH	18.1
184	148	ALSISAR	18.0
184	56	BANERA	18.0
184	227	BARGAON	18.0
184	209	DHOND	18.0
184	144	JHALRAPATAN	18.0
184	72	KESHORAIPATAN	18.0
184	181	MERTA	18.0
184	118	NOHAR	18.0
184	65	SUWANA	18.0
	LOW (16-18)		
193	173	SANGOD	17.9
194	203	BAMANWAS	17.8
194	172	LADPURA	17.8
196	150	CHIRAWA	17.7
196	199	KHAMNOR*	17.7
196	185	RIYAN	17.7
199	31	ANTA	17.6
199	81	CHHOTI SADRI	17.6
199	59	KOTRI	17.6
199	192	RANI STATION	17.6
203	154	SURAJGARH	17.5
204	62	RAIPUR	17.4
205	153	NAWALGARH	17.3
206	32	ATRU	17.2
206	77	BEGUN	17.2
206	145	KHANPUR	17.2
209	33	BARAN	17.1
209	82	CHITTAURGARH	17.1
209	86	NIMBAHERA	17.1
209	147	PIRAWA	17.1
209	113	RAISINGHNAGAR	17.1
209	174	SULTANPUR	17.1
215	76	BARI SADRI	17.0
215	84	GANGRAR	17.0
215	16	NIMRANA	17.0
218	10	BEHROR	16.9
218	78	BHADESAR	16.9
218	143	DAG	16.9
218	117	HANUMANGARH	16.9
218	171	ITAWA	16.9
218	63	SAHARA	16.9
224	116	BHADRA	16.8
224	228	BHINDER	16.8
224	151	JHUNJHUNUN	16.8
227	149	BUHANA	16.6
227	83	DUNGLA	16.6
229	235	MAVLI	16.4
229	112	PADAMPUR	16.4
231	88	RASHMI	16.3
232	111	KARANPUR	16.0
	VERY-LOW (<16)		
233	110	GANGANAGAR	15.8
233	201	RAILMAGRA	15.8
235	114	SADULSHAHAR	15.6
236	80	BHOPALSAGAR	15.5
237	85	KAPASAN	15.2
		RAJASTHAN	**19.80**
		% AGE OF AAPs	**44.30**

BOLD: Equal/Above Average Panchayat Samities (AAPs)

Source: General Annex VII, Col. 16.

ANNEX-2.3

RANKING OF PSS BY TOTAL NO. OF REVENUE VILLAGES: RAJASTHAN, 2001

(Descending Order)

RANK	P. CODE	PANCHAYAT SAMITIES NAME	NO.
1	2	3	4
	VERY HIGH (>250)		
1	117	HANUMANGARH	1152
2	109	ANUPGARH	1131
3	118	NOHAR	538
4	115	SURATGARH	467
5	113	RAISINGHNAGAR	407
6	87	PRATAPGARH	358
7	142	BAKANI	326
8	40	BAYTOO	323
9	97	LALSOT	321
10	144	JHALRAPATAN	316
11	39	BARMER	309
12	234	KOTRA	304
13	133	SAM	303
14	146	MANOHARTHANA	302
15	61	MANDALGARH	299
16	121	CHAKSU	287
17	228	BHINDER	284
18	110	GANGANAGAR	273
19	74	TALERA	267
20	42	DHORIMANNA	261
21	44	SINDHARI	259
22	232	JHADOL	258
23	77	BEGUN	254
24	225	TONK	253
25	233	KHERWARA	252
25	114	SADULSHAHAR	252
27	43	SHEO	251
28	229	DHARIAWAD	250
	HIGH (200-250)		
29	112	PADAMPUR	247
30	66	BIKANER	244
31	124	JAMWA RAMGARH	241
32	111	KARANPUR	237
33	37	SHAHBAD	236
34	236	SALUMBAR	234
35	38	BALOTRA	233
35	96	DAUSA	233
37	102	DHAULPUR	232
38	143	DAG	231
39	58	JAHAZPUR	230
40	82	CHITTAURGARH	229
40	122	DUDU	229
42	72	KESHORAIPATAN	227
42	51	NAGAR PAHARI	227
44	168	SAPOTRA	224
45	26	GHATOL	223
45	30	TALWARA	223
47	68	KOLAYAT	221
48	108	SIMALWARA	220
49	147	PIRAWA	218
50	120	BASSI	215
50	116	BHADRA	215
50	90	RAJGARH	215
53	95	DANDIKUI	213
54	79	BHAINSRORGARH	212
54	226	UNIARA	212
56	173	SANGOD	211
57	27	KUSHALGARH	210
58	48	KAMAN	209
59	145	KHANPUR	207
60	140	SANCHORE	206
61	21	TIJARA	205
62	55	ASIND	204
63	166	KARAULI	203
63	36	KISHANGANJ	203
65	103	RAJAKHERA	203
66	223	NIWAI	201
67	3	JAWAJA	200
	MEDIUM (150-200)		
68	28	PEEPALKHOON	197
69	119	AMBER	196
69	101	BASERI	196
71	178	KUCHAMAN	193
72	34	CHHABRA	192
73	60	MANDAL	191
74	199	KHAMNOR*	190
75	41	CHOHTAN	189
76	29	SAJJANGARH	187
77	212	LACHHMANGARH	186
78	237	SARAD	185
79	92	SARDARSHAHAR	184
80	172	LADPURA	182
81	73	NAINWA	181
82	204	BONLI	180
82	35	CHHIPABAROD	180
82	230	GIRWA	180
82	206	KHANDAR	180
86	75	ARNOD	179
86	134	SANKRA	179
88	46	BAYANA	177
88	53	SEWAR	177
90	69	LUNKARANSAR	176
91	105	BICHHIWARA	175
91	59	KOTRI	175
91	162	OSIAN	175
94	71	HINDOLI	174
95	18	RAMGARH	173
96	176	DIDWANA	172
97	100	BARI	171
97	221	DEOLI	171
97	127	PHAGI	171
97	174	SULTANPUR	171
101	25	GARHI	170
101	86	NIMBAHERA	170
103	171	ITAWA	169
104	78	BHADESAR	168
105	24	BAGIDORA	165
106	200	KUMBHALGARH	164
107	207	SAWAI MADHOPUR	162
108	11	KATHUMAR	160
109	170	CHECHAT	159
109	106	DUNGARPUR	159
109	20	THANAGAZI	159
112	52	RUPBAS	158
112	107	SAGWARA	158
114	208	DANTA RAMGARH	157
115	31	ANTA	156
116	132	JAISALMER	155
116	130	SHAHPURA	155
116	93	SUJANGARH	155
116	22	UMREN	155
120	183	NAGAUR	154
121	76	BARI SADRI	153
122	175	DEGANA	152
122	98	MAHWA	152
124	81	CHHOTI SADRI	151
124	213	NEEM KA THANA	151
124	54	WEIR	151
127	203	BAMANWAS	150
	LOW (100-150)		
128	235	MAVLI	149
128	169	TODABHIM	149
130	231	GOGUNDA	148
131	17	RAJGARH	147
131	129	SANGANER	147
133	104	ASPUR	146
134	151	JHUNJHUNUN	145
135	128	SAMBHAR	144
136	210	FATEHPUR	143
136	6	MASOODA	143
138	189	MARWAR JUN.	142
138	15	MANDAWAR	142
140	12	KISHANGARH BAS	140
140	14	LACHHMANGARH	140
142	99	SIKRAI	139
143	32	ATRU	138
143	222	MALPURA	138
143	65	SUWANA	138
146	196	AMET	137
146	177	JAYAL	137
146	160	LUNI	137
146	70	NOKHA	137
150	202	RAJSAMAND	135
151	198	DEOGARH	134
152	197	BHIM	133
153	9	BANSURE	132
154	47	DEEG	132
155	211	KHANDELA	131
156	23	ANANDPURI	129
156	1	ARAIN	129
158	2	BHINAY	128
158	84	GANGRAR	128
158	7	PISANGAN	128
161	185	RIYAN	128
162	165	HINDAUN	127
163	149	BUHANA	126
163	218	REODAR	126
165	148	ALSISAR	125
165	156	BALESAR	125
165	157	BAP	125
168	49	KUMHER	124
169	205	GANGAPUR	122
169	182	MUNDWA	122
169	154	SURAJGARH	122
172	126	KOTPUTLI	121
172	94	TARANAGAR	121
172	131	VIRATNAGAR	121
175	180	MAKRANA	119
176	224	TODARAISINGH	118
177	50	NADBAI	117
178	13	KOTKASIM	116
178	45	SIWANA	116
180	181	MERTA	115
180	194	SOJAT	115
182	5	KISHANGARH	114
183	135	AHORE	113
183	191	RAIPUR	113
185	85	KAPASAN	111
185	163	PHALODI	111
187	184	PARBATSAR	110
188	209	DHOND	109
189	83	DUNGLA	108
189	188	JAITARAN	108
191	227	BARGAON	107
191	161	MANDOR	107
191	164	SHERGARH	107
194	89	CHURU	106
195	63	SAHARA	104
196	33	BARAN	102
196	19	RENI	102
198	91	RATANGARH	101
199	123	GOVINDGARH	100
199	4	KEKRI	100
199	217	PINDWARA	100
	VERY LOW (<100)		
202	179	LADNU	98
203	67	DUNGARGARH	97
204	8	SRINAGAR	96
205	167	NADOTI	95
205	214	PIPRALI	95
207	201	RAILMAGRA	94
208	62	RAIPUR	92
209	186	BALI	91
210	10	BEHROR	90
210	159	BILARA	90
210	153	NAWALGARH	90
213	88	RASHMI	89
214	16	NIMRANA	87
215	158	BHOPALGARH	86
215	152	KHETRI*	86
215	64	SHAHPURA	86
218	56	BANERA	85
218	80	BHOPALSAGAR	85
218	139	RANIWARA	85
218	220	SIROHI	85
222	150	CHIRAWA	84
223	190	PALI	82
224	216	ABU ROAD	81
224	136	BHINMAL	81
224	155	UDAIPURWATI	81
227	193	ROHAT	79
228	187	DESURI	78
229	141	SAYLA	77
230	192	RANI STATION	76
231	138	JASWANTPURA	75
232	125	JHOTWARA	73
233	57	HURDA	72
234	219	SHEOGANJ	70
235	137	JALOR	69
236	215	SRI MADHOPUR	66
237	195	SUMERPUR	65
RAJASTHAN		TOTAL	41353
		AVERAGE	174.50
		% AGE OF AAPs	38.40

BOLD: Equal/Above Average Panchayat Samities (AAPs)

Source : General Annex VII, Col. 3.

ANNEX-2.4

RANKING OF PSS BY TOTAL NO. OF INHABITED VILLAGES, 2001

RANK	P. CODE	PANCHAYAT SAMITIES NAME	NUMBER
1	2	3	4
	VERY HIGH (>250)		
1	**109**	**ANUPGARH**	**1090**
2	**117**	**HANUMANGARH**	**1074**
3	**118**	**NOHAR**	**501**
4	**115**	**SURATGARH**	**433**
5	**113**	**RAISINGHNAGAR**	**367**
6	**87**	**PRATAPGARH**	**330**
7	**40**	**BAYTOO**	**323**
8	**39**	**BARMER**	**307**
9	**234**	**KOTRA**	**302**
10	**97**	**LALSOT**	**300**
11	**142**	**BAKANI**	**289**
12	**144**	**JHALRAPATAN**	**285**
13	**146**	**MANOHARTHANA**	**284**
14	**61**	**MANDALGARH**	**281**
14	**133**	**SAM**	**281**
16	**228**	**BHINDER**	**279**
17	**121**	**CHAKSU**	**267**
18	**74**	**TALERA**	**262**
19	**42**	**DHORIMANNA**	**261**
20	**44**	**SINDHARI**	**259**
21	**232**	**JHADOL**	**258**
22	**110**	**GANGANAGAR**	**257**
23	**43**	**SHEO**	**250**
23	**233**	**KHERWARA**	**250**
	HIGH (200-250)		
25	**229**	**DHARIAWAD**	**249**
26	**112**	**PADAMPUR**	**239**
27	**225**	**TONK**	**238**
28	**114**	**SADULSHAHAR**	**237**
29	**236**	**SALUMBAR**	**234**
30	**124**	**JAMWA RAMGARH**	**233**
31	**38**	**BALOTRA**	**231**
32	**102**	**DHAULPUR**	**229**
33	**72**	**KESHORAIPATAN**	**223**
33	**96**	**DAUSA**	**223**
35	**77**	**BEGUN**	**222**
36	**143**	**DAG**	**221**
37	**26**	**GHATOL**	**220**
37	**108**	**SIMALWARA**	**220**
39	**66**	**BIKANER**	**219**
39	**122**	**DUDU**	**219**
41	**82**	**CHITTAURGARH**	**218**
42	**58**	**JAHAZPUR**	**217**
43	**51**	**NAGAR PAHARI**	**216**
44	**30**	**TALWARA**	**213**
44	**90**	**RAJGARH**	**213**
46	**95**	**BANDIKUI**	**211**
47	**120**	**BASSI**	**210**
47	**168**	**SAPOTRA**	**210**
49	**27**	**KUSHALGARH**	**209**
50	**111**	**KARANPUR**	**207**
51	**147**	**PIRAWA**	**205**
52	**55**	**ASIND**	**204**
52	**140**	**SANCHORE**	**204**
54	**21**	**TIJARA**	**202**
	MEDIUM (150-200)		
55	**3**	**JAWAJA**	**199**
55	**103**	**RAJAKHERA**	**199**
57	**116**	**BHADRA**	**198**
58	**173**	**SANGOD**	**197**
59	**68**	**KOLAYAT**	**196**
59	**226**	**UNIARA**	**196**
61	**166**	**KARAULI**	**195**
62	**48**	**KAMAN**	**194**
63	**145**	**KHANPUR**	**193**
63	**178**	**KUCHAMAN**	**193**
65	**119**	**AMBER**	**192**
66	**223**	**NIWAI**	**191**
67	**101**	**BASERI**	**190**
68	**60**	**MANDAL**	**188**
69	**28**	**PEEPALKHOONT**	**187**
69	**41**	**CHOHTAN**	**187**
69	**199**	**KHAMNOR**	**187**
72	**34**	**CHHABRA**	**186**
73	**29**	**SAJJANGARH**	**185**
73	**237**	**SARADA**	**185**
75	**14**	**LACHHMANGARH**	**184**
76	**36**	**KISHANGANJ**	**180**
76	**73**	**NAINWA**	**180**
78	**230**	**GIRWA**	**179**
79	**75**	**ARNOD**	**178**

RANK	P. CODE	PANCHAYAT SAMITIES NAME	NUMBER
1	2	3	4
80	**134**	**SANKRA**	**176**
81	**59**	**KOTRI**	**175**
81	**105**	**BICHHIWARA**	**175**
81	**162**	**OSIAN**	**175**
84	**71**	**HINDOLI**	**174**
85	**18**	**RAMGARH**	**173**
85	**35**	**CHHIPABAROD**	**173**
87	**92**	**SARDARSHAHAR**	**170**
87	**176**	**DIDWANA**	**170**
89	**127**	**PHAGI**	**169**
90	**25**	**GARHI**	**168**
90	**100**	**BARI**	**168**
92	37	SHAHBAD	167
93	24	BAGIDORA	165
93	221	DEOLI	165
95	200	KUMBHALGARH	164
96	78	BHADESAR	163
96	171	ITAWA	163
96	174	SULTANPUR	163
99	46	BAYANA	161
100	69	LUNKARANSAR	160
101	106	DUNGARPUR	159
101	204	BONLI	159
103	11	KATHUMAR	158
104	53	SEWAR	157
104	107	SAGWARA	157
104	208	DANTA RAMGARH	157
107	207	SAWAI MADHOPUR	156
108	93	SUJANGARH	155
108	206	KHANDAR	155
110	79	BHAINSRORGARH	154
111	86	NIMBAHERA	152
111	98	MAHWA	152
113	64	SHAHPURA	151
113	213	NEEM KA THANA	151
115	183	NAGAUR	150
	LOW (100-150)		
116	22	UMREN	149
116	235	MAVLI	149
118	20	THANAGAZI	148
118	31	ANTA	148
118	175	DEGANA	148
121	231	GOGUNDA	147
122	54	WEIR	146
123	151	JHUNJHUNUN	145
123	172	LADPURA	145
125	128	SAMBHAR	144
125	169	TODABHIM	144
125	170	CHECHAT	144
128	76	BARI SADRI	143
128	104	ASPUR	143
128	129	SANGANER	143
128	132	JAISALMER	143
128	210	FATEHPUR	143
133	15	MANDAWAR	142
133	52	RUPBAS	142
133	189	MARWAR JUN.	142
136	81	CHHOTI SADRI	141
137	17	RAJGARH	140
137	212	LACHHMANGARH	140
139	6	MASOODA	139
139	99	SIKRAI	139
141	70	NOKHA	137
142	32	ATRU	136
142	65	SUWANA	136
142	177	JAYAL	136
142	196	AMET	136
142	203	BAMANWAS	136
147	12	KISHANGARH BAS	135
147	160	LUNI	135
149	197	BHIM	132
149	202	RAJSAMAND	132
151	9	BANSURE	131
151	198	DEOGARH	131
153	222	MALPURA	130
154	23	ANANDPURI	129
155	2	BHINAY	128
155	7	PISANGAN	128
157	84	GANGRAR	127
158	149	BUHANA	126
158	211	KHANDELA	126
158	218	REODAR	126

RANK	P. CODE	PANCHAYAT SAMITIES NAME	NUMBER
1	2	3	4
161	1	ARAIN	125
161	156	BALESAR	125
161	157	BAP	125
161	185	RIYAN	125
165	148	ALSISAR	124
166	154	SURAJGARH	122
167	126	KOTPUTLI	121
167	165	HINDAUN	121
167	182	MUNDWA	121
170	131	VIRATNAGAR	120
171	47	DEEG	119
171	180	MAKRANA	119
173	49	KUMHER	117
174	13	KOTKASIM	115
174	45	SIWANA	115
174	194	SOJAT	115
177	50	NADBAI	114
178	205	GANGAPUR	113
179	224	TODARAISINGH	112
180	5	KISHANGARH	111
180	163	PHALODI	111
180	181	MERTA	111
183	94	TARANAGAR	110
183	135	AHORE	110
183	184	PARBATSAR	110
186	191	RAIPUR	109
186	209	DHOND	109
188	85	KAPASAN	107
188	164	SHERGARH	107
188	227	BARGAON	107
191	89	CHURU	105
191	161	MANDOR	105
193	188	JAITARAN	103
194	19	RENI	102
194	83	DUNGLA	102
196	91	RATANGARH	101
197	123	GOVINDGARH	100
	VERY LOW (<100)		
198	4	KEKRI	99
198	33	BARAN	99
198	63	SAHARA	99
198	217	PINDWARA	99
202	179	LADNU	97
203	8	SRINAGAR	96
204	214	PIPRALI	94
205	67	DUNGARGARH	92
206	186	BALI	91
206	201	RAILMAGRA	91
208	10	BEHROR	90
209	62	RAIPUR	89
209	159	BILARA	89
211	153	NAWALGARH	88
212	130	SHAHPURA	86
212	158	BHOPALGARH	86
214	16	NIMRANA	85
214	152	KHETRI	85
214	167	NADOTI	85
217	139	RANIWARA	84
217	150	CHIRAWA	84
219	56	BANERA	83
219	80	BHOPALSAGAR	83
219	220	SIROHI	83
222	88	RASHMI	81
222	155	UDAIPURWATI	81
224	136	BHINMAL	80
224	190	PALI	80
226	193	ROHAT	79
227	187	DESURI	78
227	216	ABU ROAD	78
229	141	SAYLA	77
230	192	RANI STATION	76
231	138	JASWANTPURA	74
232	125	JHOTWARA	73
233	57	HURDA	70
234	219	SHEOGANJ	69
235	137	JALOR	68
236	215	SRI MADHOPUR	66
237	195	SUMERPUR	63
RAJASTHAN		**TOTAL**	**39753**
		AVERAGE	**167.70**
		% AGE OF AAPs	**38.40**

BOLD: Equal/Above Average Panchayat Samities (AAPs) *Source*: General Annex IX, Col. 3.

ANNEX-2.5

RANKING OF PSS BY TOTAL NO. OF GRAM PANCHAYATS: RAJASTHAN, 2001

(Descending Order)

RANK	P. CODE	PANCHAYAT SAMITIES NAME	No.
1	2	3	4
	VERY HIGH (>50)		
1	117	**HANUMANGARH**	121
2	109	**ANUPGARH**	88
3	118	**NOHAR**	81
4	162	**OSIAN**	67
5	66	**BIKANER**	63
5	140	**SANCHORE**	63
7	233	**KHERWARA**	62
8	74	**TALERA**	61
9	213	**NEEM KA THANA**	59
10	108	**SIMALWARA**	58
11	176	**DIDWANA**	57
12	122	**DUDU**	56
13	25	**GARHI**	55
13	178	**KUCHAMAN**	55
13	90	**RAJGARH**	55
13	168	**SAPOTRA**	55
13	30	**TALWARA**	55
18	38	**BALOTRA**	54
19	26	**GHATOL**	53
19	70	**NOKHA**	53
21	228	**BHINDER**	52
21	96	**DAUSA**	52
23	41	**CHOHTAN**	51
23	165	**HINDAUN**	51
23	93	**SUJANGARH**	51
26	39	**BARMER**	50
26	61	**MANDALGARH**	50
26	225	**TONK**	50
	HIGH (40-50)		
29	104	**ASPUR**	49
29	116	**BHADRA**	49
29	229	**DHARIAWAD**	49
29	51	**NAGAR PAHARI**	49
29	87	**PRATAPGARH**	49
29	133	**SAM**	49
35	119	**AMBER**	48
35	105	**BICHHIWARA**	48
35	102	**DHAULPUR**	48
35	230	**GIRWA**	48
35	144	**JHALRAPATAN**	48
35	236	**SALUMBAR**	48
35	92	**SARDARSHAHAR**	48
42	40	**BAYTOO**	47
42	42	**DHORIMANNA**	47
42	189	**MARWAR JUN.**	47
42	97	**LALSOT**	47
42	235	**MAVLI**	47
42	183	**NAGAUR**	47
42	113	**RAISINGHNAGAR**	47
42	207	**SAWAI MADHOPUR**	47
50	72	**KESHORAIPATAN**	46
50	60	**MANDAL**	46
50	107	**SAGWARA**	46
50	237	**SARAD**	46
50	44	**SINDHARI**	46
50	54	**WEIR**	46
56	46	**BAYANA**	45
56	208	**DANTA RAMGARH**	45
56	177	**JAYAL**	45
56	232	**JHADOL**	45
56	166	**KARAULI**	45
56	7	**PISANGAN**	45
56	52	**RUPBAS**	45
56	43	**SHEO**	45
64	65	**ASIND**	44
64	95	**BANDIKUI**	44
64	110	**GANGANAGAR**	44
64	48	**KAMAN**	44
64	212	**LACHHMANGARH**	44
64	147	**PIRAWA**	44
64	128	**SAMBHAR**	44
64	169	**TODABHIM**	44
72	175	**DEGANA**	43
72	209	**DHOND**	43
72	124	**JAMWA RAMGARH**	43
75	142	**BAKANI**	42
75	149	**BUHANA**	42
75	123	**GOVINDGARH**	42
75	126	**KOTPUTLI**	42
79	135	**AHORE**	41
79	24	**BAGIDORA**	41
79	204	**BONLI**	41
79	71	**HINDOLI**	41
79	11	**KATHUMAR**	41
79	199	**KHAMNOR***	41
79	98	**MAHWA**	41
79	223	**NIWAI**	41
79	99	**SIKRAI**	41
88	143	**DAG**	40
88	221	**DEOLI**	40
88	231	**GOGUNDA**	40
88	132	**JAISALMER**	40
88	211	**KHANDELA**	40
88	15	**MANDAWAR**	40
88	146	**MANOHARTHANA**	40
88	45	**SIWANA**	40
	MEDIUM (30-40)		
96	186	**BALI**	39
96	120	**BASSI**	39
96	82	**CHITTAURGARH**	39
96	145	**KHANPUR**	39
96	160	**LUNI**	39
96	182	**MUNDWA**	39
96	103	**RAJAKHERA**	39
96	134	**SANKRA**	39
104	31	ANTA	38
104	159	BILARA	38
104	205	GANGAPUR	38
104	152	KHETRI*	38
104	185	RIYAN	38
104	141	SAYLA	38
104	130	SHAHPURA	38
104	194	SOJAT	38
104	115	SURATGARH	38
104	21	TIJARA	38
114	58	JAHAZPUR	37
114	68	KOLAYAT	37
114	200	KUMBHALGARH	37
114	14	LACHHMANGARH	37
114	50	NADBAI	37
114	163	PHALODI	37
114	18	RAMGARH	37
114	218	REODAR	37
114	8	SRINAGAR	37
114	154	SURAJGARH	37
114	155	UDAIPURWATI	37
114	131	VIRATNAGAR	37
126	203	BAMANWAS	36
126	9	BANSURE	36
126	158	BHOPALGARH	36
126	170	CHECHAT	36
126	47	DEEG	36
126	106	DUNGARPUR	36
126	151	JHUNJHUNUN	36
126	234	KOTRA	36
126	49	KUMHER	36
126	69	LUNKARANSAR	36
126	180	MAKRANA	36
126	222	MALPURA	36
126	112	PADAMPUR	36
126	28	PEEPALKHOON	36
126	214	PIPRALI	36
126	173	SANGOD	36
126	22	UMREN	36
143	101	BASERI	35
143	2	BHINAY	35
143	136	BHINMAL	35
143	121	CHAKSU	35
143	89	CHURU	35
143	210	FATEHPUR	35
143	3	JAWAJA	35
143	111	KARANPUR	35
143	206	KHANDAR	35
143	153	NAWALGARH	35
143	86	NIMBAHERA	35
143	184	PARBATSAR	35
143	191	RAIPUR	35
143	20	THANAGAZI	35
157	148	ALSISAR	34
157	32	ATRU	34
157	181	MERTA	34
157	217	PINDWARA	34
157	215	SRI MADHOPUR	34
157	65	SUWANA	34
163	156	BALESAR	33
163	188	JAITARAN	33
163	59	KOTRI	33
163	73	NAINWA	33
163	16	NIMRANA	33
163	53	SEWAR	33
163	174	SULTANPUR	33
163	226	UNIARA	33
171	157	BAP	32
171	36	KISHANGANJ	32
171	179	LADNU	32
171	6	MASOODA	32
171	91	RATANGARH	32
171	114	SADULSHAHAR	32
171	164	SHERGARH	32
178	100	BARI	31
178	77	BEGUN	31
178	4	KEKRI*	31
178	5	KISHANGARH	31
178	127	PHAGI	31
178	220	SIROHI	31
178	224	TODARAISINGH	31
185	1	ARAIN	30
185	75	ARNOD	30
185	197	BHIM	30
185	35	CHHIPABAROD	30
185	67	DUNGARGARH	30
185	171	ITAWA	30
185	17	RAJGARH	30
185	139	RANIWARA	30
185	29	SAJJANGARH	30
185	64	SHAHPURA	30
	LOW (20-30)		
195	10	BEHROR	29
195	150	CHIRAWA	29
195	138	JASWANTPURA	29
195	12	KISHANGARH BAS	29
195	27	KUSHALGARH	29
195	167	NADOTI	29
195	201	RAILMAGRA	29
195	202	RAJSAMAND	29
195	192	RANI STATION	29
195	195	SUMERPUR	29
205	137	JALOR	28
205	63	SAHARA	28
205	94	TARANAGAR	28
208	33	BARAN	27
208	34	CHHABRA	27
208	172	LADPURA	27
208	37	SHAHBAD	27
212	23	ANANDPURI	26
212	56	BANERA	26
212	83	DUNGLA	26
212	19	RENI	26
216	216	ABU ROAD	25
216	227	BARGAON	25
216	78	BHADESAR	25
216	161	MANDOR	25
216	129	SANGANER	25
221	81	CHHOTI SADRI	24
221	187	DESURI	24
221	13	KOTKASIM	24
221	219	SHEOGANJ	24
225	76	BARI SADRI	23
225	79	BHAINSRORGARH	23
225	85	KAPASAN	23
225	190	PALI	23
225	88	RASHMI	23
225	193	ROHAT	23
231	62	RAIPUR	22
232	84	GANGRAR	21
233	196	AMET	20
233	57	HURDA	20
	VERY LOW (<20)		
235	80	BHOPALSAGAR	19
235	198	DEOGARH	19
237	125	JHOTWARA	16
RAJASTHAN		**TOTAL**	**9187**
		AVERAGE	**38.80**
		% AGE OF AAPs	**43.50**

BOLD: Equal/Above Average Panchayat Samities (AAPs)   *Source*: Gen Annex VII, Col. 4.

ANNEX-2.6

RANKING OF PSS BY SEX-RATIO (0-6 POPULATION): RAJASTHAN, 2001

(Descending Order)

RANK	P. CODE	PANCHAYAT SAMITIES NAME	SEX-RATIO POP.
1	2	3	4
		VERY HIGH (>1000)	
1	27	KUSHALGARH	1007
		HIGH (950-1000)	
2	56	BANERA	996
2	234	KOTRA	996
4	23	ANANDPURI	990
4	232	JHADOL	990
6	28	PEEPALKHOONT	987
7	29	SAJJANGARH	983
8	105	BICHHIWARA	978
8	108	SIMALWARA	978
10	229	DHARIAWAD	972
11	61	MANDALGARH	970
11	216	ABU ROAD	970
13	60	MANDAL	969
14	24	BAGIDORA	968
14	63	SAHARA	968
16	164	SHERGARH	966
16	231	GOGUNDA	966
18	62	RAIPUR	965
19	55	ASIND	964
20	233	KHERWARA	963
21	196	AMET	962
22	64	SHAHPURA	961
23	59	KOTRI	960
23	75	ARNOD	960
25	143	DAG	958
26	30	TALWARA	955
27	36	KISHANGANJ	954
27	106	DUNGARPUR	954
27	230	GIRWA	954
30	26	GHATOL	953
31	77	BEGUN	951
32	1	ARAIN	950
32	6	MASOODA	950
32	146	MANOHARTHANA	950
		MEDIUM (900-950)	
35	85	KAPASAN	949
35	237	SARADA	949
37	222	MALPURA	948
38	179	LADNU	947
38	197	BHIM	947
38	202	RAJSAMAND	947
41	2	BHINAY	946
41	76	BARI SADRI	946
41	147	PIRAWA	946
41	217	PINDWARA	946
45	88	RASHMI	945
45	186	BALI	945
47	42	DHORIMANNA	944
47	107	SAGWARA	944
47	200	KUMBHALGARH	944
47	201	RAILMAGRA	944
51	65	SUWANA	943
52	171	ITAWA	942
52	191	RAIPUR	942
54	25	GARHI	941
54	78	BHADESAR	941
54	87	PRATAPGARH	941
54	218	REODAR	941
54	236	SALUMBAR	941
59	96	DAUSA	940
60	125	JHOTWARA	938
61	92	SARDARSHAHAR	937
62	38	BALOTRA	936
62	81	CHHOTI SADRI	936
62	189	MARWAR JUN.	936
62	224	TODARAISINGH	936
66	145	KHANPUR	935
67	4	KEKRI	934
68	41	CHOHTAN	933
68	67	DUNGARGARH	933
68	142	BAKANI	933
68	170	CHECHAT	933
68	225	TONK	933
73	82	CHITTAURGARH	932
73	160	LUNI	932
73	221	DEOLI	932
76	137	JALOR	931
76	194	SOJAT	931
78	57	HURDA	930
78	198	DEOGARH	930
80	97	LALSOT	929
80	228	BHINDER	929
82	70	NOKHA	928
82	72	KESHORAIPATAN	928
82	104	ASPUR	928
82	136	BHINMAL	928
82	141	SAYLA	928
82	144	JHALRAPATAN	928
82	227	BARGAON	928
89	5	KISHANGARH	927
89	80	BHOPALSAGAR	927
89	128	SAMBHAR	927
89	162	OSIAN	927
93	177	JAYAL	926
93	183	NAGAUR	926
95	58	JAHAZPUR	925
95	140	SANCHORE	925
95	163	PHALODI	925
98	44	SINDHARI	924
98	190	PALI	924
100	7	PISANGAN	923
100	45	SIWANA	923
100	93	SUJANGARH	923
100	131	VIRATNAGAR	923
100	182	MUNDWA	923
105	159	BILARA	922
105	188	JAITARAN	922
105	235	MAVLI	922
108	69	LUNKARANSAR	921
108	124	JAMWA RAMGARH	921
108	127	PHAGI	921
108	156	BALESAR	921
112	39	BARMER	920
112	172	LADPURA	920
112	176	DIDWANA	920
112	192	RANI STATION	920
112	223	NIWAI	920
117	34	CHHABRA	919
117	37	SHAHBAD	919
117	66	BIKANER	919
117	74	TALERA	919
117	203	BAMANWAS	919
122	83	DUNGLA	918
122	135	AHORE	918
122	158	BHOPALGARH	918
125	84	GANGRAR	917
125	175	DEGANA	917
127	20	THANAGAZI	916
127	94	TARANAGAR	916
127	119	AMBER	916
127	157	BAP	916
131	12	KISHANGARH BAS	915
131	32	ATRU	915
131	35	CHHIPABAROD	915
131	40	BAYTOO	915
131	187	DESURI	915
136	120	BASSI	914
136	180	MAKRANA	914
136	193	ROHAT	914
139	79	BHAINSRORGARH	912
139	122	DUDU	912
139	199	KHAMNOR	912
142	3	JAWAJA	911
142	71	HINDOLI	911
142	138	JASWANTPURA	911
142	204	BONLI	911
146	33	BARAN	910
147	18	RAMGARH	909
147	22	UMREN	909
147	48	KAMAN	909
150	8	SRINAGAR	908
150	174	SULTANPUR	908
152	31	ANTA	907
153	73	NAINWA	906
153	121	CHAKSU	906
153	129	SANGANER	906
153	139	RANIWARA	906
153	161	MANDOR	906
153	173	SANGOD	906
159	123	GOVINDGARH	905
160	68	KOLAYAT	904
160	86	NIMBAHERA	904
160	130	SHAHPURA	904
163	21	TIJARA	903
163	184	PARBATSAR	903
163	195	SUMERPUR	903
166	178	KUCHAMAN	902
166	207	SAWAI MADHOPUR	902
168	14	LACHHMANGARH	901
168	226	UNIARA	901
170	95	BANDIKUI	900
170	118	NOHAR	900
		LOW (850-900)	
172	9	BANSURE	899
172	17	RAJGARH	899
172	91	RATANGARH	899
172	185	RIYAN	899
172	219	SHEOGANJ	899
177	168	SAPOTRA	898
178	155	UDAIPURWATI	897
179	19	RENI	896
180	115	SURATGARH	895
180	213	NEEM KA THANA	895
182	181	MERTA	893
183	89	CHURU	892
183	211	KHANDELA	892
185	11	KATHUMAR	891
185	53	SEWAR	891
185	215	SRI MADHOPUR	891
188	51	NAGAR PAHARI	890
188	134	SANKRA	890
188	206	KHANDAR	890
191	208	DANTA RAMGARH	888
192	50	NADBAI	886
192	99	SIKRAI	886
192	109	ANUPGARH	886
192	205	GANGAPUR	886
196	90	RAJGARH	883
197	132	JAISALMER	880
198	47	DEEG	879
199	49	KUMHER	878
199	54	WEIR	878
201	148	ALSISAR	877
201	166	KARAULI	877
203	210	FATEHPUR	875
204	116	BHADRA	874
204	152	KHETRI	874
204	167	NADOTI	874
204	220	SIROHI	874
208	214	PIPRALI	873
209	98	MAHWA	871
209	102	DHAULPUR	871
211	212	LACHHMANGARH	867
212	126	KOTPUTLI	866
213	209	DHOND	865
214	101	BASERI	864
214	103	RAJAKHERA	864
216	117	HANUMANGARH	861
216	153	NAWALGARH	861
218	13	KOTKASIM	860
219	15	MANDAWAR	859
219	151	JHUNJHUNUN	859
221	46	BAYANA	858
221	52	RUPBAS	858
223	165	HINDAUN	856
224	150	CHIRAWA	854
225	113	RAISINGHNAGAR	853
226	43	SHEO	851
		VERY LOW (<850)	
227	16	NIMRANA	849
227	100	BARI	849
227	154	SURAJGARH	849
227	169	TODABHIM	849
231	10	BEHROR	842
232	112	PADAMPUR	841
233	149	BUHANA	840
234	133	SAM	837
235	111	KARANPUR	831
236	110	GANGANAGAR	823
237	114	SADULSHAHAR	814
		RAJASTHAN	914
		% AGE OF AAPs	58.23

BOLD: Equal/Above Average Panchayat Samities (AAPs)

Source: General Annex VII, Col. 18.

ANNEX-2.7

RANKING OF PSS BY SEX-RATIO (TOTAL POPULATION): RAJASTHAN, 2001

(Descending Order)

RANK	P. CODE	PANCHAYAT SAMITIES NAME	SEX-RATIO TOTAL POP.
1	2	3	4
	VERY HIGH (>1000)		
1	107	**SAGWARA**	1074
2	104	**ASPUR**	1071
3	63	**SAHARA**	1070
4	187	**DESURI**	1054
5	62	**RAIPUR**	1042
5	198	**DEOGARH**	1042
7	192	**RANI STATION**	1040
8	60	**MANDAL**	1033
8	200	**KUMBHALGARH**	1033
10	106	**DUNGARPUR**	1032
11	236	**SALUMBAR**	1025
12	197	**BHIM**	1024
13	88	**RASHMI**	1020
14	135	**AHORE**	1019
14	201	**RAILMAGRA**	1019
16	55	**ASIND**	1018
16	237	**SARADA**	1018
18	220	**SIROHI**	1013
19	186	**BALI**	1012
20	189	**MARWAR JUNCTION**	1011
21	194	**SOJAT**	1009
22	199	**KHAMNOR**	1005
23	80	**BHOPALSAGAR**	1003
23	83	**DUNGLA**	1003
23	233	**KHERWARA**	1003
26	105	**BICHHIWARA**	1001
27	196	**AMET**	1000
	HIGH (950-1000)		
28	76	**BARI SADRI**	999
29	137	**JALOR**	997
30	108	**SIMALWARA**	996
31	138	**JASWANTPURA**	995
31	195	**SUMERPUR**	995
31	229	**DHARIAWAD**	995
34	210	**FATEHPUR**	994
35	85	**KAPASAN**	992
36	26	**GHATOL**	989
36	148	**ALSISAR**	989
38	27	**KUSHALGARH**	987
39	176	**DIDWANA**	985
39	191	**RAIPUR**	985
41	3	**JAWAJA**	983
41	24	**BAGIDORA**	983
41	56	**BANERA**	983
41	228	**BHINDER**	983
45	231	**GOGUNDA**	981
46	175	**DEGANA**	980
47	78	**BHADESAR**	979
47	179	**LADNU**	979
47	190	**PALI**	979
47	234	**KOTRA**	979
51	232	**JHADOL**	978
52	141	**SAYLA**	977
52	151	**JHUNJHUNUN**	977
54	25	**GARHI**	976
55	91	**RATANGARH**	975
55	235	**MAVLI**	975
57	136	**BHINMAL**	974
57	202	**RAJSAMAND**	974
59	29	**SAJJANGARH**	973
59	30	**TALWARA**	973
61	212	**LACHHMANGARH**	972
62	84	**GANGRAR**	971
63	75	**ARNOD**	970
64	86	**NIMBAHERA**	969
65	93	**SUJANGARH**	968
65	153	**NAWALGARH**	968
65	188	**JAITARAN**	968
68	28	**PEEPALKHOONT**	967
68	208	**DANTA RAMGARH**	967
70	81	**CHHOTI SADRI**	966
71	65	**SUWANA**	965
71	77	**BEGUN**	965
71	193	**ROHAT**	965
71	211	**KHANDELA**	965
75	23	**ANANDPURI**	964
75	219	**SHEOGANJ**	964
77	82	**CHITTAURGARH**	963
77	155	**UDAIPURWATI**	963
79	1	**ARAIN**	961
79	209	**DHOND**	961
81	230	**GIRWA**	960
82	2	**BHINAY**	959
82	89	**CHURU**	959
84	87	**PRATAPGARH**	958
84	150	**CHIRAWA**	958
84	177	**JAYAL**	958
87	4	**KEKRI**	957
87	180	**MAKRANA**	957
89	59	**KOTRI**	955
90	6	**MASOODA**	954
90	217	**PINDWARA**	954
92	92	**SARDARSHAHAR**	953
93	64	**SHAHPURA**	951
93	224	**TODARAISINGH**	951
95	214	**PIPRALI**	950
95	215	**SRI MADHOPUR**	950
	MEDIUM (900-950)		
97	57	**HURDA**	949
97	143	**DAG**	949
99	67	**DUNGARGARH**	947
99	182	**MUNDWA**	947
101	183	**NAGAUR**	945
101	218	**REODAR**	945
103	149	**BUHANA**	944
103	222	**MALPURA**	944
105	7	**PISANGAN**	943
105	158	**BHOPALGARH**	943
105	185	**RIYAN**	943
105	227	**BARGAON**	943
109	94	**TARANAGAR**	940
109	152	**KHETRI**	940
109	184	**PARBATSAR**	940
112	147	**PIRAWA**	939
113	140	**SANCHORE**	938
114	5	**KISHANGARH**	935
114	216	**ABU ROAD**	935
116	90	**RAJGARH**	933
116	128	**SAMBHAR**	933
116	139	**RANIWARA**	933
116	178	**KUCHAMAN**	933
120	221	**DEOLI**	932
120	225	**TONK**	932
122	159	**BILARA**	931
123	154	**SURAJGARH**	930
124	58	JAHAZPUR	929
124	61	MANDALGARH	929
126	160	LUNI	928
127	122	DUDU	927
127	142	BAKANI	927
129	16	NIMRANA	926
129	144	JHALRAPATAN	926
131	8	SRINAGAR	925
132	38	BALOTRA	924
132	44	SINDHARI	924
132	146	MANOHARTHANA	924
132	181	MERTA	924
132	213	NEEM KA THANA	924
137	162	OSIAN	923
138	45	SIWANA	922
139	36	KISHANGANJ	919
139	123	GOVINDGARH	919
139	223	NIWAI	919
142	15	MANDAWAR	918
142	127	PHAGI	918
144	10	BEHROR	917
144	31	ANTA	917
146	35	CHHIPABAROD	916
146	97	LALSOT	916
146	173	SANGOD	916
146	226	UNIARA	916
150	72	KESHORAIPATAN	915
150	121	CHAKSU	915
150	125	JHOTWARA	915
153	129	SANGANER	914
153	145	KHANPUR	914
153	156	BALESAR	914
153	163	PHALODI	914
157	70	NOKHA	913
157	113	RAISINGHNAGAR	913
157	174	SULTANPUR	913
160	42	DHORIMANNA	912
160	69	LUNKARANSAR	912
162	164	SHERGARH	911
163	73	NAINWA	910
163	120	BASSI	910
165	12	KISHANGARH BAS	909
165	131	VIRATNAGAR	909
165	161	MANDOR	909
168	124	JAMWA RAMGARH	908
169	13	KOTKASIM	907
169	96	DAUSA	907
171	74	TALERA	906
171	112	PADAMPUR	906
171	119	AMBER	906
171	126	KOTPUTLI	906
171	171	ITAWA	906
176	32	ATRU	905
176	170	CHECHAT	905
176	204	BONLI	905
179	9	BANSURE	904
179	33	BARAN	904
179	40	BAYTOO	904
179	207	SAWAI MADHOPUR	904
183	79	BHAINSRORGARH	903
183	118	NOHAR	903
183	172	LADPURA	903
186	20	THANAGAZI	902
186	130	SHAHPURA	902
188	71	HINDOLI	901
	LOW (850-900)		
189	95	BANDIKUI	899
189	99	SIKRAI	899
189	157	BAP	899
192	116	BHADRA	898
193	111	KARANPUR	897
194	37	SHAHBAD	896
195	18	RAMGARH	895
195	117	HANUMANGARH	895
197	34	CHHABRA	894
197	109	ANUPGARH	894
199	14	LACHHMANGARH	892
200	17	RAJGARH	890
201	167	NADOTI	889
202	66	BIKANER	888
203	22	UMREN	886
203	110	GANGANAGAR	886
205	48	KAMAN	883
206	19	RENI	882
206	203	BAMANWAS	882
208	68	KOLAYAT	877
209	51	NAGAR PAHARI	876
209	134	SANKRA	876
211	205	GANGAPUR	875
212	41	CHOHTAN	872
212	98	MAHWA	872
214	206	KHANDAR	871
215	11	KATHUMAR	868
216	21	TIJARA	860
217	169	TODABHIM	858
218	49	KUMHER	857
219	53	SEWAR	855
220	39	BARMER	853
221	114	SADULSHAHAR	851
	VERY LOW (<850)		
222	47	DEEG	849
222	168	SAPOTRA	849
224	54	WEIR	847
225	52	RUPBAS	843
225	165	HINDAUN	843
227	43	SHEO	842
228	50	NADBAI	840
229	115	SURATGARH	839
229	166	KARAULI	839
231	102	DHAULPUR	836
232	101	BASERI	825
233	103	RAJAKHERA	816
234	132	JAISALMER	811
235	46	BAYANA	807
236	100	BARI	796
237	133	SAM	787
RAJASTHAN			**930**
		% AGE OF AAPs	**51.90**

BOLD: Equal/Above Average Panchayat Samities (AAPs)

Source: General Annex VII, Col. 17.

ANNEX-3.1

RANKING OF PSS BY PERCENTAGE OF RURAL POPULATION SERVED BY MEDICAL AMENITIES: RAJASTHAN, 1991

(Descending Order)

RANK	P. CODE	PANCHAYAT SAMITIES NAME	%
1	2	3	4
	VERY HIGH (>60)		
1	123	GOVINDGARH	78.48
2	159	BILARA	75.35
3	56	BANERA	74.52
4	186	BALI	73.69
5	153	NAWALGARH	73.61
6	192	RANI STATION	72.90
7	57	HURDA	72.82
8	195	SUMERPUR	71.11
9	209	DHOND	70.61
10	187	DESURI	69.91
11	4	KEKRI	66.66
12	7	PISANGAN	66.45
13	156	BALESAR	65.93
14	152	KHETRI	64.87
15	63	SAHARA	64.86
16	208	DANTA RAMGARH	64.52
17	107	SAGWARA	64.03
18	137	JALOR	63.83
19	66	BIKANER	62.59
20	141	SAYLA	62.45
21	155	UDAIPURWATI	62.41
22	219	SHEOGANJ	62.27
23	67	DUNGARGARH	61.86
24	117	HANUMANGARH	61.81
25	135	AHORE	61.62
25	214	PIPRALI	61.62
27	5	KISHANGARH	61.56
28	230	GIRWA	61.35
29	213	NEEM KA THANA	61.28
30	2	BHINAY	61.21
31	199	KHAMNOR	61.20
32	60	MANDAL	60.90
33	181	MERTA	60.84
34	188	JAITARAN	60.77
35	58	JAHAZPUR	60.42
36	201	RAILMAGRA	60.35
	HIGH (50-60)		
37	221	DEOLI	59.57
38	237	SARADA	59.24
39	62	RAIPUR	58.84
40	49	KUMHER	58.39
41	235	MAVLI	58.29
42	116	BHADRA	58.13
43	158	BHOPALGARH	57.94
44	25	GARHI	57.70
45	130	SHAHPURA	57.66
46	222	MALPURA	57.64
47	211	KHANDELA	57.41
48	205	GANGAPUR	57.32
49	88	RASHMI	57.13
50	183	NAGAUR	56.47
51	189	KHARCHI/MARWAR JUN.	56.45
52	164	SHERGARH	56.34
53	131	VIRATNAGAR	55.76
54	55	ASIND	55.33
55	150	CHIRAWA	55.30
56	102	DHAULPUR	54.95
57	148	ALSISAR	54.82
58	94	TARANAGAR	54.77
59	160	LUNI	54.43
60	217	PINDWARA	54.31
61	64	SHAHPURA	54.26
62	20	THANAGAZI	54.16
63	91	RATANGARH	54.03
64	6	MASOODA	53.89
65	179	LADNU	53.60
66	118	NOHAR	53.42
67	110	GANGANAGAR	53.05
68	65	SUWANA	52.81
69	194	SOJAT	52.75
70	215	SRI MADHOPUR	52.56
71	80	BHOPALSAGAR	52.38
72	190	PALI	52.13
73	70	NOKHA	51.78
74	10	BEHROR	51.70
74	185	RIYAN	51.70
76	220	SIROHI	51.63
77	61	MANDALGARH	51.48
78	114	SADULSHAHAR	51.17
79	69	KOTRI	51.05
80	203	BAMANWAS	50.75
81	167	NADOTI	50.63
82	178	KUCHAMAN	50.62
83	30	TALWARA	50.26
	MEDIUM (40-50)		
84	104	ASPUR	49.97
85	16	NIMRANA	49.90
86	165	HINDAUN	49.73
87	1	ARAIN	49.69
88	32	ATRU	49.63
89	24	BAGIDORA	49.32
90	177	JAYAL	49.20
91	101	BASERI	48.81
92	105	BICHHIWARA	48.60
93	224	TODARAISINGH	48.57
94	170	CHECHAT	48.55
95	93	SUJANGARH	48.32
96	8	SRINAGAR	48.26
97	197	BHIM	47.94
98	175	DEGANA	47.79
99	210	FATEHPUR	47.62
100	17	RAJGARH	47.48
101	126	KOTPUTLI	47.34
102	207	SAWAI MADHOPUR	47.33
103	54	WEIR	47.23
103	180	MAKRANA	47.23
105	212	LACHHMANGARH	47.16
106	182	MUNDWA	46.95
107	206	KHANDAR	46.80
108	228	BHINDER	46.70
109	151	JHUNJHUNUN	46.68
110	127	PHAGI	46.57
111	128	SAMBHAR	46.52
112	124	JAMWA RAMGARH	46.40
113	138	JASWANTPURA	46.36
114	236	SALUMBAR	46.31
115	202	RAJSAMAND	45.94
116	232	JHADOL	45.76
117	45	SIWANA	45.72
118	168	SAPOTRA	45.68
119	184	PARBATSAR	45.59
120	122	DUDU	45.57
121	120	BASSI	45.36
122	31	ANTA	45.34
123	171	ITAWA	45.23
124	69	LUNKARANSAR	44.96
125	169	TODABHIM	44.80
126	28	PEEPALKHOONT	44.79
127	15	MANDAWAR	44.44
128	68	KOLAYAT	44.43
129	227	BARGAON	44.27
130	172	LADPURA	44.19
131	11	KATHUMAR	44.10
132	46	BAYANA	44.02
133	9	BANSURE	43.66
134	176	DIDWANA	43.15
135	225	TONK	43.08
136	174	SULTANPUR	42.97
137	204	BONLI	42.81
138	99	SIKRAI	42.43
139	26	GHATOL	42.31
140	162	OSIAN	42.29
141	52	RUPBAS	42.28
142	73	NAINWA	42.07
143	96	DAUSA	41.91
144	149	BUHANA	41.81
145	233	KHERWARA	41.44
146	108	SIMALWARA	41.42
147	115	SURATGARH	41.22
148	196	AMET	41.18
149	13	KOTKASIM	40.96
150	19	RENI	40.87
151	106	DUNGARPUR	40.56
152	22	UMREN	40.52
153	112	PADAMPUR	40.47
154	85	KAPASAN	40.30
155	119	AMBER	40.10
156	223	NIWAI	40.04
157	132	JAISALMER	40.03
	LOW (30-40)		
158	200	KUMBHALGARH	39.80
159	75	ARNOD	39.79
160	113	RAISINGHNAGAR	39.53
161	12	KISHANGARH BAS	39.46
161	23	ANANDPURI	39.46
163	84	GANGRAR	39.45
164	145	KHANPUR	39.25
165	98	MAHWA	39.16
166	129	SANGANER	39.08
167	218	REODAR	38.66
168	226	UNIARA	38.55
169	72	KESHORAIPATAN	38.22
170	173	SANGOD	38.03
171	166	KARAULI	37.77
172	142	BAKANI	37.62
173	36	KISHANGANJ	37.27
173	136	BHINMAL	37.27
175	121	CHAKSU	37.06
176	89	CHURU	37.04
177	125	JHOTWARA	37.02
177	143	DAG	37.02
179	231	GOGUNDA	36.94
180	18	RAMGARH	36.72
181	78	BHADESAR	36.66
182	163	PHALODI	36.59
183	83	DUNGLA	36.47
184	41	CHOHTAN	36.45
185	100	BARI	36.22
186	191	RAIPUR	36.11
187	140	SANCHORE	35.96
188	139	RANIWARA	35.35
189	154	SURAJGARH	35.21
190	95	BANDIKUI	35.14
190	147	PIRAWA	35.14
192	74	TALERA	34.98
193	77	BEGUN	34.91
194	229	DHARIAWAD	34.79
195	38	BALOTRA	34.77
196	193	ROHAT	34.73
197	50	NADBAI	34.37
198	111	KARANPUR	34.03
199	53	SEWAR	33.86
200	14	LACHHMANGARH	33.66
201	90	RAJGARH	33.61
202	3	JAWAJA	33.60
203	76	BARI SADRI	33.53
204	82	CHITTAURGARH	33.39
205	144	JHALRAPATAN	33.21
206	87	PRATAPGARH	33.18
207	47	DEEG	33.08
208	92	SARDARSHAHAR	33.05
209	134	SANKRA	32.92
210	33	BARAN	31.62
211	97	LALSOT	31.00
212	133	SAM	30.42
213	21	TIJARA	30.22
	VERY LOW (<30)		
214	48	KAMAN	29.99
215	35	CHHIPABAROD	29.30
216	37	SHAHBAD	29.04
217	198	DEOGARH	28.25
218	146	MANOHARTHANA	28.21
219	103	RAJAKHERA	28.16
220	161	MANDOR	27.67
221	71	HINDOLI	26.47
222	157	BAP	26.40
223	86	NIMBAHERA	25.09
224	44	SINDHARI	25.07
225	51	NAGAR PAHARI	24.36
226	34	CHHABRA	24.20
227	234	KOTRA	23.73
228	79	BHAINSRORGARH	23.52
229	29	SAJJANGARH	23.46
230	109	ANUPGARH	23.07
231	43	SHEO	21.26
232	42	DHORIMANNA	20.23
233	39	BARMER	20.21
234	81	CHHOTI SADRI	20.08
235	27	KUSHALGARH	16.90
236	40	BAYTOO	15.49
237	216	ABU ROAD	4.41
RAJASTHAN			**46.17**
		%age of AAPs	**48.10**

BOLD: Equal/Above Average Panchayat Samities (AAPs)

Source: General Annex II, Col. 3.

ANNEX-3.2

RANKING OF PSS BY PERCENTAGE OF INHABITED VILLAGES HAVING MEDICAL AMENITIES: RAJASTHAN, 1991

(Descending Order)

RANK	*P. CODE*	*PANCHAYAT SAMITIES NAME*	*%*
1	2	3	4
	VERY HIGH (>50)		
1	153	**NAWALGARH**	54.29
2	209	**DHOND**	50.93
	HIGH (40-50)		
3	159	**BILARA**	48.10
4	123	**GOVINDGARH**	47.37
5	195	**SUMERPUR**	46.03
6	164	**SHERGARH**	46.00
7	137	**JALOR**	45.45
8	7	**PISANGAN**	44.74
9	192	**RANI STATION**	43.84
10	56	**BANERA**	42.68
11	156	**BALESAR**	42.65
12	186	**BALI**	41.57
13	213	**NEEM KA THANA**	41.26
14	152	**KHETRI**	41.25
15	57	**HURDA**	41.18
16	102	**DHAULPUR**	40.38
	MEDIUM (30-40)		
17	67	**DUNGARGARH**	40.00
18	187	**DESURI**	39.47
19	215	**SRI MADHOPUR**	39.34
20	130	**SHAHPURA**	39.24
21	2	**BHINAY**	39.17
22	141	**SAYLA**	38.96
23	25	**GARHI**	38.04
24	4	**KEKRI**	37.23
25	155	**UDAIPURWATI**	37.04
25	208	**DANTA RAMGARH**	37.04
27	91	**RATANGARH**	34.37
28	188	**JAITARAN**	33.70
29	199	**KHAMNOR**	33.33
30	235	**MAVLI**	33.11
31	5	**KISHANGARH**	32.73
32	107	**SAGWARA**	32.68
33	8	**SRINAGAR**	32.63
34	49	**KUMHER**	32.43
35	135	**AHORE**	32.41
36	158	**BHOPALGARH**	32.14
37	165	**HINDAUN**	31.93
38	211	**KHANDELA**	31.90
39	63	**SAHARA**	31.87
39	214	**PIPRALI**	31.87
41	205	**GANGAPUR**	31.30
42	194	**SOJAT**	31.25
43	237	**SARADA**	31.12
44	126	**KOTPUTLI**	31.09
45	58	**JAHAZPUR**	30.94
46	45	**SIWANA**	30.93
47	222	**MALPURA**	30.89
48	160	**CHIRAWA**	30.49
49	219	**SHEOGANJ**	30.30
50	104	**ASPUR**	30.28
51	179	**LADNU**	30.21
	LOW (20-30)		
52	210	**FATEHPUR**	29.79
53	217	**PINDWARA**	29.59
54	178	**KUCHAMAN**	29.45
55	16	**NIMRANA**	29.41
56	62	**RAIPUR**	29.07
57	10	**BEHROR**	28.89
57	201	**RAILMAGRA**	28.89
59	221	**DEOLI**	28.66
60	183	**NAGAUR**	28.57
61	66	**BIKANER**	28.39
62	64	**SHAHPURA**	28.19
63	60	**MANDAL**	27.85
63	106	**DUNGARPUR**	27.85
65	70	**NOKHA**	27.78
65	138	**JASWANTPURA**	27.78
65	184	**PARBATSAR**	27.78
68	230	**GIRWA**	27.67
69	93	**SUJANGARH**	27.45
70	167	**NADOTI**	27.38
71	191	**RAIPUR**	27.18
72	6	**MASOODA**	27.01
73	110	**GANGANAGAR**	26.97
74	54	**WEIR**	26.76
74	169	**TODABHIM**	26.76
76	55	**ASIND**	26.60
77	160	**LUNI**	26.56
78	212	**LACHHMANGARH**	26.47
79	24	**BAGIDORA**	26.28
79	189	**KHARCHI/MARWAR JUN.**	26.28
81	131	**VIRATNAGAR**	26.27
82	190	**PALI**	26.25
83	15	**MANDAWAR**	26.06
84	181	**MERTA**	26.04
85	185	**RIYAN**	25.83
86	162	**OSIAN**	25.75
87	220	**SIROHI**	25.61
88	163	**PHALODI**	25.58
89	88	**RASHMI**	25.32
90	89	**CHURU**	24.75
91	105	**BICHHIWARA**	24.71
92	59	**KOTRI**	24.66
92	175	**DEGANA**	24.66
94	149	**BUHANA**	24.59
95	182	**MUNDWA**	24.55
96	65	**SUWANA**	24.43
97	120	**BASSI**	24.40
98	151	**JHUNJHUNUN**	24.36
99	30	**TALWARA**	24.30
100	46	**BAYANA**	23.90
101	224	**TODARAISINGH**	23.85
102	232	**JHADOL**	23.83
103	1	**ARAIN**	23.77
104	177	**JAYAL**	23.48
105	94	**TARANAGAR**	23.42
106	52	**RUPBAS**	23.40
107	236	**SALUMBAR**	23.38
108	154	**SURAJGARH**	23.33
109	128	**SAMBHAR**	23.08
109	216	**ABU ROAD**	23.08
111	100	**BARI**	23.02
112	148	**ALSISAR**	23.01
113	101	**BASERI**	22.95
114	140	**SANCHORE**	22.78
115	176	**DIDWANA**	22.75
116	28	**PEEPALKHOONT**	22.58
117	32	**ATRU**	22.22
118	197	**BHIM**	22.02
119	233	**KHERWARA**	21.99
120	113	**RAISINGHNAGAR**	21.81
121	124	**JAMWA RAMGARH**	21.65
122	20	**THANAGAZI**	21.62
123	134	**SANKRA**	21.54
124	136	**BHINMAL**	21.52
125	85	**KAPASAN**	21.50
126	92	**SARDARSHAHAR**	21.18
127	23	**ANANDPURI**	21.14
128	119	**AMBER**	21.13
129	200	**KUMBHALGARH**	21.12
130	50	**NADBAI**	21.05
131	227	**BARGAON**	20.98
132	11	**KATHUMAR**	20.89
133	180	**MAKRANA**	20.83
134	53	SEWAR	20.13
134	207	SAWAI MADHOPUR	20.13
136	12	KISHANGARH BAS	20.00
136	13	KOTKASIM	20.00
136	22	UMREN	20.00
136	202	RAJSAMAND	20.00
	VERY LOW (<20)		
140	170	CHECHAT	19.86
141	9	BANSURE	19.85
142	203	BAMANWAS	19.70
143	3	JAWAJA	19.69
144	61	MANDALGARH	19.63
145	90	RAJGARH	19.51
146	116	BHADRA	19.47
147	166	KARAULI	19.39
148	139	RANIWARA	19.28
149	69	LUNKARANSAR	19.23
150	196	AMET	19.12
151	193	ROHAT	18.99
152	99	SIKRAI	18.84
153	48	KAMAN	18.72
154	168	SAPOTRA	18.66
155	112	PADAMPUR	18.64
156	41	CHOHTAN	18.56
157	172	LADPURA	18.49
157	231	GOGUNDA	18.49
159	127	PHAGI	18.45
160	225	TONK	18.15
161	18	RAMGARH	18.13
162	122	DUDU	18.10
163	80	BHOPALSAGAR	18.07
164	206	KHANDAR	17.95
165	121	CHAKSU	17.83
165	204	BONLI	17.83
167	31	ANTA	17.69
168	118	NOHAR	17.68
169	108	SIMALWARA	17.35
170	218	REODAR	17.21
171	68	KOLAYAT	17.16
172	147	PIRAWA	17.00
173	174	SULTANPUR	16.87
174	74	TALERA	16.86
175	125	JHOTWARA	16.67
176	17	RAJGARH	16.18
177	171	ITAWA	16.15
178	157	BAP	16.13
179	129	SANGANER	16.10
180	26	GHATOL	16.06
180	132	JAISALMER	16.06
182	96	DAUSA	15.84
183	72	KESHORAIPATAN	15.74
184	19	RENI	15.69
185	103	RAJAKHERA	15.65
186	143	DAG	15.45
187	98	MAHWA	15.33
188	33	BARAN	15.31
189	117	HANUMANGARH	15.30
190	161	MANDOR	15.24
191	47	DEEG	15.00
192	73	NAINWA	14.86
193	114	SADULSHAHAR	14.85
194	38	BALOTRA	14.81
195	228	BHINDER	14.77
196	146	MANOHARTHANA	14.60
197	144	JHALRAPATAN	14.54
198	111	KARANPUR	14.50
199	95	BANDIKUI	14.49
200	145	KHANPUR	14.21
201	29	SAJJANGARH	13.74
202	14	LACHHMANGARH	13.69
203	115	SURATGARH	13.68
204	173	SANGOD	13.64
205	142	BAKANI	13.48
206	87	PRATAPGARH	13.44
207	42	DHORIMANNA	13.10
208	226	UNIARA	13.09
209	21	TIJARA	13.07
210	75	ARNOD	12.87
211	83	DUNGLA	12.75
212	84	GANGRAR	12.60
213	223	NIWAI	12.57
214	44	SINDHARI	12.50
215	35	CHHIPABAROD	12.02
216	51	NAGAR PAHARI	11.98
217	36	KISHANGANJ	11.93
218	77	BEGUN	11.87
219	71	HINDOLI	11.49
220	198	DEOGARH	11.45
221	39	BARMER	11.32
222	34	CHHABRA	11.05
223	229	DHARIAWAD	10.98
224	43	SHEO	10.78
225	78	BHADESAR	10.56
226	76	BARI SADRI	10.42
227	133	SAM	9.96
228	97	LALSOT	9.90
229	27	KUSHALGARH	9.62
230	37	SHAHBAD	8.80
231	82	CHITTAURGARH	7.80
232	234	KOTRA	7.62
233	109	ANUPGARH	7.61
234	79	BHAINSRORGARH	7.33
234	86	NIMBAHERA	7.33
236	40	BAYTOO	6.85
237	81	CHHOTI SADRI	6.38
		RAJASTHAN	**20.68**
		%age of AAPs	**56.11**

BOLD: Equal/Above Average Panchayat Samities (AAPs)

Source: General Annex III, Col. 3.

ANNEX-3.3

RANKING OF PSS BY TOTAL NO. OF MEDICAL INSTITUTIONS: RAJASTHAN, 1991

(Descending Order)

RANK	P. CODE	PANCHAYAT SAMITIES NAME	%
1	2	3	4
	VERY HIGH (>80)		
1	**25**	**GARHI**	**104**
2	**61**	**MANDALGARH**	**100**
3	**104**	**ASPUR**	**88**
4	**208**	**DANTA RAMGARH**	**81**
	HIGH (60-80)		
5	**232**	**JHADOL**	**79**
5	**233**	**KHERWARA**	**79**
7	**7**	**PISANGAN**	**78**
8	**107**	**SAGWARA**	**74**
9	**60**	**MANDAL**	**72**
9	**30**	**TALWARA**	**72**
11	**237**	**SARADA**	**71**
12	**105**	**BICHHIWARA**	**68**
13	**26**	**GHATOL**	**66**
14	**209**	**DHOND**	**65**
14	**213**	**NEEM KA THANA**	**65**
16	**228**	**BHINDER**	**64**
16	**143**	**DAG**	**64**
16	**58**	**JAHAZPUR**	**64**
16	**235**	**MAVLI**	**64**
20	**24**	**BAGIDORA**	**62**
20	**106**	**DUNGARPUR**	**62**
20	**5**	**KISHANGARH**	**62**
23	**123**	**GOVINDGARH**	**61**
23	**52**	**RUPBAS**	**61**
25	**178**	**KUCHAMAN**	**60**
25	**113**	**RAISINGHNAGAR**	**60**
	MEDIUM (40-60)		
27	**32**	**ATRU**	**59**
27	**186**	**BALI**	**59**
27	**2**	**BHINAY**	**59**
27	**199**	**KHAMNOR**	**59**
27	**189**	**KHARCHI/MARWAR JUN.**	**59**
27	**59**	**KOTRI**	**59**
27	**98**	**MAHWA**	**59**
27	**207**	**SAWAI MADHOPUR**	**59**
27	**115**	**SURATGARH**	**59**
36	**162**	**OSIAN**	**58**
36	**87**	**PRATAPGARH**	**58**
36	**54**	**WEIR**	**58**
39	**176**	**DIDWANA**	**57**
39	**57**	**HURDA**	**57**
39	**144**	**JHALRAPATAN**	**57**
39	**74**	**TALERA**	**57**
43	**175**	**DEGANA**	**56**
43	**236**	**SALUMBAR**	**56**
43	**64**	**SHAHPURA**	**56**
43	**93**	**SUJANGARH**	**56**
47	**230**	**GIRWA**	**55**
47	**4**	**KEKRI**	**55**
47	**118**	**NOHAR**	**55**
50	**135**	**AHORE**	**54**
50	**187**	**DESURI**	**54**
50	**205**	**GANGAPUR**	**54**
50	**117**	**HANUMANGARH**	**54**
54	**177**	**JAYAL**	**53**
54	**191**	**RAIPUR**	**53**
56	**221**	**DEOLI**	**52**
56	**90**	**RAJGARH**	**52**
56	**192**	**RANI STATION**	**52**
56	**128**	**SAMBHAR**	**52**
56	**225**	**TONK**	**52**
61	**66**	**BIKANER**	**51**
61	**159**	**BILARA**	**51**
61	**124**	**JAMWA RAMGARH**	**51**
61	**108**	**SIMALWARA**	**51**
65	**122**	**DUDU**	**50**
65	**151**	**JHUNJHUNUN**	**50**
65	**126**	**KOTPUTLI**	**50**
65	**147**	**PIRAWA**	**50**
69	**56**	**BANERA**	**49**
69	**89**	**CHURU**	**49**
69	**231**	**GOGUNDA**	**49**
69	**141**	**SAYLA**	**49**
73	**102**	**DHAULPUR**	**48**
73	**152**	**KHETRI**	**48**
73	**153**	**NAWALGARH**	**48**
76	**171**	**ITAWA**	**47**
76	**137**	**JALOR**	**47**
76	**163**	**PHALODI**	**47**
76	**140**	**SANCHORE**	**47**

RANK	P. CODE	PANCHAYAT SAMITIES NAME	%
1	2	3	4
80	**200**	**KUMBHALGARH**	**46**
80	**217**	**PINDWARA**	**46**
82	**212**	**LACHHMANGARH**	**45**
82	**160**	**LUNI**	**45**
82	**51**	**NAGAR PAHARI**	**45**
82	**134**	**SANKRA**	**45**
82	**130**	**SHAHPURA**	**45**
82	**45**	**SIWANA**	**45**
88	**121**	**CHAKSU**	**44**
88	**71**	**HINDOLI**	**44**
88	**166**	**KARAULI**	**44**
88	**11**	**KATHUMAR**	**44**
88	**202**	**RAJSAMAND**	**44**
88	**63**	**SAHARA**	**44**
94	**75**	**ARNOD**	**43**
94	**77**	**BEGUN**	**43**
94	**188**	**JAITARAN**	**43**
94	**72**	**KESHORAIPATAN**	**43**
94	**181**	**MERTA**	**43**
94	**73**	**NAINWA**	**43**
94	**70**	**NOKHA**	**43**
94	**184**	**PARBATSAR**	**43**
94	**168**	**SAPOTRA**	**43**
94	**194**	**SOJAT**	**43**
94	**195**	**SUMERPUR**	**43**
105	55	ASIND	42
105	42	DHORIMANNA	42
105	206	KHANDAR	42
105	222	MALPURA	42
105	214	PIPRALI	42
105	114	SADULSHAHAR	42
105	65	SUWANA	42
105	169	TODABHIM	42
113	156	BALESAR	41
113	3	JAWAJA	41
113	183	NAGAUR	41
113	129	SANGANER	41
113	155	UDAIPURWATI	41
118	31	ANTA	40
118	38	BALOTRA	40
118	116	BHADRA	40
118	197	BHIM	40
118	204	BONLI	40
118	96	DAUSA	40
118	210	FATEHPUR	40
118	179	LADNU	40
118	180	MAKRANA	40
118	164	SHERGARH	40
118	20	THANAGAZI	40
	LOW (20-40)		
129	120	BASSI	39
129	10	BEHROR	39
129	170	CHECHAT	39
129	229	DHARIAWAD	39
129	36	KISHANGANJ	39
129	68	KOLAYAT	39
129	15	MANDAWAR	39
129	6	MASOODA	39
129	44	SINDHARI	39
138	148	ALSISAR	38
138	62	RAIPUR	38
138	17	RAJGARH	38
138	218	REODAR	38
138	99	SIKRAI	38
143	80	BHOPALSAGAR	37
143	138	JASWANTPURA	37
143	69	LUNKARANSAR	37
143	88	RASHMI	37
143	185	RIYAN	37
143	215	SRI MADHOPUR	37
149	9	BANSURE	36
149	158	BHOPALGARH	36
149	110	GANGANAGAR	36
149	167	NADOTI	36
149	91	RATANGARH	36
149	133	SAM	36
149	174	SULTANPUR	36
149	131	VIRATNAGAR	36
157	227	BARGAON	35
157	39	BARMER	35
157	49	KUMHER	35
157	146	MANOHARTHANA	35

RANK	P. CODE	PANCHAYAT SAMITIES NAME	%
1	2	3	4
157	223	NIWAI	35
157	127	PHAGI	35
157	201	RAILMAGRA	35
157	18	RAMGARH	35
157	8	SRINAGAR	35
166	23	ANANDPURI	34
166	1	ARAIN	34
166	100	BARI	34
166	149	BUHANA	34
166	150	CHIRAWA	34
166	165	HINDAUN	34
166	182	MUNDWA	34
166	173	SANGOD	34
174	119	AMBER	33
174	203	BAMANWAS	33
174	14	LACHHMANGARH	33
174	28	PEEPALKHOONT	33
174	94	TARANAGAR	33
174	22	UMREN	33
180	46	BAYANA	32
180	211	KHANDELA	32
180	234	KOTRA	32
180	27	KUSHALGARH	32
180	112	PADAMPUR	32
185	196	AMET	31
185	142	BAKANI	31
185	95	BANDIKUI	31
185	172	LADPURA	31
189	101	BASERI	30
189	41	CHOHTAN	30
189	132	JAISALMER	30
189	97	LALSOT	30
189	220	SIROHI	30
194	34	CHHABRA	29
194	35	CHHIPABAROD	29
194	85	KAPASAN	29
194	145	KHANPUR	29
194	190	PALI	29
199	109	ANUPGARH	28
199	67	DUNGARGARH	28
199	16	NIMRANA	28
199	29	SAJJANGARH	28
199	154	SURAJGARH	28
199	21	TIJARA	28
199	226	UNIARA	28
206	33	BARAN	26
206	76	BARI SADRI	26
206	78	BHADESAR	26
206	84	GANGRAR	26
206	13	KOTKASIM	26
206	53	SEWAR	26
206	219	SHEOGANJ	26
213	40	BAYTOO	25
213	92	SARDARSHAHAR	25
215	50	NADBAI	24
215	19	RENI	24
217	216	ABU ROAD	23
217	136	BHINMAL	23
217	82	CHITTAURGARH	23
217	47	DEEG	23
217	103	RAJAKHERA	23
222	125	JHOTWARA	22
223	83	DUNGLA	21
223	37	SHAHBAD	21
223	224	TODARAISINGH	21
226	193	ROHAT	20
226	43	SHEO	20
	VERY LOW (< 20)		
228	81	CHHOTI SADRI	18
228	12	KISHANGARH BAS	18
228	161	MANDOR	18
231	48	KAMAN	17
232	79	BHAINSRORGARH	16
232	86	NIMBAHERA	16
232	139	RANIWARA	16
235	157	BAP	13
235	198	DEOGARH	13
237	111	KARANPUR	12
RAJASTHAN		**TOTAL**	**10050**
		AVERAGE	**42.41**
		%age of AAPs	**43.88**

BOLD: Equal/Above Average Panchayat Samities (AAPs) *Source*: General Annex IV, Col. 10.

ANNEX-3.4

RANKING OF PSS BY PERCENTAGE OF RURAL POPULATION SERVED BY EDUCATION AMENITIES: RAJASTHAN, 1991

(Descending Order)

RANK	P. CODE	PANCHAYAT SAMITIES NAME	%
1	2	3	4
	PERFECT (100)		
1	153	NAWALGARH	100.00
1	164	SHERGARH	100.00
	VERY HIGH (95-100)		
3	139	RANIWARA	99.98
4	130	SHAHPURA	99.96
5	215	SRI MADHOPUR	99.93
6	141	SAYLA	99.91
7	186	BALI	99.86
8	8	SRINAGAR	99.84
9	210	FATEHPUR	99.76
10	7	PISANGAN	99.74
11	159	BILARA	99.73
12	216	ABU ROAD	99.71
13	154	SURAJGARH	99.67
14	137	JALOR	99.66
15	102	DHAULPUR	99.64
16	4	KEKRI	99.60
17	194	SOJAT	99.51
18	156	BALESAR	99.43
19	49	KUMHER	99.42
20	192	RANI STATION	99.39
21	155	UDAIPURWATI	99.38
22	2	BHINAY	99.35
23	123	GOVINDGARH	99.34
24	175	DEGANA	99.32
25	57	HURDA	99.29
26	89	CHURU	99.24
27	214	PIPRALI	99.23
28	193	ROHAT	99.17
29	190	PALI	99.15
29	212	LACHHMANGARH	99.15
31	10	BEHROR	99.14
32	217	PINDWARA	99.13
33	1	ARAIN	99.06
33	33	BARAN	99.06
35	160	LUNI	99.04
36	149	BUHANA	99.00
37	107	SAGWARA	98.99
38	15	MANDAWAR	98.94
38	135	AHORE	98.94
38	158	BHOPALGARH	98.94
41	185	RIYAN	98.92
42	148	ALSISAR	98.87
42	205	GANGAPUR	98.87
44	54	WEIR	98.86
44	138	JASWANTPURA	98.86
46	220	SIROHI	98.84
47	161	MANDOR	98.81
48	219	SHEOGANJ	98.80
49	182	MUNDWA	98.76
49	211	KHANDELA	98.76
51	179	LADNU	98.74
52	235	MAVLI	98.60
53	50	NADBAI	98.55
54	70	NOKHA	98.50
55	66	BIKANER	98.48
56	16	NIMRANA	98.47
56	209	DHOND	98.47
58	150	CHIRAWA	98.43
59	195	SUMERPUR	98.36
60	52	RUPBAS	98.35
61	208	DANTA RAMGARH	98.34
62	140	SANCHORE	98.33
63	180	MAKRANA	98.30
64	88	RASHMI	98.29
65	62	RAIPUR	98.27
66	178	KUCHAMAN	98.26
67	136	BHINMAL	98.24
68	152	KHETRI	98.21
69	53	SEWAR	98.18
70	11	KATHUMAR	98.16
71	65	SUWANA	98.14
72	187	DESURI	98.10
73	218	REODAR	98.09
74	64	SHAHPURA	98.07
75	151	JHUNJHUNUN	98.06
76	9	BANSURE	98.03
76	184	PARBATSAR	98.03
78	45	SIWANA	98.01
79	177	JAYAL	97.99
80	69	LUNKARANSAR	97.98
81	46	BAYANA	97.91
82	126	KOTPUTLI	97.87
83	25	GARHI	97.85
84	165	HINDAUN	97.83
85	63	SAHARA	97.82
86	213	NEEM KA THANA	97.70
87	93	SUJANGARH	97.69
88	207	SAWAI MADHOPUR	97.68
89	91	RATANGARH	97.66
90	47	DEEG	97.64
91	67	DUNGARGARH	97.62
91	222	MALPURA	97.62
93	176	DIDWANA	97.60
94	188	JAITARAN	97.54
95	202	RAJSAMAND	97.51
96	183	NAGAUR	97.38
97	181	MERTA	97.35
98	56	BANERA	97.32
99	203	BAMANWAS	97.30
100	128	SAMBHAR	97.29
101	163	PHALODI	97.26
102	231	GOGUNDA	97.17
103	94	TARANAGAR	97.08
104	201	RAILMAGRA	97.04
105	105	BICHHIWARA	97.03
106	20	THANAGAZI	96.97
107	199	KHAMNOR	96.90
108	90	RAJGARH	96.82
108	147	PIRAWA	96.82
110	106	DUNGARPUR	96.75
111	60	MANDAL	96.74
112	23	ANANDPURI	96.69
113	92	SARDARSHAHAR	96.60
114	227	BARGAON	96.55
115	59	KOTRI	96.26
116	101	BASERI	96.25
117	5	KISHANGARH	96.24
117	71	HINDOLI	96.24
117	169	TODABHIM	96.24
120	103	RAJAKHERA	96.21
121	230	GIRWA	95.96
122	99	SIKRAI	95.87
123	204	BONLI	95.86
124	98	MAHWA	95.78
125	58	JAHAZPUR	95.72
126	237	SARADA	95.70
127	26	GHATOL	95.51
128	172	LADPURA	95.43
129	221	DEOLI	95.39
130	14	LACHHMANGARH	95.38
131	189	KHARCHI/MARWAR JUN	95.37
132	6	MASOODA	95.36
133	31	ANTA	95.29
134	191	RAIPUR	95.25
135	13	KOTKASIM	95.15
136	197	BHIM	95.03
	HIGH (90-95)		
137	122	DUDU	94.97
138	233	KHERWARA	94.95
139	12	KISHANGARH BAS	94.84
140	125	JHOTWARA	94.81
141	83	DUNGLA	94.79
142	124	JAMWA RAMGARH	94.75
143	134	SANKRA	94.69
144	167	NADOTI	94.53
145	73	NAINWA	94.52
146	132	JAISALMER	94.45
147	116	BHADRA	94.23
148	68	KOLAYAT	94.12
149	17	RAJGARH	94.10
150	80	BHOPALSAGAR	94.01
151	51	NAGAR PAHARI	93.95
152	19	RENI	93.94
153	55	ASIND	93.89
154	22	UMREN	93.88
155	223	NIWAI	93.73
156	24	BAGIDORA	93.58
157	168	SAPOTRA	93.49
158	18	RAMGARH	93.48
159	127	PHAGI	93.40
160	108	SIMALWARA	93.24
161	85	KAPASAN	93.20
162	86	NIMBAHERA	93.17
163	120	BASSI	93.16
164	72	KESHORAIPATAN	93.11
165	3	JAWAJA	93.02
166	100	BARI	92.99
167	200	KUMBHALGARH	92.88
168	21	TIJARA	92.70
169	112	PADAMPUR	92.63
170	131	VIRATNAGAR	92.62
171	174	SULTANPUR	92.60
172	119	AMBER	92.59
173	111	KARANPUR	92.46
174	170	CHECHAT	92.39
175	30	TALWARA	92.30
176	104	ASPUR	92.25
177	48	KAMAN	92.16
178	96	DAUSA	91.84
179	38	BALOTRA	91.72
180	43	SHEO	91.67
181	32	ATRU	91.66
182	224	TODARAISINGH	91.58
183	225	TONK	91.48
184	84	GANGRAR	91.41
185	166	KARAULI	91.38
186	81	CHHOTI SADRI	91.21
187	228	BHINDER	91.20
188	171	ITAWA	91.19
189	74	TALERA	90.99
190	133	SAM	90.78
191	82	CHITTAURGARH	90.65
192	232	JHADOL	90.58
193	41	CHOHTAN	90.54
194	157	BAP	90.26
195	196	AMET	90.05
196	162	OSIAN	90.02
	MEDIUM (85-90)		
197	129	SANGANER	89.88
198	145	KHANPUR	89.75
199	97	LALSOT	89.73
200	143	DAG	89.62
201	206	KHANDAR	89.45
202	75	ARNOD	89.30
203	34	CHHABRA	89.27
204	35	CHHIPABAROD	88.85
205	118	NOHAR	88.34
206	110	GANGANAGAR	87.95
207	95	BANDIKUI	87.60
208	226	UNIARA	87.49
209	61	MANDALGARH	87.08
210	229	DHARIAWAD	86.99
211	76	BARI SADRI	86.91
212	78	BHADESAR	86.85
213	27	KUSHALGARH	85.70
214	37	SHAHBAD	85.51
214	114	SADULSHAHAR	85.51
216	144	JHALRAPATAN	85.26
217	29	SAJJANGARH	85.12
218	28	PEEPALKHOONT	85.08
	LOW (<85)		
219	236	SALUMBAR	84.64
220	87	PRATAPGARH	84.47
221	77	BEGUN	83.91
222	36	KISHANGANJ	83.73
223	173	SANGOD	83.71
224	39	BARMER	83.65
225	113	RAISINGHNAGAR	82.59
226	79	BHAINSRORGARH	81.15
227	142	BAKANI	80.66
228	198	DEOGARH	80.52
229	44	SINDHARI	79.53
230	121	CHAKSU	78.13
231	42	DHORIMANNA	77.69
232	117	HANUMANGARH	76.20
233	40	BAYTOO	74.35
234	146	MANOHARTHANA	74.31
235	115	SURATGARH	74.25
236	234	KOTRA	72.73
237	109	ANUPGARH	56.53
	RAJASTHAN		93.90
	%age of AAPs		64.13

BOLD: Equal/Above Average Panchayat Samities (AAPs)

Source: General Annex II, Col. 5.

ANNEX-3.5

RANKING OF PSS BY PERCENTAGE OF INHABITED VILLAGES HAVING EDUCATION AMENITIES: RAJASTHAN, 1991

(Descending Order)

RANK	P. CODE	PANCHAYAT SAMITIES NAME	%
1	2	3	4
	PERFECT (100)		
1	153	NAWALGARH	100.00
2	164	SHERGARH	100.00
	VERY HIGH (90-100)		
3	210	FATEHPUR	99.29
4	139	RANIWARA	98.80
5	130	SHAHPURA	98.73
6	141	SAYLA	98.70
7	215	SRI MADHOPUR	98.36
8	154	SURAJGARH	98.33
9	8	SRINAGAR	97.89
9	212	LACHHMANGARH	97.79
11	67	DUNGARGARH	97.78
12	186	BALI	97.75
13	158	BHOPALGARH	97.62
14	155	UDAIPURWATI	97.53
15	165	HINDAUN	97.48
16	159	BILARA	97.47
16	193	ROHAT	97.47
18	209	DHOND	97.22
19	161	MANDOR	97.14
20	156	BALESAR	97.06
21	137	JALOR	96.97
22	4	KEKRI	96.81
23	149	BUHANA	96.72
24	148	ALSISAR	96.46
25	194	SOJAT	96.43
26	102	DHAULPUR	96.15
26	216	ABU ROAD	96.15
28	89	CHURU	96.04
29	45	SIWANA	95.88
30	2	BHINAY	95.82
31	15	MANDAWAR	95.77
32	7	PISANGAN	95.61
33	49	KUMHER	95.50
34	184	PARBATSAR	95.37
35	195	SUMERPUR	95.24
36	175	DEGANA	95.21
36	176	DIDWANA	95.21
38	150	CHIRAWA	95.12
39	52	RUPBAS	95.04
40	152	KHETRI	95.00
40	190	PALI	95.00
42	126	KOTPUTLI	94.96
43	90	RAJGARH	94.63
44	160	LUNI	94.58
45	138	JASWANTPURA	94.44
46	1	ARAIN	94.26
47	16	NIMRANA	94.12
47	57	HURDA	94.12
49	33	BARAN	93.88
50	136	BHINMAL	93.67
51	54	WEIR	93.66
52	64	SHAHPURA	93.29
53	178	KUCHAMAN	93.15
53	192	RANI STATION	93.15
55	11	KATHUMAR	93.04
56	162	OSIAN	92.81
57	123	GOVINDGARH	92.63
58	135	AHORE	92.59
59	177	JAYAL	92.42
59	219	SHEOGANJ	92.42
59	140	SANCHORE	92.22
59	201	RAILMAGRA	92.22
63	107	SAGWARA	92.16
64	235	MAVLI	91.89
65	163	PHALODI	91.86
66	182	MUNDWA	91.82
67	183	NAGAUR	91.73
68	151	JHUNJHUNUN	91.67
68	185	RIYAN	91.67
70	205	GANGAPUR	91.30
71	63	SAHARA	91.21
72	9	BANSURE	90.84
73	180	MAKRANA	90.83
74	62	RAIPUR	90.70
75	91	RATANGARH	90.63
75	179	LADNU	90.63
77	92	SARDARSHAHAR	90.59
78	56	BANERA	90.24
79	188	JAITARAN	90.22
80	218	REODAR	90.16
81	214	PIPRALI	90.11
82	5	KISHANGARH	90.00
82	10	BEHROR	90.00
82	202	RAJSAMAND	90.00
	HIGH (80-90)		
85	88	RASHMI	89.87
86	131	VIRATNAGAR	89.83
87	103	RAJAKHERA	89.80
88	231	GOGUNDA	89.73
89	213	NEEM KA THANA	89.51
90	69	LUNKARANSAR	89.23
91	189	KHARCHI/MARWAR JUN.	89.05
92	207	SAWAI MADHOPUR	88.96
93	70	NOKHA	88.89
93	208	DANTA RAMGARH	88.89
95	211	KHANDELA	88.79
96	217	PINDWARA	88.78
97	50	NADBAI	88.60
98	65	SUWANA	88.55
99	134	SANKRA	88.46
100	104	ASPUR	88.03
101	25	GARHI	87.73
102	59	KOTRI	87.61
103	147	PIRAWA	87.50
104	106	DUNGARPUR	87.34
105	128	SAMBHAR	87.21
106	66	BIKANER	87.10
107	14	LACHHMANGARH	86.96
108	187	DESURI	86.84
109	105	BICHHIWARA	86.78
110	169	TODABHIM	86.62
111	220	SIROHI	86.59
112	23	ANANDPURI	86.18
113	46	BAYANA	86.16
114	47	DEEG	85.83
115	93	SUJANGARH	85.62
116	94	TARANAGAR	85.59
117	60	MANDAL	85.44
118	181	MERTA	85.42
119	222	MALPURA	85.37
120	73	NAINWA	85.14
121	200	KUMBHALGARH	84.47
122	53	SEWAR	84.42
122	124	JAMWA RAMGARH	84.42
124	13	KOTKASIM	84.35
125	19	RENI	84.31
126	204	BONLI	84.07
127	98	MAHWA	84.00
128	99	SIKRAI	83.33
128	100	BARI	83.33
128	167	NADOTI	83.33
131	237	SARADA	83.12
132	12	KISHANGARH BAS	82.96
133	71	HINDOLI	82.76
134	197	BHIM	82.57
135	191	RAIPUR	82.52
136	18	RAMGARH	81.87
137	31	ANTA	81.63
138	51	NAGAR PAHARI	81.57
139	122	DUDU	81.43
140	83	DUNGLA	81.37
141	233	KHERWARA	81.33
142	101	BASERI	81.15
143	43	SHEO	80.84
144	157	BAP	80.65
145	127	PHAGI	80.36
146	203	BAMANWAS	80.30
	MEDIUM (70-80)		
147	74	TALERA	79.69
148	41	CHOHTAN	79.64
149	6	MASOODA	79.56
150	80	BHOPALSAGAR	79.52
151	85	KAPASAN	79.44
152	120	BASSI	78.95
153	132	JAISALMER	78.83
154	72	KESHORAIPATAN	78.70
155	230	GIRWA	78.62
156	58	JAHAZPUR	78.45
157	21	TIJARA	78.39
158	24	BAGIDORA	78.10
159	172	LADPURA	78.08
160	199	KHAMNOR	78.03
161	26	GHATOL	77.98
162	20	THANAGAZI	77.70
163	227	BARGAON	77.62
164	22	UMREN	77.33
165	108	SIMALWARA	77.17
166	32	ATRU	77.04
167	3	JAWAJA	76.68
168	166	KARAULI	76.53
169	17	RAJGARH	76.47
169	48	KAMAN	76.47
169	125	JHOTWARA	76.47
172	221	DEOLI	76.43
173	174	SULTANPUR	75.63
174	55	ASIND	75.37
175	119	AMBER	75.26
176	223	NIWAI	74.87
177	143	DAG	74.55
178	111	KARANPUR	74.00
179	170	CHECHAT	73.97
180	38	BALOTRA	73.54
181	224	TODARAISINGH	73.39
182	86	NIMBAHERA	73.33
183	35	CHHIPABAROD	73.22
184	30	TALWARA	72.43
185	168	SAPOTRA	71.29
186	112	PADAMPUR	71.19
187	171	ITAWA	70.19
	LOW (<70)		
188	68	KOLAYAT	69.82
189	225	TONK	69.76
190	96	DAUSA	69.68
191	232	JHADOL	69.53
192	145	KHANPUR	69.47
193	95	BANDIKUI	69.08
194	81	CHHOTI SADRI	68.79
195	42	DHORIMANNA	68.65
196	34	CHHABRA	68.60
197	84	GANGRAR	68.50
198	196	AMET	68.38
199	27	KUSHALGARH	67.79
200	39	BARMER	67.17
201	206	KHANDAR	66.67
201	236	SALUMBAR	66.67
203	82	CHITTAURGARH	66.06
204	44	SINDHARI	65.83
205	129	SANGANER	65.37
206	228	BHINDER	64.02
207	29	SAJJANGARH	63.74
208	78	BHADESAR	63.35
209	97	LALSOT	63.14
210	144	JHALRAPATAN	63.12
210	173	SANGOD	62.12
212	76	BARI SADRI	61.11
213	110	GANGANAGAR	60.17
214	40	BAYTOO	60.08
215	226	UNIARA	59.69
216	61	MANDALGARH	59.63
217	198	DEOGARH	59.54
218	75	ARNOD	59.06
219	229	DHARIAWAD	58.94
220	37	SHAHBAD	58.49
221	133	SAM	58.17
222	87	PRATAPGARH	57.50
223	113	RAISINGHNAGAR	56.94
224	36	KISHANGANJ	56.82
225	28	PEEPALKHOONT	55.91
226	77	BEGUN	54.34
227	121	CHAKSU	53.10
228	116	BHADRA	52.63
229	79	BHAINSRORGARH	51.33
230	146	MANOHARTHANA	50.36
231	142	BAKANI	50.35
232	234	KOTRA	44.04
233	118	NOHAR	42.53
234	114	SADULSHAHAR	34.22
235	115	SURATGARH	30.44
236	109	ANUPGARH	27.89
237	117	HANUMANGARH	25.76
		RAJASTHAN	74.97
		%age of AAPs	73.80

BOLD: Equal/Above Average Panchayat Samities (AAPs)

Source: General Annex III, Col. 5.

ANNEX-3.6

RANKING OF PSS BY TOTAL NO. OF PRIMARY SCHOOLS: RAJASTHAN, 1991

(Descending Order)

RANK	P. CODE	PANCHAYAT SAMITIES NAME	No.
1	2	3	4
	MEDIUM (>=200)		
1	109	**ANUPGARH**	293
2	162	**OSIAN**	230
3	118	**NOHAR**	213
4	115	**SURATGARH**	213
5	233	**KHERWARA**	206
6	74	**TALERA**	205
	LOW (100-200)		
7	140	**SANCHORE**	198
8	113	**RAISINGHNAGAR**	196
8	108	**SIMALWARA**	196
10	124	**JAMWA RAMGARH**	194
11	208	**DANTA RAMGARH**	192
12	90	**RAJGARH**	191
13	39	**BARMER**	186
14	97	**LALSOT**	184
15	51	**NAGAR PAHARI**	183
15	213	**NEEM KA THANA**	183
17	122	**DUDU**	182
17	26	**GHATOL**	182
17	30	**TALWARA**	182
20	102	**DHAULPUR**	180
21	66	**BIKANER**	177
22	228	**BHINDER**	176
22	168	**SAPOTRA**	176
24	72	**KESHORAIPATAN**	174
25	120	**BASSI**	173
26	212	**LACHHMANGARH**	172
26	7	**PISANGAN**	172
26	225	**TONK**	172
29	117	**HANUMANGARH**	171
30	112	**PADAMPUR**	170
30	44	**SINDHARI**	170
32	3	**JAWAJA**	169
32	87	**PRATAPGARH**	169
34	42	**DHORIMANNA**	167
35	151	**JHUNJHUNUN**	166
36	176	**DIDWANA**	165
36	144	**JHALRAPATAN**	165
38	96	**DAUSA**	163
39	147	**PIRAWA**	162
40	230	**GIRWA**	161
41	110	**GANGANAGAR**	160
41	160	**LUNI**	160
43	55	**ASIND**	157
43	166	**KARAULI**	157
45	61	**MANDALGARH**	156
45	235	**MAVLI**	156
47	46	**BAYANA**	155
47	143	**DAG**	155
49	60	**MANDAL**	155
50	70	**NOKHA**	154
51	119	**AMBER**	153
51	232	**JHADOL**	153
51	223	**NIWAI**	153
51	107	**SAGWARA**	153
55	54	**WEIR**	152
56	149	**BUHANA**	150
56	52	**RUPBAS**	150
56	21	**TIJARA**	150
59	69	**LUNKARANSAR**	149
59	133	**SAM**	149
61	95	**BANDIKUI**	148
61	105	**BICHHIWARA**	148
61	82	**CHITTAURGARH**	148
61	111	**KARANPUR**	148
61	200	**KUMBHALGARH**	148
61	73	**NAINWA**	148
61	128	**SAMBHAR**	148
68	25	**GARHI**	147
68	103	**RAJAKHERA**	147
68	155	**UDAIPURWATI**	147
71	40	**BAYTOO**	146
71	71	**HINDOLI**	146
71	178	**KUCHAMAN**	146
71	14	**LACHHMANGARH**	146
71	183	**NAGAUR**	146
71	237	**SARAD**	146
71	92	**SARDARSHAHAR**	146
71	130	**SHAHPURA**	146
79	121	**CHAKSU**	145
79	229	**DHARIAWAD**	145
79	106	**DUNGARPUR**	145
79	126	**KOTPUTLI**	145
79	207	**SAWAI MADHOPUR**	145
84	41	**CHOHTAN**	143
85	123	**GOVINDGARH**	142
85	48	**KAMAN**	142
85	93	**SUJANGARH**	142
88	11	**KATHUMAR**	141
88	153	**NAWALGARH**	141
88	43	**SHEO**	141
91	9	**BANSURE**	140
91	210	**FATEHPUR**	140
91	114	**SADULSHAHAR**	140
94	175	**DEGANA**	139
94	129	**SANGANER**	139
96	38	**BALOTRA**	138
96	53	**SEWAR**	138
96	22	**UMREN**	138
99	15	**MANDAWAR**	137
100	58	**JAHAZPUR**	136
100	20	**THANAGAZI**	136
102	203	**BAMANWAS**	135
102	101	**BASERI**	135
104	127	**PHAGI**	134
105	68	**KOLAYAT**	133
106	204	**BONLI**	132
106	98	**MAHWA**	132
106	222	**MALPURA**	132
106	18	**RAMGARH**	132
106	236	**SALUMBAR**	132
111	165	**HINDAUN**	131
111	169	**TODABHIM**	131
113	177	**JAYAL**	130
113	27	**KUSHALGARH**	130
113	154	**SURAJGARH**	130
116	104	ASPUR	129
116	158	BHOPALGARH	129
118	146	MANOHARTHANA	128
119	142	BAKANI	126
119	34	CHHABRA	126
119	211	KHANDELA	126
119	234	KOTRA	126
123	148	ALSISAR	125
123	227	BARGAON	125
123	145	KHANPUR	125
126	209	DHOND	124
126	202	RAJSAMAND	124
128	205	GANGAPUR	123
128	182	MUNDWA	123
128	65	SUWANA	123
131	189	KHARCHI/MARWAR JUN.	122
131	131	VIRATNAGAR	122
133	24	BAGIDORA	121
133	2	BHINAY	121
133	152	KHETRI*	121
133	59	KOTRI	121
133	49	KUMHER	121
133	6	MASOODA	121
133	134	SANKRA	121
140	35	CHHIPABAROD	120
140	221	DEOLI	120
140	173	SANGOD	120
143	31	ANTA	119
143	1	ARAIN	119
143	174	SULTANPUR	119
146	185	RIYAN	118
146	99	SIKRAI	118
148	4	KEKRI*	117
148	5	KISHANGARH	117
148	12	KISHANGARH BAS	117
148	214	PIPRALI	117
152	100	BARI	116
152	116	BHADRA	116
152	231	GOGUNDA	116
152	163	PHALODI	116
156	199	KHAMNOR*	115
157	197	BHIM	114
158	135	AHORE	112
158	180	MAKRANA	112
158	218	REODAR	112
161	77	BEGUN	111
161	47	DEEG	111
161	206	KHANDAR	111
161	184	PARBATSAR	111
165	28	PEEPALKHOON	110
166	171	ITAWA	109
166	17	RAJGARH	109
168	170	CHECHAT	108
168	13	KOTKASIM	108
170	132	JAISALMER	107
170	172	LADPURA	107
172	50	NADBAI	106
172	86	NIMBAHERA	106
172	29	SAJJANGARH	106
172	194	SOJAT	106
172	226	UNIARA	106
177	159	BILARA	105
177	19	RENI	105
179	32	ATRU	104
179	215	SRI MADHOPUR	104
181	161	MANDOR	103
182	75	ARNOD	102
182	156	BALESAR	102
182	45	SIWANA	102
182	8	SRINAGAR	102
186	10	BEHROR	100
	VERY LOW (<100)		
187	78	BHADESAR	99
187	94	TARANAGAR	99
189	89	CHURU	98
189	191	RAIPUR	98
191	81	CHHOTI SADRI	97
191	36	KISHANGANJ	97
193	67	DUNGARGARH	96
194	23	ANANDPURI	95
194	150	CHIRAWA	95
194	179	LADNU	95
194	64	SHAHPURA	95
198	196	AMET	93
198	136	BHINMAL	93
198	181	MERTA	93
201	141	SAYLA	91
202	33	BARAN	90
202	125	JHOTWARA	90
202	63	SAHARA	90
202	37	SHAHBAD	90
206	186	BALI	89
206	188	JAITARAN	89
206	91	RATANGARH	89
209	84	GANGRAR	88
210	157	BAP	87
210	167	NADOTI	87
210	16	NIMRANA	87
210	224	TODARAISINGH	87
214	80	BHOPALSAGAR	83
214	164	SHERGARH	83
216	217	PINDWARA	82
216	139	RANIWARA	82
218	56	BANERA	81
218	76	BARI SADRI	81
220	62	RAIPUR	80
221	83	DUNGLA	78
221	201	RAILMAGRA	78
223	79	BHAINSRORGARH	77
223	192	RANI STATION	77
225	216	ABU ROAD	76
226	190	PALI	75
227	198	DEOGARH	74
227	57	HURDA	74
227	85	KAPASAN	74
230	193	ROHAT	73
231	137	JALOR	72
232	138	JASWANTPURA	71
232	220	SIROHI	71
234	187	DESURI	69
235	88	RASHMI	68
236	219	SHEOGANJ	64
237	195	SUMERPUR	55
RAJASTHAN		**TOTAL**	**30667**
		AVERAGE	**129.4**
		%age of AAPs	**48.50**

BOLD: Equal/Above Average Panchayat Samities (AAPs)

Source: General Annex V, Col. 3.

ANNEX-3.7

RANKING OF PSS BY PERCENTAGE OF RURAL POPULATION SERVED BY DRINKING WATER AMENITIES: RAJASTHAN, 1991

(Descending Order)

RANK	P. CODE	PANCHAYAT SAMITIES NAME	%
1	2	3	4
	PERFECT (100)		
1	23	**ANANDPURI**	100.00
1	31	**ANTA**	100.00
1	1	**ARAIN**	100.00
1	75	**ARNOD**	100.00
1	55	**ASIND**	100.00
1	32	**ATRU**	100.00
1	24	**BAGIDORA**	100.00
1	95	**BANDIKUI**	100.00
1	56	**BANERA**	100.00
1	9	**BANSURE**	100.00
1	33	**BARAN**	100.00
1	100	**BARI**	100.00
1	76	**BARI SADRI**	100.00
1	101	**BASERI**	100.00
1	46	**BAYANA**	100.00
1	77	**BEGUN**	100.00
1	10	**BEHROR**	100.00
1	78	**BHADESAR**	100.00
1	79	**BHAINSRORGARH**	100.00
1	2	**BHINAY**	100.00
1	80	**BHOPALSAGAR**	100.00
1	105	**BICHHIWARA**	100.00
1	34	**CHHABRA**	100.00
1	35	**CHHIPABAROD**	100.00
1	81	**CHHOTI SADRI**	100.00
1	82	**CHITTAURGARH**	100.00
1	41	**CHOHTAN**	100.00
1	96	**DAUSA**	100.00
1	47	**DEEG**	100.00
1	102	**DHAULPUR**	100.00
1	42	**DHORIMANNA**	100.00
1	83	**DUNGLA**	100.00
1	84	**GANGRAR**	100.00
1	25	**GARHI**	100.00
1	26	**GHATOL**	100.00
1	71	**HINDOLI**	100.00
1	57	**HURDA**	100.00
1	58	**JAHAZPUR**	100.00
1	85	**KAPASAN**	100.00
1	11	**KATHUMAR**	100.00
1	4	**KEKRI**	100.00
1	72	**KESHORAIPATAN**	100.00
1	5	**KISHANGARH**	100.00
1	12	**KISHANGARH BAS**	100.00
1	13	**KOTKASIM**	100.00
1	59	**KOTRI**	100.00
1	14	**LACHHMANGARH**	100.00
1	97	**LALSOT**	100.00
1	98	**MAHWA**	100.00
1	60	**MANDAL**	100.00
1	61	**MANDALGARH**	100.00
1	15	**MANDAWAR**	100.00
1	6	**MASOODA**	100.00
1	50	**NADBAI**	100.00
1	51	**NAGAR PAHARI**	100.00
1	73	**NAINWA**	100.00
1	16	**NIMRANA**	100.00
1	28	**PEEPALKHOONT**	100.00
1	7	**PISANGAN**	100.00
1	87	**PRATAPGARH**	100.00
1	62	**RAIPUR**	100.00
1	103	**RAJAKHERA**	100.00
1	17	**RAJGARH**	100.00
1	18	**RAMGARH**	100.00
1	88	**RASHMI**	100.00
1	19	**RENI**	100.00
1	52	**RUPBAS**	100.00
1	63	**SAHARA**	100.00
1	29	**SAJJANGARH**	100.00
1	64	**SHAHPURA**	100.00
1	99	**SIKRAI**	100.00
1	45	**SIWANA**	100.00
1	8	**SRINAGAR**	100.00
1	65	**SUWANA**	100.00
1	74	**TALERA**	100.00
1	30	**TALWARA**	100.00
1	94	**TARANAGAR**	100.00
1	20	**THANAGAZI**	100.00
1	21	**TIJARA**	100.00
1	22	**UMREN**	100.00
1	54	**WEIR**	100.00
1	216	**ABU ROAD**	100.00
1	135	**AHORE**	100.00
1	148	**ALSISAR**	100.00
1	196	**AMET**	100.00
1	109	**ANUPGARH**	100.00
1	142	**BAKANI**	100.00
1	186	**BALI**	100.00
1	203	**BAMANWAS**	100.00
1	120	**BASSI**	100.00
1	116	**BHADRA**	100.00
1	197	**BHIM**	100.00
1	136	**BHINMAL**	100.00
1	159	**BILARA**	100.00
1	149	**BUHANA**	100.00
1	143	**DAG**	100.00
1	208	**DANTA RAMGARH**	100.00
1	175	**DEGANA**	100.00
1	198	**DEOGARH**	100.00
1	187	**DESURI**	100.00
1	176	**DIDWANA**	100.00
1	106	**DUNGARPUR**	100.00
1	210	**FATEHPUR**	100.00
1	110	**GANGANAGAR**	100.00
1	205	**GANGAPUR**	100.00
1	123	**GOVINDGARH**	100.00
1	117	**HANUMANGARH**	100.00
1	165	**HINDAUN**	100.00
1	171	**ITAWA**	100.00
1	188	**JAITARAN**	100.00
1	137	**JALOR**	100.00
1	124	**JAMWA RAMGARH**	100.00
1	138	**JASWANTPURA**	100.00
1	177	**JAYAL**	100.00
1	144	**JHALRAPATAN**	100.00
1	125	**JHOTWARA**	100.00
1	111	**KARANPUR**	100.00
1	166	**KARAULI**	100.00
1	199	**KHAMNOR**	100.00
1	206	**KHANDAR**	100.00
1	211	**KHANDELA**	100.00
1	145	**KHANPUR**	100.00
1	189	**KHARCHI/MARWAR JUN.**	100.00
1	152	**KHETRI**	100.00
1	126	**KOTPUTLI**	100.00
1	200	**KUMBHALGARH**	100.00
1	179	**LADNU**	100.00
1	172	**LADPURA**	100.00
1	160	**LUNI**	100.00
1	180	**MAKRANA**	100.00
1	146	**MANOHARTHANA**	100.00
1	181	**MERTA**	100.00
1	182	**MUNDWA**	100.00
1	167	**NADOTI**	100.00
1	183	**NAGAUR**	100.00
1	153	**NAWALGARH**	100.00
1	112	**PADAMPUR**	100.00
1	190	**PALI**	100.00
1	214	**PIPRALI**	100.00
1	147	**PIRAWA**	100.00
1	201	**RAILMAGRA**	100.00
1	191	**RAIPUR**	100.00
1	113	**RAISINGHNAGAR**	100.00
1	202	**RAJSAMAND**	100.00
1	192	**RANI STATION**	100.00
1	139	**RANIWARA**	100.00
1	218	**REODAR**	100.00
1	193	**ROHAT**	100.00
1	107	**SAGWARA**	100.00
1	129	**SANGANER**	100.00
1	173	**SANGOD**	100.00
1	134	**SANKRA**	100.00
1	207	**SAWAI MADHOPUR**	100.00
1	219	**SHEOGANJ**	100.00
1	108	**SIMALWARA**	100.00
1	220	**SIROHI**	100.00
1	194	**SOJAT**	100.00
1	215	**SRI MADHOPUR**	100.00
1	174	**SULTANPUR**	100.00
1	195	**SUMERPUR**	100.00
1	115	**SURATGARH**	100.00
1	169	**TODABHIM**	100.00
1	155	**UDAIPURWATI**	100.00
1	227	**BARGAON**	100.00
1	228	**BHINDER**	100.00
1	221	**DEOLI**	100.00
1	229	**DHARIAWAD**	100.00
1	230	**GIRWA**	100.00
1	231	**GOGUNDA**	100.00
1	232	**JHADOL**	100.00
1	233	**KHERWARA**	100.00
1	234	**KOTRA**	100.00
1	222	**MALPURA**	100.00
1	235	**MAVLI**	100.00
1	223	**NIWAI**	100.00
1	236	**SALUMBAR**	100.00
1	237	**SARADA**	100.00
1	224	**TODARAISINGH**	100.00
1	225	**TONK**	100.00
1	226	**UNIARA**	100.00
	VERY HIGH (98-100)		
181	121	**CHAKSU**	99.98
182	104	**ASPUR**	99.97
183	130	**SHAHPURA**	99.96
184	91	**RATANGARH**	99.94
185	141	**SAYLA**	99.92
186	133	**SAM**	99.91
187	36	**KISHANGANJ**	99.90
188	170	**CHECHAT**	99.89
188	53	**SEWAR**	99.89
190	86	**NIMBAHERA**	99.88
191	162	**OSIAN**	99.86
191	128	**SAMBHAR**	99.86
191	48	**KAMAN**	99.86
194	119	**AMBER**	99.85
195	204	**BONLI**	99.83
195	178	**KUCHAMAN**	99.83
197	69	**LUNKARANSAR**	99.81
198	157	**BAP**	99.79
199	209	**DHOND**	99.76
200	131	**VIRATNAGAR**	99.75
200	27	**KUSHALGARH**	99.75
202	212	**LACHHMANGARH**	99.73
202	122	**DUDU**	99.73
202	118	**NOHAR**	99.73
202	114	**SADULSHAHAR**	99.73
206	44	**SINDHARI**	99.71
207	127	**PHAGI**	99.70
208	151	**JHUNJHUNUN**	99.68
208	38	**BALOTRA**	99.68
210	92	SARDARSHAHAR	99.67
211	150	CHIRAWA	99.65
212	185	RIYAN	99.58
213	168	SAPOTRA	99.54
214	156	BALESAR	99.52
215	37	SHAHBAD	99.45
216	70	NOKHA	99.43
216	49	KUMHER	99.43
218	217	PINDWARA	99.42
219	213	NEEM KA THANA	99.34
219	158	BHOPALGARH	99.34
221	184	PARBATSAR	99.27
222	43	SHEO	99.24
223	93	SUJANGARH	99.18
223	67	DUNGARGARH	99.18
225	3	JAWAJA	99.08
226	154	SURAJGARH	98.87
227	132	JAISALMER	98.50
228	66	BIKANER	98.42
229	161	MANDOR	98.37
230	140	SANCHORE	98.29
231	89	CHURU	98.21
	HIGH (96-98)		
232	68	KOLAYAT	97.53
233	39	BARMER	97.29
234	40	BAYTOO	96.39
	MEDIUM (94-96)		
235	90	RAJGARH	95.52
236	164	SHERGARH	95.15
	LOW (<94)		
237	163	PHALODI	93.03
		RAJASTHAN	**99.68**
		%age of AAPs	**88.19**

BOLD: Equal/Above Average Panchayat Samities (AAPs) *Source:* General Annex II, Col. 4.

ANNEX-3.8

RANKING OF PSS BY PERCENTAGE OF INHABITATED VILLAGES HAVING DRINKING WATER AMENITIES: RAJASTHAN (1991)

(Descending Order)

RANK	PANCHAYAT SAMITIES P. CODE	PANCHAYAT SAMITIES NAME	%
1	2	3	4
		PERFECT (100)	
1	1	ARAIN	100.00
1	2	BHINAY	100.00
1	4	KEKRI	100.00
1	5	KISHANGARH	100.00
1	6	MASOODA	100.00
1	7	PISANGAN	100.00
1	8	SRINAGAR	100.00
1	9	BANSURE	100.00
1	10	BEHROR	100.00
1	11	KATHUMAR	100.00
1	12	KISHANGARH BAS	100.00
1	13	KOTKASIM	100.00
1	14	LACHHMANGARH	100.00
1	15	MANDAWAR	100.00
1	16	NIMRANA	100.00
1	17	RAJGARH	100.00
1	18	RAMGARH	100.00
1	19	RENI	100.00
1	20	THANAGAZI	100.00
1	21	TIJARA	100.00
1	22	UMREN	100.00
1	23	ANANDPURI	100.00
1	24	BAGIDORA	100.00
1	25	GARHI	100.00
1	26	GHATOL	100.00
1	28	PEEPALKHOONT	100.00
1	29	SAJJANGARH	100.00
1	30	TALWARA	100.00
1	31	ANTA	100.00
1	32	ATRU	100.00
1	33	BARAN	100.00
1	34	CHHABRA	100.00
1	35	CHHIPABAROD	100.00
1	41	CHOHTAN	100.00
1	42	DHORIMANNA	100.00
1	45	SIWANA	100.00
1	46	BAYANA	100.00
1	47	DEEG	100.00
1	50	NADBAI	100.00
1	51	NAGAR PAHARI	100.00
1	52	RUPBAS	100.00
1	54	WEIR	100.00
1	55	ASIND	100.00
1	56	BANERA	100.00
1	57	HURDA	100.00
1	58	JAHAZPUR	100.00
1	59	KOTRI	100.00
1	60	MANDAL	100.00
1	61	MANDALGARH	100.00
1	62	RAIPUR	100.00
1	63	SAHARA	100.00
1	64	SHAHPURA	100.00
1	65	SUWANA	100.00
1	71	HINDOLI	100.00
1	72	KESHORAIPATAN	100.00
1	73	NAINWA	100.00
1	74	TALERA	100.00
1	75	ARNOD	100.00
1	76	BARI SADRI	100.00
1	77	BEGUN	100.00
1	78	BHADESAR	100.00
1	79	BHAINSRORGARH	100.00
1	80	BHOPALSAGAR	100.00
1	81	CHHOTI SADRI	100.00
1	82	CHITTAURGARH	100.00
1	83	DUNGLA	100.00
1	84	GANGRAR	100.00
1	85	KAPASAN	100.00
1	87	PRATAPGARH	100.00
1	88	RASHMI	100.00
1	95	BANDIKUI	100.00
1	96	DAUSA	100.00
1	97	LALSOT	100.00
1	98	MAHWA	100.00
1	99	SIKRAI	100.00
1	100	BARI	100.00
1	101	BASERI	100.00
1	102	DHAULPUR	100.00
1	103	RAJAKHERA	100.00
1	105	BICHHIWARA	100.00
1	106	DUNGARPUR	100.00
1	107	SAGWARA	100.00
1	108	SIMALWARA	100.00
1	109	ANUPGARH	100.00
1	110	GANGANAGAR	100.00
1	111	KARANPUR	100.00
1	112	PADAMPUR	100.00
1	113	RAISINGHNAGAR	100.00
1	115	SURATGARH	100.00
1	116	BHADRA	100.00
1	117	HANUMANGARH	100.00
1	120	BASSI	100.00
1	123	GOVINDGARH	100.00
1	124	JAMWA RAMGARH	100.00
1	125	JHOTWARA	100.00
1	126	KOTPUTLI	100.00
1	129	SANGANER	100.00
1	134	SANKRA	100.00
1	135	AHORE	100.00
1	136	BHINMAL	100.00
1	137	JALOR	100.00
1	138	JASWANTPURA	100.00
1	139	RANIWARA	100.00
1	142	BAKANI	100.00
1	143	DAG	100.00
1	144	JHALRAPATAN	100.00
1	145	KHANPUR	100.00
1	146	MANOHARTHANA	100.00
1	147	PIRAWA	100.00
1	148	ALSISAR	100.00
1	149	BUHANA	100.00
1	152	KHETRI	100.00
1	153	NAWALGARH	100.00
1	155	UDAIPURWATI	100.00
1	156	BALESAR	100.00
1	158	BHOPALGARH	100.00
1	159	BILARA	100.00
1	160	LUNI	100.00
1	165	HINDAUN	100.00
1	166	KARAULI	100.00
1	167	NADOTI	100.00
1	169	TODABHIM	100.00
1	171	ITAWA	100.00
1	172	LADPURA	100.00
1	173	SANGOD	100.00
1	174	SULTANPUR	100.00
1	175	DEGANA	100.00
1	176	DIDWANA	100.00
1	177	JAYAL	100.00
1	179	LADNU	100.00
1	180	MAKRANA	100.00
1	181	MERTA	100.00
1	182	MUNDWA	100.00
1	183	NAGAUR	100.00
1	186	BALI	100.00
1	187	DESURI	100.00
1	188	JAITARAN	100.00
1	189	KHARCHI/MARWAR JUN.	100.00
1	190	PALI	100.00
1	191	RAIPUR	100.00
1	192	RANI STATION	100.00
1	193	ROHAT	100.00
1	194	SOJAT	100.00
1	195	SUMERPUR	100.00
1	196	AMET	100.00
1	197	BHIM	100.00
1	198	DEOGARH	100.00
1	199	KHAMNOR	100.00
1	200	KUMBHALGARH	100.00
1	201	RAILMAGRA	100.00
1	202	RAJSAMAND	100.00
1	203	BAMANWAS	100.00
1	205	GANGAPUR	100.00
1	206	KHANDAR	100.00
1	207	SAWAI MADHOPUR	100.00
1	208	DANTA RAMGARH	100.00
1	210	FATEHPUR	100.00
1	211	KHANDELA	100.00
1	214	PIPRALI	100.00
1	215	SRI MADHOPUR	100.00
1	216	ABU ROAD	100.00
1	218	REODAR	100.00
1	219	SHEOGANJ	100.00
1	220	SIROHI	100.00
1	221	DEOLI	100.00
1	222	MALPURA	100.00
1	223	NIWAI	100.00
1	224	TODARAISINGH	100.00
1	225	TONK	100.00
1	226	UNIARA	100.00
1	227	BARGAON	100.00
1	228	BHINDER	100.00
1	229	DHARIAWAD	100.00
1	230	GIRWA	100.00
1	231	GOGUNDA	100.00
1	232	JHADOL	100.00
1	233	KHERWARA	100.00
1	234	KOTRA	100.00
1	235	MAVLI	100.00
1	236	SALUMBAR	100.00
1	237	SARADA	100.00
		VERY HIGH (95-100)	
182	121	CHAKSU	99.61
183	133	SAM	99.60
184	44	SINDHARI	99.58
185	122	DUDU	99.52
186	119	AMBER	99.48
187	38	BALOTRA	99.47
187	48	KAMAN	99.47
187	114	SADULSHAHAR	99.47
190	36	KISHANGANJ	99.43
191	92	SARDARSHAHAR	99.41
192	118	NOHAR	99.37
193	151	JHUNJHUNUN	99.36
193	204	BONLI	99.36
195	170	CHECHAT	99.31
196	104	ASPUR	99.30
196	213	NEEM KA THANA	99.30
198	212	LACHHMANGARH	99.26
199	69	LUNKARANSAR	99.23
200	185	RIYAN	99.17
201	131	VIRATNAGAR	99.15
202	184	PARBATSAR	99.07
202	209	DHOND	99.07
204	161	MANDOR	99.05
205	27	KUSHALGARH	99.04
205	168	SAPOTRA	99.04
207	90	RAJGARH	99.02
208	217	PINDWARA	98.98
209	157	BAP	98.92
210	127	PHAGI	98.81
211	162	OSIAN	98.80
212	150	CHIRAWA	98.78
213	130	SHAHPURA	98.73
214	53	SEWAR	98.70
214	141	SAYLA	98.70
216	86	NIMBAHERA	98.67
217	178	KUCHAMAN	98.63
218	128	SAMBHAR	98.60
219	3	JAWAJA	98.45
220	70	NOKHA	98.41
221	43	SHEO	98.20
221	49	KUMHER	98.20
221	94	TARANAGAR	98.20
224	91	RATANGARH	97.92
225	67	DUNGARGARH	97.78
225	140	SANCHORE	97.78
227	163	PHALODI	97.67
228	154	SURAJGARH	97.50
229	37	SHAHBAD	96.86
230	68	KOLAYAT	96.45
231	66	BIKANER	96.13
232	89	CHURU	96.04
233	164	SHERGARH	96.00
234	132	JAISALMER	95.62
235	39	BARMER	95.09
		HIGH (<95)	
236	40	BAYTOO	94.35
237	93	SUJANGARH	93.46
		RAJASTHAN	99.63
		%age of AAPs	76.40

BOLD: Equal/Above Average Panchayat Samities (AAPs)

Source: General Annex III, Col. 4.

ANNEX-3.9

RANKING OF PSS BY PERCENTAGE OF RURAL POPULATION SERVED BY PUCCA ROAD AMENITIES: RAJASTHAN, 1991

(Descending Order)

RANK	P. CODE	PANCHAYAT SAMITIES NAME	%
1	2	3	4
		VERY HIGH (>80)	
1	219	**SHEOGANJ**	98.01
2	195	**SUMERPUR**	87.74
3	155	**UDAIPURWATI**	83.25
		HIGH (60-80)	
4	158	**BHOPALGARH**	79.73
5	159	**BILARA**	77.71
6	117	**HANUMANGARH**	75.79
7	125	**JHOTWARA**	75.19
8	7	**PISANGAN**	75.18
9	172	**LADPURA**	74.97
10	216	**ABU ROAD**	73.83
11	8	**SRINAGAR**	71.81
12	160	**LUNI**	71.73
13	110	**GANGANAGAR**	71.40
14	114	**SADULSHAHAR**	70.57
15	151	**JHUNJHUNUN**	70.30
16	130	**SHAHPURA**	69.72
17	153	**NAWALGARH**	69.44
18	217	**PINDWARA**	68.95
19	214	**PIPRALI**	68.81
20	123	**GOVINDGARH**	67.16
21	150	**CHIRAWA**	66.65
22	186	**BALI**	66.07
23	220	**SIROHI**	66.05
24	80	**BHOPALSAGAR**	65.40
25	137	**JALOR**	64.94
26	218	**REODAR**	64.81
27	161	**MANDOR**	64.26
28	181	**MERTA**	63.84
29	49	**KUMHER**	63.22
30	164	**SHERGARH**	62.89
31	190	**PALI**	62.32
32	152	**KHETRI**	62.31
33	57	**HURDA**	62.07
34	65	**SUWANA**	61.51
34	120	**BASSI**	61.51
36	230	**GIRWA**	61.28
37	129	**SANGANER**	61.05
38	53	**SEWAR**	60.67
39	101	**BASERI**	60.56
40	201	**RAILMAGRA**	60.30
41	107	**SAGWARA**	60.25
42	197	**BHIM**	60.06
43	66	**BIKANER**	60.00
		MEDIUM (40-60)	
44	30	**TALWARA**	59.56
45	6	**MASOODA**	59.51
46	25	**GARHI**	59.48
47	235	**MAVLI**	59.18
48	24	**BAGIDORA**	59.05
49	131	**VIRATNAGAR**	58.97
50	215	**SRI MADHOPUR**	58.77
51	105	**BICHHIWARA**	58.76
52	139	**RANIWARA**	58.53
53	185	**RIYAN**	58.40
54	141	**SAYLA**	58.32
55	162	**OSIAN**	57.89
56	119	**AMBER**	57.57
57	208	**DANTA RAMGARH**	57.35
58	115	**SURATGARH**	57.34
59	187	**DESURI**	57.32
60	68	**KOLAYAT**	56.99
61	3	**JAWAJA**	56.92
62	111	**KARANPUR**	56.84
63	5	**KISHANGARH**	56.80
64	20	**THANAGAZI**	56.25
65	4	**KEKRI**	56.23
66	109	**ANUPGARH**	55.68
67	17	**RAJGARH**	55.58
68	165	**HINDAUN**	55.31
69	228	**BHINDER**	54.96
70	148	**ALSISAR**	54.93
71	88	**RASHMI**	54.92
72	132	**JAISALMER**	54.67
73	67	**DUNGARGARH**	54.62
74	227	**BARGAON**	54.57
75	189	**KHARCHI/MARWAR JUN.**	54.49
76	138	**JASWANTPURA**	54.35
77	2	**BHINAY**	54.30
78	128	**SAMBHAR**	54.29
79	69	**LUNKARANSAR**	54.02
80	47	**DEEG**	53.77
81	194	**SOJAT**	53.56
82	211	**KHANDELA**	53.51
83	126	**KOTPUTLI**	53.49
84	12	**KISHANGARH BAS**	53.29
84	56	**BANERA**	53.29
84	64	**SHAHPURA**	53.29
87	52	**RUPBAS**	53.20
88	106	**DUNGARPUR**	53.17
89	167	**NADOTI**	52.95
90	43	**SHEO**	52.70
91	209	**DHOND**	52.68
92	102	**DHAULPUR**	52.65
93	18	**RAMGARH**	52.36
94	70	**NOKHA**	52.29
95	16	**NIMRANA**	52.25
96	237	**SARADA**	51.71
97	113	**RAISINGHNAGAR**	51.38
98	104	**ASPUR**	51.20
99	112	**PADAMPUR**	51.18
100	124	**JAMWA RAMGARH**	50.93
101	156	**BALESAR**	50.89
102	122	**DUDU**	50.46
103	163	**PHALODI**	50.31
104	203	**BAMANWAS**	50.14
105	9	**BANSURE**	49.59
106	169	**TODABHIM**	49.57
107	170	**CHECHAT**	49.46
108	154	**SURAJGARH**	49.19
109	54	**WEIR**	49.05
110	134	**SANKRA**	48.92
111	149	**BUHANA**	48.81
112	15	**MANDAWAR**	48.61
113	38	**BALOTRA**	48.60
114	26	**GHATOL**	48.55
115	199	**KHAMNOR**	48.45
116	202	**RAJSAMAND**	48.26
117	182	MUNDWA	47.85
118	213	NEEM KA THANA	47.73
119	94	TARANAGAR	47.70
120	14	LACHHMANGARH	47.48
121	116	BHADRA	47.44
122	63	SAHARA	47.41
123	60	MANDAL	46.93
124	50	NADBAI	46.51
125	127	PHAGI	46.47
126	10	BEHROR	46.41
127	175	DEGANA	46.16
128	61	MANDALGARH	46.04
129	39	BARMER	46.00
130	74	TALERA	45.82
131	108	SIMALWARA	45.52
132	11	KATHUMAR	45.42
133	82	CHITTAURGARH	45.17
134	222	MALPURA	45.15
135	205	GANGAPUR	45.02
136	192	RANI STATION	44.43
137	23	ANANDPURI	44.38
138	77	BEGUN	44.37
139	135	AHORE	44.36
140	99	SIKRAI	44.26
141	58	JAHAZPUR	44.23
142	13	KOTKASIM	44.12
143	96	DAUSA	43.96
144	236	SALUMBAR	43.91
145	55	ASIND	43.62
146	22	UMREN	43.41
147	46	BAYANA	43.22
148	98	MAHWA	43.14
149	78	BHADESAR	43.04
150	86	NIMBAHERA	42.87
151	191	RAIPUR	42.68
152	59	KOTRI	42.57
153	200	KUMBHALGARH	42.14
154	19	RENI	42.11
155	89	CHURU	41.65
156	177	JAYAL	41.60
157	90	RAJGARH	41.20
158	76	BARI SADRI	41.15
159	45	SIWANA	40.98
160	206	KHANDAR	40.69
161	136	BHINMAL	40.64
162	198	DEOGARH	40.34
163	231	GOGUNDA	40.13
		LOW (20-40)	
164	51	NAGAR PAHARI	39.78
165	79	BHAINSRORGARH	39.55
166	173	SANGOD	38.99
167	103	RAJAKHERA	38.87
167	142	BAKANI	38.87
169	21	TIJARA	38.57
170	33	BARAN	38.47
171	62	RAIPUR	38.20
172	140	SANCHORE	38.18
173	229	DHARIAWAD	37.89
174	171	ITAWA	37.61
175	168	SAPOTRA	37.54
176	212	LACHHMANGARH	37.38
177	118	NOHAR	37.22
178	44	SINDHARI	37.19
179	221	DEOLI	37.15
180	31	ANTA	37.02
181	144	JHALRAPATAN	36.92
182	28	PEEPALKHOONT	36.75
183	97	LALSOT	36.70
184	85	KAPASAN	36.67
185	174	SULTANPUR	36.39
186	204	BONLI	36.28
187	193	ROHAT	36.26
188	233	KHERWARA	36.09
189	73	NAINWA	35.42
190	207	SAWAI MADHOPUR	35.37
191	100	BARI	35.05
192	37	SHAHBAD	34.95
193	32	ATRU	34.85
194	41	CHOHTAN	34.84
195	224	TODARAISINGH	34.54
196	84	GANGRAR	34.50
197	196	AMET	34.17
198	83	DUNGLA	33.99
199	92	SARDARSHAHAR	33.71
200	36	KISHANGANJ	33.70
201	91	RATANGARH	33.55
202	226	UNIARA	33.35
203	145	KHANPUR	33.22
204	184	PARBATSAR	33.20
205	179	LADNU	33.19
206	1	ARAIN	33.04
207	232	JHADOL	33.00
208	183	NAGAUR	32.85
209	71	HINDOLI	32.55
210	81	CHHOTI SADRI	32.39
211	188	JAITARAN	32.30
212	143	DAG	32.18
213	166	KARAULI	32.14
214	75	ARNOD	31.82
215	29	SAJJANGARH	31.53
216	93	SUJANGARH	31.30
217	48	KAMAN	30.99
218	225	TONK	30.92
219	234	KOTRA	30.72
220	133	SAM	30.11
221	42	DHORIMANNA	29.64
222	72	KESHORAIPATAN	29.43
223	223	NIWAI	29.38
224	178	KUCHAMAN	28.74
225	121	CHAKSU	28.30
226	87	PRATAPGARH	27.99
227	95	BANDIKUI	27.56
228	210	FATEHPUR	24.68
229	146	MANOHARTHANA	23.14
230	27	KUSHALGARH	21.96
231	35	CHHIPABAROD	21.67
232	157	BAP	20.79
		VERY LOW (<20)	
233	180	MAKRANA	19.99
234	40	BAYTOO	19.60
235	34	CHHABRA	13.71
236	147	PIRAWA	12.43
237	176	DIDWANA	4.84
		RAJASTHAN	**48.21**
		%age of AAPs	**48.9**

BOLD: Equal/Above Average Panchayat Samities (AAPs)   *Source*: General Annex II, Col. 9.

ANNEX-3.10

RANKING OF PSS BY PERCENTAGE OF INHABITED VILLAGES HAVING PUCCA ROAD AMENITIES: RAJASTHAN, 1991

(Descending Order)

RANK	P. CODE	PANCHAYAT SAMITIES NAME	%
1	2	3	4
		VERY HIGH (>70)	
1	195	**SUMERPUR**	74.60
		HIGH (60-70)	
2	158	**BHOPALGARH**	63.10
3	172	**LADPURA**	60.96
4	155	**UDAIPURWATI**	60.49
		MEDIUM (50-60)	
5	159	**BILARA**	59.49
6	7	**PISANGAN**	58.77
7	151	**JHUNJHUNUN**	56.41
8	216	**ABU ROAD**	56.41
9	8	**SRINAGAR**	55.79
10	110	**GANGANAGAR**	54.36
11	125	**JHOTWARA**	50.98
		LOW (40-50)	
12	130	**SHAHPURA**	49.37
13	153	**NAWALGARH**	48.57
14	137	**JALOR**	48.48
15	160	**LUNI**	48.44
16	164	**SHERGARH**	48.00
17	217	**PINDWARA**	47.96
18	117	**HANUMANGARH**	47.34
19	186	**BALI**	47.19
20	161	**MANDOR**	46.67
21	106	**DUNGARPUR**	46.20
22	197	**BHIM**	45.87
23	131	**VIRATNAGAR**	45.76
24	162	**OSIAN**	45.51
25	66	**BIKANER**	45.16
26	214	**PIPRALI**	45.05
27	3	**JAWAJA**	44.56
28	120	**BASSI**	44.50
29	126	**KOTPUTLI**	44.45
30	141	**SAYLA**	44.16
31	49	**KUMHER**	44.14
32	22	**UMREN**	44.00
33	150	**CHIRAWA**	43.90
34	102	**DHAULPUR**	42.95
35	152	**KHETRI**	42.50
35	190	**PALI**	42.50
37	219	**SHEOGANJ**	42.42
38	139	**RANIWARA**	42.17
39	165	**HINDAUN**	42.02
40	163	**PHALODI**	41.86
41	138	**JASWANTPURA**	41.67
42	220	**SIROHI**	41.46
43	201	**RAILMAGRA**	41.11
44	113	**RAISINGHNAGAR**	41.08
45	123	**GOVINDGARH**	41.05
46	80	**BHOPALSAGAR**	40.96
47	5	**KISHANGARH**	40.91
47	53	**SEWAR**	40.91
49	105	**BICHHIWARA**	40.80
50	25	**GARHI**	40.49
51	52	**RUPBAS**	40.43
52	12	**KISHANGARH BAS**	40.00
52	67	**DUNGARGARH**	40.00
52	111	**KARANPUR**	40.00
		VERY LOW (<40)	
55	114	**SADULSHAHAR**	39.79
56	24	**BAGIDORA**	39.42
57	4	**KEKRI**	39.36
58	215	**SRI MADHOPUR**	39.34
58	218	**REODAR**	39.34
60	30	**TALWARA**	39.25
61	235	**MAVLI**	39.19
62	154	**SURAJGARH**	39.17
63	65	**SUWANA**	38.93
64	43	**SHEO**	38.92
65	209	**DHOND**	38.89
66	16	**NIMRANA**	38.82
67	211	**KHANDELA**	38.79
68	89	**CHURU**	38.61
69	167	**NADOTI**	38.10
70	6	**MASOODA**	37.96
71	20	**THANAGAZI**	37.16
72	237	**SARADA**	37.01
73	112	**PADAMPUR**	36.86
74	57	**HURDA**	36.76
75	2	**BHINAY**	36.67
76	169	**TODABHIM**	36.62
77	107	**SAGWARA**	36.60
78	128	**SAMBHAR**	36.36
79	115	**SURATGARH**	36.18
80	129	**SANGANER**	36.10
81	101	**BASERI**	36.07
82	230	**GIRWA**	35.85
83	185	**RIYAN**	35.83
84	70	**NOKHA**	35.71
85	208	**DANTA RAMGARH**	35.56
86	156	**BALESAR**	35.29
87	15	**MANDAWAR**	35.21
88	119	**AMBER**	35.05
89	132	**JAISALMER**	35.04
90	90	**RAJGARH**	34.63
91	134	**SANKRA**	34.62
92	149	**BUHANA**	34.43
93	213	**NEEM KA THANA**	34.27
94	50	**NADBAI**	34.21
94	187	**DESURI**	34.21
96	88	**RASHMI**	34.18
97	18	**RAMGARH**	33.92
98	205	**GANGAPUR**	33.91
99	10	**BEHROR**	33.33
99	38	**BALOTRA**	33.33
99	100	**BARI**	33.33
99	103	**RAJAKHERA**	33.33
99	181	**MERTA**	33.33
104	14	**LACHHMANGARH**	33.15
105	54	**WEIR**	33.10
106	69	**LUNKARANSAR**	33.08
107	194	**SOJAT**	33.04
108	189	**KHARCHI/MARWAR JUN.**	32.85
109	39	**BARMER**	32.83
110	182	**MUNDWA**	32.73
111	176	**DIDWANA**	32.34
112	227	**BARGAON**	32.17
113	148	**ALSISAR**	31.86
114	11	**KATHUMAR**	31.65
115	136	**BHINMAL**	31.65
116	124	**JAMWA RAMGARH**	31.60
117	175	**DEGANA**	31.51
118	46	**BAYANA**	31.45
119	183	**NAGAUR**	30.83
120	170	**CHECHAT**	30.82
121	63	**SAHARA**	30.77
122	68	**KOLAYAT**	30.77
123	92	**SARDARSHAHAR**	30.59
124	99	**SIKRAI**	30.43
125	199	**KHAMNOR**	30.30
126	26	**GHATOL**	30.28
127	104	**ASPUR**	30.28
128	179	**LADNU**	30.21
129	231	**GOGUNDA**	30.14
130	47	**DEEG**	30.00
130	202	**RAJSAMAND**	30.00
132	228	**BHINDER**	29.92
133	74	**TALERA**	29.89
134	200	**KUMBHALGARH**	29.81
135	17	RAJGARH	29.41
136	56	BANERA	29.27
137	108	SIMALWARA	29.22
138	140	SANCHORE	28.89
139	23	ANANDPURI	28.46
140	116	BHADRA	28.42
141	64	SHAHPURA	28.19
142	229	DHARIAWAD	28.05
143	13	KOTKASIM	27.83
144	77	BEGUN	27.40
145	203	BAMANWAS	27.27
146	60	MANDAL	27.22
147	212	LACHHMANGARH	27.21
148	122	DUDU	27.14
149	21	TIJARA	26.63
150	42	DHORIMANNA	26.59
151	193	ROHAT	26.58
152	51	NAGAR PAHARI	26.27
153	94	TARANAGAR	26.13
154	192	RANI STATION	26.03
155	157	BAP	25.81
156	98	MAHWA	25.33
157	9	BANSURE	25.19
158	144	JHALRAPATAN	25.18
159	135	AHORE	25.00
160	196	AMET	25.00
161	233	KHERWARA	24.90
162	45	SIWANA	24.74
163	29	SAJJANGARH	24.73
164	55	ASIND	24.63
165	96	DAUSA	24.43
165	198	DEOGARH	24.43
167	191	RAIPUR	24.27
168	78	BHADESAR	24.22
169	81	CHHOTI SADRI	24.11
170	236	SALUMBAR	23.81
171	41	CHOHTAN	23.35
172	79	BHAINSRORGARH	23.33
173	58	JAHAZPUR	23.20
174	91	RATANGARH	22.92
175	93	SUJANGARH	22.88
176	210	FATEHPUR	22.70
177	127	PHAGI	22.62
178	61	MANDALGARH	22.59
179	118	NOHAR	22.53
180	44	SINDHARI	22.50
181	82	CHITTAURGARH	22.48
182	33	BARAN	22.45
183	85	KAPASAN	22.43
184	173	SANGOD	22.22
185	206	KHANDAR	21.79
186	168	SAPOTRA	21.53
187	28	PEEPALKHOONT	21.51
188	225	TONK	21.37
189	184	PARBATSAR	21.30
190	178	KUCHAMAN	21.23
191	166	KARAULI	20.92
192	72	KESHORAIPATAN	20.83
193	86	NIMBAHERA	20.67
194	19	RENI	20.59
195	83	DUNGLA	20.59
196	142	BAKANI	20.57
197	59	KOTRI	20.55
198	222	MALPURA	20.33
199	97	LALSOT	20.14
200	71	HINDOLI	20.11
201	62	RAIPUR	19.77
202	48	KAMAN	19.25
203	27	KUSHALGARH	19.23
204	1	ARAIN	18.85
205	76	BARI SADRI	18.75
206	32	ATRU	18.52
207	221	DEOLI	18.47
208	31	ANTA	18.37
209	174	SULTANPUR	18.12
210	226	UNIARA	17.80
211	234	KOTRA	17.55
212	177	JAYAL	17.42
213	188	JAITARAN	17.39
214	145	KHANPUR	17.37
215	73	NAINWA	17.14
216	171	ITAWA	16.77
217	232	JHADOL	16.41
218	87	PRATAPGARH	16.25
219	133	SAM	15.94
220	204	BONLI	15.92
221	146	MANOHARTHANA	15.69
222	224	TODARAISINGH	15.60
223	207	SAWAI MADHOPUR	15.58
224	143	DAG	15.45
225	95	BANDIKUI	14.98
226	36	KISHANGANJ	14.70
227	84	GANGRAR	14.17
228	37	SHAHBAD	13.84
229	121	CHAKSU	13.57
230	75	ARNOD	13.45
231	35	CHHIPABAROD	12.57
232	223	NIWAI	12.57
233	34	CHHABRA	12.21
234	40	BAYTOO	11.69
235	109	ANUPGARH	11.64
236	147	PIRAWA	8.50
237	180	MAKRANA	8.33
		RAJASTHAN	**29.66**
		%age of AAPs	**56.60**

BOLD: Equal/Above Average Panchayat Samities (AAPs) *Source*: General Annex III, Col. 9.

ANNEX-3.11

RANKING OF PSS BY PERCENTAGE OF RURAL POPULATION SERVED BY POWER AMENITIES: RAJASTHAN, 1991

(Descending Order)

RANK	P. CODE	PANCHAYAT SAMITIES NAME	%
1	2	3	4
	PERFECT (100)		
1	57	HURDA	100.00
1	123	GOVINDGARH	100.00
1	150	CHIRAWA	100.00
1	153	NAWALGARH	100.00
1	195	SUMERPUR	100.00
1	201	RAILMAGRA	100.00
1	209	DHOND	100.00
	VERY HIGH (75-100)		
8	16	NIMRANA	99.99
9	129	SANGANER	99.94
10	125	JHOTWARA	99.92
11	12	KISHANGARH BAS	99.82
12	10	BEHROR	99.77
13	215	SRI MADHOPUR	99.76
14	139	RANIWARA	99.74
15	220	SIROHI	99.68
16	159	BILARA	99.59
16	192	RANI STATION	99.59
16	211	KHANDELA	99.59
19	178	KUCHAMAN	99.58
20	130	SHAHPURA	99.54
21	9	BANSURE	99.32
22	212	LACHHMANGARH	99.30
23	131	VIRATNAGAR	99.18
24	155	UDAIPURWATI	99.11
25	54	WEIR	99.09
26	7	PISANGAN	99.02
27	124	JAMWA RAMGARH	99.01
28	137	JALOR	98.77
29	128	SAMBHAR	98.71
30	184	PARBATSAR	98.68
31	85	KAPASAN	98.59
32	80	BHOPALSAGAR	98.43
33	135	AHORE	98.30
34	119	AMBER	98.01
35	181	MERTA	97.96
36	170	CHECHAT	97.92
37	111	KARANPUR	97.91
38	56	BANERA	97.74
38	138	JASWANTPURA	97.74
40	210	FATEHPUR	97.62
41	151	JHUNJHUNUN	97.59
42	65	SUWANA	97.57
43	63	SAHARA	97.50
44	141	SAYLA	97.38
45	190	PALI	97.32
46	218	REODAR	97.24
47	15	MANDAWAR	97.08
48	187	DESURI	96.47
49	91	RATANGARH	96.21
50	95	BANDIKUI	96.02
51	154	SURAJGARH	95.91
52	185	RIYAN	95.87
53	22	UMREN	95.59
54	193	ROHAT	94.98
55	165	HINDAUN	94.97
56	188	JAITARAN	94.95
57	49	KUMHER	94.74
58	86	NIMBAHERA	94.73
59	4	KEKRI	94.58
60	8	SRINAGAR	94.48
61	208	DANTA RAMGARH	94.24
62	199	KHAMNOR	94.22
63	152	KHETRI	94.15
64	227	BARGAON	93.85
65	64	SHAHPURA	93.70
66	186	BALI	93.69
67	126	KOTPUTLI	93.58
68	213	NEEM KA THANA	93.39
69	81	CHHOTI SADRI	93.32
70	158	BHOPALGARH	93.15
71	110	GANGANAGAR	93.11
72	156	BALESAR	93.05
73	33	BARAN	92.87
74	60	MANDAL	92.72
75	62	RAIPUR	92.67
76	149	BUHANA	92.29
77	5	KISHANGARH	92.28
78	189	KHARCHI/MARWAR JUN.	91.71
79	70	NOKHA	91.41
80	180	MAKRANA	90.66
81	205	GANGAPUR	90.65
82	161	MANDOR	90.45
83	67	DUNGARGARH	90.27
84	144	JHALRAPATAN	90.24
85	45	SIWANA	90.23
86	194	SOJAT	90.21
87	25	GARHI	90.16
88	89	CHURU	89.99
89	235	MAVLI	89.54
90	167	NADOTI	89.21
91	228	BHINDER	89.10
92	6	MASOODA	88.78
93	18	RAMGARH	88.68
94	136	BHINMAL	88.50
95	61	MANDALGARH	88.47
96	147	PIRAWA	88.43
97	223	NIWAI	88.31
98	204	BONLI	88.02
99	176	DIDWANA	87.87
100	58	JAHAZPUR	87.71
101	50	NADBAI	87.60
102	55	ASIND	87.27
103	82	CHITTAURGARH	86.91
104	32	ATRU	86.89
105	77	BEGUN	86.83
106	69	LUNKARANSAR	86.80
107	114	SADULSHAHAR	86.71
108	172	LADPURA	86.66
109	71	HINDOLI	86.26
110	96	DAUSA	86.02
111	196	AMET	86.00
112	73	NAINWA	85.91
113	53	SEWAR	85.68
114	173	SANGOD	85.45
115	59	KOTRI	85.41
116	120	BASSI	85.38
117	13	KOTKASIM	84.95
118	175	DEGANA	83.96
119	36	KISHANGANJ	83.90
120	217	PINDWARA	83.82
121	148	ALSISAR	83.48
122	2	BHINAY	83.15
123	145	KHANPUR	83.13
124	84	GANGRAR	83.01
124	160	LUNI	83.01
126	222	MALPURA	82.89
127	162	OSIAN	82.44
128	20	THANAGAZI	82.39
129	117	HANUMANGARH	82.33
130	88	RASHMI	81.47
131	93	SUJANGARH	81.40
132	174	SULTANPUR	81.21
133	230	GIRWA	81.16
134	19	RENI	80.84
135	83	DUNGLA	80.62
136	182	MUNDWA	80.57
137	21	TIJARA	80.50
138	197	BHIM	80.18
139	66	BIKANER	80.10
140	76	BARI SADRI	79.58
141	74	TALERA	79.43
142	17	RAJGARH	79.08
143	31	ANTA	78.99
144	94	TARANAGAR	78.86
145	104	ASPUR	78.67
146	105	BICHHIWARA	78.26
147	203	BAMANWAS	77.86
148	164	SHERGARH	77.72
149	191	RAIPUR	77.13
150	231	GOGUNDA	76.94
151	68	KOLAYAT	76.59
152	79	BHAINSRORGARH	76.44
153	216	ABU ROAD	76.11
154	112	PADAMPUR	75.74
155	179	LADNU	75.53
156	163	PHALODI	75.41
157	237	SARADA	75.39
158	1	ARAIN	75.23
	HIGH (50-75)		
159	207	SAWAI MADHOPUR	74.47
160	198	DEOGARH	73.96
161	127	PHAGI	73.50
162	47	DEEG	72.50
163	103	RAJAKHERA	72.47
164	46	BAYANA	72.19
165	75	ARNOD	72.13
166	226	UNIARA	70.80
167	34	CHHABRA	70.79
168	97	LALSOT	70.32
169	99	SIKRAI	70.09
170	169	TODABHIM	69.77
171	183	NAGAUR	68.65
172	78	BHADESAR	68.60
173	26	GHATOL	68.35
174	142	BAKANI	68.18
175	107	SAGWARA	68.11
176	121	CHAKSU	67.92
177	11	KATHUMAR	67.66
178	92	SARDARSHAHAR	65.90
179	229	DHARIAWAD	65.53
180	37	SHAHBAD	65.45
181	219	SHEOGANJ	65.25
182	30	TALWARA	63.92
183	236	SALUMBAR	63.88
184	14	LACHHMANGARH	63.11
185	225	TONK	62.37
186	113	RAISINGHNAGAR	62.02
187	221	DEOLI	61.79
188	177	JAYAL	61.73
189	52	RUPBAS	61.63
190	38	BALOTRA	61.52
191	3	JAWAJA	61.43
192	108	SIMALWARA	61.29
193	140	SANCHORE	60.02
194	98	MAHWA	59.28
195	24	BAGIDORA	58.17
196	72	KESHORAIPATAN	58.07
197	87	PRATAPGARH	57.96
197	168	SAPOTRA	57.96
199	106	DUNGARPUR	57.59
200	166	KARAULI	55.68
201	116	BHADRA	54.97
202	48	KAMAN	54.12
203	233	KHERWARA	50.08
	MEDIUM (25-50)		
204	42	DHORIMANNA	49.91
205	224	TODARAISINGH	49.23
206	118	NOHAR	48.94
207	102	DHAULPUR	48.88
208	23	ANANDPURI	48.42
209	90	RAJGARH	48.25
210	143	DAG	46.85
211	232	JHADOL	46.34
212	35	CHHIPABAROD	46.26
213	171	ITAWA	44.90
214	51	NAGAR PAHARI	44.80
215	206	KHANDAR	43.50
216	115	SURATGARH	43.31
217	27	KUSHALGARH	41.36
218	146	MANOHARTHANA	40.79
219	122	DUDU	40.58
220	132	JAISALMER	38.59
221	214	PIPRALI	38.37
222	101	BASERI	37.45
223	29	SAJJANGARH	35.33
224	44	SINDHARI	34.02
225	157	BAP	33.77
226	43	SHEO	33.15
227	234	KOTRA	29.21
228	28	PEEPALKHOONT	28.32
229	41	CHOHTAN	28.30
230	200	KUMBHALGARH	26.08
231	202	RAJSAMAND	26.00
232	40	BAYTOO	25.00
	LOW (<25)		
233	109	ANUPGARH	23.09
234	100	BARI	22.36
235	39	BARMER	21.99
236	134	SANKRA	19.51
237	133	SAM	1.51
		RAJASTHAN	77.09
		%age of AAPs	62.9

BOLD: Equal/Above Average Panchayat Samities (AAPs) *Source*: General Annex II, Col. 10.

ANNEX-3.12

RANKING OF PSS BY PERCENTAGE OF INHABITED VILLAGES HAVING POWER AMENITIES: RAJASTHAN, 1991

(Descending Order)

RANK	P. CODE	PANCHAYAT SAMITIES NAME	%
1	2	3	4
		PERFECT (100)	
1	57	HURDA	100.00
1	123	GOVINDGARH	100.00
1	150	CHIRAWA	100.00
1	153	NAWALGARH	100.00
1	195	SUMERPUR	100.00
1	201	RAILMAGRA	100.00
1	209	DHOND	100.00
		VERY HIGH (95-100)	
8	125	JHOTWARA	99.02
9	16	NIMRANA	98.82
10	130	SHAHPURA	98.73
10	159	BILARA	98.73
12	212	LACHHMANGARH	98.53
13	12	KISHANGARH BAS	98.52
14	215	SRI MADHOPUR	98.36
15	129	SANGANER	98.05
16	9	BANSURE	97.71
17	139	RANIWARA	97.59
18	220	SIROHI	97.56
19	119	AMBER	97.42
20	178	KUCHAMAN	97.26
21	184	PARBATSAR	97.22
22	85	KAPASAN	97.20
22	128	SAMBHAR	97.20
22	63	SAHARA	96.70
25	10	BEHROR	96.67
25	154	SURAJGARH	96.67
27	155	UDAIPURWATI	96.30
28	54	WEIR	95.77
29	131	VIRATNAGAR	95.76
30	210	FATEHPUR	95.74
31	124	JAMWA RAMGARH	95.67
32	137	JALOR	95.45
		HIGH (90-95)	
33	151	JHUNJHUNUN	94.87
34	211	KHANDELA	94.83
35	192	RANI STATION	94.52
36	138	JASWANTPURA	94.44
37	15	MANDAWAR	94.37
38	141	SAYLA	93.51
39	170	CHECHAT	93.15
40	80	BHOPALSAGAR	92.77
41	208	DANTA RAMGARH	92.59
42	165	HINDAUN	92.44
43	65	SUWANA	92.37
44	7	PISANGAN	92.11
45	135	AHORE	91.67
46	149	BUHANA	90.98
46	218	REODAR	90.98
48	181	MERTA	90.63
49	158	BHOPALGARH	90.48
50	95	BANDIKUI	90.34
51	56	BANERA	90.24
52	190	PALI	90.00
		MEDIUM (85-90)	
53	199	KHAMNOR	89.39
54	219	SHEOGANJ	89.39
55	185	RIYAN	89.17
56	152	KHETRI	88.75
57	193	ROHAT	88.61
58	91	RATANGARH	88.54
59	8	SRINAGAR	88.42
60	187	DESURI	88.16
61	110	GANGANAGAR	87.55
62	49	KUMHER	87.39
62	126	KOTPUTLI	87.39
64	111	KARANPUR	87.00
65	188	JAITARAN	86.96
66	33	BARAN	86.73
67	22	UMREN	86.67
68	186	BALI	86.52
69	213	NEEM KA THANA	86.01
70	156	BALESAR	85.29
71	180	MAKRANA	85.00
		LOW (<85)	
72	45	SIWANA	84.54
73	4	KEKRI	84.04
74	227	BARGAON	83.92
75	64	SHAHPURA	83.89
76	5	KISHANGARH	83.64
77	81	CHHOTI SADRI	82.98
78	214	PIPRALI	82.42
79	194	SOJAT	82.14
80	70	NOKHA	81.75
81	205	GANGAPUR	81.74
82	60	MANDAL	81.01
82	136	BHINMAL	81.01
84	59	KOTRI	80.82
85	86	KOTRI	80.67
86	89	CHURU	80.20
87	50	NADBAI	79.82
88	161	MANDOR	79.05
89	147	PIRAWA	79.00
90	189	KHARCHI/MARWAR JUN.	78.83
91	202	RAJSAMAND	78.46
92	62	RAIPUR	77.91
93	176	DIDWANA	77.84
94	18	RAMGARH	77.78
94	67	DUNGARGARH	77.78
96	13	KOTKASIM	77.39
97	204	BONLI	77.07
98	235	MAVLI	77.03
99	144	JHALRAPATAN	76.60
100	167	NADOTI	76.19
101	69	LUNKARANSAR	76.15
102	173	SANGOD	74.75
103	25	GARHI	74.23
104	6	MASOODA	73.72
105	71	HINDOLI	73.56
106	172	LADPURA	73.29
107	175	DEGANA	73.29
108	73	NAINWA	73.14
109	162	OSIAN	73.05
110	53	SEWAR	72.73
110	120	BASSI	72.73
112	32	ATRU	72.59
112	61	MANDALGARH	72.59
114	66	BIKANER	71.61
115	148	ALSISAR	70.80
116	196	AMET	70.59
117	164	SHERGARH	70.00
117	182	MUNDWA	70.00
119	55	ASIND	69.95
120	223	NIWAI	69.63
121	84	GANGRAR	69.29
122	96	DAUSA	69.23
123	93	SUJANGARH	68.63
124	58	JAHAZPUR	68.51
125	231	GOGUNDA	68.49
126	2	BHINAY	68.33
127	222	MALPURA	68.29
128	77	BEGUN	67.12
129	19	RENI	66.67
129	122	DUDU	66.67
131	163	PHALODI	66.28
132	105	BICHHIWARA	66.09
133	36	KISHANGANJ	65.34
134	103	RAJAKHERA	65.31
134	217	PINDWARA	65.31
136	21	TIJARA	64.32
137	160	LUNI	64.06
138	79	BHAINSRORGARH	64.00
139	145	KHANPUR	63.68
140	74	TALERA	63.60
141	107	SAGWARA	63.40
142	88	RASHMI	63.29
143	174	SULTANPUR	63.12
144	82	CHITTAURGARH	62.84
145	83	DUNGLA	62.75
146	17	RAJGARH	62.50
146	179	LADNU	62.50
148	112	PADAMPUR	62.29
149	230	GIRWA	62.26
150	200	KUMBHALGARH	62.11
151	216	ABU ROAD	61.54
152	35	CHHIPABAROD	60.66
153	191	RAIPUR	60.19
154	31	ANTA	59.86
155	92	SARDARSHAHAR	59.41
156	104	ASPUR	59.15
157	46	BAYANA	59.12
158	237	SARADA	59.09
159	1	ARAIN	59.02
160	197	BHIM	58.72
161	169	TODABHIM	57.75
162	78	BHADESAR	57.14
163	117	HANUMANGARH	57.00
164	76	BARI SADRI	56.94
165	121	CHAKSU	56.59
166	203	BAMANWAS	56.09
167	127	PHAGI	55.95
168	94	TARANAGAR	55.86
169	47	DEEG	55.83
170	198	DEOGARH	55.73
171	207	SAWAI MADHOPUR	55.19
172	99	SIKRAI	53.62
173	108	SIMALWARA	51.60
174	97	LALSOT	50.85
175	140	SANCHORE	50.56
176	183	NAGAUR	50.38
177	11	KATHUMAR	49.37
178	20	THANAGAZI	49.32
179	52	RUPBAS	48.23
180	3	JAWAJA	47.67
181	236	SALUMBAR	47.62
182	113	RAISINGHNAGAR	47.03
183	68	KOLAYAT	46.75
184	142	BAKANI	46.45
185	14	LACHHMANGARH	46.20
186	106	DUNGARPUR	45.57
187	98	MAHWA	44.00
188	72	KESHORAIPATAN	43.98
189	75	ARNOD	43.86
190	114	SADULSHAHAR	43.24
191	177	JAYAL	43.18
192	229	DHARIAWAD	43.09
193	168	SAPOTRA	42.11
194	166	KARAULI	41.84
195	26	GHATOL	41.74
196	38	BALOTRA	41.27
196	42	DHORIMANNA	41.27
198	226	UNIARA	40.84
199	87	PRATAPGARH	40.63
200	90	RAJGARH	40.00
201	225	TONK	39.92
202	30	TALWARA	37.85
203	233	KHERWARA	36.51
204	37	SHAHBAD	35.85
205	102	DHAULPUR	33.97
205	206	KHANDAR	33.97
207	143	DAG	33.18
208	224	TODARAISINGH	33.03
209	228	BHINDER	32.58
210	23	ANANDPURI	32.52
211	221	DEOLI	32.48
212	24	BAGIDORA	32.12
213	48	KAMAN	31.55
214	27	KUSHALGARH	31.25
214	232	JHADOL	31.25
216	157	BAP	29.03
217	51	NAGAR PAHARI	28.57
218	116	BHADRA	28.42
219	34	CHHABRA	27.91
220	146	MANOHARTHANA	26.64
221	29	SAJJANGARH	23.08
222	132	JAISALMER	22.63
223	171	ITAWA	21.12
224	101	BASERI	20.49
225	43	SHEO	20.36
226	44	SINDHARI	20.00
226	115	SURATGARH	20.00
228	234	KOTRA	18.87
229	118	NOHAR	17.05
230	100	BARI	16.67
231	41	CHOHTAN	16.17
232	40	BAYTOO	15.32
233	28	PEEPALKHOONT	13.44
234	109	ANUPGARH	11.64
235	39	BARMER	10.57
236	134	SANKRA	10.00
237	133	SAM	0.40
		RAJASTHAN	59.78
		%age of AAPs	68.80

BOLD: Equal/Above Average Panchayat Samities (AAPs) *Source*: General Annex III, Col. 10.

ANNEX-3.13

RANKING OF PSS BY PERCENTAGE OF RURAL POPULATION SERVED BY POST & TELEGRAPH AMENITIES: RAJASTHAN, 1991

(Descending Order)

RANK	P. CODE	PANCHAYAT SAMITIES NAME	%
1	2	3	4
	VERY HIGH (>70)		
1	**195**	**SUMERPUR**	**82.52**
2	**153**	**NAWALGARH**	**81.64**
3	**217**	**PINDWARA**	**80.37**
4	**123**	**GOVINDGARH**	**79.30**
5	**214**	**PIPRALI**	**78.90**
6	**192**	**RANI STATION**	**78.51**
7	**220**	**SIROHI**	**78.48**
8	**155**	**UDAIPURWATI**	**77.88**
9	**215**	**SRI MADHOPUR**	**76.68**
10	**159**	**BILARA**	**75.33**
11	**162**	**OSIAN**	**73.83**
12	**67**	**DUNGARGARH**	**73.38**
13	**164**	**SHERGARH**	**72.50**
14	**4**	**KEKRI**	**72.09**
15	**180**	**MAKRANA**	**71.56**
16	**91**	**RATANGARH**	**71.34**
17	**7**	**PISANGAN**	**71.21**
18	**208**	**DANTA RAMGARH**	**71.13**
19	**141**	**SAYLA**	**70.70**
20	**5**	**KISHANGARH**	**70.48**
	HIGH (60-70)		
21	**158**	**BHOPALGARH**	**69.95**
22	**150**	**CHIRAWA**	**69.64**
23	**149**	**BUHANA**	**68.75**
24	**211**	**KHANDELA**	**68.66**
25	**45**	**SIWANA**	**68.24**
26	**219**	**SHEOGANJ**	**67.83**
27	**135**	**AHORE**	**67.49**
28	**189**	**KHARCHI/MARWAR JUN.**	**67.14**
29	**191**	**RAIPUR**	**66.87**
30	**186**	**BALI**	**66.52**
31	**194**	**SOJAT**	**66.37**
32	**179**	**LADNU**	**65.98**
33	**209**	**DHOND**	**65.57**
34	**63**	**SAHARA**	**65.50**
35	**237**	**SARADA**	**65.45**
36	**152**	**KHETRI**	**65.33**
37	**116**	**BHADRA**	**65.30**
38	**156**	**BALESAR**	**65.29**
39	**110**	**GANGANAGAR**	**65.27**
40	**178**	**KUCHAMAN**	**65.16**
41	**188**	**JAITARAN**	**64.99**
42	**70**	**NOKHA**	**64.79**
43	**230**	**GIRWA**	**64.67**
44	**210**	**FATEHPUR**	**64.49**
45	**213**	**NEEM KA THANA**	**64.40**
46	**2**	**BHINAY**	**64.12**
47	**94**	**TARANAGAR**	**63.34**
48	**137**	**JALOR**	**63.27**
49	**93**	**SUJANGARH**	**62.75**
50	**126**	**KOTPUTLI**	**62.23**
51	**105**	**BICHHIWARA**	**62.22**
52	**182**	**MUNDWA**	**61.68**
53	**16**	**NIMRANA**	**61.42**
54	**10**	**BEHROR**	**61.31**
55	**185**	**RIYAN**	**61.17**
56	**38**	**BALOTRA**	**61.05**
57	**181**	**MERTA**	**60.97**
58	**160**	**LUNI**	**60.79**
59	**54**	**WEIR**	**60.69**
60	**138**	**JASWANTPURA**	**60.58**
61	**136**	**BHINMAL**	**60.49**
62	**184**	**PARBATSAR**	**60.16**
	MEDIUM (50-60)		
63	**111**	**KARANPUR**	**59.98**
64	**167**	**NADOTI**	**59.77**
65	**132**	**JAISALMER**	**59.47**
66	**187**	**DESURI**	**59.39**
67	**148**	**ALSISAR**	**59.37**
68	**205**	**GANGAPUR**	**59.11**
69	**176**	**DIDWANA**	**59.09**
70	**41**	**CHOHTAN**	**59.00**
71	**177**	**JAYAL**	**58.95**
72	**46**	**BAYANA**	**58.64**
73	**222**	**MALPURA**	**58.59**
74	**49**	**KUMHER**	**58.56**
75	**202**	**RAJSAMAND**	**58.55**
76	**227**	**BARGAON**	**58.16**
77	**56**	**BANERA**	**58.04**
78	**212**	**LACHHMANGARH**	**57.96**
79	**163**	**PHALODI**	**57.81**
80	**6**	**MASOODA**	**57.57**
81	**114**	**SADULSHAHAR**	**56.76**
82	**139**	**RANIWARA**	**56.69**
83	**107**	**SAGWARA**	**56.66**
84	**32**	**ATRU**	**56.57**
85	**161**	**MANDOR**	**56.44**
86	**130**	**SHAHPURA**	**56.36**
87	**207**	**SAWAI MADHOPUR**	**56.12**
88	**88**	**RASHMI**	**56.04**
89	**235**	**MAVLI**	**55.93**
90	**201**	**RAILMAGRA**	**55.84**
91	**190**	**PALI**	**55.72**
92	**125**	**JHOTWARA**	**55.62**
93	**62**	**RAIPUR**	**55.55**
94	**197**	**BHIM**	**55.52**
95	**68**	**KOLAYAT**	**55.51**
96	**221**	**DEOLI**	**55.41**
97	**19**	**RENI**	**54.90**
98	**8**	**SRINAGAR**	**54.55**
99	**122**	**DUDU**	**54.51**
100	**50**	**NADBAI**	**54.45**
100	**199**	**KHAMNOR**	**54.45**
102	**154**	**SURAJGARH**	**54.23**
103	**55**	**ASIND**	**53.56**
104	**134**	**SANKRA**	**53.05**
105	**66**	**BIKANER**	**53.04**
106	**1**	**ARAIN**	**53.01**
107	**17**	**RAJGARH**	**52.99**
108	**117**	**HANUMANGARH**	**52.89**
109	**65**	**SUWANA**	**52.86**
110	**183**	**NAGAUR**	**52.73**
111	**104**	**ASPUR**	**52.63**
112	**101**	**BASERI**	**52.49**
113	**216**	**ABU ROAD**	**52.46**
114	**151**	**JHUNJHUNUN**	**52.43**
115	69	LUNKARANSAR	51.89
116	168	SAPOTRA	51.81
117	203	BAMANWAS	51.68
118	60	MANDAL	51.25
119	102	DHAULPUR	50.93
120	98	MAHWA	50.85
120	165	HINDAUN	50.85
122	96	DAUSA	50.76
123	169	TODABHIM	50.48
124	80	BHOPALSAGAR	50.34
125	127	PHAGI	50.27
126	64	SHAHPURA	50.19
127	31	ANTA	50.07
128	118	NOHAR	50.06
129	171	ITAWA	50.02
	LOW (40-50)		
130	175	DEGANA	49.97
131	157	BAP	49.95
132	218	REODAR	49.93
133	58	JAHAZPUR	49.81
134	59	KOTRI	49.69
135	20	THANAGAZI	49.58
136	204	BONLI	49.38
137	128	SAMBHAR	49.34
138	92	SARDARSHAHAR	49.11
139	9	BANSURE	49.09
140	22	UMREN	49.07
141	90	RAJGARH	49.06
142	57	HURDA	48.91
143	119	AMBER	48.81
144	12	KISHANGARH BAS	48.70
144	15	MANDAWAR	48.70
144	99	SIKRAI	48.70
147	174	SULTANPUR	48.58
148	133	SAM	48.57
149	82	CHITTAURGARH	48.53
150	25	GARHI	47.91
151	52	RUPBAS	47.87
152	231	GOGUNDA	47.45
153	112	PADAMPUR	47.18
154	131	VIRATNAGAR	46.85
155	103	RAJAKHERA	46.81
156	75	ARNOD	46.66
157	108	SIMALWARA	46.63
158	170	CHECHAT	46.61
159	233	KHERWARA	46.25
160	140	SANCHORE	45.48
161	13	KOTKASIM	45.28
162	61	MANDALGARH	45.23
163	83	DUNGLA	45.17
164	47	DEEG	45.10
165	226	UNIARA	45.03
166	86	NIMBAHERA	45.02
167	39	BARMER	44.92
168	51	NAGAR PAHARI	44.77
169	11	KATHUMAR	44.71
169	26	GHATOL	44.71
171	72	KESHORAIPATAN	44.40
172	124	JAMWA RAMGARH	43.82
173	200	KUMBHALGARH	43.65
174	106	DUNGARPUR	43.57
174	223	NIWAI	43.57
176	129	SANGANER	43.54
177	206	KHANDAR	43.45
178	89	CHURU	43.21
179	228	BHINDER	43.15
180	84	GANGRAR	42.92
181	225	TONK	42.64
182	78	BHADESAR	42.57
183	173	SANGOD	42.48
184	30	TALWARA	42.39
185	33	BARAN	42.22
186	120	BASSI	42.11
187	166	KARAULI	41.94
188	100	BARI	41.80
189	73	NAINWA	41.67
190	48	KAMAN	41.58
191	14	LACHHMANGARH	41.57
192	85	KAPASAN	41.34
193	18	RAMGARH	41.31
194	53	SEWAR	40.48
195	3	JAWAJA	40.24
196	74	TALERA	40.08
196	81	CHHOTI SADRI	40.08
196	196	AMET	40.08
	VERY LOW (<40)		
199	142	BAKANI	39.76
200	236	SALUMBAR	39.58
201	71	HINDOLI	39.42
202	229	DHARIAWAD	39.40
203	76	BARI SADRI	39.08
204	193	ROHAT	38.53
205	44	SINDHARI	38.31
206	43	SHEO	38.22
207	95	BANDIKUI	38.18
208	42	DHORIMANNA	37.75
209	143	DAG	37.71
210	172	LADPURA	37.45
211	21	TIJARA	37.39
212	40	BAYTOO	37.35
213	97	LALSOT	36.67
214	24	BAGIDORA	36.56
215	37	SHAHBAD	36.42
215	147	PIRAWA	36.42
217	198	DEOGARH	35.37
218	36	KISHANGANJ	35.20
219	145	KHANPUR	34.86
220	113	RAISINGHNAGAR	34.69
221	115	SURATGARH	34.60
222	144	JHALRAPATAN	34.38
223	87	PRATAPGARH	34.14
224	77	BEGUN	33.65
225	23	ANANDPURI	32.92
226	232	JHADOL	32.84
227	35	CHHIPABAROD	31.35
228	234	KOTRA	30.62
229	121	CHAKSU	29.70
230	28	PEEPALKHOONT	27.46
231	109	ANUPGARH	27.35
232	34	CHHABRA	25.35
233	146	MANOHARTHANA	24.65
234	79	BHAINSRORGARH	23.76
235	29	SAJJANGARH	22.56
236	27	KUSHALGARH	7.35
237	224	TODARAISINGH	0.44
		RAJASTHAN	**52.19**
		%age of AAP	**48.10**

BOLD: Equal/Above Average Panchayat Samities (AAPs) *Source*: General Annex II, Col. 6.

ANNEX-3.14

RANKING OF PSS BY PERCENTAGE OF INHABITED VILLAGES HAVING POST & TELEGRAPH AMENITIES: RAJASTHAN, 1991

(Descending Order)

RANK	PANCHAYAT SAMITIES P. CODE	PANCHAYAT SAMITIES NAME	%
1	2	3	4
	VERY HIGH (>35)		
1	195	**SUMERPUR**	60.32
2	164	**SHERGARH**	56.00
3	153	**NAWALGARH**	55.71
4	155	**UDAIPURWATI**	55.56
5	67	**DUNGARGARH**	53.33
6	215	**SRI MADHOPUR**	52.46
7	192	**RANI STATION**	52.05
8	7	**PISANGAN**	51.75
9	214	**PIPRALI**	51.65
10	159	**BILARA**	49.37
11	91	**RATANGARH**	48.96
12	220	**SIROHI**	48.78
13	123	**GOVINDGARH**	46.32
14	210	**FATEHPUR**	46.10
15	156	**BALESAR**	45.59
16	45	**SIWANA**	44.33
17	211	**KHANDELA**	43.97
18	208	**DANTA RAMGARH**	43.70
19	209	**DHOND**	43.52
20	141	**SAYLA**	42.86
21	149	**BUHANA**	42.62
22	4	**KEKRI**	42.55
23	162	**OSIAN**	42.51
24	152	**KHETRI**	42.50
25	136	**BHINMAL**	41.77
26	158	**BHOPALGARH**	41.67
26	180	**MAKRANA**	41.67
28	150	**CHIRAWA**	41.46
29	213	**NEEM KA THANA**	40.56
30	179	**LADNU**	39.58
31	163	**PHALODI**	39.53
32	110	**GANGANAGAR**	39.42
33	137	**JALOR**	39.39
34	186	**BALI**	39.33
35	194	**SOJAT**	39.29
36	2	**BHINAY**	39.17
37	178	**KUCHAMAN**	39.04
38	111	**KARANPUR**	39.00
39	16	**NIMRANA**	38.82
40	212	**LACHHMANGARH**	38.24
41	5	**KISHANGARH**	38.18
42	70	**NOKHA**	38.10
43	126	**KOTPUTLI**	37.82
44	93	**SUJANGARH**	37.25
45	188	**JAITARAN**	36.96
46	189	**KHARCHI/MARWAR JUN.**	36.50
47	134	**SANKRA**	36.15
48	135	**AHORE**	36.11
49	54	**WEIR**	35.92
	HIGH (30-35)		
50	191	**RAIPUR**	34.95
51	139	**RANIWARA**	34.94
52	219	**SHEOGANJ**	34.85
53	8	**SRINAGAR**	34.74
54	41	**CHOHTAN**	34.73
54	176	**DIDWANA**	34.73
56	138	**JASWANTPURA**	34.72
57	167	**NADOTI**	34.52
58	161	**MANDOR**	34.29
59	184	**PARBATSAR**	34.26
60	154	**SURAJGARH**	34.17
61	63	**SAHARA**	34.07
62	9	**BANSURE**	33.66
63	38	**BALOTRA**	32.80
64	182	**MUNDWA**	32.73
65	46	**BAYANA**	32.70
66	237	**SARADA**	32.52
67	185	**RIYAN**	32.50
67	190	**PALI**	32.50
69	207	**SAWAI MADHOPUR**	32.47
70	94	**TARANAGAR**	32.43
71	202	**RAJSAMAND**	32.31
72	10	**BEHROR**	32.22
73	92	**SARDARSHAHAR**	31.76
74	130	**SHAHPURA**	31.65
75	151	**JHUNJHUNUN**	31.41
76	132	**JAISALMER**	31.39
77	205	**GANGAPUR**	31.30
78	90	**RAJGARH**	30.73
79	160	**LUNI**	30.47
80	104	**ASPUR**	30.28
81	187	**DESURI**	30.26
82	165	**HINDAUN**	30.25
83	181	**MERTA**	30.21
	MEDIUM (25-30)		
84	103	**RAJAKHERA**	29.93
85	50	**NADBAI**	29.82
86	230	**GIRWA**	29.56
87	169	**TODABHIM**	28.87
88	177	**JAYAL**	28.79
89	125	**JHOTWARA**	28.43
90	235	**MAVLI**	28.38
91	148	**ALSISAR**	28.32
92	216	**ABU ROAD**	28.21
93	105	**BICHHIWARA**	28.16
94	157	**BAP**	27.96
95	49	**KUMHER**	27.93
96	89	**CHURU**	27.72
97	197	**BHIM**	27.52
98	15	**MANDAWAR**	27.46
99	32	**ATRU**	27.41
100	106	**DUNGARPUR**	27.22
101	102	**DHAULPUR**	26.92
102	56	**BANERA**	26.83
103	201	**RAILMAGRA**	26.67
104	217	**PINDWARA**	26.53
105	199	**KHAMNOR**	26.52
106	57	**HURDA**	26.47
107	1	**ARAIN**	26.23
108	140	**SANCHORE**	26.11
109	39	**BARMER**	26.04
110	175	**DEGANA**	26.03
111	203	**BAMANWAS**	25.76
112	233	**KHERWARA**	25.73
113	62	**RAIPUR**	25.58
114	52	**RUPBAS**	25.53
115	19	**RENI**	25.49
115	107	**SAGWARA**	25.49
117	100	**BARI**	25.40
118	231	**GOGUNDA**	25.34
119	12	**KISHANGARH BAS**	25.19
	LOW (20-25)		
120	64	**SHAHPURA**	24.83
121	183	**NAGAUR**	24.81
122	69	**LUNKARANSAR**	24.62
123	66	**BIKANER**	24.52
124	128	**SAMBHAR**	24.48
125	222	**MALPURA**	24.39
126	200	**KUMBHALGARH**	24.22
127	42	**DHORIMANNA**	24.21
128	88	**RASHMI**	24.05
129	22	**UMREN**	24.00
130	168	**SAPOTRA**	23.92
131	99	**SIKRAI**	23.91
132	227	**BARGAON**	23.78
133	65	**SUWANA**	23.66
134	6	MASOODA	23.36
135	43	SHEO	23.35
136	55	ASIND	23.15
137	101	BASERI	22.95
137	218	REODAR	22.95
139	122	DUDU	22.86
140	193	ROHAT	22.78
141	25	GARHI	22.70
142	98	MAHWA	22.67
143	47	DEEG	22.50
144	112	PADAMPUR	22.46
145	166	KARAULI	22.45
146	60	MANDAL	22.15
147	44	SINDHARI	22.08
148	17	RAJGARH	22.06
149	224	TODARAISINGH	22.02
150	59	KOTRI	21.92
150	108	SIMALWARA	21.92
152	68	KOLAYAT	21.89
153	40	BAYTOO	21.77
154	119	AMBER	21.65
155	11	KATHUMAR	21.52
156	33	BARAN	21.43
157	3	JAWAJA	21.24
158	131	VIRATNAGAR	21.19
159	116	BHADRA	21.05
160	204	BONLI	21.02
161	221	DEOLI	21.02
162	20	THANAGAZI	20.95
163	51	NAGAR PAHARI	20.74
164	174	SULTANPUR	20.62
165	127	PHAGI	20.24
166	13	KOTKASIM	20.00
166	129	SANGANER	20.00
	VERY LOW (<20)		
168	133	SAM	19.92
169	96	DAUSA	19.91
170	31	ANTA	19.73
171	30	TALWARA	19.63
172	14	LACHHMANGARH	19.57
173	58	JAHAZPUR	19.34
174	18	RAMGARH	19.30
175	83	DUNGLA	18.63
176	206	KHANDAR	18.59
177	72	KESHORAIPATAN	18.52
178	48	KAMAN	18.18
179	113	RAISINGHNAGAR	17.85
180	124	JAMWA RAMGARH	17.75
181	196	AMET	17.65
182	74	TALERA	17.62
183	21	TIJARA	17.59
184	198	DEOGARH	17.56
185	147	PIRAWA	17.50
186	171	ITAWA	17.39
187	120	BASSI	17.22
188	170	CHECHAT	17.12
189	225	TONK	16.94
190	80	BHOPALSAGAR	16.87
191	85	KAPASAN	16.82
192	73	NAINWA	16.57
193	26	GHATOL	16.51
194	53	SEWAR	16.23
195	173	SANGOD	16.16
196	82	CHITTAURGARH	16.06
197	86	NIMBAHERA	16.00
198	95	BANDIKUI	15.94
199	75	ARNOD	15.79
200	81	CHHOTI SADRI	15.60
201	236	SALUMBAR	15.58
202	78	BHADESAR	15.53
203	71	HINDOLI	15.52
204	114	SADULSHAHAR	15.38
205	223	NIWAI	15.18
206	84	GANGRAR	14.96
207	228	BHINDER	14.77
208	23	ANANDPURI	14.63
209	24	BAGIDORA	14.60
210	61	MANDALGARH	14.44
211	226	UNIARA	14.14
212	117	HANUMANGARH	14.01
213	144	JHALRAPATAN	13.83
214	172	LADPURA	13.70
215	118	NOHAR	13.68
216	143	DAG	13.64
217	229	DHARIAWAD	13.41
218	76	BARI SADRI	13.19
219	87	PRATAPGARH	12.81
220	37	SHAHBAD	12.58
221	97	LALSOT	12.29
222	234	KOTRA	12.25
223	145	KHANPUR	12.11
224	142	BAKANI	12.06
225	232	JHADOL	11.72
226	35	CHHIPABAROD	11.48
227	36	KISHANGANJ	11.36
228	34	CHHABRA	11.05
229	146	MANOHARTHANA	10.22
230	77	BEGUN	10.05
231	28	PEEPALKHOONT	9.68
232	115	SURATGARH	9.41
233	121	CHAKSU	9.30
234	109	ANUPGARH	8.45
235	79	BHAINSRORGARH	8.00
236	29	SAJJANGARH	7.14
237	27	KUSHALGARH	5.29
		RAJASTHAN	**23.37**
		%age of AAPs	**56.10**

BOLD: Equal/Above Average Panchayat Samities (AAPs) *Source*: General Annex III, Col. 6.

ANNEX-3.15

RANKING OF PSS BY PERCENTAGE OF RURAL POPULATION SERVED BY MARKET / HAT AMENITIES: RAJASTHAN, 1991

(Descending Order)

RANK	P. CODE	PANCHAYAT SAMITIES NAME	%
1	2	3	4
	VERY HIGH (>6)		
1	**171**	**ITAWA**	**37.48**
2	**164**	**SHERGARH**	**35.33**
3	**174**	**SULTANPUR**	**30.13**
4	**204**	**BONLI**	**28.82**
5	**32**	**ATRU**	**25.89**
6	**31**	**ANTA**	**25.62**
7	**36**	**KISHANGANJ**	**24.98**
8	**173**	**SANGOD**	**22.16**
9	**170**	**CHECHAT**	**20.61**
10	**142**	**BAKANI**	**19.97**
11	**74**	**TALERA**	**18.07**
12	**102**	**DHAULPUR**	**18.03**
13	**75**	**ARNOD**	**17.59**
14	**167**	**NADOTI**	**17.46**
15	**73**	**NAINWA**	**17.19**
16	**206**	**KHANDAR**	**17.09**
17	**145**	**KHANPUR**	**17.06**
18	**28**	**PEEPALKHOONT**	**16.13**
19	**187**	**DESURI**	**14.70**
20	**143**	**DAG**	**14.37**
21	**207**	**SAWAI MADHOPUR**	**13.64**
22	**37**	**SHAHBAD**	**13.58**
23	**35**	**CHHIPABAROD**	**13.51**
23	**153**	**NAWALGARH**	**13.51**
25	**147**	**PIRAWA**	**13.04**
26	**72**	**KESHORAIPATAN**	**12.93**
27	**177**	**JAYAL**	**11.32**
28	**165**	**HINDAUN**	**11.12**
29	**203**	**BAMANWAS**	**10.76**
30	**185**	**RIYAN**	**10.75**
31	**226**	**UNIARA**	**10.70**
32	**52**	**RUPBAS**	**10.62**
33	**223**	**NIWAI**	**10.31**
34	**18**	**RAMGARH**	**9.68**
35	**168**	**SAPOTRA**	**9.37**
36	**47**	**DEEG**	**9.30**
37	**148**	**ALSISAR**	**8.83**
38	**33**	**BARAN**	**8.70**
39	**172**	**LADPURA**	**8.70**
40	**26**	**GHATOL**	**8.63**
41	**146**	**MANOHARTHANA**	**8.38**
42	**214**	**PIPRALI**	**8.18**
43	**94**	**TARANAGAR**	**8.02**
44	**144**	**JHALRAPATAN**	**7.87**
45	**151**	**JHUNJHUNUN**	**7.85**
46	**189**	**KHARCHI/MARWAR JUN.**	**7.63**
47	**34**	**CHHABRA**	**7.41**
48	**205**	**GANGAPUR**	**7.34**
49	**133**	**SAM**	**7.25**
50	**54**	**WEIR**	**7.06**
51	**169**	**TODABHIM**	**6.91**
52	**192**	**RANI STATION**	**6.86**
53	**9**	**BANSURE**	**6.74**
54	**219**	**SHEOGANJ**	**6.51**
55	**79**	**BHAINSRORGARH**	**6.42**
56	**57**	**HURDA**	**6.22**
	HIGH (4-6)		
57	**156**	**BALESAR**	**5.56**
58	**99**	**SIKRAI**	**5.18**
59	**103**	**RAJAKHERA**	**5.06**
60	**12**	**KISHANGARH BAS**	**5.00**
61	**22**	**UMREN**	**4.90**
62	**97**	**LALSOT**	**4.88**
63	**129**	**SANGANER**	**4.81**
64	**27**	**KUSHALGARH**	**4.70**
65	**50**	**NADBAI**	**4.41**
66	**98**	**MAHWA**	**4.40**
67	**118**	**NOHAR**	**4.27**
	MEDIUM (2-4)		
68	**40**	**BAYTOO**	**3.94**
69	**194**	**SOJAT**	**3.76**
70	**166**	**KARAULI**	**3.68**
71	**183**	**NAGAUR**	**3.55**
72	**88**	**RASHMI**	**3.45**
73	29	SAJJANGARH	3.37
74	176	DIDWANA	3.36
75	45	SIWANA	3.20
76	181	MERTA	3.17
77	184	PARBATSAR	3.05
78	218	REODAR	2.66
79	71	HINDOLI	2.32
		LOW (<2)	
80	180	MAKRANA	1.99
81	68	KOLAYAT	1.92
82	100	BARI	1.90
83	46	BAYANA	1.54
84	95	BANDIKUI	1.53
85	58	JAHAZPUR	1.51
86	163	PHALODI	1.36
87	112	PADAMPUR	1.34
88	132	JAISALMER	1.31
89	51	NAGAR PAHARI	1.13
90	84	GANGRAR	1.08
91	87	PRATAPGARH	0.83
92	208	DANTA RAMGARH	0.75
93	124	JAMWA RAMGARH	0.72
94	236	SALUMBAR	0.71
95	104	ASPUR	0.66
96	30	TALWARA	0.60
97	230	GIRWA	0.59
98	157	BAP	0.49
99	44	SINDHARI	0.47
	ABSENCE (0)		
	1	ARAIN	
	2	BHINAY	
	3	JAWAJA	
	4	KEKRI	
	5	KISHANGARH	
	6	MASOODA	
	7	PISANGAN	
	8	SRINAGAR	
	10	BEHROR	
	11	KATHUMAR	
	13	KOTKASIM	
	14	LACHHMANGARH	
	15	MANDAWAR	
	16	NIMRANA	
	17	RAJGARH	
	19	RENI	
	20	THANAGAZI	
	21	TIJARA	
	23	ANANDPURI	
	24	BAGIDORA	
	25	GARHI	
	38	BALOTRA	
	39	BARMER	
	41	CHOHTAN	
	42	DHORIMANNA	
	43	SHEO	
	48	KAMAN	
	49	KUMHER	
	53	SEWAR	
	55	ASIND	
	56	BANERA	
	59	KOTRI	
	60	MANDAL	
	61	MANDALGARH	
	62	RAIPUR	
	63	SAHARA	
	64	SHAHPURA	
	65	SUWANA	
	66	BIKANER	
	67	DUNGARGARH	
	69	LUNKARANSAR	
	70	NOKHA	
	76	BARI SADRI	
	77	BEGUN	
	78	BHADESAR	
	80	BHOPALSAGAR	
	81	CHHOTI SADRI	
	82	CHITTAURGARH	
	83	DUNGLA	
	85	KAPASAN	
	86	NIMBAHERA	
	89	CHURU	
	90	RAJGARH	
	91	RATANGARH	
	92	SARDARSHAHAR	
	93	SUJANGARH	
	96	DAUSA	
	101	BASERI	
	105	BICHHIWARA	
	106	DUNGARPUR	
	107	SAGWARA	
	108	SIMALWARA	
	109	ANUPGARH	
	110	GANGANAGAR	
	111	KARANPUR	
	113	RAISINGHNAGAR	
	114	SADULSHAHAR	
	115	SURATGARH	
	116	BHADRA	
	117	HANUMANGARH	
	119	AMBER	
	120	BASSI	
	121	CHAKSU	
	122	DUDU	
	123	GOVINDGARH	
	125	JHOTWARA	
	126	KOTPUTLI	
	127	PHAGI	
	128	SAMBHAR	
	130	SHAHPURA	
	131	VIRATNAGAR	
	134	SANKRA	
	135	AHORE	
	136	BHINMAL	
	137	JALOR	
	138	JASWANTPURA	
	139	RANIWARA	
	140	SANCHORE	
	141	SAYLA	
	149	BUHANA	
	150	CHIRAWA	
	152	KHETRI	
	154	SURAJGARH	
	155	UDAIPURWATI	
	158	BHOPALGARH	
	159	BILARA	
	160	LUNI	
	161	MANDOR	
	162	OSIAN	
	175	DEGANA	
	178	KUCHAMAN	
	179	LADNU	
	182	MUNDWA	
	186	BALI	
	188	JAITARAN	
	190	PALI	
	191	RAIPUR	
	193	ROHAT	
	195	SUMERPUR	
	196	AMET	
	197	BHIM	
	198	DEOGARH	
	199	KHAMNOR	
	200	KUMBHALGARH	
	201	RAILMAGRA	
	202	RAJSAMAND	
	209	DHOND	
	210	FATEHPUR	
	211	KHANDELA	
	212	LACHHMANGARH	
	213	NEEM KA THANA	
	215	SRI MADHOPUR	
	216	ABU ROAD	
	217	PINDWARA	
	220	SIROHI	
	221	DEOLI	
	222	MALPURA	
	224	TODARAISINGH	
	225	TONK	
	227	BARGAON	
	228	BHINDER	
	229	DHARIAWAD	
	231	GOGUNDA	
	232	JHADOL	
	233	KHERWARA	
	234	KOTRA	
	235	MAVLI	
	237	SARADA	
RAJASTHAN			**3.40**
%age of AAPs			**30.40**

BOLD: Equal/Above Average Panchayat Samities (AAPs)　*Source*: General Annex II, Col. 7.

ANNEX-3.16

RANKING OF PSS BY PERCENTAGE OF INHABITED VILLAGES HAVING MARKET / HAT AMENITIES: RAJASTHAN, 1991

(Descending Order)

RANK	P. CODE	PANCHAYAT SAMITIES NAME	%
1	2	3	4
	VERY HIGH (>3)		
1	**164**	**SHERGARH**	**28.00**
2	**171**	**ITAWA**	**9.32**
3	**204**	**BONLI**	**8.28**
4	**57**	**HURDA**	**7.35**
5	**174**	**SULTANPUR**	**6.87**
6	**32**	**ATRU**	**6.67**
7	**187**	**DESURI**	**6.58**
8	**102**	**DHAULPUR**	**5.77**
9	**74**	**TALERA**	**5.36**
10	**151**	**JHUNJHUNUN**	**5.13**
11	**36**	**KISHANGANJ**	**5.11**
12	**173**	**SANGOD**	**5.05**
13	**31**	**ANTA**	**4.76**
13	**167**	**NADOTI**	**4.76**
15	**214**	**PIPRALI**	**4.40**
16	**165**	**HINDAUN**	**4.20**
17	**185**	**RIYAN**	**4.17**
18	**75**	**ARNOD**	**4.09**
19	**147**	**PIRAWA**	**4.00**
20	**206**	**KHANDAR**	**3.85**
21	**35**	**CHHIPABAROD**	**3.83**
22	**28**	**PEEPALKHOONT**	**3.76**
23	**72**	**KESHORAIPATAN**	**3.70**
24	**143**	**DAG**	**3.64**
25	**73**	**NAINWA**	**3.43**
26	**170**	**CHECHAT**	**3.42**
27	**133**	**SAM**	**3.19**
27	**142**	**BAKANI**	**3.19**
29	**145**	**KHANPUR**	**3.16**
30	**37**	**SHAHBAD**	**3.14**
31	**177**	**JAYAL**	**3.03**
31	**219**	**SHEOGANJ**	**3.03**
	HIGH (2-3)		
33	**146**	**MANOHARTHANA**	**2.92**
34	**34**	**CHHABRA**	**2.91**
35	**27**	**KUSHALGARH**	**2.88**
36	**153**	**NAWALGARH**	**2.86**
37	**52**	**RUPBAS**	**2.84**
38	**54**	**WEIR**	**2.82**
38	**169**	**TODABHIM**	**2.82**
40	**192**	**RANI STATION**	**2.74**
41	**50**	**NADBAI**	**2.62**
42	**207**	**SAWAI MADHOPUR**	**2.60**
43	**47**	**DEEG**	**2.50**
44	**203**	**BAMANWAS**	**2.27**
45	**186**	**BALI**	**2.25**
46	**189**	**KHARCHI/MARWAR JUN.**	**2.19**
47	**144**	**JHALRAPATAN**	**2.13**
48	**223**	**NIWAI**	**2.09**
49	**181**	**MERTA**	**2.08**
50	**45**	**SIWANA**	**2.06**
51	**172**	**LADPURA**	**2.05**
52	**33**	**BARAN**	**2.04**
53	**79**	**BHAINSRORGARH**	**2.00**
53	**98**	**MAHWA**	**2.00**
	MEDIUM (1-2)		
55	**168**	**SAPOTRA**	**1.91**
56	**184**	**PARBATSAR**	**1.85**
57	**205**	**GANGAPUR**	**1.74**
58	**226**	**UNIARA**	**1.57**
59	**156**	**BALESAR**	**1.47**
60	**132**	**JAISALMER**	**1.46**
61	**26**	**GHATOL**	**1.38**
62	**103**	**RAJAKHERA**	**1.36**
63	**88**	**RASHMI**	**1.27**
64	**40**	**BAYTOO**	**1.21**
65	**18**	**RAMGARH**	**1.17**
66	**163**	**PHALODI**	**1.16**
67	**29**	**SAJJANGARH**	**1.10**
68	**157**	**BAP**	**1.08**
69	**166**	**KARAULI**	**1.02**
	LOW (<1)		
70	129	SANGANER	0.98
71	51	NAGAR PAHARI	0.92
72	94	TARANAGAR	0.90
73	194	SOJAT	0.89
74	148	ALSISAR	0.88
75	118	NOHAR	0.84
76	180	MAKRANA	0.83
77	218	REODAR	0.82
78	84	GANGRAR	0.79
79	100	BARI	0.79
80	9	BANSURE	0.76
81	183	NAGAUR	0.75
82	12	KISHANGARH BAS	0.74
83	208	DANTA RAMGARH	0.74
84	99	SIKRAI	0.72
85	104	ASPUR	0.70
86	97	LALSOT	0.68
87	22	UMREN	0.67
88	46	BAYANA	0.63
88	87	PRATAPGARH	0.63
88	230	GIRWA	0.63
91	176	DIDWANA	0.60
92	68	KOLAYAT	0.59
93	71	HINDOLI	0.57
94	58	JAHAZPUR	0.55
95	95	BANDIKUI	0.48
96	30	TALWARA	0.47
97	124	JAMWA RAMGARH	0.43
97	236	SALUMBAR	0.43
99	44	SINDHARI	0.42
99	112	PADAMPUR	0.42
	ABSENCE (0)		
	1	ARAIN	
	2	BHINAY	
	3	JAWAJA	
	4	KEKRI	
	5	KISHANGARH	
	6	MASOODA	
	7	PISANGAN	
	8	SRINAGAR	
	10	BEHROR	
	11	KATHUMAR	
	13	KOTKASIM	
	14	LACHHMANGARH	
	15	MANDAWAR	
	16	NIMRANA	
	17	RAJGARH	
	19	RENI	
	20	THANAGAZI	
	21	TIJARA	
	23	ANANDPURI	
	24	BAGIDORA	
	25	GARHI	
	38	BALOTRA	
	39	BARMER	
	41	CHOHTAN	
	42	DHORIMANNA	
	43	SHEO	
	48	KAMAN	
	49	KUMHER	
	53	SEWAR	
	55	ASIND	
	56	BANERA	
	59	KOTRI	
	60	MANDAL	
	61	MANDALGARH	
	62	RAIPUR	
	63	SAHARA	
	64	SHAHPURA	
	65	SUWANA	
	66	BIKANER	
	67	DUNGARGARH	
	69	LUNKARANSAR	
	70	NOKHA	
	76	BARI SADRI	
	77	BEGUN	
	78	BHADESAR	
	80	BHOPALSAGAR	
	81	CHHOTI SADRI	
	82	CHITTAURGARH	
	83	DUNGLA	
	85	KAPASAN	
	86	NIMBAHERA	
	89	CHURU	
	90	RAJGARH	
	91	RATANGARH	
	92	SARDARSHAHAR	
	93	SUJANGARH	
	96	DAUSA	
	101	BASERI	
	105	BICHHIWARA	
	106	DUNGARPUR	
	107	SAGWARA	
	108	SIMALWARA	
	109	ANUPGARH	
	110	GANGANAGAR	
	111	KARANPUR	
	113	RAISINGHNAGAR	
	114	SADULSHAHAR	
	115	SURATGARH	
	116	BHADRA	
	117	HANUMANGARH	
	119	AMBER	
	120	BASSI	
	121	CHAKSU	
	122	DUDU	
	123	GOVINDGARH	
	125	JHOTWARA	
	126	KOTPUTLI	
	127	PHAGI	
	128	SAMBHAR	
	130	SHAHPURA	
	131	VIRATNAGAR	
	134	SANKRA	
	135	AHORE	
	136	BHINMAL	
	137	JALOR	
	138	JASWANTPURA	
	139	RANIWARA	
	140	SANCHORE	
	141	SAYLA	
	149	BUHANA	
	150	CHIRAWA	
	152	KHETRI	
	154	SURAJGARH	
	155	UDAIPURWATI	
	158	BHOPALGARH	
	159	BILARA	
	160	LUNI	
	161	MANDOR	
	162	OSIAN	
	175	DEGANA	
	178	KUCHAMAN	
	179	LADNU	
	182	MUNDWA	
	188	JAITARAN	
	190	PALI	
	191	RAIPUR	
	193	ROHAT	
	195	SUMERPUR	
	196	AMET	
	197	BHIM	
	198	DEOGARH	
	199	KHAMNOR	
	200	KUMBHALGARH	
	201	RAILMAGRA	
	202	RAJSAMAND	
	209	DHOND	
	210	FATEHPUR	
	211	KHANDELA	
	212	LACHHMANGARH	
	213	NEEM KA THANA	
	215	SRI MADHOPUR	
	216	ABU ROAD	
	217	PINDWARA	
	220	SIROHI	
	221	DEOLI	
	222	MALPURA	
	224	TODARAISINGH	
	225	TONK	
	227	BARGAON	
	228	BHINDER	
	229	DHARIAWAD	
	231	GOGUNDA	
	232	JHADOL	
	233	KHERWARA	
	234	KOTRA	
	235	MAVLI	
	237	SARADA	
RAJASTHAN			**1.02**
%age of AAPs			**29.10**

BOLD: Equal/Above Average Panchayat Samities (AAPs)

Source: General Annex III, Col. 7.

ANNEX-3.17

RANKING OF PSS BY PERCENTAGE OF RURAL POP. SERVED BY COMMUNICATION AMENITIES: RAJASTHAN, 1991

(Descending Order)

RANK	P. CODE	PANCHAYAT SAMITIES NAME	%
1	2	3	4
	VERY HIGH (>80)		
1	162	**OSIAN**	97.07
2	159	**BILARA**	93.18
3	141	**SAYLA**	90.36
4	158	**BHOPALGARH**	89.94
5	195	**SUMERPUR**	89.47
6	137	**JALOR**	87.47
7	181	**MERTA**	86.95
8	135	**AHORE**	85.53
9	160	**LUNI**	84.48
10	164	**SHERGARH**	84.37
11	179	**LADNU**	82.42
12	153	**NAWALGARH**	82.12
13	192	**RANI STATION**	81.60
	HIGH (60-80)		
14	208	**DANTA RAMGARH**	79.79
15	202	**RAJSAMAND**	79.59
16	38	**BALOTRA**	79.52
17	209	**DHOND**	79.24
18	190	**PALI**	78.93
19	189	**KHARCHI/MARWAR JUN.**	78.51
20	186	**BALI**	78.23
21	45	**SIWANA**	77.92
22	176	**DIDWANA**	77.27
23	138	**JASWANTPURA**	77.22
24	156	**BALESAR**	76.73
25	152	**KHETRI**	76.23
26	182	**MUNDWA**	75.83
27	194	**SOJAT**	75.74
28	57	**HURDA**	75.25
29	175	**DEGANA**	74.88
30	88	**RASHMI**	74.66
31	150	**CHIRAWA**	74.51
32	139	**RANIWARA**	74.22
33	155	**UDAIPURWATI**	74.18
34	62	**RAIPUR**	73.60
35	136	**BHINMAL**	73.55
36	178	**KUCHAMAN**	73.52
37	199	**KHAMNOR**	73.47
38	177	**JAYAL**	72.14
39	91	**RATANGARH**	71.97
40	151	**JHUNJHUNUN**	71.94
41	185	**RIYAN**	71.26
42	215	**SRI MADHOPUR**	71.13
43	180	**MAKRANA**	70.89
44	201	**RAILMAGRA**	70.88
45	89	**CHURU**	70.79
46	60	**MANDAL**	70.56
47	114	**SADULSHAHAR**	70.23
48	183	**NAGAUR**	70.18
49	117	**HANUMANGARH**	70.17
50	184	**PARBATSAR**	70.02
51	163	**PHALODI**	69.30
52	148	**ALSISAR**	69.19
53	219	**SHEOGANJ**	68.78
54	123	**GOVINDGARH**	68.43
55	107	**SAGWARA**	68.22
56	140	**SANCHORE**	68.06
57	94	**TARANAGAR**	67.99
58	188	**JAITARAN**	67.83
59	235	**MAVLI**	67.80
60	116	**BHADRA**	67.75
61	210	**FATEHPUR**	67.65
62	93	**SUJANGARH**	67.26
63	212	**LACHHMANGARH**	66.81
64	220	**SIROHI**	66.36
65	92	**SARDARSHAHAR**	66.08
66	67	**DUNGARGARH**	65.87
67	237	**SARADA**	65.67
68	193	**ROHAT**	65.36
69	70	**NOKHA**	65.35
70	68	**KOLAYAT**	65.20
71	196	**AMET**	64.89
72	80	**BHOPALSAGAR**	64.52
73	66	**BIKANER**	64.48
74	217	**PINDWARA**	64.47
75	134	**SANKRA**	64.28
76	187	**DESURI**	63.88
77	110	**GANGANAGAR**	63.86
78	63	**SAHARA**	63.69
79	115	**SURATGARH**	63.60
80	65	**SUWANA**	62.94
81	230	**GIRWA**	62.26
82	55	**ASIND**	62.25
83	120	**BASSI**	61.74
84	211	**KHANDELA**	61.45
85	149	**BUHANA**	61.11
86	161	**MANDOR**	60.65
87	154	**SURAJGARH**	60.27
88	200	**KUMBHALGARH**	60.14
	MEDIUM (40-60)		
89	8	**SRINAGAR**	59.60
90	5	**KISHANGARH**	59.56
91	113	**RAISINGHNAGAR**	59.22
92	2	**BHINAY**	58.74
93	218	**REODAR**	58.62
94	132	**JAISALMER**	58.49
95	25	**GARHI**	58.44
96	56	**BANERA**	58.35
97	197	**BHIM**	57.60
98	104	**ASPUR**	57.58
99	157	**BAP**	57.50
100	167	**NADOTI**	57.40
101	118	**NOHAR**	57.25
102	64	**SHAHPURA**	56.82
103	125	**JHOTWARA**	56.78
104	84	**GANGRAR**	56.69
105	69	**LUNKARANSAR**	56.67
106	119	**AMBER**	56.63
107	90	**RAJGARH**	56.58
108	228	**BHINDER**	56.36
109	112	**PADAMPUR**	56.19
110	227	**BARGAON**	56.11
111	128	**SAMBHAR**	56.07
112	206	**KHANDAR**	55.00
113	105	**BICHHIWARA**	54.76
114	109	**ANUPGARH**	54.75
115	82	**CHITTAURGARH**	54.54
116	30	**TALWARA**	54.48
117	231	**GOGUNDA**	54.38
118	191	**RAIPUR**	54.34
119	6	**MASOODA**	54.18
120	111	KARANPUR	53.36
121	213	NEEM KA THANA	53.35
122	59	KOTRI	53.22
123	198	DEOGARH	52.87
124	79	BHAINSRORGARH	52.81
125	224	TODARAISINGH	52.54
126	20	THANAGAZI	52.39
127	129	SANGANER	51.91
128	7	PISANGAN	51.72
129	124	JAMWA RAMGARH	51.70
130	43	SHEO	51.52
131	233	KHERWARA	51.19
132	85	KAPASAN	50.33
133	78	BHADESAR	49.21
134	229	DHARIAWAD	49.07
135	236	SALUMBAR	48.94
136	127	PHAGI	48.89
137	96	DAUSA	48.71
138	24	BAGIDORA	48.64
139	108	SIMALWARA	48.10
140	1	ARAIN	47.98
141	133	SAM	47.90
142	106	DUNGARPUR	47.52
143	122	DUDU	47.38
144	86	NIMBAHERA	47.04
145	15	MANDAWAR	46.83
146	126	KOTPUTLI	46.70
147	9	BANSURE	46.67
148	76	BARI SADRI	46.57
149	216	ABU ROAD	46.46
150	52	RUPBAS	46.01
151	83	DUNGLA	45.90
152	10	BEHROR	45.34
153	41	CHOHTAN	44.91
154	73	NAINWA	44.81
155	44	SINDHARI	44.61
156	204	BONLI	43.95
157	22	UMREN	43.74
158	61	MANDALGARH	43.47
159	205	GANGAPUR	43.46
160	171	ITAWA	43.33
161	50	NADBAI	43.18
162	221	DEOLI	42.69
163	77	BEGUN	42.62
164	81	CHHOTI SADRI	42.41
165	36	KISHANGANJ	42.28
166	232	JHADOL	42.14
167	99	SIKRAI	42.06
168	3	JAWAJA	41.93
169	226	UNIARA	41.75
170	165	HINDAUN	41.39
171	58	JAHAZPUR	40.85
172	101	BASERI	40.78
173	32	ATRU	40.55
174	87	PRATAPGARH	40.11
	LOW (20-40)		
175	170	CHECHAT	39.88
176	16	NIMRANA	39.77
177	130	SHAHPURA	39.76
178	174	SULTANPUR	39.37
179	26	GHATOL	39.34
180	13	KOTKASIM	38.80
181	207	SAWAI MADHOPUR	38.35
182	203	BAMANWAS	38.19
183	40	BAYTOO	38.04
184	131	VIRATNAGAR	38.00
185	31	ANTA	37.92
186	75	ARNOD	37.71
187	71	HINDOLI	37.56
188	143	DAG	37.38
189	234	KOTRA	37.04
190	173	SANGOD	37.01
191	72	KESHORAIPATAN	36.97
192	12	KISHANGARH BAS	36.76
193	39	BARMER	36.34
194	23	ANANDPURI	36.27
195	42	DHORIMANNA	35.75
196	168	SAPOTRA	35.10
197	19	RENI	34.76
198	74	TALERA	34.60
199	223	NIWAI	34.33
200	18	RAMGARH	34.24
201	17	RAJGARH	34.23
202	222	MALPURA	34.12
203	97	LALSOT	34.05
204	14	LACHHMANGARH	33.99
205	142	BAKANI	33.97
206	121	CHAKSU	33.80
207	11	KATHUMAR	33.55
208	144	JHALRAPATAN	33.44
209	46	BAYANA	31.94
210	49	KUMHER	31.15
211	54	WEIR	30.76
212	145	KHANPUR	30.23
213	95	BANDIKUI	29.68
214	53	SEWAR	29.20
215	4	KEKRI	29.04
216	37	SHAHBAD	28.16
217	33	BARAN	27.23
218	51	NAGAR PAHARI	27.13
219	35	CHHIPABAROD	26.72
220	225	TONK	26.38
221	166	KARAULI	26.16
222	28	PEEPALKHOONT	25.91
223	214	PIPRALI	25.86
224	169	TODABHIM	25.80
225	172	LADPURA	25.09
226	21	TIJARA	24.20
227	147	PIRAWA	23.58
228	29	SAJJANGARH	22.31
229	102	DHAULPUR	21.89
230	146	MANOHARTHANA	20.80
	VERY LOW (<20)		
231	100	BARI	19.90
232	27	KUSHALGARH	18.68
233	98	MAHWA	17.30
234	48	KAMAN	16.43
235	34	CHHABRA	12.50
236	103	RAJAKHERA	11.05
237	47	DEEG	10.81
		RAJASTHAN	**53.43**
		%age of AAPs	**50.20**

BOLD: Equal/Above Average Panchayat Samities (AAPs) *Source*: General Annex II, Col. 8.

ANNEX-3.18

RANKING OF PSS BY PERCENTAGE OF INHABITED VILLAGES HAVING COMMUNICATION AMENITIES: RAJASTHAN, 1991

(Descending Order)

RANK	*P. CODE*	*PANCHAYAT SAMITIES NAME*	*%*
1	2	3	4
	VERY HIGH (>75)		
1	**158**	**BHOPALGARH**	**79.76**
2	**195**	**SUMERPUR**	**79.37**
3	**141**	**SAYLA**	**77.92**
	HIGH (60-75)		
4	**137**	**JALOR**	**72.73**
5	**164**	**SHERGARH**	**72.00**
6	**153**	**NAWALGARH**	**70.00**
7	**209**	**DHOND**	**69.44**
8	**179**	**LADNU**	**68.75**
9	**190**	**PALI**	**67.50**
10	**136**	**BHINMAL**	**65.82**
11	**192**	**RANI STATION**	**65.75**
12	**135**	**AHORE**	**65.74**
13	**162**	**OSIAN**	**65.27**
14	**160**	**LUNI**	**64.84**
15	**138**	**JASWANTPURA**	**63.89**
16	**176**	**DIDWANA**	**62.87**
17	**38**	**BALOTRA**	**62.43**
18	**159**	**BILARA**	**60.76**
19	**208**	**DANTA RAMGARH**	**60.74**
20	**181**	**MERTA**	**60.42**
21	**89**	**CHURU**	**60.40**
22	**139**	**RANIWARA**	**60.24**
	HIGH (45-60)		
23	**45**	**SIWANA**	**59.79**
24	**175**	**DEGANA**	**59.59**
25	**151**	**JHUNJHUNUN**	**58.97**
26	**212**	**LACHHMANGARH**	**58.82**
27	**186**	**BALI**	**58.43**
28	**182**	**MUNDWA**	**58.18**
29	**210**	**FATEHPUR**	**58.16**
30	**194**	**SOJAT**	**58.04**
31	**155**	**UDAIPURWATI**	**58.02**
32	**178**	**KUCHAMAN**	**57.53**
33	**180**	**MAKRANA**	**57.50**
34	**156**	**BALESAR**	**57.35**
35	**91**	**RATANGARH**	**57.29**
36	**163**	**PHALODI**	**56.98**
37	**57**	**HURDA**	**55.88**
37	**92**	**SARDARSHAHAR**	**55.88**
39	**193**	**ROHAT**	**55.70**
40	**183**	**NAGAUR**	**55.64**
41	**152**	**KHETRI**	**55.00**
42	**140**	**SANCHORE**	**54.44**
43	**189**	**KHARCHI/MARWAR JUN.**	**54.01**
44	**196**	**AMET**	**53.68**
45	**150**	**CHIRAWA**	**53.66**
46	**67**	**DUNGARGARH**	**53.33**
46	**201**	**RAILMAGRA**	**53.33**
48	**184**	**PARBATSAR**	**51.85**
49	**7**	**PISANGAN**	**51.75**
50	**134**	**SANKRA**	**51.54**
51	**148**	**ALSISAR**	**51.33**
52	**202**	**RAJSAMAND**	**50.77**
53	**60**	**MANDAL**	**50.00**
53	**62**	**RAIPUR**	**50.00**
53	**199**	**KHAMNOR**	**50.00**
56	**93**	**SUJANGARH**	**49.67**
57	**161**	**MANDOR**	**49.52**
58	**214**	**PIPRALI**	**49.45**
59	**237**	**SARADA**	**49.35**
60	**188**	**JAITARAN**	**48.91**
61	**88**	**RASHMI**	**48.10**
62	**235**	**MAVLI**	**47.97**
63	**215**	**SRI MADHOPUR**	**47.54**
64	**90**	**RAJGARH**	**47.32**
65	**70**	**NOKHA**	**46.83**
66	**185**	**RIYAN**	**46.67**
67	**220**	**SIROHI**	**46.34**
68	**8**	**SRINAGAR**	**46.32**
69	**149**	**BUHANA**	**45.90**
70	**197**	**BHIM**	**45.87**
71	**154**	**SURAJGARH**	**45.83**
72	**177**	**JAYAL**	**45.45**
72	**219**	**SHEOGANJ**	**45.45**
74	**113**	**RAISINGHNAGAR**	**45.33**
75	**157**	**BAP**	**45.16**
76	**65**	**SUWANA**	**45.04**
	LOW (30-45)		
77	**211**	**KHANDELA**	**43.97**
78	**217**	**PINDWARA**	**43.88**
79	**5**	**KISHANGARH**	**43.64**
80	**200**	**KUMBHALGARH**	**43.48**
81	**187**	**DESURI**	**43.42**
82	**94**	**TARANAGAR**	**43.24**
83	**66**	**BIKANER**	**43.23**
84	**110**	**GANGANAGAR**	**42.74**
85	**112**	**PADAMPUR**	**41.95**
86	**107**	**SAGWARA**	**41.83**
87	**125**	**JHOTWARA**	**41.18**
88	**231**	**GOGUNDA**	**40.41**
89	**123**	**GOVINDGARH**	**40.00**
90	**80**	**BHOPALSAGAR**	**39.76**
91	**68**	**KOLAYAT**	**39.64**
92	**63**	**SAHARA**	**39.56**
93	**55**	**ASIND**	**39.41**
94	**167**	**NADOTI**	**39.29**
95	**64**	**SHAHPURA**	**38.93**
96	**120**	**BASSI**	**38.76**
97	**132**	**JAISALMER**	**38.69**
98	**233**	**KHERWARA**	**38.59**
99	**227**	**BARGAON**	**38.46**
100	**2**	**BHINAY**	**38.33**
101	**128**	**SAMBHAR**	**37.76**
102	**43**	**SHEO**	**37.72**
103	**218**	**REODAR**	**37.70**
104	**69**	**LUNKARANSAR**	**37.69**
105	**25**	**GARHI**	**37.42**
106	**111**	**KARANPUR**	**37.00**
107	**106**	**DUNGARPUR**	**36.71**
108	**198**	**DEOGARH**	**36.64**
109	**213**	**NEEM KA THANA**	**36.36**
110	**109**	**ANUPGARH**	**36.15**
111	**104**	**ASPUR**	**35.92**
112	**116**	**BHADRA**	**35.79**
113	**119**	**AMBER**	**35.57**
114	**114**	**SADULSHAHAR**	**35.54**
115	**30**	**TALWARA**	**35.51**
116	**126**	**KOTPUTLI**	**35.29**
117	**105**	**BICHHIWARA**	**35.06**
118	**59**	**KOTRI**	**34.25**
119	**52**	**RUPBAS**	**34.04**
120	**230**	**GIRWA**	**33.96**
121	**15**	**MANDAWAR**	**33.80**
122	115	SURATGARH	33.09
123	10	BEHROR	32.22
124	216	ABU ROAD	32.05
125	191	RAIPUR	32.04
126	228	BHINDER	31.82
127	85	KAPASAN	31.78
128	84	GANGRAR	31.50
129	6	MASOODA	31.39
130	117	HANUMANGARH	31.24
131	124	JAMWA RAMGARH	31.17
132	236	SALUMBAR	30.74
133	129	SANGANER	30.73
134	81	CHHOTI SADRI	30.50
135	56	BANERA	30.49
136	20	THANAGAZI	30.41
137	229	DHARIAWAD	30.08
138	44	SINDHARI	30.00
	VERY LOW (<30)		
139	50	NADBAI	29.82
140	3	JAWAJA	29.53
141	16	NIMRANA	29.41
142	78	BHADESAR	29.19
143	206	KHANDAR	28.85
144	79	BHAINSRORGARH	28.67
145	118	NOHAR	28.63
146	165	HINDAUN	28.57
147	83	DUNGLA	28.43
148	41	CHOHTAN	28.14
149	232	JHADOL	27.73
150	222	MALPURA	27.64
151	42	DHORIMANNA	27.38
152	86	NIMBAHERA	27.33
153	1	ARAIN	27.05
154	24	BAGIDORA	27.01
155	205	GANGAPUR	26.96
156	82	CHITTAURGARH	26.15
157	39	BARMER	26.04
158	108	SIMALWARA	26.03
159	22	UMREN	26.00
160	96	DAUSA	25.34
161	87	PRATAPGARH	25.31
162	122	DUDU	25.24
163	77	BEGUN	25.11
164	40	BAYTOO	25.00
165	133	SAM	24.70
166	99	SIKRAI	24.64
167	131	VIRATNAGAR	24.58
168	9	BANSURE	24.43
169	23	ANANDPURI	24.39
170	46	BAYANA	23.90
171	72	KESHORAIPATAN	23.61
172	127	PHAGI	23.21
173	58	JAHAZPUR	23.20
174	12	KISHANGARH BAS	22.96
174	32	ATRU	22.96
176	101	BASERI	22.95
177	130	SHAHPURA	22.78
178	13	KOTKASIM	22.61
179	26	GHATOL	22.48
180	73	NAINWA	22.29
181	74	TALERA	22.22
182	234	KOTRA	22.19
183	170	CHECHAT	21.92
184	204	BONLI	21.66
185	76	BARI SADRI	21.53
186	61	MANDALGARH	21.48
187	143	DAG	20.91
188	171	ITAWA	20.50
189	203	BAMANWAS	20.45
190	221	DEOLI	20.38
191	75	ARNOD	19.88
192	17	RAJGARH	19.85
193	173	SANGOD	19.70
194	14	LACHHMANGARH	19.57
195	169	TODABHIM	19.01
196	11	KATHUMAR	18.99
197	71	HINDOLI	18.39
198	33	BARAN	18.37
199	224	TODARAISINGH	18.35
200	226	UNIARA	18.32
201	54	WEIR	18.31
202	36	KISHANGANJ	18.18
203	144	JHALRAPATAN	18.09
204	49	KUMHER	18.02
205	168	SAPOTRA	17.70
206	21	TIJARA	17.59
207	18	RAMGARH	17.54
208	53	SEWAR	17.53
208	207	SAWAI MADHOPUR	17.53
210	174	SULTANPUR	17.50
211	172	LADPURA	17.12
212	31	ANTA	17.01
213	97	LALSOT	16.72
214	166	KARAULI	16.33
215	4	KEKRI	16.17
216	29	SAJJANGARH	15.93
217	19	RENI	15.69
218	51	NAGAR PAHARI	15.67
219	223	NIWAI	15.18
220	121	CHAKSU	14.73
221	142	BAKANI	14.54
222	28	PEEPALKHOONT	14.52
223	100	BARI	14.29
224	95	BANDIKUI	13.53
225	27	KUSHALGARH	13.46
226	147	PIRAWA	13.00
227	34	CHHABRA	12.79
228	146	MANOHARTHANA	12.77
229	145	KHANPUR	12.63
230	35	CHHIPABAROD	11.48
231	225	TONK	10.89
232	102	DHAULPUR	10.26
233	48	KAMAN	9.63
234	37	SHAHBAD	9.43
235	103	RAJAKHERA	7.48
236	98	MAHWA	7.33
237	47	DEEG	6.67
		RAJASTHAN	**33.20**
		%age of AAPs	**51.10**

BOLD: Equal/Above Average Panchayat Samities (AAPs)

Source: General Annex III, Col. 8.

ANNEX-4.1

RANKING OF PSS BY PERCENTAGE OF RURAL POP. SERVED BY MEDICAL AMENITIES: RAJASTHAN, 2001

(Descending Order)

RANK	P. CODE	PANCHAYAT SAMITIES NAME	%
1	2	3	4
	VERY HIGH (>60)		
1	220	**SIROHI**	88.10
2	159	**BILARA**	86.10
3	91	**RATANGARH**	85.90
4	135	**AHORE**	83.20
5	186	**BALI**	82.70
6	195	**SUMERPUR**	82.10
6	192	**RANI STATION**	82.10
8	67	**DUNGARGARH**	80.70
9	155	**UDAIPURWATI**	80.10
10	123	**GOVINDGARH**	79.40
11	152	**KHETRI**	78.80
12	160	**LUNI**	78.70
13	209	**DHOND**	78.20
14	141	**SAYLA**	77.80
15	188	**JAITARAN**	77.70
16	114	**SADULSHAHAR**	77.20
17	158	**BHOPALGARH**	77.10
18	56	**BANERA**	76.70
19	214	**PIPRALI**	76.60
20	89	**CHURU**	76.40
21	116	**BHADRA**	76.30
22	50	**NADBAI**	76.20
23	217	**PINDWARA**	76.10
24	49	**KUMHER**	75.50
25	219	**SHEOGANJ**	74.50
25	211	**KHANDELA**	74.50
27	179	**LADNU**	73.40
28	137	**JALOR**	73.20
29	4	**KEKRI**	73.10
30	107	**SAGWARA**	72.90
31	191	**RAIPUR**	72.80
32	194	**SOJAT**	72.60
32	130	**SHAHPURA**	72.60
34	7	**PISANGAN**	72.40
34	181	**MERTA**	72.40
36	187	**DESURI**	72.10
37	208	**DANTA RAMGARH**	72.00
38	162	**OSIAN**	71.60
38	213	**NEEM KA THANA**	71.60
40	205	**GANGAPUR**	71.10
41	139	**RANIWARA**	71.00
41	201	**RAILMAGRA**	71.00
41	189	**KHARCHI/MARWAR JUN.**	71.00
44	215	**SRI MADHOPUR**	70.90
45	57	**HURDA**	70.70
46	45	**SIWANA**	70.30
47	138	**JASWANTPURA**	70.10
48	235	**MAVLI**	69.80
49	149	**BUHANA**	69.40
50	25	**GARHI**	68.90
51	185	**RIYAN**	68.60
51	177	**JAYAL**	68.60
53	5	**KISHANGARH**	68.40
53	105	**BICHHIWARA**	68.40
55	94	**TARANAGAR**	68.00
55	16	**NIMRANA**	68.00
57	104	**ASPUR**	67.50
58	10	**BEHROR**	67.30
59	47	**DEEG**	67.00
60	93	**SUJANGARH**	66.90
61	150	**CHIRAWA**	66.80
62	182	**MUNDWA**	66.50
63	218	**REODAR**	66.20
64	153	**NAWALGARH**	66.10
64	180	**MAKRANA**	66.10
66	190	**PALI**	66.00
67	184	**PARBATSAR**	65.60
68	88	**RASHMI**	65.20
69	175	**DEGANA**	65.00
70	174	**SULTANPUR**	64.80
70	165	**HINDAUN**	64.80
72	207	**SAWAI MADHOPUR**	64.50
73	230	**GIRWA**	64.00
74	63	**SAHARA**	63.90
74	110	**GANGANAGAR**	63.90
76	136	**BHINMAL**	63.80
77	128	**SAMBHAR**	63.60
78	210	**FATEHPUR**	63.40
79	169	**TODABHIM**	63.30
80	156	**BALESAR**	62.90
81	183	**NAGAUR**	62.10
81	151	**JHUNJHUNUN**	62.10
83	8	**SRINAGAR**	61.90
83	83	**DUNGLA**	61.90
85	117	**HANUMANGARH**	61.80
86	28	**PEEPALKHOONT**	61.50
87	100	**BARI**	61.10
88	20	**THANAGAZI**	61.00
88	176	**DIDWANA**	61.00
90	237	**SARADA**	60.60
91	106	**DUNGARPUR**	60.50
	HIGH (50-60)		
92	112	**PADAMPUR**	59.60
92	167	**NADOTI**	59.60
94	225	**TONK**	59.20
95	65	**SUWANA**	59.10
96	119	**AMBER**	59.00
97	19	**RENI**	58.60
97	148	**ALSISAR**	58.60
99	108	**SIMALWARA**	58.50
100	221	**DEOLI**	58.20
101	172	**LADPURA**	58.10
102	164	**SHERGARH**	58.00
102	122	**DUDU**	58.00
104	2	**BHINAY**	57.90
105	168	**SAPOTRA**	57.80
105	132	**JAISALMER**	57.80
107	203	**BAMANWAS**	57.30
108	62	**RAIPUR**	57.00
108	1	**ARAIN**	57.00
110	131	**VIRATNAGAR**	56.70
110	224	**TODARAISINGH**	56.70
112	212	LACHHMANGARH	56.50
113	170	CHECHAT	56.30
113	120	BASSI	56.30
115	199	KHAMNOR	56.20
115	124	JAMWA RAMGARH	56.20
117	58	JAHAZPUR	56.10
118	30	TALWARA	55.90
118	161	MANDOR	55.90
120	52	RUPBAS	55.60
121	206	KHANDAR	55.50
122	64	SHAHPURA	55.10
122	166	KARAULI	55.10
124	90	RAJGARH	55.00
125	163	PHALODI	54.80
126	22	UMREN	54.70
127	178	KUCHAMAN	54.50
128	111	KARANPUR	54.30
129	14	LACHHMANGARH	54.20
130	53	SEWAR	54.10
130	228	BHINDER	54.10
130	38	BALOTRA	54.10
133	26	GHATOL	54.00
133	204	BONLI	54.00
135	70	NOKHA	53.90
136	69	LUNKARANSAR	53.70
137	171	ITAWA	53.40
138	193	ROHAT	53.10
139	129	SANGANER	53.00
140	54	WEIR	52.80
140	55	ASIND	52.80
142	60	MANDAL	52.70
142	71	HINDOLI	52.70
142	96	DAUSA	52.70
145	6	MASOODA	52.50
146	15	MANDAWAR	52.10
147	222	MALPURA	51.90
148	125	JHOTWARA	51.70
149	24	BAGIDORA	51.50
150	11	KATHUMAR	51.40
151	202	RAJSAMAND	51.30
152	95	BANDIKUI	51.00
153	236	SALUMBAR	50.90
153	9	BANSURE	50.90
155	61	MANDALGARH	50.50
156	80	BHOPALSAGAR	50.00
	MEDIUM (40-50)		
157	231	GOGUNDA	49.70
158	216	ABU ROAD	49.70
159	134	SANKRA	49.50
160	68	KOLAYAT	49.20
161	32	ATRU	49.10
162	59	KOTRI	49.00
163	31	ANTA	48.90
164	233	KHERWARA	48.80
165	140	SANCHORE	48.40
165	86	NIMBAHERA	48.40
167	197	BHIM	48.30
168	232	JHADOL	48.20
169	226	UNIARA	48.10
169	23	ANANDPURI	48.10
171	154	SURAJGARH	47.80
171	98	MAHWA	47.80
171	200	KUMBHALGARH	47.80
174	66	BIKANER	47.70
175	92	SARDARSHAHAR	47.60
176	133	SAM	47.30
176	223	NIWAI	47.30
178	41	CHOHTAN	47.10
179	126	KOTPUTLI	46.90
179	145	KHANPUR	46.90
179	84	GANGRAR	46.90
179	227	BARGAON	46.90
183	29	SAJJANGARH	46.60
184	18	RAMGARH	46.40
185	173	SANGOD	46.30
186	17	RAJGARH	46.10
186	48	KAMAN	46.10
186	46	BAYANA	46.10
189	118	NOHAR	45.80
190	76	BARI SADRI	45.70
191	33	BARAN	45.40
192	157	BAP	45.00
193	36	KISHANGANJ	44.90
194	196	AMET	44.80
195	113	RAISINGHNAGAR	44.70
196	82	CHITTAURGARH	43.60
197	127	PHAGI	43.50
198	74	TALERA	43.40
199	73	NAINWA	43.30
199	229	DHARIAWAD	43.30
201	115	SURATGARH	42.40
202	87	PRATAPGARH	42.20
202	101	BASERI	42.20
204	3	JAWAJA	41.90
205	77	BEGUN	41.60
206	99	SIKRAI	41.40
207	72	KESHORAIPATAN	41.30
208	51	NAGAR PAHARI	41.20
209	97	LALSOT	40.50
210	13	KOTKASIM	40.30
	LOW (30-40)		
211	102	DHAULPUR	37.90
211	109	ANUPGARH	37.90
213	78	BHADESAR	37.30
214	234	KOTRA	36.70
215	21	TIJARA	36.60
216	37	SHAHBAD	36.30
217	44	SINDHARI	36.20
217	12	KISHANGARH BAS	36.20
219	198	DEOGARH	35.20
220	143	DAG	34.90
221	27	KUSHALGARH	34.70
222	79	BHAINSRORGARH	34.10
222	142	BAKANI	34.10
224	75	ARNOD	33.80
225	147	PIRAWA	33.20
225	144	JHALRAPATAN	33.20
227	121	CHAKSU	31.40
227	39	BARMER	31.40
229	42	DHORIMANNA	30.80
230	43	SHEO	30.30
231	81	CHHOTI SADRI	30.20
	VERY LOW (<30)		
232	35	CHHIPABAROD	28.80
233	103	RAJAKHERA	28.10
234	40	BAYTOO	27.40
235	85	KAPASAN	24.30
236	146	MANOHARTHANA	21.10
237	34	CHHABRA	14.80
		RAJASTHAN	**56.64**
		%age of AAPs	**46.84**

BOLD: Equal/Above Average Panchayat Samities (AAPs)   *Source*: General Annex VIII, Col. 4.

ANNEX-4.2

RANKING OF PSS BY PERCENTAGE OF INHABITED VILLAGES HAVING MEDICAL AMENITIES: RAJASTHAN, 2001

(Descending Order)

RANK	P. CODE	PANCHAYAT SAMITIES NAME	%
1	2	3	4
		VERY HIGH (>=50)	
1	159	**BILARA**	69.7
2	91	**RATANGARH**	65.3
3	155	**UDAIPURWATI**	64.2
4	195	**SUMERPUR**	61.9
4	89	**CHURU**	61.9
6	209	**DHOND**	61.5
7	67	**DUNGARGARH**	60.9
8	137	**JALOR**	60.3
9	220	**SIROHI**	60.2
10	192	**RANI STATION**	59.2
11	135	**AHORE**	57.3
12	186	**BALI**	57.1
13	50	**NADBAI**	57.0
14	152	**KHETRI**	56.5
15	141	**SAYLA**	55.8
16	49	**KUMHER**	54.7
17	215	**SRI MADHOPUR**	54.5
18	162	**OSIAN**	52.6
19	188	**JAITARAN**	52.4
20	158	**BHOPALGARH**	52.3
21	160	**LUNI**	51.9
22	100	**BARI**	51.8
23	139	**RANIWARA**	51.2
24	211	**KHANDELA**	50.8
25	194	**SOJAT**	50.4
25	165	**HINDAUN**	50.4
27	149	**BUHANA**	50.0
27	214	**PIPRALI**	50.0
		HIGH (40-50)	
29	219	**SHEOGANJ**	49.3
30	213	**NEEM KA THANA**	49.0
30	107	**SAGWARA**	49.0
30	123	**GOVINDGARH**	49.0
33	25	**GARHI**	48.8
34	138	**JASWANTPURA**	48.6
35	104	**ASPUR**	48.3
36	16	**NIMRANA**	48.2
37	7	**PISANGAN**	47.7
37	130	**SHAHPURA**	47.7
39	4	**KEKRI**	47.5
39	136	**BHINMAL**	47.5
41	56	**BANERA**	47.0
42	205	**GANGAPUR**	46.9
43	106	**DUNGARPUR**	46.5
44	208	**DANTA RAMGARH**	45.9
45	153	**NAWALGARH**	45.5
45	184	**PARBATSAR**	45.5
45	217	**PINDWARA**	45.5
48	47	**DEEG**	45.4
48	179	**LADNU**	45.4
50	191	**RAIPUR**	45.0
51	180	**MAKRANA**	44.5
52	210	**FATEHPUR**	44.1
53	105	**BICHHIWARA**	44.0
54	187	**DESURI**	43.6
55	150	**CHIRAWA**	42.9
56	189	**KHARCHI/MARWAR JUN.**	42.3
57	8	**SRINAGAR**	41.7
57	169	**TODABHIM**	41.7
59	235	**MAVLI**	41.6
60	57	**HURDA**	41.4
61	93	**SUJANGARH**	41.3
62	128	**SAMBHAR**	41.0
63	45	**SIWANA**	40.9
64	151	**JHUNJHUNUN**	40.7
65	10	**BEHROR**	40.0
65	190	**PALI**	40.0
		MEDIUM (30-40)	
67	175	**DEGANA**	39.9
68	177	**JAYAL**	39.7
69	201	**RAILMAGRA**	39.6
70	183	**NAGAUR**	39.3
71	112	**PADAMPUR**	38.9
72	182	**MUNDWA**	38.8
73	52	**RUPBAS**	38.7
74	156	**BALESAR**	38.4
74	185	**RIYAN**	38.4
76	176	**DIDWANA**	38.2
77	5	**KISHANGARH**	37.8
78	119	**AMBER**	37.5
79	174	**SULTANPUR**	36.8
80	131	**VIRATNAGAR**	36.7
81	163	**PHALODI**	36.0
82	116	**BHADRA**	35.9
82	207	**SAWAI MADHOPUR**	35.9
84	218	**REODAR**	35.7
85	90	**RAJGARH**	35.7
86	124	**JAMWA RAMGARH**	35.6
87	193	**ROHAT**	35.4
87	166	**KARAULI**	35.4
89	167	**NADOTI**	35.3
90	15	**MANDAWAR**	35.2
90	161	**MANDOR**	35.2
92	181	**MERTA**	35.1
93	92	**SARDARSHAHAR**	34.7
94	216	**ABU ROAD**	34.6
94	164	**SHERGARH**	34.6
96	237	**SARADA**	34.1
97	140	**SANCHORE**	33.8
98	94	**TARANAGAR**	33.6
98	212	**LACHHMANGARH**	33.6
100	83	**DUNGLA**	33.3
101	154	**SURAJGARH**	32.8
102	28	**PEEPALKHOONT**	32.6
103	230	**GIRWA**	32.4
104	108	**SIMALWARA**	32.3
104	148	**ALSISAR**	32.3
106	126	**KOTPUTLI**	32.2
107	178	**KUCHAMAN**	32.1
108	2	**BHINAY**	32.0
109	120	**BASSI**	31.9
110	22	**UMREN**	31.5
111	19	**RENI**	31.4
112	63	**SAHARA**	31.3
112	170	**CHECHAT**	31.3
114	231	**GOGUNDA**	31.3
115	110	**GANGANAGAR**	31.1
116	14	**LACHHMANGARH**	31.0
116	168	**SAPOTRA**	31.0
118	88	**RASHMI**	30.9
119	233	**KHERWARA**	30.8
120	1	**ARAIN**	30.4
120	11	**KATHUMAR**	30.4
122	206	**KHANDAR**	30.3
122	24	**BAGIDORA**	30.3
122	62	**RAIPUR**	30.3
125	65	**SUWANA**	30.1
125	132	**JAISALMER**	30.1
125	134	**SANKRA**	30.1
		LOW (20-30)	
128	199	**KHAMNOR**	29.9
129	227	**BARGAON**	29.9
130	9	**BANSURE**	29.8
130	46	**BAYANA**	29.8
130	64	**SHAHPURA**	29.8
133	172	**LADPURA**	29.7
134	98	**MAHWA**	29.6
135	54	**WEIR**	29.5
136	203	**BAMANWAS**	29.4
137	53	**SEWAR**	29.3
138	70	**NOKHA**	29.2
139	20	THANAGAZI	29.1
140	71	HINDOLI	28.7
141	29	SAJJANGARH	28.6
141	30	TALWARA	28.6
143	225	TONK	28.2
144	69	LUNKARANSAR	28.1
145	236	SALUMBAR	27.8
146	58	JAHAZPUR	27.6
147	41	CHOHTAN	27.3
147	48	KAMAN	27.3
149	197	BHIM	27.3
149	221	DEOLI	27.3
151	23	ANANDPURI	27.1
152	204	BONLI	27.0
152	114	SADULSHAHAR	27.0
154	38	BALOTRA	26.8
154	224	TODARAISINGH	26.8
156	111	KARANPUR	26.6
157	113	RAISINGHNAGAR	26.4
158	33	BARAN	26.3
159	200	KUMBHALGARH	26.2
160	125	JHOTWARA	26.0
161	32	ATRU	25.7
162	3	JAWAJA	25.6
162	122	DUDU	25.6
162	232	JHADOL	25.6
165	27	KUSHALGARH	25.4
166	95	BANDIKUI	25.1
167	26	GHATOL	25.0
167	55	ASIND	25.0
169	18	RAMGARH	24.9
170	157	BAP	24.8
171	222	MALPURA	24.6
172	51	NAGAR PAHARI	24.5
173	202	RAJSAMAND	24.2
174	61	MANDALGARH	23.8
174	129	SANGANER	23.8
176	6	MASOODA	23.0
177	59	KOTRI	22.9
177	60	MANDAL	22.9
179	66	BIKANER	22.8
180	96	DAUSA	22.4
181	102	DHAULPUR	22.3
181	173	SANGOD	22.3
183	228	BHINDER	22.2
184	42	DHORIMANNA	21.5
185	44	SINDHARI	21.2
186	86	NIMBAHERA	21.1
187	223	NIWAI	20.9
188	21	TIJARA	20.8
189	196	AMET	20.6
190	74	TALERA	20.2
190	171	ITAWA	20.2
		VERY LOW (<20)	
192	39	BARMER	19.9
193	84	GANGRAR	19.7
194	31	ANTA	19.6
195	68	KOLAYAT	19.4
196	12	KISHANGARH BAS	19.3
196	17	RAJGARH	19.3
196	72	KESHORAIPATAN	19.3
196	80	BHOPALSAGAR	19.3
200	13	KOTKASIM	19.1
201	36	KISHANGANJ	18.9
201	76	BARI SADRI	18.9
201	115	SURATGARH	18.9
201	117	HANUMANGARH	18.9
201	127	PHAGI	18.9
206	87	PRATAPGARH	18.8
207	99	SIKRAI	18.7
207	145	KHANPUR	18.7
209	101	BASERI	18.4
210	229	DHARIAWAD	18.1
211	40	BAYTOO	18.0
212	73	NAINWA	17.8
213	43	SHEO	17.2
214	103	RAJAKHERA	17.1
214	133	SAM	17.1
216	109	ANUPGARH	16.8
217	77	BEGUN	16.7
218	226	UNIARA	16.3
219	118	NOHAR	16.2
220	79	BHAINSRORGARH	15.6
220	82	CHITTAURGARH	15.6
222	143	DAG	15.4
223	198	DEOGARH	15.3
224	144	JHALRAPATAN	15.1
225	142	BAKANI	14.9
226	97	LALSOT	14.3
227	234	KOTRA	14.2
228	147	PIRAWA	13.2
229	37	SHAHBAD	12.6
230	75	ARNOD	12.4
231	78	BHADESAR	11.7
232	81	CHHOTI SADRI	11.3
233	35	CHHIPABAROD	11.0
234	146	MANOHARTHANA	10.9
235	85	KAPASAN	10.3
236	121	CHAKSU	10.1
237	34	CHHABRA	7.5
		RAJASTHAN	**29.20**
		%age of AAPs	**58.23**

BOLD: Equal/Above Average Panchayat Samities (AAPs)   *Source*: General Annex IX, Col. 4.

ANNEX-4.3

RANKING OF PSS BY TOTAL NO. OF MEDICAL INSTITUTIONS: RAJASTHAN, 2001

(Descending Order)

RANK	P. CODE	PANCHAYAT SAMITIES NAME	%
1	2	3	4
		VERY HIGH (>=80)	
1	104	**ASPUR**	137
1	117	**HANUMANGARH**	137
3	208	**DANTA RAMGARH**	121
4	162	**OSIAN**	117
5	107	**SAGWARA**	113
6	25	**GARHI**	111
6	237	**SARADA**	111
8	61	**MANDALGARH**	109
9	232	**JHADOL**	107
9	118	**NOHAR**	107
9	108	**SIMALWARA**	107
12	236	**SALUMBAR**	106
13	194	**SOJAT**	103
14	213	**NEEM KA THANA**	101
15	105	**BICHHIWARA**	97
15	209	**DHOND**	97
15	220	**SIROHI**	97
18	149	**BUHANA**	96
18	233	**KHERWARA**	96
20	106	**DUNGARPUR**	95
20	230	**GIRWA**	95
22	225	**TONK**	94
23	200	**KUMBHALGARH**	91
24	175	**DEGANA**	90
24	30	**TALWARA**	90
26	228	**BHINDER**	88
27	109	**ANUPGARH**	86
27	26	**GHATOL**	86
27	199	**KHAMNOR**	86
27	178	**KUCHAMAN**	86
27	91	**RATANGARH**	86
27	44	**SINDHARI**	86
27	155	**UDAIPURWATI**	86
34	214	**PIPRALI**	85
34	90	**RAJGARH**	85
34	140	**SANCHORE**	85
37	55	**ASIND**	84
37	122	**DUDU**	84
37	210	**FATEHPUR**	84
37	151	**JHUNJHUNUN**	84
41	159	**BILARA**	82
41	176	**DIDWANA**	82
41	235	**MAVLI**	82
44	89	**CHURU**	81
44	58	**JAHAZPUR**	81
44	7	**PISANGAN**	81
47	186	**BALI**	80
47	211	**KHANDELA**	80
47	87	**PRATAPGARH**	80
47	168	**SAPOTRA**	80
		HIGH (60-80)	
51	207	**SAWAI MADHOPUR**	79
52	189	**KHARCHI/MARWAR JUN.**	78
53	218	**REODAR**	75
53	93	**SUJANGARH**	75
55	183	**NAGAUR**	74
56	135	**AHORE**	73
56	229	**DHARIAWAD**	73
56	28	**PEEPALKHOONT**	73
56	192	**RANI STATION**	73
56	185	**RIYAN**	73
61	96	**DAUSA**	72
61	153	**NAWALGARH**	72
61	201	**RAILMAGRA**	72
64	67	**DUNGARGARH**	71
65	38	**BALOTRA**	70
65	124	**JAMWA RAMGARH**	70
65	179	**LADNU**	70
65	160	**LUNI**	70
69	120	**BASSI**	69
69	40	**BAYTOO**	69
69	110	**GANGANAGAR**	69
69	188	**JAITARAN**	69
69	177	**JAYAL**	69
69	27	**KUSHALGARH**	69
69	94	**TARANAGAR**	69
76	184	**PARBATSAR**	68
77	114	**SADULSHAHAR**	67
77	169	**TODABHIM**	67
79	152	**KHETRI**	66
79	45	**SIWANA**	66
81	148	**ALSISAR**	65
81	156	**BALESAR**	65
81	39	**BARMER**	65
81	116	**BHADRA**	65
81	231	**GOGUNDA**	65
81	123	**GOVINDGARH**	65
81	15	**MANDAWAR**	65
81	52	**RUPBAS**	65
89	66	**BIKANER**	64
89	134	**SANKRA**	64
89	92	**SARDARSHAHAR**	64
89	130	**SHAHPURA**	64
89	115	**SURATGARH**	64
94	77	**BEGUN**	63
94	158	**BHOPALGARH**	63
94	204	**BONLI**	63
94	133	**SAM**	63
94	128	**SAMBHAR**	63
94	65	**SUWANA**	63
100	24	**BAGIDORA**	62
100	102	**DHAULPUR**	62
100	64	**SHAHPURA**	62
103	2	**BHINAY**	61
103	42	**DHORIMANNA**	61
103	165	**HINDAUN**	61
103	126	**KOTPUTLI**	61
103	223	**NIWAI**	61
108	71	HINDOLI	60
108	132	JAISALMER	60
108	3	JAWAJA	60
108	234	KOTRA	60
108	74	TALERA	60
		MEDIUM (40-60)	
113	166	KARAULI	59
113	72	KESHORAIPATAN	59
113	212	LACHHMANGARH	59
113	180	MAKRANA	59
117	217	PINDWARA	58
118	119	AMBER	57
118	4	KEKRI	57
118	5	KISHANGARH	57
118	60	MANDAL	57
118	181	MERTA	57
118	182	MUNDWA	57
118	191	RAIPUR	57
118	29	SAJJANGARH	57
118	173	SANGOD	57
118	195	SUMERPUR	57
128	100	BARI	56
129	56	BANERA	55
129	221	DEOLI	55
129	137	JALOR	55
129	145	KHANPUR	55
129	219	SHEOGANJ	55
134	41	CHOHTAN	54
134	187	DESURI	54
134	69	LUNKARANSAR	54
134	73	NAINWA	54
134	20	THANAGAZI	54
139	163	PHALODI	53
139	141	SAYLA	53
141	227	BARGAON	52
141	197	BHIM	52
141	150	CHIRAWA	52
141	82	CHITTAURGARH	52
141	205	GANGAPUR	52
141	11	KATHUMAR	52
141	49	KUMHER	52
141	6	MASOODA	52
141	113	RAISINGHNAGAR	52
141	54	WEIR	52
151	206	KHANDAR	51
151	222	MALPURA	51
151	129	SANGANER	51
151	131	VIRATNAGAR	51
155	1	ARAIN	50
155	203	BAMANWAS	50
155	138	JASWANTPURA	50
155	97	LALSOT	50
155	8	SRINAGAR	50
155	154	SURAJGARH	50
155	22	UMREN	50
162	59	KOTRI	49
162	63	SAHARA	49
164	23	ANANDPURI	48
165	9	BANSURE	47
165	43	SHEO	47
165	215	SRI MADHOPUR	47
168	111	KARANPUR	46
168	172	LADPURA	46
168	202	RAJSAMAND	46
171	101	BASERI	45
171	143	DAG	45
171	112	PADAMPUR	45
171	19	RENI	45
175	144	JHALRAPATAN	44
175	14	LACHHMANGARH	44
175	167	NADOTI	44
175	193	ROHAT	44
175	174	SULTANPUR	44
175	21	TIJARA	44
181	171	ITAWA	43
181	68	KOLAYAT	43
181	98	MAHWA	43
181	70	NOKHA	43
181	147	PIRAWA	43
181	62	RAIPUR	43
187	31	ANTA	42
188	57	HURDA	40
188	37	SHAHBAD	40
		LOW (20-40)	
190	10	BEHROR	39
190	127	PHAGI	39
190	224	TODARAISINGH	39
193	32	ATRU	38
193	136	BHINMAL	38
193	51	NAGAR PAHARI	38
193	86	NIMBAHERA	38
193	88	RASHMI	38
193	164	SHERGARH	38
193	99	SIKRAI	38
200	95	BANDIKUI	37
200	121	CHAKSU	37
200	50	NADBAI	37
203	142	BAKANI	36
203	190	PALI	36
203	18	RAMGARH	36
206	12	KISHANGARH BAS	35
206	17	RAJGARH	35
206	139	RANIWARA	35
206	53	SEWAR	35
210	196	AMET	34
210	170	CHECHAT	34
210	83	DUNGLA	34
210	16	NIMRANA	34
214	216	ABU ROAD	33
215	226	UNIARA	32
216	157	BAP	31
216	47	DEEG	31
216	125	JHOTWARA	31
219	75	ARNOD	30
219	46	BAYANA	30
219	36	KISHANGANJ	30
222	35	CHHIPABAROD	29
222	84	GANGRAR	29
224	80	BHOPALSAGAR	28
224	48	KAMAN	28
226	161	MANDOR	27
227	103	RAJAKHERA	25
228	79	BHAINSRORGARH	24
228	81	CHHOTI SADRI	24
230	78	BHADESAR	23
231	33	BARAN	22
232	198	DEOGARH	20
		VERY LOW (<20)	
233	146	MANOHARTHANA	19
234	13	KOTKASIM	17
235	76	BARI SADRI	14
235	34	CHHABRA	14
235	85	KAPASAN	14
RAJASTHAN		TOTAL	14231
		AVERAGE	60
		%age of AAPs	45.15

BOLD: Equal/Above Average Panchayat Samities (AAPs) *Source:* General Annex X, Col. 11.

ANNEX-4.4

RANKING OF PSS BY PERCENTAGE OF RURAL POP. SERVED BY EDUCATION AMENITIES: RAJASTHAN, 2001

(Descending Order)

RANK	P. CODE	PANCHAYAT SAMITIES NAME	%
1	2	3	4
	PERFECT (100)		
1	216	**ABU ROAD**	100.00
1	2	**BHINAY**	100.00
1	136	**BHINMAL**	100.00
1	158	**BHOPALGARH**	100.00
1	150	**CHIRAWA**	100.00
1	47	**DEEG**	100.00
1	209	**DHOND**	100.00
1	106	**DUNGARPUR**	100.00
1	137	**JALOR**	100.00
1	11	**KATHUMAR**	100.00
1	152	**KHETRI**	100.00
1	126	**KOTPUTLI**	100.00
1	153	**NAWALGARH**	100.00
1	16	**NIMRANA**	100.00
1	7	**PISANGAN**	100.00
1	139	**RANIWARA**	100.00
1	130	**SHAHPURA**	100.00
1	194	**SOJAT**	100.00
1	215	**SRI MADHOPUR**	100.00
1	154	**SURAJGARH**	100.00
1	155	**UDAIPURWATI**	100.00
	VERY HIGH (95-100)		
22	186	**BALI**	99.90
22	56	**BANERA**	99.90
22	9	**BANSURE**	99.90
22	175	**DEGANA**	99.90
22	67	**DUNGARGARH**	99.90
22	25	**GARHI**	99.90
22	188	**JAITARAN**	99.90
22	138	**JASWANTPURA**	99.90
22	151	**JHUNJHUNUN**	99.90
22	5	**KISHANGARH**	99.90
22	49	**KUMHER**	99.90
22	214	**PIPRALI**	99.90
22	192	**RANI STATION**	99.90
22	193	**ROHAT**	99.90
22	8	**SRINAGAR**	99.90
37	1	**ARAIN**	99.80
37	4	**KEKRI**	99.80
37	52	**RUPBAS**	99.80
37	94	**TARANAGAR**	99.80
37	105	**BICHHIWARA**	99.80
37	107	**SAGWARA**	99.80
37	141	**SAYLA**	99.80
37	149	**BUHANA**	99.80
37	180	**MAKRANA**	99.80
37	184	**PARBATSAR**	99.80
37	219	**SHEOGANJ**	99.80
37	222	**MALPURA**	99.80
49	33	**BARAN**	99.70
49	50	**NADBAI**	99.70
49	51	**NAGAR PAHARI**	99.70
49	63	**SAHARA**	99.70
49	65	**SUWANA**	99.70
49	90	**RAJGARH**	99.70
49	128	**SAMBHAR**	99.70
49	160	**LUNI**	99.70
49	162	**OSIAN**	99.70
49	197	**BHIM**	99.70
49	208	**DANTA RAMGARH**	99.70
49	212	**LACHHMANGARH**	99.70
61	13	**KOTKASIM**	99.60
61	44	**SINDHARI**	99.60
61	54	**WEIR**	99.60
61	108	**SIMALWARA**	99.60
61	135	**AHORE**	99.60
61	176	**DIDWANA**	99.60
61	201	**RAILMAGRA**	99.60
61	210	**FATEHPUR**	99.60
69	14	**LACHHMANGARH**	99.50
69	15	**MANDAWAR**	99.50
69	62	**RAIPUR**	99.50
69	80	**BHOPALSAGAR**	99.50
69	123	**GOVINDGARH**	99.50
69	131	**VIRATNAGAR**	99.50
69	159	**BILARA**	99.50
69	177	**JAYAL**	99.50
69	205	**GANGAPUR**	99.50
69	231	**GOGUNDA**	99.50
79	26	**GHATOL**	99.40
79	45	**SIWANA**	99.40

RANK	P. CODE	PANCHAYAT SAMITIES NAME	%
1	2	3	4
79	48	**KAMAN**	99.40
79	64	**SHAHPURA**	99.40
79	207	**SAWAI MADHOPUR**	99.40
79	211	**KHANDELA**	99.40
79	217	**PINDWARA**	99.40
79	220	**SIROHI**	99.40
87	10	**BEHROR**	99.30
87	140	**SANCHORE**	99.30
87	169	**TODABHIM**	99.30
87	187	**DESURI**	99.30
87	191	**RAIPUR**	99.30
92	24	**BAGIDORA**	99.20
92	46	**BAYANA**	99.20
92	104	**ASPUR**	99.20
92	161	**MANDOR**	99.20
92	167	**NADOTI**	99.20
92	189	**KHARCHI/MARWAR JUN.**	99.20
98	32	**ATRU**	99.10
98	41	**CHOHTAN**	99.10
98	53	**SEWAR**	99.10
98	74	**TALERA**	99.10
98	86	**NIMBAHERA**	99.10
98	91	**RATANGARH**	99.10
98	127	**PHAGI**	99.10
98	195	**SUMERPUR**	99.10
106	27	**KUSHALGARH**	99.00
106	31	**ANTA**	99.00
106	60	**MANDAL**	99.00
106	99	**SIKRAI**	99.00
106	165	**HINDAUN**	99.00
106	179	**LADNU**	99.00
106	183	**NAGAUR**	99.00
106	213	**NEEM KA THANA**	99.00
106	218	**REODAR**	99.00
115	29	**SAJJANGARH**	98.90
115	83	**DUNGLA**	98.90
115	95	**BANDIKUI**	98.90
115	178	**KUCHAMAN**	98.90
115	190	**PALI**	98.90
115	202	**RAJSAMAND**	98.90
115	203	**BAMANWAS**	98.90
115	230	**GIRWA**	98.90
115	237	**SARADA**	98.90
124	19	**RENI**	98.80
124	73	**NAINWA**	98.80
126	55	**ASIND**	98.70
126	57	**HURDA**	98.70
126	148	**ALSISAR**	98.70
126	166	**KARAULI**	98.70
126	181	**MERTA**	98.70
126	182	**MUNDWA**	98.70
126	185	**RIYAN**	98.70
126	204	**BONLI**	98.70
126	235	**MAVLI**	98.70
135	30	**TALWARA**	98.60
136	12	**KISHANGARH BAS**	98.50
136	89	**CHURU**	98.50
136	93	**SUJANGARH**	98.50
136	119	**AMBER**	98.50
136	122	**DUDU**	98.50
136	200	**KUMBHALGARH**	98.50
136	224	**TODARAISINGH**	98.50
143	18	**RAMGARH**	98.40
143	163	**PHALODI**	98.40
143	170	**CHECHAT**	98.40
143	174	**SULTANPUR**	98.40
147	6	**MASOODA**	98.30
147	20	**THANAGAZI**	98.30
147	92	**SARDARSHAHAR**	98.30
147	120	**BASSI**	98.30
147	199	**KHAMNOR**	98.30
152	23	**ANANDPURI**	98.20
152	72	**KESHORAIPATAN**	98.20
154	68	**KOLAYAT**	98.10
154	88	**RASHMI**	98.10
154	125	**JHOTWARA**	98.10
157	59	**KOTRI**	98.00
157	70	**NOKHA**	98.00
157	168	**SAPOTRA**	98.00
160	134	**SANKRA**	97.90
160	172	**LADPURA**	97.90
162	42	**DHORIMANNA**	97.80

RANK	P. CODE	PANCHAYAT SAMITIES NAME	%
1	2	3	4
162	102	**DHAULPUR**	97.80
162	225	**TONK**	97.80
165	132	**JAISALMER**	97.70
165	206	**KHANDAR**	97.70
165	227	**BARGAON**	97.70
165	236	**SALUMBAR**	97.70
169	103	RAJAKHERA	97.60
169	173	SANGOD	97.60
171	71	HINDOLI	97.50
172	101	BASERI	97.40
172	196	AMET	97.40
174	22	UMREN	97.30
174	85	KAPASAN	97.30
174	147	PIRAWA	97.30
174	221	DEOLI	97.30
178	232	JHADOL	97.20
179	3	JAWAJA	97.10
179	38	BALOTRA	97.10
179	84	GANGRAR	97.10
179	96	DAUSA	97.10
179	229	DHARIAWAD	97.10
184	28	PEEPALKHOONT	97.00
184	223	NIWAI	97.00
186	124	JAMWA RAMGARH	96.90
187	82	CHITTAURGARH	96.60
187	198	DEOGARH	96.60
187	233	KHERWARA	96.60
190	97	LALSOT	96.30
190	143	DAG	96.30
190	171	ITAWA	96.30
193	21	TIJARA	96.20
193	98	MAHWA	96.20
193	111	KARANPUR	96.20
196	37	SHAHBAD	96.10
196	66	BIKANER	96.10
196	69	LUNKARANSAR	96.10
196	129	SANGANER	96.10
200	17	RAJGARH	95.90
200	43	SHEO	95.90
202	144	JHALRAPATAN	95.60
203	78	BHADESAR	95.50
203	100	BARI	95.50
205	81	CHHOTI SADRI	95.40
206	58	JAHAZPUR	95.30
206	61	MANDALGARH	95.30
206	164	SHERGARH	95.30
209	133	SAM	95.10
210	156	BALESAR	95.00
	HIGH (90-95)		
211	87	PRATAPGARH	94.80
211	228	BHINDER	94.80
213	75	ARNOD	94.70
214	36	KISHANGANJ	94.60
215	35	CHHIPABAROD	94.30
215	226	UNIARA	94.30
217	76	BARI SADRI	94.10
217	114	SADULSHAHAR	94.10
219	34	CHHABRA	93.70
219	112	PADAMPUR	93.70
221	121	CHAKSU	93.50
222	110	GANGANAGAR	93.20
222	116	BHADRA	93.20
224	234	KOTRA	93.10
225	146	MANOHARTHANA	92.80
226	145	KHANPUR	92.60
227	40	BAYTOO	92.30
227	113	RAISINGHNAGAR	92.30
229	39	BARMER	92.10
230	157	BAP	91.70
231	77	BEGUN	91.40
	MEDIUM (85-90)		
232	79	BHAINSRORGARH	88.80
233	118	NOHAR	87.90
234	142	BAKANI	87.00
235	117	HANUMANGARH	85.50
	LOW (<85)		
236	115	SURATGARH	78.90
237	109	ANUPGARH	78.10
		RAJASTHAN	**97.65**
		%age of AAPs	**70.89**

BOLD: Equal/Above Average Panchayat Samities (AAPs)   *Source*: General Annex VIII, Col. 6.

ANNEX-4.5

RANKING OF PSS BY PERCENTAGE OF INHABITED VILLAGES HAVING EDUCATION AMENITIES, 2001

(Descending Order)

RANK	P. CODE	PANCHAYAT SAMITIES NAME	%
1	2	3	4
	PERFECT (100)		
1	2	BHINAY	100.0
1	126	KOTPUTLI	100.0
1	136	BHINMAL	100.0
1	137	JALOR	100.0
1	152	KHETRI	100.0
1	153	NAWALGARH	100.0
1	154	SURAJGARH	100.0
1	155	UDAIPURWATI	100.0
1	158	BHOPALGARH	100.0
1	194	SOJAT	100.0
1	209	DHOND	100.0
	VERY HIGH (95-100)		
12	106	DUNGARPUR	99.4
13	9	BANSURE	99.2
13	149	BUHANA	99.2
13	165	HINDAUN	99.2
16	161	MANDOR	99.0
17	16	NIMRANA	98.8
17	130	SHAHPURA	98.8
17	150	CHIRAWA	98.8
20	193	ROHAT	98.7
20	216	ABU ROAD	98.7
20	11	KATHUMAR	98.7
20	192	RANI STATION	98.7
24	212	LACHHMANGARH	98.6
25	44	SINDHARI	98.5
25	215	SRI MADHOPUR	98.5
27	195	SUMERPUR	98.4
28	49	KUMHER	98.3
29	5	KISHANGARH	98.2
29	176	DIDWANA	98.2
31	184	PARBATSAR	98.2
32	89	CHURU	98.1
32	90	RAJGARH	98.1
34	4	KEKRI	98.0
35	210	FATEHPUR	97.9
35	8	SRINAGAR	97.9
35	15	MANDAWAR	97.9
35	52	RUPBAS	97.9
35	151	JHUNJHUNUN	97.9
40	14	LACHHMANGARH	97.8
40	62	RAIPUR	97.8
40	67	DUNGARGARH	97.8
40	159	BILARA	97.8
44	7	PISANGAN	97.7
44	105	BICHHIWARA	97.7
44	222	MALPURA	97.7
47	25	GARHI	97.6
47	139	RANIWARA	97.6
49	47	DEEG	97.5
49	107	SAGWARA	97.5
51	13	KOTKASIM	97.4
51	45	SIWANA	97.4
51	141	SAYLA	97.4
54	138	JASWANTPURA	97.3
54	175	DEGANA	97.3
56	51	NAGAR PAHARI	97.2
57	65	SUWANA	97.1
57	92	SARDARSHAHAR	97.1
59	177	JAYAL	97.1
60	33	BARAN	97.0
60	197	BHIM	97.0
62	178	KUCHAMAN	96.9
63	214	PIPRALI	96.8
63	108	SIMALWARA	96.8
65	201	RAILMAGRA	96.7
65	186	BALI	96.7
67	140	SANCHORE	96.6
67	162	OSIAN	96.6
67	180	MAKRANA	96.6
67	231	GOGUNDA	96.6
71	128	SAMBHAR	96.5
71	189	KHARCHI/MARWAR JUN.	96.5
73	24	BAGIDORA	96.4
74	41	CHOHTAN	96.3
74	190	PALI	96.3
76	188	JAITARAN	96.1
77	1	ARAIN	96.0
77	63	SAHARA	96.0
77	148	ALSISAR	96.0
80	48	KAMAN	95.9
81	42	DHORIMANNA	95.8
81	104	ASPUR	95.8
83	57	HURDA	95.7
84	135	AHORE	95.5
85	191	RAIPUR	95.4
86	167	NADOTI	95.3
87	102	DHAULPUR	95.2
88	19	RENI	95.1
88	169	TODABHIM	95.1
90	91	RATANGARH	95.0
	HIGH (90-95)		
91	134	SANKRA	94.9
91	207	SAWAI MADHOPUR	94.9
93	160	LUNI	94.8
94	50	NADBAI	94.7
94	64	SHAHPURA	94.7
94	74	TALERA	94.7
94	183	NAGAUR	94.7
94	205	GANGAPUR	94.7
99	235	MAVLI	94.6
100	54	WEIR	94.5
101	27	KUSHALGARH	94.3
101	208	DANTA RAMGARH	94.3
103	219	SHEOGANJ	94.2
103	182	MUNDWA	94.2
105	32	ATRU	94.1
105	127	PHAGI	94.1
105	237	SARADA	94.1
108	56	BANERA	94.0
108	103	RAJAKHERA	94.0
110	73	NAINWA	93.9
111	166	KARAULI	93.8
112	59	KOTRI	93.7
112	71	HINDOLI	93.7
112	163	PHALODI	93.7
115	18	RAMGARH	93.6
115	185	RIYAN	93.6
115	187	DESURI	93.6
118	213	NEEM KA THANA	93.4
119	131	VIRATNAGAR	93.3
120	60	MANDAL	93.1
121	83	DUNGLA	93.1
122	29	SAJJANGARH	93.0
122	123	GOVINDGARH	93.0
124	93	SUJANGARH	92.9
125	80	BHOPALSAGAR	92.8
125	99	SIKRAI	92.8
125	179	LADNU	92.8
125	181	MERTA	92.8
129	230	GIRWA	92.7
129	94	TARANAGAR	92.7
129	200	KUMBHALGARH	92.7
132	31	ANTA	92.6
133	227	BARGAON	92.5
134	202	RAJSAMAND	92.4
134	95	BANDIKUI	92.4
136	217	PINDWARA	91.9
136	12	KISHANGARH BAS	91.9
136	46	BAYANA	91.9
136	120	BASSI	91.9
136	236	SALUMBAR	91.9
141	204	BONLI	91.8
142	55	ASIND	91.7
142	119	AMBER	91.7
144	220	SIROHI	91.6
145	26	GHATOL	91.4
145	174	SULTANPUR	91.4
147	69	LUNKARANSAR	91.3
147	211	KHANDELA	91.3
147	218	REODAR	91.3
150	43	SHEO	91.2
150	70	NOKHA	91.2
152	10	BEHROR	91.1
152	101	BASERI	91.1
154	198	DEOGARH	90.8
155	23	ANANDPURI	90.7
155	85	KAPASAN	90.7
157	6	MASOODA	90.6
158	122	DUDU	90.4
158	125	JHOTWARA	90.4
160	170	CHECHAT	90.3
161	39	BARMER	90.2
162	21	TIJARA	90.1
162	30	TALWARA	90.1
162	72	KESHORAIPATAN	90.1
	MEDIUM (85-90)		
165	225	TONK	89.9
166	196	AMET	89.7
166	164	SHERGARH	89.7
168	233	KHERWARA	89.6
169	86	NIMBAHERA	89.5
170	100	BARI	89.3
171	53	SEWAR	89.2
172	172	LADPURA	89.0
173	147	PIRAWA	88.8
173	173	SANGOD	88.8
175	38	BALOTRA	88.7
176	98	MAHWA	88.2
177	132	JAISALMER	88.1
178	124	JAMWA RAMGARH	88.0
179	168	SAPOTRA	87.6
180	203	BAMANWAS	87.5
181	206	KHANDAR	87.1
182	40	BAYTOO	87.0
183	223	NIWAI	86.9
183	3	JAWAJA	86.9
185	66	BIKANER	86.8
186	224	TODARAISINGH	86.6
186	22	UMREN	86.6
188	232	JHADOL	86.4
188	88	RASHMI	86.4
188	143	DAG	86.4
188	156	BALESAR	86.4
189	229	DHARIAWAD	86.3
193	28	PEEPALKHOONT	85.0
	LOW (<85)		
194	221	DEOLI	84.8
194	58	JAHAZPUR	84.8
196	199	KHAMNOR	84.5
197	96	DAUSA	84.3
198	171	ITAWA	84.0
199	81	CHHOTI SADRI	83.7
200	84	GANGRAR	83.5
200	144	JHALRAPATAN	83.5
202	129	SANGANER	83.2
203	17	RAJGARH	82.9
204	111	KARANPUR	82.6
205	20	THANAGAZI	82.4
205	157	BAP	82.4
207	37	SHAHBAD	82.0
208	36	KISHANGANJ	81.7
209	78	BHADESAR	81.6
210	226	UNIARA	80.6
211	82	CHITTAURGARH	80.3
211	87	PRATAPGARH	80.3
213	34	CHHABRA	80.1
214	146	MANOHARTHANA	79.9
215	228	BHINDER	79.6
216	112	PADAMPUR	79.5
217	145	KHANPUR	79.3
218	35	CHHIPABAROD	78.6
219	68	KOLAYAT	77.0
219	97	LALSOT	77.0
221	61	MANDALGARH	76.9
222	234	KOTRA	76.8
223	76	BARI SADRI	76.2
224	75	ARNOD	75.8
225	121	CHAKSU	74.2
226	113	RAISINGHNAGAR	72.2
227	79	BHAINSRORGARH	70.1
228	77	BEGUN	69.8
229	110	GANGANAGAR	69.3
230	133	SAM	66.2
231	142	BAKANI	63.3
232	116	BHADRA	58.1
233	118	NOHAR	50.5
234	109	ANUPGARH	49.4
234	114	SADULSHAHAR	49.4
236	115	SURATGARH	49.0
237	117	HANUMANGARH	36.6
	RAJASTHAN		86.30
	%age of AAPs		81.00

BOLD: Equal/Above Average Panchayat Samities (AAPs)   *Source*: General Annex IX, Col. 6.

ANNEX-4.6

RANKING OF PSS BY TOTAL NO. OF PRIMARY SCHOOLS : RAJASTHAN, 2000

(Descending Order)

RANK	P. CODE	PANCHAYAT SAMITIES NAME	NO.
1	2	3	4
		VERY HIGH (>=400)	**80**
1	162	**OSIAN**	585
2	109	**ANUPGARH**	563
3	117	**HANUMANGARH**	523
4	39	**BARMER**	472
5	40	**BAYTOO**	420
6	44	**SINDHARI**	400
		HIGH (300-400)	
7	140	**SANCHORE**	378
8	38	**BALOTRA**	375
9	233	**KHERWARA**	374
10	42	**DHORIMANNA**	371
11	66	**BIKANER**	348
12	97	**LALSOT**	337
12	118	**NOHAR**	337
14	213	**NEEM KA THANA**	335
15	41	**CHOHTAN**	334
16	108	**SIMALWARA**	333
17	43	**SHEO**	331
18	122	**DUDU**	330
19	178	**KUCHAMAN**	327
20	74	**TALERA**	321
21	183	**NAGAUR**	318
22	232	**JHADOL**	317
22	199	**KHAMNOR***	317
24	166	**KARAULI**	314
25	236	**SALUMBAR**	311
26	95	**BANDIKUI**	308
27	26	**GHATOL**	308
28	163	**PHALODI**	308
29	119	**AMBER**	306
29	105	**BICHHIWARA**	306
29	129	**SANGANER**	306
29	168	**SAPOTRA**	306
33	208	**DANTA RAMGARH**	302
34	87	**PRATAPGARH**	301
		MEDIUM (200-300)	
35	25	**GARHI**	298
36	107	**SAGWARA**	297
37	134	**SANKRA**	293
38	30	**TALWARA**	293
39	176	**DIDWANA**	288
40	230	**GIRWA**	287
40	124	**JAMWA RAMGARH**	287
42	96	**DAUSA**	282
43	165	**HINDAUN**	277
44	133	**SAM**	272
45	229	**DHARIAWAD**	270
45	68	**KOLAYAT**	270
47	237	**SARAD**	270
48	235	**MAVLI**	267
49	197	**BHIM**	261
50	102	**DHAULPUR**	260
51	70	**NOKHA**	259
52	144	**JHALRAPATAN**	258
52	115	**SURATGARH**	258
54	101	**BASERI**	256
54	128	**SAMBHAR**	256
56	60	**MANDAL**	255
57	120	**BASSI**	254
57	160	**LUNI**	254
59	228	**BHINDER**	253
59	234	**KOTRA**	253
59	223	**NIWAI**	253
59	93	**SUJANGARH**	253
59	225	**TONK**	253
64	51	**NAGAR PAHARI**	252
65	121	**CHAKSU**	251
65	71	**HINDOLI**	251
67	104	**ASPUR**	248
67	9	**BANSURE**	248
69	209	**DHOND**	247
70	158	**BHOPALGARH**	246
70	155	**UDAIPURWATI**	246
72	211	**KHANDELA**	241
72	152	**KHETRI***	241
72	126	**KOTPUTLI**	241
72	146	**MANOHARTHANA**	241
76	212	**LACHHMANGARH**	240
76	131	**VIRATNAGAR**	240
78	90	**RAJGARH**	239
78	45	**SIWANA**	239
106		**DUNGARPUR**	237
81	123	**GOVINDGARH**	234
82	113	**RAISINGHNAGAR**	233
83	61	**MANDALGARH**	232
84	153	**NAWALGARH**	228
85	28	**PEEPALKHOON**	227
85	18	**RAMGARH**	227
87	203	**BAMANWAS**	226
87	27	**KUSHALGARH**	226
89	55	**ASIND**	224
89	20	**THANAGAZI**	224
91	3	**JAWAJA**	221
91	14	**LACHHMANGARH**	221
93	72	**KESHORAIPATAN**	220
94	182	**MUNDWA**	217
94	22	**UMREN**	217
96	204	**BONLI**	216
97	69	**LUNKARANSAR**	215
97	222	**MALPURA**	215
97	169	**TODABHIM**	215
100	177	**JAYAL**	214
101	98	**MAHWA**	212
102	46	BAYANA	211
102	151	JHUNJHUNUN	211
104	142	BAKANI	210
104	191	RAIPUR	210
104	207	SAWAI MADHOPUR	210
104	21	TIJARA	210
108	99	SIKRAI	209
109	7	PISANGAN	207
110	29	SAJJANGARH	206
111	200	KUMBHALGARH	204
111	215	SRI MADHOPUR	204
113	149	BUHANA	202
114	143	DAG	201
114	11	KATHUMAR	201
116	175	DEGANA	200
		LOW (100-200)	
117	127	PHAGI	199
118	214	PIPRALI	197
118	103	RAJAKHERA	197
120	205	GANGAPUR	195
120	231	GOGUNDA	195
120	184	PARBATSAR	195
123	180	MAKRANA	193
123	174	SULTANPUR	193
125	116	BHADRA	192
125	159	BILARA	192
125	226	UNIARA	192
128	58	JAHAZPUR	191
128	164	SHERGARH	191
130	59	KOTRI	190
130	202	RAJSAMAND	190
132	173	SANGOD	189
133	24	BAGIDORA	187
133	206	KHANDAR	187
133	73	NAINWA	187
136	100	BARI	186
137	112	PADAMPUR	185
138	156	BALESAR	184
138	36	KISHANGANJ	184
140	189	KHARCHI/MARWAR JUN.	183
141	157	BAP	181
141	147	PIRAWA	181
143	82	CHITTAURGARH	180
143	171	ITAWA	180
143	48	KAMAN	180
143	64	SHAHPURA	180
143	54	WEIR	180
148	6	MASOODA	179
149	130	SHAHPURA	178
150	110	GANGANAGAR	177
151	154	SURAJGARH	176
152	217	PINDWARA	175
153	148	ALSISAR	173
153	186	BALI	173
153	145	KHANPUR	173
156	132	JAISALMER	172
157	139	RANIWARA	171
157	92	SARDARSHAHAR	171
159	210	FATEHPUR	169
160	75	ARNOD	168
161	50	CHIRAWA	167
162	170	CHECHAT	166
162	17	RAJGARH	166
164	65	SUWANA	166
165	15	MANDAWAR	164
166	23	ANANDPURI	163
166	221	DEOLI	163
166	12	KISHANGARH BAS	163
169	185	RIYAN	162
170	188	JAITARAN	161
171	35	CHHIPABAROD	160
171	161	MANDOR	160
171	181	MERTA	160
171	19	RENI	160
175	52	RUPBAS	158
176	227	BARGAON	156
176	34	CHHABRA	156
178	5	KISHANGARH	155
179	77	BEGUN	153
180	31	ANTA	152
181	218	REODAR	150
182	136	BHINMAL	149
182	172	LADPURA	149
184	141	SAYLA	148
184	53	SEWAR	148
186	111	KARANPUR	147
186	49	KUMHER	147
188	37	SHAHBAD	146
189	10	BEHROR	145
189	78	BHADESAR	145
189	86	NIMBAHERA	145
192	57	HURDA	144
193	47	DEEG	142
193	67	DUNGARGARH	142
193	194	SOJAT	142
196	196	AMET	140
197	2	BHINAY	138
198	32	ATRU	137
199	135	AHORE	136
199	4	KEKRI*	136
201	179	LADNU	135
202	125	JHOTWARA	132
202	8	SRINAGAR	132
204	167	NADOTI	130
205	76	BARI SADRI	129
206	16	NIMRANA	128
206	201	RAILMAGRA	128
208	216	ABU ROAD	126
208	1	ARAIN	126
208	89	CHURU	126
211	91	RATANGARH	125
212	81	CHHOTI SADRI	124
212	63	SAHARA	124
214	33	BARAN	123
215	79	BHAINSRORGARH	122
216	198	DEOGARH	120
217	84	GANGRAR	119
217	94	TARANAGAR	119
219	56	BANERA	118
220	224	TODARAISINGH	118
221	62	RAIPUR	117
222	138	JASWANTPURA	115
222	114	SADULSHAHAR	115
224	83	DUNGLA	114
224	13	KOTKASIM	114
224	50	NADBAI	114
227	220	SIROHI	112
228	190	PALI	107
229	137	JALOR	102
230	85	KAPASAN	100
		VERY LOW (<100)	
231	88	RASHMI	97
232	80	BHOPALSAGAR	93
233	193	ROHAT	92
234	195	SUMERPUR	86
235	187	DESURI	85
236	192	RANI STATION	81
237	219	SHEOGANJ	76
RAJASTHAN		**TOTAL**	**50219**
		AVERAGE	**212**
		%age of AAPs	**42.60**

BOLD: Equal/Above Average Panchayat Samities (AAPs)

Source: General Annex XIII, Col. 7.

ANNEX-4.7

RANKING OF PSS BY PERCENTAGE OF RURAL POP. SERVED BY DRINKING WATER AMENITIES: RAJASTHAN, 2001

(Descending Order)

RANK	P. CODE	PANCHAYAT SAMITIES NAME	%
1	2	3	4
	PERFECT (100)		
1	3	**JAWAJA**	100.00
1	4	**KEKRI**	100.00
1	6	**MASOODA**	100.00
1	7	**PISANGAN**	100.00
1	8	**SRINAGAR**	100.00
1	13	**KOTKASIM**	100.00
1	14	**LACHHMANGARH**	100.00
1	15	**MANDAWAR**	100.00
1	18	**RAMGARH**	100.00
1	25	**GARHI**	100.00
1	29	**SAJJANGARH**	100.00
1	31	**ANTA**	100.00
1	32	**ATRU**	100.00
1	33	**BARAN**	100.00
1	47	**DEEG**	100.00
1	50	**NADBAI**	100.00
1	65	**SUWANA**	100.00
1	77	**BEGUN**	100.00
1	78	**BHADESAR**	100.00
1	83	**DUNGLA**	100.00
1	84	**GANGRAR**	100.00
1	85	**KAPASAN**	100.00
1	86	**NIMBAHERA**	100.00
1	88	**RASHMI**	100.00
1	99	**SIKRAI**	100.00
1	104	**ASPUR**	100.00
1	107	**SAGWARA**	100.00
1	119	**AMBER**	100.00
1	123	**GOVINDGARH**	100.00
1	126	**KOTPUTLI**	100.00
1	130	**SHAHPURA**	100.00
1	153	**NAWALGARH**	100.00
1	165	**HINDAUN**	100.00
1	173	**SANGOD**	100.00
1	174	**SULTANPUR**	100.00
1	186	**BALI**	100.00
1	191	**RAIPUR**	100.00
1	192	**RANI STATION**	100.00
1	196	**AMET**	100.00
1	198	**DEOGARH**	100.00
1	202	**RAJSAMAND**	100.00
1	207	**SAWAI MADHOPUR**	100.00
1	210	**FATEHPUR**	100.00
1	213	**NEEM KA THANA**	100.00
1	228	**BHINDER**	100.00
1	235	**MAVLI**	100.00
1	237	**SARADA**	100.00
	VERY HIGH (98-100)		
48	9	**BANSURE**	99.90
48	10	**BEHROR**	99.90
48	21	**TIJARA**	99.90
48	26	**GHATOL**	99.90
48	49	**KUMHER**	99.90
48	76	**BARI SADRI**	99.90
48	98	**MAHWA**	99.90
48	120	**BASSI**	99.90
48	218	**REODAR**	99.90
57	16	**NIMRANA**	99.80
57	52	**RUPBAS**	99.80
57	56	**BANERA**	99.80
57	60	**MANDAL**	99.80
57	81	**CHHOTI SADRI**	99.80
57	137	**JALOR**	99.80
57	155	**UDAIPURWATI**	99.80
57	171	**ITAWA**	99.80
57	201	**RAILMAGRA**	99.80
57	224	**TODARAISINGH**	99.80
67	20	**THANAGAZI**	99.70
67	36	**KISHANGANJ**	99.70
67	80	**BHOPALSAGAR**	99.70
67	97	**LALSOT**	99.70
67	108	**SIMALWARA**	99.70
67	124	**JAMWA RAMGARH**	99.70
67	127	**PHAGI**	99.70
67	131	**VIRATNAGAR**	99.70
67	147	**PIRAWA**	99.70
67	179	**LADNU**	99.70
67	199	**KHAMNOR**	99.70
67	221	**DEOLI**	99.70
79	1	**ARAIN**	99.60
79	5	**KISHANGARH**	99.60
79	12	**KISHANGARH BAS**	99.60
79	54	**WEIR**	99.60
79	61	**MANDALGARH**	99.60
79	74	**TALERA**	99.60
79	79	**BHAINSRORGARH**	99.60
79	220	**SIROHI**	99.60
79	236	**SALUMBAR**	99.60
88	82	**CHITTAURGARH**	99.50
88	129	**SANGANER**	99.50
88	172	**LADPURA**	99.50
88	215	**SRI MADHOPUR**	99.50
88	222	**MALPURA**	99.50
93	37	**SHAHBAD**	99.40
93	105	**BICHHIWARA**	99.40
93	145	**KHANPUR**	99.40
93	159	**BILARA**	99.40
93	214	**PIPRALI**	99.40
98	55	**ASIND**	99.30
98	170	**CHECHAT**	99.30
98	206	**KHANDAR**	99.30
98	209	**DHOND**	99.30
98	211	**KHANDELA**	99.30
98	227	**BARGAON**	99.30
104	2	**BHINAY**	99.20
104	63	**SAHARA**	99.20
104	87	**PRATAPGARH**	99.20
104	141	**SAYLA**	99.20
104	152	**KHETRI**	99.20
104	200	**KUMBHALGARH**	99.20
110	162	**OSIAN**	99.10
110	212	**LACHHMANGARH**	99.10
112	22	**UMREN**	99.00
112	59	**KOTRI**	99.00
112	102	**DHAULPUR**	99.00
112	121	**CHAKSU**	99.00
112	197	**BHIM**	99.00
112	217	**PINDWARA**	99.00
118	28	**PEEPALKHOONT**	98.90
118	46	**BAYANA**	98.90
118	53	**SEWAR**	98.90
118	57	**HURDA**	98.90
118	95	**BANDIKUI**	98.90
118	208	**DANTA RAMGARH**	98.90
124	51	**NAGAR PAHARI**	98.80
124	135	**AHORE**	98.80
124	225	**TONK**	98.80
127	58	**JAHAZPUR**	98.70
127	71	**HINDOLI**	98.70
127	233	**KHERWARA**	98.70
130	19	**RENI**	98.60
130	96	**DAUSA**	98.60
130	110	**GANGANAGAR**	98.60
130	143	**DAG**	98.60
130	150	**CHIRAWA**	98.60
130	216	**ABU ROAD**	98.60
130	223	**NIWAI**	98.60
137	138	**JASWANTPURA**	98.50
137	204	**BONLI**	98.50
139	62	**RAIPUR**	98.40
139	232	**JHADOL**	98.40
141	30	**TALWARA**	98.30
141	103	**RAJAKHERA**	98.30
141	187	**DESURI**	98.30
141	205	**GANGAPUR**	98.30
145	27	**KUSHALGARH**	98.20
145	169	**TODABHIM**	98.20
145	226	**UNIARA**	98.20
148	11	**KATHUMAR**	98.10
148	35	**CHHIPABAROD**	98.10
148	101	**BASERI**	98.10
148	146	**MANOHARTHANA**	98.10
152	230	**GIRWA**	98.00
	HIGH (96-98)		
153	24	**BAGIDORA**	97.90
153	144	**JHALRAPATAN**	97.90
153	189	**KHARCHI/MARWAR JUN.**	97.90
156	75	**ARNOD**	97.80
156	142	**BAKANI**	97.80
156	229	**DHARIAWAD**	97.80
159	23	**ANANDPURI**	97.70
159	45	**SIWANA**	97.70
159	167	**NADOTI**	97.70
159	188	**JAITARAN**	97.70
163	231	**GOGUNDA**	97.60
164	73	**NAINWA**	97.50
164	156	**BALESAR**	97.50
166	72	**KESHORAIPATAN**	97.40
167	106	**DUNGARPUR**	97.10
167	122	**DUDU**	97.10
169	64	**SHAHPURA**	97.00
170	168	**SAPOTRA**	96.90
170	219	**SHEOGANJ**	96.90
172	184	**PARBATSAR**	96.70
173	100	**BARI**	96.50
174	34	**CHHABRA**	96.40
175	182	**MUNDWA**	96.30
176	193	**ROHAT**	96.10
	MEDIUM (94-96)		
177	17	**RAJGARH**	95.90
178	166	**KARAULI**	95.80
179	70	**NOKHA**	95.70
179	158	**BHOPALGARH**	95.70
181	128	**SAMBHAR**	95.60
181	163	**PHALODI**	95.60
183	194	**SOJAT**	95.50
184	139	RANIWARA	95.30
185	181	MERTA	95.10
186	117	HANUMANGARH	94.90
187	111	KARANPUR	94.80
187	151	JHUNJHUNUN	94.80
189	160	LUNI	94.50
190	125	JHOTWARA	94.40
191	195	SUMERPUR	94.30
192	112	PADAMPUR	94.20
193	185	RIYAN	94.10
194	190	PALI	94.00
	LOW (<94)		
195	176	DIDWANA	93.70
196	48	KAMAN	93.40
196	149	BUHANA	93.40
198	203	BAMANWAS	93.20
199	91	RATANGARH	93.00
199	161	MANDOR	93.00
201	113	RAISINGHNAGAR	92.80
202	234	KOTRA	92.40
203	40	BAYTOO	91.20
204	42	DHORIMANNA	90.90
205	178	KUCHAMAN	89.90
206	93	SUJANGARH	89.60
207	154	SURAJGARH	88.80
208	164	SHERGARH	88.70
209	67	DUNGARGARH	88.30
210	175	DEGANA	86.70
211	148	ALSISAR	86.20
212	140	SANCHORE	85.90
213	116	BHADRA	85.60
214	136	BHINMAL	85.40
215	41	CHOHTAN	85.30
216	90	RAJGARH	85.20
217	134	SANKRA	84.10
218	109	ANUPGARH	83.90
219	133	SAM	83.50
220	44	SINDHARI	83.40
221	94	TARANAGAR	82.40
222	38	BALOTRA	82.00
223	43	SHEO	81.00
224	114	SADULSHAHAR	79.50
225	115	SURATGARH	78.70
226	183	NAGAUR	78.30
227	180	MAKRANA	77.50
228	39	BARMER	77.00
229	69	LUNKARANSAR	76.20
230	89	CHURU	75.90
231	66	BIKANER	74.30
232	118	NOHAR	73.50
233	68	KOLAYAT	73.20
234	177	JAYAL	73.00
235	132	JAISALMER	70.80
236	157	BAP	66.40
237	92	SARDARSHAHAR	52.50
		RAJASTHAN	**95.40**
		%age of AAPs	**77.22**

BOLD: Equal/Above Average Panchayat Samities (AAPs)

Source: General Annex VIII, Col. 5.

ANNEX-4.8

RANKING OF PSS BY PERCENTAGE OF INHABITED VILLAGES HAVING DRINKING WATER AMENITIES, 2001

(Descending Order)

RANK	P. CODE	PANCHAYAT SAMITIES NAME	%
1	2	3	4
		PERFECT (100)	
1	**3**	**JAWAJA**	**100.0**
1	**4**	**KEKRI**	**100.0**
1	**6**	**MASOODA**	**100.0**
1	**7**	**PISANGAN**	**100.0**
1	**8**	**SRINAGAR**	**100.0**
1	**13**	**KOTKASIM**	**100.0**
1	**14**	**LACHHMANGARH**	**100.0**
1	**15**	**MANDAWAR**	**100.0**
1	**29**	**SAJJANGARH**	**100.0**
1	**32**	**ATRU**	**100.0**
1	**50**	**NADBAI**	**100.0**
1	**65**	**SUWANA**	**100.0**
1	**78**	**BHADESAR**	**100.0**
1	**83**	**DUNGLA**	**100.0**
1	**84**	**GANGRAR**	**100.0**
1	**85**	**KAPASAN**	**100.0**
1	**104**	**ASPUR**	**100.0**
1	**119**	**AMBER**	**100.0**
1	**123**	**GOVINDGARH**	**100.0**
1	**126**	**KOTPUTLI**	**100.0**
1	**130**	**SHAHPURA**	**100.0**
1	**153**	**NAWALGARH**	**100.0**
1	**165**	**HINDAUN**	**100.0**
1	**191**	**RAIPUR**	**100.0**
1	**192**	**RANI STATION**	**100.0**
1	**196**	**AMET**	**100.0**
1	**198**	**DEOGARH**	**100.0**
1	**210**	**FATEHPUR**	**100.0**
1	**228**	**BHINDER**	**100.0**
1	**235**	**MAVLI**	**100.0**
		VERY HIGH (95-100)	
31	**74**	**TALERA**	**99.6**
32	**26**	**GHATOL**	**99.5**
32	**108**	**SIMALWARA**	**99.5**
32	**120**	**BASSI**	**99.5**
32	**173**	**SANGOD**	**99.5**
32	**237**	**SARADA**	**99.5**
37	**25**	**GARHI**	**99.4**
37	**107**	**SAGWARA**	**99.4**
37	**174**	**SULTANPUR**	**99.4**
40	**31**	**ANTA**	**99.3**
40	**76**	**BARI SADRI**	**99.3**
40	**86**	**NIMBAHERA**	**99.3**
40	**99**	**SIKRAI**	**99.3**
40	**172**	**LADPURA**	**99.3**
45	**202**	**RAJSAMAND**	**99.2**
45	**2**	**BHINAY**	**99.2**
45	**47**	**DEEG**	**99.2**
48	**236**	**SALUMBAR**	**99.1**
48	**5**	**KISHANGARH**	**99.1**
48	**49**	**KUMHER**	**99.1**
48	**82**	**CHITTAURGARH**	**99.1**
48	**143**	**DAG**	**99.1**
48	**209**	**DHOND**	**99.1**
48	**227**	**BARGAON**	**99.1**
55	**33**	**BARAN**	**99.0**
55	**63**	**SAHARA**	**99.0**
57	**199**	**KHAMNOR**	**98.9**
57	**201**	**RAILMAGRA**	**98.9**
57	**59**	**KOTRI**	**98.9**
57	**60**	**MANDAL**	**98.9**
57	**71**	**HINDOLI**	**98.9**
57	**105**	**BICHHIWARA**	**98.9**
57	**159**	**BILARA**	**98.9**
57	**186**	**BALI**	**98.9**
65	**18**	**RAMGARH**	**98.8**
65	**80**	**BHOPALSAGAR**	**98.8**
65	**88**	**RASHMI**	**98.8**
65	**155**	**UDAIPURWATI**	**98.8**
65	**221**	**DEOLI**	**98.8**
65	**200**	**KUMBHALGARH**	**98.8**
71	**207**	**SAWAI MADHOPUR**	**98.7**
71	**98**	**MAHWA**	**98.7**
71	**187**	**DESURI**	**98.7**
74	**52**	**RUPBAS**	**98.6**
74	**54**	**WEIR**	**98.6**
74	**57**	**HURDA**	**98.6**
74	**77**	**BEGUN**	**98.6**
74	**95**	**BANDIKUI**	**98.6**
74	**212**	**LACHHMANGARH**	**98.6**
75	**9**	**BANSURE**	**98.5**
75	**21**	**TIJARA**	**98.5**
75	**55**	**ASIND**	**98.5**
75	**103**	**RAJAKHERA**	**98.5**
75	**137**	**JALOR**	**98.5**
75	**197**	**BHIM**	**98.5**
86	**211**	**KHANDELA**	**98.4**
86	**1**	**ARAIN**	**98.4**
86	**145**	**KHANPUR**	**98.4**
89	**36**	**KISHANGANJ**	**98.3**
89	**124**	**JAMWA RAMGARH**	**98.3**
91	**224**	**TODARAISINGH**	**98.2**
91	**171**	**ITAWA**	**98.2**
91	**184**	**PARBATSAR**	**98.2**
94	**27**	**KUSHALGARH**	**98.1**
95	**213**	**NEEM KA THANA**	**98.0**
95	**147**	**PIRAWA**	**98.0**
95	**233**	**KHERWARA**	**98.0**
95	**229**	**DHARIAWAD**	**98.0**
99	**225**	**TONK**	**97.9**
100	**10**	**BEHROR**	**97.8**
100	**62**	**RAIPUR**	**97.8**
100	**96**	**DAUSA**	**97.8**
100	**102**	**DHAULPUR**	**97.8**
104	**30**	**TALWARA**	**97.7**
104	**51**	**NAGAR PAHARI**	**97.7**
104	**232**	**JHADOL**	**97.7**
107	**218**	**REODAR**	**97.6**
107	**16**	**NIMRANA**	**97.6**
107	**24**	**BAGIDORA**	**97.6**
107	**56**	**BANERA**	**97.6**
107	**87**	**PRATAPGARH**	**97.6**
107	**127**	**PHAGI**	**97.6**
107	**152**	**KHETRI**	**97.6**
114	**61**	**MANDALGARH**	**97.5**
115	**79**	**BHAINSRORGARH**	**97.4**
115	**141**	**SAYLA**	**97.4**
117	**97**	**LALSOT**	**97.3**
118	**58**	**JAHAZPUR**	**97.2**
118	**75**	**ARNOD**	**97.2**
118	**81**	**CHHOTI SADRI**	**97.2**
121	**19**	**RENI**	**97.1**
122	**12**	**KISHANGARH BAS**	**97.0**
122	**215**	**SRI MADHOPUR**	**97.0**
124	**222**	**MALPURA**	**96.9**
124	**23**	**ANANDPURI**	**96.9**
126	**208**	**DANTA RAMGARH**	**96.8**
126	**214**	**PIPRALI**	**96.8**
126	**144**	**JHALRAPATAN**	**96.8**
129	**230**	**GIRWA**	**96.6**
129	**20**	**THANAGAZI**	**96.6**
129	**162**	**OSIAN**	**96.6**
132	**179**	**SANGANER**	**96.5**
132	**146**	**MANOHARTHANA**	**96.5**
132	**169**	**TODABHIM**	**96.5**
132	**189**	**KHARCHI/MARWAR JUN.**	**96.5**
136	**150**	**CHIRAWA**	**96.4**
137	**223**	**NIWAI**	**96.3**
137	**46**	**BAYANA**	**96.3**
137	**121**	**CHAKSU**	**96.3**
140	**53**	**SEWAR**	**96.2**
140	**142**	**BAKANI**	**96.2**
142	**206**	**KHANDAR**	**96.1**
143	**22**	**UMREN**	**96.0**
143	**35**	**CHHIPABAROD**	**96.0**
143	**64**	**SHAHPURA**	**96.0**
143	**217**	**PINDWARA**	**96.0**
147	**231**	**GOGUNDA**	**95.9**
147	**138**	**JASWANTPURA**	**95.9**
147	**179**	**LADNU**	**95.9**
150	**101**	**BASERI**	**95.8**
150	**131**	**VIRATNAGAR**	**95.8**
150	**170**	**CHECHAT**	**95.8**
153	**28**	**PEEPALKHOONT**	**95.7**
154	**45**	**SIWANA**	**95.7**
155	**11**	**KATHUMAR**	**95.6**
156	**106**	**DUNGARPUR**	**95.6**
157	**204**	**BONLI**	**95.6**
158	**135**	**AHORE**	**95.5**
159	**220**	**SIROHI**	**95.2**
160	**72**	**KESHORAIPATAN**	**95.1**
161	**73**	**NAINWA**	**95.0**
		HIGH (90-95)	
162	**216**	**ABU ROAD**	**94.9**
163	**205**	**GANGAPUR**	**94.7**
164	**34**	**CHHABRA**	**94.6**
165	**226**	**UNIARA**	**94.4**
166	**182**	**MUNDWA**	**94.2**
167	**167**	**NADOTI**	**94.1**
168	**139**	**RANIWARA**	**94.0**
169	**193**	**ROHAT**	**93.7**
170	**37**	**SHAHBAD**	**93.4**
171	**168**	**SAPOTRA**	**93.3**
172	**151**	**JHUNJHUNUN**	**93.1**
173	**158**	**BHOPALGARH**	**93.0**
174	**166**	**KARAULI**	**92.8**
175	**122**	**DUDU**	**92.7**
176	**190**	**PALI**	**92.5**
177	**100**	**BARI**	**92.3**
178	**195**	**SUMERPUR**	**92.1**
179	**156**	**BALESAR**	**92.0**
180	**181**	**MERTA**	**91.9**
181	161	MANDOR	91.4
182	194	SOJAT	91.3
183	219	SHEOGANJ	91.3
184	188	JAITARAN	91.3
185	128	SAMBHAR	91.0
186	17	RAJGARH	90.7
187	110	GANGANAGAR	90.7
188	125	JHOTWARA	90.4
189	48	KAMAN	90.2
190	112	PADAMPUR	90.0
191	176	DIDWANA	90.0
		MEDIUM (85-90)	
192	70	NOKHA	89.8
193	160	LUNI	89.6
194	42	DHORIMANNA	89.3
195	111	KARANPUR	88.4
196	113	RAISINGHNAGAR	88.3
197	163	PHALODI	88.3
198	203	BAMANWAS	88.2
199	149	BUHANA	88.1
200	185	RIYAN	88.0
201	116	BHADRA	87.9
202	40	BAYTOO	87.3
203	91	RATANGARH	87.1
204	93	SUJANGARH	85.8
		LOW (<85)	
205	234	KOTRA	84.8
206	117	HANUMANGARH	84.6
207	67	DUNGARGARH	83.7
208	140	SANCHORE	82.8
209	136	BHINMAL	82.5
210	164	SHERGARH	82.2
211	154	SURAJGARH	82.0
212	178	KUCHAMAN	81.3
213	90	RAJGARH	81.2
214	44	SINDHARI	79.5
215	134	SANKRA	79.5
216	175	DEGANA	76.4
217	148	ALSISAR	75.0
218	43	SHEO	74.4
219	41	CHOHTAN	74.3
220	38	BALOTRA	72.7
221	109	ANUPGARH	72.7
222	180	MAKRANA	72.3
223	89	CHURU	70.5
224	39	BARMER	70.4
225	66	BIKANER	70.3
226	183	NAGAUR	70.0
227	115	SURATGARH	69.5
228	118	NOHAR	67.9
229	94	TARANAGAR	67.3
230	69	LUNKARANSAR	66.3
231	177	JAYAL	65.4
232	133	SAM	64.4
233	132	JAISALMER	61.5
234	114	SADULSHAHAR	53.6
235	157	BAP	52.8
236	68	KOLAYAT	52.0
237	92	SARDARSHAHAR	47.1
		RAJASTHAN	**91.70**
		%age of AAPs	**75.95**

BOLD: Equal/Above Average Panchayat Samities (AAPs)

Source: General Annex IX, Col. 5.

ANNEX-4.9

RANKING OF PSS BY PERCENTAGE OF RURAL POP. SERVED BY PUCCA ROAD AMENITIES: RAJASTHAN, 2001

(Descending Order)

RANK	P. CODE	PANCHAYAT SAMITIES NAME	%
1	2	3	4
		VERY HIGH (>80)	
1	195	**SUMERPUR**	**99.80**
2	186	**BALI**	**95.10**
3	110	**GANGANAGAR**	**94.80**
4	53	**SEWAR**	**94.00**
5	158	**BHOPALGARH**	**93.20**
6	114	**SADULSHAHAR**	**92.20**
7	137	**JALOR**	**91.80**
8	172	**LADPURA**	**91.60**
9	111	**KARANPUR**	**91.10**
10	117	**HANUMANGARH**	**91.00**
11	91	**RATANGARH**	**90.90**
12	215	**SRI MADHOPUR**	**90.40**
13	123	**GOVINDGARH**	**90.10**
13	150	**CHIRAWA**	**90.10**
15	66	**BIKANER**	**90.00**
16	155	**UDAIPURWATI**	**89.90**
16	159	**BILARA**	**89.90**
18	181	**MERTA**	**89.80**
19	8	**SRINAGAR**	**89.60**
20	89	**CHURU**	**89.50**
20	116	**BHADRA**	**89.50**
22	153	**NAWALGARH**	**88.90**
23	165	**HINDAUN**	**88.40**
24	16	**NIMRANA**	**88.30**
25	130	**SHAHPURA**	**88.10**
25	220	**SIROHI**	**88.10**
27	214	**PIPRALI**	**88.00**
28	141	**SAYLA**	**87.90**
29	219	**SHEOGANJ**	**87.50**
30	22	**UMREN**	**87.40**
31	3	**JAWAJA**	**86.90**
32	17	**RAJGARH**	**86.80**
32	192	**RANI STATION**	**86.80**
34	7	**PISANGAN**	**86.30**
35	131	**VIRATNAGAR**	**86.00**
36	49	**KUMHER**	**85.90**
37	152	**KHETRI**	**85.30**
38	126	**KOTPUTLI**	**85.20**
39	217	**PINDWARA**	**85.00**
40	160	**LUNI**	**84.70**
41	162	**OSIAN**	**84.50**
42	185	**RIYAN**	**84.30**
42	201	**RAILMAGRA**	**84.30**
44	138	**JASWANTPURA**	**84.00**
44	209	**DHOND**	**84.00**
46	20	**THANAGAZI**	**83.90**
47	190	**PALI**	**83.30**
48	99	**SIKRAI**	**83.20**
48	125	**JHOTWARA**	**83.20**
50	169	**TODABHIM**	**82.80**
51	11	**KATHUMAR**	**82.60**
52	4	**KEKRI**	**82.50**
53	120	**BASSI**	**82.40**
54	19	**RENI**	**82.10**
55	189	**KHARCHI/MARWAR JUN.**	**81.70**
56	10	**BEHROR**	**81.50**
57	18	**RAMGARH**	**81.30**
57	194	**SOJAT**	**81.30**
59	47	**DEEG**	**81.20**
59	69	**LUNKARANSAR**	**81.20**
61	216	**ABU ROAD**	**80.90**
62	187	**DESURI**	**80.80**
63	135	**AHORE**	**80.60**
64	191	**RAIPUR**	**80.50**
65	25	**GARHI**	**80.40**
66	132	**JAISALMER**	**80.30**
67	5	**KISHANGARH**	**80.20**
67	6	**MASOODA**	**80.20**
69	149	**BUHANA**	**80.10**
69	188	**JAITARAN**	**80.10**
		HIGH (60-80)	
71	57	**HURDA**	**79.70**
71	124	**JAMWA RAMGARH**	**79.70**
73	21	**TIJARA**	**79.50**
73	70	**NOKHA**	**79.50**
73	136	**BHINMAL**	**79.50**
73	151	**JHUNJHUNUN**	**79.50**
77	67	**DUNGARGARH**	**79.30**
78	50	**NADBAI**	**79.10**
79	68	**KOLAYAT**	**79.00**
80	65	**SUWANA**	**78.80**
81	139	**RANIWARA**	**78.60**
81	199	**KHAMNOR**	**78.60**
83	88	**RASHMI**	**78.20**
83	104	**ASPUR**	**78.20**
83	107	**SAGWARA**	**78.20**
83	122	**DUDU**	**78.20**
87	161	**MANDOR**	**77.70**
87	218	**REODAR**	**77.70**
89	148	**ALSISAR**	**77.50**
90	184	**PARBATSAR**	**77.40**
91	33	**BARAN**	**77.30**
91	176	**DIDWANA**	**77.30**
93	112	**PADAMPUR**	**77.00**
93	179	**LADNU**	**77.00**
95	109	**ANUPGARH**	**76.60**
96	9	**BANSURE**	**76.50**
96	208	**DANTA RAMGARH**	**76.50**
98	15	**MANDAWAR**	**76.30**
98	222	**MALPURA**	**76.30**
98	230	**GIRWA**	**76.30**
101	46	**BAYANA**	**76.20**
101	163	**PHALODI**	**76.20**
103	52	**RUPBAS**	**76.00**
103	197	**BHIM**	**76.00**
105	95	**BANDIKUI**	**75.90**
106	86	**NIMBAHERA**	**75.80**
106	154	**SURAJGARH**	**75.80**
108	237	**SARADA**	**75.70**
109	129	**SANGANER**	**75.30**
110	45	**SIWANA**	**75.20**
110	96	**DAUSA**	**75.20**
112	128	**SAMBHAR**	**75.10**
112	167	**NADOTI**	**75.10**
112	205	**GANGAPUR**	**75.10**
112	235	**MAVLI**	**75.10**
116	14	**LACHHMANGARH**	**75.00**
116	213	**NEEM KA THANA**	**75.00**
118	170	**CHECHAT**	**74.70**
118	227	**BARGAON**	**74.70**
120	119	**AMBER**	**74.50**
121	63	**SAHARA**	**74.30**
122	90	**RAJGARH**	**74.00**
123	102	**DHAULPUR**	**73.60**
123	182	**MUNDWA**	**73.60**
123	193	**ROHAT**	**73.60**
123	202	**RAJSAMAND**	**73.60**
127	94	**TARANAGAR**	**73.50**
128	12	KISHANGARH BAS	73.30
129	174	SULTANPUR	73.00
130	177	JAYAL	72.70
131	13	KOTKASIM	72.60
132	30	TALWARA	72.50
133	60	MANDAL	72.40
133	108	SIMALWARA	72.40
135	56	BANERA	72.10
135	103	RAJAKHERA	72.10
135	118	NOHAR	72.10
138	140	SANCHORE	72.00
139	2	BHINAY	71.90
140	115	SURATGARH	71.80
141	48	KAMAN	71.70
142	51	NAGAR PAHARI	71.60
143	211	KHANDELA	71.50
144	183	NAGAUR	71.30
145	225	TONK	71.20
146	166	KARAULI	71.00
147	98	MAHWA	70.40
148	175	DEGANA	70.30
149	101	BASERI	70.20
150	113	RAISINGHNAGAR	70.10
151	156	BALESAR	69.90
152	74	TALERA	69.70
152	168	SAPOTRA	69.70
154	38	BALOTRA	69.60
154	157	BAP	69.60
156	31	ANTA	69.40
156	93	SUJANGARH	69.40
158	206	KHANDAR	69.30
159	26	GHATOL	68.40
160	41	CHOHTAN	68.30
161	105	BICHHIWARA	67.80
162	233	KHERWARA	67.30
163	180	MAKRANA	67.00
164	32	ATRU	66.90
165	106	DUNGARPUR	66.80
166	82	CHITTAURGARH	66.50
167	223	NIWAI	66.10
168	61	MANDALGARH	66.00
168	71	HINDOLI	66.00
168	178	KUCHAMAN	66.00
171	224	TODARAISINGH	65.90
172	97	LALSOT	65.00
172	133	SAM	65.00
174	171	ITAWA	64.70
175	55	ASIND	64.50
176	127	PHAGI	64.30
177	1	ARAIN	64.10
177	231	GOGUNDA	64.10
179	54	WEIR	63.80
180	203	BAMANWAS	63.70
181	228	BHINDER	63.50
182	24	BAGIDORA	62.90
183	92	SARDARSHAHAR	62.60
184	79	BHAINSRORGARH	62.50
185	80	BHOPALSAGAR	62.40
186	212	LACHHMANGARH	62.10
187	36	KISHANGANJ	62.00
188	204	BONLI	61.90
189	229	DHARIAWAD	61.60
190	164	SHERGARH	61.20
191	173	SANGOD	60.60
192	78	BHADESAR	60.30
192	210	FATEHPUR	60.30
194	221	DEOLI	60.10
		MEDIUM (40-60)	
195	200	KUMBHALGARH	59.90
196	87	PRATAPGARH	59.80
197	23	ANANDPURI	59.10
198	73	NAINWA	58.80
198	84	GANGRAR	58.80
200	236	SALUMBAR	58.50
201	83	DUNGLA	58.30
201	207	SAWAI MADHOPUR	58.30
203	72	KESHORAIPATAN	57.90
204	226	UNIARA	57.80
205	42	DHORIMANNA	57.60
206	37	SHAHBAD	57.40
206	100	BARI	57.40
208	58	JAHAZPUR	57.00
208	81	CHHOTI SADRI	57.00
210	39	BARMER	56.90
211	59	KOTRI	56.70
212	75	ARNOD	56.60
212	76	BARI SADRI	56.60
214	64	SHAHPURA	56.30
214	196	AMET	56.30
216	62	RAIPUR	56.10
217	134	SANKRA	55.90
218	77	BEGUN	55.40
219	145	KHANPUR	54.20
220	44	SINDHARI	53.90
221	35	CHHIPABAROD	53.50
222	29	SAJJANGARH	53.00
223	85	KAPASAN	52.80
224	198	DEOGARH	52.30
225	232	JHADOL	51.50
226	43	SHEO	50.90
227	144	JHALRAPATAN	50.70
228	121	CHAKSU	50.10
229	28	PEEPALKHOONT	47.20
230	234	KOTRA	46.80
231	27	KUSHALGARH	46.50
232	142	BAKANI	46.10
233	40	BAYTOO	44.20
234	147	PIRAWA	44.00
235	143	DAG	40.90
		LOW (<40)	
236	34	CHHABRA	36.40
237	146	MANOHARTHANA	31.10
		RAJASTHAN	**73.48**
		%age of AAPs	**53.59**

BOLD: Equal/Above Average Panchayat Samities (AAPs) *Source*: General Annex VIII, Col. 8.

ANNEX-4.10

RANKING OF PSS BY PERCENTAGE OF INHABITED VILLAGES HAVING PUCCA ROAD AMENITIES: RAJASTHAN, 2001

(Descending Order)

RANK	*P. CODE*	*PANCHAYAT SAMITIES NAME*	*%*
1	2	3	4
	VERY HIGH (>=70)		
1	195	**SUMERPUR**	**98.4**
2	186	**BALI**	**87.9**
3	111	**KARANPUR**	**83.1**
3	110	**GANGANAGAR**	**82.1**
5	165	**HINDAUN**	**81.8**
6	158	**BHOPALGARH**	**81.4**
7	53	**SEWAR**	**80.3**
8	89	**CHURU**	**80.0**
8	172	**LADPURA**	**80.0**
10	159	**BILARA**	**78.7**
11	137	**JALOR**	**77.9**
12	126	**KOTPUTLI**	**77.7**
13	215	**SRI MADHOPUR**	**77.3**
14	91	**RATANGARH**	**77.2**
15	155	**UDAIPURWATI**	**76.5**
16	153	**NAWALGARH**	**76.1**
17	8	**SRINAGAR**	**76.0**
18	66	**BIKANER**	**74.9**
19	49	**KUMHER**	**74.4**
20	141	**SAYLA**	**74.0**
21	150	**CHIRAWA**	**73.8**
22	214	**PIPRALI**	**73.4**
22	209	**DHOND**	**73.4**
24	130	**SHAHPURA**	**73.3**
25	16	**NIMRANA**	**72.9**
26	123	**GOVINDGARH**	**72.0**
27	22	**UMREN**	**71.1**
28	152	**KHETRI**	**70.6**
29	162	**OSIAN**	**70.3**
	HIGH (60-70)		
30	192	**RANI STATION**	**69.7**
31	11	**KATHUMAR**	**69.6**
31	114	**SADULSHAHAR**	**69.6**
33	7	**PISANGAN**	**69.5**
34	169	**TODABHIM**	**69.4**
35	3	**JAWAJA**	**68.8**
35	136	**BHINMAL**	**68.8**
37	17	**RAJGARH**	**68.6**
38	125	**JHOTWARA**	**68.5**
38	181	**MERTA**	**68.5**
40	120	**BASSI**	**68.1**
41	185	**RIYAN**	**68.0**
42	10	**BEHROR**	**67.8**
43	131	**VIRATNAGAR**	**67.5**
43	190	**PALI**	**67.5**
45	21	**TIJARA**	**67.3**
46	149	**BUHANA**	**66.7**
46	219	**SHEOGANJ**	**66.7**
48	138	**JASWANTPURA**	**66.2**
49	197	**BHIM**	**65.9**
50	4	**KEKRI**	**65.7**
50	217	**PINDWARA**	**65.7**
52	151	**JHUNJHUNUN**	**65.5**
53	216	**ABU ROAD**	**65.4**
54	220	**SIROHI**	**65.1**
55	112	**PADAMPUR**	**64.9**
56	154	**SURAJGARH**	**64.8**
57	18	**RAMGARH**	**64.7**
57	19	**RENI**	**64.7**
57	99	**SIKRAI**	**64.7**
60	117	**HANUMANGARH**	**64.5**
61	201	**RAILMAGRA**	**63.7**
62	103	**RAJAKHERA**	**63.3**
63	5	**KISHANGARH**	**63.1**
63	116	**BHADRA**	**63.1**
65	124	**JAMWA RAMGARH**	**62.7**
66	69	**LUNKARANSAR**	**62.5**
67	20	**THANAGAZI**	**62.2**
67	104	**ASPUR**	**62.2**
69	139	**RANIWARA**	**61.9**
69	161	**MANDOR**	**61.9**
69	179	**LADNU**	**61.9**
72	46	**BAYANA**	**61.5**
73	25	**GARHI**	**61.3**
74	67	**DUNGARGARH**	**60.9**
74	184	**PARBATSAR**	**60.9**
74	194	**SOJAT**	**60.9**
77	132	**JAISALMER**	**60.8**
77	193	**ROHAT**	**60.8**
79	15	**MANDAWAR**	**60.6**
79	52	**RUPBAS**	**60.6**
79	70	**NOKHA**	**60.6**
82	47	**DEEG**	**60.5**
	MEDIUM (50-60)		
83	208	**DANTA RAMGARH**	**59.9**
84	106	**DUNGARPUR**	**59.7**
84	109	**ANUPGARH**	**59.7**
86	163	**PHALODI**	**59.5**
87	102	**DHAULPUR**	**59.4**
88	160	**LUNI**	**59.3**
89	90	**RAJGARH**	**59.2**
89	188	**JAITARAN**	**59.2**
91	57	**HURDA**	**58.6**
92	135	**AHORE**	**58.2**
92	176	**DIDWANA**	**58.2**
94	50	**NADBAI**	**57.9**
95	95	**BANDIKUI**	**57.8**
96	170	**CHECHAT**	**57.6**
97	115	**SURATGARH**	**57.5**
98	65	**SUWANA**	**57.4**
99	9	**BANSURE**	**57.3**
99	107	**SAGWARA**	**57.3**
101	12	**KISHANGARH BAS**	**57.0**
101	189	**KHARCHI/MARWAR JUN.**	**57.0**
103	113	**RAISINGHNAGAR**	**56.9**
103	191	**RAIPUR**	**56.9**
105	93	**SUJANGARH**	**56.8**
105	237	**SARADA**	**56.8**
107	33	**BARAN**	**56.6**
108	148	**ALSISAR**	**56.5**
109	187	**DESURI**	**56.4**
110	6	**MASOODA**	**56.1**
111	14	**LACHHMANGARH**	**56.0**
112	30	**TALWARA**	**55.9**
113	140	**SANCHORE**	**55.4**
114	167	**NADOTI**	**55.3**
114	183	**NAGAUR**	**55.3**
116	211	**KHANDELA**	**54.8**
116	218	**REODAR**	**54.8**
118	48	**KAMAN**	**54.6**
119	199	**KHAMNOR**	**54.5**
119	129	**SANGANER**	**54.5**
119	182	**MUNDWA**	**54.5**
122	157	**BAP**	**54.4**
123	205	**GANGAPUR**	**54.0**
124	2	**BHINAY**	**53.9**
124	13	**KOTKASIM**	**53.9**
124	86	**NIMBAHERA**	**53.9**
127	213	**NEEM KA THANA**	**53.6**
127	119	**AMBER**	**53.6**
129	41	**CHOHTAN**	**53.5**
129	128	**SAMBHAR**	**53.5**
131	227	**BARGAON**	**53.3**
132	156	**BALESAR**	**52.8**
133	175	**DEGANA**	**52.7**
134	122	**DUDU**	**52.5**
135	51	**NAGAR PAHARI**	**52.3**
135	166	**KARAULI**	**52.3**
137	235	MAVLI	51.7
138	96	DAUSA	51.6
138	101	BASERI	51.6
140	202	RAJSAMAND	51.5
140	63	SAHARA	51.5
142	230	GIRWA	51.4
143	45	SIWANA	51.3
144	92	SARDARSHAHAR	51.2
145	71	HINDOLI	51.1
146	105	BICHHIWARA	50.9
147	74	TALERA	50.8
148	68	KOLAYAT	50.5
149	118	NOHAR	50.3
	LOW (40-50)		
150	210	FATEHPUR	49.7
151	225	TONK	49.6
152	100	BARI	49.4
153	222	MALPURA	49.2
154	94	TARANAGAR	49.1
154	108	SIMALWARA	49.1
154	174	SULTANPUR	49.1
157	178	KUCHAMAN	48.2
158	168	SAPOTRA	48.1
159	233	KHERWARA	48.0
160	24	BAGIDORA	47.9
160	39	BARMER	47.9
162	177	JAYAL	47.8
163	231	GOGUNDA	47.6
164	54	WEIR	47.3
165	212	LACHHMANGARH	47.1
165	42	DHORIMANNA	47.1
165	206	KHANDAR	47.1
168	88	RASHMI	46.9
169	38	BALOTRA	46.8
169	60	MANDAL	46.8
171	98	MAHWA	46.7
172	133	SAM	46.3
173	180	MAKRANA	46.2
174	26	GHATOL	45.9
175	56	BANERA	45.8
176	23	ANANDPURI	45.0
177	29	SAJJANGARH	44.9
178	31	ANTA	44.6
178	229	DHARIAWAD	44.6
180	80	BHOPALSAGAR	43.4
180	203	BAMANWAS	43.4
182	196	AMET	42.6
182	32	ATRU	42.6
184	164	SHERGARH	42.1
184	200	KUMBHALGARH	42.1
186	223	NIWAI	41.9
187	27	KUSHALGARH	41.6
187	173	SANGOD	41.6
189	134	SANKRA	40.9
190	1	ARAIN	40.8
190	127	PHAGI	40.8
192	44	SINDHARI	40.5
193	87	PRATAPGARH	40.3
193	204	BONLI	40.3
	VERY LOW (<40)		
195	55	ASIND	39.7
195	97	LALSOT	39.7
197	85	KAPASAN	39.3
198	72	KESHORAIPATAN	39.0
198	82	CHITTAURGARH	39.0
200	228	BHINDER	38.4
201	36	KISHANGANJ	38.3
201	79	BHAINSRORGARH	38.3
203	144	JHALRAPATAN	37.9
204	77	BEGUN	37.8
205	61	MANDALGARH	37.7
206	78	BHADESAR	37.4
207	236	SALUMBAR	37.2
208	76	BARI SADRI	37.1
209	43	SHEO	36.8
210	224	TODARAISINGH	36.6
211	64	SHAHPURA	36.4
212	40	DAYTOO	36.2
212	81	CHHOTI SADRI	36.2
212	84	GANGRAR	36.2
215	58	JAHAZPUR	35.5
216	207	SAWAI MADHOPUR	34.6
217	198	DEOGARH	34.4
218	35	CHHIPABAROD	34.1
219	73	NAINWA	33.9
220	171	ITAWA	33.7
221	75	ARNOD	33.1
222	226	UNIARA	32.7
223	83	DUNGLA	32.4
224	221	DEOLI	32.1
225	59	KOTRI	32.0
226	232	JHADOL	31.4
227	121	CHAKSU	30.3
227	37	SHAHBAD	29.3
229	234	KOTRA	29.1
230	62	RAIPUR	28.1
231	145	KHANPUR	27.5
232	28	PEEPALKHOONT	26.2
233	34	CHHABRA	25.8
234	142	BAKANI	24.6
235	147	PIRAWA	23.4
236	143	DAG	23.1
237	146	MANOHARTHANA	21.8
		RAJASTHAN	**52.30**
		%age of AAPs	**57.40**

BOLD: Equal/Above Average Panchayat Samities (AAPs) *Source:* General Annex IX, Col. 8.

ANNEX-4.11

RANKING OF PSS BY PERCENTAGE OF RURAL POP. SERVED BY POWER AMENITIES: RAJASTHAN, 2001

(Descending Order)

RANK	P. CODE	PANCHAYAT SAMITIES NAME	%
1	2	3	4
		PERFECT (100)	
1	9	**BANSURE**	100.00
1	16	**NIMRANA**	100.00
1	19	**RENI**	100.00
1	33	**BARAN**	100.00
1	56	**BANERA**	100.00
1	63	**SAHARA**	100.00
1	78	**BHADESAR**	100.00
1	89	**CHURU**	100.00
1	95	**BANDIKUI**	100.00
1	124	**JAMWA RAMGARH**	100.00
1	129	**SANGANER**	100.00
1	131	**VIRATNAGAR**	100.00
1	138	**JASWANTPURA**	100.00
1	150	**CHIRAWA**	100.00
1	153	**NAWALGARH**	100.00
1	154	**SURAJGARH**	100.00
1	159	**BILARA**	100.00
1	178	**KUCHAMAN**	100.00
1	181	**MERTA**	100.00
1	184	**PARBATSAR**	100.00
1	195	**SUMERPUR**	100.00
1	196	**AMET**	100.00
1	201	**RAILMAGRA**	100.00
1	202	**RAJSAMAND**	100.00
1	208	**DANTA RAMGARH**	100.00
1	209	**DHOND**	100.00
1	210	**FATEHPUR**	100.00
1	215	**SRI MADHOPUR**	100.00
1	235	**MAVLI**	100.00
		VERY HIGH (75-100)	
30	10	**BEHROR**	99.90
30	62	**RAIPUR**	99.90
30	81	**CHHOTI SADRI**	99.90
30	86	**NIMBAHERA**	99.90
30	91	**RATANGARH**	99.90
30	128	**SAMBHAR**	99.90
30	147	**PIRAWA**	99.90
30	151	**JHUNJHUNUN**	99.90
30	170	**CHECHAT**	99.90
30	175	**DEGANA**	99.90
30	192	**RANI STATION**	99.90
30	211	**KHANDELA**	99.90
42	53	**SEWAR**	99.80
42	83	**DUNGLA**	99.80
42	88	**RASHMI**	99.80
42	93	**SUJANGARH**	99.80
42	193	**ROHAT**	99.80
42	212	**LACHHMANGARH**	99.80
42	214	**PIPRALI**	99.80
42	218	**REODAR**	99.80
50	18	**RAMGARH**	99.70
50	67	**DUNGARGARH**	99.70
50	84	**GANGRAR**	99.70
50	120	**BASSI**	99.70
50	137	**JALOR**	99.70
50	139	**RANIWARA**	99.70
50	152	**KHETRI**	99.70
50	165	**HINDAUN**	99.70
50	220	**SIROHI**	99.70
59	32	**ATRU**	99.60
59	65	**SUWANA**	99.60
59	119	**AMBER**	99.60
59	190	**PALI**	99.60
63	110	**GANGANAGAR**	99.50
63	123	**GOVINDGARH**	99.50
63	130	**SHAHPURA**	99.50
63	135	**AHORE**	99.50
67	6	**MASOODA**	99.40
67	125	**JHOTWARA**	99.40
67	158	**BHOPALGARH**	99.40
67	176	**DIDWANA**	99.40
71	5	**KISHANGARH**	99.30
71	173	**SANGOD**	99.30
71	180	**MAKRANA**	99.30
74	76	**BARI SADRI**	99.20
74	80	**BHOPALSAGAR**	99.20
74	185	**RIYAN**	99.20
74	187	**DESURI**	99.20
78	50	**NADBAI**	99.10
78	54	**WEIR**	99.10
78	155	**UDAIPURWATI**	99.10
78	162	**OSIAN**	99.10
78	198	**DEOGARH**	99.10
78	200	**KUMBHALGARH**	99.10
84	13	**KOTKASIM**	98.90
84	49	**KUMHER**	98.90
84	57	**HURDA**	98.90
87	85	**KAPASAN**	98.80
87	149	**BUHANA**	98.80
87	194	**SOJAT**	98.80
87	199	**KHAMNOR**	98.80
91	105	**BICHHIWARA**	98.70
91	114	**SADULSHAHAR**	98.70
91	148	**ALSISAR**	98.70
94	11	**KATHUMAR**	98.60
94	82	**CHITTAURGARH**	98.60
94	219	**SHEOGANJ**	98.60
97	111	**KARANPUR**	98.50
97	172	**LADPURA**	98.50
97	228	**BHINDER**	98.50
100	22	**UMREN**	98.40
101	14	**LACHHMANGARH**	98.30
101	141	**SAYLA**	98.30
101	161	**MANDOR**	98.30
104	7	**PISANGAN**	98.20
104	12	**KISHANGARH BAS**	98.20
104	213	**NEEM KA THANA**	98.20
107	15	**MANDAWAR**	98.10
107	179	**LADNU**	98.10
107	205	**GANGAPUR**	98.10
110	45	**SIWANA**	98.00
111	21	**TIJARA**	97.90
111	70	**NOKHA**	97.90
113	4	**KEKRI**	97.80
113	112	**PADAMPUR**	97.80
113	188	**JAITARAN**	97.80
116	8	**SRINAGAR**	97.60
116	145	**KHANPUR**	97.60
116	174	**SULTANPUR**	97.60
116	189	**KHARCHI/MARWAR JUN.**	97.60
120	47	**DEEG**	97.40
120	177	**JAYAL**	97.40
122	2	**BHINAY**	97.30
122	31	**ANTA**	97.30
122	55	**ASIND**	97.30
122	116	**BHADRA**	97.30
126	227	**BARGAON**	97.20
127	77	**BEGUN**	97.10
127	94	**TARANAGAR**	97.10
129	25	**GARHI**	97.00
129	73	**NAINWA**	97.00
129	224	**TODARAISINGH**	97.00
132	1	**ARAIN**	96.90
133	96	**DAUSA**	96.80
134	144	**JHALRAPATAN**	96.70
135	127	**PHAGI**	96.60
136	186	**BALI**	96.50
137	182	**MUNDWA**	96.40
138	126	**KOTPUTLI**	96.20
139	3	**JAWAJA**	96.10
140	61	**MANDALGARH**	96.00
141	223	**NIWAI**	95.90
142	20	**THANAGAZI**	95.50
143	64	**SHAHPURA**	95.20
143	99	**SIKRAI**	95.20
145	58	**JAHAZPUR**	95.10
145	117	**HANUMANGARH**	95.10
145	160	**LUNI**	95.10
145	222	**MALPURA**	95.10
149	17	**RAJGARH**	95.00
149	60	**MANDAL**	95.00
149	197	**BHIM**	95.00
152	122	**DUDU**	94.90
153	71	**HINDOLI**	94.70
153	98	**MAHWA**	94.70
153	191	**RAIPUR**	94.70
156	226	**UNIARA**	94.50
157	92	**SARDARSHAHAR**	94.40
158	36	**KISHANGANJ**	94.30
159	103	**RAJAKHERA**	94.10
160	51	**NAGAR PAHARI**	93.90
161	34	**CHHABRA**	93.80
161	204	**BONLI**	93.80
163	136	**BHINMAL**	93.70
164	106	**DUNGARPUR**	93.60
165	59	**KOTRI**	93.40
165	74	**TALERA**	93.40
167	52	**RUPBAS**	92.80
168	104	**ASPUR**	92.60
169	107	**SAGWARA**	92.50
170	79	**BHAINSRORGARH**	92.30
171	183	**NAGAUR**	91.90
171	230	**GIRWA**	91.90
173	35	**CHHIPABAROD**	91.80
173	169	**TODABHIM**	91.80
175	72	KESHORAIPATAN	91.40
176	46	BAYANA	91.00
176	167	NADOTI	91.00
178	156	BALESAR	90.80
179	171	ITAWA	90.30
180	97	LALSOT	90.20
181	163	PHALODI	90.10
182	90	RAJGARH	90.00
183	69	LUNKARANSAR	89.60
184	231	GOGUNDA	89.20
185	217	PINDWARA	89.00
186	48	KAMAN	88.40
186	121	CHAKSU	88.40
188	207	SAWAI MADHOPUR	88.20
189	108	SIMALWARA	87.80
190	225	TONK	87.60
191	229	DHARIAWAD	86.90
192	37	SHAHBAD	86.40
193	113	RAISINGHNAGAR	86.30
194	140	SANCHORE	86.00
194	142	BAKANI	86.00
196	203	BAMANWAS	85.90
197	30	TALWARA	85.80
198	143	DAG	85.10
199	166	KARAULI	84.60
200	216	ABU ROAD	84.50
201	26	GHATOL	84.40
201	221	DEOLI	84.40
203	237	SARADA	83.10
204	87	PRATAPGARH	82.60
204	236	SALUMBAR	82.60
206	102	DHAULPUR	82.30
207	75	ARNOD	81.60
208	157	BAP	81.40
209	68	KOLAYAT	80.10
210	206	KHANDAR	79.80
211	164	SHERGARH	79.50
212	38	BALOTRA	77.70
212	42	DHORIMANNA	77.70
214	23	ANANDPURI	75.40
		HIGH (50-75)	
215	146	MANOHARTHANA	74.30
216	41	CHOHTAN	73.10
217	232	JHADOL	72.30
218	168	SAPOTRA	72.10
219	118	NOHAR	72.00
220	66	BIKANER	71.90
221	109	ANUPGARH	69.00
222	233	KHERWARA	68.90
223	29	SAJJANGARH	66.90
224	24	BAGIDORA	64.60
225	101	BASERI	63.60
226	132	JAISALMER	62.90
227	27	KUSHALGARH	57.80
228	100	BARI	57.20
229	44	SINDHARI	56.90
230	115	SURATGARH	56.50
231	134	SANKRA	55.20
232	43	SHEO	54.30
233	39	BARMER	51.50
		MEDIUM (<50)	
234	28	PEEPALKHOONT	41.00
235	133	SAM	39.50
236	40	BAYTOO	35.00
237	234	KOTRA	33.30
		RAJASTHAN	**91.57**
		%age of AAPs	**73.41**

BOLD: Equal/Above Average Panchayat Samities (AAPs) *Source*: General Annex VIII, Col. 7.

ANNEX-4.12

RANKING OF PSS BY PERCENTAGE OF INHABITED VILLAGES HAVING POWER AMENITIES, 2001

(Descending Order)

RANK	P. CODE	PANCHAYAT SAMITIES NAME	%
1	2	3	4
	PERFECT (100)		
1	9	BANSURE	100.0
1	19	RENI	100.0
1	56	BANERA	100.0
1	63	SAHARA	100.0
1	78	BHADESAR	100.0
1	89	CHURU	100.0
1	129	SANGANER	100.0
1	138	JASWANTPURA	100.0
1	150	CHIRAWA	100.0
1	153	NAWALGARH	100.0
1	154	SURAJGARH	100.0
1	159	BILARA	100.0
1	178	KUCHAMAN	100.0
1	184	PARBATSAR	100.0
1	195	SUMERPUR	100.0
1	196	AMET	100.0
1	201	RAILMAGRA	100.0
1	209	DHOND	100.0
1	210	FATEHPUR	100.0
1	215	SRI MADHOPUR	100.0
1	235	MAVLI	100.0
	VERY HIGH (95-100)		
22	95	BANDIKUI	99.5
22	119	AMBER	99.5
22	147	PIRAWA	99.5
25	208	DANTA RAMGARH	99.4
26	128	SAMBHAR	99.3
26	151	JHUNJHUNUN	99.3
26	212	LACHHMANGARH	99.3
29	202	RAJSAMAND	99.2
29	131	VIRATNAGAR	99.2
29	149	BUHANA	99.2
29	165	HINDAUN	99.2
33	13	KOTKASIM	99.1
33	124	JAMWA RAMGARH	99.1
35	33	BARAN	99.0
35	83	DUNGLA	99.0
35	123	GOVINDGARH	99.0
38	214	PIPRALI	98.9
38	10	BEHROR	98.9
38	62	RAIPUR	98.9
38	67	DUNGARGARH	98.9
42	16	NIMRANA	98.8
42	130	SHAHPURA	98.8
42	152	KHETRI	98.8
42	155	UDAIPURWATI	98.8
42	200	KUMBHALGARH	98.8
47	193	ROHAT	98.7
47	93	SUJANGARH	98.7
47	192	RANI STATION	98.7
50	57	HURDA	98.6
50	120	BASSI	98.6
50	125	JHOTWARA	98.6
50	175	DEGANA	98.6
54	32	ATRU	98.5
54	65	SUWANA	98.5
54	137	JALOR	98.5
57	181	MERTA	98.2
58	53	SEWAR	98.1
59	86	NIMBAHERA	98.0
59	173	SANGOD	98.0
61	54	WEIR	97.9
61	76	BARI SADRI	97.9
61	170	CHECHAT	97.9
64	6	MASOODA	97.8
65	18	RAMGARH	97.7
65	158	BHOPALGARH	97.7
67	218	REODAR	97.6
67	80	BHOPALSAGAR	97.6
67	139	RANIWARA	97.6
67	148	ALSISAR	97.6
67	176	DIDWANA	97.6
67	220	SIROHI	97.6
73	88	RASHMI	97.5
73	180	MAKRANA	97.5
73	190	PALI	97.5
76	49	KUMHER	97.4
76	50	NADBAI	97.4
78	15	MANDAWAR	97.2
78	81	CHHOTI SADRI	97.2
78	85	KAPASAN	97.2
81	161	MANDOR	97.1
82	12	KISHANGARH BAS	97.0
82	91	RATANGARH	97.0
84	198	DEOGARH	96.9
84	8	SRINAGAR	96.9
84	84	GANGRAR	96.9
87	185	RIYAN	96.8
87	199	KHAMNOR	96.8
89	105	BICHHIWARA	96.6
89	162	OSIAN	96.6
91	5	KISHANGARH	96.4
91	135	AHORE	96.4
93	141	SAYLA	96.1
94	211	KHANDELA	96.0
95	14	LACHHMANGARH	95.7
95	194	SOJAT	95.7
97	11	KATHUMAR	95.6
98	228	BHINDER	95.0
	HIGH (90-95)		
99	187	DESURI	94.9
100	21	TIJARA	94.6
101	172	LADPURA	94.5
102	110	GANGANAGAR	94.2
103	45	SIWANA	93.9
104	205	GANGAPUR	93.8
104	179	LADNU	93.8
106	189	KHARCHI/MARWAR JUN.	93.7
107	177	JAYAL	93.4
107	182	MUNDWA	93.4
109	73	NAINWA	93.3
109	145	KHANPUR	93.3
111	7	PISANGAN	93.0
111	3	JAWAJA	93.0
111	2	BHINAY	93.0
114	112	PADAMPUR	92.9
115	1	ARAIN	92.8
115	111	KARANPUR	92.8
115	219	SHEOGANJ	92.8
118	31	ANTA	92.6
118	55	ASIND	92.6
118	126	KOTPUTLI	92.6
121	227	BARGAON	92.5
122	127	PHAGI	92.3
122	186	BALI	92.3
124	174	SULTANPUR	92.0
125	4	KEKRI	91.9
125	96	DAUSA	91.9
127	82	CHITTAURGARH	91.7
128	144	JHALRAPATAN	91.6
129	99	SIKRAI	91.4
129	213	NEEM KA THANA	91.4
131	22	UMREN	91.3
132	70	NOKHA	91.2
132	92	SARDARSHAHAR	91.2
132	106	DUNGARPUR	91.2
135	25	GARHI	91.1
136	47	DEEG	90.8
137	51	NAGAR PAHARI	90.7
137	64	SHAHPURA	90.7
139	188	JAITARAN	90.3
140	71	HINDOLI	90.2
140	197	BHIM	90.2
	MEDIUM (85-90)		
142	223	NIWAI	89.5
143	103	RAJAKHERA	89.4
144	122	DUDU	89.0
145	160	LUNI	88.9
146	60	MANDAL	88.8
146	98	MAHWA	88.8
148	61	MANDALGARH	88.6
149	94	TARANAGAR	88.2
150	191	RAIPUR	88.1
151	58	JAHAZPUR	88.0
152	77	BEGUN	87.8
153	34	CHHABRA	87.6
154	136	BHINMAL	87.5
154	169	TODABHIM	87.5
156	52	RUPBAS	87.3
157	204	BONLI	86.8
158	224	TODARAISINGH	86.6
158	74	TALERA	86.6
160	114	SADULSHAHAR	86.5
161	230	GIRWA	86.0
162	59	KOTRI	85.1
162	79	BHAINSRORGARH	85.1
164	231	GOGUNDA	85.0
164	17	RAJGARH	85.0
	LOW (<85)		
166	183	NAGAUR	84.7
167	222	MALPURA	84.6
168	46	BAYANA	84.5
169	36	KISHANGANJ	84.4
170	90	RAJGARH	84.0
171	35	CHHIPABAROD	83.8
172	163	PHALODI	83.8
173	104	ASPUR	82.5
174	107	SAGWARA	82.2
175	72	KESHORAIPATAN	81.6
176	97	LALSOT	80.7
177	226	UNIARA	80.1
178	117	HANUMANGARH	80.0
179	156	BALESAR	79.2
180	48	KAMAN	78.9
181	207	SAWAI MADHOPUR	78.8
181	167	NADOTI	78.8
183	121	CHAKSU	78.3
184	20	THANAGAZI	75.7
185	108	SIMALWARA	75.5
185	140	SANCHORE	75.5
187	237	SARADA	75.1
187	102	DHAULPUR	75.1
189	69	LUNKARANSAR	75.0
190	217	PINDWARA	74.7
191	225	TONK	74.4
192	236	SALUMBAR	73.9
193	143	DAG	73.8
194	203	BAMANWAS	73.5
195	216	ABU ROAD	73.1
196	113	RAISINGHNAGAR	73.0
197	229	DHARIAWAD	71.9
198	116	BHADRA	71.7
199	171	ITAWA	71.2
200	142	BAKANI	70.2
201	87	PRATAPGARH	70.0
202	42	DHORIMANNA	69.7
203	166	KARAULI	69.2
204	157	BAP	68.8
205	26	GHATOL	68.6
206	30	TALWARA	68.5
207	164	SHERGARH	65.4
208	221	DEOLI	64.2
209	75	ARNOD	64.0
210	233	KHERWARA	63.6
211	37	SHAHBAD	63.5
212	23	ANANDPURI	62.8
212	38	BALOTRA	62.8
214	206	KHANDAR	62.6
215	146	MANOHARTHANA	61.6
216	66	BIKANER	61.2
217	232	JHADOL	55.4
218	41	CHOHTAN	55.1
219	68	KOLAYAT	54.1
220	29	SAJJANGARH	52.4
221	168	SAPOTRA	51.9
222	24	BAGIDORA	50.9
223	27	KUSHALGARH	50.7
224	132	JAISALMER	49.7
225	101	BASERI	48.9
226	109	ANUPGARH	48.5
227	100	BARI	46.4
228	118	NOHAR	43.9
229	43	SHEO	42.0
230	44	SINDHARI	41.7
231	134	SANKRA	40.3
232	115	SURATGARH	38.1
233	39	BARMER	35.8
234	40	BAYTOO	26.9
235	28	PEEPALKHOONT	24.1
236	234	KOTRA	21.5
237	133	SAM	14.6
		RAJASTHAN	81.20
		%age of AAPs	73.84

BOLD: Equal/Above Average Panchayat Samities (AAPs) *Source*: General Annex IX, Col. 7.

ANNEX-4.13

RANKING OF PSS BY PERCENTAGE OF RURAL POP. SERVED BY POST OFFICE AMENITIES: RAJASTHAN, 2001

RANK	P. CODE	PANCHAYAT SAMITIES NAME	%
1	2	3	4
	VERY HIGH (>=70)		
1	**220**	**SIROHI**	**78.30**
2	**192**	**RANI STATION**	**77.90**
3	**67**	**DUNGARGARH**	**77.30**
4	**155**	**UDAIPURWATI**	**77.00**
5	**215**	**SRI MADHOPUR**	**75.70**
6	**195**	**SUMERPUR**	**74.80**
6	**219**	**SHEOGANJ**	**73.80**
8	**209**	**DHOND**	**73.40**
9	**123**	**GOVINDGARH**	**72.80**
10	**153**	**NAWALGARH**	**72.40**
11	**214**	**PIPRALI**	**72.30**
12	**158**	**BHOPALGARH**	**72.00**
13	**135**	**AHORE**	**71.90**
14	**45**	**SIWANA**	**71.80**
14	**152**	**KHETRI**	**71.80**
16	**181**	**MERTA**	**71.50**
16	**186**	**BALI**	**71.50**
18	**70**	**NOKHA**	**71.40**
18	**191**	**RAIPUR**	**71.40**
	HIGH (60-70)		
20	**188**	**JAITARAN**	**69.40**
20	**211**	**KHANDELA**	**69.40**
22	**150**	**CHIRAWA**	**69.30**
23	**4**	**KEKRI**	**68.40**
24	**184**	**PARBATSAR**	**67.70**
25	**208**	**DANTA RAMGARH**	**67.50**
26	**116**	**BHADRA**	**66.90**
27	**137**	**JALOR**	**66.70**
28	**217**	**PINDWARA**	**66.50**
29	**187**	**DESURI**	**65.90**
30	**179**	**LADNU**	**65.10**
31	**180**	**MAKRANA**	**64.80**
32	**185**	**RIYAN**	**64.70**
33	**189**	**KHARCHI/MARWAR JUN.**	**64.50**
34	**162**	**OSIAN**	**64.40**
35	**130**	**SHAHPURA**	**64.30**
36	**176**	**DIDWANA**	**64.20**
37	**216**	**ABU ROAD**	**64.00**
38	**210**	**FATEHPUR**	**63.90**
39	**177**	**JAYAL**	**63.80**
40	**6**	**MASOODA**	**63.30**
41	**88**	**RASHMI**	**62.90**
41	**136**	**BHINMAL**	**62.90**
41	**149**	**BUHANA**	**62.90**
44	**107**	**SAGWARA**	**62.70**
45	**212**	**LACHHMANGARH**	**62.50**
46	**159**	**BILARA**	**62.40**
47	**50**	**NADBAI**	**62.30**
48	**148**	**ALSISAR**	**62.00**
49	**141**	**SAYLA**	**61.90**
50	**138**	**JASWANTPURA**	**61.80**
50	**194**	**SOJAT**	**61.80**
52	**139**	**RANIWARA**	**61.70**
53	**47**	**DEEG**	**61.60**
53	**57**	**HURDA**	**61.60**
55	**63**	**SAHARA**	**61.40**
55	**89**	**CHURU**	**61.40**
57	**5**	**KISHANGARH**	**61.30**
57	**218**	**REODAR**	**61.30**
59	**105**	**BICHHIWARA**	**61.10**
60	**2**	**BHINAY**	**61.00**
60	**213**	**NEEM KA THANA**	**61.00**
62	**203**	**BAMANWAS**	**60.70**
63	**94**	**TARANAGAR**	**60.30**
64	**56**	**BANERA**	**60.20**
64	**169**	**TODABHIM**	**60.20**
66	**16**	**NIMRANA**	**60.00**
66	**38**	**BALOTRA**	**60.00**
	MEDIUM (50-60)		
68	**91**	**RATANGARH**	**59.40**
69	**93**	**SUJANGARH**	**59.30**
70	**154**	**SURAJGARH**	**59.20**
71	**7**	**PISANGAN**	**58.70**
72	**122**	**DUDU**	**58.30**
73	**54**	**WEIR**	**58.20**
74	**207**	**SAWAI MADHOPUR**	**58.00**
75	**1**	**ARAIN**	**57.90**
76	**110**	**GANGANAGAR**	**57.70**
77	**131**	**VIRATNAGAR**	**57.50**
78	**132**	**JAISALMER**	**57.40**
79	**160**	**LUNI**	**57.00**

RANK	P. CODE	PANCHAYAT SAMITIES NAME	%
1	2	3	4
80	**175**	**DEGANA**	**56.90**
81	**151**	**JHUNJHUNUN**	**56.80**
82	**10**	**BEHROR**	**56.70**
83	**165**	**HINDAUN**	**56.40**
84	**32**	**ATRU**	**56.30**
85	**178**	**KUCHAMAN**	**56.30**
86	**166**	**KARAULI**	**56.10**
86	**182**	**MUNDWA**	**56.10**
88	**190**	**PALI**	**55.90**
89	**41**	**CHOHTAN**	**55.40**
90	**25**	**GARHI**	**55.30**
90	**205**	**GANGAPUR**	**55.30**
90	**221**	**DEOLI**	**55.30**
93	**49**	**KUMHER**	**55.20**
94	**20**	**THANAGAZI**	**55.10**
95	**163**	**PHALODI**	**55.00**
96	**222**	**MALPURA**	**54.80**
97	**19**	**RENI**	**54.60**
98	**224**	**TODARAISINGH**	**54.00**
98	**227**	**BARGAON**	**54.00**
100	**167**	**NADOTI**	**53.90**
101	**104**	**ASPUR**	**53.80**
102	**11**	**KATHUMAR**	**53.70**
103	**201**	**RAILMAGRA**	**53.60**
104	**117**	**HANUMANGARH**	**53.50**
105	**8**	**SRINAGAR**	**53.40**
105	**204**	**BONLI**	**53.40**
107	**237**	**SARADA**	**53.30**
108	**128**	**SAMBHAR**	**52.90**
109	**171**	**ITAWA**	**52.80**
110	**17**	**RAJGARH**	**52.60**
110	**126**	**KOTPUTLI**	**52.60**
110	**202**	**RAJSAMAND**	**52.60**
113	**161**	**MANDOR**	**52.20**
114	**31**	**ANTA**	**52.10**
114	**168**	**SAPOTRA**	**52.10**
116	**164**	**SHERGARH**	**51.50**
117	96	DAUSA	51.30
118	68	KOLAYAT	51.00
118	83	DUNGLA	51.00
118	114	SADULSHAHAR	51.00
121	62	RAIPUR	50.90
121	183	NAGAUR	50.90
123	15	MANDAWAR	50.40
123	86	NIMBAHERA	50.40
125	9	BANSURE	50.10
125	60	MANDAL	50.10
127	55	ASIND	50.00
127	75	ARNOD	50.00
	LOW (40-50)		
129	90	RAJGARH	49.70
130	147	PIRAWA	49.60
131	108	SIMALWARA	49.10
132	92	SARDARSHAHAR	49.00
133	174	SULTANPUR	48.80
134	53	SEWAR	48.60
135	133	SAM	48.50
136	65	SUWANA	48.40
137	226	UNIARA	48.30
138	82	CHITTAURGARH	48.20
139	52	RUPBAS	48.00
140	118	NOHAR	47.70
140	156	BALESAR	47.70
140	223	NIWAI	47.70
143	235	MAVLI	47.60
144	106	DUNGARPUR	47.30
145	80	BHOPALSAGAR	47.20
146	99	SIKRAI	47.20
147	69	LUNKARANSAR	47.10
147	231	GOGUNDA	47.10
149	22	UMREN	46.80
149	197	BHIM	46.80
151	98	MAHWA	46.60
152	230	GIRWA	46.50
153	64	SHAHPURA	46.10
153	206	KHANDAR	46.10
155	61	MANDALGARH	45.70
156	71	HINDOLI	45.60
156	84	GANGRAR	45.60
158	26	GHATOL	45.40
158	33	BARAN	45.40
160	157	BAP	45.30

RANK	P. CODE	PANCHAYAT SAMITIES NAME	%
1	2	3	4
161	59	KOTRI	45.10
162	140	SANCHORE	45.00
163	73	NAINWA	44.90
163	111	KARANPUR	44.90
165	51	NAGAR PAHARI	44.80
166	120	BASSI	44.50
166	173	SANGOD	44.50
168	145	KHANPUR	44.40
168	225	TONK	44.40
170	199	KHAMNOR	44.20
171	14	LACHHMANGARH	44.00
172	72	KESHORAIPATAN	43.40
172	134	SANKRA	43.40
174	119	AMBER	43.20
175	58	JAHAZPUR	42.70
176	129	SANGANER	42.60
177	193	ROHAT	42.10
177	228	BHINDER	42.10
179	12	KISHANGARH BAS	42.00
179	46	BAYANA	42.00
181	76	BARI SADRI	41.30
181	95	BANDIKUI	41.30
181	124	JAMWA RAMGARH	41.30
184	42	DHORIMANNA	41.10
185	127	PHAGI	40.60
186	87	PRATAPGARH	40.50
187	48	KAMAN	40.40
188	143	DAG	40.10
189	66	BIKANER	40.00
	VERY LOW (<40)		
190	43	SHEO	39.60
191	102	DHAULPUR	39.40
192	13	KOTKASIM	39.20
192	200	KUMBHALGARH	39.20
194	236	SALUMBAR	39.00
195	103	RAJAKHERA	38.90
196	81	CHHOTI SADRI	38.80
197	85	KAPASAN	38.60
198	100	BARI	38.10
199	97	LALSOT	38.00
200	44	SINDHARI	37.80
200	125	JHOTWARA	37.80
202	39	BARMER	37.70
203	112	PADAMPUR	37.60
204	196	AMET	37.50
204	229	DHARIAWAD	37.50
206	24	BAGIDORA	36.70
207	3	JAWAJA	36.20
208	35	CHHIPABAROD	35.20
209	77	BEGUN	34.90
210	74	TALERA	34.70
210	172	LADPURA	34.70
212	23	ANANDPURI	34.50
213	18	RAMGARH	34.10
214	232	JHADOL	33.50
215	101	BASERI	33.30
216	113	RAISINGHNAGAR	33.20
217	37	SHAHBAD	33.00
217	78	BHADESAR	33.00
219	28	PEEPALKHOONT	32.50
220	170	CHECHAT	32.20
221	233	KHERWARA	31.20
222	30	TALWARA	31.10
222	121	CHAKSU	31.10
224	142	BAKANI	30.70
225	144	JHALRAPATAN	30.50
226	115	SURATGARH	29.00
227	21	TIJARA	28.20
228	36	KISHANGANJ	28.10
229	198	DEOGARH	27.10
230	234	KOTRA	26.70
231	146	MANOHARTHANA	26.10
232	40	BAYTOO	25.40
233	79	BHAINSRORGARH	24.10
234	109	ANUPGARH	22.80
235	34	CHHABRA	20.90
236	29	SAJJANGARH	17.10
237	27	KUSHALGARH	11.40
		RAJASTHAN	**51.32**
		%age of AAPs	**48.95**

BOLD: Equal/Above Average Panchayat Samities (AAPs) *Source*: General Annex VIII, Col. 9.

ANNEX-4.14

RANKING OF PSS BY PERCENTAGE OF INHABITED VILLAGES HAVING POST OFFICE AMENITIES: RAJASTHAN, 2001

(Descending Order)

RANK	*P. CODE*	*PANCHAYAT SAMITIES NAME*	*%*
1	2	3	4
	VERY HIGH (>35)		
1	215	**SRI MADHOPUR**	59.1
2	67	**DUNGARGARH**	54.3
3	152	**KHETRI**	54.1
4	155	**UDAIPURWATI**	53.1
5	209	**DHOND**	52.3
6	153	**NAWALGARH**	51.1
7	195	**SUMERPUR**	50.8
8	192	**RANI STATION**	50.0
9	211	**KHANDELA**	46.8
10	158	**BHOPALGARH**	46.5
11	220	**SIROHI**	45.8
12	136	**BHINMAL**	45.0
13	210	**FATEHPUR**	44.8
14	214	**PIPRALI**	44.7
15	123	**GOVINDGARH**	44.0
16	70	**NOKHA**	43.1
17	89	**CHURU**	42.9
17	149	**BUHANA**	42.9
17	186	**BALI**	42.9
20	135	**AHORE**	42.7
21	162	**OSIAN**	42.3
22	219	**SHEOGANJ**	42.0
23	176	**DIDWANA**	41.8
23	184	**PARBATSAR**	41.8
25	141	**SAYLA**	41.6
26	16	**NIMRANA**	41.2
26	137	**JALOR**	41.2
28	208	**DANTA RAMGARH**	40.8
29	212	**LACHHMANGARH**	40.7
30	180	**MAKRANA**	40.3
31	45	**SIWANA**	40.0
32	91	**RATANGARH**	39.6
33	4	**KEKRI**	39.4
34	139	**RANIWARA**	39.3
34	150	**CHIRAWA**	39.3
34	154	**SURAJGARH**	39.3
37	179	**LADNU**	39.2
38	7	**PISANGAN**	39.1
38	213	**NEEM KA THANA**	39.1
40	216	**ABU ROAD**	38.5
41	50	**NADBAI**	37.7
42	93	**SUJANGARH**	37.4
43	130	**SHAHPURA**	37.2
43	165	**HINDAUN**	37.2
45	159	**BILARA**	37.1
46	191	**RAIPUR**	36.7
47	8	**SRINAGAR**	36.5
47	138	**JASWANTPURA**	36.5
49	94	**TARANAGAR**	36.4
50	188	**JAITARAN**	35.9
50	189	**KHARCHI/MARWAR JUN.**	35.9
52	185	**RIYAN**	35.2
53	175	**DEGANA**	35.1
	HIGH (30-35)		
54	194	**SOJAT**	34.8
55	169	**TODABHIM**	34.7
56	177	**JAYAL**	34.6
56	187	**DESURI**	34.6
58	2	**BHINAY**	34.4
59	54	**WEIR**	34.2
59	163	**PHALODI**	34.2
61	126	**KOTPUTLI**	33.9
62	107	**SAGWARA**	33.8
63	104	**ASPUR**	33.6
64	151	**JHUNJHUNUN**	33.1
64	182	**MUNDWA**	33.1
66	105	**BICHHIWARA**	32.6
67	5	**KISHANGARH**	32.4
67	92	**SARDARSHAHAR**	32.4
67	181	**MERTA**	32.4
70	41	**CHOHTAN**	32.1
71	38	**BALOTRA**	32.0
72	148	**ALSISAR**	31.5
73	217	**PINDWARA**	31.3
74	47	**DEEG**	31.1
75	218	**REODAR**	31.0
76	203	**BAMANWAS**	30.9
77	167	**NADOTI**	30.6
78	1	**ARAIN**	30.4
78	160	**LUNI**	30.4
80	15	**MANDAWAR**	30.3
81	57	**HURDA**	30.0
	MEDIUM (25-30)		
82	90	**RAJGARH**	29.6
82	156	**BALESAR**	29.6
84	178	**KUCHAMAN**	29.5
85	205	**GANGAPUR**	29.2
85	128	**SAMBHAR**	29.2
87	10	**BEHROR**	28.9
87	56	**BANERA**	28.9
87	106	**DUNGARPUR**	28.9
90	207	**SAWAI MADHOPUR**	28.8
90	190	**PALI**	28.8
92	166	**KARAULI**	28.7
92	183	**NAGAUR**	28.7
94	11	**KATHUMAR**	28.5
95	19	**RENI**	28.4
96	49	**KUMHER**	28.2
97	237	**SARADA**	28.1
98	25	**GARHI**	28.0
98	42	**DHORIMANNA**	28.0
98	132	**JAISALMER**	28.0
101	32	**ATRU**	27.9
101	231	**GOGUNDA**	27.9
103	161	**MANDOR**	27.6
104	131	**VIRATNAGAR**	27.5
105	63	**SAHARA**	27.3
106	88	**RASHMI**	27.2
107	164	**SHERGARH**	27.1
108	6	**MASOODA**	26.6
109	140	**SANCHORE**	26.5
110	157	**BAP**	26.4
110	201	**RAILMAGRA**	26.4
112	227	**BARGAON**	26.2
113	52	**RUPBAS**	26.1
114	9	**BANSURE**	26.0
115	62	**RAIPUR**	25.8
116	134	**SANKRA**	25.6
117	193	**ROHAT**	25.3
117	33	**BARAN**	25.3
119	197	**BHIM**	25.0
119	224	**TODARAISINGH**	25.0
	LOW (20-25)		
121	103	**RAJAKHERA**	24.6
122	204	**BONLI**	24.5
122	64	**SHAHPURA**	24.5
122	99	**SIKRAI**	24.5
125	100	**BARI**	24.4
126	168	**SAPOTRA**	24.3
127	202	**RAJSAMAND**	24.2
128	51	**NAGAR PAHARI**	24.1
129	43	**SHEO**	24.0
130	110	**GANGANAGAR**	23.7
130	116	**BHADRA**	23.7
130	122	**DUDU**	23.7
133	108	**SIMALWARA**	23.6
134	230	**GIRWA**	23.5
135	39	BARMER	23.1
135	222	MALPURA	23.1
137	12	KISHANGARH BAS	23.0
137	20	THANAGAZI	23.0
137	71	HINDOLI	23.0
140	235	MAVLI	22.8
141	111	KARANPUR	22.7
142	53	SEWAR	22.3
143	22	UMREN	22.1
143	55	ASIND	22.1
143	65	SUWANA	22.1
146	44	SINDHARI	22.0
146	147	PIRAWA	22.0
148	69	LUNKARANSAR	21.9
149	102	DHAULPUR	21.8
150	46	BAYANA	21.7
150	98	MAHWA	21.7
152	96	DAUSA	21.5
153	17	RAJGARH	21.4
153	119	AMBER	21.4
155	200	KUMBHALGARH	21.3
156	221	DEOLI	21.2
157	31	ANTA	20.9
158	14	LACHHMANGARH	20.7
159	206	KHANDAR	20.6
159	83	DUNGLA	20.6
	VERY LOW (<20)		
161	199	KHAMNOR	19.8
162	75	ARNOD	19.7
163	95	BANDIKUI	19.4
164	172	LADPURA	19.3
165	236	SALUMBAR	19.2
166	3	JAWAJA	19.1
166	26	GHATOL	19.1
166	48	KAMAN	19.1
166	86	NIMBAHERA	19.1
170	72	KESHORAIPATAN	18.8
170	233	KHERWARA	18.8
172	66	BIKANER	18.7
173	60	MANDAL	18.6
174	133	SAM	18.5
175	68	KOLAYAT	18.4
175	171	ITAWA	18.4
175	174	SULTANPUR	18.4
178	13	KOTKASIM	18.3
178	73	NAINWA	18.3
180	85	KAPASAN	17.8
180	173	SANGOD	17.8
182	120	BASSI	17.6
182	124	JAMWA RAMGARH	17.6
184	84	GANGRAR	17.3
184	223	NIWAI	17.3
186	143	DAG	17.2
187	59	KOTRI	17.1
188	24	BAGIDORA	17.0
188	87	PRATAPGARH	17.0
190	80	BHOPALSAGAR	16.9
191	225	TONK	16.8
191	129	SANGANER	16.8
193	170	CHECHAT	16.7
194	23	ANANDPURI	16.3
194	113	RAISINGHNAGAR	16.3
196	196	AMET	16.2
197	40	BAYTOO	16.1
198	112	PADAMPUR	15.9
199	58	JAHAZPUR	15.7
200	35	CHHIPABAROD	15.6
200	74	TALERA	15.6
200	81	CHHOTI SADRI	15.6
203	118	NOHAR	15.6
204	145	KHANPUR	15.5
205	82	CHITTAURGARH	15.1
205	125	JHOTWARA	15.1
207	97	LALSOT	15.0
208	61	MANDALGARH	14.9
209	127	PHAGI	14.8
209	226	UNIARA	14.8
211	232	JHADOL	14.7
211	101	BASERI	14.7
213	229	DHARIAWAD	14.5
214	144	JHALRAPATAN	14.4
215	228	BHINDER	14.3
216	76	BARI SADRI	14.0
216	77	BEGUN	14.0
218	18	RAMGARH	13.9
218	21	TIJARA	13.9
220	37	SHAHBAD	13.2
221	30	TALWARA	13.1
222	114	SADULSHAHAR	12.7
223	198	DEOGARH	11.5
224	117	HANUMANGARH	11.0
225	121	CHAKSU	10.9
226	34	CHHABRA	10.8
227	28	PEEPALKHOONT	10.7
228	146	MANOHARTHANA	10.6
229	115	SURATGARH	9.7
229	142	BAKANI	9.7
231	27	KUSHALGARH	9.6
232	234	KOTRA	9.3
233	78	BHADESAR	9.2
234	79	BHAINSRORGARH	9.1
235	36	KISHANGANJ	8.9
236	29	SAJJANGARH	7.6
237	109	ANUPGARH	7.3
		RAJASTHAN	**23.30**
		%age of AAPs	**56.50**

BOLD: Equal/Above Average Panchayat Samities (AAPs) *Source*: General Annex IX, Col. 9.

ANNEX-4.15

RANKING OF PSS BY PERCENTAGE OF RURAL POP. SERVED BY AGRICULTURAL CREDIT SOCIETIES, 2001

RANK	P. CODE	PANCHAYAT SAMITIES NAME	%
1	2	3	4
	VERY HIGH (>=40)		
1	**47**	**DEEG**	**66.80**
2	**116**	**BHADRA**	**63.00**
3	**141**	**SAYLA**	**62.90**
4	**49**	**KUMHER**	**59.90**
5	**123**	**GOVINDGARH**	**59.10**
6	**135**	**AHORE**	**56.60**
7	**177**	**JAYAL**	**53.10**
8	**181**	**MERTA**	**53.00**
9	**153**	**NAWALGARH**	**52.90**
10	**150**	**CHIRAWA**	**51.80**
11	**57**	**HURDA**	**51.40**
12	**179**	**LADNU**	**51.30**
13	**159**	**BILARA**	**51.20**
14	**194**	**SOJAT**	**51.10**
15	**195**	**SUMERPUR**	**50.60**
16	**94**	**TARANAGAR**	**50.10**
17	**167**	**NADOTI**	**49.60**
18	**186**	**BALI**	**49.30**
19	**188**	**JAITARAN**	**49.20**
20	**88**	**RASHMI**	**48.60**
21	**114**	**SADULSHAHAR**	**48.40**
22	**174**	**SULTANPUR**	**48.10**
23	**110**	**GANGANAGAR**	**47.80**
24	**189**	**KHARCHI/MARWAR JUN.**	**47.60**
25	**190**	**PALI**	**47.50**
26	**45**	**SIWANA**	**47.00**
27	**171**	**ITAWA**	**46.90**
28	**191**	**RAIPUR**	**46.80**
29	**53**	**SEWAR**	**46.30**
30	**80**	**BHOPALSAGAR**	**45.90**
31	**215**	**SRI MADHOPUR**	**45.40**
32	**207**	**SAWAI MADHOPUR**	**44.90**
33	**86**	**NIMBAHERA**	**44.70**
34	**148**	**ALSISAR**	**44.50**
35	**117**	**HANUMANGARH**	**43.80**
36	**137**	**JALOR**	**43.70**
37	**14**	**LACHHMANGARH**	**43.10**
37	**224**	**TODARAISINGH**	**43.10**
39	**192**	**RANI STATION**	**42.90**
40	**204**	**BONLI**	**42.20**
41	**33**	**BARAN**	**42.00**
42	**185**	**RIYAN**	**41.80**
43	**73**	**NAINWA**	**41.50**
44	**226**	**UNIARA**	**41.30**
45	**31**	**ANTA**	**41.10**
45	**208**	**DANTA RAMGARH**	**41.10**
	HIGH (30-40)		
47	**63**	**SAHARA**	**39.80**
48	**70**	**NOKHA**	**39.70**
49	**203**	**BAMANWAS**	**39.60**
50	**187**	**DESURI**	**39.40**
51	**127**	**PHAGI**	**39.20**
52	**182**	**MUNDWA**	**39.20**
53	**56**	**BANERA**	**39.10**
54	**163**	**PHALODI**	**39.00**
55	**162**	**OSIAN**	**38.70**
56	**82**	**CHITTAURGARH**	**38.60**
57	**205**	**GANGAPUR**	**38.50**
58	**65**	**SUWANA**	**38.30**
59	**22**	**UMREN**	**38.10**
60	**60**	**MANDAL**	**37.80**
61	**62**	**RAIPUR**	**37.70**
61	**160**	**LUNI**	**37.70**
63	**218**	**REODAR**	**37.40**
64	**130**	**SHAHPURA**	**37.20**
64	**158**	**BHOPALGARH**	**37.20**
64	**221**	**DEOLI**	**37.20**
67	**72**	**KESHORAIPATAN**	**37.10**
68	**91**	**RATANGARH**	**36.90**
69	**219**	**SHEOGANJ**	**36.60**
70	**214**	**PIPRALI**	**36.40**
71	**83**	**DUNGLA**	**36.10**
72	**52**	**RUPBAS**	**35.80**
73	**89**	**CHURU**	**35.60**
73	**193**	**ROHAT**	**35.60**
75	**81**	**CHHOTI SADRI**	**35.40**
76	**2**	**BHINAY**	**35.30**
77	**6**	**MASOODA**	**35.30**
77	**61**	**MANDALGARH**	**35.30**
79	**118**	**NOHAR**	**35.10**
80	**122**	**DUDU**	**35.00**
80	**161**	**MANDOR**	**35.00**
82	**76**	**BARI SADRI**	**34.80**
83	**180**	**MAKRANA**	**34.40**
84	**201**	**RAILMAGRA**	**34.10**
85	**55**	**ASIND**	**33.80**
86	**211**	**KHANDELA**	**33.70**
87	**32**	**ATRU**	**33.60**
87	**220**	**SIROHI**	**33.60**
89	**112**	**PADAMPUR**	**33.40**
90	**173**	**SANGOD**	**33.30**
90	**175**	**DEGANA**	**33.30**
92	**225**	**TONK**	**33.20**
93	**115**	**SURATGARH**	**33.10**
94	**157**	**BAP**	**33.00**
94	**169**	**TODABHIM**	**33.00**
96	**213**	**NEEM KA THANA**	**32.90**
97	**67**	**DUNGARGARH**	**32.80**
98	**4**	**KEKRI**	**32.60**
99	**140**	**SANCHORE**	**32.50**
100	**13**	**KOTKASIM**	**32.40**
100	**113**	**RAISINGHNAGAR**	**32.40**
102	**64**	**SHAHPURA**	**32.30**
102	**136**	**BHINMAL**	**32.30**
104	**59**	**KOTRI**	**32.20**
105	**184**	**PARBATSAR**	**32.20**
106	**109**	**ANUPGARH**	**32.10**
107	**132**	**JAISALMER**	**32.00**
108	**120**	**BASSI**	**31.80**
108	**222**	**MALPURA**	**31.80**
110	**19**	**RENI**	**31.60**
111	**7**	**PISANGAN**	**31.30**
112	**128**	**SAMBHAR**	**31.20**
113	**66**	**BIKANER**	**31.00**
114	**18**	**RAMGARH**	**30.90**
115	**223**	**NIWAI**	**30.50**
116	**15**	**MANDAWAR**	**30.30**
117	**206**	**KHANDAR**	**30.10**
	MEDIUM (20-30)		
118	**58**	**JAHAZPUR**	**29.90**
118	**68**	**KOLAYAT**	**29.90**
120	41	CHOHTAN	29.80
121	20	THANAGAZI	29.70
122	147	PIRAWA	29.60
122	165	HINDAUN	29.60
124	152	KHETRI	29.50
125	11	KATHUMAR	29.30
126	35	CHHIPABAROD	28.90
127	154	SURAJGARH	28.80
128	5	KISHANGARH	28.50
129	84	GANGRAR	28.40
130	25	GARHI	28.20
131	202	RAJSAMAND	28.00
132	69	LUNKARANSAR	27.50
132	90	RAJGARH	27.50
134	99	SIKRAI	27.30
135	178	KUCHAMAN	27.00
136	199	KHAMNOR	27.00
137	85	KAPASAN	26.70
137	216	ABU ROAD	26.70
139	38	BALOTRA	26.30
139	125	JHOTWARA	26.30
139	129	SANGANER	26.30
139	134	SANKRA	26.30
143	176	DIDWANA	26.30
144	144	JHALRAPATAN	26.20
145	78	BHADESAR	26.00
145	217	PINDWARA	26.00
147	92	SARDARSHAHAR	25.80
147	96	DAUSA	25.80
147	138	JASWANTPURA	25.80
150	155	UDAIPURWATI	25.60
151	36	KISHANGANJ	25.40
152	1	ARAIN	25.30
152	149	BUHANA	25.30
152	151	JHUNJHUNUN	25.30
155	51	NAGAR PAHARI	25.10
156	139	RANIWARA	25.00
157	145	KHANPUR	24.70
158	111	KARANPUR	24.30
159	10	BEHROR	24.10
160	164	SHERGARH	23.90
161	143	DAG	23.50
162	77	BEGUN	23.30
163	93	SUJANGARH	23.10
164	131	VIRATNAGAR	23.00
165	121	CHAKSU	22.70
166	209	DHOND	22.60
167	210	FATEHPUR	22.50
168	30	TALWARA	22.20
168	98	MAHWA	22.20
170	183	NAGAUR	22.00
171	119	AMBER	21.90
172	71	HINDOLI	21.80
173	230	GIRWA	21.70
174	107	SAGWARA	21.60
175	97	LALSOT	21.50
176	34	CHHABRA	21.20
177	102	DHAULPUR	21.10
177	235	MAVLI	21.10
179	42	DHORIMANNA	21.00
180	168	SAPOTRA	20.80
181	95	BANDIKUI	20.60
182	79	BHAINSRORGARH	20.40
183	124	JAMWA RAMGARH	20.10
	LOW (10-20)		
184	44	SINDHARI	19.60
185	74	TALERA	19.50
186	8	SRINAGAR	19.20
186	75	ARNOD	19.20
188	43	SHEO	19.10
188	172	LADPURA	19.10
190	24	BAGIDORA	18.90
190	37	SHAHBAD	18.90
192	26	GHATOL	18.40
192	198	DEOGARH	18.40
194	101	BASERI	18.20
195	21	TIJARA	17.80
196	9	BANSURE	17.30
197	12	KISHANGARH BAS	17.10
198	126	KOTPUTLI	17.00
199	170	CHECHAT	16.90
200	104	ASPUR	16.40
201	39	BARMER	16.10
201	108	SIMALWARA	16.10
203	237	SARADA	15.60
204	156	BALESAR	15.30
205	105	BICHHIWARA	14.40
206	196	AMET	14.40
207	17	RAJGARH	14.30
207	40	BAYTOO	14.30
209	212	LACHHMANGARH	14.20
210	50	NADBAI	14.00
210	197	BHIM	14.00
212	133	SAM	13.80
212	200	KUMBHALGARH	13.80
214	228	BHINDER	13.20
215	146	MANOHARTHANA	12.90
216	87	PRATAPGARH	12.50
217	232	JHADOL	12.40
218	16	NIMRANA	12.30
219	28	PEEPALKHOONT	12.20
220	46	BAYANA	11.90
221	29	SAJJANGARH	11.50
222	142	BAKANI	11.20
223	236	SALUMBAR	11.10
224	23	ANANDPURI	10.90
225	229	DHARIAWAD	10.20
226	166	KARAULI	10.00
	VERY LOW (<10)		
227	227	BARGAON	9.70
228	54	WEIR	9.60
229	234	KOTRA	9.50
230	3	JAWAJA	8.70
231	48	KAMAN	8.20
232	233	KHERWARA	7.40
233	103	RAJAKHERA	7.30
234	100	BARI	6.70
235	231	GOGUNDA	6.10
236	27	KUSHALGARH	4.60
237	106	DUNGARPUR	2.10
	RAJASTHAN		**29.90**
	%age of AAPs		**50.21**

BOLD: Equal/Above Average Panchayat Samities (AAPs)

Source: General Annex VIII, Col. 13.

ANNEX-4.16

RANKING OF PSS BY PERCENTAGE OF INHABITED VILLAGES HAVING AGRICULTURAL CREDIT SOCIETIES, 2001

(Descending Order)

RANK	P. CODE	PANCHAYAT SAMITIES NAME	%
1	2	3	4
		VERY HIGH (>=20)	
1	47	**DEEG**	53.8
2	141	**SAYLA**	40.3
3	49	**KUMHER**	37.6
4	159	**BILARA**	33.7
5	153	**NAWALGARH**	33.0
6	179	**LADNU**	32.0
7	135	**AHORE**	31.8
8	150	**CHIRAWA**	31.0
9	177	**JAYAL**	30.9
10	167	**NADOTI**	30.6
11	195	**SUMERPUR**	30.2
12	123	**GOVINDGARH**	30.0
13	53	**SEWAR**	28.7
14	182	**MUNDWA**	28.1
15	194	**SOJAT**	27.8
15	116	**BHADRA**	27.8
17	190	**PALI**	27.5
18	185	**RIYAN**	25.6
19	33	**BARAN**	25.3
20	14	**LACHHMANGARH**	25.0
21	136	**BHINMAL**	25.0
22	89	**CHURU**	24.8
23	57	**HURDA**	24.3
24	94	**TARANAGAR**	23.6
24	208	**DANTA RAMGARH**	23.6
26	163	**PHALODI**	23.4
27	175	**DEGANA**	23.0
28	161	**MANDOR**	22.9
29	215	**SRI MADHOPUR**	22.7
30	157	**BAP**	22.4
31	188	**JAITARAN**	22.3
32	137	**JALOR**	22.1
33	91	**RATANGARH**	21.8
33	189	**KHARCHI/MARWAR JUN.**	21.8
35	162	**OSIAN**	21.7
36	140	**SANCHORE**	21.6
36	181	**MERTA**	21.6
38	52	**RUPBAS**	21.1
39	165	**HINDAUN**	20.7
40	80	**BHOPALSAGAR**	20.5
41	193	**ROHAT**	20.3
42	22	**UMREN**	20.1
43	45	**SIWANA**	20.0
		HIGH (15-20)	
44	110	**GANGANAGAR**	19.8
44	186	**BALI**	19.8
46	192	**RANI STATION**	19.7
47	224	**TODARAISINGH**	19.6
47	205	**GANGAPUR**	19.5
47	207	**SAWAI MADHOPUR**	19.2
50	15	**MANDAWAR**	19.0
51	70	**NOKHA**	19.0
52	158	**BHOPALGARH**	18.6
53	88	**RASHMI**	18.5
53	148	**ALSISAR**	18.5
55	174	**SULTANPUR**	18.4
56	191	**RAIPUR**	18.3
57	169	**TODABHIM**	18.1
58	113	**RAISINGHNAGAR**	18.0
59	203	**BAMANWAS**	17.6
59	152	**KHETRI**	17.6
61	130	**SHAHPURA**	17.4
62	155	**UDAIPURWATI**	17.3
63	171	**ITAWA**	17.2
64	92	**SARDARSHAHAR**	17.1
64	176	**DIDWANA**	17.1
66	32	**ATRU**	16.9
66	66	**BIKANER**	16.9
66	90	**RAJGARH**	16.9
69	19	**RENI**	16.7
69	218	**REODAR**	16.7
71	127	**PHAGI**	16.6
72	114	**SADULSHAHAR**	16.5
73	86	**NIMBAHERA**	16.4
73	154	**SURAJGARH**	16.4
73	204	**BONLI**	16.4
76	67	**DUNGARGARH**	16.3
76	112	**PADAMPUR**	16.3
78	31	**ANTA**	16.2
79	73	**NAINWA**	16.1
80	128	**SAMBHAR**	16.0
81	214	**PIPRALI**	16.0
82	211	**KHANDELA**	15.9
83	13	**KOTKASIM**	15.7
83	56	**BANERA**	15.7
83	72	**KESHORAIPATAN**	15.7
83	220	**SIROHI**	15.7
87	7	**PISANGAN**	15.6
87	160	**LUNI**	15.6
89	109	**ANUPGARH**	15.5
89	122	**DUDU**	15.5
91	65	**SUWANA**	15.4
91	210	**FATEHPUR**	15.4
93	4	**KEKRI**	15.2
		MEDIUM (10-15)	
94	138	**JASWANTPURA**	14.9
95	183	**NAGAUR**	14.7
95	209	**DHOND**	14.7
97	11	**KATHUMAR**	14.6
97	62	**RAIPUR**	14.6
97	213	**NEEM KA THANA**	14.6
100	111	**KARANPUR**	14.5
100	115	**SURATGARH**	14.5
102	41	**CHOHTAN**	14.4
103	149	**BUHANA**	14.3
103	180	**MAKRANA**	14.3
103	201	**RAILMAGRA**	14.3
106	134	**SANKRA**	14.2
107	216	**ABU ROAD**	14.1
107	2	**BHINAY**	14.1
107	63	**SAHARA**	14.1
110	132	**JAISALMER**	14.0
111	83	**DUNGLA**	13.7
112	223	**NIWAI**	13.6
112	184	**PARBATSAR**	13.6
114	81	**CHHOTI SADRI**	13.5
115	18	**RAMGARH**	13.3
116	64	**SHAHPURA**	13.2
116	173	**SANGOD**	13.2
118	222	**MALPURA**	13.1
119	219	**SHEOGANJ**	13.0
120	93	**SUJANGARH**	12.9
121	187	**DESURI**	12.8
122	221	**DEOLI**	12.7
123	5	**KISHANGARH**	12.6
124	178	KUCHAMAN	12.4
125	42	DHORIMANNA	12.3
126	99	SIKRAI	12.2
127	59	KOTRI	12.0
128	199	KHAMNOR	11.8
128	225	TONK	11.8
130	226	UNIARA	11.7
130	78	BHADESAR	11.7
130	147	PIRAWA	11.7
130	172	LADPURA	11.7
134	126	KOTPUTLI	11.6
135	39	BARMER	11.4
135	61	MANDALGARH	11.4
137	25	GARHI	11.3
138	55	ASIND	11.3
139	1	ARAIN	11.2
139	60	MANDAL	11.2
139	98	MAHWA	11.2
142	82	CHITTAURGARH	11.0
142	118	NOHAR	11.0
144	143	DAG	10.9
144	144	JHALRAPATAN	10.9
146	6	MASOODA	10.8
147	68	KOLAYAT	10.7
147	139	RANIWARA	10.7
149	16	NIMRANA	10.6
149	51	NAGAR PAHARI	10.6
151	8	SRINAGAR	10.4
151	35	CHHIPABAROD	10.4
153	206	KHANDAR	10.3
153	85	KAPASAN	10.3
153	151	JHUNJHUNUN	10.3
153	164	SHERGARH	10.3
157	217	PINDWARA	10.1
157	58	JAHAZPUR	10.1
159	10	BEHROR	10.0
159	102	DHAULPUR	10.0
		LOW (5-10)	
161	202	RAJSAMAND	9.8
162	76	BARI SADRI	9.8
163	44	SINDHARI	9.7
164	12	KISHANGARH BAS	9.6
164	125	JHOTWARA	9.6
166	235	MAVLI	9.4
167	36	KISHANGANJ	8.9
168	43	SHEO	8.8
169	38	BALOTRA	8.7
169	40	BAYTOO	8.7
171	34	CHHABRA	8.6
171	120	BASSI	8.6
171	124	JAMWA RAMGARH	8.6
171	168	SAPOTRA	8.6
175	30	TALWARA	8.5
175	95	BANDIKUI	8.5
177	74	TALERA	8.4
177	101	BASERI	8.4
179	107	SAGWARA	8.3
179	170	CHECHAT	8.3
181	117	HANUMANGARH	8.2
182	69	LUNKARANSAR	8.1
183	156	BALESAR	8.0
184	24	BAGIDORA	7.9
185	119	AMBER	7.8
186	129	SANGANER	7.7
187	71	HINDOLI	7.5
187	131	VIRATNAGAR	7.5
189	77	BEGUN	7.2
189	96	DAUSA	7.2
191	212	LACHHMANGARH	7.1
191	84	GANGRAR	7.1
193	50	NADBAI	7.0
194	21	TIJARA	6.9
195	20	THANAGAZI	6.8
196	230	GIRWA	6.7
196	145	KHANPUR	6.7
198	79	BHAINSRORGARH	6.5
199	104	ASPUR	6.3
200	46	BAYANA	6.2
201	9	BANSURE	6.1
201	200	KUMBHALGARH	6.1
203	237	SARADA	5.9
203	26	GHATOL	5.9
203	29	SAJJANGARH	5.9
206	97	LALSOT	5.7
206	105	BICHHIWARA	5.7
208	121	CHAKSU	5.6
209	54	WEIR	5.5
210	198	DEOGARH	5.3
211	48	KAMAN	5.2
212	75	ARNOD	5.1
		VERY LOW (<5)	
213	87	PRATAPGARH	4.8
214	23	ANANDPURI	4.7
215	166	KARAULI	4.6
216	197	BHIM	4.5
217	228	BHINDER	4.3
217	17	RAJGARH	4.3
217	133	SAM	4.3
220	37	SHAHBAD	4.2
220	100	BARI	4.2
220	146	MANOHARTHANA	4.2
223	108	SIMALWARA	4.1
223	231	GOGUNDA	4.1
225	3	JAWAJA	4.0
225	233	KHERWARA	4.0
227	232	JHADOL	3.9
228	236	SALUMBAR	3.8
228	142	BAKANI	3.8
230	196	AMET	3.7
231	103	RAJAKHERA	3.5
232	28	PEEPALKHOONT	3.2
233	27	KUSHALGARH	2.9
234	234	KOTRA	2.6
235	106	DUNGARPUR	2.5
236	229	DHARIAWAD	2.4
237	227	BARGAON	1.9
		RAJASTHAN	**12.60**
		%age of AAPs	**51.90**

BOLD: Equal/Above Average Panchayat Samities (AAPs)

Source: General Annex IX, Col. 13.

ANNEX-4.17

RANKING OF PSS BY PERCENTAGE OF RURAL POP. SERVED BY TRANSPORT COMMUNICATIONS AMENITIES, 2001

RANK	P. CODE	PANCHAYAT SAMITIES NAME	%
1	2	3	4
	VERY HIGH (>=80)		
1	158	**BHOPALGARH**	**98.40**
2	141	**SAYLA**	**95.00**
3	192	**RANI STATION**	**94.50**
4	179	**LADNU**	**93.90**
5	220	**SIROHI**	**93.60**
6	209	**DHOND**	**93.40**
7	195	**SUMERPUR**	**91.40**
8	135	**AHORE**	**90.90**
9	186	**BALI**	**90.60**
10	181	**MERTA**	**90.50**
11	136	**BHINMAL**	**90.10**
12	162	**OSIAN**	**89.70**
13	194	**SOJAT**	**88.70**
14	190	**PALI**	**88.50**
15	155	**UDAIPURWATI**	**88.30**
16	175	**DEGANA**	**88.30**
17	116	**BHADRA**	**87.60**
18	153	**NAWALGARH**	**87.50**
19	212	**LACHHMANGARH**	**87.40**
20	70	**NOKHA**	**87.20**
21	150	**CHIRAWA**	**87.00**
22	187	**DESURI**	**86.30**
23	177	**JAYAL**	**85.90**
24	138	**JASWANTPURA**	**85.60**
25	182	**MUNDWA**	**85.20**
26	38	**BALOTRA**	**85.00**
27	159	**BILARA**	**84.70**
28	45	**SIWANA**	**84.50**
29	180	**MAKRANA**	**84.10**
30	67	**DUNGARGARH**	**83.90**
31	160	**LUNI**	**83.70**
32	184	**PARBATSAR**	**83.50**
33	193	**ROHAT**	**83.10**
34	110	**GANGANAGAR**	**83.00**
35	137	**JALOR**	**82.80**
36	214	**PIPRALI**	**82.60**
37	189	**KHARCHI/MARWAR JUN.**	**82.40**
38	93	**SUJANGARH**	**82.30**
39	114	**SADULSHAHAR**	**82.10**
40	208	**DANTA RAMGARH**	**82.00**
41	185	**RIYAN**	**81.40**
41	210	**FATEHPUR**	**81.40**
43	111	**KARANPUR**	**81.30**
44	92	**SARDARSHAHAR**	**80.90**
45	68	**KOLAYAT**	**80.70**
46	88	**RASHMI**	**80.60**
46	91	**RATANGARH**	**80.60**
48	176	**DIDWANA**	**80.00**
	HIGH (70-80)		
49	151	**JHUNJHUNUN**	**79.60**
50	123	**GOVINDGARH**	**79.50**
51	161	**MANDOR**	**79.30**
52	117	**HANUMANGARH**	**79.20**
52	132	**JAISALMER**	**79.20**
54	139	**RANIWARA**	**78.40**
55	57	**HURDA**	**78.30**
55	201	**RAILMAGRA**	**78.30**
57	7	**PISANGAN**	**77.90**
58	148	**ALSISAR**	**77.80**
58	196	**AMET**	**77.80**
60	215	**SRI MADHOPUR**	**77.60**
61	66	**BIKANER**	**76.90**
62	62	**RAIPUR**	**76.80**
63	107	**SAGWARA**	**76.30**
63	183	**NAGAUR**	**76.30**
63	211	**KHANDELA**	**76.30**
66	80	**BHOPALSAGAR**	**76.20**
67	41	**CHOHTAN**	**76.10**
68	133	**SAM**	**75.50**
69	152	**KHETRI**	**75.10**
70	199	**KHAMNOR**	**75.10**
71	163	**PHALODI**	**74.90**
72	118	**NOHAR**	**74.80**
73	129	**SANGANER**	**74.70**
73	157	**BAP**	**74.70**
75	134	**SANKRA**	**74.60**
76	113	**RAISINGHNAGAR**	**73.70**
77	140	**SANCHORE**	**73.60**
78	94	**TARANAGAR**	**73.50**
78	219	**SHEOGANJ**	**73.50**
80	5	**KISHANGARH**	**73.30**
81	191	**RAIPUR**	**73.10**
82	124	**JAMWA RAMGARH**	**72.80**
83	8	**SRINAGAR**	**72.70**
84	115	**SURATGARH**	**72.10**
85	63	**SAHARA**	**72.00**
86	154	**SURAJGARH**	**71.50**
87	90	**RAJGARH**	**71.30**
88	104	**ASPUR**	**71.00**
88	149	**BUHANA**	**71.00**
90	202	**RAJSAMAND**	**70.40**
91	10	**BEHROR**	**70.30**
92	69	**LUNKARANSAR**	**70.20**
	MEDIUM (60-70)		
93	178	**KUCHAMAN**	**69.80**
93	188	**JAITARAN**	**69.80**
95	60	**MANDAL**	**69.70**
95	156	**BALESAR**	**69.70**
97	125	**JHOTWARA**	**69.60**
98	230	**GIRWA**	**69.40**
99	235	**MAVLI**	**69.30**
100	25	**GARHI**	**69.10**
100	89	**CHURU**	**69.10**
102	128	**SAMBHAR**	**69.00**
103	44	**SINDHARI**	**68.50**
104	120	**BASSI**	**68.40**
105	9	**BANSURE**	**68.30**
106	65	**SUWANA**	**67.20**
107	30	**TALWARA**	**67.10**
108	200	**KUMBHALGARH**	**66.90**
109	237	**SARADA**	**66.70**
110	82	**CHITTAURGARH**	**66.40**
111	227	**BARGAON**	**66.20**
112	55	**ASIND**	**66.00**
112	197	**BHIM**	**66.00**
112	218	**REODAR**	**66.00**
115	16	**NIMRANA**	**65.90**
116	112	**PADAMPUR**	**65.60**
117	122	**DUDU**	**65.20**
118	56	**BANERA**	**65.00**
119	39	**BARMER**	**64.50**
120	119	**AMBER**	**63.80**
121	6	**MASOODA**	**63.70**
122	109	**ANUPGARH**	**63.50**
123	20	**THANAGAZI**	**63.40**
124	85	**KAPASAN**	**63.30**
125	4	**KEKRI**	**63.20**
126	231	**GOGUNDA**	**63.20**
127	2	BHINAY	62.70
128	79	BHAINSRORGARH	61.90
129	167	NADOTI	61.80
130	236	SALUMBAR	61.70
131	86	NIMBAHERA	61.40
132	105	BICHHIWARA	61.00
133	198	DEOGARH	60.70
134	42	DHORIMANNA	60.60
135	43	SHEO	60.10
135	84	GANGRAR	60.10
	LOW (50-60)		
137	217	PINDWARA	59.10
138	83	DUNGLA	58.40
139	131	VIRATNAGAR	58.30
140	130	SHAHPURA	58.10
141	216	ABU ROAD	58.00
142	76	BARI SADRI	57.70
143	228	BHINDER	57.20
144	164	SHERGARH	57.00
145	206	KHANDAR	56.70
146	229	DHARIAWAD	56.70
147	213	NEEM KA THANA	56.60
147	222	MALPURA	56.60
149	232	JHADOL	56.40
150	205	GANGAPUR	56.10
151	59	KOTRI	55.80
151	108	SIMALWARA	55.80
153	127	PHAGI	55.40
154	26	GHATOL	54.90
155	126	KOTPUTLI	54.80
156	106	DUNGARPUR	54.50
157	64	SHAHPURA	54.20
158	87	PRATAPGARH	54.00
159	15	MANDAWAR	53.90
159	61	MANDALGARH	53.90
161	166	KARAULI	53.60
162	165	HINDAUN	53.50
163	31	ANTA	53.20
164	1	ARAIN	53.00
165	96	DAUSA	52.80
166	40	BAYTOO	52.60
167	52	RUPBAS	52.30
168	77	BEGUN	52.00
169	171	ITAWA	51.60
170	24	BAGIDORA	51.20
171	203	BAMANWAS	51.00
	VERY LOW (<50)		
172	168	SAPOTRA	49.70
173	50	NADBAI	49.00
174	14	LACHHMANGARH	48.90
175	78	BHADESAR	48.80
176	32	ATRU	48.50
177	73	NAINWA	48.50
178	204	BONLI	48.50
179	207	SAWAI MADHOPUR	47.20
180	169	TODABHIM	47.00
181	233	KHERWARA	46.90
182	170	CHECHAT	46.40
183	72	KESHORAIPATAN	45.90
184	75	ARNOD	45.80
185	224	TODARAISINGH	44.80
186	221	DEOLI	44.70
187	173	SANGOD	44.50
188	223	NIWAI	44.00
189	29	SAJJANGARH	43.90
190	226	UNIARA	43.70
191	101	BASERI	43.10
192	234	KOTRA	43.10
193	81	CHHOTI SADRI	43.00
194	13	KOTKASIM	42.90
195	36	KISHANGANJ	42.90
196	58	JAHAZPUR	42.70
197	145	KHANPUR	42.60
198	46	BAYANA	42.30
199	71	HINDOLI	42.30
200	3	JAWAJA	40.70
200	11	KATHUMAR	40.70
200	174	SULTANPUR	40.70
203	18	RAMGARH	40.30
204	74	TALERA	39.60
205	23	ANANDPURI	39.30
206	97	LALSOT	38.90
207	95	BANDIKUI	38.80
208	99	SIKRAI	38.50
209	17	RAJGARH	38.30
209	143	DAG	38.30
211	54	WEIR	38.20
212	28	PEEPALKHOONT	38.10
213	33	BARAN	38.00
214	121	CHAKSU	37.50
215	19	RENI	36.70
215	147	PIRAWA	36.70
217	37	SHAHBAD	36.00
218	47	DEEG	35.60
219	35	CHHIPABAROD	35.30
220	12	KISHANGARH BAS	35.10
221	22	UMREN	34.60
222	49	KUMHER	33.50
223	144	JHALRAPATAN	33.20
224	102	DHAULPUR	32.90
225	225	TONK	32.80
226	21	TIJARA	31.50
227	53	SEWAR	30.50
228	100	BARI	30.20
229	172	LADPURA	30.00
230	142	BAKANI	29.80
231	51	NAGAR PAHARI	27.90
232	27	KUSHALGARH	26.20
233	146	MANOHARTHANA	24.10
234	48	KAMAN	22.80
235	98	MAHWA	20.50
236	103	RAJAKHERA	19.80
237	34	CHHABRA	13.10
		RAJASTHAN	**63.15**
		%age of AAPs	**53.30**

BOLD: Equal/Above Average Panchayat Samities (AAPs)

Source: General Annex VIII, Col. 11.

ANNEX-4.18

RANKING OF PSS BY PERCENTAGE OF INHABITED VILLAGES HAVING TRANSPORT COMMUNICATIONS AMENITIES: RAJASTHAN, 2001

(Descending Order)

RANK	P. CODE	PANCHAYAT SAMITIES NAME	%
1	2	3	4
	VERY HIGH (>=75)		
1	**158**	**BHOPALGARH**	**93.0**
2	**192**	**RANI STATION**	**89.5**
3	**209**	**DHOND**	**89.0**
4	**141**	**SAYLA**	**87.0**
5	**179**	**LADNU**	**86.6**
6	**195**	**SUMERPUR**	**84.1**
7	**136**	**BHINMAL**	**80.0**
8	**153**	**NAWALGARH**	**79.5**
9	**162**	**OSIAN**	**79.4**
10	**175**	**DEGANA**	**79.1**
10	**186**	**BALI**	**79.1**
12	**190**	**PALI**	**78.8**
13	**194**	**SOJAT**	**77.4**
14	**135**	**AHORE**	**75.5**
15	**155**	**UDAIPURWATI**	**75.3**
16	**212**	**LACHHMANGARH**	**75.0**
	HIGH (60-75)		
17	**137**	**JALOR**	**73.5**
17	**220**	**SIROHI**	**73.5**
19	**210**	**FATEHPUR**	**73.4**
20	**159**	**BILARA**	**73.0**
21	**150**	**CHIRAWA**	**72.6**
22	**70**	**NOKHA**	**72.3**
23	**193**	**ROHAT**	**72.2**
24	**182**	**MUNDWA**	**71.9**
25	**67**	**DUNGARGARH**	**71.7**
26	**138**	**JASWANTPURA**	**71.6**
27	**92**	**SARDARSHAHAR**	**70.6**
27	**180**	**MAKRANA**	**70.6**
29	**187**	**DESURI**	**70.5**
30	**177**	**JAYAL**	**69.9**
31	**91**	**RATANGARH**	**69.3**
32	**111**	**KARANPUR**	**69.1**
33	**93**	**SUJANGARH**	**69.0**
34	**183**	**NAGAUR**	**68.7**
35	**151**	**JHUNJHUNUN**	**68.3**
36	**184**	**PARBATSAR**	**67.3**
37	**38**	**BALOTRA**	**66.7**
38	**176**	**DIDWANA**	**66.5**
39	**196**	**AMET**	**66.2**
39	**45**	**SIWANA**	**65.2**
39	**160**	**LUNI**	**65.2**
42	**208**	**DANTA RAMGARH**	**65.0**
43	**161**	**MANDOR**	**64.8**
44	**152**	**KHETRI**	**64.7**
45	**181**	**MERTA**	**64.0**
46	**215**	**SRI MADHOPUR**	**63.6**
47	**139**	**RANIWARA**	**61.9**
48	**66**	**BIKANER**	**61.6**
49	**41**	**CHOHTAN**	**61.5**
50	**149**	**BUHANA**	**61.1**
51	**7**	**PISANGAN**	**60.9**
52	**185**	**RIYAN**	**60.8**
53	**201**	**RAILMAGRA**	**60.4**
53	**163**	**PHALODI**	**60.4**
55	**134**	**SANKRA**	**60.2**
56	**89**	**CHURU**	**60.0**
	MEDIUM (45-60)		
57	**189**	**KHARCHI/MARWAR JUN.**	**59.9**
58	**148**	**ALSISAR**	**59.7**
59	**214**	**PIPRALI**	**59.6**
60	**8**	**SRINAGAR**	**59.4**
61	**140**	**SANCHORE**	**59.3**
62	**90**	**RAJGARH**	**59.2**
63	**110**	**GANGANAGAR**	**59.1**
64	**211**	**KHANDELA**	**58.7**
65	**57**	**HURDA**	**58.6**
66	**113**	**RAISINGHNAGAR**	**58.3**
67	**154**	**SURAJGARH**	**58.2**
68	**123**	**GOVINDGARH**	**58.0**
69	**132**	**JAISALMER**	**56.6**
70	**69**	**LUNKARANSAR**	**56.3**
71	**157**	**BAP**	**56.0**
72	**44**	**SINDHARI**	**55.6**
73	**156**	**BALESAR**	**55.2**
74	**62**	**RAIPUR**	**55.1**
75	**114**	**SADULSHAHAR**	**54.9**
76	**104**	**ASPUR**	**54.5**
77	**5**	**KISHANGARH**	**54.1**
78	**112**	**PADAMPUR**	**54.0**
79	**219**	**SHEOGANJ**	**53.6**
80	**124**	**JAMWA RAMGARH**	**53.6**
81	**116**	**BHADRA**	**53.5**
82	**10**	**BEHROR**	**53.3**
83	**68**	**KOLAYAT**	**53.1**
83	**88**	**RASHMI**	**53.1**
85	**80**	**BHOPALSAGAR**	**53.0**
86	**107**	**SAGWARA**	**52.9**
87	**202**	**RAJSAMAND**	**52.3**
88	**125**	**JHOTWARA**	**52.1**
89	**237**	**SARADA**	**51.9**
90	**16**	**NIMRANA**	**51.8**
90	**39**	**BARMER**	**51.8**
92	**115**	**SURATGARH**	**51.7**
93	**197**	**BHIM**	**51.5**
93	**65**	**SUWANA**	**51.5**
95	**200**	**KUMBHALGARH**	**51.2**
96	**178**	**KUCHAMAN**	**50.8**
97	**63**	**SAHARA**	**50.5**
98	**231**	**GOGUNDA**	**50.3**
98	**129**	**SANGANER**	**50.3**
100	**199**	**KHAMNOR**	**49.7**
101	**42**	**DHORIMANNA**	**49.4**
101	**109**	**ANUPGARH**	**49.4**
103	**118**	**NOHAR**	**49.3**
103	**128**	**SAMBHAR**	**49.3**
105	**235**	**MAVLI**	**49.0**
106	**25**	**GARHI**	**48.8**
106	**43**	**SHEO**	**48.8**
108	**230**	**GIRWA**	**48.6**
109	**85**	**KAPASAN**	**47.7**
109	**191**	**RAIPUR**	**47.7**
111	**188**	**JAITARAN**	**47.6**
112	**126**	**KOTPUTLI**	**47.1**
113	**9**	**BANSURE**	**46.6**
114	**94**	**TARANAGAR**	**46.4**
115	**106**	**DUNGARPUR**	**45.9**
116	**119**	**AMBER**	**45.8**
116	**227**	**BARGAON**	**45.8**
118	**30**	**TALWARA**	**45.5**
119	**218**	**REODAR**	**45.2**
120	**55**	**ASIND**	**45.1**
121	**198**	**DEOGARH**	**45.0**
	LOW (30-45)		
122	**60**	**MANDAL**	**44.7**
123	**133**	**SAM**	**44.5**
124	**120**	**BASSI**	**44.3**
125	**2**	**BHINAY**	**43.8**
126	**40**	**BAYTOO**	**43.3**
127	**6**	**MASOODA**	**43.2**
128	**165**	**HINDAUN**	**43.0**
129	**236**	**SALUMBAR**	**42.7**
130	56	BANERA	42.2
131	105	BICHHIWARA	41.7
132	15	MANDAWAR	41.5
133	216	ABU ROAD	41.0
134	130	SHAHPURA	40.7
135	108	SIMALWARA	40.5
136	217	PINDWARA	40.4
137	232	JHADOL	40.3
138	166	KARAULI	40.0
138	167	NADOTI	40.0
140	117	HANUMANGARH	39.9
141	4	KEKRI	39.4
141	52	RUPBAS	39.4
143	213	NEEM KA THANA	39.1
144	79	BHAINSRORGARH	39.0
145	82	CHITTAURGARH	39.0
146	86	NIMBAHERA	38.8
147	228	BHINDER	38.7
148	229	DHARIAWAD	38.6
149	20	THANAGAZI	38.5
150	206	KHANDAR	37.4
150	164	SHERGARH	37.4
152	76	BARI SADRI	37.1
153	26	GHATOL	36.4
153	64	SHAHPURA	36.4
155	205	GANGAPUR	36.3
156	122	DUDU	36.1
157	233	KHERWARA	35.6
158	83	DUNGLA	35.3
159	29	SAJJANGARH	35.1
160	131	VIRATNAGAR	35.0
161	77	BEGUN	34.2
162	24	BAGIDORA	33.9
162	84	GANGRAR	33.9
162	87	PRATAPGARH	33.9
165	222	MALPURA	33.8
165	31	ANTA	33.8
167	50	NADBAI	33.3
168	14	LACHHMANGARH	32.1
169	3	JAWAJA	31.7
170	203	BAMANWAS	31.6
171	81	CHHOTI SADRI	31.2
172	169	TODABHIM	30.6
173	1	ARAIN	30.4
174	127	PHAGI	30.2
	VERY LOW (<30)		
175	11	KATHUMAR	29.7
175	59	KOTRI	29.7
177	72	KESHORAIPATAN	29.6
178	78	BHADESAR	28.8
179	32	ATRU	28.7
180	61	MANDALGARH	28.5
181	168	SAPOTRA	28.1
182	46	BAYANA	28.0
183	23	ANANDPURI	27.9
184	170	CHECHAT	27.8
185	75	ARNOD	27.0
186	96	DAUSA	26.9
187	173	SANGOD	26.4
188	101	BASERI	26.3
189	234	KOTRA	26.2
190	13	KOTKASIM	26.1
190	73	NAINWA	26.1
192	204	BONLI	25.8
193	33	BARAN	25.3
194	53	SEWAR	24.8
194	74	TALERA	24.8
196	54	WEIR	24.7
197	58	JAHAZPUR	24.4
198	17	RAJGARH	24.3
199	71	HINDOLI	24.1
200	100	BARI	23.8
201	207	SAWAI MADHOPUR	23.7
201	12	KISHANGARH BAS	23.7
201	95	BANDIKUI	22.7
201	171	ITAWA	22.7
205	172	LADPURA	22.1
206	18	RAMGARH	22.0
206	27	KUSHALGARH	22.0
208	221	DEOLI	21.8
208	21	TIJARA	21.8
210	99	SIKRAI	21.6
211	22	UMREN	21.5
212	28	PEEPALKHOONT	21.4
213	47	DEEG	21.0
214	143	DAG	20.4
215	147	PIRAWA	20.0
216	226	UNIARA	19.9
216	223	NIWAI	19.9
218	102	DHAULPUR	19.7
219	224	TODARAISINGH	19.6
219	174	SULTANPUR	19.6
221	19	RENI	18.6
222	35	CHHIPABAROD	18.5
223	121	CHAKSU	18.4
224	36	KISHANGANJ	18.3
225	144	JHALRAPATAN	18.2
226	49	KUMHER	17.9
227	97	LALSOT	17.3
228	103	RAJAKHERA	17.1
229	145	KHANPUR	16.6
230	51	NAGAR PAHARI	16.2
231	225	TONK	15.1
232	142	BAKANI	14.9
233	146	MANOHARTHANA	14.8
234	37	SHAHBAD	14.4
235	48	KAMAN	12.9
236	98	MAHWA	9.9
237	34	CHHABRA	9.7
		RAJASTHAN	**42.70**
		%age of AAPs	**54.40**

BOLD: Equal/Above Average Panchayat Samities (AAPs)

Source: General Annex IX, Col. 11.

ANNEX-4.19

RANKING OF PSS BY PERCENTAGE OF RURAL POP. SERVED BY TELEPHONE AMENITIES: RAJASTHAN, 2001

RANK	P. CODE	PANCHAYAT SAMITIES NAME	%
1	2	3	4
	VERY HIGH (>=80)		
1	91	**RATANGARH**	98.00
2	195	**SUMERPUR**	97.70
3	192	**RANI STATION**	96.60
4	153	**NAWALGARH**	96.30
5	186	**BALI**	95.90
6	1	**ARAIN**	94.80
7	189	**KHARCHI/MARWAR JUN.**	94.10
8	194	**SOJAT**	94.00
8	220	**SIROHI**	94.00
10	190	**PALI**	93.70
11	150	**CHIRAWA**	93.40
12	141	**SAYLA**	92.70
13	202	**RAJSAMAND**	92.40
13	114	**SADULSHAHAR**	92.20
15	151	**JHUNJHUNUN**	92.10
16	57	**HURDA**	92.00
17	110	**GANGANAGAR**	91.90
18	63	**SAHARA**	91.80
19	210	**FATEHPUR**	91.70
20	209	**DHOND**	91.50
21	235	**MAVLI**	91.00
22	187	**DESURI**	89.90
22	214	**PIPRALI**	89.90
24	56	**BANERA**	89.50
25	215	**SRI MADHOPUR**	89.30
26	4	**KEKRI**	89.20
27	8	**SRINAGAR**	88.30
28	208	**DANTA RAMGARH**	87.90
29	159	**BILARA**	87.80
30	7	**PISANGAN**	87.30
31	5	**KISHANGARH**	87.10
32	160	**LUNI**	86.80
33	219	**SHEOGANJ**	86.50
34	111	**KARANPUR**	86.40
35	177	**JAYAL**	85.50
36	212	**LACHHMANGARH**	85.20
37	135	**AHORE**	84.30
38	158	**BHOPALGARH**	84.20
39	155	**UDAIPURWATI**	84.10
40	191	**RAIPUR**	83.90
41	154	**SURAJGARH**	83.60
42	161	**MANDOR**	82.70
43	136	**BHINMAL**	82.60
44	45	**SIWANA**	82.50
44	67	**DUNGARGARH**	82.50
46	50	**NADBAI**	82.30
47	62	**RAIPUR**	82.20
48	180	**MAKRANA**	82.00
49	112	**PADAMPUR**	81.90
50	125	**JHOTWARA**	81.70
50	138	**JASWANTPURA**	81.70
52	213	**NEEM KA THANA**	81.40
53	137	**JALOR**	81.30
54	207	**SAWAI MADHOPUR**	80.70
55	218	**REODAR**	80.20
56	188	**JAITARAN**	80.10
	HIGH (70-80)		
57	123	**GOVINDGARH**	79.90
58	49	**KUMHER**	79.40
58	181	**MERTA**	79.40
60	165	**HINDAUN**	79.10
61	172	**LADPURA**	78.50
62	6	**MASOODA**	78.40
62	10	**BEHROR**	78.40
62	22	**UMREN**	78.40
65	12	**KISHANGARH BAS**	78.30
66	193	**ROHAT**	78.10
67	20	**THANAGAZI**	77.50
68	128	**SAMBHAR**	77.40
69	88	**RASHMI**	77.30
69	148	**ALSISAR**	77.30
71	65	**SUWANA**	76.80
71	175	**DEGANA**	76.80
73	116	**BHADRA**	76.60
74	38	**BALOTRA**	76.00
75	129	**SANGANER**	75.80
76	2	**BHINAY**	75.50
77	217	**PINDWARA**	75.20
78	126	**KOTPUTLI**	74.40
79	117	**HANUMANGARH**	74.30
79	201	**RAILMAGRA**	74.30
81	113	**RAISINGHNAGAR**	74.10
82	199	**KHAMNOR**	74.00
83	82	**CHITTAURGARH**	73.80
84	184	**PARBATSAR**	73.50
85	204	**BONLI**	73.30
85	211	**KHANDELA**	73.30
87	162	**OSIAN**	73.10
88	47	**DEEG**	72.70
89	15	**MANDAWAR**	72.60
90	84	**GANGRAR**	72.50
91	11	**KATHUMAR**	72.40
92	53	**SEWAR**	72.20
93	55	**ASIND**	71.90
94	89	**CHURU**	71.80
95	94	**TARANAGAR**	71.80
96	32	**ATRU**	71.40
97	130	**SHAHPURA**	71.30
98	80	**BHOPALSAGAR**	70.80
99	134	**SANKRA**	70.80
100	14	**LACHHMANGARH**	70.20
	MEDIUM (60-70)		
101	223	**NIWAI**	69.90
102	83	**DUNGLA**	69.80
103	196	**AMET**	69.70
104	152	**KHETRI**	69.60
105	170	**CHECHAT**	69.40
106	198	**DEOGARH**	69.30
107	18	**RAMGARH**	68.70
108	122	**DUDU**	68.60
109	3	**JAWAJA**	67.90
110	60	**MANDAL**	67.60
111	107	**SAGWARA**	67.00
112	96	**DAUSA**	66.30
113	221	**DEOLI**	66.30
114	133	**SAM**	66.10
115	176	**DIDWANA**	65.80
116	132	**JAISALMER**	64.90
117	19	**RENI**	64.70
118	216	**ABU ROAD**	64.20
119	118	**NOHAR**	64.10
120	183	**NAGAUR**	64.00
121	9	BANSURE	63.60
122	139	RANIWARA	63.50
123	61	MANDALGARH	63.40
124	90	RAJGARH	63.30
124	98	MAHWA	63.30
126	149	BUHANA	63.10
126	222	MALPURA	63.10
128	54	WEIR	62.60
129	230	GIRWA	62.20
130	64	SHAHPURA	62.10
131	179	LADNU	61.80
132	227	BARGAON	61.60
133	185	RIYAN	61.40
134	81	CHHOTI SADRI	60.80
135	33	BARAN	60.70
135	145	KHANPUR	60.70
137	52	RUPBAS	60.50
138	228	BHINDER	60.00
	LOW (50-60)		
139	178	KUCHAMAN	59.90
140	25	GARHI	59.60
141	42	DHORIMANNA	58.80
141	119	AMBER	58.80
143	197	BHIM	58.70
144	13	KOTKASIM	58.60
145	231	GOGUNDA	58.50
146	144	JHALRAPATAN	58.00
147	44	SINDHARI	57.90
148	31	ANTA	57.70
148	58	JAHAZPUR	57.70
148	104	ASPUR	57.40
148	169	TODABHIM	57.40
152	70	NOKHA	57.30
152	115	SURATGARH	57.30
154	173	SANGOD	57.10
154	224	TODARAISINGH	57.10
156	16	NIMRANA	57.00
157	163	PHALODI	56.60
158	21	TIJARA	56.30
159	120	BASSI	55.70
160	171	ITAWA	55.60
161	205	GANGAPUR	55.50
162	51	NAGAR PAHARI	55.40
162	93	SUJANGARH	55.40
164	226	UNIARA	54.70
165	156	BALESAR	54.60
166	59	KOTRI	54.40
167	109	ANUPGARH	54.30
167	225	TONK	54.30
169	92	SARDARSHAHAR	54.20
169	174	SULTANPUR	54.20
171	41	CHOHTAN	54.10
172	131	VIRATNAGAR	53.90
173	140	SANCHORE	53.80
174	17	RAJGARH	53.60
175	106	DUNGARPUR	53.20
176	206	KHANDAR	52.90
177	36	KISHANGANJ	52.80
178	237	SARADA	52.70
179	147	PIRAWA	51.40
180	69	LUNKARANSAR	51.30
181	85	KAPASAN	51.10
182	95	BANDIKUI	50.30
183	77	BEGUN	50.20
184	127	PHAGI	50.00
	VERY LOW (<50)		
185	30	TALWARA	49.40
186	40	BAYTOO	49.30
187	164	SHERGARH	49.10
187	200	KUMBHALGARH	49.10
189	203	BAMANWAS	49.00
190	71	HINDOLI	48.60
191	43	SHEO	48.10
191	233	KHERWARA	48.10
193	108	SIMALWARA	47.40
194	66	BIKANER	47.10
194	86	NIMBAHERA	47.10
194	105	BICHHIWARA	47.10
194	229	DHARIAWAD	47.10
198	35	CHHIPABAROD	46.70
199	101	BASERI	45.40
200	73	NAINWA	44.80
201	78	BHADESAR	44.50
202	182	MUNDWA	44.30
203	97	LALSOT	44.10
204	24	BAGIDORA	43.90
205	99	SIKRAI	43.40
206	74	TALERA	43.30
206	143	DAG	43.30
208	157	BAP	42.50
209	76	BARI SADRI	41.80
210	39	BARMER	41.60
210	102	DHAULPUR	41.60
210	103	RAJAKHERA	41.60
213	236	SALUMBAR	41.00
214	26	GHATOL	40.90
215	37	SHAHBAD	37.90
216	68	KOLAYAT	37.60
217	124	JAMWA RAMGARH	37.00
218	34	CHHABRA	36.90
219	167	NADOTI	36.10
220	142	BAKANI	33.20
221	232	JHADOL	32.10
222	100	BARI	30.60
223	72	KESHORAIPATAN	30.40
224	121	CHAKSU	30.00
225	48	KAMAN	29.90
226	146	MANOHARTHANA	29.50
227	168	SAPOTRA	29.40
228	166	KARAULI	28.90
229	46	BAYANA	27.80
230	87	PRATAPGARH	24.20
231	75	ARNOD	23.80
232	28	PEEPALKHOONT	23.50
233	29	SAJJANGARH	22.60
234	27	KUSHALGARH	21.10
235	23	ANANDPURI	13.00
236	79	BHAINSRORGARH	12.10
237	234	KOTRA	11.20
		RAJASTHAN	**63.99**
		%age of AAPs	**50.63**

BOLD: Equal/Above Average Panchayat Samities (AAPs)

Source: General Annex VIII, Col. 10.

ANNEX-4.20

RANKING OF PSS BY PERCENTAGE OF INHABITED VILLAGES HAVING TELEPHONE AMENITIES: RAJASTHAN, 2001

(Descending Order)

RANK	P. CODE	PANCHAYAT SAMITIES NAME	%
1	2	3	4
		VERY HIGH (>75)	
1	195	**SUMERPUR**	93.7
2	91	**RATANGARH**	93.1
3	153	**NAWALGARH**	90.9
4	1	**ARAIN**	89.6
5	186	**BALI**	89.0
6	192	**RANI STATION**	88.2
7	151	**JHUNJHUNUN**	87.6
8	190	**PALI**	87.5
9	209	**DHOND**	87.2
10	150	**CHIRAWA**	86.9
11	4	**KEKRI**	85.9
12	210	**FATEHPUR**	85.3
13	194	**SOJAT**	85.2
14	202	**RAJSAMAND**	84.8
15	189	**KHARCHI/MARWAR JUN.**	84.5
16	141	**SAYLA**	84.4
17	57	**HURDA**	84.3
18	235	**MAVLI**	81.2
19	137	**JALOR**	80.9
20	215	**SRI MADHOPUR**	80.3
21	7	**PISANGAN**	79.7
22	154	**SURAJGARH**	78.7
23	212	**LACHHMANGARH**	78.6
24	220	**SIROHI**	78.3
25	67	**DUNGARGARH**	77.2
26	187	**DESURI**	76.9
27	177	**JAYAL**	76.5
28	50	**NADBAI**	76.3
29	63	**SAHARA**	75.8
30	155	**UDAIPURWATI**	75.3
30	159	**BILARA**	75.3
		HIGH (60-75)	
32	111	**KARANPUR**	74.9
33	160	**LUNI**	74.8
34	56	**BANERA**	74.7
35	8	**SRINAGAR**	74.0
36	136	**BHINMAL**	73.8
37	110	**GANGANAGAR**	73.5
38	208	**DANTA RAMGARH**	73.2
39	193	**ROHAT**	72.2
40	5	**KISHANGARH**	72.1
41	2	**BHINAY**	71.9
42	161	**MANDOR**	71.4
43	214	**PIPRALI**	71.3
44	165	**HINDAUN**	71.1
45	112	**PADAMPUR**	70.3
46	158	**BHOPALGARH**	69.8
47	135	**AHORE**	68.2
48	219	**SHEOGANJ**	66.7
49	126	**KOTPUTLI**	66.1
50	12	**KISHANGARH BAS**	65.9
51	138	**JASWANTPURA**	64.9
51	207	**SAWAI MADHOPUR**	64.7
53	180	**MAKRANA**	64.7
54	148	**ALSISAR**	64.5
55	218	**REODAR**	64.3
56	6	**MASOODA**	63.3
57	125	**JHOTWARA**	63.0
58	175	**DEGANA**	62.8
59	45	**SIWANA**	62.6
60	128	**SAMBHAR**	62.5
61	38	**BALOTRA**	62.3
62	123	**GOVINDGARH**	62.0
63	213	**NEEM KA THANA**	61.6
63	201	**RAILMAGRA**	61.5
65	49	**KUMHER**	61.5
66	47	**DEEG**	61.3
67	53	**SEWAR**	61.1
68	89	**CHURU**	61.0
69	134	**SANKRA**	60.8
70	62	**RAIPUR**	60.7
70	162	**OSIAN**	60.6
72	191	**RAIPUR**	60.6
73	10	**BEHROR**	60.0
		MEDIUM (45-60)	
74	32	**ATRU**	59.6
75	198	**DEOGARH**	59.5
76	172	**LADPURA**	59.3
77	15	**MANDAWAR**	59.2
77	188	**JAITARAN**	59.2
79	22	**UMREN**	59.1
79	184	**PARBATSAR**	59.1
81	196	**AMET**	58.8
81	65	**SUWANA**	58.8
83	11	**KATHUMAR**	58.2
84	3	**JAWAJA**	57.8
84	181	**MERTA**	56.8
84	130	**SHAHPURA**	55.8
87	113	**RAISINGHNAGAR**	55.6
87	217	**PINDWARA**	55.6
89	204	**BONLI**	55.3
90	211	**KHANDELA**	54.8
91	90	**RAJGARH**	54.5
92	129	**SANGANER**	53.8
93	199	**KHAMNOR**	53.5
94	55	**ASIND**	53.4
95	183	**NAGAUR**	53.3
96	152	**KHETRI**	52.9
97	114	**SADULSHAHAR**	51.9
98	14	**LACHHMANGARH**	51.6
99	149	**BUHANA**	50.8
100	20	**THANAGAZI**	50.7
101	33	**BARAN**	50.5
102	42	**DHORIMANNA**	50.2
103	83	**DUNGLA**	50.0
103	170	**CHECHAT**	50.0
105	84	**GANGRAR**	49.6
106	88	**RASHMI**	49.4
107	139	**RANIWARA**	48.8
108	216	**ABU ROAD**	48.7
109	169	**TODABHIM**	48.6
110	44	**SINDHARI**	48.3
111	52	**RUPBAS**	47.9
111	54	**WEIR**	47.9
113	145	**KHANPUR**	47.7
114	122	**DUDU**	47.5
115	156	**BALESAR**	47.2
116	176	**DIDWANA**	46.5
117	223	**NIWAI**	46.1
117	221	**DEOLI**	46.1
119	82	**CHITTAURGARH**	45.9
120	80	**BHOPALSAGAR**	45.8
121	98	**MAHWA**	45.4
122	230	**GIRWA**	45.3
123	18	**RAMGARH**	45.1
124	9	**BANSURE**	45.0
124	64	**SHAHPURA**	45.0
124	163	**PHALODI**	45.0
		LOW (30-45)	
127	132	**JAISALMER**	44.8
128	60	**MANDAL**	44.7
129	224	**TODARAISINGH**	44.6
129	93	**SUJANGARH**	44.5
131	94	**TARANAGAR**	44.5
131	119	**AMBER**	44.3
133	179	**LADNU**	44.3
134	144	JHALRAPATAN	43.2
135	70	NOKHA	43.1
135	107	SAGWARA	42.7
137	178	KUCHAMAN	42.5
138	205	GANGAPUR	42.5
139	92	SARDARSHAHAR	42.4
140	197	BHIM	41.7
140	173	SANGOD	41.6
140	16	NIMRANA	41.2
143	19	RENI	41.2
143	31	ANTA	41.2
145	227	BARGAON	41.1
145	25	GARHI	41.1
147	40	BAYTOO	40.9
148	106	DUNGARPUR	40.9
149	231	GOGUNDA	40.8
150	140	SANCHORE	40.7
151	104	ASPUR	40.6
152	58	JAHAZPUR	40.1
153	13	KOTKASIM	40.0
154	51	NAGAR PAHARI	39.8
155	116	BHADRA	39.4
156	133	SAM	39.1
157	96	DAUSA	39.0
158	222	MALPURA	38.5
159	185	RIYAN	38.4
160	237	SARADA	37.8
161	118	NOHAR	37.1
162	21	TIJARA	36.6
163	41	CHOHTAN	36.4
164	61	MANDALGARH	36.3
165	81	CHHOTI SADRI	36.2
165	174	SULTANPUR	36.2
167	117	HANUMANGARH	35.8
168	69	LUNKARANSAR	35.6
168	233	KHERWARA	35.6
170	59	KOTRI	35.4
171	43	SHEO	35.2
172	200	KUMBHALGARH	33.5
173	103	RAJAKHERA	33.2
174	225	TONK	32.8
175	203	BAMANWAS	32.4
176	66	BIKANER	32.0
177	206	KHANDAR	31.6
178	228	BHINDER	31.5
179	120	BASSI	31.4
179	182	MUNDWA	31.4
181	30	TALWARA	31.0
181	71	HINDOLI	31.0
183	95	BANDIKUI	30.8
183	164	SHERGARH	30.8
183	115	SURATGARH	30.3
186	36	KISHANGANJ	30.0
		VERY LOW (<30)	
187	109	ANUPGARH	29.9
188	147	PIRAWA	29.8
189	127	PHAGI	29.6
189	157	BAP	29.6
191	77	BEGUN	29.3
191	102	DHAULPUR	29.3
193	108	SIMALWARA	29.1
194	74	TALERA	29.0
194	85	KAPASAN	29.0
196	17	RAJGARH	28.6
197	39	BARMER	28.3
197	131	VIRATNAGAR	28.3
199	226	UNIARA	28.1
200	105	BICHHIWARA	27.4
201	35	CHHIPABAROD	27.2
202	171	ITAWA	27.0
203	73	NAINWA	26.7
204	86	NIMBAHERA	26.3
205	26	GHATOL	25.5
206	229	DHARIAWAD	25.3
206	101	BASERI	25.3
208	34	CHHABRA	24.7
209	99	SIKRAI	24.5
210	236	SALUMBAR	24.4
211	143	DAG	24.0
212	24	BAGIDORA	22.4
213	46	BAYANA	21.7
214	37	SHAHBAD	21.6
215	124	JAMWA RAMGARH	21.0
216	68	KOLAYAT	20.4
217	27	KUSHALGARH	19.6
218	97	LALSOT	19.3
219	78	BHADESAR	19.0
219	100	BARI	19.0
221	167	NADOTI	18.8
222	48	KAMAN	18.0
223	142	BAKANI	17.6
224	72	KESHORAIPATAN	17.0
225	146	MANOHARTHANA	16.2
226	76	BARI SADRI	15.4
227	121	CHAKSU	15.4
228	232	JHADOL	15.1
229	166	KARAULI	14.4
230	168	SAPOTRA	14.3
231	29	SAJJANGARH	13.0
231	87	PRATAPGARH	12.4
233	28	PEEPALKHOONT	12.3
234	23	ANANDPURI	10.1
235	75	ARNOD	9.0
236	234	KOTRA	5.3
237	79	BHAINSRORGARH	1.9
		RAJASTHAN	**43.60**
		%age of AAPs	**56.10**

BOLD: Equal/Above Average Panchayat Samities (AAPs) *Source*: General Annex IX, Col. 10.

ANNEX-4.21

RANKING OF PSS BY PERCENTAGE OF RURAL POP. SERVED BY BANK AMENITIES : RAJASTHAN, 2001

RANK	P. CODE	PANCHAYAT SAMITIES NAME	%
1	2	3	4
	VERY HIGH (>=25)		
1	190	**PALI**	41.20
2	192	**RANI STATION**	39.90
3	187	**DESURI**	39.60
4	188	**JAITARAN**	38.50
5	220	**SIROHI**	37.10
6	80	**BHOPALSAGAR**	36.90
7	181	**MERTA**	36.70
8	57	**HURDA**	35.10
9	191	**RAIPUR**	34.60
10	186	**BALI**	34.10
11	110	**GANGANAGAR**	33.90
12	214	**PIPRALI**	33.30
13	123	**GOVINDGARH**	33.00
14	94	**TARANAGAR**	32.60
14	189	**KHARCHI/MARWAR JUN.**	32.60
16	222	**MALPURA**	32.40
17	174	**SULTANPUR**	32.20
18	31	**ANTA**	31.40
19	66	**BIKANER**	31.30
20	49	**KUMHER**	31.00
21	70	**NOKHA**	30.80
22	219	**SHEOGANJ**	30.40
23	195	**SUMERPUR**	29.70
23	207	**SAWAI MADHOPUR**	29.70
25	67	**DUNGARGARH**	29.50
25	158	**BHOPALGARH**	29.50
25	171	**ITAWA**	29.50
28	194	**SOJAT**	29.20
29	5	**KISHANGARH**	29.00
30	69	**LUNKARANSAR**	29.00
31	159	**BILARA**	28.90
32	135	**AHORE**	28.50
33	91	**RATANGARH**	28.20
34	107	**SAGWARA**	28.00
35	45	**SIWANA**	27.70
36	204	**BONLI**	27.60
36	208	**DANTA RAMGARH**	27.60
38	2	**BHINAY**	27.40
38	185	**RIYAN**	27.40
40	148	**ALSISAR**	27.20
41	65	**SUWANA**	27.10
41	227	**BARGAON**	27.10
43	167	**NADOTI**	26.80
44	1	**ARAIN**	26.30
44	19	**RENI**	26.30
44	25	**GARHI**	26.30
44	215	**SRI MADHOPUR**	26.30
48	137	**JALOR**	26.10
49	114	**SADULSHAHAR**	25.80
50	116	**BHADRA**	25.60
51	68	**KOLAYAT**	25.40
52	32	**ATRU**	25.20
	HIGH (20-25)		
53	180	**MAKRANA**	24.90
54	4	**KEKRI**	24.80
54	61	**MANDALGARH**	24.80
54	99	**SIKRAI**	24.80
57	96	**DAUSA**	24.70
58	13	**KOTKASIM**	24.40
59	56	**BANERA**	24.20
60	10	**BEHROR**	24.10
60	205	**GANGAPUR**	24.10
62	221	**DEOLI**	23.80
63	201	**RAILMAGRA**	23.50
64	117	**HANUMANGARH**	23.40
64	150	**CHIRAWA**	23.40
64	179	**LADNU**	23.40
64	213	**NEEM KA THANA**	23.40
68	217	**PINDWARA**	23.20
69	36	**KISHANGANJ**	23.00
70	16	**NIMRANA**	22.80
71	193	**ROHAT**	22.70
72	76	**BARI SADRI**	22.60
72	131	**VIRATNAGAR**	22.60
72	141	**SAYLA**	22.50
72	161	**MANDOR**	22.50
76	20	**THANAGAZI**	22.40
77	104	**ASPUR**	22.40
78	38	**BALOTRA**	22.20
78	130	**SHAHPURA**	22.20
78	184	**PARBATSAR**	22.20
81	74	**TALERA**	22.10
82	218	**REODAR**	22.00
83	78	**BHADESAR**	21.90
84	7	**PISANGAN**	21.80
85	235	**MAVLI**	21.70
86	226	**UNIARA**	21.60
87	122	**DUDU**	21.50
88	8	**SRINAGAR**	21.40
89	50	**NADBAI**	21.30
89	95	**BANDIKUI**	21.30
91	11	**KATHUMAR**	20.90
91	119	**AMBER**	20.90
91	138	**JASWANTPURA**	20.90
91	163	**PHALODI**	20.90
95	82	**CHITTAURGARH**	20.80
96	60	**MANDAL**	20.70
96	84	**GANGRAR**	20.70
96	209	**DHOND**	20.70
99	62	**RAIPUR**	20.60
99	63	**SAHARA**	20.60
101	53	**SEWAR**	20.50
101	89	**CHURU**	20.50
101	132	**JAISALMER**	20.50
101	202	**RAJSAMAND**	20.50
105	24	**BAGIDORA**	20.40
105	97	**LALSOT**	20.40
105	173	**SANGOD**	20.40
108	176	**DIDWANA**	20.30
109	162	**OSIAN**	20.20
109	230	**GIRWA**	20.20
111	73	**NAINWA**	20.10
112	55	**ASIND**	20.00
112	223	**NIWAI**	20.00
	MEDIUM (15-20)		
114	211	**KHANDELA**	19.60
115	120	**BASSI**	19.50
116	9	**BANSURE**	19.40
116	93	**SUJANGARH**	19.40
116	182	**MUNDWA**	19.40
119	228	**BHINDER**	19.30
120	51	NAGAR PAHARI	19.20
120	170	CHECHAT	19.20
122	145	KHANPUR	19.10
123	147	PIRAWA	18.80
124	178	KUCHAMAN	18.70
125	118	NOHAR	18.60
126	54	WEIR	18.50
126	160	LUNI	18.50
126	237	SARADA	18.50
129	168	SAPOTRA	18.40
130	124	JAMWA RAMGARH	18.20
131	26	GHATOL	18.10
132	83	DUNGLA	18.00
133	18	RAMGARH	17.90
134	127	PHAGI	17.90
135	139	RANIWARA	17.90
136	30	TALWARA	17.70
137	112	PADAMPUR	17.60
137	136	BHINMAL	17.60
137	155	UDAIPURWATI	17.60
140	175	DEGANA	17.30
140	177	JAYAL	17.30
142	6	MASOODA	17.20
142	157	BAP	17.20
144	108	SIMALWARA	17.00
144	143	DAG	17.00
144	203	BAMANWAS	17.00
147	128	SAMBHAR	16.90
147	212	LACHHMANGARH	16.90
149	52	RUPBAS	16.70
149	172	LADPURA	16.70
149	225	TONK	16.70
152	22	UMREN	16.40
153	142	BAKANI	16.30
154	121	CHAKSU	16.20
155	216	ABU ROAD	16.10
156	15	MANDAWAR	16.00
156	71	HINDOLI	16.00
158	21	TIJARA	15.70
158	129	SANGANER	15.70
160	14	LACHHMANGARH	15.60
161	153	NAWALGARH	15.50
162	75	ARNOD	15.40
163	47	DEEG	15.30
163	77	BEGUN	15.30
	LOW (10-15)		
165	102	DHAULPUR	14.80
165	144	JHALRAPATAN	14.80
167	37	SHAHBAD	14.70
167	90	RAJGARH	14.70
169	59	KOTRI	14.30
170	64	SHAHPURA	14.20
170	133	SAM	14.20
170	140	SANCHORE	14.20
173	72	KESHORAIPATAN	14.10
173	197	BHIM	14.10
175	46	BAYANA	13.80
175	86	NIMBAHERA	13.80
175	198	DEOGARH	13.80
178	17	RAJGARH	13.70
179	199	KHAMNOR	13.30
180	152	KHETRI	13.00
181	28	PEEPALKHOONT	12.90
181	164	SHERGARH	12.90
183	101	BASERI	12.80
183	126	KOTPUTLI	12.80
185	12	KISHANGARH BAS	12.60
185	224	TODARAISINGH	12.60
187	3	JAWAJA	12.50
188	35	CHHIPABAROD	12.40
188	58	JAHAZPUR	12.40
188	166	KARAULI	12.40
191	125	JHOTWARA	12.30
191	200	KUMBHALGARH	12.30
193	81	CHHOTI SADRI	12.10
194	165	HINDAUN	12.00
195	134	SANKRA	11.80
195	183	NAGAUR	11.80
197	85	KAPASAN	11.60
197	105	BICHHIWARA	11.60
199	196	AMET	11.40
200	156	BALESAR	11.30
201	236	SALUMBAR	11.20
202	33	BARAN	11.10
203	206	KHANDAR	11.00
204	92	SARDARSHAHAR	10.80
205	48	KAMAN	10.50
206	231	GOGUNDA	10.40
207	41	CHOHTAN	10.20
207	106	DUNGARPUR	10.20
209	169	TODABHIM	10.00
	VERY LOW (<10)		
210	43	SHEO	9.60
211	87	PRATAPGARH	9.50
212	98	MAHWA	9.40
212	210	FATEHPUR	9.40
214	154	SURAJGARH	9.30
215	42	DHORIMANNA	8.90
215	109	ANUPGARH	8.90
215	232	JHADOL	8.90
218	79	BHAINSRORGARH	8.80
219	40	BAYTOO	8.60
220	234	KOTRA	8.40
221	29	SAJJANGARH	8.10
221	229	DHARIAWAD	8.10
223	115	SURATGARH	8.00
224	149	BUHANA	7.90
225	44	SINDHARI	7.60
226	111	KARANPUR	7.20
227	23	ANANDPURI	7.10
228	88	RASHMI	7.00
229	151	JHUNJHUNUN	6.10
230	100	BARI	6.00
231	233	KHERWARA	5.50
232	113	RAISINGHNAGAR	5.40
233	39	BARMER	4.70
234	146	MANOHARTHANA	4.70
235	27	KUSHALGARH	3.80
235	34	CHHABRA	3.80
237	103	RAJAKHERA	3.30
		RAJASTHAN	**19.30**
		%age of AAPs	**50.21**

BOLD: Equal/Above Average Panchayat Samities (AAPs) *Source*: General Annex VIII, Col. 12.

ANNEX-4.22

RANKING OF PSS BY PERCENTAGE OF INHABITED VILLAGES HAVING BANK AMENITIES: RAJASTHAN, 2001

(Descending Order)

RANK	P. CODE	PANCHAYAT SAMITIES NAME	%
1	2	3	4
	VERY HIGH (>=7)		
1	190	PALI	17.5
2	192	RANI STATION	15.8
3	49	KUMHER	14.5
4	215	SRI MADHOPUR	13.6
5	220	SIROHI	13.3
6	70	NOKHA	13.1
7	67	DUNGARGARH	13.0
8	189	KHARCHI/MARWAR JUN.	12.7
8	195	SUMERPUR	12.7
10	188	JAITARAN	12.6
11	194	SOJAT	12.2
12	66	BIKANER	11.9
12	91	RATANGARH	11.9
14	16	NIMRANA	11.8
15	50	NADBAI	11.4
15	57	HURDA	11.4
17	123	GOVINDGARH	11.0
18	163	PHALODI	10.8
19	214	PIPRALI	10.6
19	205	GANGAPUR	10.6
21	158	BHOPALGARH	10.5
22	1	ARAIN	10.4
22	141	SAYLA	10.4
24	187	DESURI	10.3
25	219	SHEOGANJ	10.1
25	193	ROHAT	10.1
25	25	GARHI	10.1
25	31	ANTA	10.1
25	159	BILARA	10.1
25	191	RAIPUR	10.1
25	209	DHOND	10.1
32	135	AHORE	10.0
32	136	BHINMAL	10.0
34	213	NEEM KA THANA	9.9
34	5	KISHANGARH	9.9
34	181	MERTA	9.9
34	186	BALI	9.9
38	208	DANTA RAMGARH	9.6
39	89	CHURU	9.5
40	8	SRINAGAR	9.4
40	69	LUNKARANSAR	9.4
40	167	NADOTI	9.4
43	130	SHAHPURA	9.3
44	222	MALPURA	9.2
45	94	TARANAGAR	9.1
46	216	ABU ROAD	9.0
47	107	SAGWARA	8.9
48	137	JALOR	8.8
49	2	BHINAY	8.6
49	7	PISANGAN	8.6
49	110	GANGANAGAR	8.6
52	227	BARGAON	8.4
52	80	BHOPALSAGAR	8.4
52	104	ASPUR	8.4
52	180	MAKRANA	8.4
56	207	SAWAI MADHOPUR	8.3
57	68	KOLAYAT	8.2
58	65	SUWANA	8.1
59	162	OSIAN	8.0
60	24	BAGIDORA	7.9
61	10	BEHROR	7.8
61	19	RENI	7.8
61	45	SIWANA	7.8
64	93	SUJANGARH	7.7
65	11	KATHUMAR	7.6
65	53	SEWAR	7.6
65	116	BHADRA	7.6
68	155	UDAIPURWATI	7.4
68	174	SULTANPUR	7.4
68	175	DEGANA	7.4
68	182	MUNDWA	7.4
72	124	JAMWA RAMGARH	7.3
72	184	PARBATSAR	7.3
74	4	KEKRI	7.1
74	176	DIDWANA	7.1
74	217	PINDWARA	7.1
77	237	SARADA	7.0
77	13	KOTKASIM	7.0
77	15	MANDAWAR	7.0
77	132	JAISALMER	7.0
	HIGH (6-7)		
81	140	SANCHORE	6.9
81	172	LADPURA	6.9
83	119	AMBER	6.8
83	138	JASWANTPURA	6.8
83	153	NAWALGARH	6.8
86	230	GIRWA	6.7
86	161	MANDOR	6.7
88	203	BAMANWAS	6.6
89	74	TALERA	6.5
89	99	SIKRAI	6.5
89	148	ALSISAR	6.5
92	157	BAP	6.4
92	185	RIYAN	6.4
94	211	KHANDELA	6.3
94	204	BONLI	6.3
96	179	LADNU	6.2
97	38	BALOTRA	6.1
98	235	MAVLI	6.0
98	61	MANDALGARH	6.0
	MEDIUM (5-6)		
100	60	MANDAL	5.9
100	160	LUNI	5.9
102	96	DAUSA	5.8
103	212	LACHHMANGARH	5.7
103	95	BANDIKUI	5.7
103	105	BICHHIWARA	5.7
103	134	SANKRA	5.7
103	178	KUCHAMAN	5.7
108	46	BAYANA	5.6
108	62	RAIPUR	5.6
108	218	REODAR	5.6
111	26	GHATOL	5.5
111	54	WEIR	5.5
111	201	RAILMAGRA	5.5
114	21	TIJARA	5.4
114	22	UMREN	5.4
114	112	PADAMPUR	5.4
117	202	RAJSAMAND	5.3
117	9	BANSURE	5.3
117	92	SARDARSHAHAR	5.3
120	30	TALWARA	5.2
120	90	RAJGARH	5.2
122	32	ATRU	5.1
122	51	NAGAR PAHARI	5.1
122	177	JAYAL	5.1
125	106	DUNGARPUR	5.0
125	122	DUDU	5.0
125	126	KOTPUTLI	5.0
125	131	VIRATNAGAR	5.0
	LOW (4-5)		
129	55	ASIND	4.9
129	83	DUNGLA	4.9
129	128	SAMBHAR	4.9
132	221	DEOLI	4.8
132	37	SHAHBAD	4.8
132	56	BANERA	4.8
132	139	RANIWARA	4.8
132	150	CHIRAWA	4.8
132	168	SAPOTRA	4.8
138	223	NIWAI	4.7
138	20	THANAGAZI	4.7
138	101	BASERI	4.7
138	152	KHETRI	4.7
138	164	SHERGARH	4.7
138	183	NAGAUR	4.7
144	18	RAMGARH	4.6
145	197	BHIM	4.5
145	108	SIMALWARA	4.5
147	12	KISHANGARH BAS	4.4
147	73	NAINWA	4.4
147	147	PIRAWA	4.4
150	6	MASOODA	4.3
150	17	RAJGARH	4.3
150	120	BASSI	4.3
150	171	ITAWA	4.3
154	225	TONK	4.2
154	47	DEEG	4.2
154	129	SANGANER	4.2
154	144	JHALRAPATAN	4.2
154	169	TODABHIM	4.2
159	170	CHECHAT	4.2
159	210	FATEHPUR	4.2
161	154	SURAJGARH	4.1
161	165	HINDAUN	4.1
161	166	KARAULI	4.1
161	173	SANGOD	4.1
161	231	GOGUNDA	4.1
166	3	JAWAJA	4.0
166	63	SAHARA	4.0
166	71	HINDOLI	4.0
166	72	KESHORAIPATAN	4.0
166	97	LALSOT	4.0
166	156	BALESAR	4.0
	VERY LOW (<4)		
172	36	KISHANGANJ	3.9
172	87	PRATAPGARH	3.9
172	102	DHAULPUR	3.9
172	206	KHANDAR	3.9
176	236	SALUMBAR	3.8
176	29	SAJJANGARH	3.8
176	42	DHORIMANNA	3.8
176	114	SADULSHAHAR	3.8
176	118	NOHAR	3.8
181	199	KHAMNOR	3.7
181	28	PEEPALKHOONT	3.7
181	78	BHADESAR	3.7
184	117	HANUMANGARH	3.6
184	127	PHAGI	3.6
184	143	DAG	3.6
184	228	BHINDER	3.6
184	224	TODARAISINGH	3.6
189	44	SINDHARI	3.5
189	52	RUPBAS	3.5
189	76	BARI SADRI	3.5
189	81	CHHOTI SADRI	3.5
193	75	ARNOD	3.4
193	121	CHAKSU	3.4
195	14	LACHHMANGARH	3.3
195	27	KUSHALGARH	3.3
195	64	SHAHPURA	3.3
195	98	MAHWA	3.3
199	41	CHOHTAN	3.2
199	58	JAHAZPUR	3.2
199	77	BEGUN	3.2
199	115	SURATGARH	3.2
203	23	ANANDPURI	3.1
203	84	GANGRAR	3.1
203	142	BAKANI	3.1
203	145	KHANPUR	3.1
203	226	UNIARA	3.1
203	198	DEOGARH	3.1
209	200	KUMBHALGARH	3.0
209	33	BARAN	3.0
209	100	BARI	3.0
212	196	AMET	2.9
212	35	CHHIPABAROD	2.9
214	40	BAYTOO	2.8
214	82	CHITTAURGARH	2.8
214	85	KAPASAN	2.8
214	133	SAM	2.8
214	233	KHERWARA	2.8
219	232	JHADOL	2.7
219	125	JHOTWARA	2.7
221	234	KOTRA	2.6
221	48	KAMAN	2.6
221	86	NIMBAHERA	2.6
224	88	RASHMI	2.5
225	43	SHEO	2.4
225	111	KARANPUR	2.4
225	149	BUHANA	2.4
228	59	KOTRI	2.3
229	151	JHUNJHUNUN	2.1
230	229	DHARIAWAD	2.0
230	39	BARMER	2.0
230	103	RAJAKHERA	2.0
233	79	BHAINSRORGARH	1.9
234	34	CHHABRA	1.6
234	113	RAISINGHNAGAR	1.6
236	146	MANOHARTHANA	1.4
237	109	ANUPGARH	1.2
		RAJASTHAN	5.30
		%age of AAPs	50.20

BOLD: Equal/Above Average Panchayat Samities (AAPs)

Source: General Annex IX, Col. 12.

ANNEX-5.1

RANKING OF PSS BY HEALTH STATUS INDEX, 1991

(Descending Order)

RANK	PANCHAYAT SAMITIES P. CODE	NAME	HEALTH STATUS INDEX
1	2	3	4
	HIGH (0.7-0.8)		
1	195	**SUMERPUR**	0.7291
2	153	**NAWALGARH**	0.7268
3	186	**BALI**	0.7016
	MEDIUM (0.6-0.7)		
4	159	**BILARA**	0.6991
5	155	**UDAIPURWATI**	0.6990
6	123	**GOVINDGARH**	0.6956
7	7	**PISANGAN**	0.6908
8	192	**RANI STATION**	0.6903
9	209	**DHOND**	0.6902
10	187	**DESURI**	0.6901
11	137	**JALOR**	0.6843
12	57	**HURDA**	0.6838
13	63	**SAHARA**	0.6710
14	56	**BANERA**	0.6704
15	150	**CHIRAWA**	0.6659
16	201	**RAILMAGRA**	0.6649
17	4	**KEKRI**	0.6643
18	220	**SIROHI**	0.6633
19	199	**KHAMNOR**	0.6589
20	130	**SHAHPURA**	0.6583
21	151	**JHUNJHUNUN**	0.6581
22	25	**GARHI**	0.6575
23	219	**SHEOGANJ**	0.6573
24	208	**DANTA RAMGARH**	0.6572
25	141	**SAYLA**	0.6559
26	152	**KHETRI**	0.6536
27	215	**SRI MADHOPUR**	0.6531
28	107	**SAGWARA**	0.6529
29	158	**BHOPALGARH**	0.6515
30	16	**NIMRANA**	0.6495
31	135	**AHORE**	0.6464
32	235	**MAVLI**	0.6439
33	211	**KHANDELA**	0.6414
34	8	**SRINAGAR**	0.6389
35	217	**PINDWARA**	0.6370
36	10	**BEHROR**	0.6358
37	60	**MANDAL**	0.6350
38	156	**BALESAR**	0.6346
39	62	**RAIPUR**	0.6344
40	104	**ASPUR**	0.6338
41	181	**MERTA**	0.6336
42	2	**BHINAY**	0.6324
42	65	**SUWANA**	0.6324
44	148	**ALSISAR**	0.6323
45	194	**SOJAT**	0.6321
45	67	**DUNGARGARH**	0.6321
45	80	**BHOPALSAGAR**	0.6321
48	189	**KHARCHI/MARWAR JUN.**	0.6316
49	213	**NEEM KA THANA**	0.6307
50	88	**RASHMI**	0.6300
51	197	**BHIM**	0.6298
52	237	**SARADA**	0.6290
53	5	**KISHANGARH**	0.6251
54	190	**PALI**	0.6250
55	185	**RIYAN**	0.6201
56	230	**GIRWA**	0.6200
57	212	**LACHHMANGARH**	0.6191
58	138	**JASWANTPURA**	0.6173
59	160	**LUNI**	0.6169
60	64	**SHAHPURA**	0.6149
61	110	**GANGANAGAR**	0.6146
62	15	**MANDAWAR**	0.6119
63	131	**VIRATNAGAR**	0.6116
64	210	**FATEHPUR**	0.6105
65	149	**BUHANA**	0.6085
66	55	**ASIND**	0.6084
67	6	**MASOODA**	0.6080
68	188	**JAITARAN**	0.6074
69	128	**SAMBHAR**	0.6069
70	105	**BICHHIWARA**	0.6058
70	164	**SHERGARH**	0.6058
72	49	**KUMHER**	0.6056
72	126	**KOTPUTLI**	0.6056
74	218	**REODAR**	0.6033
75	227	**BARGAON**	0.6000
75	91	**RATANGARH**	0.6000
	LOW (0.5-0.6)		
77	70	**NOKHA**	0.5996
78	172	**LADPURA**	0.5989
79	222	**MALPURA**	0.5976
80	125	**JHOTWARA**	0.5975
81	58	**JAHAZPUR**	0.5956
82	178	**KUCHAMAN**	0.5941
83	228	**BHINDER**	0.5931
84	175	**DEGANA**	0.5928
85	214	**PIPRALI**	0.5924
86	154	**SURAJGARH**	0.5913
87	66	**BIKANER**	0.5909
88	179	**LADNU**	0.5893
89	12	**KISHANGARH BAS**	0.5884
90	30	**TALWARA**	0.5883
90	117	**HANUMANGARH**	0.5883
92	184	**PARBATSAR**	0.5875
93	94	**TARANAGAR**	0.5871
94	111	**KARANPUR**	0.5860
95	45	**SIWANA**	0.5856
96	106	**DUNGARPUR**	0.5854
97	139	**RANIWARA**	0.5850
98	119	**AMBER**	0.5838
99	59	**KOTRI**	0.5834
99	124	**JAMWA RAMGARH**	0.5834
101	85	**KAPASAN**	0.5823
102	205	**GANGAPUR**	0.5807
103	120	**BASSI**	0.5804
104	114	**SADULSHAHAR**	0.5791
105	89	**CHURU**	0.5789
106	24	**BAGIDORA**	0.5788
107	170	**CHECHAT**	0.5786
108	165	**HINDAUN**	0.5779
108	129	**SANGANER**	0.5779
110	9	**BANSURE**	0.5763
111	20	**THANAGAZI**	0.5759
112	182	**MUNDWA**	0.5729
113	167	**NADOTI**	0.5728
114	69	**LUNKARANSAR**	0.5726
115	54	**WEIR**	0.5688
116	13	**KOTKASIM**	0.5676
117	162	**OSIAN**	0.5654
118	112	**PADAMPUR**	0.5653
119	191	**RAIPUR**	0.5626
120	180	**MAKRANA**	0.5624
121	93	**SUJANGARH**	0.5623
122	26	**GHATOL**	0.5620
123	193	**ROHAT**	0.5615
124	1	**ARAIN**	0.5614
125	161	**MANDOR**	0.5600
126	3	JAWAJA	0.5583
127	236	SALUMBAR	0.5577
128	183	NAGAUR	0.5574
129	61	MANDALGARH	0.5573
130	231	GOGUNDA	0.5571
131	196	AMET	0.5557
132	221	DEOLI	0.5542
133	17	RAJGARH	0.5535
134	136	BHINMAL	0.5534
134	32	ATRU	0.5534
136	177	JAYAL	0.5524
137	216	ABU ROAD	0.5513
138	18	RAMGARH	0.5513
139	233	KHERWARA	0.5497
140	203	BAMANWAS	0.5488
141	22	UMREN	0.5484
142	33	BARAN	0.5476
143	31	ANTA	0.5471
143	82	CHITTAURGARH	0.5471
145	86	NIMBAHERA	0.5469
146	176	DIDWANA	0.5458
147	83	DUNGLA	0.5454
147	116	BHADRA	0.5454
149	127	PHAGI	0.5430
150	108	SIMALWARA	0.5415
151	163	PHALODI	0.5410
152	53	SEWAR	0.5408
153	223	NIWAI	0.5405
154	68	KOLAYAT	0.5398
155	76	BARI SADRI	0.5369
156	174	SULTANPUR	0.5368
157	96	DAUSA	0.5366
157	77	BEGUN	0.5366
159	204	BONLI	0.5364
160	113	RAISINGHNAGAR	0.5363
161	84	GANGRAR	0.5329
162	207	SAWAI MADHOPUR	0.5300
163	75	ARNOD	0.5296
164	173	SANGOD	0.5283
165	99	SIKRAI	0.5281
166	169	TODABHIM	0.5275
167	50	NADBAI	0.5265
168	202	RAJSAMAND	0.5263
169	23	ANANDPURI	0.5258
170	19	RENI	0.5256
171	198	DEOGARH	0.5253
172	144	JHALRAPATAN	0.5251
173	102	DHAULPUR	0.5250
174	73	NAINWA	0.5245
175	81	CHHOTI SADRI	0.5213
175	145	KHANPUR	0.5213
177	78	BHADESAR	0.5203
178	74	TALERA	0.5193
179	52	RUPBAS	0.5175
179	95	BANDIKUI	0.5175
181	224	TODARAISINGH	0.5175
182	147	PIRAWA	0.5164
183	11	KATHUMAR	0.5148
184	92	SARDARSHAHAR	0.5138
185	122	DUDU	0.5128
186	21	TIJARA	0.5110
187	140	SANCHORE	0.5099
188	38	BALOTRA	0.5096
189	232	JHADOL	0.5095
190	36	KISHANGANJ	0.5074
191	90	RAJGARH	0.5073
192	229	DHARIAWAD	0.5053
193	14	LACHHMANGARH	0.5046
194	118	NOHAR	0.5045
195	200	KUMBHALGARH	0.5039
196	47	DEEG	0.5026
197	71	HINDOLI	0.5024
198	225	TONK	0.5010
	VERY LOW (< 0.5)		
199	46	BAYANA	0.4991
200	226	UNIARA	0.4976
201	142	BAKANI	0.4975
202	98	MAHWA	0.4950
203	97	LALSOT	0.4869
204	171	ITAWA	0.4865
205	87	PRATAPGARH	0.4854
206	72	KESHORAIPATAN	0.4853
207	101	BASERI	0.4841
208	143	DAG	0.4819
209	28	PEEPALKHOONT	0.4813
210	168	SAPOTRA	0.4799
211	121	CHAKSU	0.4794
212	79	BHAINSRORGARH	0.4724
213	206	KHANDAR	0.4703
214	115	SURATGARH	0.4686
215	37	SHAHBAD	0.4635
216	103	RAJAKHERA	0.4591
217	48	KAMAN	0.4556
218	166	KARAULI	0.4519
219	29	SAJJANGARH	0.4466
220	132	JAISALMER	0.4439
221	34	CHHABRA	0.4429
222	134	SANKRA	0.4409
223	51	NAGAR PAHARI	0.4408
224	35	CHHIPABAROD	0.4383
225	41	CHOHTAN	0.4328
226	27	KUSHALGARH	0.4296
227	42	DHORIMANNA	0.4263
228	44	SINDHARI	0.4238
229	146	MANOHARTHANA	0.4163
230	43	SHEO	0.4160
231	157	BAP	0.4145
232	234	KOTRA	0.4090
233	109	ANUPGARH	0.3974
234	100	BARI	0.3966
235	39	BARMER	0.3928
236	40	BAYTOO	0.3656
237	133	SAM	0.3460
		RAJASTHAN	**0.5588**
		%age of AAPs	**63.71**

BOLD: Equal/Above Average Panchayat Samities (AAPs)

Source: Annex 6.1 , Col. 4.

ANNEX-6.1

PANCHAYAT SAMITI-WISE CHANGED PATTERN OF HEALTH STATUS INDEX (1991-01)

P. Code	*Panchayat Samities*	*Health Status Index 1991*		*2001*		*Differences (1991-01)*		*% Increase in HSI Value*	*Remarks*
		Rank	*Value*	*Rank*	*Value*	*Rank*	*Value*		
1	2	3	4	5	6	7	8	9	10
1	ARAIN	124	0.5614	127	0.6736	-3	0.1122	20	B
2	BHINAY	42	0.6324	117	0.6771	-75	0.0447	7	B
3	JAWAJA	126	0.5583	68	0.7191	58	0.1608	29	A
4	KEKRI	17	0.6643	48	0.7348	-31	0.0705	11	B
5	KISHANGARH	53	0.6251	70	0.7172	-17	0.0921	15	B
6	MASOODA	67	0.6080	110	0.6824	-43	0.0744	12	B
7	PISANGAN	7	0.6908	42	0.7417	-35	0.0509	7	B
8	SRINAGAR	34	0.6389	73	0.7157	-39	0.0768	12	B
	AJMER DISTRICT		**0.6243**		**0.7075**		**0.0832**	**13**	
9	BANSURE	110	0.5763	119	0.6769	-9	0.1006	17	B
10	BEHROR	36	0.6358	26	0.7615	10	0.1257	20	A
11	KATHUMAR	183	0.5148	136	0.6646	47	0.1498	29	A
12	KISHANGARH BAS	89	0.5884	171	0.6348	-82	0.0464	8	B
13	KOTKASIM	116	0.5676	142	0.6614	-26	0.0938	17	B
14	LACHHMANGARH	193	0.5046	133	0.6672	60	0.1626	32	A
15	MANDAWAR	62	0.6119	83	0.7037	-21	0.0918	15	B
16	NIMRANA	30	0.6495	33	0.7520	-3	0.1025	16	B
17	RAJGARH	133	0.5535	165	0.6404	-32	0.0869	16	B
18	RAMGARH	138	0.5513	147	0.6569	-9	0.1056	19	B
19	RENI	170	0.5256	115	0.6785	55	0.1529	29	A
20	THANAGAZI	111	0.5759	130	0.6726	-19	0.0967	17	B
21	TIJARA	186	0.5110	189	0.6187	-3	0.1077	21	B
22	UMREN	141	0.5484	125	0.6751	16	0.1267	23	A
	ALWAR		**0.5616**		**0.6725**		**0.1109**	**20**	
23	ANANDPURI	169	0.5258	192	0.6167	-23	0.0909	17	B
24	BAGIDORA	106	0.5788	184	0.6251	-78	0.0463	8	B
25	GARHI	22	0.6575	38	0.7465	-16	0.0890	14	B
26	GHATOL	122	0.5620	151	0.6555	-29	0.0935	17	B
27	KUSHALGARH	226	0.4296	222	0.5633	4	0.1337	31	A
28	PEEPALKHOONT	209	0.4813	219	0.5685	-10	0.0872	18	B
29	SAJJANGARH	219	0.4466	203	0.6021	16	0.1555	35	A
30	TALWARA	90	0.5883	134	0.6660	-44	0.0777	13	B
	BANSWARA		**0.5475**		**0.6405**		**0.0930**	**17**	
31	ANTA	143	0.5471	143	0.6603	0	0.1132	21	C
32	ATRU	134	0.5534	140	0.6619	-6	0.1085	20	B
33	BARAN	142	0.5476	124	0.6753	18	0.1277	23	A
34	CHHABRA	221	0.4429	230	0.5216	-9	0.0787	18	B
35	CHHIPABAROD	224	0.4383	220	0.5674	4	0.1291	29	A
36	KISHANGANJ	190	0.5074	185	0.6249	5	0.1175	23	A
37	SHAHBAD	215	0.4635	214	0.5809	1	0.1174	25	A
	BARAN		**0.5025**		**0.6148**		**0.1123**	**22**	
38	BALOTRA	188	0.5096	187	0.6194	1	0.1098	22	A
39	BARMER	235	0.3928	236	0.4930	-1	0.1002	26	B
40	BAYTOO	236	0.3656	234	0.4950	2	0.1294	35	A
41	CHOHTAN	225	0.4328	211	0.5880	14	0.1552	36	A
42	DHORIMANNA	227	0.4263	206	0.6006	21	0.1743	41	A
43	SHEO	230	0.4160	235	0.4938	-5	0.0778	19	B
44	SINDHARI	228	0.4238	224	0.5611	4	0.1373	32	A
45	SIWANA	95	0.5856	67	0.7197	28	0.1341	23	A
	BARMER		**0.4418**		**0.5715**		**0.1297**	**29**	
46	BAYANA	199	0.4991	199	0.6120	0	0.1129	23	C
47	DEEG	196	0.5026	93	0.6939	103	0.1913	38	A
48	KAMAN	217	0.4556	195	0.6137	22	0.1581	35	A
49	KUMHER	72	0.6056	45	0.7390	27	0.1334	22	A
50	NADBAI	167	0.5265	54	0.7286	113	0.2021	38	A
51	NAGAR PAHARI	223	0.4408	179	0.6301	44	0.1893	43	A
52	RUPBAS	179	0.5175	132	0.6699	47	0.1524	29	A
53	SEWAR	152	0.5408	104	0.6895	48	0.1487	27	A
54	WEIR	115	0.5688	170	0.6374	-55	0.0686	12	B
	BHARATPUR		**0.5134**		**0.6617**		**0.1483**	**29**	
55	ASIND	66	0.6084	122	0.6764	-56	0.0680	11	B
56	BANERA	14	0.6704	39	0.7464	-25	0.0760	11	B
57	HURDA	12	0.6838	58	0.7243	-46	0.0405	6	B
58	JAHAZPUR	81	0.5956	166	0.6404	-85	0.0448	8	B
59	KOTRI	99	0.5834	181	0.6281	-82	0.0447	8	B

P. Code	*Panchayat Samities*	*Health Status Index 1991*		*2001*		*Differences (1991-01)*		*% Increase in HSI Value*	*Remarks*
		Rank	*Value*	*Rank*	*Value*	*Rank*	*Value*		
1	2	3	4	5	6	7	8	9	10
60	MANDAL	37	0.6350	103	0.6896	-66	0.0546	9	B
61	MANDALGARH	129	0.5573	169	0.6374	-40	0.0801	14	B
62	RAIPUR	39	0.6344	97	0.6919	-58	0.0575	9	B
63	SAHARA	13	0.6710	44	0.7396	-31	0.0686	10	B
64	SHAHPURA	60	0.6149	157	0.6464	-97	0.0315	5	B
65	SUWANA	42	0.6324	88	0.6972	-46	0.0648	10	B
	BHILWARA		**0.6175**		**0.6749**		**0.0574**	**9**	
66	BIKANER	87	0.5909	209	0.5913	-122	0.0004	0	B
67	DUNGARGARH *	45	0.6321	27	0.7612	18	0.1291	20	A
68	KOLAYAT	154	0.5398	217	0.5752	-63	0.0354	7	B
69	LUNKARANSAR	114	0.5726	180	0.6284	-66	0.0558	10	B
70	NOKHA	77	0.5996	138	0.6635	-61	0.0639	11	B
	BIKANER **		**0.5781**		**0.6136**		**0.0355**	**6**	
71	HINDOLI	197	0.5024	168	0.6375	29	0.1351	27	A
72	KESHORAIPATAN	206	0.4853	196	0.6136	10	0.1283	26	A
73	NAINWA	174	0.5245	198	0.6122	-24	0.0877	17	B
74	TALERA	178	0.5193	173	0.6318	5	0.1125	22	A
	BUNDI		**0.4968**		**0.6247**		**0.1279**	**26**	
75	ARNOD	163	0.5296	210	0.5903	-47	0.0607	11	B
76	BARI SADRI	155	0.5369	163	0.6427	-8	0.1058	20	B
77	BEGUN	157	0.5366	188	0.6188	-31	0.0822	15	B
78	BHADESAR	177	0.5203	182	0.6269	-5	0.1066	20	B
79	BHAINSRORGARH	212	0.4724	213	0.5819	-1	0.1095	23	B
80	BHOPALSAGAR	45	0.6321	128	0.6731	-83	0.0410	6	B
81	CHHOTI SADRI	175	0.5213	197	0.6124	-22	0.0911	17	B
82	CHITTAURGARH	143	0.5471	160	0.6443	-17	0.0972	18	B
83	DUNGLA	147	0.5454	91	0.6959	56	0.1505	28	A
84	GANGRAR	161	0.5329	158	0.6454	3	0.1125	21	A
85	KAPASAN	101	0.5823	204	0.6016	-103	0.0193	3	B
86	NIMBAHERA	145	0.5469	116	0.6775	29	0.1306	24	A
87	PRATAPGARH	205	0.4854	190	0.6185	15	0.1331	27	A
88	RASHMI	50	0.6300	63	0.7226	-13	0.0926	15	B
	CHITTAURGARH		**0.5391**		**0.6365**		**0.0974**	**18**	
89	CHURU	105	0.5789	19	0.7716	86	0.1927	33	A
90	RAJGARH	191	0.5073	98	0.6918	93	0.1845	36	A
91	RATANGARH	76	0.6000	2	0.8164	74	0.2164	36	A
92	SARDARSHAHAR	184	0.5138	191	0.6175	-7	0.1037	20	B
93	SUJANGARH	121	0.5623	60	0.7240	61	0.1617	29	A
94	TARANAGAR	93	0.5871	75	0.7154	18	0.1283	22	A
	CHURU ***		**0.5611**		**0.7191**		**0.1580**	**28**	
95	BANDIKUI	179	0.5175	118	0.6771	61	0.1596	31	A
96	DAUSA	157	0.5366	149	0.6561	8	0.1195	22	A
97	LALSOT	203	0.4869	201	0.6088	2	0.1219	25	A
98	MAHWA	202	0.4950	154	0.6485	48	0.1535	31	A
99	SIKRAI	165	0.5281	150	0.6557	15	0.1276	24	A
	DAUSA		**0.5129**		**0.6487**		**0.1358**	**26**	
100	BARI	234	0.3966	212	0.5844	22	0.1878	47	A
101	BASERI	207	0.4841	221	0.5663	-14	0.0822	17	B
102	DHAULPUR	173	0.5250	208	0.5947	-35	0.0697	13	B
103	RAJAKHERA	216	0.4591	215	0.5785	1	0.1194	26	A
	DHAULPUR		**0.4735**		**0.5827**		**0.1092**	**23**	
104	ASPUR	40	0.6338	24	0.7632	16	0.1294	20	A
105	BICHHIWARA	70	0.6058	55	0.7266	15	0.1208	20	A
106	DUNGARPUR	96	0.5854	65	0.7214	31	0.1360	23	A
107	SAGWARA	28	0.6529	14	0.7802	14	0.1273	19	A
108	SIMALWARA	150	0.5415	107	0.6858	43	0.1443	27	A
	DUNGARPUR		**0.5975**		**0.7324**		**0.1349**	**23**	
109	ANUPGARH	233	0.3974	225	0.5610	8	0.1636	41	A
110	GANGANAGAR	61	0.6146	76	0.7151	-15	0.1005	16	B
111	KARANPUR	94	0.5860	95	0.6928	-1	0.1068	18	B
112	PADAMPUR	118	0.5653	90	0.6968	28	0.1315	23	A
113	RAISINGHNAGAR	160	0.5363	164	0.6419	-4	0.1056	20	B
114	SADULSHAHAR	104	0.5791	111	0.6817	-7	0.1026	18	B
115	SURATGARH	214	0.4686	231	0.5150	-17	0.0464	10	B
	GANGANAGAR		**0.5109**		**0.6183**		**0.1074**	**21**	
116	BHADRA	147	0.5454	69	0.7173	78	0.1719	32	A
117	HANUMANGARH	90	0.5883	129	0.6726	-39	0.0843	14	B
118	NOHAR	194	0.5045	216	0.5785	-22	0.0740	15	B
	HANUMANGARH		**0.5483**		**0.6510**		**0.1027**	**19**	
119	AMBER	98	0.5838	101	0.6910	-3	0.1072	18	B
120	BASSI	103	0.5804	102	0.6905	1	0.1101	19	A
121	CHAKSU	211	0.4794	222	0.5633	-11	0.0839	18	B
122	DUDU	185	0.5128	120	0.6766	65	0.1638	32	A
123	GOVINDGARH	6	0.6956	20	0.7682	-14	0.0726	10	B
124	JAMWA RAMGARH	99	0.5834	87	0.6978	12	0.1144	20	A

P. Code	Panchayat Samities	Health Status Index 1991		Health Status Index 2001		Differences (1991-01)		% Increase in HSI Value	Remarks
		Rank	Value	Rank	Value	Rank	Value		
1	2	3	4	5	6	7	8	9	10
125	JHOTWARA	80	0.5975	106	0.6887	-26	0.0912	15	B
126	KOTPUTLI	72	0.6056	80	0.7073	-8	0.1017	17	B
127	PHAGI	149	0.5430	161	0.6441	-12	0.1011	19	B
128	SAMBHAR	69	0.6069	59	0.7241	10	0.1172	19	A
129	SANGANER	108	0.5779	126	0.6740	-18	0.0961	17	B
130	SHAHPURA	20	0.6583	34	0.7487	-14	0.0904	14	B
131	VIRATNAGAR	63	0.6116	64	0.7225	-1	0.1109	18	B
	JAIPUR		**0.5860**		**0.6925**		**0.1065**	**18**	
132	JAISALMER	220	0.4439	227	0.5541	-7	0.1102	25	B
133	SAM	237	0.3460	237	0.4749	0	0.1289	37	C
134	SANKRA	222	0.4409	229	0.5487	-7	0.1078	24	B
	JAISALMER		**0.4085**		**0.5238**		**0.1153**	**28**	
135	AHORE	31	0.6464	8	0.7941	23	0.1477	23	A
136	BHINMAL	134	0.5534	92	0.6954	42	0.1420	26	A
137	JALOR	11	0.6843	12	0.7826	-1	0.0983	14	B
138	JASWANTPURA	58	0.6173	41	0.7441	17	0.1268	21	A
139	RANIWARA	97	0.5850	62	0.7228	35	0.1378	24	A
140	SANCHORE	187	0.5099	172	0.6339	15	0.1240	24	A
141	SAYLA	25	0.6559	25	0.7621	0	0.1062	16	C
	JALOR		**0.5948**		**0.7190**		**0.1242**	**21**	
142	BAKANI	201	0.4975	228	0.5525	-27	0.0550	11	B
143	DAG	208	0.4819	218	0.5723	-10	0.0904	19	B
144	JHALRAPATAN	172	0.5251	207	0.5985	-35	0.0734	14	B
145	KHANPUR	175	0.5213	176	0.6309	-1	0.1096	21	B
146	MANOHARTHANA	229	0.4163	232	0.5097	-3	0.0934	22	B
147	PIRAWA	182	0.5164	193	0.6153	-11	0.0989	19	B
	JHALAWAR		**0.4944**		**0.5804**		**0.0860**	**17**	
148	ALSISAR	44	0.6323	52	0.7316	-8	0.0993	16	B
149	BUHANA	65	0.6085	21	0.7669	44	0.1584	26	A
150	CHIRAWA	15	0.6659	15	0.7770	0	0.1111	17	C
151	JHUNJHUNUN	21	0.6581	29	0.7596	-8	0.1015	15	B
152	KHETRI	26	0.6536	11	0.7827	15	0.1291	20	A
153	NAWALGARH	2	0.7268	17	0.7741	-15	0.0473	7	B
154	SURAJGARH	86	0.5913	94	0.6928	-8	0.1015	17	B
155	UDAIPURWATI	5	0.6990	1	0.8307	4	0.1317	19	A
	JHUNJHUNUN		**0.6531**		**0.7645**		**0.1114**	**17**	
156	BALESAR	38	0.6346	153	0.6530	-115	0.0184	3	B
157	BAP	231	0.4145	226	0.5588	5	0.1443	35	A
158	BHOPALGARH	29	0.6515	36	0.7479	-7	0.0964	15	B
159	BILARA	4	0.6991	10	0.7828	-6	0.0837	12	B
160	LUNI	59	0.6169	46	0.7390	13	0.1221	20	A
161	MANDOR	125	0.5600	144	0.6600	-19	0.1000	18	B
162	OSIAN	117	0.5654	53	0.7313	64	0.1659	29	A
163	PHALODI	151	0.5410	146	0.6584	5	0.1174	22	A
164	SHERGARH	70	0.6058	202	0.6050	-132	-0.0008	0	D
	JODHPUR		**0.5715**		0.6891		**0.1176**	**21**	
165	HINDAUN	108	0.5779	50	0.7326	58	0.1547	27	A
166	KARAULI	218	0.4519	183	0.6265	35	0.1746	39	A
167	NADOTI	113	0.5728	113	0.6804	0	0.1076	19	C
168	SAPOTRA	210	0.4799	194	0.6140	16	0.1341	28	A
169	TODABHIM	166	0.5275	108	0.6843	58	0.1568	30	A
	KARAULI		**0.5174**		**0.6658**		**0.1484**	**29**	
170	CHECHAT	107	0.5786	89	0.6970	18	0.1184	20	A
171	ITAWA	204	0.4865	162	0.6437	42	0.1572	32	A
172	LADPURA	78	0.5989	78	0.7114	0	0.1125	19	C
173	SANGOD	164	0.5283	145	0.6599	19	0.1316	25	A
174	SULTANPUR	156	0.5368	72	0.7159	84	0.1791	33	A
	KOTA		**0.5440**		**0.6844**		**0.1404**	**26**	
175	DEGANA	84	0.5928	81	0.7072	3	0.1144	19	A
176	DIDWANA	146	0.5458	51	0.7325	95	0.1867	34	A
177	JAYAL	136	0.5524	112	0.6812	24	0.1288	23	A
178	KUCHAMAN	82	0.5941	123	0.6762	-41	0.0821	14	B
179	LADNU	88	0.5893	30	0.7543	58	0.1650	28	A
180	MAKRANA	120	0.5624	85	0.7008	35	0.1384	25	A
181	MERTA	41	0.6336	66	0.7209	-25	0.0873	14	B
182	MUNDWA	112	0.5729	99	0.6914	13	0.1185	21	A
183	NAGAUR	128	0.5574	139	0.6631	-11	0.1057	19	B
184	PARBATSAR	92	0.5875	56	0.7254	36	0.1379	23	A
185	RIYAN	55	0.6201	71	0.7160	-16	0.0959	15	B
	NAGAUR		**0.5796**		**0.7044**		**0.1248**	**22**	
186	BALI	3	0.7016	6	0.8057	-3	0.1041	15	B
187	DESURI	10	0.6901	16	0.7745	-6	0.0844	12	B
188	JAITARAN	68	0.6074	37	0.7466	31	0.1392	23	A
189	KHARCHI/MARWAR JUN.	48	0.6316	35	0.7486	13	0.1170	19	A
190	PALI	54	0.6250	57	0.7246	-3	0.0996	16	B
191	RAIPUR	119	0.5626	43	0.7404	76	0.1778	32	A

P. Code	Panchayat Samities	Health Status Index 1991		Health Status Index 2001		Differences (1991-01)		% Increase in HSI Value	Remarks
		Rank	Value	Rank	Value	Rank	Value		
1	2	3	4	5	6	7	8	9	10
192	RANI STATION	8	0.6903	3	0.8148	5	0.1245	18	A
193	ROHAT	123	0.5615	100	0.6911	23	0.1296	23	A
194	SOJAT	45	0.6321	28	0.7603	17	0.1282	20	A
195	SUMERPUR	1	0.7291	4	0.8076	-3	0.0785	11	B
	PALI		**0.6448**		**0.7612**		**0.1164**	**18**	
196	AMET	131	0.5557	148	0.6562	-17	0.1005	18	B
197	BHIM	51	0.6298	84	0.7011	-33	0.0713	11	B
198	DEOGARH	171	0.5253	156	0.6475	15	0.1222	23	A
199	KHAMNOR	19	0.6589	74	0.7155	-55	0.0566	9	B
200	KUMBHALGARH	195	0.5039	114	0.6803	81	0.1764	35	A
201	RAILMAGRA	16	0.6649	23	0.7650	-7	0.1001	15	B
202	RAJSAMAND	168	0.5263	105	0.6890	63	0.1627	31	A
	RAJSAMAND		**0.5825**		**0.6962**		**0.1137**	**20**	
203	BAMANWAS	140	0.5488	174	0.6316	-34	0.0828	15	B
204	BONLI	159	0.5364	167	0.6376	-8	0.1012	19	B
205	GANGAPUR	102	0.5807	86	0.6992	16	0.1185	20	A
206	KHANDAR	213	0.4703	200	0.6089	13	0.1386	29	A
207	SAWAI MADHOPUR	162	0.5300	159	0.6450	3	0.1150	22	A
	SAWAI MADHOPUR		**0.5343**		**0.6448**		**0.1105**	**21**	
208	DANTA RAMGARH	24	0.6572	22	0.7667	2	0.1095	17	A
209	DHOND	9	0.6902	7	0.7978	2	0.1076	16	A
210	FATEHPUR	64	0.6105	32	0.7534	32	0.1429	23	A
211	KHANDELA	33	0.6414	18	0.7736	15	0.1322	21	A
212	LACHHMANGARH	57	0.6191	61	0.7233	-4	0.1042	17	B
213	NEEM KA THANA	49	0.6307	40	0.7444	9	0.1137	18	A
214	PIPRALI	85	0.5924	9	0.7841	76	0.1917	32	A
215	SRI MADHOPUR	27	0.6531	13	0.7825	14	0.1294	20	A
	SIKAR		**0.6347**		**0.7633**		**0.1286**	**20**	
216	ABU ROAD	137	0.5513	141	0.6618	-4	0.1105	20	B
217	PINDWARA	35	0.6370	47	0.7379	-12	0.1009	16	B
218	REODAR	74	0.6033	79	0.7079	-5	0.1046	17	B
219	SHEOGANJ	23	0.6573	31	0.7538	-8	0.0965	15	B
220	SIROHI	18	0.6633	5	0.8059	13	0.1426	21	A
	SIROHI		**0.6234**		**0.7320**		**0.1086**	**17**	
221	DEOLI	132	0.5542	178	0.6302	-46	0.0760	14	B
222	MALPURA	79	0.5976	137	0.6640	-58	0.0664	11	B
223	NIWAI	153	0.5405	175	0.6309	-22	0.0904	17	B
224	TODARAISINGH	181	0.5175	131	0.6713	50	0.1538	30	A
225	TONK	198	0.5010	155	0.6480	43	0.1470	29	A
226	UNIARA	200	0.4976	205	0.6007	-5	0.1031	21	B
	TONK		**0.5351**		**0.6404**		**0.1053**	**20**	
227	BARGAON *	75	0.6000	96	0.6920	-21	0.0920	15	B
228	BHINDER	83	0.5931	109	0.6841	-26	0.0910	15	B
229	DHARIAWAD	192	0.5053	186	0.6205	6	0.1152	23	A
230	GIRWA	56	0.6200	82	0.7056	-26	0.0856	14	B
231	GOGUNDA	130	0.5571	135	0.6659	-5	0.1088	20	B
232	JHADOL	189	0.5095	177	0.6309	12	0.1214	24	A
233	KHERWARA	139	0.5497	152	0.6541	-13	0.1044	19	B
234	KOTRA	232	0.4090	233	0.4951	-1	0.0861	21	B
235	MAVLI	32	0.6439	49	0.7348	-17	0.0909	14	B
236	SALUMBAR	127	0.5577	121	0.6766	6	0.1189	21	A
237	SARADA	52	0.6290	77	0.7122	-25	0.0832	13	B
	UDAIPUR		**0.5625**		**0.6599**		**0.0974**	**17**	
	RAJASTHAN		**0.5588**		**0.6684**		**0.1096**	**20**	

Note: A Improvement in Both HSI Value and Rank
B Increase in HSI Value but Rank Deteriorated
C Increase in HSI Value but Rank Remained Constant
D Decrease in Both HSI Value and Rank
* Dungargarh PS shifted from Churu to Bikaner District on 1st April 2001
** Excluding data of Dungargarh PS
*** Including data of Dungargarh PS

Source: Hemlata Joshi. 2007. *'Health Status Index: Rajasthan* (Spatio-Temporal Appraisal at Panchayat Samiti/Block Level), Publised Research Report, IDS Jaipur, Concept Publishing Company, New Delhi.

ANNEX-6.2

RANKING OF PSS BY HEALTH STATUS INDEX, 2001

(Descending Order)

RANK	PANCHAYAT SAMITIES P. CODE	PANCHAYAT SAMITIES NAME	HEALTH STATUS INDEX
1	2	3	4
	VERY HIGH (>0.8)		
1	**155**	**UDAIPURWATI**	**0.8307**
2	**91**	**RATANGARH**	**0.8164**
3	**192**	**RANI STATION**	**0.8148**
4	**195**	**SUMERPUR**	**0.8076**
5	**220**	**SIROHI**	**0.8059**
6	**186**	**BALI**	**0.8057**
	HIGH (0.7-0.8)		
7	**209**	**DHOND**	**0.7978**
8	**135**	**AHORE**	**0.7941**
9	**214**	**PIPRALI**	**0.7841**
10	**159**	**BILARA**	**0.7828**
11	**152**	**KHETRI**	**0.7827**
12	**137**	**JALOR**	**0.7826**
13	**215**	**SRI MADHOPUR**	**0.7825**
14	**107**	**SAGWARA**	**0.7802**
15	**150**	**CHIRAWA**	**0.7770**
16	**187**	**DESURI**	**0.7745**
17	**153**	**NAWALGARH**	**0.7741**
18	**211**	**KHANDELA**	**0.7736**
19	**89**	**CHURU**	**0.7716**
20	**123**	**GOVINDGARH**	**0.7682**
21	**149**	**BUHANA**	**0.7669**
22	**208**	**DANTA RAMGARH**	**0.7667**
23	**201**	**RAILMAGRA**	**0.7650**
24	**104**	**ASPUR**	**0.7632**
25	**141**	**SAYLA**	**0.7621**
26	**10**	**BEHROR**	**0.7615**
27	**67**	**DUNGARGARH**	**0.7612**
28	**194**	**SOJAT**	**0.7603**
29	**151**	**JHUNJHUNUN**	**0.7596**
30	**179**	**LADNU**	**0.7543**
31	**219**	**SHEOGANJ**	**0.7538**
32	**210**	**FATEHPUR**	**0.7534**
33	**16**	**NIMRANA**	**0.7520**
34	**130**	**SHAHPURA**	**0.7487**
35	**189**	**MARWAR JUN.**	**0.7486**
36	**158**	**BHOPALGARH**	**0.7479**
37	**188**	**JAITARAN**	**0.7466**
38	**25**	**GARHI**	**0.7465**
39	**56**	**BANERA**	**0.7464**
40	**213**	**NEEM KA THANA**	**0.7444**
41	**138**	**JASWANTPURA**	**0.7441**
42	**7**	**PISANGAN**	**0.7417**
43	**191**	**RAIPUR**	**0.7404**
44	**63**	**SAHARA**	**0.7396**
45	**49**	**KUMHER**	**0.7390**
46	**160**	**LUNI**	**0.7390**
47	**217**	**PINDWARA**	**0.7379**
48	**4**	**KEKRI**	**0.7348**
49	**235**	**MAVLI**	**0.7348**
50	**165**	**HINDAUN**	**0.7326**
51	**176**	**DIDWANA**	**0.7325**
52	**148**	**ALSISAR**	**0.7316**
53	**162**	**OSIAN**	**0.7313**
54	**50**	**NADBAI**	**0.7286**
55	**105**	**BICHHIWARA**	**0.7266**
56	**184**	**PARBATSAR**	**0.7254**
57	**190**	**PALI**	**0.7246**
58	**57**	**HURDA**	**0.7243**
59	**128**	**SAMBHAR**	**0.7241**
60	**93**	**SUJANGARH**	**0.7240**
61	**212**	**LACHHMANGARH**	**0.7233**
62	**139**	**RANIWARA**	**0.7228**
63	**88**	**RASHMI**	**0.7226**
64	**131**	**VIRATNAGAR**	**0.7225**
65	**106**	**DUNGARPUR**	**0.7214**
66	**181**	**MERTA**	**0.7209**
67	**45**	**SIWANA**	**0.7197**
68	**3**	**JAWAJA**	**0.7191**
69	**116**	**BHADRA**	**0.7173**
70	**5**	**KISHANGARH**	**0.7172**
71	**185**	**RIYAN**	**0.7160**
72	**174**	**SULTANPUR**	**0.7159**
73	**8**	**SRINAGAR**	**0.7157**
74	**199**	**KHAMNOR**	**0.7155**
75	**94**	**TARANAGAR**	**0.7154**
76	**110**	**GANGANAGAR**	**0.7151**
77	**237**	**SARADA**	**0.7122**
78	**172**	**LADPURA**	**0.7114**
79	**218**	**REODAR**	**0.7079**
80	**126**	**KOTPUTLI**	**0.7073**
81	**175**	**DEGANA**	**0.7072**
82	**230**	**GIRWA**	**0.7056**
83	**15**	**MANDAWAR**	**0.7037**
84	**197**	**BHIM**	**0.7011**
85	**180**	**MAKRANA**	**0.7008**
	MEDIUM (0.6-0.7)		
86	**205**	**GANGAPUR**	**0.6992**
87	**124**	**JAMWA RAMGARH**	**0.6978**
88	**65**	**SUWANA**	**0.6972**
89	**170**	**CHECHAT**	**0.6970**
90	**112**	**PADAMPUR**	**0.6968**
91	**83**	**DUNGLA**	**0.6959**
92	**136**	**BHINMAL**	**0.6954**
93	**47**	**DEEG**	**0.6939**
94	**154**	**SURAJGARH**	**0.6928**
95	**111**	**KARANPUR**	**0.6928**
96	**227**	**BARGAON**	**0.6920**
97	**62**	**RAIPUR**	**0.6919**
98	**90**	**RAJGARH**	**0.6918**
99	**182**	**MUNDWA**	**0.6914**
100	**193**	**ROHAT**	**0.6911**
101	**119**	**AMBER**	**0.6910**
102	**120**	**BASSI**	**0.6905**
103	**60**	**MANDAL**	**0.6896**
104	**53**	**SEWAR**	**0.6895**
105	**202**	**RAJSAMAND**	**0.6890**
106	**125**	**JHOTWARA**	**0.6887**
107	**108**	**SIMALWARA**	**0.6858**
108	**169**	**TODABHIM**	**0.6843**
109	**228**	**BHINDER**	**0.6841**
110	**6**	**MASOODA**	**0.6824**
111	**114**	**SADULSHAHAR**	**0.6817**
112	**177**	**JAYAL**	**0.6812**
113	**167**	**NADOTI**	**0.6804**
114	**200**	**KUMBHALGARH**	**0.6803**
115	**19**	**RENI**	**0.6785**
116	**86**	**NIMBAHERA**	**0.6775**
117	**2**	**BHINAY**	**0.6771**
118	**95**	**BANDIKUI**	**0.6771**
119	**9**	**BANSURE**	**0.6769**
120	**122**	**DUDU**	**0.6766**
121	**236**	**SALUMBAR**	**0.6766**
122	**55**	**ASIND**	**0.6764**
123	**178**	**KUCHAMAN**	**0.6762**
124	**33**	**BARAN**	**0.6753**
125	**22**	**UMREN**	**0.6751**
126	**129**	**SANGANER**	**0.6740**
127	**1**	**ARAIN**	**0.6736**
128	**80**	**BHOPALSAGAR**	**0.6731**
129	**117**	**HANUMANGARH**	**0.6726**
130	**20**	**THANAGAZI**	**0.6726**
131	**224**	**TODARAISINGH**	**0.6713**
132	**52**	**RUPBAS**	**0.6699**
133	14	LACHHMANGARH	0.6672
134	30	TALWARA	0.6660
135	231	GOGUNDA	0.6659
136	11	KATHUMAR	0.6646
137	222	MALPURA	0.6640
138	70	NOKHA	0.6635
139	183	NAGAUR	0.6631
140	32	ATRU	0.6619
141	216	ABU ROAD	0.6618
142	13	KOTKASIM	0.6614
143	31	ANTA	0.6603
144	161	MANDOR	0.6600
145	173	SANGOD	0.6599
146	163	PHALODI	0.6584
147	18	RAMGARH	0.6569
148	196	AMET	0.6562
149	96	DAUSA	0.6561
150	99	SIKRAI	0.6557
151	26	GHATOL	0.6555
152	233	KHERWARA	0.6541
153	156	BALESAR	0.6530
154	98	MAHWA	0.6485
155	225	TONK	0.6480
156	198	DEOGARH	0.6475
157	64	SHAHPURA	0.6464
158	84	GANGRAR	0.6454
159	207	SAWAI MADHOPUR	0.6450
160	82	CHITTAURGARH	0.6443
161	127	PHAGI	0.6441
162	171	ITAWA	0.6437
163	76	BARI SADRI	0.6427
164	113	RAISINGHNAGAR	0.6419
165	17	RAJGARH	0.6404
166	58	JAHAZPUR	0.6404
167	204	BONLI	0.6376
168	71	HINDOLI	0.6375
169	61	MANDALGARH	0.6374
170	54	WEIR	0.6374
171	12	KISHANGARH BAS	0.6348
172	140	SANCHORE	0.6339
173	74	TALERA	0.6318
174	203	BAMANWAS	0.6316
175	223	NIWAI	0.6309
176	145	KHANPUR	0.6309
177	232	JHADOL	0.6309
178	221	DEOLI	0.6302
179	51	NAGAR PAHARI	0.6301
180	69	LUNKARANSAR	0.6284
181	59	KOTRI	0.6281
182	78	BHADESAR	0.6269
183	166	KARAULI	0.6265
184	24	BAGIDORA	0.6251
185	36	KISHANGANJ	0.6249
186	229	DHARIAWAD	0.6205
187	38	BALOTRA	0.6194
188	77	BEGUN	0.6188
189	21	TIJARA	0.6187
190	87	PRATAPGARH	0.6185
191	92	SARDARSHAHAR	0.6175
192	23	ANANDPURI	0.6167
193	147	PIRAWA	0.6153
194	168	SAPOTRA	0.6140
195	48	KAMAN	0.6137
196	72	KESHORAIPATAN	0.6136
197	81	CHHOTI SADRI	0.6124
198	73	NAINWA	0.6122
199	46	BAYANA	0.6120
200	206	KHANDAR	0.6089
201	97	LALSOT	0.6088
202	164	SHERGARH	0.6050
203	29	SAJJANGARH	0.6021
204	85	KAPASAN	0.6016
205	226	UNIARA	0.6007
206	42	DHORIMANNA	0.6006
	LOW (0.5-0.6)		
207	144	JHALRAPATAN	0.5985
208	102	DHAULPUR	0.5947
209	66	BIKANER	0.5913
210	75	ARNOD	0.5903
211	41	CHOHTAN	0.5880
212	100	BARI	0.5844
213	79	BHAINSRORGARH	0.5819
214	37	SHAHBAD	0.5809
215	103	RAJAKHERA	0.5785
216	118	NOHAR	0.5785
217	68	KOLAYAT	0.5752
218	143	DAG	0.5723
219	28	PEEPALKHOONT	0.5685
220	35	CHHIPABAROD	0.5674
221	101	BASERI	0.5663
222	27	KUSHALGARH	0.5633
222	121	CHAKSU	0.5633
224	44	SINDHARI	0.5611
225	109	ANUPGARH	0.5610
226	157	BAP	0.5588
227	132	JAISALMER	0.5541
228	142	BAKANI	0.5525
229	134	SANKRA	0.5487
230	34	CHHABRA	0.5216
231	115	SURATGARH	0.5150
232	146	MANOHARTHANA	0.5097
	VERY LOW (< 0.5)		
233	234	KOTRA	0.4951
234	40	BAYTOO	0.4950
235	43	SHEO	0.4938
236	39	BARMER	0.4930
237	133	SAM	0.4749
		RAJASTHAN	**0.6684**
		%age of AAPs	**55.70**

BOLD: Above Average Panchayat Samities (AAPs) *Source*: Annex 6.1, Col. 6.

ANNEX-6.3

RANKING OF PSS BY POPULATION SERVED PER MEDICAL INSTITUTION: RAJASTHAN, 2001

(Descending Order)

RANK	PANCHAYAT SAMITIES P. CODE	PANCHAYAT SAMITIES NAME	POP. SERVED PER MEDICAL INSTITUTION
1	2	3	4
		VERY HIGH/WORST (>=5000)	
1	146	**MANOHARTHANA**	**8496**
2	103	**RAJAKHERA**	**7672**
3	48	**KAMAN**	**7576**
4	95	**BANDIKUI**	**7217**
5	34	**CHHABRA**	**7105**
6	13	**KOTKASIM**	**6923**
7	70	**NOKHA**	**6496**
8	46	**BAYANA**	**6388**
9	76	**BARI SADRI**	**6346**
10	51	**NAGAR PAHARI**	**6219**
11	18	**RAMGARH**	**6117**
12	85	**KAPASAN**	**6038**
13	66	**BIKANER**	**5856**
14	161	**MANDOR**	**5602**
15	99	**SIKRAI**	**5573**
16	21	**TIJARA**	**5159**
17	14	**LACHHMANGARH**	**5133**
18	157	**BAP**	**5074**
19	97	**LALSOT**	**5027**
		HIGH/WORSE (4000-5000)	
20	47	**DEEG**	**4996**
21	136	**BHINMAL**	**4862**
22	109	**ANUPGARH**	**4858**
23	68	**KOLAYAT**	**4831**
24	53	**SEWAR**	**4790**
25	12	**KISHANGARH BAS**	**4786**
26	33	**BARAN**	**4688**
27	144	**JHALRAPATAN**	**4679**
28	78	**BHADESAR**	**4669**
29	139	**RANIWARA**	**4667**
30	119	**AMBER**	**4597**
31	117	**HANUMANGARH**	**4585**
32	9	**BANSURE**	**4561**
33	36	**KISHANGANJ**	**4507**
34	215	**SRI MADHOPUR**	**4489**
35	101	**BASERI**	**4484**
36	22	**UMREN**	**4436**
37	35	**CHHIPABAROD**	**4409**
38	121	**CHAKSU**	**4355**
39	50	**NADBAI**	**4354**
40	163	**PHALODI**	**4338**
41	74	**TALERA**	**4315**
42	165	**HINDAUN**	**4302**
43	164	**SHERGARH**	**4280**
44	123	**GOVINDGARH**	**4243**
45	102	**DHAULPUR**	**4233**
46	142	**BAKANI**	**4231**
47	16	**NIMRANA**	**4216**
48	41	**CHOHTAN**	**4181**
49	81	**CHHOTI SADRI**	**4169**
50	98	**MAHWA**	**4167**
51	127	**PHAGI**	**4144**
52	226	**UNIARA**	**4141**
53	17	**RAJGARH**	**4135**
54	42	**DHORIMANNA**	**4114**
55	11	**KATHUMAR**	**4071**
56	131	**VIRATNAGAR**	**4047**
57	69	**LUNKARANSAR**	**4025**
57	140	**SANCHORE**	**4025**
		MEDIUM/NORMAL (3000-4000)	
59	147	**PIRAWA**	**3998**
60	75	**ARNOD**	**3995**
61	141	**SAYLA**	**3984**
62	198	**DEOGARH**	**3893**
63	54	**WEIR**	**3888**
64	170	**CHECHAT**	**3885**
65	43	**SHEO**	**3799**
66	38	**BALOTRA**	**3794**
67	96	**DAUSA**	**3776**
68	166	**KARAULI**	**3773**
69	126	**KOTPUTLI**	**3745**
70	143	**DAG**	**3715**
71	39	**BARMER**	**3663**
72	171	**ITAWA**	**3620**
73	162	**OSIAN**	**3608**
74	10	**BEHROR**	**3577**
75	124	**JAMWA RAMGARH**	**3573**
76	86	**NIMBAHERA**	**3663**
77	31	**ANTA**	**3542**
78	20	**THANAGAZI**	**3518**
79	154	**SURAJGARH**	**3516**
80	92	**SARDARSHAHAR**	**3484**
81	216	**ABU ROAD**	**3479**
82	176	**DIDWANA**	**3476**
83	222	**MALPURA**	**3469**
84	60	**MANDAL**	**3465**
84	182	**MUNDWA**	**3465**
86	205	**GANGAPUR**	**3446**
87	174	**SULTANPUR**	**3422**
88	118	**NOHAR**	**3418**
89	8	**SRINAGAR**	**3403**
90	116	**BHADRA**	**3394**
91	180	**MAKRANA**	**3384**
92	93	**SUJANGARH**	**3376**
93	79	**BHAINSRORGARH**	**3349**
94	32	**ATRU**	**3343**
95	212	**LACHHMANGARH**	**3339**
96	115	**SURATGARH**	**3334**
97	204	**BONLI**	**3331**
98	120	**BASSI**	**3328**
99	128	**SAMBHAR**	**3326**
100	160	**LUNI**	**3273**
101	177	**JAYAL**	**3260**
102	152	**KHETRI**	**3250**
103	52	**RUPBAS**	**3248**
104	122	**DUDU**	**3244**
105	45	**SIWANA**	**3237**
106	82	**CHITTAURGARH**	**3230**
107	181	**MERTA**	**3218**
108	158	**BHOPALGARH**	**3211**
109	191	**RAIPUR**	**3193**
110	217	**PINDWARA**	**3186**
111	71	**HINDOLI**	**3155**
112	90	**RAJGARH**	**3146**
113	172	**LADPURA**	**3145**
114	213	**NEEM KA THANA**	**3139**
115	178	**KUCHAMAN**	**3118**
116	221	**DEOLI**	**3078**
117	6	**MASOODA**	**3069**
118	234	**KOTRA**	**3058**
119	84	**GANGRAR**	**3057**
120	202	**RAJSAMAND**	**3055**
121	40	**BAYTOO**	**3048**
122	15	MANDAWAR	3040
123	183	NAGAUR	3038
124	59	KOTRI	3035
125	19	RENI	3033
126	72	KESHORAIPATAN	3028
127	113	RAISINGHNAGAR	3026
128	153	NAWALGARH	3023
		LOW/BETTER (2000-3000)	
129	203	BAMANWAS	2989
130	49	KUMHER	2983
131	206	KHANDAR	2944
132	150	CHIRAWA	2939
133	7	PISANGAN	2919
134	168	SAPOTRA	2906
135	169	TODABHIM	2897
136	73	NAINWA	2893
137	125	JHOTWARA	2869
138	167	NADOTI	2866
139	24	BAGIDORA	2850
140	130	SHAHPURA	2836
141	224	TODARAISINGH	2824
142	145	KHANPUR	2789
142	229	DHARIAWAD	2789
144	44	SINDHARI	2751
145	184	PARBATSAR	2741
146	155	UDAIPURWATI	2736
147	207	SAWAI MADHOPUR	2732
148	211	KHANDELA	2732
149	223	NIWAI	2710
150	188	JAITARAN	2709
151	37	SHAHBAD	2704
152	112	PADAMPUR	2697
153	5	KISHANGARH	2693
154	100	BARI	2689
155	156	BALESAR	2680
156	26	GHATOL	2678
157	1	ARAIN	2668
158	233	KHERWARA	2649
159	83	DUNGLA	2646
159	197	BHIM	2646
161	3	JAWAJA	2632
162	65	SUWANA	2603
163	80	BHOPALSAGAR	2596
164	196	AMET	2593
165	134	SANKRA	2584
166	173	SANGOD	2578
167	67	DUNGARGARH	2575
167	129	SANGANER	2575
169	138	JASWANTPURA	2568
170	110	GANGANAGAR	2558
171	2	BHINAY	2543
172	87	PRATAPGARH	2515
173	190	PALI	2498
174	4	KEKRI	2472
175	185	RIYAN	2461
176	105	BICHHIWARA	2434
177	135	AHORE	2429
178	214	PIPRALI	2424
179	195	SUMERPUR	2421
180	64	SHAHPURA	2403
181	137	JALOR	2397
182	230	GIRWA	2396
183	227	BARGAON	2381
184	30	TALWARA	2375
185	235	MAVLI	2368
186	29	SAJJANGARH	2359
187	218	REODAR	2338
188	193	ROHAT	2332
188	231	GOGUNDA	2332
190	189	MARWAR JUN.	2326
191	23	ANANDPURI	2317
192	210	FATEHPUR	2303
193	186	BALI	2298
194	228	BHINDER	2294
195	55	ASIND	2290
196	57	HURDA	2277
197	179	LADNU	2258
198	108	SIMALWARA	2253
199	111	KARANPUR	2241
200	159	BILARA	2202
201	133	SAM	2201
202	94	TARANAGAR	2188
202	114	SADULSHAHAR	2188
204	148	ALSISAR	2176
205	225	TONK	2174
206	208	DANTA RAMGARH	2167
207	209	DHOND	2164
208	25	GARHI	2140
209	132	JAISALMER	2130
210	149	BUHANA	2129
211	175	DEGANA	2112
212	151	JHUNJHUNUN	2103
213	28	PEEPALKHOONT	2072
214	58	JAHAZPUR	2071
215	27	KUSHALGARH	2014
216	199	KHAMNOR	2005
217	63	SAHARA	2001
		VERY LOW/BEST (<2000)	
218	88	RASHMI	1982
219	62	RAIPUR	1962
220	56	BANERA	1931
221	237	SARADA	1912
222	187	DESURI	1893
223	89	CHURU	1879
224	236	SALUMBAR	1855
225	91	RATANGARH	1838
226	61	MANDALGARH	1834
227	106	DUNGARPUR	1815
228	219	SHEOGANJ	1812
229	232	JHADOL	1811
230	107	SAGWARA	1705
231	77	BEGUN	1619
232	201	RAILMAGRA	1534
233	194	SOJAT	1513
234	192	RANI STATION	1459
235	200	KUMBHALGARH	1443
236	104	ASPUR	1347
237	220	SIROHI	1295
		RAJASTHAN	**3042**
		%age of AAPs	**51.05**

BOLD: Equal/Above Average Panchayat Samities (AAPs)

Source: General Annex X, Col. 13.

ANNEX-6.4

RANKING OF PSS BY POPULATION SERVED PER BED: RAJASTHAN, 2001

(Descending Order)

RANK	PANCHAYAT SAMITIES P. CODE	PANCHAYAT SAMITIES NAME	POPULATION SERVED PER BED
1	2	3	4
	VERY HIGH/WORST (>4000)		
1	53	**SEWAR**	6985
2	8	**SRINAGAR**	6544
3	132	**JAISALMER**	5325
4	5	**KISHANGARH**	5116
5	39	**BARMER**	4960
6	125	**JHOTWARA**	4941
7	144	**JHALRAPATAN**	4902
8	163	**PHALODI**	4789
9	82	**CHITTAURGARH**	4666
10	38	**BALOTRA**	4427
11	183	**NAGAUR**	4408
12	64	**SHAHPURA**	4381
13	207	**SAWAI MADHOPUR**	4316
14	33	**BARAN**	4298
15	120	**BASSI**	4253
16	161	**MANDOR**	4202
17	184	**PARBATSAR**	4143
18	92	**SARDARSHAHAR**	4129
19	22	**UMREN**	4107
20	18	**RAMGARH**	4078
21	109	**ANUPGARH**	4017
	HIGH/WORSE (3000-4000)		
22	102	**DHAULPUR**	3977
23	152	**KHETRI**	3972
24	51	**NAGAR PAHARI**	3939
25	99	**SIKRAI**	3922
26	204	**BONLI**	3886
27	87	**PRATAPGARH**	3870
28	97	**LALSOT**	3809
29	126	**KOTPUTLI**	3808
30	190	**PALI**	3747
31	166	**KARAULI**	3710
32	117	**HANUMANGARH**	3569
33	103	**RAJAKHERA**	3552
34	48	**KAMAN**	3536
35	168	**SAPOTRA**	3523
36	122	**DUDU**	3494
37	217	**PINDWARA**	3422
38	101	**BASERI**	3363
39	50	**NADBAI**	3356
40	44	**SINDHARI**	3285
41	165	**HINDAUN**	3280
42	169	**TODABHIM**	3235
43	11	**KATHUMAR**	3207
44	52	**RUPBAS**	3199
45	40	**BAYTOO**	3187
46	128	**SAMBHAR**	3175
47	20	**THANAGAZI**	3166
48	71	**HINDOLI**	3155
49	95	**BANDIKUI**	3105
50	74	**TALERA**	3082
51	123	**GOVINDGARH**	3064
52	65	**SUWANA**	3037
53	105	**BICHHIWARA**	3027
	MEDIUM/NORMAL (2000-3000)		
54	127	**PHAGI**	2993
55	60	**MANDAL**	2992
56	121	**CHAKSU**	2984
57	43	**SHEO**	2976
58	30	**TALWARA**	2968
59	110	**GANGANAGAR**	2942
60	141	**SAYLA**	2933
61	162	**OSIAN**	2932
62	55	**ASIND**	2914
63	41	**CHOHTAN**	2894
64	130	**SHAHPURA**	2836
65	116	**BHADRA**	2828
66	231	**GOGUNDA**	2807
67	29	**SAJJANGARH**	2801
68	69	**LUNKARANSAR**	2786
69	206	**KHANDAR**	2780
70	234	**KOTRA**	2780
71	203	**BAMANWAS**	2767
72	226	**UNIARA**	2761
73	212	**LACHHMANGARH**	2736
74	68	**KOLAYAT**	2734
75	164	**SHERGARH**	2711
76	137	**JALOR**	2690
77	135	**AHORE**	2687
78	70	**NOKHA**	2686
79	9	**BANSURE**	2679
80	177	**JAYAL**	2678
81	115	**SURATGARH**	2667
82	35	**CHHIPABAROD**	2664
83	214	**PIPRALI**	2642
84	175	**DEGANA**	2640
85	167	**NADOTI**	2627
86	157	**BAP**	2622
87	218	**REODAR**	2617
88	106	**DUNGARPUR**	2612
89	158	**BHOPALGARH**	2594
90	171	**ITAWA**	2594
91	49	**KUMHER**	2585
92	21	**TIJARA**	2579
93	227	**BARGAON**	2579
94	6	**MASOODA**	2574
95	66	**BIKANER**	2567
96	221	**DEOLI**	2565
97	145	**KHANPUR**	2556
98	142	**BAKANI**	2539
99	230	**GIRWA**	2529
100	19	**RENI**	2528
101	28	**PEEPALKHOONT**	2521
102	119	**AMBER**	2520
103	140	**SANCHORE**	2516
104	179	**LADNU**	2508
105	36	**KISHANGANJ**	2504
106	176	**DIDWANA**	2500
107	209	**DHOND**	2499
108	185	**RIYAN**	2495
109	180	**MAKRANA**	2465
110	24	**BAGIDORA**	2455
111	13	**KOTKASIM**	2452
112	155	**UDAIPURWATI**	2451
113	173	**SANGOD**	2449
114	182	**MUNDWA**	2439
115	149	**BUHANA**	2433
116	211	**KHANDELA**	2428
117	205	**GANGAPUR**	2422
118	46	**BAYANA**	2395
119	16	**NIMRANA**	2389
120	147	**PIRAWA**	2387
121	81	**CHHOTI SADRI**	2383
122	148	**ALSISAR**	2357
123	233	**KHERWARA**	2355
124	32	**ATRU**	2353
125	15	**MANDAWAR**	2352
126	2	**BHINAY**	2350
127	67	**DUNGARGARH**	2344
128	23	ANANDPURI	2317
129	118	NOHAR	2315
130	133	SAM	2311
131	139	RANIWARA	2269
132	12	KISHANGARH BAS	2263
133	26	GHATOL	2258
134	154	SURAJGARH	2254
135	178	KUCHAMAN	2253
136	160	LUNI	2246
137	78	BHADESAR	2237
138	45	SIWANA	2226
139	114	SADULSHAHAR	2222
140	93	SUJANGARH	2221
141	75	ARNOD	2219
142	100	BARI	2215
143	56	BANERA	2213
144	156	DALESAR	2177
145	191	RAIPUR	2167
146	189	MARWAR JUN.	2160
147	124	JAMWA RAMGARH	2156
148	83	DUNGLA	2142
149	193	ROHAT	2137
150	236	SALUMBAR	2137
151	72	KESHORAIPATAN	2126
152	150	CHIRAWA	2123
153	84	GANGRAR	2110
154	94	TARANAGAR	2097
155	174	SULTANPUR	2091
156	219	SHEOGANJ	2076
157	134	SANKRA	2067
158	42	DHORIMANNA	2057
159	14	LACHHMANGARH	2053
160	224	TODARAISINGH	2039
161	3	JAWAJA	2024
162	1	ARAIN	2021
	LOW/BETTER (1000-2000)		
163	194	SOJAT	1999
164	229	DHARIAWAD	1996
165	129	SANGANER	1989
166	232	JHADOL	1978
167	192	RANI STATION	1972
168	7	PISANGAN	1970
169	113	RAISINGHNAGAR	1967
170	237	SARADA	1965
171	138	JASWANTPURA	1946
172	47	DEEG	1936
173	222	MALPURA	1923
174	104	ASPUR	1922
175	223	NIWAI	1922
176	199	KHAMNOR	1916
177	90	RAJGARH	1910
178	108	SIMALWARA	1884
179	27	KUSHALGARH	1878
180	153	NAWALGARH	1876
181	54	WEIR	1872
182	98	MAHWA	1866
183	197	BHIM	1859
184	25	GARHI	1856
185	151	JHUNJHUNUN	1841
186	201	RAILMAGRA	1841
187	112	PADAMPUR	1839
188	196	AMET	1837
189	200	KUMBHALGARH	1824
190	181	MERTA	1816
191	213	NEEM KA THANA	1801
192	235	MAVLI	1798
193	88	RASHMI	1793
194	131	VIRATNAGAR	1779
195	59	KOTRI	1770
196	91	RATANGARH	1757
197	146	MANOHARTHANA	1755
198	220	SIROHI	1744
199	73	NAINWA	1698
200	86	NIMBAHERA	1692
201	17	RAJGARH	1683
202	208	DANTA RAMGARH	1681
203	79	BHAINSRORGARH	1675
204	215	SRI MADHOPUR	1648
205	195	SUMERPUR	1643
206	96	DAUSA	1638
207	143	DAG	1608
208	136	BHINMAL	1593
209	89	CHURU	1585
210	62	RAIPUR	1562
211	186	BALI	1532
212	61	MANDALGARH	1526
213	111	KARANPUR	1516
214	80	BHOPALSAGAR	1514
215	210	FATEHPUR	1512
216	225	TONK	1481
217	34	CHHABRA	1463
218	188	JAITARAN	1460
219	198	DEOGARH	1442
220	107	SAGWARA	1311
221	170	CHECHAT	1270
222	228	BHINDER	1261
223	4	KEKRI	1258
224	85	KAPASAN	1243
225	31	ANTA	1240
226	76	BARI SADRI	1201
227	187	DESURI	1189
228	37	SHAHBAD	1176
229	216	ABU ROAD	1172
230	57	HURDA	1153
231	58	JAHAZPUR	1141
232	77	BEGUN	1109
233	159	BILARA	1101
234	10	BEHROR	1073
	VERY LOW/BEST (<1000)		
235	202	RAJSAMAND	997
236	63	SAHARA	891
237	172	LADPURA	851
		RAJASTHAN	**2342**
		%age of AAPs	**53.59**

BOLD: Equal/Above Average Panchayat Samities (AAPs)

Source: General Annex XI, Col. 10.

ANNEX-6.5

RANKING OF PSS BY POPULATION SERVED PER DOCTOR: RAJASTHAN, 2001

(Descending Order)

RANK	PANCHAYAT SAMITIES P. CODE	PANCHAYAT SAMITIES NAME	POPULATION SERVED PER DOCTOR
1	2	3	4
	VERY HIGH/WORST (>25,000)		
1	8	**SRINAGAR**	56714
2	207	**SAWAI MADHOPUR**	53953
3	53	**SEWAR**	41910
4	134	**SANKRA**	33075
5	163	**PHALODI**	32842
6	121	**CHAKSU**	32228
7	234	**KOTRA**	30584
8	48	**KAMAN**	30306
9	64	**SHAHPURA**	29791
10	125	**JHOTWARA**	29649
11	44	**SINDHARI**	29568
12	51	**NAGAR PAHARI**	29541
13	168	**SAPOTRA**	29064
14	101	**BASERI**	28825
15	221	**DEOLI**	28212
16	23	**ANANDPURI**	27802
17	184	**PARBATSAR**	26630
18	102	**DHAULPUR**	26246
19	157	**BAP**	26215
20	119	**AMBER**	26203
21	144	**JHALRAPATAN**	25734
22	5	**KISHANGARH**	25579
23	28	**PEEPALKHOONT**	25212
24	117	**HANUMANGARH**	25125
	HIGH/WORSE (20,000-25,000)		
25	18	**RAMGARH**	24469
26	169	**TODABHIM**	24262
27	55	**ASIND**	24043
28	152	**KHETRI**	23830
29	39	**BARMER**	23808
30	13	**KOTKASIM**	23537
31	40	**BAYTOO**	23372
32	204	**BONLI**	23315
33	133	**SAM**	23113
34	183	**NAGAUR**	22482
35	92	**SARDARSHAHAR**	22298
36	22	**UMREN**	22179
37	161	**MANDOR**	21608
38	74	**TALERA**	21576
39	203	**BAMANWAS**	21347
40	103	**RAJAKHERA**	21312
41	132	**JAISALMER**	21300
42	122	**DUDU**	20963
43	128	**SAMBHAR**	20953
44	114	**SADULSHAHAR**	20947
45	26	**GHATOL**	20940
46	126	**KOTPUTLI**	20770
47	217	**PINDWARA**	20534
48	38	**BALOTRA**	20430
49	127	**PHAGI**	20201
50	50	**NADBAI**	20139
51	87	**PRATAPGARH**	20123
	MEDIUM/NORMAL (15,000-20,000)		
52	123	**GOVINDGARH**	19699
53	24	**BAGIDORA**	19637
54	30	**TALWARA**	19430
55	156	**BALESAR**	19353
56	97	**LALSOT**	19336
57	99	**SIKRAI**	19253
58	52	**RUPBAS**	19195
59	162	**OSIAN**	19190
60	95	**BANDIKUI**	19073
61	142	**BAKANI**	19041
62	71	**HINDOLI**	18929
63	68	**KOLAYAT**	18886
64	88	**RASHMI**	18832
65	131	**VIRATNAGAR**	18765
66	129	**SANGANER**	18757
67	233	**KHERWARA**	18164
68	105	**BICHHIWARA**	18163
68	109	**ANUPGARH**	18163
70	130	**SHAHPURA**	18150
71	140	**SANCHORE**	18006
72	60	**MANDAL**	17955
73	9	**BANSURE**	17863
74	43	**SHEO**	17854
75	115	**SURATGARH**	17782
76	227	**DARGAON**	17686
77	120	**BASSI**	17665
78	141	**SAYLA**	17596
79	218	**REODAR**	17534
80	165	**HINDAUN**	17494
81	21	**TIJARA**	17460
82	70	**NOKHA**	17459
83	41	**CHOHTAN**	17366
84	33	**BARAN**	17190
85	19	**RENI**	17061
86	66	**BIKANER**	17036
87	36	**KISHANGANJ**	16902
88	158	**BHOPALGARH**	16860
89	82	**CHITTAURGARH**	16796
90	12	**KISHANGARH BAS**	16750
91	69	**LUNKARANSAR**	16719
92	11	**KATHUMAR**	16284
93	164	**SHERGARH**	16266
94	209	**DHOND**	16148
95	14	**LACHHMANGARH**	16131
96	135	**AHORE**	16122
97	79	**BHAINSRORGARH**	16076
98	177	**JAYAL**	16067
99	110	**GANGANAGAR**	16047
100	35	**CHHIPABAROD**	15982
101	6	**MASOODA**	15960
102	32	**ATRU**	15880
103	179	**LADNU**	15803
104	106	**DUNGARPUR**	15671
105	211	**KHANDELA**	15611
106	27	**KUSHALGARH**	15441
107	78	**BHADESAR**	15342
108	145	**KHANPUR**	15337
109	15	**MANDAWAR**	15199
110	231	**GOGUNDA**	15158
111	212	**LACHHMANGARH**	15156
112	100	**BARI**	15060
113	206	**KHANDAR**	15014
114	176	**DIDWANA**	15002
	LOW/BETTER (10,000-15,000)		
115	83	**DUNGLA**	14996
116	190	**PALI**	14990
117	75	**ARNOD**	14980
118	29	**SAJJANGARH**	14940
119	65	**SUWANA**	14909
120	59	**KOTRI**	14870
121	166	**KARAULI**	14841
122	84	**GANGRAR**	14773
123	42	**DHORIMANNA**	14761
124	46	**BAYANA**	14741
125	151	**JHUNJHUNUN**	14724
126	226	**UNIARA**	14723
127	214	**PIPRALI**	14719
128	116	**BHADRA**	14705
129	137	**JALOR**	14647
130	118	**NOHAR**	14630
131	229	**DHARIAWAD**	14543
132	80	**BHOPALSAGAR**	14535
133	16	NIMRANA	14333
134	160	LUNI	14319
135	81	CHHOTI SADRI	14295
136	61	MANDALGARH	14281
137	45	SIWANA	14243
138	148	ALSISAR	14142
139	182	MUNDWA	14109
140	49	KUMHER	14102
141	47	DEEG	14078
142	236	SALUMBAR	14044
143	150	CHIRAWA	13895
144	232	JHADOL	13844
145	205	GANGAPUR	13785
146	149	BUHANA	13627
147	139	RANIWARA	13612
148	20	THANAGAZI	13570
149	154	SURAJGARH	13525
150	173	SANGOD	13359
151	93	SUJANGARH	13327
152	56	BANERA	13278
153	237	SARADA	13261
154	147	PIRAWA	13223
155	136	BHINMAL	13197
156	25	GARHI	13196
157	124	JAMWA RAMGARH	13165
158	7	PISANGAN	13137
159	73	NAINWA	13019
160	191	RAIPUR	13000
161	171	ITAWA	12971
162	2	BHINAY	12926
163	138	JASWANTPURA	12841
164	185	RIYAN	12831
165	223	NIWAI	12715
166	76	BARI SADRI	12692
167	175	DEGANA	12672
168	167	NADOTI	12609
169	196	AMET	12595
170	146	MANOHARTHANA	12417
171	104	ASPUR	12301
172	181	MERTA	12229
173	67	DUNGARGARH	12188
174	112	PADAMPUR	12136
175	235	MAVLI	12134
176	1	ARAIN	12126
177	108	SIMALWARA	12055
178	225	TONK	12021
179	230	GIRWA	11980
180	200	KUMBHALGARH	11941
181	222	MALPURA	11795
182	155	UDAIPURWATI	11764
183	174	SULTANPUR	11584
184	193	ROHAT	11400
185	213	NEEM KA THANA	11323
186	113	RAISINGHNAGAR	11238
187	228	BHINDER	11213
188	178	KUCHAMAN	11173
189	90	RAJGARH	11142
190	224	TODARAISINGH	11013
191	63	SAHARA	10894
192	189	MARWAR JUN.	10673
193	197	BHIM	10583
194	85	KAPASAN	10566
195	62	RAIPUR	10544
196	3	JAWAJA	10527
197	180	MAKRANA	10509
198	220	SIROHI	10466
199	194	SOJAT	10393
200	54	WEIR	10110
201	208	DANTA RAMGARH	10084
202	96	DAUSA	10071
203	94	TARANAGAR	10067
	VERY LOW/BEST (<10,000)		
204	219	SHEOGANJ	9966
205	98	MAHWA	9954
206	192	RANI STATION	9682
207	170	CHECHAT	9434
208	72	KESHORAIPATAN	9401
209	111	KARANPUR	9372
210	201	RAILMAGRA	9203
211	57	HURDA	9109
212	37	SHAHBAD	9012
213	216	ABU ROAD	8832
214	195	SUMERPUR	8625
215	153	NAWALGARH	8371
216	186	BALI	8355
217	17	RAJGARH	8040
218	89	CHURU	8009
219	58	JAHAZPUR	7990
220	86	NIMBAHERA	7964
221	91	RATANGARH	7905
222	77	BEGUN	7847
223	215	SRI MADHOPUR	7814
224	188	JAITARAN	7789
225	107	SAGWARA	7707
226	34	CHHABRA	7652
227	4	KEKRI	7417
228	10	BEHROR	6975
229	143	DAG	6966
230	210	FATEHPUR	6910
231	187	DESURI	6816
232	31	ANTA	6468
233	199	KHAMNOR	6385
234	202	RAJSAMAND	5855
235	159	BILARA	5310
236	172	LADPURA	5168
237	198	DEOGARH	4867
	RAJASTHAN		**14445**
	%age of AAPs		**55.70**

BOLD: Equal/Above Average Panchayat Samities (AAPs)

Source: General Annex XI, Col. 9.

ANNEX-6.6

RANKING OF PSS BY AREA SERVED PER MEDICAL INSTITUTION: RAJASTHAN, 2001

(Descending Order)

RANK	PANCHAYAT SAMITIES P. CODE	NAME	AREA SERVED PER MEDICAL INSTITUTION (sq. kms.)
1	2	3	4
	VERY HIGH/WORST (>40)		
1	**133**	**SAM**	**335.10**
2	**132**	**JAISALMER**	**214.16**
3	**68**	**KOLAYAT**	**170.20**
4	**157**	**BAP**	**142.94**
5	**43**	**SHEO**	**140.77**
6	**66**	**BIKANER**	**139.76**
7	**69**	**LUNKARANSAR**	**115.07**
8	**70**	**NOKHA**	**87.62**
9	**134**	**SANKRA**	**85.73**
10	**163**	**PHALODI**	**61.09**
11	**41**	**CHOHTAN**	**60.49**
12	**92**	**SARDARSHAHAR**	**59.60**
13	**115**	**SURATGARH**	**59.24**
14	**39**	**BARMER**	**58.67**
15	**79**	**BHAINSRORGARH**	**57.08**
16	**34**	**CHHABRA**	**55.98**
17	**38**	**BALOTRA**	**55.50**
18	**164**	**SHERGARH**	**51.97**
19	**146**	**MANOHARTHANA**	**48.56**
20	**36**	**KISHANGANJ**	**48.35**
21	**161**	**MANDOR**	**47.01**
22	**40**	**BAYTOO**	**46.78**
23	**42**	**DHORIMANNA**	**43.74**
24	**67**	**DUNGARGARH**	**42.29**
25	**109**	**ANUPGARH**	**41.21**
26	**118**	**NOHAR**	**40.23**
	HIGH/WORSE (30-40)		
27	**182**	**MUNDWA**	**38.32**
28	**37**	**SHAHBAD**	**36.71**
29	**44**	**SINDHARI**	**36.23**
30	**190**	**PALI**	**36.02**
31	**162**	**OSIAN**	**35.76**
32	**140**	**SANCHORE**	**35.39**
33	**136**	**BHINMAL**	**35.20**
34	**93**	**SUJANGARH**	**34.61**
35	**85**	**KAPASAN**	**34.47**
36	**76**	**BARI SADRI**	**33.89**
37	**183**	**NAGAUR**	**32.17**
38	**193**	**ROHAT**	**31.92**
39	**74**	**TALERA**	**31.38**
40	**226**	**UNIARA**	**30.83**
41	**177**	**JAYAL**	**30.26**
42	**144**	**JHALRAPATAN**	**30.21**
43	**45**	**SIWANA**	**30.03**
	MEDIUM/NORMAL (20-30)		
44	**198**	**DEOGARH**	**29.46**
45	**17**	**RAJGARH**	**28.83**
45	**81**	**CHHOTI SADRI**	**28.83**
47	**127**	**PHAGI**	**28.55**
48	**156**	**BALESAR**	**28.52**
49	**35**	**CHHIPABAROD**	**28.43**
50	**172**	**LADPURA**	**28.42**
51	**160**	**LUNI**	**28.32**
52	**222**	**MALPURA**	**28.22**
53	**139**	**RANIWARA**	**28.11**
54	**33**	**BARAN**	**27.85**
55	**158**	**BHOPALGARH**	**27.67**
56	**141**	**SAYLA**	**27.54**
57	**46**	**BAYANA**	**26.66**
58	**206**	**KHANDAR**	**26.52**
59	**116**	**BHADRA**	**26.36**
60	**216**	**ABU ROAD**	**26.00**
61	**90**	**RAJGARH**	**25.85**
62	**94**	**TARANAGAR**	**25.84**
63	**113**	**RAISINGHNAGAR**	**25.30**
64	**224**	**TODARAISINGH**	**25.27**
65	**143**	**DAG**	**25.12**
66	**142**	**BAKANI**	**24.60**
67	**168**	**SAPOTRA**	**24.53**
68	**181**	**MERTA**	**24.51**
69	**1**	**ARAIN**	**24.04**
70	78	BHADESAR	23.50
71	75	ARNOD	23.38
72	147	PIRAWA	23.28
73	103	RAJAKHERA	22.88
74	170	CHECHAT	22.67
75	32	ATRU	22.62
76	221	DEOLI	22.46
77	71	HINDOLI	22.32
78	101	BASERI	22.25
79	31	ANTA	22.20
80	114	SADULSHAHAR	22.16
81	122	DUDU	22.09
82	135	AHORE	21.87
83	72	KESHORAIPATAN	21.82
84	86	NIMBAHERA	21.39
85	138	JASWANTPURA	21.38
86	73	NAINWA	21.11
87	121	CHAKSU	20.72
87	174	SULTANPUR	20.72
89	166	KARAULI	20.67
90	171	ITAWA	20.63
91	60	MANDAL	20.27
92	13	KOTKASIM	20.26
	LOW/BETTER (10-20)		
93	2	BHINAY	19.94
94	48	KAMAN	19.88
95	234	KOTRA	19.86
96	20	THANAGAZI	19.64
97	217	PINDWARA	19.63
98	176	DIDWANA	19.61
99	179	LADNU	19.59
100	5	KISHANGARH	19.42
101	59	KOTRI	19.39
102	89	CHURU	19.25
103	137	JALOR	19.18
104	84	GANGRAR	19.16
105	91	RATANGARH	19.10
106	180	MAKRANA	18.75
107	112	PADAMPUR	18.72
108	188	JAITARAN	18.69
109	173	SANGOD	18.35
110	159	BILARA	18.29
111	64	SHAHPURA	18.18
112	8	SRINAGAR	17.95
113	87	PRATAPGARH	17.85
114	189	MARWAR JUN.	17.83
115	111	KARANPUR	17.62
116	4	KEKRI	17.43
117	212	LACHHMANGARH	17.41
118	191	RAIPUR	17.31
119	18	RAMGARH	17.14
120	186	BALI	17.12
121	145	KHANPUR	17.09
122	97	LALSOT	17.08
123	185	RIYAN	16.98
124	22	UMREN	16.97
125	223	NIWAI	16.89
126	6	MASOODA	16.83
127	178	KUCHAMAN	16.70
128	51	NAGAR PAHARI	16.36
129	95	BANDIKUI	16.24
130	219	SHEOGANJ	16.22
131	175	DEGANA	16.19
132	229	DHARIAWAD	16.13
133	204	BONLI	16.02
134	195	SUMERPUR	16.00
135	47	DEEG	15.82
136	194	SOJAT	15.80
137	184	PARBATSAR	15.75
138	82	CHITTAURGARH	15.65
139	154	SURAJGARH	15.63
140	207	SAWAI MADHOPUR	15.60
141	57	HURDA	15.43
142	187	DESURI	15.35
143	77	BEGUN	15.20
144	225	TONK	15.06
145	7	PISANGAN	14.86
145	196	AMET	14.86
147	117	HANUMANGARH	14.85
148	119	AMBER	14.73
148	210	FATEHPUR	14.73
150	167	NADOTI	14.68
151	21	TIJARA	14.63
152	203	BAMANWAS	14.58
153	83	DUNGLA	14.52
154	218	REODAR	14.49
155	124	JAMWA RAMGARH	14.45
156	12	KISHANGARH BAS	14.44
157	80	BHOPALSAGAR	14.22
158	230	GIRWA	14.20
159	100	BARI	14.18
160	9	BANSURE	14.14
161	14	LACHHMANGARH	14.07
162	231	GOGUNDA	13.41
163	232	JHADOL	13.35
164	99	SIKRAI	13.23
165	55	ASIND	13.22
166	65	SUWANA	13.21
166	128	SAMBHAR	13.21
168	53	SEWAR	13.09
169	197	BHIM	13.03
170	63	SAHARA	12.92
171	61	MANDALGARH	12.77
172	58	JAHAZPUR	12.76
173	131	VIRATNAGAR	12.73
174	96	DAUSA	12.61
175	28	PEEPALKHOONT	12.50
176	227	BARGAON	12.46
177	125	JHOTWARA	12.42
178	205	GANGAPUR	12.40
179	110	GANGANAGAR	12.39
180	202	RAJSAMAND	12.38
181	56	BANERA	12.30
182	152	KHETRI	12.06
182	215	SRI MADHOPUR	12.06
184	62	RAIPUR	11.99
185	88	RASHMI	11.83
186	213	NEEM KA THANA	11.75
187	50	NADBAI	11.67
188	148	ALSISAR	11.49
189	129	SANGANER	11.45
190	220	SIROHI	11.24
191	233	KHERWARA	11.22
192	228	BHINDER	11.19
193	16	NIMRANA	11.13
194	54	WEIR	11.08
195	3	JAWAJA	11.03
196	98	MAHWA	11.01
197	11	KATHUMAR	10.87
197	126	KOTPUTLI	10.87
199	192	RANI STATION	10.45
200	165	HINDAUN	10.35
201	123	GOVINDGARH	10.25
	VERY LOW/BEST (<10)		
202	211	KHANDELA	9.80
203	151	JHUNJHUNUN	9.77
204	235	MAVLI	9.74
205	237	SARADA	9.71
206	155	UDAIPURWATI	9.66
207	209	DHOND	9.41
208	150	CHIRAWA	9.40
209	214	PIPRALI	9.38
210	102	DHAULPUR	9.31
211	27	KUSHALGARH	9.29
212	153	NAWALGARH	9.24
213	208	DANTA RAMGARH	9.22
214	120	BASSI	9.14
215	26	GHATOL	9.11
216	15	MANDAWAR	8.88
217	19	RENI	8.71
218	236	SALUMBAR	8.70
219	10	BEHROR	8.63
220	108	SIMALWARA	8.54
221	200	KUMBHALGARH	8.53
222	49	KUMHER	8.47
223	30	TALWARA	8.34
224	24	BAGIDORA	8.32
225	52	RUPBAS	8.29
226	169	TODABHIM	7.80
227	105	BICHHIWARA	7.69
228	201	RAILMAGRA	7.56
229	23	ANANDPURI	7.12
230	29	SAJJANGARH	7.06
231	199	KHAMNOR	6.92
232	149	BUHANA	6.81
233	130	SHAHPURA	6.38
234	25	GARHI	6.34
235	106	DUNGARPUR	6.05
236	107	SAGWARA	5.41
237	104	ASPUR	5.05
	RAJASTHAN		**23.6**
	%age of AAPs		**29.11**

BOLD: Equal/Above Average Panchayat Samities (AAPs)

Source: General Annex X, Col. 11.

ANNEX-7.1

RANKING OF PANCHAYAT SAMITIES BY EDI: RAJ, 1991

(Descending Order)

RANK	PANCHAYAT SAMITIES P. CODE	PANCHAYAT SAMITIES NAME	EDI
1	2	3	4
	HIGH (0.4-0.5)		
1	16	**NIMRANA**	0.465
2	10	**BEHROR**	0.440
3	13	**KOTKASIM**	0.415
4	149	**BUHANA**	0.409
5	15	**MANDAWAR**	0.406
5	151	**JHUNJHUNUN**	0.406
	MEDIUM (0.3-0.4)		
7	110	**GANGANAGAR**	0.393
8	112	**PADAMPUR**	0.380
8	150	**CHIRAWA**	0.380
10	153	**NAWALGARH**	0.375
11	154	**SURAJGARH**	0.361
12	111	**KARANPUR**	0.360
13	148	**ALSISAR**	0.359
14	49	**KUMHER**	0.356
15	52	**RUPBAS**	0.346
16	152	**KHETRI**	0.343
17	114	**SADULSHAHAR**	0.340
18	155	**UDAIPURWATI**	0.338
19	50	**NADBAI**	0.337
19	4	**KEKRI**	0.337
21	174	**SULTANPUR**	0.335
22	215	**SRI MADHOPUR**	0.332
22	113	**RAISINGHNAGAR**	0.332
22	53	**SEWAR**	0.332
25	173	**SANGOD**	0.327
26	123	**GOVINDGARH**	0.325
27	54	**WEIR**	0.320
28	31	**ANTA**	0.319
28	214	**PIPRALI**	0.319
30	12	**KISHANGARH BAS**	0.318
31	125	**JHOTWARA**	0.314
32	33	**BARAN**	0.313
32	213	**NEEM KA THANA**	0.313
34	211	**KHANDELA**	0.310
34	7	**PISANGAN**	0.310
34	145	**KHANPUR**	0.310
37	32	**ATRU**	0.308
37	212	**LACHHMANGARH**	0.308
37	98	**MAHWA**	0.308
40	209	**DHOND**	0.307
41	172	**LADPURA**	0.305
41	129	**SANGANER**	0.305
41	116	**BHADRA**	0.305
44	208	**DANTA RAMGARH**	0.304
44	170	**CHECHAT**	0.304
46	3	**JAWAJA**	0.303
47	210	**FATEHPUR**	0.301
	LOW (0.2-0.3)		
48	130	**SHAHPURA**	0.299
49	95	**BANDIKUI**	0.291
50	57	**HURDA**	0.290
50	47	**DEEG**	0.290
52	126	**KOTPUTLI**	0.287
53	128	**SAMBHAR**	0.285
54	117	**HANUMANGARH**	0.284
55	171	**ITAWA**	0.279
56	115	**SURATGARH**	0.278
57	192	**RANI STATION**	0.276
58	11	**KATHUMAR**	0.275
58	6	**MASOODA**	0.275
58	107	**SAGWARA**	0.275
59	17	**RAJGARH**	0.275
62	90	**RAJGARH**	0.274
62	18	**RAMGARH**	0.274
64	119	**AMBER**	0.273
64	167	**NADOTI**	0.273
64	205	**GANGAPUR**	0.273
67	109	**ANUPGARH**	0.272
68	131	**VIRATNAGAR**	0.271
69	21	**TIJARA**	0.270
70	227	**BARGAON**	0.269
70	165	**HINDAUN**	0.269
72	9	**BANSURE**	0.267
72	25	**GARHI**	0.267
74	201	**RAILMAGRA**	0.266
74	14	**LACHHMANGARH**	0.266
74	46	**BAYANA**	0.266
77	8	**SRINAGAR**	0.265
77	19	**RENI**	0.265
77	169	**TODABHIM**	0.265
80	86	**NIMBAHERA**	0.264
80	102	**DHAULPUR**	0.264
82	195	**SUMERPUR**	0.262
82	2	**BHINAY**	0.262
84	122	**DUDU**	0.260
85	233	**KHERWARA**	0.258
86	235	**MAVLI**	0.257
87	202	**RAJSAMAND**	0.256
87	22	**UMREN**	0.256
87	120	**BASSI**	0.256
90	96	**DAUSA**	0.255
90	186	**BALI**	0.255
90	179	**LADNU**	0.255
93	187	**DESURI**	0.254
94	194	**SOJAT**	0.254
95	81	**CHHOTI SADRI**	0.251
95	203	**BAMANWAS**	0.251
95	199	**KHAMNOR**	0.251
98	101	**BASERI**	0.250
99	5	**KISHANGARH**	0.248
100	181	**MERTA**	0.246
101	197	**BHIM**	0.245
101	180	**MAKRANA**	0.245
103	189	**KHARCHI/MARWAR JUN.**	0.244
103	221	**DEOLI**	0.244
105	72	**KESHORAIPATAN**	0.243
105	124	**JAMWA RAMGARH**	0.243
107	178	**KUCHAMAN**	0.242
107	176	**DIDWANA**	0.242
107	118	**NOHAR**	0.242
110	223	**NIWAI**	0.241
110	207	**SAWAI MADHOPUR**	0.241
112	204	BONLI	0.238
112	51	NAGAR PAHARI	0.238
114	80	BHOPALSAGAR	0.236
114	89	CHURU	0.236
116	159	BILARA	0.235
116	99	SIKRAI	0.235
118	160	LUNI	0.234
119	1	ARAIN	0.233
119	127	PHAGI	0.233
121	147	PIRAWA	0.232
121	228	BHINDER	0.232
123	97	LALSOT	0.230
123	103	RAJAKHERA	0.230
123	144	JHALRAPATAN	0.230
126	135	AHORE	0.226
127	161	MANDOR	0.225
127	75	ARNOD	0.225
127	104	ASPUR	0.225
130	82	CHITTAURGARH	0.224
130	220	SIROHI	0.224
132	37	SHAHBAD	0.222
133	121	CHAKSU	0.221
134	191	RAIPUR	0.220
134	230	GIRWA	0.220
136	88	RASHMI	0.219
136	224	TODARAISINGH	0.219
138	237	SARADA	0.218
138	87	PRATAPGARH	0.218
140	20	THANAGAZI	0.217
140	175	DEGANA	0.217
142	222	MALPURA	0.216
142	168	SAPOTRA	0.216
144	83	DUNGLA	0.215
145	185	RIYAN	0.213
145	74	TALERA	0.213
145	158	BHOPALGARH	0.213
148	190	PALI	0.212
148	76	BARI SADRI	0.212
150	106	DUNGARPUR	0.211
150	184	PARBATSAR	0.211
152	94	TARANAGAR	0.210
153	77	BEGUN	0.209
154	78	BHADESAR	0.208
154	36	KISHANGANJ	0.208
156	84	GANGRAR	0.207
157	91	RATANGARH	0.206
158	56	BANERA	0.205
158	193	ROHAT	0.205
158	137	JALOR	0.205
161	66	BIKANER	0.203
162	226	UNIARA	0.203
163	58	JAHAZPUR	0.202
164	59	KOTRI	0.201
164	69	LUNKARANSAR	0.201
166	63	SAHARA	0.200
166	132	JAISALMER	0.200
	VERY LOW (<0.2)		
168	188	JAITARAN	0.199
168	105	BICHHIWARA	0.199
168	225	TONK	0.199
168	62	RAIPUR	0.199
172	79	BHAINSRORGARH	0.198
173	100	BARI	0.197
173	35	CHHIPABAROD	0.197
175	24	BAGIDORA	0.195
176	108	SIMALWARA	0.194
177	65	SUWANA	0.193
178	166	KARAULI	0.192
179	55	ASIND	0.191
180	183	NAGAUR	0.190
181	219	SHEOGANJ	0.188
181	206	KHANDAR	0.188
183	217	PINDWARA	0.187
184	60	MANDAL	0.186
184	162	OSIAN	0.186
186	34	CHHABRA	0.185
186	142	BAKANI	0.185
188	177	JAYAL	0.184
189	200	KUMBHALGARH	0.183
189	156	BALESAR	0.183
189	231	GOGUNDA	0.183
189	73	NAINWA	0.183
193	48	KAMAN	0.182
194	68	KOLAYAT	0.181
194	93	SUJANGARH	0.181
196	67	DUNGARGARH	0.179
196	196	AMET	0.179
196	38	BALOTRA	0.179
199	85	KAPASAN	0.178
200	61	MANDALGARH	0.177
200	182	MUNDWA	0.177
200	163	PHALODI	0.177
203	30	TALWARA	0.176
203	236	SALUMBAR	0.176
205	45	SIWANA	0.174
205	71	HINDOLI	0.174
205	198	DEOGARH	0.174
208	70	NOKHA	0.173
209	26	GHATOL	0.170
209	92	SARDARSHAHAR	0.170
211	218	REODAR	0.169
211	143	DAG	0.169
213	64	SHAHPURA	0.167
214	23	ANANDPURI	0.165
215	134	SANKRA	0.162
216	164	SHERGARH	0.159
217	138	JASWANTPURA	0.157
218	232	JHADOL	0.156
219	141	SAYLA	0.153
219	133	SAM	0.153
219	157	BAP	0.153
222	139	RANIWARA	0.151
222	40	BAYTOO	0.151
224	216	ABU ROAD	0.148
225	39	BARMER	0.141
226	43	SHEO	0.140
227	29	SAJJANGARH	0.138
227	140	SANCHORE	0.138
229	136	BHINMAL	0.127
230	44	SINDHARI	0.123
231	42	DHORIMANNA	0.122
232	146	MANOHARTHANA	0.117
233	229	DHARIAWAD	0.103
234	27	KUSHALGARH	0.097
235	41	CHOHTAN	0.090
236	28	PEEPALKHOONT	0.085
237	234	KOTRA	0.066
		RAJASTHAN	**0.241**
		%age of AAPs	**46.84**

BOLD: Equal/Above Average Panchayat Samities (AAPs)

Source: Annex 8.1, Col. 5.

ANNEX-7.2

RANKING OF PSS BY POPULATION SERVED PER PRIMARY SCHOOL : RAJASTHAN, 1991

(Descending Order)

RANK	PANCHAYAT SAMITIES P. CODE	NAME	Population (No.)
1	2	3	4
	VERY HIGH (>=1500)		
1	195	SUMERPUR	2097
2	117	HANUMANGARH	1953
3	141	SAYLA	1816
4	186	BALI	1677
5	215	SRI MADHOPUR	1613
6	136	BHINMAL	1572
7	217	PINDWARA	1561
8	116	BHADRA	1558
9	181	MERTA	1533
10	188	JAITARAN	1515
11	139	RANIWARA	1502
	HIGH (1250-1500)		
12	137	JALOR	1499
12	165	HINDAUN	1499
14	138	JASWANTPURA	1498
15	220	SIROHI	1490
16	114	SADULSHAHAR	1488
17	152	KHETRI	1486
18	123	GOVINDGARH	1482
19	91	RATANGARH	1410
20	178	KUCHAMAN	1405
21	214	PIPRALI	1403
22	211	KHANDELA	1401
23	180	MAKRANA	1395
24	38	BALOTRA	1392
24	163	PHALODI	1392
24	67	DUNGARGARH	1392
27	16	NIMRANA	1383
28	213	NEEM KA THANA	1382
29	209	DHOND	1381
30	93	SUJANGARH	1369
31	164	SHERGARH	1362
32	99	SIKRAI	1361
32	118	NOHAR	1361
34	177	JAYAL	1359
34	176	DIDWANA	1359
36	70	NOKHA	1357
37	130	SHAHPURA	1349
37	159	BILARA	1349
39	191	RAIPUR	1348
40	119	AMBER	1342
41	135	AHORE	1341
42	162	OSIAN	1332
43	45	SIWANA	1319
44	140	SANCHORE	1315
45	150	CHIRAWA	1312
46	66	BIKANER	1311
47	8	SRINAGAR	1298
48	179	LADNU	1297
49	115	SURATGARH	1288
50	184	PARBATSAR	1287
51	153	NAWALGARH	1286
51	201	RAILMAGRA	1286
53	25	GARHI	1282
54	96	DAUSA	1276
54	155	UDAIPURWATI	1276
56	131	VIRATNAGAR	1273
57	189	MARWAR JUN.	1269
58	95	BANDIKUI	1260
59	89	CHURU	1258
60	94	TARANAGAR	1254
	MEDIUM (1000-1250)		
61	219	SHEOGANJ	1248
62	204	BONLI	1246
63	183	NAGAUR	1242
63	182	MUNDWA	1242
65	194	SOJAT	1239
66	187	DESURI	1237
67	126	KOTPUTLI	1225
67	18	RAMGARH	1225
69	236	SALUMBAR	1224
70	192	RANI STATION	1222
70	105	BICHHIWARA	1222
72	158	BHOPALGARH	1213
73	185	RIYAN	1211
74	50	NADBAI	1204
75	11	KATHUMAR	1203
76	92	SARDARSHAHAR	1198
77	41	CHOHTAN	1197
78	207	SAWAI MADHOPUR	1195
79	205	GANGAPUR	1193
80	157	BAP	1191
81	15	MANDAWAR	1183
82	218	REODAR	1180
83	22	UMREN	1179
84	169	TODABHIM	1178
85	237	SARADA	1172
86	167	NADOTI	1169
87	9	BANSURE	1168
88	171	ITAWA	1166
89	12	KISHANGARH BAS	1163
90	90	RAJGARH	1159
91	122	DUDU	1157
92	149	BUHANA	1152
92	156	BALESAR	1152
94	10	BEHROR	1150
95	125	JHOTWARA	1145
96	104	ASPUR	1136
97	24	BAGIDORA	1134
98	47	DEEG	1132
99	221	DEOLI	1130
100	190	PALI	1127
101	222	MALPURA	1124
101	210	FATEHPUR	1124
103	101	BASERI	1120
104	102	DHAULPUR	1117
104	36	KISHANGANJ	1117
104	170	CHECHAT	1117
107	193	ROHAT	1114
108	98	MAHWA	1111
109	52	RUPBAS	1110
109	175	DEGANA	1110
111	129	SANGANER	1107
112	230	GIRWA	1100
113	128	SAMBHAR	1096
114	212	LACHHMANGARH	1089
115	56	BANERA	1087
115	161	MANDOR	1087
115	48	KAMAN	1087
118	154	SURAJGARH	1086
119	42	DHORIMANNA	1084
120	229	DHARIAWAD	1076
121	206	KHANDAR	1075
121	208	DANTA RAMGARH	1075
123	49	KUMHER	1067
124	216	ABU ROAD	1061
125	166	KARAULI	1060
125	20	THANAGAZI	1060
127	54	WEIR	1056
128	65	SUWANA	1055
129	235	MAVLI	1054
130	6	MASOODA	1053
131	107	SAGWARA	1050
131	69	LUNKARANSAR	1050
133	231	GOGUNDA	1049
134	74	TALERA	1044
134	5	KISHANGARH	1044
134	224	TODARAISINGH	1044
137	160	LUNI	1042
138	174	SULTANPUR	1041
139	86	NIMBAHERA	1040
139	40	BAYTOO	1040
141	71	HINDOLI	1039
142	31	ANTA	1037
143	168	SAPOTRA	1036
144	234	KOTRA	1035
144	2	BHINAY	1035
146	32	ATRU	1033
147	17	RAJGARH	1032
148	142	BAKANI	1030
149	103	RAJAKHERA	1027
150	14	LACHHMANGARH	1025
151	172	LADPURA	1024
152	173	SANGOD	1022
153	97	LALSOT	1019
154	110	GANGANAGAR	1015
155	100	BARI	1012
156	7	PISANGAN	1010
157	21	TIJARA	1008
158	19	RENI	1007
158	59	KOTRI	1007
160	28	PEEPALKHOONT	1006
161	109	ANUPGARH	1004
162	61	MANDALGARH	1003
	LOW (750-1000)		
163	68	KOLAYAT	997
164	55	ASIND	994
165	51	NAGAR PAHARI	993
166	227	BARGAON	988
166	144	JHALRAPATAN	988
166	83	DUNGLA	988
169	44	SINDHARI	987
170	57	HURDA	986
171	85	KAPASAN	985
171	146	MANOHARTHANA	985
173	124	JAMWA RAMGARH	984
174	4	KEKRI	983
175	225	TONK	982
176	46	BAYANA	979
177	58	JAHAZPUR	977
178	226	UNIARA	976
179	199	KHAMNOR	975
180	127	PHAGI	974
181	29	SAJJANGARH	973
182	53	SEWAR	968
182	88	RASHMI	968
184	108	SIMALWARA	967
184	26	GHATOL	967
186	233	KHERWARA	966
187	228	BHINDER	962
188	232	JHADOL	961
189	134	SANKRA	956
190	76	BARI SADRI	950
191	60	MANDAL	948
191	145	KHANPUR	948
191	151	JHUNJHUNUN	948
194	63	SAHARA	946
195	87	PRATAPGARH	942
196	120	BASSI	923
196	37	SHAHBAD	923
198	1	ARAIN	922
199	39	BARMER	920
200	106	DUNGARPUR	919
201	82	CHITTAURGARH	917
202	197	BHIM	913
203	78	BHADESAR	904
204	30	TALWARA	902
204	148	ALSISAR	902
206	33	BARAN	899
207	223	NIWAI	898
208	75	ARNOD	896
209	143	DAG	895
210	23	ANANDPURI	894
211	62	RAIPUR	892
212	203	BAMANWAS	891
213	13	KOTKASIM	883
214	81	CHHOTI SADRI	875
214	202	RAJSAMAND	875
216	121	CHAKSU	867
217	198	DEOGARH	862
217	43	SHEO	862
219	72	KESHORAIPATAN	857
220	35	CHHIPABAROD	855
221	84	GANGRAR	853
222	79	BHAINSRORGARH	830
223	64	SHAHPURA	826
224	73	NAINWA	822
225	147	PIRAWA	802
226	27	KUSHALGARH	784
227	77	BEGUN	773
228	80	BHOPALSAGAR	772
229	196	AMET	769
230	200	KUMBHALGARH	767
231	132	JAISALMER	751
	VERY LOW (<750)		
232	3	JAWAJA	710
233	113	RAISINGHNAGAR	657
234	34	CHHABRA	648
235	133	SAM	637
236	111	KARANPUR	623
236	112	PADAMPUR	623
		RAJASTHAN	**1106**
		%age of AAPs	**46.84**

BOLD: Equal/Above Average Panchayat Samities (AAPs)

Source: General Annex V, Col. 9.

ANNEX-7.3

RANKING OF PSS BY AREA SERVED PER PRIMARY SCHOOL: RAJASTHAN, 1991

(Descending Order)

RANK	PANCHAYAT SAMITIES P. CODE	PANCHAYAT SAMITIES NAME	Area (Sq. Kms.)
1	2	3	4.00
	VERY HIGH (>=10)		
1	**132**	**JAISALMER**	**141.7**
2	**131**	**VIRATNAGAR**	**120.1**
3	**68**	**KOLAYAT**	**55.0**
4	**156**	**BALESAR**	**50.9**
5	**66**	**BIKANER**	**50.5**
6	**43**	**SHEO**	**46.9**
7	**133**	**SAM**	**45.3**
8	**69**	**LUNKARANSAR**	**41.7**
9	**67**	**DUNGARGARH**	**31.3**
10	**38**	**BALOTRA**	**28.2**
11	**162**	**OSIAN**	**27.9**
12	**92**	**SARDARSHAHAR**	**26.1**
13	**70**	**NOKHA**	**24.5**
14	**163**	**PHALODI**	**23.8**
15	**41**	**CHOHTAN**	**22.8**
16	**40**	**BAYTOO**	**22.1**
17	**39**	**BARMER**	**20.5**
18	**117**	**HANUMANGARH**	**20.2**
19	**45**	**SIWANA**	**19.4**
20	**192**	**RANI STATION**	**19.2**
21	**91**	**RATANGARH**	**18.5**
22	**44**	**SINDHARI**	**18.3**
22	**93**	**SUJANGARH**	**18.3**
24	**161**	**MANDOR**	**18.2**
24	**155**	**UDAIPURWATI**	**18.2**
26	**94**	**TARANAGAR**	**18.0**
27	**114**	**SADULSHAHAR**	**17.8**
27	**79**	**BHAINSRORGARH**	**17.8**
27	**181**	**MERTA**	**17.8**
30	**189**	**MARWAR JUN.**	**17.3**
31	**194**	**SOJAT**	**16.6**
32	**37**	**SHAHBAD**	**16.3**
32	**182**	**MUNDWA**	**16.3**
34	**176**	**DIDWANA**	**16.1**
35	**140**	**SANCHORE**	**16.0**
35	**42**	**DHORIMANNA**	**16.0**
37	**89**	**CHURU**	**15.9**
38	**185**	**RIYAN**	**15.4**
38	**219**	**SHEOGANJ**	**15.4**
38	**193**	**ROHAT**	**15.4**
41	**139**	**RANIWARA**	**15.2**
42	**137**	**JALOR**	**15.1**
43	**180**	**MAKRANA**	**15.0**
43	**36**	**KISHANGANJ**	**15.0**
45	**115**	**SURATGARH**	**14.8**
46	**136**	**BHINMAL**	**14.7**
47	**187**	**DESURI**	**14.5**
48	**178**	**KUCHAMAN**	**14.4**
48	**135**	**AHORE**	**14.4**
50	**158**	**BHOPALGARH**	**14.3**
50	**134**	**SANKRA**	**14.3**
52	**218**	**REODAR**	**13.9**
52	**216**	**ABU ROAD**	**13.9**
54	**157**	**BAP**	**13.5**
55	**159**	**BILARA**	**12.4**
56	**160**	**LUNI**	**12.3**
57	**171**	**ITAWA**	**12.2**
57	**205**	**GANGAPUR**	**12.2**
59	**186**	**BALI**	**12.0**
59	**138**	**JASWANTPURA**	**12.0**
61	**116**	**BHADRA**	**11.9**
62	**90**	**RAJGARH**	**11.5**
63	**188**	**JAITARAN**	**11.4**
64	**223**	**NIWAI**	**11.3**
64	**215**	**SRI MADHOPUR**	**11.3**
66	**167**	**NADOTI**	**11.2**
67	**221**	**DEOLI**	**10.9**
68	113	RAISINGHNAGAR	10.6
69	184	PARBATSAR	10.5
69	174	SULTANPUR	10.5
71	220	SIROHI	10.3
72	121	CHAKSU	10.2
73	1	ARAIN	10.1
73	190	PALI	10.1
73	2	BHINAY	10.1
	HIGH (7.5-10.0)		
76	191	RAIPUR	9.9
76	179	LADNU	9.9
78	177	JAYAL	9.8
78	175	DEGANA	9.8
80	217	PINDWARA	9.7
80	183	NAGAUR	9.7
82	5	KISHANGARH	9.5
82	233	KHERWARA	9.5
84	231	GOGUNDA	9.3
84	225	TONK	9.3
84	17	RAJGARH	9.3
87	74	TALERA	9.2
87	71	HINDOLI	9.2
89	61	MANDALGARH	8.9
90	209	DHOND	8.8
90	8	SRINAGAR	8.8
92	172	LADPURA	8.7
93	77	BEGUN	8.6
94	206	KHANDAR	8.5
94	4	KEKRI	8.5
94	87	PRATAPGARH	8.5
97	229	DHARIAWAD	8.4
97	56	BANERA	8.4
99	57	HURDA	8.3
99	126	KOTPUTLI	8.3
99	28	PEEPALKHOONT	8.3
99	32	ATRU	8.3
103	224	TODARAISINGH	8.2
104	170	CHECHAT	8.1
104	228	BHINDER	8.1
106	143	DAG	8.1
107	197	BHIM	8.0
108	59	KOTRI	7.9
109	31	ANTA	7.8
109	20	THANAGAZI	7.8
109	165	HINDAUN	7.8
112	64	SHAHPURA	7.7
112	73	NAINWA	7.7
112	86	NIMBAHERA	7.7
112	173	SANGOD	7.7
112	203	BAMANWAS	7.7
117	58	JAHAZPUR	7.6
118	144	JHALRAPATAN	7.5
118	230	GIRWA	7.5
118	60	MANDAL	7.5
	MEDIUM (5.0-7.5)		
121	166	KARAULI	7.4
121	101	BASERI	7.4
121	72	KESHORAIPATAN	7.4
121	236	SALUMBAR	7.4
121	208	DANTA RAMGARH	7.4
126	142	BAKANI	7.3
127	6	MASOODA	7.2
127	145	KHANPUR	7.2
129	169	TODABHIM	7.1
129	81	CHHOTI SADRI	7.1
129	55	ASIND	7.1
132	63	SAHARA	7.0
132	141	SAYLA	7.0
132	211	KHANDELA	7.0
132	237	SARADA	7.0
132	7	PISANGAN	7.0
132	200	KUMBHALGARH	7.0
132	235	MAVLI	7.0
139	75	ARNOD	6.9
139	35	CHHIPABAROD	6.9
141	100	BARI	6.8
141	213	NEEM KA THANA	6.8
141	33	BARAN	6.8
141	65	SUWANA	6.8
145	222	MALPURA	6.7
145	112	PADAMPUR	6.7
147	88	RASHMI	6.6
147	151	JHUNJHUNUN	6.6
149	85	KAPASAN	6.5
149	212	LACHHMANGARH	6.5
151	62	RAIPUR	6.4
152	83	DUNGLA	6.3
152	84	GANGRAR	6.3
154	34	CHHABRA	6.2
154	210	FATEHPUR	6.2
154	146	MANOHARTHANA	6.2
154	22	UMREN	6.2
158	153	NAWALGARH	6.0
158	147	PIRAWA	6.0
160	196	AMET	5.9
160	76	BARI SADRI	5.9
162	207	SAWAI MADHOPUR	5.8
163	154	SURAJGARH	5.7
164	127	PHAGI	5.6
164	227	BARGAON	5.6
164	96	DAUSA	5.6
167	82	CHITTAURGARH	5.5
167	118	NOHAR	5.5
167	110	GANGANAGAR	5.5
167	78	BHADESAR	5.5
167	214	PIPRALI	5.5
172	195	SUMERPUR	5.4
172	202	RAJSAMAND	5.4
172	104	ASPUR	5.4
175	109	ANUPGARH	5.3
175	130	SHAHPURA	5.3
175	120	BASSI	5.3
178	199	KHAMNOR	5.2
178	204	BONLI	5.2
178	232	JHADOL	5.2
178	123	GOVINDGARH	5.2
178	226	UNIARA	5.2
178	198	DEOGARH	5.2
178	46	BAYANA	5.2
178	149	BUHANA	5.2
186	234	KOTRA	5.1
187	105	BICHHIWARA	5.0
187	111	KARANPUR	5.0
	LOW (2.5-5.0)		
189	150	CHIRAWA	4.9
189	27	KUSHALGARH	4.9
191	164	SHERGARH	4.8
191	80	BHOPALSAGAR	4.8
191	25	GARHI	4.8
191	9	BANSURE	4.8
195	152	KHETRI	4.7
195	122	DUDU	4.7
195	18	RAMGARH	4.7
195	108	SIMALWARA	4.7
199	97	LALSOT	4.6
199	201	RAILMAGRA	4.6
199	125	JHOTWARA	4.6
202	47	DEEG	4.4
202	148	ALSISAR	4.4
202	16	NIMRANA	4.4
205	12	KISHANGARH BAS	4.3
205	26	GHATOL	4.3
205	21	TIJARA	4.3
205	129	SANGANER	4.3
205	124	JAMWA RAMGARH	4.3
205	24	BAGIDORA	4.3
205	99	SIKRAI	4.3
212	15	MANDAWAR	4.2
212	128	SAMBHAR	4.2
214	30	TALWARA	4.1
214	50	NADBAI	4.1
214	95	BANDIKUI	4.1
217	11	KATHUMAR	4.0
217	107	SAGWARA	4.0
217	168	SAPOTRA	4.0
217	106	DUNGARPUR	4.0
221	3	JAWAJA	3.9
221	48	KAMAN	3.9
221	103	RAJAKHERA	3.9
224	29	SAJJANGARH	3.8
224	54	WEIR	3.8
226	19	RENI	3.7
226	119	AMBER	3.7
228	49	KUMHER	3.6
228	14	LACHHMANGARH	3.6
228	23	ANANDPURI	3.6
228	52	RUPBAS	3.6
228	98	MAHWA	3.6
233	51	NAGAR PAHARI	3.4
233	10	BEHROR	3.4
235	53	SEWAR	3.3
236	102	DHAULPUR	3.2
236	13	KOTKASIM	3.2
		RAJASTHAN	**10.9**
		%age of AAPs	**28.27**

BOLD: Equal/Above Average Panchayat Samities (AAPs)

Source: General Annex V, Col. 13.

ANNEX-8.1

PANCHAYAT SAMITI-WISE VARIATION IN EDUCATION INDEX: RAJASTHAN, 1991 & 2001

P. Code	*Panchayat Samities/District*	*1991*			*2001*		
		Total Literacy Index (A)	*Female Literacy Index (B)*	***EDI/3 (2*A+1*B)***	*Total Literacy Index (A)*	*Female Literacy Index (B)*	***EDI (2*A+1*B)/3***
1	*2*	*3*	*4*	*5*	*6*	*7*	*8*
1	ARAIN	0.2911	0.1169	0.2330	0.4652	0.2830	0.4045
2	BHINAY	0.3267	0.1327	0.2620	0.4266	0.2123	0.3552
3	JAWAJA	0.3937	0.1226	0.3033	0.7441	0.5802	0.6895
4	KEKRI	0.4052	0.1992	0.3365	0.4714	0.2557	0.3995
5	KISHANGARH	0.3083	0.1273	0.2480	0.5312	0.3386	0.4670
6	MASOODA	0.3522	0.1208	0.2751	0.5463	0.3193	0.4706
7	PISANGAN	0.3838	0.1622	0.3099	0.5288	0.3164	0.4580
8	SRINAGAR	0.3341	0.1278	0.2653	0.5225	0.3031	0.4494
	AJMER DISTRICT	**0.3510**	**0.1396**	**0.2805**	**0.5309**	**0.3272**	**0.4630**
9	BANSURE	0.3366	0.1273	0.2668	0.5815	0.3951	0.5194
10	BEHROR	0.5165	0.2857	0.4396	0.9319	0.7218	0.8619
11	KATHUMAR	0.3558	0.1144	0.2753	0.5735	0.3676	0.5049
12	KISHANGARH BAS	0.3822	0.1894	0.3179	0.5590	0.3623	0.4934
13	KOTKASIM	0.4901	0.2632	0.4145	0.6969	0.5273	0.6404
14	LACHHMANGARH	0.3382	0.1217	0.2660	0.5640	0.3448	0.4909
15	MANDAWAR	0.4819	0.2529	0.4056	0.6929	0.5237	0.6365
16	NIMRANA	0.5372	0.3195	0.4646	0.5684	0.4539	0.5302
17	RAJGARH	0.3515	0.1221	0.2750	0.5494	0.3272	0.4753
18	RAMGARH	0.3390	0.1438	0.2739	0.5382	0.3260	0.4675
19	RENI	0.3419	0.1120	0.2653	0.5724	0.3518	0.4989
20	THANAGAZI	0.2809	0.0893	0.2170	0.4807	0.2620	0.4078
21	TIJARA	0.3341	0.1427	0.2703	0.5314	0.3281	0.4636
22	UMREN	0.3240	0.1192	0.2557	0.5352	0.3240	0.4648
	ALWAR	**0.3802**	**0.1673**	**0.3092**	**0.5888**	**0.3916**	**0.5231**
23	ANANDPURI	0.2116	0.0708	0.1647	0.4052	0.2402	0.3502
24	BAGIDORA	0.2393	0.1060	0.1949	0.4104	0.2403	0.3537
25	GARHI	0.3192	0.1614	0.2666	0.5198	0.3471	0.4622
26	GHATOL	0.2147	0.0810	0.1701	0.3995	0.2170	0.3387
27	KUSHALGARH	0.1256	0.0391	0.0968	0.3361	0.1810	0.2844
28	PEEPALKHOONT	0.1123	0.0295	0.0847	0.2577	0.1187	0.2114
29	SAJJANGARH	0.1744	0.0661	0.1383	0.3751	0.2112	0.3205
30	TALWARA	0.2194	0.0887	0.1758	0.4559	0.2647	0.3922
	BANSWARA	**0.2146**	**0.0887**	**0.1726**	**0.4078**	**0.2378**	**0.3511**
31	ANTA	0.3947	0.1680	0.3191	0.6346	0.4501	0.5731
32	ATRU	0.3837	0.1578	0.3084	0.6342	0.4382	0.5689
33	BARAN	0.3904	0.1568	0.3125	0.6552	0.4645	0.5916
34	CHHABRA	0.2462	0.0636	0.1853	0.5362	0.3277	0.4667
35	CHHIPABAROD	0.2599	0.0712	0.1970	0.4883	0.2771	0.4179
36	KISHANGANJ	0.2563	0.1110	0.2079	0.5288	0.3583	0.4720
37	SHAHBAD	0.2784	0.1092	0.2220	0.5299	0.3403	0.4667
	BARAN	**0.3193**	**0.1225**	**0.2537**	**0.5743**	**0.3821**	**0.5102**
38	BALOTRA	0.2331	0.0693	0.1785	0.5513	0.3697	0.4908
39	BARMER	0.1938	0.0342	0.1406	0.5485	0.3653	0.4874
40	BAYTOO	0.2022	0.0470	0.1505	0.5826	0.4293	0.5315
41	CHOHTAN	0.1238	0.0223	0.0900	0.5066	0.3517	0.4550
42	DHORIMANNA	0.1676	0.0304	0.1219	0.6775	0.5672	0.6407
43	SHEO	0.1934	0.0332	0.1400	0.5763	0.3980	0.5169
44	SINDHARI	0.1707	0.0289	0.1234	0.6088	0.4642	0.5606
45	SIWANA	0.2259	0.0706	0.1741	0.5954	0.4356	0.5421
	BARMER	**0.1879**	**0.0420**	**0.1393**	**0.5814**	**0.4243**	**0.5290**
46	BAYANA	0.3498	0.0971	0.2656	0.5727	0.3374	0.4943
47	DEEG	0.3746	0.1200	0.2897	0.5854	0.3634	0.5114
48	KAMAN	0.2427	0.0606	0.1820	0.4768	0.2620	0.4052
49	KUMHER	0.4521	0.1638	0.3560	0.6752	0.4609	0.6038
50	NADBAI	0.4344	0.1421	0.3370	0.6876	0.4683	0.6145
51	NAGAR PAHARI	0.3075	0.0975	0.2375	0.5896	0.3812	0.5201
52	RUPBAS	0.4338	0.1696	0.3457	0.6772	0.4727	0.6090
53	SEWAR	0.4256	0.1438	0.3317	0.6789	0.4666	0.6081
54	WEIR	0.4110	0.1385	0.3202	0.6168	0.3831	0.5389
	BHARATPUR	**0.3784**	**0.1248**	**0.2939**	**0.6144**	**0.3962**	**0.5417**
55	ASIND	0.2438	0.0841	0.1906	0.4193	0.2293	0.3560
56	BANERA	0.2569	0.1015	0.2051	0.5012	0.3187	0.4404
57	HURDA	0.3428	0.1851	0.2902	0.5188	0.3211	0.4529
58	JAHAZPUR	0.2583	0.0883	0.2016	0.4911	0.2967	0.4263
59	KOTRI	0.2360	0.1321	0.2014	0.3948	0.2253	0.3383
60	MANDAL	0.2339	0.0905	0.1861	0.4319	0.2462	0.3700
61	MANDALGARH	0.2212	0.0899	0.1774	0.4350	0.2594	0.3765

P. Code	Panchayat Samities/District	1991			2001		
		Total Literacy Index (A)	Female Literacy Index (B)	**EDI /3 (2*A+1*B)**	Total Literacy Index (A)	Female Literacy Index (B)	**EDI (2*A+1*B)/3**
1	2	3	4	5	6	7	8
62	RAIPUR	0.2489	0.0979	0.1986	0.4258	0.2421	0.3646
63	SAHARA	0.2497	0.1014	0.2003	0.4413	0.2644	0.3823
64	SHAHPURA	0.2115	0.0773	0.1668	0.4282	0.2459	0.3674
65	SUWANA	0.2422	0.0930	0.1925	0.4587	0.2641	0.3938
	BHILWARA	**0.2448**	**0.0996**	**0.1964**	**0.4459**	**0.2609**	**0.3842**
66	BIKANER	0.2546	0.1003	0.2032	0.4702	0.3023	0.4142
67	DUNGARGARH *	0.2290	0.0803	0.1794	0.5836	0.4171	0.5281
68	KOLAYAT	0.2280	0.0866	0.1809	0.4134	0.2464	0.3577
69	LUNKARANSAR	0.2493	0.1030	0.2005	0.4662	0.3034	0.4119
70	NOKHA	0.2269	0.0659	0.1732	0.4890	0.2878	0.4219
	BIKANER **	**0.2407**	**0.0884**	**0.1899**	**0.4633**	**0.2883**	**0.4050**
71	HINDOLI	0.2216	0.0786	0.1739	0.4691	0.2760	0.4047
72	KESHORAIPATAN	0.3093	0.1094	0.2427	0.5621	0.3689	0.4977
73	NAINWA	0.2357	0.0767	0.1827	0.5100	0.2968	0.4389
74	TALERA	0.2674	0.1040	0.2129	0.5211	0.3439	0.4620
	BUNDI	**0.2602**	**0.0939**	**0.2048**	**0.5159**	**0.3241**	**0.4520**
75	ARNOD	0.2732	0.1277	0.2247	0.4708	0.2972	0.4129
76	BARI SADRI	0.2699	0.0948	0.2115	0.4501	0.2513	0.3838
77	BEGUN	0.2705	0.0863	0.2091	0.4887	0.2876	0.4217
78	BHADESAR	0.2633	0.0978	0.2081	0.4753	0.2833	0.4113
79	BHAINSRORGARH	0.2505	0.0927	0.1979	0.4637	0.2793	0.4022
80	BHOPALSAGAR	0.2943	0.1183	0.2356	0.5110	0.3238	0.4486
81	CHHOTI SADRI	0.3163	0.1203	0.2510	0.5183	0.3189	0.4518
82	CHITTAURGARH	0.2809	0.1115	0.2244	0.5036	0.3158	0.4410
83	DUNGLA	0.2736	0.0984	0.2152	0.4793	0.2862	0.4149
84	GANGRAR	0.2599	0.0999	0.2066	0.4718	0.2823	0.4086
85	KAPASAN	0.2317	0.0706	0.1780	0.4525	0.2530	0.3860
86	NIMBAHERA	0.3356	0.1220	0.2644	0.5436	0.3244	0.4705
87	PRATAPGARH	0.2725	0.1090	0.2180	0.5253	0.3545	0.4684
88	RASHMI	0.2740	0.1098	0.2193	0.4397	0.2464	0.3753
	CHITTAURGARH	**0.2780**	**0.1055**	**0.2205**	**0.4911**	**0.2998**	**0.4273**
89	CHURU	0.3001	0.1063	0.2355	0.6667	0.5287	0.6207
90	RAJGARH	0.3423	0.1374	0.2740	0.7199	0.5975	0.6791
91	RATANGARH	0.2654	0.0885	0.2064	0.6528	0.5180	0.6079
92	SARDARSHAHAR	0.2238	0.0613	0.1696	0.5970	0.4360	0.5433
93	SUJANGARH	0.2338	0.0752	0.1809	0.6265	0.4874	0.5801
94	TARANAGAR	0.2696	0.0904	0.2099	0.7211	0.6168	0.6863
	CHURU ***	**0.2689**	**0.0931**	**0.2103**	**0.6529**	**0.5145**	**0.6068**
95	BANDIKUI	0.3727	0.1289	0.2914	0.6622	0.4843	0.6029
96	DAUSA	0.3342	0.0978	0.2554	0.5837	0.3615	0.5096
97	LALSOT	0.2982	0.0942	0.2302	0.5424	0.3230	0.4693
98	MAHWA	0.3926	0.1392	0.3081	0.6500	0.4515	0.5838
99	SIKRAI	0.3067	0.0905	0.2346	0.6237	0.4363	0.5612
	DAUSA	**0.3396**	**0.1090**	**0.2627**	**0.6102**	**0.4083**	**0.5429**
100	BARI	0.2624	0.0668	0.1972	0.5687	0.3684	0.5019
101	BASERI	0.3156	0.1199	0.2504	0.6187	0.4282	0.5552
102	DHAULPUR	0.3384	0.1153	0.2640	0.5946	0.3912	0.5268
103	RAJAKHERA	0.3046	0.0802	0.2298	0.5795	0.3801	0.5130
	DHAULPUR	**0.3101**	**0.0989**	**0.2397**	**0.5922**	**0.3937**	**0.5260**
104	ASPUR	0.2727	0.1288	0.2247	0.4421	0.2761	0.3868
105	BICHHIWARA	0.2505	0.0965	0.1992	0.4594	0.2792	0.3993
106	DUNGARPUR	0.2654	0.1029	0.2112	0.4667	0.2756	0.4030
107	SAGWARA	0.3298	0.1657	0.2751	0.5091	0.3361	0.4514
108	SIMALWARA	0.2387	0.1032	0.1935	0.4152	0.2464	0.3589
	DUNGARPUR	**0.2701**	**0.1192**	**0.2198**	**0.4569**	**0.2819**	**0.3986**
109	ANUPGARH	0.3205	0.1746	0.2719	0.5842	0.4463	0.5382
110	GANGANAGAR	0.4463	0.2849	0.3925	0.6442	0.5158	0.6014
111	KARANPUR	0.4012	0.2783	0.3602	0.6149	0.4994	0.5764
112	PADAMPUR	0.4288	0.2831	0.3802	0.6303	0.5058	0.5888
113	RAISINGHNAGAR	0.3812	0.2331	0.3318	0.6534	0.5313	0.6127
114	SADULSHAHAR	0.3965	0.2283	0.3404	0.6241	0.4816	0.5766
115	SURATGARH	0.3355	0.1632	0.2781	0.5358	0.4006	0.4907
	GANGANAGAR	**0.3740**	**0.2186**	**0.3222**	**0.6039**	**0.4727**	**0.5602**
116	BHADRA	0.3737	0.1676	0.3050	0.6765	0.5287	0.6272
117	HANUMANGARH	0.3333	0.1858	0.2841	0.6165	0.4867	0.5732
118	NOHAR	0.3025	0.1206	0.2419	0.6467	0.5061	0.5998
	HANUMANGARH	**0.3314**	**0.1581**	**0.2736**	**0.6365**	**0.5001**	**0.5910**
119	AMBER	0.3539	0.1114	0.2731	0.5982	0.3811	0.5258
120	BASSI	0.3347	0.0972	0.2555	0.5907	0.3696	0.5170
121	CHAKSU	0.2914	0.0799	0.2209	0.5193	0.2966	0.4451
122	DUDU	0.3267	0.1258	0.2597	0.5631	0.3678	0.4980
123	GOVINDGARH	0.4089	0.1566	0.3248	0.6624	0.4739	0.5996
124	JAMWA RAMGARH	0.3175	0.0924	0.2425	0.6287	0.4393	0.5656
125	JHOTWARA	0.3923	0.1560	0.3135	0.6668	0.4973	0.6103
126	KOTPUTLI	0.3609	0.1391	0.2870	0.7222	0.5970	0.6805
127	PHAGI	0.2946	0.1094	0.2329	0.6092	0.4383	0.5522
128	SAMBHAR	0.3639	0.1262	0.2847	0.6688	0.5035	0.6137

P. Code	Panchayat Samities/District	1991 Total Literacy Index (A)	1991 Female Literacy Index (B)	1991 EDI /3 (2*A+1*B)	2001 Total Literacy Index (A)	2001 Female Literacy Index (B)	2001 EDI (2*A+1*B)/3
1	2	3	4	5	6	7	8
129	SANGANER	0.3846	0.1463	0.3052	0.6286	0.4338	0.5637
130	SHAHPURA	0.3792	0.1389	0.2991	0.6503	0.4669	0.5892
131	VIRATNAGAR	0.3436	0.1245	0.2706	0.6838	0.5278	0.6318
	JAIPUR	**0.3505**	**0.1232**	**0.2747**	**0.6296**	**0.4442**	**0.5678**
132	JAISALMER	0.2686	0.0638	0.2003	0.4732	0.2772	0.4079
133	SAM	0.2121	0.0348	0.1530	0.4496	0.2398	0.3797
134	SANKRA	0.2202	0.0458	0.1621	0.4855	0.3003	0.4238
	JAISALMER	**0.2310**	**0.0471**	**0.1697**	**0.4702**	**0.2745**	**0.4050**
135	AHORE	0.2844	0.1089	0.2259	0.5184	0.3528	0.4632
136	BHINMAL	0.1750	0.0320	0.1273	0.4007	0.1950	0.3321
137	JALOR	0.2603	0.0938	0.2048	0.4438	0.2719	0.3865
138	JASWANTPURA	0.2073	0.0549	0.1565	0.3916	0.2068	0.3300
139	RANIWARA	0.2023	0.0482	0.1509	0.4743	0.2845	0.4110
140	SANCHORE	0.1917	0.0299	0.1378	0.4600	0.2609	0.3936
141	SAYLA	0.1979	0.0636	0.1531	0.4262	0.2310	0.3611
	JALOR	**0.2136**	**0.0585**	**0.1619**	**0.4481**	**0.2588**	**0.3850**
142	BAKANI	0.2337	0.0879	0.1851	0.4247	0.2385	0.3626
143	DAG	0.2107	0.0843	0.1686	0.4608	0.2758	0.3991
144	JHALRAPATAN	0.2935	0.1025	0.2298	0.5717	0.3766	0.5067
145	KHANPUR	0.3897	0.1491	0.3095	0.6617	0.4717	0.5984
146	MANOHARTHANA	0.1592	0.0318	0.1167	0.4747	0.2818	0.4104
147	PIRAWA	0.2963	0.1029	0.2318	0.6533	0.4901	0.5989
	JHALAWAR	**0.2632**	**0.0929**	**0.2064**	**0.5413**	**0.3551**	**0.4792**
148	ALSISAR	0.4312	0.2157	0.3594	0.7389	0.6172	0.6983
149	BUHANA	0.4866	0.2530	0.4087	0.7741	0.6448	0.7310
150	CHIRAWA	0.4537	0.2333	0.3802	0.7451	0.6132	0.7011
151	JHUNJHUNUN	0.4820	0.2525	0.4055	0.7666	0.6303	0.7212
152	KHETRI	0.4200	0.1890	0.3430	0.6585	0.5040	0.6070
153	NAWALGARH	0.4531	0.2194	0.3752	0.6968	0.5378	0.6438
154	SURAJGARH	0.4334	0.2170	0.3613	0.7067	0.5594	0.6576
155	UDAIPURWATI	0.4125	0.1891	0.3380	0.7766	0.6795	0.7442
	JHUNJHUNUN	**0.4465**	**0.2204**	**0.3711**	**0.7324**	**0.5980**	**0.6876**
156	BALESAR	0.2498	0.0492	0.1829	0.4304	0.1980	0.3529
157	BAP	0.2030	0.0525	0.1528	0.4336	0.2467	0.3713
158	BHOPALGARH	0.2840	0.0697	0.2126	0.4627	0.2341	0.3865
159	BILARA	0.3093	0.0877	0.2354	0.5045	0.2818	0.4303
160	LUNI	0.3034	0.0937	0.2335	0.5482	0.3407	0.4790
161	MANDOR	0.2999	0.0752	0.2250	0.4430	0.2208	0.3689
162	OSIAN	0.2487	0.0592	0.1855	0.4750	0.2745	0.4082
163	PHALODI	0.2361	0.0578	0.1767	0.4750	0.2745	0.4082
164	SHERGARH	0.2174	0.0428	0.1592	0.4170	0.1948	0.3429
	JODHPUR	**0.2624**	**0.0662**	**0.1970**	**0.4688**	**0.2510**	**0.3962**
165	HINDAUN	0.3541	0.0975	0.2686	0.7389	0.5783	0.6854
166	KARAULI	0.2536	0.0699	0.1924	0.5754	0.3589	0.5032
167	NADOTI	0.3543	0.1097	0.2728	0.6504	0.4614	0.5874
168	SAPOTRA	0.2747	0.0974	0.2156	0.5830	0.3787	0.5149
169	TODABHIM	0.3531	0.0886	0.2649	0.6229	0.3972	0.5477
	KARAULI	**0.3151**	**0.0917**	**0.2406**	**0.6362**	**0.4384**	**0.5703**
170	CHECHAT	0.3745	0.1630	0.3040	0.6860	0.5235	0.6318
171	ITAWA	0.3491	0.1378	0.2787	0.6248	0.4458	0.5651
172	LADPURA	0.3740	0.1679	0.3053	0.6601	0.4908	0.6037
173	SANGOD	0.4050	0.1718	0.3273	0.6982	0.5314	0.6426
174	SULTANPUR	0.4122	0.1801	0.3348	0.7014	0.5427	0.6485
	KOTA	**0.3830**	**0.1639**	**0.3100**	**0.6734**	**0.5060**	**0.6176**
175	DEGANA	0.2784	0.0940	0.2169	0.5358	0.3532	0.4749
176	DIDWANA	0.3089	0.1087	0.2422	0.6362	0.4646	0.5790
177	JAYAL	0.2403	0.0725	0.1844	0.5112	0.3219	0.4481
178	KUCHAMAN	0.3072	0.1125	0.2423	0.6254	0.4552	0.5687
179	LADNU	0.3201	0.1241	0.2548	0.6068	0.4238	0.5458
180	MAKRANA	0.3079	0.1196	0.2451	0.6181	0.4492	0.5618
181	MERTA	0.3124	0.1116	0.2455	0.5485	0.3444	0.4805
182	MUNDWA	0.2341	0.0630	0.1771	0.4501	0.2444	0.3815
183	NAGAUR	0.2493	0.0707	0.1898	0.4984	0.3080	0.4349
184	PARBATSAR	0.2632	0.1051	0.2105	0.5592	0.3908	0.5031
185	RIYAN	0.2725	0.0950	0.2133	0.5192	0.3230	0.4538
	NAGAUR	**0.2814**	**0.0975**	**0.2201**	**0.5592**	**0.3758**	**0.4981**
186	BALI	0.3057	0.1535	0.2550	0.5034	0.3453	0.4507
187	DESURI	0.3136	0.1359	0.2544	0.5035	0.3437	0.4502
188	JAITARAN	0.2604	0.0775	0.1994	0.4677	0.2668	0.4007
189	KHARCHI/MARWAR JUN.	0.3101	0.1118	0.2440	0.4999	0.3073	0.4357
190	PALI	0.2745	0.0873	0.2121	0.4879	0.2938	0.4232
191	RAIPUR	0.2862	0.0887	0.2204	0.5037	0.2966	0.4347
192	RANI STATION	0.3349	0.1577	0.2758	0.5273	0.3643	0.4730
193	ROHAT	0.2700	0.0750	0.2050	0.5124	0.3091	0.4446
194	SOJAT	0.3257	0.1114	0.2543	0.5202	0.3178	0.4527
195	SUMERPUR	0.3247	0.1379	0.2624	0.5269	0.3536	0.4691
	PALI	**0.3013**	**0.1147**	**0.2391**	**0.5039**	**0.3176**	**0.4418**

P. Code	Panchayat Samities/District	1991			2001		
		Total Literacy Index (A)	Female Literacy Index (B)	**EDI /3 (2*A+1*B)**	Total Literacy Index (A)	Female Literacy Index (B)	**EDI (2*A+1*B)/3**
1	2	3	4	5	6	7	8
196	AMET	0.2293	0.0780	0.1789	0.4911	0.3090	0.4304
197	BHIM	0.3202	0.0956	0.2453	0.5650	0.3315	0.4872
198	DEOGARH	0.2272	0.0664	0.1736	0.4946	0.3144	0.4345
199	KHAMNOR	0.3074	0.1366	0.2505	0.5041	0.3430	0.4504
200	KUMBHALGARH	0.2333	0.0829	0.1832	0.4645	0.2821	0.4037
201	RAILMAGRA	0.3257	0.1469	0.2661	0.5497	0.3675	0.4890
202	RAJSAMAND	0.3170	0.1334	0.2558	0.5523	0.3625	0.4890
	RAJSAMAND	**0.2851**	**0.1094**	**0.2265**	**0.5193**	**0.3322**	**0.4569**
203	BAMANWAS	0.3266	0.0985	0.2506	0.6011	0.3871	0.5298
204	BONLI	0.3045	0.1038	0.2376	0.5318	0.3075	0.4570
205	GANGAPUR	0.3534	0.1106	0.2725	0.5827	0.3437	0.5030
206	KHANDAR	0.2453	0.0726	0.1877	0.4338	0.2053	0.3576
207	SAWAI MADHOPUR	0.3157	0.0902	0.2405	0.5083	0.2474	0.4213
	SAWAI MADHOPUR	**0.3109**	**0.0959**	**0.2392**	**0.5324**	**0.2969**	**0.4539**
208	DANTA RAMGARH	0.3804	0.1519	0.3042	0.7018	0.5574	0.6537
209	DHOND	0.3865	0.1471	0.3067	0.6864	0.5247	0.6325
210	FATEHPUR	0.3757	0.1518	0.3011	0.7452	0.6222	0.7042
211	KHANDELA	0.3932	0.1445	0.3103	0.7293	0.5938	0.6841
212	LACHHMANGARH	0.3850	0.1549	0.3083	0.7449	0.6157	0.7018
213	NEEM KA THANA	0.3902	0.1571	0.3125	0.6760	0.5147	0.6222
214	PIPRALI	0.3983	0.1589	0.3185	0.7010	0.5418	0.6479
215	SRI MADHOPUR	0.4143	0.1677	0.3321	0.6677	0.5128	0.6161
	SIKAR	**0.3903**	**0.1542**	**0.3116**	**0.7039**	**0.5570**	**0.6549**
216	ABU ROAD	0.1853	0.0737	0.1481	0.4355	0.2641	0.3784
217	PINDWARA	0.2276	0.1060	0.1871	0.5273	0.3565	0.4704
218	REODAR	0.2126	0.0823	0.1692	0.4832	0.3024	0.4229
219	SHEOGANJ	0.2403	0.0836	0.1881	0.4951	0.3275	0.4392
220	SIROHI	0.2822	0.1074	0.2239	0.4875	0.3051	0.4267
	SIROHI	**0.2305**	**0.0923**	**0.1844**	**0.4897**	**0.3147**	**0.4314**
221	DEOLI	0.3096	0.1112	0.2435	0.4581	0.2345	0.3836
222	MALPURA	0.2733	0.1013	0.2160	0.4692	0.2649	0.4011
223	NIWAI	0.2994	0.1246	0.2411	0.5097	0.2916	0.4370
224	TODARAISINGH	0.2851	0.0871	0.2191	0.5288	0.3267	0.4614
225	TONK	0.2651	0.0670	0.1991	0.4548	0.2193	0.3763
226	UNIARA	0.2665	0.0758	0.2029	0.4671	0.2256	0.3866
	TONK	**0.2829**	**0.0948**	**0.2202**	**0.4777**	**0.2562**	**0.4039**
227	BARGAON	0.3297	0.1481	0.2692	0.6651	0.5066	0.6123
228	BHINDER	0.2917	0.1116	0.2317	0.6082	0.4449	0.5538
229	DHARIAWAD	0.1293	0.0490	0.1025	0.3522	0.1821	0.2955
230	GIRWA	0.2720	0.1172	0.2204	0.5793	0.4048	0.5211
231	GOGUNDA	0.2301	0.0885	0.1829	0.5012	0.3232	0.4419
232	JHADOL	0.1981	0.0718	0.1560	0.5926	0.4343	0.5398
233	KHERWARA	0.3211	0.1306	0.2576	0.5578	0.3617	0.4924
234	KOTRA	0.0867	0.0257	0.0664	0.2452	0.1114	0.2006
235	MAVLI	0.3158	0.1393	0.2570	0.5372	0.3543	0.4762
236	SALUMBAR	0.2210	0.0845	0.1755	0.5738	0.4144	0.5207
237	SARADA	0.2695	0.1159	0.2183	0.5534	0.3682	0.4917
	UDAIPUR	**0.2474**	**0.1008**	**0.1985**	**0.5252**	**0.3546**	**0.4683**
	RAJASTHAN	**0.3039**	**0.1161**	**0.2413**	**0.5592**	**0.3774**	**0.4986**

Note: * Dungargarh PS shifted from Churu to Bikaner district on 1st April 2001
** Excluding data of Dungargarh PS; *** Including data of Dungargarh PS.
Source: Calculated from data given in General Annex-I (Col. 11 & 13) and General Annex- 7 (Col. 19 & 21)

ANNEX-8.2

PANCHAYAT SAMITI-WISE CHANGED PATTERN OF EDUCATION INDEX (1991-01)

P. Code	*Panchayat Samities*	*Education Index 1991*		*2001*		*Differences (1991-2001)*		*% Increase in EDI Value*	*Remarks*
		Rank	*Value*	*Rank*	*Value*	*Rank*	*Value*		
1	2	3	4	5	6	7	8	9	10
1	ARAIN	119	0.2330	185	0.4045	-66	0.1715	73.6	B
2	BHINAY	82	0.2620	224	0.3552	-142	0.0932	35.6	B
3	JAWAJA	46	0.3033	9	0.6895	37	0.3862	127.3	A
4	KEKRI	19	0.3365	193	0.3995	-174	0.0630	18.7	B
5	KISHANGARH	99	0.2480	127	0.4670	-28	0.2190	88.3	B
6	MASOODA	58	0.2751	120	0.4706	-62	0.1955	71.1	B
7	PISANGAN	34	0.3099	136	0.4580	-102	0.1481	47.8	B
8	SRINAGAR	77	0.2653	147	0.4494	-70	0.1841	69.4	B
	AJMER DISTRICT		**0.2805**		**0.4630**		**0.1825**	**65.1**	
9	BANSURE	72	0.2668	86	0.5194	-14	0.2526	94.7	B
10	BEHROR	2	0.4396	1	0.8619	1	0.4223	96.1	A
11	KATHUMAR	58	0.2753	94	0.5049	-36	0.2296	83.4	B
12	KISHANGARH BAS	30	0.3179	103	0.4934	-73	0.1755	55.2	B
13	KOTKASIM	3	0.4145	22	0.6404	-19	0.2259	54.5	B
14	LACHHMANGARH	74	0.2660	106	0.4909	-32	0.2249	84.5	B
15	MANDAWAR	5	0.4056	23	0.6365	-18	0.2309	56.9	B
16	NIMRANA	1	0.4646	78	0.5302	-77	0.0656	14.1	B
17	RAJGARH	59	0.2750	116	0.4753	-57	0.2003	72.8	B
18	RAMGARH	62	0.2739	125	0.4675	-63	0.1936	70.7	B
19	RENI	77	0.2653	99	0.4989	-22	0.2336	88.1	B
20	THANAGAZI	140	0.2170	181	0.4078	-41	0.1908	87.9	B
21	TIJARA	69	0.2703	131	0.4636	-62	0.1933	71.5	B
22	UMREN	87	0.2557	130	0.4648	-43	0.2091	81.8	B
	ALWAR		**0.3092**		**0.5231**		**0.2139**	**69.2**	
23	ANANDPURI	214	0.1647	227	0.3502	-13	0.1855	112.6	B
24	BAGIDORA	175	0.1949	225	0.3537	-50	0.1588	81.5	B
25	GARHI	72	0.2666	133	0.4622	-61	0.1956	73.4	B
26	GHATOL	209	0.1701	229	0.3387	-20	0.1686	99.1	B
27	KUSHALGARH	234	0.0968	235	0.2844	-1	0.1876	193.8	B
28	PEEPALKHOONT	236	0.0847	236	0.2114	0	0.1267	149.6	C
29	SAJJANGARH	227	0.1383	233	0.3205	-6	0.1822	131.7	B
30	TALWARA	203	0.1758	198	0.3922	5	0.2164	123.1	A
	BANSWARA		**0.1726**		**0.3511**		**0.1785**	**103.4**	
31	ANTA	28	0.3191	58	0.5731	-30	0.2540	79.6	B
32	ATRU	37	0.3084	59	0.5689	-22	0.2605	84.5	B
33	BARAN	32	0.3125	48	0.5916	-16	0.2791	89.3	B
34	CHHABRA	186	0.1853	127	0.4667	59	0.2814	151.9	A
35	CHHIPABAROD	173	0.1970	172	0.4179	1	0.2209	112.1	A
36	KISHANGANJ	154	0.2079	119	0.4720	35	0.2641	127.0	A
37	SHAHBAD	132	0.2220	127	0.4667	5	0.2447	110.2	A
	BARAN		**0.2537**		**0.5102**		**0.2565**	**101.1**	
38	BALOTRA	196	0.1785	106	0.4908	90	0.3123	175.0	A
39	BARMER	225	0.1406	111	0.4874	114	0.3468	246.7	A
40	BAYTOO	222	0.1505	77	0.5315	145	0.3810	253.2	A
41	CHOHTAN	235	0.0900	138	0.4550	97	0.3650	405.6	A
42	DHORIMANNA	231	0.1219	21	0.6407	210	0.5188	425.6	A
43	SHEO	226	0.1400	87	0.5169	139	0.3769	269.2	A
44	SINDHARI	230	0.1234	65	0.5606	165	0.4372	354.3	A
45	SIWANA	205	0.1741	73	0.5421	132	0.3680	211.4	A
	BARMER		**0.1393**		**0.5290**		**0.3897**	**279.8**	
46	BAYANA	74	0.2656	102	0.4943	-28	0.2287	86.1	B
47	DEEG	50	0.2897	91	0.5114	-41	0.2217	76.5	B
48	KAMAN	193	0.1820	185	0.4052	8	0.2232	122.6	A
49	KUMHER	14	0.3560	40	0.6038	-26	0.2478	69.6	B
50	NADBAI	19	0.3370	31	0.6145	-12	0.2775	82.3	B
51	NAGAR PAHARI	112	0.2375	85	0.5201	27	0.2826	119.0	A
52	RUPBAS	15	0.3457	36	0.6090	-21	0.2633	76.2	B
53	SEWAR	22	0.3317	37	0.6081	-15	0.2764	83.3	B
54	WEIR	27	0.3202	75	0.5389	-48	0.2187	68.3	B
	BHARATPUR		**0.2939**		**0.5417**		**0.2478**	**84.3**	
55	ASIND	179	0.1906	223	0.3560	-44	0.1654	86.8	B
56	BANERA	158	0.2051	154	0.4404	4	0.2353	114.7	A
57	HURDA	50	0.2902	140	0.4529	-90	0.1627	56.1	B
58	JAHAZPUR	163	0.2016	165	0.4263	-2	0.2247	111.5	B
59	KOTRI	164	0.2014	230	0.3383	-66	0.1369	68.0	B
60	MANDAL	184	0.1861	214	0.3700	-30	0.1839	98.8	B

P. Code	Panchayat Samities	Education Index 1991		Education Index 2001		Differences (1991-2001)		% Increase in EDI Value	Remarks
		Rank	Value	Rank	Value	Rank	Value		
1	2	3	4	5	6	7	8	9	10
61	MANDALGARH	200	0.1774	210	0.3765	-10	0.1991	112.2	B
62	RAIPUR	168	0.1986	217	0.3646	-49	0.1660	83.6	B
63	SAHARA	166	0.2003	206	0.3823	-40	0.1820	90.9	B
64	SHAHPURA	213	0.1668	216	0.3674	-3	0.2006	120.3	B
65	SUWANA	177	0.1925	196	0.3938	-19	0.2013	104.6	B
	BHILWARA		**0.1964**		**0.3842**		**0.1878**	**95.6**	
66	BIKANER	161	0.2032	174	0.4142	-13	0.2110	103.8	B
67	DUNGARGARH *	196	0.1794	80	0.5281	116	0.3487	194.4	A
68	KOLAYAT	194	0.1809	221	0.3577	-27	0.1768	97.7	B
69	LUNKARANSAR	164	0.2005	176	0.4119	-12	0.2114	105.4	B
70	NOKHA	208	0.1732	169	0.4219	39	0.2487	143.6	A
	BIKANER **		**0.1899**		**0.4050**		**0.2151**	**113.3**	
71	HINDOLI	205	0.1739	185	0.4047	20	0.2308	132.7	A
72	KESHORAIPATAN	105	0.2427	100	0.4977	5	0.2550	105.1	A
73	NAINWA	189	0.1827	155	0.4389	34	0.2562	140.2	A
74	TALERA	145	0.2129	133	0.4620	12	0.2491	117.0	A
	BUNDI		**0.2048**		**0.4520**		**0.2472**	**120.7**	
75	ARNOD	127	0.2247	175	0.4129	-48	0.1882	83.8	B
76	BARI SADRI	148	0.2115	204	0.3838	-56	0.1723	81.5	B
77	BEGUN	153	0.2091	169	0.4217	-16	0.2126	101.7	B
78	BHADESAR	154	0.2081	177	0.4113	-23	0.2032	97.6	B
79	BHAINSRORGARH	172	0.1979	190	0.4022	-18	0.2043	103.2	B
80	BHOPALSAGAR	114	0.2356	147	0.4486	-33	0.2130	90.4	B
81	CHHOTI SADRI	95	0.2510	142	0.4518	-47	0.2008	80.0	B
82	CHITTAURGARH	130	0.2244	153	0.4410	-23	0.2166	96.5	B
83	DUNGLA	144	0.2152	173	0.4149	-29	0.1997	92.8	B
84	GANGRAR	156	0.2066	180	0.4086	-24	0.2020	97.8	B
85	KAPASAN	199	0.1780	203	0.3860	-4	0.2080	116.9	B
86	NIMBAHERA	80	0.2644	120	0.4705	-40	0.2061	78.0	B
87	PRATAPGARH	138	0.2180	125	0.4684	13	0.2504	114.9	A
88	RASHMI	136	0.2193	212	0.3753	-76	0.1560	71.1	B
	CHITTAURGARH		**0.2205**		**0.4273**		**0.2068**	**93.8**	
89	CHURU	114	0.2355	29	0.6207	85	0.3852	163.6	A
90	RAJGARH	62	0.2740	14	0.6791	48	0.4051	147.8	A
91	RATANGARH	157	0.2064	37	0.6079	120	0.4015	194.5	A
92	SARDARSHAHAR	209	0.1696	72	0.5433	137	0.3737	220.3	A
93	SUJANGARH	194	0.1809	53	0.5801	141	0.3992	220.7	A
94	TARANAGAR	152	0.2099	10	0.6863	142	0.4764	227.0	A
	CHURU ***		**0.2103**		**0.6068**		**0.3965**	**188.5**	
95	BANDIKUI	49	0.2914	42	0.6029	7	0.3115	106.9	A
96	DAUSA	90	0.2554	92	0.5096	-2	0.2542	99.5	B
97	LALSOT	123	0.2302	123	0.4693	0	0.2391	103.9	C
98	MAHWA	37	0.3081	52	0.5838	-15	0.2757	89.5	B
99	SIKRAI	116	0.2346	65	0.5612	51	0.3266	139.2	A
	DAUSA		**0.2627**		**0.5429**		**0.2802**	**106.7**	
100	BARI	173	0.1972	98	0.5019	75	0.3047	154.5	A
101	BASERI	98	0.2504	67	0.5552	31	0.3048	121.7	A
102	DHAULPUR	80	0.2640	81	0.5268	-1	0.2628	99.5	B
103	RAJAKHERA	123	0.2298	90	0.5130	33	0.2832	123.2	A
	DHAULPUR		**0.2397**		**0.5260**		**0.2863**	**119.4**	
104	ASPUR	127	0.2247	199	0.3868	-72	0.1621	72.1	B
105	BICHHIWARA	168	0.1992	194	0.3993	-26	0.2001	100.5	B
106	DUNGARPUR	150	0.2112	189	0.4030	-39	0.1918	90.8	B
107	SAGWARA	58	0.2751	143	0.4514	-85	0.1763	64.1	B
108	SIMALWARA	176	0.1935	220	0.3589	-44	0.1654	85.5	B
	DUNGARPUR		**0.2198**		**0.3986**		**0.1788**	**81.3**	
109	ANUPGARH	67	0.2719	76	0.5382	-9	0.2663	97.9	B
110	GANGANAGAR	7	0.3925	43	0.6014	-36	0.2089	53.2	B
111	KARANPUR	12	0.3602	56	0.5764	-44	0.2162	60.0	B
112	PADAMPUR	8	0.3802	49	0.5888	-41	0.2086	54.9	B
113	RAISINGHNAGAR	22	0.3318	33	0.6127	-11	0.2809	84.7	B
114	SADULSHAHAR	17	0.3404	55	0.5766	-38	0.2362	69.4	B
115	SURATGARH	56	0.2781	106	0.4907	-50	0.2126	76.4	B
	GANGANAGAR		**0.3222**		**0.5602**		**0.2380**	**73.9**	
116	BHADRA	41	0.3050	27	0.6272	14	0.3222	105.6	A
117	HANUMANGARH	54	0.2841	57	0.5732	-3	0.2891	101.8	B
118	NOHAR	107	0.2419	44	0.5998	63	0.3579	148.0	A
	HANUMANGARH		**0.2736**		**0.5910**		**0.3174**	**116.0**	
119	AMBER	64	0.2731	82	0.5258	-18	0.2527	92.5	B
120	BASSI	87	0.2555	87	0.5170	0	0.2615	102.3	C
121	CHAKSU	133	0.2209	150	0.4451	-17	0.2242	101.5	B
122	DUDU	84	0.2597	100	0.4980	-16	0.2383	91.8	B
123	GOVINDGARH	26	0.3248	44	0.5996	-18	0.2748	84.6	D
124	JAMWA RAMGARH	103	0.2425	61	0.5656	44	0.3231	133.2	A

P. Code	*Panchayat Samities*	*Education Index 1991*		*2001*		*Differences (1991-2001)*		*% Increase in EDI Value*	*Remarks*
		Rank	*Value*	*Rank*	*Value*	*Rank*	*Value*		
1	2	3	4	5	6	7	8	9	10
125	JHOTWARA	31	0.3135	35	0.6103	-4	0.2968	94.7	B
126	KOTPUTLI	52	0.2870	13	0.6805	39	0.3935	137.1	A
127	PHAGI	119	0.2329	69	0.5522	50	0.3193	137.1	A
128	SAMBHAR	53	0.2847	32	0.6137	21	0.3290	115.6	A
129	SANGANER	41	0.3052	63	0.5637	-22	0.2585	84.7	B
130	SHAHPURA	48	0.2991	49	0.5892	-1	0.2901	97.0	B
131	VIRATNAGAR	68	0.2706	25	0.6318	43	0.3612	133.5	A
	JAIPUR		**0.2747**		**0.5678**		**0.2931**	**106.7**	
132	JAISALMER	166	0.2003	181	0.4079	-15	0.2076	103.6	B
133	SAM	219	0.1530	208	0.3797	11	0.2267	148.2	A
134	SANKRA	215	0.1621	166	0.4238	49	0.2617	161.4	A
	JAISALMER		**0.1697**		**0.4050**		**0.2353**	**138.7**	
135	AHORE	126	0.2259	132	0.4632	-6	0.2373	105.0	B
136	BHINMAL	229	0.1273	231	0.3321	-2	0.2048	160.9	B
137	JALOR	158	0.2048	199	0.3865	-41	0.1817	88.7	B
138	JASWANTPURA	217	0.1565	232	0.3300	-15	0.1735	110.9	B
139	RANIWARA	222	0.1509	177	0.4110	45	0.2601	172.4	A
140	SANCHORE	227	0.1378	196	0.3936	31	0.2558	185.6	A
141	SAYLA	219	0.1531	219	0.3611	0	0.2080	135.9	C
	JALOR		**0.1619**		**0.3850**		**0.2231**	**137.8**	
142	BAKANI	186	0.1851	218	0.3626	-32	0.1775	95.9	B
143	DAG	211	0.1686	194	0.3991	17	0.2305	136.7	A
144	JHALRAPATAN	123	0.2298	93	0.5067	30	0.2769	120.5	A
145	KHANPUR	34	0.3095	47	0.5984	-13	0.2889	93.3	B
146	MANOHARTHANA	232	0.1167	179	0.4104	53	0.2937	251.7	A
147	PIRAWA	121	0.2318	46	0.5989	75	0.3671	158.4	A
	JHALAWAR		**0.2064**		**0.4792**		**0.2728**	**132.2**	
148	ALSISAR	13	0.3594	8	0.6983	5	0.3389	94.3	A
149	BUHANA	4	0.4087	3	0.7310	1	0.3223	78.9	A
150	CHIRAWA	8	0.3802	7	0.7011	1	0.3209	84.4	A
151	JHUNJHUNUN	5	0.4055	4	0.7212	1	0.3157	77.9	A
152	KHETRI	16	0.3430	39	0.6070	-23	0.2640	77.0	B
153	NAWALGARH	10	0.3752	19	0.6438	-9	0.2686	71.6	B
154	SURAJGARH	11	0.3613	15	0.6576	-4	0.2963	82.0	B
155	UDAIPURWATI	18	0.3380	2	0.7442	16	0.4062	120.2	A
	JHUNJHUNUN		**0.3711**		**0.6876**		**0.3165**	**85.3**	
156	BALESAR	189	0.1829	226	0.3529	-37	0.1700	92.9	B
157	BAP	219	0.1528	213	0.3713	6	0.2185	143.0	A
158	BHOPALGARH	145	0.2126	199	0.3865	-54	0.1739	81.8	B
159	BILARA	116	0.2354	162	0.4303	-46	0.1949	82.8	B
160	LUNI	118	0.2335	114	0.4790	4	0.2455	105.1	A
161	MANDOR	127	0.2250	215	0.3689	-88	0.1439	64.0	B
162	OSIAN	184	0.1855	181	0.4082	3	0.2227	120.1	A
163	PHALODI	200	0.1767	181	0.4082	19	0.2315	131.0	A
164	SHERGARH	216	0.1592	228	0.3429	-12	0.1837	115.4	B
	JODHPUR		**0.1970**		**0.3962**		**0.1992**	**101.1**	
165	HINDAUN	70	0.2686	11	0.6854	59	0.4168	155.2	A
166	KARAULI	178	0.1924	95	0.5032	83	0.3108	161.5	A
167	NADOTI	64	0.2728	51	0.5874	13	0.3146	115.3	A
168	SAPOTRA	142	0.2156	89	0.5149	53	0.2993	138.8	A
169	TODABHIM	77	0.2649	70	0.5477	7	0.2828	106.8	A
	KARAULI		**0.2406**		**0.5703**		**0.3297**	**137.0**	
170	CHECHAT	44	0.3040	25	0.6318	19	0.3278	107.8	A
171	ITAWA	55	0.2787	62	0.5651	-7	0.2864	102.8	B
172	LADPURA	41	0.3053	40	0.6037	1	0.2984	97.7	A
173	SANGOD	25	0.3273	20	0.6426	5	0.3153	96.3	A
174	SULTANPUR	21	0.3348	17	0.6485	4	0.3137	93.7	A
	KOTA		**0.3100**		**0.6176**		**0.3076**	**99.2**	
175	DEGANA	140	0.2169	116	0.4749	24	0.2580	118.9	A
176	DIDWANA	107	0.2422	54	0.5790	53	0.3368	139.1	A
177	JAYAL	188	0.1844	149	0.4481	39	0.2637	143.0	A
178	KUCHAMAN	107	0.2423	59	0.5687	48	0.3264	134.7	A
179	LADNU	90	0.2548	71	0.5458	19	0.2910	114.2	A
180	MAKRANA	101	0.2451	64	0.5618	37	0.3167	129.2	A
181	MERTA	100	0.2455	113	0.4805	-13	0.2350	95.7	B
182	MUNDWA	200	0.1771	206	0.3815	-6	0.2044	115.4	B
183	NAGAUR	180	0.1898	159	0.4349	21	0.2451	129.1	A
184	PARBATSAR	150	0.2105	95	0.5031	55	0.2926	139.0	A
185	RIYAN	145	0.2133	139	0.4538	6	0.2405	112.8	A
	NAGAUR		**0.2201**		**0.4981**		**0.2780**	**126.3**	
186	BALI	90	0.2550	143	0.4507	-53	0.1957	76.7	B
187	DESURI	93	0.2544	145	0.4502	-52	0.1958	77.0	B
188	JAITARAN	168	0.1994	191	0.4007	-23	0.2013	101.0	B
189	KHARCHI/MARWAR JUN.	103	0.2440	158	0.4357	-55	0.1917	78.6	B
190	PALI	148	0.2121	167	0.4232	-19	0.2111	99.5	B

P. Code	Panchayat Samities	Education Index 1991 Rank	Education Index 1991 Value	Education Index 2001 Rank	Education Index 2001 Value	Differences (1991-2001) Rank	Differences (1991-2001) Value	% Increase in EDI Value	Remarks
191	RAIPUR	134	0.2204	159	0.4347	-25	0.2143	97.2	B
192	RANI STATION	57	0.2758	118	0.4730	-61	0.1972	71.5	B
1	2	3	4	5	6	7	8	9	10
193	ROHAT	158	0.2050	150	0.4446	8	0.2396	116.9	A
194	SOJAT	94	0.2543	140	0.4527	-46	0.1984	78.0	B
195	SUMERPUR	82	0.2624	123	0.4691	-41	0.2067	78.8	B
	PALI		**0.2391**		**0.4418**		**0.2027**	**84.8**	
196	AMET	196	0.1789	162	0.4304	34	0.2515	140.6	A
197	BHIM	101	0.2453	111	0.4872	-10	0.2419	98.6	B
198	DEOGARH	205	0.1736	159	0.4345	46	0.2609	150.3	A
199	KHAMNOR	95	0.2505	145	0.4504	-50	0.1999	79.8	B
200	KUMBHALGARH	189	0.1832	188	0.4037	1	0.2205	120.4	A
201	RAILMAGRA	74	0.2661	109	0.4890	-35	0.2229	83.8	B
202	RAJSAMAND	87	0.2558	109	0.4890	-22	0.2332	91.2	B
	RAJSAMAND		**0.2265**		**0.4569**		**0.2304**	**101.7**	
203	BAMANWAS	95	0.2506	78	0.5298	17	0.2792	111.4	A
204	BONLI	112	0.2376	137	0.4570	-25	0.2194	92.3	B
205	GANGAPUR	64	0.2725	95	0.5030	-31	0.2305	84.6	B
206	KHANDAR	181	0.1877	221	0.3576	-40	0.1699	90.5	B
207	SAWAI MADHOPUR	110	0.2405	171	0.4213	-61	0.1808	75.2	B
	SAWAI MADHOPUR		**0.2392**		**0.4539**		**0.2147**	**89.8**	
208	DANTA RAMGARH	44	0.3042	16	0.6537	28	0.3495	114.9	A
209	DHOND	40	0.3067	24	0.6325	16	0.3258	106.2	A
210	FATEHPUR	47	0.3011	5	0.7042	42	0.4031	133.9	A
211	KHANDELA	34	0.3103	12	0.6841	22	0.3738	120.5	A
212	LACHHMANGARH	37	0.3083	6	0.7018	31	0.3935	127.6	A
213	NEEM KA THANA	32	0.3125	28	0.6222	4	0.3097	99.1	A
214	PIPRALI	28	0.3185	18	0.6479	10	0.3294	103.4	A
215	SRI MADHOPUR	22	0.3321	30	0.6161	-8	0.2840	85.5	B
	SIKAR		**0.3116**		**0.6549**		**0.3433**	**110.2**	
216	ABU ROAD	224	0.1481	209	0.3784	15	0.2303	155.5	A
217	PINDWARA	183	0.1871	122	0.4704	61	0.2833	151.4	A
218	REODAR	211	0.1692	167	0.4229	44	0.2537	149.9	A
219	SHEOGANJ	181	0.1881	155	0.4392	26	0.2511	133.5	A
220	SIROHI	130	0.2239	164	0.4267	-34	0.2028	90.6	B
	SIROHI		**0.1844**		**0.4314**		**0.2470**	**133.9**	
221	DEOLI	103	0.2435	204	0.3836	-101	0.1401	57.5	B
222	MALPURA	142	0.2160	191	0.4011	-49	0.1851	85.7	B
223	NIWAI	110	0.2411	157	0.4370	-47	0.1959	81.3	B
224	TODARAISINGH	136	0.2191	135	0.4614	1	0.2423	110.6	A
225	TONK	168	0.1991	211	0.3763	-43	0.1772	89.0	B
226	UNIARA	162	0.2029	199	0.3866	-37	0.1837	90.5	B
	TONK		**0.2202**		**0.4039**		**0.1837**	**83.4**	
227	BARGAON	70	0.2692	34	0.6123	36	0.3431	127.5	A
228	BHINDER	121	0.2317	68	0.5538	53	0.3221	139.0	A
229	DHARIAWAD	233	0.1025	234	0.2955	-1	0.1930	188.3	B
230	GIRWA	134	0.2204	83	0.5211	51	0.3007	136.4	A
231	GOGUNDA	189	0.1829	152	0.4419	37	0.2590	141.6	A
232	JHADOL	218	0.1560	74	0.5398	144	0.3838	246.0	A
233	KHERWARA	85	0.2576	104	0.4924	-19	0.2348	91.1	B
234	KOTRA	237	0.0664	237	0.2006	0	0.1342	202.1	C
235	MAVLI	86	0.2570	115	0.4762	-29	0.2192	85.3	B
236	SALUMBAR	203	0.1755	83	0.5207	120	0.3452	196.7	A
237	SARADA	138	0.2183	104	0.4917	34	0.2734	125.2	A
	UDAIPUR		**0.1985**		**0.4683**		**0.2698**	**135.9**	
	RAJASTHAN		**0.2413**		**0.4986**		**0.2573**	**106.6**	

* Dungargarh PS shifted from Churu to Bikaner District on 1st April 2001
** Excluding data of Dungargarh PS
*** Including data of Dungargarh PS
Source: Annex 8.1

Note:
A Improvement in both EDI Value and Rank
B Increase in EDI Value but Rank Deteriorated
C Increase in EDI Value but Rank Remained Constant
D Decrease in Both EDI Value and Rank

ANNEX-8.3

RANKING OF PSS BY EDI, 2001

(Descending Order)

RANK	PANCHAYAT SAMITIES P. CODE	PANCHAYAT SAMITIES NAME	EDI
1	2	3	4
	VERY HIGH (>0.5)		
1	**10**	**BEHROR**	**0.862**
2	**155**	**UDAIPURWATI**	**0.744**
3	**149**	**BUHANA**	**0.731**
4	**151**	**JHUNJHUNUN**	**0.721**
5	**210**	**FATEHPUR**	**0.704**
6	**212**	**LACHHMANGARH**	**0.702**
7	**150**	**CHIRAWA**	**0.701**
8	**148**	**ALSISAR**	**0.698**
9	**3**	**JAWAJA**	**0.690**
10	**94**	**TARANAGAR**	**0.686**
11	**165**	**HINDAUN**	**0.685**
12	**211**	**KHANDELA**	**0.684**
13	**126**	**KOTPUTLI**	**0.681**
14	**90**	**RAJGARH**	**0.679**
15	**154**	**SURAJGARH**	**0.658**
16	**208**	**DANTA RAMGARH**	**0.654**
17	**174**	**SULTANPUR**	**0.649**
18	**214**	**PIPRALI**	**0.648**
19	**153**	**NAWALGARH**	**0.644**
20	**173**	**SANGOD**	**0.643**
21	**42**	**DHORIMANNA**	**0.641**
22	**13**	**KOTKASIM**	**0.640**
23	**15**	**MANDAWAR**	**0.637**
24	**209**	**DHOND**	**0.633**
25	**131**	**VIRATNAGAR**	**0.632**
25	**170**	**CHECHAT**	**0.632**
27	**116**	**BHADRA**	**0.627**
28	**213**	**NEEM KA THANA**	**0.622**
29	**89**	**CHURU**	**0.621**
30	**215**	**SRI MADHOPUR**	**0.616**
31	**50**	**NADBAI**	**0.615**
32	**128**	**SAMBHAR**	**0.614**
33	**113**	**RAISINGHNAGAR**	**0.613**
34	**227**	**BARGAON**	**0.612**
35	**125**	**JHOTWARA**	**0.610**
36	**52**	**RUPBAS**	**0.609**
37	**53**	**SEWAR**	**0.608**
37	**91**	**RATANGARH**	**0.608**
39	**152**	**KHETRI**	**0.607**
40	**49**	**KUMHER**	**0.604**
40	**172**	**LADPURA**	**0.604**
42	**95**	**BANDIKUI**	**0.603**
43	**110**	**GANGANAGAR**	**0.601**
44	**118**	**NOHAR**	**0.600**
44	**123**	**GOVINDGARH**	**0.600**
46	**147**	**PIRAWA**	**0.599**
47	**145**	**KHANPUR**	**0.598**
48	**33**	**BARAN**	**0.592**
49	**130**	**SHAHPURA**	**0.589**
49	**112**	**PADAMPUR**	**0.589**
51	**167**	**NADOTI**	**0.587**
52	**98**	**MAHWA**	**0.584**
53	**93**	**SUJANGARH**	**0.580**
54	**176**	**DIDWANA**	**0.579**
55	**114**	**SADULSHAHAR**	**0.577**
56	**111**	**KARANPUR**	**0.576**
57	**117**	**HANUMANGARH**	**0.573**
57	**31**	**ANTA**	**0.573**
59	**32**	**ATRU**	**0.569**
59	**178**	**KUCHAMAN**	**0.569**
61	**124**	**JAMWA RAMGARH**	**0.566**
62	**171**	**ITAWA**	**0.565**
63	**129**	**SANGANER**	**0.564**
64	**180**	**MAKRANA**	**0.562**
65	**99**	**SIKRAI**	**0.561**
65	**44**	**SINDHARI**	**0.561**
67	**101**	**BASERI**	**0.555**
68	**228**	**BHINDER**	**0.554**
69	**127**	**PHAGI**	**0.552**
70	**169**	**TODABHIM**	**0.548**
71	**179**	**LADNU**	**0.546**
72	**92**	**SARDARSHAHAR**	**0.543**
73	**45**	**SIWANA**	**0.542**
74	**232**	**JHADOL**	**0.540**
75	**54**	**WEIR**	**0.539**
76	**109**	**ANUPGARH**	**0.538**
77	**40**	**BAYTOO**	**0.532**
78	**16**	**NIMRANA**	**0.530**
78	**203**	**BAMANWAS**	**0.530**
80	**67**	**DUNGARGARH**	**0.528**
81	**102**	**DHAULPUR**	**0.527**
82	**119**	**AMBER**	**0.526**
83	**230**	**GIRWA**	**0.521**
83	**236**	**SALUMBAR**	**0.521**
85	**51**	**NAGAR PAHARI**	**0.520**
86	**9**	**BANSURE**	**0.519**
87	**120**	**BASSI**	**0.517**
87	**43**	**SHEO**	**0.517**
89	**168**	**SAPOTRA**	**0.515**
90	**103**	**RAJAKHERA**	**0.513**
91	**47**	**DEEG**	**0.511**
92	**96**	**DAUSA**	**0.510**
93	**144**	**JHALRAPATAN**	**0.507**
94	**11**	**KATHUMAR**	**0.505**
95	**166**	**KARAULI**	**0.503**
95	**184**	**PARBATSAR**	**0.503**
95	**205**	**GANGAPUR**	**0.503**
98	**100**	**BARI**	**0.502**
	HIGH (0.4-0.5)		
99	**19**	**RENI**	**0.499**
100	122	DUDU	0.498
100	72	KESHORAIPATAN	0.498
102	46	BAYANA	0.494
103	12	KISHANGARH BAS	0.493
104	233	KHERWARA	0.492
104	237	SARADA	0.492
106	14	LACHHMANGARH	0.491
106	38	BALOTRA	0.491
106	115	SURATGARH	0.491
109	201	RAILMAGRA	0.489
109	202	RAJSAMAND	0.489
111	39	BARMER	0.487
111	197	BHIM	0.487
113	181	MERTA	0.481
114	160	LUNI	0.479
115	235	MAVLI	0.476
116	17	RAJGARH	0.475
116	175	DEGANA	0.475
118	192	RANI STATION	0.473
119	36	KISHANGANJ	0.472
120	6	MASOODA	0.471
120	86	NIMBAHERA	0.471
122	217	PINDWARA	0.470
123	97	LALSOT	0.469
123	195	SUMERPUR	0.469
125	87	PRATAPGARH	0.468
125	18	RAMGARH	0.468
127	5	KISHANGARH	0.467
127	34	CHHABRA	0.467
127	37	SHAHBAD	0.467
130	22	UMREN	0.465
131	21	TIJARA	0.464
132	135	AHORE	0.463
133	25	GARHI	0.462
133	74	TALERA	0.462
135	224	TODARAISINGH	0.461
136	7	PISANGAN	0.458
137	204	BONLI	0.457
138	41	CHOHTAN	0.455
139	185	RIYAN	0.454
140	57	HURDA	0.453
140	194	SOJAT	0.453
142	81	CHHOTI SADRI	0.452
143	107	SAGWARA	0.451
143	186	BALI	0.451
145	199	KHAMNOR	0.450
145	187	DESURI	0.450
147	8	SRINAGAR	0.449
147	80	BHOPALSAGAR	0.449
149	177	JAYAL	0.448
150	121	CHAKSU	0.445
150	193	ROHAT	0.445
152	231	GOGUNDA	0.442
153	82	CHITTAURGARH	0.441
154	56	BANERA	0.440
155	219	SHEOGANJ	0.439
155	73	NAINWA	0.439
157	223	NIWAI	0.437
158	189	MARWAR JUN.	0.436
159	183	NAGAUR	0.435
159	191	RAIPUR	0.435
159	198	DEOGARH	0.435
162	196	AMET	0.430
162	159	BILARA	0.430
164	220	SIROHI	0.427
165	58	JAHAZPUR	0.426
166	134	SANKRA	0.424
167	190	PALI	0.423
167	218	REODAR	0.423
169	70	NOKHA	0.422
169	77	BEGUN	0.422
171	207	SAWAI MADHOPUR	0.421
172	35	CHHIPABAROD	0.418
173	83	DUNGLA	0.415
174	66	BIKANER	0.414
175	75	ARNOD	0.413
176	69	LUNKARANSAR	0.412
177	78	BHADESAR	0.411
177	139	RANIWARA	0.411
179	146	MANOHARTHANA	0.410
180	84	GANGRAR	0.409
181	162	OSIAN	0.408
181	163	PHALODI	0.408
181	132	JAISALMER	0.408
181	20	THANAGAZI	0.408
185	48	KAMAN	0.405
185	71	HINDOLI	0.405
185	1	ARAIN	0.405
188	200	KUMBHALGARH	0.404
189	106	DUNGARPUR	0.403
190	79	BHAINSRORGARH	0.402
191	222	MALPURA	0.401
191	188	JAITARAN	0.401
193	4	KEKRI	0.400
	MEDIUM (0.3-0.4)		
194	105	BICHHIWARA	0.399
194	143	DAG	0.399
196	65	SUWANA	0.394
196	140	SANCHORE	0.394
198	30	TALWARA	0.392
199	104	ASPUR	0.387
199	226	UNIARA	0.387
199	137	JALOR	0.387
199	158	BHOPALGARH	0.387
203	85	KAPASAN	0.386
204	76	BARI SADRI	0.384
204	221	DEOLI	0.384
206	63	SAHARA	0.382
206	182	MUNDWA	0.382
208	133	SAM	0.380
209	216	ABU ROAD	0.378
210	61	MANDALGARH	0.377
211	225	TONK	0.376
212	88	RASHMI	0.375
213	157	BAP	0.371
214	60	MANDAL	0.370
215	161	MANDOR	0.369
216	64	SHAHPURA	0.367
217	62	RAIPUR	0.365
218	142	BAKANI	0.363
219	141	SAYLA	0.361
220	108	SIMALWARA	0.359
221	68	KOLAYAT	0.358
221	206	KHANDAR	0.358
223	55	ASIND	0.356
224	2	BHINAY	0.355
225	24	BAGIDORA	0.354
226	156	BALESAR	0.353
227	23	ANANDPURI	0.350
228	164	SHERGARH	0.343
229	26	GHATOL	0.339
230	59	KOTRI	0.338
231	136	BHINMAL	0.332
232	138	JASWANTPURA	0.330
233	29	SAJJANGARH	0.321
	LOW (0.2-0.3)		
234	229	DHARIAWAD	0.296
235	27	KUSHALGARH	0.284
236	28	PEEPALKHOONT	0.211
237	234	KOTRA	0.201
	RAJASTHAN		**0.499**
	%age of AAPs		**41.77**

BOLD: Equal/Above Average Panchayat Samities (AAPs)

Source: Annex- 8.1.

ANNEX-9.1

RANKING OF PANCHAYAT SAMITIES BY GEDI, 1991

(Descending Order)

RANK	PANCHAYAT SAMITIES P. CODE	NAME	GEDI
1	2	3	4
	VERY HIGH (>0.3)		
1	16	**NIMRANA**	0.452
2	10	**BEHROR**	0.418
3	110	**GANGANAGAR**	0.393
4	13	**KOTKASIM**	0.391
5	112	**PADAMPUR**	0.383
6	149	**BUHANA**	0.379
7	15	**MANDAWAR**	0.378
8	151	**JHUNJHUNUN**	0.375
9	111	**KARANPUR**	0.366
10	150	**CHIRAWA**	0.350
11	153	**NAWALGARH**	0.335
12	114	**SADULSHAHAR**	0.331
13	154	**SURAJGARH**	0.330
14	113	**RAISINGHNAGAR**	0.327
15	148	**ALSISAR**	0.325
16	4	**KEKRI**	0.303
	HIGH (0.25-0.3)		
17	152	**KHETRI**	0.299
18	155	**UDAIPURWATI**	0.295
19	12	**KISHANGARH BAS**	0.289
20	174	**SULTANPUR**	0.288
21	52	**RUPBAS**	0.286
22	49	**KUMHER**	0.281
23	173	**SANGOD**	0.276
24	57	**HURDA**	0.273
25	117	**HANUMANGARH**	0.272
25	215	**SRI MADHOPUR**	0.272
27	31	**ANTA**	0.270
28	172	**LADPURA**	0.266
28	116	**BHADRA**	0.266
30	170	**CHECHAT**	0.261
31	7	**PISANGAN**	0.260
32	109	**ANUPGARH**	0.259
32	123	**GOVINDGARH**	0.259
34	214	**PIPRALI**	0.258
35	32	**ATRU**	0.257
35	125	**JHOTWARA**	0.257
35	33	**BARAN**	0.257
38	213	**NEEM KA THANA**	0.256
39	115	**SURATGARH**	0.253
40	53	**SEWAR**	0.252
41	50	**NADBAI**	0.251
	MEDIUM (0.20-0.25)		
42	212	**LACHHMANGARH**	0.249
43	107	**SAGWARA**	0.248
44	145	**KHANPUR**	0.247
45	208	**DANTA RAMGARH**	0.246
46	210	**FATEHPUR**	0.244
47	54	**WEIR**	0.243
47	129	**SANGANER**	0.243
49	25	**GARHI**	0.242
49	192	**RANI STATION**	0.242
51	209	**DHOND**	0.240
52	211	**KHANDELA**	0.239
53	98	**MAHWA**	0.238
54	18	**RAMGARH**	0.233
54	227	**BARGAON**	0.233
56	130	**SHAHPURA**	0.232
57	21	**TIJARA**	0.230
57	186	**BALI**	0.230
59	126	**KOTPUTLI**	0.229
60	201	**RAILMAGRA**	0.228
61	171	**ITAWA**	0.227
62	90	**RAJGARH**	0.222
63	95	**BANDIKUI**	0.220
64	195	**SUMERPUR**	0.219
64	235	**MAVLI**	0.219
66	2	**BHINAY**	0.215
67	187	**DESURI**	0.213
67	47	**DEEG**	0.213
67	199	**KHAMNOR**	0.213
70	128	**SAMBHAR**	0.212
70	9	**BANSURE**	0.212
72	202	**RAJSAMAND**	0.211
72	8	**SRINAGAR**	0.211
74	131	**VIRATNAGAR**	0.210
75	3	**JAWAJA**	0.209
76	17	**RAJGARH**	0.208
76	233	**KHERWARA**	0.208
76	122	**DUDU**	0.208
79	14	**LACHHMANGARH**	0.206
79	5	**KISHANGARH**	0.206
81	101	**BASERI**	0.205
81	6	**MASOODA**	0.205
83	102	**DHAULPUR**	0.202
83	86	**NIMBAHERA**	0.202
85	179	**LADNU**	0.201
85	22	**UMREN**	0.201
85	11	**KATHUMAR**	0.201
88	223	**NIWAI**	0.200
	LOW (0.15-0.2)		
89	118	**NOHAR**	0.198
90	75	**ARNOD**	0.197
90	81	**CHHOTI SADRI**	0.197
92	104	**ASPUR**	0.195
92	180	**MAKRANA**	0.195
92	205	**GANGAPUR**	0.195
95	19	**RENI**	0.194
95	167	**NADOTI**	0.194
97	119	**AMBER**	0.192
97	59	**KOTRI**	0.192
99	80	BHOPALSAGAR	0.190
99	1	ARAIN	0.190
101	181	MERTA	0.188
102	178	KUCHAMAN	0.187
103	221	DEOLI	0.186
103	230	GIRWA	0.186
103	194	SOJAT	0.186
106	189	KHARCHI/MAR.	0.185
106	72	KESHORAIPATAN	0.185
108	228	BHINDER	0.182
108	127	PHAGI	0.182
108	237	SARADA	0.182
111	176	DIDWANA	0.181
112	37	SHAHBAD	0.180
112	82	CHITTAURGARH	0.180
112	46	BAYANA	0.180
115	165	HINDAUN	0.179
116	204	BONLI	0.178
116	36	KISHANGANJ	0.178
118	135	AHORE	0.177
118	89	CHURU	0.177
120	87	PRATAPGARH	0.176
121	88	RASHMI	0.176
122	144	JHALRAPATAN	0.174
122	203	BAMANWAS	0.174
124	220	SIROHI	0.173
124	147	PIRAWA	0.173
124	96	DAUSA	0.173
124	74	TALERA	0.173
128	51	NAGAR PAHARI	0.172
129	120	BASSI	0.171
130	184	PARBATSAR	0.170
131	222	MALPURA	0.168
132	168	SAPOTRA	0.167
132	69	LUNKARANSAR	0.167
134	24	BAGIDORA	0.166
134	66	BIKANER	0.166
136	106	DUNGARPUR	0.165
137	169	TODABHIM	0.164
137	217	PINDWARA	0.164
137	84	GANGRAR	0.164
137	56	BANERA	0.164
141	97	LALSOT	0.163
141	160	LUNI	0.163
141	108	SIMALWARA	0.163
144	124	JAMWA RAMGARH	0.162
144	83	DUNGLA	0.162
144	197	BHIM	0.162
147	78	BHADESAR	0.161
148	63	SAHARA	0.160
148	207	SAWAI MADHOPUR	0.160
150	185	RIYAN	0.159
150	99	SIKRAI	0.159
152	175	DEGANA	0.158
152	76	BARI SADRI	0.158
154	62	RAIPUR	0.157
155	105	BICHHIWARA	0.156
155	79	BHAINSRORGARH	0.156
157	137	JALOR	0.155
157	159	BILARA	0.155
157	20	THANAGAZI	0.155
160	191	RAIPUR	0.152
160	94	TARANAGAR	0.152
160	65	SUWANA	0.152
163	224	TODARAISINGH	0.150
163	103	RAJAKHERA	0.150
163	91	RATANGARH	0.150
	VERY LOW (0.1-0.15)		
166	190	PALI	0.149
166	58	JAHAZPUR	0.149
168	60	MANDAL	0.147
168	77	BEGUN	0.147
168	61	MANDALGARH	0.147
171	142	BAKANI	0.146
172	68	KOLAYAT	0.145
173	231	GOGUNDA	0.144
174	30	TALWARA	0.142
174	121	CHAKSU	0.142
176	219	SHEOGANJ	0.140
176	55	ASIND	0.140
178	200	KUMBHALGARH	0.137
179	143	DAG	0.136
179	236	SALUMBAR	0.136
181	161	MANDOR	0.135
182	67	DUNGARGARH	0.134
182	218	REODAR	0.134
182	226	UNIARA	0.134
182	71	HINDOLI	0.134
186	188	JAITARAN	0.133
186	73	NAINWA	0.133
188	26	GHATOL	0.132
188	193	ROHAT	0.132
190	196	AMET	0.130
190	206	KHANDAR	0.130
192	166	KARAULI	0.128
192	93	SUJANGARH	0.128
192	64	SHAHPURA	0.128
195	100	BARI	0.127
196	35	CHHIPABAROD	0.126
196	158	BHOPALGARH	0.126
198	183	NAGAUR	0.124
196	177	JAYAL	0.124
200	132	JAISALMER	0.122
200	45	SIWANA	0.122
202	85	KAPASAN	0.121
203	38	BALOTRA	0.120
203	225	TONK	0.120
203	216	ABU ROAD	0.120
206	23	ANANDPURI	0.119
206	232	JHADOL	0.119
208	34	CHHABARA	0.116
209	70	NOKHA	0.115
210	198	DEOGARH	0.112
210	48	KAMAN	0.112
210	182	MUNDWA	0.112
213	141	SAYLA	0.109
214	29	SAJJANGARH	0.108
214	92	SARDARSHAHAR	0.108
216	162	OSIAN	0.107
217	163	PHALODI	0.105
	EXTREMELY LOW (<0.1)		
218	156	BALESAR	0.097
218	138	JASWANTPURA	0.097
220	157	BAP	0.096
221	134	SANKRA	0.087
221	139	RANIWARA	0.087
223	40	BAYTOO	0.085
224	164	SHERGARH	0.081
225	229	DHARIAWAD	0.080
226	133	SAM	0.070
227	27	KUSHALGARH	0.067
228	39	BARMER	0.066
229	43	SHEO	0.065
230	136	BHINMAL	0.060
231	146	MANOHARTHANA	0.059
232	140	SANCHORE	0.057
232	42	DHORIMANNA	0.057
234	44	SINDHARI	0.055
235	28	PEEPALKHOONT	0.051
236	234	KOTRA	0.045
237	41	CHOHTAN	0.042
		RAJASTHAN	**0.192**
		%age of AAPs	**41.40**

BOLD: Equal/Above Average Panchayat Samities (AAPs)

Source: Annex-10.1, Col. 7.

ANNEX 10.1

PANCHAYAT SAMITI-WISE VARIATION IN GEDI RAJASTHAN: (1991-2001)

P. Code	*Panchayat Samities Name*	*1991*					*2001*				
		Female Pop. Index	*Male Pop. Index*	*FLI*	*MLI*	***GEDI***	*Female Pop. Index*	*Male Pop. Index*	*FLI*	*MLI*	***GEDI***
1	*2*	*3*	*4*	*5*	*6*	*7*	*8*	*9*	*10*	*11*	*12*
1	ARAIN	0.485	0.515	0.117	0.455	0.190	0.490	0.510	0.283	0.641	0.396
2	BHINAY	0.484	0.516	0.133	0.509	0.215	0.490	0.510	0.212	0.633	0.321
3	JAWAJA	0.497	0.503	0.123	0.670	0.209	0.496	0.504	0.580	0.909	0.709
4	KEKRI	0.485	0.515	0.199	0.599	0.303	0.489	0.511	0.256	0.680	0.376
5	KISHANGARH	0.477	0.523	0.127	0.474	0.206	0.483	0.517	0.339	0.712	0.465
6	MASOODA	0.479	0.521	0.121	0.565	0.205	0.488	0.512	0.319	0.764	0.454
7	PISANGAN	0.480	0.520	0.162	0.590	0.260	0.485	0.515	0.316	0.731	0.446
8	SRINAGAR	0.480	0.520	0.128	0.525	0.211	0.480	0.520	0.303	0.726	0.435
	AJMER	**0.483**	**0.517**	**0.140**	**0.550**	**0.227**	**0.487**	**0.513**	**0.327**	**0.726**	**0.455**
9	BANSURE	0.468	0.532	0.127	0.519	0.212	0.475	0.525	0.395	0.750	0.526
10	BEHROR	0.483	0.517	0.286	0.733	0.418	0.478	0.522	0.722	0.898	0.804
11	KATHUMAR	0.456	0.544	0.114	0.555	0.201	0.465	0.535	0.368	0.751	0.506
12	KISHANGARH BAS	0.474	0.526	0.189	0.555	0.289	0.476	0.524	0.362	0.738	0.494
13	KOTKASIM	0.473	0.527	0.263	0.693	0.391	0.476	0.524	0.527	0.853	0.659
14	LACHHMANGARH	0.469	0.531	0.122	0.527	0.206	0.471	0.529	0.345	0.759	0.485
15	MANDAWAR	0.478	0.522	0.253	0.692	0.378	0.479	0.521	0.524	0.851	0.655
16	NIMRANA	0.486	0.514	0.320	0.745	0.452	0.481	0.519	0.454	0.676	0.547
17	RAJGARH	0.469	0.531	0.122	0.551	0.208	0.471	0.529	0.327	0.747	0.465
18	RAMGARH	0.468	0.532	0.144	0.507	0.233	0.472	0.528	0.326	0.728	0.460
19	RENI	0.467	0.533	0.112	0.540	0.194	0.469	0.531	0.352	0.766	0.494
20	THANAGAZI	0.471	0.529	0.089	0.448	0.155	0.474	0.526	0.262	0.678	0.387
21	TIJARA	0.470	0.530	0.143	0.502	0.230	0.463	0.537	0.328	0.704	0.460
22	UMREN	0.464	0.536	0.119	0.499	0.201	0.470	0.530	0.324	0.721	0.458
	ALWAR	**0.470**	**0.530**	**0.167**	**0.568**	**0.267**	**0.472**	**0.528**	**0.392**	**0.765**	**0.528**
23	ANANDPURI	0.491	0.509	0.071	0.346	0.119	0.491	0.509	0.240	0.564	0.339
24	BAGIDORA	0.493	0.507	0.106	0.368	0.166	0.496	0.504	0.240	0.578	0.340
25	GARHI	0.493	0.507	0.161	0.474	0.242	0.494	0.506	0.347	0.693	0.464
26	GHATOL	0.496	0.504	0.081	0.347	0.132	0.497	0.503	0.217	0.583	0.317
27	KUSHALGARH	0.491	0.509	0.039	0.209	0.067	0.497	0.503	0.181	0.488	0.265
28	PEEPALKHOONT	0.491	0.509	0.030	0.192	0.051	0.492	0.508	0.119	0.392	0.184
29	SAJJANGARH	0.489	0.511	0.066	0.278	0.108	0.493	0.507	0.211	0.534	0.304
30	TALWARA	0.497	0.503	0.089	0.349	0.142	0.493	0.507	0.265	0.642	0.377
	BANSWARA	**0.493**	**0.507**	**0.089**	**0.337**	**0.142**	**0.494**	**0.506**	**0.238**	**0.575**	**0.338**
31	ANTA	0.476	0.524	0.168	0.600	0.270	0.478	0.522	0.450	0.804	0.584
32	ATRU	0.472	0.528	0.158	0.583	0.257	0.475	0.525	0.438	0.811	0.578
33	BARAN	0.475	0.525	0.157	0.602	0.257	0.475	0.525	0.465	0.827	0.604
34	CHHABARA	0.469	0.531	0.064	0.406	0.116	0.472	0.528	0.328	0.721	0.461
35	CHHIPABAROD	0.475	0.525	0.071	0.429	0.126	0.478	0.522	0.277	0.683	0.402
36	KISHANGANJ	0.474	0.526	0.111	0.386	0.178	0.479	0.521	0.358	0.684	0.476
37	SHAHBAD	0.467	0.533	0.109	0.424	0.180	0.473	0.527	0.340	0.698	0.466
	BARAN	**0.473**	**0.527**	**0.123**	**0.494**	**0.203**	**0.476**	**0.524**	**0.382**	**0.748**	**0.514**
38	BALOTRA	0.479	0.521	0.069	0.383	0.120	0.480	0.520	0.370	0.719	0.495
39	BARMER	0.461	0.539	0.034	0.330	0.066	0.460	0.540	0.365	0.702	0.493
40	BAYTOO	0.479	0.521	0.047	0.346	0.085	0.475	0.525	0.429	0.723	0.546
41	CHOHTAN	0.466	0.534	0.022	0.212	0.042	0.466	0.534	0.352	0.639	0.463
42	DHORIMANNA	0.477	0.523	0.030	0.292	0.057	0.477	0.523	0.567	0.777	0.660
43	SHEO	0.452	0.548	0.033	0.326	0.065	0.457	0.543	0.398	0.726	0.527
44	SINDHARI	0.478	0.522	0.029	0.301	0.055	0.480	0.520	0.464	0.742	0.576
45	SIWANA	0.484	0.516	0.071	0.373	0.122	0.480	0.520	0.436	0.744	0.555
	BARMER	**0.473**	**0.527**	**0.042**	**0.318**	**0.077**	**0.472**	**0.528**	**0.424**	**0.722**	**0.542**
46	BAYANA	0.440	0.560	0.097	0.545	0.180	0.447	0.553	0.337	0.760	0.487
47	DEEG	0.450	0.550	0.120	0.578	0.213	0.459	0.541	0.363	0.774	0.509
48	KAMAN	0.463	0.537	0.061	0.398	0.112	0.469	0.531	0.262	0.665	0.386
49	KUMHER	0.452	0.548	0.164	0.686	0.281	0.461	0.539	0.461	0.858	0.614
50	NADBAI	0.450	0.550	0.142	0.671	0.251	0.456	0.544	0.468	0.874	0.626
51	NAGAR PAHARI	0.459	0.541	0.098	0.483	0.172	0.467	0.533	0.381	0.772	0.522
52	RUPBAS	0.450	0.550	0.170	0.646	0.286	0.457	0.543	0.473	0.850	0.623
53	SEWAR	0.451	0.549	0.144	0.653	0.252	0.461	0.539	0.467	0.859	0.619
54	WEIR	0.452	0.548	0.139	0.632	0.243	0.458	0.542	0.383	0.813	0.537
	BHARATPUR	**0.452**	**0.548**	**0.125**	**0.584**	**0.219**	**0.460**	**0.540**	**0.396**	**0.800**	**0.545**
55	ASIND	0.497	0.503	0.084	0.403	0.140	0.505	0.495	0.229	0.616	0.332
56	BANERA	0.488	0.512	0.102	0.404	0.164	0.496	0.504	0.319	0.680	0.436
57	HURDA	0.482	0.518	0.185	0.489	0.273	0.487	0.513	0.321	0.708	0.446
58	JAHAZPUR	0.478	0.522	0.088	0.413	0.149	0.482	0.518	0.297	0.673	0.418
59	KOTRI	0.482	0.518	0.132	0.332	0.192	0.488	0.512	0.225	0.557	0.324
60	MANDAL	0.499	0.501	0.091	0.378	0.147	0.508	0.492	0.246	0.628	0.351
61	MANDALGARH	0.474	0.526	0.090	0.338	0.147	0.482	0.518	0.259	0.597	0.366
62	RAIPUR	0.504	0.496	0.098	0.404	0.157	0.510	0.490	0.242	0.622	0.345
63	SAHARA	0.510	0.490	0.101	0.407	0.160	0.517	0.483	0.264	0.636	0.368
64	SHAHPURA	0.485	0.515	0.077	0.337	0.128	0.487	0.513	0.246	0.601	0.353

P. Code	Panchayat Samities Name	1991 Female Pop. Index	1991 Male Pop. Index	1991 FLI	1991 MLI	1991 GEDI	2001 Female Pop. Index	2001 Male Pop. Index	2001 FLI	2001 MLI	2001 GEDI
1	2	3	4	5	6	7	8	9	10	11	12
65	SUWANA	0.490	0.510	0.093	0.385	0.152	0.491	0.509	0.264	0.648	0.378
	BHILWARA	**0.489**	**0.511**	**0.100**	**0.384**	**0.160**	**0.495**	**0.505**	**0.261**	**0.629**	**0.370**
66	BIKANER	0.466	0.534	0.100	0.388	0.166	0.470	0.530	0.302	0.618	0.414
67	DUNGARGARH*	0.483	0.517	0.080	0.368	0.134	0.486	0.514	0.417	0.742	0.538
68	KOLAYAT	0.467	0.533	0.087	0.351	0.145	0.467	0.533	0.246	0.559	0.351
69	LUNKARANSAR	0.475	0.525	0.103	0.380	0.167	0.477	0.523	0.303	0.614	0.412
70	NOKHA	0.481	0.519	0.066	0.376	0.115	0.477	0.523	0.288	0.671	0.411
	BIKANER **	**0.472**	**0.528**	**0.088**	**0.376**	**0.148**	**0.473**	**0.527**	**0.288**	**0.619**	**0.401**
71	HINDOLI	0.471	0.529	0.079	0.348	0.134	0.474	0.526	0.276	0.643	0.394
72	KESHORAIPATAN	0.473	0.527	0.109	0.488	0.185	0.478	0.522	0.369	0.739	0.500
73	NAINWA	0.470	0.530	0.077	0.376	0.133	0.477	0.523	0.297	0.704	0.426
74	TALERA	0.468	0.532	0.104	0.410	0.173	0.475	0.525	0.344	0.682	0.465
	BUNDI	**0.470**	**0.530**	**0.094**	**0.407**	**0.159**	**0.476**	**0.524**	**0.324**	**0.690**	**0.449**
75	ARNOD	0.492	0.508	0.128	0.414	0.197	0.492	0.508	0.297	0.640	0.408
76	BARI SADRI	0.495	0.505	0.095	0.443	0.158	0.500	0.500	0.251	0.652	0.362
77	BEGUN	0.487	0.513	0.086	0.444	0.147	0.491	0.509	0.288	0.683	0.408
78	BHADESAR	0.488	0.512	0.098	0.422	0.161	0.495	0.505	0.283	0.665	0.399
79	BHAINSRORGARH	0.471	0.529	0.093	0.390	0.156	0.475	0.525	0.279	0.631	0.394
80	BHOPALSAGAR	0.492	0.508	0.118	0.467	0.190	0.501	0.499	0.324	0.702	0.443
81	CHHOTI SADRI	0.489	0.511	0.120	0.504	0.197	0.491	0.509	0.319	0.713	0.444
82	CHITTAURGARH	0.490	0.510	0.112	0.444	0.180	0.491	0.509	0.316	0.687	0.436
83	DUNGLA	0.494	0.506	0.098	0.446	0.162	0.501	0.499	0.286	0.676	0.402
84	GANGRAR	0.484	0.516	0.100	0.409	0.164	0.493	0.507	0.282	0.658	0.397
85	KAPASAN	0.495	0.505	0.071	0.390	0.121	0.498	0.502	0.253	0.652	0.365
86	NIMBAHERA	0.490	0.510	0.122	0.540	0.202	0.492	0.508	0.324	0.759	0.457
87	PRATAPGARH	0.488	0.512	0.109	0.428	0.176	0.489	0.511	0.355	0.690	0.472
88	RASHMI	0.501	0.499	0.110	0.441	0.176	0.505	0.495	0.246	0.640	0.354
	CHITTAURGARH	**0.490**	**0.510**	**0.106**	**0.444**	**0.173**	**0.493**	**0.507**	**0.300**	**0.679**	**0.418**
89	CHURU	0.489	0.511	0.106	0.490	0.177	0.490	0.510	0.529	0.802	0.640
90	RAJGARH	0.485	0.515	0.137	0.537	0.222	0.483	0.517	0.598	0.836	0.701
91	RATANGARH	0.484	0.516	0.089	0.434	0.150	0.494	0.506	0.518	0.787	0.626
92	SARDARSHAHAR	0.483	0.517	0.061	0.377	0.108	0.488	0.512	0.436	0.751	0.555
93	SUJANGARH	0.485	0.515	0.075	0.384	0.128	0.492	0.508	0.487	0.763	0.597
94	TARANAGAR	0.487	0.513	0.090	0.440	0.152	0.485	0.515	0.617	0.820	0.707
	CHURU ***	**0.485**	**0.515**	**0.093**	**0.436**	**0.156**	**0.488**	**0.512**	**0.515**	**0.786**	**0.625**
95	BANDIKUI	0.471	0.529	0.129	0.587	0.220	0.473	0.527	0.484	0.822	0.618
96	DAUSA	0.470	0.530	0.098	0.542	0.173	0.476	0.524	0.362	0.783	0.504
97	LALSOT	0.472	0.528	0.094	0.478	0.163	0.478	0.522	0.323	0.744	0.458
98	MAHWA	0.461	0.539	0.139	0.607	0.238	0.466	0.534	0.452	0.824	0.595
99	SIKRAI	0.472	0.528	0.091	0.498	0.159	0.473	0.527	0.436	0.793	0.572
	DAUSA	**0.470**	**0.530**	**0.109**	**0.542**	**0.189**	**0.474**	**0.526**	**0.408**	**0.792**	**0.548**
100	BARI	0.433	0.567	0.067	0.407	0.127	0.443	0.557	0.368	0.726	0.507
101	BASERI	0.441	0.559	0.120	0.466	0.205	0.452	0.548	0.428	0.774	0.567
102	DHAULPUR	0.444	0.556	0.115	0.512	0.202	0.455	0.545	0.391	0.763	0.532
103	RAJAKHERA	0.440	0.560	0.080	0.475	0.150	0.449	0.551	0.380	0.739	0.519
	DHAULPUR	**0.440**	**0.560**	**0.099**	**0.471**	**0.177**	**0.451**	**0.549**	**0.394**	**0.753**	**0.533**
104	ASPUR	0.513	0.487	0.129	0.427	0.195	0.517	0.483	0.276	0.627	0.378
105	BICHHIWARA	0.494	0.506	0.097	0.401	0.156	0.500	0.500	0.279	0.642	0.389
106	DUNGARPUR	0.505	0.495	0.103	0.433	0.165	0.508	0.492	0.276	0.668	0.388
107	SAGWARA	0.505	0.495	0.166	0.499	0.248	0.518	0.482	0.336	0.701	0.449
108	SIMALWARA	0.491	0.509	0.103	0.369	0.163	0.499	0.501	0.246	0.585	0.347
	DUNGARPUR	**0.501**	**0.499**	**0.119**	**0.423**	**0.186**	**0.508**	**0.492**	**0.282**	**0.641**	**0.389**
109	ANUPGARH	0.465	0.535	0.175	0.446	0.259	0.472	0.528	0.446	0.708	0.554
110	GANGANAGAR	0.462	0.538	0.285	0.583	0.393	0.470	0.530	0.516	0.759	0.622
111	KARANPUR	0.475	0.525	0.278	0.513	0.366	0.473	0.527	0.499	0.720	0.595
112	PADAMPUR	0.475	0.525	0.283	0.562	0.383	0.475	0.525	0.506	0.745	0.608
113	RAISINGHNAGAR	0.478	0.522	0.233	0.517	0.327	0.477	0.523	0.531	0.767	0.633
114	SADULSHAHAR	0.463	0.537	0.228	0.541	0.331	0.460	0.540	0.482	0.746	0.596
115	SURATGARH	0.460	0.540	0.163	0.480	0.253	0.456	0.544	0.401	0.647	0.505
	GANGANAGAR	**0.466**	**0.534**	**0.219**	**0.509**	**0.314**	**0.469**	**0.531**	**0.473**	**0.720**	**0.578**
116	BHADRA	0.475	0.525	0.168	0.561	0.266	0.473	0.527	0.529	0.810	0.647
117	HANUMANGARH	0.471	0.529	0.186	0.464	0.272	0.472	0.528	0.487	0.734	0.592
118	NOHAR	0.476	0.524	0.121	0.469	0.198	0.475	0.525	0.506	0.774	0.618
	HANUMANGARH	**0.474**	**0.526**	**0.158**	**0.487**	**0.245**	**0.473**	**0.527**	**0.500**	**0.760**	**0.610**
119	AMBER	0.476	0.524	0.111	0.571	0.192	0.475	0.525	0.381	0.795	0.524
120	BASSI	0.474	0.526	0.097	0.548	0.171	0.477	0.523	0.370	0.792	0.513
121	CHAKSU	0.476	0.524	0.080	0.482	0.142	0.478	0.522	0.297	0.724	0.429
122	DUDU	0.478	0.522	0.126	0.509	0.208	0.481	0.519	0.368	0.745	0.499
123	GOVINDGARH	0.478	0.522	0.157	0.639	0.259	0.479	0.521	0.474	0.837	0.612
124	JAMWA RAMGARH	0.475	0.525	0.092	0.519	0.162	0.476	0.524	0.439	0.801	0.575
125	JHOTWARA	0.469	0.531	0.156	0.598	0.257	0.478	0.522	0.497	0.821	0.626
126	KOTPUTLI	0.477	0.523	0.139	0.563	0.229	0.475	0.525	0.597	0.837	0.703
127	PHAGI	0.475	0.525	0.109	0.461	0.182	0.479	0.521	0.438	0.767	0.564
128	SAMBHAR	0.482	0.518	0.126	0.584	0.212	0.483	0.517	0.504	0.824	0.630
129	SANGANER	0.472	0.528	0.146	0.594	0.243	0.478	0.522	0.434	0.807	0.572
130	SHAHPURA	0.476	0.524	0.139	0.596	0.232	0.474	0.526	0.467	0.816	0.602
131	VIRATNAGAR	0.474	0.526	0.125	0.539	0.210	0.476	0.524	0.528	0.825	0.651
	JAIPUR	**0.476**	**0.524**	**0.123**	**0.555**	**0.208**	**0.478**	**0.522**	**0.444**	**0.800**	**0.579**
132	JAISALMER	0.438	0.562	0.064	0.425	0.122	0.448	0.552	0.277	0.632	0.402
133	SAM	0.443	0.557	0.035	0.352	0.070	0.440	0.560	0.240	0.612	0.364
134	SANKRA	0.462	0.538	0.046	0.369	0.087	0.467	0.533	0.300	0.647	0.420

P. Code	Panchayat Samities Name	1991					2001				
		Female Pop. Index	Male Pop. Index	FLI	MLI	GEDI	Female Pop. Index	Male Pop. Index	FLI	MLI	GEDI
1	2	3	4	5	6	7	8	9	10	11	12
	JAISALMER	**0.449**	**0.551**	**0.047**	**0.379**	**0.091**	**0.453**	**0.547**	**0.275**	**0.631**	**0.397**
135	AHORE	0.496	0.504	0.109	0.464	0.177	0.505	0.495	0.353	0.693	0.466
136	BHINMAL	0.482	0.518	0.032	0.309	0.060	0.494	0.506	0.195	0.605	0.297
137	JALOR	0.492	0.508	0.094	0.424	0.155	0.499	0.501	0.272	0.620	0.378
138	JASWANTPURA	0.490	0.510	0.055	0.355	0.097	0.499	0.501	0.207	0.582	0.306
139	RANIWARA	0.479	0.521	0.048	0.344	0.087	0.483	0.517	0.285	0.653	0.402
140	SANCHORE	0.480	0.520	0.030	0.342	0.057	0.484	0.516	0.261	0.648	0.377
141	SAYLA	0.489	0.511	0.064	0.327	0.109	0.494	0.506	0.231	0.620	0.338
	JALOR	**0.486**	**0.514**	**0.059**	**0.362**	**0.103**	**0.492**	**0.508**	**0.259**	**0.635**	**0.370**
142	BAKANI	0.479	0.521	0.088	0.366	0.146	0.481	0.519	0.239	0.598	0.347
143	DAG	0.484	0.516	0.084	0.328	0.136	0.487	0.513	0.276	0.636	0.389
144	JHALRAPATAN	0.479	0.521	0.103	0.469	0.174	0.481	0.519	0.377	0.753	0.509
145	KHANPUR	0.473	0.527	0.149	0.605	0.247	0.477	0.523	0.472	0.835	0.611
146	MANOHARTHANA	0.478	0.522	0.032	0.275	0.059	0.480	0.520	0.282	0.653	0.400
147	PIRAWA	0.482	0.518	0.103	0.475	0.173	0.484	0.516	0.490	0.807	0.615
	JHALAWAR	**0.479**	**0.521**	**0.093**	**0.419**	**0.156**	**0.482**	**0.518**	**0.355**	**0.715**	**0.480**
148	ALSISAR	0.495	0.505	0.216	0.646	0.325	0.497	0.503	0.617	0.862	0.720
149	BUHANA	0.483	0.517	0.253	0.708	0.379	0.486	0.514	0.645	0.899	0.755
150	CHIRAWA	0.487	0.513	0.233	0.666	0.350	0.489	0.511	0.613	0.875	0.724
151	JHUNJHUNUN	0.491	0.509	0.253	0.709	0.375	0.494	0.506	0.630	0.903	0.744
152	KHETRI	0.473	0.527	0.189	0.626	0.299	0.484	0.516	0.504	0.805	0.624
153	NAWALGARH	0.490	0.510	0.219	0.681	0.335	0.492	0.508	0.538	0.854	0.663
154	SURAJGARH	0.478	0.522	0.217	0.633	0.330	0.482	0.518	0.559	0.846	0.678
155	UDAIPURWATI	0.487	0.513	0.189	0.627	0.295	0.491	0.509	0.680	0.872	0.766
	JHUNJHUNUN	**0.485**	**0.515**	**0.220**	**0.662**	**0.336**	**0.489**	**0.511**	**0.598**	**0.864**	**0.709**
156	BALESAR	0.436	0.564	0.049	0.398	0.097	0.478	0.522	0.198	0.643	0.310
157	BAP	0.469	0.531	0.053	0.335	0.096	0.473	0.527	0.247	0.604	0.359
158	BHOPALGARH	0.482	0.518	0.070	0.486	0.126	0.485	0.515	0.234	0.680	0.353
159	BILARA	0.479	0.521	0.088	0.514	0.155	0.482	0.518	0.282	0.714	0.411
160	LUNI	0.479	0.521	0.094	0.495	0.163	0.481	0.519	0.341	0.741	0.474
161	MANDOR	0.475	0.525	0.075	0.503	0.135	0.476	0.524	0.221	0.649	0.338
162	OSIAN	0.478	0.522	0.059	0.421	0.107	0.480	0.520	0.275	0.656	0.394
163	PHALODI	0.478	0.522	0.058	0.398	0.105	0.477	0.523	0.275	0.656	0.395
164	SHERGARH	0.472	0.528	0.043	0.373	0.081	0.477	0.523	0.195	0.616	0.303
	JODHPUR	**0.474**	**0.526**	**0.066**	**0.438**	**0.120**	**0.479**	**0.521**	**0.251**	**0.669**	**0.372**
165	HINDAUN	0.454	0.546	0.098	0.566	0.179	0.457	0.543	0.578	0.875	0.709
166	KARAULI	0.450	0.550	0.070	0.401	0.128	0.456	0.544	0.359	0.755	0.502
167	NADOTI	0.463	0.537	0.110	0.566	0.194	0.471	0.529	0.461	0.819	0.600
168	SAPOTRA	0.453	0.547	0.097	0.418	0.167	0.459	0.541	0.379	0.753	0.518
169	TODABHIM	0.457	0.543	0.089	0.576	0.164	0.462	0.538	0.397	0.820	0.549
	KARAULI	**0.455**	**0.545**	**0.092**	**0.499**	**0.165**	**0.460**	**0.540**	**0.438**	**0.805**	**0.581**
170	CHECHAT	0.469	0.531	0.163	0.560	0.261	0.475	0.525	0.524	0.832	0.650
171	ITAWA	0.471	0.529	0.138	0.537	0.227	0.475	0.525	0.446	0.786	0.577
172	LADPURA	0.473	0.527	0.168	0.557	0.266	0.474	0.526	0.491	0.815	0.621
173	SANGOD	0.475	0.525	0.172	0.614	0.276	0.478	0.522	0.531	0.851	0.661
174	SULTANPUR	0.472	0.528	0.180	0.618	0.288	0.477	0.523	0.543	0.847	0.668
	KOTA	**0.472**	**0.528**	**0.164**	**0.577**	**0.264**	**0.476**	**0.524**	**0.506**	**0.826**	**0.635**
175	DEGANA	0.490	0.510	0.094	0.458	0.158	0.495	0.505	0.353	0.718	0.475
176	DIDWANA	0.495	0.505	0.109	0.509	0.181	0.496	0.504	0.465	0.808	0.592
177	JAYAL	0.488	0.512	0.073	0.402	0.124	0.489	0.511	0.322	0.695	0.444
178	KUCHAMAN	0.486	0.514	0.113	0.492	0.187	0.483	0.517	0.455	0.787	0.582
179	LADNU	0.494	0.506	0.124	0.515	0.201	0.495	0.505	0.424	0.787	0.553
180	MAKRANA	0.488	0.512	0.120	0.489	0.195	0.489	0.511	0.449	0.782	0.574
181	MERTA	0.479	0.521	0.112	0.497	0.188	0.480	0.520	0.344	0.739	0.476
182	MUNDWA	0.482	0.518	0.063	0.395	0.112	0.486	0.514	0.244	0.647	0.359
183	NAGAUR	0.483	0.517	0.071	0.417	0.124	0.486	0.514	0.308	0.680	0.429
184	PARBATSAR	0.485	0.515	0.105	0.413	0.170	0.485	0.515	0.391	0.722	0.512
185	RIYAN	0.484	0.516	0.095	0.440	0.159	0.485	0.515	0.323	0.707	0.448
	NAGAUR	**0.487**	**0.513**	**0.098**	**0.458**	**0.164**	**0.488**	**0.512**	**0.376**	**0.737**	**0.502**
186	BALI	0.497	0.503	0.154	0.459	0.230	0.503	0.497	0.345	0.666	0.454
187	DESURI	0.502	0.498	0.136	0.497	0.213	0.513	0.487	0.344	0.678	0.452
188	JAITARAN	0.487	0.513	0.078	0.436	0.133	0.492	0.508	0.267	0.665	0.384
189	KHARCHI/MAR.	0.496	0.504	0.112	0.509	0.185	0.503	0.497	0.307	0.699	0.426
190	PALI	0.483	0.517	0.087	0.452	0.149	0.495	0.505	0.294	0.682	0.412
191	RAIPUR	0.490	0.510	0.089	0.480	0.152	0.496	0.504	0.297	0.710	0.420
192	RANI STATION	0.501	0.499	0.158	0.519	0.242	0.510	0.490	0.364	0.702	0.476
193	ROHAT	0.486	0.514	0.075	0.457	0.132	0.491	0.509	0.309	0.713	0.434
194	SOJAT	0.494	0.506	0.111	0.540	0.186	0.502	0.498	0.318	0.728	0.442
195	SUMERPUR	0.493	0.507	0.138	0.510	0.219	0.499	0.501	0.354	0.704	0.471
	PALI	**0.493**	**0.507**	**0.115**	**0.486**	**0.187**	**0.500**	**0.500**	**0.318**	**0.694**	**0.436**
196	AMET	0.493	0.507	0.078	0.377	0.130	0.500	0.500	0.309	0.675	0.424
197	BHIM	0.511	0.489	0.096	0.565	0.162	0.506	0.494	0.332	0.810	0.469
198	DEOGARH	0.503	0.497	0.066	0.392	0.112	0.510	0.490	0.314	0.689	0.428
199	KHAMNOR	0.504	0.496	0.137	0.483	0.213	0.501	0.499	0.343	0.670	0.453
200	KUMBHALGARH	0.498	0.502	0.083	0.384	0.137	0.508	0.492	0.282	0.657	0.392
201	RAILMAGRA	0.497	0.503	0.147	0.504	0.228	0.505	0.495	0.368	0.738	0.490
202	RAJSAMAND	0.496	0.504	0.133	0.498	0.211	0.494	0.506	0.363	0.739	0.489
	RAJSAMAND	**0.500**	**0.500**	**0.109**	**0.464**	**0.177**	**0.503**	**0.497**	**0.332**	**0.712**	**0.452**
203	BAMANWAS	0.464	0.536	0.099	0.523	0.174	0.469	0.531	0.387	0.788	0.530
204	BONLI	0.469	0.531	0.104	0.481	0.178	0.475	0.525	0.308	0.735	0.443
205	GANGAPUR	0.461	0.539	0.111	0.560	0.195	0.467	0.533	0.344	0.791	0.492

P. Code	Panchayat Samities Name	1991 Female Pop. Index	1991 Male Pop. Index	1991 FLI	1991 MLI	1991 GEDI	2001 Female Pop. Index	2001 Male Pop. Index	2001 FLI	2001 MLI	2001 GEDI
1	2	3	4	5	6	7	8	9	10	11	12
206	KHANDAR	0.462	0.538	0.073	0.392	0.130	0.466	0.534	0.205	0.632	0.321
207	SAWAI MADHOPUR	0.470	0.530	0.090	0.515	0.160	0.475	0.525	0.247	0.745	0.381
	SAWAI MADHOPUR	**0.466**	**0.534**	**0.096**	**0.497**	**0.169**	**0.471**	**0.529**	**0.297**	**0.741**	**0.435**
208	DANTA RAMGARH	0.487	0.513	0.152	0.598	0.246	0.492	0.508	0.557	0.844	0.673
209	DHOND	0.492	0.508	0.147	0.622	0.240	0.490	0.510	0.525	0.846	0.651
210	FATEHPUR	0.499	0.501	0.152	0.607	0.244	0.498	0.502	0.622	0.871	0.726
211	KHANDELA	0.486	0.514	0.145	0.631	0.239	0.491	0.509	0.594	0.860	0.705
212	LACHHMANGARH	0.496	0.504	0.155	0.617	0.249	0.493	0.507	0.616	0.874	0.724
213	NEEM KA THANA	0.478	0.522	0.157	0.604	0.256	0.480	0.520	0.515	0.827	0.641
214	PIPRALI	0.486	0.514	0.159	0.629	0.258	0.487	0.513	0.542	0.855	0.667
215	SRI MADHOPUR	0.484	0.516	0.168	0.646	0.272	0.487	0.513	0.513	0.820	0.635
	SIKAR	**0.488**	**0.512**	**0.154**	**0.618**	**0.250**	**0.489**	**0.511**	**0.557**	**0.847**	**0.675**
216	ABU ROAD	0.485	0.515	0.074	0.289	0.120	0.483	0.517	0.264	0.594	0.370
217	PINDWARA	0.491	0.509	0.106	0.347	0.164	0.488	0.512	0.357	0.690	0.474
218	REODAR	0.486	0.514	0.082	0.337	0.134	0.486	0.514	0.302	0.655	0.418
219	SHEOGANJ	0.490	0.510	0.084	0.394	0.140	0.491	0.509	0.328	0.661	0.441
220	SIROHI	0.502	0.498	0.107	0.465	0.173	0.503	0.497	0.305	0.679	0.420
	SIROHI	**0.491**	**0.509**	**0.092**	**0.366**	**0.149**	**0.490**	**0.510**	**0.315**	**0.659**	**0.429**
221	DEOLI	0.479	0.521	0.111	0.491	0.186	0.483	0.517	0.235	0.668	0.353
222	MALPURA	0.482	0.518	0.101	0.434	0.168	0.486	0.514	0.265	0.662	0.383
223	NIWAI	0.484	0.516	0.125	0.463	0.200	0.479	0.521	0.292	0.710	0.421
224	TODARAISINGH	0.486	0.514	0.087	0.474	0.150	0.488	0.512	0.327	0.722	0.454
225	TONK	0.478	0.522	0.067	0.445	0.120	0.482	0.518	0.219	0.674	0.337
226	UNIARA	0.477	0.523	0.076	0.439	0.134	0.478	0.522	0.226	0.691	0.348
	TONK	**0.481**	**0.519**	**0.095**	**0.457**	**0.161**	**0.482**	**0.518**	**0.256**	**0.685**	**0.379**
227	BARGAON	0.483	0.517	0.148	0.499	0.233	0.485	0.515	0.507	0.815	0.630
228	BHINDER	0.493	0.507	0.112	0.469	0.182	0.496	0.504	0.445	0.771	0.565
229	DHARIAWAD	0.490	0.510	0.049	0.206	0.080	0.499	0.501	0.182	0.523	0.270
230	GIRWA	0.485	0.515	0.117	0.417	0.186	0.490	0.510	0.405	0.747	0.528
231	GOGUNDA	0.494	0.506	0.089	0.368	0.144	0.495	0.505	0.323	0.677	0.439
232	JHADOL	0.488	0.512	0.072	0.318	0.119	0.494	0.506	0.434	0.747	0.551
233	KHERWARA	0.506	0.494	0.131	0.518	0.208	0.501	0.499	0.362	0.757	0.489
234	KOTRA	0.488	0.512	0.026	0.144	0.045	0.495	0.505	0.111	0.376	0.172
235	MAVLI	0.490	0.510	0.139	0.486	0.219	0.494	0.506	0.354	0.718	0.476
236	SALUMBAR	0.500	0.500	0.085	0.359	0.136	0.506	0.494	0.414	0.742	0.530
237	SARADA	0.503	0.497	0.116	0.426	0.182	0.504	0.496	0.368	0.746	0.491
	UDAIPUR	**0.493**	**0.507**	**0.101**	**0.390**	**0.162**	**0.497**	**0.503**	**0.355**	**0.695**	**0.471**
	RAJASTHAN	**0.479**	**0.521**	**0.116**	**0.476**	**0.192**	**0.482**	**0.518**	**0.377**	**0.730**	**0.503**

Note: # For calculaton of GEDI, please see 'Methodology' (Chapter I)
* Dungargarh PS shifted from Churu to Bikaner district on 1st April 2001
** Excluding data of Dungargarh PS; *** Including data of Dungargarh PS.

Source: Calculated from data given in : 1. General Annex I, col. 6, 8, 12 and 13
2. General Annex VII Col. 7, 9, 20, 21

ANNEX 10.2

PANCHAYAT SAMITI-WISE CHANGED PATTERN OF GEDI (1991-01): RAJASTHAN

P. Code	*Panchayat Samities*	*GEDI 1991 Rank*	*GEDI 1991 Value*	*GEDI 2001 Rank*	*GEDI 2001 Value*	*Differences in GEDI Rank*	*Differences in GEDI Value*	*% Increase in GEDI Value*	*Remarks*
1	*2*	*3*	*4*	*5*	*6*	*7*	*8*	*9*	*10*
1	ARAIN	100	0.190	181	0.396	-81	0.206	108.4	B
2	BHINAY	66	0.215	226	0.321	-160	0.106	49.3	B
3	JAWAJA	75	0.209	9	0.709	66	0.500	239.2	A
4	KEKRI	16	0.303	200	0.376	-184	0.073	24.1	B
5	KISHANGARH	79	0.206	124	0.465	-45	0.259	125.7	B
6	MASOODA	81	0.205	135	0.454	-54	0.249	121.5	B
7	PISANGAN	31	0.260	142	0.446	-111	0.186	71.5	B
8	SRINAGAR	72	0.211	153	0.435	-81	0.224	106.2	B
	AJMER								
9	BANSURE	70	0.212	85	0.526	-15	0.314	148.1	B
10	BEHROR	2	0.418	1	0.804	1	0.386	92.3	A
11	KATHUMAR	85	0.201	95	0.506	-10	0.305	151.7	B
12	KISHANGARH BAS	19	0.289	102	0.494	-83	0.205	70.9	B
13	KOTKASIM	4	0.391	22	0.659	-18	0.268	68.5	B
14	LACHHMANGARH	79	0.206	111	0.485	-32	0.279	135.4	B
15	MANDAWAR	7	0.378	23	0.655	-16	0.277	73.3	B
16	NIMRANA	1	0.452	76	0.547	-75	0.095	21.0	B
17	RAJGARH	76	0.208	124	0.465	-48	0.257	123.6	B
18	RAMGARH	54	0.233	130	0.460	-76	0.227	97.4	B
19	RENI	95	0.194	102	0.494	-7	0.300	154.6	B
20	THANAGAZI	157	0.155	190	0.387	-33	0.232	149.7	B
21	TIJARA	57	0.230	130	0.460	-73	0.230	100.0	B
22	UMREN	85	0.201	132	0.458	-47	0.257	127.9	B
	ALWAR								
23	ANANDPURI	206	0.119	220	0.339	-14	0.220	184.9	B
24	BAGIDORA	134	0.166	219	0.340	-85	0.174	104.8	B
25	GARHI	49	0.242	127	0.464	-78	0.222	91.7	B
26	GHATOL	188	0.132	228	0.317	-40	0.185	140.2	B
27	KUSHALGARH	227	0.067	235	0.265	-8	0.198	295.5	B
28	PEEPALKHOONT	235	0.051	236	0.184	-1	0.133	260.8	B
29	SAJJANGARH	214	0.108	231	0.304	-17	0.196	181.5	B
30	TALWARA	174	0.142	198	0.377	-24	0.235	165.5	B
	BANSWARA								
31	ANTA	27	0.270	58	0.584	-31	0.314	116.3	B
32	ATRU	35	0.257	60	0.578	-25	0.321	124.9	B
33	BARAN	35	0.257	49	0.604	-14	0.347	135.0	B
34	CHHABARA	208	0.116	129	0.461	79	0.345	297.4	A
35	CHHIPABAROD	196	0.126	174	0.402	22	0.276	219.0	A
36	KISHANGANJ	116	0.178	112	0.476	4	0.298	167.4	A
37	SHAHBAD	112	0.180	122	0.466	-10	0.286	158.9	B
	BARAN								
38	BALOTRA	203	0.120	101	0.495	102	0.375	312.5	A
39	BARMER	228	0.066	104	0.493	124	0.427	647.0	A
40	BAYTOO	223	0.085	77	0.546	146	0.461	542.4	A
41	CHOHTAN	237	0.042	128	0.463	109	0.421	1002.4	A
42	DHORIMANNA	232	0.057	21	0.660	211	0.603	1057.9	A
43	SHEO	229	0.065	84	0.527	145	0.462	710.8	A
44	SINDHARI	234	0.055	62	0.576	172	0.521	947.3	A
45	SIWANA	200	0.122	70	0.555	130	0.433	354.9	A
	BARMER								
46	DAYANA	112	0.180	110	0.487	2	0.307	170.6	A
47	DEEG	67	0.213	92	0.509	-25	0.296	139.0	B
48	KAMAN	210	0.112	191	0.386	19	0.274	244.6	A
49	KUMHER	22	0.281	45	0.614	-23	0.333	118.5	B
50	NADBAI	41	0.251	34	0.626	7	0.375	149.4	A
51	NAGAR PAHARI	128	0.172	87	0.522	41	0.350	203.5	A
52	RUPBAS	21	0.286	38	0.623	-17	0.337	117.8	B
53	SEWAR	40	0.252	41	0.619	-1	0.367	145.6	B
54	WEIR	47	0.243	79	0.537	-32	0.294	121.0	B
	BHARATPUR								
55	ASIND	176	0.140	224	0.332	-48	0.192	137.1	B
56	BANERA	137	0.164	151	0.436	-14	0.272	165.9	B
57	HURDA	24	0.273	143	0.446	-119	0.173	63.4	B
58	JAHAZPUR	166	0.149	165	0.418	1	0.269	180.5	A
59	KOTRI	97	0.192	225	0.324	-128	0.132	68.8	B
60	MANDAL	168	0.147	213	0.351	-45	0.204	138.8	B

P. Code	Panchayat Samities	GEDI 1991 Rank	GEDI 1991 Value	GEDI 2001 Rank	GEDI 2001 Value	Differences in GEDI Rank	Differences in GEDI Value	% Increase in GEDI Value	Remarks
1	2	3	4	5	6	7	8	9	10
61	MANDALGARH	169	0.147	203	0.366	-34	0.219	149.0	B
62	RAIPUR	154	0.157	218	0.345	-64	0.188	119.7	B
63	SAHARA	148	0.160	202	0.368	-54	0.208	130.0	B
64	SHAHPURA	192	0.128	210	0.353	-18	0.225	175.8	B
65	SUWANA	160	0.152	195	0.378	-35	0.226	148.7	B
	BHILWARA								
66	BIKANER	134	0.166	167	0.414	-33	0.248	149.4	B
67	DUNGARGARH*	182	0.134	78	0.538	104	0.404	301.5	A
68	KOLAYAT	172	0.145	213	0.351	-41	0.206	142.1	B
69	LUNKARANSAR	132	0.167	168	0.412	-36	0.245	146.7	B
70	NOKHA	209	0.115	170	0.411	39	0.296	257.4	A
	BIKANER **								
71	HINDOLI	182	0.134	183	0.394	-1	0.260	194.0	B
72	KESHORAIPATAN	106	0.185	99	0.500	7	0.315	170.3	A
73	NAINWA	186	0.133	158	0.426	28	0.293	220.3	A
74	TALERA	124	0.173	124	0.465	0	0.292	168.8	C
	BUNDI								
75	ARNOD	90	0.197	172	0.408	-82	0.211	107.1	B
76	BARI SADRI	152	0.158	206	0.362	-54	0.204	129.1	B
77	BEGUN	169	0.147	172	0.408	-3	0.261	177.6	B
78	BHADESAR	147	0.161	179	0.399	-32	0.238	147.8	B
79	BHAINSRORGARH	155	0.156	183	0.394	-28	0.238	152.6	B
80	BHOPALSAGAR	99	0.190	146	0.443	-47	0.253	133.2	B
81	CHHOTI SADRI	91	0.197	144	0.444	-53	0.247	125.4	B
82	CHITTAURGARH	112	0.180	151	0.436	-39	0.256	142.2	B
83	DUNGLA	144	0.162	174	0.402	-30	0.240	148.1	B
84	GANGRAR	137	0.164	180	0.397	-43	0.233	142.1	B
85	KAPASAN	202	0.121	204	0.365	-2	0.244	201.7	B
86	NIMBAHERA	83	0.202	134	0.457	-51	0.255	126.2	B
87	PRATAPGARH	120	0.176	119	0.472	1	0.296	168.2	A
88	RASHMI	120	0.176	209	0.354	-89	0.178	101.1	B
	CHITTAURGARH								
89	CHURU	118	0.177	29	0.640	89	0.463	261.6	A
90	RAJGARH	62	0.222	14	0.701	48	0.479	215.8	A
91	RATANGARH	163	0.150	34	0.626	129	0.476	317.3	A
92	SARDARSHAHAR	214	0.108	70	0.555	144	0.447	413.9	A
93	SUJANGARH	192	0.128	52	0.597	140	0.469	366.4	A
94	TARANAGAR	160	0.152	11	0.707	149	0.555	365.1	A
	CHURU ***								
95	BANDIKUI	63	0.220	42	0.618	21	0.398	180.9	A
96	DAUSA	124	0.173	97	0.504	27	0.331	191.3	A
97	LALSOT	141	0.163	132	0.458	9	0.295	181.0	A
98	MAHWA	53	0.238	54	0.595	-1	0.357	150.0	B
99	SIKRAI	150	0.159	65	0.572	85	0.413	259.7	A
	DAUSA								
100	BARI	195	0.127	94	0.507	101	0.380	299.2	A
101	BASERI	81	0.205	67	0.567	14	0.362	176.6	A
102	DHAULPUR	83	0.202	80	0.532	3	0.330	163.4	A
103	RAJAKHERA	163	0.150	88	0.519	75	0.369	246.0	A
	DHAULPUR								
104	ASPUR	92	0.195	195	0.378	-103	0.183	93.8	B
105	BICHHIWARA	155	0.156	187	0.389	-32	0.233	149.4	B
106	DUNGARPUR	136	0.165	189	0.388	-53	0.223	135.2	B
107	SAGWARA	43	0.248	140	0.449	-97	0.201	81.0	B
108	SIMALWARA	141	0.163	216	0.347	-75	0.184	112.9	B
	DUNGARPUR								
109	ANUPGARH	32	0.259	72	0.554	-40	0.295	113.9	B
110	GANGANAGAR	3	0.393	39	0.622	-36	0.229	58.3	B
111	KARANPUR	9	0.366	54	0.595	-45	0.229	62.6	B
112	PADAMPUR	5	0.383	48	0.608	-43	0.225	58.7	B
113	RAISINGHNAGAR	14	0.327	31	0.633	-17	0.306	93.6	B
114	SADULSHAHAR	12	0.331	53	0.596	-41	0.265	80.1	B
115	SURATGARH	39	0.253	96	0.505	-57	0.252	99.6	B
	GANGANAGAR								
116	BHADRA	28	0.266	27	0.647	1	0.381	143.2	A
117	HANUMANGARH	25	0.272	56	0.592	-31	0.320	117.6	B
118	NOHAR	89	0.198	42	0.618	47	0.420	212.1	A
	HANUMANGARH								
119	AMBER	97	0.192	86	0.524	11	0.332	172.9	A
120	BASSI	129	0.171	90	0.513	39	0.342	200.0	A
121	CHAKSU	174	0.142	155	0.429	19	0.287	202.1	A
122	DUDU	78	0.208	100	0.499	-22	0.291	139.9	B
123	GOVINDGARH	32	0.259	46	0.612	-14	0.353	136.3	B
124	JAMWA RAMGARH	144	0.162	63	0.575	81	0.413	254.9	A
125	JHOTWARA	35	0.257	34	0.626	1	0.369	143.6	A

P. Code	Panchayat Samities	GEDI 1991 Rank	GEDI 1991 Value	GEDI 2001 Rank	GEDI 2001 Value	Differences in GEDI Rank	Differences in GEDI Value	% Increase in GEDI Value	Remarks
1	2	3	4	5	6	7	8	9	10
126	KOTPUTLI	59	0.229	13	0.703	46	0.474	207.0	A
127	PHAGI	108	0.182	69	0.564	39	0.382	209.9	A
128	SAMBHAR	70	0.212	32	0.630	38	0.418	197.2	A
129	SANGANER	47	0.243	65	0.572	-18	0.329	135.4	B
130	SHAHPURA	56	0.232	50	0.602	6	0.370	159.5	A
131	VIRATNAGAR	74	0.210	24	0.651	50	0.441	210.0	A
	JAIPUR								
132	JAISALMER	200	0.122	174	0.402	26	0.280	229.5	A
133	SAM	226	0.070	205	0.364	21	0.294	420.0	A
134	SANKRA	221	0.087	162	0.420	59	0.333	382.8	A
	JAISALMER								
135	AHORE	118	0.177	122	0.466	-4	0.289	163.3	B
136	BHINMAL	230	0.060	233	0.297	-3	0.237	395.0	B
137	JALOR	157	0.155	195	0.378	-38	0.223	143.9	B
138	JASWANTPURA	218	0.097	230	0.306	-12	0.209	215.5	B
139	RANIWARA	221	0.087	174	0.402	47	0.315	362.1	A
140	SANCHORE	232	0.057	198	0.377	34	0.320	561.4	A
141	SAYLA	213	0.109	221	0.338	-8	0.229	210.1	B
	JALOR								
142	BAKANI	171	0.146	216	0.347	-45	0.201	137.7	B
143	DAG	179	0.136	187	0.389	-8	0.253	186.0	B
144	JHALRAPATAN	122	0.174	92	0.509	30	0.335	192.5	A
145	KHANPUR	44	0.247	47	0.611	-3	0.364	147.4	B
146	MANOHARTHANA	231	0.059	178	0.400	53	0.341	578.0	A
147	PIRAWA	124	0.173	44	0.615	80	0.442	255.5	A
	JHALAWAR								
148	ALSISAR	15	0.325	8	0.720	7	0.395	121.5	A
149	BUHANA	6	0.379	3	0.755	3	0.376	99.2	A
150	CHIRAWA	10	0.350	6	0.724	4	0.374	106.9	A
151	JHUNJHUNUN	8	0.375	4	0.744	4	0.369	98.4	A
152	KHETRI	17	0.299	37	0.624	-20	0.325	108.7	B
153	NAWALGARH	11	0.335	19	0.663	-8	0.328	97.9	B
154	SURAJGARH	13	0.330	15	0.678	-2	0.348	105.5	B
155	UDAIPURWATI	18	0.295	2	0.766	16	0.471	159.7	A
	JHUNJHUNUN								
156	BALESAR	218	0.097	229	0.310	-11	0.213	219.6	B
157	BAP	220	0.096	207	0.359	13	0.263	274.0	A
158	BHOPALGARH	196	0.126	210	0.353	-14	0.227	180.2	B
159	BILARA	157	0.155	170	0.411	-13	0.256	165.2	B
160	LUNI	141	0.163	117	0.474	24	0.311	190.8	A
161	MANDOR	181	0.135	221	0.338	-40	0.203	150.4	B
162	OSIAN	216	0.107	183	0.394	33	0.287	268.2	A
163	PHALODI	217	0.105	182	0.395	35	0.290	276.2	A
164	SHERGARH	224	0.081	232	0.303	-8	0.222	274.1	B
	JODHPUR								
165	HINDAUN	115	0.179	9	0.709	106	0.530	296.1	A
166	KARAULI	192	0.128	98	0.502	94	0.374	292.2	A
167	NADOTI	95	0.194	51	0.600	44	0.406	209.3	A
168	SAPOTRA	132	0.167	89	0.518	43	0.351	210.2	A
169	TODABHIM	137	0.164	75	0.549	62	0.385	234.8	A
	KARAULI								
170	CHECHAT	30	0.261	26	0.650	4	0.389	149.0	A
171	ITAWA	61	0.227	61	0.577	0	0.350	154.2	C
172	LADPURA	28	0.266	40	0.621	-12	0.355	133.5	B
173	SANGOD	23	0.276	20	0.661	3	0.385	139.5	A
174	SULTANPUR	20	0.288	17	0.668	3	0.380	131.9	A
	KOTA								
175	DEGANA	152	0.158	116	0.475	36	0.317	200.6	A
176	DIDWANA	111	0.181	56	0.592	55	0.411	227.1	A
177	JAYAL	198	0.124	144	0.444	54	0.320	258.1	A
178	KUCHAMAN	102	0.187	59	0.582	43	0.395	211.2	A
179	LADNU	85	0.201	73	0.553	12	0.352	175.1	A
180	MAKRANA	92	0.195	64	0.574	28	0.379	194.4	A
181	MERTA	101	0.188	112	0.476	-11	0.288	153.2	B
182	MUNDWA	210	0.112	207	0.359	3	0.247	220.5	A
183	NAGAUR	198	0.124	155	0.429	43	0.305	246.0	A
184	PARBATSAR	130	0.170	91	0.512	39	0.342	201.2	A
185	RIYAN	150	0.159	141	0.448	9	0.289	181.8	A
	NAGAUR								
186	BALI	57	0.230	135	0.454	-78	0.224	97.4	B
187	DESURI	67	0.213	139	0.452	-72	0.239	112.2	B
188	JAITARAN	186	0.133	192	0.384	-6	0.251	188.7	B
189	KHARCHI/MARWAR JUN.	106	0.185	158	0.426	-52	0.241	130.3	B
190	PALI	166	0.149	169	0.412	-3	0.263	176.5	B
191	RAIPUR	160	0.152	162	0.420	-2	0.268	176.3	B

P. Code	Panchayat Samities	GEDI 1991 Rank	GEDI 1991 GEDI	GEDI 2001 Rank	GEDI 2001 GEDI	Differences in GEDI Rank	Differences in GEDI Value	% Increase in GEDI Value	Remarks
1	2	3	4	5	6	7	8	9	10
192	RANI STATION	49	0.242	112	0.476	-63	0.234	96.7	B
193	ROHAT	188	0.132	154	0.434	34	0.302	228.8	A
194	SOJAT	105	0.186	148	0.442	-43	0.256	137.6	B
195	SUMERPUR	64	0.219	120	0.471	-56	0.252	115.1	B
	PALI								
196	AMET	190	0.130	160	0.424	30	0.294	226.2	A
197	BHIM	144	0.162	121	0.469	23	0.307	189.5	A
198	DEOGARH	210	0.112	157	0.428	53	0.316	282.1	A
199	KHAMNOR	67	0.213	138	0.453	-71	0.240	112.7	B
200	KUMBHALGARH	178	0.137	186	0.392	-8	0.255	186.1	B
201	RAILMAGRA	60	0.228	107	0.490	-47	0.262	114.9	B
202	RAJSAMAND	72	0.211	108	0.489	-36	0.278	131.8	B
	RAJSAMAND								
203	BAMANWAS	122	0.174	81	0.530	41	0.356	204.6	A
204	BONLI	116	0.178	146	0.443	-30	0.265	148.9	B
205	GANGAPUR	94	0.195	105	0.492	-11	0.297	152.3	B
206	KHANDAR	190	0.130	226	0.321	-36	0.191	146.9	B
207	SAWAI MADHOPUR	148	0.160	194	0.381	-46	0.221	138.1	B
	SAWAI MADHOPUR								
208	DANTA RAMGARH	45	0.246	16	0.673	29	0.427	173.6	A
209	DHOND	51	0.240	24	0.651	27	0.411	171.3	A
210	FATEHPUR	46	0.244	5	0.726	41	0.482	197.5	A
211	KHANDELA	52	0.239	12	0.705	40	0.466	195.0	A
212	LACHHMANGARH	42	0.249	6	0.724	36	0.475	190.8	A
213	NEEM KA THANA	38	0.256	28	0.641	10	0.385	150.4	A
214	PIPRALI	34	0.258	18	0.667	16	0.409	158.5	A
215	SRI MADHOPUR	25	0.272	30	0.635	-5	0.363	133.5	B
	SIKAR								
216	ABU ROAD	203	0.120	201	0.370	2	0.250	208.3	A
217	PINDWARA	137	0.164	117	0.474	20	0.310	189.0	A
218	REODAR	182	0.134	165	0.418	17	0.284	211.9	A
219	SHEOGANJ	176	0.140	149	0.441	27	0.301	215.0	A
220	SIROHI	124	0.173	162	0.420	-38	0.247	142.8	B
	SIROHI								
221	DEOLI	103	0.186	210	0.353	-107	0.167	89.8	B
222	MALPURA	131	0.168	193	0.383	-62	0.215	128.0	B
223	NIWAI	88	0.200	161	0.421	-73	0.221	110.5	B
224	TODARAISINGH	163	0.150	135	0.454	28	0.304	202.7	A
225	TONK	203	0.120	223	0.337	-20	0.217	180.8	B
226	UNIARA	182	0.134	215	0.348	-33	0.214	159.7	B
	TONK								
227	BARGAON	54	0.233	32	0.630	22	0.397	170.4	A
228	BHINDER	108	0.182	68	0.565	40	0.383	210.4	A
229	DHARIAWAD	225	0.080	234	0.270	-9	0.190	237.5	B
230	GIRWA	103	0.186	83	0.528	20	0.342	183.9	A
231	GOGUNDA	173	0.144	150	0.439	23	0.295	204.9	A
232	JHADOL	206	0.119	74	0.551	132	0.432	363.0	A
233	KHERWARA	76	0.208	108	0.489	-32	0.281	135.1	B
234	KOTRA	236	0.045	237	0.172	-1	0.127	282.2	B
235	MAVLI	64	0.219	112	0.476	-48	0.257	117.4	B
236	SALUMBAR	179	0.136	81	0.530	98	0.394	289.7	A
237	SARADA	108	0.182	106	0.491	2	0.309	169.8	A
	UDAIPUR								
	RAJASTHAN		**0.192**		**0.503**	**0**	**0.311**	**162.0**	

Note: For calculaton of GEDI, please see 'Methodology' (Chapter I)
* Dungargarh PS shifted from Churu to Bikaner district on 1st April 2001
** Excluding data of Dungargarh PS; *** Including data of Dungargarh PS.
Source: Annex 10.1

A Improvement in both GEDI Value and Rank
B Increase in GEDI Value but Rank Deteriorated
C Increase in GEDI Value but Rank Remained Constant
D Decrease in Both GEDI Value and Rank

ANNEX-10.3

RANKING OF PSS BY GEDI, 2001

(Descending Order)

RANK	PANCHAYAT SAMITIES P. CODE	NAME	GEDI
1	2	3	4
	VERY HIGH (>=0.8)		
1	**10**	**BEHROR**	**0.804**
	HIGH (0.6-0.8)		
2	**155**	**UDAIPURWATI**	**0.766**
3	**149**	**BUHANA**	**0.755**
4	**151**	**JHUNJHUNUN**	**0.744**
5	**210**	**FATEHPUR**	**0.726**
6	**150**	**CHIRAWA**	**0.724**
6	**212**	**LACHHMANGARH**	**0.724**
8	**148**	**ALSISAR**	**0.720**
9	**3**	**JAWAJA**	**0.709**
9	**165**	**HINDAUN**	**0.709**
11	**94**	**TARANAGAR**	**0.707**
12	**211**	**KHANDELA**	**0.705**
13	**126**	**KOTPUTLI**	**0.703**
14	**90**	**RAJGARH**	**0.701**
15	**154**	**SURAJGARH**	**0.678**
16	**208**	**DANTA RAMGARH**	**0.673**
17	**174**	**SULTANPUR**	**0.668**
18	**214**	**PIPRALI**	**0.667**
19	**153**	**NAWALGARH**	**0.663**
20	**173**	**SANGOD**	**0.661**
21	**42**	**DHORIMANNA**	**0.660**
22	**13**	**KOTKASIM**	**0.659**
23	**15**	**MANDAWAR**	**0.655**
24	**131**	**VIRATNAGAR**	**0.651**
24	**209**	**DHOND**	**0.651**
26	**170**	**CHECHAT**	**0.650**
27	**116**	**BHADRA**	**0.647**
28	**213**	**NEEM KA THANA**	**0.641**
29	**89**	**CHURU**	**0.640**
30	**215**	**SRI MADHOPUR**	**0.635**
31	**113**	**RAISINGHNAGAR**	**0.633**
32	**128**	**SAMBHAR**	**0.630**
32	**227**	**BARGAON**	**0.630**
34	**50**	**NADBAI**	**0.626**
34	**91**	**RATANGARH**	**0.626**
34	**125**	**JHOTWARA**	**0.626**
37	**152**	**KHETRI**	**0.624**
38	**52**	**RUPBAS**	**0.623**
39	**110**	**GANGANAGAR**	**0.622**
40	**172**	**LADPURA**	**0.621**
41	**53**	**SEWAR**	**0.619**
42	**95**	**BANDIKUI**	**0.618**
42	**118**	**NOHAR**	**0.618**
44	**147**	**PIRAWA**	**0.615**
45	**49**	**KUMHER**	**0.614**
46	**123**	**GOVINDGARH**	**0.612**
47	**145**	**KHANPUR**	**0.611**
48	**112**	**PADAMPUR**	**0.608**
49	**33**	**BARAN**	**0.604**
50	**130**	**SHAHPURA**	**0.602**
51	**167**	**NADOTI**	**0.600**
	MEDIUM (0.4-0.6)		
52	**93**	**SUJANGARH**	**0.597**
53	**114**	**SADULSHAHAR**	**0.596**
54	**98**	**MAHWA**	**0.595**
54	**111**	**KARANPUR**	**0.595**
56	**117**	**HANUMANGARH**	**0.592**
56	**176**	**DIDWANA**	**0.592**
58	**31**	**ANTA**	**0.584**
59	**178**	**KUCHAMAN**	**0.582**
60	**32**	**ATRU**	**0.578**
61	**171**	**ITAWA**	**0.577**
62	**44**	**SINDHARI**	**0.576**
63	**124**	**JAMWA RAMGARH**	**0.575**
64	**180**	**MAKRANA**	**0.574**
65	**99**	**SIKRAI**	**0.572**
65	**129**	**SANGANER**	**0.572**
67	**101**	**BASERI**	**0.567**
68	**228**	**BHINDER**	**0.565**
69	**127**	**PHAGI**	**0.564**
70	**45**	**SIWANA**	**0.555**
70	**92**	**SARDARSHAHAR**	**0.555**
72	**109**	**ANUPGARH**	**0.554**
73	**179**	**LADNU**	**0.553**
74	**232**	**JHADOL**	**0.551**
75	**169**	**TODABHIM**	**0.549**
76	**16**	**NIMRANA**	**0.547**
77	**40**	**BAYTOO**	**0.546**
78	**67**	**DUNGARGARH**	**0.538**
79	**54**	**WEIR**	**0.537**
80	**102**	**DHAULPUR**	**0.532**
81	**203**	**BAMANWAS**	**0.530**
81	**236**	**SALUMBAR**	**0.530**
83	**230**	**GIRWA**	**0.528**
84	**43**	**SHEO**	**0.527**
85	**9**	**BANSURE**	**0.526**
86	**119**	**AMBER**	**0.524**
87	**51**	**NAGAR PAHARI**	**0.522**
88	**103**	**RAJAKHERA**	**0.519**
89	**168**	**SAPOTRA**	**0.518**
90	**120**	**BASSI**	**0.513**
91	**184**	**PARBATSAR**	**0.512**
92	**47**	**DEEG**	**0.509**
92	**144**	**JHALRAPATAN**	**0.509**
94	**100**	**BARI**	**0.507**
95	**11**	**KATHUMAR**	**0.506**
96	**115**	**SURATGARH**	**0.505**
97	**96**	**DAUSA**	**0.504**
98	166	KARAULI	0.502
99	72	KESHORAIPATAN	0.500
100	122	DUDU	0.499
101	38	BALOTRA	0.495
102	12	KISHANGARH BAS	0.494
102	19	RENI	0.494
104	39	BARMER	0.493
105	205	GANGAPUR	0.492
106	237	SARADA	0.491
107	201	RAILMAGRA	0.490
108	202	RAJSAMAND	0.489
108	233	KHERWARA	0.489
110	46	BAYANA	0.487
111	14	LACHHMANGARH	0.485
112	36	KISHANGANJ	0.476
112	181	MERTA	0.476
112	192	RANI STATION	0.476
112	235	MAVLI	0.476
116	175	DEGANA	0.475
117	160	LUNI	0.474
117	217	PINDWARA	0.474
119	87	PRATAPGARH	0.472
120	195	SUMERPUR	0.471
121	197	BHIM	0.469
122	37	SHAHBAD	0.466
122	135	AHORE	0.466
124	5	KISHANGARH	0.465
124	17	RAJGARH	0.465
124	74	TALERA	0.465
127	25	GARHI	0.464
128	41	CHOHTAN	0.463
129	34	CHHADRA	0.461
130	18	RAMGARH	0.460
130	21	TIJARA	0.460
132	22	UMREN	0.458
132	97	LALSOT	0.458
134	86	NIMBAHERA	0.457
135	6	MASOODA	0.454
135	186	BALI	0.454
135	224	TODARAISINGH	0.454
138	199	KHAMNOR	0.453
139	187	DESURI	0.452
140	107	SAGWARA	0.449
141	185	RIYAN	0.448
142	7	PISANGAN	0.446
143	57	HURDA	0.446
144	81	CHHOTI SADRI	0.444
144	177	JAYAL	0.444
146	80	BHOPALSAGAR	0.443
146	204	BONLI	0.443
148	194	SOJAT	0.442
149	219	SHEOGANJ	0.441
150	231	GOGUNDA	0.439
151	56	BANERA	0.436
151	82	CHITTAURGARH	0.436
153	8	SRINAGAR	0.435
154	193	ROHAT	0.434
155	121	ROHAT	0.429
155	183	NAGAUR	0.429
157	198	DEOGARH	0.428
158	73	NAINWA	0.426
158	189	MARWAR JUN.	0.426
160	196	AMET	0.424
161	223	NIWAI	0.421
162	134	SANKRA	0.420
162	191	RAIPUR	0.420
162	220	SIROHI	0.420
165	58	JAHAZPUR	0.418
167	66	BIKANER	0.414
168	69	LUNKARANSAR	0.412
168	190	PALI	0.412
170	70	NOKHA	0.411
170	159	BILARA	0.411
172	75	ARNOD	0.408
172	77	BEGUN	0.408
174	35	CHHIPABAROD	0.402
174	83	DUNGLA	0.402
174	132	JAISALMER	0.402
174	139	RANIWARA	0.402
178	146	MANOHARTHANA	0.400
	LOW (0.2-0.4)		
179	78	BHADESAR	0.399
180	84	GANGRAR	0.397
181	1	ARIAN	0.396
182	163	PHALODI	0.395
183	71	HINDOLI	0.394
183	79	BHAINSRORGARH	0.394
183	162	OSIAN	0.394
186	200	KUMBHALGARH	0.392
187	105	BICHHIWARA	0.389
187	143	DAG	0.389
189	106	DUNGARPUR	0.388
190	20	THANAGAZI	0.387
191	48	KAMAN	0.386
192	188	JAITARAN	0.384
193	222	MALPURA	0.383
194	207	SAWAI MADHOPUR	0.381
195	65	SUWANA	0.378
195	104	ASPUR	0.378
195	137	JALOR	0.378
198	30	TALWARA	0.377
198	140	SANCHORE	0.377
200	4	KEKRI	0.376
201	216	ABU ROAD	0.370
202	63	SAHARA	0.368
203	61	MANDALGARH	0.366
204	85	KAPASAN	0.365
205	133	SAM	0.364
206	76	BARI SADRI	0.362
207	157	BAP	0.359
207	182	MUNDWA	0.359
209	88	RASHMI	0.354
210	64	SHAHPURA	0.353
210	158	BHOPALGARH	0.353
210	221	DEOLI	0.353
213	60	MANDAL	0.351
213	68	KOLAYAT	0.351
215	226	UNIARA	0.348
216	108	SIMALWARA	0.347
216	142	BAKANI	0.347
218	62	RAIPUR	0.345
219	24	BAGIDORA	0.340
220	23	ANANDPURI	0.339
221	141	SAYLA	0.338
221	161	MANDOR	0.338
223	225	TONK	0.337
224	55	ASIND	0.332
225	59	KOTRI	0.324
226	2	BHINAY	0.321
226	206	KHANDAR	0.321
228	26	GHATOL	0.317
229	156	BALESAR	0.310
230	138	JASWANTPURA	0.306
231	29	SAJJANGARH	0.304
232	164	SHERGARH	0.303
233	136	BHINMAL	0.297
234	229	DHARIAWAD	0.270
235	27	KUSHALGARH	0.265
	VERY LOW (<0.2)		
236	28	PEEPALKHOONT	0.184
237	234	KOTRA	0.172
		RAJASTHAN	**0.503**
		%age of AAPs	**40.90**

BOLD: Equal/Above Average Panchayat Samities (AAPs)

Source: Annex 10.1, Col. 9.

ANNEX-11.1

RANKING OF PANCHAYAT SAMITIES BY INI, 1991-92 (BASED ON RURAL AND URBAN INCOME RATIO 1.29:1)

(Descending Order)

RANK	PANCHAYAT SAMITIES P. CODE	NAME	VALUE
1	2	3	4
	HIGH (0.6-0.8)		
1	**173**	**SANGOD**	**0.7641**
2	**170**	**CHECHAT**	**0.7566**
3	**121**	**CHAKSU**	**0.7213**
4	**171**	**ITAWA**	**0.7208**
5	**172**	**LADPURA**	**0.7063**
6	**174**	**SULTANPUR**	**0.6906**
7	**111**	**KARANPUR**	**0.6903**
8	**127**	**PHAGI**	**0.6783**
9	**120**	**BASSI**	**0.6678**
10	**113**	**RAISINGHNAGAR**	**0.6440**
11	**119**	**AMBER**	**0.6402**
12	**122**	**DUDU**	**0.6373**
13	**124**	**JAMWA RAMGARH**	**0.6367**
14	**116**	**BHADRA**	**0.6240**
15	**129**	**SANGANER**	**0.6205**
16	**35**	**CHHIPABAROD**	**0.6156**
17	**118**	**NOHAR**	**0.6089**
	MEDIUM (0.4-0.6)		
18	**1**	**ARAIN**	**0.5804**
19	**126**	**KOTPUTLI**	**0.5721**
20	**109**	**ANUPGARH**	**0.5703**
21	**130**	**SHAHPURA**	**0.5673**
22	**125**	**JHOTWARA**	**0.5648**
23	**2**	**BHINAY**	**0.5632**
24	**128**	**SAMBHAR**	**0.5631**
25	**115**	**SURATGARH**	**0.5494**
26	**110**	**GANGANAGAR**	**0.5475**
27	**131**	**VIRATNAGAR**	**0.5411**
28	**114**	**SADULSHAHAR**	**0.5398**
29	**123**	**GOVINDGARH**	**0.5390**
30	**4**	**KEKRI**	**0.5382**
31	**70**	**NOKHA**	**0.5317**
32	**117**	**HANUMANGARH**	**0.5304**
33	**8**	**SRINAGAR**	**0.5302**
34	**6**	**MASOODA**	**0.5260**
35	**7**	**PISANGAN**	**0.5211**
36	**5**	**KISHANGARH**	**0.5184**
37	**66**	**BIKANER**	**0.5144**
38	**112**	**PADAMPUR**	**0.5074**
39	**68**	**KOLAYAT**	**0.5057**
40	**69**	**LUNKARANSAR**	**0.4899**
41	**3**	**JAWAJA**	**0.4662**
42	**71**	**HINDOLI**	**0.4589**
43	**73**	**NAINWA**	**0.4545**
44	**217**	**PINDWARA**	**0.4525**
45	**158**	**BHOPALGARH**	**0.4513**
46	**159**	**BILARA**	**0.4505**
47	**85**	**KAPASAN**	**0.4498**
48	**84**	**GANGRAR**	**0.4436**
49	**37**	**SHAHBAD**	**0.4385**
50	**78**	**BHADESAR**	**0.4363**
51	**81**	**CHHOTI SADRI**	**0.4352**
52	**76**	**BARI SADRI**	**0.4321**
53	**77**	**BEGUN**	**0.4301**
54	**82**	**CHITTAURGARH**	**0.4271**
55	**164**	**SHERGARH**	**0.4267**
56	**218**	**REODAR**	**0.4254**
57	**88**	**RASHMI**	**0.4243**
58	**83**	**DUNGLA**	**0.4238**
59	**36**	**KISHANGANJ**	**0.4214**
60	**86**	**NIMBAHERA**	**0.4198**
61	**228**	**BHINDER**	**0.4195**
62	**63**	**SAHARA**	**0.4194**
63	**160**	**LUNI**	**0.4180**
64	**19**	**RENI**	**0.4169**
65	**236**	**SALUMBAR**	**0.4142**
66	**216**	**ABU ROAD**	**0.4133**
67	**194**	**SOJAT**	**0.4132**
68	**60**	**MANDAL**	**0.4120**
69	**72**	**KESHORAIPATAN**	**0.4118**
70	**234**	**KOTRA**	**0.4101**
71	**80**	**BHOPALSAGAR**	**0.4093**
72	**74**	**TALERA**	**0.4092**
73	**232**	**JHADOL**	**0.4091**
74	**193**	**ROHAT**	**0.4087**
75	**65**	**SUWANA**	**0.4075**
76	**188**	**JAITARAN**	**0.4047**
77	**56**	**BANERA**	**0.4035**
78	**61**	**MANDALGARH**	**0.4024**
79	**224**	**TODARAISINGH**	**0.4008**
	LOW (0.2-0.4)		
80	**55**	**ASIND**	**0.3997**
81	**59**	**KOTRI**	**0.3995**
82	**64**	**SHAHPURA**	**0.3992**
83	**33**	**BARAN**	**0.3991**
84	**32**	**ATRU**	**0.3976**
85	**17**	**RAJGARH**	**0.3952**
86	**227**	**BARGAON**	**0.3930**
87	**204**	**BONLI**	**0.3926**
88	**229**	**DHARIAWAD**	**0.3918**
89	**79**	**BHAINSRORGARH**	**0.3913**
90	**190**	**PALI**	**0.3905**
91	**87**	**PRATAPGARH**	**0.3892**
91	**163**	**PHALODI**	**0.3892**
93	**75**	**ARNOD**	**0.3871**
94	**156**	**BALESAR**	**0.3868**
95	**161**	**MANDOR**	**0.3854**
96	**134**	**SANKRA**	**0.3832**
97	162	OSIAN	0.3812
98	47	DEEG	0.3799
99	191	RAIPUR	0.3793
100	57	HURDA	0.3788
101	221	DEOLI	0.3782
102	223	NIWAI	0.3770
103	219	SHEOGANJ	0.3764
104	200	KUMBHALGARH	0.3751
105	48	KAMAN	0.3748
106	231	GOGUNDA	0.3734
107	235	MAVLI	0.3722
108	157	BAP	0.3700
109	206	KHANDAR	0.3678
110	14	LACHHMANGARH	0.3676
111	189	KHARCHI/MARWAR JUN.	0.3655
112	225	TONK	0.3648
113	222	MALPURA	0.3643
114	201	RAILMAGRA	0.3634
115	10	BEHROR	0.3628
116	220	SIROHI	0.3591
117	237	SARADA	0.3588
118	31	ANTA	0.3575
119	199	KHAMNOR	0.3571
119	230	GIRWA	0.3571
121	11	KATHUMAR	0.3557
122	226	UNIARA	0.3548
123	34	CHHABRA	0.3547
124	146	MANOHARTHANA	0.3543
125	20	THANAGAZI	0.3526
126	58	JAHAZPUR	0.3491
127	142	BAKANI	0.3485
127	233	KHERWARA	0.3485
129	21	TIJARA	0.3484
130	203	BAMANWAS	0.3477
131	207	SAWAI MADHOPUR	0.3471
132	196	AMET	0.3449
133	62	RAIPUR	0.3445
134	186	BALI	0.3421
135	192	RANI STATION	0.3403
136	168	SAPOTRA	0.3385
137	147	PIRAWA	0.3319
138	49	KUMHER	0.3310
139	166	KARAULI	0.3279
140	99	SIKRAI	0.3270
141	96	DAUSA	0.3263
142	135	AHORE	0.3256
143	9	BANSURE	0.3232
144	50	NADBAI	0.3217
145	197	BHIM	0.3216
146	167	NADOTI	0.3195
147	67	DUNGARGARH	0.3190
147	195	SUMERPUR	0.3190
149	198	DEOGARH	0.3178
150	51	NAGAR PAHARI	0.3162
151	22	UMREN	0.3140
152	187	DESURI	0.3128
153	54	WEIR	0.3110
154	94	TARANAGAR	0.3096
154	210	FATEHPUR	0.3096
156	46	BAYANA	0.3086
157	144	JHALRAPATAN	0.3085
158	133	SAM	0.3080
159	205	GANGAPUR	0.3059
160	185	RIYAN	0.3053
161	132	JAISALMER	0.3028
162	97	LALSOT	0.3020
163	12	KISHANGARH BAS	0.2991
164	98	MAHWA	0.2970
165	53	SEWAR	0.2956
165	202	RAJSAMAND	0.2956
167	18	RAMGARH	0.2928
168	13	KOTKASIM	0.2903
168	169	TODABHIM	0.2903
170	182	MUNDWA	0.2900
171	95	BANDIKUI	0.2861
172	90	RAJGARH	0.2839
173	212	LACHHMANGARH	0.2832
174	165	HINDAUN	0.2823
175	175	DEGANA	0.2800
176	15	MANDAWAR	0.2791
177	184	PARBATSAR	0.2783
178	23	ANANDPURI	0.2717
178	101	BASERI	0.2717
180	177	JAYAL	0.2705
181	181	MERTA	0.2678
182	100	BARI	0.2662
183	93	SUJANGARH	0.2658
184	91	RATANGARH	0.2646
185	24	BAGIDORA	0.2614
186	29	SAJJANGARH	0.2605
187	16	NIMRANA	0.2597
188	27	KUSHALGARH	0.2570
189	52	RUPBAS	0.2567
190	28	PEEPALKHOONT	0.2545
191	183	NAGAUR	0.2491
192	179	LADNU	0.2474
193	140	SANCHORE	0.2440
194	136	BHINMAL	0.2434
195	89	CHURU	0.2426
196	145	KHANPUR	0.2397
197	92	SARDARSHAHAR	0.2394
198	138	JASWANTPURA	0.2275
199	180	MAKRANA	0.2249
200	143	DAG	0.2245
201	26	GHATOL	0.2242
202	139	RANIWARA	0.2220
203	176	DIDWANA	0.2201
204	102	DHAULPUR	0.2141
205	209	DHOND	0.2139
206	214	PIPRALI	0.2138
207	25	GARHI	0.2123
208	211	KHANDELA	0.2116
209	137	JALOR	0.2108
210	103	RAJAKHERA	0.2093
210	141	SAYLA	0.2093
212	178	KUCHAMAN	0.2056
	VERY LOW (<0.2)		
213	208	DANTA RAMGARH	0.1897
214	30	TALWARA	0.1881
215	149	BUHANA	0.1840
216	40	BAYTOO	0.1724
217	154	SURAJGARH	0.1688
218	44	SINDHARI	0.1609
219	151	JHUNJHUNUN	0.1589
220	148	ALSISAR	0.1561
221	41	CHOHTAN	0.1519
222	213	NEEM KA THANA	0.1504
223	42	DHORIMANNA	0.1456
224	215	SRI MADHOPUR	0.1418
225	38	BALOTRA	0.1338
226	155	UDAIPURWATI	0.1303
227	39	BARMER	0.1273
228	108	SIMALWARA	0.1179
229	150	CHIRAWA	0.1141
230	106	DUNGARPUR	0.1017
231	152	KHETRI	0.1000
232	105	BICHHIWARA	0.0893
233	43	SHEO	0.0885
234	45	SIWANA	0.0784
235	107	SAGWARA	0.0660
236	153	NAWALGARH	0.0635
237	104	ASPUR	0.0319
		RAJASTHAN	**0.3813**
		%age of AAPs	**40.51**

BOLD: Equal/Above Average Panchayat Samities (AAPs)

Source : Annex 12.1, Col. 6.

ANNEX-11.2

RANKING OF PANCHAYAT SAMITIES BY PCI, 1991-92 (BASED ON RURAL AND URBAN INCOME RATIO 1.29:1)

(Descending Order)

RANK	PANCHAYAT SAMITIES P. CODE	NAME	PCI
1	2	3	4
	VERY HIGH (>8000)		
1	173	**SANGOD**	10261
2	170	**CHECHAT**	10096
3	121	**CHAKSU**	9362
4	171	**ITAWA**	9353
5	172	**LADPURA**	9066
6	174	**SULTANPUR**	8767
7	111	**KARANPUR**	8761
8	127	**PHAGI**	8540
9	120	**BASSI**	8349
	HIGH (6000-8000)		
10	113	**RAISINGHNAGAR**	7935
11	119	**AMBER**	7870
12	122	**DUDU**	7821
13	124	**JAMWA RAMGARH**	7812
14	116	**BHADRA**	7602
15	129	**SANGANER**	7545
16	35	**CHHIPABAROD**	7467
17	118	**NOHAR**	7361
18	1	**ARAIN**	6925
19	126	**KOTPUTLI**	6803
20	109	**ANUPGARH**	6777
21	130	**SHAHPURA**	6733
22	125	**JHOTWARA**	6698
23	2	**BHINAY**	6675
24	128	**SAMBHAR**	6674
25	115	**SURATGARH**	6481
26	110	**GANGANAGAR**	6454
27	131	**VIRATNAGAR**	6367
28	114	**SADULSHAHAR**	6349
29	123	**GOVINDGARH**	6338
30	4	**KEKRI**	6327
31	70	**NOKHA**	6240
32	117	**HANUMANGARH**	6223
33	8	**SRINAGAR**	6220
34	6	**MASOODA**	6164
35	7	**PISANGAN**	6100
36	5	**KISHANGARH**	6064
37	66	**BIKANER**	6013
	MEDIUM (4000-6000)		
38	112	**PADAMPUR**	5924
39	68	**KOLAYAT**	5902
40	69	**LUNKARANSAR**	5706
41	3	**JAWAJA**	5424
42	71	**HINDOLI**	5339
43	73	**NAINWA**	5289
44	217	**PINDWARA**	5267
45	158	**BHOPALGARH**	5253
46	159	**BILARA**	5244
47	85	**KAPASAN**	5237
48	84	**GANGRAR**	5168
49	37	**SHAHBAD**	5111
50	78	**BHADESAR**	5087
51	81	**CHHOTI SADRI**	5075
52	76	**BARI SADRI**	5042
53	77	**BEGUN**	5020
54	82	**CHITTAURGARH**	4988
55	164	**SHERGARH**	4984
56	218	**REODAR**	4970
57	88	**RASHMI**	4958
58	83	**DUNGLA**	4953
59	36	**KISHANGANJ**	4928
60	86	**NIMBAHERA**	4911
61	228	**BHINDER**	4908
62	63	**SAHARA**	4907
63	160	**LUNI**	4892
64	19	**RENI**	4881
65	236	**SALUMBAR**	4852
66	216	**ABU ROAD**	4843
67	194	**SOJAT**	4842
68	60	**MANDAL**	4830
69	72	**KESHORAIPATAN**	4828
70	234	**KOTRA**	4810
71	80	**BHOPALSAGAR**	4802
72	74	**TALERA**	4802
73	232	**JHADOL**	4800
74	193	**ROHAT**	4796
75	65	**SUWANA**	4783
76	188	**JAITARAN**	4755
77	56	**BANERA**	4743
78	61	**MANDALGARH**	4731
79	224	**TODARAISINGH**	4715

RANK	PANCHAYAT SAMITIES P. CODE	NAME	PCI
1	2	3	4
80	55	**ASIND**	4704
81	59	**KOTRI**	4702
82	64	**SHAHPURA**	4699
83	33	**BARAN**	4698
84	32	**ATRU**	4683
85	17	**RAJGARH**	4659
86	227	**BARGAON**	4637
87	204	**BONLI**	4633
88	229	**DHARIAWAD**	4625
89	79	**BHAINSRORGARH**	4620
90	190	**PALI**	4612
91	87	**PRATAPGARH**	4600
91	163	**PHALODI**	4600
93	75	**ARNOD**	4579
94	156	**BALESAR**	4576
95	161	**MANDOR**	4562
96	134	**SANKRA**	4541
97	162	OSIAN	4522
98	47	DEEG	4509
99	191	RAIPUR	4503
100	57	HURDA	4498
101	221	DEOLI	4493
102	223	NIWAI	4481
103	219	SHEOGANJ	4475
104	200	KUMBHALGARH	4463
105	48	KAMAN	4460
106	231	GOGUNDA	4447
107	235	MAVLI	4435
108	157	BAP	4414
109	206	KHANDAR	4394
110	14	LACHHMANGARH	4392
111	189	KHARCHI/MARWAR JUN.	4372
112	225	TONK	4366
113	222	MALPURA	4361
114	201	RAILMAGRA	4353
115	10	BEHROR	4347
116	220	SIROHI	4313
117	237	SARADA	4310
118	31	ANTA	4298
119	199	KHAMNOR	4294
119	230	GIRWA	4294
121	11	KATHUMAR	4281
122	226	UNIARA	4273
123	34	CHHABRA	4272
124	146	MANOHARTHANA	4269
125	20	THANAGAZI	4253
126	58	JAHAZPUR	4221
127	142	BAKANI	4216
127	233	KHERWARA	4216
129	21	TIJARA	4215
130	203	BAMANWAS	4209
131	207	SAWAI MADHOPUR	4203
132	196	AMET	4184
133	62	RAIPUR	4180
134	186	BALI	4159
135	192	RANI STATION	4143
136	168	SAPOTRA	4127
137	147	PIRAWA	4069
138	49	KUMHER	4061
139	166	KARAULI	4034
140	99	SIKRAI	4026
141	96	DAUSA	4020
142	135	AHORE	4014
	LOW (2000-4000)		
143	9	BANSURE	3994
144	50	NADBAI	3981
145	197	BHIM	3980
146	167	NADOTI	3962
147	67	DUNGARGARH	3958
147	195	SUMERPUR	3958
149	198	DEOGARH	3948
150	51	NAGAR PAHARI	3934
151	22	UMREN	3916
152	187	DESURI	3906
153	54	WEIR	3891
154	94	TARANAGAR	3879
154	210	FATEHPUR	3879
156	46	BAYANA	3871
157	144	JHALRAPATAN	3870
158	133	SAM	3866
159	205	GANGAPUR	3849
160	185	RIYAN	3844

RANK	PANCHAYAT SAMITIES P. CODE	NAME	PCI
1	2	3	4
161	132	JAISALMER	3823
162	97	LALSOT	3817
163	12	KISHANGARH BAS	3793
164	98	MAHWA	3776
165	53	SEWAR	3765
165	202	RAJSAMAND	3765
167	18	RAMGARH	3742
168	13	KOTKASIM	3722
168	169	TODABHIM	3722
170	182	MUNDWA	3720
171	95	BANDIKUI	3689
172	90	RAJGARH	3672
173	212	LACHHMANGARH	3666
174	165	HINDAUN	3659
175	175	DEGANA	3641
176	15	MANDAWAR	3634
177	184	PARBATSAR	3628
178	23	ANANDPURI	3577
178	101	BASERI	3577
180	177	JAYAL	3568
181	181	MERTA	3547
182	100	BARI	3535
183	93	SUJANGARH	3532
184	91	RATANGARH	3523
185	24	BAGIDORA	3499
186	29	SAJJANGARH	3492
187	16	NIMRANA	3486
188	27	KUSHALGARH	3466
189	52	RUPBAS	3464
190	28	PEEPALKHOONT	3448
191	183	NAGAUR	3408
192	179	LADNU	3396
193	140	SANCHORE	3371
194	136	BHINMAL	3367
195	89	CHURU	3361
196	145	KHANPUR	3340
197	92	SARDARSHAHAR	3338
198	138	JASWANTPURA	3254
199	180	MAKRANA	3236
200	143	DAG	3233
201	26	GHATOL	3231
202	139	RANIWARA	3216
203	176	DIDWANA	3203
204	102	DHAULPUR	3162
205	209	DHOND	3161
206	214	PIPRALI	3160
207	25	GARHI	3150
208	211	KHANDELA	3145
209	137	JALOR	3140
210	103	RAJAKHERA	3130
210	141	SAYLA	3130
212	178	KUCHAMAN	3105
213	208	DANTA RAMGARH	3001
214	30	TALWARA	2991
215	149	BUHANA	2965
216	40	BAYTOO	2892
217	154	SURAJGARH	2870
218	44	SINDHARI	2822
219	151	JHUNJHUNUN	2810
220	148	ALSISAR	2793
221	41	CHOHTAN	2768
222	213	NEEM KA THANA	2759
223	42	DHORIMANNA	2731
224	215	SRI MADHOPUR	2709
225	38	BALOTRA	2663
226	155	UDAIPURWATI	2643
227	39	BARMER	2626
228	108	SIMALWARA	2574
229	150	CHIRAWA	2553
230	106	DUNGARPUR	2486
231	152	KHETRI	2477
232	105	BICHHIWARA	2421
233	43	SHEO	2417
234	45	SIWANA	2365
235	107	SAGWARA	2303
236	153	NAWALGARH	2291
237	104	ASPUR	2141
		RAJASTHAN	**4523**
		%age of AAPs	**40.51**

BOLD: Equal/Above Average Panchayat Samities (AAPs)

Source: Annex-12.1, Col. 3.

ANNEX-12.1

PANCHAYAT SAMITI-WISE CHANGED PATTERN OF INCOME INDEX (1991-1998)

P. Code	Panchayat Samities	PCI		INI (1991-92)		INI (1998-99)		Difference (1991-1998)		% Increase in INI Value	Remarks
		1991-92	1998-99	Rank	Value	Rank	Value	Rank	Value		
1	2	3	4	5	6	7	8	9	10	11	12
1	ARAIN	6925	11067	18	0.5804	18	0.7994	0	0.2190	38	C
2	BHINAY	6675	10635	23	0.5632	21	0.7808	2	0.2176	39	A
3	JAWAJA	5424	8075	41	0.4662	41	0.6521	0	0.1859	40	C
4	KEKRI	6327	10112	30	0.5382	23	0.7573	7	0.2191	41	A
5	KISHANGARH	6064	9498	36	0.5184	28	0.7280	8	0.2096	40	A
6	MASOODA	6164	9658	34	0.5260	26	0.7359	8	0.2099	40	A
7	PISANGAN	6100	8786	35	0.5211	35	0.6916	0	0.1705	33	C
8	SRINAGAR	6220	9506	33	0.5302	27	0.7284	6	0.1982	37	A
	AJMER DISTRICT	**6224**	**9580**		**0.5305**		**0.7321**		**0.2016**	**38**	
9	BANSURE	3994	5746	143	0.3232	137	0.4932	6	0.1700	53	A
10	BEHROR	4347	6717	115	0.3628	72	0.5662	43	0.2034	56	A
11	KATHUMAR	4281	6461	121	0.3557	88	0.5480	33	0.1923	54	A
12	KISHANGARH BAS	3793	5778	163	0.2991	135	0.4958	28	0.1967	66	A
13	KOTKASIM	3722	5699	168	0.2903	140	0.4893	28	0.1990	69	A
14	LACHHMANGARH	4392	6500	110	0.3676	86	0.5508	24	0.1832	50	A
15	MANDAWAR	3634	5649	176	0.2791	142	0.4853	34	0.2062	74	A
16	NIMRANA	3486	5533	187	0.2597	152	0.4756	35	0.2159	83	A
17	RAJGARH	4659	6795	85	0.3952	70	0.5716	15	0.1764	45	A
18	RAMGARH	3742	5196	167	0.2928	174	0.4462	-7	0.1534	52	B
19	RENI	4881	7195	64	0.4169	60	0.5982	4	0.1813	43	A
20	THANAGAZI	4253	6120	125	0.3526	113	0.5227	12	0.1701	48	A
21	TIJARA	4215	5289	129	0.3484	170	0.4545	-41	0.1061	30	B
22	UMREN	3916	5411	151	0.3140	160	0.4651	-9	0.1511	48	B
	ALWAR	**4081**	**5959**		**0.3333**		**0.5102**		**0.1769**	**53**	
23	ANANDPURI	3577	4977	178	0.2717	184	0.4261	-6	0.1544	57	B
24	BAGIDORA	3499	4796	185	0.2614	190	0.4088	-5	0.1474	56	B
25	GARHI	3150	4461	207	0.2123	208	0.3749	-1	0.1626	77	B
26	GHATOL	3231	4404	201	0.2242	211	0.3688	-10	0.1446	64	B
27	KUSHALGARH	3466	4514	188	0.2570	205	0.3805	-17	0.1235	48	B
28	PEEPALKHOONT	3448	4472	190	0.2545	207	0.3760	-17	0.1215	48	B
29	SAJJANGARH	3492	4746	186	0.2605	196	0.4038	-10	0.1433	55	B
30	TALWARA	2991	4101	214	0.1881	221	0.3356	-7	0.1475	78	B
	BANSWARA	**3312**	**4514**		**0.2357**		**0.3805**		**0.1448**	**61**	
31	ANTA	4298	6698	118	0.3575	73	0.5648	45	0.2073	58	A
32	ATRU	4683	7411	84	0.3976	55	0.6121	29	0.2145	54	A
33	BARAN	4698	6937	83	0.3991	64	0.5812	19	0.1821	46	A
34	CHHABRA	4272	8273	123	0.3547	40	0.6635	83	0.3088	87	A
35	CHHIPABAROD	7467	8974	16	0.6156	33	0.7015	-17	0.0859	14	B
36	KISHANGANJ	4928	7419	59	0.4214	54	0.6125	5	0.1911	45	A
37	SHAHBAD	5111	7383	49	0.4385	56	0.6103	-7	0.1718	39	B
	BARAN	**4980**	**7562**		**0.4263**		**0.6215**		**0.1952**	**46**	
38	BALOTRA	2663	3719	225	0.1338	229	0.2899	-4	0.1561	117	B
39	BARMER	2626	3559	227	0.1273	230	0.2693	-3	0.1420	112	B
40	BAYTOO	2892	4087	216	0.1724	222	0.3340	-6	0.1616	94	B
41	CHOHTAN	2768	4053	221	0.1519	223	0.3301	-2	0.1782	117	B
42	DHORIMANNA	2731	3774	223	0.1456	228	0.2968	-5	0.1512	104	B
43	SHEO	2417	3182	233	0.0885	234	0.2170	-1	0.1285	145	B
44	SINDHARI	2822	3927	218	0.1609	227	0.3154	-9	0.1545	96	B
45	SIWANA	2365	2885	234	0.0784	236	0.1712	-2	0.0928	118	B
	BARMER	**2678**	**3669**		**0.1364**		**0.2835**		**0.1471**	**108**	
46	BAYANA	3871	5715	156	0.3086	139	0.4906	17	0.1820	59	A
47	DEEG	4509	6766	98	0.3799	71	0.5695	27	0.1896	50	A
48	KAMAN	4460	6050	105	0.3748	119	0.5173	-14	0.1425	38	B
49	KUMHER	4061	6329	138	0.3310	100	0.5383	38	0.2073	63	A
50	NADBAI	3981	5879	144	0.3217	131	0.5039	13	0.1822	57	A
51	NAGAR PAHARI	3934	5610	150	0.3162	144	0.4820	6	0.1658	52	A
52	RUPBAS	3464	5073	189	0.2567	179	0.4350	10	0.1783	69	A
53	SEWAR	3765	5583	165	0.2956	146	0.4798	19	0.1842	62	A
54	WEIR	3891	5721	153	0.3110	138	0.4912	5	0.1802	58	A
	BHARATPUR	**3978**	**5818**		**0.3214**		**0.4990**		**0.1776**	**55**	
55	ASIND	4704	6317	80	0.3997	101	0.5374	-21	0.1377	34	B
56	BANERA	4743	6439	77	0.4035	90	0.5464	-13	0.1429	35	B
57	HURDA	4498	5947	100	0.3788	125	0.5093	-25	0.1305	34	B
58	JAHAZPUR	4221	5517	126	0.3491	154	0.4742	-28	0.1251	36	B
59	KOTRI	4702	6431	81	0.3995	91	0.5458	-10	0.1463	37	B
60	MANDAL	4830	5914	68	0.4120	130	0.5067	-62	0.0947	23	B
61	MANDALGARH	4731	6113	78	0.4024	115	0.5222	-37	0.1198	30	B

P. Code	*Panchayat Samities*	*PCI*		*INI (1991-92)*		*INI (1998-99)*		*Difference (1991-1998)*		*% Increase in INI Value*	*Remarks*
		1991-92	*1998-99*	*Rank*	*Value*	*Rank*	*Value*	*Rank*	*Value*		
1	*2*	*3*	*4*	*5*	*6*	*7*	*8*	*9*	*10*	*11*	*12*
62	RAIPUR	4180	5814	133	0.3445	133	0.4987	0	0.1542	45	C
63	SAHARA	4907	7072	62	0.4194	62	0.5902	0	0.1708	41	C
64	SHAHPURA	4699	6295	82	0.3992	102	0.5358	-20	0.1366	34	B
65	SUWANA	4783	6223	75	0.4075	106	0.5304	-31	0.1229	30	B
	BHILWARA	**4654**	**6163**		**0.3947**		**0.5259**		**0.1312**	**33**	
66	BIKANER	6013	8753	37	0.5144	36	0.6899	1	0.1755	34	A
67	DUNGARGARH *	3958	7031	147	0.3190	63	0.5875	84	0.2685	84	A
68	KOLAYAT	5902	8895	39	0.5057	34	0.6973	5	0.1916	38	A
69	LUNKARANSAR	5706	9666	40	0.4899	25	0.7362	15	0.2463	50	A
70	NOKHA	6240	10989	31	0.5317	19	0.7962	12	0.2645	50	A
	BIKANER **	**5992**	**9543**		**0.5128**		**0.7302**		**0.2174**	**42**	
71	HINDOLI	5339	6846	42	0.4589	69	0.5750	-27	0.1161	25	B
72	KESHORAIPATAN	4828	6462	69	0.4118	87	0.5481	-18	0.1363	33	B
73	NAINWA	5289	6614	43	0.4545	81	0.5590	-38	0.1045	23	B
74	TALERA	4801	6350	72	0.4092	97	0.5399	-25	0.1307	32	B
	BUNDI	**5029**	**6548**		**0.4309**		**0.5542**		**0.1233**	**29**	
75	ARNOD	4579	6340	93	0.3871	99	0.5392	-6	0.1521	39	B
76	BARI SADRI	5042	7865	52	0.4321	42	0.6399	10	0.2078	48	A
77	BEGUN	5020	7696	53	0.4301	48	0.6298	5	0.1997	46	A
78	BHADESAR	5087	7677	50	0.4363	49	0.6286	1	0.1923	44	A
79	BHAINSRORGARH	4620	6671	89	0.3913	77	0.5629	12	0.1716	44	A
80	BHOPALSAGAR	4802	7516	71	0.4093	51	0.6187	20	0.2094	51	A
81	CHHOTI SADRI	5075	7813	51	0.4352	45	0.6368	6	0.2016	46	A
82	CHITTAURGARH	4988	7300	54	0.4271	57	0.6050	-3	0.1779	42	B
83	DUNGLA	4953	7740	58	0.4238	47	0.6323	11	0.2085	49	A
84	GANGRAR	5168	7865	48	0.4436	42	0.6399	6	0.1963	44	A
85	KAPASAN	5237	8304	47	0.4498	39	0.6653	8	0.2155	48	A
86	NIMBAHERA	4911	7283	60	0.4198	58	0.6039	2	0.1841	44	A
87	PRATAPGARH	4600	6591	91	0.3892	82	0.5573	9	0.1681	43	A
88	RASHMI	4958	7808	57	0.4243	46	0.6364	11	0.2121	50	A
	CHITTAURGARH	**4914**	**7366**		**0.4201**		**0.6092**		**0.1891**	**45**	
89	CHURU	3361	4786	195	0.2426	193	0.4078	2	0.1652	68	A
90	RAJGARH	3672	5330	172	0.2839	169	0.4580	3	0.1741	61	A
91	RATANGARH	3523	4911	184	0.2646	186	0.4198	-2	0.1552	59	B
92	SARDARSHAHAR	3338	4595	197	0.2394	201	0.3887	-4	0.1493	62	B
93	SUJANGARH	3532	4759	183	0.2658	195	0.4051	-12	0.1393	52	B
94	TARANAGAR	3879	5606	154	0.3096	145	0.4817	9	0.1721	56	A
	CHURU ***	**3597**	**5187**		**0.2743**		**0.4453**		**0.1710**	**62**	
95	BANDIKUI	3689	5373	171	0.2861	162	0.4618	9	0.1757	61	A
96	DAUSA	4020	6414	141	0.3263	95	0.5445	46	0.2182	67	A
97	LALSOT	3817	5929	162	0.3020	127	0.5079	35	0.2059	68	A
98	MAHWA	3776	6431	164	0.2970	91	0.5458	73	0.2488	84	A
99	SIKRAI	4026	6376	140	0.3270	96	0.5417	44	0.2147	66	A
	DAUSA	**3869**	**6071**		**0.3084**		**0.5189**		**0.2105**	**68**	
100	BARI	3535	4709	182	0.2662	198	0.4002	-16	0.1340	50	B
101	BASERI	3577	4592	178	0.2717	203	0.3884	-25	0.1167	43	B
102	DHAULPUR	3162	4152	204	0.2141	220	0.3414	-16	0.1273	59	B
103	RAJAKHERA	3130	4216	210	0.2093	218	0.3485	-8	0.1392	67	B
	DHAULPUR	**3326**	**4381**		**0.2377**		**0.3665**		**0.1288**	**54**	
104	ASPUR	2141	2882	237	0.0319	237	0.1708	0	0.1389	435	C
105	BICHHIWARA	2421	3160	232	0.0893	235	0.2138	-3	0.1245	139	B
106	DUNGARPUR	2486	3279	230	0.1017	232	0.2310	-2	0.1293	127	B
107	SAGWARA	2303	3253	235	0.0660	233	0.2274	2	0.1614	245	A
108	SIMALWARA	2574	3419	228	0.1179	231	0.2506	-3	0.1327	113	B
	DUNGARPUR	**2389**	**3202**		**0.0830**		**0.2199**		**0.1369**	**165**	
109	ANUPGARH	6777	6899	20	0.5703	66	0.5787	-46	0.0084	1	B
110	GANGANAGAR	6454	8575	26	0.5475	38	0.6802	-12	0.1327	24	B
111	KARANPUR	8761	11327	7	0.6903	16	0.8103	-9	0.1200	17	B
112	PADAMPUR	5924	7443	38	0.5074	53	0.6141	-15	0.1067	21	B
113	RAISINGHNAGAR	7935	9357	10	0.6440	29	0.7210	-19	0.0770	12	B
114	SADULSHAHAR	6349	12989	28	0.5398	7	0.8743	21	0.3345	62	A
115	SURATGARH	6481	12004	25	0.5494	10	0.8374	15	0.2880	52	A
	GANGANAGAR	**6785**	**9278**		**0.5709**		**0.7171**		**0.1462**	**26**	
116	BHADRA	7602	11543	14	0.6240	14	0.8191	0	0.1951	31	C
117	HANUMANGARH	6223	6145	32	0.5304	112	0.5245	-80	-0.0059	-1	D
118	NOHAR	7361	10838	17	0.6089	20	0.7896	-3	0.1807	30	B
	HANUMANGARH	**6943**	**8540**		**0.5816**		**0.6784**		**0.0968**	**17**	
119	AMBER	7870	11872	11	0.6402	11	0.8323	0	0.1921	30	C
120	BASSI	8349	11148	9	0.6678	17	0.8029	-8	0.1351	20	B
121	CHAKSU	9362	14029	3	0.7213	5	0.9103	-2	0.1890	26	B
122	DUDU	7821	11747	12	0.6373	12	0.8273	0	0.1900	30	C
123	GOVINDGARH	6338	9326	29	0.5390	30	0.7195	-1	0.1805	33	B
124	JAMWA RAMGARH	7812	11532	13	0.6367	15	0.8187	-2	0.1820	29	B
125	JHOTWARA	6698	15215	22	0.5648	2	0.9482	20	0.3834	68	A
126	KOTPUTLI	6803	10217	19	0.5721	22	0.7621	-3	0.1900	33	B
127	PHAGI	8540	13281	8	0.6783	6	0.8847	2	0.2064	30	A

P. Code	Panchayat Samities	PCI		INI (1991-92)		INI (1998-99)		Difference (1991-1998)		% Increase in INI Value	Remarks
		1991-92	1998-99	Rank	Value	Rank	Value	Rank	Value		
1	2	3	4	5	6	7	8	9	10	11	12
128	SAMBHAR	6674	9967	24	0.5631	24	0.7506	0	0.1875	33	C
129	SANGANER	7545	17233	15	0.6205	1	1.0065	14	0.3860	62	A
130	SHAHPURA	6733	9229	21	0.5673	31	0.7147	-10	0.1474	26	B
131	VIRATNAGAR	6367	9216	27	0.5411	32	0.7139	-5	0.1728	32	B
	JAIPUR	**7425**	**11411**		**0.6129**		**0.8138**		**0.2009**	**33**	
132	JAISALMER	3823	4960	161	0.3028	185	0.4245	-24	0.1217	40	B
133	SAM	3866	5343	158	0.3080	167	0.4592	-9	0.1512	49	B
134	SANKRA	4541	6453	96	0.3832	89	0.5474	7	0.1642	43	A
	JAISALMER	**4122**	**5657**		**0.3380**		**0.4859**		**0.1479**	**44**	
135	AHORE	4014	5557	142	0.3256	150	0.4775	-8	0.1519	47	B
136	BHINMAL	3367	4437	194	0.2434	210	0.3724	-16	0.1290	53	B
137	JALOR	3140	4239	209	0.2108	217	0.3511	-8	0.1403	67	B
138	JASWANTPURA	3254	4329	198	0.2275	213	0.3609	-15	0.1334	59	B
139	RANIWARA	3216	3979	202	0.2220	226	0.3215	-24	0.0995	45	B
140	SANCHORE	3371	4202	193	0.2440	219	0.3470	-26	0.1030	42	B
141	SAYLA	3130	4013	210	0.2093	225	0.3255	-15	0.1162	56	B
	JALOR	**3368**	**4373**		**0.2435**		**0.3656**		**0.1221**	**50**	
142	BAKANI	4216	5973	127	0.3485	123	0.5113	4	0.1628	47	A
143	DAG	3233	4448	200	0.2245	209	0.3736	-9	0.1491	66	B
144	JHALRAPATAN	3870	5087	157	0.3085	178	0.4363	-21	0.1278	41	B
145	KHANPUR	3340	4262	196	0.2397	216	0.3536	-20	0.1139	48	B
146	MANOHARTHANA	4269	5505	124	0.3543	155	0.4732	-31	0.1189	34	B
147	PIRAWA	4069	5092	137	0.3319	177	0.4367	-40	0.1048	32	B
	JHALAWAR	**3836**	**5062**		**0.3044**		**0.4339**		**0.1295**	**43**	
148	ALSISAR	2793	5355	220	0.1561	163	0.4603	57	0.3042	195	A
149	BUHANA	2965	6004	215	0.1840	121	0.5137	94	0.3297	179	A
150	CHIRAWA	2553	5136	229	0.1141	176	0.4407	53	0.3266	286	A
151	JHUNJHUNUN	2810	5828	219	0.1589	132	0.4998	87	0.3409	215	A
152	KHETRI	2477	4997	231	0.1000	182	0.4279	49	0.3279	328	A
153	NAWALGARH	2291	4594	236	0.0635	202	0.3886	34	0.3251	512	A
154	SURAJGARH	2870	5526	217	0.1688	153	0.4749	64	0.3061	181	A
155	UDAIPURWATI	2643	5059	226	0.1303	180	0.4337	46	0.3034	233	A
	JHUNJHUNUN	**2664**	**5298**		**0.1340**		**0.4552**		**0.3212**	**240**	
156	BALESAR	4576	6212	94	0.3868	110	0.5296	-16	0.1428	37	B
157	BAP	4414	8691	108	0.3700	37	0.6866	71	0.3166	86	A
158	BHOPALGARH	5253	7445	45	0.4513	52	0.6143	-7	0.1630	36	B
159	BILARA	5244	7654	46	0.4505	50	0.6272	-4	0.1767	39	B
160	LUNI	4892	6696	63	0.4180	74	0.5647	-11	0.1467	35	B
161	MANDOR	4562	6032	95	0.3854	120	0.5159	-25	0.1305	34	B
162	OSIAN	4522	6103	97	0.3812	116	0.5213	-19	0.1401	37	B
163	PHALODI	4600	4733	91	0.3892	197	0.4025	-106	0.0133	3	B
164	SHERGARH	4984	6424	55	0.4267	94	0.5453	-39	0.1186	28	B
	JODHPUR	**4774**	**6424**		**0.4066**		**0.5453**		**0.1387**	**34**	
165	HINDAUN	3659	4538	174	0.2823	204	0.3829	-30	0.1006	36	B
166	KARAULI	4034	4992	139	0.3279	183	0.4275	-44	0.0996	30	B
167	NADOTI	3962	5411	146	0.3195	160	0.4651	-14	0.1456	46	B
168	SAPOTRA	4127	5347	136	0.3385	166	0.4595	-30	0.1210	36	B
169	TODABHIM	3722	4886	168	0.2903	187	0.4175	-19	0.1272	44	B
	KARAULI	**3898**	**4992**		**0.3119**		**0.4275**		**0.1156**	**37**	
170	CHECHAT	10096	15164	2	0.7566	3	0.9466	-1	0.1900	25	B
171	ITAWA	9353	12790	4	0.7208	8	0.8671	-4	0.1463	20	B
172	LADPURA	9066	11616	5	0.7063	13	0.8221	-8	0.1158	16	B
173	SANGOD	10261	14340	1	0.7641	4	0.9205	-3	0.1564	20	B
174	SULTANPUR	8767	12075	6	0.6906	9	0.8402	-3	0.1496	22	B
	KOTA	**9514**	**13161**		**0.7288**		**0.8805**		**0.1517**	**21**	
175	DEGANA	3641	5041	175	0.2800	181	0.4320	-6	0.1520	54	B
176	DIDWANA	3203	4311	203	0.2201	215	0.3589	-12	0.1388	63	B
177	JAYAL	3568	4791	180	0.2705	192	0.4082	-12	0.1377	51	B
178	KUCHAMAN	3105	4053	212	0.2056	223	0.3301	-11	0.1245	61	B
179	LADNU	3396	4514	192	0.2474	205	0.3805	-13	0.1331	54	B
180	MAKRANA	3236	4328	199	0.2249	214	0.3608	-15	0.1359	60	B
181	MERTA	3547	4707	181	0.2678	199	0.3999	-18	0.1321	49	B
182	MUNDWA	3720	4807	170	0.2900	189	0.4098	-19	0.1198	41	B
183	NAGAUR	3408	4794	191	0.2491	191	0.4085	0	0.1594	64	C
184	PARBATSAR	3628	4763	177	0.2783	194	0.4055	-17	0.1272	46	B
185	RIYAN	3844	5245	160	0.3053	172	0.4505	-12	0.1452	48	B
	NAGAUR	**3464**	**4649**		**0.2567**		**0.3942**		**0.1375**	**54**	
186	BALI	4159	5413	134	0.3421	159	0.4652	-25	0.1231	36	B
187	DESURI	3906	5210	152	0.3128	173	0.4474	-21	0.1346	43	B
188	JAITARAN	4755	5506	76	0.4047	155	0.4732	-79	0.0685	17	B
189	KHARCHI/MAR. JUN.	4372	5998	111	0.3655	122	0.5132	-11	0.1477	40	B
190	PALI	4612	6853	90	0.3905	68	0.5755	22	0.1850	47	A
191	RAIPUR	4503	5271	99	0.3793	171	0.4529	-72	0.0736	19	B
192	RANI STATION	4143	6092	135	0.3403	117	0.5206	18	0.1803	53	A
193	ROHAT	4796	6092	74	0.4087	117	0.5206	-43	0.1119	27	B
194	SOJAT	4842	6565	67	0.4132	85	0.5554	-18	0.1422	34	B
195	SUMERPUR	3958	5350	147	0.3190	165	0.4599	-18	0.1409	44	B
	PALI	**4410**	**5771**		**0.3695**		**0.4953**		**0.1258**	**34**	

P. Code	Panchayat Samities	PCI		INI (1991-92)		INI (1998-99)		Difference (1991-1998)		% Increase in INI Value	Remarks
		1991-92	1998-99	Rank	Value	Rank	Value	Rank	Value		
1	2	3	4	5	6	7	8	9	10	11	12
196	AMET	4184	6247	132	0.3449	105	0.5323	27	0.1874	54	A
197	BHIM	3980	5562	145	0.3216	149	0.4779	-4	0.1563	49	B
198	DEOGARH	3948	5947	149	0.3178	125	0.5093	24	0.1915	60	A
199	KHAMNOR	4294	5146	119	0.3571	175	0.4417	-56	0.0846	24	B
200	KUMBHALGARH	4463	7114	104	0.3751	61	0.5930	43	0.2179	58	A
201	RAILMAGRA	4353	7272	114	0.3634	59	0.6033	55	0.2399	66	A
202	RAJSAMAND	3765	5353	165	0.2956	164	0.4601	1	0.1645	56	A
	RAJSAMAND	**4153**	**6013**		**0.3415**		**0.5144**		**0.1729**	**51**	
203	BAMANWAS	4209	5921	130	0.3477	129	0.5072	1	0.1595	46	A
204	BONLI	4633	6343	87	0.3926	98	0.5394	-11	0.1468	37	B
205	GANGAPUR	3849	5506	159	0.3059	155	0.4732	4	0.1673	55	A
206	KHANDAR	4394	6576	109	0.3678	84	0.5563	25	0.1885	51	A
207	SAWAI MADHOPUR	4203	5624	131	0.3471	143	0.4831	-12	0.1360	39	B
	SAWAI MADHOPUR	**4261**	**5958**		**0.3535**		**0.5101**		**0.1566**	**44**	
208	DANTA RAMGARH	3001	4867	213	0.1897	188	0.4156	25	0.2259	119	A
209	DHOND	3161	5335	205	0.2139	168	0.4585	37	0.2446	114	A
210	FATEHPUR	3879	6632	154	0.3096	80	0.5601	74	0.2505	81	A
211	KHANDELA	3145	5565	208	0.2116	148	0.4783	60	0.2667	126	A
212	LACHHMANGARH	3666	6216	173	0.2832	108	0.5299	65	0.2467	87	A
213	NEEM KA THANA	2759	4634	222	0.1504	200	0.3927	22	0.2423	161	A
214	PIPRALI	3160	5582	206	0.2138	147	0.4797	59	0.2659	124	A
215	SRI MADHOPUR	2709	4402	224	0.1418	212	0.3687	12	0.2269	160	A
	SIKAR	**3153**	**5335**		**0.2127**		**0.4585**		**0.2458**	**116**	
216	ABU ROAD	4843	6223	66	0.4133	106	0.5304	-40	0.1171	28	B
217	PINDWARA	5267	6677	44	0.4525	76	0.5634	-32	0.1109	25	B
218	REODAR	4970	6866	56	0.4254	67	0.5764	-11	0.1510	35	B
219	SHEOGANJ	4475	6581	103	0.3764	83	0.5566	20	0.1802	48	A
220	SIROHI	4313	6664	116	0.3591	78	0.5624	38	0.2033	57	A
	SIROHI	**4815**	**6627**		**0.4106**		**0.5598**		**0.1492**	**36**	
221	DEOLI	4493	6175	101	0.3782	111	0.5268	-10	0.1486	39	B
222	MALPURA	4361	6279	113	0.3643	103	0.5346	10	0.1703	47	A
223	NIWAI	4481	6427	102	0.3770	93	0.5455	9	0.1685	45	A
224	TODARAISINGH	4715	6680	79	0.4008	75	0.5636	4	0.1628	41	A
225	TONK	4366	6216	112	0.3648	108	0.5299	4	0.1651	45	A
226	UNIARA	4273	5748	122	0.3548	136	0.4933	-14	0.1385	39	B
	TONK	**4435**	**6245**		**0.3722**		**0.5321**		**0.1599**	**43**	
227	BARGAON,	4637	7839	86	0.3930	44	0.6384	42	0.2454	62	A
228	BHINDER,	4908	6902	61	0.4195	65	0.5789	-4	0.1594	38	B
229	DHARIAWAD,	4625	5927	88	0.3918	128	0.5076	-40	0.1158	30	B
230	GIRWA,	4294	5549	119	0.3571	151	0.4769	-32	0.1198	34	B
231	GOGUNDA,	4447	5948	106	0.3734	124	0.5094	-18	0.1360	36	B
232	JHADOL,	4800	6121	73	0.4091	113	0.5227	-40	0.1136	28	B
233	KHERWARA,	4216	5504	127	0.3485	158	0.4731	-31	0.1246	36	B
234	KOTRA,	4810	5694	70	0.4101	141	0.4889	-71	0.0788	19	B
235	MAVLI,	4435	6255	107	0.3722	104	0.5328	3	0.1606	43	A
236	SALUMBAR,	4852	6653	65	0.4142	79	0.5617	-14	0.1475	36	B
237	SARADA,	4310	5812	117	0.3588	134	0.4985	-17	0.1397	39	B
	UDAIPUR	**4556**	**6121**		**0.3847**		**0.5227**		**0.1380**	**36**	
	RAJASTHAN	**4523**	**6432**		**0.3813**		**0.5458**		**0.1645**	**43**	

Note: *Dungargarh PS shifted from Churu to Bikaner District on 1st April 2001
** Excluding data of Dungargarh PS
*** Including data of Dungargarh PS
A Improvement in Both INI Value and Rank
B Increase in INI Value but Rank Deteriorated
C Increase in INI Value but Rank Remained Constant
D Decrease in Both INI Value and Rank

Source: Hemlata Joshi. 2005. *'Economic Development Index*, Rajasthan (Spatio-Temporal and Gender Appraisal at Panchayat Samiti / Block Level), Published Research Report, IDSJ, University Book House, Jaipur.

ANNEX-12.2

RANKING OF PSS BY INI (1998-99) (BASED ON RURAL AND URBAN INCOME RATIO 1.29:1)

(Descending Order)

RANK	PANCHAYAT SAMITIES P. CODE	NAME	VALUE
1	2	3	4
	VERY HIGH (>0.8)		
1	**129**	**SANGANER**	**1.0065**
2	**125**	**JHOTWARA**	**0.9482**
3	**170**	**CHECHAT**	**0.9466**
4	**173**	**SANGOD**	**0.9205**
5	**121**	**CHAKSU**	**0.9103**
6	**127**	**PHAGI**	**0.8847**
7	**114**	**SADULSHAHAR**	**0.8743**
8	**171**	**ITAWA**	**0.8671**
9	**174**	**SULTANPUR**	**0.8402**
10	**115**	**SURATGARH**	**0.8374**
11	**119**	**AMBER**	**0.8323**
12	**122**	**DUDU**	**0.8273**
13	**172**	**LADPURA**	**0.8221**
14	**116**	**BHADRA**	**0.8191**
15	**124**	**JAMWA RAMGARH**	**0.8187**
16	**111**	**KARANPUR**	**0.8103**
17	**120**	**BASSI**	**0.8029**
	HIGH (0.6-0.8)		
18	**1**	**ARAIN**	**0.7994**
19	**70**	**NOKHA**	**0.7962**
20	**118**	**NOHAR**	**0.7896**
21	**2**	**BHINAY**	**0.7808**
22	**126**	**KOTPUTLI**	**0.7621**
23	**4**	**KEKRI**	**0.7573**
24	**128**	**SAMBHAR**	**0.7506**
25	**69**	**LUNKARANSAR**	**0.7362**
26	**6**	**MASOODA**	**0.7359**
27	**8**	**SRINAGAR**	**0.7284**
28	**5**	**KISHANGARH**	**0.7280**
29	**113**	**RAISINGHNAGAR**	**0.7210**
30	**123**	**GOVINDGARH**	**0.7195**
31	**130**	**SHAHPURA**	**0.7147**
32	**131**	**VIRATNAGAR**	**0.7139**
33	**35**	**CHHIPABAROD**	**0.7015**
34	**68**	**KOLAYAT**	**0.6973**
35	**7**	**PISANGAN**	**0.6916**
36	**66**	**BIKANER**	**0.6899**
37	**157**	**BAP**	**0.6866**
38	**110**	**GANGANAGAR**	**0.6802**
39	**85**	**KAPASAN**	**0.6653**
40	**34**	**CHHABRA**	**0.6635**
41	**3**	**JAWAJA**	**0.6521**
42	**76**	**BARI SADRI**	**0.6399**
42	**84**	**GANGRAR**	**0.6399**
44	**227**	**BARGAON**	**0.6384**
45	**81**	**CHHOTI SADRI**	**0.6368**
46	**88**	**RASHMI**	**0.6364**
47	**83**	**DUNGLA**	**0.6323**
48	**77**	**BEGUN**	**0.6298**
49	**78**	**BHADESAR**	**0.6286**
50	**159**	**BILARA**	**0.6272**
51	**80**	**BHOPALSAGAR**	**0.6187**
52	**158**	**BHOPALGARH**	**0.6143**
53	**112**	**PADAMPUR**	**0.6141**
54	**36**	**KISHANGANJ**	**0.6125**
55	**32**	**ATRU**	**0.6121**
56	**37**	**SHAHBAD**	**0.6103**
57	**82**	**CHITTAURGARH**	**0.6050**
58	**86**	**NIMBAHERA**	**0.6039**
59	**201**	**RAILMAGRA**	**0.6033**
	MEDIUM (0.4-0.6)		
60	**19**	**RENI**	**0.5982**
61	**200**	**KUMBHALGARH**	**0.5930**
62	**63**	**SAHARA**	**0.5902**
63	**67**	**DUNGARGARH**	**0.5875**
64	**33**	**BARAN**	**0.5812**
65	**228**	**BHINDER**	**0.5789**
66	**109**	**ANUPGARH**	**0.5787**
67	**218**	**REODAR**	**0.5764**
68	**190**	**PALI**	**0.5755**
69	**71**	**HINDOLI**	**0.5750**
70	**17**	**RAJGARH**	**0.5716**
71	**47**	**DEEG**	**0.5695**
72	**10**	**BEHROR**	**0.5662**
73	**31**	**ANTA**	**0.5648**
74	**160**	**LUNI**	**0.5647**
75	**224**	**TODARAISINGH**	**0.5636**
76	**217**	**PINDWARA**	**0.5634**
77	**79**	**BHAINSRORGARH**	**0.5629**
78	**220**	**SIROHI**	**0.5624**
79	**236**	**SALUMBAR**	**0.5617**

RANK	PANCHAYAT SAMITIES P. CODE	NAME	VALUE
1	2	3	4
80	**210**	**FATEHPUR**	**0.5601**
81	**73**	**NAINWA**	**0.5590**
82	**87**	**PRATAPGARH**	**0.5573**
83	**219**	**SHEOGANJ**	**0.5566**
84	**206**	**KHANDAR**	**0.5563**
85	**194**	**SOJAT**	**0.5554**
86	**14**	**LACHHMANGARH**	**0.5508**
87	**72**	**KESHORAIPATAN**	**0.5481**
88	**11**	**KATHUMAR**	**0.5480**
89	**134**	**SANKRA**	**0.5474**
90	**56**	**BANERA**	**0.5464**
91	**59**	**KOTRI**	**0.5458**
91	**98**	**MAHWA**	**0.5458**
93	223	NIWAI	0.5455
94	164	SHERGARH	0.5453
95	96	DAUSA	0.5445
96	99	SIKRAI	0.5417
97	74	TALERA	0.5399
98	204	BONLI	0.5394
99	75	ARNOD	0.5392
100	49	KUMHER	0.5383
101	55	ASIND	0.5374
102	64	SHAHPURA	0.5358
103	222	MALPURA	0.5346
104	235	MAVLI	0.5328
105	196	AMET	0.5323
106	65	SUWANA	0.5304
106	216	ABU ROAD	0.5304
108	212	LACHHMANGARH	0.5299
108	225	TONK	0.5299
110	156	BALESAR	0.5296
111	221	DEOLI	0.5268
112	117	HANUMANGARH	0.5245
113	20	THANAGAZI	0.5227
113	232	JHADOL	0.5227
115	61	MANDALGARH	0.5222
116	162	OSIAN	0.5213
117	192	RANI STATION	0.5206
117	193	ROHAT	0.5206
119	48	KAMAN	0.5173
120	161	MANDOR	0.5159
121	149	BUHANA	0.5137
122	189	MARWAR JUN.	0.5132
123	142	BAKANI	0.5113
124	231	GOGUNDA	0.5094
125	57	HURDA	0.5093
125	198	DEOGARH	0.5093
127	97	LALSOT	0.5079
128	229	DHARIAWAD	0.5076
129	203	BAMANWAS	0.5072
130	60	MANDAL	0.5067
131	50	NADBAI	0.5039
132	151	JHUNJHUNUN	0.4998
133	62	RAIPUR	0.4987
134	237	SARADA	0.4985
135	12	KISHANGARH BAS	0.4958
136	226	UNIARA	0.4933
137	9	BANSURE	0.4932
138	54	WEIR	0.4912
139	46	BAYANA	0.4906
140	13	KOTKASIM	0.4893
141	234	KOTRA	0.4889
142	15	MANDAWAR	0.4853
143	207	SAWAI MADHOPUR	0.4831
144	51	NAGAR PAHARI	0.4820
145	94	TARANAGAR	0.4817
146	53	SEWAR	0.4798
147	214	PIPRALI	0.4797
148	211	KHANDELA	0.4783
149	197	BHIM	0.4779
150	135	AHORE	0.4775
151	230	GIRWA	0.4769
152	16	NIMRANA	0.4756
153	154	SURAJGARH	0.4749
154	58	JAHAZPUR	0.4742
155	146	MANOHARTHANA	0.4732
155	188	JAITARAN	0.4732
155	205	GANGAPUR	0.4732
158	233	KHERWARA	0.4731
159	186	BALI	0.4652
160	22	UMREN	0.4651
160	167	NADOTI	0.4651

RANK	PANCHAYAT SAMITIES P. CODE	NAME	VALUE
1	2	3	4
162	95	BANDIKUI	0.4618
163	148	ALSISAR	0.4603
164	202	RAJSAMAND	0.4601
165	195	SUMERPUR	0.4599
166	168	SAPOTRA	0.4595
167	133	SAM	0.4592
168	209	DHOND	0.4585
169	90	RAJGARH	0.4580
170	21	TIJARA	0.4545
171	191	RAIPUR	0.4529
172	185	RIYAN	0.4505
173	187	DESURI	0.4474
174	18	RAMGARH	0.4462
175	199	KHAMNOR	0.4417
176	150	CHIRAWA	0.4407
177	147	PIRAWA	0.4367
178	144	JHALRAPATAN	0.4363
179	52	RUPBAS	0.4350
180	155	UDAIPURWATI	0.4337
181	175	DEGANA	0.4320
182	152	KHETRI	0.4279
183	166	KARAULI	0.4275
184	23	ANANDPURI	0.4261
185	132	JAISALMER	0.4245
186	91	RATANGARH	0.4198
187	169	TODABHIM	0.4175
188	208	DANTA RAMGARH	0.4156
189	182	MUNDWA	0.4098
190	24	BAGIDORA	0.4088
191	183	NAGAUR	0.4085
192	177	JAYAL	0.4082
193	89	CHURU	0.4078
194	184	PARBATSAR	0.4055
195	93	SUJANGARH	0.4051
196	29	SAJJANGARH	0.4038
197	163	PHALODI	0.4025
198	100	BARI	0.4002
	LOW (0.2-0.4)		
199	181	MERTA	0.3999
200	213	NEEM KA THANA	0.3927
201	92	SARDARSHAHAR	0.3887
202	153	NAWALGARH	0.3886
203	101	BASERI	0.3884
204	165	HINDAUN	0.3829
205	27	KUSHALGARH	0.3805
206	179	LADNU	0.3805
207	28	PEEPALKHOONT	0.3760
208	25	GARHI	0.3749
209	143	DAG	0.3736
210	136	BHINMAL	0.3724
211	26	GHATOL	0.3688
212	215	SRI MADHOPUR	0.3687
213	138	JASWANTPURA	0.3609
214	180	MAKRANA	0.3608
215	176	DIDWANA	0.3589
216	145	KHANPUR	0.3536
217	137	JALOR	0.3511
218	103	RAJAKHERA	0.3485
219	140	SANCHORE	0.3470
220	102	DHAULPUR	0.3414
221	30	TALWARA	0.3356
222	40	BAYTOO	0.3340
223	41	CHOHTAN	0.3301
223	178	KUCHAMAN	0.3301
225	141	SAYLA	0.3255
226	139	RANIWARA	0.3215
227	44	SINDHARI	0.3154
228	42	DHORIMANNA	0.2968
229	38	BALOTRA	0.2899
230	39	BARMER	0.2693
231	108	SIMALWARA	0.2506
232	106	DUNGARPUR	0.2310
233	107	SAGWARA	0.2274
234	43	SHEO	0.2170
235	105	BICHHIWARA	0.2138
	VERY LOW (<0.2)		
236	45	SIWANA	0.1712
237	104	ASPUR	0.1708
	RAJASTHAN		**0.5458**
	%age of AAPs		**38.80**

BOLD: Equal/Above Average Panchayat Samities (AAPs)

Source: Annex 12.1, Col. 8.

ANNEX-12.3

RANKING OF PSS BY PCI (1998-99) (BASED ON RURAL AND URBAN INCOME RATIO 1.29:1)

(Descending Order)

RANK	PANCHAYAT SAMITIES P. CODE	NAME	PCI
1	2	3	4
	VERY HIGH (>8000)		
1	129	**SANGANER**	17233
2	125	**JHOTWARA**	15215
3	170	**CHECHAT**	15164
4	173	**SANGOD**	14340
5	121	**CHAKSU**	14029
6	127	**PHAGI**	13281
7	114	**SADULSHAHAR**	12989
8	171	**ITAWA**	12790
9	174	**SULTANPUR**	12075
10	115	**SURATGARH**	12004
11	119	**AMBER**	11872
12	122	**DUDU**	11747
13	172	**LADPURA**	11616
14	116	**BHADRA**	11543
15	124	**JAMWA RAMGARH**	11532
16	111	**KARANPUR**	11327
17	120	**BASSI**	11148
18	1	**ARAIN**	11067
19	70	**NOKHA**	10989
20	118	**NOHAR**	10838
21	2	**BHINAY**	10635
22	126	**KOTPUTLI**	10217
23	4	**KEKRI**	10112
24	128	**SAMBHAR**	9967
25	69	**LUNKARANSAR**	9666
26	6	**MASOODA**	9658
27	8	**SRINAGAR**	9506
28	5	**KISHANGARH**	9498
29	113	**RAISINGHNAGAR**	9357
30	123	**GOVINDGARH**	9326
31	130	**SHAHPURA**	9229
32	131	**VIRATNAGAR**	9216
33	35	**CHHIPABAROD**	8974
34	68	**KOLAYAT**	8895
35	7	**PISANGAN**	8786
36	66	**BIKANER**	8753
37	157	**BAP**	8691
38	110	**GANGANAGAR**	8575
39	85	**KAPASAN**	8304
40	34	**CHHABRA**	8273
41	3	**JAWAJA**	8075
	HIGH (6000-8000)		
42	76	**BARI SADRI**	7865
43	84	**GANGRAR**	7865
44	227	**BARGAON**	7839
45	81	**CHHOTI SADRI**	7813
46	88	**RASHMI**	7808
47	83	**DUNGLA**	7740
48	77	**BEGUN**	7696
49	78	**BHADESAR**	7677
50	159	**BILARA**	7654
51	80	**BHOPALSAGAR**	7516
52	158	**BHOPALGARH**	7445
53	112	**PADAMPUR**	7443
54	36	**KISHANGANJ**	7419
55	32	**ATRU**	7411
56	37	**SHAHBAD**	7383
57	82	**CHITTAURGARH**	7300
58	86	**NIMBAHERA**	7283
59	201	**RAILMAGRA**	7272
60	19	**RENI**	7195
61	200	**KUMBHALGARH**	7114
62	63	**SAHARA**	7072
63	67	**DUNGARGARH**	7031
64	33	**BARAN**	6937
65	228	**BHINDER**	6902
66	109	**ANUPGARH**	6899
67	218	**REODAR**	6866
68	190	**PALI**	6853
69	71	**HINDOLI**	6846
70	17	**RAJGARH**	6795
71	47	**DEEG**	6766
72	10	**BEHROR**	6717
73	31	**ANTA**	6698
74	160	**LUNI**	6696
75	224	**TODARAISINGH**	6680
76	217	**PINDWARA**	6677
77	79	**BHAINSRORGARH**	6671
78	220	**SIROHI**	6664
79	236	**SALUMBAR**	6653
80	210	**FATEHPUR**	6632
81	73	**NAINWA**	6614
82	87	**PRATAPGARH**	6591
83	219	**SHEOGANJ**	6581
84	206	**KHANDAR**	6576
85	194	**SOJAT**	6565
86	14	**LACHHMANGARH**	6500
87	72	**KESHORAIPATAN**	6462
88	11	**KATHUMAR**	6461
89	134	**SANKRA**	6453
90	56	**BANERA**	6439
91	59	KOTRI	6431
92	98	MAHWA	6431
93	223	NIWAI	6427
94	164	SHERGARH	6424
95	96	DAUSA	6414
96	99	SIKRAI	6376
97	74	TALERA	6350
98	204	BONLI	6343
99	75	ARNOD	6340
100	49	KUMHER	6329
101	55	ASIND	6317
102	64	SHAHPURA	6295
103	222	MALPURA	6279
104	235	MAVLI	6255
105	196	AMET	6247
106	65	SUWANA	6223
106	216	ABU ROAD	6223
108	212	LACHHMANGARH	6216
108	225	TONK	6216
110	156	BALESAR	6212
111	221	DEOLI	6175
112	117	HANUMANGARH	6145
113	232	JHADOL	6121
114	20	THANAGAZI	6120
115	61	MANDALGARH	6113
116	162	OSIAN	6103
117	192	RANI STATION	6092
117	193	ROHAT	6092
119	48	KAMAN	6050
120	161	MANDOR	6032
121	149	BUHANA	6004
	MEDIUM (4000-6000)		
122	189	MARWAR JUN.	5998
123	142	BAKANI	5973
124	231	GOGUNDA	5948
125	57	HURDA	5947
125	198	DEOGARH	5947
127	97	LALSOT	5929
128	229	DHARIAWAD	5927
129	203	BAMANWAS	5921
130	60	MANDAL	5914
131	50	NADBAI	5879
132	151	JHUNJHUNUN	5828
133	62	RAIPUR	5814
134	237	SARADA	5812
135	12	KISHANGARH BAS	5778
136	226	UNIARA	5748
137	9	BANSURE	5746
138	54	WEIR	5721
139	46	BAYANA	5715
140	13	KOTKASIM	5699
141	234	KOTRA	5694
142	15	MANDAWAR	5649
143	207	SAWAI MADHOPUR	5624
144	51	NAGAR PAHARI	5610
145	94	TARANAGAR	5606
146	53	SEWAR	5583
147	214	PIPRALI	5582
148	211	KHANDELA	5565
149	197	BHIM	5562
150	135	AHORE	5557
151	230	GIRWA	5549
152	16	NIMRANA	5533
153	154	SURAJGARH	5526
154	58	JAHAZPUR	5517
155	188	JAITARAN	5506
156	205	GANGAPUR	5506
157	146	MANOHARTHANA	5505
158	233	KHERWARA	5504
159	186	BALI	5413
160	22	UMREN	5411
160	167	NADOTI	5411
162	95	BANDIKUI	5373
163	148	ALSISAR	5355
164	202	RAJSAMAND	5353
165	195	SUMERPUR	5350
166	168	SAPOTRA	5347
167	133	SAM	5343
168	209	DHOND	5335
169	90	RAJGARH	5330
170	21	TIJARA	5289
171	191	RAIPUR	5271
172	185	RIYAN	5245
173	187	DESURI	5210
174	18	RAMGARH	5196
175	199	KHAMNOR	5146
176	150	CHIRAWA	5136
177	147	PIRAWA	5092
178	144	JHALRAPATAN	5087
179	52	RUPBAS	5073
180	155	UDAIPURWATI	5059
181	175	DEGANA	5041
182	152	KHETRI	4997
183	166	KARAULI	4992
184	23	ANANDPURI	4977
185	132	JAISALMER	4960
186	91	RATANGARH	4911
187	169	TODABHIM	4886
188	208	DANTA RAMGARH	4867
189	182	MUNDWA	4807
190	24	BAGIDORA	4796
191	183	NAGAUR	4794
192	177	JAYAL	4791
193	89	CHURU	4786
194	184	PARBATSAR	4763
195	93	SUJANGARH	4759
196	29	SAJJANGARH	4746
197	163	PHALODI	4733
198	100	BARI	4709
199	181	MERTA	4707
200	213	NEEM KA THANA	4634
201	92	SARDARSHAHAR	4595
202	153	NAWALGARH	4594
203	101	BASERI	4592
204	165	HINDAUN	4538
205	27	KUSHALGARH	4514
205	179	LADNU	4514
207	28	PEEPALKHOONT	4472
208	25	GARHI	4461
209	143	DAG	4448
210	136	BHINMAL	4437
211	26	GHATOL	4404
212	215	SRI MADHOPUR	4402
213	138	JASWANTPURA	4329
214	180	MAKRANA	4328
215	176	DIDWANA	4311
216	145	KHANPUR	4262
217	137	JALOR	4239
218	103	RAJAKHERA	4216
219	140	SANCHORE	4202
220	102	DHAULPUR	4152
221	30	TALWARA	4101
222	40	BAYTOO	4087
223	41	CHOHTAN	4053
223	178	KUCHAMAN	4053
225	141	SAYLA	4013
	LOW (2000-4000)		
226	139	RANIWARA	3979
227	44	SINDHARI	3927
228	42	DHORIMANNA	3774
229	38	BALOTRA	3719
230	39	BARMER	3559
231	108	SIMALWARA	3419
232	106	DUNGARPUR	3279
233	107	SAGWARA	3253
234	43	SHEO	3182
235	105	BICHHIWARA	3160
236	45	SIWANA	2885
237	104	ASPUR	2882
		RAJASTHAN	**6432**
		%age of AAPs	**38.00**

BOLD: Equal/Above Average Panchayat Samities (AAPs)

Source: Annex 12.1, Col. 4.

ANNEX-13.1

RANKING OF PSS BY GINI (1991-92)

(Descending Order)

RANK	PANCHAYAT SAMITIES P. CODE	NAME	GINI
1	2	3	4
	VERY HIGH (>=0.75)		
1	173	**SANGOD**	**0.8196**
2	121	**CHAKSU**	**0.8113**
3	170	**CHECHAT**	**0.8040**
4	111	**KARANPUR**	**0.7926**
5	171	**ITAWA**	**0.7877**
6	120	**BASSI**	**0.7871**
7	127	**PHAGI**	**0.7861**
8	172	**LADPURA**	**0.7758**
9	119	**AMBER**	**0.7735**
10	116	**BHADRA**	**0.7719**
11	113	**RAISINGHNAGAR**	**0.7705**
12	124	**JAMWA RAMGARH**	**0.7681**
13	122	**DUDU**	**0.7639**
13	174	**SULTANPUR**	**0.7639**
15	118	**NOHAR**	**0.7606**
16	1	**ARAIN**	**0.7555**
16	129	**SANGANER**	**0.7555**
	HIGH (0.70-0.75)		
18	2	**BHINAY**	**0.7479**
19	4	**KEKRI**	**0.7368**
20	130	**SHAHPURA**	**0.7342**
21	126	**KOTPUTLI**	**0.7330**
22	8	**SRINAGAR**	**0.7328**
23	70	**NOKHA**	**0.7313**
24	6	**MASOODA**	**0.7311**
25	7	**PISANGAN**	**0.7290**
26	35	**CHHIPABAROD**	**0.7288**
27	5	**KISHANGARH**	**0.7250**
28	128	**SAMBHAR**	**0.7197**
29	125	**JHOTWARA**	**0.7159**
30	66	**BIKANER**	**0.7123**
31	3	**JAWAJA**	**0.7095**
32	123	**GOVINDGARH**	**0.7072**
33	158	**BHOPALGARH**	**0.7070**
34	109	**ANUPGARH**	**0.7060**
35	68	**KOLAYAT**	**0.7059**
36	85	**KAPASAN**	**0.7058**
37	159	**BILARA**	**0.7053**
38	34	**CHHABRA**	**0.7030**
39	81	**CHHOTI SADRI**	**0.7025**
40	84	**GANGRAR**	**0.7018**
41	76	**BARI SADRI**	**0.7010**
42	78	**BHADESAR**	**0.7007**
	MEDIUM (0.65-0.70)		
43	71	**HINDOLI**	**0.6985**
44	73	**NAINWA**	**0.6984**
45	19	**RENI**	**0.6980**
46	217	**PINDWARA**	**0.6978**
46	131	**VIRATNAGAR**	**0.6976**
48	82	**CHITTAURGARH**	**0.6971**
49	69	**LUNKARANSAR**	**0.6967**
50	83	**DUNGLA**	**0.6961**
51	88	**RASHMI**	**0.6955**
52	77	**BEGUN**	**0.6951**
53	86	**NIMBAHERA**	**0.6934**
54	63	**SAHARA**	**0.6933**
54	228	**BHINDER**	**0.6914**
56	164	**SHERGARH**	**0.6909**
57	194	**SOJAT**	**0.6897**
58	60	**MANDAL**	**0.6888**
59	234	**KOTRA**	**0.6880**
60	232	**JHADOL**	**0.6879**
61	17	**RAJGARH**	**0.6875**
62	80	**BHOPALSAGAR**	**0.6868**
63	115	**SURATGARH**	**0.6862**
64	236	**SALUMBAR**	**0.6857**
65	37	**SHAHBAD**	**0.6853**
66	193	**ROHAT**	**0.6851**
67	55	**ASIND**	**0.6845**
68	160	**LUNI**	**0.6842**
69	188	**JAITARAN**	**0.6835**
70	204	**BONLI**	**0.6822**
71	218	**REODAR**	**0.6820**
71	65	**SUWANA**	**0.6816**
73	56	**BANERA**	**0.6814**
74	64	**SHAHPURA**	**0.6811**
75	75	**ARNOD**	**0.6809**
75	59	**KOTRI**	**0.6807**
77	87	**PRATAPGARH**	**0.6805**
78	61	**MANDALGARH**	**0.6800**
79	224	**TODARAISINGH**	**0.6798**
79	79	**BHAINSRORGARH**	**0.6785**
79	10	**BEHROR**	**0.6762**
79	229	**DHARIAWAD**	**0.6761**
83	47	**DEEG**	**0.6759**
83	14	**LACHHMANGARH**	**0.6741**
85	223	**NIWAI**	**0.6737**
86	36	**KISHANGANJ**	**0.6735**
87	227	**BARGAON**	**0.6726**
87	191	**RAIPUR**	**0.6724**
89	221	**DEOLI**	**0.6717**
90	163	**PHALODI**	**0.6700**
91	117	**HANUMANGARH**	**0.6698**
91	156	**BALESAR**	**0.6698**
93	146	**MANOHARTHANA**	**0.6697**
94	134	**SANKRA**	**0.6696**
95	190	**PALI**	**0.6696**
96	57	**HURDA**	**0.6694**
97	72	**KESHORAIPATAN**	**0.6686**
98	110	**GANGANAGAR**	**0.6682**
99	11	KATHUMAR	0.6678
100	48	KAMAN	0.6666
101	225	TONK	0.6660
102	189	KHARCHI	0.6658
103	200	KUMBHALGARH	0.6651
103	233	KHERWARA	0.6651
105	161	MANDOR	0.6648
106	142	BAKANI	0.6646
107	206	KHANDAR	0.6642
108	235	MAVLI	0.6637
109	216	ABU ROAD	0.6635
110	21	TIJARA	0.6634
111	33	BARAN	0.6633
112	32	ATRU	0.6629
113	162	OSIAN	0.6628
113	20	THANAGAZI	0.6626
115	231	GOGUNDA	0.6625
116	201	RAILMAGRA	0.6614
116	222	MALPURA	0.6614
118	74	TALERA	0.6611
119	203	BAMANWAS	0.6606
120	237	SARADA	0.6592
121	197	BHIM	0.6589
122	58	JAHAZPUR	0.6588
122	226	UNIARA	0.6588
124	207	SAWAI MADHOPUR	0.6587
125	114	SADULSHAHAR	0.6576
126	135	AHORE	0.6573
127	67	DUNGARGARH	0.6569
128	199	KHAMNOR	0.6568
129	94	TARANAGAR	0.6547
129	230	GIRWA	0.6527
131	147	PIRAWA	0.6525
132	210	FATEHPUR	0.6510
133	99	SIKRAI	0.6500
133	219	SHEOGANJ	0.6500
	LOW (0.60-0.65)		
135	157	BAP	0.6499
136	167	NADOTI	0.6489
137	185	RIYAN	0.6488
138	62	RAIPUR	0.6486
139	96	DAUSA	0.6483
139	192	RANI STATION	0.6483
139	220	SIROHI	0.6483
142	9	BANSURE	0.6479
143	49	KUMHER	0.6473
144	168	SAPOTRA	0.6451
145	90	RAJGARH	0.6449
146	22	UMREN	0.6425
147	112	PADAMPUR	0.6422
147	196	AMET	0.6422
149	186	BALI	0.6407
150	182	MUNDWA	0.6405
151	23	ANANDPURI	0.6404
151	144	JHALRAPATAN	0.6402
153	166	KARAULI	0.6400
154	50	NADBAI	0.6375
155	13	KOTKASIM	0.6367
155	175	DEGANA	0.6367
157	198	DEOGARH	0.6357
158	212	LACHHMANGARH	0.6353
159	24	BAGIDORA	0.6352
159	205	GANGAPUR	0.6352
161	12	KISHANGARH BAS	0.6341
161	29	SAJJANGARH	0.6341
163	98	MAHWA	0.6338
164	184	PARBATSAR	0.6334
165	27	KUSHALGARH	0.6330
166	177	JAYAL	0.6329
167	169	TODABHIM	0.6319
168	28	PEEPALKHOONT	0.6296
168	93	SUJANGARH	0.6293
170	91	RATANGARH	0.6291
171	97	LALSOT	0.6290
172	54	WEIR	0.6289
173	51	NAGAR PAHARI	0.6276
174	181	MERTA	0.6272
175	15	MANDAWAR	0.6264
176	31	ANTA	0.6262
176	95	BANDIKUI	0.6262
178	187	DESURI	0.6248
179	195	SUMERPUR	0.6244
180	18	RAMGARH	0.6233
181	179	LADNU	0.6228
182	16	NIMRANA	0.6210
183	89	CHURU	0.6206
184	165	HINDAUN	0.6198
184	183	NAGAUR	0.6198
186	136	BHINMAL	0.6153
186	26	GHATOL	0.6148
188	140	SANCHORE	0.6130
189	53	SEWAR	0.6125
189	202	RAJSAMAND	0.6122
189	46	BAYANA	0.6116
192	92	SARDARSHAHAR	0.6096
193	25	GARHI	0.6092
194	145	KHANPUR	0.6074
195	176	DIDWANA	0.6070
196	138	JASWANTPURA	0.6043
197	180	MAKRANA	0.6017
198	40	BAYTOO	0.6016
199	149	BUHANA	0.6008
	VERY LOW (<0.60)		
200	211	KHANDELA	0.5970
201	30	TALWARA	0.5963
201	139	RANIWARA	0.5957
203	137	JALOR	0.5938
204	44	SINDHARI	0.5931
205	151	JHUNJHUNUN	0.5900
206	178	KUCHAMAN	0.5898
207	141	SAYLA	0.5890
208	214	PIPRALI	0.5864
209	154	SURAJGARH	0.5855
210	148	ALSISAR	0.5851
210	209	DHOND	0.5851
212	42	DHORIMANNA	0.5849
213	133	SAM	0.5833
214	41	CHOHTAN	0.5808
215	38	BALOTRA	0.5795
216	132	JAISALMER	0.5792
217	108	SIMALWARA	0.5767
218	39	BARMER	0.5732
219	106	DUNGARPUR	0.5700
220	155	UDAIPURWATI	0.5647
221	105	BICHHIWARA	0.5640
222	208	DANTA RAMGARH	0.5605
223	52	RUPBAS	0.5565
224	101	BASERI	0.5531
225	107	SAGWARA	0.5500
226	143	DAG	0.5498
227	45	SIWANA	0.5482
228	150	CHIRAWA	0.5480
229	43	SHEO	0.5451
230	152	KHETRI	0.5418
231	213	NEEM KA THANA	0.5369
232	215	SRI MADHOPUR	0.5279
233	100	BARI	0.5261
234	104	ASPUR	0.5246
235	153	NAWALGARH	0.5166
236	102	DHAULPUR	0.3662
237	103	RAJAKHERA	0.2323
	RAJASTHAN		**0.6680**
	%age of AAPs		**41.35**

BOLD: Equal/Above Average Panchayat Samities (AAPs)

Source: Annex-14.1, Col. 4.

ANNEX-14.1

PANCHAYAT SAMITI-WISE CHANGED PATTERN OF GINI: RAJASTHAN (1991-98)

P. Code	*Panchayat Samities*	*1991-92*		*1998-99*		*Difference (1991-98)*		*% Increase in GINI*	*Remarks*
		Rank	*Value*	*Rank*	*Value*	*Rank*	*Value*		
1	2	3	4	5	6	7	8	9	10
1	ARAIN	16	0.7555	15	0.8428	1	0.0873	11.6	A
2	BHINAY	18	0.7479	19	0.8380	-1	0.0901	12.0	B
3	JAWAJA	31	0.7095	39	0.7856	-8	0.0761	10.7	B
4	KEKRI	19	0.7368	22	0.8273	-3	0.0905	12.3	B
5	KISHANGARH	27	0.7250	26	0.8078	1	0.0828	11.4	A
6	MASOODA	24	0.7311	24	0.8187	0	0.0876	12.0	C
7	PISANGAN	25	0.7290	33	0.7925	-8	0.0635	8.7	B
8	SRINAGAR	22	0.7328	41	0.7830	-19	0.0502	6.9	B
	AJMER DISTRICT		**0.7336**		**0.8125**		**0.0789**	**10.8**	
9	BANSURE	142	0.6479	132	0.7236	10	0.0757	11.7	A
10	BEHROR	79	0.6762	64	0.7551	15	0.0789	11.7	A
11	KATHUMAR	99	0.6678	75	0.7493	24	0.0815	12.2	A
12	KISHANGARH BAS	161	0.6341	125	0.7257	36	0.0916	14.4	A
13	KOTKASIM	155	0.6367	128	0.7245	27	0.0878	13.8	A
14	LACHHMANGARH	83	0.6741	76	0.7491	7	0.0750	11.1	A
15	MANDAWAR	175	0.6264	131	0.7237	44	0.0973	15.5	A
16	NIMRANA	182	0.6210	140	0.7195	42	0.0985	15.9	A
17	RAJGARH	61	0.6875	65	0.7539	-4	0.0664	9.7	B
18	RAMGARH	180	0.6233	163	0.7055	17	0.0822	13.2	A
19	RENI	45	0.6980	55	0.7646	-10	0.0666	9.5	B
20	THANAGAZI	113	0.6626	100	0.7370	13	0.0744	11.2	A
21	TIJARA	110	0.6634	159	0.7104	-49	0.0470	7.1	B
22	UMREN	146	0.6425	148	0.7150	-2	0.0725	11.3	B
	ALWAR		**0.6558**		**0.7322**		**0.0764**	**11.6**	
23	ANANDPURI	151	0.6404	165	0.7013	-14	0.0609	9.5	B
24	BAGIDORA	159	0.6352	180	0.6942	-21	0.0590	9.3	B
25	GARHI	193	0.6092	213	0.6673	-20	0.0581	9.5	B
26	GHATOL	186	0.6148	202	0.6782	-16	0.0634	10.3	B
27	KUSHALGARH	165	0.6330	195	0.6836	-30	0.0506	8.0	B
28	PEEPALKHOONT	168	0.6296	199	0.6807	-31	0.0511	8.1	B
29	SAJJANGARH	161	0.6341	182	0.6933	-21	0.0592	9.3	B
30	TALWARA	201	0.5963	215	0.6644	-14	0.0681	11.4	B
	BANSWARA		**0.6217**		**0.6817**		**0.0600**	**9.7**	
31	ANTA	176	0.6262	79	0.7473	97	0.1211	19.3	A
32	ATRU	112	0.6629	57	0.7627	55	0.0998	15.1	A
33	BARAN	111	0.6633	74	0.7499	37	0.0866	13.1	A
34	CHHABRA	38	0.7030	32	0.7930	6	0.0900	12.8	A
35	CHHIPABAROD	26	0.7288	28	0.8072	-2	0.0784	10.8	B
36	KISHANGANJ	86	0.6735	52	0.7668	34	0.0933	13.9	A
37	SHAHBAD	65	0.6853	53	0.7667	12	0.0814	11.9	A
	BARAN		**0.6794**		**0.7710**		**0.0916**	**13.5**	
38	BALOTRA	215	0.5795	228	0.6438	-13	0.0643	11.1	B
39	BARMER	218	0.5732	230	0.6360	-12	0.0628	11.0	B
40	BAYTOO	198	0.6016	214	0.6654	-16	0.0638	10.6	B
41	CHOHTAN	214	0.5808	218	0.6615	-4	0.0807	13.9	B
42	DHORIMANNA	212	0.5849	226	0.6501	-14	0.0652	11.1	B
43	SHEO	229	0.5451	235	0.6132	-6	0.0681	12.5	B
44	SINDHARI	204	0.5931	224	0.6570	-20	0.0639	10.8	B
45	SIWANA	227	0.5482	237	0.5875	-10	0.0393	7.2	B
	BARMER		**0.5787**		**0.6420**		**0.0633**	**10.9**	
46	BAYANA	189	0.6116	142	0.7186	47	0.1070	17.5	A
47	DEEG	83	0.6759	60	0.7571	23	0.0812	12.0	A
48	KAMAN	100	0.6666	102	0.7356	-2	0.0690	10.4	B
49	KUMHER	143	0.6473	111	0.7307	32	0.0834	12.9	A
50	NADBAI	154	0.6375	119	0.7289	35	0.0914	14.3	A
51	NAGAR PAHARI	173	0.6276	137	0.7203	36	0.0927	14.8	A
52	RUPBAS	223	0.5565	176	0.6961	47	0.1396	25.1	A
53	SEWAR	189	0.6125	191	0.6886	-2	0.0761	12.4	B
54	WEIR	172	0.6289	123	0.7266	49	0.0977	15.5	A
	BHARATPUR		**0.6329**		**0.7236**		**0.0907**	**14.3**	
55	ASIND	67	0.6845	88	0.7427	-21	0.0582	8.5	B
56	BANERA	73	0.6814	89	0.7421	-16	0.0607	8.9	B
57	HURDA	96	0.6694	136	0.7206	-40	0.0512	7.6	B
58	JAHAZPUR	122	0.6588	154	0.7139	-32	0.0551	8.4	B
59	KOTRI	75	0.6807	93	0.7398	-18	0.0591	8.7	B
60	MANDAL	58	0.6888	130	0.7240	-72	0.0352	5.1	B

P. Code	*Panchayat Samities*	*1991-92*		*1998-99*		*Difference (1991-98)*		*% Increase in GINI*	*Remarks*
		Rank	*Value*	*Rank*	*Value*	*Rank*	*Value*		
1	2	3	4	5	6	7	8	9	10
61	MANDALGARH	78	0.6800	107	0.7329	-29	0.0529	7.8	B
62	RAIPUR	138	0.6486	152	0.7142	-14	0.0656	10.1	B
63	SAHARA	54	0.6933	58	0.7608	-4	0.0675	9.7	B
64	SHAHPURA	74	0.6811	96	0.7387	-22	0.0576	8.5	B
65	SUWANA	71	0.6816	97	0.7385	-26	0.0569	8.3	B
	BHILWARA		**0.6788**		**0.7341**		**0.0553**	**8.1**	
66	BIKANER	30	0.7123	36	0.7899	-6	0.0776	10.9	B
67	DUNGARGARH *	127	0.6569	54	0.7652	73	0.1083	16.5	A
68	KOLAYAT	35	0.7059	34	0.7905	1	0.0846	12.0	A
69	LUNKARANSAR	49	0.6967	25	0.8156	24	0.1189	17.1	A
70	NOKHA	23	0.7313	14	0.8429	9	0.1116	15.3	A
	BIKANER **		**0.7144**		**0.8102**		**0.0958**	**13.4**	
71	HINDOLI	43	0.6985	59	0.7576	-16	0.0591	8.5	B
72	KESHORAIPATAN	97	0.6686	91	0.7409	6	0.0723	10.8	A
73	NAINWA	44	0.6984	73	0.7501	-29	0.0517	7.4	B
74	TALERA	118	0.6611	99	0.7379	19	0.0768	11.6	A
	BUNDI		**0.6803**		**0.7470**		**0.0667**	**9.8**	
75	ARNOD	75	0.6809	82	0.7448	-7	0.0639	9.4	B
76	BARI SADRI	41	0.7010	40	0.7847	1	0.0837	11.9	A
77	BEGUN	52	0.6951	45	0.7793	7	0.0842	12.1	A
78	BHADESAR	42	0.7007	46	0.7780	-4	0.0773	11.0	B
79	BHAINSRORGARH	79	0.6785	77	0.7490	2	0.0705	10.4	A
80	BHOPALSAGAR	62	0.6868	50	0.7718	12	0.0850	12.4	A
81	CHHOTI SADRI	39	0.7025	42	0.7829	-3	0.0804	11.4	B
82	CHITTAURGARH	48	0.6971	56	0.7636	-8	0.0665	9.5	B
83	DUNGLA	50	0.6961	43	0.7813	7	0.0852	12.2	A
84	GANGRAR	40	0.7018	47	0.7771	-7	0.0753	10.7	B
85	KAPASAN	36	0.7058	35	0.7903	1	0.0845	12.0	A
86	NIMBAHERA	53	0.6934	51	0.7692	2	0.0758	10.9	A
87	PRATAPGARH	77	0.6805	67	0.7523	10	0.0718	10.6	A
88	RASHMI	51	0.6955	44	0.7810	7	0.0855	12.3	A
	CHITTAURGARH		**0.6937**		**0.7704**		**0.0767**	**11.1**	
89	CHURU	183	0.6206	184	0.6928	-1	0.0722	11.6	B
90	RAJGARH	145	0.6449	149	0.7149	-4	0.0700	10.9	B
91	RATANGARH	170	0.6291	174	0.6977	-4	0.0686	10.9	B
92	SARDARSHAHAR	192	0.6096	193	0.6869	-1	0.0773	12.7	B
93	SUJANGARH	168	0.6293	187	0.6907	-19	0.0614	9.8	B
94	TARANAGAR	129	0.6547	134	0.7214	-5	0.0667	10.2	B
	CHURU ***		**0.6355**		**0.7082**		**0.0727**	**11.4**	
95	BANDIKUI	176	0.6262	157	0.7129	19	0.0867	13.8	A
96	DAUSA	139	0.6483	83	0.7447	56	0.0964	14.9	A
97	LALSOT	171	0.6290	114	0.7302	57	0.1012	16.1	A
98	MAHWA	163	0.6338	110	0.7316	53	0.0978	15.4	A
99	SIKRAI	133	0.6500	87	0.7433	46	0.0933	14.4	A
	DAUSA		**0.6379**		**0.7335**		**0.0956**	**15.0**	
100	BARI	233	0.5261	190	0.6899	43	0.1638	31.1	A
101	BASERI	224	0.5531	203	0.6776	21	0.1245	22.5	A
102	DHAULPUR	236	0.3662	223	0.6574	13	0.2912	79.5	A
103	RAJAKHERA	237	0.2323	221	0.6595	16	0.4272	183.9	A
	DHAULPUR		**0.4605**		**0.6674**		**0.2069**	**44.9**	C
104	ASPUR	234	0.5246	236	0.5969	-2	0.0723	13.8	B
105	BICHHIWARA	221	0.5640	234	0.6168	-13	0.0528	9.4	B
106	DUNGARPUR	219	0.5700	232	0.6227	-13	0.0527	9.2	B
107	SAGWARA	225	0.5500	233	0.6202	-8	0.0702	12.8	B
108	SIMALWARA	217	0.5767	231	0.6334	-14	0.0567	9.8	B
	DUNGARPUR		**0.5590**		**0.6189**		**0.0599**	**10.7**	
109	ANUPGARH	34	0.7060	103	0.7352	-69	0.0292	4.1	B
110	GANGANAGAR	98	0.6682	70	0.7510	28	0.0828	12.4	A
111	KARANPUR	4	0.7926	17	0.8403	-13	0.0477	6.0	B
112	PADAMPUR	147	0.6422	105	0.7349	42	0.0927	14.4	A
113	RAISINGHNAGAR	11	0.7705	37	0.7898	-26	0.0193	2.5	B
114	SADULSHAHAR	125	0.6576	7	0.8635	118	0.2059	31.3	A
115	SURATGARH	63	0.6862	17	0.8403	46	0.1541	22.5	A
	GANGANAGAR		**0.7060**		**0.7902**	**0**	**0.0842**	**11.9**	
116	BHADRA	10	0.7719	8	0.8532	2	0.0813	10.5	A
117	HANUMANGARH	91	0.6698	173	0.6989	-82	0.0291	4.3	B
118	NOHAR	15	0.7606	20	0.8342	-5	0.0736	9.7	B
	HANUMANGARH		**0.7366**		**0.7855**		**0.0489**	**6.6**	C
119	AMBER	9	0.7735	13	0.8443	-4	0.0708	9.2	B
120	BASSI	6	0.7871	16	0.8416	-10	0.0545	6.9	B
121	CHAKSU	2	0.8113	3	0.8874	-1	0.0761	9.4	B
122	DUDU	13	0.7639	10	0.8500	3	0.0861	11.3	A
123	GOVINDGARH	32	0.7072	31	0.7983	1	0.0911	12.9	A
124	JAMWA RAMGARH	12	0.7681	9	0.8520	3	0.0839	10.9	A
125	JHOTWARA	29	0.7159	2	0.8875	27	0.1716	24.0	A

P. Code	Panchayat Samities	1991-92		1998-99		Difference (1991-98)		% Increase in GINI	Remarks
		Rank	Value	Rank	Value	Rank	Value		
1	2	3	4	5	6	7	8	9	10
126	KOTPUTLI	21	0.7330	21	0.8281	0	0.0951	13.0	C
127	PHAGI	7	0.7861	6	0.8712	1	0.0851	10.8	A
128	SAMBHAR	28	0.7197	29	0.8043	-1	0.0846	11.8	B
129	SANGANER	16	0.7555	1	0.9081	15	0.1526	20.2	A
130	SHAHPURA	20	0.7342	30	0.8029	-10	0.0687	9.4	B
131	VIRATNAGAR	46	0.6976	27	0.8077	19	0.1101	15.8	A
	JAIPUR		**0.7540**		**0.8426**		**0.0886**	**11.8**	
132	JAISALMER	216	0.5792	216	0.6626	0	0.0834	14.4	C
133	SAM	213	0.5833	200	0.6802	13	0.0969	16.6	A
134	SANKRA	94	0.6696	92	0.7399	2	0.0703	10.5	A
	JAISALMER		**0.6273**		**0.7073**		**0.0800**	**12.8**	
135	AHORE	126	0.6573	144	0.7167	-18	0.0594	9.0	B
136	BHINMAL	186	0.6153	198	0.6818	-12	0.0665	10.8	B
137	JALOR	203	0.5938	227	0.6481	-24	0.0543	9.1	B
138	JASWANTPURA	196	0.6043	211	0.6688	-15	0.0645	10.7	B
139	RANIWARA	201	0.5957	220	0.6601	-19	0.0644	10.8	B
140	SANCHORE	188	0.6130	208	0.6712	-20	0.0582	9.5	B
141	SAYLA	207	0.5890	218	0.6615	-11	0.0725	12.3	B
	JALOR		**0.6127**		**0.6751**		**0.0624**	**10.2**	
142	BAKANI	106	0.6646	117	0.7295	-11	0.0649	9.8	B
143	DAG	226	0.5498	222	0.6587	4	0.1089	19.8	A
144	JHALRAPATAN	151	0.6402	170	0.7004	-19	0.0602	9.4	B
145	KHANPUR	194	0.6074	212	0.6674	-18	0.0600	9.9	B
146	MANOHARTHANA	93	0.6697	135	0.7210	-42	0.0513	7.7	B
147	PIRAWA	131	0.6525	166	0.7011	-35	0.0486	7.4	B
	JHALAWAR		**0.6373**		**0.6982**		**0.0609**	**9.6**	
148	ALSISAR	210	0.5851	162	0.7057	48	0.1206	20.6	A
149	BUHANA	199	0.6008	106	0.7338	93	0.1330	22.1	A
150	CHIRAWA	228	0.5480	171	0.6998	57	0.1518	27.7	A
151	JHUNJHUNUN	205	0.5900	133	0.7216	72	0.1316	22.3	A
152	KHETRI	230	0.5418	172	0.6991	58	0.1573	29.0	A
153	NAWALGARH	235	0.5166	201	0.6786	34	0.1620	31.4	A
154	SURAJGARH	209	0.5855	151	0.7145	58	0.1290	22.0	A
155	UDAIPURWATI	220	0.5647	175	0.6964	45	0.1317	23.3	A
	JHUNJHUNUN		**0.5690**		**0.7065**		**0.1375**	**24.2**	
156	BALESAR	91	0.6698	126	0.7255	-35	0.0557	8.3	B
157	BAP	135	0.6499	38	0.7879	97	0.1380	21.2	A
158	BHOPALGARH	33	0.7070	49	0.7730	-16	0.0660	9.3	B
159	BILARA	37	0.7053	48	0.7754	-11	0.0701	9.9	B
160	LUNI	68	0.6842	84	0.7446	-16	0.0604	8.8	B
161	MANDOR	105	0.6648	139	0.7197	-34	0.0549	8.3	B
162	OSIAN	113	0.6628	107	0.7329	6	0.0701	10.6	A
163	PHALODI	90	0.6700	204	0.6773	-114	0.0073	1.1	B
164	SHERGARH	56	0.6909	109	0.7318	-53	0.0409	5.9	B
	JODHPUR		**0.6792**		**0.7390**		**0.0598**	**8.8**	
165	HINDAUN	184	0.6198	194	0.6840	-10	0.0642	10.4	B
166	KARAULI	153	0.6400	185	0.6918	-32	0.0518	8.1	B
167	NADOTI	136	0.6489	155	0.7137	-19	0.0648	10.0	B
168	SAPOTRA	144	0.6451	160	0.7079	-16	0.0628	9.7	B
169	TODABHIM	167	0.6319	177	0.6959	-10	0.0640	10.1	B
	KARAULI		**0.6365**		**0.6974**		**0.0609**	**9.6**	
170	CHECHAT	3	0.8040	4	0.8872	-1	0.0832	10.3	B
171	ITAWA	5	0.7877	11	0.8466	-6	0.0589	7.5	B
172	LADPURA	8	0.7758	23	0.8267	-15	0.0509	6.6	D
173	SANGOD	1	0.8196	5	0.8842	-4	0.0646	7.9	B
174	SULTANPUR	13	0.7639	12	0.8453	1	0.0814	10.7	A
	KOTA		**0.7923**		**0.8594**		**0.0671**	**8.5**	
175	DEGANA	155	0.6367	167	0.7010	-12	0.0643	10.1	B
176	DIDWANA	195	0.6070	217	0.6618	-22	0.0548	9.0	B
177	JAYAL	166	0.6329	179	0.6945	-13	0.0616	9.7	B
178	KUCHAMAN	206	0.5898	229	0.6420	-23	0.0522	8.9	B
179	LADNU	181	0.6228	205	0.6771	-24	0.0543	8.7	B
180	MAKRANA	197	0.6017	225	0.6525	-28	0.0508	8.4	B
181	MERTA	174	0.6272	197	0.6819	-23	0.0547	8.7	B
182	MUNDWA	150	0.6405	181	0.6935	-31	0.0530	8.3	B
183	NAGAUR	184	0.6198	183	0.6931	1	0.0733	11.8	A
184	PARBATSAR	164	0.6334	210	0.6697	-46	0.0363	5.7	B
185	RIYAN	137	0.6488	168	0.7008	-31	0.0520	8.0	B
	NAGAUR		**0.6231**		**0.6809**		**0.0578**	**9.3**	
186	BALI	149	0.6407	164	0.7015	-15	0.0608	9.5	B
187	DESURI	178	0.6248	178	0.6953	0	0.0705	11.3	C
188	JAITARAN	69	0.6835	147	0.7158	-78	0.0323	4.7	B
189	KHARCHI/MARWAR JUN.	102	0.6658	124	0.7258	-22	0.0600	9.0	B
190	PALI	95	0.6696	72	0.7502	23	0.0806	12.0	A
191	RAIPUR	87	0.6724	169	0.7007	-82	0.0283	4.2	B
192	RANI STATION	139	0.6483	128	0.7245	11	0.0762	11.8	A

P. Code	Panchayat Samities	1991-92		1998-99		Difference (1991-98)		% Increase in GINI	Remarks
		Rank	Value	Rank	Value	Rank	Value		
1	2	3	4	5	6	7	8	9	10
1193	ROHAT	66	0.6851	112	0.7304	-46	0.0453	6.6	B
194	SOJAT	57	0.6897	81	0.7456	-24	0.0559	8.1	B
195	SUMERPUR	179	0.6244	186	0.6912	-7	0.0668	10.7	B
	PALI		**0.6634**		**0.7175**		**0.0541**	**8.2**	
196	AMET	147	0.6422	189	0.6903	-42	0.0481	7.5	B
197	BHIM	121	0.6589	145	0.7163	-24	0.0574	8.7	B
198	DEOGARH	157	0.6357	115	0.7299	42	0.0942	14.8	A
199	KHAMNOR	128	0.6568	196	0.6822	-68	0.0254	3.9	B
200	KUMBHALGARH	103	0.6651	61	0.7568	42	0.0917	13.8	A
201	RAILMAGRA	116	0.6614	66	0.7527	50	0.0913	13.8	A
202	RAJSAMAND	189	0.6122	206	0.6768	-17	0.0646	10.6	B
	RAJSAMAND		**0.6507**		**0.7179**		**0.0672**	**10.3**	
203	BAMANWAS	119	0.6606	118	0.7291	1	0.0685	10.4	A
204	BONLI	70	0.6822	85	0.7443	-15	0.0621	9.1	B
205	GANGAPUR	159	0.6352	152	0.7142	7	0.0790	12.4	A
206	KHANDAR	107	0.6642	71	0.7505	36	0.0863	13.0	A
207	SAWAI MADHOPUR	124	0.6587	138	0.7198	-14	0.0611	9.3	B
	SAWAI MADHOPUR		**0.6617**		**0.7301**		**0.0684**	**10.3**	
208	DANTA RAMGARH	222	0.5605	192	0.6874	30	0.1269	22.6	A
209	DHOND	210	0.5851	161	0.7075	49	0.1224	20.9	A
210	FATEHPUR	132	0.6510	62	0.7561	70	0.1051	16.1	A
211	KHANDELA	200	0.5970	156	0.7132	44	0.1162	19.5	A
212	LACHHMANGARH	158	0.6353	90	0.7420	68	0.1067	16.8	A
213	NEEM KA THANA	231	0.5369	207	0.6748	24	0.1379	25.7	A
214	PIPRALI	208	0.5864	146	0.7161	62	0.1297	22.1	A
215	SRI MADHOPUR	232	0.5279	209	0.6698	23	0.1419	26.9	A
	SIKAR		**0.5885**		**0.7080**		**0.1195**	**20.3**	
216	ABU ROAD	109	0.6635	120	0.7284	-11	0.0649	9.8	B
217	PINDWARA	46	0.6978	86	0.7441	-40	0.0463	6.6	B
218	REODAR	71	0.6820	69	0.7517	2	0.0697	10.2	A
219	SHEOGANJ	133	0.6500	122	0.7268	11	0.0768	11.8	A
220	SIROHI	139	0.6483	97	0.7385	42	0.0902	13.9	A
	SIROHI		**0.6726**		**0.7407**		**0.0681**	**10.1**	
221	DEOLI	89	0.6717	101	0.7361	-12	0.0644	9.6	B
222	MALPURA	116	0.6614	103	0.7352	13	0.0738	11.2	A
223	NIWAI	85	0.6737	78	0.7474	7	0.0737	10.9	A
224	TODARAISINGH	79	0.6798	68	0.7521	11	0.0723	10.6	A
225	TONK	101	0.6660	93	0.7398	8	0.0738	11.1	A
226	UNIARA	122	0.6588	121	0.7271	1	0.0683	10.4	A
	TONK		**0.6682**		**0.7399**		**0.0717**	**10.7**	
227	BARGAON	87	0.6726	63	0.7557	24	0.0831	12.4	A
228	BHINDER	54	0.6914	95	0.7393	-41	0.0479	6.9	B
229	DHARIAWAD	79	0.6761	113	0.7303	-34	0.0542	8.0	B
230	GIRWA	129	0.6527	188	0.6906	-59	0.0379	5.8	B
231	GOGUNDA	115	0.6625	127	0.7249	-12	0.0624	9.4	B
232	JHADOL	60	0.6879	116	0.7298	-56	0.0419	6.1	B
233	KHERWARA	103	0.6651	150	0.7148	-47	0.0497	7.5	B
234	KOTRA	59	0.6880	141	0.7193	-82	0.0313	4.5	B
235	MAVLI	108	0.6637	143	0.7169	-35	0.0532	8.0	B
236	SALUMBAR	64	0.6857	80	0.7469	-16	0.0612	8.9	B
237	SARADA	120	0.6592	158	0.7117	-38	0.0525	8.0	B
	UDAIPUR		**0.6734**		**0.7263**		**0.0529**	**7.9**	
	RAJASTHAN		**0.6680**		**0.7390**		**0.0710**	**10.6**	

Note: * Dungargarh PS shifted from Churu to Bikaner district on 1st April 2001
** Excluding data of Dungargarh PS; *** Including data of Dungargarh PS.

Source: Hemlata Joshi. 2005. *'Economic Development Index, Rajasthan* (Spatio-Temporal & Gender Appraisal at Panchayat Samiti / Block Level), Published Research Report, IDSJ, University Book House, Jaipur.

ANNEX-14.2

RANKING OF PANCHAYAT SAMITIES BY GINI, 1998-99

(Descending Order)

RANK	PANCHAYAT SAMITIES P. CODE	NAME	GINI
1	2	3	4
	VERY HIGH (>=0.75)		
1	**129**	**SANGANER**	**0.9081**
2	**125**	**JHOTWARA**	**0.8875**
3	**121**	**CHAKSU**	**0.8874**
4	**170**	**CHECHAT**	**0.8872**
5	**173**	**SANGOD**	**0.8842**
6	**127**	**PHAGI**	**0.8712**
7	**114**	**SADULSHAHAR**	**0.8635**
8	**116**	**BHADRA**	**0.8532**
9	**124**	**JAMWA RAMGARH**	**0.8520**
10	**122**	**DUDU**	**0.8500**
11	**171**	**ITAWA**	**0.8466**
12	**174**	**SULTANPUR**	**0.8453**
13	**119**	**AMBER**	**0.8443**
14	**70**	**NOKHA**	**0.8429**
15	**1**	**ARAIN**	**0.8428**
16	**120**	**BASSI**	**0.8416**
17	**111**	**KARANPUR**	**0.8403**
17	**115**	**SURATGARH**	**0.8403**
19	**2**	**BHINAY**	**0.8380**
20	**118**	**NOHAR**	**0.8342**
21	**126**	**KOTPUTLI**	**0.8281**
22	**4**	**KEKRI**	**0.8273**
23	**172**	**LADPURA**	**0.8267**
24	**6**	**MASOODA**	**0.8187**
25	**69**	**LUNKARANSAR**	**0.8156**
26	**5**	**KISHANGARH**	**0.8078**
27	**131**	**VIRATNAGAR**	**0.8077**
28	**35**	**CHHIPABAROD**	**0.8072**
29	**128**	**SAMBHAR**	**0.8043**
30	**130**	**SHAHPURA**	**0.8029**
31	**123**	**GOVINDGARH**	**0.7983**
32	**34**	**CHHABRA**	**0.7930**
33	**7**	**PISANGAN**	**0.7925**
34	**68**	**KOLAYAT**	**0.7905**
35	**85**	**KAPASAN**	**0.7903**
36	**66**	**BIKANER**	**0.7899**
37	**113**	**RAISINGHNAGAR**	**0.7898**
38	**157**	**BAP**	**0.7879**
39	**3**	**JAWAJA**	**0.7856**
40	**76**	**BARI SADRI**	**0.7847**
41	**8**	**SRINAGAR**	**0.7830**
42	**81**	**CHHOTI SADRI**	**0.7829**
43	**83**	**DUNGLA**	**0.7813**
44	**88**	**RASHMI**	**0.7810**
45	**77**	**BEGUN**	**0.7793**
46	**78**	**BHADESAR**	**0.7780**
47	**84**	**GANGRAR**	**0.7771**
48	**159**	**BILARA**	**0.7754**
49	**158**	**BHOPALGARH**	**0.7730**
50	**80**	**BHOPALSAGAR**	**0.7718**
51	**86**	**NIMBAHERA**	**0.7692**
52	**36**	**KISHANGANJ**	**0.7668**
53	**37**	**SHAHBAD**	**0.7667**
54	**67**	**DUNGARGARH**	**0.7652**
55	**19**	**RENI**	**0.7646**
56	**82**	**CHITTAURGARH**	**0.7636**
57	**32**	**ATRU**	**0.7627**
58	**63**	**SAHARA**	**0.7608**
59	**71**	**HINDOLI**	**0.7576**
60	**47**	**DEEG**	**0.7571**
61	**200**	**KUMBHALGARH**	**0.7568**
62	**210**	**FATEHPUR**	**0.7561**
63	**227**	**BARGAON**	**0.7557**
64	**10**	**BEHROR**	**0.7551**
65	**17**	**RAJGARH**	**0.7539**
66	**201**	**RAILMAGRA**	**0.7527**
67	**87**	**PRATAPGARH**	**0.7523**
68	**224**	**TODARAISINGH**	**0.7521**
69	**218**	**REODAR**	**0.7517**
70	**110**	**GANGANAGAR**	**0.7510**
71	**206**	**KHANDAR**	**0.7505**
72	**190**	**PALI**	**0.7502**
73	**73**	**NAINWA**	**0.7501**
	HIGH (0.70-0.75)		
74	**33**	**BARAN**	**0.7499**
75	**11**	**KATHUMAR**	**0.7493**
76	**14**	**LACHHMANGARH**	**0.7491**
77	**79**	**BHAINSRORGARH**	**0.7490**
78	**223**	**NIWAI**	**0.7474**
79	**31**	**ANTA**	**0.7473**
80	**236**	**SALUMBAR**	**0.7469**
81	**194**	**SOJAT**	**0.7456**
82	**75**	**ARNOD**	**0.7448**
83	**96**	**DAUSA**	**0.7447**
84	**160**	**LUNI**	**0.7446**
85	**204**	**BONLI**	**0.7443**
86	**217**	**PINDWARA**	**0.7441**
87	**99**	**SIKRAI**	**0.7433**
88	**55**	**ASIND**	**0.7427**
89	**56**	**BANERA**	**0.7421**
90	**212**	**LACHHMANGARH**	**0.7420**
91	**72**	**KESHORAIPATAN**	**0.7409**
92	**134**	**SANKRA**	**0.7399**
93	**59**	**KOTRI**	**0.7398**
93	**225**	**TONK**	**0.7398**
95	**228**	**BHINDER**	**0.7393**
96	64	SHAHPURA	0.7387
97	65	SUWANA	0.7385
97	220	SIROHI	0.7385
99	74	TALERA	0.7379
100	20	THANAGAZI	0.7370
101	221	DEOLI	0.7361
102	48	KAMAN	0.7356
103	109	ANUPGARH	0.7352
103	222	MALPURA	0.7352
105	112	PADAMPUR	0.7349
106	149	BUHANA	0.7338
107	61	MANDALGARH	0.7329
107	162	OSIAN	0.7329
109	164	SHERGARH	0.7318
110	98	MAHWA	0.7316
111	49	KUMHER	0.7307
112	193	ROHAT	0.7304
113	229	DHARIAWAD	0.7303
114	97	LALSOT	0.7302
115	198	DEOGARH	0.7299
116	232	JHADOL	0.7298
117	142	BAKANI	0.7295
118	203	BAMANWAS	0.7291
119	50	NADBAI	0.7289
120	216	ABU ROAD	0.7284
121	226	UNIARA	0.7271
122	219	SHEOGANJ	0.7268
123	54	WEIR	0.7266
124	189	MARWAR JUN.	0.7258
125	12	KISHANGARH BAS	0.7257
126	156	BALESAR	0.7255
127	231	GOGUNDA	0.7249
128	13	KOTKASIM	0.7245
128	192	RANI STATION	0.7245
130	60	MANDAL	0.7240
131	15	MANDAWAR	0.7237
132	9	DANSURE	0.7236
133	151	JHUNJHUNUN	0.7216
134	94	TARANAGAR	0.7214
135	146	MANOHARTHANA	0.7210
136	57	HURDA	0.7206
137	51	NAGAR PAHARI	0.7203
138	207	SAWAI MADHOPUR	0.7198
139	161	MANDOR	0.7197
140	16	NIMRANA	0.7195
141	234	KOTRA	0.7193
142	46	BAYANA	0.7186
143	235	MAVLI	0.7169
144	135	AHORE	0.7167
145	197	BHIM	0.7163
146	214	PIPRALI	0.7161
147	188	JAITARAN	0.7158
148	22	UMREN	0.7150
149	90	RAJGARH	0.7149
150	233	KHERWARA	0.7148
151	154	SURAJGARH	0.7145
152	62	RAIPUR	0.7142
152	205	GANGAPUR	0.7142
154	58	JAHAZPUR	0.7139
155	167	NADOTI	0.7137
156	211	KHANDELA	0.7132
157	95	BANDIKUI	0.7129
158	237	SARADA	0.7117
159	21	TIJARA	0.7104
160	168	SAPOTRA	0.7079
161	209	DHOND	0.7075
162	148	ALSISAR	0.7057
163	18	RAMGARH	0.7055
164	186	BALI	0.7015
165	23	ANANDPURI	0.7013
166	147	PIRAWA	0.7011
167	175	DEGANA	0.7010
168	185	RIYAN	0.7008
169	191	RAIPUR	0.7007
170	144	JHALRAPATAN	0.7004
	MEDIUM (0.65-0.70)		
171	150	CHIRAWA	0.6998
172	152	KHETRI	0.6991
173	117	HANUMANGARH	0.6989
174	91	RATANGARH	0.6977
175	155	UDAIPURWATI	0.6964
176	52	RUPBAS	0.6961
177	169	TODABHIM	0.6959
178	187	DESURI	0.6953
179	177	JAYAL	0.6945
180	24	BAGIDORA	0.6942
181	182	MUNDWA	0.6935
182	29	SAJJANGARH	0.6933
183	183	NAGAUR	0.6931
184	89	CHURU	0.6928
185	166	KARAULI	0.6918
186	195	SUMERPUR	0.6912
187	93	SUJANGARH	0.6907
188	230	GIRWA	0.6906
189	196	AMET	0.6903
190	100	BARI	0.6899
191	53	SEWAR	0.6886
192	208	DANTA RAMGARH	0.6874
193	92	SARDARSHAHAR	0.6869
194	165	HINDAUN	0.6840
195	27	KUSHALGARH	0.6836
196	199	KHAMNOR	0.6822
197	181	MERTA	0.6819
198	136	BHINMAL	0.6818
199	28	PEEPALKHOONT	0.6807
200	133	SAM	0.6802
201	153	NAWALGARH	0.6786
202	26	GHATOL	0.6782
203	101	BASERI	0.6776
204	163	PHALODI	0.6773
205	179	LADNU	0.6771
206	202	RAJSAMAND	0.6768
207	213	NEEM KA THANA	0.6748
208	140	SANCHORE	0.6712
209	215	SRI MADHOPUR	0.6698
210	184	PARBATSAR	0.6697
211	138	JASWANTPURA	0.6688
212	145	KHANPUR	0.6674
213	25	GARHI	0.6673
214	40	BAYTOO	0.6654
215	30	TALWARA	0.6644
216	132	JAISALMER	0.6626
217	176	DIDWANA	0.6618
218	41	CHOHTAN	0.6615
218	141	SAYLA	0.6615
220	139	RANIWARA	0.6601
221	103	RAJAKHERA	0.6595
222	143	DAG	0.6587
223	102	DHAULPUR	0.6574
224	44	SINDHARI	0.6570
225	180	MAKRANA	0.6525
226	42	DHORIMANNA	0.6501
	LOW (0.60-0.65)		
227	137	JALOR	0.6481
228	38	BALOTRA	0.6438
229	178	KUCHAMAN	0.6420
230	39	BARMER	0.6360
231	108	SIMALWARA	0.6334
232	106	DUNGARPUR	0.6227
233	107	SAGWARA	0.6202
234	105	BICHHIWARA	0.6168
235	43	SHEO	0.6132
	VERY LOW (< 0.60)		
236	104	ASPUR	0.5969
237	45	SIWANA	0.5875
		RAJASTHAN	**0.7390**
		%age of AAPs	**40.10**

BOLD: Equal/Above Average Panchayat Samities (AAPs)

Source: Annex 14.1, Col. 6.

ANNEX 15.1

PANCHAYAT SAMITI-WISE VARIATION IN GENDER EMPOWERMENT MEASURE, 2001

P. Code	Panchayat Samiti	Female and Male Share of Total Pop.		Female and Male Share of PS Members		Female and Male Share of Sarpanchs		Female and Male Share of Teachers in Govt. Pr. and UPS		Female and Male Share of Govt. Doctors		Female and Male Estimated Income Index		EDEP for PS Repre#	Indexed EDEP for PS Repre#	EDEP for GP Repre#	Indexed EDEP for GP Repre#	EDEP for Political Repre# (A)	EDEP for Position as Teachers in Govt. Pr. and UPS	Indexed EDEP for Teachers in Govt. Pr. and UPS	EDEP for Position as Doctors in Govt. Hospital	Indexed EDEP for Doctors in Govt. Hosp.	EDEP for Socio-Eco Parti.## (B)	EDEP for Income (C)	GEM (A+B+C)/3
		Female	Male	Female (%)	Male (%)	Female (%)	Male (%)	Female (%)	Male (%)	Female (%)	Male (%)	Female	Male												
1	2	3	4	5	6	7	8	9	10	11	12	13	14	15	16	17	18	19	20	21	22	23	24	25	26
1	ARAIN	0.490	0.510	41.2	58.8	33.3	66.7	13.9	86.1	9.1	90.9	0.795	0.895	48.6	0.972	44.7	0.894	0.933	24.4	0.488	16.9	0.339	0.413	0.843	0.730
2	BHINAY	0.490	0.510	42.1	57.9	34.3	65.7	19.7	80.3	0.0	100.0	0.796	0.883	48.9	0.978	45.4	0.908	0.943	32.3	0.645	0.0	0.000	0.323	0.838	0.701
3	JAWAJA	0.496	0.504	42.1	57.9	37.1	62.9	44.8	55.2	0.0	100.0	0.739	0.838	48.8	0.976	46.8	0.936	0.956	50.0	1.000	0.0	0.000	0.500	0.786	0.747
4	KEKRI	0.489	0.511	31.6	68.4	32.3	67.7	26.4	73.6	15.8	84.2	0.782	0.876	43.6	0.872	44.1	0.882	0.877	40.0	0.800	27.0	0.541	0.670	0.827	0.792
5	KISHANGARH	0.483	0.517	31.6	68.4	32.3	67.7	52.6	47.4	0.0	100.0	0.745	0.877	43.8	0.876	44.3	0.886	0.881	50.0	1.000	0.0	0.000	0.500	0.808	0.730
6	MASOODA	0.488	0.512	47.4	52.6	34.4	65.6	37.1	62.9	20.0	80.0	0.772	0.869	49.9	0.998	45.5	0.910	0.954	47.6	0.952	32.3	0.645	0.799	0.819	0.857
7	PISANGAN	0.485	0.515	33.3	66.7	35.6	64.4	48.0	52.0	16.7	83.3	0.729	0.864	44.9	0.898	46.3	0.926	0.912	50.0	1.000	28.6	0.571	0.786	0.793	0.830
8	SRINAGAR	0.480	0.520	30.0	70.0	32.4	67.6	53.7	46.3	0.0	100.0	0.688	0.897	42.7	0.854	44.4	0.888	0.871	50.0	1.000	0.0	0.000	0.500	0.783	0.718
	AJMER DISTRICT	**0.487**	**0.513**	**37.1**	**62.9**	**34.1**	**65.9**	**39.1**	**60.9**	**9.6**	**90.4**	**0.757**	**0.874**	**47.0**	**0.940**	**45.3**	**0.906**	**0.923**	**47.6**	**0.952**	**17.9**	**0.357**	**0.655**	**0.813**	**0.797**
9	BANSURE	0.475	0.525	36.0	64.0	32.4	67.6	14.0	86.0	16.7	83.3	0.674	0.775	46.7	0.934	44.6	0.892	0.913	25.0	0.500	28.6	0.571	0.536	0.724	0.724
10	BEHROR	0.478	0.522	36.8	63.2	37.9	62.1	18.2	81.8	10.0	90.0	0.714	0.797	47.1	0.942	47.6	0.952	0.947	30.3	0.606	18.5	0.370	0.488	0.755	0.730
11	KATHUMAR	0.465	0.535	44.0	56.0	41.0	59.0	5.9	94.1	0.0	100.0	0.710	0.787	49.7	0.994	49.0	0.980	0.987	11.9	0.238	0.0	0.000	0.119	0.749	0.618
12	KISHANGARH BAS	0.476	0.524	42.9	57.1	39.3	60.7	43.4	56.6	10.0	90.0	0.680	0.773	49.3	0.986	48.2	0.964	0.975	50.0	1.000	18.9	0.377	0.689	0.726	0.796
13	KOTKASIM	0.476	0.524	33.3	66.7	36.4	63.6	15.6	84.4	0.0	100.0	0.681	0.769	45.1	0.902	46.9	0.938	0.920	27.0	0.541	0.0	0.000	0.270	0.725	0.638
14	LACHHMANGARH	0.471	0.529	33.3	66.7	34.1	65.9	12.3	87.7	28.6	71.4	0.708	0.790	45.3	0.906	45.8	0.916	0.911	22.7	0.455	41.7	0.833	0.644	0.749	0.768
15	MANDAWAR	0.479	0.521	32.0	68.0	34.2	65.8	13.8	86.2	15.4	84.6	0.684	0.765	44.2	0.884	45.6	0.912	0.898	24.4	0.488	27.0	0.541	0.514	0.724	0.712
16	NIMRANA	0.481	0.519	31.6	68.4	31.3	68.8	19.3	80.7	10.0	90.0	0.679	0.762	43.8	0.876	43.6	0.872	0.874	32.3	0.645	18.5	0.370	0.508	0.720	0.700
17	RAJGARH	0.471	0.529	35.3	64.7	34.5	65.5	12.8	87.2	11.1	88.9	0.704	0.805	46.5	0.930	46.0	0.920	0.925	23.3	0.465	20.8	0.417	0.441	0.754	0.707
18	RAMGARH	0.472	0.528	44.0	56.0	37.8	62.2	31.0	69.0	0.0	100.0	0.657	0.756	49.6	0.992	47.7	0.954	0.973	43.5	0.870	0.0	0.000	0.435	0.706	0.704
19	RENI	0.469	0.531	35.3	64.7	38.5	61.5	10.5	89.5	0.0	100.0	0.715	0.814	46.5	0.930	48.0	0.960	0.945	19.6	0.392	0.0	0.000	0.196	0.765	0.635
20	THANAGAZI	0.474	0.526	38.1	61.9	34.3	65.7	11.1	88.9	28.6	71.4	0.692	0.783	47.8	0.956	45.8	0.916	0.936	20.4	0.408	41.7	0.833	0.621	0.737	0.765
21	TIJARA	0.463	0.537	36.0	64.0	42.1	57.9	23.9	76.1	0.0	100.0	0.665	0.755	47.1	0.942	49.3	0.986	0.964	38.5	0.769	0.0	0.000	0.385	0.710	0.686
22	UMREN	0.470	0.530	32.0	68.0	38.9	61.1	34.9	65.1	30.0	70.0	0.671	0.759	44.5	0.890	48.2	0.964	0.927	45.5	0.909	43.5	0.870	0.889	0.715	0.844
	ALWAR	**0.472**	**0.528**	**36.6**	63.4	**36.6**	**63.4**	**19.1**	**80.9**	**12.4**	**87.6**	**0.688**	**0.777**	47.1	0.942	47.1	0.942	0.942	**32.3**	**0.645**	**22.7**	**0.455**	**0.550**	**0.732**	0.741
23	ANANDPURI	0.491	0.509	40.0	60.0	38.5	61.5	9.5	90.5	0.0	100.0	0.665	0.741	48.2	0.964	47.6	0.952	0.958	17.5	0.351	0.0	0.000	0.176	0.701	0.612
24	BAGIDORA	0.496	0.504	38.1	61.9	46.2	53.8	19.1	80.9	11.1	88.9	0.656	0.736	47.3	0.946	49.7	0.994	0.970	31.3	0.625	20.0	0.400	0.513	0.694	0.726
25	GARHI	0.494	0.506	37.9	62.1	36.5	63.5	18.8	81.2	27.8	72.2	0.604	0.744	47.2	0.944	45.5	0.930	0.937	30.3	0.606	40.0	0.800	0.703	0.667	0.769
26	GHATOL	0.497	0.503	40.7	59.3	37.7	62.3	18.8	81.2	9.1	90.9	0.639	0.722	48.3	0.966	47.0	0.940	0.953	30.3	0.606	16.7	0.333	0.470	0.678	0.700
27	KUSHALGARH	0.497	0.503	35.3	64.7	41.4	58.6	13.8	86.2	11.1	88.9	0.647	0.724	45.8	0.916	43.6	0.972	0.944	23.8	0.476	20.0	0.400	0.438	0.684	0.689
28	PEEPALKHOONT	0.492	0.508	35.3	64.7	36.1	63.9	33.8	66.3	0.0	100.0	0.640	0.726	45.9	0.918	46.3	0.926	0.922	45.5	0.909	0.0	0.000	0.455	0.681	0.686
29	SAJJANGARH	0.493	0.507	35.3	64.7	50.0	50.0	11.9	88.1	11.1	88.9	0.658	0.732	45.9	0.918	50.0	1.000	0.959	21.3	0.426	20.0	0.400	0.413	0.693	0.688
30	TALWARA	0.493	0.507	32.0	68.0	34.5	65.5	32.0	68.0	18.2	81.8	0.623	0.710	43.7	0.874	45.4	0.908	0.891	43.5	0.870	30.3	0.606	0.738	0.664	0.764
	BANSWARA	**0.494**	**0.506**	**36.9**	**63.1**	**39.4**	**60.6**	**21.0**	**79.0**	**14.3**	**85.7**	**0.640**	**0.729**	**46.7**	**0.934**	**47.9**	**0.958**	**0.946**	**33.3**	**0.667**	**25.0**	**0.500**	**0.583**	**0.682**	**0.737**
31	ANTA	0.478	0.522	31.6	68.4	36.8	63.2	24.9	75.1	13.0	87.0	0.690	0.809	43.9	0.878	47.1	0.942	0.910	38.5	0.769	23.3	0.465	0.617	0.747	0.758
32	ATRU	0.475	0.525	35.3	64.7	32.4	67.6	13.8	86.2	12.5	87.5	0.700	0.830	46.4	0.928	44.6	0.892	0.910	24.4	0.488	22.7	0.455	0.471	0.763	0.715
33	BARAN	0.475	0.525	33.3	66.7	34.6	65.4	27.6	72.4	16.7	83.3	0.685	0.820	45.2	0.904	46.0	0.920	0.912	41.7	0.833	28.6	0.571	0.702	0.750	0.788
34	CHHABRA	0.472	0.528	46.7	53.3	37.0	63.0	13.2	86.8	7.7	92.3	0.751	0.835	50.0	1.000	47.3	0.946	0.973	23.8	0.476	14.9	0.299	0.387	0.793	0.718
35	CHHIPABAROD	0.478	0.522	31.6	68.4	33.3	66.7	18.5	81.5	25.0	75.0	0.765	0.850	43.9	0.878	45.1	0.902	0.890	31.3	0.625	38.5	0.769	0.697	0.807	0.798
36	KISHANGANJ	0.479	0.521	41.2	58.8	35.5	64.5	11.1	88.9	25.0	75.0	0.711	0.826	48.8	0.976	46.4	0.928	0.952	20.4	0.408	38.5	0.769	0.589	0.767	0.769
37	SHAHBAD	0.473	0.527	33.3	66.7	33.3	66.7	12.7	87.3	25.0	75.0	0.712	0.823	45.2	0.904	45.2	0.904	0.904	23.3	0.465	38.5	0.769	0.617	0.767	0.763
	BARAN	**0.476**	**0.524**	**35.9**	**64.1**	**34.7**	**65.3**	**18.8**	**81.2**	**16.7**	**83.3**	**0.717**	**0.828**	**46.7**	**0.934**	**46.0**	**0.920**	**0.927**	**31.3**	**0.625**	**28.6**	**0.571**	**0.598**	**0.771**	**0.765**
38	BALOTRA	0.480	0.520	48.3	51.7	37.0	63.0	15.2	84.8	23.1	76.9	0.595	0.697	50.0	1.000	47.1	0.942	0.971	26.3	0.526	35.7	0.714	0.620	0.644	0.745
39	BARMER	0.460	0.540	32.0	68.0	36.0	64.0	24.9	75.1	0.0	100.0	0.585	0.687	44.8	0.896	47.1	0.942	0.919	38.5	0.769	0.0	0.000	0.385	0.636	0.647
40	BAYTOO	0.475	0.525	47.8	52.2	38.3	61.7	6.8	93.2	11.1	88.9	0.627	0.705	50.0	1.000	47.8	0.956	0.978	13.3	0.267	20.4	0.408	0.338	0.665	0.660
41	CHOHTAN	0.466	0.534	36.0	64.0	38.0	62.0	3.4	96.6	0.0	100.0	0.615	0.708	47.0	0.940	47.9	0.958	0.949	7.0	0.140	0.0	0.000	0.070	0.662	0.560
42	DHORIMANNA	0.477	0.523	33.3	66.7	36.2	63.8	3.5	96.5	5.9	94.1	0.610	0.692	45.1	0.902	46.8	0.936	0.919	7.0	0.141	11.6	0.233	0.187	0.650	0.585
43	SHEO	0.457	0.543	36.8	63.2	35.6	64.4	5.5	94.5	0.0	100.0	0.558	0.669	47.6	0.952	47.0	0.940	0.946	11.2	0.225	0.0	0.000	0.112	0.613	0.557
44	SINDHARI	0.480	0.520	32.0	68.0	41.3	58.7	4.7	95.3	12.5	87.5	0.616	0.700	44.2	0.884	48.8	0.976	0.930	9.3	0.185	22.7	0.455	0.320	0.657	0.636
45	SIWANA	0.480	0.520	32.0	68.0	32.5	67.5	11.6	88.4	20.0	80.0	0.523	0.663	44.2	0.884	44.5	0.890	0.887	21.3	0.426	32.3	0.645	0.535	0.588	0.670
	BARMER	**0.472**	**0.528**	**37.4**	**62.6**	**36.9**	**63.1**	**12.8**	**87.2**	**9.5**	**90.5**	**0.594**	**0.693**	**47.5**	**0.950**	**47.3**	**0.946**	**0.948**	**23.3**	**0.465**	**17.9**	**0.357**	**0.411**	**0.642**	**0.667**
46	BAYANA	0.447	0.553	39.1	60.9	40.9	59.1	8.1	91.9	7.7	92.3	0.659	0.776	48.8	0.976	49.3	0.986	0.981	16.4	0.328	15.6	0.313	0.320	0.719	0.673
47	DEEG	0.459	0.541	33.3	66.7	42.9	57.1	11.2	88.8	0.0	100.0	0.716	0.796	45.7	0.914	49.6	0.992	0.953	21.3	0.426	0.0	0.000	0.213	0.757	0.641
48	KAMAN	0.469	0.531	39.1	60.9	40.9	59.1	7.8	92.2	0.0	100.0	0.692	0.779	48.3	0.966	48.9	0.978	0.972	15.2	0.303	0.0	0.000	0.152	0.736	0.620
49	KUMHER	0.461	0.539	52.6	47.4	42.9	57.1	18.1	81.9	0.0	100.0	0.661	0.804	49.7	0.994	49.5	0.990	0.992	31.3	0.625	0.0	0.000	0.313	0.731	0.678

1	2	3	4	5	6	7	8	9	10	11	12	13	14	15	16	17	18	19	20	21	22	23	24	25	26
50	NADBAI	0.456	0.544	36.8	63.2	35.1	64.9	15.8	84.2	12.5	87.5	0.681	0.775	47.6	0.952	46.8	0.936	0.944	28.6	0.571	23.3	0.465	0.518	0.729	0.730
51	NAGAR PAHARI	0.467	0.533	37.0	63.0	32.7	67.3	12.8	87.2	12.5	87.5	0.674	0.767	47.4	0.948	45.0	0.900	0.924	23.3	0.465	23.3	0.465	0.465	0.720	0.703
52	RUPBAS	0.457	0.543	33.3	66.7	35.6	64.4	7.7	92.3	9.1	90.9	0.636	0.757	45.7	0.914	47.0	0.940	0.927	15.4	0.308	17.9	0.357	0.332	0.696	0.652
53	SEWAR	0.461	0.539	33.3	66.7	39.4	60.6	19.8	80.2	50.0	50.0	0.596	0.795	45.6	0.912	48.6	0.972	0.942	33.3	0.667	50.0	1.000	0.833	0.689	0.821
54	WEIR	0.458	0.542	52.0	48.0	46.7	53.3	13.8	86.2	5.0	95.0	0.686	0.765	49.8	0.996	50.1	1.002	0.999	25.6	0.513	10.3	0.206	0.360	0.727	0.695
	BHARATPUR	**0.460**	**0.540**	**39.7**	**60.3**	**39.5**	**60.5**	**12.7**	**87.3**	**7.5**	**92.5**	**0.669**	**0.778**	**48.7**	**0.974**	**48.6**	**0.972**	**0.973**	**23.8**	**0.476**	**14.9**	**0.299**	**0.387**	**0.724**	**0.695**
55	ASIND	0.505	0.495	34.8	65.2	38.6	61.4	21.5	78.5	37.5	62.5	0.701	0.791	45.2	0.904	47.3	0.946	0.925	33.3	0.667	47.6	0.952	0.810	0.743	0.826
56	BANERA	0.496	0.504	33.3	66.7	30.8	69.2	35.2	64.8	12.5	87.5	0.691	0.800	44.5	0.890	42.8	0.856	0.873	45.5	0.909	22.2	0.444	0.677	0.742	0.764
57	HURDA	0.487	0.513	33.3	66.7	40.0	60.0	25.5	74.5	40.0	60.0	0.657	0.794	44.8	0.896	48.3	0.966	0.931	38.5	0.769	47.6	0.952	0.861	0.721	0.837
58	JAHAZPUR	0.482	0.518	38.1	61.9	37.8	62.2	25.9	74.1	23.8	76.2	0.661	0.771	47.6	0.952	47.4	0.948	0.950	38.5	0.769	37.0	0.741	0.755	0.714	0.806
59	KOTRI	0.488	0.512	31.6	68.4	33.3	66.7	27.2	72.8	20.0	80.0	0.684	0.802	43.6	0.872	44.8	0.896	0.884	40.0	0.800	32.3	0.645	0.723	0.740	0.782
60	MANDAL	0.508	0.492	40.0	60.0	30.4	69.6	37.4	62.6	36.4	63.6	0.669	0.791	47.8	0.956	42.1	0.842	0.899	47.6	0.952	45.5	0.909	0.931	0.724	0.851
61	MANDALGARH	0.482	0.518	36.0	64.0	36.0	64.0	30.9	69.1	42.9	57.1	0.680	0.790	46.5	0.930	46.5	0.930	0.930	43.5	0.870	50.0	1.000	0.935	0.733	0.866
62	RAIPUR	0.510	0.490	33.3	66.7	31.8	68.2	30.7	69.3	37.5	62.5	0.650	0.796	44.1	0.882	43.1	0.862	0.872	41.7	0.833	47.6	0.952	0.893	0.714	0.826
63	SAHARA	0.517	0.483	46.7	53.3	32.1	67.9	38.1	61.9	22.2	77.8	0.715	0.817	49.7	0.994	43.1	0.862	0.928	47.6	0.952	34.5	0.690	0.821	0.761	0.837
64	SHAHPURA	0.487	0.513	31.6	68.4	31.6	68.4	33.8	66.2	40.0	60.0	0.688	0.794	43.6	0.872	43.6	0.872	0.872	45.5	0.909	47.6	0.952	0.931	0.739	0.847
65	SUWANA	0.491	0.509	42.1	57.9	29.4	70.6	48.6	51.4	18.2	81.8	0.692	0.790	48.9	0.978	41.8	0.836	0.907	50.0	1.000	30.3	0.606	0.803	0.739	0.816
	BHILWARA	**0.495**	**0.505**	**36.5**	**63.5**	**33.9**	**66.1**	**32.0**	**68.0**	**29.6**	**70.4**	**0.682**	**0.793**	**46.5**	**0.930**	**45.0**	**0.900**	**0.915**	**43.5**	**0.870**	**41.7**	**0.833**	**0.852**	**0.734**	**0.834**
66	BIKANER	0.470	0.530	34.3	65.7	33.9	66.1	16.8	83.2	18.2	81.8	0.7201	0.864	45.9	0.918	45.7	0.914	0.916	29.4	0.588	31.3	0.625	0.607	0.790	0.771
67	DUNGARGARH *	0.486	0.514	38.1	61.9	33.3	66.7	35.2	64.8	20.0	80.0	0.7298	0.802	47.5	0.950	44.8	0.896	0.923	45.5	0.909	32.3	0.645	0.777	0.765	0.822
68	KOLAYAT	0.467	0.533	38.1	61.9	32.4	67.6	15.9	84.1	45.5	54.5	0.7175	0.868	47.9	0.958	44.8	0.896	0.927	27.8	0.556	50.0	1.000	0.778	0.791	0.832
69	LUNKARANSAR	0.477	0.523	43.5	56.5	33.3	66.7	21.5	78.5	23.1	76.9	0.7607	0.873	49.5	0.990	45.1	0.902	0.946	34.5	0.690	37.0	0.741	0.715	0.816	0.826
70	NOKHA	0.477	0.523	32.3	67.7	34.0	66.0	29.7	70.3	6.3	93.8	0.7976	0.889	44.5	0.890	45.6	0.912	0.901	41.7	0.833	12.3	0.247	0.540	0.843	0.761
	BIKANER **	**0.473**	**0.527**	**36.6**	**63.4**	**33.5**	**-0.2**	**23.5**	**76.5**	**20.8**	**79.2**	**0.7492**	**0.874**	**47.1**	**0.942**	**-0.4**	**-0.008**	**0.467**	**37.0**	**0.741**	**34.5**	**0.690**	**0.715**	**0.810**	**0.664**
71	HINDOLI	0.474	0.526	34.8	65.2	36.6	63.4	22.1	77.9	0.0	100.0	0.714	0.802	46.1	0.922	47.1	0.942	0.932	35.7	0.714	0.0	0.000	0.357	0.758	0.682
72	KESHORAIPATAN	0.478	0.522	43.5	56.5	32.6	67.4	33.6	66.4	10.5	89.5	0.684	0.802	49.4	0.988	44.6	0.892	0.940	45.5	0.909	19.6	0.392	0.651	0.741	0.777
73	NAINWA	0.477	0.523	31.6	68.4	33.3	66.7	26.7	73.3	8.3	91.7	0.703	0.799	44.0	0.880	45.1	0.902	0.891	40.0	0.800	15.9	0.318	0.559	0.750	0.733
74	TALERA	0.475	0.525	32.3	67.7	32.8	67.2	30.6	69.4	16.7	83.3	0.681	0.799	44.5	0.890	44.9	0.898	0.894	43.5	0.870	28.6	0.571	0.721	0.738	0.784
	BUNDI	**0.476**	**0.524**	**35.4**	**64.6**	**33.7**	**66.3**	**29.4**	**70.6**	**9.4**	**90.6**	**0.697**	**0.799**	**46.4**	**0.928**	**45.4**	**0.908**	**0.918**	**41.7**	**0.833**	**17.9**	**0.357**	**0.595**	**0.747**	**0.753**
75	ARNOD	0.492	0.508	33.3	66.7	41.4	58.6	17.2	82.8	0.0	100.0	0.705	0.788	44.7	0.894	48.7	0.974	0.934	28.6	0.571	0.0	0.000	0.286	0.745	0.655
76	BARI SADRI	0.500	0.500	33.3	66.7	34.8	65.2	15.3	84.7	14.3	85.7	0.747	0.826	44.4	0.888	45.4	0.908	0.898	25.6	0.513	24.4	0.488	0.500	0.785	0.728
77	BEGUN	0.491	0.509	40.0	60.0	32.3	67.7	36.1	63.9	0.0	100.0	0.739	0.823	48.2	0.964	44.0	0.880	0.922	45.5	0.909	0.0	0.000	0.455	0.779	0.719
78	BHADESAR	0.495	0.505	33.3	66.7	36.0	64.0	23.8	76.2	57.1	42.9	0.735	0.825	44.6	0.892	46.2	0.924	0.908	37.0	0.741	50.0	1.000	0.870	0.778	0.852
79	BHAINSRORGARH	0.475	0.525	33.3	66.7	40.9	59.1	45.6	54.4	40.0	60.0	0.697	0.804	45.2	0.904	48.8	0.976	0.940	50.0	1.000	47.6	0.952	0.976	0.749	0.888
80	BHOPALSAGAR	0.501	0.499	33.3	66.7	31.6	68.4	24.3	75.7	20.0	80.0	0.725	0.826	44.4	0.888	43.2	0.864	0.876	37.0	0.741	32.3	0.645	0.693	0.772	0.780
81	CHHOTI SADRI	0.491	0.509	33.3	66.7	33.3	66.7	25.6	74.4	14.3	85.7	0.744	0.825	44.7	0.894	44.7	0.894	0.894	38.5	0.769	25.0	0.500	0.635	0.783	0.771
82	CHITTAURGARH	0.491	0.509	33.3	66.7	35.9	64.1	29.3	70.7	20.0	80.0	0.709	0.825	44.7	0.894	46.3	0.926	0.910	41.7	0.833	32.3	0.645	0.739	0.764	0.804
83	DUNGLA	0.501	0.499	40.0	60.0	34.6	65.4	16.5	83.5	33.3	66.7	0.744	0.823	48.0	0.960	45.2	0.904	0.932	27.8	0.556	43.5	0.870	0.713	0.781	0.809
84	GANGRAR	0.493	0.507	40.0	60.0	38.1	61.9	27.5	72.5	0.0	100.0	0.723	0.838	48.1	0.962	47.3	0.946	0.954	40.0	0.800	0.0	0.000	0.400	0.777	0.710
85	KAPASAN	0.498	0.502	33.3	66.7	34.8	65.2	25.2	74.8	25.0	75.0	0.744	0.843	44.5	0.890	45.4	0.908	0.899	38.5	0.769	37.0	0.741	0.755	0.790	0.815
86	NIMBAHERA	0.492	0.508	35.3	64.7	37.1	62.9	36.2	63.8	17.6	82.4	0.729	0.813	45.9	0.918	46.9	0.938	0.928	45.5	0.909	29.4	0.588	0.749	0.769	0.815
87	PRATAPGARH	0.489	0.511	30.4	69.6	35.4	64.6	29.8	70.2	20.0	80.0	0.714	0.793	42.7	0.854	46.0	0.920	0.887	41.7	0.833	32.3	0.645	0.739	0.752	0.793
88	RASHMI	0.505	0.495	33.3	66.7	47.8	52.2	21.7	78.3	0.0	100.0	0.739	0.829	44.3	0.886	49.9	0.998	0.942	33.3	0.667	0.0	0.000	0.333	0.781	0.685
	CHITTAURGARH	**0.493**	**0.507**	**34.5**	**65.5**	**36.6**	**63.4**	**28.3**	**71.7**	**17.7**	**82.3**	**0.727**	**0.818**	**45.4**	**0.908**	**46.6**	**0.932**	**0.920**	**41.7**	**0.833**	**29.4**	**0.588**	**0.711**	**0.770**	**0.800**
89	CHURU	0.490	0.510	42.1	57.9	37.1	62.9	21.1	78.9	26.3	73.7	0.6512	0.738	48.9	0.978	46.9	0.938	0.958	33.3	0.667	38.5	0.769	0.718	0.693	0.790
91	RATANGARH	0.494	0.506	31.6	68.4	38.7	61.3	12.6	87.4	5.0	95.0	0.6567	0.743	43.4	0.868	47.6	0.952	0.910	22.2	0.444	9.6	0.192	0.318	0.698	0.642
92	SARDARSHAHAR	0.488	0.512	32.0	68.0	33.3	66.7	11.0	89.0	20.0	80.0	0.6484	0.728	43.9	0.878	44.8	0.896	0.887	20.0	0.400	32.3	0.645	0.523	0.687	0.699
93	SUJANGARH	0.492	0.508	37.9	62.1	33.3	66.7	18.8	81.2	15.8	84.2	0.647	0.739	47.3	0.946	44.7	0.894	0.920	31.3	0.625	27.0	0.541	0.583	0.691	0.731
94	TARANAGAR	0.485	0.515	36.8	63.2	32.1	67.9	17.3	82.7	13.3	86.7	0.6793	0.766	46.9	0.938	44.1	0.882	0.910	29.4	0.588	23.8	0.476	0.532	0.721	0.721
	CHURU ***	**0.488**	**0.512**	**38.2**	**61.8**	**34.3**	**132.4**	**17.2**	**82.8**	**15.0**	**85.0**	**0.6691**	**0.750**	**47.5**	**0.950**	**55.3**	**1.106**	**1.028**	**28.6**	**0.571**	**25.6**	**0.513**	**0.542**	**0.708**	**0.759**
95	BANDIKUI	0.473	0.527	34.6	65.4	46.2	53.8	15.4	84.6	7.1	92.9	0.668	0.759	46.0	0.920	49.9	0.998	0.959	27.0	0.541	13.9	0.278	0.409	0.713	0.694
96	DAUSA	0.476	0.524	30.0	70.0	43.1	56.9	15.1	84.9	3.7	96.3	0.699	0.792	42.8	0.856	49.4	0.988	0.922	26.3	0.526	7.5	0.149	0.338	0.745	0.668
97	LALSOT	0.478	0.522	51.9	48.1	46.8	53.2	7.8	92.2	15.4	84.6	0.684	0.779	49.8	0.996	49.9	0.998	0.997	14.9	0.299	27.0	0.541	0.420	0.730	0.716
98	MAHWA	0.466	0.534	34.8	65.2	36.6	63.4	10.5	89.5	11.1	88.9	0.659	0.809	46.3	0.926	47.3	0.946	0.936	20.0	0.400	20.8	0.417	0.408	0.732	0.692
99	SIKRAI	0.473	0.527	36.0	64.0	36.6	63.4	4.4	95.6	27.3	72.7	0.696	0.792	46.8	0.936	47.1	0.942	0.939	8.9	0.177	40.0	0.800	0.489	0.743	0.724
	DAUSA	**0.474**	**0.526**	**37.4**	**62.6**	**42.0**	**58.0**	**11.0**	**89.0**	**10.8**	**89.2**	**0.684**	**0.785**	**47.4**	**0.948**	**49.1**	**0.982**	**0.965**	**20.4**	**0.408**	**20.0**	**0.400**	**0.404**	**0.734**	**0.701**
100	BARI	0.443	0.557	31.6	68.4	35.5	64.5	7.6	92.4	30.0	70.0	0.645	0.731	45.1	0.902	47.4	0.948	0.925	15.6	0.313	43.5	0.870	0.591	0.690	0.735
101	BASERI	0.452	0.548	34.8	65.2	40.0	60.0	5.5	94.5	0.0	100.0	0.616	0.739	46.7	0.934	48.9	0.978	0.956	11.4	0.227	0.0	0.000	0.114	0.678	0.582
102	DHAULPUR	0.455	0.545	41.4	58.6	33.3	66.7	18.3	81.7	10.0	90.0	0.593	0.723	49.3	0.986	45.8	0.916	0.951	31.3	0.625	19.2	0.385	0.505	0.657	0.704
103	RAJAKHERA	0.449	0.551	43.5	56.5	31.7	68.3	10.5	89.5	11.1	88.9	0.593	0.726	49.8	0.996	45.0	0.900	0.948	20.4	0.408	21.3	0.426	0.417	0.660	0.675
	DHAULPUR	**0.451**	**0.549**	**38.3**	**61.7**	**34.8**	**65.2**	**11.3**	**88.7**	**13.9**	**86.1**	**0.603**	**0.732**	**48.4**	**0.968**	**46.8**	**0.936**	**0.952**	**21.7**	**0.435**	**25.6**	**0.513**	**0.474**	**0.667**	**0.698**
104	ASPUR	0.517	0.483	34.8	65.2	33.3	66.7	16.0	84.0	6.7	93.3	0.552	0.655	44.9	0.898	43.9	0.878	0.888	26.3	0.526	12.2	0.244	0.385	0.597	0.623
105	BICHHIWARA	0.500	0.500	33.3	66.7	35.4	64.6	20.6	79.4	0.0	100.0	0.576	0.664	44.4	0.888	45.7	0.914	0.901	32.3	0.645	0.0	0.000	0.323	0.617	0.613
106	DUNGARPUR	0.508	0.492	33.3	66.7	30.6	69.4	24.8	75.2	36.4	63.6	0.580	0.674	44.2	0.884	42.2	0.844	0.864	37.0	0.741	45.5	0.909	0.825	0.623	0.771
107	SAGWARA	0.518	0.482	32.0	68.0	35.7	64.3	20.7	79.3	16.0	84.0	0.576	0.676	43.0	0.860	45.4	0.908	0.884	32.3	0.645	26.3	0.526	0.586	0.620	0.697
108	SIMALWARA	0.499	0.501	34.5	65.5	32.8	67.2	23.9	76.1	5.0	95.0	0.598	0.673	45.2	0.904	44.1	0.882	0.893	37.0	0.741	9.5	0.191	0.466	0.633	0.664
	DUNGARPUR	**0.508**	**0.492**	**33.6**	**66.4**	**33.6**	**66.4**	**21.6**	**78.4**	**11.9**	**88.1**	**0.578**	**0.668**	**44.4**	**0.888**	**44.4**	**0.888**	**0.888**	**33.3**	**0.667**	**20.8**	**0.417**	**0.542**	**0.619**	**0.683**
109	ANUPGARH	0.472	0.528	46.3	53.7	36.8	63.2	13.8	86.3	26.1	73.9	0.652	0.830	49.9	0.998	47.2	0.944	0.971	25.0	0.500	40.0	0.800	0.650	0.735	0.785
110	GANGANAGAR	0.470	0.530	44.0	56.0	37.2	62.3	55.5	44.5	45.5	54.5	0.642	0.883	49.6	0.992	47.5	0.950	0.971	50.0	1.000	50.0	1.000	1.000	0.751	0.907
111	KARANPUR	0.473	0.527	33.3	66.7	31.4	68.5	35.7	64.3	18.2	81.8	0.777	0.907	45.2	0.904	44.0	0.880	0.892	47.6	0.952	31.3	0.625	0.789	0.840	0.840

P. Code	Panchayat Samiti	Female and Male Share of Total Pop. Female	Female and Male Share of Total Pop. Male	Female and Male Share of PS Members Female (%)	Female and Male Share of PS Members Male (%)	Female and Male Share of Sarpanchs Female (%)	Female and Male Share of Sarpanchs Male (%)	Female and Male Share of Teachers in Govt. Pr. and UPS Female (%)	Female and Male Share of Teachers in Govt. Pr. and UPS Male (%)	Female and Male Share of Govt. Doctors Female (%)	Female and Male Share of Govt. Doctors Male (%)	Female and Male Estimated Income Index Female	Female and Male Estimated Income Index Male	EDEP for PS Repre#	Indexed EDEP for PS Repre#	EDEP for GP Repre#	Indexed EDEP for GP Repre#	EDEP for Political Repre# (A)	EDEP for Position as Teachers in Govt. Pr. and UPS	Indexed EDEP for Teachers in Govt. Pr. and UPS	EDEP for Position as Doctors in Govt. Hospital	Indexed EDEP for Doctors in Govt. Hosp.	EDEP for Socio-Eco Parti.## (B)	EDEP for Income (C)	GEM (A+B+C)/3
1	2	3	4	5	6	7	8	9	10	11	12	13	14	15	16	17	18	19	20	21	22	23	24	25	26
112	PADAMPUR	0.475	0.525	35.3	64.7	33.3	66.7	32.4	67.6	10.0	90.0	0.638	0.853	46.4	0.928	45.2	0.904	0.916	45.5	0.909	18.9	0.377	0.643	0.735	0.765
113	RAISINGHNAGAR	0.477	0.523	31.6	68.4	33.3	66.7	16.9	83.1	21.4	78.6	0.705	0.887	44.0	0.880	45.1	0.902	0.891	28.6	0.571	34.5	0.690	0.631	0.790	0.770
114	SADULSHAHAR	0.460	0.540	31.6	68.4	34.4	65.6	15.7	84.3	28.6	71.4	0.795	0.932	44.5	0.890	46.3	0.926	0.908	27.8	0.556	41.7	0.833	0.695	0.864	0.822
115	SURATGARH	0.456	0.544	34.8	65.2	34.2	65.8	25.6	74.4	33.3	66.7	0.756	0.926	46.6	0.932	46.3	0.926	0.929	40.0	0.800	45.5	0.909	0.855	0.840	0.875
	GANGANAGAR	**0.469**	**0.531**	**38.4**	**61.6**	**34.8**	**65.2**	**29.8**	**70.2**	**26.1**	**73.9**	**0.706**	**0.883**	**48.0**	**0.960**	**46.3**	**0.926**	**0.943**	**43.5**	**0.870**	**40.0**	**0.800**	**0.835**	**0.790**	**0.856**
116	BHADRA	0.473	0.527	37.0	63.0	41.7	58.3	16.2	83.8	6.7	93.3	0.810	0.896	47.3	0.946	49.1	0.982	0.964	28.6	0.571	13.2	0.263	0.417	0.853	0.745
117	HANUMANGARH	0.472	0.528	41.7	58.3	33.3	66.7	31.9	68.1	20.0	80.0	0.601	0.819	49.1	0.982	45.3	0.906	0.944	43.5	0.870	33.3	0.667	0.768	0.699	0.804
118	NOHAR	0.475	0.525	36.6	63.4	33.3	66.7	9.7	90.3	8.0	92.0	0.774	0.897	47.0	0.940	45.2	0.904	0.922	18.2	0.364	15.4	0.308	0.336	0.834	0.697
	HANUMANGARH	**0.473**	**0.527**	**39.3**	**60.7**	**34.9**	**65.1**	**21.8**	**78.2**	**12.3**	**87.7**	**0.717**	**0.859**	**48.3**	**0.966**	**46.2**	**0.924**	**0.945**	**35.7**	**0.714**	**22.7**	**0.455**	**0.584**	**0.786**	**0.772**
119	AMBER	0.475	0.525	34.5	65.5	34.8	65.2	22.3	77.7	40.0	60.0	0.773	0.921	45.9	0.918	46.1	0.922	0.920	35.7	0.714	47.6	0.952	0.833	0.844	0.866
120	BASSI	0.477	0.523	36.0	64.0	31.6	68.4	22.2	77.8	15.4	84.6	0.787	0.899	46.7	0.934	44.0	0.880	0.907	35.7	0.714	27.0	0.541	0.627	0.842	0.792
121	CHAKSU	0.478	0.522	31.6	68.4	35.3	64.7	34.1	65.9	0.0	100.0	0.843	0.933	43.9	0.878	46.3	0.926	0.902	45.5	0.909	0.0	0.000	0.455	0.887	0.748
122	DUDU	0.481	0.519	33.3	66.7	34.5	65.5	23.7	76.3	23.1	76.9	0.794	0.910	45.0	0.900	45.7	0.914	0.907	37.0	0.741	35.7	0.714	0.728	0.850	0.828
123	GOVINDGARH	0.479	0.521	32.3	67.7	34.1	65.9	12.4	87.6	28.6	71.4	0.726	0.879	44.4	0.888	45.6	0.912	0.900	22.2	0.444	41.7	0.833	0.639	0.798	0.779
124	JAMWA RAMGARH	0.476	0.524	37.9	62.1	32.6	67.4	18.2	81.8	15.8	84.2	0.807	0.898	47.6	0.952	44.7	0.894	0.923	30.3	0.606	27.8	0.556	0.581	0.852	0.785
125	JHOTWARA	0.478	0.522	33.3	66.7	31.3	68.8	44.2	55.8	33.3	66.7	0.814	0.968	45.1	0.902	43.7	0.874	0.888	50.0	1.000	45.5	0.909	0.955	0.888	0.910
126	KOTPUTLI	0.475	0.525	33.3	66.7	38.1	61.9	8.6	91.4	36.4	63.6	0.779	0.878	45.2	0.904	47.7	0.954	0.929	16.4	0.328	47.6	0.952	0.640	0.828	0.799
127	PHAGI	0.479	0.521	33.3	66.7	32.3	67.7	24.5	75.5	0.0	100.0	0.812	0.934	45.1	0.902	44.4	0.888	0.895	38.5	0.769	0.0	0.000	0.385	0.871	0.717
128	SAMBHAR	0.483	0.517	32.0	68.0	34.1	65.9	12.5	87.5	20.0	80.0	0.723	0.898	44.1	0.882	45.4	0.908	0.895	22.2	0.444	32.3	0.645	0.545	0.804	0.748
129	SANGANER	0.478	0.522	40.0	60.0	32.0	68.0	50.9	49.1	71.4	28.6	0.830	0.993	48.4	0.968	44.2	0.884	0.926	50.0	1.000	40.0	0.800	0.900	0.908	0.911
130	SHAHPURA	0.474	0.526	34.8	65.2	31.0	69.0	9.5	90.5	40.0	60.0	0.740	0.870	46.1	0.922	43.6	0.872	0.897	17.9	0.357	47.6	0.952	0.655	0.803	0.785
131	VIRATNAGAR	0.476	0.524	31.8	68.2	32.4	67.6	8.8	91.2	18.2	81.8	0.755	0.863	44.1	0.882	44.6	0.892	0.887	16.7	0.333	30.3	0.606	0.470	0.808	0.721
	JAIPUR	**0.478**	**0.522**	**34.1**	**65.9**	**33.7**	**66.3**	**20.5**	**79.5**	**25.4**	**74.6**	**0.782**	**0.907**	**45.6**	**0.912**	**45.3**	**0.906**	**0.909**	**33.3**	**0.667**	**38.5**	**0.769**	**0.718**	**0.843**	**0.823**
132	JAISALMER	0.448	0.552	33.3	66.7	32.5	67.5	25.3	74.7	0.0	100.0	0.564	0.775	46.0	0.920	45.5	0.910	0.915	40.0	0.800	0.0	0.000	0.400	0.663	0.659
133	SAM	0.440	0.560	33.3	66.7	32.7	67.3	4.5	95.5	0.0	100.0	0.582	0.784	46.3	0.926	45.9	0.918	0.922	9.6	0.192	0.0	0.000	0.096	0.680	0.566
134	SANKRA	0.467	0.533	52.6	47.4	33.3	66.7	9.2	90.8	20.0	80.0	0.680	0.802	49.7	0.994	45.4	0.908	0.951	17.5	0.351	33.3	0.667	0.509	0.740	0.733
	JAISALMER	**0.453**	**0.547**	**40.8**	**59.2**	**32.8**	**67.2**	**14.2**	**85.8**	**5.9**	**94.1**	**0.632**	**0.785**	**49.2**	**0.984**	**45.6**	**0.912**	**0.948**	**26.3**	**0.526**	**12.0**	**0.241**	**0.384**	**0.707**	**0.680**
135	AHORE	0.505	0.495	34.8	65.2	36.6	63.4	19.5	80.5	9.1	90.9	0.670	0.772	45.2	0.904	46.3	0.926	0.915	31.3	0.625	16.4	0.328	0.477	0.717	0.703
136	BHINMAL	0.494	0.506	34.8	65.2	34.3	65.7	15.5	84.5	21.4	78.6	0.648	0.719	45.5	0.910	45.2	0.904	0.907	26.3	0.526	33.3	0.667	0.597	0.682	0.728
137	JALOR	0.499	0.501	35.3	64.7	35.7	64.3	29.3	70.7	22.2	77.8	0.574	0.745	45.7	0.914	45.9	0.918	0.916	41.7	0.833	34.5	0.690	0.762	0.648	0.775
138	JASWANTPURA	0.499	0.501	35.3	64.7	34.5	65.5	11.1	88.9	10.0	90.0	0.617	0.731	45.7	0.914	45.2	0.904	0.909	19.6	0.392	18.2	0.364	0.378	0.669	0.652
139	RANIWARA	0.483	0.517	42.1	57.9	33.3	66.7	7.3	92.7	0.0	100.0	0.620	0.702	49.0	0.980	44.9	0.898	0.939	13.9	0.278	0.0	0.000	0.139	0.660	0.579
140	SANCHORE	0.484	0.516	35.1	64.9	36.5	63.5	4.0	96.0	15.8	84.2	0.634	0.710	46.0	0.920	46.8	0.936	0.928	7.9	0.159	27.0	0.541	0.350	0.671	0.650
141	SAYLA	0.494	0.506	40.0	60.0	32.4	67.6	20.8	79.2	16.7	83.3	0.623	0.704	48.1	0.962	44.0	0.880	0.921	33.3	0.667	27.8	0.556	0.611	0.662	0.731
	JALOR	**0.492**	**0.508**	**36.6**	**63.4**	**35.0**	**65.0**	**15.7**	**84.3**	**13.8**	**86.2**	**0.631**	**0.725**	**46.6**	**0.932**	**45.7**	**0.914**	**0.923**	**27.0**	**0.541**	**23.8**	**0.476**	**0.508**	**0.675**	**0.702**
142	BAKANI	0.481	0.519	36.8	63.2	31.7	68.3	11.7	88.3	0.0	100.0	0.679	0.784	47.0	0.940	43.9	0.878	0.909	21.3	0.426	0.0	0.000	0.213	0.730	0.617
143	DAG	0.487	0.513	38.1	61.9	32.5	67.5	17.8	82.2	8.3	91.7	0.584	0.750	47.5	0.950	44.3	0.886	0.918	29.4	0.588	15.6	0.313	0.450	0.659	0.676
144	JHALRAPATAN	0.481	0.519	32.0	68.0	35.4	64.6	34.5	65.5	12.5	87.5	0.650	0.755	44.1	0.882	46.2	0.924	0.903	45.5	0.909	22.7	0.455	0.682	0.700	0.762
145	KHANPUR	0.477	0.523	31.6	68.4	34.2	65.8	14.4	85.6	20.0	80.0	0.616	0.723	44.0	0.880	45.7	0.914	0.897	25.6	0.513	33.3	0.667	0.590	0.667	0.718
146	MANOHARTHANA	0.480	0.520	33.3	66.7	35.9	64.1	14.8	85.2	15.4	84.6	0.688	0.755	45.0	0.900	46.5	0.930	0.915	25.6	0.513	27.0	0.541	0.527	0.721	0.721
147	PIRAWA	0.484	0.516	33.3	66.7	35.7	64.3	13.8	86.2	15.4	84.6	0.652	0.754	44.9	0.898	46.3	0.926	0.912	24.4	0.488	26.3	0.526	0.507	0.701	0.707
	JHALAWAR	**0.482**	**0.518**	**34.1**	**65.9**	**34.3**	**65.7**	**21.2**	**78.8**	**11.8**	**88.2**	**0.645**	**0.756**	**45.5**	**0.910**	**45.6**	**0.912**	**0.911**	**34.5**	**0.690**	**21.3**	**0.426**	**0.558**	**0.698**	**0.722**
148	ALSISAR	0.497	0.503	31.6	68.4	36.4	63.6	21.8	78.2	10.0	90.0	0.649	0.772	43.3	0.866	46.4	0.928	0.897	34.5	0.690	18.2	0.364	0.527	0.706	0.710
149	BUHANA	0.486	0.514	48.0	52.0	36.6	63.4	19.0	81.0	6.7	93.3	0.691	0.779	50.0	1.000	46.8	0.936	0.968	31.3	0.625	12.8	0.256	0.441	0.734	0.714
150	CHIRAWA	0.489	0.511	36.8	63.2	34.5	65.5	38.4	61.6	9.1	90.9	0.646	0.760	46.8	0.936	45.5	0.910	0.923	47.6	0.952	16.9	0.339	0.646	0.700	0.756
151	JHUNJHUNUN	0.494	0.506	34.8	65.2	37.8	62.2	26.6	73.4	8.3	91.7	0.666	0.786	45.5	0.910	47.2	0.944	0.927	40.0	0.800	15.4	0.308	0.554	0.722	0.734
152	KHETRI	0.484	0.516	32.1	67.9	36.1	63.9	20.3	79.7	11.1	88.9	0.654	0.748	44.1	0.882	46.5	0.930	0.906	33.3	0.667	20.4	0.408	0.538	0.699	0.714
153	NAWALGARH	0.492	0.508	37.0	63.0	37.1	62.9	28.2	71.8	19.2	80.8	0.624	0.742	46.8	0.936	46.9	0.938	0.937	40.0	0.800	31.3	0.625	0.713	0.679	0.776
154	SURAJGARH	0.482	0.518	33.3	66.7	35.1	64.9	36.8	63.2	7.7	92.3	0.662	0.771	45.0	0.900	46.1	0.922	0.911	47.6	0.952	14.7	0.294	0.623	0.715	0.750
155	UDAIPURWATI	0.491	0.509	42.3	57.7	32.4	67.6	8.4	91.6	10.0	90.0	0.642	0.759	48.9	0.978	44.1	0.882	0.930	15.6	0.313	18.2	0.364	0.338	0.696	0.655
	JHUNJHUNUN	**0.489**	**0.511**	**37.2**	**62.8**	**35.5**	**64.5**	**24.3**	**75.7**	**11.2**	**88.8**	**0.654**	**0.765**	**47.0**	**0.940**	**46.1**	**0.922**	**0.931**	**37.0**	**0.741**	**20.4**	**0.408**	**0.575**	**0.707**	**0.737**
156	BALESAR	0.478	0.522	36.8	63.2	36.4	63.6	32.4	67.6	0.0	100.0	0.656	0.804	47.1	0.942	46.9	0.938	0.940	45.5	0.909	0.0	0.000	0.455	0.726	0.707
157	BAP	0.473	0.527	35.3	64.7	35.5	64.5	0.0	100.0	33.3	66.7	0.719	0.864	46.4	0.928	46.5	0.930	0.929	0.0	0.000	45.5	0.909	0.455	0.788	0.724
158	BHOPALGARH	0.485	0.515	34.8	65.2	33.3	66.7	10.7	89.3	25.0	75.0	0.731	0.817	45.8	0.916	44.9	0.898	0.907	19.6	0.392	38.5	0.769	0.581	0.773	0.754
159	BILARA	0.482	0.518	33.3	66.7	37.8	62.2	19.6	80.4	32.4	67.6	0.727	0.827	45.0	0.900	47.4	0.948	0.924	32.3	0.645	43.5	0.870	0.757	0.775	0.819
160	LUNI	0.481	0.519	32.0	68.0	30.8	69.2	48.9	51.1	12.5	87.5	0.683	0.813	44.1	0.882	43.3	0.866	0.874	50.0	1.000	22.7	0.455	0.727	0.745	0.782
161	MANDOR	0.476	0.524	41.2	58.8	36.0	64.0	22.8	77.2	14.3	85.7	0.649	0.799	48.9	0.978	46.7	0.934	0.956	35.7	0.714	25.6	0.513	0.614	0.720	0.763
162	OSIAN	0.480	0.520	37.2	62.8	34.3	65.7	35.3	64.7	22.7	77.3	0.681	0.788	47.2	0.944	45.6	0.912	0.928	45.5	0.909	35.7	0.714	0.812	0.733	0.824
163	PHALODI	0.477	0.523	44.0	56.0	35.1	64.9	9.9	90.1	14.3	85.7	0.609	0.754	49.6	0.992	46.2	0.924	0.958	18.5	0.370	25.6	0.513	0.442	0.677	0.692
164	SHERGARH	0.477	0.523	35.3	64.7	37.5	62.5	11.3	88.7	10.0	90.0	0.662	0.810	46.3	0.926	47.4	0.948	0.937	20.8	0.417	18.5	0.370	0.394	0.732	0.687
	JODHPUR	**0.479**	**0.521**	**36.7**	**63.3**	**35.0**	**65.0**	**24.9**	**75.1**	**22.2**	**77.8**	**0.680**	**0.803**	**47.0**	**0.940**	**46.1**	**0.922**	**0.931**	**38.5**	**0.769**	**35.7**	**0.714**	**0.742**	**0.739**	**0.804**
165	HINDAUN	0.457	0.543	41.4	58.6	37.3	62.7	10.4	89.6	6.7	93.3	0.642	0.724	49.2	0.984	47.8	0.956	0.970	20.0	0.400	13.5	0.270	0.335	0.684	0.663
166	KARAULI	0.456	0.544	32.0	68.0	35.6	64.4	14.8	85.2	0.0	100.0	0.628	0.756	44.9	0.898	47.0	0.940	0.919	27.0	0.541	0.0	0.000	0.270	0.692	0.627
167	NADOTI	0.471	0.529	35.3	64.7	31.0	69.0	15.4	84.6	0.0	100.0	0.666	0.762	46.5	0.930	43.7	0.874	0.902	27.0	0.541	0.0	0.000	0.270	0.714	0.629

1	2	3	4	5	6	7	8	9	10	11	12	13	14	15	16	17	18	19	20	21	22	23	24	25	26
168	SAPOTRA	0.459	0.541	33.3	66.7	30.9	69.1	9.2	90.8	0.0	100.0	0.652	0.763	45.7	0.914	44.1	0.882	0.898	17.9	0.357	0.0	0.000	0.179	0.708	0.595
169	TODABHIM	0.462	0.538	47.8	52.2	46.5	53.5	4.6	95.4	0.0	100.0	0.650	0.741	50.1	1.002	50.0	1.000	1.001	9.4	0.189	0.0	0.000	0.094	0.696	0.597
	KARAULI	**0.460**	**0.540**	**38.0**	**62.0**	**36.3**	**63.7**	**10.9**	**89.1**	**1.8**	**98.2**	**0.646**	**0.749**	**48.0**	**0.960**	**47.3**	**0.946**	**0.953**	**20.8**	**0.417**	**3.8**	**0.077**	**0.247**	**0.697**	**0.632**
170	CHECHAT	0.475	0.525	39.1	60.9	50.0	50.0	27.2	72.8	35.7	64.3	0.813	0.967	48.1	0.962	50.0	1.000	0.981	40.0	0.800	47.6	0.952	0.876	0.887	0.915
171	ITAWA	0.475	0.525	36.8	63.2	33.3	66.7	19.4	80.6	8.3	91.7	0.760	0.944	47.1	0.942	45.2	0.904	0.923	32.3	0.645	15.9	0.318	0.481	0.847	0.750
172	LADPURA	0.474	0.526	35.3	64.7	33.3	66.7	67.8	32.2	35.7	64.3	0.738	0.928	46.4	0.928	45.2	0.904	0.916	43.5	0.870	47.6	0.952	0.911	0.827	0.885
173	SANGOD	0.478	0.522	31.6	68.4	37.1	62.9	17.0	83.0	18.2	81.8	0.823	0.949	43.9	0.878	47.2	0.944	0.911	29.4	0.588	30.3	0.606	0.597	0.884	0.797
174	SULTANPUR	0.477	0.523	36.8	63.2	33.3	66.7	35.1	64.9	30.8	69.2	0.772	0.926	47.1	0.942	45.1	0.902	0.922	45.5	0.909	43.5	0.870	0.889	0.845	0.886
	KOTA	**0.476**	**0.524**	**36.1**	**63.9**	**34.4**	**65.6**	**47.9**	**52.1**	**28.2**	**71.8**	**0.783**	**0.943**	**46.8**	**0.936**	**45.8**	**0.916**	**0.926**	**50.0**	**1.000**	**41.7**	**0.833**	**0.917**	**0.859**	**0.901**
175	DEGANA	0.495	0.505	32.0	68.0	30.2	69.8	9.8	90.2	13.3	86.7	0.657	0.751	43.7	0.874	42.3	0.846	0.860	17.9	0.357	23.3	0.465	0.411	0.701	0.657
176	DIDWANA	0.496	0.504	33.3	66.7	33.3	66.7	7.3	92.7	10.5	89.5	0.599	0.738	44.5	0.890	44.5	0.890	0.890	13.7	0.274	18.9	0.377	0.326	0.662	0.626
177	JAYAL	0.489	0.511	40.7	59.3	33.3	66.7	11.5	88.5	35.7	64.3	0.658	0.734	48.5	0.970	44.8	0.896	0.933	20.8	0.417	45.5	0.909	0.663	0.695	0.763
178	KUCHAMAN	0.483	0.517	38.7	61.3	38.5	61.5	12.0	88.0	16.7	83.3	0.567	0.733	47.8	0.956	47.7	0.954	0.955	21.7	0.435	28.6	0.571	0.503	0.642	0.700
179	LADNU	0.495	0.505	31.6	68.4	40.6	59.4	13.2	86.8	0.0	100.0	0.625	0.737	43.4	0.868	48.3	0.966	0.917	23.3	0.465	0.0	0.000	0.233	0.677	0.609
180	MAKRANA	0.489	0.511	32.0	68.0	52.8	47.2	9.5	90.5	15.8	84.2	0.577	0.747	43.9	0.878	49.8	0.996	0.937	17.5	0.351	27.0	0.541	0.446	0.653	0.678
181	MERTA	0.480	0.520	33.3	66.7	34.4	65.6	12.9	87.1	13.3	86.7	0.624	0.746	45.0	0.900	45.7	0.914	0.907	23.3	0.465	23.8	0.476	0.471	0.682	0.687
182	MUNDWA	0.486	0.514	34.8	65.2	36.8	63.2	6.9	93.1	14.3	85.7	0.652	0.738	45.8	0.916	46.9	0.938	0.927	13.2	0.263	25.0	0.500	0.382	0.694	0.667
183	NAGAUR	0.486	0.514	33.3	66.7	32.0	68.0	14.4	85.6	10.0	90.0	0.652	0.737	44.8	0.896	44.0	0.880	0.888	25.0	0.500	18.5	0.370	0.435	0.693	0.672
184	PARBATSAR	0.485	0.515	38.1	61.9	37.5	62.5	17.9	82.1	28.6	71.4	0.593	0.764	47.5	0.950	47.2	0.944	0.947	30.3	0.606	41.7	0.833	0.720	0.670	0.779
185	RIYAN	0.485	0.515	33.3	66.7	33.3	66.7	13.2	86.8	14.3	85.7	0.641	0.768	44.9	0.898	44.9	0.898	0.898	23.3	0.465	25.0	0.500	0.483	0.701	0.694
	NAGAUR	**0.488**	**0.512**	**34.8**	**65.2**	**36.2**	**63.8**	**11.7**	**88.3**	**15.5**	**84.5**	**0.626**	**0.744**	**45.7**	**0.914**	**46.5**	**0.930**	**0.922**	**20.8**	**0.417**	**26.3**	**0.526**	**0.472**	**0.681**	**0.691**
186	BALI	0.503	0.497	39.1	60.9	35.9	64.1	20.9	79.1	22.7	77.3	0.637	0.782	47.6	0.952	45.9	0.918	0.935	33.3	0.667	34.5	0.690	0.678	0.702	0.772
187	DESURI	0.513	0.487	40.0	60.0	33.3	66.7	11.0	89.0	6.7	93.3	0.634	0.775	47.8	0.956	44.0	0.880	0.918	19.2	0.385	12.2	0.244	0.314	0.695	0.643
188	JAITARAN	0.492	0.508	34.8	65.2	34.4	65.6	14.0	86.0	16.7	83.3	0.669	0.768	45.6	0.912	45.4	0.908	0.910	24.4	0.488	27.8	0.556	0.522	0.716	0.716
189	MARWAR JUN.	0.503	0.497	36.0	64.0	32.6	67.4	15.9	84.1	5.9	94.1	0.670	0.793	46.0	0.920	43.9	0.878	0.899	26.3	0.526	11.0	0.220	0.373	0.726	0.666
190	PALI	0.495	0.505	33.3	66.7	34.8	65.2	37.9	62.1	0.0	100.0	0.693	0.817	44.6	0.892	45.5	0.910	0.901	47.6	0.952	0.0	0.000	0.476	0.750	0.709
191	RAIPUR	0.496	0.504	42.9	57.1	45.7	54.3	21.6	78.4	7.1	92.9	0.641	0.771	49.0	0.980	49.7	0.994	0.987	34.5	0.690	13.3	0.267	0.478	0.701	0.722
192	RANI STATION	0.510	0.490	33.3	66.7	34.5	65.5	20.8	79.2	0.0	100.0	0.663	0.802	44.1	0.882	44.9	0.898	0.890	32.3	0.645	0.0	0.000	0.323	0.725	0.646
193	ROHAT	0.491	0.509	33.3	66.7	34.8	65.2	14.7	85.3	11.1	88.9	0.676	0.792	44.7	0.894	45.6	0.912	0.903	25.6	0.513	20.0	0.400	0.456	0.730	0.697
194	SOJAT	0.502	0.498	33.3	66.7	35.1	64.9	12.9	87.1	13.3	86.7	0.696	0.804	44.4	0.888	45.5	0.910	0.899	22.2	0.444	23.3	0.465	0.455	0.746	0.700
195	SUMERPUR	0.499	0.501	36.8	63.2	39.3	60.7	22.9	77.1	12.5	87.5	0.617	0.786	46.5	0.930	47.7	0.954	0.942	35.7	0.714	21.7	0.435	0.575	0.691	0.736
	PALI	**0.500**	**0.500**	**36.5**	**63.5**	**36.1**	**63.9**	**20.0**	**80.0**	**11.4**	**88.6**	**0.660**	**0.787**	**46.4**	**0.928**	**46.1**	**0.922**	**0.925**	**32.3**	**0.645**	**20.0**	**0.400**	**0.523**	**0.718**	**0.722**
196	AMET	0.500	0.500	33.3	66.7	35.0	65.0	27.5	72.5	14.3	85.7	0.590	0.832	44.4	0.888	45.5	0.910	0.899	40.0	0.800	24.4	0.488	0.644	0.690	0.744
197	BHIM	0.506	0.494	35.3	64.7	34.5	65.5	18.6	81.4	15.4	84.6	0.669	0.773	45.5	0.910	45.0	0.900	0.905	30.3	0.606	25.6	0.513	0.560	0.716	0.727
198	DEOGARH	0.510	0.490	40.0	60.0	38.9	61.1	23.7	76.3	6.3	93.8	0.685	0.783	47.8	0.956	47.3	0.946	0.951	35.7	0.714	11.6	0.233	0.474	0.730	0.718
199	KHAMNOR	0.501	0.499	33.3	66.7	35.0	65.0	19.5	80.5	14.8	85.2	0.606	0.781	44.4	0.888	45.5	0.910	0.899	31.3	0.625	25.0	0.500	0.563	0.682	0.715
200	KUMBHALGARH	0.508	0.492	35.3	64.7	32.4	67.6	40.2	59.8	9.1	90.9	0.701	0.825	45.5	0.910	43.6	0.872	0.891	47.6	0.952	16.4	0.328	0.640	0.757	0.763
201	RAILMAGRA	0.505	0.495	35.3	64.7	37.9	62.1	23.0	77.0	8.3	91.7	0.684	0.838	45.5	0.910	47.0	0.940	0.925	35.7	0.714	15.2	0.303	0.509	0.753	0.729
202	RAJSAMAND	0.494	0.506	35.3	64.7	34.5	65.5	25.1	74.9	0.0	100.0	0.587	0.795	45.8	0.916	45.4	0.908	0.912	38.5	0.769	0.0	0.000	0.385	0.677	0.658
	RAJSAMAND	**0.503**	**0.497**	**35.3**	**64.7**	**35.1**	**64.9**	**24.0**	**76.0**	**9.1**	**90.9**	**0.650**	**0.803**	**45.6**	**0.912**	**45.5**	**0.910**	**0.911**	**37.0**	**0.741**	**16.4**	**0.328**	**0.534**	**0.718**	**0.721**
203	BAMANWAS	0.469	0.531	52.6	47.4	37.1	62.9	8.0	92.0	14.3	85.7	0.680	0.779	49.7	0.994	47.4	0.948	0.971	15.6	0.313	25.6	0.513	0.413	0.729	0.704
204	BONLI	0.475	0.525	30.4	69.6	34.1	65.9	13.3	86.7	0.0	100.0	0.701	0.788	43.2	0.864	45.7	0.914	0.889	23.8	0.476	0.0	0.000	0.238	0.744	0.624
205	GANGAPUR	0.467	0.533	34.8	65.2	34.2	65.8	16.7	83.3	15.4	84.6	0.660	0.769	46.3	0.926	46.0	0.920	0.923	29.4	0.588	27.0	0.541	0.564	0.714	0.734
206	KHANDAR	0.466	0.534	31.6	68.4	34.3	65.7	10.1	89.9	20.0	80.0	0.706	0.794	44.3	0.886	46.1	0.922	0.904	19.2	0.385	33.3	0.667	0.526	0.751	0.727
207	SAWAI MADHOPUR	0.475	0.525	40.0	60.0	40.0	60.0	29.9	70.1	25.0	75.0	0.672	0.770	48.5	0.970	48.5	0.970	0.970	43.5	0.870	38.5	0.769	0.819	0.720	0.836
	SAWAI MADHOPUR	**0.471**	**0.529**	**37.6**	**62.4**	**36.1**	**63.9**	**18.5**	**81.5**	**14.0**	**86.0**	**0.681**	**0.780**	**47.6**	**0.952**	**46.9**	**0.938**	**0.945**	**31.3**	**0.625**	**25.0**	**0.500**	**0.563**	**0.730**	**0.746**
208	DANTA RAMGARH	0.492	0.508	32.3	67.7	35.6	64.4	12.0	88.0	19.2	80.8	0.629	0.755	44.0	0.880	46.1	0.922	0.901	21.3	0.426	31.3	0.625	0.525	0.687	0.705
209	DHOND	0.490	0.510	32.0	68.0	32.6	67.4	17.6	82.4	0.0	100.0	0.655	0.767	43.8	0.876	44.3	0.886	0.881	29.4	0.588	0.0	0.000	0.294	0.708	0.628
210	FATEHPUR	0.498	0.502	34.8	65.2	34.3	65.7	9.6	90.4	21.4	78.6	0.727	0.788	45.4	0.908	45.1	0.902	0.905	17.5	0.351	33.3	0.667	0.509	0.756	0.723
211	KHANDELA	0.491	0.509	40.7	59.3	38.5	61.5	8.0	92.0	0.0	100.0	0.657	0.776	48.4	0.968	47.6	0.952	0.960	14.9	0.299	0.0	0.000	0.149	0.713	0.608
212	LACHHMANGARH	0.493	0.507	47.8	52.2	37.8	62.2	10.1	89.9	0.0	100.0	0.705	0.782	49.9	0.998	47.2	0.944	0.971	18.5	0.370	0.0	0.000	0.185	0.742	0.633
213	NEEM KA THANA	0.480	0.520	32.4	67.6	35.6	64.4	13.0	87.0	0.0	100.0	0.610	0.748	44.4	0.888	46.4	0.928	0.908	23.3	0.465	0.0	0.000	0.233	0.675	0.605
214	PIPRALI	0.487	0.513	40.0	60.0	36.1	63.9	23.0	77.0	7.1	92.9	0.664	0.774	48.3	0.966	46.5	0.930	0.948	35.7	0.714	13.5	0.270	0.492	0.716	0.719
215	SRI MADHOPUR	0.487	0.513	40.0	60.0	35.3	64.7	8.1	91.9	7.4	92.6	0.613	0.735	48.3	0.966	46.0	0.920	0.943	15.2	0.303	14.1	0.282	0.292	0.670	0.635
	SIKAR	**0.489**	**0.511**	**37.0**	**63.0**	**35.7**	**64.3**	**12.6**	**87.4**	**8.6**	**91.4**	**0.657**	**0.765**	**46.9**	**0.938**	**46.2**	**0.924**	**0.931**	**22.2**	**0.444**	**16.1**	**0.323**	**0.384**	**0.708**	**0.674**
216	ABU ROAD	0.483	0.517	46.7	53.3	32.0	68.0	19.1	80.9	15.4	84.6	0.663	0.803	49.9	0.998	44.1	0.882	0.940	31.3	0.625	27.0	0.541	0.583	0.728	0.750
217	PINDWARA	0.488	0.512	38.1	61.9	32.4	67.6	19.2	80.8	22.2	77.8	0.684	0.812	47.4	0.948	44.2	0.884	0.916	31.3	0.625	34.5	0.690	0.657	0.744	0.773
218	REODAR	0.486	0.514	33.3	66.7	35.1	64.9	22.4	77.6	10.0	90.0	0.696	0.814	44.8	0.896	45.9	0.918	0.907	35.7	0.714	18.5	0.370	0.542	0.752	0.734
219	SHEOGANJ	0.491	0.509	33.3	66.7	33.3	66.7	20.1	79.9	10.0	90.0	0.648	0.824	44.7	0.894	44.7	0.894	0.894	32.3	0.645	18.2	0.364	0.504	0.727	0.708
220	SIROHI	0.503	0.497	35.3	64.7	35.5	64.5	20.3	79.7	8.3	91.7	0.672	0.821	45.6	0.912	45.7	0.914	0.913	32.3	0.645	15.2	0.303	0.474	0.739	0.709
	SIROHI	**0.490**	**0.510**	**37.1**	**62.9**	**33.8**	**66.2**	**20.0**	**80.0**	**13.0**	**87.0**	**0.677**	**0.814**	**46.9**	**0.938**	**45.0**	**0.900**	**0.919**	**32.3**	**0.645**	**22.7**	**0.455**	**0.550**	**0.741**	**0.737**
221	DEOLI	0.483	0.517	38.1	61.9	33.3	66.7	25.4	74.6	16.7	83.3	0.687	0.789	47.6	0.952	44.9	0.898	0.925	38.5	0.769	28.6	0.571	0.670	0.736	0.777
222	MALPURA	0.486	0.514	34.8	65.2	33.3	66.7	24.3	75.7	13.3	86.7	0.678	0.799	45.8	0.916	44.8	0.896	0.906	37.0	0.741	23.8	0.476	0.609	0.735	0.750
223	NIWAI	0.479	0.521	33.3	66.7	34.1	65.9	25.4	74.6	15.4	84.6	0.708	0.788	45.1	0.902	45.6	0.912	0.907	38.5	0.769	27.0	0.541	0.655	0.747	0.770
224	TODARAISINGH	0.488	0.512	33.3	66.7	32.3	67.7	11.0	89.0	0.0	100.0	0.708	0.800	44.8	0.896	44.1	0.882	0.889	20.0	0.400	0.0	0.000	0.200	0.752	0.614
225	TONK	0.482	0.518	40.0	60.0	36.0	64.0	28.5	71.5	11.8	88.2	0.696	0.786	48.3	0.966	46.5	0.930	0.948	41.7	0.833	21.3	0.426	0.629	0.740	0.772
226	UNIARA	0.478	0.522	41.2	58.8	33.3	66.7	21.6	78.4	33.3	66.7	0.686	0.769	48.8	0.976	45.1	0.902	0.939	34.5	0.690	45.5	0.909	0.799	0.727	0.822
	TONK	**0.482**	**0.518**	**36.9**	**63.1**	**33.9**	**66.1**	**23.8**	**76.2**	**14.3**	**85.7**	**0.694**	**0.789**	**47.0**	**0.940**	**45.3**	**0.906**	**0.923**	**37.0**	**0.741**	**25.0**	**0.500**	**0.620**	**0.740**	**0.761**
227	BARGAON	0.485	0.515	33.3	66.7	40.0	60.0	48.1	51.9	28.6	71.4	0.671	0.858	44.9	0.898	48.3	0.966	0.932	50.0	1.000	41.7	0.833	0.917	0.756	0.868
228	BHINDER	0.496	0.504	32.0	68.0	31.4	68.6	17.8	82.2	33.3	66.7	0.665	0.831	43.6	0.872	43.2	0.864	0.868	29.4	0.588	45.5	0.909	0.749	0.739	0.785

P. Code	Panchayat Samiti	Female and Male Share of Total Pop.		Female and Male Share of PS Members		Female and Male Share of Sarpanchs		Female and Male Share of Teachers in Govt. Pr. and UPS		Female and Male Share of Govt. Doctors		Female and Male Estimated Income Index		EDEP for PS Repre#	Indexed EDEP for PS Repre#	EDEP for GP Repre#	Indexed EDEP for GP Repre#	EDEP for Political Repre# (A)	EDEP for Position as Teachers in Govt. Pr. and UPS	Indexed EDEP for Teachers in Govt. Pr. and UPS	EDEP for Position as Doctors in Govt. Hospital	Indexed EDEP for Doctors in Govt. Hosp.	EDEP for Socio-Eco Parti.## (B)	EDEP for Income (C)	GEM (A+B+C)/3
		Female	Male	Female (%)	Male (%)	Female (%)	Male (%)	Female (%)	Male (%)	Female (%)	Male (%)	Female	Male												
1	2	3	4	5	6	7	8	9	10	11	12	13	14	15	16	17	18	19	20	21	22	23	24	25	26
229	DHARIAWAD	0.499	0.501	36.0	64.0	37.5	62.5	9.2	90.8	14.3	85.7	0.686	0.780	46.1	0.922	45.9	0.938	0.930	16.7	0.333	24.4	0.488	0.411	0.730	0.690
230	GIRWA	0.490	0.510	40.7	59.3	36.2	63.8	22.0	78.0	26.3	73.7	0.606	0.797	48.5	0.970	45.4	0.928	0.949	34.5	0.690	38.5	0.769	0.730	0.691	0.790
231	GOGUNDA	0.495	0.505	31.6	68.4	32.5	67.5	33.0	67.0	10.0	90.0	0.668	0.791	43.4	0.868	44.0	0.880	0.874	43.5	0.870	18.2	0.364	0.617	0.725	0.739
232	JHADOL	0.494	0.506	34.8	65.2	33.3	66.7	14.9	85.1	21.4	78.6	0.673	0.795	45.5	0.910	44.6	0.892	0.901	25.6	0.513	33.3	0.667	0.590	0.730	0.740
233	KHERWARA	0.501	0.499	37.9	62.1	37.1	62.9	21.8	78.2	21.4	78.6	0.667	0.770	47.0	0.940	46.6	0.932	0.936	34.5	0.690	33.3	0.667	0.678	0.715	0.776
234	KOTRA	0.495	0.505	33.3	66.7	33.3	66.7	8.7	91.3	33.3	66.7	0.667	0.779	44.6	0.892	44.6	0.892	0.892	16.1	0.323	45.5	0.909	0.616	0.719	0.742
235	MAVLI	0.494	0.506	32.0	68.0	38.3	61.7	36.2	63.8	25.0	75.0	0.638	0.816	43.7	0.874	47.4	0.948	0.911	45.5	0.909	37.0	0.741	0.825	0.717	0.818
236	SALUMBAR	0.506	0.494	32.0	68.0	35.4	64.6	29.2	70.8	14.3	85.7	0.694	0.810	43.3	0.866	45.6	0.912	0.889	41.7	0.833	24.4	0.488	0.661	0.747	0.766
237	SARADA	0.504	0.496	29.2	70.8	30.4	69.6	23.3	76.7	18.8	81.3	0.644	0.797	41.2	0.824	42.2	0.844	0.834	35.7	0.714	30.3	0.606	0.660	0.712	0.735
	UDAIPUR	**0.497**	**0.503**	**34.1**	**65.9**	**34.9**	**65.1**	**24.4**	**75.6**	**22.3**	**77.7**	**0.664**	**0.800**	**45.0**	**0.900**	**45.5**	**0.910**	**0.905**	**37.0**	**0.741**	**34.5**	**0.690**	**0.715**	**0.726**	**0.782**
	RAJASTHAN	**0.482**	**0.518**	**36.5**	**63.5**	**35.5**	**64.4**	**21.5**	**78.5**	**15.1**	**84.9**	**0.685**	**0.798**	**46.8**	**0.936**	**46.3**	**0.926**	**0.931**	**34.5**	**0.690**	**26.3**	**0.526**	**0.608**	**0.739**	**0.759**

Note: For calculation of GEM. Please see Methodology

Repre.- Representation ## Parti.- Participation

* Dungargarh PS shifted from Churu to Bikaner district on 1st April 2001,

** Excluding data of Dungargarh PS;

*** Including data of Dungargarh PS.

Source: Calculated from Data given in General Annex -VII, XI, XIII, XIV and Annex 14.1.

ANNEX-15.2

RANKING OF PSS BY GEM : RAJASTHAN, 2001

(Descending Order)

RANK	*PANCHAYAT SAMITIES P. CODE*	*NAME*	*GEM*
1	2	3	4
	VERY HIGH (>=0.9)		
1	**170**	**CHECHAT**	**0.915**
2	**129**	**SANGANER**	**0.911**
3	**125**	**JHOTWARA**	**0.910**
4	**110**	**GANGANAGAR**	**0.907**
	HIGH (0.8-0.9)		
5	**79**	**BHAINSRORGARH**	**0.888**
6	**174**	**SULTANPUR**	**0.886**
7	**172**	**LADPURA**	**0.885**
8	**115**	**SURATGARH**	**0.875**
9	**227**	**BARGAON**	**0.868**
10	**61**	**MANDALGARH**	**0.866**
10	**119**	**AMBER**	**0.866**
12	**6**	**MASOODA**	**0.857**
13	**78**	**BHADESAR**	**0.852**
14	**60**	**MANDAL**	**0.851**
15	**64**	**SHAHPURA**	**0.847**
16	**22**	**UMREN**	**0.844**
17	**111**	**KARANPUR**	**0.840**
18	**57**	**HURDA**	**0.837**
18	**63**	**SAHARA**	**0.837**
20	**207**	**SAWAI MADHOPUR**	**0.836**
21	**68**	**KOLAYAT**	**0.832**
22	**7**	**PISANGAN**	**0.830**
23	**122**	**DUDU**	**0.828**
24	**55**	**ASIND**	**0.826**
24	**62**	**RAIPUR**	**0.826**
24	**69**	**LUNKARANSAR**	**0.826**
27	**162**	**OSIAN**	**0.824**
28	**67**	**DUNGARGARH**	**0.822**
28	**114**	**SADULSHAHAR**	**0.822**
28	**226**	**UNIARA**	**0.822**
31	**53**	**SEWAR**	**0.821**
32	**159**	**BILARA**	**0.819**
33	**235**	**MAVLI**	**0.818**
34	**65**	**SUWANA**	**0.816**
35	**85**	**KAPASAN**	**0.815**
35	**86**	**NIMBAHERA**	**0.815**
37	**83**	**DUNGLA**	**0.809**
38	**58**	**JAHAZPUR**	**0.806**
39	**82**	**CHITTAURGARH**	**0.804**
39	**117**	**HANUMANGARH**	**0.804**
	MEDIUM (0.7-0.8)		
41	**126**	**KOTPUTLI**	**0.799**
42	**35**	**CHHIPABAROD**	**0.798**
43	**173**	**SANGOD**	**0.797**
44	**12**	**KISHANGARH BAS**	**0.796**
45	**87**	**PRATAPGARH**	**0.793**
46	**4**	**KEKRI**	**0.792**
46	**120**	**BASSI**	**0.792**
48	**89**	**CHURU**	**0.790**
48	**230**	**GIRWA**	**0.790**
50	**33**	**BARAN**	**0.788**
51	**109**	**ANUPGARH**	**0.785**
51	**124**	**JAMWA RAMGARH**	**0.785**
51	**130**	**SHAHPURA**	**0.785**
51	**228**	**BHINDER**	**0.785**
55	**74**	**TALERA**	**0.784**
56	**59**	**KOTRI**	**0.782**
56	**160**	**LUNI**	**0.782**
58	**80**	**BHOPALSAGAR**	**0.780**
59	**123**	**GOVINDGARH**	**0.779**
59	**184**	**PARBATSAR**	**0.779**
61	**72**	**KESHORAIPATAN**	**0.777**
61	**221**	**DEOLI**	**0.777**
63	**153**	**NAWALGARH**	**0.776**
63	**233**	**KHERWARA**	**0.776**
65	**137**	**JALOR**	**0.775**
66	**217**	**PINDWARA**	**0.773**
67	**186**	**BALI**	**0.772**
67	**225**	**TONK**	**0.772**
69	**66**	**BIKANER**	**0.771**
69	**81**	**CHHOTI SADRI**	**0.771**
69	**106**	**DUNGARPUR**	**0.771**
72	**113**	**RAISINGHNAGAR**	**0.770**
72	**223**	**NIWAI**	**0.770**
74	**25**	**GARHI**	**0.769**
74	**36**	**KISHANGANJ**	**0.769**
76	**14**	**LACHHMANGARH**	**0.768**
77	**236**	**SALUMBAR**	**0.766**
78	**20**	**THANAGAZI**	**0.766**
78	**112**	**PADAMPUR**	**0.765**
80	**30**	**TALWARA**	**0.764**
80	**56**	**BANERA**	**0.764**
82	**37**	**SHAHBAD**	**0.763**
82	**161**	**MANDOR**	**0.763**
82	**177**	**JAYAL**	**0.763**
82	**200**	**KUMBHALGARH**	**0.763**
86	**144**	**JHALRAPATAN**	**0.762**
87	**70**	**NOKHA**	**0.761**
88	31	ANTA	0.758
89	150	CHIRAWA	0.756
90	158	BHOPALGARH	0.754
91	154	SURAJGARH	0.750
91	171	ITAWA	0.750
91	216	ABU ROAD	0.750
91	222	MALPURA	0.750
95	121	CHAKSU	0.748
95	128	SAMBHAR	0.748
97	3	JAWAJA	0.747
98	38	BALOTRA	0.745
98	116	BHADRA	0.745
100	196	AMET	0.744
101	234	KOTRA	0.742
102	232	JHADOL	0.740
103	231	GOGUNDA	0.739
104	195	SUMERPUR	0.736
105	100	BARI	0.735
105	237	SARADA	0.735
107	90	RAJGARH	0.734
107	151	JHUNJHUNUN	0.734
107	205	GANGAPUR	0.734
107	218	REODAR	0.734
111	73	NAINWA	0.733
111	134	SANKRA	0.733
113	93	SUJANGARH	0.731
113	141	SAYLA	0.731
115	5	KISHANGARH	0.730
116	1	ARAIN	0.730
116	10	BEHROR	0.730
116	50	NADBAI	0.730
119	201	RAILMAGRA	0.7[illegible]
120	76	BARI SADRI	0.728
120	136	BHINMAL	0.728
122	197	BHIM	0.727
122	206	KHANDAR	0.727
124	24	BAGIDORA	0.726
125	9	BANSURE	0.724
125	99	SIKRAI	0.724
125	157	BAP	0.724
128	210	FATEHPUR	0.723
129	191	RAIPUR	0.722
130	94	TARANAGAR	0.721
130	131	VIRATNAGAR	0.721
130	146	MANOHARTHANA	0.721
133	77	BEGUN	0.719
133	214	PIPRALI	0.719
135	8	SRINAGAR	0.718
135	34	CHHABRA	0.718
135	145	KHANPUR	0.718
135	198	DEOGARH	0.718
139	127	PHAGI	0.717
140	97	LALSOT	0.716
140	188	JAITARAN	0.716
142	32	ATRU	0.715
142	199	KHAMNOR	0.715
144	149	BUHANA	0.714
144	152	KHETRI	0.714
146	15	MANDAWAR	0.712
147	84	GANGRAR	0.710
147	148	ALSISAR	0.710
149	190	PALI	0.709
149	220	SIROHI	0.709
151	219	SHEOGANJ	0.708
152	17	RAJGARH	0.707
152	147	PIRAWA	0.707
152	156	BALESAR	0.707
155	208	DANTA RAMGARH	0.705
156	18	RAMGARH	0.704
156	102	DHAULPUR	0.704
156	203	BAMANWAS	0.704
159	51	NAGAR PAHARI	0.703
159	135	AHORE	0.703
161	2	BHINAY	0.701
162	16	NIMRANA	0.700
162	26	GHATOL	0.700
162	178	KUCHAMAN	0.700
162	194	SOJAT	0.700
	LOW (0.6-0.7)		
166	92	SARDARSHAHAR	0.699
167	107	SAGWARA	0.697
167	118	NOHAR	0.697
167	193	ROHAT	0.697
170	54	WEIR	0.695
171	95	BANDIKUI	0.694
171	185	RIYAN	0.694
173	98	MAHWA	0.692
173	163	PHALODI	0.692
175	229	DHARIAWAD	0.690
176	27	KUSHALGARH	0.689
177	29	SAJJANGARH	0.688
178	164	SHERGARH	0.687
178	181	MERTA	0.687
180	21	TIJARA	0.686
180	28	PEEPALKHOONT	0.686
182	88	RASHMI	0.685
183	71	HINDOLI	0.682
184	49	KUMHER	0.678
184	180	MAKRANA	0.678
186	143	DAG	0.676
187	103	RAJAKHERA	0.675
188	46	BAYANA	0.673
189	183	NAGAUR	0.672
190	45	SIWANA	0.670
191	96	DAUSA	0.668
192	182	MUNDWA	0.667
193	189	MARWAR JUN.	0.666
194	108	SIMALWARA	0.664
195	165	HINDAUN	0.663
196	40	BAYTOO	0.660
197	132	JAISALMER	0.659
198	202	RAJSAMAND	0.658
199	175	DEGANA	0.657
200	75	ARNOD	0.655
200	155	UDAIPURWATI	0.655
202	52	RUPBAS	0.652
202	138	JASWANTPURA	0.652
204	140	SANCHORE	0.650
205	39	BARMER	0.647
206	192	RANI STATION	0.646
207	187	DESURI	0.643
208	91	RATANGARH	0.642
209	47	DEEG	0.641
210	13	KOTKASIM	0.638
211	44	SINDHARI	0.636
212	19	RENI	0.635
212	215	SRI MADHOPUR	0.635
214	212	LACHHMANGARH	0.633
215	167	NADOTI	0.629
216	209	DHOND	0.628
217	166	KARAULI	0.627
218	176	DIDWANA	0.626
219	204	BONLI	0.624
220	104	ASPUR	0.623
221	48	KAMAN	0.620
222	11	KATHUMAR	0.618
223	142	BAKANI	0.617
224	224	TODARAISINGH	0.614
225	105	BICHHIWARA	0.613
226	23	ANANDPURI	0.612
227	179	LADNU	0.609
228	211	KHANDELA	0.608
229	213	NEEM KA THANA	0.605
	VERY LOW (<0.6)		
230	169	TODABHIM	0.597
231	168	SAPOTRA	0.595
232	42	DHORIMANNA	0.585
233	101	BASERI	0.582
234	139	RANIWARA	0.579
235	133	SAM	0.566
236	41	CHOHTAN	0.560
237	43	SHEO	0.557
		RAJASTHAN	**0.759**
		%age of AAPs	**36.70**

BOLD: Equal/Above Average Panchayat Samities (AAPs)

Source: Annex-15.1, Col. 26.

ANNEX-16.1

RANKING OF PSS BY HDI, 1991

RANK	PANCHAYAT SAMITIES P. CODE	NAME	HDI
1	2	3	4
	HIGH (>= 0.5)		
1	**170**	**CHECHAT**	**0.5464**
2	**111**	**KARANPUR**	**0.5455**
3	**173**	**SANGOD**	**0.5399**
4	**172**	**LADPURA**	**0.5368**
5	**174**	**SULTANPUR**	**0.5207**
6	**123**	**GOVINDGARH**	**0.5198**
7	**110**	**GANGANAGAR**	**0.5182**
8	**4**	**KEKRI**	**0.5130**
9	**130**	**SHAHPURA**	**0.5082**
10	**7**	**PISANGAN**	**0.5073**
11	**113**	**RAISINGHNAGAR**	**0.5040**
12	**120**	**BASSI**	**0.5012**
12	**129**	**SANGANER**	**0.5012**
	MEDIUM (0.4 - 0.5)		
14	**119**	**AMBER**	**0.4990**
15	**171**	**ITAWA**	**0.4953**
16	**125**	**JHOTWARA**	**0.4919**
17	**116**	**BHADRA**	**0.4915**
18	**126**	**KOTPUTLI**	**0.4882**
19	**124**	**JAMWA RAMGARH**	**0.4875**
20	**114**	**SADULSHAHAR**	**0.4864**
21	**2**	**BHINAY**	**0.4859**
22	**128**	**SAMBHAR**	**0.4849**
23	**127**	**PHAGI**	**0.4847**
24	**112**	**PADAMPUR**	**0.4843**
25	**10**	**BEHROR**	**0.4794**
26	**8**	**SRINAGAR**	**0.4781**
27	**131**	**VIRATNAGAR**	**0.4744**
28	**121**	**CHAKSU**	**0.4739**
29	**122**	**DUDU**	**0.4699**
30	**6**	**MASOODA**	**0.4697**
31	**117**	**HANUMANGARH**	**0.4676**
32	**5**	**KISHANGARH**	**0.4638**
33	**159**	**BILARA**	**0.4617**
34	**1**	**ARAIN**	**0.4583**
35	**16**	**NIMRANA**	**0.4579**
36	**118**	**NOHAR**	**0.4518**
37	**57**	**HURDA**	**0.4509**
38	**3**	**JAWAJA**	**0.4426**
39	**158**	**BHOPALGARH**	**0.4385**
40	**195**	**SUMERPUR**	**0.4368**
41	**66**	**BIKANER**	**0.4362**
42	**192**	**RANI STATION**	**0.4355**
43	**70**	**NOKHA**	**0.4348**
44	**194**	**SOJAT**	**0.4332**
45	**186**	**BALI**	**0.4329**
46	**15**	**MANDAWAR**	**0.4322**
47	**115**	**SURATGARH**	**0.4320**
48	**201**	**RAILMAGRA**	**0.4315**
49	**49**	**KUMHER**	**0.4309**
50	**63**	**SAHARA**	**0.4302**
51	**56**	**BANERA**	**0.4263**
52	**80**	**BHOPALSAGAR**	**0.4257**
53	**217**	**PINDWARA**	**0.4255**
54	**88**	**RASHMI**	**0.4245**
55	**235**	**MAVLI**	**0.4244**
56	**13**	**KOTKASIM**	**0.4241**
57	**160**	**LUNI**	**0.4228**
58	**199**	**KHAMNOR**	**0.4222**
59	**69**	**LUNKARANSAR**	**0.4210**
60	**227**	**BARGAON**	**0.4207**
61	**32**	**ATRU**	**0.4198**
62	**33**	**BARAN**	**0.4197**
63	**187**	**DESURI**	**0.4191**
64	**35**	**CHHIPABAROD**	**0.4170**
65	**220**	**SIROHI**	**0.4154**
66	**228**	**BHINDER**	**0.4148**
67	**189**	**KHARCHI/MARWAR JUN.**	**0.4137**
68	**109**	**ANUPGARH**	**0.4132**
69	**60**	**MANDAL**	**0.4110**
70	**65**	**SUWANA**	**0.4108**
71	**86**	**NIMBAHERA**	**0.4104**
72	**190**	**PALI**	**0.4092**
73	**68**	**KOLAYAT**	**0.4088**
74	**17**	**RAJGARH**	**0.4079**
74	**31**	**ANTA**	**0.4079**
76	**151**	**JHUNJHUNUN**	**0.4075**
77	**219**	**SHEOGANJ**	**0.4073**
78	**210**	**FATEHPUR**	**0.4071**
79	**188**	**JAITARAN**	**0.4038**
80	**209**	**DHOND**	**0.4036**
81	**212**	**LACHHMANGARH**	**0.4035**
82	**85**	**KAPASAN**	**0.4034**
83	**19**	**RENI**	**0.4026**
84	**81**	**CHHOTI SADRI**	**0.4025**
85	**237**	**SARADA**	**0.4020**
86	**12**	**KISHANGARH BAS**	**0.4018**
87	**156**	**BALESAR**	**0.4014**
88	**149**	**BUHANA**	**0.4004**
89	**54**	**WEIR**	**0.4000**
	LOW (0.3 - 0.4)		
90	**55**	**ASIND**	**0.3996**
91	**82**	**CHITTAURGARH**	**0.3995**
92	**135**	**AHORE**	**0.3993**
92	**218**	**REODAR**	**0.3993**
94	**230**	**GIRWA**	**0.3992**
95	**197**	**BHIM**	**0.3989**
96	**164**	**SHERGARH**	**0.3972**
97	**50**	**NADBAI**	**0.3951**
98	**59**	**KOTRI**	**0.3948**
98	**83**	**DUNGLA**	**0.3948**
100	**84**	**GANGRAR**	**0.3944**
101	64	SHAHPURA	0.3936
102	76	BARI SADRI	0.3935
103	222	MALPURA	0.3926
104	62	RAIPUR	0.3925
105	221	DEOLI	0.3920
106	77	BEGUN	0.3919
107	193	ROHAT	0.3917
108	47	DEEG	0.3907
109	161	MANDOR	0.3901
110	53	SEWAR	0.3894
111	155	UDAIPURWATI	0.3891
112	204	BONLI	0.3889
113	9	BANSURE	0.3888
114	153	NAWALGARH	0.3885
115	167	NADOTI	0.3884
116	78	BHADESAR	0.3882
117	211	KHANDELA	0.3878
118	191	RAIPUR	0.3874
119	73	NAINWA	0.3872
120	150	CHIRAWA	0.3867
121	205	GANGAPUR	0.3864
122	223	NIWAI	0.3862
123	233	KHERWARA	0.3853
124	208	DANTA RAMGARH	0.3837
125	148	ALSISAR	0.3826
126	236	SALUMBAR	0.3825
127	203	BAMANWAS	0.3824
128	181	MERTA	0.3823
129	58	JAHAZPUR	0.3821
130	11	KATHUMAR	0.3819
131	20	THANAGAZI	0.3818
132	74	TALERA	0.3805
132	75	ARNOD	0.3805
134	72	KESHORAIPATAN	0.3799
135	185	RIYAN	0.3796
136	14	LACHHMANGARH	0.3794
137	224	TODARAISINGH	0.3791
138	61	MANDALGARH	0.3790
139	36	KISHANGANJ	0.3789
140	25	GARHI	0.3788
141	71	HINDOLI	0.3784
142	162	OSIAN	0.3774
143	67	DUNGARGARH	0.3768
144	21	TIJARA	0.3766
145	165	HINDAUN	0.3763
146	215	SRI MADHOPUR	0.3757
147	214	PIPRALI	0.3749
148	37	SHAHBAD	0.3747
149	154	SURAJGARH	0.3738
150	52	RUPBAS	0.3733
151	96	DAUSA	0.3728
152	18	RAMGARH	0.3727
152	22	UMREN	0.3727
154	207	SAWAI MADHOPUR	0.3725
155	231	GOGUNDA	0.3711
156	216	ABU ROAD	0.3709
157	163	PHALODI	0.3690
158	94	TARANAGAR	0.3689
159	98	MAHWA	0.3667
160	137	JALOR	0.3666
161	152	KHETRI	0.3655
162	95	BANDIKUI	0.3650
163	213	NEEM KA THANA	0.3645
164	87	PRATAPGARH	0.3642
165	179	LADNU	0.3638
166	99	SIKRAI	0.3632
166	175	DEGANA	0.3632
168	169	TODABHIM	0.3609
169	147	PIRAWA	0.3600
170	196	AMET	0.3598
171	202	RAJSAMAND	0.3592
172	184	PARBATSAR	0.3588
173	232	JHADOL	0.3582
174	46	BAYANA	0.3578
175	91	RATANGARH	0.3570
176	145	KHANPUR	0.3568
177	90	RAJGARH	0.3551
178	225	TONK	0.3550
179	144	JHALRAPATAN	0.3545
180	200	KUMBHALGARH	0.3541
181	79	BHAINSRORGARH	0.3539
182	89	CHURU	0.3523
183	226	UNIARA	0.3518
184	178	KUCHAMAN	0.3473
185	182	MUNDWA	0.3467
186	24	BAGIDORA	0.3450
187	168	SAPOTRA	0.3447
188	180	MAKRANA	0.3441
189	142	BAKANI	0.3437
190	206	KHANDAR	0.3419
191	97	LALSOT	0.3397
192	141	SAYLA	0.3394
193	198	DEOGARH	0.3389
194	48	KAMAN	0.3375
195	93	SUJANGARH	0.3363
196	176	DIDWANA	0.3360
197	177	JAYAL	0.3358
198	101	BASERI	0.3354
199	102	DHAULPUR	0.3344
200	138	JASWANTPURA	0.3338
201	229	DHARIAWAD	0.3332
202	183	NAGAUR	0.3321
203	51	NAGAR PAHARI	0.3315
204	107	SAGWARA	0.3313
205	134	SANKRA	0.3287
206	34	CHHABRA	0.3276
207	166	KARAULI	0.3241
208	23	ANANDPURI	0.3207
209	139	RANIWARA	0.3193
210	26	GHATOL	0.3188
211	30	TALWARA	0.3174
212	132	JAISALMER	0.3157
213	157	BAP	0.3124
214	136	BHINMAL	0.3080
215	92	SARDARSHAHAR	0.3076
	VERY LOW (<0.3)		
216	103	RAJAKHERA	0.2994
216	106	DUNGARPUR	0.2994
218	105	BICHHIWARA	0.2981
219	140	SANCHORE	0.2972
220	104	ASPUR	0.2968
221	146	MANOHARTHANA	0.2958
222	234	KOTRA	0.2952
223	143	DAG	0.2917
224	100	BARI	0.2867
225	108	SIMALWARA	0.2843
226	29	SAJJANGARH	0.2818
227	45	SIWANA	0.2794
228	38	BALOTRA	0.2740
229	28	PEEPALKHOONT	0.2735
230	133	SAM	0.2690
231	27	KUSHALGARH	0.2611
232	44	SINDHARI	0.2360
233	42	DHORIMANNA	0.2313
234	40	BAYTOO	0.2295
235	41	CHOHTAN	0.2249
236	39	BARMER	0.2202
237	43	SHEO	0.2148
		RAJASTHAN	**0.3938**
		%age of AAPs	**42.2**

BOLD: Equal/Above Average Panchayat Samities (AAPs)

Source: Annex 17.1, Col. 6.

ANNEX-17.1

PS-WISE VARIATION IN HUMAN DEVELOPMENT INDEX : RAJASTHAN (1991 & 2001)

P. Code	Panchayat Samiti	1991				2001			
		HSI	EDI	INI	HDI (Col. 3+4+5)/3	HSI	EDI	INI	HDI (Col. 7+8+9)/3
1	2	3	4	5	6	7	8	9	10
1	ARIAN	0.5614	0.2330	0.5804	0.4583	0.6736	0.4045	0.7994	0.6258
2	BHINAY	0.6324	0.2620	0.5632	0.4859	0.6771	0.3552	0.7808	0.6044
3	JAWAJA	0.5583	0.3033	0.4662	0.4426	0.7191	0.6895	0.6521	0.6869
4	KEKRI	0.6643	0.3365	0.5382	0.5130	0.7348	0.3995	0.7573	0.6305
5	KISHANGARH	0.6251	0.2480	0.5184	0.4638	0.7172	0.4670	0.7280	0.6374
6	MASOODA	0.6080	0.2751	0.5260	0.4697	0.6824	0.4706	0.7359	0.6296
7	PISANGAN	0.6908	0.3099	0.5211	0.5073	0.7417	0.4580	0.6916	0.6304
8	SRINAGAR	0.6389	0.2653	0.5302	0.4781	0.7157	0.4494	0.7284	0.6312
	AJMER DISTRICT	**0.6243**	**0.2805**	**0.5305**	**0.4784**	**0.7075**	**0.4630**	**0.7321**	**0.6342**
9	BANSURE	0.5763	0.2668	0.3232	0.3888	0.6769	0.5194	0.4932	0.5631
10	BEHROR	0.6358	0.4396	0.3628	0.4794	0.7615	0.8619	0.5662	0.7298
11	KATHUMAR	0.5148	0.2753	0.3557	0.3819	0.6646	0.5049	0.5480	0.5725
12	KISHANGARH BAS	0.5884	0.3179	0.2991	0.4018	0.6348	0.4934	0.4958	0.5414
13	KOTKASIM	0.5676	0.4145	0.2903	0.4241	0.6614	0.6404	0.4893	0.5970
14	LACHHMANGARH	0.5046	0.2660	0.3676	0.3794	0.6672	0.4909	0.5508	0.5696
15	MANDAWAR	0.6119	0.4056	0.2791	0.4322	0.7037	0.6365	0.4853	0.6085
16	NIMRANA	0.6495	0.4646	0.2597	0.4579	0.7520	0.5302	0.4756	0.5859
17	RAJGARH	0.5535	0.2750	0.3952	0.4079	0.6404	0.4753	0.5716	0.5624
18	RAMGARH	0.5513	0.2739	0.2928	0.3727	0.6569	0.4675	0.4462	0.5235
19	RENI	0.5256	0.2653	0.4169	0.4026	0.6785	0.4989	0.5982	0.5919
20	THANAGAZI	0.5759	0.2170	0.3526	0.3818	0.6726	0.4078	0.5227	0.5344
21	TIJARA	0.5110	0.2703	0.3484	0.3766	0.6187	0.4636	0.4545	0.5123
22	UMREN	0.5484	0.2557	0.3140	0.3727	0.6751	0.4648	0.4651	0.5350
	ALWAR	**0.5616**	**0.3092**	**0.3333**	**0.4014**	**0.6725**	**0.5231**	**0.5102**	**0.5686**
23	ANANDPURI	0.5258	0.1647	0.2717	0.3207	0.6167	0.3502	0.4261	0.4643
24	BAGIDORA	0.5788	0.1949	0.2614	0.3450	0.6251	0.3537	0.4088	0.4625
25	GARHI	0.6575	0.2666	0.2123	0.3788	0.7465	0.4622	0.3749	0.5279
26	GHATOL	0.5620	0.1701	0.2242	0.3188	0.6555	0.3387	0.3688	0.4543
27	KUSHALGARH	0.4296	0.0968	0.2570	0.2611	0.5633	0.2844	0.3805	0.4094
28	PEEPALKHOONT	0.4813	0.0847	0.2545	0.2735	0.5685	0.2114	0.3760	0.3853
29	SAJJANGARH	0.4466	0.1383	0.2605	0.2818	0.6021	0.3205	0.4038	0.4421
30	TALWARA	0.5883	0.1758	0.1881	0.3174	0.6660	0.3922	0.3356	0.4646
	BANSWARA	**0.5475**	**0.1726**	**0.2357**	**0.3186**	**0.6405**	**0.3511**	**0.3805**	**0.4574**
31	ANTA	0.5471	0.3191	0.3575	0.4079	0.6603	0.5731	0.5648	0.5994
32	ATRU	0.5534	0.3084	0.3976	0.4198	0.6619	0.5689	0.6121	0.6143
33	BARAN	0.5476	0.3125	0.3991	0.4197	0.6753	0.5916	0.5812	0.6160
34	CHHABRA	0.4429	0.1853	0.3547	0.3276	0.5216	0.4667	0.6635	0.5506
35	CHHIPABAROD	0.4383	0.1970	0.6156	0.4170	0.5674	0.4179	0.7015	0.5623
36	KISHANGANJ	0.5074	0.2079	0.4214	0.3789	0.6249	0.4720	0.6125	0.5698
37	SHAHBAD	0.4635	0.2220	0.4385	0.3747	0.5809	0.4667	0.6103	0.5526
	BARAN	**0.5025**	**0.2537**	**0.4263**	**0.3912**	**0.6148**	**0.5102**	**0.6215**	**0.5822**
38	BALOTRA	0.5096	0.1785	0.1338	0.2740	0.6194	0.4908	0.2899	0.4667
39	BARMER	0.3928	0.1406	0.1273	0.2202	0.4930	0.4874	0.2693	0.4166
40	BAYTOO	0.3656	0.1505	0.1724	0.2295	0.4950	0.5315	0.3340	0.4535
41	CHOHTAN	0.4328	0.0900	0.1519	0.2249	0.5880	0.4550	0.3301	0.4577
42	DHORIMANNA	0.4263	0.1219	0.1456	0.2313	0.6006	0.6407	0.2968	0.5127
43	SHEO	0.4160	0.1400	0.0885	0.2148	0.4938	0.5169	0.2170	0.4092
44	SINDHARI	0.4238	0.1234	0.1609	0.2360	0.5611	0.5606	0.3154	0.4790
45	SIWANA	0.5856	0.1741	0.0784	0.2794	0.7197	0.5421	0.1712	0.4777
	BARMER	**0.4418**	**0.1393**	**0.1364**	**0.2392**	**0.5715**	**0.5290**	**0.2835**	**0.4613**
46	BAYANA	0.4991	0.2656	0.3086	0.3578	0.6120	0.4943	0.4906	0.5323
47	DEEG	0.5026	0.2897	0.3799	0.3907	0.6939	0.5114	0.5695	0.5916
48	KAMAN	0.4556	0.1820	0.3748	0.3375	0.6137	0.4052	0.5173	0.5121
49	KUMHER	0.6056	0.3560	0.3310	0.4309	0.7390	0.6038	0.5383	0.6270
50	NADBAI	0.5265	0.3370	0.3217	0.3951	0.7286	0.6145	0.5039	0.6157
51	NAGAR PAHARI	0.4408	0.2375	0.3162	0.3315	0.6301	0.5201	0.4820	0.5441
52	RUPBAS	0.5175	0.3457	0.2567	0.3733	0.6699	0.6090	0.4350	0.5713
53	SEWAR	0.5408	0.3317	0.2956	0.3894	0.6895	0.6081	0.4798	0.5925
54	WEIR	0.5688	0.3202	0.3110	0.4000	0.6374	0.5389	0.4912	0.5558
	BHARATPUR	**0.5134**	**0.2939**	**0.3214**	**0.3762**	**0.6617**	**0.5417**	**0.4990**	**0.5674**
55	ASIND	0.6084	0.1906	0.3997	0.3996	0.6764	0.3560	0.5374	0.5233
56	BANERA	0.6704	0.2051	0.4035	0.4263	0.7464	0.4404	0.5464	0.5777
57	HURDA	0.6838	0.2902	0.3788	0.4509	0.7243	0.4529	0.5093	0.5622
58	JAHAZPUR	0.5956	0.2016	0.3491	0.3821	0.6404	0.4263	0.4742	0.5136
59	KOTRI	0.5834	0.2014	0.3995	0.3948	0.6281	0.3383	0.5458	0.5041
60	MANDAL	0.6350	0.1861	0.4120	0.4110	0.6896	0.3700	0.5067	0.5221
61	MANDALGARH	0.5573	0.1774	0.4024	0.3790	0.6374	0.3765	0.5222	0.5120

P. Code	Panchayat Samiti	1991				2001			
		HSI	EDI	INI	**HDI (Col. 3+4+5)/3**	HSI	EDI	INI	**HDI (Col. 7+8+9)/3**
1	2	3	4	5	6	7	8	9	10
62	RAIPUR	0.6344	0.1986	0.3445	0.3925	0.6919	0.3646	0.4987	0.5184
63	SAHARA	0.6710	0.2003	0.4194	0.4302	0.7396	0.3823	0.5902	0.5707
64	SHAHPURA	0.6149	0.1668	0.3992	0.3936	0.6464	0.3674	0.5358	0.5165
65	SUWANA	0.6324	0.1925	0.4075	0.4108	0.6972	0.3938	0.5304	0.5405
	BHILWARA	**0.6175**	**0.1964**	**0.3947**	**0.4029**	**0.6749**	**0.3842**	**0.5259**	**0.5284**
66	BIKANER	0.5909	0.2032	0.5144	0.4362	0.5913	0.4142	0.6899	0.5651
67	DUNGARGARH *	0.6321	0.1794	0.3190	0.3768	0.7612	0.5281	0.5875	0.6256
68	KOLAYAT	0.5398	0.1809	0.5057	0.4088	0.5752	0.3577	0.6973	0.5434
69	LUNKARANSAR	0.5726	0.2005	0.4899	0.4210	0.6284	0.4119	0.7362	0.5922
70	NOKHA	0.5996	0.1732	0.5317	0.4348	0.6635	0.4219	0.7962	0.6272
	BIKANER **	**0.5781**	**0.1899**	**0.5128**	**0.4269**	**0.6136**	**0.4050**	**0.7302**	**0.5829**
71	HINDOLI	0.5024	0.1739	0.4589	0.3784	0.6375	0.4047	0.5750	0.5391
72	KESHORAIPATAN	0.4853	0.2427	0.4118	0.3799	0.6136	0.4977	0.5481	0.5531
73	NAINWA	0.5245	0.1827	0.4545	0.3872	0.6122	0.4389	0.5590	0.5367
74	TALERA	0.5193	0.2129	0.4092	0.3805	0.6318	0.4620	0.5399	0.5446
	BUNDI	**0.4968**	**0.2048**	**0.4309**	**0.3775**	**0.6247**	**0.4520**	**0.5542**	**0.5436**
75	ARNOD	0.5296	0.2247	0.3871	0.3805	0.5903	0.4129	0.5392	0.5141
76	BARI SADRI	0.5369	0.2115	0.4321	0.3935	0.6427	0.3838	0.6399	0.5555
77	BEGUN	0.5366	0.2091	0.4301	0.3919	0.6188	0.4217	0.6298	0.5568
78	BHADESAR	0.5203	0.2081	0.4363	0.3882	0.6269	0.4113	0.6286	0.5556
79	BHAINSRORGARH	0.4724	0.1979	0.3913	0.3539	0.5819	0.4022	0.5629	0.5157
80	BHOPALSAGAR	0.6321	0.2356	0.4093	0.4257	0.6731	0.4486	0.6187	0.5801
81	CHHOTI SADRI	0.5213	0.2510	0.4352	0.4025	0.6124	0.4518	0.6368	0.5670
82	CHITTAURGARH	0.5471	0.2244	0.4271	0.3995	0.6443	0.4410	0.6050	0.5634
83	DUNGLA	0.5454	0.2152	0.4238	0.3948	0.6959	0.4149	0.6323	0.5811
84	GANGRAR	0.5329	0.2066	0.4436	0.3944	0.6454	0.4086	0.6399	0.5647
85	KAPASAN	0.5823	0.1780	0.4498	0.4034	0.6016	0.3860	0.6653	0.5510
86	NIMBAHERA	0.5469	0.2644	0.4198	0.4104	0.6775	0.4705	0.6039	0.5840
87	PRATAPGARH	0.4854	0.2180	0.3892	0.3642	0.6185	0.4684	0.5573	0.5480
88	RASHMI	0.6300	0.2193	0.4243	0.4245	0.7226	0.3753	0.6364	0.5781
	CHITTAURGARH	**0.5391**	**0.2205**	**0.4201**	**0.3932**	**0.6365**	**0.4273**	**0.6092**	**0.5577**
89	CHURU	0.5789	0.2355	0.2426	0.3523	0.7716	0.6207	0.4078	0.6000
90	RAJGARH	0.5073	0.2740	0.2839	0.3551	0.6918	0.6791	0.4580	0.6096
91	RATANGARH	0.6000	0.2064	0.2646	0.3570	0.8164	0.6079	0.4198	0.6147
92	SARDARSHAHAR	0.5138	0.1696	0.2394	0.3076	0.6175	0.5433	0.3887	0.5165
93	SUJANGARH	0.5623	0.1809	0.2658	0.3363	0.7240	0.5801	0.4051	0.5697
94	TARANAGAR	0.5871	0.2099	0.3096	0.3689	0.7154	0.6863	0.4817	0.6278
	CHURU ***	**0.5611**	**0.2103**	**0.2743**	**0.3486**	**0.7191**	**0.6068**	**0.4453**	**0.5904**
95	BANDIKUI	0.5175	0.2914	0.2861	0.3650	0.6771	0.6029	0.4618	0.5806
96	DAUSA	0.5366	0.2554	0.3263	0.3728	0.6561	0.5096	0.5445	0.5701
97	LALSOT	0.4869	0.2302	0.3020	0.3397	0.6088	0.4693	0.5079	0.5287
98	MAHWA	0.4950	0.3081	0.2970	0.3667	0.6485	0.5838	0.5458	0.5927
99	SIKRAI	0.5281	0.2346	0.3270	0.3632	0.6557	0.5612	0.5417	0.5862
	DAUSA	**0.5129**	**0.2627**	**0.3084**	**0.3613**	**0.6487**	**0.5429**	**0.5189**	**0.5702**
100	BARI	0.3966	0.1972	0.2662	0.2867	0.5844	0.5019	0.4002	0.4955
101	BASERI	0.4841	0.2504	0.2717	0.3354	0.5663	0.5552	0.3884	0.5033
102	DHAULPUR	0.5250	0.2640	0.2141	0.3344	0.5947	0.5268	0.3414	0.4876
103	RAJAKHERA	0.4591	0.2298	0.2093	0.2994	0.5785	0.5130	0.3485	0.4800
	DHAULPUR	**0.4735**	**0.2397**	**0.2377**	**0.3170**	**0.5827**	**0.5260**	**0.3665**	**0.4917**
104	ASPUR	0.6338	0.2247	0.0319	0.2968	0.7632	0.3868	0.1708	0.4403
105	BICHHIWARA	0.6058	0.1992	0.0893	0.2981	0.7266	0.3993	0.2138	0.4466
106	DUNGARPUR	0.5854	0.2112	0.1017	0.2994	0.7214	0.4030	0.2310	0.4518
107	SAGWARA	0.6529	0.2751	0.0660	0.3313	0.7802	0.4514	0.2274	0.4863
108	SIMALWARA	0.5415	0.1935	0.1179	0.2843	0.6858	0.3589	0.2506	0.4318
	DUNGARPUR	**0.5975**	**0.2198**	**0.0830**	**0.3001**	**0.7324**	**0.3986**	**0.2199**	**0.4503**
109	ANUPGARH	0.3974	0.2719	0.5703	0.4132	0.5610	0.5382	0.5787	0.5593
110	GANGANAGAR	0.6146	0.3925	0.5475	0.5182	0.7151	0.6014	0.6802	0.6656
111	KARANPUR	0.5860	0.3602	0.6903	0.5455	0.6928	0.5764	0.8103	0.6932
112	PADAMPUR	0.5653	0.3802	0.5074	0.4843	0.6968	0.5888	0.6141	0.6332
113	RAISINGHNAGAR	0.5363	0.3318	0.6440	0.5040	0.6419	0.6127	0.7210	0.6585
114	SADULSHAHAR	0.5791	0.3404	0.5398	0.4864	0.6817	0.5766	0.8743	0.7109
115	SURATGARH	0.4686	0.2781	0.5494	0.4320	0.5150	0.4907	0.8374	0.6144
	GANGANAGAR	**0.5109**	**0.3222**	**0.5709**	**0.4680**	**0.6183**	**0.5602**	**0.7171**	**0.6319**
116	BHADRA	0.5454	0.3050	0.6240	0.4915	0.7173	0.6272	0.8191	0.7212
117	HANUMANGARH	0.5883	0.2841	0.5304	0.4676	0.6726	0.5732	0.5245	0.5901
118	NOHAR	0.5045	0.2419	0.6089	0.4518	0.5785	0.5998	0.7896	0.6560
	HANUMANGARH	**0.5483**	**0.2736**	**0.5816**	**0.4678**	**0.6510**	**0.5910**	**0.6784**	**0.6402**
119	AMBER	0.5838	0.2731	0.6402	0.4990	0.6910	0.5258	0.8323	0.6831
120	BASSI	0.5804	0.2555	0.6678	0.5012	0.6905	0.5170	0.8029	0.6701
121	CHAKSU	0.4794	0.2209	0.7213	0.4739	0.5633	0.4451	0.9103	0.6396
122	DUDU	0.5128	0.2597	0.6373	0.4699	0.6766	0.4980	0.8273	0.6673
123	GOVINDGARH	0.6956	0.3248	0.5390	0.5198	0.7682	0.5996	0.7195	0.6958
124	JAMWA RAMGARH	0.5834	0.2425	0.6367	0.4875	0.6978	0.5656	0.8187	0.6940
125	JHOTWARA	0.5075	0.2125	0.5618	0.4919	0.6007	0.6103	0.9482	0.7491
126	KOTPUTLI	0.6056	0.2870	0.5721	0.4882	0.7073	0.6805	0.7621	0.7166
127	PHAGI	0.5430	0.2329	0.6783	0.4847	0.6441	0.5522	0.8847	0.6937

P. Code	*Panchayat Samiti*	*1991*				*2001*			
		HSI	*EDI*	*INI*	***HDI (Col. 3+4+5)/3***	*HSI*	*EDI*	*INI*	***HDI (Col. 7+8+9)/3***
1	*2*	*3*	*4*	*5*	*6*	*7*	*8*	*9*	*10*
128	SAMBHAR	0.6069	0.2847	0.5631	0.4849	0.7241	0.6137	0.7506	0.6961
129	SANGANER	0.5779	0.3052	0.6205	0.5012	0.6740	0.5637	1.0065	0.7481
130	SHAHPURA	0.6583	0.2991	0.5673	0.5082	0.7487	0.5892	0.7147	0.6842
131	VIRATNAGAR	0.6116	0.2706	0.5411	0.4744	0.7225	0.6318	0.7139	0.6894
	JAIPUR	**0.5860**	**0.2747**	**0.6129**	**0.4912**	**0.6925**	**0.5678**	**0.8138**	**0.6914**
132	JAISALMER	0.4439	0.2003	0.3028	0.3157	0.5541	0.4079	0.4245	0.4621
133	SAM	0.3460	0.1530	0.3080	0.2690	0.4749	0.3797	0.4592	0.4379
134	SANKRA	0.4409	0.1621	0.3832	0.3287	0.5487	0.4238	0.5474	0.5066
	JAISALMER	**0.4085**	**0.1697**	**0.3380**	**0.3054**	**0.5238**	**0.4050**	**0.4859**	**0.4716**
135	AHORE	0.6464	0.2259	0.3256	0.3993	0.7941	0.4632	0.4775	0.5783
136	BHINMAL	0.5534	0.1273	0.2434	0.3080	0.6954	0.3321	0.3724	0.4666
137	JALOR	0.6843	0.2048	0.2108	0.3666	0.7826	0.3865	0.3511	0.5067
138	JASWANTPURA	0.6173	0.1565	0.2275	0.3338	0.7441	0.3300	0.3609	0.4783
139	RANIWARA	0.5850	0.1509	0.2220	0.3193	0.7228	0.4110	0.3215	0.4851
140	SANCHORE	0.5099	0.1378	0.2440	0.2972	0.6339	0.3936	0.3470	0.4582
141	SAYLA	0.6559	0.1531	0.2093	0.3394	0.7621	0.3611	0.3255	0.4829
	JALOR	**0.5948**	**0.1619**	**0.2435**	**0.3334**	**0.7190**	**0.3850**	**0.3656**	**0.4899**
142	BAKANI	0.4975	0.1851	0.3485	0.3437	0.5525	0.3626	0.5113	0.4755
143	DAG	0.4819	0.1686	0.2245	0.2917	0.5723	0.3991	0.3736	0.4484
144	JHALRAPATAN	0.5251	0.2298	0.3085	0.3545	0.5985	0.5067	0.4363	0.5138
145	KHANPUR	0.5213	0.3095	0.2397	0.3568	0.6309	0.5984	0.3536	0.5276
146	MANOHARTHANA	0.4163	0.1167	0.3543	0.2958	0.5097	0.4104	0.4732	0.4644
147	PIRAWA	0.5164	0.2318	0.3319	0.3600	0.6153	0.5989	0.4367	0.5503
	JHALAWAR	**0.4944**	**0.2064**	**0.3044**	**0.3351**	**0.5804**	**0.4792**	**0.4339**	**0.4978**
148	ALSISAR	0.6323	0.3594	0.1561	0.3826	0.7316	0.6983	0.4603	0.6301
149	BUHANA	0.6085	0.4087	0.1840	0.4004	0.7669	0.7310	0.5137	0.6705
150	CHIRAWA	0.6659	0.3802	0.1141	0.3867	0.7770	0.7011	0.4407	0.6396
151	JHUNJHUNUN	0.6581	0.4055	0.1589	0.4075	0.7596	0.7212	0.4998	0.6602
152	KHETRI	0.6536	0.3430	0.1000	0.3655	0.7827	0.6070	0.4279	0.6059
153	NAWALGARH	0.7268	0.3752	0.0635	0.3885	0.7741	0.6438	0.3886	0.6022
154	SURAJGARH	0.5913	0.3613	0.1688	0.3738	0.6928	0.6576	0.4749	0.6084
155	UDAIPURWATI	0.6990	0.3380	0.1303	0.3891	0.8307	0.7442	0.4337	0.6695
	JHUNJHUNUN	**0.6531**	**0.3711**	**0.1340**	**0.3861**	**0.7645**	**0.6876**	**0.4552**	**0.6358**
156	BALESAR	0.6346	0.1829	0.3868	0.4014	0.6530	0.3529	0.5296	0.5119
157	BAP	0.4145	0.1528	0.3700	0.3124	0.5588	0.3713	0.6866	0.5389
158	BHOPALGARH	0.6515	0.2126	0.4513	0.4385	0.7479	0.3865	0.6143	0.5829
159	BILARA	0.6991	0.2354	0.4505	0.4617	0.7828	0.4303	0.6272	0.6134
160	LUNI	0.6169	0.2335	0.4180	0.4228	0.7390	0.4790	0.5647	0.5942
161	MANDOR	0.5600	0.2250	0.3854	0.3901	0.6600	0.3689	0.5159	0.5149
162	OSIAN	0.5654	0.1855	0.3812	0.3774	0.7313	0.4082	0.5213	0.5536
163	PHALODI	0.5410	0.1767	0.3892	0.3690	0.6584	0.4082	0.4025	0.4897
164	SHERGARH	0.6058	0.1592	0.4267	0.3972	0.6050	0.3429	0.5453	0.4977
	JODHPUR	**0.5715**	**0.1970**	**0.4066**	**0.3917**	0.6891	**0.3962**	**0.5453**	**0.5435**
165	HINDAUN	0.5779	0.2686	0.2823	0.3763	0.7326	0.6854	0.3829	0.6003
166	KARAULI	0.4519	0.1924	0.3279	0.3241	0.6265	0.5032	0.4275	0.5191
167	NADOTI	0.5728	0.2728	0.3195	0.3884	0.6804	0.5874	0.4651	0.5776
168	SAPOTRA	0.4799	0.2156	0.3385	0.3447	0.6140	0.5149	0.4595	0.5295
169	TODABHIM	0.5275	0.2649	0.2903	0.3609	0.6843	0.5477	0.4175	0.5498
	KARAULI	**0.5174**	**0.2406**	**0.3119**	**0.3566**	**0.6658**	**0.5703**	**0.4275**	**0.5545**
170	CHECHAT	0.5786	0.3040	0.7566	0.5464	0.6970	0.6318	0.9466	0.7585
171	ITAWA	0.4865	0.2787	0.7208	0.4953	0.6437	0.5651	0.8671	0.6920
172	LADPURA	0.5989	0.3053	0.7063	0.5368	0.7114	0.6037	0.8221	0.7124
173	SANGOD	0.5283	0.3273	0.7641	0.5399	0.6599	0.6426	0.9205	0.7410
174	SULTANPUR	0.5368	0.3348	0.6906	0.5207	0.7159	0.6485	0.8402	0.7349
	KOTA	**0.5440**	**0.3100**	**0.7288**	**0.5276**	**0.6844**	**0.6176**	**0.8805**	**0.7275**
175	DEGANA	0.5928	0.2169	0.2800	0.3632	0.7072	0.4749	0.4320	0.5380
176	DIDWANA	0.5458	0.2422	0.2201	0.3360	0.7325	0.5790	0.3589	0.5568
177	JAYAL	0.5524	0.1844	0.2705	0.3358	0.6812	0.4481	0.4082	0.5125
178	KUCHAMAN	0.5941	0.2423	0.2056	0.3473	0.6762	0.5687	0.3301	0.5250
179	LADNU	0.5893	0.2548	0.2474	0.3638	0.7543	0.5458	0.3805	0.5602
180	MAKRANA	0.5624	0.2451	0.2249	0.3441	0.7008	0.5618	0.3608	0.5411
181	MERTA	0.6336	0.2455	0.2678	0.3823	0.7209	0.4805	0.3999	0.5338
182	MUNDWA	0.5729	0.1771	0.2900	0.3467	0.6914	0.3815	0.4098	0.4943
183	NAGAUR	0.5574	0.1898	0.2491	0.3321	0.6631	0.4349	0.4085	0.5022
184	PARBATSAR	0.5875	0.2105	0.2783	0.3588	0.7254	0.5031	0.4055	0.5447
185	RIYAN	0.6201	0.2133	0.3053	0.3796	0.7160	0.4538	0.4505	0.5401
	NAGAUR	**0.5796**	**0.2201**	**0.2567**	**0.3521**	**0.7044**	**0.4981**	**0.3942**	**0.5322**
186	BALI	0.7016	0.2550	0.3421	0.4329	0.8057	0.4507	0.4652	0.5739
187	DESURI	0.6901	0.2544	0.3128	0.4191	0.7745	0.4502	0.4474	0.5574
188	JAITARAN	0.6074	0.1994	0.4047	0.4038	0.7466	0.4007	0.4732	0.5402
189	MARWAR JUN.	0.6316	0.2440	0.3655	0.4137	0.7486	0.4357	0.5132	0.5658
190	PALI	0.6250	0.2121	0.3905	0.4092	0.7246	0.4232	0.5755	0.5744
191	RAIPUR	0.5626	0.2204	0.3793	0.3874	0.7404	0.4347	0.4529	0.5427
192	RANI STATION	0.6903	0.2758	0.3403	0.4355	0.8148	0.4730	0.5206	0.6028
193	ROHAT	0.5615	0.2050	0.4087	0.3917	0.6911	0.4446	0.5206	0.5521
194	SOJAT	0.6321	0.2543	0.4132	0.4332	0.7603	0.4527	0.5554	0.5895

P. Code	Panchayat Samiti	1991				2001			
		HSI	EDI	INI	**HDI** (Col. 3+4+5)/3	HSI	EDI	INI	**HDI** (Col. 7+8+9)/3
1	2	3	4	5	6	7	8	9	10
195	SUMERPUR	0.7291	0.2624	0.3190	0.4368	0.8076	0.4691	0.4599	0.5789
	PALI	**0.6448**	**0.2391**	**0.3695**	**0.4178**	**0.7612**	**0.4418**	**0.4953**	**0.5661**
196	AMET	0.5557	0.1789	0.3449	0.3598	0.6562	0.4304	0.5323	0.5396
197	BHIM	0.6298	0.2453	0.3216	0.3989	0.7011	0.4872	0.4779	0.5554
198	DEOGARH	0.5253	0.1736	0.3178	0.3389	0.6475	0.4345	0.5093	0.5304
199	KHAMNOR	0.6589	0.2505	0.3571	0.4222	0.7155	0.4504	0.4417	0.5359
200	KUMBHALGARH	0.5039	0.1832	0.3751	0.3541	0.6803	0.4037	0.5930	0.5590
201	RAILMAGRA	0.6649	0.2661	0.3634	0.4315	0.7650	0.4890	0.6033	0.6191
202	RAJSAMAND	0.5263	0.2558	0.2956	0.3592	0.6890	0.4890	0.4601	0.5461
	RAJSAMAND	**0.5825**	**0.2265**	**0.3415**	**0.3835**	**0.6962**	**0.4569**	**0.5144**	**0.5558**
203	BAMANWAS	0.5488	0.2506	0.3477	0.3824	0.6316	0.5298	0.5072	0.5562
204	BONLI	0.5364	0.2376	0.3926	0.3889	0.6376	0.4570	0.5394	0.5447
205	GANGAPUR	0.5807	0.2725	0.3059	0.3864	0.6992	0.5030	0.4732	0.5585
206	KHANDAR	0.4703	0.1877	0.3678	0.3419	0.6089	0.3576	0.5563	0.5076
207	SAWAI MADHOPUR	0.5300	0.2405	0.3471	0.3725	0.6450	0.4213	0.4831	0.5165
	SAWAI MADHOPUR	**0.5343**	**0.2392**	**0.3535**	**0.3757**	**0.6448**	**0.4539**	**0.5101**	**0.5363**
208	DANTA RAMGARH	0.6572	0.3042	0.1897	0.3837	0.7667	0.6537	0.4156	0.6120
209	DHOND	0.6902	0.3067	0.2139	0.4036	0.7978	0.6325	0.4585	0.6296
210	FATEHPUR	0.6105	0.3011	0.3096	0.4071	0.7534	0.7042	0.5601	0.6726
211	KHANDELA	0.6414	0.3103	0.2116	0.3878	0.7736	0.6841	0.4783	0.6453
212	LACHHMANGARH	0.6191	0.3083	0.2832	0.4035	0.7233	0.7018	0.5299	0.6517
213	NEEM KA THANA	0.6307	0.3125	0.1504	0.3645	0.7444	0.6222	0.3927	0.5865
214	PIPRALI	0.5924	0.3185	0.2138	0.3749	0.7841	0.6479	0.4797	0.6372
215	SRI MADHOPUR	0.6531	0.3321	0.1418	0.3757	0.7825	0.6161	0.3687	0.5891
	SIKAR	**0.6347**	**0.3116**	**0.2127**	**0.3863**	**0.7633**	**0.6549**	**0.4585**	**0.6256**
216	ABU ROAD	0.5513	0.1481	0.4133	0.3709	0.6618	0.3784	0.5304	0.5235
217	PINDWARA	0.6370	0.1871	0.4525	0.4255	0.7379	0.4704	0.5634	0.5905
218	REODAR	0.6033	0.1692	0.4254	0.3993	0.7079	0.4229	0.5764	0.5691
219	SHEOGANJ	0.6573	0.1881	0.3764	0.4073	0.7538	0.4392	0.5566	0.5832
220	SIROHI	0.6633	0.2239	0.3591	0.4154	0.8059	0.4267	0.5624	0.5983
	SIROHI	**0.6234**	**0.1844**	**0.4106**	0.4061	**0.7320**	**0.4314**	**0.5598**	**0.5744**
221	DEOLI	0.5542	0.2435	0.3782	0.3920	0.6302	0.3836	0.5268	0.5135
222	MALPURA	0.5976	0.2160	0.3643	0.3926	0.6640	0.4011	0.5346	0.5332
223	NIWAI	0.5405	0.2411	0.3770	0.3862	0.6309	0.4370	0.5455	0.5378
224	TODARAISINGH	0.5175	0.2191	0.4008	0.3791	0.6713	0.4614	0.5636	0.5655
225	TONK	0.5010	0.1991	0.3648	0.3550	0.6480	0.3763	0.5299	0.5181
226	UNIARA	0.4976	0.2029	0.3548	0.3518	0.6007	0.3866	0.4933	0.4935
	TONK	**0.5351**	**0.2202**	**0.3722**	**0.3758**	**0.6404**	**0.4039**	**0.5321**	**0.5254**
227	BARGAON	0.6000	0.2692	0.3930	0.4207	0.6920	0.6123	0.6384	0.6476
228	BHINDER	0.5931	0.2317	0.4195	0.4148	0.6841	0.5538	0.5789	0.6056
229	DHARIAWAD	0.5053	0.1025	0.3918	0.3332	0.6205	0.2955	0.5076	0.4745
230	GIRWA	0.6200	0.2204	0.3571	0.3992	0.7056	0.5211	0.4769	0.5679
231	GOGUNDA	0.5571	0.1829	0.3734	0.3711	0.6659	0.4419	0.5094	0.5391
232	JHADOL	0.5095	0.1560	0.4091	0.3582	0.6309	0.5398	0.5227	0.5645
233	KHERWARA	0.5497	0.2576	0.3485	0.3853	0.6541	0.4924	0.4731	0.5399
234	KOTRA	0.4090	0.0664	0.4101	0.2952	0.4951	0.2006	0.4889	0.3949
235	MAVLI	0.6439	0.2570	0.3722	0.4244	0.7348	0.4762	0.5328	0.5813
236	SALUMBAR	0.5577	0.1755	0.4142	0.3825	0.6766	0.5207	0.5617	0.5863
237	SARADA	0.6290	0.2183	0.3588	0.4020	0.7122	0.4917	0.4985	0.5675
	UDAIPUR	**0.5625**	**0.1985**	**0.3847**	**0.3819**	**0.6599**	**0.4683**	**0.5227**	**0.5503**
	RAJASTHAN	**0.5588**	**0.2413**	**0.3813**	**0.3938**	**0.6684**	**0.4986**	**0.5458**	**0.5709**

Note: For Calculation of HDI Please See Methodology (Chapter I).
* Dungargarh PS shifted from Churu to Bikaner district on 1st April 2001
** Excluding data of Dungargarh PS;
*** Including data of Dungargarh PS.
Source: Computed from data given in Annex 6.1, 8.1, 12.1

ANNEX-17.2

PANCHAYAT SAMITI-WISE CHANGED PATTERN OF HUMAN DEVELOPMENT INDEX (1991-01)

P. Code	*Panchayat Samities*	*HDI 1991*		*HDI 2001*		*Difference (1991-01)*		*% Increase in HDI Value*	*Remarks*
		RANK	*VALUE*	*RANK*	*VALUE*	*RANK*	*VALUE*		
1	*2*	*3*	*4*	*5*	*6*	*7*	*8*	*9*	***10***
1	ARAIN	34	0.4583	47	0.6258	-13	0.1675	37	B
2	BHINAY	21	0.4859	62	0.6044	-41	0.1185	24	B
3	JAWAJA	38	0.4426	18	0.6869	20	0.2443	55	A
4	KEKRI	8	0.5130	39	0.6305	-31	0.1175	23	B
5	KISHANGARH	32	0.4638	35	0.6374	-3	0.1736	37	B
6	MASOODA	30	0.4697	42	0.6296	-12	0.1599	34	B
7	PISANGAN	10	0.5073	40	0.6304	-30	0.1231	24	B
8	SRINAGAR	26	0.4781	38	0.6312	-12	0.1531	32	B
	AJMER DISTRICT		**0.4784**		**0.6342**		**0.1558**	**33**	
9	BANSURE	113	0.3888	115	0.5631	-2	0.1743	45	B
10	BEHROR	25	0.4794	6	0.7298	19	0.2504	52	A
11	KATHUMAR	130	0.3819	98	0.5725	32	0.1906	50	A
12	KISHANGARH BAS	86	0.4018	147	0.5414	-61	0.1396	35	B
13	KOTKASIM	56	0.4241	69	0.5970	-13	0.1729	41	B
14	LACHHMANGARH	136	0.3794	103	0.5696	33	0.1902	50	A
15	MANDAWAR	46	0.4322	58	0.6085	-12	0.1763	41	B
16	NIMRANA	35	0.4579	83	0.5859	-48	0.1280	28	B
17	RAJGARH	74	0.4079	116	0.5624	-42	0.1545	38	B
18	RAMGARH	152	0.3727	172	0.5235	-20	0.1508	40	B
19	RENI	83	0.4026	74	0.5919	9	0.1893	47	A
20	THANAGAZI	131	0.3818	162	0.5344	-31	0.1526	40	B
21	TIJARA	144	0.3766	190	0.5123	-46	0.1357	36	B
22	UMREN	152	0.3727	161	0.5350	-9	0.1623	44	B
	ALWAR		**0.4014**		**0.5686**		**0.1672**	**42**	
23	ANANDPURI	208	0.3207	218	0.4643	-10	0.1436	45	B
24	BAGIDORA	186	0.3450	220	0.4625	-34	0.1175	34	B
25	GARHI	140	0.3788	169	0.5279	-29	0.1491	39	B
26	GHATOL	210	0.3188	224	0.4543	-14	0.1355	43	B
27	KUSHALGARH	231	0.2611	234	0.4094	-3	0.1483	57	B
28	PEEPALKHOONT	229	0.2735	237	0.3853	-8	0.1118	41	B
29	SAJJANGARH	226	0.2818	229	0.4421	-3	0.1603	57	B
30	TALWARA	211	0.3174	217	0.4646	-6	0.1472	46	B
	BANSWARA		**0.3186**		**0.4574**		**0.1388**	**44**	
31	ANTA	74	0.4079	67	0.5994	7	0.1915	47	A
32	ATRU	61	0.4198	54	0.6143	7	0.1945	46	A
33	BARAN	62	0.4197	50	0.6160	12	0.1963	47	A
34	CHHABRA	206	0.3276	136	0.5506	70	0.2230	68	A
35	CHHIPABAROD	64	0.4170	116	0.5623	-52	0.1453	35	B
36	KISHANGANJ	139	0.3789	102	0.5698	37	0.1909	50	A
37	SHAHBAD	148	0.3747	133	0.5526	15	0.1779	47	A
	BARAN		**0.3942**		**0.5822**		**0.1880**	**48**	
38	BALOTRA	228	0.2740	215	0.4667	13	0.1927	70	A
39	BARMER	236	0.2202	233	0.4166	3	0.1964	89	A
40	BAYTOO	234	0.2295	225	0.4535	9	0.2240	98	A
41	CHOHTAN	235	0.2249	223	0.4577	12	0.2328	104	A
42	DHORIMANNA	233	0.2313	188	0.5127	45	0.2814	122	A
43	SHEO	237	0.2148	234	0.4092	3	0.1944	91	A
44	SINDHARI	232	0.2360	210	0.4790	22	0.2430	103	A
45	SIWANA	227	0.2794	212	0.4777	15	0.1983	71	A
	BARMER		**0.2392**		**0.4613**		**0.2221**	**93**	
46	BAYANA	174	0.3578	165	0.5323	9	0.1745	49	A
47	DEEG	108	0.3907	75	0.5916	33	0.2009	51	A
48	KAMAN	194	0.3375	191	0.5121	3	0.1746	52	A
49	KUMHER	49	0.4309	46	0.6270	3	0.1961	46	A
50	NADBAI	97	0.3951	51	0.6157	46	0.2206	56	A
51	NAGAR PAHARI	203	0.3315	144	0.5441	59	0.2126	64	A
52	RUPBAS	150	0.3733	99	0.5713	51	0.1980	53	A
53	SEWAR	110	0.3894	72	0.5925	38	0.2031	52	A
54	WEIR	89	0.4000	127	0.5558	-38	0.1558	39	B
	BHARATPUR		**0.3762**		**0.5674**		**0.1912**	**51**	
55	ASIND	90	0.3996	174	0.5233	-84	0.1237	31	B
56	BANERA	51	0.4263	94	0.5777	-43	0.1514	36	B
57	HURDA	37	0.4509	118	0.5622	-81	0.1113	25	B
58	JAHAZPUR	129	0.3821	187	0.5136	-58	0.1315	34	B
59	KOTRI	98	0.3948	197	0.5041	-99	0.1093	28	B
60	MANDAL	69	0.4110	175	0.5221	-106	0.1111	27	B
61	MANDALGARH	138	0.3790	191	0.5120	-53	0.1330	35	B

P. Code	Panchayat Samities	HDI 1991		HDI 2001		Difference (1991-01)		% Increase in HDI Value	Remarks
		RANK	VALUE	RANK	VALUE	RANK	VALUE		
1	2	3	4	5	6	7	8	9	10
62	RAIPUR	104	0.3925	177	0.5184	-73	0.1259	32	B
63	SAHARA	50	0.4302	100	0.5707	-50	0.1405	33	B
64	SHAHPURA	101	0.3936	179	0.5165	-78	0.1229	31	B
65	SUWANA	70	0.4108	149	0.5405	-79	0.1297	32	B
	BHILWARA		**0.4029**		**0.5284**		**0.1255**	**31**	
66	BIKANER	41	0.4362	111	0.5651	-70	0.1289	30	B
67	DUNGARGARH *	143	0.3768	48	0.6256	95	0.2488	66	A
68	KOLAYAT	73	0.4088	145	0.5434	-72	0.1346	33	B
69	LUNKARANSAR	59	0.4210	73	0.5922	-14	0.1712	41	B
70	NOKHA	43	0.4348	45	0.6272	-2	0.1924	44	B
	BIKANER **		**0.4269**		**0.5829**		**0.1560**	**37**	
71	HINDOLI	141	0.3784	154	0.5391	-13	0.1607	42	B
72	KESHORAIPATAN	134	0.3799	132	0.5531	2	0.1732	46	A
73	NAINWA	119	0.3872	159	0.5367	-40	0.1495	39	B
74	TALERA	132	0.3805	142	0.5446	-10	0.1641	43	B
	BUNDI		**0.3775**		**0.5436**		**0.1661**	**44**	
75	ARNOD	132	0.3805	184	0.5141	-52	0.1336	35	B
76	BARI SADRI	102	0.3935	128	0.5555	-26	0.1620	41	B
77	BEGUN	106	0.3919	124	0.5568	-18	0.1649	42	B
78	BHADESAR	116	0.3882	128	0.5556	-12	0.1674	43	B
79	BHAINSRORGARH	181	0.3539	182	0.5157	-1	0.1618	46	B
80	BHOPALSAGAR	52	0.4257	90	0.5801	-38	0.1544	36	B
81	CHHOTI SADRI	84	0.4025	108	0.5670	-24	0.1645	41	B
82	CHITTAURGARH	91	0.3995	114	0.5634	-23	0.1639	41	B
83	DUNGLA	98	0.3948	88	0.5811	10	0.1863	47	A
84	GANGRAR	100	0.3944	112	0.5647	-12	0.1703	43	B
85	KAPASAN	82	0.4034	135	0.5510	-53	0.1476	37	B
86	NIMBAHERA	71	0.4104	84	0.5840	-13	0.1736	42	B
87	PRATAPGARH	164	0.3642	139	0.5480	25	0.1838	50	A
88	RASHMI	54	0.4245	93	0.5781	-39	0.1536	36	B
	CHITTAURGARH		**0.3932**		**0.5577**		**0.1645**	**42**	
89	CHURU	182	0.3523	66	0.6000	116	0.2477	70	A
90	RAJGARH	177	0.3551	57	0.6096	120	0.2545	72	A
91	RATANGARH	175	0.3570	52	0.6147	123	0.2577	72	A
92	SARDARSHAHAR	215	0.3076	179	0.5165	36	0.2089	68	A
93	SUJANGARH	195	0.3363	103	0.5697	92	0.2334	69	A
94	TARANAGAR	158	0.3689	44	0.6278	114	0.2589	70	A
	CHURU ***		**0.3486**		**0.5904**		**0.2418**	**69**	
95	BANDIKUI	162	0.3650	89	0.5806	73	0.2156	59	A
96	DAUSA	151	0.3728	101	0.5701	50	0.1973	53	A
97	LALSOT	191	0.3397	168	0.5287	23	0.1890	56	A
98	MAHWA	159	0.3667	71	0.5927	88	0.2260	62	A
99	SIKRAI	166	0.3632	82	0.5862	84	0.2230	61	A
	DAUSA		**0.3613**		**0.5702**		**0.2089**	**58**	
100	BARI	224	0.2867	201	0.4955	23	0.2088	73	A
101	BASERI	198	0.3354	198	0.5033	0	0.1679	50	C
102	DHAULPUR	199	0.3344	205	0.4876	-6	0.1532	46	B
103	RAJAKHERA	216	0.2994	209	0.4800	7	0.1806	60	A
	DHAULPUR		**0.3170**		**0.4917**		**0.1747**	**55**	
104	ASPUR	220	0.2968	230	0.4403	-10	0.1435	48	B
105	BICHHIWARA	218	0.2981	228	0.4466	-10	0.1485	50	B
106	DUNGARPUR	216	0.2994	226	0.4518	-10	0.1524	51	B
107	SAGWARA	204	0.3313	206	0.4863	-2	0.1550	47	B
108	SIMALWARA	225	0.2843	232	0.4318	-7	0.1475	52	B
	DUNGARPUR		**0.3001**		**0.4503**		**0.1502**	**50**	
109	ANUPGARH	68	0.4132	120	0.5593	-52	0.1461	35	B
110	GANGANAGAR	7	0.5182	26	0.6656	-19	0.1474	28	B
111	KARANPUR	2	0.5455	15	0.6932	-13	0.1477	27	B
112	PADAMPUR	24	0.4843	37	0.6332	-13	0.1489	31	B
113	RAISINGHNAGAR	11	0.5040	28	0.6585	-17	0.1545	31	B
114	SADULSHAHAR	20	0.4864	10	0.7109	10	0.2245	46	A
115	SURATGARH	47	0.4320	53	0.6144	-6	0.1824	42	B
	GANGANAGAR		**0.4680**		**0.6319**		**0.1639**	**35**	
116	BHADRA	17	0.4915	7	0.7212	10	0.2297	47	A
117	HANUMANGARH	31	0.4676	77	0.5901	-46	0.1225	26	B
118	NOHAR	36	0.4518	29	0.6560	7	0.2042	45	A
	HANUMANGARH		**0.4678**		**0.6402**		**0.1724**	**37**	
119	AMBER	14	0.4990	20	0.6831	-6	0.1841	37	B
120	BASSI	12	0.5012	23	0.6701	-11	0.1689	34	B
121	CHAKSU	28	0.4739	34	0.6396	-6	0.1657	35	B
122	DUDU	29	0.4699	25	0.6673	4	0.1974	42	A
123	GOVINDGARH	6	0.5198	12	0.6958	-6	0.1760	34	D
124	JAMWA RAMGARH	19	0.4875	13	0.6940	6	0.2065	42	A
125	JHOTWARA	16	0.4919	2	0.7491	14	0.2572	52	A
126	KOTPUTLI	18	0.4882	8	0.7166	10	0.2284	47	A
127	PHAGI	23	0.4847	14	0.6937	9	0.2090	43	A

P. Code	Panchayat Samities	HDI 1991 RANK	HDI 1991 VALUE	HDI 2001 RANK	HDI 2001 VALUE	Difference (1991-01) RANK	Difference (1991-01) VALUE	% Increase in HDI Value	Remarks
1	2	3	4	5	6	7	8	9	10
128	SAMBHAR	22	0.4849	11	0.6961	11	0.2112	44	A
129	SANGANER	12	0.5012	3	0.7481	9	0.2469	49	A
130	SHAHPURA	9	0.5082	19	0.6842	-10	0.1760	35	B
131	VIRATNAGAR	27	0.4744	17	0.6894	10	0.2150	45	A
	JAIPUR		**0.4912**		**0.6914**		**0.2002**	**41**	
132	JAISALMER	212	0.3157	221	0.4621	-9	0.1464	46	B
133	SAM	230	0.2690	231	0.4379	-1	0.1689	63	B
134	SANKRA	205	0.3287	196	0.5066	9	0.1779	54	A
	JAISALMER		**0.3054**		**0.4716**		**0.1662**	**54**	
135	AHORE	92	0.3993	92	0.5783	0	0.1790	45	C
136	BHINMAL	214	0.3080	216	0.4666	-2	0.1586	51	B
137	JALOR	160	0.3666	195	0.5067	-35	0.1401	38	B
138	JASWANTPURA	200	0.3338	211	0.4783	-11	0.1445	43	B
139	RANIWARA	209	0.3193	207	0.4851	2	0.1658	52	A
140	SANCHORE	219	0.2972	222	0.4582	-3	0.1610	54	B
141	SAYLA	192	0.3394	208	0.4829	-16	0.1435	42	B
	JALOR		**0.3334**		**0.4899**		**0.1565**	**47**	
142	BAKANI	189	0.3437	213	0.4755	-24	0.1318	38	B
143	DAG	223	0.2917	227	0.4484	-4	0.1567	54	B
144	JHALRAPATAN	179	0.3545	185	0.5138	-6	0.1593	45	B
145	KHANPUR	176	0.3568	170	0.5276	6	0.1708	48	A
146	MANOHARTHANA	221	0.2958	218	0.4644	3	0.1686	57	A
147	PIRAWA	169	0.3600	137	0.5503	32	0.1903	53	A
	JHALAWAR		**0.3351**		**0.4978**		**0.1627**	**49**	
148	ALSISAR	125	0.3826	41	0.6301	84	0.2475	65	A
149	BUHANA	88	0.4004	22	0.6705	66	0.2701	67	A
150	CHIRAWA	120	0.3867	33	0.6396	87	0.2529	65	A
151	JHUNJHUNUN	76	0.4075	27	0.6602	49	0.2527	62	A
152	KHETRI	161	0.3655	60	0.6059	101	0.2404	66	A
153	NAWALGARH	114	0.3885	64	0.6022	50	0.2137	55	A
154	SURAJGARH	149	0.3738	59	0.6084	90	0.2346	63	A
155	UDAIPURWATI	111	0.3891	24	0.6695	87	0.2804	72	A
	JHUNJHUNUN		**0.3861**		**0.6358**		**0.2497**	**65**	
156	BALESAR	87	0.4014	193	0.5119	-106	0.1105	28	B
157	BAP	213	0.3124	156	0.5389	57	0.2265	73	A
158	BHOPALGARH	39	0.4385	85	0.5829	-46	0.1444	33	B
159	BILARA	33	0.4617	55	0.6134	-22	0.1517	33	B
160	LUNI	57	0.4228	70	0.5942	-13	0.1714	41	B
161	MANDOR	109	0.3901	183	0.5149	-74	0.1248	32	B
162	OSIAN	142	0.3774	131	0.5536	11	0.1762	47	A
163	PHALODI	157	0.3690	204	0.4897	-47	0.1207	33	B
164	SHERGARH	96	0.3972	200	0.4977	-104	0.1005	25	B
	JODHPUR		**0.3917**		**0.5435**		**0.1518**	**39**	
165	HINDAUN	145	0.3763	65	0.6003	80	0.2240	60	A
166	KARAULI	207	0.3241	176	0.5191	31	0.1950	60	A
167	NADOTI	115	0.3884	95	0.5776	20	0.1892	49	A
168	SAPOTRA	187	0.3447	167	0.5295	20	0.1848	54	A
169	TODABHIM	168	0.3609	138	0.5498	30	0.1889	52	A
	KARAULI		**0.3566**		**0.5545**		**0.1979**	**55**	
170	CHECHAT	1	0.5464	1	0.7585	0	0.2121	39	C
171	ITAWA	15	0.4953	16	0.6920	-1	0.1967	40	B
172	LADPURA	4	0.5368	9	0.7124	-5	0.1756	33	B
173	SANGOD	3	0.5399	4	0.7410	-1	0.2011	37	B
174	SULTANPUR	5	0.5207	5	0.7349	0	0.2142	41	C
	KOTA		**0.5276**		**0.7275**		**0.1999**	**38**	
175	DEGANA	166	0.3632	157	0.5380	9	0.1748	48	A
176	DIDWANA	196	0.3360	125	0.5568	71	0.2208	66	A
177	JAYAL	197	0.3358	189	0.5125	8	0.1767	53	A
178	KUCHAMAN	184	0.3473	171	0.5250	13	0.1777	51	A
179	LADNU	165	0.3638	119	0.5602	46	0.1964	54	A
180	MAKRANA	188	0.3441	147	0.5411	41	0.1970	57	A
181	MERTA	128	0.3823	163	0.5338	-35	0.1515	40	B
182	MUNDWA	185	0.3467	202	0.4943	-17	0.1476	43	B
183	NAGAUR	202	0.3321	199	0.5022	3	0.1701	51	A
184	PARBATSAR	172	0.3588	142	0.5447	30	0.1859	52	A
185	RIYAN	135	0.3796	151	0.5401	-16	0.1605	42	B
	NAGAUR		**0.3521**		**0.5322**		**0.1801**	**51**	
186	BALI	45	0.4329	97	0.5739	-52	0.1410	33	B
187	DESURI	63	0.4191	123	0.5574	-60	0.1383	33	B
188	JAITARAN	79	0.4038	150	0.5402	-71	0.1364	34	B
189	MARWAR JUN.	67	0.4137	109	0.5658	-42	0.1521	37	B
190	PALI	72	0.4092	96	0.5744	-24	0.1652	40	B
191	RAIPUR	118	0.3874	146	0.5427	-28	0.1553	40	B
192	RANI STATION	42	0.4355	63	0.6028	-21	0.1673	38	B
193	ROHAT	107	0.3917	134	0.5521	-27	0.1604	41	B
194	SOJAT	44	0.4332	78	0.5895	-34	0.1563	36	B

P. Code	Panchayat Samities	HDI 1991		HDI 2001		Difference (1991-01)		% Increase in HDI Value	Remarks
		RANK	VALUE	RANK	VALUE	RANK	VALUE		
1	2	3	4	5	6	7	8	9	10
195	SUMERPUR	40	0.4368	91	0.5789	-51	0.1421	33	B
	PALI		**0.4178**		**0.5661**		**0.1483**	**35**	
196	AMET	170	0.3598	153	0.5396	17	0.1798	50	A
197	BHIM	95	0.3989	130	0.5554	-35	0.1565	39	B
198	DEOGARH	193	0.3389	166	0.5304	27	0.1915	57	A
199	KHAMNOR	58	0.4222	160	0.5359	-102	0.1137	27	B
200	KUMBHALGARH	180	0.3541	121	0.5590	59	0.2049	58	A
201	RAILMAGRA	48	0.4315	49	0.6191	-1	0.1876	43	B
202	RAJSAMAND	171	0.3592	140	0.5461	31	0.1869	52	A
	RAJSAMAND		**0.3835**		**0.5558**		**0.1723**	**45**	
203	BAMANWAS	127	0.3824	126	0.5562	1	0.1738	45	A
204	BONLI	112	0.3889	141	0.5447	-29	0.1558	40	B
205	GANGAPUR	121	0.3864	122	0.5585	-1	0.1721	45	B
206	KHANDAR	190	0.3419	194	0.5076	-4	0.1657	48	B
207	SAWAI MADHOPUR	154	0.3725	179	0.5165	-25	0.1440	39	B
	SAWAI MADHOPUR		**0.3757**		**0.5363**		**0.1606**	**43**	
208	DANTA RAMGARH	124	0.3837	56	0.6120	68	0.2283	59	A
209	DHOND	80	0.4036	42	0.6296	38	0.2260	56	A
210	FATEHPUR	78	0.4071	21	0.6726	57	0.2655	65	A
211	KHANDELA	117	0.3878	32	0.6453	85	0.2575	66	A
212	LACHHMANGARH	81	0.4035	30	0.6517	51	0.2482	62	A
213	NEEM KA THANA	163	0.3645	80	0.5865	83	0.2220	61	A
214	PIPRALI	147	0.3749	36	0.6372	111	0.2623	70	A
215	SRI MADHOPUR	146	0.3757	79	0.5891	67	0.2134	57	A
	SIKAR		**0.3863**		**0.6256**		**0.2393**	**62**	
216	ABU ROAD	156	0.3709	172	0.5235	-16	0.1526	41	B
217	PINDWARA	53	0.4255	76	0.5905	-23	0.1650	39	B
218	REODAR	92	0.3993	105	0.5691	-13	0.1698	43	B
219	SHEOGANJ	77	0.4073	85	0.5832	-8	0.1759	43	B
220	SIROHI	65	0.4154	68	0.5983	-3	0.1829	44	B
	SIROHI		0.4061		**0.5744**		**0.1683**	**41**	
221	DEOLI	105	0.3920	186	0.5135	-81	0.1215	31	B
222	MALPURA	103	0.3926	164	0.5332	-61	0.1406	36	B
223	NIWAI	122	0.3862	158	0.5378	-36	0.1516	39	B
224	TODARAISINGH	137	0.3791	110	0.5655	27	0.1864	49	A
225	TONK	178	0.3550	178	0.5181	0	0.1631	46	C
226	UNIARA	183	0.3518	203	0.4935	-20	0.1417	40	B
	TONK		**0.3758**		**0.5254**		**0.1496**	**40**	
227	BARGAON	60	0.4207	31	0.6476	29	0.2269	54	A
228	BHINDER	66	0.4148	61	0.6056	5	0.1908	46	A
229	DHARIAWAD	201	0.3332	214	0.4745	-13	0.1413	42	B
230	GIRWA	94	0.3992	106	0.5679	-12	0.1687	42	B
231	GOGUNDA	155	0.3711	155	0.5391	0	0.1680	45	C
232	JHADOL	173	0.3582	113	0.5645	60	0.2063	58	A
233	KHERWARA	123	0.3853	152	0.5399	-29	0.1546	40	B
234	KOTRA	222	0.2952	236	0.3949	-14	0.0997	34	B
235	MAVLI	55	0.4244	87	0.5813	-32	0.1569	37	B
236	SALUMBAR	126	0.3825	81	0.5863	45	0.2038	53	A
237	SARADA	85	0.4020	107	0.5675	-22	0.1655	41	B
	UDAIPUR		**0.3819**		**0.5503**		**0.1684**	**44**	
	RAJASTHAN		**0.3938**		**0.5709**		**0.1771**	**45**	

Note: A Improvement in both HDI Value and Rank
B Increase in HDI Value but Rank Deteriorated
C Increase in HDI Value but Rank Remained Constant
* Dungargarh PS shifted from Churu to Bikaner District on 1st April 2001
** Excluding data of Dungargarh PS
*** Including data of Dungargarh PS

Source: Annex 17.1

ANNEX-17.3

RANKING OF PANCHAYAT SAMITIES BY HDI VALUE, 2001

RANK	PANCHAYAT SAMITIES P. CODE	NAME	HDI
1	2	3	4
	VERY HIGH (>= 0.6)		
1	170	**CHECHAT**	**0.7585**
2	125	**JHOTWARA**	**0.7491**
3	129	**SANGANER**	**0.7481**
4	173	**SANGOD**	**0.7410**
5	174	**SULTANPUR**	**0.7349**
6	10	**BEHROR**	**0.7298**
7	116	**BHADRA**	**0.7212**
8	126	**KOTPUTLI**	**0.7166**
9	172	**LADPURA**	**0.7124**
10	114	**SADULSHAHAR**	**0.7109**
11	128	**SAMBHAR**	**0.6961**
12	123	**GOVINDGARH**	**0.6958**
13	124	**JAMWA RAMGARH**	**0.6940**
14	127	**PHAGI**	**0.6937**
15	111	**KARANPUR**	**0.6932**
16	171	**ITAWA**	**0.6920**
17	131	**VIRATNAGAR**	**0.6894**
18	3	**JAWAJA**	**0.6869**
19	130	**SHAHPURA**	**0.6842**
20	119	**AMBER**	**0.6831**
21	210	**FATEHPUR**	**0.6726**
22	149	**BUHANA**	**0.6705**
23	120	**BASSI**	**0.6701**
24	155	**UDAIPURWATI**	**0.6695**
25	122	**DUDU**	**0.6673**
26	110	**GANGANAGAR**	**0.6656**
27	151	**JHUNJHUNUN**	**0.6602**
28	113	**RAISINGHNAGAR**	**0.6585**
29	118	**NOHAR**	**0.6560**
30	212	**LACHHMANGARH**	**0.6517**
31	227	**BARGAON**	**0.6476**
32	211	**KHANDELA**	**0.6453**
33	150	**CHIRAWA**	**0.6396**
33	121	**CHAKSU**	**0.6396**
35	5	**KISHANGARH**	**0.6374**
36	214	**PIPRALI**	**0.6372**
37	112	**PADAMPUR**	**0.6332**
38	8	**SRINAGAR**	**0.6312**
39	4	**KEKRI**	**0.6305**
40	7	**PISANGAN**	**0.6304**
41	148	**ALSISAR**	**0.6301**
42	6	**MASOODA**	**0.6296**
42	209	**DHOND**	**0.6296**
44	94	**TARANAGAR**	**0.6278**
45	70	**NOKHA**	**0.6272**
46	49	**KUMHER**	**0.6270**
47	1	**ARAIN**	**0.6258**
48	67	**DUNGARGARH**	**0.6256**
49	201	**RAILMAGRA**	**0.6191**
50	33	**BARAN**	**0.6160**
51	50	**NADBAI**	**0.6157**
52	91	**RATANGARH**	**0.6147**
53	115	**SURATGARH**	**0.6144**
54	32	**ATRU**	**0.6143**
55	159	**BILARA**	**0.6134**
56	208	**DANTA RAMGARH**	**0.6120**
57	90	**RAJGARH**	**0.6096**
58	15	**MANDAWAR**	**0.6085**
59	154	**SURAJGARH**	**0.6084**
60	152	**KHETRI**	**0.6059**
61	228	**BHINDER**	**0.6056**
62	2	**BHINAY**	**0.6044**
63	192	**RANI STATION**	**0.6028**
64	153	**NAWALGARH**	**0.6022**
65	165	**HINDAUN**	**0.6003**
66	89	**CHURU**	**0.6000**
	HIGH (0.5 - 0.6)		
67	31	**ANTA**	**0.5994**
68	220	**SIROHI**	**0.5983**
69	13	**KOTKASIM**	**0.5970**
70	160	**LUNI**	**0.5942**
71	98	**MAHWA**	**0.5927**
72	53	**SEWAR**	**0.5925**
73	69	**LUNKARANSAR**	**0.5922**
74	19	**RENI**	**0.5919**
75	47	**DEEG**	**0.5916**
76	217	**PINDWARA**	**0.5905**
77	117	**HANUMANGARH**	**0.5901**
78	194	**SOJAT**	**0.5895**
79	215	**SRI MADHOPUR**	**0.5891**

RANK	PANCHAYAT SAMITIES P. CODE	NAME	HDI
1	2	3	4
80	213	**NEEM KA THANA**	**0.5865**
81	236	**SALUMBAR**	**0.5863**
82	99	**SIKRAI**	**0.5862**
83	16	**NIMRANA**	**0.5859**
84	86	**NIMBAHERA**	**0.5840**
85	158	**BHOPALGARH**	**0.5829**
85	219	**SHEOGANJ**	**0.5832**
87	235	**MAVLI**	**0.5813**
88	83	**DUNGLA**	**0.5811**
89	95	**BANDIKUI**	**0.5806**
90	80	**BHOPALSAGAR**	**0.5801**
91	195	**SUMERPUR**	**0.5789**
92	135	**AHORE**	**0.5783**
93	88	**RASHMI**	**0.5781**
94	56	**BANERA**	**0.5777**
95	167	**NADOTI**	**0.5776**
96	190	**PALI**	**0.5744**
97	186	**BALI**	**0.5739**
98	11	**KATHUMAR**	**0.5725**
99	52	**RUPBAS**	**0.5713**
100	63	SAHARA	0.5707
101	96	DAUSA	0.5701
102	36	KISHANGANJ	0.5698
103	14	LACHHMANGARH	0.5696
103	93	SUJANGARH	0.5697
105	218	REODAR	0.5691
106	230	GIRWA	0.5679
107	237	SARADA	0.5675
108	81	CHHOTI SADRI	0.5670
109	189	MARWAR JUN.	0.5658
110	224	TODARAISINGH	0.5655
111	66	BIKANER	0.5651
112	84	GANGRAR	0.5647
113	232	JHADOL	0.5645
114	82	CHITTAURGARH	0.5634
115	9	BANSURE	0.5631
116	17	RAJGARH	0.5624
116	35	CHHIPABAROD	0.5623
118	57	HURDA	0.5622
119	179	LADNU	0.5602
120	109	ANUPGARH	0.5593
121	200	KUMBHALGARH	0.5590
122	205	GANGAPUR	0.5585
123	187	DESURI	0.5574
124	77	BEGUN	0.5568
125	176	DIDWANA	0.5568
126	203	BAMANWAS	0.5562
127	54	WEIR	0.5558
128	76	BARI SADRI	0.5555
128	78	BHADESAR	0.5556
130	197	BHIM	0.5554
131	162	OSIAN	0.5536
132	72	KESHORAIPATAN	0.5531
133	37	SHAHBAD	0.5526
134	193	ROHAT	0.5521
135	85	KAPASAN	0.5510
136	34	CHHABRA	0.5506
137	147	PIRAWA	0.5503
138	169	TODABHIM	0.5498
139	87	PRATAPGARH	0.5480
140	202	RAJSAMAND	0.5461
141	204	BONLI	0.5447
142	74	TALERA	0.5446
142	184	PARBATSAR	0.5447
144	51	NAGAR PAHARI	0.5441
145	68	KOLAYAT	0.5434
146	191	RAIPUR	0.5427
147	12	KISHANGARH BAS	0.5414
147	180	MAKRANA	0.5411
149	65	SUWANA	0.5405
150	188	JAITARAN	0.5402
151	185	RIYAN	0.5401
152	233	KHERWARA	0.5399
153	196	AMET	0.5396
154	71	HINDOLI	0.5391
155	231	GOGUNDA	0.5391
156	157	BAP	0.5389
157	175	DEGANA	0.5380
158	223	NIWAI	0.5378
159	73	NAINWA	0.5367
160	199	KHAMNOR	0.5359

RANK	PANCHAYAT SAMITIES P. CODE	NAME	HDI
1	2	3	4
161	22	UMREN	0.5350
162	20	THANAGAZI	0.5344
163	181	MERTA	0.5338
164	222	MALPURA	0.5332
165	46	BAYANA	0.5323
166	198	DEOGARH	0.5304
167	168	SAPOTRA	0.5295
168	97	LALSOT	0.5287
169	25	GARHI	0.5279
170	145	KHANPUR	0.5276
171	178	KUCHAMAN	0.5250
172	18	RAMGARH	0.5235
172	216	ABU ROAD	0.5235
174	55	ASIND	0.5233
175	60	MANDAL	0.5221
176	166	KARAULI	0.5191
177	62	RAIPUR	0.5184
178	225	TONK	0.5181
179	64	SHAHPURA	0.5165
179	92	SARDARSHAHAR	0.5165
179	207	SAWAI MADHOPUR	0.5165
182	79	BHAINSRORGARH	0.5157
183	161	MANDOR	0.5149
184	75	ARNOD	0.5141
185	144	JHALRAPATAN	0.5138
186	221	DEOLI	0.5135
187	58	JAHAZPUR	0.5136
188	42	DHORIMANNA	0.5127
189	177	JAYAL	0.5125
190	21	TIJARA	0.5123
191	48	KAMAN	0.5121
191	61	MANDALGARH	0.5120
193	156	BALESAR	0.5119
194	206	KHANDAR	0.5076
195	137	JALOR	0.5067
196	134	SANKRA	0.5066
197	59	KOTRI	0.5041
198	101	BASERI	0.5033
199	183	NAGAUR	0.5022
	MEDIUM (0.4 - 0.5)		
200	164	SHERGARH	0.4977
201	100	BARI	0.4955
202	182	MUNDWA	0.4943
203	226	UNIARA	0.4935
204	163	PHALODI	0.4897
205	102	DHAULPUR	0.4876
206	107	SAGWARA	0.4863
207	139	RANIWARA	0.4851
208	141	SAYLA	0.4829
209	103	RAJAKHERA	0.4800
210	44	SINDHARI	0.4790
211	138	JASWANTPURA	0.4783
212	45	SIWANA	0.4777
213	142	BAKANI	0.4755
214	229	DHARIAWAD	0.4745
215	38	BALOTRA	0.4667
216	136	BHINMAL	0.4666
217	30	TALWARA	0.4646
218	23	ANANDPURI	0.4643
218	146	MANOHARTHANA	0.4644
220	24	BAGIDORA	0.4625
221	132	JAISALMER	0.4621
222	140	SANCHORE	0.4582
223	41	CHOHTAN	0.4577
224	26	GHATOL	0.4543
225	40	BAYTOO	0.4535
226	106	DUNGARPUR	0.4518
227	143	DAG	0.4484
228	105	BICHHIWARA	0.4466
229	29	SAJJANGARH	0.4421
230	104	ASPUR	0.4403
231	133	SAM	0.4379
232	108	SIMALWARA	0.4318
233	39	BARMER	0.4166
234	27	KUSHALGARH	0.4094
234	43	SHEO	0.4092
	LOW (< 0.4)		
236	234	KOTRA	0.3949
237	28	PEEPALKHOONT	0.3853
		RAJASTHAN	**0.5709**
		%age of APPs	**41.8**

BOLD: Equal/Above Average Panchayat Samities (AAPs)

Source: Annex 17.1, Col. 10.

ANNEX-18.1

RANKING OF PSS BY % INCREASE IN HUMAN DEVELOPMENT INDEX: RAJASTHAN (1991-01)

(Descending Order)

RANK	*PANCHAYAT SAMITIES* *P. CODE*	*NAME*	*%*
1	2	3	4
	VERY HIGH (>100)		
1	**42**	**DHORIMANNA**	**122**
2	**41**	**CHOHTAN**	**104**
3	**44**	**SINDHARI**	**103**
	HIGH (75-100)		
4	**40**	**BAYTOO**	**98**
5	**43**	**SHEO**	**91**
6	**39**	**BARMER**	**89**
	MEDIUM (50-75)		
7	**100**	**BARI**	**73**
7	**157**	**BAP**	**73**
9	**90**	**RAJGARH**	**72**
9	**91**	**RATANGARH**	**72**
9	**155**	**UDAIPURWATI**	**72**
12	**45**	**SIWANA**	**71**
13	**38**	**BALOTRA**	**70**
13	**89**	**CHURU**	**70**
13	**94**	**TARANAGAR**	**70**
13	**214**	**PIPRALI**	**70**
17	**93**	**SUJANGARH**	**69**
18	**34**	**CHHABRA**	**68**
18	**92**	**SARDARSHAHAR**	**68**
20	**149**	**BUHANA**	**67**
21	**67**	**DUNGARGARH**	**66**
21	**152**	**KHETRI**	**66**
21	**176**	**DIDWANA**	**66**
21	**211**	**KHANDELA**	**66**
25	**148**	**ALSISAR**	**65**
25	**150**	**CHIRAWA**	**65**
25	**210**	**FATEHPUR**	**65**
28	**51**	**NAGAR PAHARI**	**64**
29	**133**	**SAM**	**63**
29	**154**	**SURAJGARH**	**63**
31	**98**	**MAHWA**	**62**
31	**151**	**JHUNJHUNUN**	**62**
31	**212**	**LACHHMANGARH**	**62**
34	**99**	**SIKRAI**	**61**
34	**213**	**NEEM KA THANA**	**61**
36	**103**	**RAJAKHERA**	**60**
36	**165**	**HINDAUN**	**60**
36	**166**	**KARAULI**	**60**
39	**95**	**BANDIKUI**	**59**
39	**208**	**DANTA RAMGARH**	**59**
41	**200**	**KUMBHALGARH**	**58**
41	**232**	**JHADOL**	**58**
43	**27**	**KUSHALGARH**	**57**
43	**29**	**SAJJANGARH**	**57**
43	**146**	**MANOHARTHANA**	**57**
43	**180**	**MAKRANA**	**57**
43	**198**	**DEOGARH**	**57**
43	**215**	**SRI MADHOPUR**	**57**
49	**50**	**NADBAI**	**56**
49	**97**	**LALSOT**	**56**
51	**209**	**DHOND**	**56**
51	**3**	**JAWAJA**	**55**
53	**153**	**NAWALGARH**	**55**
53	**134**	**SANKRA**	**54**
53	**140**	**SANCHORE**	**54**
53	**143**	**DAG**	**54**
53	**168**	**SAPOTRA**	**54**
53	**179**	**LADNU**	**54**
53	**227**	**BARGAON**	**54**
60	**52**	**RUPBAS**	**53**
60	**96**	**DAUSA**	**53**
60	**147**	**PIRAWA**	**53**
60	**177**	**JAYAL**	**53**
60	**236**	**SALUMBAR**	**53**
65	**10**	**BEHROR**	**52**
65	**48**	**KAMAN**	**52**
65	**53**	**SEWAR**	**52**
65	**108**	**SIMALWARA**	**52**
65	**125**	**JHOTWARA**	**52**
65	**139**	**RANIWARA**	**52**
65	**169**	**TODABHIM**	**52**
65	**184**	**PARBATSAR**	**52**
65	**202**	**RAJSAMAND**	**52**
74	**47**	**DEEG**	**51**
74	**106**	**DUNGARPUR**	**51**
74	**136**	**BHINMAL**	**51**
74	**178**	**KUCHAMAN**	**51**
74	**183**	**NAGAUR**	**51**
79	**11**	**KATHUMAR**	**50**
79	**14**	**LACHHMANGARH**	**50**
79	**36**	**KISHANGANJ**	**50**
79	**87**	**PRATAPGARH**	**50**
79	**101**	**BASERI**	**50**
79	**105**	**BICHHIWARA**	**50**
79	**196**	**AMET**	**50**
	LOW (25-50)		
86	**46**	**BAYANA**	**49**
86	**129**	**SANGANER**	**49**
86	**167**	**NADOTI**	**49**
86	**224**	**TODARAISINGH**	**49**
90	**104**	**ASPUR**	**48**
90	**145**	**KHANPUR**	**48**
90	**175**	**DEGANA**	**48**
90	**206**	**KHANDAR**	**48**
94	**19**	**RENI**	**47**
94	**31**	**ANTA**	**47**
94	**33**	**BARAN**	**47**
94	**37**	**SHAHBAD**	**47**
94	**83**	**DUNGLA**	**47**
94	**107**	**SAGWARA**	**47**
94	**116**	**BHADRA**	**47**
94	**126**	**KOTPUTLI**	**47**
94	**162**	**OSIAN**	**47**
103	**30**	**TALWARA**	**46**
103	**32**	**ATRU**	**46**
103	**49**	**KUMHER**	**46**
103	**72**	**KESHORAIPATAN**	**46**
103	**79**	**BHAINSRORGARH**	**46**
103	**102**	**DHAULPUR**	**46**
103	**114**	**SADULSHAHAR**	**46**
103	**132**	**JAISALMER**	**46**
103	**225**	**TONK**	**46**
103	**228**	**BHINDER**	**46**
113	**9**	**BANSURE**	**45**
113	**23**	**ANANDPURI**	**45**
113	**118**	**NOHAR**	**45**
113	**131**	**VIRATNAGAR**	**45**
113	**135**	**AHORE**	**45**
113	**144**	**JHALRAPATAN**	**45**
113	**203**	**BAMANWAS**	**45**
113	**205**	**GANGAPUR**	**45**
113	**231**	**GOGUNDA**	**45**
122	22	UMREN	44
122	70	NOKHA	44
122	128	SAMBHAR	44
122	220	SIROHI	44
126	26	GHATOL	43
126	74	TALERA	43
126	78	BHADESAR	43
126	84	GANGRAR	43
126	127	PHAGI	43
126	138	JASWANTPURA	43
126	182	MUNDWA	43
126	201	RAILMAGRA	43
126	218	REODAR	43
126	219	SHEOGANJ	43
136	71	HINDOLI	42
136	77	BEGUN	42
136	86	NIMBAHERA	42
136	115	SURATGARH	42
136	122	DUDU	42
136	124	JAMWA RAMGARH	42
136	141	SAYLA	42
136	185	RIYAN	42
136	229	DHARIAWAD	42
136	230	GIRWA	42
146	13	KOTKASIM	41
146	15	MANDAWAR	41
146	28	PEEPALKHOONT	41
146	69	LUNKARANSAR	41
146	76	BARI SADRI	41
146	81	CHHOTI SADRI	41
146	82	CHITTAURGARH	41
146	160	LUNI	41
146	174	SULTANPUR	41
146	193	ROHAT	41
146	216	ABU ROAD	41
146	237	SARADA	41
158	18	RAMGARH	40
158	20	THANAGAZI	40
158	171	ITAWA	40
158	181	MERTA	40
158	190	PALI	40
158	191	RAIPUR	40
158	204	BONLI	40
158	226	UNIARA	40
158	233	KHERWARA	40
167	25	GARHI	39
167	54	WEIR	39
167	73	NAINWA	39
167	170	CHECHAT	39
167	197	BHIM	39
167	207	SAWAI MADHOPUR	39
167	217	PINDWARA	39
167	223	NIWAI	39
175	17	RAJGARH	38
175	137	JALOR	38
175	142	BAKANI	38
175	192	RANI STATION	38
179	1	ARAIN	37
179	5	KISHANGARH	37
179	85	KAPASAN	37
179	119	AMBER	37
179	173	SANGOD	37
179	189	MARWAR JUN.	37
179	235	MAVLI	37
186	21	TIJARA	36
186	56	BANERA	36
186	80	BHOPALSAGAR	36
186	88	RASHMI	36
186	194	SOJAT	36
186	222	MALPURA	36
192	12	KISHANGARH BAS	35
192	35	CHHIPABAROD	35
192	61	MANDALGARH	35
192	75	ARNOD	35
192	109	ANUPGARH	35
192	121	CHAKSU	35
192	130	SHAHPURA	35
199	6	MASOODA	34
199	24	BAGIDORA	34
199	58	JAHAZPUR	34
199	120	BASSI	34
199	123	GOVINDGARH	34
199	188	JAITARAN	34
199	234	KOTRA	34
206	63	SAHARA	33
206	68	KOLAYAT	33
206	158	BHOPALGARH	33
206	159	BILARA	33
206	163	PHALODI	33
206	172	LADPURA	33
206	186	BALI	33
206	187	DESURI	33
206	195	SUMERPUR	33
215	8	SRINAGAR	32
215	62	RAIPUR	32
215	65	SUWANA	32
215	161	MANDOR	32
219	55	ASIND	31
219	64	SHAHPURA	31
219	112	PADAMPUR	31
219	113	RAISINGHNAGAR	31
219	221	DEOLI	31
224	66	BIKANER	30
225	16	NIMRANA	28
225	59	KOTRI	28
225	110	GANGANAGAR	28
225	156	BALESAR	28
229	60	MANDAL	27
229	111	KARANPUR	27
229	199	KHAMNOR	27
232	117	HANUMANGARH	26
233	57	HURDA	25
233	164	SHERGARH	25
	VERY LOW (<25)		
235	2	BHINAY	24
235	7	PISANGAN	24
237	4	KEKRI	23
	RAJASTHAN		**45**
	%age of AAPs		**51**

BOLD: Equal/Above Average Panchayat Samities (AAPs)

Source: Annex- 17.2, Col. 9.

ANNEX-18.2

RANKING OF PSS BY INCREASED VALUE OF HDI : RAJASTHAN (1991-01)

(Descending Order)

RANK	PANCHAYAT SAMITIES P. CODE	PANCHAYAT SAMITIES NAME	VALUE
1	2	3	4
		VERY HIGH (>0.25)	
1	**42**	**DHORIMANNA**	**0.2814**
2	**155**	**UDAIPURWATI**	**0.2804**
3	**149**	**BUHANA**	**0.2701**
4	**210**	**FATEHPUR**	**0.2655**
5	**214**	**PIPRALI**	**0.2623**
6	**94**	**TARANAGAR**	**0.2589**
7	**91**	**RATANGARH**	**0.2577**
8	**211**	**KHANDELA**	**0.2575**
9	**125**	**JHOTWARA**	**0.2572**
10	**90**	**RAJGARH**	**0.2545**
11	**150**	**CHIRAWA**	**0.2529**
12	**151**	**JHUNJHUNUN**	**0.2527**
13	**10**	**BEHROR**	**0.2504**
		HIGH (0.20-0.25)	
14	**67**	**DUNGARGARH**	**0.2488**
15	**212**	**LACHHMANGARH**	**0.2482**
16	**89**	**CHURU**	**0.2477**
17	**148**	**ALSISAR**	**0.2475**
18	**129**	**SANGANER**	**0.2469**
19	**3**	**JAWAJA**	**0.2443**
20	**44**	**SINDHARI**	**0.2430**
21	**152**	**KHETRI**	**0.2404**
22	**154**	**SURAJGARH**	**0.2346**
23	**93**	**SUJANGARH**	**0.2334**
24	**41**	**CHOHTAN**	**0.2328**
25	**116**	**BHADRA**	**0.2297**
26	**126**	**KOTPUTLI**	**0.2284**
27	**208**	**DANTA RAMGARH**	**0.2283**
28	**227**	**BARGAON**	**0.2269**
29	**157**	**BAP**	**0.2265**
30	**98**	**MAHWA**	**0.2260**
30	**209**	**DHOND**	**0.2260**
32	**114**	**SADULSHAHAR**	**0.2245**
33	**40**	**BAYTOO**	**0.2240**
33	**165**	**HINDAUN**	**0.2240**
35	**34**	**CHHABRA**	**0.2230**
35	**99**	**SIKRAI**	**0.2230**
37	**213**	**NEEM KA THANA**	**0.2220**
38	**176**	**DIDWANA**	**0.2208**
39	**50**	**NADBAI**	**0.2206**
40	**95**	**BANDIKUI**	**0.2156**
41	**131**	**VIRATNAGAR**	**0.2150**
42	**174**	**SULTANPUR**	**0.2142**
43	**153**	**NAWALGARH**	**0.2137**
44	**215**	**SRI MADHOPUR**	**0.2134**
45	**51**	**NAGAR PAHARI**	**0.2126**
46	**170**	**CHECHAT**	**0.2121**
47	**128**	**SAMBHAR**	**0.2112**
48	**127**	**PHAGI**	**0.2090**
49	**92**	**SARDARSHAHAR**	**0.2089**
50	**100**	**BARI**	**0.2088**
51	**124**	**JAMWA RAMGARH**	**0.2065**
52	**232**	**JHADOL**	**0.2063**
53	**200**	**KUMBHALGARH**	**0.2049**
54	**118**	**NOHAR**	**0.2042**
55	**236**	**SALUMBAR**	**0.2038**
56	**53**	**SEWAR**	**0.2031**
57	**173**	**SANGOD**	**0.2011**
58	**47**	**DEEG**	**0.2009**
		MEDIUM (0.15-0.20)	
59	**45**	**SIWANA**	**0.1983**
60	**52**	**RUPBAS**	**0.1980**
61	**122**	**DUDU**	**0.1974**
62	**96**	**DAUSA**	**0.1973**
63	**180**	**MAKRANA**	**0.1970**
64	**171**	**ITAWA**	**0.1967**
65	**39**	**BARMER**	**0.1964**
66	**179**	**LADNU**	**0.1964**
67	**33**	**BARAN**	**0.1963**
68	**49**	**KUMHER**	**0.1961**
69	**166**	**KARAULI**	**0.1950**
70	**32**	**ATRU**	**0.1945**
71	**43**	**SHEO**	**0.1944**
72	**38**	**BALOTRA**	**0.1927**
73	**70**	**NOKHA**	**0.1924**
74	**31**	**ANTA**	**0.1915**
75	**198**	**DEOGARH**	**0.1915**
76	**36**	**KISHANGANJ**	**0.1909**
77	**228**	**BHINDER**	**0.1908**
78	**11**	**KATHUMAR**	**0.1906**
79	**147**	**PIRAWA**	**0.1903**
80	**14**	**LACHHMANGARH**	**0.1902**
81	**19**	**RENI**	**0.1893**
82	**167**	**NADOTI**	**0.1892**
83	**97**	**LALSOT**	**0.1890**
84	**169**	**TODABHIM**	**0.1889**
85	**201**	**RAILMAGRA**	**0.1876**
86	**202**	**RAJSAMAND**	**0.1869**
87	**224**	**TODARAISINGH**	**0.1864**
88	**83**	**DUNGLA**	**0.1863**
89	**184**	**PARBATSAR**	**0.1859**
90	**168**	**SAPOTRA**	**0.1848**
91	**119**	**AMBER**	**0.1841**
92	**87**	**PRATAPGARH**	**0.1838**
93	**220**	**SIROHI**	**0.1829**
94	**115**	**SURATGARH**	**0.1824**
95	**103**	**RAJAKHERA**	**0.1806**
96	**196**	**AMET**	**0.1798**
97	**135**	**AHORE**	**0.1790**
98	**37**	**SHAHBAD**	**0.1779**
98	**134**	**SANKRA**	**0.1779**
100	**178**	**KUCHAMAN**	**0.1777**
101	177	JAYAL	0.1767
102	15	MANDAWAR	0.1763
103	162	OSIAN	0.1762
104	123	GOVINDGARH	0.1760
104	130	SHAHPURA	0.1760
106	219	SHEOGANJ	0.1759
107	172	LADPURA	0.1756
108	175	DEGANA	0.1748
109	48	KAMAN	0.1746
110	46	BAYANA	0.1745
111	9	BANSURE	0.1743
112	203	BAMANWAS	0.1738
113	5	KISHANGARH	0.1736
113	86	NIMBAHERA	0.1736
115	72	KESHORAIPATAN	0.1732
116	13	KOTKASIM	0.1729
117	205	GANGAPUR	0.1721
118	160	LUNI	0.1714
119	69	LUNKARANSAR	0.1712
120	145	KHANPUR	0.1708
121	84	GANGRAR	0.1703
122	183	NAGAUR	0.1701
123	218	REODAR	0.1698
124	120	BASSI	0.1689
125	133	SAM	0.1689
126	230	GIRWA	0.1687
127	146	MANOHARTHANA	0.1686
128	231	GOGUNDA	0.1680
129	101	BASERI	0.1679
130	1	ARAIN	0.1675
131	78	BHADESAR	0.1674
132	192	RANI STATION	0.1673
133	139	RANIWARA	0.1658
134	121	CHAKSU	0.1657
134	206	KHANDAR	0.1657
136	237	SARADA	0.1655
137	190	PALI	0.1652
138	217	PINDWARA	0.1650
139	77	BEGUN	0.1649
140	81	CHHOTI SADRI	0.1645
141	74	TALERA	0.1641
142	82	CHITTAURGARH	0.1639
143	225	TONK	0.1631
144	22	UMREN	0.1623
145	76	BARI SADRI	0.1620
146	79	BHAINSRORGARH	0.1618
147	140	SANCHORE	0.1610
148	71	HINDOLI	0.1607
149	185	RIYAN	0.1605
150	193	ROHAT	0.1604
151	29	SAJJANGARH	0.1603
152	6	MASOODA	0.1599
153	144	JHALRAPATAN	0.1593
154	136	BHINMAL	0.1586
155	235	MAVLI	0.1569
156	143	MAVLI	0.1567
157	197	BHIM	0.1565
158	194	SOJAT	0.1563
159	54	WEIR	0.1558
159	204	BONLI	0.1558
161	191	RAIPUR	0.1553
162	107	SAGWARA	0.1550
163	233	KHERWARA	0.1546
164	17	RAJGARH	0.1545
164	113	RAISINGHNAGAR	0.1545
166	80	BHOPALSAGAR	0.1544
167	88	RASHMI	0.1536
168	102	DHAULPUR	0.1532
169	8	SRINAGAR	0.1531
170	20	THANAGAZI	0.1526
170	216	ABU ROAD	0.1526
172	106	DUNGARPUR	0.1524
173	189	MARWAR. JUN.	0.1521
174	159	BILARA	0.1517
175	223	NIWAI	0.1516
176	181	MERTA	0.1515
177	56	BANERA	0.1514
178	18	RAMGARH	0.1508
		LOW (0.10-0.15)	
179	73	NAINWA	0.1495
180	25	GARHI	0.1491
181	112	PADAMPUR	0.1489
182	105	BICHHIWARA	0.1485
183	27	KUSHALGARH	0.1483
184	111	KARANPUR	0.1477
185	85	KAPASAN	0.1476
186	182	MUNDWA	0.1476
187	108	SIMALWARA	0.1475
188	110	GANGANAGAR	0.1474
189	30	TALWARA	0.1472
190	132	JAISALMER	0.1464
191	109	ANUPGARH	0.1461
192	35	CHHIPABAROD	0.1453
193	138	JASWANTPURA	0.1445
194	158	BHOPALGARH	0.1444
195	207	SAWAI MADHOPUR	0.1440
196	23	ANANDPURI	0.1436
197	104	ASPUR	0.1435
197	141	SAYLA	0.1435
199	195	SUMERPUR	0.1421
200	226	UNIARA	0.1417
201	229	DHARIAWAD	0.1413
202	186	BALI	0.1410
203	222	MALPURA	0.1406
204	63	SAHARA	0.1405
205	137	JALOR	0.1401
206	12	KISHANGARH BAS	0.1396
207	187	DESURI	0.1383
208	188	JAITARAN	0.1364
209	21	TIJARA	0.1357
210	26	GHATOL	0.1355
211	68	KOLAYAT	0.1346
212	75	ARNOD	0.1336
213	61	MANDALGARH	0.1330
214	142	BAKANI	0.1318
215	58	JAHAZPUR	0.1315
216	65	SUWANA	0.1297
217	66	BIKANER	0.1289
218	16	NIMRANA	0.1280
219	62	RAIPUR	0.1259
220	161	MANDOR	0.1248
221	55	ASIND	0.1237
222	7	PISANGAN	0.1231
223	64	SHAHPURA	0.1229
224	117	HANUMANGARH	0.1225
225	221	DEOLI	0.1215
226	163	PHALODI	0.1207
227	2	BHINAY	0.1185
228	4	KEKRI	0.1175
228	24	BAGIDORA	0.1175
230	199	KHAMNOR	0.1137
231	28	PEEPALKHOONT	0.1118
232	57	HURDA	0.1113
233	60	MANDAL	0.1111
234	156	BALESAR	0.1105
235	59	KOTRI	0.1093
236	164	SHERGARH	0.1005
		VERY LOW (<0.10)	
237	234	KOTRA	0.0997
		RAJASTHAN	**0.1771**
		%age of AAPs	**42.20**

BOLD: Equal/Above Average Panchayat Samities (AAPs) *Source*: Annex-17.2, Col. 8.

ANNEX-18.3

RANKING OF PANCHAYAT SAMITIES BY DIFFERENCE IN HDI RANK (1991-01)

(Descending Order)

RANK	PANCHAYAT SAMITIES P. CODE	NAME	RANK DIFFERENCE
1	2	3	4
	(>=50)		
1	91	RATANGARH	123
2	90	RAJGARH	120
3	89	CHURU	116
4	94	TARANAGAR	114
5	214	PIPRALI	111
6	152	KHETRI	101
7	67	DUNGARGARH	95
8	93	SUJANGARH	92
9	154	SURAJGARH	90
10	98	MAHWA	88
11	150	CHIRAWA	87
11	155	UDAIPURWATI	87
13	211	KHANDELA	85
14	99	SIKRAI	84
14	148	ALSISAR	84
16	213	NEEM KA THANA	83
17	165	HINDAUN	80
18	95	BANDIKUI	73
19	176	DIDWANA	71
20	34	CHHABRA	70
21	208	DANTA RAMGARH	68
22	215	SRI MADHOPUR	67
23	149	BUHANA	66
24	232	JHADOL	60
25	51	NAGAR PAHARI	59
25	200	KUMBHALGARH	59
27	157	BAP	57
27	210	FATEHPUR	57
29	52	RUPBAS	51
29	212	LACHHMANGARH	51
31	96	DAUSA	50
31	153	NAWALGARH	50
	(25-50)		
33	151	JHUNJHUNUN	49
34	50	NADBAI	46
34	179	LADNU	46
36	42	DHORIMANNA	45
36	236	SALUMBAR	45
38	180	MAKRANA	41
39	53	SEWAR	38
39	209	DHOND	38
41	36	KISHANGANJ	37
42	92	SARDARSHAHAR	36
43	14	LACHHMANGARH	33
43	47	DEEG	33
45	11	KATHUMAR	32
45	147	PIRAWA	32
47	166	KARAULI	31
47	202	RAJSAMAND	31
49	169	TODABHIM	30
49	184	PARBATSAR	30
51	227	BARGAON	29
52	198	DEOGARH	27
52	224	TODARAISINGH	27
54	87	PRATAPGARH	25
	(0-25)		
55	97	LALSOT	23
55	100	BARI	23
57	44	SINDHARI	22
58	3	JAWAJA	20
58	167	NADOTI	20
58	168	SAPOTRA	20
61	10	BEHROR	19
62	196	AMET	17
63	37	SHAHBAD	15
63	45	SIWANA	15
65	125	JHOTWARA	14
66	38	BALOTRA	13
66	178	KUCHAMAN	13
68	33	BARAN	12
68	41	CHOHTAN	12
70	128	SAMBHAR	11
70	162	OSIAN	11
72	83	DUNGLA	10
72	114	SADULSHAHAR	10
72	116	BHADRA	10
72	126	KOTPUTLI	10
72	131	VIRATNAGAR	10
77	19	RENI	9
77	40	BAYTOO	9
77	46	BAYANA	9
77	127	PHAGI	9
77	129	SANGANER	9
77	134	SANKRA	9
77	175	DEGANA	9
84	177	JAYAL	8
85	31	ANTA	7
85	32	ATRU	7
85	103	RAJAKHERA	7
85	118	NOHAR	7
89	124	JAMWA RAMGARH	6
89	145	KHANPUR	6
91	228	BHINDER	5
92	122	DUDU	4
93	39	BARMER	3
93	43	SHEO	3
93	48	KAMAN	3
93	49	KUMHER	3
93	146	MANOHARTHANA	3
93	183	NAGAUR	3
99	72	KESHORAIPATAN	2
99	139	RANIWARA	2
101	203	BAMANWAS	1
102	101	BASERI	0
102	135	AHORE	0
102	170	CHECHAT	0
102	174	SULTANPUR	0
102	225	TONK	0
102	231	GOGUNDA	0
	(0 to -25)		
108	79	BHAINSRORGARH	-1
108	133	SAM	-1
108	171	ITAWA	-1
108	173	SANGOD	-1
108	201	RAILMAGRA	-1
108	205	GANGAPUR	-1
114	9	BANSURE	-2
114	70	NOKHA	-2
114	107	SAGWARA	-2
114	136	BHINMAL	-2
118	5	KISHANGARH	-3
118	27	KUSHALGARH	-3
118	29	SAJJANGARH	-3
118	140	SANCHORE	-3
118	220	SIROHI	-3
123	143	DAG	-4
123	206	KHANDAR	-4
125	172	LADPURA	-5
126	30	TALWARA	-6
126	102	DHAULPUR	-6
126	115	SURATGARH	-6
126	119	AMBER	-6
126	121	CHAKSU	-6
126	123	GOVINDGARH	-6
126	144	JHALRAPATAN	-6
133	108	SIMALWARA	-7
134	28	PEEPALKHOONT	-8
134	219	SHEOGANJ	-8
136	22	UMREN	-9
136	132	JAISALMER	-9
138	23	ANANDPURI	-10
138	74	TALERA	-10
138	104	ASPUR	-10
138	105	BICHHIWARA	-10
138	106	DUNGARPUR	-10
138	130	SHAHPURA	-10
144	120	BASSI	-11
144	138	JASWANTPURA	-11
146	6	MASOODA	-12
146	8	SRINAGAR	-12
146	15	MANDAWAR	-12
146	78	BHADESAR	-12
146	84	GANGRAR	-12
146	230	GIRWA	-12
152	1	ARAIN	-13
152	13	KOTKASIM	-13
152	71	HINDOLI	-13
152	86	NIMBAHERA	-13
152	111	KARANPUR	-13
152	112	PADAMPUR	-13
152	160	LUNI	-13
152	218	REODAR	-13
152	229	DHARIAWAD	-13
161	26	GHATOL	-14
162	69	LUNKARANSAR	-14
163	234	KOTRA	-14
164	141	SAYLA	-16
164	185	RIYAN	-16
164	216	ABU ROAD	-16
167	113	RAISINGHNAGAR	-17
167	182	MUNDWA	-17
169	77	BEGUN	-18
170	110	GANGANAGAR	-19
171	18	RAMGARH	-20
171	226	UNIARA	-20
173	192	RANI STATION	-21
174	159	BILARA	-22
174	237	SARADA	-22
176	82	CHITTAURGARH	-23
176	217	PINDWARA	-23
178	81	CHHOTI SADRI	-24
178	142	BAKANI	-24
178	190	PALI	-24
181	207	SAWAI MADHOPUR	-25
	(-25 to -50)		
182	76	BARI SADRI	-26
183	193	ROHAT	-27
184	191	RAIPUR	-28
185	25	GARHI	-29
185	204	BONLI	-29
185	233	KHERWARA	-29
188	7	PISANGAN	-30
189	4	KEKRI	-31
189	20	THANAGAZI	-31
191	235	MAVLI	-32
192	24	BAGIDORA	-34
192	194	SOJAT	-34
194	137	JALOR	-35
194	181	MERTA	-35
194	197	BHIM	-35
197	223	NIWAI	-36
198	54	WEIR	-38
198	80	BHOPALSAGAR	-38
200	88	RASHMI	-39
201	73	NAINWA	-40
202	2	BHINAY	-41
203	17	RAJGARH	-42
203	189	MARWAR JUN.	-42
205	56	BANERA	-43
206	21	TIJARA	-46
206	117	HANUMANGARH	-46
206	158	BHOPALGARH	-46
209	163	PHALODI	-47
210	16	NIMRANA	-48
	(> -50)		
211	63	SAHARA	-50
212	195	SUMERPUR	-51
213	35	CHHIPABAROD	-52
213	75	ARNOD	-52
213	109	ANUPGARH	-52
213	186	BALI	-52
217	61	MANDALGARH	-53
217	85	KAPASAN	-53
219	58	JAHAZPUR	-58
220	187	DESURI	-60
221	12	KISHANGARH BAS	-61
221	222	MALPURA	-61
223	66	BIKANER	-70
224	188	JAITARAN	-71
225	68	KOLAYAT	-72
226	62	RAIPUR	-73
227	161	MANDOR	-74
228	64	SHAHPURA	-78
229	65	SUWANA	-79
230	57	HURDA	-81
230	221	DEOLI	-81
232	55	ASIND	-84
233	59	KOTRI	-99
234	199	KHAMNOR	-102
235	164	SHERGARH	-104
236	60	MANDAL	-106
236	156	BALESAR	-106

Source: Annex-17.2, Col. 7.

ANNEX-18.4

RANKING OF PSS BY % INCREASE/DECREASE IN HEALTH STATUS INDEX: RAJASTHAN (1991-01)

(Descending Order)

RANK	PANCHAYAT SAMITIES P. CODE	PANCHAYAT SAMITIES NAME	%
1	2	3	4
	VERY HIGH (>40)		
1	100	**BARI**	47
2	51	**NAGAR PAHARI**	43
3	42	**DHORIMANNA**	41
3	109	**ANUPGARH**	41
	HIGH (30-40)		
5	166	**KARAULI**	39
6	47	**DEEG**	38
6	50	**NADBAI**	38
8	133	**SAM**	37
9	41	**CHOHTAN**	36
9	90	**RAJGARH**	36
9	91	**RATANGARH**	36
12	29	**SAJJANGARH**	35
12	40	**BAYTOO**	35
12	48	**KAMAN**	35
12	157	**BAP**	35
12	200	**KUMBHALGARH**	35
17	176	**DIDWANA**	34
18	89	**CHURU**	33
18	174	**SULTANPUR**	33
20	14	**LACHHMANGARH**	32
20	44	**SINDHARI**	32
20	116	**BHADRA**	32
20	122	**DUDU**	32
20	171	**ITAWA**	32
20	191	**RAIPUR**	32
20	214	**PIPRALI**	32
27	27	**KUSHALGARH**	31
27	95	**BANDIKUI**	31
27	98	**MAHWA**	31
27	202	**RAJSAMAND**	31
31	169	**TODABHIM**	30
31	224	**TODARAISINGH**	30
	MEDIUM (20-30)		
33	3	**JAWAJA**	29
33	11	**KATHUMAR**	29
33	19	**RENI**	29
33	35	**CHHIPABAROD**	29
33	52	**RUPBAS**	29
33	93	**SUJANGARH**	29
33	162	**OSIAN**	29
33	206	**KHANDAR**	29
33	225	**TONK**	29
42	53	**SEWAR**	28
42	83	**DUNGLA**	28
42	168	**SAPOTRA**	28
42	179	**LADNU**	28
46	71	**HINDOLI**	27
46	87	**PRATAPGARH**	27
46	108	**SIMALWARA**	27
46	165	**HINDAUN**	27
50	39	**BARMER**	26
50	72	**KESHORAIPATAN**	26
50	103	**RAJAKHERA**	26
50	136	**BHINMAL**	26
50	149	**BUHANA**	26
55	37	**SHAHBAD**	25
55	97	**LALSOT**	25
55	132	**JAISALMER**	25
55	173	**SANGOD**	25
55	180	**MAKRANA**	25
60	86	**NIMBAHERA**	24
60	99	**SIKRAI**	24
60	134	**SANKRA**	24
60	139	**RANIWARA**	24
60	140	**SANCHORE**	24
60	232	**JHADOL**	24
66	22	**UMREN**	23
66	33	**BARAN**	23
66	36	**KISHANGANJ**	23
66	45	**SIWANA**	23
66	46	**BAYANA**	23
66	79	**BHAINSRORGARH**	23
66	106	**DUNGARPUR**	23
66	112	**PADAMPUR**	23
66	135	**AHORE**	23
66	177	**JAYAL**	23
66	184	**PARBATSAR**	23
66	188	**JAITARAN**	23
66	193	**ROHAT**	23
66	198	**DEOGARH**	23
66	210	**FATEHPUR**	23
66	229	**DHARIAWAD**	23
82	38	**BALOTRA**	22
82	49	**KUMHER**	22
82	74	**TALERA**	22
82	94	**TARANAGAR**	22
82	96	**DAUSA**	22
82	146	**MANOHARTHANA**	22
82	163	**PHALODI**	22
82	207	**SAWAI MADHOPUR**	22
90	21	**TIJARA**	21
90	31	**ANTA**	21
90	78	**BHADESAR**	21
90	84	**GANGRAR**	21
90	138	**JASWANTPURA**	21
90	145	**KHANPUR**	21
90	182	**MUNDWA**	21
90	211	**KHANDELA**	21
90	220	**SIROHI**	21
90	226	**UNIARA**	21
90	234	**KOTRA**	21
90	236	**SALUMBAR**	21
102	1	**ARAIN**	20
102	10	**BEHROR**	20
102	32	**ATRU**	20
102	67	**DUNGARGARH**	20
102	76	**BARI SADRI**	20
102	92	**SARDARSHAHAR**	20
102	104	**ASPUR**	20
102	105	**BICHHIWARA**	20
102	113	**RAISINGHNAGAR**	20
102	124	**JAMWA RAMGARH**	20
102	152	**KHETRI**	20
102	160	**LUNI**	20
102	170	**CHECHAT**	20
102	194	**SOJAT**	20
102	205	**GANGAPUR**	20
102	215	**SRI MADHOPUR**	20
102	216	**ABU ROAD**	20
102	231	**GOGUNDA**	20
	LOW (10-20)		
120	18	RAMGARH	19
120	43	SHEO	19
120	107	SAGWARA	19
120	120	BASSI	19
120	127	PHAGI	19
120	128	SAMBHAR	19
120	143	DAG	19
120	147	PIRAWA	19
120	155	UDAIPURWATI	19
120	167	NADOTI	19
120	172	LADPURA	19
120	175	DEGANA	19
120	183	NAGAUR	19
120	189	MARWAR JUN.	19
120	204	MARWAR JUN	19
120	233	KHERWARA	19
136	28	PEEPALKHOONT	18
136	34	CHHABRA	18
136	82	CHITTAURGARH	18
136	111	KARANPUR	18
136	114	SADULSHAHAR	18
136	119	AMBER	18
136	121	CHAKSU	18
136	131	VIRATNAGAR	18
136	161	MANDOR	18
136	192	RANI STATION	18
136	196	AMET	18
136	213	NEEM KA THANA	18
148	9	BANSURE	17
148	13	KOTKASIM	17
148	20	THANAGAZI	17
148	23	ANANDPURI	17
148	26	GHATOL	17
148	73	NAINWA	17
148	81	CHHOTI SADRI	17
148	101	BASERI	17
148	126	KOTPUTLI	17
148	129	SANGANER	17
148	150	CHIRAWA	17
148	154	SURAJGARH	17
148	208	DANTA RAMGARH	17
148	212	LACHHMANGARH	17
148	218	REODAR	17
148	223	NIWAI	17
164	16	NIMRANA	16
164	17	RAJGARH	16
164	110	GANGANAGAR	16
164	141	SAYLA	16
164	148	ALSISAR	16
164	190	PALI	16
164	209	DHOND	16
164	217	PINDWARA	16
172	5	KISHANGARH	15
172	15	MANDAWAR	15
172	77	BEGUN	15
172	88	RASHMI	15
172	118	NOHAR	15
172	125	JHOTWARA	15
172	151	JHUNJHUNUN	15
172	158	BHOPALGARH	15
172	185	RIYAN	15
172	186	BALI	15
172	201	RAILMAGRA	15
172	203	BAMANWAS	15
172	219	SHEOGANJ	15
172	227	BARGAON	15
172	228	BHINDER	15
187	25	GARHI	14
187	61	MANDALGARH	14
187	117	HANUMANGARH	14
187	130	SHAHPURA	14
187	137	JALOR	14
187	144	JHALRAPATAN	14
187	178	KUCHAMAN	14
187	181	MERTA	14
187	221	DEOLI	14
187	230	GIRWA	14
187	235	MAVLI	14
198	30	TALWARA	13
198	102	DHAULPUR	13
198	237	SARADA	13
201	6	MASOODA	12
201	8	SRINAGAR	12
201	54	WEIR	12
201	159	BILARA	12
201	187	DESURI	12
206	4	KEKRI	11
206	55	ASIND	11
206	56	BANERA	11
206	70	NOKHA	11
206	75	ARNOD	11
206	142	BAKANI	11
206	195	SUMERPUR	11
206	197	BHIM	11
206	222	MALPURA	11
215	63	SAHARA	10
215	65	SUWANA	10
215	69	LUNKARANSAR	10
215	115	SURATGARH	10
215	123	GOVINDGARH	10
	VERY LOW (<10)		
220	60	MANDAL	9
220	62	RAIPUR	9
220	199	KHAMNOR	9
223	12	KISHANGARH BAS	8
223	24	BAGIDORA	8
223	58	JAHAZPUR	8
223	59	KOTRI	8
227	2	BHINAY	7
227	7	PISANGAN	7
227	68	KOLAYAT	7
227	153	NAWALGARH	7
231	57	HURDA	6
231	80	BHOPALSAGAR	6
233	64	SHAHPURA	5
234	85	KAPASAN	3
234	156	BALESAR	3
236	66	BIKANER *	0
	DECREASE (-)		
236	164	SHERGARH **	0
		RAJASTHAN	**20**
		%age of AAPs	**50.21**

Note: * Bikaner PS Registered the Lowest 0.07% Increase in HSI

** Shergarh PS of Jodhpur District is the only PS which Regisered Decrease (-0.13%) in HSI.

BOLD: Equal/Above Average Panchayat Samities (AAPs)

Source: Annex 6.1, Col. 9.

ANNEX-18.5

RANKING OF PSS BY DIFFERENCE IN HEALTH STATUS INDEX VALUE: RAJASTHAN (1991-01)

(Descending Order)

RANK	PANCHAYAT SAMITIES P. CODE	NAME	VALUE
1	2	3	4
	VERY HIGH (>0.20)		
1	**91**	**RATANGARH**	**0.2164**
2	**50**	**NADBAI**	**0.2021**
	HIGH (0.15-0.20)		
3	**89**	**CHURU**	**0.1927**
4	**214**	**PIPRALI**	**0.1917**
5	**47**	**DEEG**	**0.1913**
6	**51**	**NAGAR PAHARI**	**0.1893**
7	**100**	**BARI**	**0.1878**
8	**176**	**DIDWANA**	**0.1867**
9	**90**	**RAJGARH**	**0.1845**
10	**174**	**SULTANPUR**	**0.1791**
11	**191**	**RAIPUR**	**0.1778**
12	**200**	**KUMBHALGARH**	**0.1764**
13	**166**	**KARAULI**	**0.1746**
14	**42**	**DHORIMANNA**	**0.1743**
15	**116**	**BHADRA**	**0.1719**
16	**162**	**OSIAN**	**0.1659**
17	**179**	**LADNU**	**0.1650**
18	**122**	**DUDU**	**0.1638**
19	**109**	**ANUPGARH**	**0.1636**
20	**202**	**RAJSAMAND**	**0.1627**
21	**14**	**LACHHMANGARH**	**0.1626**
22	**93**	**SUJANGARH**	**0.1617**
23	**3**	**JAWAJA**	**0.1608**
24	**95**	**BANDIKUI**	**0.1596**
25	**149**	**BUHANA**	**0.1584**
26	**48**	**KAMAN**	**0.1581**
27	**171**	**ITAWA**	**0.1572**
28	**169**	**TODABHIM**	**0.1568**
29	**29**	**SAJJANGARH**	**0.1555**
30	**41**	**CHOHTAN**	**0.1552**
31	**165**	**HINDAUN**	**0.1547**
32	**224**	**TODARAISINGH**	**0.1538**
33	**98**	**MAHWA**	**0.1535**
34	**19**	**RENI**	**0.1529**
35	**52**	**RUPBAS**	**0.1524**
36	**83**	**DUNGLA**	**0.1505**
	MEDIUM (0.10-0.15)		
37	**11**	**KATHUMAR**	**0.1498**
38	**53**	**SEWAR**	**0.1487**
39	**135**	**AHORE**	**0.1477**
40	**225**	**TONK**	**0.1470**
41	**108**	**SIMALWARA**	**0.1443**
41	**157**	**BAP**	**0.1443**
43	**210**	**FATEHPUR**	**0.1429**
44	**220**	**SIROHI**	**0.1426**
45	**136**	**BHINMAL**	**0.1420**
46	**188**	**JAITARAN**	**0.1392**
47	**206**	**KHANDAR**	**0.1386**
48	**180**	**MAKRANA**	**0.1384**
49	**184**	**PARBATSAR**	**0.1379**
50	**139**	**RANIWARA**	**0.1378**
51	**44**	**SINDHARI**	**0.1373**
52	**106**	**DUNGARPUR**	**0.1360**
53	**71**	**HINDOLI**	**0.1351**
54	**45**	**SIWANA**	**0.1341**
54	**168**	**SAPOTRA**	**0.1341**
56	**27**	**KUSHALGARH**	**0.1337**
57	**49**	**KUMHER**	**0.1334**
58	**87**	**PRATAPGARH**	**0.1331**
59	**211**	**KHANDELA**	**0.1322**
60	**155**	**UDAIPURWATI**	**0.1317**
61	**173**	**SANGOD**	**0.1316**
62	**112**	**PADAMPUR**	**0.1315**
63	**86**	**NIMBAHERA**	**0.1306**
64	**193**	**ROHAT**	**0.1296**
65	**40**	**BAYTOO**	**0.1294**
65	**104**	**ASPUR**	**0.1294**
65	**215**	**SRI MADHOPUR**	**0.1294**
68	**35**	**CHHIPABAROD**	**0.1291**
68	**67**	**DUNGARGARH**	**0.1291**
68	**152**	**KHETRI**	**0.1291**
71	**133**	**SAM**	**0.1289**
72	**177**	**JAYAL**	**0.1288**
73	**72**	**KESHORAIPATAN**	**0.1283**
73	**94**	**TARANAGAR**	**0.1283**
75	**194**	**SOJAT**	**0.1282**
76	**33**	**BARAN**	**0.1277**
77	**99**	**SIKRAI**	**0.1276**
78	**107**	**SAGWARA**	**0.1273**
79	**138**	**JASWANTPURA**	**0.1268**

RANK	PANCHAYAT SAMITIES P. CODE	NAME	VALUE
1	2	3	4
80	**22**	**UMREN**	**0.1267**
81	**10**	**BEHROR**	**0.1257**
82	**192**	**RANI STATION**	**0.1245**
83	**140**	**SANCHORE**	**0.1240**
84	**198**	**DEOGARH**	**0.1222**
85	**160**	**LUNI**	**0.1221**
86	**97**	**LALSOT**	**0.1219**
87	**232**	**JHADOL**	**0.1214**
88	**105**	**BICHHIWARA**	**0.1208**
89	**96**	**DAUSA**	**0.1195**
90	**103**	**RAJAKHERA**	**0.1194**
91	**236**	**SALUMBAR**	**0.1189**
92	**182**	**MUNDWA**	**0.1185**
92	**205**	**GANGAPUR**	**0.1185**
94	**170**	**CHECHAT**	**0.1184**
95	**36**	**KISHANGANJ**	**0.1175**
96	**37**	**SHAHBAD**	**0.1174**
96	**163**	**PHALODI**	**0.1174**
98	**128**	**SAMBHAR**	**0.1172**
99	**189**	**MARWAR JUN.**	**0.1170**
100	**229**	**DHARIAWAD**	**0.1152**
101	**207**	**SAWAI MADHOPUR**	**0.1150**
102	**124**	**JAMWA RAMGARH**	**0.1144**
102	**175**	**DEGANA**	**0.1144**
104	**213**	**NEEM KA THANA**	**0.1137**
105	**31**	**ANTA**	**0.1132**
106	**46**	**BAYANA**	**0.1129**
107	**74**	**TALERA**	**0.1125**
107	**84**	**GANGRAR**	**0.1125**
107	**172**	**LADPURA**	**0.1125**
110	**1**	**ARAIN**	**0.1122**
111	**150**	**CHIRAWA**	**0.1111**
112	**131**	**VIRATNAGAR**	**0.1109**
113	**216**	**ABU ROAD**	**0.1105**
114	**132**	**JAISALMER**	**0.1102**
115	**120**	**BASSI**	**0.1101**
116	**38**	**BALOTRA**	**0.1098**
117	**145**	**KHANPUR**	**0.1096**
118	79	BHAINSRORGARH	0.1095
118	208	DANTA RAMGARH	0.1095
120	231	GOGUNDA	0.1088
121	32	ATRU	0.1085
122	134	SANKRA	0.1078
123	21	TIJARA	0.1077
124	167	NADOTI	0.1076
124	209	DHOND	0.1076
126	119	AMBER	0.1072
127	111	KARANPUR	0.1068
128	78	BHADESAR	0.1066
129	141	SAYLA	0.1062
130	76	BARI SADRI	0.1058
131	183	NAGAUR	0.1057
132	18	RAMGARH	0.1056
132	113	RAISINGHNAGAR	0.1056
134	218	REODAR	0.1046
135	233	KHERWARA	0.1044
136	212	LACHHMANGARH	0.1042
137	186	BALI	0.1041
138	92	SARDARSHAHAR	0.1037
139	226	UNIARA	0.1031
140	114	SADULSHAHAR	0.1026
141	16	NIMRANA	0.1025
142	126	KOTPUTLI	0.1017
143	151	JHUNJHUNUN	0.1015
143	154	SURAJGARH	0.1015
145	204	BONLI	0.1012
146	127	PHAGI	0.1011
147	217	PINDWARA	0.1009
148	9	BANSURE	0.1006
149	110	GANGANAGAR	0.1005
149	196	AMET	0.1005
151	39	BARMER	0.1002
152	201	RAILMAGRA	0.1001
153	161	MANDOR	0.1000
	LOW (0.05-0.10)		
154	190	PALI	0.0996
155	148	ALSISAR	0.0993
156	147	PIRAWA	0.0989
157	137	JALOR	0.0983
158	82	CHITTAURGARH	0.0972
159	20	THANAGAZI	0.0967
160	219	SHEOGANJ	0.0965

RANK	PANCHAYAT SAMITIES P. CODE	NAME	VALUE
1	2	3	4
161	158	BHOPALGARH	0.0964
162	129	SANGANER	0.0961
163	185	RIYAN	0.0959
164	13	KOTKASIM	0.0938
165	26	GHATOL	0.0935
166	146	MANOHARTHANA	0.0934
167	88	RASHMI	0.0926
168	5	KISHANGARH	0.0921
169	227	BARGAON	0.0920
170	15	MANDAWAR	0.0918
171	125	JHOTWARA	0.0912
172	81	CHHOTI SADRI	0.0911
173	228	BHINDER	0.0910
174	23	ANANDPURI	0.0909
174	235	MAVLI	0.0909
176	130	SHAHPURA	0.0904
176	143	DAG	0.0904
176	223	NIWAI	0.0904
179	25	GARHI	0.0890
180	73	NAINWA	0.0877
181	181	MERTA	0.0873
182	28	PEEPALKHOONT	0.0872
183	17	RAJGARH	0.0869
184	234	KOTRA	0.0861
185	230	GIRWA	0.0856
186	187	DESURI	0.0844
187	117	HANUMANGARH	0.0843
188	121	CHAKSU	0.0839
189	159	BILARA	0.0837
190	237	SARADA	0.0832
191	203	BAMANWAS	0.0828
192	77	BEGUN	0.0822
192	101	BASERI	0.0822
194	178	KUCHAMAN	0.0821
195	61	MANDALGARH	0.0801
196	34	CHHABRA	0.0787
197	195	SUMERPUR	0.0785
198	43	SHEO	0.0778
199	30	TALWARA	0.0777
200	8	SRINAGAR	0.0768
201	56	BANERA	0.0760
201	221	DEOLI	0.0760
203	6	MASOODA	0.0744
204	118	NOHAR	0.0740
205	144	JHALRAPATAN	0.0734
206	123	GOVINDGARH	0.0726
207	197	BHIM	0.0713
208	4	KEKRI	0.0705
209	102	DHAULPUR	0.0697
210	54	WEIR	0.0686
210	63	SAHARA	0.0686
212	55	ASIND	0.0680
213	222	MALPURA	0.0664
214	65	SUWANA	0.0648
215	70	NOKHA	0.0639
216	75	ARNOD	0.0607
217	62	RAIPUR	0.0575
218	199	KHAMNOR	0.0566
219	69	LUNKARANSAR	0.0558
220	142	BAKANI	0.0550
221	60	MANDAL	0.0546
222	7	PISANGAN	0.0509
	VERY LOW (<0.05)		
223	153	NAWALGARH	0.0473
224	12	KISHANGARH BAS	0.0464
224	115	SURATGARH	0.0464
226	24	BAGIDORA	0.0463
227	58	JAHAZPUR	0.0448
228	2	BHINAY	0.0447
228	59	KOTRI	0.0447
230	80	BHOPALSAGAR	0.0410
231	57	HURDA	0.0405
232	68	KOLAYAT	0.0354
233	64	SHAHPURA	0.0315
234	85	KAPASAN	0.0193
235	156	BALESAR	0.0184
236	66	BIKANER	0.0004
237	164	SHERGARH	-0.0008
	RAJASTHAN		**0.1096**
	%age of AAPs		**49.37**

BOLD: Equal/Above Average Panchayat Samities (AAPs)

Source: Annex 6.1, Col. 8.

ANNEX-18.6

RANKING OF PSS BY DIFFERENCE IN HSI RANK, 1991-01

(Descending Order)

RANK	PANCHAYAT SAMITIES P. CODE	PANCHAYAT SAMITIES NAME	DIFFERENCE
1	2	3	4
	VERY HIGH (>=50)		
1	50	NADBAI	113
2	47	DEEG	103
3	176	DIDWANA	95
4	90	RAJGARH	93
5	89	CHURU	86
6	174	SULTANPUR	84
7	200	KUMBHALGARH	81
8	116	BHADRA	78
9	191	RAIPUR	76
9	214	PIPRALI	76
11	91	RATANGARH	74
12	122	DUDU	65
13	162	OSIAN	64
14	202	RAJSAMAND	63
15	93	SUJANGARH	61
15	95	BANDIKUI	61
17	14	LACHHMANGARH	60
18	3	JAWAJA	58
18	165	HINDAUN	58
18	169	TODABHIM	58
18	179	LADNU	58
22	83	DUNGLA	56
23	19	RENI	55
24	224	TODARAISINGH	50
	HIGH (25-50)		
25	53	SEWAR	48
25	98	MAHWA	48
27	11	KATHUMAR	47
27	52	RUPBAS	47
29	51	NAGAR PAHARI	44
29	149	BUHANA	44
31	108	SIMALWARA	43
31	225	TONK	43
33	136	BHINMAL	42
33	171	ITAWA	42
35	184	PARBATSAR	36
36	139	RANIWARA	35
36	166	KARAULI	35
36	180	MAKRANA	35
39	210	FATEHPUR	32
40	106	DUNGARPUR	31
40	188	JAITARAN	31
42	71	HINDOLI	29
42	86	NIMBAHERA	29
44	45	SIWANA	28
44	112	PADAMPUR	28
46	49	KUMHER	27
	MEDIUM (0-25)		
47	177	JAYAL	24
48	135	AHORE	23
48	193	ROHAT	23
50	48	KAMAN	22
50	100	BARI	22
52	42	DHORIMANNA	21
53	173	SANGOD	19
54	33	BARAN	18
54	67	DUNGARGARH	18
54	94	TARANAGAR	18
54	170	CHECHAT	18
58	138	JASWANTPURA	17
58	194	SOJAT	17
60	22	UMREN	16
60	29	SAJJANGARH	16
60	104	ASPUR	16
60	168	SAPOTRA	16
60	205	GANGAPUR	16
65	87	PRATAPGARH	15
65	99	SIKRAI	15
65	105	BICHHIWARA	15
65	140	SANCHORE	15
65	152	KHETRI	15
65	198	DEOGARH	15
65	211	KHANDELA	15
72	41	CHOHTAN	14
72	107	SAGWARA	14
72	215	SRI MADHOPUR	14
75	160	LUNI	13
75	182	MUNDWA	13
75	189	MARWAR JUN.	13
75	206	KHANDAR	13
75	220	SIROHI	13
80	124	JAMWA RAMGARH	12
80	232	JHADOL	12
82	10	BEHROR	10
82	72	KESHORAIPATAN	10
82	128	SAMBHAR	10
85	213	NEEM KA THANA	9
86	96	DAUSA	8
86	109	ANUPGARH	8
88	229	DHARIAWAD	6
88	236	SALUMBAR	6
90	36	KISHANGANJ	5
90	74	TALERA	5
90	157	BAP	5
90	163	PHALODI	5
90	192	RANI STATION	5
95	27	KUSHALGARH	4
95	35	CHHIPABAROD	4
95	44	SINDHARI	4
95	155	UDAIPURWATI	4
99	84	GANGRAR	3
99	175	DEGANA	3
99	207	SAWAI MADHOPUR	3
102	40	BAYTOO	2
102	97	LALSOT	2
102	208	DANTA RAMGARH	2
102	209	DHOND	2
106	37	SHAHBAD	1
106	38	BALOTRA	1
106	103	RAJAKHERA	1
106	120	BASSI	1
110	31	ANTA	0
110	46	BAYANA	0
110	133	SAM	0
110	141	SAYLA	0
110	150	CHIRAWA	0
110	167	NADOTI	0
110	172	LADPURA	0
	LOW (0 to -25)		
117	39	BARMER	-1
117	79	BHAINSRORGARH	-1
117	111	KARANPUR	-1
117	131	VIRATNAGAR	-1
117	137	JALOR	-1
117	145	KHANPUR	-1
117	234	KOTRA	-1
124	1	ARAIN	-3
124	16	NIMRANA	-3
124	21	TIJARA	-3
124	119	AMBER	-3
124	146	MANOHARTHANA	-3
124	186	BALI	-3
124	190	PALI	-3
124	195	SUMERPUR	-3
132	113	RAISINGHNAGAR	-4
132	212	LACHHMANGARH	-4
132	216	ABU ROAD	-4
135	43	SHEO	-5
135	78	BHADESAR	5
135	218	REODAR	-5
135	226	UNIARA	-5
135	231	GOGUNDA	-5
140	32	ATRU	-6
140	159	BILARA	-6
140	187	DESURI	-6
143	92	SARDARSHAHAR	-7
143	114	SADULSHAHAR	-7
143	132	JAISALMER	-7
143	134	SANKRA	-7
143	158	BHOPALGARH	-7
143	201	RAILMAGRA	-7
149	76	BARI SADRI	-8
149	126	KOTPUTLI	-8
149	148	ALSISAR	-8
149	151	JHUNJHUNUN	-8
149	154	SURAJGARH	-8
149	204	BONLI	-8
149	219	SHEOGANJ	-8
156	9	BANSURE	-9
156	18	RAMGARH	-9
156	34	CHHABRA	-9
159	28	PEEPALKHOONT	-10
159	143	DAG	-10
161	121	CHAKSU	-11
161	147	PIRAWA	-11
161	183	NAGAUR	-11
164	127	PHAGI	-12
164	217	PINDWARA	-12
166	88	RASHMI	-13
166	233	KHERWARA	-13
168	101	BASERI	-14
168	123	GOVINDGARH	-14
168	130	SHAHPURA	-14
171	110	GANGANAGAR	-15
171	153	NAWALGARH	-15
173	25	GARHI	-16
173	185	RIYAN	-16
175	5	KISHANGARH	-17
175	82	CHITTAURGARH	-17
175	115	SURATGARH	-17
175	196	AMET	-17
175	235	MAVLI	-17
180	129	SANGANER	-18
181	20	THANAGAZI	-19
181	161	MANDOR	-19
183	15	MANDAWAR	-21
183	227	BARGAON	-21
185	81	CHHOTI SADRI	-22
185	118	NOHAR	-22
185	223	NIWAI	-22
188	23	ANANDPURI	-23
189	73	NAINWA	-24
190	56	BANERA	-25
190	181	MERTA	-25
190	237	SARADA	-25
	VERY LOW (-25 to -50)		
193	13	KOTKASIM	-26
193	125	JHOTWARA	-26
193	228	BHINDER	-26
193	230	GIRWA	-26
197	142	BAKANI	-27
198	26	GHATOL	-29
199	4	KEKRI	-31
199	63	SAHARA	-31
199	77	BEGUN	-31
202	17	RAJGARH	-32
203	197	BHIM	-33
204	203	BAMANWAS	-34
205	7	PISANGAN	-35
205	102	DHAULPUR	-35
205	144	JHALRAPATAN	-35
208	8	SRINAGAR	-39
208	117	HANUMANGARH	-39
210	61	MANDALGARH	-40
211	178	KUCHAMAN	-41
212	6	MASOODA	-43
213	30	TALWARA	-44
214	57	HURDA	-46
214	65	SUWANA	-46
214	221	DEOLI	-46
217	75	ARNOD	-47
	EXTREMELY LOW (> -50)		
218	54	WEIR	-55
218	199	KHAMNOR	-55
220	55	ASIND	-56
221	62	RAIPUR	-58
221	222	MALPURA	-58
223	70	NOKHA	-61
224	68	KOLAYAT	-63
225	60	MANDAL	-66
225	69	LUNKARANSAR	-66
227	2	BHINAY	-75
228	24	BAGIDORA	-78
229	12	KISHANGARH BAS	-82
229	59	KOTRI	-82
231	80	BHOPALSAGAR	-83
232	58	JAHAZPUR	-85
233	64	SHAHPURA	-97
234	85	KAPASAN	-103
235	156	BALESAR	-115
236	66	BIKANER	-122
237	164	SHERGARH	-132

BOLD: Equal/Above Average Panchayat Samities (AAPs)

Source: Annex 6.1, Col. 7.

ANNEX-18.7

RANKING OF PSS BY % INCREASE IN EDI VALUE: RAJASTHAN (1991-01)

RANK	PANCHAYAT SAMITIES P. CODE	NAME	%
1	2	3	4
	VERY HIGH (>=200)		
1	42	**DHORIMANNA**	425.6
2	41	**CHOHTAN**	405.6
3	44	**SINDHARI**	354.3
4	43	**SHEO**	269.2
5	40	**BAYTOO**	253.2
6	146	**MANOHARTHANA**	251.7
7	39	**BARMER**	246.7
8	232	**JHADOL**	246.0
9	94	**TARANAGAR**	227.0
10	93	**SUJANGARH**	220.7
11	92	**SARDARSHAHAR**	220.3
12	45	**SIWANA**	211.4
13	234	**KOTRA**	202.1
	HIGH (150-200)		
14	236	**SALUMBAR**	196.7
15	91	**RATANGARH**	194.5
16	67	**DUNGARGARH**	194.4
17	27	**KUSHALGARH**	193.8
18	229	**DHARIAWAD**	188.3
19	140	**SANCHORE**	185.6
20	38	**BALOTRA**	175.0
21	139	**RANIWARA**	172.4
22	89	**CHURU**	163.6
23	166	**KARAULI**	161.5
24	134	**SANKRA**	161.4
25	136	**BHINMAL**	160.9
26	147	**PIRAWA**	158.4
27	216	**ABU ROAD**	155.5
28	165	**HINDAUN**	155.2
29	100	**BARI**	154.5
30	34	**CHHABRA**	151.9
31	217	**PINDWARA**	151.4
32	198	**DEOGARH**	150.3
	MEDIUM (100-150)		
33	218	**REODAR**	149.9
34	28	**PEEPALKHOONT**	149.6
35	133	**SAM**	148.2
36	118	**NOHAR**	148.0
37	90	**RAJGARH**	147.8
38	70	**NOKHA**	143.6
39	177	**JAYAL**	143.0
39	157	**BAP**	143.0
41	231	**GOGUNDA**	141.6
42	196	**AMET**	140.6
43	73	**NAINWA**	140.2
44	99	**SIKRAI**	139.2
45	176	**DIDWANA**	139.1
46	228	**BHINDER**	139.0
46	184	**PARBATSAR**	139.0
48	168	**SAPOTRA**	138.8
49	126	**KOTPUTLI**	137.1
49	127	**PHAGI**	137.1
51	143	**DAG**	136.7
52	230	**GIRWA**	136.4
53	141	**SAYLA**	135.9
54	178	**KUCHAMAN**	134.7
55	210	**FATEHPUR**	133.9
56	219	**SHEOGANJ**	133.5
56	131	**VIRATNAGAR**	133.5
58	124	**JAMWA RAMGARH**	133.2
59	71	**HINDOLI**	132.7
60	29	**SAJJANGARH**	131.7
61	163	**PHALODI**	131.0
62	180	**MAKRANA**	129.2
63	183	**NAGAUR**	129.1
64	212	**LACHHMANGARH**	127.6
65	227	**BARGAON**	127.5
66	3	**JAWAJA**	127.3
67	36	**KISHANGANJ**	127.0
68	237	**SARADA**	125.2
69	103	**RAJAKHERA**	123.2
70	30	**TALWARA**	123.1
71	48	**KAMAN**	122.6
72	101	**BASERI**	121.7
73	144	**JHALRAPATAN**	120.5
73	211	**KHANDELA**	120.5
75	200	**KUMBHALGARH**	120.4
76	64	**SHAHPURA**	120.3
77	155	**UDAIPURWATI**	120.2
78	162	**OSIAN**	120.1
79	51	**NAGAR PAHARI**	119.0
80	175	**DEGANA**	118.9
81	74	**TALERA**	117.0
82	193	**ROHAT**	116.9
82	85	**KAPASAN**	116.9
84	128	**SAMBHAR**	115.6
85	182	**MUNDWA**	115.4
85	164	**SHERGARH**	115.4
87	167	**NADOTI**	115.3
88	208	**DANTA RAMGARH**	114.9
88	87	**PRATAPGARH**	114.9
90	56	**BANERA**	114.7
91	179	**LADNU**	114.2
92	185	**RIYAN**	112.8
93	23	**ANANDPURI**	112.6
94	61	**MANDALGARH**	112.2
95	35	**CHHIPABAROD**	112.1
96	58	**JAHAZPUR**	111.5
97	203	**BAMANWAS**	111.4
98	138	**JASWANTPURA**	110.9
99	224	**TODARAISINGH**	110.6
100	37	**SHAHBAD**	110.2
101	170	**CHECHAT**	107.8
102	95	**BANDIKUI**	106.9
103	169	**TODABHIM**	106.8
104	209	DHOND	106.2
105	116	BHADRA	105.6
106	69	LUNKARANSAR	105.4
107	160	LUNI	105.1
107	72	KESHORAIPATAN	105.1
109	135	AHORE	105.0
110	65	SUWANA	104.6
111	97	LALSOT	103.9
112	66	BIKANER	103.8
113	132	JAISALMER	103.6
114	214	PIPRALI	103.4
115	79	BHAINSRORGARH	103.2
116	171	ITAWA	102.8
117	120	BASSI	102.3
118	117	HANUMANGARH	101.8
119	77	BEGUN	101.7
120	121	CHAKSU	101.5
121	188	JAITARAN	101.0
122	105	BICHHIWARA	100.5
	LOW (50-100)		
123	102	DHAULPUR	99.5
123	96	DAUSA	99.5
123	190	PALI	99.5
126	26	GHATOL	99.1
126	213	NEEM KA THANA	99.1
128	60	MANDAL	98.8
129	197	BHIM	98.6
130	109	ANUPGARH	97.9
131	84	GANGRAR	97.8
132	172	LADPURA	97.7
132	68	KOLAYAT	97.7
134	78	BHADESAR	97.6
135	191	RAIPUR	97.2
136	130	SHAHPURA	97.0
137	82	CHITTAURGARH	96.5
138	173	SANGOD	96.3
139	10	BEHROR	96.1
140	142	BAKANI	95.9
141	181	MERTA	95.7
141	9	BANSURE	94.7
141	125	JHOTWARA	94.7
144	148	ALSISAR	94.3
145	174	SULTANPUR	93.7
146	145	KHANPUR	93.3
147	156	BALESAR	92.9
148	83	DUNGLA	92.8
149	119	AMBER	92.5
150	204	BONLI	92.3
151	122	DUDU	91.8
152	202	RAJSAMAND	91.2
153	233	KHERWARA	91.1
154	63	SAHARA	90.9
155	106	DUNGARPUR	90.8
156	220	SIROHI	90.6
157	226	UNIARA	90.5
157	206	KHANDAR	90.5
159	80	BHOPALSAGAR	90.4
160	98	MAHWA	89.5
161	33	BARAN	89.3
162	225	TONK	89.0
163	137	JALOR	88.7
164	5	KISHANGARH	88.3
165	19	RENI	88.1
166	20	THANAGAZI	87.9
167	55	ASIND	86.8
168	46	BAYANA	86.1
169	222	MALPURA	85.7
170	215	SRI MADHOPUR	85.5
170	108	SIMALWARA	85.5
172	235	MAVLI	85.3
173	129	SANGANER	84.7
173	113	RAISINGHNAGAR	84.7
175	123	GOVINDGARH	84.6
175	205	GANGAPUR	84.6
177	14	LACHHMANGARH	84.5
177	32	ATRU	84.5
179	150	CHIRAWA	84.4
180	201	RAILMAGRA	83.8
180	75	ARNOD	83.8
182	62	RAIPUR	83.6
183	11	KATHUMAR	83.4
184	53	SEWAR	83.3
185	159	BILARA	82.8
186	50	NADBAI	82.3
187	154	SURAJGARH	82.0
188	158	BHOPALGARH	81.8
188	22	UMREN	81.8
190	24	BAGIDORA	81.5
190	76	BARI SADRI	81.5
192	223	NIWAI	81.3
193	81	CHHOTI SADRI	80.0
194	199	KHAMNOR	79.8
195	31	ANTA	79.6
196	149	BUHANA	78.9
197	195	SUMERPUR	78.8
198	189	MARWAR JUN.	78.6
199	194	SOJAT	78.0
199	86	NIMBAHERA	78.0
201	151	JHUNJHUNUN	77.9
202	152	KHETRI	77.0
202	187	DESURI	77.0
204	186	BALI	76.7
205	47	DEEG	76.5
206	115	SURATGARH	76.4
207	52	RUPBAS	76.2
208	207	SAWAI MADHOPUR	75.2
209	1	ARAIN	73.6
210	25	GARHI	73.4
211	17	RAJGARH	72.8
212	104	ASPUR	72.1
213	153	NAWALGARH	71.6
214	21	TIJARA	71.5
214	192	RANI STATION	71.5
216	88	RASHMI	71.1
216	6	MASOODA	71.1
218	18	RAMGARH	70.7
219	49	KUMHER	69.6
220	8	SRINAGAR	69.4
220	114	SADULSHAHAR	69.4
222	54	WEIR	68.3
223	59	KOTRI	68.0
224	107	SAGWARA	64.1
225	161	MANDOR	64.0
226	111	KARANPUR	60.0
227	221	DEOLI	57.5
228	15	MANDAWAR	56.9
229	57	HURDA	56.1
230	12	KISHANGARH BAS	55.2
231	112	PADAMPUR	54.9
232	13	KOTKASIM	54.5
233	110	GANGANAGAR	53.2
	VERY LOW (<50)		
234	7	PISANGAN	47.8
235	2	BHINAY	35.6
236	4	KEKRI	18.7
237	16	NIMRANA	14.1
		RAJASTHAN	**106.6**
		%age of AAPs	**43.50**

BOLD: Equal/Above Average Panchayat Samities (AAPs)

Source: Annex- 8.2, Col. 9.

ANNEX-18.8

RANKING OF PSS BY INCREASED VALUE OF EDI: RAJASTHAN (1991-01)

(Descending Order)

RANK	PANCHAYAT SAMITIES P. CODE	PANCHAYAT SAMITIES NAME	VALUE
1	2	3	4
	VERY HIGH (>=0.4)		
1	**42**	**DHORIMANNA**	**0.5188**
2	**94**	**TARANAGAR**	**0.4764**
3	**44**	**SINDHARI**	**0.4372**
4	**10**	**BEHROR**	**0.4223**
5	**165**	**HINDAUN**	**0.4168**
6	**155**	**UDAIPURWATI**	**0.4062**
7	**90**	**RAJGARH**	**0.4051**
8	**210**	**FATEHPUR**	**0.4031**
9	**91**	**RATANGARH**	**0.4015**
	HIGH (0.3-0.4)		
10	**93**	**SUJANGARH**	**0.3992**
11	**126**	**KOTPUTLI**	**0.3935**
12	**212**	**LACHHMANGARH**	**0.3935**
13	**3**	**JAWAJA**	**0.3862**
14	**89**	**CHURU**	**0.3852**
15	**232**	**JHADOL**	**0.3838**
16	**40**	**BAYTOO**	**0.3810**
17	**43**	**SHEO**	**0.3769**
18	**211**	**KHANDELA**	**0.3738**
19	**92**	**SARDARSHAHAR**	**0.3737**
20	**45**	**SIWANA**	**0.3680**
21	**147**	**PIRAWA**	**0.3671**
22	**41**	**CHOHTAN**	**0.3650**
23	**131**	**VIRATNAGAR**	**0.3612**
24	**118**	**NOHAR**	**0.3579**
25	**208**	**DANTA RAMGARH**	**0.3495**
26	**67**	**DUNGARGARH**	**0.3487**
27	**39**	**BARMER**	**0.3468**
28	**236**	**SALUMBAR**	**0.3452**
29	**227**	**BARGAON**	**0.3431**
30	**148**	**ALSISAR**	**0.3389**
31	**176**	**DIDWANA**	**0.3368**
32	**214**	**PIPRALI**	**0.3294**
33	**128**	**SAMBHAR**	**0.3290**
34	**170**	**CHECHAT**	**0.3278**
35	**99**	**SIKRAI**	**0.3266**
36	**178**	**KUCHAMAN**	**0.3264**
37	**209**	**DHOND**	**0.3258**
38	**124**	**JAMWA RAMGARH**	**0.3231**
39	**149**	**BUHANA**	**0.3223**
40	**116**	**BHADRA**	**0.3222**
41	**228**	**BHINDER**	**0.3221**
42	**150**	**CHIRAWA**	**0.3209**
43	**127**	**PHAGI**	**0.3193**
44	**180**	**MAKRANA**	**0.3167**
45	**151**	**JHUNJHUNUN**	**0.3157**
46	**173**	**SANGOD**	**0.3153**
47	**167**	**NADOTI**	**0.3146**
48	**174**	**SULTANPUR**	**0.3137**
49	**38**	**BALOTRA**	**0.3123**
50	**95**	**BANDIKUI**	**0.3115**
51	**166**	**KARAULI**	**0.3108**
52	**213**	**NEEM KA THANA**	**0.3097**
53	**101**	**BASERI**	**0.3048**
54	**100**	**BARI**	**0.3047**
55	**230**	**GIRWA**	**0.3007**
	MEDIUM (0.2-0.3)		
56	**168**	**SAPOTRA**	**0.2993**
57	**172**	**LADPURA**	**0.2984**
58	**125**	**JHOTWARA**	**0.2968**
59	**154**	**SURAJGARH**	**0.2963**
60	**146**	**MANOHARTHANA**	**0.2937**
61	**184**	**PARBATSAR**	**0.2926**
62	**179**	**LADNU**	**0.2910**
63	**130**	**SHAHPURA**	**0.2901**
64	**117**	**HANUMANGARH**	**0.2891**
65	**145**	**KHANPUR**	**0.2889**
66	**171**	**ITAWA**	**0.2864**
67	**215**	**SRI MADHOPUR**	**0.2840**
68	**217**	**PINDWARA**	**0.2833**
69	**103**	**RAJAKHERA**	**0.2832**
70	**169**	**TODABHIM**	**0.2828**
71	**51**	**NAGAR PAHARI**	**0.2826**
72	**34**	**CHHABRA**	**0.2814**
73	**113**	**RAISINGHNAGAR**	**0.2809**
74	**203**	**BAMANWAS**	**0.2792**
75	**33**	**BARAN**	**0.2791**
76	**50**	**NADBAI**	**0.2775**
77	**144**	**JHALRAPATAN**	**0.2769**
78	**53**	**SEWAR**	**0.2764**
79	**98**	**MAHWA**	**0.2757**
80	**123**	**GOVINDGARH**	**0.2748**
81	**237**	**SARADA**	**0.2734**
82	**153**	**NAWALGARH**	**0.2686**
83	**109**	**ANUPGARH**	**0.2663**
84	**36**	**KISHANGANJ**	**0.2641**
85	**152**	**KHETRI**	**0.2640**
86	**177**	**JAYAL**	**0.2637**
87	**52**	**RUPBAS**	**0.2633**
88	**102**	**DHAULPUR**	**0.2628**
89	**134**	**SANKRA**	**0.2617**
90	**120**	**BASSI**	**0.2615**
91	**198**	**DEOGARH**	**0.2609**
92	**32**	**ATRU**	**0.2605**
93	**139**	**RANIWARA**	**0.2601**
94	**231**	**GOGUNDA**	**0.2590**
95	**129**	**SANGANER**	**0.2585**
96	**175**	**DEGANA**	**0.2580**
97	73	NAINWA	0.2562
98	140	SANCHORE	0.2558
99	72	KESHORAIPATAN	0.2550
100	96	DAUSA	0.2542
101	31	ANTA	0.2540
102	218	REODAR	0.2537
103	119	AMBER	0.2527
104	9	BANSURE	0.2526
105	196	AMET	0.2515
106	219	SHEOGANJ	0.2511
107	87	PRATAPGARH	0.2504
108	74	TALERA	0.2491
109	70	NOKHA	0.2487
110	49	KUMHER	0.2478
111	160	LUNI	0.2455
112	183	NAGAUR	0.2451
113	37	SHAHBAD	0.2447
114	224	TODARAISINGH	0.2423
115	197	BHIM	0.2419
116	185	RIYAN	0.2405
117	193	ROHAT	0.2396
118	97	LALSOT	0.2391
119	122	DUDU	0.2383
120	135	AHORE	0.2373
121	114	SADULSHAHAR	0.2362
122	56	BANERA	0.2353
123	181	MERTA	0.2350
124	233	KHERWARA	0.2348
125	19	RENI	0.2336
126	202	RAJSAMAND	0.2332
127	163	PHALODI	0.2315
128	15	MANDAWAR	0.2309
129	71	HINDOLI	0.2308
130	143	DAG	0.2305
131	205	GANGAPUR	0.2305
132	216	ABU ROAD	0.2303
133	11	KATHUMAR	0.2296
134	46	BAYANA	0.2287
135	133	SAM	0.2267
136	13	KOTKASIM	0.2259
137	14	LACHHMANGARH	0.2249
138	58	JAHAZPUR	0.2247
139	121	CHAKSU	0.2242
140	48	KAMAN	0.2232
141	201	RAILMAGRA	0.2229
142	162	OSIAN	0.2227
143	47	DEEG	0.2217
144	35	CHHIPABAROD	0.2209
145	200	KUMBHALGARH	0.2205
146	204	BONLI	0.2194
147	235	MAVLI	0.2192
148	5	KISHANGARH	0.2190
149	54	WEIR	0.2187
150	157	BAP	0.2185
151	82	CHITTAURGARH	0.2166
152	30	TALWARA	0.2164
153	111	KARANPUR	0.2162
154	191	RAIPUR	0.2143
155	80	BHOPALSAGAR	0.2130
156	77	BEGUN	0.2126
157	115	SURATGARH	0.2126
158	69	LUNKARANSAR	0.2114
159	190	PALI	0.2111
160	66	BIKANER	0.2110
161	22	UMREN	0.2091
162	110	GANGANAGAR	0.2089
163	112	PADAMPUR	0.2086
164	85	KAPASAN	0.2080
165	141	SAYLA	0.2080
166	132	JAISALMER	0.2076
167	195	SUMERPUR	0.2067
168	86	NIMBAHERA	0.2061
169	136	BHINMAL	0.2048
170	182	MUNDWA	0.2044
171	79	BHAINSRORGARH	0.2043
172	78	BHADESAR	0.2032
173	220	SIROHI	0.2028
174	84	GANGRAR	0.2020
175	188	JAITARAN	0.2013
176	65	SUWANA	0.2013
177	81	CHHOTI SADRI	0.2008
178	64	SHAHPURA	0.2006
179	17	RAJGARH	0.2003
180	105	BICHHIWARA	0.2001
	LOW (0.1-0.2)		
181	199	KHAMNOR	0.1999
182	83	DUNGLA	0.1997
183	61	MANDALGARH	0.1991
184	194	SOJAT	0.1984
185	192	RANI STATION	0.1972
186	223	NIWAI	0.1959
187	187	DESURI	0.1958
188	186	BALI	0.1957
189	25	GARHI	0.1956
190	6	MASOODA	0.1955
191	159	BILARA	0.1949
192	18	RAMGARH	0.1936
193	21	TIJARA	0.1933
194	229	DHARIAWAD	0.1930
195	106	DUNGARPUR	0.1918
196	189	MARWAR JUN.	0.1917
197	20	THANAGAZI	0.1908
198	75	ARNOD	0.1882
199	27	KUSHALGARH	0.1876
200	23	ANANDPURI	0.1855
201	222	MALPURA	0.1851
202	8	SRINAGAR	0.1841
203	60	MANDAL	0.1839
204	226	UNIARA	0.1837
205	164	SHERGARH	0.1837
206	29	SAJJANGARH	0.1822
207	63	SAHARA	0.1820
208	137	JALOR	0.1817
209	207	SAWAI MADHOPUR	0.1808
210	142	BAKANI	0.1775
211	225	TONK	0.1772
212	68	KOLAYAT	0.1768
213	107	SAGWARA	0.1763
214	12	KISHANGARH BAS	0.1755
215	158	BHOPALGARH	0.1739
216	138	JASWANTPURA	0.1735
217	76	BARI SADRI	0.1723
218	1	ARAIN	0.1715
219	156	BALESAR	0.1700
220	206	KHANDAR	0.1699
221	26	GHATOL	0.1686
222	62	RAIPUR	0.1660
223	55	ASIND	0.1654
224	108	SIMALWARA	0.1654
225	57	HURDA	0.1627
226	104	ASPUR	0.1621
227	24	BAGIDORA	0.1588
228	88	RASHMI	0.1560
229	7	PISANGAN	0.1481
230	161	MANDOR	0.1439
231	221	DEOLI	0.1401
232	59	KOTRI	0.1369
233	234	KOTRA	0.1342
234	28	PEEPALKHOONT	0.1267
	LOW (<0.1)		
235	2	BHINAY	0.0932
236	16	NIMRANA	0.0656
237	4	KEKRI	0.0630
		RAJASTHAN	**0.2573**
		%age of AAPs	**40.50**

BOLD: Equal/Above Average Panchayat Samities (AAPs)

Source: Annex- 8.2, Col. 8.

ANNEX-18.9

RANKING OF PSS BY DIFFERENCE IN EDI RANK: RAJASTHAN (1991-01)

(Descending Order)

RANK	PANCHAYAT SAMITIES P. CODE	PANCHAYAT SAMITIES NAME	RANK DIFFERENCE
1	2	3	4
	(>=50)		
1	42	DHORIMANNA	210
2	44	SINDHARI	165
3	40	BAYTOO	145
4	232	JHADOL	144
5	94	TARANAGAR	142
6	93	SUJANGARH	141
7	43	SHEO	139
8	92	SARDARSHAHAR	137
9	45	SIWANA	132
10	91	RATANGARH	120
11	236	SALUMBAR	120
12	67	DUNGARGARH	116
13	39	BARMER	114
14	41	CHOHTAN	97
15	38	BALOTRA	90
16	89	CHURU	85
17	166	KARAULI	83
18	100	BARI	75
19	147	PIRAWA	75
20	118	NOHAR	63
21	217	PINDWARA	61
22	34	CHHABRA	59
23	165	HINDAUN	59
24	184	PARBATSAR	55
25	146	MANOHARTHANA	53
26	168	SAPOTRA	53
27	176	DIDWANA	53
28	228	BHINDER	53
29	99	SIKRAI	51
30	230	GIRWA	51
31	127	PHAGI	50
	(25-50)		
32	134	SANKRA	49
33	90	RAJGARH	48
34	178	KUCHAMAN	48
35	198	DEOGARH	46
36	139	RANIWARA	45
37	124	JAMWA RAMGARH	44
38	218	REODAR	44
39	131	VIRATNAGAR	43
40	210	FATEHPUR	42
41	70	NOKHA	39
42	126	KOTPUTLI	39
43	177	JAYAL	39
44	3	JAWAJA	37
45	180	MAKRANA	37
46	231	GOGUNDA	37
47	227	BARGAON	36
48	36	KISHANGANJ	35
49	73	NAINWA	34
50	196	AMET	34
51	237	SARADA	34
52	103	RAJAKHERA	33
53	101	BASERI	31
54	140	SANCHORE	31
55	212	LACHHMANGARH	31
56	144	JHALRAPATAN	30
57	208	DANTA RAMGARH	28
58	51	NAGAR PAHARI	27
59	219	SHEOGANJ	26
	(0-25)		
60	175	DEGANA	24
61	211	KHANDELA	22
62	128	SAMBHAR	21
63	183	NAGAUR	21
64	71	HINDOLI	20
65	163	PHALODI	19
66	170	CHECHAT	19
67	179	LADNU	19
68	143	DAG	17
69	203	BAMANWAS	17
70	155	UDAIPURWATI	16
71	209	DHOND	16
72	216	ABU ROAD	15
73	116	BHADRA	14
74	87	PRATAPGARH	13
75	167	NADOTI	13
76	74	TALERA	12
77	133	SAM	11
78	214	PIPRALI	10
79	48	KAMAN	8
80	193	ROHAT	8
81	95	BANDIKUI	7
82	169	TODABHIM	7
83	157	BAP	6
84	185	RIYAN	6
85	30	TALWARA	5
86	37	SHAHBAD	5
87	72	KESHORAIPATAN	5
88	148	ALSISAR	5
89	173	SANGOD	5
90	56	BANERA	4
91	160	LUNI	4
92	174	SULTANPUR	4
93	213	NEEM KA THANA	4
94	162	OSIAN	3
95	10	BEHROR	1
96	35	CHHIPABAROD	1
97	149	BUHANA	1
98	150	CHIRAWA	1
99	151	JHUNJHUNUN	1
100	172	LADPURA	1
101	200	KUMBHALGARH	1
102	224	TODARAISINGH	1
103	28	PEEPALKHOONT	0
104	97	LALSOT	0
105	120	BASSI	0
106	141	SAYLA	0
107	234	KOTRA	0
	(0 to -25)		
108	27	KUSHALGARH	-1
109	102	DHAULPUR	-1
110	130	SHAHPURA	-1
111	229	DHARIAWAD	-1
112	58	JAHAZPUR	-2
113	96	DAUSA	-2
114	136	BHINMAL	-2
115	64	SHAHPURA	-3
116	117	HANUMANGARH	-3
117	85	KAPASAN	-4
118	125	JHOTWARA	-4
119	154	SURAJGARH	-4
120	29	SAJJANGARH	-6
121	135	AHORE	-6
122	182	MUNDWA	-6
123	171	ITAWA	-7
124	215	SRI MADHOPUR	-8
125	109	ANUPGARH	-9
126	153	NAWALGARH	-9
127	61	MANDALGARH	-10
128	197	BHIM	-10
129	113	RAISINGHNAGAR	-11
130	50	NADBAI	-12
131	69	LUNKARANSAR	-12
132	164	SHERGARH	-12
133	23	ANANDPURI	-13
134	66	BIKANER	-13
135	145	KHANPUR	-13
136	181	MERTA	-13
137	9	BANSURE	-14
138	53	SEWAR	-15
139	98	MAHWA	-15
140	132	JAISALMER	-15
141	138	JASWANTPURA	-15
142	33	BARAN	-16
143	77	BEGUN	-16
144	122	DUDU	-16
145	121	CHAKSU	-17
146	15	MANDAWAR	-18
147	79	BHAINSRORGARH	-18
148	119	AMBER	-18
149	123	GOVINDGARH	-18
150	13	KOTKASIM	-19
151	65	SUWANA	-19
152	190	PALI	-19
153	233	KHERWARA	-19
154	26	GHATOL	-20
155	52	RUPBAS	-21
156	19	RENI	-22
157	32	ATRU	-22
158	129	SANGANER	-22
159	202	RAJSAMAND	-22
160	78	BHADESAR	-23
161	82	CHITTAURGARH	-23
162	152	KHETRI	-23
163	188	JAITARAN	-23
164	84	GANGRAR	-24
165	191	RAIPUR	-25
166	204	BONLI	-25
167	49	KUMHER	-26
	(-25 to -50)		
168	105	BICHHIWARA	-26
169	68	KOLAYAT	-27
170	5	KISHANGARH	-28
171	46	BAYANA	-28
172	83	DUNGLA	-29
173	235	MAVLI	-29
174	31	ANTA	-30
175	60	MANDAL	-30
176	205	GANGAPUR	-31
177	14	LACHHMANGARH	-32
178	142	BAKANI	-32
179	80	BHOPALSAGAR	-33
180	220	SIROHI	-34
181	201	RAILMAGRA	-35
182	11	KATHUMAR	-36
183	110	GANGANAGAR	-36
184	156	BALESAR	-37
185	226	UNIARA	-37
186	114	SADULSHAHAR	-38
187	106	DUNGARPUR	-39
188	63	SAHARA	-40
189	86	NIMBAHERA	-40
190	206	KHANDAR	-40
191	20	THANAGAZI	-41
192	47	DEEG	-41
193	112	PADAMPUR	-41
194	137	JALOR	-41
195	195	SUMERPUR	-41
196	22	UMREN	-43
197	225	TONK	-43
198	55	ASIND	-44
199	108	SIMALWARA	-44
200	111	KARANPUR	-44
201	159	BILARA	-46
202	194	SOJAT	-46
203	81	CHHOTI SADRI	-47
204	223	NIWAI	-47
205	54	WEIR	-48
206	75	ARNOD	-48
207	62	RAIPUR	-49
208	222	MALPURA	-49
209	24	BAGIDORA	-50
210	115	SURATGARH	-50
211	199	KHAMNOR	-50
	(-25 to -50)		
212	187	DESURI	-52
213	186	BALI	-53
214	158	BHOPALGARH	-54
215	189	MARWAR JUN.	-55
216	76	BARI SADRI	-56
217	17	RAJGARH	-57
218	25	GARHI	-61
219	192	RANI STATION	-61
220	207	SAWAI MADHOPUR	-61
221	6	MASOODA	-62
222	21	TIJARA	-62
223	18	RAMGARH	-63
224	1	ARAIN	-66
225	59	KOTRI	-66
226	8	SRINAGAR	-70
227	104	ASPUR	-72
228	12	KISHANGARH BAS	-73
229	88	RASHMI	-76
230	16	NIMRANA	-77
231	107	SAGWARA	-85
232	161	MANDOR	-88
233	57	HURDA	-90
234	221	DEOLI	-101
235	7	PISANGAN	-102
236	2	BHINAY	-142
237	4	KEKRI	-174

BOLD: Equal/Above Average Panchayat Samities (AAPs)

Source: Annex- 8.2, Col. 7.

ANNEX-18.10

RANKING OF PSS BY % INCREASE IN GEDI VALUE: RAJASTHAN (1991-01)

(Descending Order)

RANK	PANCHAYAT SAMITIES P. CODE	NAME	%
1	2	3	4
	VERY HIGH (>=250)		
1	**42**	**DHORIMANNA**	**1057.9**
2	**41**	**CHOHTAN**	**1002.4**
3	**44**	**SINDHARI**	**947.3**
4	**43**	**SHEO**	**710.8**
5	**39**	**BARMER**	**647.0**
6	**146**	**MANOHARTHANA**	**578.0**
7	**140**	**SANCHORE**	**561.4**
8	**40**	**BAYTOO**	**542.4**
9	**133**	**SAM**	**420.0**
10	**92**	**SARDARSHAHAR**	**413.9**
11	**136**	**BHINMAL**	**395.0**
12	**134**	**SANKRA**	**382.8**
13	**93**	**SUJANGARH**	**366.4**
14	**94**	**TARANAGAR**	**365.1**
15	**232**	**JHADOL**	**363.0**
15	**139**	**RANIWARA**	**362.1**
17	**45**	**SIWANA**	**354.9**
18	**91**	**RATANGARH**	**317.3**
19	**38**	**BALOTRA**	**312.5**
20	**67**	**DUNGARGARH**	**301.5**
21	**100**	**BARI**	**299.2**
21	**34**	**CHHABARA**	**297.4**
21	**165**	**HINDAUN**	**296.1**
24	**27**	**KUSHALGARH**	**295.5**
25	**166**	**KARAULI**	**292.2**
26	**236**	**SALUMBAR**	**289.7**
27	**234**	**KOTRA**	**282.2**
28	**198**	**DEOGARH**	**282.1**
29	**163**	**PHALODI**	**276.2**
30	**164**	**SHERGARH**	**274.1**
31	**157**	**BAP**	**274.0**
32	**162**	**OSIAN**	**268.2**
33	**89**	**CHURU**	**261.6**
34	**28**	**PEEPALKHOONT**	**260.8**
34	**99**	**SIKRAI**	**259.7**
36	**177**	**JAYAL**	**258.1**
37	**70**	**NOKHA**	**257.4**
38	**147**	**PIRAWA**	**255.5**
38	**124**	**JAMWA RAMGARH**	**254.9**
	HIGH (200-250)		
40	**103**	**RAJAKHERA**	**246.0**
40	**183**	**NAGAUR**	**246.0**
42	**48**	**KAMAN**	**244.6**
43	**3**	**JAWAJA**	**239.2**
44	**229**	**DHARIAWAD**	**237.5**
45	**169**	**TODABHIM**	**234.8**
46	**132**	**JAISALMER**	**229.5**
47	**193**	**ROHAT**	**228.8**
48	**176**	**DIDWANA**	**227.1**
49	**196**	**AMET**	**226.2**
50	**182**	**MUNDWA**	**220.5**
51	**73**	**NAINWA**	**220.3**
52	**156**	**BALESAR**	**219.6**
53	**35**	**CHHIPABAROD**	**219.0**
54	**90**	**RAJGARH**	**215.8**
55	**138**	**JASWANTPURA**	**215.5**
56	**219**	**SHEOGANJ**	**215.0**
57	**118**	**NOHAR**	**212.1**
58	**218**	**REODAR**	**211.9**
59	**178**	**KUCHAMAN**	**211.2**
60	**228**	**BHINDER**	**210.4**
61	**168**	**SAPOTRA**	**210.2**
62	**141**	**SAYLA**	**210.1**
63	**131**	**VIRATNAGAR**	**210.0**
64	**127**	**PHAGI**	**209.9**
65	**167**	**NADOTI**	**209.3**
66	**216**	**ABU ROAD**	**208.3**
67	**126**	**KOTPUTLI**	**207.0**
68	**231**	**GOGUNDA**	**204.9**
69	**203**	**BAMANWAS**	**204.6**
70	**51**	**NAGAR PAHARI**	**203.5**
71	**224**	**TODARAISINGH**	**202.7**
72	**121**	**CHAKSU**	**202.1**
73	**85**	**KAPASAN**	**201.7**
74	**184**	**PARBATSAR**	**201.2**
75	**175**	**DEGANA**	**200.6**
76	**120**	**BASSI**	**200.0**
	MEDIUM (150-200)		
77	**210**	**FATEHPUR**	**197.5**
78	**128**	**SAMBHAR**	**197.2**
79	**211**	**KHANDELA**	**195.0**
80	**180**	**MAKRANA**	**194.4**
81	**71**	**HINDOLI**	**194.0**
82	**144**	**JHALRAPATAN**	**192.5**
83	**96**	**DAUSA**	**191.3**
84	**160**	**LUNI**	**190.8**
84	**212**	**LACHHMANGARH**	**190.8**
86	**197**	**BHIM**	**189.5**
87	**217**	**PINDWARA**	**189.0**
88	**188**	**JAITARAN**	**188.7**
89	**200**	**KUMBHALGARH**	**186.1**
90	**143**	**DAG**	**186.0**
91	**23**	**ANANDPURI**	**184.9**
92	**230**	**GIRWA**	**183.9**
93	**185**	**RIYAN**	**181.8**
94	**29**	**SAJJANGARH**	**181.5**
95	**97**	**LALSOT**	**181.0**
96	**95**	**BANDIKUI**	**180.9**
97	**225**	**TONK**	**180.8**
98	**58**	**JAHAZPUR**	**180.5**
99	**158**	**BHOPALGARH**	**180.2**
100	**77**	**BEGUN**	**177.6**
101	**101**	**BASERI**	**176.6**
102	**190**	**PALI**	**176.5**
103	**191**	**RAIPUR**	**176.3**
104	**64**	**SHAHPURA**	**175.8**
105	**179**	**LADNU**	**175.1**
106	**208**	**DANTA RAMGARH**	**173.6**
107	**119**	**AMBER**	**172.9**
108	**209**	**DHOND**	**171.3**
109	**46**	**BAYANA**	**170.6**
110	**227**	**BARGAON**	**170.4**
111	**72**	**KESHORAIPATAN**	**170.3**
112	**237**	**SARADA**	**169.8**
113	**74**	**TALERA**	**168.8**
114	**87**	**PRATAPGARH**	**168.2**
115	**36**	**KISHANGANJ**	**167.4**
116	**56**	**BANERA**	**165.9**
117	**30**	**TALWARA**	**165.5**
118	**159**	**BILARA**	**165.2**
119	**102**	**DHAULPUR**	**163.4**
120	**135**	**AHORE**	**163.3**
121	155	UDAIPURWATI	159.7
121	226	UNIARA	159.7
123	130	SHAHPURA	159.5
124	37	SHAHBAD	158.9
125	214	PIPRALI	158.5
126	19	RENI	154.6
127	171	ITAWA	154.2
128	181	MERTA	153.2
129	79	BHAINSRORGARH	152.6
130	205	GANGAPUR	152.3
131	11	KATHUMAR	151.7
132	161	MANDOR	150.4
132	213	NEEM KA THANA	150.4
134	98	MAHWA	150.0
	LOW (100-150)		
135	20	THANAGAZI	149.7
136	50	NADBAI	149.4
136	66	BIKANER	149.4
136	105	BICHHIWARA	149.4
139	61	MANDALGARH	149.0
139	170	CHECHAT	149.0
141	204	BONLI	148.9
142	65	SUWANA	148.7
143	9	BANSURE	148.1
143	83	DUNGLA	148.1
145	78	BHADESAR	147.8
146	145	KHANPUR	147.4
147	206	KHANDAR	146.9
148	69	LUNKARANSAR	146.7
149	53	SEWAR	145.6
150	137	JALOR	143.9
151	125	JHOTWARA	143.6
152	116	BHADRA	143.2
153	220	SIROHI	142.8
154	82	CHITTAURGARH	142.2
155	68	KOLAYAT	142.1
155	84	GANGRAR	142.1
157	26	GHATOL	140.2
158	122	DUDU	139.9
159	173	SANGOD	139.5
160	47	DEEG	139.0
161	60	MANDAL	138.8
162	207	SAWAI MADHOPUR	138.1
163	142	BAKANI	137.7
164	194	SOJAT	137.6
165	55	ASIND	137.1
166	123	GOVINDGARH	136.3
167	14	LACHHMANGARH	135.4
167	129	SANGANER	135.4
169	106	DUNGARPUR	135.2
170	233	KHERWARA	135.1
171	33	BARAN	135.0
172	172	LADPURA	133.5
172	215	SRI MADHOPUR	133.5
174	80	BHOPALSAGAR	133.2
175	174	SULTANPUR	131.9
176	202	RAJSAMAND	131.8
177	189	MARWAR JUN.	130.3
178	63	SAHARA	130.0
179	76	BARI SADRI	129.1
180	222	MALPURA	128.0
181	22	UMREN	127.9
182	86	NIMBAHERA	126.2
183	5	KISHANGARH	125.7
184	81	CHHOTI SADRI	125.4
185	32	ATRU	124.9
186	17	RAJGARH	123.6
187	6	MASOODA	121.5
187	148	ALSISAR	121.5
189	54	WEIR	121.0
190	62	RAIPUR	119.7
191	49	KUMHER	118.5
192	52	RUPBAS	117.8
193	117	HANUMANGARH	117.6
194	235	MAVLI	117.4
195	31	ANTA	116.3
196	195	SUMERPUR	115.1
197	201	RAILMAGRA	114.9
198	109	ANUPGARH	113.9
199	108	SIMALWARA	112.9
200	199	KHAMNOR	112.7
201	187	DESURI	112.2
202	223	NIWAI	110.5
203	152	KHETRI	108.7
204	1	ARAIN	108.4
205	75	ARNOD	107.1
206	150	CHIRAWA	106.9
207	8	SRINAGAR	106.2
208	154	SURAJGARH	105.5
209	24	BAGIDORA	104.8
210	88	RASHMI	101.1
211	21	TIJARA	100.0
	VERY LOW (<100)		
212	115	SURATGARH	99.6
213	149	BUHANA	99.2
214	151	JHUNJHUNUN	98.4
215	153	NAWALGARH	97.9
216	18	RAMGARH	97.4
216	186	BALI	97.4
218	192	RANI STATION	96.7
219	104	ASPUR	93.8
220	113	RAISINGHNAGAR	93.6
221	10	BEHROR	92.3
222	25	GARHI	91.7
223	221	DEOLI	89.8
224	107	SAGWARA	81.0
225	114	SADULSHAHAR	80.1
226	15	MANDAWAR	73.3
227	7	PISANGAN	71.5
228	12	KISHANGARH BAS	70.9
229	59	KOTRI	68.8
230	13	KOTKASIM	68.5
231	57	HURDA	63.4
232	111	KARANPUR	62.6
233	112	PADAMPUR	58.7
234	110	GANGANAGAR	58.3
235	2	BHINAY	49.3
236	4	KEKRI	24.1
237	16	NIMRANA	21.0
	RAJASTHAN		**162**
	%age of AAPs		**50.6**

BOLD: Equal/Above Average Panchayat Samities (AAPs)

Source: Annex- 10.2. Col. 9.

ANNEX-18.11

RANKING OF PSS BY INCREASED VALUE OF GEDI : RAJASTHAN (1991-01)

(Descending Order)

RANK	PANCHAYAT SIMITIES PCODE	NAME	VALUE
1	2	3	4
	VERY HIGH (>=0.5)		
1	42	**DHORIMANNA**	0.603
2	94	**TARANAGAR**	0.555
3	165	**HINDAUN**	0.530
4	44	**SINDHARI**	0.521
5	3	**JAWAJA**	0.500
	HIGH (0.4 - 0.5)		
6	210	**FATEHPUR**	0.482
7	90	**RAJGARH**	0.479
8	91	**RATANGARH**	0.476
9	212	**LACHHMANGARH**	0.475
10	126	**KOTPUTLI**	0.474
11	155	**UDAIPURWATI**	0.471
12	93	**SUJANGARH**	0.469
13	211	**KHANDELA**	0.466
14	89	**CHURU**	0.463
15	43	**SHEO**	0.462
16	40	**BAYTOO**	0.461
17	92	**SARDARSHAHAR**	0.447
18	147	**PIRAWA**	0.442
19	131	**VIRATNAGAR**	0.441
20	45	**SIWANA**	0.433
21	232	**JHADOL**	0.432
22	39	**BARMER**	0.427
22	208	**DANTA RAMGARH**	0.427
24	41	**CHOHTAN**	0.421
25	118	**NOHAR**	0.42
26	128	**SAMBHAR**	0.418
27	99	**SIKRAI**	0.413
27	124	**JAMWA RAMGARH**	0.413
29	176	**DIDWANA**	0.411
29	209	**DHOND**	0.411
31	214	**PIPRALI**	0.409
32	167	**NADOTI**	0.406
33	67	**DUNGARGARH**	0.404
	MEDIUM (0.3 - 0.4)		
34	95	**BANDIKUI**	0.398
35	227	**BARGAON**	0.397
36	178	**KUCHAMAN**	0.395
36	148	**ALSISAR**	0.395
38	236	**SALUMBAR**	0.394
39	170	**CHECHAT**	0.389
40	10	**BEHROR**	0.386
41	213	**NEEM KA THANA**	0.385
41	173	**SANGOD**	0.385
41	169	**TODABHIM**	0.385
44	228	**BHINDER**	0.383
45	127	**PHAGI**	0.382
46	116	**BHADRA**	0.381
47	174	**SULTANPUR**	0.380
47	100	**BARI**	0.380
49	180	**MAKRANA**	0.379
50	149	**BUHANA**	0.376
51	50	**NADBAI**	0.375
51	38	**BALOTRA**	0.375
53	150	**CHIRAWA**	0.374
53	166	**KARAULI**	0.374
55	130	**SHAHPURA**	0.370
56	125	**JHOTWARA**	0.369
56	103	**RAJAKHERA**	0.369
56	151	**JHUNJHUNUN**	0.369
59	53	**SEWAR**	0.367
60	145	**KHANPUR**	0.364
61	215	**SRI MADHOPUR**	0.363
62	101	**BASERI**	0.362
63	98	**MAHWA**	0.357
64	203	**BAMANWAS**	0.356
65	172	**LADPURA**	0.355
66	123	**GOVINDGARH**	0.353
67	179	**LADNU**	0.352
68	168	**SAPOTRA**	0.351
69	51	**NAGAR PAHARI**	0.350
69	171	**ITAWA**	0.350
71	154	**SURAJGARH**	0.348
72	33	**BARAN**	0.347
73	34	**CHHABARA**	0.345
74	230	**GIRWA**	0.342
74	120	**BASSI**	0.342
74	184	**PARBATSAR**	0.342
77	146	**MANOHARTHANA**	0.341
78	52	**RUPBAS**	0.337
79	144	**JHALRAPATAN**	0.335
80	134	**SANKRA**	0.333
80	49	**KUMHER**	0.333
82	119	**AMBER**	0.332
83	96	**DAUSA**	0.331
84	102	**DHAULPUR**	0.330
85	129	**SANGANER**	0.329
86	153	**NAWALGARH**	0.328
87	152	**KHETRI**	0.325
88	32	**ATRU**	0.321
89	140	**SANCHORE**	0.320
89	177	**JAYAL**	0.320
89	117	**HANUMANGARH**	0.320
92	175	**DEGANA**	0.317
93	198	**DEOGARH**	0.316
94	72	**KESHORAIPATAN**	0.315
94	139	**RANIWARA**	0.315
96	31	**ANTA**	0.314
96	9	**BANSURE**	0.314
98	160	**LUNI**	0.311
99	217	PINDWARA	0.310
100	237	SARADA	0.309
101	197	BHIM	0.307
101	46	BAYANA	0.307
103	113	RAISINGHNAGAR	0.306
104	11	KATHUMAR	0.305
104	183	NAGAUR	0.305
106	224	TODARAISINGH	0.304
107	193	ROHAT	0.302
108	219	SHEOGANJ	0.301
109	19	RENI	0.300
	LOW (0.2 - 0.3)		
110	36	KISHANGANJ	0.298
111	205	GANGAPUR	0.297
112	47	DEEG	0.296
112	87	PRATAPGARH	0.296
112	70	NOKHA	0.296
115	97	LALSOT	0.295
115	109	ANUPGARH	0.295
115	231	GOGUNDA	0.295
118	54	WEIR	0.294
118	133	SAM	0.294
118	196	AMET	0.294
121	73	NAINWA	0.293
122	74	TALERA	0.292
123	122	DUDU	0.291
124	163	PHALODI	0.290
125	135	AHORE	0.289
125	185	RIYAN	0.289
127	181	MERTA	0.288
128	162	OSIAN	0.287
128	121	CHAKSU	0.287
130	37	SHAHBAD	0.286
131	218	REODAR	0.284
132	233	KHERWARA	0.281
133	132	JAISALMER	0.280
134	14	LACHHMANGARH	0.279
135	202	RAJSAMAND	0.278
136	15	MANDAWAR	0.277
137	35	CHHIPABAROD	0.276
138	48	KAMAN	0.274
139	56	BANERA	0.272
140	58	JAHAZPUR	0.269
141	13	KOTKASIM	0.268
141	191	RAIPUR	0.268
143	114	SADULSHAHAR	0.265
143	204	BONLI	0.265
145	157	BAP	0.263
145	190	PALI	0.263
147	201	RAILMAGRA	0.262
148	77	BEGUN	0.261
149	71	HINDOLI	0.260
150	5	KISHANGARH	0.259
151	235	MAVLI	0.257
151	22	UMREN	0.257
151	17	RAJGARH	0.257
154	194	SOJAT	0.256
154	82	CHITTAURGARH	0.256
154	159	BILARA	0.256
157	86	NIMBAHERA	0.255
157	200	KUMBHALGARH	0.255
159	80	BHOPALSAGAR	0.253
159	143	DAG	0.253
161	195	SUMERPUR	0.252
161	115	SURATGARH	0.252
163	188	JAITARAN	0.251
164	216	ABU ROAD	0.250
165	6	MASOODA	0.249
166	66	BIKANER	0.248
167	81	CHHOTI SADRI	0.247
167	182	MUNDWA	0.247
167	220	SIROHI	0.247
170	69	LUNKARANSAR	0.245
171	85	KAPASAN	0.244
172	189	MARWAR JUN.	0.241
173	199	DUNGLA	0.240
173	83	KHAMNOR	0.240
175	187	DESURI	0.239
176	79	BHADESAR	0.238
176	78	BHAINSRORGARH	0.238
178	136	BHINMAL	0.237
179	30	TALWARA	0.235
180	192	RANI STATION	0.234
181	84	GANGRAR	0.233
181	105	BICHHIWARA	0.233
183	20	THANAGAZI	0.232
184	21	TIJARA	0.230
185	141	GANGANAGAR	0.229
185	111	KARANPUR	0.229
185	110	SAYLA	0.229
188	18	RAMGARH	0.227
188	158	BHOPALGARH	0.227
190	65	SUWANA	0.226
191	112	SHAHPURA	0.225
191	64	PADAMPUR	0.225
193	8	SRINAGAR	0.224
193	186	BALI	0.224
195	106	DUNGARPUR	0.223
195	137	JALOR	0.223
197	164	GARHI	0.222
197	25	SHERGARH	0.222
199	207	SAWAI MADHOPUR	0.221
199	223	NIWAI	0.221
201	23	ANANDPURI	0.220
202	61	MANDALGARH	0.219
203	225	TONK	0.217
204	222	MALPURA	0.215
205	226	UNIARA	0.214
206	156	BALESAR	0.213
207	75	ARNOD	0.211
208	138	JASWANTPURA	0.209
209	63	SAHARA	0.208
210	1	ARAIN	0.206
210	68	KOLAYAT	0.206
212	12	KISHANGARH BAS	0.205
213	76	MANDAL	0.204
213	60	BARI SADRI	0.204
215	161	MANDOR	0.203
216	107	SAGWARA	0.201
216	142	BAKANI	0.201
	VERY LOW (< 0.2)		
218	27	KUSHALGARH	0.198
219	29	SAJJANGARH	0.196
220	55	ASIND	0.192
221	206	KHANDAR	0.191
222	229	DHARIAWAD	0.190
223	62	RAIPUR	0.188
224	7	PISANGAN	0.186
225	26	GHATOL	0.185
226	108	SIMALWARA	0.184
227	104	ASPUR	0.183
228	88	RASHMI	0.178
229	24	BAGIDORA	0.174
230	57	HURDA	0.173
231	221	DEOLI	0.167
232	28	PEEPALKHOONT	0.133
233	59	KOTRI	0.132
234	234	KOTRA	0.127
235	2	BHINAY	0.106
236	16	NIMRANA	0.095
237	4	KEKRI	0.073
		RAJASTHAN	**0.311**
		%age of AAPs	**41.40**

BOLD: Equal/Above Average Panchayat Samities (AAPs)

Source: Annex- 10.2 Col. 8.

ANNEX-18.12

RANKING OF PSS BY DIFFERENCE IN GEDI RANK: RAJASTHAN (1991-01)

(Descending Order)

RANK	*PANCHAYAT SIMITIES RANK PCODE*	*NAME*	*RANK DIFF.*
1	2	3	4
	(> =50)		
1	42	DHORIMANNA	211
2	44	SINDHARI	172
3	94	TARANAGAR	149
4	40	BAYTOO	146
5	43	SHEO	145
6	92	SARDARSHAHAR	144
7	93	SUJANGARH	140
8	232	JHADOL	132
9	45	SIWANA	130
10	91	RATANGARH	129
11	39	BARMER	124
12	41	CHOHTAN	109
13	165	HINDAUN	106
14	67	DUNGARGARH	104
15	38	BALOTRA	102
16	100	BARI	101
17	236	SALUMBAR	98
18	166	KARAULI	94
19	89	CHURU	89
20	99	SIKRAI	85
21	124	JAMWA RAMGARH	81
22	147	PIRAWA	80
23	34	CHHABARA	79
24	103	RAJAKHERA	75
25	3	JAWAJA	66
26	169	TODABHIM	62
27	134	SANKRA	59
28	176	DIDWANA	55
29	177	JAYAL	54
30	146	MANOHARTHANA	53
30	198	DEOGARH	53
32	131	VIRATNAGAR	50
	(25 to 50)		
33	90	RAJGARH	48
34	118	NOHAR	47
34	139	RANIWARA	47
36	126	KOTPUTLI	46
37	167	NADOTI	44
38	168	SAPOTRA	43
38	178	KUCHAMAN	43
38	183	NAGAUR	43
41	51	NAGAR PAHARI	41
41	203	BAMANWAS	41
41	210	FATEHPUR	41
44	211	KHANDELA	40
44	228	BHINDER	40
46	70	NOKHA	39
46	120	BASSI	39
46	127	PHAGI	39
46	184	PARBATSAR	39
50	128	SAMBHAR	38
51	175	DEGANA	36
51	212	LACHHMANGARH	36
53	163	PHALODI	35
54	140	SANCHORE	34
54	193	ROHAT	34
56	162	OSIAN	33
57	144	JHALRAPATAN	30
57	196	AMET	30
59	208	DANTA RAMGARH	29
60	73	NAINWA	28
60	180	MAKRANA	28
60	224	TODARAISINGH	28
63	96	DAUSA	27
63	209	DHOND	27
63	219	SHEOGANJ	27
66	132	JAISALMER	26
	(0 to 25)		
67	160	LUNI	24
68	197	BHIM	23
68	231	GOGUNDA	23
70	35	CHHIPABAROD	22
70	227	BARGAON	22
72	95	BANDIKUI	21
72	133	SAM	21
74	217	PINDWARA	20
74	230	GIRWA	20
76	48	KAMAN	19
76	121	CHAKSU	19
78	218	REODAR	17
79	155	UDAIPURWATI	16
80	214	PIPRALI	16
81	101	BASERI	14
82	157	BAP	13
83	179	LADNU	12
84	119	AMBER	11
85	213	NEEM KA THANA	10
86	97	LALSOT	9
86	185	RIYAN	9
88	50	NADBAI	7
88	72	KESHORAIPATAN	7
88	148	ALSISAR	7
91	130	SHAHPURA	6
92	36	KISHANGANJ	4
92	150	CHIRAWA	4
92	151	JHUNJHUNUN	4
92	170	CHECHAT	4
96	102	DHAULPUR	3
96	149	BUHANA	3
96	173	SANGOD	3
96	174	SULTANPUR	3
96	182	MUNDWA	3
101	46	BAYANA	2
101	216	ABU ROAD	2
101	237	SARADA	2
104	10	BEHROR	1
104	58	JAHAZPUR	1
104	87	PRATAPGARH	1
104	116	BHADRA	1
104	125	JHOTWARA	1
109	74	TALERA	0
109	171	ITAWA	0
	(0 to -25)		
111	28	PEEPALKHOONT	-1
111	53	SEWAR	-1
111	71	HINDOLI	-1
111	98	MAHWA	-1
111	234	KOTRA	-1
116	85	KAPASAN	-2
116	154	SURAJGARH	-2
116	191	RAIPUR	-2
119	77	BEGUN	-3
119	136	BHINMAL	-3
119	145	KHANPUR	-3
119	190	PALI	-3
123	135	AHORE	-4
124	215	SRI MADHOPUR	-5
125	188	JAITARAN	-6
126	19	RENI	-7
127	27	KUSHALGARH	-8
127	141	SAYLA	-8
127	143	DAG	-8
127	153	NAWALGARH	-8
127	164	SHERGARH	-8
127	200	KUMBHALGARH	-8
133	229	DHARIAWAD	-9
134	11	KATHUMAR	-10
134	37	SHAHBAD	-10
136	156	BALESAR	-11
136	181	MERTA	-11
136	205	GANGAPUR	-11
139	138	JASWANTPURA	-12
139	172	LADPURA	-12
141	159	BILARA	-13
142	23	ANANDPURI	-14
142	33	BARAN	-14
142	56	BANERA	-14
142	123	GOVINDGARH	-14
142	158	BHOPALGARH	-14
147	9	BANSURE	-15
148	15	MANDAWAR	-16
149	29	SAJJANGARH	-17
149	52	RUPBAS	-17
149	113	RAISINGHNAGAR	-17
152	13	KOTKASIM	-18
152	64	SHAHPURA	-18
152	129	SANGANER	-18
155	152	KHETRI	-20
155	225	TONK	-20
157	122	DUDU	-22
158	49	KUMHER	-23
159	30	TALWARA	-24
160	32	ATRU	-25
161	47	DEEG	-25
	(-25 to -50)		
162	79	BHAINSRORGARH	-28
163	83	DUNGLA	-30
163	204	BONLI	-30
165	31	ANTA	-31
165	117	HANUMANGARH	-31
167	14	LACHHMANGARH	-32
167	54	WEIR	-32
167	78	BHADESAR	-32
167	105	BICHHIWARA	-32
167	233	KHERWARA	-32
172	20	THANAGAZI	-33
172	66	BIKANER	-33
172	226	UNIARA	-33
175	61	MANDALGARH	-34
176	65	SUWANA	-35
177	69	LUNKARANSAR	-36
177	110	GANGANAGAR	-36
177	202	RAJSAMAND	-36
177	206	KHANDAR	-36
181	137	JALOR	-38
181	220	SIROHI	-38
183	82	CHITTAURGARH	-39
184	26	GHATOL	-40
184	109	ANUPGARH	-40
184	161	MANDOR	-40
187	68	KOLAYAT	-41
187	114	SADULSHAHAR	-41
189	84	GANGRAR	-43
189	112	PADAMPUR	-43
189	194	SOJAT	-43
192	5	KISHANGARH	-45
192	60	MANDAL	-45
192	111	KARANPUR	-45
192	142	BAKANI	-45
196	207	SAWAI MADHOPUR	-46
197	22	UMREN	-47
197	80	BHOPALSAGAR	-47
197	201	RAILMAGRA	-47
200	17	RAJGARH	-48
200	55	ASIND	-48
200	235	MAVLI	-48
	(> -50)		
203	86	NIMBAHERA	-51
204	189	MARWAR JUN.	-52
205	81	CHHOTI SADRI	-53
205	106	DUNGARPUR	-53
207	6	MASOODA	-54
207	63	SAHARA	-54
207	76	BARI SADRI	-54
210	195	SUMERPUR	-56
211	115	SURATGARH	-57
212	222	MALPURA	-62
213	192	RANI STATION	-63
214	62	RAIPUR	-64
215	199	KHAMNOR	-71
216	187	DESURI	-72
217	21	TIJARA	-73
217	223	NIWAI	-73
219	16	NIMRANA	-75
219	108	SIMALWARA	-75
221	18	RAMGARH	-76
222	25	GARHI	-78
222	186	BALI	-78
224	1	ARAIN	-81
224	8	SRINAGAR	-81
226	75	ARNOD	-82
227	12	KISHANGARH BAS	-83
228	24	BAGIDORA	-85
229	88	RASHMI	-89
230	107	SAGWARA	-97
231	104	ASPUR	-103
232	221	DEOLI	-107
233	7	PISANGAN	-111
234	57	HURDA	-119
235	59	KOTRI	-128
236	2	BHINAY	-160
237	4	KEKRI	-184

Source : Annex 10.2,Col.7.

ANNEX-18.13

RANKING OF PSS BY % INCREASE/DECREASE IN INI VALUE (1991-98)

(Descending Order)

RANK	PANCHAYAT SAMITIES P. CODE	NAME	% CHANGE
1	2	3	4
	VERY HIGH (>100)		
1	153	**NAWALGARH**	512
2	104	**ASPUR**	435
3	152	**KHETRI**	328
4	150	**CHIRAWA**	286
5	107	**SAGWARA**	245
6	155	**UDAIPURWATI**	233
7	151	**JHUNJHUNUN**	215
8	148	**ALSISAR**	195
9	154	**SURAJGARH**	181
10	149	**BUHANA**	179
11	213	**NEEM KA THANA**	161
12	215	**SRI MADHOPUR**	160
13	43	**SHEO**	145
14	105	**BICHHIWARA**	139
15	106	**DUNGARPUR**	127
16	211	**KHANDELA**	126
17	214	**PIPRALI**	124
18	208	**DANTA RAMGARH**	119
19	45	**SIWANA**	118
20	38	**BALOTRA**	117
20	41	**CHOHTAN**	117
22	209	**DHOND**	114
23	108	**SIMALWARA**	113
24	39	**BARMER**	112
25	42	**DHORIMANNA**	104
	HIGH (75-100)		
26	44	**SINDHARI**	96
27	40	**BAYTOO**	94
28	34	**CHHABRA**	87
28	212	**LACHHMANGARH**	87
30	157	**BAP**	86
31	67	**DUNGARGARH**	84
31	98	**MAHWA**	84
33	16	**NIMRANA**	83
34	210	**FATEHPUR**	81
35	30	**TALWARA**	78
36	25	**GARHI**	77
	MEDIUM (50-75)		
37	15	**MANDAWAR**	74
38	13	**KOTKASIM**	69
38	52	**RUPBAS**	69
40	89	**CHURU**	68
40	97	**LALSOT**	68
40	125	**JHOTWARA**	68
43	96	**DAUSA**	67
43	103	**RAJAKHERA**	67
43	137	**JALOR**	67
46	12	**KISHANGARH BAS**	66
46	99	**SIKRAI**	66
46	143	**DAG**	66
46	201	**RAILMAGRA**	66
50	26	**GHATOL**	64
50	183	**NAGAUR**	64
52	49	**KUMHER**	63
52	176	**DIDWANA**	63
54	53	**SEWAR**	62
54	92	**SARDARSHAHAR**	62
54	114	**SADULSHAHAR**	62
54	129	**SANGANER**	62
54	227	**BARGAON,**	62
59	90	**RAJGARH**	61
59	95	**BANDIKUI**	61
59	178	**KUCHAMAN**	61
62	180	**MAKRANA**	60
62	198	**DEOGARH**	60
64	46	**BAYANA**	59
64	91	**RATANGARH**	59
64	102	**DHAULPUR**	59
64	138	**JASWANTPURA**	59
68	31	**ANTA**	58
68	54	**WEIR**	58
68	200	**KUMBHALGARH**	58
71	23	**ANANDPURI**	57
71	50	**NADBAI**	57
71	220	**SIROHI**	57
74	10	**BEHROR**	56
74	24	**BAGIDORA**	56
74	94	**TARANAGAR**	56
74	141	**SAYLA**	56
74	202	**RAJSAMAND**	56
79	29	**SAJJANGARH**	55
79	205	**GANGAPUR**	55
81	11	**KATHUMAR**	54
81	32	**ATRU**	54
81	175	**DEGANA**	54
81	179	**LADNU**	54
81	196	**AMET**	54
86	9	**BANSURE**	53
86	136	**BHINMAL**	53
86	192	**RANI STATION**	53
89	18	**RAMGARH**	52
89	51	**NAGAR PAHARI**	52
89	93	**SUJANGARH**	52
89	115	**SURATGARH**	52
93	80	**BHOPALSAGAR**	51
93	177	**JAYAL**	51
93	206	**KHANDAR**	51
	LOW (25-50)		
96	14	**LACHHMANGARH**	50
96	47	**DEEG**	50
96	69	**LUNKARANSAR**	50
96	70	**NOKHA**	50
96	88	**RASHMI**	50
96	100	**BARI**	50
102	83	**DUNGLA**	49
102	133	**SAM**	49
102	181	**MERTA**	49
102	197	**BHIM**	49
106	20	**THANAGAZI**	48
106	22	**UMREN**	48
106	27	**KUSHALGARH**	48
106	28	**PEEPALKHOONT**	48
106	76	**BARI SADRI**	48
106	85	**KAPASAN**	48
106	145	**KHANPUR**	48
106	185	**RIYAN**	48
106	219	**SHEOGANJ**	48
115	135	**AHORE**	47
115	142	**BAKANI**	47
115	190	**PALI**	47
115	222	**MALPURA**	47
119	33	**BARAN**	46
119	77	**BEGUN**	46
119	81	**CHHOTI SADRI**	46
119	167	**NADOTI**	46
119	184	**PARBATSAR**	46
119	203	**BAMANWAS**	46
125	17	**RAJGARH**	45
125	36	**KISHANGANJ**	45
125	62	**RAIPUR**	45
125	139	**RANIWARA**	45
125	223	**NIWAI**	45
125	225	**TONK**	45
131	78	**BHADESAR**	44
131	79	**BHAINSRORGARH**	44
131	84	**GANGRAR**	44
131	86	**NIMBAHERA**	44
131	169	**TODABHIM**	44
131	195	**SUMERPUR**	44
137	19	**RENI**	43
137	87	**PRATAPGARH**	43
·137	101	**BASERI**	43
137	134	**SANKRA**	43
137	187	**DESURI**	43
137	235	**MAVLI**	43
143	82	CHITTAURGARH	42
143	140	SANCHORE	42
145	4	KEKRI	41
145	63	SAHARA	41
145	144	JHALRAPATAN	41
145	182	MUNDWA	41
145	224	TODARAISINGH	41
150	3	JAWAJA	40
150	5	KISHANGARH	40
150	6	MASOODA	40
150	132	JAISALMER	40
150	189	MARWAR JUN.	40
155	2	BHINAY	39
155	37	SHAHBAD	39
155	75	ARNOD	39
155	159	BILARA	39
155	207	SAWAI MADHOPUR	39
155	221	DEOLI	39
155	226	UNIARA	39
155	237	SARADA	39
163	1	ARAIN	38
163	48	KAMAN	38
163	68	KOLAYAT	38
163	228	BHINDER,	38
167	8	SRINAGAR	37
167	59	KOTRI	37
167	156	BALESAR	37
167	162	OSIAN	37
167	204	BONLI	37
172	58	JAHAZPUR	36
172	158	BHOPALGARH	36
172	165	HINDAUN	36
172	168	SAPOTRA	36
172	186	BALI	36
172	231	GOGUNDA,	36
172	233	KHERWARA,	36
172	236	SALUMBAR,	36
180	56	BANERA	35
180	160	LUNI	35
180	218	REODAR	35
183	55	ASIND	34
183	57	HURDA	34
183	64	SHAHPURA	34
183	66	BIKANER	34
183	146	MANOHARTHANA	34
183	161	MANDOR	34
183	194	SOJAT	34
183	230	GIRWA,	34
191	7	PISANGAN	33
191	72	KESHORAIPATAN	33
191	123	GOVINDGARH	33
191	126	KOTPUTLI	33
191	128	SAMBHAR	33
196	74	TALERA	32
196	131	VIRATNAGAR	32
196	147	PIRAWA	32
199	116	BHADRA	31
200	21	TIJARA	30
200	61	MANDALGARH	30
200	65	SUWANA	30
200	118	NOHAR	30
200	119	AMBER	30
200	122	DUDU	30
200	127	PHAGI	30
200	166	KARAULI	30
200	229	DHARIAWAD,	30
209	124	JAMWA RAMGARH	29
210	164	SHERGARH	28
210	216	ABU ROAD	28
210	232	JHADOL,	28
213	193	ROHAT	27
214	121	CHAKSU	26
214	130	SHAHPURA	26
	VERY LOW (<25)		
216	71	HINDOLI	25
216	170	CHECHAT	25
216	217	PINDWARA	25
219	110	GANGANAGAR	24
219	199	KHAMNOR	24
221	60	MANDAL	23
221	73	NAINWA	23
223	174	SULTANPUR	22
224	112	PADAMPUR	21
225	120	BASSI	20
225	171	ITAWA	20
225	173	SANGOD	20
228	191	RAIPUR	19
228	234	KOTRA,	19
230	111	KARANPUR	17
230	188	JAITARAN	17
232	172	LADPURA	16
233	35	CHHIPABAROD	14
234	113	RAISINGHNAGAR	12
235	163	PHALODI	3
236	109	ANUPGARH	1
237	117	HANUMANGARH	-1
		RAJASTHAN	**43**
		%age of AAPs	**59.92**

BOLD: Equal/Above Average Panchayat Samities (AAPs)

Source: Annex 12.1, Col. 11.

ANNEX-18.14

RANKING OF PANCHAYAT SAMITIES BY DIFFERENCE IN INI VALUE (1991-98)

(Descending Order)

RANK	PANCHAYAT SAMITIES P. CODE	NAME	VALUE
1	2	3	4
	VERY HIGH (>0.25)		
1	129	**SANGANER**	**0.3860**
2	125	**JHOTWARA**	**0.3834**
3	151	**JHUNJHUNUN**	**0.3409**
4	114	**SADULSHAHAR**	**0.3345**
5	149	**BUHANA**	**0.3297**
6	152	**KHETRI**	**0.3279**
7	150	**CHIRAWA**	**0.3266**
8	153	**NAWALGARH**	**0.3251**
9	157	**BAP**	**0.3166**
10	34	**CHHABRA**	**0.3088**
11	154	**SURAJGARH**	**0.3061**
12	148	**ALSISAR**	**0.3042**
13	155	**UDAIPURWATI**	**0.3034**
14	115	**SURATGARH**	**0.2880**
15	67	**DUNGARGARH**	**0.2685**
16	211	**KHANDELA**	**0.2667**
17	214	**PIPRALI**	**0.2659**
18	70	**NOKHA**	**0.2645**
19	210	**FATEHPUR**	**0.2505**
	HIGH (0.20-0.25)		
20	98	**MAHWA**	**0.2488**
21	212	**LACHHMANGARH**	**0.2467**
22	69	**LUNKARANSAR**	**0.2463**
23	227	**BARGAON**	**0.2454**
24	209	**DHOND**	**0.2446**
25	213	**NEEM KA THANA**	**0.2423**
26	201	**RAILMAGRA**	**0.2399**
27	215	**SRI MADHOPUR**	**0.2269**
28	208	**DANTA RAMGARH**	**0.2259**
29	4	**KEKRI**	**0.2191**
30	1	**ARAIN**	**0.2190**
31	96	**DAUSA**	**0.2182**
32	200	**KUMBHALGARH**	**0.2179**
33	2	**BHINAY**	**0.2176**
34	16	**NIMRANA**	**0.2159**
35	85	**KAPASAN**	**0.2155**
36	99	**SIKRAI**	**0.2147**
37	32	**ATRU**	**0.2145**
38	88	**RASHMI**	**0.2121**
39	6	**MASOODA**	**0.2099**
40	5	**KISHANGARH**	**0.2096**
41	80	**BHOPALSAGAR**	**0.2094**
42	83	**DUNGLA**	**0.2085**
43	76	**BARI SADRI**	**0.2078**
44	31	**ANTA**	**0.2073**
44	49	**KUMHER**	**0.2073**
46	127	**PHAGI**	**0.2064**
47	15	**MANDAWAR**	**0.2062**
48	97	**LALSOT**	**0.2059**
49	10	**BEHROR**	**0.2034**
50	220	**SIROHI**	**0.2033**
51	81	**CHHOTI SADRI**	**0.2016**
	MEDIUM (0.15-0.20)		
52	77	**BEGUN**	**0.1997**
53	13	**KOTKASIM**	**0.1990**
54	8	**SRINAGAR**	**0.1982**
55	12	**KISHANGARH BAS**	**0.1967**
56	84	**GANGRAR**	**0.1963**
57	116	**BHADRA**	**0.1951**
58	11	**KATHUMAR**	**0.1923**
58	78	**BHADESAR**	**0.1923**
60	119	**AMBER**	**0.1921**
61	68	**KOLAYAT**	**0.1916**
62	198	**DEOGARH**	**0.1915**
63	36	**KISHANGANJ**	**0.1911**
64	122	**DUDU**	**0.1900**
64	126	**KOTPUTLI**	**0.1900**
64	170	**CHECHAT**	**0.1900**
67	47	**DEEG**	**0.1896**
68	121	**CHAKSU**	**0.1890**
69	206	**KHANDAR**	**0.1885**
70	128	**SAMBHAR**	**0.1875**
71	196	**AMET**	**0.1874**
72	3	**JAWAJA**	**0.1859**
73	190	**PALI**	**0.1850**
74	53	**SEWAR**	**0.1842**
75	86	**NIMBAHERA**	**0.1841**
76	14	**LACHHMANGARH**	**0.1832**
77	50	**NADBAI**	**0.1822**
78	33	**BARAN**	**0.1821**
79	46	**BAYANA**	**0.1820**

RANK	PANCHAYAT SAMITIES P. CODE	NAME	VALUE
1	2	3	4
79	124	**JAMWA RAMGARH**	**0.1820**
81	19	**RENI**	**0.1813**
82	118	**NOHAR**	**0.1807**
83	123	**GOVINDGARH**	**0.1805**
84	192	**RANI STATION**	**0.1803**
85	54	**WEIR**	**0.1802**
85	219	**SHEOGANJ**	**0.1802**
87	52	**RUPBAS**	**0.1783**
88	41	**CHOHTAN**	**0.1782**
89	82	**CHITTAURGARH**	**0.1779**
90	159	**BILARA**	**0.1767**
91	17	**RAJGARH**	**0.1764**
92	95	**BANDIKUI**	**0.1757**
93	66	**BIKANER**	**0.1755**
94	90	**RAJGARH**	**0.1741**
95	131	**VIRATNAGAR**	**0.1728**
96	94	**TARANAGAR**	**0.1721**
97	37	**SHAHBAD**	**0.1718**
98	79	**BHAINSRORGARH**	**0.1716**
99	63	**SAHARA**	**0.1708**
100	7	**PISANGAN**	**0.1705**
101	222	**MALPURA**	**0.1703**
102	20	**THANAGAZI**	**0.1701**
103	9	**BANSURE**	**0.1700**
104	223	**NIWAI**	**0.1685**
105	87	**PRATAPGARH**	**0.1681**
106	205	**GANGAPUR**	**0.1673**
107	51	**NAGAR PAHARI**	**0.1658**
108	89	**CHURU**	**0.1652**
109	225	**TONK**	**0.1651**
110	202	**RAJSAMAND**	**0.1645**
111	134	SANKRA	0.1642
112	158	BHOPALGARH	0.1630
113	142	BAKANI	0.1628
113	224	TODARAISINGH	0.1628
115	25	GARHI	0.1626
116	40	BAYTOO	0.1616
117	107	SAGWARA	0.1614
118	235	MAVLI	0.1606
119	203	BAMANWAS	0.1595
120	183	NAGAUR	0.1594
120	228	BHINDER	0.1594
122	173	SANGOD	0.1564
123	197	BHIM	0.1563
124	38	BALOTRA	0.1561
125	91	RATANGARH	0.1552
126	44	SINDHARI	0.1545
127	23	ANANDPURI	0.1544
128	62	RAIPUR	0.1542
129	18	RAMGARH	0.1534
130	75	ARNOD	0.1521
131	175	DEGANA	0.1520
132	135	AHORE	0.1519
133	42	DHORIMANNA	0.1512
133	133	SAM	0.1512
135	22	UMREN	0.1511
136	218	REODAR	0.1510
	LOW (0.10-0.15)		
137	174	SULTANPUR	0.1496
138	92	SARDARSHAHAR	0.1493
139	143	DAG	0.1491
140	221	DEOLI	0.1486
141	189	MARWAR JUN.	0.1477
142	30	TALWARA	0.1475
142	236	SALUMBAR	0.1475
144	24	BAGIDORA	0.1474
144	130	SHAHPURA	0.1474
146	204	BONLI	0.1468
147	160	LUNI	0.1467
148	59	KOTRI	0.1463
148	171	ITAWA	0.1463
150	167	NADOTI	0.1456
151	185	RIYAN	0.1452
152	26	GHATOL	0.1446
153	29	SAJJANGARH	0.1433
154	56	BANERA	0.1429
155	156	BALESAR	0.1428
156	48	KAMAN	0.1425
157	194	SOJAT	0.1422
158	39	BARMER	0.1420
159	195	SUMERPUR	0.1409
160	137	JALOR	0.1403

RANK	PANCHAYAT SAMITIES P. CODE	NAME	VALUE
1	2	3	4
161	162	OSIAN	0.1401
162	237	SARADA	0.1397
163	93	SUJANGARH	0.1393
164	103	RAJAKHERA	0.1392
165	104	ASPUR	0.1389
166	176	DIDWANA	0.1388
167	226	UNIARA	0.1385
168	55	ASIND	0.1377
168	177	JAYAL	0.1377
170	64	SHAHPURA	0.1366
171	72	KESHORAIPATAN	0.1363
172	207	SAWAI MADHOPUR	0.1360
172	231	GOGUNDA	0.1360
174	180	MAKRANA	0.1359
175	120	BASSI	0.1351
176	187	DESURI	0.1346
177	100	BARI	0.1340
178	138	JASWANTPURA	0.1334
179	179	LADNU	0.1331
180	108	SIMALWARA	0.1327
180	110	GANGANAGAR	0.1327
182	181	MERTA	0.1321
183	74	TALERA	0.1307
184	57	HURDA	0.1305
184	161	MANDOR	0.1305
186	106	DUNGARPUR	0.1293
187	136	BHINMAL	0.1290
188	43	SHEO	0.1285
189	144	JHALRAPATAN	0.1278
190	102	DHAULPUR	0.1273
191	169	TODABHIM	0.1272
191	184	PARBATSAR	0.1272
193	58	JAHAZPUR	0.1251
194	233	KHERWARA	0.1246
195	105	BICHHIWARA	0.1245
195	178	KUCHAMAN	0.1245
197	27	KUSHALGARH	0.1235
198	186	BALI	0.1231
199	65	SUWANA	0.1229
200	132	JAISALMER	0.1217
201	28	PEEPALKHOONT	0.1215
202	168	SAPOTRA	0.1210
203	111	KARANPUR	0.1200
204	61	MANDALGARH	0.1198
204	182	MUNDWA	0.1198
204	230	GIRWA	0.1198
207	146	MANOHARTHANA	0.1189
208	164	SHERGARH	0.1186
209	216	ABU ROAD	0.1171
210	101	BASERI	0.1167
211	141	SAYLA	0.1162
212	71	HINDOLI	0.1161
213	172	LADPURA	0.1158
213	229	DHARIAWAD	0.1158
215	145	KHANPUR	0.1139
216	232	JHADOL	0.1136
217	193	ROHAT	0.1119
218	217	PINDWARA	0.1109
219	112	PADAMPUR	0.1067
220	21	TIJARA	0.1061
221	147	PIRAWA	0.1048
222	73	NAINWA	0.1045
223	140	SANCHORE	0.1030
224	165	HINDAUN	0.1006
	VERY LOW (<0.10)		
225	166	KARAULI	0.0996
226	139	RANIWARA	0.0995
227	60	MANDAL	0.0947
228	45	SIWANA	0.0928
229	35	CHHIPABAROD	0.0859
230	199	KHAMNOR	0.0846
231	234	KOTRA	0.0788
232	113	RAISINGHNAGAR	0.0770
233	191	RAIPUR	0.0736
234	188	JAITARAN	0.0685
235	163	PHALODI	0.0133
236	109	ANUPGARH	0.0084
237	117	HANUMANGARH	-0.0059
		RAJASTHAN	**0.1645**
		%age of AAPs	**46.41**

BOLD: Equal/Above Average Panchayat Samities (AAPs)

Source: Annex 12.1, Col. 10.

ANNEX-18.15

RANKING OF PSS BY DIFFERENCE IN INI RANK (1991-98)

(Descending Order)

RANK	PANCHAYAT SAMITIES P. CODE	NAME	DIFFERENCE RANK
1	2	3	4
	VERY HIGH (>=50)		
1	149	BUHANA	94
2	151	JHUNJHUNUN	87
3	67	DUNGARGARH	84
4	34	CHHABRA	83
5	210	FATEHPUR	74
6	98	MAHWA	73
7	157	BAP	71
8	212	LACHHMANGARH	65
9	154	SURAJGARH	64
10	211	KHANDELA	60
11	214	PIPRALI	59
12	148	ALSISAR	57
13	201	RAILMAGRA	55
14	150	CHIRAWA	53
	HIGH (25 to 50)		
15	152	KHETRI	49
16	96	DAUSA	46
16	155	UDAIPURWATI	46
18	31	ANTA	45
19	99	SIKRAI	44
20	10	BEHROR	43
20	200	KUMBHALGARH	43
22	227	BARGAON	42
23	49	KUMHER	38
23	220	SIROHI	38
25	209	DHOND	37
26	16	NIMRANA	35
26	97	LALSOT	35
28	15	MANDAWAR	34
28	153	NAWALGARH	34
30	11	KATHUMAR	33
31	32	ATRU	29
32	12	KISHANGARH BAS	28
32	13	KOTKASIM	28
34	47	DEEG	27
34	196	AMET	27
	MEDIUM (0 to 25)		
36	206	KHANDAR	25
36	208	DANTA RAMGARH	25
38	14	LACHHMANGARH	24
38	198	DEOGARH	24
40	190	PALI	22
40	213	NEEM KA THANA	22
42	114	SADULSHAHAR	21
43	80	BHOPALSAGAR	20
43	125	JHOTWARA	20
43	219	SHEOGANJ	20
46	33	BARAN	19
46	53	SEWAR	19
48	192	RANI STATION	18
49	46	BAYANA	17
50	17	RAJGARH	15
50	54	WEIR	15
50	69	LUNKARANSAR	15
50	115	SURATGARH	15
54	129	SANGANER	14
55	50	NADBAI	13
56	20	THANAGAZI	12
56	70	NOKHA	12
56	79	BHAINSRORGARH	12
56	215	SRI MADHOPUR	12
60	83	DUNGLA	11
60	88	RASHMI	11
62	52	RUPBAS	10
62	76	BARI SADRI	10
62	222	MALPURA	10
65	87	PRATAPGARH	9
65	94	TARANAGAR	9
65	95	BANDIKUI	9
65	223	NIWAI	9
69	5	KISHANGARH	8
69	6	MASOODA	8
69	85	KAPASAN	8
72	4	KEKRI	7
72	134	SANKRA	7
74	8	SRINAGAR	6
74	9	BANSURE	6
74	51	NAGAR PAHARI	6
74	81	CHHOTI SADRI	6
74	84	GANGRAR	6
79	36	KISHANGANJ	5
79	68	KOLAYAT	5
79	77	BEGUN	5
82	19	RENI	4
82	142	BAKANI	4
82	205	GANGAPUR	4
82	224	TODARAISINGH	4
82	225	TONK	4
87	90	RAJGARH	3
87	235	MAVLI	3
89	2	BHINAY	2
89	86	NIMBAHERA	2
89	89	CHURU	2
89	107	SAGWARA	2
89	127	PHAGI	2
94	66	BIKANER	1
94	78	BHADESAR	1
94	202	RAJSAMAND	1
94	203	BAMANWAS	1
	LOW (0 to -25)		
98	1	ARAIN	0
98	3	JAWAJA	0
98	7	PISANGAN	0
98	62	RAIPUR	0
98	63	SAHARA	0
98	104	ASPUR	0
98	116	BHADRA	0
98	119	AMBER	0
98	122	DUDU	0
98	128	SAMBHAR	0
98	183	NAGAUR	0
109	25	GARHI	-1
109	43	SHEO	-1
109	123	GOVINDGARH	-1
109	170	CHECHAT	-1
113	41	CHOHTAN	-2
113	45	SIWANA	-2
113	91	RATANGARH	-2
113	106	DUNGARPUR	-2
113	121	CHAKSU	-2
113	124	JAMWA RAMGARH	-2
119	39	BARMER	-3
119	82	CHITTAURGARH	-3
119	105	BICHHIWARA	-3
119	108	SIMALWARA	-3
119	118	NOHAR	-3
119	126	KOTPUTLI	-3
119	173	SANGOD	-3
119	174	SULTANPUR	-3
127	38	BALOTRA	-4
127	92	SARDARSHAHAR	-4
127	159	BILARA	-4
127	171	ITAWA	-4
127	197	BHIM	-4
127	228	BHINDER	-4
133	24	BAGIDORA	-5
133	42	DHORIMANNA	-5
133	131	VIRATNAGAR	-5
136	23	ANANDPURI	-6
136	40	BAYTOO	-6
136	75	ARNOD	-6
136	175	DEGANA	-6
140	18	RAMGARH	-7
140	30	TALWARA	-7
140	37	SHAHBAD	-7
140	158	BHOPALGARH	-7
144	103	RAJAKHERA	-8
144	120	BASSI	-8
144	135	AHORE	-8
144	137	JALOR	-8
144	172	LADPURA	-8
149	22	UMREN	-9
149	44	SINDHARI	-9
149	111	KARANPUR	-9
149	133	SAM	-9
149	143	DAG	-9
154	26	GHATOL	-10
154	29	SAJJANGARH	-10
154	59	KOTRI	-10
154	130	SHAHPURA	-10
154	221	DEOLI	-10
159	160	LUNI	-11
159	178	KUCHAMAN	-11
159	189	MARWAR JUN.	-11
159	204	BONLI	-11
159	218	REODAR	-11
159	93	SUJANGARH	-12
159	110	GANGANAGAR	-12
164	176	DIDWANA	-12
164	177	JAYAL	-12
164	185	RIYAN	-12
164	207	SAWAI MADHOPUR	-12
164	56	BANERA	-13
164	179	LADNU	-13
170	48	KAMAN	-14
170	167	NADOTI	-14
172	226	UNIARA	-14
172	236	SALUMBAR	-14
172	112	PADAMPUR	-15
172	138	JASWANTPURA	-15
176	141	SAYLA	-15
176	180	MAKRANA	-15
176	100	BARI	-16
176	102	DHAULPUR	-16
180	136	BHINMAL	-16
180	156	BALESAR	-16
180	27	KUSHALGARH	-17
180	28	PEEPALKHOONT	-17
184	35	CHHIPABAROD	-17
184	184	PARBATSAR	-17
184	237	SARADA	-17
184	72	KESHORAIPATAN	-18
184	181	MERTA	-18
189	194	SOJAT	-18
189	195	SUMERPUR	-18
189	231	GOGUNDA	-18
189	113	RAISINGHNAGAR	-19
189	162	OSIAN	-19
194	169	TODABHIM	-19
194	182	MUNDWA	-19
194	64	SHAHPURA	-20
194	145	KHANPUR	-20
198	55	ASIND	-21
198	144	JHALRAPATAN	-21
200	187	DESURI	-21
200	132	JAISALMER	-24
200	139	RANIWARA	-24
	VERY LOW (-25 to -50)		
203	141	SAYLA	-27
203	168	SAPOTRA	-27
205	57	HURDA	-25
205	74	TALERA	-25
205	101	BASERI	-25
205	161	MANDOR	-25
205	186	BALI	-25
210	140	SANCHORE	-26
211	71	HINDOLI	-27
212	58	JAHAZPUR	-28
213	165	HINDAUN	-30
213	168	SAPOTRA	-30
215	65	SUWANA	-31
215	146	MANOHARTHANA	-31
215	233	KHERWARA	-31
218	217	PINDWARA	-32
218	230	GIRWA	-32
220	61	MANDALGARH	-37
221	73	NAINWA	-38
222	164	SHERGARH	-39
223	147	PIRAWA	-40
223	216	ABU ROAD	-40
223	229	DHARIAWAD	-40
223	232	JHADOL	-40
227	21	TIJARA	-41
228	193	ROHAT	-43
229	166	KARAULI	-44
230	109	ANUPGARH	-46
	EXTREMELY LOW (> -50)		
231	199	KHAMNOR	-56
232	60	MANDAL	-62
233	234	KOTRA	-71
234	191	RAIPUR	-72
235	188	JAITARAN	-79
236	117	HANUMANGARH	-80
237	163	PHALODI	-106

BOLD: Equal/Above Average Panchayat Samities (AAPs)

Source: Annex 12.1, Col.9.

ANNEX-18.16

RANKING OF PSS BY % INCREASE IN GINI VALUE: RAJASTHAN (1991-01)

(Descending Order)

RANK	*PANCHAYAT SAMITIES P. CODE*	*NAME*	*%*
1	2	3	4
	VERY HIGH (>=20)		
1	103	**RAJAKHERA**	183.9
2	102	**DHAULPUR**	79.5
3	153	**NAWALGARH**	31.4
4	114	**SADULSHAHAR**	31.3
5	100	**BARI**	31.1
6	152	**KHETRI**	29.0
7	150	**CHIRAWA**	27.7
8	215	**SRI MADHOPUR**	26.9
9	213	**NEEM KA THANA**	25.7
10	52	**RUPBAS**	25.1
11	125	**JHOTWARA**	24.0
12	155	**UDAIPURWATI**	23.3
13	208	**DANTA RAMGARH**	22.6
14	101	**BASERI**	22.5
14	115	**SURATGARH**	22.5
16	151	**JHUNJHUNUN**	22.3
17	149	**BUHANA**	22.1
17	214	**PIPRALI**	22.1
19	154	**SURAJGARH**	22.0
20	157	**BAP**	21.2
21	209	**DHOND**	20.9
22	148	**ALSISAR**	20.6
23	129	**SANGANER**	20.2
	HIGH (15-20)		
24	143	**DAG**	19.8
25	211	**KHANDELA**	19.5
26	31	**ANTA**	19.3
27	46	**BAYANA**	17.5
28	69	**LUNKARANSAR**	17.1
29	212	**LACHHMANGARH**	16.8
30	133	**SAM**	16.6
31	67	**DUNGARGARH**	16.5
32	97	**LALSOT**	16.1
32	210	**FATEHPUR**	16.1
34	16	**NIMRANA**	15.9
35	131	**VIRATNAGAR**	15.8
36	15	**MANDAWAR**	15.5
36	54	**WEIR**	15.5
38	98	**MAHWA**	15.4
39	70	**NOKHA**	15.3
40	32	**ATRU**	15.1
	MEDIUM (10-15)		
41	96	**DAUSA**	14.9
42	51	**NAGAR PAHARI**	14.8
42	198	**DEOGARH**	14.8
44	12	**KISHANGARH BAS**	14.4
44	99	**SIKRAI**	14.4
44	112	**PADAMPUR**	14.4
44	132	**JAISALMER**	14.4
48	50	**NADBAI**	14.3
49	36	**KISHANGANJ**	13.9
49	41	**CHOHTAN**	13.9
49	220	**SIROHI**	13.9
52	13	**KOTKASIM**	13.8
52	95	**BANDIKUI**	13.8
52	104	**ASPUR**	13.8
52	200	**KUMBHALGARH**	13.8
52	201	**RAILMAGRA**	13.8
57	18	**RAMGARH**	13.2
58	33	**BARAN**	13.1
59	126	**KOTPUTLI**	13.0
59	206	**KHANDAR**	13.0
61	49	**KUMHER**	12.9
61	123	**GOVINDGARH**	12.9
63	34	**CHHABRA**	12.8
63	107	**SAGWARA**	12.8
65	92	**SARDARSHAHAR**	12.7
66	43	**SHEO**	12.5
67	53	**SEWAR**	12.4
67	80	**BHOPALSAGAR**	12.4
67	110	**GANGANAGAR**	12.4
67	205	**GANGAPUR**	12.4
67	227	**BARGAON**	12.4
72	4	**KEKRI**	12.3
72	88	**RASHMI**	12.3
72	141	**SAYLA**	12.3
75	11	**KATHUMAR**	12.2
75	83	**DUNGLA**	12.2
77	77	**BEGUN**	12.1
78	2	**BHINAY**	12.0
78	6	**MASOODA**	12.0
78	47	**DEEG**	12.0
78	68	**KOLAYAT**	12.0
78	85	**KAPASAN**	12.0
78	190	**PALI**	12.0
84	37	**SHAHBAD**	11.9
84	76	**BARI SADRI**	11.9
86	128	**SAMBHAR**	11.8
86	183	**NAGAUR**	11.8
86	192	**RANI STATION**	11.8
86	219	**SHEOGANJ**	11.8
90	9	**BANSURE**	11.7
90	10	**BEHROR**	11.7
92	1	**ARAIN**	11.6
92	74	**TALERA**	11.6
92	89	**CHURU**	11.6
95	5	**KISHANGARH**	11.4
95	30	**TALWARA**	11.4
95	81	**CHHOTI SADRI**	11.4
98	22	**UMREN**	11.3
98	122	**DUDU**	11.3
98	187	**DESURI**	11.3
101	20	**THANAGAZI**	11.2
101	222	**MALPURA**	11.2
103	14	**LACHHMANGARH**	11.1
103	38	**BALOTRA**	11.1
103	42	**DHORIMANNA**	11.1
103	225	**TONK**	11.1
107	39	**BARMER**	11.0
107	78	**BHADESAR**	11.0
109	66	**BIKANER**	10.9
109	86	**NIMBAHERA**	10.9
109	90	**RAJGARH**	10.9
109	91	**RATANGARH**	10.9
109	124	**JAMWA RAMGARH**	10.9
109	223	**NIWAI**	10.9
115	35	**CHHIPABAROD**	10.8
115	44	**SINDHARI**	10.8
115	72	**KESHORAIPATAN**	10.8
115	127	**PHAGI**	10.8
115	136	**BHINMAL**	10.8
115	139	**RANIWARA**	10.8
121	3	**JAWAJA**	10.7
121	84	**GANGRAR**	10.7
121	138	**JASWANTPURA**	10.7
121	174	**SULTANPUR**	10.7
121	195	**SUMERPUR**	10.7
126	40	**BAYTOO**	10.6
126	87	**PRATAPGARH**	10.6
126	162	**OSIAN**	10.6
126	202	**RAJSAMAND**	10.6
126	224	**TODARAISINGH**	10.6
131	116	BHADRA	10.5
131	134	SANKRA	10.5
133	48	KAMAN	10.4
133	79	BHAINSRORGARH	10.4
133	165	HINDAUN	10.4
133	203	BAMANWAS	10.4
133	226	UNIARA	10.4
138	26	GHATOL	10.3
138	170	CHECHAT	10.3
140	94	TARANAGAR	10.2
140	218	REODAR	10.2
142	62	RAIPUR	10.1
142	169	TODABHIM	10.1
142	175	DEGANA	10.1
145	167	NADOTI	10.0
	LOW (5-10)		
146	145	KHANPUR	9.9
146	159	BILARA	9.9
148	93	SUJANGARH	9.8
148	108	SIMALWARA	9.8
148	142	BAKANI	9.8
148	216	ABU ROAD	9.8
152	17	RAJGARH	9.7
152	63	SAHARA	9.7
152	118	NOHAR	9.7
152	168	SAPOTRA	9.7
152	177	JAYAL	9.7
157	221	DEOLI	9.6
158	19	RENI	9.5
158	23	ANANDPURI	9.5
158	25	GARHI	9.5
158	82	CHITTAURGARH	9.5
158	140	SANCHORE	9.5
158	186	BALI	9.5
164	75	ARNOD	9.4
164	105	BICHHIWARA	9.4
164	121	CHAKSU	9.4
164	130	SHAHPURA	9.4
164	144	JHALRAPATAN	9.4
164	231	GOGUNDA	9.4
170	24	BAGIDORA	9.3
170	29	SAJJANGARH	9.3
170	158	BHOPALGARH	9.3
173	207	SAWAI MADHOPUR	9.3
173	106	DUNGARPUR	9.2
173	119	AMBER	9.2
176	137	JALOR	9.1
176	204	BONLI	9.1
178	135	AHORE	9.0
178	176	DIDWANA	9.0
178	189	MARWAR JUN.	9.0
181	56	BANERA	8.9
181	178	KUCHAMAN	8.9
181	236	SALUMBAR	8.9
184	160	LUNI	8.8
185	7	PISANGAN	8.7
185	59	KOTRI	8.7
185	179	LADNU	8.7
185	181	MERTA	8.7
185	197	BHIM	8.7
190	55	ASIND	8.5
190	64	SHAHPURA	8.5
190	71	HINDOLI	8.5
193	58	JAHAZPUR	8.4
193	180	MAKRANA	8.4
195	65	SUWANA	8.3
195	156	BALESAR	8.3
195	161	MANDOR	8.3
195	182	MUNDWA	8.3
199	28	PEEPALKHOONT	8.1
199	166	KARAULI	8.1
199	194	SOJAT	8.1
202	27	KUSHALGARH	8.0
202	185	RIYAN	8.0
202	229	DHARIAWAD	8.0
202	235	MAVLI	8.0
202	237	SARADA	8.0
207	173	SANGOD	7.9
208	61	MANDALGARH	7.8
209	146	MANOHARTHANA	7.7
210	57	HURDA	7.6
211	171	ITAWA	7.5
211	196	AMET	7.5
211	233	KHERWARA	7.5
214	73	NAINWA	7.4
214	147	PIRAWA	7.4
216	45	SIWANA	7.2
217	21	TIJARA	7.1
218	8	SRINAGAR	6.9
218	120	BASSI	6.9
218	228	BHINDER	6.9
221	172	LADPURA	6.6
221	193	ROHAT	6.6
221	217	PINDWARA	6.6
224	232	JHADOL	6.1
225	111	KARANPUR	6.0
226	164	SHERGARH	5.9
227	230	GIRWA	5.8
228	184	PARBATSAR	5.7
229	60	MANDAL	5.1
	VERY LOW (<5)		
230	188	JAITARAN	4.7
231	234	KOTRA	4.5
232	117	HANUMANGARH	4.3
233	191	RAIPUR	4.2
234	109	ANUPGARH	4.1
235	199	KHAMNOR	3.9
236	113	RAISINGHNAGAR	2.5
237	163	PHALODI	1.1
		RAJASTHAN	**10.6**
		%age of AAPs	**54.9**

BOLD: Equal/Above Average Panchayat Samities (AAPs)

Source: Annex- 14.1, Col. 9.

ANNEX-18.17

RANKING OF PSS BY INCREASED VALUE OF GINI: RAJASTHAN (1991-01)

(Descending Order)

RANK	PANCHAYAT SAMITIES P. CODE	PANCHAYAT SAMITIES NAME	VALUE
1	2	3	4
	VERY HIGH (>=0.08)		
1	103	**RAJAKHERA**	0.4272
2	102	**DHAULPUR**	0.2912
3	114	**SADULSHAHAR**	0.2059
4	125	**JHOTWARA**	0.1716
5	100	**BARI**	0.1638
6	153	**NAWALGARH**	0.1620
7	152	**KHETRI**	0.1573
8	115	**SURATGARH**	0.1541
9	129	**SANGANER**	0.1526
10	150	**CHIRAWA**	0.1518
11	215	**SRI MADHOPUR**	0.1419
12	52	**RUPBAS**	0.1396
13	157	**BAP**	0.1380
14	213	**NEEM KA THANA**	0.1379
15	149	**BUHANA**	0.1330
16	155	**UDAIPURWATI**	0.1317
17	151	**JHUNJHUNUN**	0.1316
18	214	**PIPRALI**	0.1297
19	154	**SURAJGARH**	0.1290
20	208	**DANTA RAMGARH**	0.1269
21	101	**BASERI**	0.1245
22	209	**DHOND**	0.1224
23	31	**ANTA**	0.1211
24	148	**ALSISAR**	0.1206
25	69	**LUNKARANSAR**	0.1189
26	211	**KHANDELA**	0.1162
27	70	**NOKHA**	0.1116
28	131	**VIRATNAGAR**	0.1101
29	143	**DAG**	0.1089
30	67	**DUNGARGARH**	0.1083
31	46	**BAYANA**	0.1070
32	212	**LACHHMANGARH**	0.1067
33	210	**FATEHPUR**	0.1051
34	97	**LALSOT**	0.1012
35	32	**ATRU**	0.0998
36	16	**NIMRANA**	0.0985
37	98	**MAHWA**	0.0978
38	54	**WEIR**	0.0977
39	15	**MANDAWAR**	0.0973
40	133	**SAM**	0.0969
41	96	**DAUSA**	0.0964
42	126	**KOTPUTLI**	0.0951
43	198	**DEOGARH**	0.0942
44	36	**KISHANGANJ**	0.0933
44	99	**SIKRAI**	0.0933
46	51	**NAGAR PAHARI**	0.0927
46	112	**PADAMPUR**	0.0927
48	200	**KUMBHALGARH**	0.0917
49	12	**KISHANGARH BAS**	0.0916
50	50	**NADBAI**	0.0914
51	201	**RAILMAGRA**	0.0913
52	123	**GOVINDGARH**	0.0911
53	4	**KEKRI**	0.0905
54	220	**SIROHI**	0.0902
55	2	**BHINAY**	0.0901
56	34	**CHHABRA**	0.0900
57	13	**KOTKASIM**	0.0878
58	6	**MASOODA**	0.0876
59	1	**ARAIN**	0.0873
60	95	**BANDIKUI**	0.0867
61	33	**BARAN**	0.0866
62	206	**KHANDAR**	0.0863
63	122	**DUDU**	0.0861
64	88	**RASHMI**	0.0855
65	83	**DUNGLA**	0.0852
66	127	**PHAGI**	0.0851
67	80	**BHOPALSAGAR**	0.0850
68	68	**KOLAYAT**	0.0846
68	128	**SAMBHAR**	0.0846
70	85	**KAPASAN**	0.0845
71	77	**BEGUN**	0.0842
72	124	**JAMWA RAMGARH**	0.0839
73	76	**BARI SADRI**	0.0837
74	49	**KUMHER**	0.0834
74	132	**JAISALMER**	0.0834
76	170	**CHECHAT**	0.0832
77	227	**BARGAON**	0.0831
78	5	**KISHANGARH**	0.0828
78	110	**GANGANAGAR**	0.0828
80	18	**RAMGARH**	0.0822
81	11	**KATHUMAR**	0.0815
82	37	**SHAHBAD**	0.0814
83	174	**SULTANPUR**	0.0814
84	116	**BHADRA**	0.0813
85	47	**DEEG**	0.0812
86	41	**CHOHTAN**	0.0807
87	190	**PALI**	0.0806
88	81	**CHHOTI SADRI**	0.0804
	HIGH (0.06-0.08)		
89	205	**GANGAPUR**	0.0790
90	10	**BEHROR**	0.0789
91	35	**CHHIPABAROD**	0.0784
92	66	**BIKANER**	0.0776
93	78	**BHADESAR**	0.0773
93	92	**SARDARSHAHAR**	0.0773
95	74	**TALERA**	0.0768
95	219	**SHEOGANJ**	0.0768
97	192	**RANI STATION**	0.0762
98	3	**JAWAJA**	0.0761
98	53	**SEWAR**	0.0761
98	121	**CHAKSU**	0.0761
101	86	**NIMBAHERA**	0.0758
102	9	**BANSURE**	0.0757
103	84	**GANGRAR**	0.0753
104	14	**LACHHMANGARH**	0.0750
105	20	**THANAGAZI**	0.0744
106	222	**MALPURA**	0.0738
106	225	**TONK**	0.0738
108	223	**NIWAI**	0.0737
109	118	**NOHAR**	0.0736
110	183	**NAGAUR**	0.0733
111	22	**UMREN**	0.0725
111	141	**SAYLA**	0.0725
113	72	**KESHORAIPATAN**	0.0723
113	104	**ASPUR**	0.0723
113	224	**TODARAISINGH**	0.0723
116	89	**CHURU**	0.0722
117	87	**PRATAPGARH**	0.0718
118	119	AMBER	0.0708
119	79	BHAINSRORGARH	0.0705
119	187	DESURI	0.0705
121	134	SANKRA	0.0703
122	107	SAGWARA	0.0702
123	162	OSIAN	0.0701
123	159	BILARA	0.0701
125	90	RAJGARH	0.0700
126	218	REODAR	0.0697
127	48	KAMAN	0.0690
128	130	SHAHPURA	0.0687
129	91	RATANGARH	0.0686
130	203	BAMANWAS	0.0685
131	226	UNIARA	0.0683
132	30	TALWARA	0.0681
133	43	SHEO	0.0681
134	63	SAHARA	0.0675
135	195	SUMERPUR	0.0668
136	94	TARANAGAR	0.0667
137	19	RENI	0.0666
138	136	BHINMAL	0.0665
138	82	CHITTAURGARH	0.0665
140	17	RAJGARH	0.0664
141	158	BHOPALGARH	0.0660
142	62	RAIPUR	0.0656
143	42	DHORIMANNA	0.0652
144	142	BAKANI	0.0649
144	216	ABU ROAD	0.0649
146	167	NADOTI	0.0648
147	173	SANGOD	0.0646
147	202	RAJSAMAND	0.0646
149	138	JASWANTPURA	0.0645
150	139	RANIWARA	0.0644
150	221	DEOLI	0.0644
152	38	BALOTRA	0.0643
152	175	DEGANA	0.0643
154	165	HINDAUN	0.0642
155	169	TODABHIM	0.0640
156	44	SINDHARI	0.0639
156	75	ARNOD	0.0639
158	40	BAYTOO	0.0638
159	7	PISANGAN	0.0635
160	26	GHATOL	0.0634
161	39	BARMER	0.0628
161	168	SAPOTRA	0.0628
163	231	GOGUNDA	0.0624
164	204	BONLI	0.0621
165	177	JAYAL	0.0616
166	93	SUJANGARH	0.0614
167	236	SALUMBAR	0.0612
168	207	SAWAI MADHOPUR	0.0611
169	23	ANANDPURI	0.0609
170	186	BALI	0.0608
171	56	BANERA	0.0607
172	160	LUNI	0.0604
173	144	JHALRAPATAN	0.0602
174	189	MARWAR JUN.	0.0600
175	145	KHANPUR	0.0600
	MEDIUM (0.04-0.06)		
176	135	AHORE	0.0594
177	29	SAJJANGARH	0.0592
178	59	KOTRI	0.0591
179	71	HINDOLI	0.0591
180	24	BAGIDORA	0.0590
181	171	ITAWA	0.0589
182	55	ASIND	0.0582
183	140	SANCHORE	0.0582
184	25	GARHI	0.0581
185	64	SHAHPURA	0.0576
186	197	BHIM	0.0574
187	65	SUWANA	0.0569
188	108	SIMALWARA	0.0567
189	194	SOJAT	0.0559
190	156	BALESAR	0.0557
191	58	JAHAZPUR	0.0551
192	161	MANDOR	0.0549
193	176	DIDWANA	0.0548
194	181	MERTA	0.0547
195	120	BASSI	0.0545
196	137	JALOR	0.0543
196	179	LADNU	0.0543
198	229	DHARIAWAD	0.0542
199	235	MAVLI	0.0532
200	182	MUNDWA	0.0530
201	61	MANDALGARH	0.0529
202	105	BICHHIWARA	0.0528
203	106	DUNGARPUR	0.0527
204	237	SARADA	0.0525
205	178	KUCHAMAN	0.0522
206	185	RIYAN	0.0520
207	166	KARAULI	0.0518
208	73	NAINWA	0.0517
209	146	MANOHARTHANA	0.0513
210	57	HURDA	0.0512
211	28	PEEPALKHOONT	0.0511
212	172	LADPURA	0.0509
213	180	MAKRANA	0.0508
214	27	KUSHALGARH	0.0506
215	8	SRINAGAR	0.0502
216	233	KHERWARA	0.0497
217	147	PIRAWA	0.0486
218	196	AMET	0.0481
219	228	BHINDER	0.0479
220	111	KARANPUR	0.0477
221	21	TIJARA	0.0470
222	217	PINDWARA	0.0463
223	193	ROHAT	0.0453
224	232	JHADOL	0.0419
225	164	SHERGARH	0.0409
	LOW (0.02-0.04)		
226	45	SIWANA	0.0393
227	230	GIRWA	0.0379
228	184	PARBATSAR	0.0363
229	60	MANDAL	0.0352
230	188	JAITARAN	0.0323
231	234	KOTRA	0.0313
232	109	ANUPGARH	0.0292
233	117	HANUMANGARH	0.0291
234	191	RAIPUR	0.0283
235	199	KHAMNOR	0.0254
	VERY LOW (<0.02)		
236	113	RAISINGHNAGAR	0.0193
237	163	PHALODI	0.0073
	RAJASTHAN		**0.0710**
	%age of AAPs		**49.4**

BOLD: Equal/Above Average Panchayat Samities (AAPs)

Source: Annex- 14.1, Col. 8.

ANNEX-18.18

RANKING OF PSS BY DIFFERENCE IN GINI RANK 1991-01

(Descending Order)

RANK	PANCHAYAT SAMITIES P. CODE	NAME	RANK DIFF
1	2	3	4
	(>=50)		
1	114	SADULSHAHAR	118
2	31	ANTA	97
2	157	BAP	97
4	149	BUHANA	93
5	67	DUNGARGARH	73
6	151	JHUNJHUNUN	72
7	210	FATEHPUR	70
8	212	LACHHMANGARH	68
9	214	PIPRALI	62
10	152	KHETRI	58
10	154	SURAJGARH	58
12	97	LALSOT	57
12	150	CHIRAWA	57
14	96	DAUSA	56
15	32	ATRU	55
16	98	MAHWA	53
17	201	RAILMAGRA	50
	(25-50)		
18	54	WEIR	49
18	209	DHOND	49
20	148	ALSISAR	48
21	46	BAYANA	47
21	52	RUPBAS	47
23	99	SIKRAI	46
23	115	SURATGARH	46
25	155	UDAIPURWATI	45
26	15	MANDAWAR	44
26	211	KHANDELA	44
28	100	BARI	43
29	16	NIMRANA	42
29	112	PADAMPUR	42
29	198	DEOGARH	42
29	200	KUMBHALGARH	42
29	220	SIROHI	42
34	33	BARAN	37
35	12	KISHANGARH BAS	36
35	51	NAGAR PAHARI	36
35	206	KHANDAR	36
38	50	NADBAI	35
39	36	KISHANGANJ	34
39	153	NAWALGARH	34
41	49	KUMHER	32
42	208	DANTA RAMGARH	30
43	110	GANGANAGAR	28
44	13	KOTKASIM	27
44	125	JHOTWARA	27
	(0-25)		
46	11	KATHUMAR	24
46	69	LUNKARANSAR	24
46	213	NEEM KA THANA	24
46	227	BARGAON	24
50	47	DEEG	23
50	190	PALI	23
50	215	SRI MADHOPUR	23
53	101	BASERI	21
54	74	TALERA	19
54	95	BANDIKUI	19
54	131	VIRATNAGAR	19
57	18	RAMGARH	17
58	103	RAJAKHERA	16
59	10	BEHROR	15
59	129	SANGANER	15
61	20	THANAGAZI	13
61	102	DHAULPUR	13
61	133	SAM	13
61	222	MALPURA	13
65	37	SHAHBAD	12
65	80	BHOPALSAGAR	12
67	192	RANI STATION	11
67	219	SHEOGANJ	11
67	224	TODARAISINGH	11
70	9	BANSURE	10
70	87	PRATAPGARH	10
72	70	NOKHA	9
73	225	TONK	8
74	14	LACHHMANGARH	7
74	77	BEGUN	7
74	83	DUNGLA	7
74	88	RASHMI	7
74	205	GANGAPUR	7
74	223	NIWAI	7
80	34	CHHABRA	6
81	72	KESHORAIPATAN	6
81	162	OSIAN	6
83	143	DAG	4
84	122	DUDU	3
84	124	JAMWA RAMGARH	3
86	79	BHAINSRORGARH	2
86	86	NIMBAHERA	2
86	116	BHADRA	2
86	134	SANKRA	2
86	218	REODAR	2
91	1	ARAIN	1
91	5	KISHANGARH	1
91	68	KOLAYAT	1
91	76	BARI SADRI	1
91	85	KAPASAN	1
91	123	GOVINDGARH	1
91	127	PHAGI	1
91	174	SULTANPUR	1
91	183	NAGAUR	1
91	203	BAMANWAS	1
91	226	UNIARA	1
102	6	MASOODA	0
102	126	KOTPUTLI	0
102	132	JAISALMER	0
102	187	DESURI	0
	(0 to -25)		
106	2	BHINAY	-1
106	89	CHURU	-1
106	92	SARDARSHAHAR	-1
106	121	CHAKSU	-1
106	128	SAMBHAR	-1
106	170	CHECHAT	-1
112	22	UMREN	-2
112	35	CHHIPABAROD	-2
112	48	KAMAN	-2
112	53	SEWAR	-2
112	104	ASPUR	-2
117	4	KEKRI	-3
117	81	CHHOTI SADRI	-3
119	17	RAJGARH	-4
119	41	CHOHTAN	-4
119	63	SAHARA	-4
119	78	BHADESAR	-4
119	90	RAJGARH	-4
119	91	RATANGARH	-4
119	119	AMBER	-4
119	173	SANGOD	-4
127	94	TARANAGAR	-5
127	118	NOHAR	-5
129	43	SHEO	-6
129	66	BIKANER	-6
129	171	ITAWA	-6
132	75	ARNOD	-7
132	84	GANGRAR	-7
132	195	SUMERPUR	-7
135	3	JAWAJA	-8
135	7	PISANGAN	-8
135	82	CHITTAURGARH	-8
135	107	SAGWARA	-8
135	19	RENI	-10
135	45	SIWANA	-10
135	120	BASSI	-10
135	130	SHAHPURA	-10
135	165	HINDAUN	-10
135	169	TODABHIM	-10
145	141	SAYLA	-11
145	142	BAKANI	-11
145	159	BILARA	-11
145	216	ABU ROAD	-11
149	39	BARMER	-12
149	136	BHINMAL	-12
149	175	DEGANA	-12
149	221	DEOLI	-12
149	231	GOGUNDA	-12
154	38	BALOTRA	-13
154	105	BICHHIWARA	-13
154	106	DUNGARPUR	-13
154	111	KARANPUR	-13
154	177	JAYAL	-13
159	23	ANANDPURI	-14
159	30	TALWARA	-14
159	42	DHORIMANNA	-14
159	62	RAIPUR	-14
159	108	SIMALWARA	-14
159	207	SAWAI MADHOPUR	-14
165	138	JASWANTPURA	-15
165	172	LADPURA	-15
165	186	BALI	-15
165	204	BONLI	-15
169	26	GHATOL	-16
169	40	BAYTOO	-16
169	56	BANERA	-16
169	71	HINDOLI	-16
169	158	BHOPALGARH	-16
169	160	LUNI	-16
169	168	SAPOTRA	-16
169	236	SALUMBAR	-16
177	202	RAJSAMAND	-17
178	59	KOTRI	-18
178	135	AHORE	-18
178	145	KHANPUR	-18
181	8	SRINAGAR	-19
181	93	SUJANGARH	-19
181	139	RANIWARA	-19
181	144	JHALRAPATAN	-19
181	167	NADOTI	-19
186	25	GARHI	-20
186	44	SINDHARI	-20
186	140	SANCHORE	-20
189	24	BAGIDORA	-21
189	29	SAJJANGARH	-21
189	55	ASIND	-21
192	64	SHAHPURA	-22
192	176	DIDWANA	-22
192	189	MARWAR JUN.	-22
195	178	KUCHAMAN	-23
195	181	MERTA	-23
197	137	JALOR	-24
197	179	LADNU	-24
197	194	SOJAT	-24
197	197	BHIM	-24
	(-25 to -50)		
201	65	SUWANA	-26
201	113	RAISINGHNAGAR	-26
203	180	MAKRANA	-28
204	61	MANDALGARH	-29
204	73	NAINWA	-29
206	27	KUSHALGARH	-30
207	28	PEEPALKHOONT	-31
207	182	MUNDWA	-31
207	185	RIYAN	-31
210	58	JAHAZPUR	-32
210	166	KARAULI	-32
212	161	MANDOR	-34
212	229	DHARIAWAD	-34
214	147	PIRAWA	-35
214	156	BALESAR	-35
214	235	MAVLI	-35
217	237	SARADA	-38
218	57	HURDA	-40
218	217	PINDWARA	-40
220	228	BHINDER	-41
221	146	MANOHARTHANA	-42
221	196	AMET	-42
223	184	PARBATSAR	-46
223	193	ROHAT	-46
225	233	KHERWARA	-47
226	21	TIJARA	-49
	(> - 50)		
227	164	SHERGARH	-53
228	232	JHADOL	-56
229	230	GIRWA	-59
230	199	KHAMNOR	-68
231	109	ANUPGARH	-69
232	60	MANDAL	-72
233	188	JAITARAN	-78
234	117	HANUMANGARH	-82
234	191	RAIPUR	-82
234	234	KOTRA	-82
237	163	PHALODI	-114

Source: Annex- 14.1, Col.7.

ANNEX-K1

PANCHAYAT SAMITI-WISE NO. OF HOUSE HOLDS, LITERACY RATE, SCHOOLS, SC/ST POP. AND SEX-RATIO : RAJASTHAN (2001)

P. Code	Panchayat Samities	Total No. of House Holds	Literacy Rate (%)			No. of Schools		Pop Served Per Primary School	Area Served Per Primary School, 2001	SC Population				ST Population				Sex-Ratio	
			Person	Male	Female	Primary	UPS			Person Number	Person %age to Total Pop.	Male	Female	Person Number	Person %age to Total Pop.	Male	Female	SC Pop.	ST Pop.
1	2	3	4	5	6	7	8	9	10	11	12	13	14	15	16	17	18	19	20
1	ARAIN	21481	46.19	63.46	28.27	150	53	889	8.01	25639	19.22	13135	12504	3661	2.74	1873	1788	952	955
2	BHINAY	26606	42.69	62.88	21.71	153	58	1014	7.95	31404	20.25	16085	15319	7089	4.57	3673	3416	952	930
3	JAWAJA	28917	73.85	90.22	57.54	212	55	745	3.12	15781	9.99	7970	7811	941	0.60	487	454	980	932
4	KEKRI	25367	47.16	67.52	25.99	137	54	1029	7.25	32080	22.76	16526	15554	17790	12.62	9247	8543	941	924
5	KISHANGARH	24123	52.26	69.99	33.34	157	49	978	7.05	30475	19.86	15649	14826	1177	0.77	605	572	947	945
6	MASOODA	28734	54.35	75.67	32.03	190	53	840	4.61	18685	11.71	9522	9163	5106	3.20	2561	2545	962	994
7	PISANGAN	40448	52.57	72.30	31.76	209	81	1131	5.76	35254	14.91	17899	17355	2329	0.98	1128	1201	970	1065
8	SRINAGAR	28069	51.51	71.91	29.56	138	52	1233	6.51	21436	12.60	11135	10301	2,305	1.35	1180	1125	925	953
	AJMER	**223745**	**52.70**	**71.90**	**32.63**	**1346**	**455**	**971**	**6.06**	**210754**	**16.13**	**107921**	**102833**	**40398**	**3.09**	**20754**	**19644**	**953**	**947**
9	BANSURE	31023	57.57	74.37	39.01	209	72	1026	3.18	32954	15.37	17183	15771	9186	4.29	4790	4396	918	918
10	BEHROR	21796	71.88	87.60	55.03	193	75	723	1.74	21100	15.13	10905	10195	1678	1.20	884	794	935	898
11	KATHUMAR	30473	58.51	76.92	37.16	190	68	1114	2.97	51024	24.10	27186	23838	27457	12.97	14622	12835	877	878
12	KISHAN-GARH BAS	24518	55.06	72.87	35.42	158	44	1060	3.20	34824	20.79	18326	16498	100	0.06	60	40	900	667
13	KOTKASIM	18465	69.12	84.65	52.20	138	47	853	2.50	22731	19.31	11796	10935	887	0.75	490	397	927	810
14	LACHHMAN-GARH	33037	54.05	73.16	32.57	213	75	1060	2.91	42508	18.82	22520	19988	25803	11.43	13655	12148	888	890
15	MANDAWAR	30194	68.63	84.39	51.72	177	83	1116	3.26	38233	19.35	19892	18341	6137	3.11	3145	2992	922	951
16	NIMRANA	23682	74.44	88.55	59.47	136	71	1054	2.78	23159	16.16	12108	11051	2238	1.56	1120	1118	913	998
17	RAJGARH	22109	54.23	73.76	32.22	142	55	1019	7.11	26843	18.55	14077	12766	42660	29.48	22700	19960	907	879
18	RAMGARH	32265	52.38	70.81	31.71	199	59	1107	3.10	41796	18.98	22030	19766	7587	3.45	4079	3508	897	860
19	RENI	20027	56.41	75.57	34.60	127	48	1075	3.09	26020	19.06	13781	12239	50525	37.02	26916	23609	888	877
20	THANAGAZI	28427	47.47	66.83	25.92	196	69	969	5.41	27465	14.46	14399	13066	36249	19.08	19226	17023	907	885
21	TIJARA	35,919	52.93	70.19	32.57	207	53	1096	3.11	31677	13.96	16872	14805	363	0.16	197	166	877	843
22	UMREN	31909	52.92	71.47	31.83	192	66	1155	4.42	50093	22.59	26556	23537	17983	8.11	9624	8,359	886	869
	ALWAR	**383844**	**58.17**	**75.74**	**38.54**	**2477**	**885**	**1033**	**3.46**	**470427**	**18.39**	**247631**	**222796**	**228853**	**8.95**	**121508**	**107345**	**900**	**883**
23	ANANDPURI	18293	40.92	56.43	24.72	155	42	717	2.21	2228	2.00	1119	1109	96132	86.44	48824	47308	991	969
24	BAGIDORA	29814	40.84	57.46	23.99	195	60	906	2.64	8983	5.08	4541	4442	135252	76.53	68108	67144	978	986
25	GARHI	41741	52.59	69.28	35.63	252	116	943	2.79	15879	6.69	7982	7897	127998	53.89	64499	63499	989	984
26	GHATOL	42274	40.90	58.65	23.13	278	89	829	2.82	11,077	4.81	5630	5447	173515	75.33	86809	86706	967	999
27	KUSHALGARH	22120	33.40	48.50	18.00	208	39	668	3.08	1369	0.99	694	675	131281	94.47	66019	65262	973	989
28	PEEPAL-KHOONT	26953	28.01	41.72	13.74	195	41	776	4.68	5089	3.36	2606	2483	134538	88.94	68297	66241	953	970
29	SAJJANGARH	22275	37.34	53.11	21.07	193	37	697	2.09	4024	2.99	1999	2025	120281	89.46	60891	59390	1013	975
30	TALWARA	37348	45.88	64.61	26.73	268	79	797	2.80	8043	3.76	4082	3961	154933	72.49	77965	76968	970	987
	BANSWARA	**240818**	**41.28**	**57.77**	**24.43**	**1744**	**503**	**799**	**2.90**	**56692**	**4.07**	**28653**	**28039**	**1073930**	**77.03**	**541412**	**532518**	**979**	**984**
31	ANTA	24071	62.90	79.64	44.67	153	62	972	6.09	28726	19.31	14939	13787	27591	18.55	14356	13235	923	922
32	ATRU	21010	62.41	79.96	42.99	142	48	895	6.05	25995	20.46	13655	12340	23863	18.78	12510	11353	904	908
33	BARAN	16730	64.49	81.50	45.65	102	34	1011	6.01	25369	24.60	13325	12044	19558	18.96	10359	9199	904	888
34	CHHABRA	16583	52.86	71.00	32.45	190	36	524	4.12	15905	15.99	8300	7605	23177	23.30	12351	10826	916	877
35	CHHIPABAROD	21781	48.57	67.74	27.65	143	34	894	5.77	17793	13.92	9328	8465	33804	26.44	17661	16143	907	914
36	KISHANGANJ	22462	51.98	67.34	35.12	147	44	920	9.87	16780	12.41	8855	7925	46416	34.33	23890	22526	895	943
37	SHAHBAD	18578	51.73	68.27	33.16	147	45	736	9.99	17654	16.32	9380	8274	36812	34.04	18866	17946	882	951
	BARAN #	**141215**	**56.62**	**73.79**	**37.66**	**1024**	**303**	**830**	**6.77**	**148222**	**17.45**	**77782**	**70440**	**211221**	**24.86**	**109993**	**101228**	**906**	**920**
38	BALOTRA	40695	54.31	70.69	36.52	308	77	862	12.61	36477	13.73	19084	17,393	23748	8.94	12499	11249	911	900
39	BARMER	37995	53.69	68.85	35.53	345	75	690	11.05	36660	15.40	19409	17251	15576	6.54	8348	7228	889	866
40	BAYTOO	32846	58.45	72.13	43.28	355	77	593	9.09	29863	14.20	15582	14281	7317	3.48	3918	3399	917	868
41	CHOHTAN	36824	50.36	63.50	34.99	268	68	842	12.19	54635	24.20	29095	25540	20687	9.16	10959	9728	878	888
42	DHORIMANNA	38020	66.91	76.76	55.99	306	71	820	8.72	36401	14.51	19176	17225	13679	5.45	7251	6428	898	886
43	SHEO	28343	57.01	71.78	39.41	246	54	726	26.90	29317	16.42	15446	13871	6873	3.85	3699	3174	898	858
44	SINDHARI	35677	60.58	73.72	46.35	349	72	678	8.93	28751	12.15	14966	13785	7258	3.07	3845	3413	921	888
45	SIWANA	34396	58.76	73.33	42.96	186	65	1149	10.66	36721	17.19	19397	17324	20720	9.70	10880	9840	893	904
	BARMER	**284796**	**57.55**	**71.33**	**42.04**	**2363**	**559**	**770**	**12.09**	**288825**	**15.87**	**152155**	**136670**	**115858**	**6.37**	**61399**	**54459**	**898**	**887**
46	BAYANA	28877	56.92	76.39	32.40	196	62	978	4.08	53462	27.90	29216	24246	5788	3.02	3113	2675	830	859
47	DEEG	22678	58.03	76.54	36.04	151	55	1026	3.25	29023	18.74	15952	13071	750	0.48	405	345	819	852
48	KAMAN	30357	47.24	65.61	26.22	202	55	1050	2.75	17940	8.46	9542	8398	339	0.16	185	154	880	832
49	KUMHER	22866	66.83	84.90	45.61	145	55	1070	3.04	30754	19.83	16825	13929	3623	2.34	1915	1708	828	892
50	NADBAI	23774	67.16	84.80	45.89	148	54	1089	2.92	40647	25.23	22306	18341	4252	2.64	2253	1999	822	887
51	NAGAR PAHARI	33042	57.88	75.86	37.25	246	82	961	2.53	33654	14.24	18181	15473	3826	1.62	2045	1781	851	871
52	RUPBAS	31818	67.26	84.25	47.00	173	79	1221	3.12	54982	26.04	29541	25441	2219	1.05	1210	1009	861	834
53	SEWAR	24530	67.30	85.43	45.85	178	67	942	2.57	42598	25.41	22788	19810	2708	1.62	1497	1211	869	809
54	WEIR	29994	61.37	80.88	38.12	196	74	1032	2.94	56413	27.90	30677	25736	19149	9.47	10255	8894	839	867
	BHARATPUR	**247936**	**60.79**	**79.12**	**39.06**	**1635**	**583**	**1035**	**3.01**	**359473**	**21.24**	**195028**	**164445**	**42654**	**2.52**	**22878**	**19776**	**843**	**864**

P. Code	Panchayat Samities	Total No. of House Holds	Literacy Rate (%) Person	Male	Female	No. of Schools Primary	UPS	Pop Served Per Primary School	Area Served Per Primary School, 2001	SC Population Person Number	%age to Total Pop.	Male	Female	ST Population Person Number	%age to Total Pop.	Male	Female	Sex-Ratio SC Pop.	ST Pop.
1	2	3	4	5	6	7	8	9	10	11	12	13	14	15	16	17	18	19	20
55	ASIND	36844	41.60	60.92	22.89	237	72	812	4.68	27101	14.09	13511	13590	13237	6.88	6573	6664	1006	1014
56	BANERA	20019	49.99	67.49	32.11	126	36	843	5.37	16393	15.43	8326	8067	6830	6.43	3396	3434	969	1011
57	HURDA	16760	51.24	69.79	31.79	116	41	785	5.32	14315	15.72	7368	6947	6882	7.56	3568	3314	943	929
58	JAHAZPUR	31496	48.12	65.74	29.18	209	69	803	4.94	29134	17.36	15196	13938	56881	33.90	29802	27079	917	909
59	KOTRI	28264	39.26	55.09	22.66	184	51	808	5.16	25762	17.32	13290	12472	8169	5.49	4151	4018	938	968
60	MANDAL	37954	43.18	61.99	25.23	232	70	851	4.98	28588	14.47	14115	14473	9316	4.72	4538	4778	1025	1053
61	MANDALGARH	38493	43.38	59.15	26.22	237	61	844	5.88	33203	16.61	17258	15945	31624	15.82	16492	15132	924	918
62	RAIPUR	16132	42.65	61.89	24.48	111	34	760	4.64	13145	15.58	6495	6650	5343	6.33	2666	2677	1024	1004
63	SAHARA	19477	44.19	63.25	26.73	119	41	824	5.32	16507	16.84	8077	8430	6609	6.74	3291	3318	1044	1008
64	SHAHPURA	26641	42.63	59.49	24.86	177	54	842	6.37	29301	19.67	15010	14291	14649	9.83	7539	7110	952	943
65	SUWANA	32032	45.53	64.13	26.34	176	58	932	4.73	29760	18.15	14996	14764	7241	4.42	3744	3497	985	934
	BHILWARA	**304112**	**44.31**	**62.12**	**26.20**	**1924**	**587**	**831**	**5.22**	**263209**	**16.46**	**133642**	**129567**	**166781**	**10.43**	**85760**	**81021**	**970**	**945**
66	BIKANER	55163	29.92	61.20	29.92	266	93	1409	33.63	101302	27.03	53753	47549	987	0.26	543	444	885	818
67	DUNGAR-GARH *	24540	57.58	73.40	40.95	134	67	1364	22.41	45541	24.91	23630	21911	55	0.03	42	13	927	310
68	KOLAYAT	30686	24.28	55.22	24.28	187	57	1111	39.14	52951	25.49	28176	24775	552	0.27	294	258	879	878
69	LUNKARANSAR	30980	30.01	60.87	30.01	172	72	1264	36.13	48942	22.52	25605	23337	329	0.15	188	141	911	750
70	NOKHA	36938	28.22	65.68	28.22	215	78	1299	17.52	61457	22.00	32208	29249	42	0.02	28	14	908	500
	BIKANER **	**153767**	**45.72**	**61.11**	**28.44**	**840**	**300**	**1285**	**34.82**	**264652**	**24.52**	**139742**	**124910**	**1910**	**0.18**	**1053**	**857**	**894**	**814**
71	HINDOLI	33332	46.81	64.00	27.68	173	51	1094	7.74	33861	17.89	17837	16024	34309	18.13	18105	16204	898	895
72	KESHORAI-PATAN	30945	55.95	73.32	36.90	220	70	812	5.85	31597	17.69	16566	15031	50848	28.47	26545	24303	907	916
73	NAINWA	27303	50.56	69.51	29.77	199	55	785	5.73	27374	17.52	14225	13149	34873	22.32	18493	16380	924	886
74	TALERA	45298	51.98	67.82	34.44	265	80	977	7.10	50212	19.39	26447	23765	66613	25.73	34915	31698	899	908
	BUNDI	**136878**	**51.37**	**68.50**	**32.46**	**857**	**256**	**914**	**6.59**	**143044**	**18.27**	**75075**	**67969**	**186643**	**23.84**	**98058**	**88585**	**905**	**903**
75	ARNOD	22074	46.77	63.45	29.63	146	39	821	4.80	6006	5.01	3137	2869	80577	67.24	40659	39918	915	982
76	BARI SADRI	18335	44.77	64.56	25.20	113	31	786	4.20	10666	12.01	5380	5286	17389	19.57	8637	8752	983	1013
77	BEGUN	20653	48.71	68.02	28.76	166	44	615	5.77	17230	16.89	8868	8362	11856	11.62	6079	5777	943	950
78	BHADESAR	21889	47.41	66.02	28.57	145	40	741	3.73	18037	16.80	9091	8946	8369	7.79	4263	4106	984	963
79	BHAINSROR-GARH	16004	46.16	62.63	27.88	117	31	687	11.71	8691	10.81	4625	4066	28328	35.24	14645	13683	879	934
80	BHOPALSAGAR	15104	50.69	69.36	32.33	91	27	799	4.38	12362	17.01	6161	6201	9224	12.69	4681	4543	1006	971
81	CHHOTI SADRI	19688	51.44	70.56	31.80	137	40	730	5.05	11754	11.75	5940	5814	38131	38.11	19342	18789	979	971
82	CHITTAUR-GARH	33433	50.26	68.21	31.77	206	63	815	3.95	28913	17.21	14663	14250	21007	12.51	10766	10241	972	951
83	DUNGLA	18711	47.85	67.53	28.58	101	31	891	4.89	13801	15.34	6940	6861	12213	13.57	6055	6158	989	1017
84	GANGRAR	17905	46.70	65.01	28.07	114	35	778	4.87	16122	18.19	8255	7867	6171	6.96	3103	3068	953	989
85	KAPASAN	17880	44.82	64.53	25.12	110	32	768	4.39	15907	18.82	8072	7835	8903	10.53	4461	4442	971	996
86	NIMBAHERA	25753	54.29	75.48	32.73	149	43	909	5.45	22374	16.53	11417	10957	17867	13.20	9045	8822	960	975
87	PRATAPGARH	37466	52.24	68.66	35.16	300	85	671	4.76	15363	7.63	7864	7499	113195	56.25	57740	55455	954	960
88	RASHMI	15230	43.96	63.68	24.92	75	32	1004	6.00	15859	21.05	7894	7965	4411	5.86	2199	2212	1009	1006
	CHITTAUR-GARH	**300125**	**48.88**	**67.43**	**29.98**	**1970**	**573**	**769**	**5.16**	**213085**	**14.07**	**108307**	**104778**	**377641**	**24.94**	**191675**	**185966**	**967**	**970**
89	CHURU	24101	66.21	79.59	52.50	139	77	1095	11.22	35392	23.26	18356	17036	1094	0.72	582	512	928	880
90	RAJGARH	44535	71.51	83.01	59.34	268	98	998	8.20	62229	23.27	32511	29718	2730	1.02	1406	1324	914	942
91	RATANGARH	24449	64.67	77.99	51.29	138	69	1146	11.90	36413	23.03	18818	17595	584	0.37	303	281	935	927
92	SARDAR-SHAHAR	32881	59.20	74.51	43.22	195	82	1143	19.56	51167	22.95	26778	24389	722	0.32	378	344	911	910
93	SUJANGARH	37175	61.67	75.10	47.98	192	84	1319	13.52	74400	29.38	38650	35750	280	0.11	155	125	925	806
94	TARANAGAR	23707	71.57	81.32	61.27	143	63	1056	12.47	32591	21.58	17040	15551	738	0.49	388	350	913	902
	CHURU ***	**211388**	**64.66**	**77.89**	**50.93**	**1209**	**540**	**1148**	**11.24**	**337733**	**24.34**	**175783**	**161950**	**6203**	**0.45**	**3254**	**2949**	**921**	**906**
95	BANDIKUI	39385	65.40	81.31	47.71	247	81	1081	2.43	51918	19.44	27113	24805	55865	20.92	29589	26276	915	888
96	DAUSA	38145	57.69	77.53	35.61	292	104	931	3.11	61033	22.45	31764	29269	86151	31.68	45159	40992	921	908
97	LALSOT	35323	53.17	72.77	31.69	277	79	907	3.08	52916	21.05	27476	25440	104128	41.42	54429	49699	926	913
98	MAHWA	26905	64.19	81.98	43.80	177	73	1012	2.68	43372	24.21	22970	20402	46601	26.01	24933	21668	888	869
99	SIKRAI	32339	61.25	78.14	42.54	186	81	1139	2.70	47452	22.41	24611	22841	52405	24.75	27941	24464	928	876
	DAUSA #	**172097**	**60.13**	**78.20**	**40.02**	**1179**	**418**	**1002**	**2.83**	**256691**	**21.73**	**133934**	**122757**	**345150**	**29.22**	**182051**	**163099**	**917**	**896**
100	BARI	22055	56.46	71.99	36.55	179	44	841	4.44	35165	23.35	19382	15783	15165	10.07	8284	6881	814	831
101	BASERI	29300	61.30	76.77	42.27	202	59	999	4.96	42211	20.92	22996	19215	31148	15.44	16931	14217	836	840
102	DHAULPUR	37193	58.73	75.33	38.64	287	80	914	2.01	52893	20.15	28574	24319	190	0.07	97	93	851	959
103	RAJAKHERA	26979	57.20	73.03	37.46	207	67	927	2.76	37580	19.59	20637	16943	7	0.00	6	1	821	167
	DHAULPUR	**115527**	**58.59**	**74.51**	**38.89**	**875**	**250**	**922**	**3.37**	**167849**	**20.81**	**91589**	**76260**	**46510**	**5.77**	**25318**	**21192**	**833**	**837**
104	ASPUR	35901	44.71	62.74	28.48	210	70	879	3.29	10117	5.48	4990	5127	91190	49.42	44047	47143	1027	1070
105	BICHHIWARA	40921	45.84	63.51	28.31	232	68	1018	3.22	6623	2.81	3355	3268	188192	79.70	93704	94488	974	1008
106	DUNGARPUR	31210	46.54	66.24	27.89	218	67	791	2.64	4239	2.46	2103	2136	139524	80.94	68138	71386	1016	1048
107	SAGWARA	35749	51.14	69.99	34.11	226	76	853	2.71	8995	4.67	4436	4559	104695	54.34	50514	54181	1028	1073
108	SIMALWARA	42960	42.60	59.36	25.85	337	82	715	2.71	9597	3.98	4803	4794	180276	74.77	90155	90121	998	1000
	DUNGARPUR	**186741**	**46.02**	**64.06**	**28.86**	**1223**	**363**	**840**	**2.89**	**39571**	**3.85**	**19687**	**19884**	**703877**	**68.55**	**346558**	**357319**	**1010**	**1031**
109	ANUPGARH	68240	57.7	69.95	44.1	593	191	704	5.98	179037	42.86	93670	85367	1970	0.47	1097	873	911	796
110	GANGANAGAR	30484	62.8	74.14	50.2	232	91	761	3.68	60797	34.44	32004	28793	424	0.24	215	209	900	972
111	KARANPUR	17790	61.2	71.78	49.6	191	70	540	4.24	48312	46.86	25309	23003	107	0.10	69	38	909	551
112	PADAMPUR	20330	62.7	74.21	50.2	203	62	598	4.15	41498	34.19	21823	19675	302	0.25	160	142	902	888
113	RAISINGH-NAGAR	25763	64.7	75.80	52.6	294	85	535	4.47	68653	43.64	35826	32827	539	0.34	287	252	916	878
114	SADULSHAHAR	23957	62.5	74.75	48.2	162	68	905	9.16	50151	34.20	26613	23538	154	0.11	93	61	884	656
115	SURATGARH	34516	57.5	69.76	42.6	241	80	885	15.73	62707	29.39	33155	29552	487	0.23	264	223	891	845
	GANGANAGAR	**221080**	**60.46**	**72.23**	**47.19**	**1323**	**456**	**697**	**6.60**	**511155**	**38.26**	**268400**	**242755**	**3983**	**0.30**	**2185**	**1798**	904	823

P. Code	Panchayat Samities	Total No. of House Holds	Literacy Rate (%) Person	Literacy Rate (%) Male	Literacy Rate (%) Female	No. of Schools Primary	No. of Schools UPS	Pop Served Per Primary School	Area Served Per Primary School, 2001	SC Population Person Number	SC Population Person %age to Total Pop.	SC Population Male	SC Population Female	ST Population Person Number	ST Population Person %age to Total Pop.	ST Population Male	ST Population Female	Sex-Ratio SC Pop.	Sex-Ratio ST Pop.
1	2	3	4	5	6	7	8	9	10	11	12	13	14	15	16	17	18	19	20
116	BHADRA	37179	66.45	79.81	51.66	200	104	1103	8.57	45959	20.84	24324	21635	1377	0.62	732	645	889	881
117	HANUMAN-GARH	101573	57.39	69.88	43.54	562	249	1118	3.62	207548	33.04	109145	98403	2431	0.39	1309	1122	902	857
118	NOHAR	57744	62.27	75.43	47.70	314	132	1165	13.71	92967	25.42	48700	44267	746	0.20	407	339	909	833
	HANUMAN-## GARH	**196496**	**60.50**	**73.35**	**46.27**	**1076**	**485**	**1129**	**7.48**	**346474**	**28.53**	**182169**	**164305**	**4554**	**0.37**	**2448**	**2106**	**902**	**860**
119	AMBER	35308	59.17	78.43	37.85	233	80	1125	3.60	39587	15.11	20804	18783	35930	13.71	18784	17146	903	913
120	BASSI	31950	58.14	77.99	36.30	242	65	949	2.61	44013	19.17	22989	21024	72237	31.46	37712	34525	915	915
121	CHAKSU	22294	51.22	71.39	29.24	229	52	704	3.35	31977	19.84	16657	15320	38337	23.79	20030	18307	920	914
122	DUDU	39936	55.85	73.76	36.60	251	83	1086	7.39	50591	18.56	26322	24269	8240	3.02	4291	3949	922	920
123	GOVINDGARH	35914	65.53	82.87	46.73	203	83	1359	3.28	33218	12.05	17387	15831	15410	5.59	8104	7306	911	902
124	JAMWA RAMGARH	35352	62.21	79.06	43.58	254	93	985	3.98	39334	15.73	20579	18755	74675	29.85	38936	35739	911	918
125	JHOTWARA	11998	65.44	80.64	48.72	94	28	946	4.10	16373	18.41	8578	7795	4194	4.72	2146	2048	909	954
126	KOTPUTLI	32937	71.20	82.58	58.79	214	75	1068	3.10	34863	15.26	18176	16687	15898	6.96	8325	7573	918	910
127	PHAGI	22713	60.28	75.65	43.55	185	60	874	6.02	33277	20.59	17471	15806	7050	4.36	3674	3376	905	919
128	SAMBHAR	28435	66.16	81.43	49.83	199	76	1053	4.18	35091	16.75	18393	16698	8541	4.08	4440	4101	908	924
129	SANGANER	17548	61.26	78.64	42.28	150	42	875	3.89	24296	18.50	12628	11668	16516	12.58	8662	7854	924	907
130	SHAHPURA	24536	64.38	80.80	46.16	147	74	1235	2.78	27960	15.41	14639	13321	8529	4.70	4462	4067	910	911
131	VIRATNAGAR	28970	67.24	81.09	51.95	186	63	1110	3.49	30783	14.91	16031	14752	13281	6.43	7002	6279	920	897
	JAIPUR	**367891**	**62.15**	**78.88**	**43.86**	**2587**	**874**	**1028**	**4.02**	**441363**	**16.60**	**230654**	**210709**	**318838**	**11.99**	**166568**	**152270**	**914**	**914**
132	JAISALMER	21808	47.84	63.62	27.90	171	51	747	75.14	21581	16.89	11580	10001	9877	7.73	5316	4561	864	858
133	SAM	23315	44.33	60.39	23.56	214	54	648	98.65	23082	16.64	12350	10732	6539	4.72	3493	3046	869	872
134	SANKRA	25371	48.04	64.04	29.71	244	67	678	22.49	21347	12.91	11204	10143	8053	4.87	4222	3831	905	907
	JAISALMER	**70494**	**46.78**	**62.71**	**27.26**	**629**	**172**	**687**	**62.71**	**66010**	**15.29**	**35134**	**30876**	**24469**	**5.67**	**13031**	**11438**	**879**	**878**
135	AHORE	33325	51.91	68.96	35.59	144	66	1232	11.09	345[illegible]	19.50	17752	16833	21124	11.91	11108	10016	948	902
136	BHINMAL	28891	39.92	59.55	20.07	126	46	1466	10.62	23405	12.67	12147	11258	18793	10.17	9818	8975	927	914
137	JALOR	22911	45.54	63.56	27.76	101	41	1305	10.44	26097	19.80	13627	12470	13588	10.31	7110	6478	915	911
138	JASWANTPURA	22232	40.50	59.58	21.77	83	36	1547	12.88	20656	16.09	10712	9944	13355	10.40	7037	6318	928	898
139	RANIWARA	25806	47.32	64.82	28.71	127	42	1286	7.75	31736	19.43	16631	15105	23246	14.23	12149	11097	908	913
140	SANCHORE	52070	45.79	64.34	26.09	266	80	1286	11.31	61350	17.93	31984	29366	15330	4.48	8035	7295	918	908
141	SAYLA	34222	41.58	59.88	23.14	119	47	1774	12.26	42423	20.09	22038	20385	15874	7.52	8440	7434	925	881
	JALOR	**219457**	**44.81**	**63.13**	**26.18**	**966**	**358**	**1386**	**10.88**	**240252**	**17.94**	**124891**	**115361**	**121310**	**9.06**	**63697**	**57613**	**924**	**904**
142	BAKANI	26269	42.16	59.13	23.83	189	43	806	4.69	17988	11.81	9295	8693	22043	14.47	11459	10584	935	924
143	DAG	28419	45.71	62.95	27.50	197	46	849	5.74	38428	22.98	19879	18549	438	0.26	229	209	933	913
144	JHALRAPATAN	34824	56.33	73.89	37.36	254	67	811	5.23	34509	16.76	18079	16430	32698	15.88	17045	15653	909	918
145	KHANPUR	25215	65.35	82.38	46.63	168	49	913	5.60	26,644	17.37	14,005	12,639	22,818	14.88	11,920	10,898	902	914
146	MANOHAR-THANA	28582	45.24	62.88	26.00	234	38	690	3.94	14188	8.79	7387	6801	46900	29.05	24402	22498	921	922
147	PIRAWA	28933	64.70	79.94	48.44	196	58	877	5.11	29332	17.06	15211	14121	10944	6.37	5682	5262	928	926
	JHALAWAR	**172242**	**53.55**	**70.51**	**35.25**	**1238**	**301**	**818**	**5.02**	**161089**	**15.92**	**83856**	**77233**	**135841**	**13.42**	**70737**	**65104**	**921**	**920**
148	ALSISAR	23056	73.64	86.06	61.41	174	73	813	4.29	27699	19.59	14274	13425	3312	2.34	1696	1616	941	953
149	BUHANA	33399	76.75	89.15	63.91	211	102	969	3.10	34556	16.91	18022	16534	1463	0.72	741	722	917	974
150	CHIRAWA	24179	74.16	87.13	60.96	149	59	1026	3.28	25504	16.69	13137	12367	2736	1.79	1406	1330	941	946
151	JHUNJHUNUN	29229	75.66	89.14	62.21	221	98	800	3.71	35797	20.26	18528	17269	5333	3.02	2718	2615	932	962
152	KHETRI	33236	65.97	81.12	50.11	220	83	975	3.62	25997	12.12	13429	12568	6241	2.91	3246	2995	936	923
153	NAWALGARH	33600	69.07	84.84	53.18	236	83	922	2.82	29409	13.51	15072	14337	5236	2.41	2707	2529	951	934
154	SURAJGARH	28435	69.95	83.86	55.27	161	74	1092	4.85	40486	23.03	21173	19313	1279	0.73	675	604	912	895
155	UDAIPURWATI	36122	77.06	86.60	67.32	223	106	1055	3.73	29698	12.62	15215	14483	7890	3.35	4059	3831	952	944
	JHUNJHUNUN	**241256**	**72.72**	**85.90**	**59.25**	**1595**	**678**	**952**	**3.63**	**249146**	**16.41**	**128850**	**120296**	**33490**	**2.21**	**17248**	**16242**	**934**	**942**
156	BALESAR	26009	42.67	63.56	19.77	156	41	1117	11.89	30732	17.64	16063	14669	6728	3.86	3560	3168	913	890
157	BAP	22001	44.07	61.01	25.14	131	45	1201	33.83	25347	16.11	13295	12052	4527	2.88	2415	2112	907	875
158	BHOPALGARH	33454	46.35	67.86	23.69	173	66	1169	10.08	41548	20.54	21574	19974	765	0.38	411	354	926	861
159	BILARA	31042	49.93	70.32	28.10	155	68	1165	9.67	37449	20.74	19647	17802	598	0.33	334	264	906	790
160	LUNI	35031	53.69	72.57	33.32	194	67	1181	10.22	36740	16.04	19212	17528	8719	3.81	4493	4226	912	941
161	MANDOR	23082	49.13	69.72	26.50	140	50	1080	9.07	23694	15.66	12395	11299	5194	3.43	2685	2509	912	934
162	OSIAN	61230	43.41	63.72	21.40	325	109	1299	12.88	73264	17.35	38038	35226	14566	3.45	7458	7108	926	953
163	PHALODI	32943	46.30	64.30	26.53	240	63	958	13.49	35951	15.64	18888	17063	8584	3.73	4485	4099	903	914
164	SHERGARH	24440	41.09	60.65	19.24	126	41	1291	15.67	28475	17.51	14829	13646	11737	7.22	6055	5682	920	938
	JODHPUR	**289232**	**46.21**	**65.93**	**24.75**	**1640**	**550**	**1164**	**13.52**	**333200**	**17.45**	**173941**	**159259**	**61418**	**3.22**	**31896**	**29522**	**916**	**926**
165	HINDAUN	38368	71.93	85.53	55.72	227	96	1156	2.78	81955	31.23	44310	37645	42508	16.20	22940	19568	850	853
166	KARAULI	33789	56.45	74.10	35.16	217	73	1026	5.62	50075	22.49	27029	23046	43925	19.73	23829	20096	853	843
167	NADOTI	18650	64.55	81.12	45.98	135	55	934	4.79	24236	19.22	12599	11637	29813	23.64	15768	14045	924	891
168	SAPOTRA	35264	57.30	74.21	37.11	261	84	891	7.52	49859	21.44	27069	22790	86017	36.99	46584	39433	842	846
169	TODABHIM	28806	60.98	80.21	38.63	179	70	1084	2.92	41866	21.57	22417	19449	60834	31.34	32731	28103	868	859
	KARAULI ###	**154877**	**62.39**	**79.00**	**42.77**	**1019**	**378**	**1018**	**4.89**	**247991**	**23.90**	**133424**	**114567**	**263097**	**25.35**	**141852**	**121245**	**859**	**855**
170	CHECHAT	24139	67.36	81.84	51.23	140	40	943	5.51	31280	23.68	16416	14864	18380	13.92	9597	8783	905	915
171	ITAWA	27585	61.76	77.67	44.06	190	62	819	4.67	36300	23.32	19061	17239	34987	22.48	18436	16551	904	898
172	LADPURA	24244	64.70	79.12	48.66	164	54	882	7.97	25219	17.43	13261	11958	21378	14.77	11353	10025	902	883
173	SANGOD	23894	68.64	83.69	52.25	203	60	724	5.15	32278	21.97	16862	15416	16321	11.11	8584	7737	914	901
174	SULTANPUR	25123	69.22	83.64	53.43	180	60	837	5.07	33814	22.45	17655	16159	26765	17.77	13959	12806	915	917
	KOTA	**124985**	**66.27**	**81.14**	**49.85**	**877**	**276**	**832**	**5.61**	**158891**	**21.77**	**83255**	**75636**	**117831**	**16.14**	**61929**	**55902**	**908**	**903**
175	DEGANA	31477	52.99	70.79	35.09	177	58	1074	8.23	42130	22.16	21487	20643	219	0.12	113	106	961	938
176	DIDWANA	41334	62.16	79.03	45.33	223	90	1278	7.21	55548	19.49	28420	27128	407	0.14	212	195	955	920
177	JAYAL	34701	50.83	68.90	32.12	175	63	1285	11.93	53521	23.79	27627	25894	37	0.02	25	12	937	480
178	KUCHAMAN	38869	60.80	77.00	43.59	288	90	931	4.99	53722	20.03	27919	25803	3713	1.38	1936	1777	924	918

P. Code	Panchayat Samities	Total No. of House Holds	Literacy Rate (%) Person	Male	Female	No. of Schools Primary	UPS	Pop Served Per Primary School	Area Served Per Primary School, 2001	SC Population Person Number	%age to Total Pop.	Male	Female	ST Population Person Number	%age to Total Pop.	Male	Female	Sex-Ratio SC Pop.	ST Pop.
1	2	3	4	5	6	7	8	9	10	11	12	13	14	15	16	17	18	19	20
179	LADNU	23591	59.47	77.22	41.49	124	47	1274	11.06	33870	21.43	17325	16545	174	0.11	87	87	955	1000
180	MAKRANA	29661	60.43	76.56	43.77	162	66	1233	6.83	45829	22.95	23707	22122	115	0.06	82	33	933	402
181	MERTA	30379	53.75	72.56	33.55	141	58	1301	9.91	42469	23.15	22270	20199	353	0.19	201	152	907	756
182	MUNDWA	30523	44.25	63.47	24.07	163	52	1212	13.40	39532	20.01	20445	19087	65	0.03	35	30	934	857
183	NAGAUR	32544	49.34	67.22	30.53	246	73	914	9.68	47603	21.17	24651	22952	135	0.06	75	60	931	800
184	PARBATSAR	28897	55.58	71.44	38.87	170	59	1097	6.30	35592	19.09	18384	17208	175	0.09	102	73	936	716
185	RIYAN	30577	51.43	70.10	31.82	153	59	1174	8.10	38337	21.34	19657	18680	156	0.09	91	65	950	714
	NAGAUR	**352553**	**54.99**	**72.46**	**36.85**	**2022**	**715**	**1136**	**8.58**	**488153**	**21.25**	**251892**	**236261**	**5549**	**0.24**	**2959**	**2590**	**938**	**875**
186*	BALI	34653	49.48	65.43	33.98	173	69	1062	7.92	30109	16.38	15237	14872	49417	26.89	25367	24050	976	948
187	DESURI	20172	50.66	68.06	34.67	101	41	1012	8.21	20167	19.72	10243	9924	5256	5.14	2724	2532	969	930
188	JAITARAN	33789	46.08	65.42	26.32	135	59	1385	9.55	36409	19.48	18851	17558	123	0.07	68	55	931	809
189	MARWAR JUN.	35505	49.55	68.87	30.77	170	66	1067	8.18	34491	19.01	17788	16703	4700	2.59	2433	2267	939	932
190	PALI	17064	48.02	66.89	28.99	99	32	908	13.10	17919	19.92	9198	8721	6952	7.73	3679	3273	948	890
191	RAIPUR	33763	49.80	70.02	29.51	181	44	1006	5.45	25485	14.00	12983	12502	281	0.15	141	140	963	993
192	RANI STATION	20830	52.04	69.04	36.11	101	45	1054	7.55	20687	19.42	10570	10117	4208	3.95	2192	2016	957	920
193	ROHAT	16923	50.72	70.38	30.64	85	29	1207	16.52	20289	19.78	10532	9757	5427	5.29	2874	2553	926	888
194	SOJAT	29817	51.89	72.30	32.02	135	55	1155	12.05	33376	21.41	17276	16100	143	0.09	78	65	932	833
195	SUMERPUR	26504	52.85	70.32	35.69	84	40	1643	10.86	24498	17.75	12615	11883	18631	13.50	9754	8877	942	910
	PALI	**269020**	**49.95**	**68.57**	**31.65**	**1264**	**480**	**1131**	**9.39**	**263430**	**18.43**	**135293**	**128137**	**95138**	**6.66**	**49310**	**45828**	**947**	**929**
196	AMET	16600	48.59	66.69	30.65	129	32	683	3.92	14319	16.24	7319	7000	8211	9.31	4200	4011	956	955
197	BHIM	26514	56.10	80.27	33.00	196	55	702	3.46	14090	10.24	6924	7166	2605	1.89	1327	1278	1035	963
198	DEOGARH	15661	49.09	68.26	31.24	114	24	683	5.17	14285	18.35	7085	7200	3782	4.86	1911	1871	1016	979
199	KHAMNOR	34338	52.04	70.37	34.19	245	71	704	2.43	16464	9.55	8436	8028	40401	23.44	20465	19936	952	974
200	KUMBHAL-GARH	27959	46.00	64.96	28.02	198	58	663	3.92	12045	9.17	6098	5947	36079	27.47	18402	17677	975	961
201	RAILMAGRA	21960	54.61	73.21	36.63	117	45	944	4.65	18388	16.65	9212	9176	9777	8.85	4950	4827	996	975
202	RAJSAMAND	26585	54.53	72.84	35.86	152	47	924	3.75	18247	12.99	9296	8951	21256	15.13	10754	10502	963	977
	RAJSAMAND #	**169617**	**51.88**	**71.30**	**33.02**	**1034**	**287**	**746**	**3.70**	**107838**	**12.56**	**54370**	**53468**	**122111**	**14.23**	**62009**	**60102**	**983**	**969**
203	BAMANWAS	22901	58.90	77.18	38.01	194	54	770	3.76	28506	19.08	14941	13565	47450	31.75	25234	22216	908	880
204	BONLI	31682	52.88	72.90	30.71	224	79	937	4.51	38963	18.57	20349	18614	53961	25.72	28424	25537	915	898
205	GANGAPUR	26545	57.37	77.93	33.82	157	64	1141	4.11	39473	22.03	20945	18528	43710	24.39	23469	20241	885	862
206	KHANDAR	26491	43.29	62.84	20.74	168	43	894	8.05	43207	28.78	22991	20216	16687	11.11	9064	7623	879	841
207	SAWAI MADHOPUR	33970	50.64	73.76	25.07	224	88	963	5.50	33241	15.40	17434	15807	70736	32.78	37242	33494	907	899
	SAWAI MADHOPUR	**141589**	**52.64**	**73.13**	**29.52**	**967**	**328**	**935**	**5.14**	**183390**	**20.28**	**96660**	**86730**	**232544**	**25.71**	**123433**	**109111**	**897**	**884**
208	DANTA RAMGARH	38502	69.41	83.40	55.21	280	94	936	3.98	48521	18.51	24977	23544	7174	2.74	3696	3478	943	941
209	DHOND	31763	68.14	84.04	51.97	212	80	990	4.30	37665	17.94	19393	18272	2960	1.41	1502	1458	942	971
210	FATEHPUR	30799	74.01	86.51	61.78	166	83	1166	7.45	34919	18.05	17888	17031	1461	0.76	760	701	952	922
211	KHANDELA	31455	66.56	81.81	51.05	204	84	1071	3.84	27169	12.43	14066	13103	11092	5.08	5640	5452	932	967
212	LACHHMAN-GARH	30554	74.17	86.96	61.34	206	79	956	4.99	36035	18.29	18633	17402	1520	0.77	806	714	934	886
213	NEEM KA THANA	44933	67.05	81.89	51.12	274	99	1157	4.33	42270	13.33	21891	20379	21130	6.66	11047	10083	931	913
214	PIPRALI	30592	69.39	84.74	53.52	212	78	972	3.76	31168	15.13	16094	15074	4686	2.27	2468	2218	937	899
215	SRI MADHOPUR	29037	72.35	85.31	58.91	167	65	1263	3.39	26392	12.51	13787	12605	7807	3.70	4074	3733	914	916
	SIKAR	**267635**	**69.86**	**84.10**	**55.27**	**1721**	**662**	**1055**	**4.43**	**284139**	**15.65**	**146729**	**137410**	**57830**	**3.19**	**29993**	**27837**	**936**	**928**
216	ABU ROAD	20320	43.03	58.67	26.12	95	35	1209	9.03	6258	5.45	3259	2999	76526	66.65	38864	37662	920	969
217	PINDWARA	34012	52.03	67.99	35.35	121	48	1527	9.41	20476	11.08	10552	9924	72986	39.49	36819	36167	940	982
218	REODAR	31861	47.97	64.96	30.01	144	46	1218	7.55	58325	33.26	30361	27964	20375	11.62	10609	9766	921	921
219	SHEOGANJ	19375	49.03	65.12	32.61	80	35	1246	11.15	19443	19.51	10165	9278	18205	18.27	9553	8652	913	906
220	SIROHI	24563	48.50	67.35	30.54	109	45	1152	10.00	30126	23.99	15602	14524	9093	7.24	4826	4267	931	884
	SIROHI	**130131**	**48.51**	**65.19**	**31.29**	**549**	**209**	**1275**	**9.23**	**134628**	**19.23**	**69939**	**64689**	**197185**	**28.16**	**100671**	**96514**	**925**	**959**
221	DEOLI	30142	45.69	66.25	23.65	176	45	962	7.02	33556	19.82	17333	16223	37149	21.95	19244	17905	936	930
222	MALPURA	27856	46.77	65.82	26.58	216	62	819	6.66	33644	19.02	17310	16334	6713	3.79	3498	3215	944	919
223	NIWAI	24439	50.63	70.54	28.94	227	59	728	4.54	36144	21.87	18959	17185	31712	19.18	16486	15226	906	924
224	TODARAISINGH	18019	52.55	71.55	32.65	132	49	834	7.47	22400	20.34	11532	10868	8951	8.13	4639	4312	942	930
225	TONK	31343	45.15	66.81	21.91	237	82	862	5.97	45362	22.20	23368	21994	21976	10.75	11463	10513	941	917
226	UNIARA	21813	46.43	68.17	22.81	178	50	744	5.54	22210	16.76	11555	10655	36698	27.69	19327	17371	922	899
	TONK	**153612**	**47.52**	**67.90**	**25.66**	**1166**	**347**	**822**	**6.08**	**193316**	**20.17**	**100057**	**93259**	**143199**	**14.94**	**74657**	**68542**	**932**	**918**
227	BARGAON	25146	65.86	80.59	50.29	138	44	897	4.70	8517	6.88	4444	4073	45233	36.54	23073	22160	917	960
228	BHINDER	40961	60.32	76.30	44.25	243	72	831	4.05	17043	8.44	8646	8397	40000	19.82	20282	19718	971	972
229	DHARIAWAD	38677	35.10	51.65	18.57	260	64	783	4.53	8125	3.99	4110	4015	167950	82.49	84123	83827	977	996
230	GIRWA	43928	56.83	73.40	39.60	230	74	990	5.87	10004	4.39	5199	4805	127293	55.92	64682	62611	924	968
231	GOGUNDA	30133	49.69	66.85	32.27	161	58	941	5.41	12375	8.16	6322	6053	67696	44.66	34557	33139	957	959
232	JHADOL	37648	58.70	73.92	43.08	281	59	690	5.08	4767	2.46	2454	2313	135152	69.73	68022	67130	943	987
233	KHERWARA	44216	55.27	75.01	35.82	286	88	889	3.76	10005	3.93	5034	4971	200645	78.90	100085	100560	987	1005
234	KOTRA	31449	24.21	36.96	11.11	258	43	711	4.62	1869	1.02	971	898	163903	89.32	82550	81353	925	985
235	MAVLI	38978	53.40	71.27	35.27	209	72	929	3.82	19580	10.09	10027	9553	37314	19.22	19181	18133	953	945
236	SALUMBAR	38233	56.53	72.90	40.90	251	77	783	3.67	8669	4.41	4360	4309	111040	56.48	55322	55718	988	1007
237	SARADA	39909	54.42	73.37	36.12	261	74	813	4.13	8280	3.90	4146	4134	135588	63.90	67548	68040	997	1007
	UDAIPUR	**409278**	**51.94**	**68.64**	**35.14**	**2578**	**725**	**831**	**4.47**	**109234**	**5.10**	**55713**	**53521**	**1231814**	**57.48**	**619425**	**612389**	**961**	**989**
	RAJASTHAN	**7054434**	**55.34**	**72.16**	**37.33**	**45755**	**15055**	**946**	**7.33**	**7739926**	**17.88**	**4042156**	**3697770**	**6717830**	**15.52**	**3445719**	**3272111**	**915**	**950**

Note: * Dungargarh PS shifted from Churu to Bikaner district on 1st April 2001 ** Excluding data of Dungargarh PS; *** Including data of Dungargarh PS.
Came in force from April, 1991; ## Came in force from July 1994 ### Came in force from July 1997.

Source: 1. Primary Census Abstract, Rajasthan, Series-9, Census of India, 2001.
2. Computed from "Village Directory", (CD 35) and "PCA" CD Directrate of Census Operations, Rajasthan, 2001.

ANNEX-K2

RANKING OF PSS BY TOTAL NO. OF HOUSE HOLDS : RAJASTHAN (2001)

(Descending Order)

RANK	PANCHAYAT SAMITIES P. CODE	NAME	NO.
1	2	3	4
	VERY HIGH (>=50,000)		
1	117	**HANUMANGARH**	101573
2	109	**ANUPGARH**	68240
3	162	**OSIAN**	61230
4	118	**NOHAR**	57744
5	66	**BIKANER**	55163
6	140	**SANCHORE**	52070
	HIGH (40,000-50,000)		
7	74	**TALERA**	45298
8	213	**NEEM KA THANA**	44933
9	90	**RAJGARH**	44535
10	233	**KHERWARA**	44216
11	230	**GIRWA**	43928
12	108	**SIMALWARA**	42960
13	26	**GHATOL**	42274
14	25	**GARHI**	41741
15	176	**DIDWANA**	41334
16	228	**BHINDER**	40961
17	105	**BICHHIWARA**	40921
18	38	**BALOTRA**	40695
19	7	**PISANGAN**	40448
	MEDIUM (30,000-40,000)		
20	122	**DUDU**	39936
21	237	**SARADA**	39909
22	95	**BANDIKUI**	39385
23	235	**MAVLI**	38978
24	178	**KUCHAMAN**	38869
25	229	**DHARIAWAD**	38677
26	208	**DANTA RAMGARH**	38502
27	67	**MANDALGARH**	38493
28	155	**HINDAUN**	38368
29	236	**SALUMBAR**	38233
30	96	**DAUSA**	38145
31	42	**DHORIMANNA**	38020
32	39	**BARMER**	37995
33	60	**MANDAL**	37954
34	232	**JHADOL**	37648
35	87	**PRATAPGARH**	37466
36	30	**TALWARA**	37348
37	102	**DHAULPUR**	37193
38	116	**BHADRA**	37179
39	93	**SUJANGARH**	37175
40	70	**NOKHA**	36938
41	55	**ASIND**	36844
42	41	**CHOHTAN**	36824
43	155	**UDAIPURWATI**	36122
44	21	**TIJARA**	35,919
45	123	**GOVINDGARH**	35914
46	104	**ASPUR**	35901
47	107	**SAGWARA**	35749
48	44	**SINDHARI**	35677
49	189	**MARWAR JUN.**	35505
50	124	**JAMWA RAMGARH**	35352
51	97	**LALSOT**	35323
52	119	**AMBER**	35308
53	168	**SAPOTRA**	35264
54	160	**LUNI**	35031
55	144	**JHALRAPATAN**	34824
56	177	**JAYAL**	34701
57	186	**BALI**	34653
58	115	**SURATGARH**	34516
59	45	**SIWANA**	34396
60	199	**KHAMNOR**	34338
61	141	**SAYLA**	34222
62	217	**PINDWARA**	34012
63	207	**SAWAI MADHOPUR**	33970
64	166	**KARAULI**	33789
64	188	**JAITARAN**	33789
66	191	**RAIPUR**	33763
67	153	**NAWALGARH**	33600
68	158	**BHOPALGARH**	33454
69	82	**CHITTAURGARH**	33433
70	149	**BUHANA**	33399
71	71	**HINDOLI**	33332
72	135	**AHORE**	33325
73	152	**KHETRI**	33236
74	51	**NAGAR PAHARI**	33042
75	14	**LACHHMANGARH**	33037
76	163	**PHALODI**	32943
77	136	**KOTPUTLI**	32937
78	92	**SARDARSHAHAR**	32881
79	40	**BAYTOO**	32846
80	183	**NAGAUR**	32544
81	99	**SIKRAI**	32339
82	18	**RAMGARH**	32265
83	65	**SUWANA**	32032
84	120	**BASSI**	31950
85	22	**UMREN**	31909
86	218	**REODAR**	31861
87	52	**RUPBAS**	31818
88	209	**DHOND**	31763
89	204	**BONLI**	31682
90	58	**JAHAZPUR**	31496
91	175	**DEGANA**	31477
92	211	**KHANDELA**	31455
93	234	**KOTRA**	31449
94	225	**TONK**	31343
95	106	**DUNGARPUR**	31210
96	159	**BILARA**	31042
97	9	**BANSURE**	31023
98	69	**LUNKARANSAR**	30980
99	72	**KESHORAIPATAN**	30945
100	210	**FATEHPUR**	30799
101	68	**KOLAYAT**	30686
102	214	**PIPRALI**	30592
103	185	**RIYAN**	30577
104	212	**LACHHMANGARH**	30554
105	182	**MUNDWA**	30523
106	110	**GANGANAGAR**	30484
107	11	**KATHUMAR**	30473
108	181	**MERTA**	30379
109	48	**KAMAN**	30357
110	15	**MANDAWAR**	30194
111	221	**DEOLI**	30142
112	231	**GOGUNDA**	30133
	LOW (20,000-30,000)		
113	54	**WEIR**	29994
114	194	**SOJAT**	29817
115	24	**BAGIDORA**	29814
116	180	MAKRANA	29661
117	101	BASERI	29300
118	151	JHUNJHUNUN	29229
119	215	SRI MADHOPUR	29037
120	131	VIRATNAGAR	28970
121	147	PIRAWA	28933
122	3	JAWAJA	28917
123	184	PARBATSAR	28897
124	136	BHINMAL	28891
125	46	BAYANA	28877
126	169	TODABHIM	28806
127	6	MASOODA	28734
128	146	MANOHARTHANA	28582
129	128	SAMBHAR	28435
129	154	SURAJGARH	28435
131	20	THANAGAZI	28427
132	143	DAG	28419
133	43	SHEO	28343
134	59	KOTRI	28264
135	8	SRINAGAR	28069
136	200	KUMBHALGARH	27959
137	222	MALPURA	27856
138	171	ITAWA	27585
139	73	NAINWA	27303
140	103	RAJAKHERA	26979
141	28	PEEPALKHOONT	26953
142	98	MAHWA	26905
143	64	SHAHPURA	26641
144	2	BHINAY	26606
145	202	RAJSAMAND	26585
146	205	GANGAPUR	26545
147	197	BHIM	26514
148	195	SUMERPUR	26504
149	206	KHANDAR	26491
150	142	BAKANI	26269
151	156	BALESAR	26009
152	139	RANIWARA	25806
153	113	RAISINGHNAGAR	25763
154	86	NIMBAHERA	25753
155	134	SANKRA	25371
156	4	KEKRI	25367
157	145	KHANPUR	25215
158	227	DARGAON	25146
159	174	SULTANPUR	25123
160	220	SIROHI	24563
161	67	DUNGARGARH	24540
162	130	SHAHPURA	24536
163	53	SEWAR	24530
164	12	KISHANGARH BAS	24518
165	91	RATANGARH	24449
166	164	SHERGARH	24440
167	223	NIWAI	24439
168	172	LADPURA	24244
169	150	CHIRAWA	24179
170	170	CHECHAT	24139
171	5	KISHANGARH	24123
172	89	CHURU	24101
173	31	ANTA	24071
174	114	SADULSHAHAR	23957
175	173	SANGOD	23894
176	50	NADBAI	23774
177	94	TARANAGAR	23707
178	16	NIMRANA	23682
179	179	LADNU	23591
180	133	SAM	23315
181	161	MANDOR	23082
182	148	ALSISAR	23056
183	137	JALOR	22911
184	203	BAMANWAS	22901
185	49	KUMHER	22866
186	127	PHAGI	22713
187	47	DEEG	22678
188	36	KISHANGANJ	22462
189	121	CHAKSU	22294
190	29	SAJJANGARH	22275
191	138	JASWANTPURA	22232
192	27	KUSHALGARH	22120
193	17	RAJGARH	22109
194	75	ARNOD	22074
195	100	BARI	22055
196	157	BAP	22001
197	201	RAILMAGRA	21960
198	78	BHADESAR	21889
199	226	UNIARA	21813
200	132	JAISALMER	21808
201	10	BEHROR	21796
202	35	CHHIPABAROD	21781
203	1	ARAIN	21481
204	32	ATRU	21010
205	192	RANI STATION	20830
206	77	BEGUN	20653
207	112	PADAMPUR	20330
208	216	ABU ROAD	20320
209	187	DESURI	20172
210	19	RENI	20027
211	56	BANERA	20019
	VERY LOW (< 20,000)		
212	81	CHHOTI SADRI	19688
213	63	SAHARA	19477
214	219	SHEOGANJ	19375
215	83	DUNGLA	18711
216	167	NADOTI	18650
217	37	SHAHBAD	18578
218	13	KOTKASIM	18465
219	76	BARI SADRI	18335
220	23	ANANDPURI	18293
221	224	TODARAISINGH	18019
222	84	GANGRAR	17905
223	85	KAPASAN	17880
224	111	KARANPUR	17790
225	129	SANGANER	17548
226	190	PALI	17064
227	193	ROHAT	16923
228	57	HURDA	16760
229	33	BARAN	16730
230	196	AMET	16600
231	34	CHHABRA	16583
232	62	RAIPUR	16132
233	79	BHAINSRORGARH	16004
234	198	DEOGARH	15661
235	88	RASHMI	15230
236	80	BHOPALSAGAR	15104
237	125	JHOTWARA	11998
RAJASTHAN		**TOTAL**	**7054434**
		AVERAGE	**29766**
		%age of AAPs	**48.52**

BOLD: Equal/Above Average Panchayat Samities (AAPs)

Source: Annex K1, Col. 3.

ANNEX-K3

RANKING OF PSS BY LITERACY RATE : RAJASTHAN (2001)

(Descending Order)

RANK	PANCHAYAT SAMITIES P. CODE	NAME	L.R.%
1	2	3	4
	VERY HIGH (>=60)		
1	**155**	**UDAIPURWATI**	**77.06**
2	**149**	**BUHANA**	**76.75**
3	**151**	**JHUNJHUNUN**	**75.66**
4	**16**	**NIMRANA**	**74.44**
5	**212**	**LACHHMANGARH**	**74.17**
6	**150**	**CHIRAWA**	**74.16**
7	**210**	**FATEHPUR**	**74.01**
8	**3**	**JAWAJA**	**73.85**
9	**148**	**ALSISAR**	**73.64**
10	**215**	**SRI MADHOPUR**	**72.35**
11	**165**	**HINDAUN**	**71.93**
12	**10**	**BEHROR**	**71.88**
13	**94**	**TARANAGAR**	**71.57**
14	**90**	**RAJGARH**	**71.51**
15	**126**	**KOTPUTLI**	**71.20**
16	**154**	**SURAJGARH**	**69.95**
17	**208**	**DANTA RAMGARH**	**69.41**
18	**214**	**PIPRALI**	**69.39**
19	**174**	**SULTANPUR**	**69.22**
20	**13**	**KOTKASIM**	**69.12**
21	**153**	**NAWALGARH**	**69.07**
22	**173**	**SANGOD**	**68.64**
23	**15**	**MANDAWAR**	**68.63**
24	**209**	**DHOND**	**68.14**
25	**170**	**CHECHAT**	**67.36**
26	**53**	**SEWAR**	**67.30**
27	**52**	**RUPBAS**	**67.26**
28	**131**	**VIRATNAGAR**	**67.24**
29	**50**	**NADBAI**	**67.16**
30	**213**	**NEEM KA THANA**	**67.05**
31	**42**	**DHORIMANNA**	**66.91**
32	**49**	**KUMHER**	**66.83**
33	**211**	**KHANDELA**	**66.56**
34	**116**	**BHADRA**	**66.45**
35	**89**	**CHURU**	**66.21**
36	**128**	**SAMBHAR**	**66.16**
37	**152**	**KHETRI**	**65.97**
38	**227**	**BARGAON**	**65.86**
39	**123**	**GOVINDGARH**	**65.53**
40	**125**	**JHOTWARA**	**65.44**
41	**95**	**BANDIKUI**	**65.40**
42	**145**	**KHANPUR**	**65.35**
43	**147**	**PIRAWA**	**64.70**
43	**172**	**LADPURA**	**64.70**
45	**91**	**RATANGARH**	**64.67**
46	**113**	**RAISINGHNAGAR**	**64.66**
47	**167**	**NADOTI**	**64.55**
48	**33**	**BARAN**	**64.49**
49	**130**	**SHAHPURA**	**64.38**
50	**98**	**MAHWA**	**64.19**
51	**31**	**ANTA**	**62.90**
52	**110**	**GANGANAGAR**	**62.80**
53	**112**	**PADAMPUR**	**62.73**
54	**114**	**SADULSHAHAR**	**62.49**
55	**32**	**ATRU**	**62.41**
56	**118**	**NOHAR**	**62.27**
57	**124**	**JAMWA RAMGARH**	**62.21**
58	**176**	**DIDWANA**	**62.16**
59	**171**	**ITAWA**	**61.76**
60	**93**	**SUJANGARH**	**61.67**
61	**54**	**WEIR**	**61.37**
62	**101**	**BASERI**	**61.30**
63	**129**	**SANGANER**	**61.26**
64	**99**	**SIKRAI**	**61.25**
65	**111**	**KARANPUR**	**61.23**
66	**169**	**TODABHIM**	**60.98**
67	**178**	**KUCHAMAN**	**60.80**
68	**44**	**SINDHARI**	**60.58**
69	**180**	**MAKRANA**	**60.43**
70	**228**	**BHINDER**	**60.32**
71	**127**	**PHAGI**	**60.28**
	HIGH (50-60)		
72	**179**	**LADNU**	**59.47**
73	**92**	**SARDARSHAHAR**	**59.20**
74	**119**	**AMBER**	**59.17**
75	**203**	**BAMANWAS**	**58.90**
76	**45**	**SIWANA**	**58.76**
77	**102**	**DHAULPUR**	**58.73**
78	**232**	**JHADOL**	**58.70**
79	**11**	**KATHUMAR**	**58.51**
80	**40**	**BAYTOO**	**58.45**
81	**120**	**BASSI**	**58.14**
82	**47**	**DEEG**	**58.03**
83	**51**	**NAGAR PAHARI**	**57.88**
84	**109**	**ANUPGARH**	**57.73**
85	**96**	**DAUSA**	**57.69**
86	**67**	**DUNGARGARH**	**57.58**
87	**9**	**BANSURE**	**57.57**
88	**115**	**SURATGARH**	**57.48**
89	**117**	**HANUMANGARH**	**57.39**
90	**205**	**GANGAPUR**	**57.37**
91	**168**	**SAPOTRA**	**57.30**
92	**103**	**RAJAKHERA**	**57.20**
93	**43**	**SHEO**	**57.01**
94	**46**	**BAYANA**	**56.92**
95	**230**	**GIRWA**	**56.83**
96	**236**	**SALUMBAR**	**56.53**
97	**100**	**BARI**	**56.46**
98	**166**	**KARAULI**	**56.45**
99	**19**	**RENI**	**56.41**
100	**144**	**JHALRAPATAN**	**56.33**
101	**197**	**BHIM**	**56.10**
102	**72**	**KESHORAIPATAN**	**55.95**
103	**122**	**DUDU**	**55.85**
104	**184**	**PARBATSAR**	**55.58**
105	233	KHERWARA	55.27
106	12	KISHANGARH BAS	55.06
107	201	RAILMAGRA	54.61
108	202	RAJSAMAND	54.53
109	237	SARADA	54.42
110	6	MASOODA	54.35
111	38	BALOTRA	54.31
112	86	NIMBAHERA	54.29
113	17	RAJGARH	54.23
114	14	LACHHMANGARH	54.05
115	181	MERTA	53.75
116	39	BARMER	53.69
116	160	LUNI	53.69
118	235	MAVLI	53.40
119	97	LALSOT	53.17
120	175	DEGANA	52.99
121	21	TIJARA	52.93
122	22	UMREN	52.92
123	204	BONLI	52.88
124	34	CHHABRA	52.86
125	195	SUMERPUR	52.85
126	25	GARHI	52.59
127	7	PISANGAN	52.57
128	224	TODARAISINGH	52.55
129	18	RAMGARH	52.38
130	5	KISHANGARH	52.26
131	87	PRATAPGARH	52.24
132	199	KHAMNOR	52.01
133	192	RANI STATION	52.04
134	217	PINDWARA	52.03
135	36	KISHANGANJ	51.98
135	74	TALERA	51.98
137	135	AHORE	51.91
138	194	SOJAT	51.89
139	37	SHAHBAD	51.73
140	8	SRINAGAR	51.51
141	81	CHHOTI SADRI	51.44
142	185	RIYAN	51.43
143	57	HURDA	51.24
144	121	CHAKSU	51.22
145	107	SAGWARA	51.14
146	177	JAYAL	50.83
147	193	ROHAT	50.72
148	80	BHOPALSAGAR	50.69
149	187	DESURI	50.66
150	207	SAWAI MADHOPUR	50.64
151	223	NIWAI	50.63
152	73	NAINWA	50.56
153	41	CHOHTAN	50.36
154	82	CHITTAURGARH	50.26
	MEDIUM (40-50)		
155	56	BANERA	49.99
156	159	BILARA	49.93
157	191	RAIPUR	49.80
158	231	GOGUNDA	49.69
159	189	MARWAR JUN.	49.55
160	186	BALI	49.48
161	183	NAGAUR	49.34
162	161	MANDOR	49.13
163	198	DEOGARH	49.09
164	219	SHEOGANJ	49.03
165	77	BEGUN	48.71
166	196	AMET	48.59
167	35	CHHIPABAROD	48.57
168	220	SIROHI	48.50
169	58	JAHAZPUR	48.12
170	134	SANKRA	48.04
171	190	PALI	48.02
172	218	REODAR	47.97
173	83	DUNGLA	47.85
174	132	JAISALMER	47.84
175	20	THANAGAZI	47.47
176	78	BHADESAR	47.41
177	139	RANIWARA	47.32
178	48	KAMAN	47.24
179	4	KEKRI	47.16
180	71	HINDOLI	46.81
181	222	MALPURA	46.77
181	75	ARNOD	46.77
183	84	GANGRAR	46.70
184	106	DUNGARPUR	46.54
185	226	UNIARA	46.43
186	158	BHOPALGARH	46.35
187	163	PHALODI	46.30
188	1	ARAIN	46.19
189	79	BHAINSRORGARH	46.16
190	188	JAITARAN	46.08
191	200	KUMBHALGARH	46.00
192	30	TALWARA	45.88
193	105	BICHHIWARA	45.84
194	140	SANCHORE	45.79
195	143	DAG	45.71
196	221	DEOLI	45.69
197	137	JALOR	45.54
198	65	SUWANA	45.53
199	146	MANOHARTHANA	45.24
200	225	TONK	45.15
201	85	KAPASAN	44.82
202	76	BARI SADRI	44.77
203	104	ASPUR	44.71
204	133	SAM	44.33
205	182	MUNDWA	44.25
206	63	SAHARA	44.19
207	157	BAP	44.07
208	88	RASHMI	43.96
209	162	OSIAN	43.41
210	61	MANDALGARH	43.38
211	206	KHANDAR	43.29
212	60	MANDAL	43.18
213	216	ABU ROAD	43.03
214	2	BHINAY	42.69
215	156	BALESAR	42.67
216	62	RAIPUR	42.65
217	64	SHAHPURA	42.63
218	108	SIMALWARA	42.60
219	142	BAKANI	42.16
220	55	ASIND	41.60
221	141	SAYLA	41.58
222	164	SHERGARH	41.09
223	23	ANANDPURI	40.92
224	26	GHATOL	40.90
225	24	BAGIDORA	40.84
226	138	JASWANTPURA	40.50
	LOW (30-40)		
227	136	BHINMAL	39.92
228	59	KOTRI	39.26
229	29	SAJJANGARH	37.34
230	229	DHARIAWAD	35.10
231	27	KUSHALGARH	33.40
232	69	LUNKARANSAR	30.01
	VERY LOW (<30)		
233	66	BIKANER	29.92
234	70	NOKHA	28.22
235	28	PEEPALKHOONT	28.01
236	68	KOLAYAT	24.28
237	234	KOTRA	24.21
		RAJASTHAN	**55.34**
		%age of AAPs	**43.88**

BOLD: Equal/Above Average Panchayat Samities (AAPs)

Source: Annex K1, Col. 4.

ANNEX-K4

RANKING OF PSS BY MALE LITERACY RATE : RAJASTHAN (2001)

(Descending Order)

RANK	PANCHAYAT SAMITIES P. CODE	NAME	M L R %
1	2	3	4
	VERY HIGH (>=80)		
1	3	**JAWAJA**	**90.22**
2	149	**BUHANA**	**89.15**
3	151	**JHUNJHUNUN**	**89.14**
4	16	**NIMRANA**	**88.55**
5	10	**BEHROR**	**87.60**
6	150	**CHIRAWA**	**87.13**
7	212	**LACHHMANGARH**	**86.96**
8	155	**UDAIPURWATI**	**86.60**
9	210	**FATEHPUR**	**86.51**
10	148	**ALSISAR**	**86.06**
11	165	**HINDAUN**	**85.53**
12	53	**SEWAR**	**85.43**
13	215	**SRI MADHOPUR**	**85.31**
14	49	**KUMHER**	**84.90**
15	153	**NAWALGARH**	**84.84**
16	50	**NADBAI**	**84.80**
17	214	**PIPRALI**	**84.74**
18	13	**KOTKASIM**	**84.65**
19	15	**MANDAWAR**	**84.39**
20	52	**RUPBAS**	**84.25**
21	209	**DHOND**	**84.04**
22	154	**SURAJGARH**	**83.86**
23	173	**SANGOD**	**83.69**
24	174	**SULTANPUR**	**83.64**
25	208	**DANTA RAMGARH**	**83.40**
26	90	**RAJGARH**	**83.01**
27	123	**GOVINDGARH**	**82.87**
28	126	**KOTPUTLI**	**82.58**
29	145	**KHANPUR**	**82.38**
30	98	**MAHWA**	**81.98**
31	213	**NEEM KA THANA**	**81.89**
32	170	**CHECHAT**	**81.84**
33	211	**KHANDELA**	**81.81**
34	33	**BARAN**	**81.50**
35	128	**SAMBHAR**	**81.43**
36	94	**TARANAGAR**	**81.32**
37	95	**BANDIKUI**	**81.31**
38	167	**NADOTI**	**81.12**
38	152	**KHETRI**	**81.12**
40	131	**VIRATNAGAR**	**81.09**
41	54	**WEIR**	**80.88**
42	130	**SHAHPURA**	**80.80**
43	125	**JHOTWARA**	**80.64**
44	227	**BARGAON**	**80.59**
45	197	**BHIM**	**80.27**
46	169	**TODABHIM**	**80.21**
	HIGH (70-80)		
47	32	**ATRU**	**79.96**
48	147	**PIRAWA**	**79.94**
49	116	**BHADRA**	**79.81**
50	31	**ANTA**	**79.64**
51	89	**CHURU**	**79.59**
52	172	**LADPURA**	**79.12**
53	124	**JAMWA RAMGARH**	**79.06**
54	176	**DIDWANA**	**79.03**
55	129	**SANGANER**	**78.64**
56	119	**AMBER**	**78.43**
57	99	**SIKRAI**	**78.14**
58	120	**BASSI**	**77.99**
58	91	**RATANGARH**	**77.99**
60	205	**GANGAPUR**	**77.93**
61	171	**ITAWA**	**77.67**
62	96	**DAUSA**	**77.53**
63	179	**LADNU**	**77.22**
64	203	**BAMANWAS**	**77.18**
65	178	**KUCHAMAN**	**77.00**
66	11	**KATHUMAR**	**76.92**
67	101	**BASERI**	**76.77**
68	42	**DHORIMANNA**	**76.76**
69	180	**MAKRANA**	**76.56**
70	47	**DEEG**	**76.54**
71	46	**BAYANA**	**76.39**
72	228	**BHINDER**	**76.30**
73	51	**NAGAR PAHARI**	**75.86**
74	113	**RAISINGHNAGAR**	**75.80**
75	6	**MASOODA**	**75.67**
76	127	**PHAGI**	**75.65**
77	19	**RENI**	**75.57**
78	86	**NIMBAHERA**	**75.46**
79	118	**NOHAR**	**75.43**
80	102	**DHAULPUR**	**75.33**
81	93	**SUJANGARH**	**75.10**

RANK	PANCHAYAT SAMITIES P. CODE	NAME	M L R %
1	2	3	4
82	233	**KHERWARA**	**75.01**
83	114	**SADULSHAHAR**	**74.75**
84	92	**SARDARSHAHAR**	**74.51**
85	9	**BANSURE**	**74.37**
86	112	**PADAMPUR**	**74.21**
86	168	**SAPOTRA**	**74.21**
88	110	**GANGANAGAR**	**74.14**
89	166	**KARAULI**	**74.10**
90	232	**JHADOL**	**73.92**
91	144	**JHALRAPATAN**	**73.89**
92	122	**DUDU**	**73.76**
92	17	**RAJGARH**	**73.76**
92	207	**SAWAI MADHOPUR**	**73.76**
95	44	**SINDHARI**	**73.72**
96	67	**DUNGARGARH**	**73.40**
96	230	**GIRWA**	**73.40**
98	237	**SARADA**	**73.37**
99	45	**SIWANA**	**73.33**
100	72	**KESHORAIPATAN**	**73.32**
101	201	**RAILMAGRA**	**73.21**
102	14	**LACHHMANGARH**	**73.16**
103	103	**RAJAKHERA**	**73.03**
104	236	**SALUMBAR**	**72.90**
104	204	**BONLI**	**72.90**
106	12	**KISHANGARH BAS**	**72.87**
107	202	**RAJSAMAND**	**72.84**
108	97	**LALSOT**	**72.77**
109	160	**LUNI**	**72.57**
110	181	**MERTA**	**72.56**
111	7	**PISANGAN**	**72.30**
111	194	**SOJAT**	**72.30**
113	40	BAYTOO	72.13
114	100	BARI	71.99
115	8	SRINAGAR	71.91
116	111	KARANPUR	71.78
116	43	SHEO	71.78
118	224	TODARAISINGH	71.55
119	22	UMREN	71.47
120	184	PARBATSAR	71.44
121	121	CHAKSU	71.39
122	235	MAVLI	71.27
123	34	CHHABRA	71.00
124	18	RAMGARH	70.81
125	175	DEGANA	70.79
126	38	BALOTRA	70.69
127	81	CHHOTI SADRI	70.56
128	223	NIWAI	70.54
129	193	ROHAT	70.38
130	199	KHAMNOR	70.37
131	195	SUMERPUR	70.32
132	159	BILARA	70.32
133	21	TIJARA	70.19
134	185	RIYAN	70.10
135	191	RAIPUR	70.02
	MEDIUM (60-70)		218
136	5	KISHANGARH	69.99
136	107	SAGWARA	69.99
138	109	ANUPGARH	69.95
139	117	HANUMANGARH	69.88
140	57	HURDA	69.79
141	115	SURATGARH	69.76
142	161	MANDOR	69.72
143	73	NAINWA	69.51
144	80	BHOPALSAGAR	69.36
145	25	GARHI	69.28
146	192	RANI STATION	69.04
147	135	AHORE	68.96
148	177	JAYAL	68.90
149	189	MARWAR JUN.	68.87
150	39	BARMER	68.85
151	87	PRATAPGARH	68.66
152	37	SHAHBAD	68.27
153	198	DEOGARH	68.26
154	82	CHITTAURGARH	68.21
155	226	UNIARA	68.17
156	187	DESURI	68.06
157	77	BEGUN	68.02
158	217	PINDWARA	67.99
159	158	BHOPALGARH	67.86
160	74	TALERA	67.82
161	35	CHHIPABAROD	67.74
162	83	DUNGLA	67.53
163	4	KEKRI	67.52

RANK	PANCHAYAT SAMITIES P. CODE	NAME	M L R %
1	2	3	4
164	56	BANERA	67.49
165	220	SIROHI	67.35
166	36	KISHANGANJ	67.34
167	183	NAGAUR	67.22
168	190	PALI	66.89
169	231	GOGUNDA	66.85
170	20	THANAGAZI	66.83
171	225	TONK	66.81
172	196	AMET	66.69
173	221	DEOLI	66.25
174	106	DUNGARPUR	66.24
175	78	BHADESAR	66.02
176	222	MALPURA	65.82
177	58	JAHAZPUR	65.74
178	70	NOKHA	65.68
179	48	KAMAN	65.61
180	186	BALI	65.43
181	188	JAITARAN	65.42
182	219	SHEOGANJ	65.12
183	84	GANGRAR	65.01
184	218	REODAR	64.96
184	200	KUMBHALGARH	64.96
186	139	RANIWARA	64.82
187	30	TALWARA	64.61
188	76	BARI SADRI	64.56
189	85	KAPASAN	64.53
190	140	SANCHORE	64.34
191	163	PHALODI	64.30
192	65	SUWANA	64.13
193	134	SANKRA	64.04
194	71	HINDOLI	64.00
195	162	OSIAN	63.72
196	88	RASHMI	63.68
197	132	JAISALMER	63.62
198	156	BALESAR	63.56
198	137	JALOR	63.56
200	105	BICHHIWARA	63.51
201	41	CHOHTAN	63.50
202	182	MUNDWA	63.47
203	1	ARAIN	63.46
204	75	ARNOD	63.45
205	63	SAHARA	63.25
206	143	DAG	62.95
207	2	BHINAY	62.88
207	146	MANOHARTHANA	62.88
209	206	KHANDAR	62.84
210	104	ASPUR	62.74
211	79	BHAINSRORGARH	62.63
212	60	MANDAL	61.99
213	62	RAIPUR	61.89
214	66	BIKANER	61.20
215	157	BAP	61.01
216	55	ASIND	60.92
217	69	LUNKARANSAR	60.87
164	SHERGARH		60.65
219	133	SAM	60.39
	LOW (50-60)		
220	141	SAYLA	59.88
221	138	JASWANTPURA	59.58
222	136	BHINMAL	59.55
223	64	SHAHPURA	59.49
224	108	SIMALWARA	59.36
225	61	MANDALGARH	59.15
226	142	BAKANI	59.13
227	216	ABU ROAD	58.67
228	26	GHATOL	58.65
229	24	BAGIDORA	57.46
230	23	ANANDPURI	56.43
231	68	KOLAYAT	55.22
232	59	KOTRI	55.09
233	29	SAJJANGARH	53.11
234	229	DHARIAWAD	51.65
	VERY LOW (<50)		
235	27	KUSHALGARH	48.50
236	28	PEEPALKHOONT	41.72
237	234	KOTRA	36.96
		RAJASTHAN	**72.16**
		%age of AAPs	**47.26**

BOLD: Equal/Above Average Panchayat Samities (AAPs)

Source: Annex K1, Col. 5.

ANNEX-K5

RANKING OF PSS BY FEMALE LITERACY RATE : RAJASTHAN (2001)

(Descending Order)

RANK	PANCHAYAT SAMITIES P. CODE	PANCHAYAT SAMITIES NAME	FLR %
1	2	3	4
		VERY HIGH (>=60)	
1	155	**UDAIPURWATI**	67.32
2	149	**BUHANA**	63.91
3	151	**JHUNJHUNUN**	62.21
4	210	**FATEHPUR**	61.78
5	148	**ALSISAR**	61.41
6	212	**LACHHMANGARH**	61.34
7	94	**TARANAGAR**	61.27
8	150	**CHIRAWA**	60.96
		HIGH (45-60)	
9	16	**NIMRANA**	59.47
10	90	**RAJGARH**	59.34
11	215	**SRI MADHOPUR**	58.91
12	126	**KOTPUTLI**	58.79
13	3	**JAWAJA**	57.54
14	42	**DHORIMANNA**	55.99
15	165	**HINDAUN**	55.72
16	154	**SURAJGARH**	55.27
17	208	**DANTA RAMGARH**	55.21
18	10	**BEHROR**	55.03
19	214	**PIPRALI**	53.52
20	174	**SULTANPUR**	53.43
21	153	**NAWALGARH**	53.18
22	113	**RAISINGHNAGAR**	52.62
23	89	**CHURU**	52.50
24	173	**SANGOD**	52.25
25	13	**KOTKASIM**	52.20
26	209	**DHOND**	51.97
27	131	**VIRATNAGAR**	51.95
28	15	**MANDAWAR**	51.72
29	116	**BHADRA**	51.66
30	91	**RATANGARH**	51.29
31	170	**CHECHAT**	51.23
32	213	**NEEM KA THANA**	51.12
33	211	**KHANDELA**	51.05
34	227	**BARGAON**	50.29
35	112	**PADAMPUR**	50.25
36	110	**GANGANAGAR**	50.18
37	152	**KHETRI**	50.11
38	128	**SAMBHAR**	49.83
39	111	**KARANPUR**	49.65
40	125	**JHOTWARA**	48.72
41	172	**LADPURA**	48.66
42	147	**PIRAWA**	48.44
43	114	**SADULSHAHAR**	48.20
44	93	**SUJANGARH**	47.98
45	95	**BANDIKUI**	47.71
46	118	**NOHAR**	47.70
47	52	**RUPBAS**	47.00
48	123	**GOVINDGARH**	46.73
49	145	**KHANPUR**	46.63
50	44	**SINDHARI**	46.35
51	130	**SHAHPURA**	46.16
52	167	**NADOTI**	45.98
53	50	**NADBAI**	45.89
54	53	**SEWAR**	45.85
55	33	**BARAN**	45.65
56	49	**KUMHER**	45.61
57	176	**DIDWANA**	45.33
		MEDIUM (30-45)	
58	31	**ANTA**	44.67
59	228	**BHINDER**	44.25
60	109	**ANUPGARH**	44.08
61	171	**ITAWA**	44.06
62	98	**MAHWA**	43.80
63	180	**MAKRANA**	43.77
64	178	**KUCHAMAN**	43.59
65	124	**JAMWA RAMGARH**	43.58
66	127	**PHAGI**	43.55
67	117	**HANUMANGARH**	43.54
68	40	**BAYTOO**	43.28
69	92	**SARDARSHAHAR**	43.22
70	232	**JHADOL**	43.08
71	32	**ATRU**	42.99
72	45	**SIWANA**	42.96
73	115	**SURATGARH**	42.64
74	99	**SIKRAI**	42.54
75	129	**SANGANER**	42.28
76	101	**BASERI**	42.27
77	179	**LADNU**	41.49
78	67	**DUNGARGARH**	40.95
79	236	**SALUMBAR**	40.90
80	230	**GIRWA**	39.60
81	43	**SHEO**	39.41
82	9	**BANSURE**	39.01
83	184	**PARBATSAR**	38.87
84	102	**DHAULPUR**	38.64
85	169	**TODABHIM**	38.63
86	54	**WEIR**	38.12
87	203	**BAMANWAS**	38.01
88	119	**AMBER**	37.85
89	103	**RAJAKHERA**	37.46
90	144	**JHALRAPATAN**	37.36
91	51	NAGAR PAHARI	37.25
92	11	KATHUMAR	37.16
93	168	SAPOTRA	37.11
94	72	KESHORAIPATAN	36.90
95	201	RAILMAGRA	36.63
96	122	DUDU	36.60
97	100	BARI	36.55
98	38	BALOTRA	36.52
99	120	BASSI	36.30
100	237	SARADA	36.12
101	192	RANI STATION	36.11
102	47	DEEG	36.04
103	202	RAJSAMAND	35.86
104	233	KHERWARA	35.82
105	195	SUMERPUR	35.69
106	25	GARHI	35.63
107	96	DAUSA	35.61
108	135	AHORE	35.59
109	39	BARMER	35.53
110	12	KISHANGARH BAS	35.42
111	217	PINDWARA	35.35
112	235	MAVLI	35.27
113	87	PRATAPGARH	35.16
113	166	KARAULI	35.16
115	36	KISHANGANJ	35.12
116	175	DEGANA	35.09
117	41	CHOHTAN	34.99
118	187	DESURI	34.67
119	19	RENI	34.60
120	74	TALERA	34.44
121	199	KHAMNOR	34.19
122	107	SAGWARA	34.11
123	186	BALI	33.98
124	205	GANGAPUR	33.82
125	181	MERTA	33.55
126	5	KISHANGARH	33.34
127	160	LUNI	33.32
128	37	SHAHBAD	33.16
129	197	BHIM	33.00
130	86	NIMBAHERA	32.73
131	224	TODARAISINGH	32.65
132	219	SHEOGANJ	32.61
133	21	TIJARA	32.57
133	14	LACHHMANGARH	32.57
135	34	CHHABRA	32.45
136	46	BAYANA	32.40
137	80	BHOPALSAGAR	32.33
138	231	GOGUNDA	32.27
139	17	RAJGARH	32.22
140	177	JAYAL	32.12
141	56	BANERA	32.11
142	6	MASOODA	32.03
143	194	SOJAT	32.02
144	22	UMREN	31.83
145	185	RIYAN	31.82
146	81	CHHOTI SADRI	31.80
147	57	HURDA	31.79
148	82	CHITTAURGARH	31.77
149	7	PISANGAN	31.76
150	18	RAMGARH	31.71
151	97	LALSOT	31.69
152	198	DEOGARH	31.24
153	189	MARWAR JUN.	30.77
154	204	BONLI	30.71
155	196	AMET	30.65
156	193	ROHAT	30.64
157	220	SIROHI	30.54
158	183	NAGAUR	30.53
159	218	REODAR	30.01
159	69	LUNKARANSAR	30.01
		LOW (15-30)	
161	66	BIKANER	29.92
162	73	NAINWA	29.77
163	134	SANKRA	29.71
164	75	ARNOD	29.63
165	8	SRINAGAR	29.56
166	191	RAIPUR	29.51
167	121	CHAKSU	29.24
168	58	JAHAZPUR	29.18
169	190	PALI	28.99
170	223	NIWAI	28.94
171	77	BEGUN	28.76
172	139	RANIWARA	28.71
173	83	DUNGLA	28.58
174	78	BHADESAR	28.57
175	104	ASPUR	28.48
176	105	BICHHIWARA	28.31
177	1	ARAIN	28.27
178	70	NOKHA	28.22
179	159	BILARA	28.10
180	84	GANGRAR	28.07
181	200	KUMBHALGARH	28.02
182	132	JAISALMER	27.90
183	106	DUNGARPUR	27.89
184	79	BHAINSRORGARH	27.88
185	137	JALOR	27.76
186	71	HINDOLI	27.68
187	35	CHHIPABAROD	27.65
188	143	DAG	27.50
189	30	TALWARA	26.73
189	63	SAHARA	26.73
191	222	MALPURA	26.58
192	163	PHALODI	26.53
193	161	MANDOR	26.50
194	65	SUWANA	26.34
195	188	JAITARAN	26.32
196	61	MANDALGARH	26.22
196	48	KAMAN	26.22
198	216	ABU ROAD	26.12
199	140	SANCHORE	26.09
200	146	MANOHARTHANA	26.00
201	4	KEKRI	25.99
202	20	THANAGAZI	25.92
203	108	SIMALWARA	25.85
204	60	MANDAL	25.23
205	76	BARI SADRI	25.20
206	157	BAP	25.14
207	85	KAPASAN	25.12
208	207	SAWAI MADHOPUR	25.07
209	88	RASHMI	24.92
210	64	SHAHPURA	24.86
211	23	ANANDPURI	24.72
212	62	RAIPUR	24.48
213	68	KOLAYAT	24.28
214	182	MUNDWA	24.07
215	24	BAGIDORA	23.99
216	142	BAKANI	23.83
217	158	BHOPALGARH	23.69
218	221	DEOLI	23.65
219	133	SAM	23.56
220	141	SAYLA	23.14
221	26	GHATOL	23.13
222	55	ASIND	22.89
223	226	UNIARA	22.81
224	59	KOTRI	22.66
225	225	TONK	21.91
226	138	JASWANTPURA	21.77
227	2	DHINAY	21.71
228	162	OSIAN	21.40
229	29	SAJJANGARH	21.07
230	206	KHANDAR	20.74
231	136	BHINMAL	20.07
232	156	BALESAR	19.77
233	164	SHERGARH	19.24
234	229	DHARIAWAD	18.57
235	27	KUSHALGARH	18.00
		VERY LOW (<15)	
236	28	PEEPALKHOONT	13.74
237	234	KOTRA	11.11
		RAJASTHAN	**37.33**
		%age of AAPs	**37.97**

BOLD: Equal/Above Average Panchayat Samities (AAPs)

Source: Annex K1, Col. 6.

ANNEX-K6

RANKING OF PSS BY GENDER GAP IN LITERACY RATE : RAJASTHAN (2001)

(Descending Order)

RANK	PANCHAYAT SAMITIES P. CODE	NAME	MLF-FLR
1	2	3	4
	VERY HIGH (>=40)		
1	207	**SAWAI MADHOPUR**	48.68
2	197	**BHIM**	47.27
3	226	**UNIARA**	45.36
4	225	**TONK**	44.90
5	158	**BHOPALGARH**	44.18
6	205	**GANGAPUR**	44.12
7	46	**BAYANA**	43.99
8	156	**BALESAR**	43.79
9	6	**MASOODA**	43.64
10	161	**MANDOR**	43.22
11	54	**WEIR**	42.76
12	86	**NIMBAHERA**	42.75
13	221	**DEOLI**	42.60
14	8	**SRINAGAR**	42.35
15	162	**OSIAN**	42.32
16	159	**BILARA**	42.22
17	204	**BONLI**	42.19
18	121	**CHAKSU**	42.15
19	206	**KHANDAR**	42.10
20	96	**DAUSA**	41.92
21	120	**BASSI**	41.70
22	223	**NIWAI**	41.60
23	169	**TODABHIM**	41.58
24	17	**RAJGARH**	41.54
25	4	**KEKRI**	41.52
26	164	**SHERGARH**	41.41
27	2	**BHINAY**	41.18
28	97	**LALSOT**	41.08
29	19	**RENI**	40.97
30	20	**THANAGAZI**	40.91
31	14	**LACHHMANGARH**	40.58
31	119	**AMBER**	40.58
33	7	**PISANGAN**	40.54
34	191	**RAIPUR**	40.52
35	47	**DEEG**	40.50
36	194	**SOJAT**	40.28
37	35	**CHHIPABAROD**	40.09
	HIGH (35-40)		
38	11	**KATHUMAR**	39.76
39	73	**NAINWA**	39.74
39	193	**ROHAT**	39.74
41	22	**UMREN**	39.63
42	53	**SEWAR**	39.57
43	136	**BHINMAL**	39.48
44	85	**KAPASAN**	39.41
45	182	**MUNDWA**	39.40
46	48	**KAMAN**	39.39
47	76	**BARI SADRI**	39.36
48	49	**KUMHER**	39.29
49	77	**BEGUN**	39.26
50	160	**LUNI**	39.25
51	222	**MALPURA**	39.24
52	233	**KHERWARA**	39.18
53	203	**BAMANWAS**	39.17
54	188	**JAITARAN**	39.10
54	18	**RAMGARH**	39.10
56	181	**MERTA**	39.01
57	166	**KARAULI**	38.95
57	83	**DUNGLA**	38.95
59	50	**NADBAI**	38.91
60	224	**TODARAISINGH**	38.89
61	81	**CHHOTI SADRI**	38.76
61	88	**RASHMI**	38.76
63	51	**NAGAR PAHARI**	38.61
64	34	**CHHABRA**	38.55
65	106	**DUNGARPUR**	38.35
66	185	**RIYAN**	38.28
67	140	**SANCHORE**	38.25
68	98	**MAHWA**	38.18
69	189	**MARWAR JUN.**	38.10
70	55	**ASIND**	38.03
71	57	**HURDA**	38.00
72	190	**PALI**	37.90
73	30	**TALWARA**	37.88
74	138	**JASWANTPURA**	37.81
75	65	**SUWANA**	37.79
76	163	**PHALODI**	37.77
77	21	**TIJARA**	37.61
78	70	**NOKHA**	37.46
79	78	**BHADESAR**	37.45
79	12	**KISHANGARH BAS**	37.45
81	62	**RAIPUR**	37.41
82	237	**SARADA**	37.25
82	52	**RUPBAS**	37.25
84	122	**DUDU**	37.16
85	168	**SAPOTRA**	37.10
86	80	**BHOPALSAGAR**	37.03
87	198	**DEOGARH**	37.02
88	202	**RAJSAMAND**	36.99
89	32	**ATRU**	36.97
90	84	**GANGRAR**	36.94
91	200	**KUMBHALGARH**	36.93
92	146	**MANOHARTHANA**	36.87
93	133	**SAM**	36.82
94	220	**SIROHI**	36.80
95	177	**JAYAL**	36.78
96	60	**MANDAL**	36.76
97	141	**SAYLA**	36.74
98	183	**NAGAUR**	36.70
98	102	**DHAULPUR**	36.70
100	5	**KISHANGARH**	36.65
101	201	**RAILMAGRA**	36.59
102	58	**JAHAZPUR**	36.56
103	144	**JHALRAPATAN**	36.53
104	63	**SAHARA**	36.52
105	82	**CHITTAURGARH**	36.44
106	72	**KESHORAIPATAN**	36.43
107	129	**SANGANER**	36.36
108	71	**HINDOLI**	36.32
109	199	**KHAMNOR**	36.18
110	123	**GOVINDGARH**	36.14
111	139	**RANIWARA**	36.10
112	196	**AMET**	36.04
113	235	**MAVLI**	36.00
114	157	**BAP**	35.87
114	107	**SAGWARA**	35.87
116	33	**BARAN**	35.84
117	137	**JALOR**	35.80
118	145	**KHANPUR**	35.76
119	179	**LADNU**	35.73
120	132	**JAISALMER**	35.72
121	175	**DEGANA**	35.70
122	99	**SIKRAI**	35.60
123	103	**RAJAKHERA**	35.57
124	26	**GHATOL**	35.52
125	124	**JAMWA RAMGARH**	35.48
126	143	**DAG**	35.45
127	100	**BARI**	35.44
128	56	**BANERA**	35.38
129	9	**BANSURE**	35.36
130	142	**BAKANI**	35.29
131	105	**BICHHIWARA**	35.20
132	1	**ARAIN**	35.18
133	167	**NADOTI**	35.14
134	37	**SHAHBAD**	35.11
	MEDIUM (30-35)		
135	31	**ANTA**	34.97
136	218	**REODAR**	34.95
137	79	BHAINSRORGARH	34.75
138	130	SHAHPURA	34.64
139	195	SUMERPUR	34.63
139	64	SHAHPURA	34.63
141	231	GOGUNDA	34.58
142	101	BASERI	34.50
143	134	SANKRA	34.33
144	104	ASPUR	34.26
145	38	BALOTRA	34.18
146	75	ARNOD	33.82
147	230	GIRWA	33.80
148	176	DIDWANA	33.70
149	25	GARHI	33.65
150	171	ITAWA	33.60
150	95	BANDIKUI	33.60
152	108	SIMALWARA	33.51
152	87	PRATAPGARH	33.51
154	24	BAGIDORA	33.48
155	178	KUCHAMAN	33.41
156	187	DESURI	33.39
157	74	TALERA	33.38
158	135	AHORE	33.37
159	39	BARMER	33.32
160	229	DHARIAWAD	33.09
161	61	MANDALGARH	32.93
161	192	RANI STATION	32.93
163	180	MAKRANA	32.79
164	3	JAWAJA	32.68
164	15	MANDAWAR	32.68
166	217	PINDWARA	32.63
167	10	BEHROR	32.58
168	184	PARBATSAR	32.56
168	216	ABU ROAD	32.56
170	219	SHEOGANJ	32.51
171	67	DUNGARGARH	32.46
172	13	KOTKASIM	32.45
173	59	KOTRI	32.44
174	43	SHEO	32.36
175	36	KISHANGANJ	32.22
176	127	PHAGI	32.10
177	209	DHOND	32.07
178	228	BHINDER	32.05
179	29	SAJJANGARH	32.04
180	236	SALUMBAR	32.00
181	125	JHOTWARA	31.92
182	23	ANANDPURI	31.71
183	153	NAWALGARH	31.66
184	128	SAMBHAR	31.61
185	147	PIRAWA	31.50
186	186	BALI	31.44
186	173	SANGOD	31.44
188	92	SARDARSHAHAR	31.29
189	66	BIKANER	31.28
190	214	PIPRALI	31.22
191	152	KHETRI	31.01
192	68	KOLAYAT	30.94
193	69	LUNKARANSAR	30.86
194	232	JHADOL	30.84
195	213	NEEM KA THANA	30.77
196	211	KHANDELA	30.76
197	170	CHECHAT	30.60
198	27	KUSHALGARH	30.51
199	172	LADPURA	30.47
200	45	SIWANA	30.37
201	227	BARGAON	30.29
202	174	SULTANPUR	30.21
	LOW (25-30)		
203	165	HINDAUN	29.82
204	131	VIRATNAGAR	29.13
205	16	NIMRANA	29.08
206	40	BAYTOO	28.86
207	154	SURAJGARH	28.59
208	41	CHOHTAN	28.51
209	208	DANTA RAMGARH	28.18
210	116	BHADRA	28.14
211	28	PEEPALKHOONT	27.98
212	118	NOHAR	27.73
213	44	SINDHARI	27.38
214	115	SURATGARH	27.12
215	93	SUJANGARH	27.11
216	89	CHURU	27.09
217	151	JHUNJHUNUN	26.93
218	91	RATANGARH	26.69
219	114	SADULSHAHAR	26.56
220	215	SRI MADHOPUR	26.40
221	117	HANUMANGARH	26.34
222	150	CHIRAWA	26.17
223	109	ANUPGARH	25.87
224	234	KOTRA	25.85
225	212	LACHHMANGARH	25.62
226	149	BUHANA	25.24
	VERY LOW (<25)		
227	210	FATEHPUR	24.73
228	148	ALSISAR	24.65
229	112	PADAMPUR	23.96
229	110	GANGANAGAR	23.96
231	126	KOTPUTLI	23.79
232	90	RAJGARH	23.67
233	113	RAISINGHNAGAR	23.18
234	111	KARANPUR	22.13
235	42	DHORIMANNA	20.77
236	94	TARANAGAR	20.06
237	155	UDAIPURWATI	19.28
		RAJASTHAN	**34.83**
		%age of AAPs	**57.38**

BOLD: Equal/Above Average Panchayat Samities (AAPs)

Source: Computed from data given in Annex K1, Col. 5 and 6.

ANNEX-K7

RANKING OF PSS BY NO OF PRIMARY SCHOOLS : RAJASTHAN (2001)

(Descending Order)

RANK	PANCHAYAT SAMITIES P. CODE	NAME	NO. OF RAJASTHAN
1	2	3	4
	VERY HIGH (>=300)		
1	**109**	**ANUPGARH**	**593**
2	**117**	**HANUMANGARH**	**562**
3	**40**	**BAYTOO**	**355**
4	**44**	**SINDHARI**	**349**
5	**39**	**BARMER**	**345**
6	**108**	**SIMALWARA**	**337**
7	**162**	**OSIAN**	**325**
8	**118**	**NOHAR**	**314**
9	**38**	**BALOTRA**	**308**
10	**42**	**DHORIMANNA**	**306**
11	**87**	**PRATAPGARH**	**300**
	HIGH (250-300)		
12	**113**	**RAISINGHNAGAR**	**294**
13	**96**	**DAUSA**	**292**
14	**178**	**KUCHAMAN**	**288**
15	**102**	**DHAULPUR**	**287**
16	**233**	**KHERWARA**	**286**
17	**232**	**JHADOL**	**281**
18	**208**	**DANTA RAMGARH**	**280**
19	**26**	**GHATOL**	**278**
20	**97**	**LALSOT**	**277**
21	**213**	**NEEM KA THANA**	**274**
22	**30**	**TALWARA**	**268**
22	**41**	**CHOHTAN**	**268**
22	**90**	**RAJGARH**	**268**
25	**66**	**BIKANER**	**266**
25	**140**	**SANCHORE**	**266**
27	**74**	**TALERA**	**265**
28	**168**	**SAPOTRA**	**261**
28	**237**	**SARADA**	**261**
30	**229**	**DHARIAWAD**	**260**
31	**234**	**KOTRA**	**258**
32	**124**	**JAMWA RAMGARH**	**254**
32	**144**	**JHALRAPATAN**	**254**
34	**25**	**GARHI**	**252**
35	**122**	**DUDU**	**251**
35	**236**	**SALUMBAR**	**251**
	MEDIUM (200-250)		
37	**95**	**BANDIKUI**	**247**
38	**43**	**SHEO**	**246**
38	**51**	**NAGAR PAHARI**	**246**
38	**183**	**NAGAUR**	**246**
41	**199**	**KHAMNOR**	**245**
42	**134**	**SANKRA**	**244**
43	**228**	**BHINDER**	**243**
44	**120**	**BASSI**	**242**
45	**115**	**SURATGARH**	**241**
46	**163**	**PHALODI**	**240**
47	**55**	**ASIND**	**237**
47	**61**	**MANDALGARH**	**237**
47	**225**	**TONK**	**237**
50	**153**	**NAWALGARH**	**236**
51	**146**	**MANOHARTHANA**	**234**
52	**119**	**AMBER**	**233**
53	**60**	**MANDAL**	**232**
53	**105**	**BICHHIWARA**	**232**
53	**110**	**GANGANAGAR**	**232**
56	**230**	**GIRWA**	**230**
57	**121**	**CHAKSU**	**229**
58	**165**	**HINDAUN**	**227**
58	**223**	**NIWAI**	**227**
60	**107**	**SAGWARA**	**226**
61	**204**	**BONLI**	**224**
61	**207**	**SAWAI MADHOPUR**	**224**
63	**155**	**UDAIPURWATI**	**223**
63	**176**	**DIDWANA**	**223**
65	**151**	**JHUNJHUNUN**	**221**
66	**72**	**KESHORAIPATAN**	**220**
66	**152**	**KHETRI**	**220**
68	**106**	**DUNGARPUR**	**218**
69	**166**	**KARAULI**	**217**
70	**222**	**MALPURA**	**216**
71	**70**	**NOKHA**	**215**
72	**126**	**KOTPUTLI**	**214**
72	**133**	**SAM**	**214**
74	**14**	**LACHHMANGARH**	**213**
75	**3**	**JAWAJA**	**212**
75	**209**	**DHOND**	**212**
75	**214**	**PIPRALI**	**212**
78	**149**	**BUHANA**	**211**
79	**104**	**ASPUR**	**210**
80	**7**	**PISANGAN**	**209**
80	**9**	**BANSURE**	**209**
80	**58**	**JAHAZPUR**	**209**
80	**235**	**MAVLI**	**209**
84	**27**	**KUSHALGARH**	**208**
85	**21**	**TIJARA**	**207**
85	**103**	**RAJAKHERA**	**207**
87	**82**	**CHITTAURGARH**	**206**
87	**212**	**LACHHMANGARH**	**206**
88	**211**	**KHANDELA**	**204**
89	**112**	**PADAMPUR**	**203**
89	**123**	**GOVINDGARH**	**203**
89	**173**	**SANGOD**	**203**
92	**48**	**KAMAN**	**202**
92	**101**	**BASERI**	**202**
94	**116**	**BHADRA**	**200**
	LOW (150-200)		
95	**18**	**RAMGARH**	**199**
95	**73**	**NAINWA**	**199**
95	**128**	**SAMBHAR**	**199**
95	**200**	**KUMBHALGARH**	**198**
99	**143**	**DAG**	**197**
100	**20**	**THANAGAZI**	**196**
100	**46**	**BAYANA**	**196**
100	**54**	**WEIR**	**196**
100	**147**	**PIRAWA**	**196**
100	**197**	**BHIM**	**196**
105	**24**	**BAGIDORA**	**195**
105	**28**	**PEEPALKHOONT**	**195**
105	**92**	**SARDARSHAHAR**	**195**
108	**160**	**LUNI**	**194**
108	**203**	**BAMANWAS**	**194**
110	**10**	**BEHROR**	**193**
110	**29**	**SAJJANGARH**	**193**
112	22	UMREN	192
112	93	SUJANGARH	192
114	111	KARANPUR	191
115	6	MASOODA	190
115	11	KATHUMAR	190
115	34	CHHABRA	190
115	171	ITAWA	190
119	142	BAKANI	189
120	68	KOLAYAT	187
121	45	SIWANA	186
121	99	SIKRAI	186
121	131	VIRATNAGAR	186
124	127	PHAGI	185
125	59	KOTRI	184
126	191	RAIPUR	181
127	174	SULTANPUR	180
128	100	BARI	179
128	169	TODABHIM	179
130	53	SEWAR	178
130	226	UNIARA	178
132	15	MANDAWAR	177
132	64	SHAHPURA	177
132	98	MAHWA	177
132	175	DEGANA	177
136	65	SUWANA	176
136	221	DEOLI	176
138	177	JAYAL	175
139	148	ALSISAR	174
140	52	RUPBAS	173
140	71	HINDOLI	173
140	158	BHOPALGARH	173
140	186	BALI	173
144	69	LUNKARANSAR	172
145	132	JAISALMER	171
146	184	PARBATSAR	170
146	189	MARWAR JUN.	170
148	145	KHANPUR	168
148	206	KHANDAR	168
150	215	SRI MADHOPUR	167
151	77	BEGUN	166
151	210	FATEHPUR	166
153	172	LADPURA	164
154	182	MUNDWA	163
155	114	SADULSHAHAR	162
155	180	MAKRANA	162
157	154	SURAJGARH	161
157	231	GOGUNDA	161
159	12	KISHANGARH BAS	158
160	5	KISHANGARH	157
160	205	GANGAPUR	157
162	156	BALESAR	156
163	23	ANANDPURI	155
163	159	BILARA	155
165	2	BHINAY	153
165	31	ANTA	153
165	185	RIYAN	153
168	202	RAJSAMAND	152
169	47	DEEG	151
170	1	ARAIN	150
170	129	SANGANER	150
	VERY LOW (<150)		
172	86	NIMBAHERA	149
172	150	CHIRAWA	149
174	50	NADBAI	148
175	36	KISHANGANJ	147
175	37	SHAHBAD	147
175	130	SHAHPURA	147
178	75	ARNOD	146
179	49	KUMHER	145
180	78	BHADESAR	145
181	135	AHORE	144
181	218	REODAR	144
183	35	CHHIPABAROD	143
183	94	TARANAGAR	143
185	17	RAJGARH	142
185	32	ATRU	142
187	181	MERTA	141
188	161	MANDOR	140
188	170	CHECHAT	140
190	89	CHURU	139
191	8	SRINAGAR	138
191	13	KOTKASIM	138
191	91	RATANGARH	138
191	227	BARGAON	138
195	4	KEKRI	137
195	81	CHHOTI SADRI	137
197	16	NIMRANA	136
198	167	NADOTI	135
198	188	JAITARAN	135
198	194	SOJAT	135
201	67	DUNGARGARH	134
202	224	TODARAISINGH	132
203	157	BAP	131
204	196	AMET	129
205	19	RENI	127
205	139	RANIWARA	127
207	56	BANERA	126
207	136	BHINMAL	126
207	164	SHERGARH	126
210	179	LADNU	124
211	217	PINDWARA	121
212	63	SAHARA	119
212	141	SAYLA	119
214	79	BHAINSRORGARH	117
214	201	RAILMAGRA	117
216	57	HURDA	116
217	84	GANGRAR	114
217	198	DEOGARH	114
219	76	BARI SADRI	113
220	62	RAIPUR	111
221	85	KAPASAN	110
222	220	SIROHI	109
223	33	BARAN	102
224	83	DUNGLA	101
224	137	JALOR	101
224	187	DESURI	101
224	192	RANI STATION	101
228	190	PALI	99
229	216	ABU ROAD	95
230	125	JHOTWARA	94
231	80	BHOPALSAGAR	91
232	193	ROHAT	85
233	195	SUMERPUR	84
234	138	JASWANTPURA	83
235	219	SHEOGANJ	80
236	88	RASHMI	75
RAJASTHAN		**TOTAL**	**45755**
		AVERAGE	**193**
		% AGE OF AAPs	**46**

BOLD: Equal/Above Average Panchayat Samities (AAPs)

Source: Annex K1, Col. 7.

ANNEX-K8

RANKING OF PSS BY POPULATION SERVED PER PRIMARY SCHOOL : RAJASTHAN (2001)

(Descending Order)

RANK	PANCHAYAT SAMITIES P. CODE	PANCHAYAT SAMITIES NAME	POP.
1	2	3	4
	VERY HIGH (>=1500)		
1	141	SAYLA	1774
2	195	SUMERPUR	1643
3	138	JASWANTPURA	1547
4	217	PINDWARA	1527
	HIGH (1250-1500)		
5	136	BHINMAL	1466
6	66	BIKANER	1409
7	188	JAITARAN	1385
8	67	DUNGARGARH	1364
9	123	GOVINDGARH	1359
10	93	SUJANGARH	1319
11	137	JALOR	1305
12	181	MERTA	1301
13	70	NOKHA	1299
13	162	OSIAN	1299
15	164	SHERGARH	1291
16	139	RANIWARA	1286
16	140	SANCHORE	1286
18	177	JAYAL	1285
19	176	DIDWANA	1278
20	179	LADNU	1274
21	69	LUNKARANSAR	1264
22	215	SRI MADHOPUR	1263
	MEDIUM (1000-1250)		
23	219	SHEOGANJ	1246
24	130	SHAHPURA	1235
25	8	SRINAGAR	1233
25	180	MAKRANA	1233
27	135	AHORE	1232
28	52	RUPBAS	1221
29	218	REODAR	1218
30	182	MUNDWA	1212
31	216	ABU ROAD	1209
32	193	ROHAT	1207
33	157	BAP	1201
34	160	LUNI	1181
35	185	RIYAN	1174
36	158	BHOPALGARH	1169
37	210	FATEHPUR	1166
38	118	NOHAR	1165
38	159	BILARA	1165
40	213	NEEM KA THANA	1157
41	165	HINDAUN	1156
42	22	UMREN	1155
42	194	SOJAT	1155
44	220	SIROHI	1152
45	45	SIWANA	1149
46	91	RATANGARH	1146
47	92	SARDARSHAHAR	1143
48	205	GANGAPUR	1141
49	99	SIKRAI	1139
50	7	PISANGAN	1131
51	119	AMBER	1125
52	117	HANUMANGARH	1118
53	156	BALESAR	1117
54	15	MANDAWAR	1116
55	11	KATHUMAR	1114
56	68	KOLAYAT	1111
57	131	VIRATNAGAR	1110
58	18	RAMGARH	1107
59	116	BHADRA	1103
60	184	PARBATSAR	1097
61	21	TIJARA	1096
62	89	CHURU	1095
63	71	HINDOLI	1094
64	154	SURAJGARH	1092
65	50	NADBAI	1089
66	122	DUDU	1086
67	169	TODABHIM	1084
68	95	BANDIKUI	1081
69	161	MANDOR	1080
70	19	RENI	1075
71	175	DEGANA	1074
72	211	KHANDELA	1071
73	49	KUMHER	1070
74	126	KOTPUTLI	1068
75	189	MARWAR JUN.	1067
76	186	BALI	1062
77	14	LACHHMANGARH	1060
77	12	KISHANGARH BAS	1060
79	94	TARANAGAR	1056
80	155	UDAIPURWATI	1055

RANK	PANCHAYAT SAMITIES P. CODE	PANCHAYAT SAMITIES NAME	POP.
1	2	3	4
81	192	RANI STATION	1054
81	16	NIMRANA	1054
83	128	SAMBHAR	1053
84	48	KAMAN	1050
85	54	WEIR	1032
86	4	KEKRI	1029
87	166	KARAULI	1026
87	150	CHIRAWA	1026
87	9	BANSURE	1026
87	47	DEEG	1026
91	17	RAJGARH	1019
92	105	BICHHIWARA	1018
93	2	BHINAY	1014
94	187	DESURI	1012
94	98	MAHWA	1012
96	33	BARAN	1011
97	191	RAIPUR	1006
98	88	RASHMI	1004
	LOW (750-1000)		
99	101	BASERI	999
100	90	RAJGARH	998
101	209	DHOND	990
101	230	GIRWA	990
103	124	JAMWA RAMGARH	985
104	46	BAYANA	978
104	5	KISHANGARH	978
106	74	TALERA	977
107	152	KHETRI	975
108	31	ANTA	972
108	214	PIPRALI	972
110	20	THANAGAZI	969
110	149	BUHANA	969
112	207	SAWAI MADHOPUR	963
113	221	DEOLI	962
114	51	NAGAR PAHARI	961
115	163	PHALODI	958
116	212	LACHHMANGARH	956
117	120	BASSI	949
118	125	JHOTWARA	946
119	201	RAILMAGRA	944
120	170	CHECHAT	943
120	25	GARHI	943
122	53	SEWAR	942
123	231	GOGUNDA	941
124	204	BONLI	937
125	208	DANTA RAMGARH	936
126	167	NADOTI	934
127	65	SUWANA	932
128	96	DAUSA	931
128	178	KUCHAMAN	931
130	235	MAVLI	929
131	103	RAJAKHERA	927
132	202	RAJSAMAND	924
133	153	NAWALGARH	922
134	36	KISHANGANJ	920
135	102	DHAULPUR	914
135	183	NAGAUR	914
137	145	KHANPUR	913
138	86	NIMBAHERA	909
139	190	PALI	908
140	97	LALSOT	907
141	24	BAGIDORA	906
142	114	SADULSHAHAR	905
143	227	BARGAON	897
144	32	ATRU	895
145	35	CHHIPABAROD	894
145	206	KHANDAR	894
147	168	SAPOTRA	891
147	83	DUNGLA	891
149	1	ARAIN	889
149	233	KHERWARA	889
151	115	SURATGARH	885
152	172	LADPURA	882
153	104	ASPUR	879
154	147	PIRAWA	877
155	129	SANGANER	875
156	127	PHAGI	874
157	38	BALOTRA	862
157	225	TONK	862
159	13	KOTKASIM	853
159	107	SAGWARA	853
161	60	MANDAL	851
162	143	DAG	849

RANK	PANCHAYAT SAMITIES P. CODE	PANCHAYAT SAMITIES NAME	POP.
1	2	3	4
163	61	MANDALGARH	844
164	56	BANERA	843
165	41	CHOHTAN	842
165	64	SHAHPURA	842
167	100	BARI	841
168	6	MASOODA	840
169	174	SULTANPUR	837
170	224	TODARAISINGH	834
171	228	BHINDER	831
172	26	GHATOL	829
173	63	SAHARA	824
174	75	ARNOD	821
175	42	DHORIMANNA	820
176	171	ITAWA	819
176	222	MALPURA	819
178	82	CHITTAURGARH	815
179	237	SARADA	813
179	148	ALSISAR	813
181	72	KESHORAIPATAN	812
181	55	ASIND	812
183	144	JHALRAPATAN	811
184	59	KOTRI	808
185	142	BAKANI	806
186	58	JAHAZPUR	803
187	151	JHUNJHUNUN	800
188	80	BHOPALSAGAR	799
189	30	TALWARA	797
190	106	DUNGARPUR	791
191	76	BARI SADRI	786
192	57	HURDA	785
192	73	NAINWA	785
194	236	SALUMBAR	783
194	229	DHARIAWAD	783
196	84	GANGRAR	778
197	28	PEEPALKHOONT	776
198	203	BAMANWAS	770
199	85	KAPASAN	768
200	110	GANGANAGAR	761
201	62	RAIPUR	760
	VERY LOW (<750)		
202	132	JAISALMER	747
203	3	JAWAJA	745
204	226	UNIARA	744
205	78	BHADESAR	741
206	37	SHAHBAD	736
207	81	CHHOTI SADRI	730
208	223	NIWAI	728
209	43	SHEO	726
210	173	SANGOD	724
211	10	BEHROR	723
212	23	ANANDPURI	717
213	108	SIMALWARA	715
214	234	KOTRA	711
215	109	ANUPGARH	704
215	121	CHAKSU	704
215	199	KHAMNOR	704
218	197	BHIM	702
219	29	SAJJANGARH	697
220	39	BARMER	690
220	146	MANOHARTHANA	690
220	232	JHADOL	690
223	79	BHAINSRORGARH	687
224	196	AMET	683
224	198	DEOGARH	683
226	44	SINDHARI	678
226	134	SANKRA	678
228	87	PRATAPGARH	671
229	27	KUSHALGARH	668
230	200	KUMBHALGARH	663
231	133	SAM	648
232	77	BEGUN	615
233	112	PADAMPUR	598
234	40	BAYTOO	593
235	111	KARANPUR	540
236	113	RAISINGHNAGAR	535
237	34	CHHABRA	524
		RAJASTHAN	**946**
		%age of AAPs	**49.79**

BOLD: Equal/Above Average Panchayat Samities (AAPs) *Source*: Annex K1, Col. 9.

ANNEX-K9

RANKING OF PSS BY AREA SERVED PER PRIMARY SCHOOL : RAJASTHAN (2001)

(Descending Order)

RANK	PANCHAYAT SAMITIES P. CODE	NAME	Area (Sq. Kms.)
1	2	3	4
	VERY HIGH (>=10)		
1	133	**SAM**	98.65
2	132	**JAISALMER**	75.14
3	68	**KOLAYAT**	39.14
4	69	**LUNKARANSAR**	36.13
5	157	**BAP**	33.83
6	66	**BIKANER**	33.63
7	43	**SHEO**	26.90
8	134	**SANKRA**	22.49
9	67	**DUNGARGARH**	22.41
10	92	**SARDARSHAHAR**	19.56
11	70	**NOKHA**	17.52
12	193	**ROHAT**	16.52
13	115	**SURATGARH**	15.73
14	164	**SHERGARH**	15.67
15	118	**NOHAR**	13.71
16	93	**SUJANGARH**	13.52
17	163	**PHALODI**	13.49
18	182	**MUNDWA**	13.40
19	190	**PALI**	13.10
20	138	**JASWANTPURA**	12.88
20	162	**OSIAN**	12.88
22	38	**BALOTRA**	12.61
23	94	**TARANAGAR**	12.47
24	141	**SAYLA**	12.26
25	41	**CHOHTAN**	12.19
26	194	**SOJAT**	12.05
27	177	**JAYAL**	11.93
28	91	**RATANGARH**	11.90
29	156	**BALESAR**	11.89
30	79	**BHAINSRORGARH**	11.71
31	140	**SANCHORE**	11.31
32	89	**CHURU**	11.22
33	219	**SHEOGANJ**	11.15
34	135	**AHORE**	11.09
35	179	**LADNU**	11.06
36	39	**BARMER**	11.05
37	195	**SUMERPUR**	10.86
38	45	**SIWANA**	10.66
39	136	**BHINMAL**	10.62
40	137	**JALOR**	10.44
41	160	**LUNI**	10.22
42	158	**BHOPALGARH**	10.08
43	220	**SIROHI**	10.00
	HIGH (7.5-10.0)		
44	37	**SHAHBAD**	9.99
45	181	**MERTA**	9.91
46	36	**KISHANGANJ**	9.87
47	183	**NAGAUR**	9.68
48	159	**BILARA**	9.67
49	188	**JAITARAN**	9.55
50	217	**PINDWARA**	9.41
51	114	**SADULSHAHAR**	9.16
52	40	**BAYTOO**	9.09
53	161	**MANDOR**	9.07
54	216	**ABU ROAD**	9.03
55	44	**SINDHARI**	8.93
56	42	**DHORIMANNA**	8.72
57	116	**BHADRA**	8.57
58	175	**DEGANA**	8.23
59	187	**DESURI**	8.21
60	90	**RAJGARH**	8.20
61	189	**MARWAR JUN.**	8.18
62	185	**RIYAN**	8.10
63	206	**KHANDAR**	8.05
64	1	**ARAIN**	8.01
65	172	**LADPURA**	7.97
66	2	**BHINAY**	7.95
67	186	**BALI**	7.92
68	139	**RANIWARA**	7.75
69	71	**HINDOLI**	7.74
70	192	**RANI STATION**	7.55
70	218	**REODAR**	7.55
72	168	**SAPOTRA**	7.52
	MEDIUM (5.0-7.5)		
73	224	**TODARAISINGH**	7.47
74	210	**FATEHPUR**	7.45
75	122	**DUDU**	7.39
76	4	KEKRI	7.25
77	176	DIDWANA	7.21
78	17	RAJGARH	7.11
79	74	TALERA	7.10
80	5	KISHANGARH	7.05
81	221	DEOLI	7.02
82	180	MAKRANA	6.83
83	222	MALPURA	6.66
84	8	SRINAGAR	6.51
85	64	SHAHPURA	6.37
86	184	PARBATSAR	6.30
87	31	ANTA	6.09
88	32	ATRU	6.05
89	127	PHAGI	6.02
90	33	BARAN	6.01
91	88	RASHMI	6.00
92	109	ANUPGARH	5.98
93	225	TONK	5.97
94	61	MANDALGARH	5.88
95	230	GIRWA	5.87
96	72	KESHORAIPATAN	5.85
97	77	BEGUN	5.77
97	35	CHHIPABAROD	5.77
99	7	PISANGAN	5.76
100	143	DAG	5.74
101	73	NAINWA	5.73
102	166	KARAULI	5.62
103	145	KHANPUR	5.60
104	226	UNIARA	5.54
105	170	CHECHAT	5.51
106	207	SAWAI MADHOPUR	5.50
107	86	NIMBAHERA	5.45
107	191	RAIPUR	5.45
109	231	GOGUNDA	5.41
109	20	THANAGAZI	5.41
111	56	BANERA	5.37
112	57	HURDA	5.32
112	63	SAHARA	5.32
114	144	JHALRAPATAN	5.23
115	198	DEOGARH	5.17
116	59	KOTRI	5.16
117	173	SANGOD	5.15
118	147	PIRAWA	5.11
119	232	JHADOL	5.08
120	174	SULTANPUR	5.07
121	81	CHHOTI SADRI	5.05
	LOW (2.5-5.0)		
122	178	KUCHAMAN	4.99
122	212	LACHHMANGARH	4.99
124	60	MANDAL	4.98
125	101	BASERI	4.96
126	58	JAHAZPUR	4.94
127	83	DUNGLA	4.89
128	84	GANGRAR	4.87
129	154	SURAJGARH	4.85
130	75	ARNOD	4.80
131	167	NADOTI	4.79
132	87	PRATAPGARH	4.76
133	65	SUWANA	4.73
134	227	BARGAON	4.70
135	142	BAKANI	4.69
136	55	ASIND	4.68
136	28	PEEPALKHOONT	4.68
138	171	ITAWA	4.67
139	201	RAILMAGRA	4.65
140	62	RAIPUR	4.64
141	234	KOTRA	4.62
142	6	MASOODA	4.61
143	223	NIWAI	4.54
144	229	DHARIAWAD	4.53
145	204	BONLI	4.51
146	113	RAISINGHNAGAR	4.47
147	100	BARI	4.44
148	22	UMREN	4.42
149	85	KAPASAN	4.39
150	80	BHOPALSAGAR	4.38
151	213	NEEM KA THANA	4.33
152	209	DHOND	4.30
153	148	ALSISAR	4.29
154	111	KARANPUR	4.24
155	76	BARI SADRI	4.20
156	128	SAMBHAR	4.18
157	112	PADAMPUR	4.15
158	237	SARADA	4.13
159	34	CHHABRA	4.12
160	205	GANGAPUR	4.11
161	125	JHOTWARA	4.10
162	46	BAYANA	4.08
163	228	BHINDER	4.05
164	208	DANTA RAMGARH	3.98
164	124	JAMWA RAMGARH	3.98
166	82	CHITTAURGARH	3.95
167	146	MANOHARTHANA	3.94
168	200	KUMBHALGARH	3.92
168	196	AMET	3.92
170	129	SANGANER	3.89
171	211	KHANDELA	3.84
172	235	MAVLI	3.82
173	233	KHERWARA	3.76
173	214	PIPRALI	3.76
173	203	BAMANWAS	3.76
176	202	RAJSAMAND	3.75
177	78	BHADESAR	3.73
177	155	UDAIPURWATI	3.73
179	151	JHUNJHUNUN	3.71
180	110	GANGANAGAR	3.68
181	236	SALUMBAR	3.67
182	117	HANUMANGARH	3.62
182	152	KHETRI	3.62
184	119	AMBER	3.60
185	131	VIRATNAGAR	3.49
186	197	BHIM	3.46
187	215	SRI MADHOPUR	3.39
188	121	CHAKSU	3.35
189	104	ASPUR	3.29
190	150	CHIRAWA	3.28
190	123	GOVINDGARH	3.28
192	15	MANDAWAR	3.26
193	47	DEEG	3.25
194	105	BICHHIWARA	3.22
195	12	KISHANGARH BAS	3.20
196	9	BANSURE	3.18
197	3	JAWAJA	3.12
197	52	RUPBAS	3.12
199	96	DAUSA	3.11
199	21	TIJARA	3.11
201	18	RAMGARH	3.10
201	126	KOTPUTLI	3.10
201	149	BUHANA	3.10
204	19	RENI	3.09
205	97	LALSOT	3.08
205	27	KUSHALGARH	3.08
207	49	KUMHER	3.04
208	11	KATHUMAR	2.97
209	54	WEIR	2.94
210	169	TODABHIM	2.92
210	50	NADBAI	2.92
212	14	LACHHMANGARH	2.91
213	153	NAWALGARH	2.82
213	26	GHATOL	2.82
215	30	TALWARA	2.80
216	25	GARHI	2.79
217	165	HINDAUN	2.78
217	16	NIMRANA	2.78
217	130	SHAHPURA	2.78
220	103	RAJAKHERA	2.76
221	48	KAMAN	2.75
222	108	SIMALWARA	2.71
222	107	SAGWARA	2.71
224	99	SIKRAI	2.70
225	98	MAHWA	2.68
226	24	BAGIDORA	2.64
226	106	DUNGARPUR	2.64
228	120	BASSI	2.61
229	53	SEWAR	2.57
230	51	NAGAR PAHARI	2.53
231	13	KOTKASIM	2.50
	VERY LOW (<2.5)		
232	95	BANDIKUI	2.43
232	199	KHAMNOR	2.43
234	23	ANANDPURI	2.21
235	29	SAJJANGARH	2.09
236	102	DHAULPUR	2.01
237	10	BEHROR	1.74
	RAJASTHAN		**7.33**
	%age of AAPs		**31.65**

BOLD: Equal/Above Average Panchayat Samities (AAPs)

Source: Annex K 1, Col. 10.

ANNEX-K10

RANKING OF PSS BY NO. OF UPPER PRIMARY SCHOOLS : RAJASTHAN (2001)

(Descending Order)

RANK	PANCHAYAT SAMITIES P. CODE	PANCHAYAT SAMITIES NAME	NO.
1	2	3	4
	VERY HIGH (>=100)		
1	117	**HANUMANGARH**	249
2	109	**ANUPGARH**	191
3	118	**NOHAR**	132
4	25	**GARHI**	116
5	162	**OSIAN**	109
6	155	**UDAIPURWATI**	106
7	96	**DAUSA**	104
8	116	**BHADRA**	104
9	149	**BUHANA**	102
	HIGH (80-100)		
10	213	**NEEM KA THANA**	99
11	90	**RAJGARH**	98
11	151	**JHUNJHUNUN**	98
13	165	**HINDAUN**	96
14	208	**DANTA RAMGARH**	94
15	66	**BIKANER**	93
15	124	**JAMWA RAMGARH**	93
17	110	**GANGANAGAR**	91
18	176	**DIDWANA**	90
18	178	**KUCHAMAN**	90
20	26	**GHATOL**	89
21	207	**SAWAI MADHOPUR**	88
21	233	**KHERWARA**	88
23	87	**PRATAPGARH**	85
23	113	**RAISINGHNAGAR**	85
25	93	**SUJANGARH**	84
25	168	**SAPOTRA**	84
25	211	**KHANDELA**	84
28	15	**MANDAWAR**	83
28	122	**DUDU**	83
28	123	**GOVINDGARH**	83
28	152	**KHETRI**	83
28	153	**NAWALGARH**	83
28	210	**FATEHPUR**	83
34	51	**NAGAR PAHARI**	82
34	92	**SARDARSHAHAR**	82
34	108	**SIMALWARA**	82
34	225	**TONK**	82
38	7	**PISANGAN**	81
38	95	**BANDIKUI**	81
38	99	**SIKRAI**	81
41	74	**TALERA**	80
41	102	**DHAULPUR**	80
41	115	**SURATGARH**	80
41	119	**AMBER**	80
41	140	**SANCHORE**	80
41	209	**DHOND**	80
	MEDIUM (60-80)		
47	30	**TALWARA**	79
47	52	**RUPBAS**	79
47	97	**LALSOT**	79
47	204	**BONLI**	79
47	212	**LACHHMANGARH**	79
52	70	**NOKHA**	78
52	214	**PIPRALI**	78
54	38	**BALOTRA**	77
54	40	**BAYTOO**	77
54	89	**CHURU**	77
54	236	**SALUMBAR**	77
58	107	**SAGWARA**	76
58	128	**SAMBHAR**	76
60	10	**BEHROR**	75
60	14	**LACHHMANGARH**	75
60	39	**BARMER**	75
60	126	**KOTPUTLI**	75
64	54	**WEIR**	74
64	130	**SHAHPURA**	74
64	154	**SURAJGARH**	74
64	230	**GIRWA**	74
64	237	**SARADA**	74
69	98	**MAHWA**	73
69	148	**ALSISAR**	73
69	166	**KARAULI**	73
69	183	**NAGAUR**	73
73	9	**BANSURE**	72
73	44	**SINDHARI**	72
73	55	**ASIND**	72
73	69	**LUNKARANSAR**	72
73	228	**BHINDER**	72
73	235	**MAVLI**	72
79	16	**NIMRANA**	71
79	42	**DHORIMANNA**	71
79	199	**KHAMNOR**	71
82	60	**MANDAL**	70
828	72	**KESHORAIPATAN**	70
82	104	**ASPUR**	70
82	111	**KARANPUR**	70
82	169	**TODABHIM**	70
87	20	**THANAGAZI**	69
87	58	**JAHAZPUR**	69
87	91	**RATANGARH**	69
87	186	**BALI**	69
91	11	**KATHUMAR**	68
91	41	**CHOHTAN**	68
91	105	**BICHHIWARA**	68
91	114	**SADULSHAHAR**	68
91	159	**BILARA**	68
96	53	**SEWAR**	67
96	67	**DUNGARGARH**	67
96	103	**RAJAKHERA**	67
96	106	**DUNGARPUR**	67
96	134	**SANKRA**	67
96	144	**JHALRAPATAN**	67
96	160	**LUNI**	67
103	22	**UMREN**	66
103	135	**AHORE**	66
103	158	**BHOPALGARH**	66
103	180	**MAKRANA**	66
103	189	**MARWAR JUN.**	66
108	45	**SIWANA**	65
108	120	**BASSI**	65
108	215	**SRI MADHOPUR**	65
111	205	**GANGAPUR**	64
111	229	**DHARIAWAD**	64
113	82	CHITTAURGARH	63
113	94	TARANAGAR	63
113	131	VIRATNAGAR	63
113	163	PHALODI	63
113	177	JAYAL	63
118	31	ANTA	62
118	46	BAYANA	62
118	112	PADAMPUR	62
118	171	ITAWA	62
118	222	MALPURA	62
123	61	MANDALGARH	61
124	24	BAGIDORA	60
124	127	PHAGI	60
124	173	SANGOD	60
124	174	SULTANPUR	60
	LOW (40-60)		
128	18	RAMGARH	59
128	101	BASERI	59
128	150	CHIRAWA	59
128	184	PARBATSAR	59
128	185	RIYAN	59
128	188	JAITARAN	59
128	223	NIWAI	59
128	232	JHADOL	59
136	2	BHINAY	58
136	65	SUWANA	58
136	147	PIRAWA	58
136	175	DEGANA	58
136	181	MERTA	58
136	200	KUMBHALGARH	58
136	231	GOGUNDA	58
143	68	KOLAYAT	57
144	3	JAWAJA	55
144	17	RAJGARH	55
144	47	DEEG	55
144	48	KAMAN	55
144	49	KUMHER	55
144	73	NAINWA	55
144	167	NADOTI	55
144	194	SOJAT	55
144	197	BHIM	55
153	4	KEKRI	54
153	43	SHEO	54
153	50	NADBAI	54
153	64	SHAHPURA	54
153	133	SAM	54
153	172	LADPURA	54
153	203	BAMANWAS	54
160	1	ARAIN	53
160	6	MASOODA	53
160	21	TIJARA	53
163	8	SRINAGAR	52
163	121	CHAKSU	52
163	182	MUNDWA	52
166	59	KOTRI	51
166	71	HINDOLI	51
166	132	JAISALMER	51
169	161	MANDOR	50
169	226	UNIARA	50
171	5	KISHANGARH	49
171	145	KHANPUR	49
171	224	TODARAISINGH	49
174	19	RENI	48
174	32	ATRU	48
174	217	PINDWARA	48
177	13	KOTKASIM	47
177	141	SAYLA	47
17	179	LADNU	47
177	202	RAJSAMAND	47
181	136	BHINMAL	46
181	143	DAG	46
181	218	REODAR	46
184	37	SHAHBAD	45
184	157	BAP	45
184	192	RANI STATION	45
184	220	SIROHI	45
184	221	DEOLI	45
184	201	RAILMAGRA	45
190	12	KISHANGARH BAS	44
190	36	KISHANGANJ	44
190	77	BEGUN	44
190	100	BARI	44
190	191	RAIPUR	44
190	227	BARGAON	44
196	86	NIMBAHERA	43
196	142	BAKANI	43
196	206	KHANDAR	43
196	234	KOTRA	43
200	23	ANANDPURI	42
200	129	SANGANER	42
200	139	RANIWARA	42
203	28	PEEPALKHOONT	41
203	57	HURDA	41
203	63	SAHARA	41
203	137	JALOR	41
203	156	BALESAR	41
203	164	SHERGARH	41
203	187	DESURI	41
210	78	BHADESAR	40
210	81	CHHOTI SADRI	40
210	170	CHECHAT	40
210	195	SUMERPUR	40
	VERY LOW (<40)		
214	27	KUSHALGARH	39
214	75	ARNOD	39
216	146	MANOHARTHANA	38
217	29	SAJJANGARH	37
218	34	CHHABRA	36
218	56	BANERA	36
218	138	JASWANTPURA	36
221	84	GANGRAR	35
221	216	ABU ROAD	35
221	219	SHEOGANJ	35
224	33	BARAN	34
224	35	CHHIPABAROD	34
224	62	RAIPUR	34
227	85	KAPASAN	32
227	88	RASHMI	32
227	190	PALI	32
227	196	AMET	32
231	76	BARI SADRI	31
231	79	BHAINSRORGARH	31
231	83	DUNGLA	31
234	193	ROHAT	29
235	125	JHOTWARA	28
236	80	BHOPALSAGAR	27
237	198	DEOGARH	24
RAJASTHAN		**TOTAL**	**15055**
		AVERAGE	**63.52**
		% AGE OF AAPs	**47.26**

BOLD: Equal/Above Average Panchayat Samities (AAPs)   *Source*: Annex K1, Col. 8.

ANNEX-K11

RANKING OF PSS BY PERCENTAGE OF SC POPULATION TO TOTAL POPULATION : RAJASTHAN (2001)

(Descending Order)

RANK	PANCHAYAT SAMITIES P. CODE	NAME	%
1	2	3	4
	VERY HIGH (>=25)		
1	**111**	**KARANPUR**	**46.86**
2	**113**	**RAISINGHNAGAR**	**43.64**
3	**109**	**ANUPGARH**	**42.86**
4	**110**	**GANGANAGAR**	**34.44**
5	**114**	**SADULSHAHAR**	**34.20**
6	**112**	**PADAMPUR**	**34.19**
7	**218**	**REODAR**	**33.26**
8	**117**	**HANUMANGARH**	**33.04**
9	**165**	**HINDAUN**	**31.23**
10	**115**	**SURATGARH**	**29.39**
11	**93**	**SUJANGARH**	**29.38**
12	**206**	**KHANDAR**	**28.78**
13	**54**	**WEIR**	**27.90**
13	**46**	**BAYANA**	**27.90**
15	**66**	**BIKANER**	**27.03**
16	**52**	**RUPBAS**	**26.04**
17	**68**	**KOLAYAT**	**25.49**
18	**118**	**NOHAR**	**25.42**
19	**53**	**SEWAR**	**25.41**
20	**50**	**NADBAI**	**25.23**
	HIGH (20-25)		
21	**67**	**DUNGARGARH**	**24.91**
22	**33**	**BARAN**	**24.60**
23	**98**	**MAHWA**	**24.21**
24	**41**	**CHOHTAN**	**24.20**
25	**11**	**KATHUMAR**	**24.10**
26	**220**	**SIROHI**	**23.99**
27	**177**	**JAYAL**	**23.79**
28	**170**	**CHECHAT**	**23.68**
29	**100**	**BARI**	**23.35**
30	**171**	**ITAWA**	**23.32**
31	**90**	**RAJGARH**	**23.27**
32	**89**	**CHURU**	**23.26**
33	**181**	**MERTA**	**23.15**
34	**91**	**RATANGARH**	**23.03**
34	**154**	**SURAJGARH**	**23.03**
36	**143**	**DAG**	**22.98**
37	**180**	**MAKRANA**	**22.95**
37	**92**	**SARDARSHAHAR**	**22.95**
39	**4**	**KEKRI**	**22.76**
40	**22**	**UMREN**	**22.59**
41	**69**	**LUNKARANSAR**	**22.52**
42	**166**	**KARAULI**	**22.49**
43	**174**	**SULTANPUR**	**22.45**
43	**96**	**DAUSA**	**22.45**
45	**99**	**SIKRAI**	**22.41**
46	**225**	**TONK**	**22.20**
47	**175**	**DEGANA**	**22.16**
48	**205**	**GANGAPUR**	**22.03**
49	**70**	**NOKHA**	**22.00**
50	**173**	**SANGOD**	**21.97**
51	**223**	**NIWAI**	**21.87**
52	**94**	**TARANAGAR**	**21.58**
53	**169**	**TODABHIM**	**21.57**
54	**168**	**SAPOTRA**	**21.44**
55	**179**	**LADNU**	**21.43**
56	**194**	**SOJAT**	**21.41**
57	**185**	**RIYAN**	**21.34**
58	**183**	**NAGAUR**	**21.17**
59	**88**	**RASHMI**	**21.05**
59	**97**	**LALSOT**	**21.05**
61	**101**	**BASERI**	**20.92**
62	**116**	**BHADRA**	**20.84**
63	**12**	**KISHANGARH BAS**	**20.79**
64	**159**	**BILARA**	**20.74**
65	**127**	**PHAGI**	**20.59**
66	**158**	**BHOPALGARH**	**20.54**
67	**32**	**ATRU**	**20.46**
68	**224**	**TODARAISINGH**	**20.34**
69	**151**	**JHUNJHUNUN**	**20.26**
70	**2**	**BHINAY**	**20.25**
71	**102**	**DHAULPUR**	**20.15**
72	**141**	**SAYLA**	**20.09**
73	**178**	**KUCHAMAN**	**20.03**
74	**182**	**MUNDWA**	**20.01**
	MEDIUM (15-20)		
75	**190**	**PALI**	**19.92**
76	**5**	**KISHANGARH**	**19.86**
77	**121**	**CHAKSU**	**19.84**
78	**49**	**KUMHER**	**19.83**
79	**221**	**DEOLI**	**19.82**
80	**137**	**JALOR**	**19.80**
81	**193**	**ROHAT**	**19.78**
82	**187**	**DESURI**	**19.72**
83	**64**	**SHAHPURA**	**19.67**
84	**103**	**RAJAKHERA**	**19.59**
84	**148**	**ALSISAR**	**19.59**
86	**219**	**SHEOGANJ**	**19.51**
87	**135**	**AHORE**	**19.50**
88	**176**	**DIDWANA**	**19.49**
89	**188**	**JAITARAN**	**19.48**
90	**95**	**BANDIKUI**	**19.44**
91	**139**	**RANIWARA**	**19.43**
92	**192**	**RANI STATION**	**19.42**
93	**74**	**TALERA**	**19.39**
94	**15**	**MANDAWAR**	**19.35**
95	**13**	**KOTKASIM**	**19.31**
95	**31**	**ANTA**	**19.31**
97	**1**	**ARAIN**	**19.22**
97	**167**	**NADOTI**	**19.22**
99	**120**	**BASSI**	**19.17**
100	**184**	**PARBATSAR**	**19.09**
101	**203**	**BAMANWAS**	**19.08**
102	**19**	**RENI**	**19.06**
103	**222**	**MALPURA**	**19.02**
104	**189**	**MARWAR JUN.**	**19.01**
105	**18**	**RAMGARH**	**18.98**
106	**14**	**LACHHMANGARH**	**18.82**
106	**85**	**KAPASAN**	**18.82**
108	**47**	**DEEG**	**18.74**
109	**204**	**BONLI**	**18.57**
110	**122**	**DUDU**	**18.56**
111	**17**	**RAJGARH**	**18.55**
112	**208**	**DANTA RAMGARH**	**18.51**
113	**129**	**SANGANER**	**18.50**
114	**125**	**JHOTWARA**	**18.41**
115	**198**	**DEOGARH**	**18.35**
116	**212**	**LACHHMANGARH**	**18.29**
117	**84**	**GANGRAR**	**18.19**
118	**65**	**SUWANA**	**18.15**
119	**210**	**FATEHPUR**	**18.05**
120	**209**	**DHOND**	**17.94**
121	**140**	**SANCHORE**	**17.93**
122	**71**	**HINDOLI**	**17.89**
123	195	SUMERPUR	17.75
124	72	KESHORAIPATAN	17.69
125	156	BALESAR	17.64
126	73	NAINWA	17.52
127	164	SHERGARH	17.51
128	172	LADPURA	17.43
129	145	KHANPUR	17.37
130	58	JAHAZPUR	17.36
131	162	OSIAN	17.35
132	59	KOTRI	17.32
133	82	CHITTAURGARH	17.21
134	45	SIWANA	17.19
135	147	PIRAWA	17.06
136	80	BHOPALSAGAR	17.01
137	149	BUHANA	16.91
138	77	BEGUN	16.89
138	132	JAISALMER	16.89
140	63	SAHARA	16.84
141	78	BHADESAR	16.80
142	144	JHALRAPATAN	16.76
142	226	UNIARA	16.76
144	128	SAMBHAR	16.75
145	150	CHIRAWA	16.69
146	201	RAILMAGRA	16.65
147	133	SAM	16.64
148	61	MANDALGARH	16.61
149	86	NIMBAHERA	16.53
150	43	SHEO	16.42
151	186	BALI	16.38
152	37	SHAHBAD	16.32
153	196	AMET	16.24
154	16	NIMRANA	16.16
155	157	BAP	16.11
156	138	JASWANTPURA	16.09
157	160	LUNI	16.04
158	34	CHHABRA	15.99
159	124	JAMWA RAMGARH	15.73
160	57	HURDA	15.72
161	161	MANDOR	15.66
162	163	PHALODI	15.64
163	62	RAIPUR	15.58
164	56	BANERA	15.43
165	130	SHAHPURA	15.41
166	207	SAWAI MADHOPUR	15.40
166	39	BARMER	15.40
168	9	BANSURE	15.37
169	83	DUNGLA	15.34
170	126	KOTPUTLI	15.26
171	214	PIPRALI	15.13
171	10	BEHROR	15.13
173	119	AMBER	15.11
	LOW (10-15)		
174	131	VIRATNAGAR	14.91
174	7	PISANGAN	14.91
176	42	DHORIMANNA	14.51
177	60	MANDAL	14.47
178	20	THANAGAZI	14.46
179	51	NAGAR PAHARI	14.24
180	40	BAYTOO	14.20
181	55	ASIND	14.09
182	191	RAIPUR	14.00
183	21	TIJARA	13.96
184	35	CHHIPABAROD	13.92
185	38	BALOTRA	13.73
186	153	NAWALGARH	13.51
187	213	NEEM KA THANA	13.33
188	202	RAJSAMAND	12.99
189	134	SANKRA	12.91
190	136	BHINMAL	12.67
191	155	UDAIPURWATI	12.62
192	8	SRINAGAR	12.60
193	215	SRI MADHOPUR	12.51
194	211	KHANDELA	12.43
195	36	KISHANGANJ	12.41
196	44	SINDHARI	12.15
197	152	KHETRI	12.12
198	123	GOVINDGARH	12.05
199	76	BARI SADRI	12.01
200	142	BAKANI	11.81
201	81	CHHOTI SADRI	11.75
202	6	MASOODA	11.71
203	217	PINDWARA	11.08
204	79	BHAINSRORGARH	10.81
205	197	BHIM	10.24
206	235	MAVLI	10.09
	VERY LOW (<10)		
207	3	JAWAJA	9.99
208	199	KHAMNOR	9.55
209	200	KUMBHALGARH	9.17
210	146	MANOHARTHANA	8.79
211	48	KAMAN	8.46
212	228	BHINDER	8.44
213	231	GOGUNDA	8.16
214	87	PRATAPGARH	7.63
215	227	BARGAON	6.88
216	25	GARHI	6.69
217	104	ASPUR	5.48
218	216	ABU ROAD	5.45
219	24	BAGIDORA	5.08
220	75	ARNOD	5.01
221	26	GHATOL	4.81
222	107	SAGWARA	4.67
223	236	SALUMBAR	4.41
224	230	GIRWA	4.39
225	229	DHARIAWAD	3.99
226	108	SIMALWARA	3.98
227	233	KHERWARA	3.93
228	237	SARADA	3.90
229	30	TALWARA	3.76
230	28	PEEPALKHOONT	3.36
231	29	SAJJANGARH	2.99
232	105	BICHHIWARA	2.81
233	232	JHADOL	2.46
233	106	DUNGARPUR	2.46
235	23	ANANDPURI	2.00
236	234	KOTRA	1.02
237	27	KUSHALGARH	0.99
		RAJASTHAN	**17.88**
		%age of AAPs	**51.48**

BOLD: Equal/Above Average Panchayat Samities (AAPs) *Source*: Annex K1, Col. 12.

ANNEX-K12

RANKING OF PSS BY PERCENTAGE OF ST POPULATION TO TOTAL POPULATION : RAJASTHAN (2001)

(Descending Order)

RANK	PANCHAYAT SAMITIES P. CODE	NAME	%
1	2	3	4
	VERY HIGH (>=40)		
1	**27**	**KUSHALGARH**	**94.47**
2	**29**	**SAJJANGARH**	**89.46**
3	**234**	**KOTRA**	**89.32**
4	**28**	**PEEPALKHOONT**	**88.94**
5	**23**	**ANANDPURI**	**86.44**
6	**229**	**DHARIAWAD**	**82.49**
7	**106**	**DUNGARPUR**	**80.94**
8	**105**	**BICHHIWARA**	**79.70**
9	**233**	**KHERWARA**	**78.90**
10	**24**	**BAGIDORA**	**76.53**
11	**26**	**GHATOL**	**75.33**
12	**108**	**SIMALWARA**	**74.77**
13	**30**	**TALWARA**	**72.49**
14	**232**	**JHADOL**	**69.73**
15	**75**	**ARNOD**	**67.24**
16	**216**	**ABU ROAD**	**66.65**
17	**237**	**SARADA**	**63.90**
18	**236**	**SALUMBAR**	**56.48**
19	**87**	**PRATAPGARH**	**56.25**
20	**230**	**GIRWA**	**55.92**
21	**107**	**SAGWARA**	**54.34**
22	**25**	**GARHI**	**53.89**
23	**104**	**ASPUR**	**49.42**
24	**231**	**GOGUNDA**	**44.66**
25	**97**	**LALSOT**	**41.42**
	HIGH (30-40)		
26	**217**	**PINDWARA**	**39.49**
27	**81**	**CHHOTI SADRI**	**38.11**
28	**19**	**RENI**	**37.02**
29	**168**	**SAPOTRA**	**36.99**
30	**227**	**BARGAON**	**36.54**
31	**79**	**BHAINSRORGARH**	**35.24**
32	**36**	**KISHANGANJ**	**34.33**
33	**37**	**SHAHBAD**	**34.04**
34	**58**	**JAHAZPUR**	**33.90**
35	**207**	**SAWAI MADHOPUR**	**32.78**
36	**203**	**BAMANWAS**	**31.75**
37	**96**	**DAUSA**	**31.68**
38	**120**	**BASSI**	**31.46**
39	**169**	**TODABHIM**	**31.34**
	MEDIUM (20-30)		
40	**124**	**JAMWA RAMGARH**	**29.85**
41	**17**	**RAJGARH**	**29.48**
42	**146**	**MANOHARTHANA**	**29.05**
43	**72**	**KESHORAIPATAN**	**28.47**
44	**226**	**UNIARA**	**27.69**
45	**200**	**KUMBHALGARH**	**27.47**
46	**186**	**BALI**	**26.89**
47	**35**	**CHHIPABAROD**	**26.44**
48	**98**	**MAHWA**	**26.01**
49	**74**	**TALERA**	**25.73**
50	**204**	**BONLI**	**25.72**
51	**99**	**SIKRAI**	**24.75**
52	**205**	**GANGAPUR**	**24.39**
53	**121**	**CHAKSU**	**23.79**
54	**167**	**NADOTI**	**23.64**
55	**199**	**KHAMNOR**	**23.44**
56	**34**	**CHHABRA**	**23.30**
57	**171**	**ITAWA**	**22.48**
58	**73**	**NAINWA**	**22.32**
59	**221**	**DEOLI**	**21.95**
60	**95**	**BANDIKUI**	**20.92**
	LOW (10-20)		
61	**228**	**BHINDER**	**19.82**
62	**166**	**KARAULI**	**19.73**
63	**76**	**BARI SADRI**	**19.57**
64	**235**	**MAVLI**	**19.22**
65	**223**	**NIWAI**	**19.18**
66	**20**	**THANAGAZI**	**19.08**
67	**33**	**BARAN**	**18.96**
68	**32**	**ATRU**	**18.78**
69	**31**	**ANTA**	**18.55**
70	**219**	**SHEOGANJ**	**18.27**
71	**71**	**HINDOLI**	**18.13**
72	**174**	**SULTANPUR**	**17.77**
73	**165**	**HINDAUN**	**16.20**
74	**144**	**JHALRAPATAN**	**15.88**
75	**61**	**MANDALGARH**	**15.82**
76	101	BASERI	15.44
77	202	RAJSAMAND	15.13
78	145	KHANPUR	14.88
79	172	LADPURA	14.77
80	142	BAKANI	14.47
81	139	RANIWARA	14.23
82	170	CHECHAT	13.92
83	119	AMBER	13.71
84	83	DUNGLA	13.57
85	195	SUMERPUR	13.50
86	86	NIMBAHERA	13.20
87	11	KATHUMAR	12.97
88	80	BHOPALSAGAR	12.69
89	4	KEKRI	12.62
90	129	SANGANER	12.58
91	82	CHITTAURGARH	12.51
92	135	AHORE	11.91
93	77	BEGUN	11.62
93	218	REODAR	11.62
95	14	LACHHMANGARH	11.43
96	206	KHANDAR	11.11
96	173	SANGOD	11.11
98	225	TONK	10.75
99	85	KAPASAN	10.53
100	138	JASWANTPURA	10.40
101	137	JALOR	10.31
102	136	BHINMAL	10.17
103	100	BARI	10.07
	VERY LOW (<10)		
104	64	SHAHPURA	9.83
105	45	SIWANA	9.70
106	54	WEIR	9.47
107	196	AMET	9.31
108	41	CHOHTAN	9.16
109	38	BALOTRA	8.94
110	201	RAILMAGRA	8.85
111	224	TODARAISINGH	8.13
112	22	UMREN	8.11
113	78	BHADESAR	7.79
114	190	PALI	7.73
114	132	JAISALMER	7.73
116	57	HURDA	7.56
117	141	SAYLA	7.52
118	220	SIROHI	7.24
119	164	SHERGARH	7.22
120	84	GANGRAR	6.96
120	126	KOTPUTLI	6.96
122	55	ASIND	6.88
123	63	SAHARA	6.74
124	213	NEEM KA THANA	6.66
125	39	BARMER	6.54
126	131	VIRATNAGAR	6.43
126	56	BANERA	6.43
128	147	PIRAWA	6.37
129	62	RAIPUR	6.33
130	88	RASHMI	5.86
131	123	GOVINDGARH	5.59
132	59	KOTRI	5.49
133	42	DHORIMANNA	5.45
134	193	ROHAT	5.29
135	187	DESURI	5.14
136	211	KHANDELA	5.08
137	134	SANKRA	4.87
138	198	DEOGARH	4.86
139	60	MANDAL	4.72
139	125	JHOTWARA	4.72
139	133	SAM	4.72
142	130	SHAHPURA	4.70
143	2	BHINAY	4.57
144	140	SANCHORE	4.48
145	65	SUWANA	4.42
146	127	PHAGI	4.36
147	9	BANSURE	4.29
148	128	SAMBHAR	4.08
149	192	RANI STATION	3.95
150	156	BALESAR	3.86
151	43	SHEO	3.85
152	160	LUNI	3.81
153	222	MALPURA	3.79
154	163	PHALODI	3.73
155	215	SRI MADHOPUR	3.70
156	40	BAYTOO	3.48
157	162	OSIAN	3.45
157	18	RAMGARH	3.45
159	161	MANDOR	3.43
160	155	UDAIPURWATI	3.35
161	6	MASOODA	3.20
162	15	MANDAWAR	3.11
163	44	SINDHARI	3.07
164	122	DUDU	3.02
164	46	BAYANA	3.02
164	151	JHUNJHUNUN	3.02
167	152	KHETRI	2.91
168	157	BAP	2.88
169	1	ARAIN	2.74
169	208	DANTA RAMGARH	2.74
171	50	NADBAI	2.64
172	189	MARWAR JUN.	2.59
173	153	NAWALGARH	2.41
174	148	ALSISAR	2.34
174	49	KUMHER	2.34
176	214	PIPRALI	2.27
177	197	BHIM	1.89
178	150	CHIRAWA	1.79
179	51	NAGAR PAHARI	1.62
179	53	SEWAR	1.62
181	16	NIMRANA	1.56
182	209	DHOND	1.41
183	178	KUCHAMAN	1.38
184	8	SRINAGAR	1.35
185	10	BEHROR	1.20
186	52	RUPBAS	1.05
187	90	RAJGARH	1.02
188	7	PISANGAN	0.98
189	212	LACHHMANGARH	0.77
189	5	KISHANGARH	0.77
191	210	FATEHPUR	0.76
192	13	KOTKASIM	0.75
193	154	SURAJGARH	0.73
194	89	CHURU	0.72
194	149	BUHANA	0.72
196	116	BHADRA	0.62
197	3	JAWAJA	0.60
198	94	TARANAGAR	0.49
199	47	DEEG	0.48
200	109	ANUPGARH	0.47
201	117	HANUMANGARH	0.39
202	158	BHOPALGARH	0.38
203	91	RATANGARH	0.37
204	113	RAISINGHNAGAR	0.34
205	159	BILARA	0.33
206	92	SARDARSHAHAR	0.32
207	68	KOLAYAT	0.27
208	66	BIKANER	0.26
209	143	DAG	0.26
210	112	PADAMPUR	0.25
211	110	GANGANAGAR	0.24
212	115	SURATGARH	0.23
213	118	NOHAR	0.20
214	181	MERTA	0.19
215	21	TIJARA	0.16
215	48	KAMAN	0.16
217	191	RAIPUR	0.15
217	69	LUNKARANSAR	0.15
219	176	DIDWANA	0.14
220	175	DEGANA	0.12
221	93	SUJANGARH	0.11
221	179	LADNU	0.11
221	114	SADULSHAHAR	0.11
224	111	KARANPUR	0.10
225	184	PARBATSAR	0.09
225	194	SOJAT	0.09
225	185	RIYAN	0.09
228	102	DHAULPUR	0.07
228	188	JAITARAN	0.07
230	183	NAGAUR	0.06
230	12	KISHANGARH BAS	0.06
230	180	MAKRANA	0.06
233	182	MUNDWA	0.03
233	67	DUNGARGARH	0.03
235	177	JAYAL	0.02
235	70	NOKHA	0.02
237	103	RAJAKHERA	0.00
	RAJASTHAN		**15.52**
	%age of AAPs		**31.65**

BOLD: Equal/Above Average Panchayat Samities (AAPs)

Source: Annex K1, Col. 16.

ANNEX-K13

RANKING OF PSS BY SEX-RATIO, SC POPULATION : RAJASTHAN (2001)

(Descending Order)

RANK	PANCHAYAT SAMITIES P. CODE	NAME	SEX-RATIO
1	2	3	4
	VERY HIGH (>=1000)		
1	63	SAHARA	1044
2	197	BHIM	1035
3	107	SAGWARA	1028
4	104	ASPUR	1027
5	60	MANDAL	1025
6	62	RAIPUR	1024
7	198	DEOGARH	1016
7	106	DUNGARPUR	1016
9	29	SAJJANGARH	1013
10	88	RASHMI	1009
11	80	BHOPALSAGAR	1006
11	55	ASIND	1006
	HIGH (950-1000)		
13	108	SIMALWARA	998
14	237	SARADA	997
15	201	RAILMAGRA	996
16	23	ANANDPURI	991
17	25	GARHI	989
17	83	DUNGLA	989
19	236	SALUMBAR	988
20	233	KHERWARA	987
21	65	SUWANA	985
22	78	BHADESAR	984
23	76	BARI SADRI	983
24	3	JAWAJA	980
25	81	CHHOTI SADRI	979
26	24	BAGIDORA	978
27	229	DHARIAWAD	977
28	186	BALI	976
29	200	KUMBHALGARH	975
30	105	BICHHIWARA	974
31	27	KUSHALGARH	973
32	82	CHITTAURGARH	972
33	228	BHINDER	971
33	85	KAPASAN	971
35	30	TALWARA	970
35	7	PISANGAN	970
37	56	BANERA	969
37	187	DESURI	969
39	26	GHATOL	967
40	191	RAIPUR	963
40	202	RAJSAMAND	963
42	6	MASOODA	962
43	175	DEGANA	961
44	86	NIMBAHERA	960
45	231	GOGUNDA	957
45	192	RANI STATION	957
47	196	AMET	956
48	179	LADNU	955
48	176	DIDWANA	955
50	87	PRATAPGARH	954
51	84	GANGRAR	953
51	28	PEEPALKHOONT	953
51	235	MAVLI	953
54	2	BHINAY	952
54	64	SHAHPURA	952
54	210	FATEHPUR	952
54	1	ARAIN	952
54	155	UDAIPURWATI	952
54	199	KHAMNOR	952
60	153	NAWALGARH	951
61	185	RIYAN	950
	MEDIUM (900-950)		
62	135	AHORE	948
62	190	PALI	948
64	5	KISHANGARH	947
65	222	MALPURA	944
66	77	BEGUN	943
66	57	HURDA	943
66	208	DANTA RAMGARH	943
66	232	JHADOL	943
70	224	TODARAISINGH	942
70	209	DHOND	942
70	195	SUMERPUR	942
73	150	CHIRAWA	941
73	225	TONK	941
73	4	KEKRI	941
73	148	ALSISAR	941
77	217	PINDWARA	940
78	189	MARWAR JUN.	939
79	59	KOTRI	938
80	177	JAYAL	937
81	214	PIPRALI	937
82	184	PARBATSAR	936
82	221	DEOLI	936
82	152	KHETRI	936
85	142	BAKANI	935
85	91	RATANGARH	935
85	10	BEHROR	935
88	212	LACHHMANGARH	934
88	182	MUNDWA	934
90	180	MAKRANA	933
90	143	DAG	933
92	151	JHUNJHUNUN	932
92	194	SOJAT	932
92	211	KHANDELA	932
95	188	JAITARAN	931
95	183	NAGAUR	931
95	213	NEEM KA THANA	931
95	220	SIROHI	931
99	147	PIRAWA	928
99	138	JASWANTPURA	928
99	89	CHURU	928
99	99	SIKRAI	928
103	67	DUNGARGARH	927
103	13	KOTKASIM	927
103	136	BHINMAL	927
106	193	ROHAT	926
106	162	OSIAN	926
106	97	LALSOT	926
106	158	BHOPALGARH	926
110	8	SRINAGAR	925
110	141	SAYLA	925
110	93	SUJANGARH	925
110	234	KOTRA	925
114	73	NAINWA	924
114	230	GIRWA	924
114	178	KUCHAMAN	924
114	129	SANGANER	924
114	61	MANDALGARH	924
114	167	NADOTI	924
120	31	ANTA	923
121	226	UNIARA	922
121	15	MANDAWAR	922
121	122	DUDU	922
124	96	DAUSA	921
124	44	SINDHARI	921
124	218	REODAR	921
124	146	MANOHARTHANA	921
128	164	SHERGARH	920
128	216	ABU ROAD	920
128	131	VIRATNAGAR	920
128	121	CHAKSU	920
132	140	SANCHORE	918
132	126	KOTPUTLI	918
132	9	BANSURE	918
135	149	BUHANA	917
135	58	JAHAZPUR	917
135	227	BARGAON	917
135	40	BAYTOO	917
139	113	RAISINGHNAGAR	916
139	34	CHHABRA	916
141	174	SULTANPUR	915
141	137	JALOR	915
141	95	BANDIKUI	915
141	204	BONLI	915
141	75	ARNOD	915
141	120	BASSI	915
147	215	SRI MADHOPUR	914
147	173	SANGOD	914
147	90	RAJGARH	914
150	156	BALESAR	913
150	219	SHEOGANJ	913
150	16	NIMRANA	913
150	94	TARANAGAR	913
154	160	LUNI	912
154	154	SURAJGARH	912
154	161	MANDOR	912
157	69	LUNKARANSAR	911
157	38	BALOTRA	911
157	124	JAMWA RAMGARH	911
157	109	ANUPGARH	911
157	92	SARDARSHAHAR	911
157	123	GOVINDGARH	911
163	130	SHAHPURA	910
164	118	NOHAR	909
164	111	KARANPUR	909
164	144	JHALRAPATAN	909
164	125	JHOTWARA	909
168	139	RANIWARA	908
168	70	NOKHA	908
168	203	BAMANWAS	908
168	128	SAMBHAR	908
172	35	CHHIPABAROD	907
172	20	THANAGAZI	907
172	72	KESHORAIPATAN	907
172	181	MERTA	907
172	17	RAJGARH	907
172	207	SAWAI MADHOPUR	907
172	157	BAP	907
179	223	NIWAI	906
179	159	BILARA	906
181	170	CHECHAT	905
181	134	SANKRA	905
181	127	PHAGI	905
184	171	ITAWA	904
184	33	BARAN	904
184	32	ATRU	904
187	163	PHALODI	903
187	119	AMBER	903
189	145	KHANPUR	902
189	172	LADPURA	902
189	117	HANUMANGARH	902
189	112	PADAMPUR	902
193	12	KISHANGARH BAS	900
	LOW (850-900)		
193	110	GANGANAGAR	900
195	74	TALERA	899
196	71	HINDOLI	898
196	42	DHORIMANNA	898
196	43	SHEO	898
199	18	RAMGARH	897
200	36	KISHANGANJ	895
201	45	SIWANA	893
202	115	SURATGARH	891
203	116	BHADRA	889
203	39	BARMER	889
205	98	MAHWA	888
205	19	RENI	888
205	14	LACHHMANGARH	888
208	22	UMREN	886
209	205	GANGAPUR	885
209	66	BIKANER	885
211	114	SADULSHAHAR	884
212	37	SHAHBAD	882
213	48	KAMAN	880
214	206	KHANDAR	879
214	68	KOLAYAT	879
214	79	BHAINSRORGARH	879
217	41	CHOHTAN	878
218	21	TIJARA	877
218	11	KATHUMAR	877
220	53	SEWAR	869
220	133	SAM	869
222	169	TODABHIM	868
223	132	JAISALMER	864
224	52	RUPBAS	861
225	166	KARAULI	853
226	102	DHAULPUR	851
226	51	NAGAR PAHARI	851
	VERY LOW (<850)		
228	165	HINDAUN	850
229	168	SAPOTRA	842
230	54	WEIR	839
231	101	BASERI	836
232	46	BAYANA	830
233	49	KUMHER	828
234	50	NADBAI	822
235	103	RAJAKHERA	821
236	47	DEEG	819
237	100	BARI	814
		RAJASTHAN	915
		%age of AAPs	62

BOLD: Equal/Above Average Panchayat Samities (AAPs)

Source: Annex K1, Col. 19.

ANNEX-K14

RANKING OF PSS BY SEX-RATIO, ST POPULATION : RAJASTHAN (2001)

(Descending Order)

RANK	PANCHAYAT SAMITIES P. CODE	PANCHAYAT SAMITIES NAME	SEX - RATIO
1	2	3	4
	VERY HIGH (>=1000)		
1	**107**	**SAGWARA**	**1073**
2	**104**	**ASPUR**	**1070**
3	**7**	**PISANGAN**	**1065**
4	**60**	**MANDAL**	**1053**
5	**106**	**DUNGARPUR**	**1048**
6	**83**	**DUNGLA**	**1017**
7	**55**	**ASIND**	**1014**
8	**76**	**BARI SADRI**	**1013**
9	**56**	**BANERA**	**1011**
10	**105**	**BICHHIWARA**	**1008**
10	**63**	**SAHARA**	**1008**
12	**237**	**SARADA**	**1007**
12	**236**	**SALUMBAR**	**1007**
14	**88**	**RASHMI**	**1006**
15	**233**	**KHERWARA**	**1005**
16	**62**	**RAIPUR**	**1004**
17	**179**	**LADNU**	**1000**
	HIGH (950-1000)		
17	**108**	**SIMALWARA**	**1000**
19	**26**	**GHATOL**	**999**
20	**16**	**NIMRANA**	**998**
21	**229**	**DHARIAWAD**	**996**
21	**85**	**KAPASAN**	**996**
23	**6**	**MASOODA**	**994**
24	**191**	**RAIPUR**	**993**
25	**84**	**GANGRAR**	**989**
25	**27**	**KUSHALGARH**	**989**
27	**30**	**TALWARA**	**987**
27	**232**	**JHADOL**	**987**
29	**24**	**BAGIDORA**	**986**
30	**234**	**KOTRA**	**985**
31	**25**	**GARHI**	**984**
32	**217**	**PINDWARA**	**982**
32	**75**	**ARNOD**	**982**
34	**198**	**DEOGARH**	**979**
35	**202**	**RAJSAMAND**	**977**
36	**29**	**SAJJANGARH**	**975**
36	**86**	**NIMBAHERA**	**975**
36	**201**	**RAILMAGRA**	**975**
39	**149**	**BUHANA**	**974**
39	**199**	**KHAMNOR**	**974**
41	**228**	**BHINDER**	**972**
41	**110**	**GANGANAGAR**	**972**
43	**81**	**CHHOTI SADRI**	**971**
43	**209**	**DHOND**	**971**
43	**80**	**BHOPALSAGAR**	**971**
46	**28**	**PEEPALKHOONT**	**970**
47	**216**	**ABU ROAD**	**969**
47	**23**	**ANANDPURI**	**969**
49	**230**	**GIRWA**	**968**
49	**59**	**KOTRI**	**968**
51	**211**	**KHANDELA**	**967**
52	**78**	**BHADESAR**	**963**
52	**197**	**BHIM**	**963**
54	**151**	**JHUNJHUNUN**	**962**
55	**200**	**KUMBHALGARH**	**961**
56	**227**	**BARGAON**	**960**
56	**87**	**PRATAPGARH**	**960**
58	**231**	**GOGUNDA**	**959**
58	**102**	**DHAULPUR**	**959**
60	**196**	**AMET**	**955**
60	**1**	**ARAIN**	**955**
62	**125**	**JHOTWARA**	**954**
63	**8**	**SRINAGAR**	**953**
63	**162**	**OSIAN**	**953**
63	**148**	**ALSISAR**	**953**
66	**15**	**MANDAWAR**	**951**
66	**82**	**CHITTAURGARH**	**951**
66	**37**	**SHAHBAD**	**951**
69	**77**	**BEGUN**	**950**
	MEDIUM (900-950)		
70	186	BALI	948
71	150	CHIRAWA	946
72	5	KISHANGARH	945
72	235	MAVLI	945
74	155	UDAIPURWATI	944
75	64	SHAHPURA	943
75	36	KISHANGANJ	943
77	90	RAJGARH	942
78	208	DANTA RAMGARH	941
78	160	LUNI	941
80	164	SHERGARH	938
80	175	DEGANA	938
82	161	MANDOR	934
82	79	BHAINSRORGARH	934
82	153	NAWALGARH	934
82	65	SUWANA	934
86	3	JAWAJA	932
86	189	MARWAR JUN.	932
88	221	DEOLI	930
88	2	BHINAY	930
88	187	DESURI	930
88	224	TODARAISINGH	930
92	57	HURDA	929
93	91	RATANGARH	927
94	147	PIRAWA	926
95	4	KEKRI	924
95	128	SAMBHAR	924
95	142	BAKANI	924
95	223	NIWAI	924
99	152	KHETRI	923
100	210	FATEHPUR	922
100	146	MANOHARTHANA	922
100	31	ANTA	922
103	218	REODAR	921
104	122	DUDU	920
104	176	DIDWANA	920
104	192	RANI STATION	920
107	222	MALPURA	919
107	127	PHAGI	919
109	144	JHALRAPATAN	918
109	124	JAMWA RAMGARH	918
109	178	KUCHAMAN	918
109	9	BANSURE	918
109	61	MANDALGARH	918
114	174	SULTANPUR	917
114	225	TONK	917
116	215	SRI MADHOPUR	916
116	72	KESHORAIPATAN	916
118	120	BASSI	915
118	170	CHECHAT	915
120	145	KHANPUR	914
120	136	BHINMAL	914
120	35	CHHIPABAROD	914
120	121	CHAKSU	914
120	163	PHALODI	914
125	139	RANIWARA	913
125	97	LALSOT	913
125	119	AMBER	913
125	213	NEEM KA THANA	913
125	143	DAG	913
130	130	SHAHPURA	911
130	137	JALOR	911
132	195	SUMERPUR	910
132	92	SARDARSHAHAR	910
132	126	KOTPUTLI	910
135	58	JAHAZPUR	909
136	140	SANCHORE	908
136	74	TALERA	908
136	96	DAUSA	908
136	32	ATRU	908
140	134	SANKRA	907
140	129	SANGANER	907
142	219	SHEOGANJ	906
143	45	SIWANA	904
144	94	TARANAGAR	902
144	135	AHORE	902
144	123	GOVINDGARH	902
147	173	SANGOD	901
	LOW (850-900)		
148	38	BALOTRA	900
149	207	SAWAI MADHOPUR	899
149	226	UNIARA	899
149	214	PIPRALI	899
152	204	BONLI	898
152	10	BEHROR	898
152	138	JASWANTPURA	898
152	171	ITAWA	898
156	131	VIRATNAGAR	897
157	71	HINDOLI	895
157	154	SURAJGARH	895
159	49	KUMHER	892
160	167	NADOTI	891
161	156	BALESAR	890
161	190	PALI	890
161	14	LACHHMANGARH	890
164	193	ROHAT	888
164	95	BANDIKUI	888
164	33	BARAN	888
164	41	CHOHTAN	888
164	44	SINDHARI	888
164	112	PADAMPUR	888
170	50	NADBAI	887
171	42	DHORIMANNA	886
171	212	LACHHMANGARH	886
171	73	NAINWA	886
174	20	THANAGAZI	885
175	220	SIROHI	884
176	172	LADPURA	883
177	116	BHADRA	881
177	141	SAYLA	881
179	203	BAMANWAS	880
179	89	CHURU	880
181	17	RAJGARH	879
181	113	RAISINGHNAGAR	879
183	11	KATHUMAR	878
183	68	KOLAYAT	878
185	19	RENI	877
185	34	CHHABRA	877
187	99	SIKRAI	876
188	157	BAP	875
189	133	SAM	872
190	51	NAGAR PAHARI	871
191	98	MAHWA	869
191	22	UMREN	869
193	40	BAYTOO	868
194	54	WEIR	867
195	39	BARMER	866
196	205	GANGAPUR	862
197	158	BHOPALGARH	861
198	18	RAMGARH	860
199	46	BAYANA	859
199	169	TODABHIM	859
200	43	SHEO	858
200	132	JAISALMER	858
203	117	HANUMANGARH	857
203	182	MUNDWA	857
205	165	HINDAUN	853
206	47	DEEG	852
	VERY LOW (<850)		
207	168	SAPOTRA	846
208	115	SURATGARH	845
209	166	KARAULI	843
209	21	TIJARA	843
211	206	KHANDAR	841
212	101	BASERI	840
213	52	RUPBAS	834
214	194	SOJAT	833
214	118	NOHAR	833
216	48	KAMAN	832
217	100	BARI	831
218	66	BIKANER	818
219	13	KOTKASIM	810
220	53	SEWAR	809
220	188	JAITARAN	809
222	93	SUJANGARH	806
223	183	NAGAUR	800
224	109	ANUPGARH	796
225	159	BILARA	790
226	181	MERTA	756
227	69	LUNKARANSAR	750
228	184	PARBATSAR	716
229	185	RIYAN	714
230	12	KISHANGARH BAS	667
231	114	SADULSHAHAR	656
232	111	KARANPUR	551
233	70	NOKHA	500
234	177	JAYAL	480
235	180	MAKRANA	402
236	67	DUNGARGARH	310
237	103	RAJAKHERA	167
	RAJASTHAN		**950**
	%age of AAPs		**29**

BOLD: Equal/Above Average Panchayat Samities (AAPs)

Source: Annex K1, Col. 10.

ANNEX-K15

DISTRICT-WISE DISTRIBUTION OF CO-TERMINUS PSS : RAJASTHAN

S. No.	*Districts*	*Total No. of PSs*	*Co - Terminus PSs (With Tehsils)*		
			%ge Share to Total PSs	*No.*	*Name of Panchayat Samities*
1	2	3	4	5	6
1	Ajmer	8	37.5	3	JAWAJA, KEKRI and MASOODA
2	Alwar	14	35.7	5	BANSURE, KOTKASIM, MANDAWAR, THANAGAZI and TIJARA
3	Banswara	8	12.5	1	GARHI
4	Baran	7	85.7	6	ATRU, BARAN, CHHABRA, CHHIPABAROD, KISHANGANJ and SHAHBAD
5	Barmer	8	37.5	3	BALOTRA, SHEO and SIWANA
6	Bharatpur	9	77.8	7	BAYANA, DEEG, KUMHER, NADBAI, RUPBAS, SEWAR and WEIR
7	Bhilwara	11	90.9	10	ASIND, BANERA, HURDA, JAHAZPUR, KOTRI, MANDAL, RAIPUR, SAHARA, SHAHPURA and SUWANA
8	Bikaner *	5	60.0	3	KOLAYAT, NOKHA and DUNGARGARH *
9	Bundi	4	75.0	3	HINDOLI, NAINWA and TALERA
10	Chittaurgarh	14	71.4	10	ARNOD, BARI SADRI, BHADESAR, CHHOTI SADRI, CHITTAURGARH, DUNGLA, GANGRAR, NIMBAHERA, PRATAPGARH and RASHMI
11	Churu *	6	100.0	6	CHURU, RAJGARH, RATANGARH, SARDARSHAHAR, SUJANGARH and TARANAGAR
12	Dausa	5	100.0	5	BANDIKUI, DAUSA, LALSOT, MAHWA and SIKRAI
13	Dhaulpur	4	50.0	2	BARI and BASERI
14	Dungarpur	5	20.0	1	ASPUR
15	Ganganagar	7	57.1	4	KARANPUR, PADAMPUR, RAISINGHNAGAR and SURATGARH
16	Hanumangarh	3	33.3	1	BHADRA
17	Jaipur	13	61.5	8	AMBER, BASSI, CHAKSU, GOVINDGARH, JAMWA RAMGARH, JHOTWARA, PHAGI and SANGANER
18	Jaisalmer	3	0.0	0	—
19	Jalor	7	28.6	2	RANIWARA and SANCHORE
20	Jhalawar	6	33.3	2	KHANPUR and PIRAWA
21	Jhunjhunun	8	50.0	4	BUHANA, KHETRI, NAWALGARH and UDAIPURWATI
22	Jodhpur	9	11.1	1	BILARA
23	Karauli	5	80.0	4	HINDAUN, KARAULI, NADOTI and TODABHIM
24	Kota	5	100.0	5	CHECHAT, ITAWA, LADPURA, SANGOD and SULTANPUR
25	Nagaur	11	54.5	6	DIDWANA, JAYAL, KUCHAMAN, LADNU, MAKRANA and PARBATSAR
26	Pali	10	70.0	7	BALI, JAITARAN, RAIPUR, ROHAT, SOJAT, SUMERPUR and KHARCHI
27	Rajsamand	7	100.0	7	AMET, BHIM, DEOGARH, KHAMNOR, KUMBHALGARH, RAILMAGRA and RAJSAMAND
28	S. Madhopur	5	40.0	2	BAMANWAS and GANGAPUR
29	Sikar	8	12.5	1	NEEM KA THANA
30	Sirohi	5	100.0	5	ABU ROAD, PINDWARA, REODAR, SHEOGANJ and SIROHI
31	Tonk	6	83.3	5	DEOLI, MALPURA, NIWAI, TODARAISINGH and UNIARA
32	Udaipur	11	81.8	9	BHINDER, DHARIAWAD, GOGUNDA, JHADOL, KHERWARA, KOTRA, MAVLI, SALUMBAR and SARADA
	Rajasthan	**237**	**58.2**	**138**	

Note: Dungargarh PS shifted from Churu to Bikaner district on 1st April, 2001

Source: Compiled from information received from Directorate of Census operations, Rajasthan.

BIBLIOGRAPHY

Anand, Sudhir. and Amartya Sen. 1994. "Human Development Index: Methodology and Measurement". Occasional Paper 12. United Nations Development Programme, Human Development Report Office, New York.

Anand, Sudhir. and Amartya Sen. 1995. "Gender Inequality in Human Development: Theories and Measurement". Occasional Paper 15. United Nations Development Programme. Human Development Report Office, New York.

Anand, Sudhir. and Amartya Sen. 1997. "Concepts of Human Development and Poverty: A Multidimensional Perspective". United Nations Development Programme, Human Development Report 1997 Papers: Poverty and Human Development, New York.

Basu A.M. and Basu, K. 1991. Women's Economic Role and Child's Survival: The Case of India, *Health Transition Review,* Volume 1, No. 1.

Bhargava S.K., *et al.* 1991, "Current Status on Neonatal Care and Alternate Strategies for Reduction of Neonatal Mortality in the Decade of Nineties", *Indian Pediatrics,* 28 (12) .

Bhat, Ramesh 1993 . "The Public/Private Mix in Health Care in India", *International Journal of Health Policy and Planning,* 8 (1).

Bhatia, J. C. 1982, *'A Study of Maternal Mortality in Anantpur District,* Andhra Pradesh', Indian Institute of Management, Bangalore.

Bose, Ashish. 2002. "Towards Population Stabilisation", *NFI Bulletin,* October, The Nutritional Foundation of India, New Delhi.

Buchert, Lene. (Ed.) 1998. *"Education Reform in the South in the 1990s".* UNESCO, Paris.

Caldwell, John C. 1986. Routes to Low Mortality in Poor Countries, *Population and Development Review,* Vol. 12, No. 2.

Caldwell, John C. 1992. Old and New Factors in Health Transition, *Health Transition Review,* Volume 2, Supplementary Issue.

Central Bureau of Health, Intelligence, "Health Information India", Various Years, Directorate General of Health Services, Ministry of Health and Family Welfare, New Delhi.

Centre for Energy, 2001. "India: Raising the Sights-Better Health System for India's Poor", Health, Nutrition, Population Sector Unit, India, South Asia Region, Report No. 22304.

Centre for Policy Research, 2000. "The Report on the Restructuring of the Ministry of Health and Family Welfare", New Delhi.

Chaterjee, Meera. 1990. "Indian Women: Their Health and Productivity". Discussion paper No. 109, World Bank, Washington D.C.

Chaturwedi, A., Khanna, A. and Kothari, D. 2001. "Provision of Two-Child Norm in Panchayati Raj Act of Rajasthan: A Critical Review of Impact and Perception", FPA Working paper No 9, Forum for Population Action, Jaipur.

Chaudhary, Ranjit Roy 2001. "The Medicines Scenario in India", Background Paper, National Institute of Immunology, New Delhi.

Chiapah, Vinayagum. 1997. "Handbook on Monitoring Learning Achievement: Towards Capacity Building", United Nations Educational Scientific and Cultural Organization, Paris.

Chima, R.I. and A. Mills 1998. "Estimating the Economic Impact of Malaria in Sub-Saharan Africa: A Review of the Empirical Evidence", Mimeo, London School of Hygiene and Tropical Medicine, June.

Colombini, Manuela. "Gender-based and Sexual Violence against Women during Armed Conflict". *Journal of Health Management,* 4, 2 (2002). *"The case for Gender Equity in Health Research".* Sage Publications New Delhi, Thousand Oaks, London.

Corbett, Jenny. 1998. *"Special Educational Needs in the Twentieth Century: A Cultural Analysis",* Institute of Education Series, London, Cassell.

Cornia, Andrea and Julius, Court. 2001. "Inequality, Growth and Poverty in the Era of Liberalisation and Globalisation". *Policy Brief* 4. United Nations University and World Institute for Development Economics Research, Helsinki, Finland.

Das, Gupta, Monica, Chen Lincoln C. and Krishana, T.N. (eds.) 1998. *"Health, Poverty and Development in India",* Oxford University Press, Delhi.

Deaton, Angus. 2001. "Health, Inequality and Economics Development", NBER Working Paper No. 8313, National Bureau of Economic Research, Cambridge, Mass.

Department of Family Welfare, 2000-01. *"Bulletin on Rural Health, Family Welfare Programme in India,* Year Book", GoI, New Delhi.

DGHS. 1998. "Directory of Hospitals in India", Office of the Registrar General India, Ministry of Health and Family Welfare, GoI, New Delhi.

Directorate of Census Operation. 1991. "Primary Census Abstract of Rajasthan", Census of India-Rajasthan, Series-21, Jaipur.

Directorate of Census Operation. 1991. "District Census Handbook (All Districts)", Raj., Jaipur.

Directorate of Census Operations, Rajasthan, 2001 "Final Population Totals", Rajasthan.

Directorate of Census Operations. 1991 "Census Atlas-Rajasthan", Part-XI.

Directorate of Economics and Statistics, 2003. "District Statistical Abstract-All Districts", Jaipur.

Directorate of Economics and Statistics, 2005. *"Economic Review, 2004-05",* Jaipur.

Directorate of Medical and Health, 2005. *"Pragati Prativedan 2004-05".* GoR, Jaipur.

Directorate of Medical, Health and FP, *"Pragati Prativedan 2004-05".* GoR, Jaipur

Dubey, Amresh, Gangopadhyay, Shubhashis. 1999. "Counting the Poor: Where are the Poor in India", Servekshana Analtical Report No. 1, Department of Statistics, New Delhi.

Health Monitor. 2004. Foundation for Research in Health System, Ahmedabad.

GoI, "Tenth Five-Year Plan Document", Planning Commission, New Delhi.

GoI, 2004-05. "Economic Survey". Ministry of Finance & Economic Division, New Delhi.

GoI. 2000. National Population Policy, Department of Family Welfare, Government of India, 1954 55. New Delhi, p. 71, New Delhi.

Gopalan, Sarala and Shiva Mira. 2000. *"National Profile on Women, Health and Development",* Country Profile-India VHAI and WHO, New Delhi.

GoR. 1992. "Jan Mangal-Project Document". (Unpublished), Department of Medical & Health Services, Jaipur.

GoR. 1992. Report on the Mid-Term Evaluation of the UNFPA Assisted Area Project Phase-II (Jaipur: Department of Medical & Health).

GoR. 1997. "Population Policy for Rajasthan: Identification of Issues *-Proceedings of Workshop",* Jointly Organised By the Indian Institute of Health Management Research, Jaipur and Government of Rajasthan.

GoR. 1998. "Draft Population Policy for Rajasthan". Developed by the Indian Institute of Health Management Research, Jaipur.

Government of Madhya Pradesh. 1995 & 1998. "The Madhya Pradesh Human Development Report", Directorate of Institutional Finance, Project Office, Bhopal.

Guijt, Lrena and Shah Meena Kaul. " The Myth of Community". *Journal of Health Management,* 4, 2 (2002). *"The case for Gender Equity in Health Research"* Sage Publications, New Delhi, Thousand Oaks, London.

Gupta, R.N. 1988. "Health and Family Welfare Programme in Rajasthan—An Appraisal in M.E. Khan *et al.* (ed) *Performance of Health and Family Welfare Programme in India (Bombay:* Himalaya Publishing House.

Gupta, Indrani and Arup, Mitra. 2001. "Economic Growth, Health and Poverty: An Exploratory Study on India", Background Paper, ICRIER, New Delhi.

Haq, Mahbub Ul. 1998. *"Human Development in South Asia"*, Human Development Centre, Pakistan.

Harman, H. H. 1967. *"Modern Factor Analysis,"* University Press, Chicago, U.S.A.

Harvard Centre for Population and Development Studies 2000. "Neonatal Mortality in India: Emerging Paradoxes", Working Paper Series, 10 (13), Harvard University.

IIPS. 1993. "National Family Health Survey (NFHS-1)", International Institute of Population Sciences, Mumbai.

IIPS. 1998. "Infant and Child Mortality in India", Subject Report, International Institute of Population Sciences, Mumbai.

IIPS. 1998. "Mother's Employment and Infant and Child Mortality in India", NFHS Subject Report, December, Mumbai.

IIPS and ORC Macro. 2000. National Family Health Survey (NFHS-2), 1998-99: India International Institute for Population Sciences, Mumbai.

Indian Council of Social Service Research (ICSSR). 1981. "Health for All, An Alternative Strategy", ICSSR/ICMR Report, Committee under the Chairmanship of Ramalingaswamy, New Delhi.

Indira Gandhi Institute of Development Research. 1997. "Indian Development Report", Mumbai.

International Fund for Agricultural Development. 2001. "Rural Poverty Report 2001: The Challenge of Ending Rural Poverty". Oxford University Press, New Delhi.

International Institute for Population Sciences, "National Family Health Survey 1992-93 and 1988-89" India and Various State Reports, Mumbai.

IPU Inter-Parliamentary Union. 1995. "Women in Parliaments 1945-1995", A World Statistical Survey. Geneva.

Joshi, Hemlata. 2002. "Gender Related Educational Development Index-Raj. 2000, A Geographical Analysis at Panchayat Samiti Level", Transactions, *Institute of Indian Geographers,* Vol. 24, No. 1 & 2, pp. 41-52.

Joshi, Hemlata. 2003. *"Educational Development Index-Rajasthan Spatio-Temporal Appraisal at Panchayat Samiti/Block Level, 1991-2000",* Published Research Report, Institute of Development Studies, University Book House, Jaipur.

Joshi, Hemlata. 2005. *"Economic Development Index (Spatio-Temporal Appraisal at Panchayat Samiti/Block Level),* Published Research Report, Institute of Development Studies, University Book House, Jaipur.

Joshi, Hemlata. 2005. *"Health Status Index-Rajasthan (Spatio-Temporal Appraisal at Panchayat Samiti/Block Level),* Research Report, Institute of Development Studies, Jaipur.

Kalita, P., Choudhary, H. and Borha, M. 2004. "Factors Affecting the use of Contraception: A Case Study of Assam, based on a Multivariate Analysis", *Indian Journal of Regional Science,* Volume XXXVI, No. 2, pp. 45.

Kanjilal, Barun and Sharma, Suneeta. 1999. *Journal of Health Management,* 1, 1.

"Sustainability of Private Voluntary Health Organisation (PVHO) in India: Some Methodology Issues". Sage Publications New Delhi, Thousand Oaks, London.

Kothari, Devendra. 1989. *"Family Welfare Programme in Rajasthan: Beyond the Existing Approach".* Sponsored by the Department of Family Welfare, Ministry of Health and Family Welfare, Government of India, New Delhi. Indian Institute of Health Management Research, Jaipur.

Kothari, Devendra. 2001. "Rajasthan: Repoductive Health Needs of Women as Emerged from the Recent Findings", *FPA Working Paper No. 14,* Forum for Population Action, Jaipur.

Kothari, Devendra, Krishnaswamy, S., Maru, R.M., *et al.* 1997. "A Note on Recent Stagnation of Infant Mortality Rate in Rajasthan". Working Paper, Indian Institute of Health Management Research, Jaipur.

Kothari, Devendra, Maru, R.M., Khanna, Anoop, *et al.* 1997. "Vikalp: Managing Family Planning Programme in the Post-ICPD Era: An Experiment in Rajasthan, India". IIHMR Occasional Paper No. 2, Indian Institute of Health Management Research, Jaipur.

Lubhaya, Ram. 1998. "Target-free Approach for Family Welfare: A Review of Expenditure in Rajasthan". In the Policy Project. *Targets for Family Planning in India: An analysis of Policy Change,* Consequences and Alternative Choices. The Futures Group International, New Delhi.

Lubhaya, Ram. *Innovative approaches to population programme management in Rajasthan.*

Malhotra, Rajeev. 1998. "An Interpretation of The Capability Approach for Constructing Development and Derivational Indices–A Comparison of Alternative Estimates at Regional Level for India", Mimeograph.

Measham, Anthony, R. *et al.* 1999. "Reducing Infant Mortality and Fertility, 1975-90, Performance of all India and State Level", *EPW,* Sameeksha Trust, Mumbai.

Ministry of Health and Family Welfare, 1983. National Health Policy. GoI.

Ministry of Health and Family Welfare, 2000. National Population Policy, New Delhi.

Ministry of Human Resource Development "Annual Report". Various Years, New Delhi.

Ministry of Human Resource Development. 1997. "Women in India: A Statistical Profile", Department of Women and Child Development, Government of India, New Delhi.

Ministry of Human Resource Development. 1998. "India Nutrition Profile", Department of Women and Child Development, Government of India, New Delhi.

Morris, 1979. *"Measuring the Condition of the World's Poor-The Physical Quality of Life Index",* Oxford Pergamon Press.

National Council of Applied Economic Research. 1996. *"Human Development Profile of India: Inter-State and Inter-Group Differentials,* Volume II, Statistical Tables", National Council of Applied Economic Research, New Delhi.

National Council of Applied Economic Research. 1999. "India Human Development Report", National Council of Applied Economic Research, Oxford University Press, New Delhi.

National Council of Applied Economic Research. 2002. "West and Central India Human Development Report", Oxford University Press.

National Institute of Rural Development. 1999. "Rural Development Statistics", Hyderabad.

National Sample Survey Organisation. 1989. Morbidity and Utilisation of Medical Services 42nd Round, Department of Statistics, GoI, New Delhi.

National Sample Survey Organisation. 1992. "Morbidity and Utilisation of Medical Services", NSS 42nd Round 1986-87, *Sarvekshana,* 51st Issue, Volume-XV No. 4, Department of Statistics, New Delhi.

National Sample Survey Organisation. 1998. "The Aged in India: A Socio-Economic Profile", Department of Statistics, Ministry of Planning and Programme Implementation, New Delhi.

National Sample Survey Organisation. 1998. *Morbidity and Treatment of Ailments,* 52nd Round, July 1995-June 1996, Report No. 445, Department of Statistics, New Delhi.

National Sample Survey Organisation. 1999. *"Drinking Water, Sanitation and Hygiene in India",* 54th Round, January-June 1998, Report No. 449, Department of Statistics, New Delhi.

National Sample Survey Organisation. 2001. *"Poverty Estimates, 2001".* Department of Statistics, GoI, New Delhi.

National Sample Survey Organisation, 2001. "Employment and Unemployment Situation in India – 1999-2000", Part – I, NSS, 55th Round, July 1999-June 2000, Report No. 458, Ministry of Statistics and Programme Implementation, New Delhi.

NCERT. 2000. *"Fifth Survey of Educational Research 1988-92",* Vol. II, New Delhi.

NFHS-I. "Rajasthan: National Family Health Survey", 1992-93. International Institute of Population Sciences, Mumbai, 1991.

NFHS-II. "Rajasthan: National Family Health Survey", 1998-99. International Institute of Population Sciences, Mumbai, 2001.

OECD. 2000. "A New Economy-The Changing Roll of Innovation and Information Technology in Growth", Organization for Economic Co-operation and Development, Paris.

Office of the Registrar General India. 1987. "Child Mortality & Fertility, Rajasthan, "Occasional Paper-13, 1987, Based on 1981 Census, Demographic Division, Ministry of Home Affairs, New Delhi.

Office of the Registrar General India. 1988. *"Child Mortality Estimates of India",* Census of India, 1981, "Occasional paper No. 5 of 1988", Demographic Division, Ministry of Home Affairs, New Delhi.

Office of the Registrar General India. 1991. "Statistics in India for the Quarter Ending December 1991", Rural Health Division, Directorate General of Health Services, Ministry of Health & FW. GoI, New Delhi.

Office of the Registrar General India. 1992. *"Sample Registration Bulletin"*, Volume XXII, No. 1. Ministry of Home Affairs, New Delhi.

Office of Registrar General India. 1996. Population Projections for India and States, 1996-2016, Report of the Technical Group of Population Projections. GoI. New Delhi.

Office of the Registrar General India. 1998. "Sample Registration System-SRS, Annual Report". Vital Statistics Division , Ministry of Home Affairs, August, 1992.

Office of the Registrar General India. 1998. "Survey of Causes of Death-Rural, Series 3, No. 21, Annual Report", Ministry of Home Affairs, New Delhi, March, 1990.

Pahariya, S. *Vikalp: An Innovative Strategy for Management of Family Welfare Programme.*

Pandey, Arvind, Choe, M.K., Luther, N.Y., Sahu, D. and Chand, J. 1998. "Infant and Child Mortality in India", National Family Health Survey, Subject Reports No. 11, East-West-Center Honolulu, Hawaii.

Parikh, Kirit S. and R. Sudershana, Ed. 1993. *"Human Development and Structural Adjustment"*, Macmillan India Limited, Madras.

Planning Commission, GoI. 1951. "Recommendations of the Sub-Committee on Population Growth and Family Planning", New Delhi.

Pyle David F. *Journal of Health Management,* 1, 1 (1999). "Community Driven Strategy to Reduce Malnutrition: Experience from Tanzania and Sri Lanka". Sage Publications New Delhi, Thousand Oaks, London.

Rajvanshi Jyotsna. December 2004. "Existing System of Distribution of Nutrition its Quality Acceptability of Beneficiaries and Need for Alternative Cost Effective System". Institute of Development Studies, Jaipur.

Rao, Hemlata, G.P. Mishra Ed. 1992. *"Inter-State Disparities in Development in India,"* op. cit.7

Rao, Mohan. "Disinvesting in Health The World Bank's Prescription for Health". *Journal of Health Management,* 4, 2 (2002). "The case for Gender Equity in Health Research". Sage Publications New Delhi, Thousand Oaks, London.

RBI. 2000. *Reserve Bank of India Bulletin,* October 2000, IV (10).

Registrar General of India, SRS based Abridged Lief Tables, Various issues, New Delhi.

Registrar General of India. 1981. "Indirect Estimates of Fertility and Mortality at the District Level 1981 and Report of the Expert Committee on Population Projection, 1981-2001, Census of India-Occasional Paper No. 4 of 1994.

Registrar General of India. 1987. Fertility and Child Mortality, Estimates of Rajasthan, Census of India-Occasional Paper No. 5 of 1987.

Registrar General of India. 1997. District Level Estimates of Fertility and Child Mortality for 1991 and their Interrelations with other Variables, Occasional Paper No. 1, New Delhi.

Registrar General of India. 1998. "State Profile 1991 India", Census of India 1991, RGI, New Delhi.

Registrar General India. 1999. "Working Children in India, an Analysis of the 1991 Census Data", New Delhi.

Registrar General of India. 2001. "Census of India", Provisional Population Totals-India, Paper 1 of 2001, New Delhi.

Registrar General of India. 2001. *SRS Bulletin, Sample Registration System,* Volume 35, No. 1, Vital Statistics Division, New Delhi.

Registrar General of India. 2002. *"SRS Bulletin"* New Delhi, Volume 36, No. 2, New Delhi.

Sachdeva Arvinder, S. 2002. "Urbanisation in India: Past Trends and Future Projections", *The Asian Journal,* Vol.9, No.1 February, New Delhi.

Sangwana, Naveen and Maru, M. Rushikesh. *Journal of Health Management,* 1, 1 (1999). "The Target-Free Approach: An Overview". Sage Publications New Delhi, Thousand Oaks, London.

Sen, Amartya 1995, Mortality as an Indicator of Economic Success and Failure, Discussion Paper, DEP No. 66, Development Economics Research Programme, Sti CERD, London School of Economics, London.

Sen, Amartya 1996. "Radical Needs and Moderate Reforms", in Jean Dreze and Amartya Sen (ed.), *Indian Development: Selected Regional Perspectives,* pp. 1-32, UNI/WIDER.

Sen, Amartya 1999, *Health in Development, Bulletin of the World Health Organisation,* 77 (8), pp. 619-623, World Health Organisation, Geneva.

Sen, Gita, George Asha and Ostlin Piroska. *Journal of Health Management,* 4, 2 (2002). *"The case for Gender Equity in Health Research"*. Sage Publications New Delhi, Thousand Oaks, London.

Shankaranarayanan, R. 1997. "Health Care Auxiliaries in the Detection and Prevention of Oral Cancer". *Oral Oncology,* 149-54.

Shariff, Abusaleh. 1999. "India Human Development Report", NCAER, Oxford University Press, Delhi.

Sharma. R. Goyal, R. and Gupta, H. Rajlakshmi 2002. "An initiative for improving the status of Girl Child in Rajasthan". *FPA Working paper No. 13,* Forum for Population Action, Jaipur.

Shiva, Kumar. 1991. "Human Development Index for Indian States", *Economical and Political Weekly,* Vol. XXVI.

Singhi, N.K. 1999. "Development Debate and Human Development Index: Rajasthan", Institute of Development Studies-Jaipur.

Singhi, N.K. and Joshi, Varsha. *"Can ICDS do it: Health and Nutrition in Rajasthan".* August 1996. Working Paper No. 072. Institute of Development Studies, Jaipur.

Sisodia, P. and RVHA. 1991. *"Expenditure Targets and Achievements of Selected National Health Programmes in Rajasthan",* Jaipur

Sisodia, P. 1992. "Identification of Availability and Composition of Health Resources in Public Sector, Jaipur, IIHMR Mimeograph.

Society for International Development. 1999. "Human Development Report—Rajasthan", Jaipur.

Srinivasan, K. and Abusaleh Shariff. 1997. *"India Towards Population and Development Goals".* Delhi Oxford University Press, p. 11.

Srinivasan, Venkatesh. 2001. *"Health and Family Welfare Programmes in Developing Countries-Study of Innovations in an Indian State".* Aalekh Publishers, Jaipur.

Stuart, Gillespie and Geraldine McNeill. *Food, Health and Survival in India and Developing Countries.*

Sundaram, K. 2001. "Employment – Unemployment in the Nineties, Result From NSS 55th Round", *Economic and Political Weekly,* Volume XXXVI No. 11, March 17, 2001.

Sundaram, K.V. 1997. *"Decentralized Multilevel Planning: Principles and Practice: Asian and African Experiences",* New Delhi, Concept Pub. House, New Delhi.

Theobald, S., Elsey H. and R. Tolhurst. 2002. "Gender Mainstreaming and Sector-Wide Apporaches in Health: Key Areas for Debate". *Journal of Health Management,* 4, 2. *"The case for Gender Equity in Health Research".* Sage Publications New Delhi, Thousand Oaks, London.

Tilak, Jandhyala, B.G. 1999. "Investment in Human Capital in India: An Inter-State Analysis of Stock and Flow of Human Capital", *Journal of Indian School of Political Economy,* Volume XI, No. 1, pp. 39-75.

United Nations. 2002 c. "United Nations Population Division Database on Contraceptive Use", Department of Economics and Social Affairs, Population Division, January, New York.

United Nations. 2002 d. "World Urbanisation Prospects: The 2001 Revision, Department of Economics and Social Affairs", Population Division, New York.

UNAIDS 2000. Report on the Global HIV/AIDS Epidemic, Geneva.

UNDP. 1990 to 2005. "Human Development Report", United Nations Development Programme, Oxford University Press, New York.

UNDP. 2001. "Correspondence on State-Level Communication, Education, Energy and Electricity Data for India", United Nations Development Programme, India Country Office, New Delhi.

UNDP and GoK. 1999. "Human Development in Karnataka", United Nations Development Programme and Government of Karnataka, Bangalore, India.

UNICEF. 1994. *"The Status of the World's Children",* New Delhi: UNICEF. pp. 23-31.

UNICEF, 1995. *"The Progress of Indian States",* Delhi.

UNICEF. 2001. *"The State of the World's Children 2001",* New York: Oxford Univ. Press.

UNICEF. 2002 a. *"Correspondence on Infant and Under-Five Mortality Rates",* New York.

UNICEF. 2002 b. *"Official Summary: The State of the World Children 2002",* New York, Oxford University Press.

World Bank. 2005. "World Development Report. A Better Investment Climate for Everyone", Washington DC.

KEY TO PANCHAYAT SAMITIES

HDI RANK 2001	PANCHAYAT SAMITIES P. CODE	NAME	HDI VALUE
1	2	3	4
172	216	ABU ROAD	0.5235
92	135	AHORE	0.5783
41	148	ALSISAR	0.6301
20	119	AMBER	0.6831
153	196	AMET	0.5396
218	23	ANANDPURI	0.4643
67	31	ANTA	0.5994
120	109	ANUPGARH	0.5593
47	1	ARAIN	0.6258
184	75	ARNOD	0.5141
174	55	ASIND	0.5233
230	104	ASPUR	0.4403
54	32	ATRU	0.6143
220	24	BAGIDORA	0.4625
213	142	BAKANI	0.4755
193	156	BALESAR	0.5119
97	186	BALI	0.5739
215	38	BALOTRA	0.4667
126	203	BAMANWAS	0.5562
89	95	BANDIKUI	0.5806
94	56	BANERA	0.5777
115	9	BANSURE	0.5631
156	157	BAP	0.5389
50	33	BARAN	0.6160
31	227	BARGAON	0.6476
201	100	BARI	0.4955
128	76	BARI SADRI	0.5555
233	39	BARMER	0.4166
198	101	BASERI	0.5033
23	120	BASSI	0.6701
165	46	BAYANA	0.5323
225	40	BAYTOO	0.4535
124	77	BEGUN	0.5568
6	10	BEHROR	0.7298
128	78	BHADESAR	0.5556
7	116	BHADRA	0.7212
182	79	BHAINSRORGARH	0.5157
130	197	BHIM	0.5554
62	2	BHINAY	0.6044
61	228	BHINDER	0.6056
216	136	BHINMAL	0.4666
85	158	BHOPALGARH	0.5829
90	80	BHOPALSAGAR	0.5801
228	105	BICHHIWARA	0.4466
111	66	BIKANER	0.5651
55	159	BILARA	0.6134
141	204	BONLI	0.5447
22	149	BUHANA	0.6705
33	121	CHAKSU	0.6396
1	170	CHECHAT	0.7585
136	34	CHHABRA	0.5506
116	35	CHHIPABAROD	0.5623
108	81	CHHOTI SADRI	0.5670
33	150	CHIRAWA	0.6396
114	82	CHITTAURGARH	0.5634
223	41	CHOHTAN	0.4577
66	89	CHURU	0.6000
227	143	DAG	0.4484
56	208	DANTA RAMGARH	0.6120
101	96	DAUSA	0.5701
75	47	DEEG	0.5916
157	175	DEGANA	0.5380
166	198	DEOGARH	0.5304
186	221	DEOLI	0.5135
123	187	DESURI	0.5574
214	229	DHARIAWAD	0.4745
205	102	DHAULPUR	0.4876
42	209	DHOND	0.6296
188	42	DHORIMANNA	0.5127
125	176	DIDWANA	0.5568
25	122	DUDU	0.6673
48	67	DUNGARGARH *	0.6256
226	106	DUNGARPUR	0.4518
88	83	DUNGLA	0.5811
21	210	FATEHPUR	0.6726
26	110	GANGANAGAR	0.6656
122	205	GANGAPUR	0.5585
112	84	GANGRAR	0.5647
169	25	GARHI	0.5279

HDI RANK 2001	PANCHAYAT SAMITIES P. CODE	NAME	HDI VALUE
1	2	3	4
224	26	GHATOL	0.4543
106	230	GIRWA	0.5679
155	231	GOGUNDA	0.5391
12	123	GOVINDGARH	0.6958
77	117	HANUMANGARH	0.5901
65	165	HINDAUN	0.6003
154	71	HINDOLI	0.5391
118	57	HURDA	0.5622
16	171	ITAWA	0.6920
187	58	JAHAZPUR	0.5136
221	132	JAISALMER	0.4621
150	188	JAITARAN	0.5402
195	137	JALOR	0.5067
13	124	JAMWA RAMGARH	0.6940
211	138	JASWANTPURA	0.4783
18	3	JAWAJA	0.6869
189	177	JAYAL	0.5125
113	232	JHADOL	0.5645
185	144	JHALRAPATAN	0.5138
2	125	JHOTWARA	0.7491
27	151	JHUNJHUNUN	0.6602
191	48	KAMAN	0.5121
135	85	KAPASAN	0.5510
15	111	KARANPUR	0.6932
176	166	KARAULI	0.5191
98	11	KATHUMAR	0.5725
39	4	KEKRI	0.6305
132	72	KESHORAIPATAN	0.5531
160	199	KHAMNOR	0.5359
194	206	KHANDAR	0.5076
32	211	KHANDELA	0.6453
170	145	KHANPUR	0.5276
109	189	KHARCHI/MARWAR JUN.	0.5658
152	233	KHERWARA	0.5399
60	152	KHETRI	0.6059
102	36	KISHANGANJ	0.5698
35	5	KISHANGARH	0.6374
147	12	KISHANGARH BAS	0.5414
145	68	KOLAYAT	0.5434
69	13	KOTKASIM	0.5970
8	126	KOTPUTLI	0.7166
236	234	KOTRA	0.3949
197	59	KOTRI	0.5041
171	178	KUCHAMAN	0.5250
121	200	KUMBHALGARH	0.5590
46	49	KUMHER	0.6270
234	27	KUSHALGARH	0.4094
30	212	LACHHMANGARH	0.6517
103	14	LACHHMANGARH	0.5696
119	179	LADNU	0.5602
9	172	LADPURA	0.7124
168	97	LALSOT	0.5287
70	160	LUNI	0.5942
73	69	LUNKARANSAR	0.5922
71	98	MAHWA	0.5927
147	180	MAKRANA	0.5411
164	222	MALPURA	0.5332
175	60	MANDAL	0.5221
191	61	MANDALGARH	0.5120
58	15	MANDAWAR	0.6085
183	161	MANDOR	0.5149
218	146	MANOHARTHANA	0.4644
42	6	MASOODA	0.6296
87	235	MAVLI	0.5813
163	181	MERTA	0.5338
202	182	MUNDWA	0.4943
51	50	NADBAI	0.6157
95	167	NADOTI	0.5776
144	51	NAGAR PAHARI	0.5441
199	183	NAGAUR	0.5022
159	73	NAINWA	0.5367
64	153	NAWALGARH	0.6022
80	213	NEEM KA THANA	0.5865
84	86	NIMBAHERA	0.5840
83	16	NIMRANA	0.5859
158	223	NIWAI	0.5378
29	118	NOHAR	0.6560
45	70	NOKHA	0.6272
131	162	OSIAN	0.5536

HDI RANK 2001	PANCHAYAT SAMITIES P. CODE	NAME	HDI VALUE
1	2	3	4
37	112	PADAMPUR	0.6332
96	190	PALI	0.5744
142	184	PARBATSAR	0.5447
237	28	PEEPALKHOONT	0.3853
14	127	PHAGI	0.6937
204	163	PHALODI	0.4897
76	217	PINDWARA	0.5905
36	214	PIPRALI	0.6372
137	147	PIRAWA	0.5503
40	7	PISANGAN	0.6304
139	87	PRATAPGARH	0.5480
49	201	RAILMAGRA	0.6191
146	191	RAIPUR	0.5427
177	62	RAIPUR	0.5184
28	113	RAISINGHNAGAR	0.6585
209	103	RAJAKHERA	0.4800
57	90	RAJGARH	0.6096
116	17	RAJGARH	0.5624
140	202	RAJSAMAND	0.5461
172	18	RAMGARH	0.5235
63	192	RANI STATION	0.6028
207	139	RANIWARA	0.4851
93	88	RASHMI	0.5781
52	91	RATANGARH	0.6147
74	19	RENI	0.5919
105	218	REODAR	0.5691
151	185	RIYAN	0.5401
134	193	ROHAT	0.5521
99	52	RUPBAS	0.5713
10	114	SADULSHAHAR	0.7109
206	107	SAGWARA	0.4863
100	63	SAHARA	0.5707
229	29	SAJJANGARH	0.4421
81	236	SALUMBAR	0.5863
231	133	SAM	0.4379
11	128	SAMBHAR	0.6961
222	140	SANCHORE	0.4582
3	129	SANGANER	0.7481
4	173	SANGOD	0.7410
196	134	SANKRA	0.5066
167	168	SAPOTRA	0.5295
107	237	SARADA	0.5675
179	92	SARDARSHAHAR	0.5165
179	207	SAWAI MADHOPUR	0.5165
208	141	SAYLA	0.4829
72	53	SEWAR	0.5925
133	37	SHAHBAD	0.5526
19	130	SHAHPURA	0.6842
179	64	SHAHPURA	0.5165
234	43	SHEO	0.4092
85	219	SHEOGANJ	0.5832
200	164	SHERGARH	0.4977
82	99	SIKRAI	0.5862
232	108	SIMALWARA	0.4318
210	44	SINDHARI	0.4790
68	220	SIROHI	0.5983
212	45	SIWANA	0.4777
78	194	SOJAT	0.5895
79	215	SRI MADHOPUR	0.5891
38	8	SRINAGAR	0.6312
103	93	SUJANGARH	0.5697
5	174	SULTANPUR	0.7349
91	195	SUMERPUR	0.5789
59	154	SURAJGARH	0.6084
53	115	SURATGARH	0.6144
149	65	SUWANA	0.5405
142	74	TALERA	0.5446
217	30	TALWARA	0.4646
44	94	TARANAGAR	0.6278
162	20	THANAGAZI	0.5344
190	21	TIJARA	0.5123
138	169	TODABHIM	0.5498
110	224	TODARAISINGH	0.5655
178	225	TONK	0.5181
24	155	UDAIPURWATI	0.6695
161	22	UMREN	0.5350
203	226	UNIARA	0.4935
17	131	VIRATNAGAR	0.6894
127	54	WEIR	0.5558

Source: Annex 17.3.

INDEX